Contents

THE COUNTRIES

IRB WORLD RUGBY YEARBOOK 2012

EDITED BY PAUL MORGAN AND JOHN GRIFFITHS

Vision Sports Publishing
19-23 High Street
Kingston upon Thames
Surrey, KT1 1LL

www.visionsp.co.uk

Published by
Vision Sports Publishing in 2011

ISBN 13: 978-1907637-25-4

All pictures by Getty Images unless otherwise stated

Typeset by Palimpsest Book Production Ltd, Falkirk, Stirlingshire

Printed and bound in the UK by
Ashford Colour Press Ltd

International Rugby Board
Huguenot House
35-38 St Stephen's Green
Dublin 2, Ireland

t +353-1-240-9200
f +353-1-240-9201
e irb@irb.com

www.irb.com

THE COMBINED TEAMS

CROSS-BORDER TOURNAMENTS

THE BACK ROW

Emirates

Introduction

By Sir Maurice Flanagan

Executive Vice Chairman, Emirates Airline & Group

Any year involving a Rugby World Cup is always special, with teams, officials and fans building towards the world's biggest rugby showcase. Rugby World Cup 2011 was always going to be a very memorable occasion, hosted by such a passionate and enthusiastic rugby nation, and it certainly lived up to expectation.

For the thousands of fans from around the world who flew in to New Zealand, there was a warm and heartfelt welcome from the hosts. Emirates is extremely proud of its role as Worldwide Partner of Rugby World Cup 2011 and has enjoyed bringing fans from across the globe to New Zealand for this occasion.

The success of the New Zealand team created a fairytale for the hosts, and the celebrations will no doubt go on for a long time to come.

The tournament was an opportunity for Emirates to engage with our staff and customers around the world. One of the highlights was for Emirates to fly the Webb Ellis Cup down to New Zealand ahead of the tournament, engaging with customers in London, Dubai and Australia before arriving into Auckland.

For Emirates, the Rugby World Cup is the pinnacle of a broad portfolio of rugby around the world, which includes the IRB's Elite Panel of Referees, USA Rugby, Emirates Western Force Super 15 team and several properties in Rugby Sevens.

The Webb Ellis Cup is welcomed to New Zealand by IRB President Bernard Lapasset before the start of Rugby World Cup 2011.

The Rugby World Cup may be over for another four years, but there is no shortage of exciting rugby to focus on over the coming months. At Emirates we are excited to partner with a sport that engages fans of all nations, be it XVs or Sevens, from Dubai to Australia, and on behalf of rugby fans we would like to thank the players for making this yet another magical season of rugby around the world.

New Zealand celebrates exceptional Rugby World Cup

A message from Bernard Lapasset, Chairman of the International Rugby Board

Welcome to the 2012 *IRB World Rugby Yearbook* and the opportunity to reflect on what has been a remarkable year for our sport.

The highlight, of course, was the seventh edition of Rugby World Cup, hosted where it all began 24 years ago in New Zealand.

There was much conjecture within the New Zealand media in the build-up to the tournament as to whether a great rugby country could successfully deliver an event that both New Zealanders and the global rugby family would be proud of.

New Zealand answered with a resounding "yes". The result was quite remarkable and demonstrated the sheer passion, vision and dedication of all those involved from the organisers, the teams, the volunteers and indeed the fans who travelled to and across New Zealand in record numbers to savour the action.

Rugby World Cup 2011 will be remembered as one of the great Rugby World Cups and was a truly exceptional tournament on and off the field. It was a tournament where New Zealand's rich culture and heritage went hand in hand with rugby's traditions and values, proving that the game's premier global event is much more than 48 matches.

The tournament has written another memorable chapter in the remarkable Rugby World Cup success story, and New Zealanders should be proud of their event. They made it special by embracing the tournament the length and breadth of the country, welcoming all 20 teams and 100,000 international visitors with open arms. It was quite incredible.

I would like to extend my heartfelt thanks to Brian Roche, Martin Snedden and the Rugby New Zealand 2011 team, the New Zealand Rugby Union and the Government for their shared vision, dedication and hard work in delivering Rugby World Cup 2011 in partnership with the IRB team. Their reward was the successful hosting of what will be remembered as one of the great Rugby World Cups, a sporting and operational success. It also took our sport to new audiences and set the bar for future hosts.

And it was also a success for New Zealand. Rugby World Cup 2011 positioned the country as a major event host, a superb tourism destination and a great country. An independent study commissioned by MasterCard during the tournament has indicated that the event is due to deliver NZD$750 million (£400 million) in direct economic benefits for New Zealand and over NZD$1 billion (£500 million) in long-term benefits.

These significant economic benefits demonstrate the true value of a Rugby World Cup to a host nation, its Government, tourism and business sectors. Another great thing about New Zealand 2011 is that there will be no "white elephants". The tournament legacy is clear and long lasting.

Rugby will also benefit. Rugby World Cup 2011 will also deliver the financial platform for the International Rugby Board to continue to invest funds that are vital to the growth and prosperity of the game worldwide. Revenues from the Rugby World Cup 2011 commercial programme, including broadcast, sponsorship and travel and hospitality, will deliver an estimated £80 million net surplus boost to the game.

Rugby World Cup accounts for 95 per cent of the IRB's revenues. In the 2009–2012 investment cycle the global governing body is investing £150 million to develop and grow the sport around the world in order that future Rugby World Cups are more competitive and that more men, women and children can play the game.

We are already conducting a thorough review of the Rugby World Cup to ensure that the tournament continues to meet the strategic needs of our Unions as well as the long-term requirements for a game that continues to increase in participants in record numbers.

We will tackle the Rugby World Cup playing schedule to ensure the best possible rest periods for all teams at Rugby World Cups. Indeed, it was encouraging to hear the Tier 1 Unions give unanimous support to the IRB's review in that regard.

The hosting baton has now passed to England 2015. New Zealand has set the bar high. Planning and preparation is well underway, with Rugby World Cup Limited working in partnership with the England Rugby 2015 organising body to ensure that the rugby family is treated to another exceptional and memorable showcase event.

Rugby is experiencing unprecedented growth at present, with over 3.5 million men, women and children playing the game and the IRB continues to work to ensure the continued development of rugby on and off the field.

We have exciting opportunities ahead: Rugby World Cups in England in 2015 and Japan in 2019 when the tournament will go to Asia for the first time; Olympic Games in 2016 and 2020; an expanded HSBC Sevens World Series, with Japan joining the success story; Argentina's inclusion in the Four Nations; a 10-year tours and Tests schedule that will deliver regular Test matches between Tier 1 and 2 Unions and a global approach to player welfare best practice.

Another exciting development in 2011 was the acceleration in Olympic Games preparation as we build towards Rio 2016. We are proud of the Olympic Games opportunity, and our inclusion is much more than delivering successful Sevens events, it is about playing our part in the Olympic family.

Planning is well advanced and we have developed strong working partnerships with the International Olympic Committee and the Rio 2016 Organising Committee. Together we are committed not just to delivering exceptional Sevens events, but growing rugby and its values around the world.

We continue to work with our Member Unions to ensure that we optimise the Olympic opportunity for all and provide the blueprint for stability and growth. It was fascinating to hear, at our General Assembly in November, our Unions talking about the opportunities that have already arisen due to Olympic Games inclusion.

We have also introduced new Sevens and Women's strategic plans that will provide the blueprint for growth and stability over the next decade as we prepare for two Olympic Games, an expanded Sevens portfolio and the phenomenal growth of Women's participation worldwide.

And so attention turns to 2012. Rugby is in a very strong place, but we must not be complacent and continue to ensure that the game is able to flourish in order that more men, women and children may participate in rugby and enjoy a sport that continues to reach out to new communities worldwide.

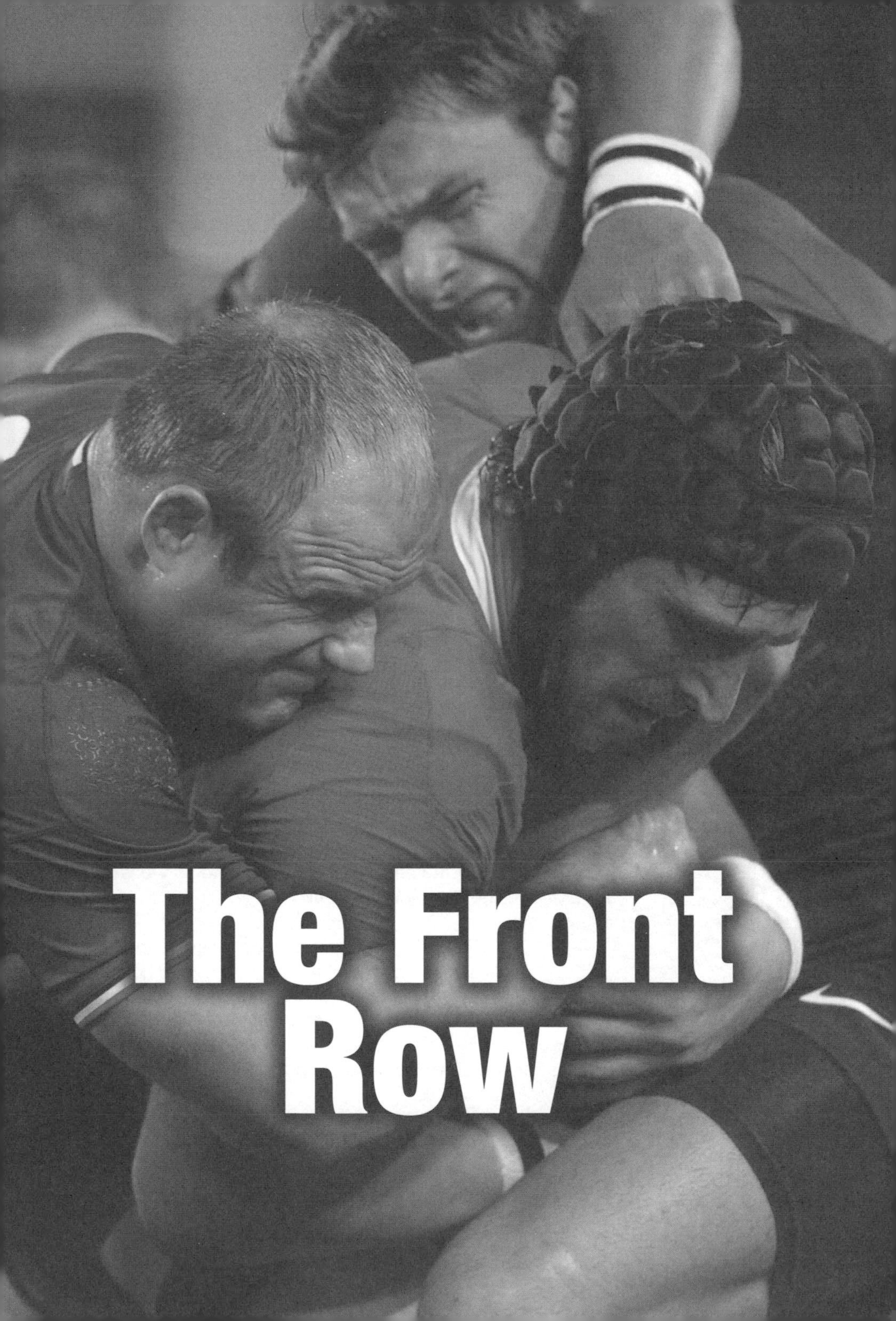

The Front Row

Four more years... as World Champions

Richie McCaw

I am so proud of the efforts of every single player and member of the management team and so grateful for the support we got from the people of New Zealand as we won the Rugby World Cup.

Crucially, every single man out there during the final showed what it means to be an All Black.

At some point one group of players was going to do it, and this group of 30 took their chance. When things happened we just kept getting up again and again and trusting in our mates beside us.

It was 30 guys and the management, and everyone played their part. It's hard to describe, but all around New Zealand people have supported us and given us so much, and it's great that we could repay them.

The celebrations continue: here I am holding up the Webb Ellis Cup at the celebration parade in Wellington.

The one-point victory in the final says a lot about the men we have in the team. It wasn't the prettiest performance, but we had to have courage and the desire to win. The boys put a lot of effort into getting into that position, over a long period of time, and we didn't want to let it go. We probably didn't play our best, but we did enough. I take my hat off to every single player.

In the semi-final against Australia we played the rugby we know we can play, and the final was about hanging in there. It wasn't really until I woke up the morning after the final that I realised what we'd done. The night after the match was a sort of relief, I suppose.

Straight after the game I found it hard to describe my emotions… I admitted to being absolutely shagged. It's hard to get it to sink in, but I am so proud of every single of one the boys, and what we have achieved. We couldn't have been under more pressure at times, but we stuck to our guns and got there in the end.

Everyone had absolutely nothing left. It was sort of a funny feeling, really. It will sink in, I'm sure.

I know some people thought – in advance of the final – that it would be an easy game for us, but within the players and management we never believed that for one minute, as it proved to be.

We went 8-0 up, and when they scored their try the big thing was not to panic, though we seemed to do that at the kick-off. We had talked about being in situations like that, and you need to keep the belief and trust. We had to dig deep, but the last thing we wanted to do was panic.

I finally get my hands on the trophy...

It is all about preparing for those kinds of situations, and we did that well in the week before the game. It is how you react. If you are a leader or captain, you have to keep the belief, and we just about managed to hang in there.

When it came to that moment, I knew we had to believe in each other and play the rugby to win. We just wanted another go to show we learned our lessons from the last four years, and I think we did.

Stephen Donald, of course, ended up scoring the vital penalty, and I think we were able to use our substitutes very well. The key was expecting things like that to happen – if you don't prepare and just hope for the best, then when things start to go against you you can't deal with it.

When we had problems someone always stood up, and then the next guy stood up, and I take my hat off to Stephen, but it's not just about one guy – everybody played as well as they can.

You've got to be warriors to win the World Cup, and there's going to be a lot of stories told about these boys as we get older. They're tough men, and I think the whole country should be very proud of every single one of them.

Yes we won the World Cup for the team and the All Blacks, but we also won it for everyone in New Zealand. It's important that everyone feels a part of it and knows they have helped in some way.

The parade and celebration in Auckland the day after we had beaten France showed the amount of support and the amount of passion there is for the All Blacks and rugby in New Zealand. We've never really underestimated that, we've always known it, but to see people come out and show their support was pretty awesome because Kiwis sometimes don't show their emotion too much, but there's plenty of it out there.

... and show it off with pride to the New Zealand fans at the stadium.

And after Auckland the players were delighted to go on a tour of the whole country, first stopping off in Christchurch. It was very important for us to go to Christchurch, where around 50,000 people turned out. Everyone in that city has been through quite a lot, so it was nice to go and put a smile on some people's faces. I hope each and every one of them is proud – it's a great time to be a Kiwi.

Although we couldn't play any games down there in Christchurch, we realised the support from all over the country, especially from that province, was huge. We went there and say "thank you" for the support and show the cup, and it meant a lot. More than 100,000 Wellingtonians packed the capital's streets when we went there and those two days were something pretty unforgettable, a time that we really didn't want to end.

It was a hell of a six weeks, and we will be the world champions for four years, so we're going to enjoy it as much as we can.

We had to get through a really tough semi-final against Australia.

Thanks for the Memories

By Paul Morgan

The All Blacks team shared their victory with the whole of New Zealand.

On the day of the first match of Rugby World Cup 2011 something magical happened. In the months leading up to the tournament the grumbles about budgets and lack of accommodation had grown louder, and from some quarters it felt like the people of New Zealand weren't looking forward to hosting the game's greatest show on earth.

But on that first day, before New Zealand played Tonga, fan power took over. In downtown Auckland representatives of all 20 nations (and some more) mingled at Queen's Wharf and kicked off a sensational party that lasted more than six weeks and covered 48 matches.

The final result was, of course, important to New Zealanders, but long before Stephen Donald kicked the winning penalty in the final against France the success of Rugby World Cup 2011 was guaranteed.

Long before one of the greatest ever All Blacks sides lifted the Webb Ellis Cup, the tournament was certain to be acclaimed as one of the best of the first seven.

The key to its success was the attitude of the people of New Zealand, who guaranteed that 2011 would be remembered as the "Friendly World Cup", and much of the praise for the country's attitude to the arrival of 100,000 overseas visitors must go to the 6,500 volunteers who transformed cities and towns across the whole country.

Thousands of people packed the streets to catch a glimpse of the Webb Ellis Cup.

The volunteers were the perfect ambassadors for a proud country and set a bar that both the London Olympics in 2012 and the next World Cup, in 2015, will do well to reach.

"New Zealand has done itself proud," said RNZ 2011 Chairman Brian Roche.

"Rugby fans, even those with a passing interest in the game, have dressed up, painted their faces and turned each match into a true festival of rugby and our country.

"Others have gone to Fanzones, enjoyed REAL New Zealand Festival events and given our visitors the best of welcomes.

"We promised a stadium of four million great fans and hosts, and without a doubt New Zealand has delivered.

"None of this would have been possible without the passion and dedication of an army of people across New Zealand.

"The Team 2011 volunteers have been at the forefront of our efforts to look after visitors and ensure they left with the best of memories of their time here while also contributing to the successful delivery of 48 matches.

"Through the past six years since we won the bid to host RWC 2011, our partners have worked tirelessly to ensure we created the best platform to deliver on the promises we made in Dublin.

"We thank those in central and local government, the NZ 2011 Office, provincial rugby unions, regional tourism and other industry organisations and of course the staff and management of our own organisation, RNZ 2011. The collective efforts of so many have ensured we have delivered an event all New Zealanders can be proud of and one that enhances our country's position on the world stage.

A young fan holds up his homemade version of the World Cup trophy at the parade in Christchurch.

"Most importantly from our position as tournament organiser, we have shown the world that our great little country can deliver a globally significant event with a host of challenges. We are confident our success stands New Zealand in good stead to attract major events in the future.

"We are proud of our achievements in meeting our ticket revenue target and successfully delivering 48 matches at 12 venues. The final was the icing on the cake of what was already one of the great Rugby World Cups."

Roche also confirmed the fact that he was part of a country that took their responsibility for hosting the World Cup very seriously.

"We made many promises in Dublin to the IRB, and throughout the tournament we've kept the focus on achieving those," he added.

"We have delivered 48 test matches, in 45 days, in 12 venues.

"We've done it, and we can reflect on everything that's been achieved."

Once the final whistle blew after the final in Eden Park, the party really picked up pace, with World Cup parades in Auckland, Christchurch and Wellington, and they captivated the hearts of everyone who witnessed them, including the country's Prime Minister, John Key.

"I don't think New Zealand's seen anything like this since we won the America's Cup in 1995. It's a remarkable outpouring of support. They think about a quarter of a million people are here, so for a city of about 1.3 million it's a lot of people turning up," said Key.

The All Blacks' final triumph and the sensational victory parades that followed were even more poignant because the 12 months before Rugby World Cup arrived had not been easy for New Zealand, with the Pike River mining disaster, the Christchurch earthquakes and then, after the Rugby World Cup tournament started, the Rena shipwreck and subsequent oil spill in the Bay of Plenty. All that in addition to the global economic downturn that especially affected small countries like New Zealand.

"Winning the World Cup means everything actually," added Prime Minister Key.

"It's been a very tough 12 months for New Zealand, with the earthquakes and the Pike River mine disaster. So this was really something that galvanised the country and brought everyone together. We're rugby mad at the best of times, and to be hosted in New Zealand was a bit of a fairytale ending really.

"I don't believe any other sport in the world could have delivered those parades. In which other sport would we have seen the fans of all 20 nations – and more – line the streets of New Zealand, arm in arm, celebrating not only the All Blacks' amazing 8–7 victory but the sport we all love?"

Wales' Mike Phillips dives over the line to score the only try of the semi-final against France.

If you ever want to see the personification of "world in union", it came less than 24 hours after Richie McCaw lifted the Webb Ellis Cup above his head, when he did it all over again in the streets of Auckland.

One man on those streets was the IRB's Head of Rugby World Cup, Kit McConnell.

"On Sunday night in Auckland, the fans I think felt a huge amount of relief and expressed themselves in a really positive way, and 200,000 people were estimated to have come out in Auckland on Monday for the parade," said McConnell.

"We have seen the same scenes in Christchurch and Wellington. And it is fantastic that the All Blacks can give something back to those communities, particularly in Christchurch, who had such a difficult time in the build-up with the earthquakes and with the fact that we had to move the matches away from the city. The fact that the All Blacks could go back there as Rugby World Cup winners and give something back to the community during the parade was something very special."

On the field it was a huge success as well, as we saw the Tier 2 nations close the gap and a compelling final that had more than 60,000 at Eden Park and millions more on television on the edge of their seats until the final whistle. McConnell explains:

Russia's Denis Simplikevich scores a try for the Tier 2 nation against Australia in Pool C.

"We saw some outstanding rugby, and that culminated in perhaps one of the great Rugby World Cup finals, which certainly had four million New Zealanders and probably people all around the world very nervous and a little bit tense going into even the last seconds.

"I think the final was a real justification of the rugby on the field, but the rugby from the first game right through the 48 games to the last has been absolutely outstanding. We have seen matches like Tonga upsetting France, who then went on to push the All Blacks to within one point in the final. We have seen Russia on their debut scoring three tries against Australia, three tries against Italy and two against Ireland and pushing the USA the whole way in that match.

"Right from the debutants through to the traditional powers of rugby, we have seen some great performances on the field, and then off the field the whole country has embraced the tournament. I don't think we have ever seen a Rugby World Cup where a whole country has come together to support the tournament, to engage with it and to welcome the 100,000 travelling fans and have those travelling fans embrace the country the same way. It has been absolutely incredible off the field."

It is was presumed by many ahead of Rugby World Cup 2011 that the tournament would never return to the Land of the Long White Cloud, but it was so successful that such a prediction could never be made again.

Even RWC 2011 Chief Executive Martin Snedden was prepared to admit before the tournament that this would be New Zealand's only chance to host it. But not afterwards.

"The Rugby World Cup is not just to make money but also for the rugby reason, and we have a lot of reasons to come back to New Zealand," said IRB Chairman Bernard Lapasset.

RWC Minister Murray McCully was similarly committed to its return, adding, "The way in which the New Zealand people went out of their way to make the visitors feel welcome was very special. Some of them took three weeks off work just to be a part of this, and I think that really epitomises what New Zealand is all about. For New Zealanders the hosting of Rugby World Cup has been a wonderful experience. An opportunity not just for rugby but to celebrate New Zealand."

Those who were part of the stadium of 4.2 million should be proud… we'll definitely be back.

In terms of the seventh Rugby World Cup final itself, we learnt:

- New Zealand join Australia and South Africa as two-time RWC winners.
- France remain the only team to have played in a RWC final without winning one. Their three final losses is a record.
- This was the lowest-scoring RWC final, surpassing the 18 points scored in 1991.
- It was the first final to have two replacements score points, and Stephen Donald became the first player to make his Rugby World Cup debut in a final.
- Jean Marc Doussain became the first player to make his Test debut in a RWC final. At 20 years and 253 days, he was the third-youngest player to play a RWC final.
- Brad Thorn, at 36 years and 262 days old, became the oldest player to win a RWC final, surpassing England's Jason Leonard who was 35 years and 100 days old when his side defeated Australia at RWC 2003.
- Tony Woodcock became only the second prop to score in a Rugby World Cup final. Tony Daly scored the only try of the match in Australia's win over England in 1991.
- Richie McCaw won his seventh RWC match as New Zealand captain, breaking Reuben Thorne's All Blacks record.

Tonga had their best-ever World Cup, beating France 19–14 to enter the top 10 of the IRB world rankings.

IRB Awards

Dusautoir honoured

By Adrian Clarke

The powerful French flanker and captain, Thierry Dusautoir, was named IRB Player of the Year.

France captain Thierry Dusautoir quickly made up for the disappointment of losing the World Cup final when he was named IRB Player of the Year at a glittering prize ceremony in Auckland just 24 hours after the Eden Park showpiece.

The Toulouse flanker became only the second-ever Frenchman to be presented with the award, following in the footsteps of former Les Bleus skipper Fabien Galthie who scooped the top gong in 2002.

It was a fitting reward for Dusautoir, who produced consistently outstanding displays for Marc Lievremont's side throughout the year, driving them on with his strong tackling, powerful ballcarrying and intelligent leadership skills.

But it was the blindside's inspirational performances during the World Cup itself that sealed the prize, as he starred in unexpected victories over England and Wales before scoring France's try in a Man-of-the-Match display for Les Tricolores in the final as they went down to a brave 8–7 defeat to the home nation.

Graham Henry capped off a successful Rugby World Cup by winning the Coach of the Year.

Dusautoir beat-off stiff competition from a six-man shortlist that featured All Blacks trio Piri Weepu, Jerome Kaino and Ma'a Nonu, as well as Australian duo Will Genia and David Pocock, and the Frenchman succeeds New Zealand captain Richie McCaw who won the big prize in both 2009 and 2010.

Elsewhere, on a special evening which also celebrated 125 years of the International Rugby Board at the Vector Arena, New Zealand unsurprisingly landed the Team of the Year award, while the man who led them to their second Webb Ellis Cup success, Graham Henry, was also named Coach of the Year.

The independent panel of judges, chaired by World Cup winner John Eales, handed the coveted IRB Young Player of the Year prize to England

Under-20s fly-half George Ford, who at 18 became the youngest-ever recipient and the first Englishman to be bestowed the honour.

The highly promising Leicester Tigers teenager played a starring role in the 2011 Junior World Championships in Italy when scoring 54 points en route to a runners-up finish with England at the tournament. This, on the back of a sensational RBS Six Nations Under-20s campaign which saw Ford amass 76 points in his country's Grand Slam winning campaign.

Promising young English fly-half, George Ford, the 2011 IRB Junior Player of the Year.

On receiving his award, the talented number 10 said: "It's a massive honour, especially when you consider the calibre of player who has won it in the past as well as the others [Sam Cane and Luke Whitelock] nominated. I couldn't believe it when I found out, to be honest, but I've got to be quick to point out that rugby is not an individual sport. All of the lads were awesome throughout the whole campaign, and I'd like to think that I'm picking the award up on behalf of them."

It was also an evening of celebration for South African Cecil Afrika who was named as the IRB International Sevens Player of the Year. The fly-half enjoyed a fabulous World Series, scoring 40 tries and a total of 385 points in the eight events, which included victories for the Blitzbokke in Las Vegas, London and Edinburgh. The 23-year-old also ended the overall competition as the top points scorer.

The IRPA Try of the Year prize was an exciting category as always, but the judges eventually plumped for Radike Samo's brilliant effort for Australia in the final Tri-Nations and Bledisloe Cup match of 2011. Shrugging off a couple

South African Cecil Afrika was named IRB International Sevens Player of the Year.

of All Black defenders on his own 10-metre line, the veteran outsprinted everyone to score a memorable individual score in a famous victory for the Wallabies.

Liverpool-born Ruth Mitchell was awarded the IRB Women's Personality of the Year prize for her services to the game. In her role as the Director of Development for the Hong Kong Rugby Board, the former player has been a driving force behind the large growth of interest in youth rugby that has been seen in the region.

The 2011 IRB Development Award went to USA Rugby for its innovative "Rookie Rugby" programme. The scheme, which involves schools, rugby organisations and local community-based projects across the States, had an initial target of introducing 100,000 children aged from six to 12 to the sport, but due to its phenomenal success many more youngsters than that are now enjoying the game in America.

Wooden Spoon saw their voluntary work with under-privileged kids for more than 25 years recognised as they received the Spirit of Rugby Award,

Radike Samo, winner of the IRPA Try of the Year Award.

and in doing so they became the first charity to receive such an accolade. While former referee and administrator Keith Lawrence, who worked for the NZRU, the IRB and as Sevens Referees Manager before retiring in 2011 was also handed the Referee Award for Distinguished Service.

This year's Vernon Pugh Award for Distinguished Service went to one of New Zealand rugby's most inspirational characters and the man who helped his country win the bid to host the 2011 Rugby World Cup, Jock Hobbs. As Chairman of NZRU and Rugby New Zealand, Hobbs oversaw considerable success on and off the pitch before standing down from his duties because of ill health.

Former Australia captain and veteran of 110 Test matches, George Smith, was honoured for his services to the game with the IRPA Special Merit Award.

The Sydney-born flanker retired from international duty in February 2010, a decade after making his debut against France in Paris. The Wallaby legend holds the distinction of becoming the youngest man to play in 100 Tests at just 29 years and 4 days, and is the most capped flanker in the history of the game.

Before the ceremony in Auckland came to a close, 19 founders, pioneers and legends of the Rugby World Cup were also inducted into the IRB Hall of Fame, and they were: Dr Roger Vanderfield, Richard Littlejohn, Sir Nicholas Shehadie, John Kendall-Carpenter, David Kirk, Sir Brian Lochore, Nick Farr-Jones, Bob Dwyer, Francois Pienaar, Kitch Christie, Rod Macqueen, Martin Johnson CBE, Sir Clive Woodward OBE, John Smit, Jake White, Gareth Rees, Agustín Pichot, Brian Lima and Jonah Lomu.

Ruth Mitchell, winner of the IRB Women's Personality of the Year.

Thierry Dusautoir, France's marauding captain and winner of the IRB Player of the Year Award, led his team all the way to the 2011 Rugby World Cup Final.

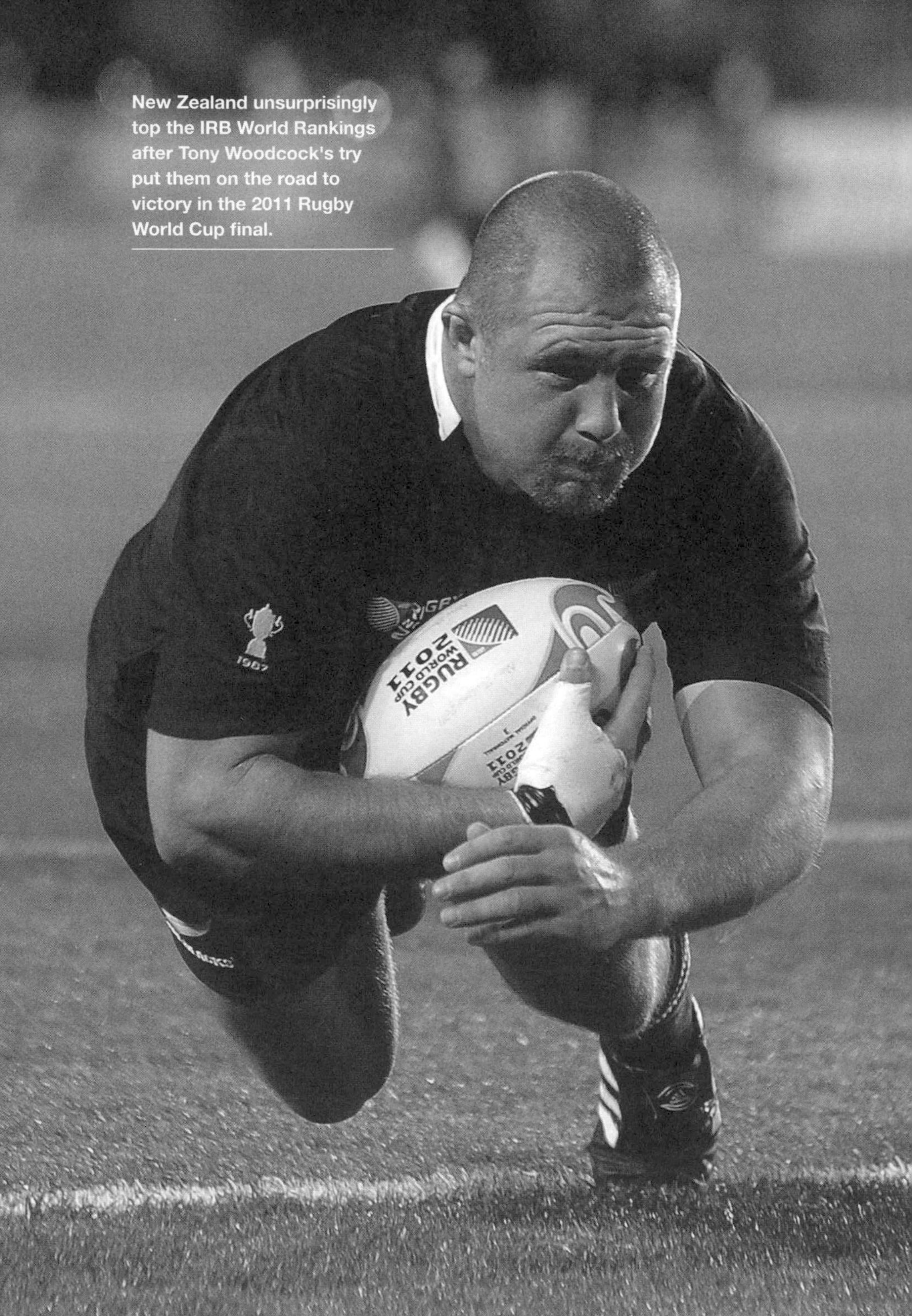

New Zealand unsurprisingly top the IRB World Rankings after Tony Woodcock's try put them on the road to victory in the 2011 Rugby World Cup final.

IRB World Rankings

All Blacks on Top

By Karen Bond

Newly-crowned world champions New Zealand retain the number one spot they have held since November 2009 despite a decrease in their rating points after suffering three defeats in the last 12 months, against South Africa and Australia in the Tri-Nations and a Bledisloe Cup tussle with the Wallabies in Hong Kong.

The All Blacks would have lost the position they have held for nearly 80 per cent of the time since the rankings were introduced in October 2003 had they again failed in their quest to lift the Webb Ellis Cup for a second time, a consequence of playing at home and with the points exchange doubled to reflect the importance of Rugby World Cup matches. Instead, Richie McCaw's men ended RWC 2011 with a 4.01-point cushion over Australia, the only other side in the top 10 to end the last year where they began it. This, though, is a far cry from the 9.21 advantage New Zealand enjoyed in October 2011 after 14 Tests unbeaten.

France's reward for reaching a third RWC final is a one-place climb to third, breaking the southern hemisphere dominance of the top three by pushing South Africa down to fourth. Wales, the other semi-finalists, also end the year one place higher in eighth, but had equalled their highest-ever ranking of fourth before finishing the tournament with defeats to France and Australia.

The biggest movers of the 20 teams involved in RWC 2011 are Tonga, who entered the top 10 for the first time after upsetting France 19–14 in their final Pool A match. Tonga now occupy ninth – equalling the highest-ever rankings of Fiji and Samoa – after beginning the year in 16th. That is a position now occupied by their fellow Pacific Islanders, Fiji, who fall six places after a disappointing year which yielded two home defeats in the IRB Pacific Nations Cup and losses to South Africa, Wales and Samoa at RWC 2011.

While Tonga's rise is impressive, nine other nations enjoyed bigger climbs than the Ikale Tahi over the last 12 months in Bulgaria, Hong Kong, Israel, Moldova, Peru, Poland, Sweden, Venezuela and Zimbabwe. The honour of being the biggest climbers in this period falls to Zimbabwe, who have rocketed up 17 places to 35th after some impressive home and away victories over the then higher-ranked Kenya and Uganda in the Victoria Cup, a sign that they will be in the mix come qualification time for RWC 2015.

Four other nations enjoyed climbs into double figures, with Peru rising 14 places to 64th, Israel 13 to 61st and Bulgaria and Sweden both 11 to 38th and 79th respectively. The majority of Peru's gain came in October 2010 after beating the higher-ranked Colombia – a win they matched in 2011 – and Venezuela in the South American B Championship. The tournament proved a costly one for hosts Colombia with defeats to Peru and Venezuela resulting in a 20-place plummet to 73rd in the rankings, totally wiping out the 12-place gain of the previous 12 months.

Tonga surged to ninth place in the rankings after an impressive Rugby World Cup 2011.

No other nation suffered a fall into double figures, although Croatia, Kenya, Madagascar and Norway all slipped eight places. This quartet were among 34 nations to fall in the IRB World Rankings in the 12 months up to the end of October 2011, with nine ending the year where they began it and the 50 others enjoying a climb.

The number of IRB Member Unions with a ranking did reduce to 93 in this time, with the Arabian Gulf Rugby Football Union ceasing to exist on 1 January 2011 as part of an exciting restructure in West Asia, meaning 57 nations began the year with a one-place elevation. They could increase again, though, in the next 12 months, with Mexico, Pakistan and the Philippines all drawing close to the requirement to earn a ranking of 10 Test matches against Full Member Unions since becoming one themselves.

The IRB World Rankings are published every Monday on www.irb.com. They are calculated using a points exchange system in which teams take points off each other based on the match result. Whatever one team gains, the other team loses. The exchanges are determined by the match result, the relative strength of the team and the margin of victory. There is also an allowance for home advantage.

Ninety-three of the IRB's Member Unions have a rating, typically between 0 and 100, with the top side in the world usually having a rating above 90 – New Zealand's was 91.43 at the time of writing. Any match that is not a full international between two countries or a Test against the Lions does not count towards the rankings. Likewise, neither does a match against a country that is not an IRB Full Member Union. For more details, visit www.irb.com.

IRB WORLD RANKINGS 01/10/10 – 31/10/11

POSITION	MEMBER UNION	RATING POINTS	MOVERS
1	New Zealand	91.43	
2	Australia	87.42	
3	France	84.70	Up 1
4	South Africa	84.34	Down 1
5	England	81.58	Up 1
6	Ireland	80.65	Down 1
7	Argentina	80.28	Up 1
8	Wales	80.18	Up 1
9	Tonga	76.63	Up 7
10	Scotland	76.20	Down 3
11	Samoa	75.81	Up 1
12	Italy	73.99	Down 1
13	Canada	72.92	Up 1
14	Georgia	71.09	Up 3
15	Japan	70.45	Down 2
16	Fiji	68.78	Down 6
17	USA	65.63	Down 2
18	Romania	63.98	Up 1
19	Namibia	61.24	Up 1
20	Portugal	60.67	Up 2
21	Russia	60.54	Down 3
22	Uruguay	60.00	Down 1
23	Spain	59.52	
24	Chile	59.43	
25	Belgium	56.50	Up 1
26	Morocco	56.13	Down 1
27	Hong Kong	54.34	Up 8
28	Brazil	54.09	
29	Moldova	54.04	Up 9
30	Poland	53.67	Up 9
31	Kazakhstan	53.62	Down 4
32	Korea	53.36	Down 1
33	Ukraine	53.22	Down 4
34	Czech Republic	52.99	Down 1
35	Zimbabwe	52.40	Up 17
36	Tunisia	52.35	Down 2
37	Germany	51.81	Down 7
38	Sweden	51.34	Up 11
39	Lithuania	50.41	Up 1
40	Kenya	49.18	Down 8
41	Paraguay	48.84	
42	Netherlands	47.71	Down 5
43	Uganda	47.69	Up 1
44	Ivory Coast	47.52	Up 1
45	Sri Lanka	47.03	Down 2
46	Papua New Guinea	46.19	Up 4
47	Bermuda	45.94	Up 7

IRB WORLD RANKINGS 01/10/10 – 31/10/11

POSITION	MEMBER UNION	RATING POINTS	MOVERS
48	Trinidad & Tobago	45.85	Down 2
49	Singapore	45.66	Up 2
50	Croatia	45.56	Down 8
51	Venezuela	45.36	Up 8
52	Senegal	45.24	Up 4
53	Malta	45.23	Down 5
54	Cook Islands	44.61	Up 1
55	Madagascar	44.31	Down 8
56	Switzerland	44.22	Up 7
57	Chinese Taipei	43.62	Up 5
58	Andorra	42.83	Up 3
59	Latvia	42.69	Down 2
60	Guyana	42.54	Up 6
61	Israel	42.02	Up 13
62	China	41.78	Up 5
63	Malaysia	41.75	Down 5
64	Peru	41.64	Up 14
65	Thailand	41.46	Down 5
66	Cayman Islands	41.23	Up 4
67	Niue Islands	41.11	Up 1
68	Denmark	40.81	Up 3
69	Serbia	41.81	Down 5
70	Slovenia	40.20	Down 5
71	Hungary	40.10	Down 2
72	Zambia	39.94	
73	Colombia	39.59	Down 20
74	St Vincent & The Grenadines	39.30	Up 1
75	India	39.19	Down 2
76	Barbados	39.13	
77	Solomon Islands	39.06	
78	Cameroon	38.33	Up 1
79	Bulgaria	37.36	Up 11
80	Austria	36.79	Up 7
81	Swaziland	36.68	Up 3
82	Botswana	36.68	Down 2
83	Jamaica	36.35	Up 2
84	Bahamas	36.33	Up 2
85	Tahiti	36.25	Up 3
86	Guam	36.24	Down 3
87	Bosnia & Herzegovina	36.18	Up 2
88	Nigeria	35.29	Up 3
89	Monaco	35.17	Up 3
90	Norway	34.81	Down 8
91	Vanuatu	34.77	Up 2
92	Luxembourg	32.26	Up 2
93	Finland	27.70	Up 2

International Tournaments

REVIEW OF THE 2011 WORLD CUP

SEVENTH TOURNAMENT IN NEW ZEALAND

THE POOL MATCHES

POOL A

9 September, Eden Park, Auckland

NEW ZEALAND 41 (4G 1PG 2T)
TONGA 10 (1G 1PG)

NEW ZEALAND: I J A Dagg; R D Kahui, M A Nonu, S Williams, I Toeava; D W Carter, Q J Cowan; T D Woodcock, A K Hore, O T Franks, B C Thorn, A J Williams, J Kaino, V V J Vito, R H McCaw (*captain*)

SUBSTITUTIONS: B J Franks for Woodcock (44 mins); P A T Weepu for Cowan (52 mins); S L Whitelock for Thorn (55 mins); C S Jane for Toeava (61 mins); C R Slade for Carter (73 mins); C R Flynn for Hore (73 mins); A F Boric for Vito (74 mins)

SCORERS *Tries*: Dagg (2), Kahui (2), Kaino, Nonu *Conversions:* Carter (3), Slade *Penalty Goal*: Carter

TONGA: V F Lilo; S V Piutau, S Hufanga, A K Ma'ilei, V Iongi; K S Morath, T Moa; S L Tonga'uiha, A A Lutui, T Filise, K P Hehea, J M L Tuineau, S M Kalamafoni, V S Ma'afu, F Maka (*captain*)

SUBSTITUTIONS: E Taukafa for Lutui (40 mins); S L N Timani for Hehea (40 mins); L A H N Fatafehi for Ma'ilei (40 mins); F K A Taumalolo for Tonga'uiha (52 mins); K Pulu for Filise (52 mins); S K Vahafolau for Maka (53 mins); S Fisilau for Hufanga (74 mins)

SCORERS *Try*: Taumalolo *Conversion:* Morath *Penalty Goal*: Morath

REFEREE G Clancy (Ireland)

10 September, North Harbour Stadium, Auckland

FRANCE 47 (4G 3PG 2T) JAPAN 21 (1G 3PG 1T)

FRANCE: C Heymans; V Clerc, A Rougerie, F Estebanez, M Médard; F Trinh-Duc, D Yachvili; F Barcella, W Servat, N Mas, J Pierre, L Nallet, T Dusautoir (*captain*), R Lakafia, I Harinordoquy

SUBSTITUTIONS: D Marty for Estebanez (46 mins); D Szarzewski for Servat (50 mins); J-B Poux for Barcella (50 mins); D Skrela for Trinh-Duc (50 mins); M Parra for Skrela (61 mins); P Papé for Pierre (72 mins); J Bonnaire for Harinordoquy (73 mins)

SCORERS *Tries*: Pierre, Trinh-Duc, Clerc, Nallet, Papé, Parra *Conversions:* Yachvili (4) *Penalty Goals*: Yachvili (3)

JAPAN: S J Webb; K Endo, K Taira, R T Nicholas, H Onozawa; J A Arlidge, F Tanaka; H Hirashima, S Horie, K Hatakeyama, L M Thompson, T Kitagawa, T Kikutani (*captain*), R Holani, M G Leitch

SUBSTITUTIONS: I Taniguchi for Holani (35 mins); N Fujita for Hatakeyama (42 mins); A Tupuailai for Taira (53 mins); A Hiwasa for Tanaka (65 mins); M C Williams for Webb (65 mins)

SCORER *Tries*: Arlidge (2) *Conversion:* Arlidge *Penalty Goals*: Arlidge (3)

REFEREE S R Walsh (Australia)

14 September, Northland Events Centre, Whangarei

TONGA 20 (2G 2PG) CANADA 25 (2G 2PG 1T)

TONGA: K S Morath; F Vainikolo, S V Piutau, L A H N Fatafehi, W F U Helu; T Moa, T T Palu; F K A Taumalolo, E Taukafa, K Pulu, S L N Timani, T Lokotui, F Maka (*captain*), S K Vahafolau, S F K Vaiomounga

SUBSTITUTIONS: V S Ma'afu for Vahafolau (49 mins); H Aulika for Pulu (51 mins); S M Kalamafoni for Timani (52 mins); A I Ma'asi for Taukafa (64 mins); V Iongi for Helu (65 mins); A N Taufa for Palu (70 mins); S L Tonga'uiha for Taumalolo (74 mins)

SCORERS *Tries*: Piutau (2) *Conversions:* Morath (2) *Penalty Goals*: Morath (2)

CANADA: J G Pritchard; C Hearn, D T H van der Merwe, R J Smith, P W Mackenzie; A H B Monro, E G Fairhurst; H A W Buydens, P D Riordan (*captain*), J A Marshall, J L Sinclair, J N Cudmore, C O'Toole, A Carpenter, A Kleeberger

SUBSTITUTIONS: T N Hotson for O'Toole (32 mins); C A Trainor for Smith (64 mins); G R O Hamilton for Riordan (temp 30 to 40 mins and 68 mins); N Dala for Sinclair (74 mins); S Franklin for Marshall (74 mins)

SCORERS *Tries*: Sinclair, Carpenter, Mackenzie *Conversions:* Pritchard (2) *Penalty Goals*: Pritchard (2)

REFEREE J I Kaplan (South Africa)

16 September, Waikato Stadium, Hamilton

NEW ZEALAND 83 (9G 4T) JAPAN 7 (1G)

NEW ZEALAND: I Toeava; C S Jane, C G Smith, M A Nonu, R D Kahui; C R Slade, A M Ellis; T D Woodcock, K F Mealamu (*captain*), O T Franks, B C Thorn, S L Whitelock, J Kaino, V V J Vito, A J Thomson

SUBSTITUTIONS: A K Hore for Mealamu (43 mins); S Williams for Jane (43 mins); A J Williams for Vito (58 mins); P A T Weepu for Toeava (61 mins); Q J Cowan for Ellis (61 mins); I F Afoa for Franks (61 mins); A F Boric for Thorn (71 mins)

SCORERS *Tries*: Kahui (2), S Williams (2), Smith, Kaino, Mealamu, Ellis, Slade, Toeava, Hore, Nonu, Thomson *Conversions:* Slade (9)

JAPAN: T Ueda; T Usuzuki, K Taira, Y Imamura, H Onozawa; M C Williams, A Hiwasa; N Kawamata, Y Aoki, N Fujita, H Ono, T Kitagawa, I Taniguchi, T Kikutani (*captain*), M G Leitch

SUBSTITUTIONS: A Tupuailai for Taira (46 mins); S J Webb for Ueda (51 mins); K Hatakeyama for Fujita (58 mins); Y Kitagawa for T Kitagawa (58 mins); S T Vatuvei for Kikutani (58 mins); H Yuhara for Aoki (63 mins); T Yoshida for Imamura (70 mins)

SCORERS *Try*: Onozawa *Conversion:* M C Williams

REFEREE N Owens (Wales)

18 September, McLean Park, Napier

FRANCE 46 (4G 5PG 1DG)
CANADA 19 (1G 2PG 2DG)

FRANCE: D Traille; V Clerc, D Marty, M Mermoz, A Rougerie (*captain*); F Trinh-Duc, M Parra; J-B Poux, W Servat, L Ducalcon, P Papé, R Millo-Chluski, F Ouedraogo, L Picamoles, J Bonnaire

SUBSTITUTIONS: F Barcella for Poux (temp 17 to 27 mins and 46 mins); G Guirado for Servat (52 mins); J Pierre for Millo-Chluski (62 mins); D Yachvili for Trinh-Duc (69 mins); M Médard for Rougerie (71 mins); I Harinordoquy for Ouedraogo (75 mins); Poux back for Ducalcon (80 mins)

SCORERS *Tries*: Clerc (3), Traille *Conversions:* Parra (4) *Penalty Goals*: Parra (5) *Dropped Goal:* Trinh-Duc

CANADA: J G Pritchard; C Hearn, D T H van der Merwe, R J Smith, P W Mackenzie; A H B Monro, E G Fairhurst; H A W Buydens, P D Riordan (*captain*), J A Marshall, J L Sinclair, J N Cudmore, C O'Toole, A Carpenter, A Kleeberger

SUBSTITUTIONS: T N Hotson for Cudmore (59 mins); G R O Hamilton for Riordan (59 mins); S T White for Fairhurst (61 mins); S Franklin for Marshall (61 mins); C A Trainor for Van der Merwe (61 mins); N Dala for O'Toole (62 mins); N S Hirayama for Monro (70 mins)

SCORERS *Try*: Smith *Conversion:* Pritchard *Penalty Goals*: Pritchard (2) *Dropped Goals:* Monro (2)

REFEREE C Joubert (South Africa)

21 September, Northland Events Centre, Whangarei

TONGA 31 (2G 4PG 1T) JAPAN 18 (1PG 3T)

TONGA: V F Lilo; F Vainikolo, S V Piutau, L A H N Fatafehi, S Hufanga; K S Morath, T Moa; S L Tonga'uiha, A A Lutui (*captain*), T Filise, T Lokotui, K P Hehea, S M Kalamafoni, V S Ma'afu, S F K Vaiomounga

SUBSTITUTIONS: F K A Taumalolo for Tonga'uiha (40 mins); H Aulika for Filise (40 mins); A I Ma'asi for Lutui (47 mins); J M L Tuineau for Hehea (64 mins); A K Ma'ilei for Hufanga (67 mins); S K Vahafolau for Vaiomounga (70 mins); S Fisilau for Moa (74 mins); Filise back for Vaiomounga (temp 61 to 70 mins)

SCORERS *Tries*: Ma'afu, Lokotui, Vainikolo *Conversions:* Morath (2) *Penalty Goals*: Morath (4)

JAPAN: S J Webb; K Endo, A Tupuailai, R T Nicholas, H Onozawa; J A Arlidge, F Tanaka; H Hirashima, S Horie, K Hatakeyama, L M Thompson, T Kitagawa, I Taniguchi, T Kikutani (*captain*), M G Leitch

SUBSTITUTIONS: A Hiwasa for Tanaka (51 mins); S T Vatuvei for Taniguchi (51 mins); H Ono for Kitagawa (56 mins); N Fujita for Hatakeyama (67 mins)

SCORERS *Tries*: Hatakeyama, Leitch, Tupuailai *Penalty Goal*: Webb

REFEREE D J Pearson (England)

YELLOW CARDS J A Arlidge (30 mins); H Aulika (60 mins); T Lokotui (78 mins)

24 September, Eden Park, Auckland

NEW ZEALAND 37 (3G 1PG 1DG 2T) FRANCE 17 (2G 1PG)

NEW ZEALAND: I J A Dagg; C S Jane, C G Smith, M A Nonu, R D Kahui; D W Carter, P A T Weepu; T D Woodcock, K F Mealamu, O T Franks, B C Thorn, S L Whitelock, J Kaino, A J Thomson, R H McCaw (*captain*)

SUBSTITUTIONS: S Williams for Jane (33 mins); A K Hore for Mealamu (55 mins); A M Ellis for Weepu (55 mins); A J Williams for Whitelock (55 mins); C R Slade for Kahui (61 mins); B J Franks for O T Franks (68 mins); A F Boric for Thomson (71 mins); O T Franks back for B J Franks (temp 73 to 76 mins)

SCORERS *Tries*: Dagg (2), Thomson, Jane, S Williams *Conversions:* Carter (3) *Penalty Goal*: Carter *Dropped Goal:* Carter

FRANCE: D Traille; V Clerc, A Rougerie, M Mermoz, M Médard; M Parra, D Yachvili; J-B Poux, D Szarzewski, L Ducalcon, P Papé, L Nallet, T Dusautoir (*captain*), L Picamoles, J Bonnaire

SUBSTITUTIONS: I Harinordoquy for Picamoles (40 mins); C Heymans for Traille (40 mins); F Barcella for Ducalcon (40 mins); W Servat for Szarzewski (52 mins); J Pierre for Papé (64 mins); F Trinh-Duc for Parra (64 mins); F Estebanez for Rougerie (68 mins)

SCORERS *Tries*: Mermoz, Trinh-Duc *Conversions:* Yachvili (2) *Penalty Goal*: Yachvili

REFEREE A C Rolland (Ireland)

27 September, McLean Park, Napier

CANADA 23 (1G 2PG 2T) JAPAN 23 (2G 3PG)

CANADA: J G Pritchard; M C Evans, D T H van der Merwe, R J Smith, P W Mackenzie; A H B Monro, E G Fairhurst; H A W Buydens, P D Riordan (*captain*), J A Marshall, J L Sinclair, J N Cudmore, C O'Toole, A Carpenter, A Kleeberger

SUBSTITUTIONS: C A Trainor for Pritchard (temp 21 to 27 mins and 40 mins); G R O Hamilton for Riordan (59 mins); J A Kyne for O'Toole (63 mins); S Franklin for Marshall (67 mins); S T White for Fairhurst (70 mins); T N Hotson for Cudmore (72 mins)

SCORERS *Tries*: Van der Merwe, Mackenzie, Monro *Conversion:* Pritchard *Penalty Goals*: Monro (2)

JAPAN: S J Webb; K Endo, A Tupuailai, R T Nicholas, H Onozawa; J A Arlidge, F Tanaka; H Hirashima, S Horie, N Fujita, L M Thompson, T Kitagawa, S T Vatuvei, T Kikutani (*captain*), M G Leitch

SUBSTITUTIONS: B B Robins for Tupuailai (12 mins); K Hatakeyama for Fujita (24 mins); A Hiwasa for Tanaka (63 mins); T Taufa for Vatuvei (63 mins); H Ono for Kitagawa (63 mins); M C Williams for Webb (72 mins)

SCORERS *Tries*: Horie, Endo *Conversions:* Arlidge (2) *Penalty Goals*: Arlidge (3)

REFEREE J I Kaplan (South Africa)

1 October, Wellington Regional Stadium, Wellington

FRANCE 14 (3PG 1T) TONGA 19 (1G 4PG)

FRANCE: M Médard; V Clerc, A Rougerie, M Mermoz, A Palisson; M Parra, D Yachvili; J-B Poux, W Servat, L Ducalcon, P Papé, L Nallet, T Dusautoir (*captain*), R Lakafia, J Bonnaire

SUBSTITUTIONS: F Barcella for Poux (temp 6 to 19 mins) and for Ducalcon (40 mins); Ducalcon back for Poux (44 mins); D Szarzewski for Servat (50 mins); I Harinordoquy for Lakafia (50 mins); F Estebanez for Rougerie (58 mins); F Trinh-Duc for Parra (58 mins); J Pierre for Papé (66 mins); C Heymans for Palisson (75 mins)

SCORERS *Try*: Clerc *Penalty Goals*: Yachvili (3)

TONGA: V F Lilo; V Iongi, S V Piutau, A K Ma'ilei, S Hufanga; K S Morath, T Moa; S L Tonga'uiha, A A Lutui, K Pulu, T Lokotui, K P Hehea, S M Kalamafoni, V S Ma'afu, F Maka (*captain*)

SUBSTITUTIONS: S K Vahafolau for Maka (temp 10 to 23 mins and 40 mins); H Aulika for Pulu (40 mins); F K A Taumalolo for Tonga'uiha (47 mins); J M L Tuineau for Hehea (57 mins); L A H N Fatafehi for Ma'ilei (60 mins); T T Palu for Hufanga (72 mins)

SCORERS *Try*: Hufanga *Conversion:* Morath *Penalty Goals*: Morath (4)

REFEREE S R Walsh (Australia)

YELLOW CARDS S Hufanga (38 mins); F Estebanez (64 mins)

2 October, Wellington Regional Stadium, Wellington

NEW ZEALAND 79 (8G 1PG 4T)
CANADA 15 (1G 1PG 1T)

NEW ZEALAND: J M Muliaina; I J A Dagg, C G Smith, S Williams, Z R Guildford; C R Slade, Q J Cowan; T D Woodcock, A K Hore (*captain*), O T Franks, S L Whitelock, A J Williams, J Kaino, K J Read, V V J Vito

SUBSTITUTIONS: I Toeava for Dagg (47 mins); P A T Weepu for Muliaina (50 mins); A F Boric for Read (50 mins); B J Franks for O T Franks (55 mins); A M Ellis for Cowan (62 mins); B C Thorn for Slade (64 mins); O T Franks back for Woodcock (72 mins); K F Mealamu for Hore (77 mins)

SCORERS *Tries*: Guildford (4), Kaino (2), Vito (2), Dagg, Muliaina, Cowan, S Williams *Conversions:* Slade (4), Weepu (4) *Penalty Goal*: Slade

CANADA: M C Evans; C A Trainor, D T H van der Merwe, R J Smith, P W Mackenzie; A H B Monro, E G Fairhurst; H A W Buydens, P D Riordan (*captain*), J A Marshall, J L Sinclair, J N Cudmore, C O'Toole, A Carpenter, A Kleeberger

SUBSTITUTIONS: S T White for Van der Merwe (30 mins); G R O Hamilton for Riordan (47 mins); S Franklin for Marshall (52 mins); T N Hotson for Cudmore (61 mins); N S Hirayama for Fairhurst (62 mins); A A Tiedemann for Buydens (62 mins); N Dala for Evans (64 mins); Cudmore back for Kleeburger (72 mins)

SCORERS *Tries*: Trainor (2) *Conversion:* Monro *Penalty Goal*: Monro

REFEREE R Poite (France)

POOL A FINAL TABLE:

	P	W	D	L	PF	PA	TF	TA	BP	PTS
New Zealand	4	4	0	0	240	49	36	6	4	**20**
France	4	2	0	2	124	96	13	9	3	**11**
Tonga	4	2	0	2	80	98	7	13	1	**9**
Canada	4	1	1	2	82	168	9	20	0	**6**
Japan	4	0	1	3	69	184	8	25	0	**2**

P=Played; W=Won; D=Draw; L=Lost; PF=Points For; PA=Points Against; TF=Tries For; TA=Tries Against; BP=Bonus Points; PTS=Points

10 September, Rugby Park Stadium, Invercargill

SCOTLAND 34 (1G 4PG 3T)
ROMANIA 24 (1G 4PG 1T)

SCOTLAND: C D Paterson; M B Evans, J A Ansbro, S F Lamont, S C J Danielli; R J H Jackson, M R L Blair; A F Jacobsen, R W Ford, G D S Cross, R J Gray, A D Kellock (*captain*), K D R Brown, R J Vernon, J A Barclay

SUBSTITUTIONS: N J Hines for Gray (52 mins); D A Parks for Jackson (52 mins); R M Rennie for Barclay (61 mins); A G Dickinson for Jacobsen (61 mins); C P Cusiter for Blair (61 mins); S Lawson for Ford (67 mins)

SCORERS *Tries*: Danielli (2), Blair, Ansbro *Conversion:* Paterson *Penalty Goals*: Paterson (4)

ROMANIA: I Dumitras; M V Lemnaru, C M Gal, T I Dimofte, S E Ciuntu; M D Dumbrava, L M Sirbu; M A Lazar, M Tincu (*captain*), P Ion, V N Ursache, C C Petre, M Macovei, D Carpo, O Tonita

SUBSTITUTIONS: F Surugiu for Sirbu (51 mins); I Cazan for Dumbrava (51 mins); F A Vlaicu for Dumitras (58 mins); B Z Suman for Tincu (67 mins); S Florea for Ion (67 mins); S S Burcea for Macovei (76 mins); V Poparlan for Petre (79 mins)

SCORERS *Tries*: Lazar, Carpo *Conversion:* Dimofte *Penalty Goals*: Dumbrava (2), Dimofte (2)

REFEREE D J Pearson (England)

Martin Hunter/Getty Images

Simon Danielli's two late tries won the game for Scotland.

10 September, Otago Stadium, Dunedin

ARGENTINA 9 (3PG) ENGLAND 13 (1G 2PG)

ARGENTINA: M Rodriguez; G O Camacho, G-P Tiesi, S Fernández, H Agulla; F Contepomi (*captain*), N Vergallo; R Roncero, M E Ledesma, J G Figallo, M Carizza, P Albacete, J-M Leguizamón, J M Fernández-Lobbe, J A F Cabello

SUBSTITUTIONS: M T Bosch for Contepomi (26 mins); J J Imhoff for Tiesi (36 mins); A Creevy for Ledesma (55 mins); M A Scelzo for Roncero (temp 16 to 18 mins) and for Figallo (57 mins); A T Campos for Cabello (68 mins); Figallo back for Roncero (77 mins); M T Galarza for Leguizamón (78 mins)

SCORERS *Penalty Goals*: Rodriguez (2), Contepomi

ENGLAND: B J Foden; C J Ashton, E M Tuilagi, M J Tindall (*captain*), D A Armitage; J P Wilkinson, R E P Wigglesworth; A J Sheridan, S G Thompson, D R Cole, L P Deacon, C L Lawes, T R Croft, N J Easter, J A W Haskell

SUBSTITUTIONS: B R Youngs for Wigglesworth (49 mins); D M Hartley for Thompson (62 mins); M J H Stevens for Sheridan (62 mins); T P Palmer for Deacon (65 mins)

SCORERS *Try*: Youngs *Conversion:* Wilkinson *Penalty Goals*: Wilkinson (2)

REFEREE B J Lawrence (New Zealand)

YELLOW CARD D R Cole (34 mins)

14 September, Rugby Park Stadium, Invercargill

SCOTLAND 15 (4PG 1DG) GEORGIA 6 (2PG)

SCOTLAND: R P Lamont; M B Evans, N J de Luca, G A Morrison, S F Lamont; D A Parks, R G M Lawson (*captain*); A F Jacobsen, R W Ford, E A Murray, N J Hines, J L Hamilton, A K Strokosch, K D R Brown, R M Rennie

SUBSTITUTIONS: R J Gray for Hines (70 mins); C D Paterson for R P Lamont (70 mins)

SCORER *Penalty Goals*: Parks (4) *Dropped Goal:* Parks

GEORGIA: R Gigauri; A Todua, D Kacharava, T Zibzibadze, I Machkhaneli; M Kvirikashvili, I Abuseridze (*captain*); D Khinchagishvili, J Bregvadze, D Zirakashvili, L Datunashvili, V Maisuradze, S Sutiashvili, D Basilaia, M Gorgodze

SUBSTITUTIONS: G Chkhaidze for Maisuradze (49 mins); D Kubriashvili for Zirakashvili (55 mins); A Giorgadze for Bregvadze (64 mins); V Kolelishvili for Basilaia (64 mins); M Urjukashvili for Todua (66 mins)

SCORER *Penalty Goals*: Kvirikashvili (2)

REFEREE G Clancy (Ireland)

17 September, Rugby Park Stadium, Invercargill

ARGENTINA 43 (5G 1PG 1T)
ROMANIA 8 (1PG 1T)

ARGENTINA: L P Gonzalez Amorosino; G O Camacho, M T Bosch, M Rodriguez, H Agulla; S Fernández, N Vergallo; R Roncero, M E Ledesma, J G Figallo, M Carizza, P Albacete, J-M Leguizamón, J M Fernández-Lobbe (*captain*), A T Campos

SUBSTITUTIONS: A Creevy for Ledesma (40 mins); J J Imhoff for Camacho (49 mins); M A Scelzo for Roncero (57 mins); G Fessia for Leguizamón (57 mins); A Lalanne for Vergallo (65 mins); N Sanchez for Fernández (74 mins); M T Galarza for Campos (temp 73 to 76 mins) and for Albacete (78 mins)

SCORERS *Tries:* Fernández, Leguizamón, Figallo, Amorosino, Imhoff, Fessia *Conversions:* Rodriguez (5) *Penalty Goal*: Rodriguez

ROMANIA: I Dumitras; M V Lemnaru, C M Gal, C Gheara, I Cazan; T I Dimofte, F Suguriu; M A Lazar, M Tincu (*captain*), P Ion, V N Ursache, C C Petre, M Macovei, D Carpo, O Tonita

SUBSTITUTIONS: V Poparlan for Petre (47 mins); F A Vlaicu for Dumitras (47 mins); S Florea for Carpo (temp 53 to 63 mins) and for Ion (63 mins); V N Calafeteanu for Suguriu (67 mins); D G Ianus for Macovei (75 mins)

SCORERS *Try*: Cazan *Penalty Goal*: Dimofte

REFEREE S R Walsh (Australia)

YELLOW CARD M A Lazar (53 mins)

Mark Kolbe/Getty Images

Argentina scored six tries against Romania, including this one from Genaro Fessia.

18 September, Otago Stadium, Dunedin

ENGLAND 41 (4G 1PG 2T) GEORGIA 10 (1G 1PG)

ENGLAND: B J Foden; C J Ashton, E M Tuilagi, S E Hape, D A Armitage; T G A L Flood, B R Youngs; M J H Stevens, D M Hartley, D R Cole, S D Shaw, T P Palmer, T A Wood, J A W Haskell, L W Moody (*captain*)

SUBSTITUTIONS: T R Croft for Moody (57 mins); S G Thompson for Wood (temp 39 to 48 mins) and for Hartley (60 mins); A R Corbisiero for Cole (62 mins); M A Banahan for Tuilagi (67 mins); J P M Simpson for Youngs (67 mins); Cole back for Stevens (74 mins)

SCORERS *Tries*: Hape (2), Ashton (2), Armitage, Tuilagi *Conversions:* Flood (4) *Penalty Goal*: Flood

GEORGIA: R Gigauri; A Todua, D Kacharava, T Zibzibadze, I Machkhaneli; M Kvirikashvili, I Abuseridze (*captain*); D Khinchagishvili, J Bregvadze, D Kubriashvili, I Zedginidze, V Maisuradze, S Sutiashvili, D Basilaia, M Gorgodze

SUBSTITUTIONS: D Zirakashvili for Kubriashvili (22 mins); G Chkhaidze for Sutiashvili (30 mins); L Khmaladze for Machkhaneli (40 mins); G Shvelidze for Khinchagishvili (56 mins); G Berishvili for Basilaia (60 mins); B Samkharadze for Abuseridze (62 mins); L Datunashvili for Zedginidze (temp 6 to 15 mins) and for Todua (67 mins)

SCORERS *Try:* Basilaia *Conversion:* Kvirikashvili *Penalty Goal*: Kvirikashvili

REFEREE J I Kaplan (South Africa)

YELLOW CARD D M Hartley (39 mins)

24 September, Otago Stadium, Dunedin

ENGLAND 67 (7G 1PG 3T) ROMANIA 3 (1PG)

ENGLAND: B J Foden; C J Ashton, E M Tuilagi, M J Tindall, M J Cueto; J P Wilkinson, B R Youngs; A R Corbisiero, S G Thompson, D R Cole, L P Deacon, T P Palmer, T R Croft, J A W Haskell, L W Moody (*captain*)

SUBSTITUTIONS: D G Wilson for Cole (40 mins); T G A L Flood for Wilkinson (40 mins); L A Mears for Thompson (50 mins); D A Armitage for Foden (51 mins); Cole back for Corbisiero (57 mins); S D Shaw for Deacon (57 mins); R E P Wigglesworth for Youngs (61 mins); T A Wood for Moody (61 mins)

SCORERS *Tries*: Cueto (3), Ashton (3), Youngs, Foden, Tuilagi, Croft *Conversions:* Flood (4), Wilkinson (3) *Penalty Goal*: Wilkinson

ROMANIA: F A Vlaicu; S E Ciuntu, I Cazan, I Dumitras, A M Apostol; M D Dumbrava, L M Sirbu; N Nere, B Z Suman, S Florea, V Poparlan, C C Petre (*captain*), S S Burcea, O Tonita, C A Ratiu

SUBSTITUTIONS: C M Gal for Cazan (40 mins); V N Calafeteanu for Sirbu (41 mins); M Tincu for Suman (50 mins); M Macovei for Petre (51 mins); D G Ianus for Ratiu (59 mins); P Ion for Florea (61 mins); C M Nicolae for Vlaicu (71 mins)

SCORER *Penalty Goal*: Dumbrava

REFEREE R Poite (France)

25 September, Wellington Regional Stadium, Wellington

ARGENTINA 13 (1G 2PG) SCOTLAND 12 (2PG 2DG)

ARGENTINA: M Rodriguez; G O Camacho, M T Bosch, F Contepomi (*captain*), H Agulla; S Fernández, N Vergallo; R Roncero, M E Ledesma, J G Figallo, M Carizza, P Albacete, J-M Leguizamón, J M Fernández-Lobbe, J A F Cabello

SUBSTITUTIONS: G Fessia for Fernández-Lobbe (30 mins); M A Scelzo for Roncero (36 mins); L P Gonzalez Amorosino for Rodriguez (68 mins); A Creevy for Ledesma (73 mins)

SCORERS *Try:* Gonzalez Amorosino *Conversion:* Contepomi *Penalty Goals*: Contepomi (2)

SCOTLAND: C D Paterson; M B Evans, N J de Luca, G A Morrison, S F Lamont; R J H Jackson, R G M Lawson (*captain*); A F Jacobsen, R W Ford, G D S Cross, R J Gray, J L Hamilton, A K Strokosch, K D R Brown, J A Barclay

SUBSTITUTIONS: N J Hines for Gray (56 mins); A G Dickinson for Jacobsen (60 mins); M R L Blair for Lawson (60 mins); D A Parks for Jackson (68 mins); D W H Hall for Ford (68 mins); Jacobsen back for Cross (73 mins); R J Vernon for Brown (77 mins)

SCORERS *Penalty Goals*: Paterson, Jackson *Dropped Goals:* Jackson, Parks

REFEREE W Barnes (England)

28 September, Arena Manawatu, Palmerston North

GEORGIA 25 (1G 6PG) ROMANIA 9 (3PG)

GEORGIA: L Khmaladze; A Todua, D Kacharava, T Zibzibadze, R Gigauri; M Kvirikashvili, I Abuseridze (*captain*); D Khinchagishvili, J Bregvadze, D Zirakashvili, I Zedginidze, V Maisuradze, G Chkhaidze, D Basilaia, M Gorgodze

SUBSTITUTIONS: L Datunashvili for Zedginidze (66 mins); G Shvelidze for Bregvadze (66 mins); V Kakovin for Khinchagishvili (67 mins); I Chkhikvadze for Gigauri (71 mins); G Berishvili for Gorgodze (73 mins); B Samkharadze for Abuseridze (74 mins); M Urjukashvili for Kvirikashvili (74 mins)

SCORERS *Try:* Gorgodze *Conversion:* Kvirikashvili *Penalty Goals*: Kvirikashvili (5), Urjukashvili

ROMANIA: I Dumitras; M V Lemnaru, C M Gal, T I Dimofte, S E Ciuntu; M D Dumbrava, F Surugiu; M A Lazar, M Tincu (*captain*), P Ion, V N Ursache, C C Petre, M Macovei, D Carpo, O Tonita

SUBSTITUTIONS: C Gheara for Ciuntu (40 mins); F A Vlaicu for Dumitras (57 mins); S Florea for Ion (67 mins); V Poparlan for Petre (67 mins); D G Ianus for Tonita (67 mins); V N Calafeteanu for Dumbrava (67 mins)

SCORERS *Penalty Goals*: Dumbrava (2), Vlaicu

REFEREE D J Pearson (England)

1 October, Eden Park, Auckland

ENGLAND 16 (1G 2PG 1DG) SCOTLAND 12 (3PG 1DG)

ENGLAND: B J Foden; C J Ashton, E M Tuilagi, M J Tindall, D A Armitage; J P Wilkinson, B R Youngs; M J H Stevens, S G Thompson, D R Cole, L P Deacon, C L Lawes, T R Croft, J A W Haskell, L W Moody (*captain*)

SUBSTITUTIONS: T P Palmer for Lawes (56 mins); N J Easter for Moody (temp 52 to 62 mins) and for Haskell (62 mins); D M Hartley for Thompson (66 mins); T G A L Flood for Tindall (70 mins); A R Corbisiero for Stevens (71 mins); R E P Wigglesworth for Youngs (72 mins); M A Banahan for Wilkinson (74 mins)

SCORERS *Try*: Ashton *Conversion:* Flood *Penalty Goals*: Wilkinson (2) *Dropped Goal:* Wilkinson

SCOTLAND: C D Paterson; M B Evans, J A Ansbro, S F Lamont, S C J Danielli; R J H Jackson, M R L Blair; A F Jacobsen, R W Ford, E A Murray, R J Gray, A D Kellock (*captain*), A K Strokosch, R J Vernon, J A Barclay

SUBSTITUTIONS: D A Parks for Jackson (4 mins); N J de Luca for Evans (40 mins); N J Hines for Strokosch (62 mins); R M Rennie for Barclay (62 mins); A G Dickinson for Jacobsen (66 mins); C P Cusiter for Blair (70 mins)

SCORERS *Penalty Goals*: Paterson (2), Parks *Dropped Goal:* Parks

REFEREE C Joubert (South Africa)

2 October, Arena Manawatu, Palmerston North

ARGENTINA 25 (2G 2PG 1T) GEORGIA 7 (1G)

ARGENTINA: L P Gonzalez Amorosino; H Agulla, M T Bosch, F Contepomi (*captain*), J J Imhoff; S Fernández, N Vergallo; M I Ayerza, M E Ledesma, J G Figallo, M T Galarza, P Albacete, J M Leguizamón, L V Senatore, J A F Cabello

SUBSTITUTIONS: A Creevy for Ledesma (62 mins); M A Scelzo for Figallo (64 mins); G Fessia for Senatore (64 mins); M Rodriguez for Agulla (65 mins); A Lalanne for Vergallo (69 mins); T Vallejos for Galarza (70 mins); A O Gosio for Contepomi (71 mins)

SCORERS *Tries:* Imhoff, Contepomi, Gosio *Conversions:* Contepomi, Bosch *Penalty Goals*: Contepomi (2)

GEORGIA: M Urjukashvili; A Todua, D Kacharava, T Zibzibadze, L Gugava; L Khmaladze, I Abuseridze (*captain*); V Kakovin, A Giorgadze, D Kubriashvili, L Datunashvili, V Maisuradze, G Chkhaidze, M Gorgodze, V Kolelishvili

SUBSTITUTIONS: G Shvelidze for Kakovin (40 mins); M Kvirikashvili for Urjukashvili (62 mins); Kakovin back for Kubriashvili (62 mins); B Samkharadze for Abuseridze (67 mins); I Zedginidze for Datunashvili (69 mins); G Nemsadze for Maisuradze (69 mins); J Bregvadze for Giorgadze (69 mins); L Malaguradze for Gugava (70 mins); Giorgadze back for Bregvadze (70 mins)

SCORERS *Try:* Khmaladze *Conversion:* Urjukashvili

REFEREE A C Rolland (Ireland)

POOL B FINAL TABLE:

	P	W	D	L	PF	PA	TF	TA	BP	PTS
England	4	4	0	0	137	34	18	1	2	**18**
Argentina	4	3	0	1	90	40	10	3	2	**14**
Scotland	4	2	0	2	73	59	4	4	3	**11**
Georgia	4	1	0	3	48	90	3	9	0	**4**
Romania	4	0	0	4	44	169	3	21	0	**0**

P=Played; W=Won; D=Draw; L=Lost; PF=Points For; PA=Points Against; TF=Tries For; TA=Tries Against; BP=Bonus Points; PTS=Points

POOL C

11 September, North Harbour Stadium, Auckland

AUSTRALIA 32 (3G 2PG 1T) ITALY 6 (2PG)

AUSTRALIA: K J Beale; A P Ashley-Cooper, A S Fainga'a, P J McCabe, D A N Ioane; Q S Cooper, S W Genia; S M Kepu, S T Moore, B E Alexander, D J Vickerman, J E Horwill (*captain*), R D Elsom, U R Samo, D W Pocock

SUBSTITUTIONS: J D O'Connor for Fainga'a (46 mins); B J McCalman for Pocock (59 mins); R A Simmons for Vickerman (59 mins); S U T Polota-Nau for Moore (60 mins); L Burgess for Genia (60 mins); J A Slipper for Alexander (65 mins); S Higginbotham for Elsom (69 mins); Moore back for Polota-Nau (temp 73 to 77 mins)

SCORERS *Tries*: Alexander, Ashley-Cooper, O'Connor, Ioane *Conversions:* O'Connor (3) *Penalty Goals*: Cooper (2)

ITALY: A Masi; T Benvenuti, G-J Canale, G Garcia, Mirco Bergamasco; L Orquera, F Semenzato; A Lo Cicero, L Ghiraldini, M-L Castrogiovanni, C-A del Fava, C van Zyl, A Zanni, S Parisse (*captain*), R Barbieri

SUBSTITUTIONS: P Derbyshire for Barbieri (51 mins); M Bortolami for Del Fava (59 mins); L McLean for Garcia (60 mins); L Cittadini for Lo Cicero (67 mins); E Gori for Semenzato (69 mins); R Bocchino for Orquera (73 mins); Lo Cicero back for Castrogiovanni (73 mins)

SCORER *Penalty Goals*: Bergamasco (2)

REFEREE A C Rolland (Ireland)

11 September, Stadium Taranaki, New Plymouth

IRELAND 22 (2G 1PG 1T) UNITED STATES 10 (1G 1PG)

IRELAND: G E A Murphy; T J Bowe, B G O'Driscoll (*captain*), G W D'Arcy, K G Earls; J J Sexton, C Murray; T G Court, R D Best, M R Ross, D P O'Callaghan, P J O'Connell, S Ferris, J P R Heaslip, S Jennings

SUBSTITUTIONS: R J R O'Gara for Sexton (50 mins); E G Reddan for Murray (50 mins); D P Leamy for Jennings (60 mins); J P Flannery for Best (60 mins); T D Buckley for Court (64 mins); A D Trimble for Murphy (66 mins)

SCORERS *Tries*: Bowe (2), Best *Conversions:* Sexton, O'Gara *Penalty Goal*: Sexton

UNITED STATES: B H Scully; T Ngwenya, P L Emerick, A Suniula, J Paterson; R P J Suniula, M Z Petri; M S MacDonald, P P Thiel, S T Pittman, J L van der Giessen, H Smith, L E Stanfill, N S Johnson, T S Clever (*captain*)

SUBSTITUTIONS: V L Malifa for R P J Suniula (58 mins); M J Moeakiola for MacDonald (62 mins); T D Usasz for Petri (66 mins); C M Biller for Thiel (67 mins)

SCORERS *Try*: Emerick *Conversion:* Paterson *Penalty Goal*: Paterson

REFEREE C Joubert (South Africa)

15 September, Stadium Taranaki, New Plymouth

RUSSIA 6 (2PG) UNITED STATES 13 (1G 2PG)

RUSSIA: I Klyuchnikov; V Ostrouchko, K Rachkov, A Makovetskiy, V Artemyev; Y Kushnarev, A Shakirov; S Popov, V Korshunov (*captain*), I Prishchepenko, A Voytov, D Antonov, A Fatakhov, V Grachev, A Garbuzov

SUBSTITUTIONS: V Gresev for Fatakhov (58 mins); A Byrnes for Antonov (59 mins); V Botvinnikov for Popov (72 mins)

SCORERS *Penalty Goals*: Kushnarev, Rachkov

UNITED STATES: C T Wyles; T Ngwenya, P L Emerick, A Suniula, J Paterson; R P J Suniula, M Z Petri; M S MacDonald, C M Biller, M J Moeakiola, J L van der Giessen, H Smith, L E Stanfill, N S Johnson, T S Clever (*captain*)

SUBSTITUTIONS: B H Scully for Paterson (37 mins); S C LaValla for Johnson (66 mins); T D Usasz for Petri (67 mins); S T Pittman for Moeakiola (temp 39 to 40 mins)

SCORERS *Try*: Petri *Conversion:* Wyles *Penalty Goals*: Wyles (2)

REFEREE D J Pearson (England)

17 September, Eden Park, Auckland

AUSTRALIA 6 (2PG) IRELAND 15 (4PG 1DG)

AUSTRALIA: K J Beale; J D O'Connor, A S Fainga'a, P J McCabe, A P Ashley-Cooper; Q S Cooper, S W Genia; S M Kepu, S U T Polota-Nau, B E Alexander, D J Vickerman, J E Horwill (*captain*), R D Elsom, U R Samo, B J McCalman

SUBSTITUTIONS: J A Slipper for Alexander (62 mins); R A Simmons for Vickerman (62 mins); W L Palu for Elsom (72 mins); S Higginbotham for Samo (73 mins); D A Mitchell for Fainga'a (73 mins)

SCORER *Penalty Goals*: O'Connor (2)

IRELAND: R D J Kearney; T J Bowe, B G O'Driscoll (*captain*), G W D'Arcy, K G Earls; J J Sexton, E G Reddan; C E Healy, R D Best, M R Ross, D P O'Callaghan, P J O'Connell, S Ferris, J P R Heaslip, S K O'Brien

SUBSTITUTIONS: R J R O'Gara for D'Arcy (49 mins); C Murray for Reddan (57 mins); A D Trimble for O'Driscoll (temp 59 to 62 mins) and for Kearney (74 mins); T G Court for Ross (76 mins)

SCORERS *Penalty Goals*: Sexton (2), O'Gara (2) *Dropped Goal:* Sexton

REFEREE B J Lawrence (New Zealand)

20 September, Trafalgar Park, Nelson

ITALY 53 (4G 5T) RUSSIA 17 (1G 2T)

ITALY: A Masi; G Toniolatti, T Benvenuti, M Pratichetti, L McLean; R Bocchino, E Gori; S Perugini, F Ongaro, L Cittadini, Q Geldenhuys, M Bortolami, P Derbyshire, S Parisse (*captain*), Mauro Bergamasco

SUBSTITUTIONS: T D'Apice for Bergamasco (temp 35 to 45 mins) and for Ongaro (45 mins); M-L Castrogiovanni for Perugini (46 mins); C van Zyl for Bortolami (46 mins); A Zanni for Parisse (56 mins); P Canavosio for Gori (56 mins); A Sgarbi for Masi (59 mins); G-J Canale for Bocchino (72 mins)

SCORERS *Tries:* Toniolatti (2), Benvenuti (2), Parisse, penalty try, Gori, McLean, Zanni *Conversions:* Bocchino (4)

RUSSIA: I Klyuchnikov; V Ostrouchko, A Kuzin, A Makovetskiy, V Artemyev; K Rachkov, A Shakirov; V Botvinnikov, V Korshunov (*captain*), I Prishchepenko, A Voytov, A Byrnes, V Grachev, V Gresev, A Garbuzov

SUBSTITUTIONS: A Yanyushkin for Shakirov (27 mins); Y Kushnarev for Klyuchnikov (32 mins); A Khrokin for Botvinnikov (53 mins); A Fatakhov for Grachev (57 mins); V Tsnobiladze for Korshunov (60 mins); D Antonov for Byrnes (65 mins); M Sidorov for Garbuzov (69 mins); Botvinnikov back for Prishchepenko (76 mins)

SCORERS *Tries*: Yanyushkin, Ostrouchko, Makovetskiy *Conversion:* Rachkov

REFEREE W Barnes (England)

YELLOW CARD F Ongaro (32 mins)

23 September, Wellington Regional Stadium, Wellington

AUSTRALIA 67 (6G 5T) UNITED STATES 5 (1T)

AUSTRALIA: K J Beale; A P Ashley-Cooper, A S Fainga'a, R G Horne, D A Mitchell; Q S Cooper, S W Genia (*captain*); J A Slipper, S U T Polota-Nau, B E Alexander, R A Simmons, N C Sharpe, R D Elsom, W L Palu, B J McCalman

SUBSTITUTIONS: B S Barnes for Beale (38 mins); U R Samo for Elsom (46 mins); P J McCabe for Horne (47 mins); L Burgess for Genia (49 mins); S M Kepu for Alexander (49 mins); D J Vickerman for Palu (53 mins); S T Moore for McCabe (65 mins)

SCORERS *Tries*: Ashley-Cooper (3), Fainga'a (2), Horne, Elsom, Beale, Mitchell, McCabe, Samo *Conversions:* Barnes (4), Cooper (2)

UNITED STATES: B H Scully; C C Hawley, T V Enosa, L Sifa, K Swiryn; V L Malifa, T D Usasz (*captain*); S T Pittman, P P Thiel, E C Fry, S C LaValla, H Smith, J I Basauri, J R Gagiano, P J Danahy

SUBSTITUTIONS: L E Stanfill for Smith (60 mins); M Z Petri for Usasz (67 mins); B R McClenahan for Thiel (71 mins); C T Wyles for Enosa (72 mins); N S Johnson for Danahy (74 mins)

SCORER *Try*: Gagiano

REFEREE N Owens (Wales)

YELLOW CARD B H Scully (73 mins)

25 September, Rotorua International Stadium, Rotorua

IRELAND 62 (7G 1PG 2T) RUSSIA 12 (1G 1T)

IRELAND: R D J Kearney; F L McFadden, K G Earls, P R Wallace, A D Trimble; R J R O'Gara, I J Boss; C E Healy, S M Cronin, T D Buckley, D P O'Callaghan, L F M Cullen (*captain*), D C Ryan, J P R Heaslip, S K O'Brien

SUBSTITUTIONS: D P Leamy for O'Callaghan (45 mins); G E A Murphy for Earls (49 mins); M R Ross for Healy (49 mins); S Jennings for O'Brien (56 mins); J J Sexton for O'Gara (66 mins); E G Reddan for Boss (66 mins)

SCORERS *Tries:* Earls (2), McFadden, O'Brien, Boss, Trimble, Kearney, Jennings, Buckley *Conversions:*O'Gara (6), Sexton *Penalty Goal*: O'Gara

RUSSIA: V Artemyev; V Ostrouchko, A Kuzin, S Trishin, D Simplikevich; K Rachkov, A Yanyushkin (*captain*); S Popov, V Tsnobiladze, A Khrokin, D Antonov, A Byrnes, A Fatakhov, V Gresev, A Garbuzov

SUBSTITUTIONS: M Sidorov for Garbuzov (45 mins); A Voytov for Antonov (49 mins); I Prishchepenko for Khrokin (49 mins); M Babaev for Ostrouchko (temp 67 to 70 mins) and for Trishin (70 mins); A Bykanov for Yanyushkin (73 mins); A Travkin for Popov (73 mins); E Matveev for Sidorov (temp 49 to 52 mins) and for Tsnobiladze (73 mins)

SCORERS *Tries*: Artemyev, Simplikevich *Conversion:* Rachkov

REFEREE C Joubert (South Africa)

YELLOW CARD K Rachkov (7 mins)

27 September, Trafalgar Park, Nelson

ITALY 27 (2G 1PG 2T) UNITED STATES 10 (1G 1PG)

ITALY: L McLean; T Benvenuti, G-J Canale, G Garcia, Mirco Bergamasco; L Orquera, F Semenzato; S Perugini, L Ghiraldini, M-L Castrogiovanni, Q Geldenhuys, C van Zyl, A Zanni, S Parisse (*captain*), Mauro Bergamasco

SUBSTITUTIONS: A Lo Cicero for Perugini (50 mins); G Toniolatti for Benvenuti (53 mins); E Gori for Semenzato (67 mins); R Bocchino for Orquera (67 mins); P Derbyshire for Mirco Bergamasco (70 mins); Perugini back for Castrogiovanni (71 mins); F Ongaro for Ghiraldini (72 mins)

SCORERS *Tries:* Parisse, Orquera, Castrogiovanni, penalty try *Conversions:* Mirco Bergamasco (2) *Penalty Goal*: Mirco Bergamasco

UNITED STATES: C T Wyles; T Ngwenya, P L Emerick, A Suniula, J Paterson; R P J Suniula, M Z Petri; M S MacDonald, C M Biller, M J Moeakiola, J L van der Giessen, H Smith, L E Stanfill, N S Johnson, T S Clever (*captain*)

SUBSTITUTIONS: P P Thiel for Biller (28 mins); B H Scully for A Suniula (45 mins); S T Pittman for Moeakiola (temp 7 to 13 mins and 55 mins);T D Usasz for Petri (63 mins); S C LaValla for Johnson (68 mins); V L Malifa for R P J Suniula (71 mins)

SCORER *Try*: Wyles *Conversion:* Wyles *Penalty Goal*: Wyles

REFEREE G Clancy (Ireland)

YELLOW CARD L E Stanfill (58 mins)

Warren Little/Getty Images

Italy's bonus-point win over the USA, which included a try for Martin Castrogiovanni, guaranteed them qualification for 2015.

1 October, Trafalgar Park, Nelson

AUSTRALIA 68 (9G 1T) RUSSIA 22 (2G 1DG 1T)

AUSTRALIA: J D O'Connor; U R Samo, A P Ashley-Cooper, B S Barnes, D A Mitchell; Q S Cooper, L Burgess; J A Slipper, S T Moore, S M Kepu, J E Horwill (*captain*), N C Sharpe, S Higginbotham, B J McCalman, D W Pocock

SUBSTITUTIONS: R S L Ma'afu for Kepu (30 mins); R A Simmons for Horwill (40 mins); R D Elsom for Pocock (40 mins); S M Fainga'a for Moore (40 mins); N J Phipps for Mitchell (53 mins); Kepu back for Slipper (69 mins)

SCORERS *Tries:* Barnes (2), Mitchell (2), Pocock (2), McCalman, Moore, Ashley-Cooper, Ma'afu *Conversions*: O'Connor (9)

RUSSIA: V Artemyev; V Ostrouchko, A Kuzin, A Makovetskiy, D Simplikevich; Y Kushnarev, A Yanyushkin; S Popov, V Korshunov (*captain*), I Prishchepenko, A Voytov, A Byrnes, A Fatakhov, V Gresev, V Grachev

SUBSTITUTIONS: K Rachkov for Kushnarev (40 mins); A Garbuzov for Grachev (50 mins); A Travkin for Prishchepenko (59 mins); M Babaev for Kuzin (59 mins); A Shakirov for Yanyushkin (63 mins); V Botvinnikov for Popov (65 mins); E Matveev for Fatakhov (72 mins)

SCORERS *Tries*: Ostrouchko, Simplikevich, Rachkov *Conversions:* Rachkov (2) *Dropped Goal:* Rachkov

REFEREE B J Lawrence (New Zealand)

2 October, Otago Stadium, Dunedin

IRELAND 36 (3G 5PG) ITALY 6 (2PG)

IRELAND: R D J Kearney; T J Bowe, B G O'Driscoll (*captain*), G W D'Arcy, K G Earls; R J R O'Gara, C Murray; C E Healy, R D Best, M R Ross, D P O'Callaghan, P J O'Connell, S Ferris, J P R Heaslip, S K O'Brien

SUBSTITUTIONS: S M Cronin for Best (53 mins); D C Ryan for O'Connell (58 mins); J J Sexton for O'Gara (66 mins); T G Court for Healy (73 mins); D P Leamy for Ferris (73 mins); E G Reddan for Murray (73 mins); A D Trimble for O'Driscoll (73 mins)

SCORERS *Tries:* Earls (2), O'Driscoll *Conversions:* O'Gara (2), Sexton *Penalty Goals*: O'Gara (4), Sexton

ITALY: A Masi; T Benvenuti, G-J Canale, G Garcia, Mirco Bergamasco; L Orquera, F Semenzato; S Perugini, L Ghiraldini, M-L Castrogiovanni, Q Geldenhuys, C van Zyl, A Zanni, S Parisse (*captain*), Mauro Bergamasco

SUBSTITUTIONS: A Lo Cicero for Castrogiovanni (34 mins); R Bocchino for Orquera (40 mins); P Derbyshire for Mauro Bergamasco (48 mins); E Gori for Semenzato (56 mins); M Bortolami for Van Zyl (60 mins); F Ongaro for Ghiraldini (60 mins); L McLean for Parisse (76 mins)

SCORER *Penalty Goals*: Mirco Bergamasco (2)

REFEREE J I Kaplan (South Africa)

POOL C FINAL TABLE:

	P	W	D	L	PF	PA	TF	TA	BP	PTS
Ireland	4	4	0	0	135	34	15	3	1	**17**
Australia	4	3	0	1	173	48	25	4	3	**15**
Italy	4	2	0	2	92	95	13	11	2	**10**
USA	4	1	0	3	38	122	4	18	0	**4**
Russia	4	0	0	4	57	196	8	29	1	**1**

P=Played; W=Won; D=Draw; L=Lost; PF=Points For; PA=Points Against; TF=Tries For; TA=Tries Against; BP=Bonus Points; PTS=Points

POOL D

10 September, Rotorua International Stadium, Rotorua

FIJI 49 (5G 3PG 1T) NAMIBIA 25 (2PG 3DG 2T)

FIJI: K Murimurivalu; V Goneva, G V Lovobalavu, S Baikeinuku, N V Nalaga; W S Luveniyali, N S K Ranuku; G D C Ma'afu, V Veikoso, D T Manu (*captain*), L Nakarawa, R W G Lewaravu, D M Waqaniburotu, N E Talei, R M M Ravulo

SUBSTITUTIONS: S K Koto for Veikoso (50 mins); A J Vulivuli for Lovobalavu (53 mins); A Qera for Talei (55 mins); V T Buatava for Ranuke (58 mins); W Nailago for Ma'afu (62 mins); S Kalou for Lewaravu (74 mins); I L R Keresoni for Goneva (78 mins)

SCORERS *Tries*: Goneva (4), Nakarawa, Nalaga *Conversions:* Baikeinuku (5) *Penalty Goals*: Baikeinuku (3)

NAMIBIA: C A Botha; H D P Dames, D van Wyk, W P van Zyl, C Marais; T A W Kotze, E A Jantjies; J H Redelinghuys, H Horn, R Larson, H van W Koll, N Esterhuyse, T du Plessis, J Nieuwenhuis, J Burger (*captain*)

SUBSTITUTIONS: R Kitshoff for Du Plessis (47 mins); E B O'Callaghan for Horn (53 mins); P-J van Lill for Esterhuyse (53 mins); D P de la Harpe for Marais (67 mins); R C A de la Harpe for Jantjies (67 mins); L P Winkler for Kotze (78 mins)

SCORERS *Tries*: Koll, Botha *Penalty Goals*: Kotze (2) *Dropped Goals*: Kotze (3)

REFEREE N Owens (Wales)

11 September, Wellington Regional Stadium, Wellington

SOUTH AFRICA 17 (2G 1PG) WALES 16 (1G 3PG)

SOUTH AFRICA: F P L Steyn; J-P R Pietersen, J Fourie, J de Villiers, B G Habana; M Steyn, P F du Preez; T Mtawarira, J W Smit (*captain*), J N du Plessis, D J Rossouw, V Matfield, S W P Burger, P J Spies, H W Brüssow

SUBSTITUTIONS: A D James for De Villiers (24 mins); G J Muller for Matfield (44 mins); G G Steenkamp for Mtawarira (55 mins); B W du Plessis for Smit (56 mins); W S Alberts for Spies (56 mins); F Hougaard for Habana (60 mins)

SCORERS *Tries*: F P L Steyn, Hougaard *Conversions:* M Steyn (2) *Penalty Goal:* M Steyn

WALES: J W Hook; G P North, J J V Davies, J H Roberts, S M Williams; R Priestland, W M Phillips; P James, H Bennett, A R Jones, L C Charteris, A-W Jones, D J Lydiate, T T Faletau, S K Warburton (*captain*)

SUBSTITUTION: B S Davies for A-W Jones (65 mins)

SCORERS *Try:* Faletau *Conversion*: Hook *Penalty Goals*: Hook (3)

REFEREE W Barnes (England)

14 September, Rotorua International Stadium, Rotorua

SAMOA 49 (5G 3PG 1T) NAMIBIA 12 (1G 1T)

SAMOA: P B Williams; S Tagicakibau, G T Pisi, S J Mapusua, A T Tuilagi; T Pisi, K F Fotuali'i; S Taulafo, M M Schwalger (*captain*), A I Perenise, D A Leo, K G Thompson, T Tuifua, G J Stowers, M Fa'asavalu

SUBSTITUTIONS: T Lavea for T Pisi (27 mins); O Treviranus for Tuifu'a (28 mins); E Fuimaono Sapolu for Mapusua (50 mins); A J Poluleuligaga for Fotuali'i (50 mins); C A I Johnston for Perenise (52 mins); T T Paulo for Schwalger (55 mins); I Tekori for Thompson (61 mins)

SCORERS *Tries*: Tuilagi (3), Fotuali'i, Williams, penalty try *Conversions:* Williams (3), T Pisi (2) *Penalty Goals*: T Pisi (2), Williams

NAMIBIA: C A Botha; H D P Dames, D van Wyk, W P van Zyl, L P Winkler; T A W Kotze, E A Jantjies; J H Redelinghuys, H Horn, R Larson, H van W Koll, H H Franken, R Kitshoff, P-J van Lill, J Burger (*captain*)

SUBSTITUTIONS: N Esterhuyse for Franken (50 mins); E B O'Callaghan for Horn (59 mins); J A du Toit for Redelinghuys (59 mins); R E van Neel for Esterhuyse (temp 55 to 66 mins) and for Van Lill (66 mins); Redelinghuys back for Larson (74 mins); D P de la Harpe for Van Wyk (temp 50 to 55 mins)

SCORERS *Tries*: Van Wyk, Kotze *Conversion*: Kotze

REFEREE R Poite (France)

YELLOW CARDS P B Williams (39 mins); R Kitshoff (65 mins)

17 September, Wellington Regional Stadium, Wellington

SOUTH AFRICA 49 (5G 3PG 1T) FIJI 3 (1PG)

SOUTH AFRICA: P Lambie; O M Ndungane, J Fourie, F P L Steyn, J-P R Pietersen; M Steyn, P F du Preez; G G Steenkamp, J W Smit (*captain*), J N du Plessis, J P Botha, D J Rossouw, S W P Burger, P J Spies, H W Brüssow

SUBSTITUTIONS: W S Alberts for Botha (40 mins); F Hougaard for Ndungane (53 mins); B W du Plessis for Smit (53 mins); T Mtawarira for Steenkamp (64 mins); R Pienaar for Du Preez (70 mins); J L de Jongh for Fourie (70 mins); Smit back for J N du Plessis (79 mins); L-F P Louw for Alberts (temp 46 to 55 mins)

SCORERS *Tries*: Steenkamp, Fourie, F P L Steyn, M Steyn, Mtawarira, Rossouw *Conversions:* M Steyn (5) *Penalty Goals:* M Steyn (2), F P L Steyn

FIJI: K Murimurivalu; V Goneva, G V Lovobalavu, S Baikeinuku, N V Nalaga; W S Luveniyali, N S K Ranuku; G D C Ma'afu, S K Koto, D T Manu (*captain*), L Nakarawa, R W G Lewaravu, D M Waqaniburotu, M S Matadigo, A Qera

SUBSTITUTIONS: S D Koyamaibole for Matadigo (49 mins); V T Buatava for Ranuku (53 mins); T D Tuapati for Koto (64 mins); N T Little for Luveniyali (64 mins); W Nailogo for Manu (70 mins); N E Talei for Lewaravu (73 mins); R S Fatiaki for Baikeinuku (73 mins)

SCORER *Penalty Goal*: Baikeinuku

REFEREE R Poite (France)

18 September, Waikato Stadium, Hamilton

WALES 17 (4PG 1T) SAMOA 10 (1G 1PG)

WALES: J W Hook; G P North, J J V Davies, J H Roberts, S M Williams; R Priestland, W M Phillips; P James, H Bennett, A R Jones, L C Charteris, A-W Jones, D J Lydiate, T T Faletau, S K Warburton (*captain*)

SUBSTITUTIONS: A T Powell for Lydiate (9 mins); S L Halfpenny for Hook (40 mins); L B Burns for Bennett (62 mins); G D Jenkins for James (62 mins); B S Davies for A-W Jones (68 mins)

SCORERS *Try:* S M Williams *Penalty Goals*: Hook (2), Priestland (2)

SAMOA: P B Williams; S Tagicakibau, G T Pisi, S J Mapusua, A T Tuilagi; T Lavea, K F Fotuali'i; S Taulafo, M M Schwalger (*captain*), A I Perenise, D A Leo, K G Thompson, O Treviranus, G J Stowers, M Fa'asavalu

SUBSTITUTIONS: J So'oialo for Tagicakibau (55 mins); I Tekori for Leo (68 mins); J I Sua for Lavea (68 mins); E Fuimaono Sapolu for Mapusua (69 mins); C A I Johnston for Perenise (69 mins); T T Paulo for Schwalger (72 mins); M Salavea for Treviranus (76 mins)

SCORERS *Try*: Perenise *Conversion:* Williams *Penalty Goal*: Williams

REFEREE A C Rolland (Ireland)

22 September, North Harbour Stadium, Auckland

SOUTH AFRICA 87 (12G 1PG) NAMIBIA 0

SOUTH AFRICA: P Lambie; G G Aplon, J Fourie, F P L Steyn, B G Habana; M Steyn, F Hougaard; G G Steenkamp, J W Smit (*captain*), C J van der Linde, J P Botha, D J Rossouw, W S Alberts, P J Spies, S W P Burger

SUBSTITUTIONS: L-F P Louw for Burger (temp 26 to 30 mins) and for Botha (49 mins); M C Ralepelle for Van der Linde (49 mins); P F du Preez for Habana (61 mins); J L de Jongh for F P L Steyn (61 mins); T Mtawarira for Steenkamp (61 mins); R Pienaar for M Steyn (61 mins); H W Brüssow for Spies (78 mins)

SCORERS *Tries*: Aplon (2), Hougaard (2), De Jongh (2), Habana, penalty try, Fourie, F P L Steyn, M Steyn, Rossouw *Conversions:* M Steyn (6), Pienaar (6) *Penalty Goal:* M Steyn

NAMIBIA: C A Botha; H D P Dames, D van Wyk, W P van Zyl, J H Bock; T A W Kotze, E A Jantjies; J H Redelinghuys, E B O'Callaghan, M Visser, H van W Koll, N Esterhuyse, T du Plessis, J Nieuwenhuis, J Burger (*captain*)

SUBSTITUTIONS: J A du Toit for Visser (39 mins); H Horn for O'Callaghan (42 mins); C Marais for Bock (45 mins); P-J van Lill for Koll (53 mins); R Kitshoff for Nieuwenhuis (54 mins); D P de la Harpe for Dames (65 mins); R C A de la Harpe for Jantjies (68 mins)

REFEREE G Clancy (Ireland)

25 September, Eden Park, Auckland

FIJI 7 (1G) SAMOA 27 (1G 4PG 1DG 1T)

FIJI: K Murimurivalu; V Goneva, G V Lovobalavu, S Baikeinuku, N V Nalaga; N T Little, N S K Ranuku; G D C Ma'afu, S K Koto, D T Manu (*captain*), S Kalou, L Nakarawa, N E Talei, S D Koyamaibole, R M M Ravulo

SUBSTITUTIONS: A Qera for Ravulo (55 mins); W S Luveniyali for Little (57 mins); V T Buatava for Ranuku (60 mins); A J Vulivali for Baikeinuku (63 mins); R Nasiga for Kalou (64 mins); S Somoca for Manu (68 mins); T D Tuapati for Luveniyali (74 mins)

SCORERS *Try*: Talei *Conversion:* Luveniyali

SAMOA: P B Williams; S Tagicakibau, G T Pisi, S J Mapusua, A T Tuilagi; T Pisi, K F Fotuali'i; S Taulafo, M M Schwalger (*captain*), C A I Johnston, D A Leo, K G Thompson, T Tuifua, G J Stowers, M Fa'asavalu

SUBSTITUTIONS: M Salavea for Fa'asavalu (40 mins); E Fuimaono Sapolu for G T Pisi (52 mins); A I Perenise for Johnston for (52 mins); F L Levi for Thompson (63 mins); J I Sua for T Pisi (63 mins); T T Paulo for Schwalger (65 mins); Johnston back for Taulafo (70 mins); Schwalger back for Paulo (74 mins)

SCORERS *Tries*: Fotouali'i, Stowers *Conversion:* Williams *Penalty Goal*: T Pisi (4) *Dropped Goal:* T Pisi

REFEREE B J Lawrence (New Zealand)

26 September, Stadium Taranaki, New Plymouth

WALES 81 (9G 1PG 3T) NAMIBIA 7 (1G)

WALES: L M Byrne; S L Halfpenny, J J V Davies, M S Williams, A G Brew; S M Jones, T D Knoyle; G D Jenkins, L B Burns, C Mitchell, B S Davies, A-W Jones, R P Jones, T T Faletau, S K Warburton (*captain*)

SUBSTITUTIONS: A T Powell for Warburton (48 mins); G P North for Brew (55 mins); L C Charteris for Faletau (56 mins); L D Williams for Knoyle (57 mins); K J Owens for Burns (61 mins); R J Bevington for Jenkins (61 mins); R Priestland for S M Jones (63 mins)

SCORERS *Tries:* M S Williams (3), North (2), Brew, Faletau, Jenkins, J J V Davies, L D Williams, Byrne, A-W Jones *Conversions:* S M Jones (6), Priestland (3) *Penalty Goal*: S M Jones

NAMIBIA: C A Botha; D van Wyk, W P van Zyl, D P de la Harpe, H D P Dames; T A W Kotze, E A Jantjies; J H Redelinghuys, H Horn, J A du Toit, H van W Koll, N Esterhuyse, T du Plessis, J Nieuwenhuis, J Burger (*captain*)

SUBSTITUTIONS: R Larson for Redelinghuys (20 mins); D G Philander for D P de la Harpe (32 mins); T C Losper for Dames (56 mins); U Kazombiaze for Koll (64 mins); E B O'Callaghan for Horn (64 mins); R C A de la Harpe for Kotze (64 mins); R Kitshoff for Du Plessis (71 mins); J Redelinghuys back for Nieuwenhuis (temp 58 to 68 mins)

SCORERS *Try*: Koll *Conversion*: Kotze

REFEREE S R Walsh (Australia)

YELLOW CARD R Larson (58 mins)

30 September, North Harbour Stadium, Auckland

SOUTH AFRICA 13 (1G 2PG) SAMOA 5 (1T)

SOUTH AFRICA: P Lambie; J-P R Pietersen, J Fourie, F P L Steyn, B G Habana; M Steyn, P F du Preez; T Mtawarira, B W du Plessis, J N du Plessis, D J Rossouw, V Matfield (*captain*), S W P Burger, P J Spies, H W Brüssow

SUBSTITUTIONS: F Hougaard for Habana (46 mins); J de Villiers for Hougaard (50 mins); G G Steenkamp for Mtawarira (61 mins); W S Alberts for Rossouw (temp 49 to 54 mins) and for Spies (61 mins); J W Smit for B W du Plessis (68 mins); B W du Plessis back for Rossouw (73 mins)

SCORERS *Try*: Habana *Conversion:* M Steyn *Penalty Goals:* F P L Steyn, M Steyn

SAMOA: P B Williams; D Lemi, S J Mapusua, E Fuimaono Sapolu, A T Tuilagi; T Pisi, K F Fotuali'i; S Taulafo, M M Schwalger (*captain*), C A I Johnston, D A Leo, K G Thompson, T Tuifua, G J Stowers, M Fa'asavalu

SUBSTITUTIONS: A I Perenise for Johnston (60 mins); I Tekori for Leo (60 mins); O Treviranus for Tuifua (73 mins); L Mulipola for Taulafo (77 mins); O Avei for Schwalger (77 mins)

SCORER *Try*: Stowers

REFEREE N Owens (Wales)

RED CARD P B Williams (69 mins) **YELLOW CARD** J W Smit (70 mins)

2 October, Waikato Stadium, Hamilton

WALES 66 (9G 1PG) FIJI 0

WALES: L M Byrne; S L Halfpenny, M S Williams, J H Roberts, G P North; R Priestland, W M Phillips; G D Jenkins, H Bennett, A R Jones, B S Davies, L C Charteris, R P Jones, T T Faletau, S K Warburton (*captain*)

SUBSTITUTIONS: L B Burns for Bennett (35 mins); A-W Jones for B S Davies (40 mins); A T Powell for Faletau (54 mins); L D Williams for Phillips (54 mins); S M Jones for Priestland (58 mins); P James for A R Jones (58 mins); J J V Davies for Roberts (64 mins); A R Jones back for Jenkins (73 mins)

SCORERS *Tries:* Roberts (2), M S Williams, North, Warburton, Burns, Halfpenny, L D Williams, J J V Davies *Conversions:* Priestland (5), S M Jones (4) *Penalty Goal*: Priestland

FIJI: I L R Keresoni; A J Vulivuli, R S Fatiaki, G V Lovobalavu, M L Tagicakibau; N T Little, V T Buatava; W Nailago, S K Koto, S Somoca, L Nakarawa, R W G Lewaravu, R Nasiga, N E Talei (*captain*), M S Matadigo

SUBSTITUTIONS: V Veikoso for Koto (40 mins); G D C Ma'afu for Somoca (51 mins); R M M Ravulo for Matadigo (54 mins); S Baikeinuku for Lovobalavu (54 mins); A Qera for Nasiga (61 mins); Somoca back for Nailago (65 mins); V Goneva for Vulivuli (69 mins); N S K Ranuku for Tagicakibau (76 mins)

REFEREE W Barnes (England)

POOL D FINAL TABLE:

	P	W	D	L	PF	PA	TF	TA	BP	PTS
South Africa	4	4	0	0	166	24	21	2	2	**18**
Wales	4	3	0	1	180	34	23	4	3	**15**
Samoa	4	2	0	2	91	49	10	5	2	**10**
Fiji	4	1	0	3	59	167	7	19	1	**5**
Namibia	4	0	0	4	44	266	5	36	0	**0**

P=Played; W=Won; D=Draw; L=Lost; PF=Points For; PA=Points Against; TF=Tries For; TA=Tries Against; BP=Bonus Points; PTS=Points

THE QUARTER-FINALS

8 October, Wellington Regional Stadium, Wellington

IRELAND 10 (1G 1PG) WALES 22 (2G 1PG 1T)

IRELAND: R D J Kearney; T J Bowe, B G O'Driscoll (*captain*), G W D'Arcy, K G Earls; R J R O'Gara, C Murray; C E Healy, R D Best, M R Ross, D P O'Callaghan, P J O'Connell, S Ferris, J P R Heaslip, S K O'Brien

SUBSTITUTIONS: E G Reddan for Murray (55 mins); J J Sexton for O'Gara (55 mins); A D Trimble for Earls (71 mins); D C Ryan for Ferris (74 mins); D P Leamy for Heaslip (74 mins);

SCORERS *Try:* Earls *Conversion:* O'Gara *Penalty Goal*: O'Gara

WALES: S L Halfpenny; S M Williams, J J V Davies, J H Roberts, G P North; R Priestland, W M Phillips; G D Jenkins, H Bennett, A R Jones, L C Charteris, A-W Jones, D J Lydiate, T T Faletau, S K Warburton (*captain*)

SUBSTITUTIONS: B S Davies for Charteris (40 mins); J W Hook for Priestland (77 mins)

SCORERS *Tries:* S M Williams, Phillips, J J V Davies *Conversions*: Priestland (2) *Penalty Goal*: Halfpenny

REFEREE C Joubert (South Africa)

Stu Forster/Getty Images

Try-scorer Mike Phillips was Man of the Match in the quarter-final victory.

8 October, Eden Park, Auckland

ENGLAND 12 (1G 1T) FRANCE 19 (2PG 1DG 2T)

ENGLAND: B J Foden; C J Ashton, E M Tuilagi, T G A L Flood, M J Cueto; J P Wilkinson, B R Youngs; M J H Stevens, S G Thompson, D R Cole, L P Deacon, T P Palmer, T R Croft, N J Easter, L W Moody (*captain*)

SUBSTITUTIONS: C L Lawes for Croft (46 mins); A R Corbisiero for Stevens (49 mins); S D Shaw for Deacon (49 mins); D M Hartley for Thompson (55 mins); Stevens back for Cole (62 mins); J A W Haskell for Moody (62 mins); R E P Wigglesworth for Youngs (64 mins); M A Banahan for Wilkinson (64 mins)

SCORERS *Tries*: Foden, Cueto *Conversion:* Wilkinson

FRANCE: M Médard; V Clerc, A Rougerie, M Mermoz, A Palisson; M Parra, D Yachvili; J-B Poux, W Servat, N Mas, P Papé, L Nallet, T Dusautoir (*captain*), I Harinordoquy, J Bonnaire

SUBSTITUTIONS: F Trinh-Duc for Yachvili (53 mins); F Barcella for Poux (55 mins); D Szarzewski for Servat (55 mins); J Pierre for Papé (64 mins); D Marty for Rougerie (68 mins); L Picamoles for Harinordoquy (72 mins); C Heymans for Mermoz (78 mins)

SCORERS *Tries*: Clerc, Médard *Penalty Goals*: Yachvili (2) *Dropped Goal:* Trinh-Duc

REFEREE S R Walsh (Australia)

9 October, Wellington Regional Stadium, Wellington

SOUTH AFRICA 9 (2PG 1DG) AUSTRALIA 11 (2PG 1T)

SOUTH AFRICA: P Lambie; J-P R Pietersen, J Fourie, J de Villiers, B G Habana; M Steyn, P F du Preez; G G Steenkamp, J W Smit (*captain*), J N du Plessis, D J Rossouw, V Matfield, S W P Burger, P J Spies, H W Brüssow

SUBSTITUTIONS: L-F P Louw for Brüssow (19 mins); B W du Plessis for J W Smit (49 mins); F Hougaard for Habana (49 mins); W S Alberts for Burger (temp 13 to 19 mins) and for Spies (63 mins)

SCORER *Penalty Goals:* M Steyn (2) *Dropped Goal:* M Steyn

AUSTRALIA: K J Beale; J D O'Connor, A P Ashley-Cooper, P J McCabe, D A N Ioane; Q S Cooper, S W Genia; S M Kepu, S T Moore, B E Alexander, D J Vickerman, J E Horwill (*captain*), R D Elsom, U R Samo, D W Pocock

SUBSTITUTIONS: B S Barnes for McCabe (52 mins); N C Sharpe for Vickerman (53 mins); S U T Polota-Nau for Moore (63 mins); J A Slipper for Kepu (68 mins); B J McCalman for Samo (72 mins); A S Fainga'a for Beale (74 mins)

SCORERS *Try*: Horwill *Penalty Goals*: O'Connor (2)

REFEREE B J Lawrence (New Zealand)

9 October, Eden Park, Auckland

NEW ZEALAND 33 (1G 7PG 1T)
ARGENTINA 10 (1G 1PG)

NEW ZEALAND: J M Muliaina; C S Jane, C G Smith, M A Nonu, S Williams; C R Slade, P A T Weepu; T D Woodcock, K F Mealamu, O T Franks, B C Thorn, S L Whitelock, J Kaino, K J Read, R H McCaw (*captain*)

SUBSTITUTIONS: A W Cruden for Slade (32 mins); I Toeava for Muliaina (40 mins); A J Williams for Whitelock (62 mins); A K Hore for Mealamu (65 mins); V V J Vito for McCaw (72 mins); Q J Cowan for Weepu (72 mins); I F Afoa for Franks (74 mins)

SCORERS *Tries*: Read, Thorn *Conversion:* Cruden *Penalty Goals*: Weepu (7)

ARGENTINA: M Rodriguez; G O Camacho, M T Bosch, F Contepomi (*captain*), H Agulla; S Fernández, N Vergallo; R Roncero, M E Ledesma, J G Figallo, M Carizza, P Albacete, J-M Leguizamón, L V Senatore, J A F Cabello

SUBSTITUTIONS: M I Ayerza for Roncero (39 mins); J J Imhoff for Agulla (49 mins); M A Scelzo for Figallo (59 mins); A T Campos for Carizza (62 mins); L P Gonzalez Amorosino for Rodriguez (68 mins); A Creevy for Ledesma (69 mins); A Lalanne for Vergallo (temp 47 to 52 mins);

SCORERS *Try:* Cabello *Conversion:* Contepomi *Penalty Goal*: Bosch

REFEREE N Owens (Wales)

YELLOW CARD N Vergallo (57 mins)

David Rogers/Getty Images

Brad Thorn capped a commanding display in the All Blacks' quarter-final victory, with a try.

THE SEMI-FINALS

15 October, Eden Park, Auckland

WALES 8 (1PG 1T) FRANCE 9 (3PG)

WALES: S L Halfpenny; S M Williams, J J V Davies, J H Roberts, G P North; J W Hook, W M Phillips; G D Jenkins, H Bennett, A R Jones, L C Charteris, A-W Jones, D J Lydiate, T T Faletau, S K Warburton (*captain*)

SUBSTITUTIONS: P James for A R Jones (9 mins); S M Jones for Hook (45 mins); R P Jones for Lydiate (55 mins); B S Davies for A-W Jones (60 mins);

SCORERS *Try:* Phillips *Penalty Goal*: Hook

FRANCE: M Médard; V Clerc, A Rougerie, M Mermoz, A Palisson; M Parra, D Yachvili; J-B Poux, W Servat, N Mas, P Papé, L Nallet, T Dusautoir (*captain*), I Harinordoquy, J Bonnaire

SUBSTITUTIONS: F Barcella for Poux (44 mins); D Szarzewski for Servat (44 mins); J Pierre for Papé (60 mins); F Ouedraogo for Bonnaire (75 mins)

SCORER *Penalty Goals*: Parra (3)

REFEREE A C Rolland (Ireland)

RED CARD S K Warburton (18 mins)

16 October, Eden Park, Auckland

AUSTRALIA 6 (1PG 1DG)
NEW ZEALAND 20 (4PG 1DG 1T)

AUSTRALIA: A P Ashley-Cooper; J D O'Connor, A S Fainga'a, P J McCabe, D A N Ioane; Q S Cooper, S W Genia; S M Kepu, S T Moore, B E Alexander, D J Vickerman, J E Horwill (*captain*), R D Elsom, U R Samo, D W Pocock

SUBSTITUTIONS: J A Slipper for Kepu (20mins); B S Barnes for McCabe (temp 34 to 40 mins and 47 mins); R A Simmons for Vickerman (temp 22 to 26 mins and 59 mins); B J McCalman for Samo (59 mins); R G Horne for Fainga'a (62 mins); S U T Polota-Nau for Moore (65 mins)

SCORERS *Penalty Goal*: O'Connor *Dropped Goal*: Cooper

NEW ZEALAND: I J A Dagg; C S Jane, C G Smith, M A Nonu, R D Kahui; A W Cruden, P A T Weepu; T D Woodcock, K F Mealamu, O T Franks, B C Thorn, S L Whitelock, J Kaino, K J Read, R H McCaw (*captain*)

SUBSTITUTIONS: A J Williams for Whitelock (56 mins); A M Ellis for Weepu (56 mins); A K Hore for Mealamu (63 mins); S Williams for Nonu (72 mins); B J Franks for O T Franks (79 mins); V V J Vito for Kaino (80 mins); Weepu back for Ellis (temp 68 to 73 mins)

SCORERS *Try*: Nonu *Penalty Goals*: Weepu (4) *Dropped Goal*: Cruden

REFEREE C Joubert (South Africa)

YELLOW CARD S Williams (75 mins)

THE BRONZE FINAL

21 October, Eden Park, Auckland

AUSTRALIA 21 (1G 2PG 1DG 1T)
WALES 18 (1G 2PG 1T)

AUSTRALIA: K J Beale; J D O'Connor, A P Ashley-Cooper, B S Barnes, D A N Ioane; Q S Cooper, S W Genia; J A Slipper, S U T Polota-Nau, R S L Ma'afu, J E Horwill (*captain*), N C Sharpe, S Higginbotham, B J McCalman, D W Pocock

SUBSTITUTIONS: R G Horne for Beale (9 mins); A S Fainga'a for Cooper (21 mins); R A Simmons for Sharpe (45 mins); S M Fainga'a for Polota-Nau (51 mins); B E Alexander for Ma'afu (59 mins); L Burgess for Genia (67 mins); U R Samo for Higginbotham (temp 30 to 34 mins) and for Horwill (70 mins)

SCORERS *Tries:* Barnes, McCalman *Conversion:* O'Connor *Penalty Goals*: O'Connor (2) *Dropped Goal*: Barnes

WALES: S L Halfpenny; G P North, J J V Davies, J H Roberts, S M Williams; J W Hook, W M Phillips; G D Jenkins (*captain*), H Bennett, P James, L C Charteris, B S Davies, D J Lydiate, R P Jones, T T Faletau

SUBSTITUTIONS: S M Jones for North (temp 32 to 36 mins) and for Hook (50 mins); A-W Jones for Charteris (53 mins); A T Powell for Lydiate (63 mins); R J Bevington for James (63 mins); L D Williams for Phillips (63 mins); L B Burns for Bennett (69 mins); M S Williams for J J V Davies (69 mins)

SCORERS *Tries:* S M Williams, Halfpenny *Conversion:* S M Jones *Penalty Goals*: Hook, S M Jones

REFEREE W Barnes (England)

THE FINAL

23 October, Eden Park, Auckland

NEW ZEALAND 8 (1PG 1T) FRANCE 7 (1G)

NEW ZEALAND: I J A Dagg; C S Jane, C G Smith, M A Nonu, R D Kahui; A W Cruden, P A T Weepu; T D Woodcock, K F Mealamu, O T Franks, B C Thorn, S L Whitelock, J Kaino, K J Read, R H McCaw (*captain*)

SUBSTITUTIONS: S R Donald for Cruden (33 mins); A J Williams for Whitelock (48 mins); A K Hore for Mealamu (48 mins); A M Ellis for Weepu (49 mins); S Williams for Nonu (75 mins)

SCORERS *Try*: Woodcock *Penalty Goal*: Donald

FRANCE: M Médard; V Clerc, A Rougerie, M Mermoz, A Palisson; M Parra, D Yachvili; J-B Poux, W Servat, N Mas, P Papé, L Nallet, T Dusautoir (*captain*), I Harinordoquy, J Bonnaire

SUBSTITUTIONS: F Trinh-Duc for Parra (temp 11 to 17 mins and 22 mins); D Traille for Clerc (45 mins); D Szarzewski for Servat (64 mins); F Barcella for Poux (64 mins); J Pierre for Papé (69 mins); J-M Doussain for Yachvili(75 mins)

SCORERS *Try*: Dusautoir *Conversion:* Trinh-Duc

REFEREE C Joubert (South Africa)

David Rogers/Getty Images

Stephen Donald kicks the penalty that separated the teams at the end of the 2011 Rugby World Cup final.

RUGBY WORLD CUP RECORDS 1987–2011

(FINAL STAGES ONLY)

OVERALL RECORDS

MOST MATCHES WON IN FINAL STAGES

37	New Zealand
33	Australia
30	France
29	England

MOST OVERALL PENALTIES IN FINAL STAGES

58	J P Wilkinson	England	1999–2011
36	A G Hastings	Scotland	1987–95
35	G Quesada	Argentina	1999–2003
33	M P Lynagh	Australia	1987–95
33	A P Mehrtens	New Zealand	1995–99

MOST OVERALL POINTS IN FINAL STAGES

277	J P Wilkinson	England	1999–2011
227	A G Hastings	Scotland	1987–95
195	M P Lynagh	Australia	1987–95
170	G J Fox	New Zealand	1987–91
163	A P Mehrtens	New Zealand	1995–99

MOST OVERALL DROPPED GOALS IN FINAL STAGES

14	J P Wilkinson	England	1999–2011
6	J H de Beer	South Africa	1999
5	C R Andrew	England	1987–95
5	G L Rees	Canada	1987–99
4	J M Hernández	Argentina	2003–07

MOST OVERALL TRIES IN FINAL STAGES

15	J T Lomu	New Zealand	1995–99
13	D C Howlett	New Zealand	2003–07
11	R Underwood	England	1987–95
11	J T Rokocoko	New Zealand	2003–07
11	C E Latham	Australia	1999–2007
11	V Clerc	France	2007–11

MOST MATCH APPEARANCES IN FINAL STAGES

22	J Leonard	England	1991–2003
20	G M Gregan	Australia	1995–2007
19	M J Catt	England	1995–2007
19	J P Wilkinson	England	1999–2011
18	M O Johnson	England	1995–2003
18	B P Lima	Samoa	1991–2007
18	R Ibañez	France	1999–2007
18	M E Ledesma	Argentina	1999–2011
18	L W Moody	England	2003–2011

MOST OVERALL CONVERSIONS IN FINAL STAGES

39	A G Hastings	Scotland	1987–95
37	G J Fox	New Zealand	1987–91
36	M P Lynagh	Australia	1987–95
35	D W Carter	New Zealand	2003–11
28	J P Wilkinson	England	1999–2011
27	P J Grayson	England	1999–2003
27	S M Jones	Wales	1999–2011

MOST POINTS IN ONE COMPETITION

126	G J Fox	New Zealand	1987
113	J P Wilkinson	England	2003
112	T Lacroix	France	1995
105	P C Montgomery	South Africa	2007
104	A G Hastings	Scotland	1995
103	F Michalak	France	2003
102	G Quesada	Argentina	1999
101	M Burke	Australia	1999

MOST TRIES IN ONE COMPETITION

8	J T Lomu	New Zealand	1999
8	B G Habana	South Africa	2007
7	M C G Ellis	New Zealand	1995
7	J T Lomu	New Zealand	1995
7	D C Howlett	New Zealand	2003
7	J M Muliaina	New Zealand	2003
7	D A Mitchell	Australia	2007

MOST CONVERSIONS IN ONE COMPETITION

30	G J Fox	New Zealand	1987
22	P C Montgomery	South Africa	2007
20	S D Culhane	New Zealand	1995
20	M P Lynagh	Australia	1987
20	L R MacDonald	New Zealand	2003
20	N J Evans	New Zealand	2007

MOST PENALTY GOALS IN ONE COMPETITION

31	G Quesada	Argentina	1999
26	T Lacroix	France	1995
23	J P Wilkinson	England	2003
21	G J Fox	New Zealand	1987
21	E J Flatley	Australia	2003
20	C R Andrew	England	1995

MOST DROPPED GOALS IN ONE COMPETITION

8	J P Wilkinson	England	2003
6	J H de Beer	South Africa	1999
5	J P Wilkinson	England	2007
4	J M Hernández	Argentina	2007

MATCH RECORDS

MOST POINTS IN A MATCH

BY A TEAM

145	New Zealand v Japan	1995
142	Australia v Namibia	2003
111	England v Uruguay	2003
108	New Zealand v Portugal	2007
101	New Zealand v Italy	1999
101	England v Tonga	1999

BY A PLAYER

45	S D Culhane	New Zealand v Japan	1995
44	A G Hastings	Scotland v Ivory Coast	1995
42	M S Rogers	Australia v Namibia	2003
36	T E Brown	New Zealand v Italy	1999
36	P J Grayson	England v Tonga	1999
34	J H de Beer	South Africa v England	1999
33	N J Evans	New Zealand v Portugal	2007
32	J P Wilkinson	England v Italy	1999

MOST CONVERSIONS IN A MATCH

BY A TEAM

20	New Zealand v Japan	1995
16	Australia v Namibia	2003
14	New Zealand v Portugal	2007
13	New Zealand v Tonga	2003
13	England v Uruguay	2003

BY A PLAYER

20	S D Culhane	New Zealand v Japan	1995
16	M S Rogers	Australia v Namibia	2003
14	N J Evans	New Zealand v Portugal	2007
12	P J Grayson	England v Tonga	1999
12	L R MacDonald	New Zealand v Tonga	2003

MOST TRIES IN A MATCH

BY A TEAM

22	Australia v Namibia	2003
21	New Zealand v Japan	1995
17	England v Uruguay	2003
16	New Zealand v Portugal	2007
14	New Zealand v Italy	1999

BY A PLAYER

6	M C G Ellis	New Zealand v Japan	1995
5	C E Latham	Australia v Namibia	2003
5	O J Lewsey	England v Uruguay	2003
4	I C Evans	Wales v Canada	1987
4	C I Green	New Zealand v Fiji	1987
4	J A Gallagher	New Zealand v Fiji	1987
4	B F Robinson	Ireland v Zimbabwe	1991
4	A G Hastings	Scotland v Ivory Coast	1995
4	C M Williams	South Africa v Western Samoa	1995
4	J T Lomu	New Zealand v England	1995
4	K G M Wood	Ireland v United States	1999
4	J M Muliaina	New Zealand v Canada	2003
4	B G Habana	South Africa v Samoa	2007
4	V Goneva	Fiji v Namibia	2011
4	Z R Guildford	New Zealand v Canada	2011

MOST PENALTY GOALS IN A MATCH

BY A TEAM

8	Australia v South Africa	1999
8	Argentina v Samoa	1999
8	Scotland v Tonga	1995
8	France v Ireland	1995

BY A PLAYER

8	M Burke	Australia v South Africa	1999
8	G Quesada	Argentina v Samoa	1999
8	A G Hastings	Scotland v Tonga	1995
8	T Lacroix	France v Ireland	1995

MOST DROPPED GOALS IN A MATCH

BY A TEAM

5	South Africa v England	1999
3	Fiji v Romania	1991
3	England v France	2003
3	Argentina v Ireland	2007
3	Namibia v Fiji	2011

BY A PLAYER

5	J H de Beer	South Africa v England	1999
3	J P Wilkinson	England v France	2003
3	J M Hernández	Argentina v Ireland	2007
3	T A W Kotze	Namibia v Fiji	2011

FIRST TOURNAMENT : 1987 IN AUSTRALIA & NEW ZEALAND

POOL 1

Australia	19	**England**	6
USA	21	**Japan**	18
England	60	**Japan**	7
Australia	47	**USA**	12
England	34	**USA**	6
Australia	42	**Japan**	23

	P	W	D	L	F	A	Pts
Australia	3	3	0	0	108	41	6
England	3	2	0	1	100	32	4
USA	3	1	0	2	39	99	2
Japan	3	0	0	3	48	123	0

POOL 3

New Zealand	70	**Italy**	6
Fiji	28	**Argentina**	9
New Zealand	74	**Fiji**	13
Argentina	25	**Italy**	16
Italy	18	**Fiji**	15
New Zealand	46	**Argentina**	15

	P	W	D	L	F	A	Pts
New Zealand	3	3	0	0	190	34	6
Fiji	3	1	0	2	56	101	2
Argentina	3	1	0	2	49	90	2
Italy	3	1	0	2	40	110	2

POOL 2

Canada	37	**Tonga**	4
Wales	13	**Ireland**	6
Wales	29	**Tonga**	16
Ireland	46	**Canada**	19
Wales	40	**Canada**	9
Ireland	32	**Tonga**	9

	P	W	D	L	F	A	Pts
Wales	3	3	0	0	82	31	6
Ireland	3	2	0	1	84	41	4
Canada	3	1	0	2	65	90	2
Tonga	3	0	0	3	29	98	0

POOL 4

Romania	21	**Zimbabwe**	20
France	20	**Scotland**	20
France	55	**Romania**	12
Scotland	60	**Zimbabwe**	21
France	70	**Zimbabwe**	12
Scotland	55	**Romania**	28

	P	W	D	L	F	A	Pts
France	3	2	1	0	145	44	5
Scotland	3	2	1	0	135	69	5
Romania	3	1	0	2	61	130	2
Zimbabwe	3	0	0	3	53	151	0

QUARTER-FINALS

New Zealand	30	**Scotland**	3
France	31	**Fiji**	16
Australia	33	**Ireland**	15
Wales	16	**England**	3

SEMI-FINALS

France	30	**Australia**	24
New Zealand	49	**Wales**	6

THIRD PLACE MATCH

Wales	22	**Australia**	21

First World Cup Final, Eden Park, Auckland, 20 June 1987

NEW ZEALAND 29 (1G 4PG 1DG 2T)
FRANCE 9 (1G 1PG)

NEW ZEALAND: J A Gallagher; J J Kirwan, J T Stanley, W T Taylor, C I Green; G J Fox, D E Kirk (captain); S C McDowell, S B T Fitzpatrick, J A Drake, M J Pierce, G W Whetton, A J Whetton, W T Shelford, M N Jones **SCORERS** *Tries:* Jones, Kirk, Kirwan *Conversion:* Fox *Penalty Goals:* Fox (4) *Dropped Goal:* Fox

FRANCE: S Blanco; D Camberabero, P Sella, D Charvet, P Lagisquet; F Mesnel, P Berbizier; P Ondarts, D Dubroca (captain), J-P Garuet, A Lorieux, J Condom, E Champ, L Rodriguez, D Erbani **SCORERS** *Try:* Berbizier *Conversion:* Camberabero *Penalty Goal:* Camberabero **REFEREE** K V J Fitzgerald (Australia)

SECOND TOURNAMENT: 1991 IN BRITAIN, IRELAND & FRANCE

POOL 1

New Zealand	18	England	12
Italy	30	USA	9
New Zealand	46	USA	6
England	36	Italy	6
England	37	USA	9
New Zealand	31	Italy	21

	P	W	D	L	F	A	Pts
New Zealand	3	3	0	0	95	39	9
England	3	2	0	1	85	33	7
Italy	3	1	0	2	57	76	5
USA	3	0	0	3	24	113	3

POOL 3

Australia	32	Argentina	19
Western Samoa	16	Wales	13
Australia	9	Western Samoa	3
Wales	16	Argentina	7
Australia	38	Wales	3
Western Samoa	35	Argentina	12

	P	W	D	L	F	A	Pts
Australia	3	3	0	0	79	25	9
Western Samoa	3	2	0	1	54	34	7
Wales	3	1	0	2	32	61	5
Argentina	3	0	0	3	38	83	3

POOL 2

Scotland	47	Japan	9
Ireland	55	Zimbabwe	11
Ireland	32	Japan	16
Scotland	51	Zimbabwe	12
Scotland	24	Ireland	15
Japan	52	Zimbabwe	8

	P	W	D	L	F	A	Pts
Scotland	3	3	0	0	122	36	9
Ireland	3	2	0	1	102	51	7
Japan	3	1	0	2	77	87	5
Zimbabwe	3	0	0	3	31	158	3

POOL 4

France	30	Romania	3
Canada	13	Fiji	3
France	33	Fiji	9
Canada	19	Romania	11
Romania	17	Fiji	15
France	19	Canada	13

	P	W	D	L	F	A	Pts
France	3	3	0	0	82	25	9
Canada	3	2	0	1	45	33	7
Romania	3	1	0	2	31	64	5
Fiji	3	0	0	3	27	63	3

QUARTER-FINALS

England	19	France	10
Scotland	28	Western Samoa	6
Australia	19	Ireland	18
New Zealand	29	Canada	13

SEMI-FINALS

England	9	Scotland	6
Australia	16	New Zealand	6

THIRD PLACE MATCH

New Zealand	13	Scotland	6

Second World Cup Final, Twickenham, 2 November 1991

AUSTRALIA 12 (1G 2PG) ENGLAND 6 (2PG)

AUSTRALIA: M C Roebuck; D I Campese, J S Little, T J Horan, R H Egerton; M P Lynagh, N C Farr-Jones (captain); A J Daly, P N Kearns, E J A McKenzie, R J McCall, J A Eales, S P Poidevin, T Coker, V Ofahengaue **SCORERS** *Try*: Daly *Conversion*: Lynagh *Penalty Goals*: Lynagh (2)

ENGLAND: J M Webb; S J Halliday, W D C Carling (captain), J C Guscott, R Underwood; C R Andrew, R J Hill; J Leonard, B C Moore, J A Probyn, P J Ackford, W A Dooley, M G Skinner, M C Teague, P J Winterbottom **SCORER** *Penalty Goals*: Webb (2)
REFEREE W D Bevan (Wales)

THIRD TOURNAMENT: 1995 IN SOUTH AFRICA

POOL A

South Africa	27	Australia	18
Canada	34	Romania	3
South Africa	21	Romania	8
Australia	27	Canada	11
Australia	42	Romania	3
South Africa	20	Canada	0

	P	W	D	L	F	A	Pts
South Africa	3	3	0	0	68	26	9
Australia	3	2	0	1	87	41	7
Canada	3	1	0	2	45	50	5
Romania	3	0	0	3	14	97	3

POOL B

Western Samoa	42	Italy	18
England	24	Argentina	18
Western Samoa	32	Argentina	26
England	27	Italy	20
Italy	31	Argentina	25
England	44	Western Samoa	22

	P	W	D	L	F	A	Pts
England	3	3	0	0	95	60	9
Western Samoa	3	2	0	1	96	88	7
Italy	3	1	0	2	69	94	5
Argentina	3	0	0	3	69	87	3

POOL C

Wales	57	Japan	10
New Zealand	43	Ireland	19
Ireland	50	Japan	28
New Zealand	34	Wales	9
New Zealand	145	Japan	17
Ireland	24	Wales	23

	P	W	D	L	F	A	Pts
New Zealand	3	3	0	0	222	45	9
Ireland	3	2	0	1	93	94	7
Wales	3	1	0	2	89	68	5
Japan	3	0	0	3	55	252	3

POOL D

Scotland	89	Ivory Coast	0
France	38	Tonga	10
France	54	Ivory Coast	18
Scotland	41	Tonga	5
Tonga	29	Ivory Coast	11
France	22	Scotland	19

	P	W	D	L	F	A	Pts
France	3	3	0	0	114	47	9
Scotland	3	2	0	1	149	27	7
Tonga	3	1	0	2	44	90	5
Ivory Coast	3	0	0	3	29	172	3

QUARTER-FINALS

France	36	Ireland	12
South Africa	42	Western Samoa	14
England	25	Australia	22
New Zealand	48	Scotland	30

SEMI-FINALS

South Africa	19	France	15
New Zealand	45	England	29

THIRD PLACE MATCH

France	19	England	9

Third World Cup Final, Ellis Park, Johannesburg, 24 June 1995

SOUTH AFRICA 15 (3PG 2DG)
NEW ZEALAND 12 (3PG 1DG) *

SOUTH AFRICA: A J Joubert; J T Small, J C Mulder, H P Le Roux, C M Williams; J T Stransky, J H van der Westhuizen; J P du Randt, C L C Rossouw, I S Swart, J J Wiese, J J Strydom, J F Pienaar (captain), M G Andrews, R J Kruger Substitutions: G L Pagel for Swart (68 mins); R A W Straeuli for Andrews (90 mins); B Venter for Small (97 mins)

SCORER *Penalty Goals*: Stransky (3) *Drop Goals*: Stransky (2)

NEW ZEALAND: G M Osborne; J W Wilson, F E Bunce, W K Little, J T Lomu; A P Mehrtens, G T M Bachop; C W Dowd, S B T Fitzpatrick (captain), O M Brown, I D Jones, R M Brooke, M R Brewer, Z V Brooke, J A Kronfeld Substitutions: J W Joseph for Brewer (40 mins); M C G Ellis for Wilson (55 mins); R W Loe for Dowd (83 mins); A D Strachan for Bachop (temp 66 to 71 mins)

SCORER *Penalty Goals*: Mehrtens (3) *Drop Goal*: Mehrtens

REFEREE E F Morrison (England)

* after extra time: 9–9 after normal time

Philip Littleton/AFP/Getty Images

One of sport's greatest moments – Nelson Mandela hands the cup to François Pienaar.

FOURTH TOURNAMENT: 1999 IN BRITAIN, IRELAND & FRANCE

POOL A

Spain	15	**Uruguay**	27
South Africa	46	**Scotland**	29
Scotland	43	**Uruguay**	12
South Africa	47	**Spain**	3
South Africa	39	**Uruguay**	3
Scotland	48	**Spain**	0

	P	W	D	L	F	A	Pts
South Africa	3	3	0	0	132	35	9
Scotland	3	2	0	1	120	58	7
Uruguay	3	1	0	2	42	97	5
Spain	3	0	0	3	18	122	3

POOL B

England	67	**Italy**	7
New Zealand	45	**Tonga**	9
England	16	**New Zealand**	30
Italy	25	**Tonga**	28
New Zealand	101	**Italy**	3
England	101	**Tonga**	10

	P	W	D	L	F	A	Pts
New Zealand	3	3	0	0	176	28	9
England	3	2	0	1	184	47	7
Tonga	3	1	0	2	47	171	5
Italy	3	0	0	3	35	196	3

POOL C

Fiji	67	**Namibia**	18
France	33	**Canada**	20
France	47	**Namibia**	13
Fiji	38	**Canada**	22
Canada	72	**Namibia**	11
France	28	**Fiji**	19

	P	W	D	L	F	A	Pts
France	3	3	0	0	108	52	9
Fiji	3	2	0	1	124	68	7
Canada	3	1	0	2	114	82	5
Namibia	3	0	0	3	42	186	3

POOL D

Wales	23	**Argentina**	18
Samoa	43	**Japan**	9
Wales	64	**Japan**	15
Argentina	32	**Samoa**	16
Wales	31	**Samoa**	38
Argentina	33	**Japan**	12

	P	W	D	L	F	A	Pts
Wales	3	2	0	1	118	71	7
Samoa	3	2	0	1	97	72	7
Argentina	3	2	0	1	83	51	7
Japan	3	0	0	3	36	140	3

POOL E

Ireland	53	**United States**	8
Australia	57	**Romania**	9
United States	25	**Romania**	27
Ireland	3	**Australia**	23
Australia	55	**United States**	19
Ireland	44	**Romania**	14

	P	W	D	L	F	A	Pts
Wales	3	2	0	1	118	71	7
Samoa	3	2	0	1	97	72	7
Argentina	3	2	0	1	83	51	7
Japan	3	0	0	3	36	140	3

PLAY-OFFS FOR QUARTER-FINAL PLACES

England	45	**Fiji**	24
Scotland	35	**Samoa**	20
Ireland	24	**Argentina**	28

QUARTER-FINALS

Wales	9	**Australia**	24
South Africa	44	**England**	21
France	47	**Argentina**	26
Scotland	18	**New Zealand**	30

SEMI-FINALS

South Africa	21	**Australia**	27
New Zealand	31	**France**	43

THIRD PLACE MATCH

South Africa	22	**New Zealand**	18

Fourth World Cup Final, Millennium Stadium, Cardiff, 6 November 1999

AUSTRALIA 35 (2G 7PG) FRANCE 12 (4PG)

AUSTRALIA: M Burke; B N Tune, D J Herbert, T J Horan, J W Roff; S J Larkham, G M Gregan; R L L Harry, M A Foley, A T Blades, D T Giffin, J A Eales (captain), M J Cockbain, R S T Kefu, D J Wilson Substitutions J S Little for Herbert (46 mins); O D A Finegan for Cockbain (52 mins); M R Connors for Wilson (73 mins); D J Crowley for Harry (75 mins); J A Paul for Foley (85 mins); C J Whitaker for Gregan (86 mins); N P Grey for Horan (86 mins)

SCORERS *Tries*: Tune, Finegan *Conversions*: Burke (2) *Penalty Goals*: Burke (7)

FRANCE: X Garbajosa; P Bernat Salles, R Dourthe, E Ntamack, C Dominici; C Lamaison, F Galthié; C Soulette, R Ibañez (captain), F Tournaire, A Benazzi, F Pelous, M Lièvremont, C Juillet, O Magne Substitutions O Brouzet for Juillet (HT); P de Villiers for Soulette (47 mins); A Costes for Magne (temp 19 to 22 mins) and for Lièvremont (67 mins); U Mola for Garbajosa (67 mins); S Glas for Dourthe (temp 49 to 55 mins and from 74 mins); S Castaignède for Galthié (76 mins); M Dal Maso for Ibañez (79 mins)

SCORER *Penalty Goals*: Lamaison (4)

REFEREE A J Watson (South Africa)

Gary M. Prior/Getty Images

The Wallabies celebrate getting their hands on the Webb Ellis Cup for the second time.

FIFTH TOURNAMENT: 2003 IN AUSTRALIA

POOL A

Australia	24	**Argentina**	8
Ireland	45	**Romania**	17
Argentina	67	**Namibia**	14
Australia	90	**Romania**	8
Ireland	64	**Namibia**	7
Argentina	50	**Romania**	3
Australia	142	**Namibia**	0
Ireland	16	**Argentina**	15
Romania	37	**Namibia**	7
Australia	17	**Ireland**	16

	P	W	D	L	F	A	Pts
Australia	4	4	0	0	273	32	18
Ireland	4	3	0	1	141	56	14
Argentina	4	2	0	2	140	57	11
Romania	4	1	0	3	65	192	5
Namibia	4	0	0	4	28	310	0

POOL B

France	61	**Fiji**	18
Scotland	32	**Japan**	11
Fiji	19	**United States**	18
France	51	**Japan**	29
Scotland	39	**United States**	15
Fiji	41	**Japan**	13
France	51	**Scotland**	9
United States	39	**Japan**	26
France	41	**United States**	14
Scotland	22	**Fiji**	20

	P	W	D	L	F	A	Pts
France	4	4	0	0	204	70	20
Scotland	4	3	0	1	102	97	14
Fiji	4	2	0	2	98	114	9
United States	4	1	0	3	86	125	6
Japan	4	0	0	4	79	163	0

POOL C

South Africa	72	**Uruguay**	6
England	84	**Georgia**	6
Samoa	60	**Uruguay**	13
England	25	**South Africa**	6
Samoa	46	**Georgia**	9
South Africa	46	**Georgia**	19
England	35	**Samoa**	22
Uruguay	24	**Georgia**	12
South Africa	60	**Samoa**	10
England	111	**Uruguay**	13

	P	W	D	L	F	A	Pts
England	4	4	0	0	255	47	19
South Africa	4	3	0	1	184	60	15
Samoa	4	2	0	2	138	117	10
Uruguay	4	1	0	3	56	255	4
Georgia	4	0	0	4	46	200	0

POOL D

New Zealand	70	**Italy**	7
Wales	41	**Canada**	10
Italy	36	**Tonga**	12
New Zealand	68	**Canada**	6
Wales	27	**Tonga**	20
Italy	19	**Canada**	14
New Zealand	91	**Tonga**	7
Wales	27	**Italy**	15
Canada	24	**Tonga**	7
New Zealand	53	**Wales**	37

	P	W	D	L	F	A	Pts
New Zealand	4	4	0	0	282	57	20
Wales	4	3	0	1	132	98	14
Italy	4	2	0	2	77	123	8
Canada	4	1	0	3	54	135	5
Tonga	4	0	0	4	46	178	1

QUARTER-FINALS

New Zealand	29	**South Africa**	9
Australia	33	**Scotland**	16
France	43	**Ireland**	21
England	28	**Wales**	17

SEMI-FINALS

Australia	22	**New Zealand**	10
England	24	**France**	7

THIRD PLACE MATCH

New Zealand	40	**France**	13

Fifth World Cup Final, Telstra Stadium, Sydney, 22 November 2003

ENGLAND 20 (4PG 1DG 1T)
AUSTRALIA 17 (4PG 1T) *

ENGLAND: J Robinson; O J Lewsey, W J H Greenwood, M J Tindall, B C Cohen; J P Wilkinson, M J S Dawson; T J Woodman, S Thompson, P J Vickery, M O Johnson (captain), B J Kay, R A Hill, L B N Dallaglio, N A Back Substitutions: M J Catt for Tindall (78 mins); J Leonard for Vickery (80 mins); I R Balshaw for Lewsey (85 mins); L W Moody for Hill (93 mins)

SCORERS *Try*: Robinson *Penalty Goals*: Wilkinson (4) *Dropped Goal*: Wilkinson

AUSTRALIA: M S Rogers; W J Sailor, S A Mortlock, E J Flatley, L Tuqiri; S J Larkham, G M Gregan (captain); W K Young, B J Cannon, A K E Baxter, J B Harrison, N C Sharpe, G B Smith, D J Lyons, P R Waugh Substitutions: D T Giffin for Sharpe (48 mins); J A Paul for Cannon (56 mins); M J Cockbain for Lyons (56 mins); J W Roff for Sailor (70 mins); M J Dunning for Young (92 mins); M J Giteau for Larkham (temp 18 to 30 mins; 55 to 63 mins; 85 to 93 mins)

SCORERS *Try*: Tuqiri *Penalty Goals*: Flatley (4)

REFEREE A J Watson (South Africa)

* after extra time: 14–14 after normal time

David Rogers/Getty Images

More than 500,000 people descended on central London to welcome home the Rugby World Cup winners in 2003.

SIXTH TOURNAMENT: 2007
IN FRANCE, WALES & SCOTLAND

POOL A

England	28	United States	10
South Africa	59	Samoa	7
United States	15	Tonga	25
England	0	South Africa	36
Samoa	15	Tonga	19
South Africa	30	Tonga	25
England	44	Samoa	22
Samoa	25	United States	21
England	36	Tonga	20
South Africa	64	United States	15

	P	W	D	L	F	A	Pts
South Africa	4	4	0	0	189	47	19
England	4	3	0	1	108	88	14
Tonga	4	2	0	2	89	96	9
Samoa	4	1	0	3	69	143	5
United States	4	0	0	4	61	142	1

POOL C

New Zealand	76	Italy	14
Scotland	56	Portugal	10
Italy	24	Romania	18
New Zealand	108	Portugal	13
Scotland	42	Romania	0
Italy	31	Portugal	5
Scotland	0	New Zealand	40
Romania	14	Portugal	10
New Zealand	85	Romania	8
Scotland	18	Italy	16

	P	W	D	L	F	A	Pts
New Zealand	4	4	0	0	309	35	20
Scotland	4	3	0	1	116	66	14
Italy	4	2	0	2	85	117	9
Romania	4	1	0	3	40	161	5
Portugal	4	0	0	4	38	209	1

POOL B

Australia	91	Japan	3
Wales	42	Canada	17
Japan	31	Fiji	35
Wales	20	Australia	32
Fiji	29	Canada	16
Wales	72	Japan	18
Australia	55	Fiji	12
Canada	12	Japan	12
Australia	37	Canada	6
Wales	34	Fiji	38

	P	W	D	L	F	A	Pts
Australia	4	4	0	0	215	41	20
Fiji	4	3	0	1	114	136	15
Wales	4	2	0	2	168	105	12
Japan	4	0	1	3	64	210	3
Canada	4	0	1	3	51	120	2

POOL D

France	12	Argentina	17
Ireland	32	Namibia	17
Argentina	33	Georgia	3
Ireland	14	Georgia	10
France	87	Namibia	10
France	25	Ireland	3
Argentina	63	Namibia	3
Georgia	30	Namibia	0
France	64	Georgia	7
Ireland	15	Argentina	30

	P	W	D	L	F	A	Pts
Argentina	4	4	0	0	143	33	18
France	4	3	0	1	188	37	15
Ireland	4	2	0	2	64	82	9
Georgia	4	1	0	3	50	111	5
Namibia	4	0	0	4	30	212	0

QUARTER-FINALS

Australia	10	England	12
New Zealand	18	France	20
South Africa	37	Fiji	20
Argentina	19	Scotland	13

SEMI-FINALS

France	9	England	14
South Africa	37	Argentina	13

BRONZE MEDAL MATCH

France	10	Argentina	34

Sixth World Cup Final, Stade de France, Paris, 20 October 2007

SOUTH AFRICA 15 (5PG) ENGLAND 6 (2PG)

SOUTH AFRICA: P C Montgomery; J–P R Pietersen, J Fourie, F P L Steyn, B G Habana; A D James, P F du Preez; J P du Randt, J W Smit (*captain*), C J van der Linde, J P Botha, V Matfield, J H Smith, D J Rossouw, S W P Burger *Substitutions:* J L van Heerden for Rossouw (72 mins); B W du Plessis for Smit (temp 71 to 76 mins)

SCORERS *Penalty Goals*: Montgomery (4), Steyn

ENGLAND: J T Robinson; P H Sackey, M Tait, M J Catt, M J Cueto; J P Wilkinson, A C T Gomarsall; A J Sheridan, M P Regan, P J Vickery (*captain*), S D Shaw, B J Kay, M E Corry, N Easter, L W Moody *Substitutions:* M J H Stevens for Vickery (40 mins); D Hipkiss for Robinson (46 mins); T Flood for Catt (50 mins); G S Chuter for Regan (62 mins); J P R Worsley for Moody (62 mins); L B N Dallaglio for Easter (64 mins); P C Richards for Worsley (70 mins)

SCORER *Penalty Goals*: Wilkinson (2)

REFEREE A C Rolland (Ireland)

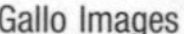

The Springboks get the party started after their win over England.

NEW ZEALAND BACK ON TOP OF THE WORLD

By Nigel Starmer-Smith

Hagen Hopkins/Getty Images

The legendary Gordon Tietjens led New Zealand to another HSBC Sevens World Series title.

The 2011 series may have concluded with the news and inception of an expanded Sevens Series, Tokyo's buzz and excitement added to the busy calendar of events, but the 2010–11 season brought familiar hands on the trophy.

The name changed, but the rugby was as good as ever. The 12th season of the IRB's Sevens World Series – now with its title sponsor and so hereafter to be known as the HSBC Sevens World Series – saw the restoration of New Zealand as champions for the first time since 2008.

An elated Gordon Tietjens, New Zealand's ever-present coach, remarked that this season's triumph was especially gratifying given the ever-increasing skills, fitness and competitiveness of all the participating nations.

New Zealand won four of the eight tournaments, taking the titles in South Africa, New Zealand, Hong Kong and Australia, and reaching the semi-finals in the other four.

Of the 44 games they played in the season, New Zealand lost just four. They also retained their remarkable record of never losing more than two in a row, and their record in finals is exemplary: they have now won 40 of their 61 cup finals since way back in 1999.

The omens were propitious for the Kiwis in the build-up to the Series when they won Gold at the Commonwealth Games in Delhi in October 2010, beating South Africa 24–17 in a thrilling final.

At the heart of that success were four players who went on to shine in the Series. Key forwards DJ Forbes, in his fourth year as captain, and the tall, long-striding Tim Mikkelson combined with the two Fijian-born backs, Lote Raikabula and the half-back Sevens genius Tomasi Cama, to create a winning formula.

Success did not come instantly in the season, and it was England who started their persistent challenge strongly in the opening tournament, the Emirates Airline Dubai Rugby Sevens.

England were led by the country's greatest Sevens exponent, Ben Gollings. Over all 12 seasons he has accumulated 2,652 points – over twice as many as the next top-scorer Waisale Serevi – and appeared in a record-equalling 70 events alongside Uale Mai of Samoa. That he will no longer be the fulcrum of England's squad will be a surprise to many, and his remarkable skills, acceleration, pace and fitness levels, and above all his Sevens acumen, will be sorely missed.

England started without a cup final to their name from the previous season and were stunned in their second pool game by European Sevens champions Portugal, who secured an historic 14–12 victory.

But in a riveting sequence of games that followed, England hit top form with Dan Caprice, Oliver Lindsay-Hague, James Rodwell and the maestro Gollings in brilliant form as they beat Fiji 26–21, Australia 24–21, New Zealand 19–14, and Samoa in the final 29–21. Competition can scarcely get more exciting than that!

In the last visit of the Series to George, the Eastern Cape town that has been so welcoming since 2002, the tables were turned as New Zealand's young recruits made their mark.

A trio of young and exceptionally quick newcomers in Frank Halai, Declan O'Donnell and Bryce Heem burst onto the scene. Of the three, 19-year-old O'Donnell was to be the star of the tournament, as he tilted both the semi-final against Fiji (26–19) and the cup final over England (22–19) New Zealand's way in dramatic style.

Early season injuries to key players took their toll on top teams as England lost Isoa Damu with a shoulder dislocation, South Africa's Cecil Afrika was ruled out with a broken jaw in George, and Forbes, New Zealand's inspirational captain, missed nearly all of Round 3 in Wellington.

However, if anything Forbes' injury seemed to galvanise the team all the more in the capital's 'Cake Tin' in front of an expectant capacity crowd, who had waited three years for a home win and remembering how Victor Vito had clinched the Cup title in 2008.

With Tomasi Cama running the show, Toby Arnold, Tim Mikkelson and the recalled Solomon King excelling, and the new star O'Donnell running in 10 tries, including a cup final hat-trick against England, New Zealand brushed aside all-comers.

A relatively comfortable triumph for the home team, but the beauty of Sevens is the uncertainty of what may follow. And so it was to prove in the contrasting environment, and marginally smaller pitch, of the University of Nevada American Football Stadium in Las Vegas.

The unheralded swift return to action of Cecil Afrika was to be a key factor in what followed. The 22-year-old was simply brilliant, with his silky running, superb tries and consistent goal-kicking, backed up by the captaincy and graft of Kyle Brown and newcomers Chris Dry, Steven Hunt and Bernardo Botha.

It was close – a draw with Samoa, then wins over Australia, England and Fiji in the final brought South Africa their first title since Adelaide 2009 during their championship season.

On to Round 5 of the Series and the majesty and splendour of Hong Kong. The tournament retains a special standing in the Series and an intensity and status that is still unsurpassed. For England it has been a second home, Gollings triumphing there four times, but not since 2006. They made the final but not without an early scare, beating Russia only 10–7. It is a sign of the times, too, as New Zealand were nearly upturned by an exciting Portugal side who only went down 19–12. Ask any coach and he'll tell you, there are no easy games any more!

The final rounds were epic as ever, with narrow margins over Samoa and Fiji, but with Forbes back at the helm New Zealand overcame a brave effort by an England team 29–17 to win the title.

In a season of farewells – including the retirement of the IRB's genial and efficient Sevens Referee Manager, Keith Lawrence – it was also goodbye to a second venue of wonderful picturesque qualities to rate alongside the Outeniqua Mountains backdrop of George, as we left behind the Adelaide Oval, memories of Moreton Bay fig trees, the grassy banks and old pavilion.

On the back of their Hong Kong heroics, New Zealand took the one cup title that had eluded them thus far, but a great finale was provided by South Africa, with a new star in Sibusiso Sithole and the outstanding performance of Cecil Afrika. It was New Zealand's day, though, with six tries by Frank Halai in the knockout rounds, and to my mind one of, if not the greatest, individual display of Sevens talent ever witnessed, coming from Tomasi Cama in the cup final.

With two rounds to play in the HSBC Sevens World Series, New Zealand led the overall title race, but Twickenham hosts England were their closest challengers and excitement was mounting. But, for reasons that are hard to fathom, England just didn't hit their straps and their challenge evaporated on day one when a rare defeat by France (another nation now embracing Sevens), a draw with Argentina and a loss to Kenya meant that they failed to qualify for the cup quarter-finals – to the dismay of the record-breaking day-one crowd at Twickenham of well over 50,000.

There were no such mistakes from New Zealand, however. The champions-in-waiting assured themselves of a ninth title in 12 seasons by securing a semi-final place with victory over Argentina 31–14, including a second consecutive hat-trick of tries for Frank Halai. Not that the celebrations lasted long – or perhaps the overall title was a distraction – Fiji winning their ensuing semi at a canter by a record margin of 42–19, one of the rare occasions throughout the season when Fiji truly did themselves justice.

The final was a triumph for Springbok coach Paul Treu. His team had lost to Fiji in their pool game the day before, so he instilled a new plan, which entailed tying in the Fijian marauders by using the short side, driving mauls and even bemusing the opposition with six-man lineouts – innovation that worked like a dream!

On to Round 8, and talk about a grand finale! The final event at Murrayfield celebrated the 100th World Series tournament since 1999 and provided some epic encounters to captivate the crowd. Both Wales and Australia rose to the occasion to underline the number of potential tournament winners in Sevens. Wales secured narrow wins over England and Spain, and France made their first semi-final of the season, while Australia revelled in rare wins over Fiji and New Zealand to face South Africa in an epic cup final.

And what a final it was – 71 points and just one between them at the final whistle. The young Australians recaptured the form of the back-end of the previous season, superbly led by Brendan Foley and leading 35–19 with less than three minutes to go, but the Boks hit back.

Adding to the spectacular form of Cecil Afrika and stalwarts Frankie Horne, Chris Dry, Kyle Brown and Branco du Preez came the flying Steven Hunt with two tries and the decisive, courageous winning run of Sithole to clinch the victory, 36–35. Surely one of the greatest Sevens encounters of all time.

So a fitting end to another magnificent season, and to round off the first century of tournaments of the HSBC Sevens World Series. Exciting changes lie ahead. With each passing season, specialist and professional squads are coming into play, while the Series is set to become bigger and better than ever. The 2011–12 season opens on Australia's Gold Coast before the well-established round in Dubai and another new venue in Port Elizabeth, the Nelson Mandela Bay Stadium. Later in the season Tokyo arrives as an additional ninth tournament, one week after Hong Kong, before the climax, again in Europe but this time ending in London.

And in the women's game, too, Sevens is taking more exciting steps en route to Rio and that first Olympic Games in 2016. Dubai hosts the first IRB-sanctioned Women's Sevens tournament in December 2011, and beyond that looms the Rugby World Cup Sevens 2013 in Moscow.

HSBC SEVENS WORLD SERIES 2010–11 RESULTS

DUBAI: 3–4 DECEMBER

England (24), **Samoa** (20), **New Zealand** (16), **Fiji** (16), **South Africa** (12), **Australia** (8), **Wales** (6), **United States** (6), **Argentina** (4)

SOUTH AFRICA: 10–11 DECEMBER

New Zealand (24), **England** (20), **Fiji** (16), **Samoa** (16), **South Africa** (12), **Argentina** (8), **Australia** (6), **Wales** (6), **Scotland** (4)

NEW ZEALAND: 4–5 FEBRUARY

New Zealand (24), **England** (20), **Samoa** (16), **Australia** (16), **Fiji** (12), **South Africa** (8), **Wales** (6), **Argentina** (6), **Kenya** (4)

USA: 12–13 FEBRUARY

South Africa (24), **Fiji** (20), **New Zealand** (16), **England** (16), **Samoa** (12), **Kenya** (8), **Australia** (6), **Argentina** (6), **Scotland** (4)

HONG KONG: 25–27 MARCH

New Zealand (30), **England** (25), **Fiji** (20), **Samoa** (20), **South Africa** (16), **Australia** (10), **Portugal** (8), **Russia** (8), **Canada** (5)

AUSTRALIA: 2–3 APRIL

New Zealand (24), **South Africa** (20), **England** (16), **Samoa** (16), **Wales** (12), **Argentina** (8), **Fiji** (6), **Australia** (6), **United States** (4)

ENGLAND: 21–22 MAY

South Africa (24), **Fiji** (20), **Wales** (16), **New Zealand** (16), **Samoa** (12), **Australia** (8), **Argentina** (6), **France** (6), **Scotland** (4)

SCOTLAND: 28–29 MAY

South Africa (24), **Australia** (20), **Wales** (16), **New Zealand** (16), **Fiji** (12), **Samoa** (8), **France** (6), **England** (6), **Kenya** (4)

FINAL STANDINGS

New Zealand – 166	**Kenya – 16**
South Africa – 140	**France – 12**
England – 127	**Scotland – 12**
Fiji – 122	**United States – 10**
Samoa – 120	**Portugal – 8**
Australia – 80	**Russia – 8**
Wales – 62	**Canada – 5**
Argentina – 38	

PREVIOUS WINNERS

1999–2000: New Zealand
2000–2001: New Zealand
2001–2002: New Zealand
2002–2003: New Zealand
2003–2004: New Zealand
2004–2005: New Zealand
2005–2006: Fiji
2006–2007: New Zealand
2007–2008: New Zealand
2008–2009: South Africa
2009–2010: Samoa
2010–2011: New Zealand

ENGLAND END EIGHT-YEAR DROUGHT

By Scott Quinnell

Dave Rogers/Getty Images

The England squad celebrate their title triumph, captain Nick Easter with the trophy.

The RBS Six Nations prior to a World Cup can often feel different to those staged in the intervening three years, but despite the obvious and understandable temptation for coaches and players alike to begin focusing on the challenge for the Rugby World Cup, I thought the Championship in 2011 was thoroughly entertaining and one which all the sides gave due respect.

England were crowned champions but were ultimately denied the

Grand Slam by Ireland. I would argue their defeat to the Irish in Dublin on the final weekend of the competition was not a total shock, but I have to confess I was surprised when I realised it was the first time England had won the title in eight years. Their problems since the 2003 World Cup have been well documented, but I was taken aback when I realised how long their barren run in the Championship had lasted.

For me, there were a number of key factors in England's revival in 2011, and not least was the change in Martin Johnson. At the start of his reign as England manager, his public persona during a game was that of a frustrated player, the man who still wanted to be in the thick of the action and who felt powerless to influence events from the touch-line.

In 2011, he seemed to have settled far more comfortably into his managerial role and was far calmer and more assured during the matches. I felt that was transmitted to his players and they responded with a series of much more convincing displays.

Johnson was also fortunate to see a number of his young players really blossom on the Championship stage.

The form of Northampton flanker Tom Wood was superb. He's a real grafter who also brings an added dimension to the lineout, and his combination with Nick Easter and James Haskell gave the English back row a lovely balance.

There was also the emergence of Chris Ashton, who was certainly a breath of fresh air in the tournament. Six tries in the opening two victories over Wales and Italy made him an overnight sensation, and he's certainly a player who seems to enjoy the limelight.

I was amused by the debate about his extravagant dives over the line before touching down. I don't think Johnson was hugely impressed, but personally I thought it was great entertainment and, as long as he continues to safely put the ball down, I don't see it as a big problem.

Of course, England will have been disappointed not to have secured the Grand Slam, but there was no disgrace in losing to a vastly experienced and pumped up Ireland side at the Aviva Stadium. Those are the kind of games England will need to win in the future, but Ireland were the superior side on the day.

France finished second in the table, and their performances posed as many questions about the team as they answered. Such is the way with the French, and it is frankly pointless to talk yet again about their inconsistency and unpredictability.

I would say, however, that there have to be questions about Marc Lièvremont's approach to selection. I really struggled to see how he could justify including the likes of Dimitri Yachvili and Sébastien Chabal during the tournament, and I also think his side conspired in their own downfall when they got their tactics horribly wrong against England at Twickenham, unsuccessfully trying to take the English on up front.

Saying that, the French were hugely convincing in their 28–9 win over Wales in Paris and remain capable of beating anyone in the world when everything clicks.

Ireland looked like a team in transition, and how Declan Kidney manages the inevitable changing of the guard will dictate how the Irish move forward over the next two or three seasons.

You could see in the levels of physical commitment and the passion they played with against England in Dublin how frustrated they were collectively with their performances earlier in the tournament, and even though it is an ageing side in some departments, they showed that they are still capable of a top-quality display.

Ireland were lucky to escape from Rome with a narrow 13–11 win at the start of the tournament courtesy of Ronan O'Gara's late drop-goal, but I'm sure it was the defeat to France at the Aviva Stadium and the reverse in Cardiff that maddened Kidney and his coaching staff.

The good news was the destructive emergence of Sean O'Brien in the back row, who alongside Jamie Heaslip was one of the players of the tournament, and Kidney certainly had a nice selection dilemma in terms of choosing between O'Gara and Johnny Sexton at fly-half.

I spoke earlier of the ageing of the current team, but Brian O'Driscoll betrayed no hint of the miles on the clock with another superb Championship. He celebrated his 32nd birthday just before the start of the tournament, but three more tries in five appearances strongly suggested retirement is still very far from his thoughts.

There was a sense of disappointment with Wales' fourth-place finish, albeit on points difference, at the end of the tournament, but I think it's important to remember they were still in with a shout of the title going into the last game against

TRIVIA

England lifted the trophy but still only had three players in *Rugby World's* Team of the Tournament as selected by the world's best-selling rugby magazine. The line-up was: Ben Foden; Chris Ashton, Brian O'Driscoll, Sean Lamont, Max Evans; Toby Flood, Mike Phillips; Alex Corbisiero, William Servat, Martin Castrogiovanni, Alan Wyn Jones, Al Kellock, Sean O'Brien, Thierry Dusautoir, Sergio Parisse. Dusautoir and Lamont, albeit in a different position, are the only survivors from the 2010 team.

France. True, it was a long shot, but I felt some of the negative reaction to the campaign was a little harsh.

There was a great deal of debate about James Hook throughout the Championship and where he was asked to play. Warren Gatland initially selected him at full-back, then fly-half, then centre before moving him back to fly-half for the last two games of the campaign and I can understand people questioning the wisdom of Gatland's decisions.

I would say that the team comes before the individual and, because James is such a talented player, there is a logic to deploying him wherever he's needed. He played at 15 initially because Lee Byrne was injured, and I also don't think there's any problem giving him game time at 10 and keeping Stephen Jones on his toes.

The highlight for Wales, however, had to be the growing maturity of Dan Lydiate and Sam Warburton in the back row. Hopefully they're going to be mainstays of the Welsh pack for years to come, and I thought Warburton was the best number seven in the Championship.

Scotland went into the Six Nations with high hopes after claiming the scalp of South Africa in the autumn, but after scoring three tries against the French in defeat in their opener their challenge began to unravel and they were only spared the Wooden Spoon after a 21–8 win over Italy at Murrayfield on the final weekend.

Paolo Bruno/Getty Images

Italy caused the shock of the tournament, beating France.

For me, Scotland's campaign all came down to the second game against Wales in Edinburgh. It was just seven days after the defeat in France, and if they could just have got a home win under their belt they may have been able to kick on. Instead, Andy Robinson's side were outplayed and they were on the ropes for the rest of the campaign.

The two Scots to catch my eye were the lock Richie Gray and the young Glasgow fly-half Ruaridh Jackson, who both had impressive tournaments in difficult circumstances. Gray was an absolute revelation with his athleticism and work rate in the loose while Jackson is a fly-half who looks capable of bringing a different dimension to the Scottish game plan and increasing the tempo of their play.

Not for the first time, it was Italy who propped up the final Six Nations table, but ironically it was Nick Mallett's side who also produced the Champagne moment of the tournament with their historic 22–21 victory over France in Rome, their first-ever Championship win over Les Bleus.

Like most neutrals, I was delighted for the Italians. The result invigorated the competition and hopefully will give Italian rugby heart as they continue the long journey to becoming consistently competitive at this level. They're not there yet, but they have definitely made real progress on the evidence of the display against France.

There has been a lot of positive spin put on the introduction of Aironi and Treviso into the Magners League and, while that will eventually bear fruit for the national side, it will still take time.

Beating the French was certainly a fitting way to draw the curtain on Mallett's reign as Italy coach in the Championship. He's done a fantastic job for the Italians, and I hope people recognise that despite the side still struggling for results.

It was also encouraging that Andrea Masi was named Player of the Tournament. So often we talk about the Italian forwards, great players like Martin Castrogiovanni and Sergio Parisse, so it was refreshing for one of the Italian back-line to receive the award. It's no secret Italy need to utilise their backs more often at Test level to take the next step forward, so hopefully Masi's success is a sign of a brighter future for the Azzurri.

FIXTURES 2012

There will be no Friday night rugby in the 2012 RBS Six Nations, with games only being played on Saturday and Sunday.

France open the tournament at home to Italy and champions England begin the defence of their title at Murrayfield, against Scotland.

The Championship will see a new venue. Rome's Stadio Olimpico will host Italy's RBS Six Nations matches. The stadium, which has already hosted the 1960 Summer Olympics, four European Cup finals and the 1990 World Cup final, will host the games against England and Scotland.

The 72,000-seater takes over from the iconic Stadio Flaminio, currently undergoing refurbishment, which has hosted the tournament for the 11 years since Italy's admission.

The full list of fixtures for 2012 is:

Saturday 4 February
France v Italy, 2.30pm and
Scotland v England, 5pm

Sunday 5 February
Ireland v Wales, 3pm

Saturday 11 February
Italy v England, 4pm and
France v Ireland, 8pm

Sunday 12 February
Wales v Scotland, 3pm

Saturday 25 February
Ireland v Italy, 1.30pm and
England v Wales, 4pm

Sunday 26 February
Scotland v France, 3pm

Saturday 10 March
Wales v Italy, 2.30pm and
Ireland v Scotland, 5pm

Sunday 11 March
France v England, 3pm

Saturday 17 March
Italy v Scotland 12.30pm,
Wales v France, 2.45pm and
England v Ireland, 5pm

* All games are live in the UK on BBC television.

RBS 6 NATIONS 2011 FINAL TABLE

	P	W	D	L	For	Against	Pts
England	5	4	0	1	132	81	**8**
France	5	3	0	2	117	91	**6**
Ireland	5	3	0	2	93	81	**6**
Wales	5	3	0	2	95	89	**6**
Scotland	5	1	0	4	82	109	**2**
Italy	5	1	0	4	70	138	**2**

Points: Win 2; Draw 1; Defeat 0.

There were 589 points scored at an average of 39.3 a match. The Championship record (803 points at an average of 53.5 a match) was set in 2000. Toby Flood was the leading individual points scorer with 50, 39 points shy of the Championship record Jonny Wilkinson set in 2001. Chris Ashton was the Championship's leading try scorer with six, two short of the all-time record shared between England's Cyril Lowe (1914) and Scotland's Ian Smith (1925).

Dave Rogers/Getty Images

Ireland ruined England's Grand Slam on the final day but Martin Johnson's side were still champions.

4 February, Millennium Stadium, Cardiff

WALES 19 (1G 4PG) ENGLAND 26 (2G 4PG)

WALES: J W Hook; M L Stoddart, J H Roberts, J J V Davies, S M Williams; S M Jones, W M Phillips; P James, M Rees (*captain*), C Mitchell, B S Davies, A–W Jones, D J Lydiate, A T Powell, S Warburton *Substitutions:* R P Jones for Powell (33 mins); L M Byrne for S M Jones (66 mins); J J Thomas for Lydiate (69 mins); D J Peel for Phillips (69 mins); J V Yapp for Lydiate (temp 52 to 56 mins) and for Mitchell (70 mins); R Hibbard for Rees (73 mins)

SCORERS *Try:* Stoddart *Conversion:* S M Jones *Penalty Goals:* S M Jones (3), Hook

ENGLAND: B J Foden; C J Ashton, M J Tindall (*captain*), S E Hape, M J Cueto; T G A L Flood, B R Youngs; A J Sheridan, D M Hartley, D R Cole, L P Deacon, T P Palmer, J A W Haskell, N J Easter, T A Wood *Substitutions:* D G Wilson for Sheridan (61 mins); J P R Worsley for Haskell (62 mins); D S Care for Youngs (62 mins); J P Wilkinson for Flood (66 mins); S G Thompson for Hartley (69 mins); S D Shaw for Deacon (69 mins)

SCORERS *Tries:* Ashton (2) *Conversions:* Flood (2) *Penalty Goals:* Flood (3), Wilkinson

REFEREE A C Rolland (Ireland)

YELLOW CARDS L P Deacon (27 mins); C Mitchell (45 mins)

5 February, Stadio Flaminio, Rome

ITALY 11 (2PG 1T) IRELAND 13 (1G 1PG 1DG)

ITALY: L McLean; A Masi, G–J Canale, A Sgarbi, Mirco Bergamasco; K Burton, E Gori; S Perugini, L Ghiraldini, M–L Castrogiovanni, S Dellape, Q Geldenhuys, A Zanni, S Parisse (*captain*), J Sole *Substitutions:* P Canavosio for Gori (10 mins); V Bernabo for Sole (50 mins); C–A del Fava for Dellape (54 mins); A Lo Cicero for Perugini (temp 35 to 40 mins and 63 mins); F Ongaro for Ghiraldini (63 mins); G Garcia for Sgarbi (69 mins); L Orquera for Burton (71 mins)

SCORERS *Try:* McLean *Penalty Goals:* Mirco Bergamasco (2)

IRELAND: L M Fitzgerald; F J McFadden, B G O'Driscoll (*captain*), G W D'Arcy, K G Earls; J Sexton, T G O'Leary; C E Healy, R D Best, M R Ross, D P O'Callaghan, P J O'Connell, D P Leamy, S K O'Brien, D P Wallace *Substitutions:* E G Reddan for O'Leary (63 mins); R J R O'Gara for Sexton (65 mins); L F M Cullen for O'Connell (73 mins); S Cronin for Best (76 mins); P Wallace for D'Arcy (76 mins); T G Court for Ross (78 mins)

SCORERS *Try:* O'Driscoll *Conversion:* Sexton *Penalty Goal:* Sexton *Dropped Goal:* O'Gara

REFEREE R Poite (France)

YELLOW CARD D P Leamy (73 mins)

5 February, Stade de France, Paris

FRANCE 34 (4G 1PG 1DG) SCOTLAND 21 (3G)

FRANCE: D Traille; Y Huget, A Rougerie, M Mermoz, M Médard; F Trinh-Duc, M Parra; T Domingo, W Servat, N Mas, J Pierre, L Nallet, T Dusautoir (*captain*), I Harinordoquy, J Bonnaire *Substitutions:* C Poitrenaud for Mermoz (44 mins); L Ducalcon for Mas (51 mins); D Yachvili for Parra (52 mins); S Chabal for Harinordoquy (55 mins); G Guirado for Servat (57 mins); J Thion for Nallet (62 mins); Mas back for Domingo (69 mins); V Clerc for Médard (73 mins)

SCORERS *Tries:* Médard, pen try, Harinordoquy, Traille *Conversions:* Parra (2), Yachvili (2) *Penalty Goal:* Yachvili *Dropped Goal:* Trinh-Duc

SCOTLAND: H F G Southwell; N Walker, J A Ansbro, N J de Luca, M B Evans; D A Parks, R G M Lawson; A F Jacobsen, R W Ford, E A Murray, R J Gray, A D Kellock (*captain*), N J Hines, K D R Brown, J A Barclay *Substitutions:* M R L Blair for Lawson (40 mins); S F Lamont for De Luca (55 mins); R J Vernon for Hines (55 mins); R M Rennie for Barclay (61 mins); R J H Jackson for Parks (69 mins); M J Low for Murray (70 mins); D W H Hall for Ford (73 mins)

SCORERS *Tries:* Kellock, Brown, Lamont *Conversions:* Parks (2), Jackson

REFEREE W Barnes (England)

12 February, Twickenham

ENGLAND 59 (8G 1PG) ITALY 13 (1G 2PG)

ENGLAND: B J Foden; C J Ashton, M J Tindall (*captain*), S E Hape, M J Cueto; T G A L Flood, B R Youngs; A Corbisiero, D M Hartley, D R Cole, L P Deacon, T P Palmer, J A W Haskell, N J Easter, T A Wood *Substitutions:* S D Shaw for Deacon (45 mins); S G Thompson for Hartley (49 mins); M A Banahan for Cueto (49 mins); D S Care for Youngs (54 mins); J P Wilkinson for Flood (54 mins); D G Wilson for Cole (61 mins); C H Fourie for Wood (61 mins)

SCORERS *Tries:* Ashton (4), Cueto, Tindall, Care, Haskell *Conversions:* Flood (5), Wilkinson (3) *Penalty Goal:* Flood

ITALY: L McLean; A Masi, G–J Canale, A Sgarbi, Mirco Bergamasco; L Orquera, F Semenzato; S Perugini, L Ghiraldini, M–L Castrogiovanni, C–A del Fava, Q Geldenhuys, V Bernabo, S Parisse (*captain*), A Zanni *Substitutions:* S Dellape for Del Fava (45 mins); R Barbieri for Bernabo (54 mins); A Lo Cicero for Bernabo (temp 49 to 54 mins) and for Castrogiovanni (56 mins); G Garcia for Sgarbi (57 mins); Castrogiovanni back for Perugini (63 mins); F Ongaro for Ghiraldini (66 mins); K Burton for McLean (78 mins); P Canavosio for Masi (temp 61 to 70 mins) and for Parisse (79 mins)

SCORERS *Try:* Ongaro *Conversion:* Mirco Bergamasco *Penalty Goals:* Mirco Bergamasco (2)

REFEREE C Joubert (South Africa)

YELLOW CARD M–L Castrogiovanni (43 mins)

12 February, Murrayfield

SCOTLAND 6 (2PG) WALES 24 (1G 4PG 1T)

SCOTLAND: H F G Southwell; N Walker, J A Ansbro, N J de Luca, M B Evans; D A Parks, R G M Lawson; A F Jacobsen, R W Ford, E A Murray, N J Hines, A D Kellock (*captain*), K D R Brown, R J Vernon, J A Barclay *Substitutions:* S F Lamont for Southwell (19 mins); M R L Blair for R G M Lawson (46 mins); M J Low for Murray (46 mins); R M Rennie for Barclay (66 mins); S Lawson for Ford (66 mins); S J MacLeod for Kellock (71 mins)

SCORER *Penalty Goals:* Parks (2)

WALES: L M Byrne; M L Stoddart, J H Roberts, J J V Davies, S M Williams; J W Hook, W M Phillips; P James, M Rees (*captain*), C Mitchell, B S Davies, A–W Jones, D J Lydiate, R P Jones, S Warburton *Substitutions:* J J Thomas for Lydiate (53 mins); S M Jones for Hook (66 mins); J V Yapp for James (66 mins); J Turnbull for A–W Jones (71 mins); T D Knoyle for Phillips (75 mins); R Hibbard for Rees (75 mins); R Priestland for Byrne (75 mins)

SCORERS *Tries:* S M Williams (2) *Conversion:* Hook *Penalty Goals:* Hook (4)

REFEREE G Clancy (Ireland)

YELLOW CARDS B S Davies (23 mins); L M Byrne (27 mins)

13 February, Aviva Stadium, Lansdowne Road, Dublin

IRELAND 22 (2G 1PG 1T) FRANCE 25 (1G 6PG)

IRELAND: L M Fitzgerald; F J McFadden, B G O'Driscoll (*captain*), G W D'Arcy, K G Earls; J Sexton, T G O'Leary; C E Healy, R D Best, M R Ross, D P O'Callaghan, P J O'Connell, S K O'Brien, J P R Heaslip, D P Wallace *Substitutions:* T G Court for Healy (56 mins); R J R O'Gara for Sexton (62 mins); E G Reddan for O'Leary (69 mins); S Cronin for Best (75 mins); L F M Cullen for O'Connell (79 mins)

SCORERS *Tries:* McFadden, O'Leary, Heaslip *Conversions:* Sexton, O'Gara *Penalty Goal:* Sexton

FRANCE: C Poitrenaud; Y Huget, A Rougerie, D Traille, M Médard; F Trinh–Duc, M Parra; T Domingo, W Servat, N Mas, J Pierre, L Nallet, T Dusautoir (*captain*), I Harinordoquy, J Bonnaire *Substitutions:* S Marconnet for Domingo (49 mins); V Clerc for Poitrenaud (50 mins); D Yachvili for Parra (53 mins); S Chabal for Bonnaire (53 mins); J Thion for Pierre (63 mins); Y Jauzion for Traille (72 mins)

SCORERS *Try:* Médard *Conversion:* Yachvili *Penalty Goals:* Parra (5), Yachvili

REFEREE D Pearson (England)

26 February, Stadio Flaminio, Rome

ITALY 16 (2PG 2T) WALES 24 (1G 3PG 1DG 1T)

ITALY: L McLean; A Masi, G–J Canale, A Sgarbi, Mirco Bergamasco; K Burton, F Semenzato; S Perugini, L Ghiraldini, M–L Castrogiovanni, S Dellape, Q Geldenhuys, A Zanni, S Parisse (*captain*), R Barbieri *Substitutions:* A Lo Cicero for Perugini (40 mins); V Bernabo for Dellape (52 mins); L Orquera for Burton (64 mins); P Canavosio for Semenzato (70 mins); Perugini back for Castrogiovanni (70 mins); M Vosawai for Barbieri (71 mins); T Benvenuti for Masi (73 mins)

SCORERS *Tries:* Canale, Parisse *Penalty Goals:* Mirco Bergamasco (2)

WALES: L M Byrne; M L Stoddart, J W Hook, J H Roberts, S M Williams; S M Jones, W M Phillips; P James, M Rees (*captain*), C Mitchell, B S Davies, A–W Jones, D J Lydiate, R P Jones, S Warburton *Substitution:* R Hibbard for Rees (77 mins)

SCORERS *Tries:* Stoddart, Warburton *Conversion:* S M Jones *Penalty Goals:* S M Jones (3) *Dropped Goal:* Hook

REFEREE W Barnes (England)

26 February, Twickenham

ENGLAND 17 (4PG 1T) FRANCE 9 (3PG)

ENGLAND: B J Foden; C J Ashton, M J Tindall (*captain*), S E Hape, M J Cueto; T G A L Flood, B R Youngs; A J Sheridan, D M Hartley, D R Cole, L P Deacon, T P Palmer, J A W Haskell, N J Easter, T A Wood *Substitutions:* A Corbisiero for Sheridan (23 mins); J P Wilkinson for Flood (50 mins); D S Care for Youngs (64 mins); S G Thompson for Hartley (66 mins); S D Shaw for Deacon (70 mins); M A Banahan for Hape (75 mins); C H Fourie for Cole (75 mins)

SCORERS *Try:* Foden *Penalty Goals:* Flood (3), Wilkinson

FRANCE: C Poitrenaud; Y Huget, A Rougerie, Y Jauzion, V Clerc; F Trinh-Duc, D Yachvili; T Domingo, W Servat, N Mas, J Pierre, L Nallet, T Dusautoir (*captain*), S Chabal, I Harinordoquy *Substitutions:* D Traille for Poitrenaud (51 mins); J Bonnaire for Chabal (51 mins); S Marconnet for Domingo (59 mins); M Parra for Yachvili (61 mins); J Thion for Pierre (61 mins); A Palisson for Trinh-Duc (66mins); G Guirado for Servat (75 mins)

SCORER *Penalty Goals:* Yachvili (3)

REFEREE G Clancy (Ireland)

27 February, Murrayfield

SCOTLAND 18 (5PG 1DG) IRELAND 21 (3G)

SCOTLAND: C D Paterson; N Walker, N J de Luca, S F Lamont, M B Evans; R J H Jackson, M R L Blair; A F Jacobsen, R W Ford, M J Low, R J Gray, A D Kellock (*captain*), K D R Brown, J W Beattie, J A Barclay *Substitutions:* D A Parks for Jackson (53 mins); S Lawson for Ford (53 mins); R J Vernon for Beattie (54 mins); R G M Lawson for Blair (60 mins); G D S Cross for Beattie (temp 45 to 54 mins) and for Low (66 mins); N J Hines for Barclay (66 mins); S C J Danielli for Walker (74 mins)

SCORERS *Penalty Goals:* Paterson (4), Parks *Dropped Goal:* Parks

IRELAND: L M Fitzgerald; T J Bowe, B G O'Driscoll (*captain*), G W D'Arcy, K G Earls; R J R O'Gara, E G Reddan; C E Healy, R D Best, M R Ross, D P O'Callaghan, P J O'Connell, S K O'Brien, J P R Heaslip, D P Wallace *Substitutions:* P A Stringer for Reddan (60 mins); S Cronin for Best (60 mins); D P Leamy for Wallace (60 mins); L F M Cullen for O'Callaghan (66 mins); J Sexton for O'Gara (67 mins); T G Court for Ross (70 mins)

SCORERS *Tries:* Heaslip, Reddan, O'Gara *Conversions:* O'Gara (3)

REFEREE N Owens (Wales)

YELLOW CARD A F Jacobsen (44 mins)

12 March, Stadio Flaminio, Rome

ITALY 22 (1G 5PG) FRANCE 21 (1G 3PG 1T)

ITALY: A Masi; T Benvenuti, G–J Canale, G Garcia, Mirco Bergamasco; L Orquera, F Semenzato; A Lo Cicero, C Festuccia, M–L Castrogiovanni, S Dellape, C–A del Fava, A Zanni, S Parisse (*captain*), R Barbieri *Substitutions:* L Ghiraldini for Festuccia (47 mins); S Perugini for Lo Cicero (47 mins); Q Geldenhuys for Dellape (51 mins); P Derbyshire for Barbieri (57 mins); K Burton for Orquera (57 mins)

SCORERS *Try:* Masi *Conversion:* Mirco Bergamasco *Penalty Goals:* Mirco Bergamasco (5)

FRANCE: M Médard; Y Huget, A Rougerie, Y Jauzion, V Clerc; F Trinh-Duc, M Parra; S Marconnet, W Servat, N Mas, J Pierre, L Nallet, T Dusautoir (*captain*), S Chabal, J Bonnaire *Substitutions:* L Ducalcon for Mas (40 mins); I Harinordoquy for Chabal (56 mins); J Thion for Nallet (50 mins); G Guirado for Servat (60 mins); D Traille for Jauzion (70 mins)

SCORERS *Tries:* Clerc, Parra *Conversion:* Parra *Penalty Goals:* Parra (3)

REFEREE B J Lawrence (New Zealand)

12 March, Millennium Stadium, Cardiff

WALES 19 (1G 4PG) IRELAND 13 (1G 2PG)

WALES: L M Byrne; S L Halfpenny, J H Roberts, J J V Davies, S M Williams; J W Hook, W M Phillips; P James, M Rees (*captain*), C Mitchell, B S Davies, A–W Jones, D J Lydiate, R P Jones, S Warburton *Substitutions:* J V Yapp for Mitchell (12 mins); J J Thomas for R P Jones (59 mins); R Hibbard for Rees (72 mins)

SCORERS *Try:* Phillips *Conversion:* Hook *Penalty Goals:* Hook (3), Halfpenny

IRELAND: L M Fitzgerald; T J Bowe, B G O'Driscoll (*captain*), G W D'Arcy, K G Earls; R J R O'Gara, E G Reddan; C E Healy, R D Best, M R Ross, D P O'Callaghan, P J O'Connell, S K O'Brien, J P R Heaslip, D P Wallace *Substitutions:* P A Stringer for Reddan (1 min); J Sexton for O'Gara (49 mins); D P Leamy for Heaslip (69 mins); T G Court for Ross (69 mins); P Wallace for Fitzgerald (72 mins); S Cronin for Best (75 mins); L F M Cullen for O'Callaghan (75 mins);

SCORERS *Try:* O'Driscoll *Conversion:* O'Gara *Penalty Goals:* O'Gara (2)

REFEREE J I Kaplan (South Africa)

13 March, Twickenham

ENGLAND 22 (1G 5PG)
SCOTLAND 16 (1G 2PG 1DG)

ENGLAND: B J Foden; C J Ashton, M J Tindall (*captain*), S E Hape, M J Cueto; T G A L Flood, B R Youngs; A Corbisiero, D M Hartley, D R Cole, L P Deacon, T P Palmer, J A W Haskell, N J Easter, T A Wood *Substitutions:* M A Banahan for Tindall (40 mins); D S Care for Youngs (54 mins); J P Wilkinson for Flood (65 mins); S G Thompson for Hartley (65 mins); T R Croft for Wood (65 mins); S D Shaw for Deacon (65 mins); P P L Doran-Jones for Cole (74 mins)

SCORERS *Try:* Croft *Conversion:* Wilkinson *Penalty Goals:* Flood (4), Wilkinson

SCOTLAND: C D Paterson; M B Evans, J A Ansbro, S F Lamont, S C J Danielli; R J H Jackson, R G M Lawson; A F Jacobsen, R W Ford, M J Low, R J Gray, A D Kellock (*captain*), N J Hines, K D R Brown, J A Barclay *Substitutions:* R J Vernon for Brown (42 mins); G D S Cross for Low (52 mins); D A Parks for Jackson (54 mins); M R L Blair for R G M Lawson (54 mins); S Lawson for Ford (65 mins); A K Strokosch for Hines (67 mins); N J de Luca for Ansbro (72 mins)

SCORERS *Try:* Evans *Conversion:* Paterson *Penalty Goals:* Paterson (2) *Dropped Goal:* Jackson

REFEREE R Poite (France) replaced by J Garces (France) (58 mins)

YELLOW CARD J A Barclay (56 mins)

19 March, Murrayfield

SCOTLAND 21 (1G 3PG 1T) ITALY 8 (1PG 1T)

SCOTLAND: C D Paterson; N Walker, J A Ansbro, S F Lamont, S C J Danielli; R J H Jackson, R G M Lawson; A F Jacobsen, R W Ford, G D S Cross, R J Gray, A D Kellock (*captain*), N J Hines, K D R Brown, J A Barclay *Substitutions:* N J de Luca for Ansbro (18 mins); A K Strokosch for Hines (53 mins); S Lawson for Ford (63 mins); E A Murray for Cross (63 mins); M R L Blair for R G M Lawson (63 mins); R J Vernon for Brown (73 mins); D A Parks for Jackson (77 mins)

SCORERS *Tries:* De Luca, Walker *Conversion:* Paterson *Penalty Goals:* Paterson (3)

ITALY: A Masi; T Benvenuti, G–J Canale, A Sgarbi, Mirco Bergamasco; K Burton, F Semenzato; S Perugini, L Ghiraldini, M–L Castrogiovanni, C–A del Fava, Q Geldenhuys, A Zanni, S Parisse (*captain*), P Derbyshire *Substitutions:* L McLean for Masi (30 mins); V Bernabo for Del Fava (52 mins); A Lo Cicero for Perugini (58 mins); R Barbieri for Derbyshire (58 mins); L Orquera for Burton (58 mins); P Canavosio for Sgarbi (67 mins); C Festuccia for Ghiraldini for (77 mins)

SCORERS *Try:* Masi *Penalty Goal:* Mirco Bergamasco

REFEREE S R Walsh (Australia)

19 March, Aviva Stadium, Lansdowne Road, Dublin

IRELAND 24 (1G 4PG 1T) ENGLAND 8 (1PG 1T)

IRELAND: K G Earls; T J Bowe, B G O'Driscoll (*captain*), G W D'Arcy, A D Trimble; J Sexton, E G Reddan; C E Healy, R D Best, M R Ross, D P O'Callaghan, P J O'Connell, S K O'Brien, J P R Heaslip, D P Wallace *Substitutions:* T G Court for Ross (57 mins); R J R O'Gara for Sexton (69 mins); D P Leamy for D P Wallace (71 mins); S Cronin for Best (78 mins); L F M Cullen for O'Connell (78 mins); P A Stringer for Reddan (78 mins); P Wallace for D'Arcy (78 mins)

SCORERS *Tries:* Bowe, O'Driscoll *Conversion:* Sexton *Penalty Goals:* Sexton (4)

ENGLAND: B J Foden; C J Ashton, M A Banahan, S E Hape, M J Cueto; T G A L Flood, B R Youngs; A Corbisiero, D M Hartley, D R Cole, L P Deacon, T P Palmer, J A W Haskell, N J Easter (*captain*), T A Wood *Substitutions:* S D Shaw for Palmer (25 mins); D S Care for Youngs (45 mins); J P Wilkinson for Flood (50 mins); S G Thompson for Hartley (50 mins); P P L Doran-Jones for Cole (50 mins); T R Croft for Deacon (54 mins); D Strettle for Cueto (65 mins)

SCORERS *Try:* Thompson *Penalty Goal:* Flood

REFEREE B J Lawrence (New Zealand)

YELLOW CARD B R Youngs (35 mins)

19 March, Stade de France, Paris

FRANCE 28 (2G 3PG 1T) WALES 9 (3PG)

FRANCE: M Médard; V Clerc, D Marty, D Traille, A Palisson; F Trinh-Duc, M Parra; T Domingo, W Servat, N Mas, J Pierre, L Nallet, T Dusautoir (*captain*), I Harinordoquy, J Bonnaire *Substitutions:* L Ducalcon for Mas (66 mins); P Papé for Pierre (66 mins); F Estebanez for Traille (69 mins); G Guirado for Servat (70 mins); A Lapandry for Harinordoquy (71 mins); J Tomas for Parra (73 mins); Y Huget for Clerc (74 mins); Mas back for Domingo (76 mins)

SCORERS *Tries:* Nallet (2), Clerc *Conversions:* Parra (2) *Penalty Goals:* Parra (3)

WALES: L M Byrne; S L Halfpenny, J H Roberts, J J V Davies, G P North; J W Hook, W M Phillips; P James, M Rees (*captain*), A R Jones, B S Davies, A–W Jones, D J Lydiate, R P Jones, S Warburton *Substitutions:* J J Thomas for Warburton (15 mins); J V Yapp for A R Jones (52 mins); S M Jones for Hook (66 mins); D J Peel for Phillips (66 mins); R Hibbard for Rees (66 mins); R J McCusker for J J Thomas (70 mins)

SCORER *Penalty Goals:* Hook (3)

REFEREE C Joubert (South Africa)

YELLOW CARD J W Hook (56 mins)

Getty Images

France only won three games, including this one against Wales, but finished second.

INTERNATIONAL CHAMPIONSHIP RECORDS 1883–2011

PREVIOUS WINNERS

1883 England	1884 England	1885 Not completed
1886 England & Scotland	1887 Scotland	1888 Not completed
1889 Not completed	1890 England & Scotland	1891 Scotland
1892 England	1893 Wales	1894 Ireland
1895 Scotland	1896 Ireland	1897 Not completed
1898 Not completed	1899 Ireland	1900 Wales
1901 Scotland	1902 Wales	1903 Scotland
1904 Scotland	1905 Wales	1906 Ireland & Wales
1907 Scotland	1908 Wales	1909 Wales
1910 England	1911 Wales	1912 England & Ireland
1913 England	1914 England	1920 England & Scotland & Wales
1921 England	1922 Wales	1923 England
1924 England	1925 Scotland	1926 Scotland & Ireland
1927 Scotland & Ireland	1928 England	1929 Scotland
1930 England	1931 Wales	1932 England & Ireland & Wales
1933 Scotland	1934 England	1935 Ireland
1936 Wales	1937 England	1938 Scotland
1939 England & Ireland & Wales	1947 England & Wales	1948 Ireland
1949 Ireland	1950 Wales	1951 Ireland
1952 Wales	1953 England	1954 England & Wales & France
1955 Wales & France	1956 Wales	1957 England
1958 England	1959 France	1960 England & France
1961 France	1962 France	1963 England
1964 Scotland & Wales	1965 Wales	1966 Wales
1967 France	1968 France	1969 Wales
1970 Wales & France	1971 Wales	1972 Not completed
1973 Five Nations tie	1974 Ireland	1975 Wales
1976 Wales	1977 France	1978 Wales
1979 Wales	1980 England	1981 France
1982 Ireland	1983 Ireland & France	1984 Scotland
1985 Ireland	1986 Scotland & France	1987 France
1988 Wales & France	1989 France	1990 Scotland
1991 England	1992 England	1993 France
1994 Wales	1995 England	1996 England
1997 France	1998 France	1999 Scotland
2000 England	2001 England	2002 France
2003 England	2004 France	2005 Wales
2006 France	2007 France	2008 Wales
2009 Ireland	2010 France	2011 England

England have won the title outright 26 times; Wales 24; France 17; Scotland 14; Ireland 11; Italy 0.

TRIPLE CROWN WINNERS

England (23 times) 1883, 1884, 1892, 1913, 1914, 1921, 1923, 1924, 1928, 1934, 1937, 1954, 1957, 1960, 1980, 1991, 1992, 1995, 1996, 1997, 1998, 2002, 2003.

Wales (19 times) 1893, 1900, 1902, 1905, 1908, 1909, 1911, 1950, 1952, 1965, 1969, 1971, 1976, 1977, 1978, 1979, 1988, 2005, 2008.

Scotland (10 times) 1891, 1895, 1901, 1903, 1907, 1925, 1933, 1938, 1984, 1990.

Ireland (10 times) 1894, 1899, 1948, 1949, 1982, 1985, 2004, 2006, 2007, 2009.

GRAND SLAM WINNERS

England (12 times) 1913, 1914, 1921, 1923, 1924, 1928, 1957, 1980, 1991, 1992, 1995, 2003.

Wales (Ten times) 1908, 1909, 1911, 1950, 1952, 1971, 1976, 1978, 2005, 2008.

France (Nine times) 1968, 1977, 1981, 1987, 1997, 1998, 2002, 2004, 2010.

Scotland (Three times) 1925, 1984, 1990.

Ireland (Twice) 1948, 2009

THE 6 NATIONS CHAMPIONSHIP 2000–11

COMPOSITE TABLE

	P	W	D	L	Pts
France	60	44	0	16	**88**
Ireland	60	42	0	18	**84**
England	60	39	1	20	**79**
Wales	60	28	2	30	**58**
Scotland	60	16	2	42	**34**
Italy	60	8	1	51	**17**

CHIEF RECORDS

RECORD	DETAIL		SET
Most team points in season	229 by England	in five matches	2001
Most team tries in season	29 by England	in five matches	2001
Highest team score	80 by England	80–23 v Italy	2001
Biggest team win	57 by England	80–23 v Italy	2001
Most team tries in match	12 by Scotland	v Wales	1887
Most appearances	56 for Ireland	C M H Gibson	1964–79
	56 for Ireland	R J R O'Gara	2000–11
Most points in matches	551 for Ireland	R J R O'Gara	2000–11
Most points in season	89 for England	J P Wilkinson	2001
Most points in match	35 for England	J P Wilkinson	v Italy, 2001
Most tries in matches	25 for Ireland	B G O'Driscoll	2000–11
Most tries in season	8 for England	C N Lowe	1914
	8 for Scotland	I S Smith	1925
Most tries in match	5 for Scotland	G C Lindsay	v Wales, 1887
Most cons in matches	89 for England	J P Wilkinson	1998–2011
Most cons in season	24 for England	J P Wilkinson	2001
Most cons in match	9 for England	J P Wilkinson	v Italy, 2001
Most pens in matches	107 for Ireland	R J R O'Gara	2000–11
Most pens in season	18 for England	S D Hodgkinson	1991
	18 for England	J P Wilkinson	2000
	18 for France	G Merceron	2002
Most pens in match	7 for England	S D Hodgkinson	v Wales, 1991
	7 for England	C R Andrew	v Scotland, 1995
	7 for England	J P Wilkinson	v France, 1999
	7 for Wales	N R Jenkins	v Italy, 2000
	7 for France	G Merceron	v Italy, 2002
	7 for Scotland	C D Paterson	v Wales, 2007
Most drops in matches	11 for England	J P Wilkinson	1998–2011
Most drops in season	5 for France	G Camberabero	1967
	5 for Italy	D Dominguez	2000
	5 for Wales	N R Jenkins	2001
	5 for England	J P Wilkinson	2003
	5 for Scotland	D A Parks	2010
Most drops in match	3 for France	P Albaladejo	v Ireland, 1960
	3 for France	J-P Lescarboura	v England, 1985
	3 for Italy	D Dominguez	v Scotland, 2000
	3 for Wales	N R Jenkins	v Scotland, 2001

RBS WOMEN'S 6 NATIONS

ENGLISH DOMINANCE CONTINUES

Dave Rogers/Getty Images

England hooker Amy Garnett reached legendary status in 2011, winning her 100th cap – the first English woman to achieve the milestone.

To describe England's march to the Six Nations title in 2011 as unstoppable would be an understatement, and even a cursory glance at the final table for the 16th instalment of the women's Championship would tell a story of utter dominance by Gary Street's side.

England completed a fifth Grand Slam in six seasons with an impressive 31–0 defeat of Ireland at Ashbourne in March, but it was the team's overall performance throughout the Championship that was truly outstanding, amassing 223 points in their five fixtures while conceding a miserly eight points over the course of the campaign.

Those meagre eight points came in the shape of an Italian try in a 68–5 win for England at Esher in February and a penalty for France in their 16–3 loss at Worcester's Sixways Stadium two weeks later. Ireland, Scotland and Wales were all beaten without troubling the scoreboard.

The Six Nations success, England's 12th title since the inaugural tournament in 1996, came just six months after the heartbreak of narrowly losing the Women's Rugby World Cup final to New Zealand, and Street was full of praise for the way his side had bounced back from their bitter disappointment.

"After the World Cup there could have been a hangover, but it is an absolute credit to the girls the way they have come back and put the work in on and off the field," he said. "We have set another Championship record in terms of points conceded, and I think that is a tremendous achievement. Not only did we score some good tries, but we defended excellently. I am absolutely delighted with this result, but most importantly the effort from the players."

England went into the tournament with a new captain – Darlington Mowden Park Sharks fly-half Katy McLean – and the 25-year-old was quick to acknowledge the significance of the imminent Championship campaign.

"This is a new start, a new four-year cycle to the next World Cup and a lot of new players have come in," she said. "I am extremely excited for them to show their potential. I will certainly do my best to support them, as well as my more-established team-mates.

"Wales is always a tough game, and it will be even tougher since we are in Wales, so as a side we need to ensure we build on our World Cup performances and set up a good marker for ourselves."

Wales made it hard for England to do that at Cross Keys and, although the home side did not score, McLean's team were made to battle for their 19–0 win, courtesy of tries from wing Fran Matthews and full-back Danielle Waterman, plus a penalty try. On the same weekend, France kicked off with a convincing 53–3 victory over Scotland at the Stade Eric Durand, while Ireland recorded a 26–5 win over Italy in Rovigo.

The second round of matches a week later saw England entertain the Italians at Esher, and Street's team stamped their authority on the tournament with an 11-try salvo, including two tries apiece from flanker Heather Fisher, Waterman and wing Katherine Merchant, as they ran out 68–5 winners. France, however, recorded a 14–12 success over Ireland at Ashbourne, and England and France, the 2005 champions, were both still in contention for the Grand Slam.

The pivotal clash in the Championship came in late February when France faced England at Sixways, and for the first time the home side were made to grind out a result as the visitors offered stubborn resistance. England scored two tries through hooker Amy Garnett and McLean, but they did not come until the final quarter of the match as the defending champions struggled to turn their superior possession into points.

"We were very sporadic today, and we managed to squander quite a few opportunities," said Street after England's 16–3 win. "It was frustrating because we got ourselves into some good positions, but we missed the try-scoring opportunities. We lacked precision at times, and that was disappointing. There is lots for us to work on, but the important thing is that we are still on track. We have now got a good focus for our game against Scotland, and we know where the improvements need to be made."

Street's side certainly did make the improvements the coach demanded in the clash with the Scots, who arrived at Twickenham short on confidence and looking for their first victory of the Championship after three successive defeats.

It was not forthcoming at Twickenham, however, as the home side ran riot. England scored 15 tries in total, with braces for Matthews, Emily Scarratt, Rochelle Clark, Maggie Alphonsi, Waterman and Fisher, which meant that only Ireland stood between them and the Grand Slam.

In truth, the result of the Friday night clash at Ashbourne was never in doubt once McLean had led by example with an early try, and when No. 8 Sarah Hunter crashed over midway through the first half England were already 12–0 in the lead.

The visitors underlined their dominance with second-half scores from Clark, Sophie Hemming and Alphonsi, and when the referee blew for full-time the English celebrations began.

RBS WOMEN'S 6 NATIONS 2011 RESULTS

4 February: **France** 53 **Scotland** 3. 6 February: **Italy** 5 **Ireland** 26, **Wales** 0 **England** 19. 11 February: **Ireland** 12 **France** 14. 12 February: **England** 68 **Italy** 5. 13 February: **Scotland** 12 **Wales** 41. 26 February: **Scotland** 5 **Ireland** 22. 27 February: **England** 16 **France** 3, **Italy** 12 **Wales** 8. 13 March: **Italy** 20 **France** 28, **Wales** 15 **Ireland** 14, **England** 89 **Scotland** 0. 18 March: **Ireland** 0 **England** 31. 19 March: **France** 15 **Wales** 0. 20 March: **Scotland** 0 **Italy** 26.

FINAL TABLE

	P	W	D	L	F	A	PTS
England	5	5	0	0	223	8	**10**
France	5	4	0	1	113	51	**8**
Ireland	5	2	0	3	74	70	**4**
Wales	5	2	0	3	64	72	**4**
Italy	5	2	0	3	68	130	**4**
Scotland	5	0	0	5	20	231	**0**

WOMEN'S GAME ON THE MARCH

By Saracens & England's Maggie Alphonsi

Phil Cole/Getty Images

Alphonsi shows her power carving through the Ireland defence in the last Women's Rugby World Cup.

I **am often** asked about the state of the women's game and, biased as I may be, I have to reply that it has never been stronger. As a sport, I believe we still have improvements we can make and complacency is never healthy, but women's rugby at the moment really is in great shape.

At all levels of the game, from club rugby up to the Test arena, there are more women playing the game, the standards rise every season and more people are watching. I am hugely positive about the future.

The Women's Rugby World Cup in 2010 was the most recent global event in my sport and, although everyone involved with the England team was devastated to lose to New Zealand in the final, the tournament was a resounding success and a superb advert for the sport.

For me, the competition began relatively quietly. Our opening pool games were well attended, but once we progressed through to the semi-final and then final the level of interest and attention we got from the media and the public was amazing. Of course, that's flattering, but the point is it reflects a sport that is capturing the public imagination and demanding the media to report on it.

The final against the Black Ferns was staged at the Twickenham Stoop and attracted a crowd of over 13,000. That's a world record for a women's rugby international and tells you everything you need to know in terms of which direction the sport is heading in.

On a personal note, I'll remember the World Cup because the supporters decided to nickname me "Maggie The Machine" and the media picked up on it. Again, that's flattering, but the real point is the tournament was obviously connecting with the fans. If you're not on the public radar, you don't get a nickname.

I read somewhere after the tournament that it was broadcast to something like 127 different countries, with a worldwide audience of more than half a million. I wasn't aware of that during the competition, but they are pretty impressive figures when you think about it. There's now women's rugby being played in more than 100 countries, from Brazil to Russia and Kenya to China, and the more global we become the better it is for the development of the game.

The IRB announced Women's Rugby World Cup 2014 will be held in France, which is fantastic news for the women's game for a number of reasons. It will be the first time France has hosted the tournament, which means we'll be breaking new ground, and they certainly have the infrastructure and experience of staging major sporting events.

Rugby World Cup 2007 in France was a big success, and it's a true rugby-loving country, so I'm confident the matches will attract the crowds just as they did in 2010.

France are traditionally one of the top three or four in the women's game based on their performances in recent World Cups, and I've no doubt they will be a real threat with home advantage and a noisy, partisan crowd cheering them on.

The greatest news for the women's game in recent years, however, has to be the International Olympic Committee's decision to introduce Sevens at the 2016 Games in Rio de Janeiro. A World Cup is a fantastic stage for the women's game, but the Olympics is the biggest of them all, and the potential impact on the game could be massive.

I would love to be part of the Olympics, but I will let my body and the selectors make the final decision. I'm not a veteran yet, but I will certainly be by 2016, and I'm not going to predict whether I'll be physically up to it by the time the Games finally come around.

My personal aspirations, though, are a minor consideration. The important thing is rugby will suddenly be on show to an enormous new audience, and the women's game will be brought to those people at the same time and on an equal footing as the men's game.

I've spoken about international rugby so far, but I would also like to talk about the domestic game in England and the strides it has also made. In particular, I think the club game and Premiership show how playing standards have improved dramatically.

In my opinion, we now train as hard as Olympic athletes to be in the best shape possible for our club games. I started playing when I was about 12, and the level of physical conditioning today is light years away from what I knew a decade ago. There is a huge amount of time and effort invested in getting as fit and strong as possible.

The England team also worked on our strength and conditioning with the English Institute Of Sport in the build-up to the World Cup, and that kind of attention to detail is increasingly common in the sport.

But I think it is in terms of tactical awareness and skill sets that we have seen the most marked progress. Put simply, I think the players understand the game better than they ever have. As an openside flanker, I spend a lot of time watching videos of Richie McCaw and David Pocock to help me refine my game and pick up as many tips as possible.

I know a lot of other players who are doing the same to improve and mature as players, and you can see it being put into practice out on the pitch. The women who play the game today are certainly fitter and stronger than they were 10 years ago but, perhaps more significantly, they are far more astute as well.

I must at this point congratulate Richmond Ladies, who were crowned RFUW Premiership champions in 2010 for a second successive season. At Saracens, we won the title for four years on the bounce, but Richmond are a class outfit who have proved themselves to be the most consistent side in England over the last two years.

The Premiership is certainly a tough nut to crack these days. There used to be three or four top teams and the rest were effectively making up the numbers, but that is definitely no longer the case. To win the title, you have to have real stamina, quality throughout the squad and perhaps a bit of luck. And that is exactly how it should be.

WALLABIES END DROUGHT

By Iain Spragg

Cameron Spencer/Getty Images

Moment of truth: the Wallabies celebrate winning the 2011 Tri-Nations, with a win over New Zealand.

It was the final year of Tri-Nations rugby. After 16 seasons, the jewel in the crown of the southern hemisphere game had already agreed to become the Four Nations in 2012 with the introduction of Argentina, and as Australia, New Zealand and South Africa bid a fond farewell to the tournament's old and hugely successful format, it was the Wallabies who emerged as its final champions.

The Australians had last held the coveted bragging rights ten years earlier but finally claimed their third crown with a pulsating 25–20 victory over the All Blacks in Brisbane, a winner-takes-all clash which would have seen the Kiwis successfully defend their title had they won.

"It's obviously a significant result for us, as we haven't done that since 2001," said Wallabies coach Robbie Deans after his side's dramatic win at Suncorp Stadium. "The momentum in the game changed and the All Blacks got back on top and looked ominous, but these blokes kept their nerve, got their hands on the ball and produced enough pressure to get the result, so that's an important step for us."

The Australians began what was a truncated campaign of four rather than six fixtures in World Cup year against the Springboks in Sydney and, inspired by 19 points from wing James O'Connor, they raced to a 39–20 triumph.

A fortnight later it was the All Blacks in Auckland. The Wallabies had won just four times in 22 previous visits to Eden Park and they were unable to improve their record in 2011, going down to a 30–14 defeat despite second-half tries from Rocky Elsom and Digby Ioane.

Unbeaten New Zealand were now favourites for the title, but the Wallabies remained in the hunt after recording a superb 14–9 win over South Africa in Durban courtesy of three second-half penalties from O'Connor and a try from centre Pat McCabe.

"Things didn't go our way early on, but we fought back," said captain Elsom after leading Australia to their third victory in five visits to King's Park. "We stuck to what we knew, and I'm very happy to come away with the win."

A week later the Springboks beat the All Blacks in Port Elizabeth, and the stage was now set for the game in Brisbane and a dramatic denouement to the last ever Tri-Nations.

Australia were the quickest out of the blocks at Suncorp Stadium and took the lead through a Quade Cooper penalty after three minutes, before really twisting the knife on 13 minutes when scrum-half Will Genia scampered over. New Zealand were reeling, and when No. 8 Radike Samo scored a spectacular long-range try for the Wallabies, the All Blacks were 18–3 adrift and almost out for the count.

The break could not come quick enough for the visitors, but they were a side reborn in the second half, levelling the match at 20–20 on the hour after tries from centres Conrad Smith and Ma'a Nonu.

It was Australia's turn to be stunned, but just as it seemed the All Blacks might snatch victory, the home side regained the initiative with a vital try from full-back Kurtley Beale. Copper missed the conversion but there was no more scoring and the Wallabies were champions.

"Any time you beat the All Blacks, you've got to give yourself a pat on the back," Cooper said after the match, only Australia's third victory over the Kiwis in their last 14 encounters. "They're not the best team in the world for no reason, and the performance we put in as a team gives us a lot of confidence moving forward."

TRI-NATIONS 2011 FINAL TABLE

	P	W	D	L	F	A	Bonus Points	Pts.
Australia	4	3	0	1	92	79	**1**	**13**
New Zealand	4	2	0	2	95	64	**2**	**10**
South Africa	4	1	0	3	54	98	**1**	**5**

Points: win 4; draw 2; four or more tries, or defeat by seven or fewer points 1

23 July, ANZ Stadium, Sydney

AUSTRALIA 39 (4G 2PG 1T) SOUTH AFRICA 20 (2G 2PG)

AUSTRALIA: K J Beale; J D O'Connor, A P Ashley-Cooper, P J McCabe, D A N Ioane; Q S Cooper, S W Genia; S M Kepu, S T Moore, B E Alexander, R A Simmons, J E Horwill, R D Elsom (*captain*), B J McCalman, D W Pocock *Substitutions:* N C Sharpe for Horwill (56 mins); S Higginbotham for Elsom (56 mins); S M Fainga'a for Moore (60 mins); A S Fainga'a for Ashley-Cooper (63 mins); M J Hodgson for Pocock (64 mins); N J Phipps for Genia (64 mins); P J M Cowan for Beale (70 mins)

SCORERS *Tries:* Alexander, Ioane, O'Connor, Moore, Ashley-Cooper *Conversions:* O'Connor (4) *Penalty Goals:* O'Connor (2)

SOUTH AFRICA: G G Aplon; B A Basson, J L de Jongh, W Olivier, L N Mvovo; M Steyn, R Pienaar; M D Greyling, J W Smit (*captain*), W Kruger, P R van der Merwe, A J Hargreaves, D J Rossouw, A F Johnson, G J Stegmann *Substitutions:* R Kankowski for Van der Merwe (33 mins); J R Deysel for Johnson (51 mins); P Lambie for Steyn (56 mins); M C Ralepelle for Greyling (56 mins); C J van der Linde for Greyling (temp 6 to 15 mins and temp 22 to 33 mins) and for Kruger (56 mins); A A Jacobs for Olivier (65 mins)

SCORER *Tries:* Ralepelle, Smit *Conversions:* Lambie (2) *Penalty Goals:* Steyn (2)

REFEREE C J Pollock (New Zealand)

30 July, Westpac Stadium, Wellington

NEW ZEALAND 40 (2G 2PG 4T)
SOUTH AFRICA 7 (1G)

NEW ZEALAND: J M Muliaina; C S Jane, C G Smith, M A Nonu, Z R Guildford; D W Carter, Q J Cowan; W W V Crockett, A K Hore, B J Franks, S L Whitelock, A J Williams, J Kaino, A J Thomson, R H McCaw (*captain*) *Substitutions:* I F Afoa for Franks (42 mins); Franks back for Afoa (48 mins); S Williams for Smith (53 mins); P A T Weepu for Cowan (55 mins); L J Messam for Kaino (55 mins); C R Slade for Nonu (66 mins); C R Flynn for Hore (71 mins); J M R A Hoeata for Whitelock (71 mins)

SCORERS *Tries*: Jane (2), Guildford (2), Crockett, Slade *Conversions*: Carter (2) *Penalty Goals:* Carter (2)

SOUTH AFRICA: M Steyn; B A Basson, A A Jacobs, J L de Jongh, L N Mvovo; P Lambie, R Pienaar; M D Greyling, J W Smit (*captain*), W Kruger, G Mostert, A J Hargreaves, J R Deysel, D J Rossouw, G J Stegmann *Substitutions:* C J van der Linde for Greyling (46 mins); M C Ralepelle for Kruger (46 mins); A F Johnson for Deysel (temp 48 to 58 mins) and for Stegmann (58 mins); C McLeod for Steyn (66 mins); W Olivier for Jacobs (66 mins); O M Ndungane for Basson (66 mins); R Kankowski for Mostert (74 mins)

SCORERS *Try:* Smit *Conversion:* Steyn

REFEREE A C Rolland (Ireland)

Phil Walter/Getty Images

Cory Jane hit the Tri-Nations with a bang, with two tries against the Springboks.

6 August, Eden Park, Auckland

NEW ZEALAND 30 (3G 2PG 1DG) AUSTRALIA 14 (2G)

NEW ZEALAND: J M Muliaina; S W Sivivatu, C G Smith, M A Nonu, H E Gear; D W Carter, P A T Weepu; W W V Crockett, K F Mealamu, O T Franks, B C Thorn, A J Williams, J Kaino, K J Read, R H McCaw (*captain*) *Substitutions:* B J Franks for Crockett (49 mins); C R Slade for Sivivatu (55 mins); A K Hore for Mealamu (59 mins); A M Ellis for Weepu (59 mins); S L Whitelock for A J Williams (65 mins); S Williams for Nonu (68 mins); A J Thomson for Kaino (70 mins)

SCORERS *Tries*: Nonu, Mealamu, Sivivatu *Conversions*: Carter (3) *Penalty Goals:* Carter (2) *Dropped Goal:* Carter

AUSTRALIA: K J Beale; J D O'Connor, A P Ashley-Cooper, P J McCabe, D A N Ioane; Q S Cooper, S W Genia; S M Kepu, S T Moore, B E Alexander, R A Simmons, J E Horwill, R D Elsom (*captain*), B J McCalman, D W Pocock *Substitutions:* D J Vickerman for Simmons (52 mins); S Higginbotham for McCalman (55 mins); S M Fainga'a for Moore (68 mins)

SCORER *Tries:* Ioane, Elsom *Conversions:* Cooper (2)

REFEREE C Joubert (South Africa)

Cameron Spencer/Getty Images

Australia's losing run at Eden Park continued with Ma'a Nonu on the scoresheet.

13 August, King's Park, Durban

SOUTH AFRICA 9 (3PG) AUSTRALIA 14 (3PG 1T)

SOUTH AFRICA: F P L Steyn; J-P R Pietersen, J Fourie, J de Villiers, B G Habana; A D James, P F du Preez; T Mtawarira, J W Smit (*captain*), J N du Plessis, J P Botha, V Matfield, D J Rossouw, P J Spies, H W Brüssow *Substitutions:* B W du Plessis for J N du Plessis (49 mins); J R Deysel for Brüssow (49 mins); G G Aplon for F P L Steyn (49 mins); G Mostert for Botha (63 mins); G G Steenkamp for Mtawarira (67 mins); M Steyn for James (67 mins); J N du Plessis back for Smit (77 mins); F Hougaard for Habana (temp 57 to 67 mins)

SCORERS *Penalty Goals:* James (2), F P L Steyn

AUSTRALIA: K J Beale; J D O'Connor, A P Ashley-Cooper, P J McCabe, D A N Ioane; Q S Cooper, S W Genia; S M Kepu, S T Moore, B E Alexander, J E Horwill, N C Sharpe, R D Elsom (*captain*), S Higginbotham, D W Pocock *Substitutions:* U R Samo for Higginbotham (59 mins); A S Fainga'a for Ashley-Cooper (59 mins)

SCORERS *Try*: McCabe *Penalty Goals:* O'Connor (3)

REFEREE B J Lawrence (New Zealand)

20 August, Nelson Mandela Bay Stadium, Port Elizabeth

SOUTH AFRICA 18 (5PG 1DG) NEW ZEALAND 5 (1T)

SOUTH AFRICA: P Lambie; J-P R Pietersen, J Fourie, J de Villiers, B G Habana; M Steyn, P F du Preez; G G Steenkamp, B W du Plessis, J N du Plessis, J P Botha, V Matfield (*captain*), W S Alberts, P J Spies, H W Brüssow *Substitutions:* F Hougaard for Lambie (20 mins); T Mtawarira for Steenkamp (40 mins); J W Smit for B W du Plessis (60 mins); A F Johnson for Brüssow (temp 11 to 25 mins) and for Alberts (67 mins); D J Rossouw for Botha (temp 46 to 56 mins and 67 mins); C J van der Linde for J N Du Plessis (69 mins)

SCORER *Penalty Goals:* M Steyn (5) *Dropped Goal:* M Steyn

NEW ZEALAND: I J A Dagg; I Toeava, R D Kahui, S Williams, H E Gear; C R Slade, Q J Cowan; T D Woodcock, K F Mealamu (*captain*), I F Afoa, S L Whitelock, A J Williams, J Kaino, L J Messam, A J Thomson *Substitutions:* B J Franks for Afoa (51 mins); A M Ellis for Cowan (53 mins); P A T Weepu for Slade (60 mins); I F Afoa back for Woodcock (60 mins); A K Hore for Mealamu (60 mins); J M R A Hoeata for A J Williams (69 mins); V V J Vito for Messam (69 mins); C S Jane for Gear (71 mins)

SCORER *Try*: Kahui

REFEREE G Clancy (Ireland)

27 August, Suncorp Stadium, Brisbane

AUSTRALIA 25 (2G 2PG 1T)
NEW ZEALAND 20 (2G 2PG)

AUSTRALIA: K J Beale; A P Ashley-Cooper, A S Fainga'a, P J McCabe, D A N Ioane; Q S Cooper, S W Genia; S M Kepu, S T Moore, B E Alexander, D J Vickerman, J E Horwill (*captain*), R D Elsom, U R Samo, D W Pocock *Substitutions:* R A Simmons for Vickerman (54 mins); B J McCalman for Samo (59 mins); S Higginbotham for Elsom (71 mins); S M Fainga'a for Moore (75 mins); R S L Ma'afu for Kepu (75 mins); L Burgess for Genia (75 mins)

SCORERS *Tries*: Genia, Samo, Beale *Conversions:* Connor (2) *Penalty Goals:* Connor (2)

NEW ZEALAND: J M Muliaina; C S Jane, C G Smith, M A Nonu, Z R Guildford; D W Carter, P A T Weepu; T D Woodcock, K F Mealamu, O T Franks, B C Thorn, S L Whitelock, A J Thomson, K J Read, R H McCaw (*captain*) *Substitutions:* V V J Vito for Read (12 mins); A J Williams for Thomson (37 mins); I Toeava for Guildford (54 mins); A M Ellis for Weepu (63 mins); A K Hore for Mealamu (73 mins); I F Afoa for Franks (73 mins)

SCORERS *Tries*: Smith, Nonu *Conversions*: Carter (2) *Penalty Goals:* Carter (2)

REFEREE W Barnes (England)

Phil Walter/Getty Images

Australia were crowned 2011 Tri-Nations champions after this win over New Zealand.

TRI-NATIONS RECORDS 1996–2011

PREVIOUS WINNERS

1996 New Zealand	1997 New Zealand	1998 South Africa	1999 New Zealand
2000 Australia	2001 Australia	2002 New Zealand	2003 New Zealand
2004 South Africa	2005 New Zealand	2006 New Zealand	2007 New Zealand
2008 New Zealand	2009 South Africa	2010 New Zealand	2011 Australia

GRAND SLAM WINNERS

New Zealand (Four times) 1996, 1997, 2003 and 2010
South Africa (Once) 1998

TEAM RECORD	DETAIL		SET
Most team points in season	184 by N Zealand	in six matches	2010
Most team tries in season	22 by N Zealand	in six matches	2010
Highest team score	61 by S Africa	61–22 v Australia (h)	1997
Biggest team win	49 by Australia	49–0 v S Africa (h)	2006
Most team tries in match	8 by S Africa	v Australia	1997
	8 by S Africa	v Australia	2008

INDIVIDUAL RECORD	DETAIL		SET
Most appearances	48 for Australia	G M Gregan	1996 to 2007
Most points in matches	461 for N Zealand	D W Carter	2003 to 2011
Most points in season	99 for N Zealand	D W Carter	2006
Most points in match	31 for S Africa	M Steyn	v N Zealand (h), 2009
Most tries in matches	16 for N Zealand	C M Cullen	1996 to 2002
Most tries in season	7 for N Zealand	C M Cullen	2000
Most tries in match	4 for S Africa	J L Nokwe	v Australia (h), 2008
Most cons in matches	61 for N Zealand	D W Carter	2003 to 2011
Most cons in season	14 for N Zealand	D W Carter	2006
Most cons in match	6 for S Africa	J H de Beer	v Australia (h),1997
Most pens in matches	100 for N Zealand	D W Carter	2003 to 2011
Most pens in season	23 for S Africa	M Steyn	2009
Most pens in match	9 for N Zealand	A P Mehrtens	v Australia (h), 1999
Most drops in matches	4 for S Africa	A S Pretorius	2002 to 2006
	4 for S Africa	M Steyn	2009 to 2011
Most drops in season	3 for S Africa	M Steyn	2009
Most drops in match	2 for S Africa	J H de Beer	v N Zealand (h), 1997
	2 for S Africa	F P L Steyn	v Australia (h), 2007

From 1996 to 2005 inclusive, each nation played four matches in a season. The nations have each played six matches since, except in 2007 and 2011 (World Cup years) when they reverted to four.

BABY BLACKS VICTORIOUS

By Karen Bond

Valerio Pennicino/Getty Images

New Zealand celebrate their fourth successive world title.

New Zealand remain the only country to lift the distinctive trophy after securing a fourth successive title, but in reality they have never come so close to tasting defeat on the Junior World Championship stage as they did against England in the final at the Stadio Plebiscito in the Italian city of Padova in late June.

The final lived up to its hype and produced a titanic battle for the title, unlike 12 months ago when New Zealand blitzed Australia with a sublime display of rugby to win 62–17 in Argentina. This time there would be no runaway win, the capacity crowd instead treated to an "intriguing and absolutely riveting" encounter in the words of commentator Nigel Starmer-Smith.

England have twice been on the receiving end of heavy final losses to New Zealand – 38–3 in 2008 and 44–28 a year later – and knew they couldn't allow their opponents to get up a head of steam or they could well suffer the same fate as Australia or even Wales, who were swept aside 92–0 in the pool stages.

The mood in the England camp was buoyant, the feeling that this was not – unlike in previous years – an invincible New Zealand outfit. Argentina had highlighted their frailties, particularly at scrum time, in their Pool A encounter, and Australia followed suit in the semi-finals, even if the scoreboard would suggest two comfortable wins for New Zealand.

England came out in determined mood, accepting the challenge of the New Zealand haka and putting the champions under intense pressure, barely allowing them out of their own half in the opening 15 minutes and getting their reward when Christian Wade raced down the touchline to open the scoring.

They were making all the running and creating plenty of opportunities, but were unable to turn their domination into points, unlike New Zealand who recovered to lead 20–10 at half-time thanks to tries by Charles Piutau and prop Ben Tameifuna. However, if the Baby Blacks, with Gareth Anscombe pulling the strings at fly-half, harboured thoughts of running away with it England had other ideas, cutting the deficit to just a single point with Henry Thomas and Wade tries.

England would have been ahead going into the last 10 minutes had TJ Perenara not somehow got his arm under the ball to deny Matt Kvesic a try, but after Anscombe kicked a penalty and lively full-back Beauden Barrett touched down to seal the 33–22 win – their 20th consecutive victory in JWC history – it was the English left ruing missed opportunities.

"The Poms rated themselves, and fairly so; they're a bloody good side and they pushed us right to the edge there, but we dug deep and held on, and to hold on in those type of conditions really meant a lot to us," admitted Anscombe, Man of the Match and the son of coach Mark and whose 100% record with the boot ultimately proved the difference on the scoreboard with both sides scoring three tries.

It was England's first defeat under coach Rob Hunter and a bitter pill for the Six Nations Grand Slam winners to swallow, the fact they had come closer to beating New Zealand than anyone in JWC history no comfort as they watched Luke Whitelock follow in the footsteps of Chris Smith, Aaron Cruden and Tyler Bleyendaal by lifting the trophy.

There was some consolation for Wade when he finished as the joint leading try-scorer with South Africa captain Arno Botha on seven, the latter scoring a hat-trick in a 104–17 defeat of Fiji in the fifth-place play-off. It was not the placing South Africa had wanted, but after missing out on the semi-finals for the first time they were a side on a mission, determined to show their potential, and 25 tries in two play-off matches went some way to doing that.

Fiji still had plenty to smile about with sixth, their best-ever finish in the tournament's four-year history. France would also leave Italy with their best-ever finish of fourth, having become the sixth different nation to play in the semi-finals after beating Australia 31–25 in an exciting tussle to top Pool B.

That encounter showcased France at their mercurial best, full of attacking flair and solid defence with the ferocity and panache that had been missing as they stuttered past Fiji and Tonga. The defeat ultimately didn't prove costly for Australia as they joined France in the semi-finals as the best runner-up across the pools, edging South Africa on points difference after they fell 26–20 to England in another epic battle.

South Africa threw everything but the kitchen sink at England in the dying minutes in search of a try that would have kept their title hopes alive, but they came up short thanks to some impressive last-ditch tackles from the English. Their absence, though, did set up two intriguing intra-hemisphere semi-finals, with New Zealand battling past Australia, while England, inspired by the tournament's youngest player, George Ford, overcame France 33–18.

Australia would avenge their earlier loss to France in the third-place play-off, not making the same mistake of starting slowly, with captain Colby Faingaa – the younger brother of Wallabies Saia and Anthony – once again a livewire in defence and attack in a 30–17 win under a blazing Padova sun.

The other matches on the final day yielded victories for Wales, Argentina and Italy, and the latter was celebrated as if it was the title the Azzurrini had won, rather than the 11th-place play-off against Tonga, with coach Andrea Cavinato thrown into the air by his jubilant players. Italy had found their return to the Junior World Championship hard, the Junior World Rugby Trophy 2010 winners losing to New Zealand, Wales and Argentina (twice) before finally discovering the scoring touch against Tonga to the delight of the Stadio Mario Battaglini crowd.

For Wales, the 38–24 victory over Ireland to match their seventh-place finish of 2010 was a positive note in a campaign of contrasting fortunes, the 92–0 mauling by New Zealand – the biggest margin of defeat by any side in Welsh rugby history – a dark day. And the 34–20 loss to Fiji on day four did little to stem the gloom. Although on the losing side, Ireland wing Andrew Conway touched down for his 10th try across two Junior World Championships, equalling the all-time record of All Black Zac Guildford.

The tournament, though, is about more than just unearthing the next generation of world stars and will certainly have left its mark on the rugby communities in the Veneto region of Italy, with fans attending matches in their tens of thousands across the three venues in Padova, Rovigo and Treviso and creating an atmosphere to savour with their enthusiasm for the exciting, attacking rugby on show.

IRB JUNIOR WORLD CHAMPIONSHIP 2011 RESULTS

POOL A

Round One: **Argentina** 8–34 **Wales**, **Italy** 7–64 **New Zealand**. Round Two: **New Zealand** 92–0 **Wales**, **Italy** 3–27 **Argentina**. Round Three: **Italy** 6–56 **Wales**, **Argentina** 15–48 **New Zealand**.

POOL B

Round One: **Australia** 54–7 **Tonga**, **France** 24–12 **Fiji**. Round Two: **Australia** 50–25 **Fiji**, **France** 27–14 **Tonga**. Round Three: **Fiji** 36–18 **Tonga**, **Australia** 25–31 **France**.

POOL C

Round One: **England** 33–25 **Ireland**, **South Africa** 33–0 **Scotland**. Round Two: **England** 39–18 **Scotland**, **Ireland** 26–42 **South Africa**. Round Three: **England** 26–20 **South Africa**, **Ireland** 30–13 **Scotland**.

POOL TABLES

POOL A

	P	W	D	L	F	A	BP	PTS
New Zealand	3	3	0	0	204	22	3	**15**
Wales	3	2	0	1	90	106	2	**10**
Argentina	3	1	0	2	50	85	0	**4**
Italy	3	0	0	3	16	147	0	**0**

POOL B

	P	W	D	L	F	A	BP	PTS
France	3	3	0	0	82	51	2	**14**
Australia	3	2	0	1	129	63	3	**11**
Fiji	3	1	0	2	73	92	1	**5**
Tonga	3	0	0	3	39	117	0	**0**

POOL C

	P	W	D	L	F	A	BP	PTS
England	3	3	0	0	98	63	2	14
South Africa	3	2	0	1	95	52	3	11
Ireland	3	1	0	2	81	88	0	4
Scotland	3	0	0	3	31	102	0	0

PLAY-OFFS – FIRST PHASE

Ninth-Place Semi-Finals	**Scotland** 30–11 **Tonga**
	Argentina 12–8 **Italy**
Fifth Place Semi-Finals	**Wales** 20–34 **Fiji**
	South Africa 57–15 **Ireland**
Semi-Finals	**England** 33–18 **France**
	New Zealand 37–7 **Australia**

PLAY-OFFS SECOND PHASE

11th-Place Play-off	**Tonga** 22–34 **Italy**
Ninth-Place Play-off	**Scotland** 14–15 **Argentina**
Seventh-Place Play-off	**Wales** 38–24 **Ireland**
Fifth-Place Play-off	**Fiji** 17–104 **South Africa**

THIRD-PLACE PLAY-OFF

26 June 2011, Stadio Plebiscito, Padova

FRANCE 17 (2G 1PG) AUSTRALIA 30 (3G 3PG)

FRANCE: G Palis; M O'Connor, JP Barraque, T Visensang, Y Artru; J Plisson, Y Lesgourgues; F Fresia, C Bourgeois, V Delmas, W Demotte, M Marie, K Chateau, P Julien, G Galan (captain).

SUBSTITUTIONS: J Come for Chateau (22 mins); L Vignon for Galan (25 mins); A Mourot for P Julien (25), T Ecohard for Lesgourgues; S Taofifenua for Fresia (50 mins); C David for Bourgeois (50 mins); JM Doussain for Barraque (64 mins).

SCORERS: *Tries:* Come, Palis *Conversions:* Barraque, Doussain *Penalty:* Barraque

AUSTRALIA: S Morahan; C Kuridrani, T Kingston, B Meakes, J Woodhouse; B Volavola, M Lucas; S Sio, S Siliva, P Alo-Emile, B Enever, G Peterson, T Postal, M Hooper, C Faingaa (captain).

SUBSTITUTIONS: J Butler for Postal (31 mins), T Postal for Butler (40 mins), L Jones for Enever (54 mins), E Bredenhann for Lucas (59 mins), R Saifoloi for Meakes (64 mins), J Butler for Peterson (68 mins), JP Pradaud for Siliva (76 mins).

SCORERS: *Tries:* Kingston, Lucas, Morahan *Conversions:* Volavola (3) *Penalty:* Volavola (3)

REFEREE: L Hodges (Wales)

FINAL

26 June 2010, Stadio Plebiscito, Padova

ENGLAND 22 (2G 1T 1PG)
NEW ZEALAND 33 (3G 4PG)

ENGLAND: B Ransom; A Short, E Daly, O Farrell, C Wade; G Ford, C Cook; M Vunipola, M Haywood, H Thomas, J Launchbury, C Matthews, S Jones, M Kvesic, A Gray (captain).

SUBSTITUTIONS: M Yarde for Short (29 mins), A Short for Yarde (35 mins), M Yarde for Short (42 mins), R Mills for Farrell (50 mins), D Robson for Cook (61 mins), W Collier for Thomas (61 mins), M Everard for Jones (73 mins), R Buchanan for Haywood (73 mins), S Twomey for Kvesic (74 mins)

SCORERS: *Tries:* Wade (2), Thomas *Conversions:* Ford (2) *Penalty:* Ford

NEW ZEALAND: B Barrett; M Scott, F Saili, L Sopoaga, C Piutau; G Anscombe, TJ Perenara; S Sakalia, C Taylor, B Tameifuna, S Luatua, B Retallick, B Shields, S Cane, L Whitelock (captain).

SUBSTITUTIONS: D Bird for Retallick (62 mins), C Axtens for Shields (66 mins), R Llewellyn for Saili (75 mins), W Naholo for Piutau (77 mins), Kainga for Tameifuna (77 mins)

SCORERS: *Tries:* Barrett, Piutau, Tameifuna *Conversions:* Anscombe (3) *Penalties*: Anscombe (4)

REFEREE: J Peyper (South Africa)

FINAL STANDINGS

1 New Zealand	2 England
3 Australia	4 France
5 South Africa	6 Fiji
7 Wales	8 Ireland
9 Argentina	10 Scotland
11 Italy	12 Tonga

SAMOA BOUNCE BACK IN GEORGIA

IRB

Samoa won an exceptional IRB Junior World Rugby Trophy in Tbilisi.

A spirited fight back from a determined Samoa side in Tbilisi saw the pre-tournament favourites defeat Japan 31–24 to claim the IRB Junior World Rugby Trophy 2011 crown and, with it, qualification back to the IRB Junior World Championship 2012 in South Africa.

Georgia, who proved exceptional hosts as they staged an IRB tournament for the first time, beat a strong Uruguay team 20–15 to take third place. The victory confirmed the growth of the country's new national sport and secured a lasting legacy, with thrilling contests, superb hospitality and future international stars on show. Eight games were shown live on www.irb.com across the four match days, with fans able to enjoy an increasingly competitive and closely-fought tournament.

Canada sealed fifth place by beating Russia 49–24 in a match featuring one of the tournament's stand-out players, Russia's 20-year-old wing Denis Simplikevich. Just four months later Simplikevich would make his Test and Rugby World Cup debut, scoring a try against Ireland and then touching down against former champions Australia. In total, nine Junior World Rugby Trophy graduates graced the game's greatest stage in New Zealand.

The final proved every bit as exciting as the pool matches which saw Samoa top Pool A and Japan, reaching their second successive final, head Pool B to set up the mouth-watering clash.

Ultimately, Samoa full-back Peter Schuster's try deep into added time proved the difference in an enthralling match that Japan had led 17–0 midway through the first half.

The Brave Blossoms began brightly, and their first try was simply executed when, from the back of a scrum, No 8 Olive Taufa popped the ball to scrum-half Keisuke Uchida, whose lovely long pass found wing Masakatasu Hikosaka to touch down.

A further try and the reliable boot of fly-half Ryodo Nakamura extended Japan's lead to 17–0 before Samoa began a stylish comeback, instigated by flanker Jordan Taufua who dived over for their first try. He was soon followed by a far more extravagant dive from centre Robert Lilomaiava after he broke cleanly through the middle. A superb chip from fly-half Patrick Fa'apale gave impressive centre Faavae Faavae a try in the corner to put the game 19–17 in Samoa's favour going into the break.

A second-half try by Samoa wing Viliamu Alauni saw the lead extended, only for Japan to claw the match back to 24–24 thanks to prop Mao Enoki who emerged from the bottom of a rolling maul to claim a try and Nakamura the conversion.

With sudden death looming, a superbly timed flat pass from captain Fa'apale put full-back Peter Schuster in for the winning try in the corner. Fa'apale added the conversion to confirm his team as champions.

John Schuster, a happy winning coach, admitted, "We were very lucky to win it. Japan played extremely well today; they had a well-structured game, forcing us into many mistakes. We feel very lucky to have won."

FINAL STANDINGS

1 Samoa	5 Canada
2 Japan	6 Russia
3 Georgia	7 USA
4 Uruguay	8 Zimbabwe

International Records and Statistics

INTERNATIONAL RECORDS

RESULTS OF INTERNATIONAL MATCHES

(UP TO 31 OCTOBER 2011)

Cap matches involving senior executive council member unions only. Years for International Championship matches are for the second half of the season: eg 1972 means season 1971–72. Years for matches against touring teams from the Southern Hemisphere refer to the actual year of the match.
Points-scoring was first introduced in 1886, when an International Board was formed by Scotland, Ireland and Wales. Points values varied among the countries until 1890, when England agreed to join the Board, and uniform values were adopted.

Northern Hemisphere seasons	Try	Conversion	Penalty goal	Dropped goal	Goal from mark
1890–91	1	2	2	3	3
1891–92 to 1892–93	2	3	3	4	4
1893–94 to 1904–05	3	2	3	4	4
1905–06 to 1947–48	3	2	3	4	3
1948–49 to 1970–71	3	2	3	3	3
1971–72 to 1991–92	4	2	3	3	3*
1992–93 onwards	5	2	3	3	–

**The goal from mark ceased to exist when the free-kick clause was introduced, 1977–78.*

WC indicates a fixture played during the Rugby World Cup finals. LC indicates a fixture played in the Latin Cup. TN indicates a fixture played in the Tri-Nations.

ENGLAND v SCOTLAND

Played 129 England won 69, Scotland won 42, Drawn 18
Highest scores England 43–3 in 2001 and 43–22 in 2005, Scotland 33–6 in 1986
Biggest wins England 43–3 in 2001, Scotland 33–6 in 1986

1871 Raeburn Place (Edinburgh) **Scotland** 1G 1T to 1T
1872 The Oval (London) **England** 1G 1DG 2T to 1DG
1873 Glasgow **Drawn** no score
1874 The Oval **England** 1DG to 1T
1875 Raeburn Place **Drawn** no score
1876 The Oval **England** 1G 1T to 0
1877 Raeburn Place **Scotland** 1 DG to 0
1878 The Oval **Drawn** no score
1879 Raeburn Place **Drawn** Scotland 1DG England 1G
1880 Manchester **England** 2G 3T to 1G
1881 Raeburn Place **Drawn** Scotland 1G 1T England 1DG 1T
1882 Manchester **Scotland** 2T to 0
1883 Raeburn Place **England** 2T to 1T
1884 Blackheath (London) **England** 1G to 1T
1885 No Match
1886 Raeburn Place **Drawn** no score
1887 Manchester **Drawn** 1T each
1888 No Match
1889 No Match
1890 Raeburn Place **England** 1G 1T to 0
1891 Richmond (London) **Scotland** 9–3
1892 Raeburn Place **England** 5–0
1893 Leeds **Scotland** 8–0
1894 Raeburn Place **Scotland** 6–0
1895 Richmond **Scotland** 6–3
1896 Glasgow **Scotland** 11–0
1897 Manchester **England** 12–3
1898 Powderhall (Edinburgh) **Drawn** 3–3
1899 Blackheath **Scotland** 5–0
1900 Inverleith (Edinburgh) **Drawn** 0–0
1901 Blackheath **Scotland** 18–3
1902 Inverleith **England** 6–3
1903 Richmond **Scotland** 10–6
1904 Inverleith **Scotland** 6–3
1905 Richmond **Scotland** 8–0
1906 Inverleith **England** 9–3
1907 Blackheath **Scotland** 8–3
1908 Inverleith **Scotland** 16–10
1909 Richmond **Scotland** 18–8
1910 Inverleith **England** 14–5
1911 Twickenham **England** 13–8
1912 Inverleith **Scotland** 8–3
1913 Twickenham **England** 3–0
1914 Inverleith **England** 16–15
1920 Twickenham **England** 13–4
1921 Inverleith **England** 18–0
1922 Twickenham **England** 11–5
1923 Inverleith **England** 8–6
1924 Twickenham **England** 19–0
1925 Murrayfield **Scotland** 14–11
1926 Twickenham **Scotland** 17–9
1927 Murrayfield **Scotland** 21–13
1928 Twickenham **England** 6–0
1929 Murrayfield **Scotland** 12–6
1930 Twickenham **Drawn** 0–0
1931 Murrayfield **Scotland** 28–19
1932 Twickenham **England** 16–3
1933 Murrayfield **Scotland** 3–0
1934 Twickenham **England** 6–3
1935 Murrayfield **Scotland** 10–7
1936 Twickenham **England** 9–8
1937 Murrayfield **England** 6–3
1938 Twickenham **Scotland** 21–16
1939 Murrayfield **England** 9–6
1947 Twickenham **England** 24–5
1948 Murrayfield **Scotland** 6–3
1949 Twickenham **England** 19–3
1950 Murrayfield **Scotland** 13–11
1951 Twickenham **England** 5–3
1952 Murrayfield **England** 19–3
1953 Twickenham **England** 26–8
1954 Murrayfield **England** 13–3
1955 Twickenham **England** 9–6
1956 Murrayfield **England** 11–6
1957 Twickenham **England** 16–3
1958 Murrayfield **Drawn** 3–3
1959 Twickenham **Drawn** 3–3
1960 Murrayfield **England** 21–12
1961 Twickenham **England** 6–0
1962 Murrayfield **Drawn** 3–3
1963 Twickenham **England** 10–8
1964 Murrayfield **Scotland** 15–6
1965 Twickenham **Drawn** 3–3
1966 Murrayfield **Scotland** 6–3

1967	Twickenham **England** 27–14	1989	Twickenham **Drawn** 12–12
1968	Murrayfield **England** 8–6	1990	Murrayfield **Scotland** 13–7
1969	Twickenham **England** 8–3	1991	Twickenham **England** 21–12
1970	Murrayfield **Scotland** 14–5	1991	Murrayfield WC **England** 9–6
1971	Twickenham **Scotland** 16–15	1992	Murrayfield **England** 25–7
1971	Murrayfield **Scotland** 26–6 Special centenary match – non-championship	1993	Twickenham **England** 26–12
		1994	Murrayfield **England** 15–14
		1995	Twickenham **England** 24–12
1972	Murrayfield **Scotland** 23–9	1996	Murrayfield **England** 18–9
1973	Twickenham **England** 20–13	1997	Twickenham **England** 41–13
1974	Murrayfield **Scotland** 16–14	1998	Murrayfield **England** 34–20
1975	Twickenham **England** 7–6	1999	Twickenham **England** 24–21
1976	Murrayfield **Scotland** 22–12	2000	Murrayfield **Scotland** 19–13
1977	Twickenham **England** 26–6	2001	Twickenham **England** 43–3
1978	Murrayfield **England** 15–0	2002	Murrayfield **England** 29–3
1979	Twickenham **Drawn** 7–7	2003	Twickenham **England** 40–9
1980	Murrayfield **England** 30–18	2004	Murrayfield **England** 35–13
1981	Twickenham **England** 23–17	2005	Twickenham **England** 43–22
1982	Murrayfield **Drawn** 9–9	2006	Murrayfield **Scotland** 18–12
1983	Twickenham **Scotland** 22–12	2007	Twickenham **England** 42–20
1984	Murrayfield **Scotland** 18–6	2008	Murrayfield **Scotland** 15–9
1985	Twickenham **England** 10–7	2009	Twickenham **England** 26–12
1986	Murrayfield **Scotland** 33–6	2010	Murrayfield **Drawn** 15–15
1987	Twickenham **England** 21–12	2011	Twickenham **England** 22–16
1988	Murrayfield **England** 9–6	2011	Auckland WC **England** 16–12

ENGLAND v IRELAND

Played 125 England won 71, Ireland won 46, Drawn 8
Highest scores England 50–18 in 2000, Ireland 43–13 in 2007
Biggest wins England 46–6 in 1997, Ireland 43–13 in 2007

1875	The Oval (London) **England** 1G 1DG 1T to 0	1891	Dublin **England** 9–0
		1892	Manchester **England** 7–0
1876	Dublin **England** 1G 1T to 0	1893	Dublin **England** 4–0
1877	The Oval **England** 2G 2T to 0	1894	Blackheath **Ireland** 7–5
1878	Dublin **England** 2G 1T to 0	1895	Dublin **England** 6–3
1879	The Oval **England** 2G 1DG 2T to 0	1896	Leeds **Ireland** 10–4
1880	Dublin **England** 1G 1T to 1T	1897	Dublin **Ireland** 13–9
1881	Manchester **England** 2G 2T to 0	1898	Richmond (London) **Ireland** 9–6
1882	Dublin **Drawn** 2T each	1899	Dublin **Ireland** 6–0
1883	Manchester **England** 1G 3T to 1T	1900	Richmond **England** 15–4
1884	Dublin **England** 1G to 0	1901	Dublin **Ireland** 10–6
1885	Manchester **England** 2T to 1T	1902	Leicester **England** 6–3
1886	Dublin **England** 1T to 0	1903	Dublin **Ireland** 6–0
1887	Dublin **Ireland** 2G to 0	1904	Blackheath **England** 19–0
1888	No Match	1905	Cork **Ireland** 17–3
1889	No Match	1906	Leicester **Ireland** 16–6
1890	Blackheath (London) **England** 3T to 0	1907	Dublin **Ireland** 17–9

1908 Richmond **England** 13–3
1909 Dublin **England** 11–5
1910 Twickenham **Drawn** 0–0
1911 Dublin **Ireland** 3–0
1912 Twickenham **England** 15–0
1913 Dublin **England** 15–4
1914 Twickenham **England** 17–12
1920 Dublin **England** 14–11
1921 Twickenham **England** 15–0
1922 Dublin **England** 12–3
1923 Leicester **England** 23–5
1924 Belfast **England** 14–3
1925 Twickenham **Drawn** 6–6
1926 Dublin **Ireland** 19–15
1927 Twickenham **England** 8–6
1928 Dublin **England** 7–6
1929 Twickenham **Ireland** 6–5
1930 Dublin **Ireland** 4–3
1931 Twickenham **Ireland** 6–5
1932 Dublin **England** 11–8
1933 Twickenham **England** 17–6
1934 Dublin **England** 13–3
1935 Twickenham **England** 14–3
1936 Dublin **Ireland** 6–3
1937 Twickenham **England** 9–8
1938 Dublin **England** 36–14
1939 Twickenham **Ireland** 5–0
1947 Dublin **Ireland** 22–0
1948 Twickenham **Ireland** 11–10
1949 Dublin **Ireland** 14–5
1950 Twickenham **England** 3–0
1951 Dublin **Ireland** 3–0
1952 Twickenham **England** 3–0
1953 Dublin **Drawn** 9–9
1954 Twickenham **England** 14–3
1955 Dublin **Drawn** 6–6
1956 Twickenham **England** 20–0
1957 Dublin **England** 6–0
1958 Twickenham **England** 6–0
1959 Dublin **England** 3–0
1960 Twickenham **England** 8–5
1961 Dublin **Ireland** 11–8
1962 Twickenham **England** 16–0
1963 Dublin **Drawn** 0–0
1964 Twickenham **Ireland** 18–5
1965 Dublin **Ireland** 5–0
1966 Twickenham **Drawn** 6–6
1967 Dublin **England** 8–3
1968 Twickenham **Drawn** 9–9
1969 Dublin **Ireland** 17–15
1970 Twickenham **England** 9–3
1971 Dublin **England** 9–6
1972 Twickenham **Ireland** 16–12
1973 Dublin **Ireland** 18–9
1974 Twickenham **Ireland** 26–21
1975 Dublin **Ireland** 12–9
1976 Twickenham **Ireland** 13–12
1977 Dublin **England** 4–0
1978 Twickenham **England** 15–9
1979 Dublin **Ireland** 12–7
1980 Twickenham **England** 24–9
1981 Dublin **England** 10–6
1982 Twickenham **Ireland** 16–15
1983 Dublin **Ireland** 25–15
1984 Twickenham **England** 12–9
1985 Dublin **Ireland** 13–10
1986 Twickenham **England** 25–20
1987 Dublin **Ireland** 17–0
1988 Twickenham **England** 35–3
1988 Dublin **England** 21–10
Non-championship match
1989 Dublin **England** 16–3
1990 Twickenham **England** 23–0
1991 Dublin **England** 16–7
1992 Twickenham **England** 38–9
1993 Dublin **Ireland** 17–3
1994 Twickenham **Ireland** 13–12
1995 Dublin **England** 20–8
1996 Twickenham **England** 28–15
1997 Dublin **England** 46–6
1998 Twickenham **England** 35–17
1999 Dublin **England** 27–15
2000 Twickenham **England** 50–18
2001 Dublin **Ireland** 20–14
2002 Twickenham **England** 45–11
2003 Dublin **England** 42–6
2004 Twickenham **Ireland** 19–13
2005 Dublin **Ireland** 19–13
2006 Twickenham **Ireland** 28–24
2007 Dublin **Ireland** 43–13
2008 Twickenham **England** 33–10
2009 Dublin **Ireland** 14–13
2010 Twickenham **Ireland** 20–16
2011 Dublin **Ireland** 24–8
2011 Dublin **England** 20–9
Non-championship match

ENGLAND v WALES

Played 122 England won 56 Wales won 54, Drawn 12
Highest scores England 62–5 in 2007, Wales 34–21 in 1967
Biggest wins England 62–5 in 2007, Wales 25–0 in 1905

1881 Blackheath (London) **England** 7G 1DG 6T to 0
1882 No Match
1883 Swansea **England** 2G 4T to 0
1884 Leeds **England** 1G 2T to 1G
1885 Swansea **England** 1G 4T to 1G 1T
1886 Blackheath **England** 1GM 2T to 1G
1887 Llanelli **Drawn** no score
1888 No Match
1889 No Match
1890 Dewsbury **Wales** 1T to 0
1891 Newport **England** 7–3
1892 Blackheath **England** 17–0
1893 Cardiff **Wales** 12–11
1894 Birkenhead **England** 24–3
1895 Swansea **England** 14–6
1896 Blackheath **England** 25–0
1897 Newport **Wales** 11–0
1898 Blackheath **England** 14–7
1899 Swansea **Wales** 26–3
1900 Gloucester **Wales** 13–3
1901 Cardiff **Wales** 13–0
1902 Blackheath **Wales** 9–8
1903 Swansea **Wales** 21–5
1904 Leicester **Drawn** 14–14
1905 Cardiff **Wales** 25–0
1906 Richmond (London) **Wales** 16–3
1907 Swansea **Wales** 22–0
1908 Bristol **Wales** 28–18
1909 Cardiff **Wales** 8–0
1910 Twickenham **England** 11–6
1911 Swansea **Wales** 15–11
1912 Twickenham **England** 8–0
1913 Cardiff **England** 12–0
1914 Twickenham **England** 10–9
1920 Swansea **Wales** 19–5
1921 Twickenham **England** 18–3
1922 Cardiff **Wales** 28–6
1923 Twickenham **England** 7–3
1924 Swansea **England** 17–9
1925 Twickenham **England** 12–6
1926 Cardiff **Drawn** 3–3
1927 Twickenham **England** 11–9
1928 Swansea **England** 10–8
1929 Twickenham **England** 8–3
1930 Cardiff **England** 11–3
1931 Twickenham **Drawn** 11–11
1932 Swansea **Wales** 12–5
1933 Twickenham **Wales** 7–3
1934 Cardiff **England** 9–0
1935 Twickenham **Drawn** 3–3
1936 Swansea **Drawn** 0–0
1937 Twickenham **England** 4–3
1938 Cardiff **Wales** 14–8
1939 Twickenham **England** 3–0
1947 Cardiff **England** 9–6
1948 Twickenham **Drawn** 3–3
1949 Cardiff **Wales** 9–3
1950 Twickenham **Wales** 11–5
1951 Swansea **Wales** 23–5
1952 Twickenham **Wales** 8–6
1953 Cardiff **England** 8–3
1954 Twickenham **England** 9–6
1955 Cardiff **Wales** 3–0
1956 Twickenham **Wales** 8–3
1957 Cardiff **England** 3–0
1958 Twickenham **Drawn** 3–3
1959 Cardiff **Wales** 5–0
1960 Twickenham **England** 14–6
1961 Cardiff **Wales** 6–3
1962 Twickenham **Drawn** 0–0
1963 Cardiff **England** 13–6
1964 Twickenham **Drawn** 6–6
1965 Cardiff **Wales** 14–3
1966 Twickenham **Wales** 11–6
1967 Cardiff **Wales** 34–21
1968 Twickenham **Drawn** 11–11
1969 Cardiff **Wales** 30–9
1970 Twickenham **Wales** 17–13
1971 Cardiff **Wales** 22–6
1972 Twickenham **Wales** 12–3
1973 Cardiff **Wales** 25–9
1974 Twickenham **England** 16–12
1975 Cardiff **Wales** 20–4
1976 Twickenham **Wales** 21–9
1977 Cardiff **Wales** 14–9
1978 Twickenham **Wales** 9–6
1979 Cardiff **Wales** 27–3

1980 Twickenham **England** 9–8
1981 Cardiff **Wales** 21–19
1982 Twickenham **England** 17–7
1983 Cardiff **Drawn** 13–13
1984 Twickenham **Wales** 24–15
1985 Cardiff **Wales** 24–15
1986 Twickenham **England** 21–18
1987 Cardiff **Wales** 19–12
1987 Brisbane WC **Wales** 16–3
1988 Twickenham **Wales** 11–3
1989 Cardiff **Wales** 12–9
1990 Twickenham **England** 34–6
1991 Cardiff **England** 25–6
1992 Twickenham **England** 24–0
1993 Cardiff **Wales** 10–9
1994 Twickenham **England** 15–8
1995 Cardiff **England** 23–9
1996 Twickenham **England** 21–15
1997 Cardiff **England** 34–13
1998 Twickenham **England** 60–26
1999 Wembley **Wales** 32–31
2000 Twickenham **England** 46–12
2001 Cardiff **England** 44–15
2002 Twickenham **England** 50–10
2003 Cardiff **England** 26–9
2003 Cardiff **England** 43–9
Non-championship match
2003 Brisbane WC **England** 28–17
2004 Twickenham **England** 31–21
2005 Cardiff **Wales** 11–9
2006 Twickenham **England** 47–13
2007 Cardiff **Wales** 27–18
2007 Twickenham **England** 62–5
Non-championship match
2008 Twickenham **Wales** 26–19
2009 Cardiff **Wales** 23–15
2010 Twickenham **England** 30–17
2011 Cardiff **England** 26–19
2011 Twickenham **England** 23–19
Non-championship match
2011 Cardiff **Wales** 19–9
Non-championship match

ENGLAND v FRANCE

Played 95 England won 51, France won 37, Drawn 7
Highest scores England 48–19 in 2001, France 37–12 in 1972
Biggest wins England 37–0 in 1911, France 37–12 in 1972 and 31–6 in 2006

1906 Paris **England** 35–8
1907 Richmond (London) **England** 41–13
1908 Paris **England** 19–0
1909 Leicester **England** 22–0
1910 Paris **England** 11–3
1911 Twickenham **England** 37–0
1912 Paris **England** 18–8
1913 Twickenham **England** 20–0
1914 Paris **England** 39–13
1920 Twickenham **England** 8–3
1921 Paris **England** 10–6
1922 Twickenham **Drawn** 11–11
1923 Paris **England** 12–3
1924 Twickenham **England** 19–7
1925 Paris **England** 13–11
1926 Twickenham **England** 11–0
1927 Paris **France** 3–0
1928 Twickenham **England** 18–8
1929 Paris **England** 16–6
1930 Twickenham **England** 11–5
1931 Paris **France** 14–13
1947 Twickenham **England** 6–3
1948 Paris **France** 15–0
1949 Twickenham **England** 8–3
1950 Paris **France** 6–3
1951 Twickenham **France** 11–3
1952 Paris **England** 6–3
1953 Twickenham **England** 11–0
1954 Paris **France** 11–3
1955 Twickenham **France** 16–9
1956 Paris **France** 14–9
1957 Twickenham **England** 9–5
1958 Paris **England** 14–0
1959 Twickenham **Drawn** 3–3
1960 Paris **Drawn** 3–3
1961 Twickenham **Drawn** 5–5
1962 Paris **France** 13–0
1963 Twickenham **England** 6–5
1964 Paris **England** 6–3
1965 Twickenham **England** 9–6
1966 Paris **France** 13–0
1967 Twickenham **France** 16–12
1968 Paris **France** 14–9
1969 Twickenham **England** 22–8

1970 Paris **France** 35–13
1971 Twickenham **Drawn** 14–14
1972 Paris **France** 37–12
1973 Twickenham **England** 14–6
1974 Paris **Drawn** 12–12
1975 Twickenham **France** 27–20
1976 Paris **France** 30–9
1977 Twickenham **France** 4–3
1978 Paris **France** 15–6
1979 Twickenham **England** 7–6
1980 Paris **England** 17–13
1981 Twickenham **France** 16–12
1982 Paris **England** 27–15
1983 Twickenham **France** 19–15
1984 Paris **France** 32–18
1985 Twickenham **Drawn** 9–9
1986 Paris **France** 29–10
1987 Twickenham **France** 19–15
1988 Paris **France** 10–9
1989 Twickenham **England** 11–0
1990 Paris **England** 26–7
1991 Twickenham **England** 21–19
1991 Paris WC **England** 19–10
1992 Paris **England** 31–13
1993 Twickenham **England** 16–15
1994 Paris **England** 18–14
1995 Twickenham **England** 31–10
1995 Pretoria WC **France 19–9**
1996 Paris **France** 15–12
1997 Twickenham **France** 23–20
1998 Paris **France** 24–17
1999 Twickenham **England** 21–10
2000 Paris **England** 15–9
2001 Twickenham **England** 48–19
2002 Paris **France** 20–15
2003 Twickenham **England** 25–17
2003 Marseilles **France** 17–16
Non-championship match
2003 Twickenham **England** 45–14
Non-championship match
2003 Sydney WC **England** 24–7
2004 Paris **France** 24–21
2005 Twickenham **France** 18–17
2006 Paris **France** 31–6
2007 Twickenham **England** 26–18
2007 Twickenham **France** 21–15
Non-championship match
2007 Marseilles **France** 22–9
Non-championship match
2007 Paris WC **England** 14–9
2008 Paris **England** 24–13
2009 Twickenham **England** 34–10
2010 Paris **France** 12–10
2011 Twickenham **England** 17–9
2011 Auckland WC **France** 19–12

ENGLAND v SOUTH AFRICA

Played 32 England won 12, South Africa won 19, Drawn 1
Highest scores England 53–3 in 2002, South Africa 58–10 in 2007
Biggest wins England 53–3 in 2002, South Africa 58–10 in 2007

1906 Crystal Palace (London) **Drawn** 3–3
1913 Twickenham **South Africa** 9–3
1932 Twickenham **South Africa** 7–0
1952 Twickenham **South Africa** 8–3
1961 Twickenham **South Africa** 5–0
1969 Twickenham **England** 11–8
1972 Johannesburg **England** 18–9
1984 *1* Port Elizabeth **South Africa** 33–15
2 Johannesburg **South Africa** 35–9
South Africa won series 2–0
1992 Twickenham **England** 33–16
1994 *1* Pretoria **England** 32–15
2 Cape Town **South Africa** 27–9
Series drawn 1–1
1995 Twickenham **South Africa** 24–14
1997 Twickenham **South Africa** 29–11
1998 Cape Town **South Africa** 18–0
1998 Twickenham **England** 13–7
1999 Paris WC **South Africa** 44–21
2000 *1* Pretoria **South Africa** 18–13
2 Bloemfontein **England** 27–22
Series drawn 1–1
2000 Twickenham **England** 25–17
2001 Twickenham **England** 29–9
2002 Twickenham **England** 53–3
2003 Perth WC **England** 25–6
2004 Twickenham **England** 32–16
2006 *1* Twickenham **England** 23–21

	2 Twickenham **South Africa** 25–14
	Series drawn 1–1
2007	*1* Bloemfontein **South Africa** 58–10
	2 Pretoria **South Africa** 55–22
	South Africa won series 2–0
2007	Paris WC **South Africa** 36–0
2007	Paris WC **South Africa** 15–6
2008	Twickenham **South Africa** 42–6
2010	Twickenham **South Africa** 21–11

ENGLAND v NEW ZEALAND

Played 34 England won 6, New Zealand won 27, Drawn 1
Highest scores England 31–28 in 2002, New Zealand 64–22 in 1998
Biggest wins England 13–0 in 1936, New Zealand 64–22 in 1998

1905	Crystal Palace (London) **New Zealand** 15–0
1925	Twickenham **New Zealand** 17–11
1936	Twickenham **England** 13–0
1954	Twickenham **New Zealand** 5–0
1963	*1* Auckland **New Zealand** 21–11
	2 Christchurch **New Zealand** 9–6
	New Zealand won series 2–0
1964	Twickenham **New Zealand** 14–0
1967	Twickenham **New Zealand** 23–11
1973	Twickenham **New Zealand** 9–0
1973	Auckland **England** 16–10
1978	Twickenham **New Zealand** 16–6
1979	Twickenham **New Zealand** 10–9
1983	Twickenham **England** 15–9
1985	*1* Christchurch **New Zealand** 18–13
	2 Wellington **New Zealand** 42–15
	New Zealand won series 2–0
1991	Twickenham WC **New Zealand** 18–12
1993	Twickenham **England** 15–9
1995	Cape Town WC **New Zealand 45–29**
1997	*1* Manchester **New Zealand** 25–8
	2 Twickenham **Drawn** 26–26
	New Zealand won series 1–0, with 1 draw
1998	*1* Dunedin **New Zealand** 64–22
	2 Auckland **New Zealand** 40–10
	New Zealand won series 2–0
1999	Twickenham WC **New Zealand** 30–16
2002	Twickenham **England** 31–28
2003	Wellington **England** 15–13
2004	*1* Dunedin **New Zealand** 36–3
	2 Auckland **New Zealand** 36–12
	New Zealand won series 2–0
2005	Twickenham **New Zealand** 23–19
2006	Twickenham **New Zealand** 41–20
2008	*1* Auckland **New Zealand** 37–20
	2 Christchurch **New Zealand** 44–12
	New Zealand won series 2–0
2008	Twickenham **New Zealand** 32–6
2009	Twickenham **New Zealand** 19–6
2010	Twickenham **New Zealand** 26–16

ENGLAND v AUSTRALIA

Played 40 England won 16, Australia won 23, Drawn 1
Highest scores England 35–18 in 2010, Australia 76–0 in 1998
Biggest wins England 20–3 in 1973, 23–6 in 1976 & 35–18 in 2010, Australia 76–0 in 1998

1909	Blackheath (London) **Australia** 9–3
1928	Twickenham **England** 18–11
1948	Twickenham **Australia** 11–0
1958	Twickenham **England** 9–6
1963	Sydney **Australia** 18–9
1967	Twickenham **Australia** 23–11
1973	Twickenham **England** 20–3
1975	*1* Sydney **Australia** 16–9
	2 Brisbane **Australia** 30–21
	Australia won series 2–0
1976	Twickenham **England** 23–6
1982	Twickenham **England** 15–11
1984	Twickenham **Australia** 19–3
1987	Sydney WC **Australia** 19–6
1988	*1* Brisbane **Australia** 22–16
	2 Sydney **Australia** 28–8
	Australia won series 2–0
1988	Twickenham **England** 28–19

1991 Sydney **Australia** 40–15
1991 Twickenham WC **Australia** 12–6
1995 Cape Town WC **England** 25–22
1997 Sydney **Australia** 25–6
1997 Twickenham **Drawn** 15–15
1998 Brisbane **Australia** 76–0
1998 Twickenham **Australia** 12–11
1999 Sydney **Australia** 22–15
2000 Twickenham **England** 22–19
2001 Twickenham **England** 21–15
2002 Twickenham **England** 32–31
2003 Melbourne **England** 25–14
2003 Sydney WC **England** 20–17 (aet)
2004 Brisbane **Australia** 51–15
2004 Twickenham **Australia** 21–19
2005 Twickenham **England** 26–16
2006 *1* Sydney **Australia** 34–3
2 Melbourne **Australia** 43–18
Australia won series 2–0
2007 Marseilles WC **England** 12–10
2008 Twickenham **Australia** 28–14
2009 Twickenham **Australia** 18–9
2010 *1* Perth **Australia** 27–17
2 Sydney **England** 21–20
Series drawn 1–1
2010 Twickenham **England** 35–18

ENGLAND v NEW ZEALAND NATIVES

Played 1 England won 1
Highest score England 7–0 in 1889, NZ Natives 0–7 in 1889
Biggest win England 7–0 in 1889, NZ Natives no win

1889 Blackheath **England** 1G 4T to 0

ENGLAND v RFU PRESIDENT'S XV

Played 1 President's XV won 1
Highest score England 11–28 in 1971, RFU President's XV 28–11 in 1971
Biggest win RFU President's XV 28–11 in 1971

1971 Twickenham **President's XV** 28–11

ENGLAND v ARGENTINA

Played 16 England won 11, Argentina won 4, Drawn 1
Highest scores England 51–0 in 1990, Argentina 33–13 in 1997
Biggest wins England 51–0 in 1990, Argentina 33–13 in 1997

1981 *1* Buenos Aires **Drawn** 19–19
2 Buenos Aires **England** 12–6
England won series 1–0 with 1 draw
1990 *1* Buenos Aires **England** 25–12
2 Buenos Aires **Argentina** 15–13
Series drawn 1–1
1990 Twickenham **England** 51–0
1995 Durban WC **England** 24–18
1996 Twickenham **England** 20–18
1997 *1* Buenos Aires **England** 46–20
2 Buenos Aires **Argentina** 33–13
Series drawn 1–1
2000 Twickenham **England** 19–0
2002 Buenos Aires **England** 26–18
2006 Twickenham **Argentina** 25–18
2009 *1* Manchester **England** 37–15
2 Salta **Argentina** 24–22
Series drawn 1–1
2009 Twickenham **England** 16–9
2011 Dunedin WC **England** 13–9

ENGLAND v ROMANIA

Played 5 England won 5
Highest scores England 134–0 in 2001, Romania 15–22 in 1985
Biggest win England 134–0 in 2001, Romania no win

1985	Twickenham **England** 22–15	2001	Twickenham **England** 134–0
1989	Bucharest **England** 58–3	2011	Dunedin WC **England** 67–3
1994	Twickenham **England** 54–3		

ENGLAND v JAPAN

Played 1 England won 1
Highest score England 60–7 in 1987, Japan 7–60 in 1987
Biggest win England 60–7 in 1987, Japan no win

1987	Sydney WC **England** 60–7

ENGLAND v UNITED STATES

Played 5 England won 5
Highest scores England 106–8 in 1999, United States 19–48 in 2001
Biggest win England 106–8 in 1999, United States no win

1987	Sydney WC **England** 34–6	2001	San Francisco **England** 48–19
1991	Twickenham WC **England** 37–9	2007	Lens WC **England** 28–10
1999	Twickenham **England** 106–8		

ENGLAND v FIJI

Played 4 England won 4
Highest scores England 58–23 in 1989, Fiji 24–45 in 1999
Biggest win England 58–23 in 1989, Fiji no win

1988	Suva **England** 25–12	1991	Suva **England** 28–12
1989	Twickenham **England** 58–23	1999	Twickenham WC **England** 45–24

ENGLAND v ITALY

Played 17 England won 17
Highest scores England 80–23 in 2001, Italy 23–80 in 2001
Biggest win England 67–7 in 1999, Italy no win

1991	Twickenham WC **England** 36–6	2000	Rome **England** 59–12
1995	Durban WC **England 27–20**	2001	Twickenham **England** 80–23
1996	Twickenham **England** 54–21	2002	Rome **England** 45–9
1998	Huddersfield **England** 23–15	2003	Twickenham **England** 40–5
1999	Twickenham WC **England** 67–7	2004	Rome **England** 50–9

2005 Twickenham **England** 39–7	2009 Twickenham **England** 36–11
2006 Rome **England** 31–16	2010 Rome **England** 17–12
2007 Twickenham **England** 20–7	2011 Twickenham **England** 59–13
2008 Rome **England** 23–19	

ENGLAND v CANADA

Played 6 England won 6
Highest scores England 70–0 in 2004, Canada 20–59 in 2001
Biggest win England 70–0 in 2004, Canada no win

1992 Wembley **England** 26–13	*2* Burnaby **England** 59–20
1994 Twickenham **England** 60–19	England won series 2–0
1999 Twickenham **England** 36–11	2004 Twickenham **England** 70–0
2001 *1* Markham **England** 22–10	

ENGLAND v SAMOA

Played 6 England won 6
Highest scores England 44–22 in 1995 and 44–22 in 2007, Samoa 22–44 in 1995, 22–35 in 2003 and 22–44 in 2007
Biggest win England 40–3 in 2005, Samoa no win

1995 Durban WC **England** 44–22	2005 Twickenham **England** 40–3
1995 Twickenham **England** 27–9	2007 Nantes WC **England** 44–22
2003 Melbourne WC **England** 35–22	2010 Twickenham **England** 26–13

ENGLAND v THE NETHERLANDS

Played 1 England won 1
Highest scores England 110–0 in 1998, The Netherlands 0–110 in 1998
Biggest win England 110–0 in 1998, The Netherlands no win

1998 Huddersfield **England** 110–0

ENGLAND v TONGA

Played 2 England won 2
Highest scores England 101–10 in 1999, Tonga 20–36 in 2007
Biggest win England 101–10 in 1999, Tonga no win

1999 Twickenham WC **England** 101–10	2007 Paris WC **England** 36–20

ENGLAND v GEORGIA

Played 2 England won 2
Highest scores England 84–6 in 2003, Georgia 10–41 in 2011
Biggest win England 84–6 in 2003, Georgia no win

2003 Perth WC **England** 84–6	2011 Dunedin WC **England** 41–10

ENGLAND v URUGUAY

Played 1 England won 1
Highest scores England 111–13 in 2003, Uruguay 13–111 in 2003
Biggest win England 111–13 in 2003, Uruguay no win

2003 Brisbane WC **England** 111–13

ENGLAND v PACIFIC ISLANDS

Played 1 England won 1
Highest scores England 39–13 in 2008, Pacific Islands 13–39 in 2008
Biggest win England 39–13 in 2008, Pacific Islands no win

2008 Twickenham **England** 39–13

SCOTLAND v IRELAND

Played 126 Scotland won 64, Ireland won 56, Drawn 5, Abandoned 1
Highest scores Scotland 38–10 in 1997, Ireland 44–22 in 2000
Biggest wins Scotland 38–10 in 1997, Ireland 36–6 in 2003

1877 Belfast **Scotland** 4G 2DG 2T to 0
1878 No Match
1879 Belfast **Scotland** 1G 1DG 1T to 0
1880 Glasgow **Scotland** 1G 2DG 2T to 0
1881 Belfast **Ireland** 1DG to 1T
1882 Glasgow **Scotland** 2T to 0
1883 Belfast **Scotland** 1G 1T to 0
1884 Raeburn Place (Edinburgh) **Scotland** 2G 2T to 1T
1885 Belfast **Abandoned** Ireland 0 Scotland 1T
1885 Raeburn Place **Scotland** 1G 2T to 0
1886 Raeburn Place **Scotland** 3G 1DG 2T to 0
1887 Belfast **Scotland** 1G 1GM 2T to 0
1888 Raeburn Place **Scotland** 1G to 0
1889 Belfast **Scotland** 1DG to 0
1890 Raeburn Place **Scotland** 1DG 1T to 0
1891 Belfast **Scotland** 14–0
1892 Raeburn Place **Scotland** 2–0
1893 Belfast **Drawn** 0–0
1894 Dublin **Ireland** 5–0
1895 Raeburn Place **Scotland** 6–0
1896 Dublin **Drawn** 0–0
1897 Powderhall (Edinburgh) **Scotland** 8–3
1898 Belfast **Scotland** 8–0
1899 Inverleith (Edinburgh) **Ireland** 9–3
1900 Dublin **Drawn** 0–0
1901 Inverleith **Scotland** 9–5
1902 Belfast **Ireland** 5–0
1903 Inverleith **Scotland** 3–0
1904 Dublin **Scotland** 19–3
1905 Inverleith **Ireland** 11–5
1906 Dublin **Scotland** 13–6
1907 Inverleith **Scotland** 15–3
1908 Dublin **Ireland** 16–11
1909 Inverleith **Scotland** 9–3
1910 Belfast **Scotland** 14–0

1911 Inverleith **Ireland** 16–10
1912 Dublin **Ireland** 10–8
1913 Inverleith **Scotland** 29–14
1914 Dublin **Ireland** 6–0
1920 Inverleith **Scotland** 19–0
1921 Dublin **Ireland** 9–8
1922 Inverleith **Scotland** 6–3
1923 Dublin **Scotland** 13–3
1924 Inverleith **Scotland** 13–8
1925 Dublin **Scotland** 14–8
1926 Murrayfield **Ireland** 3–0
1927 Dublin **Ireland** 6–0
1928 Murrayfield **Ireland** 13–5
1929 Dublin **Scotland** 16–7
1930 Murrayfield **Ireland** 14–11
1931 Dublin **Ireland** 8–5
1932 Murrayfield **Ireland** 20–8
1933 Dublin **Scotland** 8–6
1934 Murrayfield **Scotland** 16–9
1935 Dublin **Ireland** 12–5
1936 Murrayfield **Ireland** 10–4
1937 Dublin **Ireland** 11–4
1938 Murrayfield **Scotland** 23–14
1939 Dublin **Ireland** 12–3
1947 Murrayfield **Ireland** 3–0
1948 Dublin **Ireland** 6–0
1949 Murrayfield **Ireland** 13–3
1950 Dublin **Ireland** 21–0
1951 Murrayfield **Ireland** 6–5
1952 Dublin **Ireland** 12–8
1953 Murrayfield **Ireland** 26–8
1954 Belfast **Ireland** 6–0
1955 Murrayfield **Scotland** 12–3
1956 Dublin **Ireland** 14–10
1957 Murrayfield **Ireland** 5–3
1958 Dublin **Ireland** 12–6
1959 Murrayfield **Ireland** 8–3
1960 Dublin **Scotland** 6–5
1961 Murrayfield **Scotland** 16–8
1962 Dublin **Scotland** 20–6
1963 Murrayfield **Scotland** 3–0
1964 Dublin **Scotland** 6–3
1965 Murrayfield **Ireland** 16–6
1966 Dublin **Scotland** 11–3
1967 Murrayfield **Ireland** 5–3
1968 Dublin **Ireland** 14–6
1969 Murrayfield **Ireland** 16–0
1970 Dublin **Ireland** 16–11
1971 Murrayfield **Ireland** 17–5
1972 No Match
1973 Murrayfield **Scotland** 19–14
1974 Dublin **Ireland** 9–6
1975 Murrayfield **Scotland** 20–13
1976 Dublin **Scotland** 15–6
1977 Murrayfield **Scotland** 21–18
1978 Dublin **Ireland** 12–9
1979 Murrayfield **Drawn** 11–11
1980 Dublin **Ireland** 22–15
1981 Murrayfield **Scotland** 10–9
1982 Dublin **Ireland** 21–12
1983 Murrayfield **Ireland** 15–13
1984 Dublin **Scotland** 32–9
1985 Murrayfield **Ireland** 18–15
1986 Dublin **Scotland** 10–9
1987 Murrayfield **Scotland** 16–12
1988 Dublin **Ireland** 22–18
1989 Murrayfield **Scotland** 37–21
1990 Dublin **Scotland** 13–10
1991 Murrayfield **Scotland** 28–25
1991 Murrayfield WC **Scotland** 24–15
1992 Dublin **Scotland** 18–10
1993 Murrayfield **Scotland** 15–3
1994 Dublin **Drawn** 6–6
1995 Murrayfield **Scotland** 26–13
1996 Dublin **Scotland** 16–10
1997 Murrayfield **Scotland** 38–10
1998 Dublin **Scotland** 17–16
1999 Murrayfield **Scotland** 30–13
2000 Dublin **Ireland** 44–22
2001 Murrayfield **Scotland** 32–10
2002 Dublin **Ireland** 43–22
2003 Murrayfield **Ireland** 36–6
2003 Murrayfield **Ireland** 29–10
Non-championship match
2004 Dublin **Ireland** 37–16
2005 Murrayfield **Ireland** 40–13
2006 Dublin **Ireland** 15–9
2007 Murrayfield **Ireland** 19–18
2007 Murrayfield **Scotland** 31–21
Non-championship match
2008 Dublin **Ireland** 34–13
2009 Murrayfield **Ireland** 22–15
2010 Dublin **Scotland** 23–20
2011 Murrayfield **Ireland** 21–18
2011 Murrayfield **Scotland** 10–6
Non-championship match

SCOTLAND v WALES

Played 116 Scotland won 48, Wales won 65, Drawn 3
Highest scores Scotland 35–10 in 1924, Wales 46–22 in 2005
Biggest wins Scotland 35–10 in 1924, Wales 46–22 in 2005

1883 Raeburn Place (Edinburgh) **Scotland** 3G to 1G
1884 Newport **Scotland** 1DG 1T to 0
1885 Glasgow **Drawn** no score
1886 Cardiff **Scotland** 2G 1T to 0
1887 Raeburn Place **Scotland** 4G 8T to 0
1888 Newport **Wales** 1T to 0
1889 Raeburn Place **Scotland** 2T to 0
1890 Cardiff **Scotland** 1G 2T to 1T
1891 Raeburn Place **Scotland** 15–0
1892 Swansea **Scotland** 7–2
1893 Raeburn Place **Wales** 9–0
1894 Newport **Wales** 7–0
1895 Raeburn Place **Scotland** 5–4
1896 Cardiff **Wales** 6–0
1897 No Match
1898 No Match
1899 Inverleith (Edinburgh) **Scotland** 21–10
1900 Swansea **Wales** 12–3
1901 Inverleith **Scotland** 18–8
1902 Cardiff **Wales** 14–5
1903 Inverleith **Scotland** 6–0
1904 Swansea **Wales** 21–3
1905 Inverleith **Wales** 6–3
1906 Cardiff **Wales** 9–3
1907 Inverleith **Scotland** 6–3
1908 Swansea **Wales** 6–5
1909 Inverleith **Wales** 5–3
1910 Cardiff **Wales** 14–0
1911 Inverleith **Wales** 32–10
1912 Swansea **Wales** 21–6
1913 Inverleith **Wales** 8–0
1914 Cardiff **Wales** 24–5
1920 Inverleith **Scotland** 9–5
1921 Swansea **Scotland** 14–8
1922 Inverleith **Drawn** 9–9
1923 Cardiff **Scotland** 11–8
1924 Inverleith **Scotland** 35–10
1925 Swansea **Scotland** 24–14
1926 Murrayfield **Scotland** 8–5
1927 Cardiff **Scotland** 5–0
1928 Murrayfield **Wales** 13–0
1929 Swansea **Wales** 14–7
1930 Murrayfield **Scotland** 12–9
1931 Cardiff **Wales** 13–8
1932 Murrayfield **Wales** 6–0
1933 Swansea **Scotland** 11–3
1934 Murrayfield **Wales** 13–6
1935 Cardiff **Wales** 10–6
1936 Murrayfield **Wales** 13–3
1937 Swansea **Scotland** 13–6
1938 Murrayfield **Scotland** 8–6
1939 Cardiff **Wales** 11–3
1947 Murrayfield **Wales** 22–8
1948 Cardiff **Wales** 14–0
1949 Murrayfield **Scotland** 6–5
1950 Swansea **Wales** 12–0
1951 Murrayfield **Scotland** 19–0
1952 Cardiff **Wales** 11–0
1953 Murrayfield **Wales** 12–0
1954 Swansea **Wales** 15–3
1955 Murrayfield **Scotland** 14–8
1956 Cardiff **Wales** 9–3
1957 Murrayfield **Scotland** 9–6
1958 Cardiff **Wales** 8–3
1959 Murrayfield **Scotland** 6–5
1960 Cardiff **Wales** 8–0
1961 Murrayfield **Scotland** 3–0
1962 Cardiff **Scotland** 8–3
1963 Murrayfield **Wales** 6–0
1964 Cardiff **Wales** 11–3
1965 Murrayfield **Wales** 14–12
1966 Cardiff **Wales** 8–3
1967 Murrayfield **Scotland** 11–5
1968 Cardiff **Wales** 5–0
1969 Murrayfield **Wales** 17–3
1970 Cardiff **Wales** 18–9
1971 Murrayfield **Wales** 19–18
1972 Cardiff **Wales** 35–12
1973 Murrayfield **Scotland** 10–9
1974 Cardiff **Wales** 6–0
1975 Murrayfield **Scotland** 12–10
1976 Cardiff **Wales** 28–6
1977 Murrayfield **Wales** 18–9
1978 Cardiff **Wales** 22–14
1979 Murrayfield **Wales** 19–13
1980 Cardiff **Wales** 17–6
1981 Murrayfield **Scotland** 15–6

1982	Cardiff **Scotland** 34–18	1998	Wembley **Wales** 19–13
1983	Murrayfield **Wales** 19–15	1999	Murrayfield **Scotland** 33–20
1984	Cardiff **Scotland** 15–9	2000	Cardiff **Wales** 26–18
1985	Murrayfield **Wales** 25–21	2001	Murrayfield **Drawn** 28–28
1986	Cardiff **Wales** 22–15	2002	Cardiff **Scotland** 27–22
1987	Murrayfield **Scotland** 21–15	2003	Murrayfield **Scotland** 30–22
1988	Cardiff **Wales** 25–20	2003	Cardiff **Wales** 23–9
1989	Murrayfield **Scotland** 23–7		Non-championship match
1990	Cardiff **Scotland** 13–9	2004	Cardiff **Wales** 23–10
1991	Murrayfield **Scotland** 32–12	2005	Murrayfield **Wales** 46–22
1992	Cardiff **Wales** 15–12	2006	Cardiff **Wales** 28–18
1993	Murrayfield **Scotland** 20–0	2007	Murrayfield **Scotland** 21–9
1994	Cardiff **Wales** 29–6	2008	Cardiff **Wales** 30–15
1995	Murrayfield **Scotland** 26–13	2009	Murrayfield **Wales** 26–13
1996	Cardiff **Scotland** 16–14	2010	Cardiff **Wales** 31–24
1997	Murrayfield **Wales** 34–19	2011	Murrayfield **Wales** 24–6

SCOTLAND v FRANCE

Played 84 Scotland won 34, France won 47, Drawn 3
Highest scores Scotland 36–22 in 1999, France 51–16 in 1998 and 51–9 in 2003
Biggest wins Scotland 31–3 in 1912, France 51–9 in 2003

1910	Inverleith (Edinburgh) **Scotland** 27–0	1956	Murrayfield **Scotland** 12–0
1911	Paris **France** 16–15	1957	Paris **Scotland** 6–0
1912	Inverleith **Scotland** 31–3	1958	Murrayfield **Scotland** 11–9
1913	Paris **Scotland** 21–3	1959	Paris **France** 9–0
1914	No Match	1960	Murrayfield **France** 13–11
1920	Paris **Scotland** 5–0	1961	Paris **France** 11–0
1921	Inverleith **France** 3–0	1962	Murrayfield **France** 11–3
1922	Paris **Drawn** 3–3	1963	Paris **Scotland** 11–6
1923	Inverleith **Scotland** 16–3	1964	Murrayfield **Scotland** 10–0
1924	Paris **France** 12–10	1965	Paris **France** 16–8
1925	Inverleith **Scotland** 25–4	1966	Murrayfield **Drawn** 3–3
1926	Paris **Scotland** 20–6	1967	Paris **Scotland** 9–8
1927	Murrayfield **Scotland** 23–6	1968	Murrayfield **France** 8–6
1928	Paris **Scotland** 15–6	1969	Paris **Scotland** 6–3
1929	Murrayfield **Scotland** 6–3	1970	Murrayfield **France** 11–9
1930	Paris **France** 7–3	1971	Paris **France** 13–8
1931	Murrayfield **Scotland** 6–4	1972	Murrayfield **Scotland** 20–9
1947	Paris **France** 8–3	1973	Paris **France** 16–13
1948	Murrayfield **Scotland** 9–8	1974	Murrayfield **Scotland** 19–6
1949	Paris **Scotland** 8–0	1975	Paris **France** 10–9
1950	Murrayfield **Scotland** 8–5	1976	Murrayfield **France** 13–6
1951	Paris **France** 14–12	1977	Paris **France** 23–3
1952	Murrayfield **France** 13–11	1978	Murrayfield **France** 19–16
1953	Paris **France** 11–5	1979	Paris **France** 21–17
1954	Murrayfield **France** 3–0	1980	Murrayfield **Scotland** 22–14
1955	Paris **France** 15–0	1981	Paris **France** 16–9

1982 Murrayfield **Scotland** 16–7
1983 Paris **France** 19–15
1984 Murrayfield **Scotland** 21–12
1985 Paris **France** 11–3
1986 Murrayfield **Scotland** 18–17
1987 Paris **France** 28–22
1987 Christchurch WC **Drawn** 20–20
1988 Murrayfield **Scotland** 23–12
1989 Paris **France** 19–3
1990 Murrayfield **Scotland** 21–0
1991 Paris **France** 15–9
1992 Murrayfield **Scotland** 10–6
1993 Paris **France** 11–3
1994 Murrayfield **France** 20–12
1995 Paris **Scotland** 23–21
1995 Pretoria WC **France** 22–19
1996 Murrayfield **Scotland** 19–14
1997 Paris **France** 47–20
1998 Murrayfield **France** 51–16
1999 Paris **Scotland** 36–22
2000 Murrayfield **France** 28–16
2001 Paris **France** 16–6
2002 Murrayfield **France** 22–10
2003 Paris **France** 38–3
2003 Sydney WC **France** 51–9
2004 Murrayfield **France** 31–0
2005 Paris **France** 16–9
2006 Murrayfield **Scotland** 20–16
2007 Paris **France** 46–19
2008 Murrayfield **France** 27–6
2009 Paris **France** 22–13
2010 Murrayfield **France** 18–9
2011 Paris **France** 34–21

SCOTLAND v SOUTH AFRICA

Played 21 Scotland won 5, South Africa won 16, Drawn 0
Highest scores Scotland 29–46 in 1999, South Africa 68–10 in 1997
Biggest wins Scotland 21–6 in 2002, South Africa 68–10 in 1997

1906 Glasgow **Scotland** 6–0
1912 Inverleith **South Africa** 16–0
1932 Murrayfield **South Africa** 6–3
1951 Murrayfield **South Africa** 44–0
1960 Port Elizabeth **South Africa** 18–10
1961 Murrayfield **South Africa** 12–5
1965 Murrayfield **Scotland** 8–5
1969 Murrayfield **Scotland** 6–3
1994 Murrayfield **South Africa** 34–10
1997 Murrayfield **South Africa** 68–10
1998 Murrayfield **South Africa** 35–10
1999 Murrayfield WC **South Africa** 46–29
2002 Murrayfield **Scotland** 21–6
2003 *1* Durban **South Africa** 29–25
2 Johannesburg **South Africa** 28–19
South Africa won series 2–0
2004 Murrayfield **South Africa** 45–10
2006 *1* Durban **South Africa** 36–16
2 Port Elizabeth **South Africa** 29–15
South Africa won series 2–0
2007 Murrayfield **South Africa** 27–3
2008 Murrayfield **South Africa** 14–10
2010 Murrayfield **Scotland** 21–17

SCOTLAND v NEW ZEALAND

Played 28 Scotland won 0, New Zealand won 26, Drawn 2
Highest scores Scotland 31–62 in 1996, New Zealand 69–20 in 2000
Biggest wins Scotland no win, New Zealand 69–20 in 2000

1905 Inverleith (Edinburgh) **New Zealand** 12–7
1935 Murrayfield **New Zealand** 18–8
1954 Murrayfield **New Zealand** 3–0
1964 Murrayfield **Drawn** 0–0
1967 Murrayfield **New Zealand** 14–3
1972 Murrayfield **New Zealand** 14–9
1975 Auckland **New Zealand** 24–0
1978 Murrayfield **New Zealand** 18–9
1979 Murrayfield **New Zealand** 20–6
1981 *1* Dunedin **New Zealand** 11–4
2 Auckland **New Zealand** 40–15

	New Zealand won series 2–0
1983	Murrayfield **Drawn** 25–25
1987	Christchurch WC **New Zealand** 30–3
1990	*1* Dunedin **New Zealand** 31–16
	2 Auckland **New Zealand** 21–18
	New Zealand won series 2–0
1991	Cardiff WC **New Zealand** 13–6
1993	Murrayfield **New Zealand** 51–15
1995	Pretoria WC **New Zealand** 48–30
1996	*1* Dunedin **New Zealand** 62–31
	2 Auckland **New Zealand** 36–12
	New Zealand won series 2–0
1999	Murrayfield WC **New Zealand** 30–18
2000	*1* Dunedin **New Zealand** 69–20
	2 Auckland **New Zealand** 48–14
	New Zealand won series 2–0
2001	Murrayfield **New Zealand** 37–6
2005	Murrayfield **New Zealand** 29–10
2007	Murrayfield WC **New Zealand** 40–0
2008	Murrayfield **New Zealand** 32–6
2010	Murrayfield **New Zealand** 49–3

SCOTLAND v AUSTRALIA

Played 26 Scotland won 8, Australia won 18, Drawn 0
Highest scores Scotland 24–15 in 1981, Australia 45–3 in 1998
Biggest wins Scotland 24–15 in 1981, Australia 45–3 in 1998

1927	Murrayfield **Scotland** 10–8
1947	Murrayfield **Australia** 16–7
1958	Murrayfield **Scotland** 12–8
1966	Murrayfield **Scotland** 11–5
1968	Murrayfield **Scotland** 9–3
1970	Sydney **Australia** 23–3
1975	Murrayfield **Scotland** 10–3
1981	Murrayfield **Scotland** 24–15
1982	*1* Brisbane **Scotland** 12–7
	2 Sydney **Australia** 33–9
	Series drawn 1–1
1984	Murrayfield **Australia** 37–12
1988	Murrayfield **Australia** 32–13
1992	*1* Sydney **Australia** 27–12
	2 Brisbane **Australia** 37–13
	Australia won series 2–0
1996	Murrayfield **Australia** 29–19
1997	Murrayfield **Australia** 37–8
1998	*1* Sydney **Australia** 45–3
	2 Brisbane **Australia** 33–11
	Australia won series 2–0
2000	Murrayfield **Australia** 30–9
2003	Brisbane WC **Australia** 33–16
2004	*1* Melbourne **Australia** 35–15
	2 Sydney **Australia** 34–13
	Australia won series 2–0
2004	*1* Murrayfield **Australia** 31–14
	2 Glasgow **Australia** 31–17
	Australia won series 2–0
2006	Murrayfield **Australia** 44–15
2009	Murrayfield **Scotland** 9–8

SCOTLAND v SRU PRESIDENT'S XV

Played 1 Scotland won 1
Highest scores Scotland 27–16 in 1972, SRU President's XV 16–27 in 1973
Biggest win Scotland 27–16 in 1973, SRU President's XV no win

1973	Murrayfield **Scotland** 27–16

SCOTLAND v ROMANIA

Played 13 Scotland won 11 Romania won 2, Drawn 0
Highest scores Scotland 60–19 in 1999, Romania 28–55 in 1987 & 28–22 in 1984
Biggest wins Scotland 48–6 in 2006 and 42–0 in 2007, Romania 28–22 in 1984 & 18–12 in 1991

1981	Murrayfield **Scotland** 12–6	1999	Glasgow **Scotland** 60–19
1984	Bucharest **Romania** 28–22	2002	Murrayfield **Scotland** 37–10
1986	Bucharest **Scotland** 33–18	2005	Bucharest **Scotland** 39–19
1987	Dunedin WC **Scotland** 55–28	2006	Murrayfield **Scotland** 48–6
1989	Murrayfield **Scotland** 32–0	2007	Murrayfield WC **Scotland** 42–0
1991	Bucharest **Romania** 18–12	2011	Invercargill WC **Scotland** 34–24
1995	Murrayfield **Scotland** 49–16		

SCOTLAND v ZIMBABWE

Played 2 Scotland won 2
Highest scores Scotland 60–21 in 1987, Zimbabwe 21–60 in 1987
Biggest win Scotland 60–21 in 1987 & 51–12 in 1991, Zimbabwe no win

1987	Wellington WC **Scotland** 60–21	1991	Murrayfield WC **Scotland** 51–12

SCOTLAND v FIJI

Played 5 Scotland won 4, Fiji won 1
Highest scores Scotland 38–17 in 1989, Fiji 51–26 in 1998
Biggest win Scotland 38–17 in 1989, Fiji 51–26 in 1998

1989	Murrayfield **Scotland** 38–17	2003	Sydney WC **Scotland** 22–20
1998	Suva **Fiji** 51–26	2009	Murrayfield **Scotland** 23–10
2002	Murrayfield **Scotland** 36–22		

SCOTLAND v ARGENTINA

Played 13 Scotland won 4, Argentina won 9, Drawn 0
Highest scores Scotland 49–3 in 1990, Argentina 31–22 in 1999
Biggest wins Scotland 49–3 in 1990, Argentina 31–22 in 1999 and 25–16 in 2001

1990	Murrayfield **Scotland** 49–3	2008	*1* Rosario **Argentina** 21–15
1994	*1* Buenos Aires **Argentina** 16–15		*2* Buenos Aires **Scotland** 26–14
	2 Buenos Aires **Argentina** 19–17		Series drawn 1–1
	Argentina won series 2–0	2009	Murrayfield **Argentina** 9–6
1999	Murrayfield **Argentina** 31–22	2010	*1* Tucumán **Scotland** 24–16
2001	Murrayfield **Argentina** 25–16		*2* Mar del Plata **Scotland** 13–9
2005	Murrayfield **Argentina** 23–19		Scotland won series 2–0
2007	Paris WC **Argentina** 19–13	2011	Wellington WC **Argentina** 13–12

SCOTLAND v JAPAN

Played 3 Scotland won 3
Highest scores Scotland 100–8 in 2004, Japan 11–32 in 2003
Biggest win Scotland 100–8 in 2004, Japan no win

1991	Murrayfield WC **Scotland** 47–9	2004	Perth **Scotland** 100–8
2003	Townsville WC **Scotland** 32–11		

SCOTLAND v SAMOA

Played 7 Scotland won 6, Drawn 1
Highest scores Scotland 38–3 in 2004, Samoa 20–35 in 1999
Biggest win Scotland 38–3 in 2004, Samoa no win

1991	Murrayfield WC **Scotland** 28–6	2004	Wellington (NZ) **Scotland** 38–3
1995	Murrayfield **Drawn** 15–15	2005	Murrayfield **Scotland** 18–11
1999	Murrayfield WC **Scotland** 35–20	2010	Aberdeen **Scotland** 19–16
2000	Murrayfield **Scotland** 31–8		

SCOTLAND v CANADA

Played 3 Scotland won 2, Canada won 1
Highest scores Scotland 41–0 in 2008, Canada 26–23 in 2002
Biggest win Scotland 41–0 in 2008, Canada 26–23 in 2002

1995	Murrayfield **Scotland** 22–6	2008	Aberdeen **Scotland** 41–0
2002	Vancouver **Canada** 26–23		

SCOTLAND v IVORY COAST

Played 1 Scotland won 1
Highest scores Scotland 89–0 in 1995, Ivory Coast 0–89 in 1995
Biggest win Scotland 89–0 in 1995, Ivory Coast no win

1995	Rustenburg WC **Scotland** 89–0

SCOTLAND v TONGA

Played 2 Scotland won 2
Highest scores Scotland 43–20 in 2001, Tonga 20–43 in 2001
Biggest win Scotland 41–5 in 1995, Tonga no win

1995	Pretoria WC **Scotland** 41–5	2001	Murrayfield **Scotland** 43–20

SCOTLAND v ITALY

Played 18 Scotland won 12, Italy won 6
Highest scores Scotland 47–15 in 2003, Italy 37–17 in 2007
Biggest wins Scotland 47–15 in 2003, Italy 37–17 in 2007

1996 Murrayfield **Scotland** 29–22
1998 Treviso **Italy** 25–21
1999 Murrayfield **Scotland** 30–12
2000 Rome **Italy** 34–20
2001 Murrayfield **Scotland** 23–19
2002 Rome **Scotland** 29–12
2003 Murrayfield **Scotland** 33–25
2003 Murrayfield **Scotland** 47–15
Non-championship match
2004 Rome **Italy** 20–14
2005 Murrayfield **Scotland** 18–10
2006 Rome **Scotland** 13–10
2007 Murrayfield **Italy** 37–17
2007 Saint Etienne WC **Scotland** 18–16
2008 Rome **Italy** 23–20
2009 Murrayfield **Scotland** 26–6
2010 Rome **Italy** 16–12
2011 Murrayfield **Scotland** 21–8
2011 Murrayfield **Scotland** 23–12
Non-championship match

SCOTLAND v URUGUAY

Played 1 Scotland won 1
Highest scores Scotland 43–12 in 1999, Uruguay 12–43 in 1999
Biggest win Scotland 43–12 in 1999, Uruguay no win

1999 Murrayfield WC **Scotland** 43–12

SCOTLAND v SPAIN

Played 1 Scotland won 1
Highest scores Scotland 48–0 in 1999, Spain 0–48 in 1999
Biggest win Scotland 48–0 in 1999, Spain no win

1999 Murrayfield WC **Scotland** 48–0

SCOTLAND v UNITED STATES

Played 3 Scotland won 3
Highest scores Scotland 65–23 in 2002, United States 23–65 in 2002
Biggest win Scotland 53–6 in 2000, United States no win

2000 Murrayfield **Scotland** 53–6
2002 San Francisco **Scotland** 65–23
2003 Brisbane WC **Scotland** 39–15

SCOTLAND v PACIFIC ISLANDS

Played 1 Scotland won 1
Highest scores Scotland 34–22 in 2006, Pacific Islands 22–34 in 2006
Biggest win Scotland 34–22 in 2006, Pacific Islands no win

2006	Murrayfield **Scotland** 34–22

SCOTLAND v PORTUGAL

Played 1 Scotland won 1
Highest scores Scotland 56–10 in 2007, Portugal 10–56 in 2007
Biggest win Scotland 56–10 in 2007, Portugal no win

2007	Saint Etienne WC **Scotland** 56–10

SCOTLAND v GEORGIA

Played 1 Scotland won 1
Highest scores Scotland 15–6 in 2011, Georgia 6–15 in 2011
Biggest win Scotland 15–6 in 2011, Georgia no win

2011	Invercargill WC **Scotland** 15–6

IRELAND v WALES

Played 117 Ireland won 47, Wales won 64, Drawn 6
Highest scores Ireland 54–10 in 2002, Wales 34–9 in 1976
Biggest wins Ireland 54–10 in 2002, Wales 29–0 in 1907

1882	Dublin **Wales** 2G 2T to 0
1883	No Match
1884	Cardiff **Wales** 1DG 2T to 0
1885	No Match
1886	No Match
1887	Birkenhead **Wales** 1DG 1T to 3T
1888	Dublin **Ireland** 1G 1DG 1T to 0
1889	Swansea **Ireland** 2T to 0
1890	Dublin **Drawn** 1G each
1891	Llanelli **Wales** 6–4
1892	Dublin **Ireland** 9–0
1893	Llanelli **Wales** 2–0
1894	Belfast **Ireland** 3–0
1895	Cardiff **Wales** 5–3
1896	Dublin **Ireland** 8–4
1897	No Match
1898	Limerick **Wales** 11–3
1899	Cardiff **Ireland** 3–0
1900	Belfast **Wales** 3–0
1901	Swansea **Wales** 10–9
1902	Dublin **Wales** 15–0
1903	Cardiff **Wales** 18–0
1904	Belfast **Ireland** 14–12
1905	Swansea **Wales** 10–3
1906	Belfast **Ireland** 11–6
1907	Cardiff **Wales** 29–0
1908	Belfast **Wales** 11–5
1909	Swansea **Wales** 18–5
1910	Dublin **Wales** 19–3
1911	Cardiff **Wales** 16–0
1912	Belfast **Ireland** 12–5
1913	Swansea **Wales** 16–13
1914	Belfast **Wales** 11–3
1920	Cardiff **Wales** 28–4
1921	Belfast **Wales** 6–0
1922	Swansea **Wales** 11–5

1923 Dublin **Ireland** 5–4
1924 Cardiff **Ireland** 13–10
1925 Belfast **Ireland** 19–3
1926 Swansea **Wales** 11–8
1927 Dublin **Ireland** 19–9
1928 Cardiff **Ireland** 13–10
1929 Belfast **Drawn** 5–5
1930 Swansea **Wales** 12–7
1931 Belfast **Wales** 15–3
1932 Cardiff **Ireland** 12–10
1933 Belfast **Ireland** 10–5
1934 Swansea **Wales** 13–0
1935 Belfast **Ireland** 9–3
1936 Cardiff **Wales** 3–0
1937 Belfast **Ireland** 5–3
1938 Swansea **Wales** 11–5
1939 Belfast **Wales** 7–0
1947 Swansea **Wales** 6–0
1948 Belfast **Ireland** 6–3
1949 Swansea **Ireland** 5–0
1950 Belfast **Wales** 6–3
1951 Cardiff **Drawn** 3–3
1952 Dublin **Wales** 14–3
1953 Swansea **Wales** 5–3
1954 Dublin **Wales** 12–9
1955 Cardiff **Wales** 21–3
1956 Dublin **Ireland** 11–3
1957 Cardiff **Wales** 6–5
1958 Dublin **Wales** 9–6
1959 Cardiff **Wales** 8–6
1960 Dublin **Wales** 10–9
1961 Cardiff **Wales** 9–0
1962 Dublin **Drawn** 3–3
1963 Cardiff **Ireland** 14–6
1964 Dublin **Wales** 15–6
1965 Cardiff **Wales** 14–8
1966 Dublin **Ireland** 9–6
1967 Cardiff **Ireland** 3–0
1968 Dublin **Ireland** 9–6
1969 Cardiff **Wales** 24–11
1970 Dublin **Ireland** 14–0
1971 Cardiff **Wales** 23–9
1972 No Match
1973 Cardiff **Wales** 16–12
1974 Dublin **Drawn** 9–9
1975 Cardiff **Wales** 32–4
1976 Dublin **Wales** 34–9
1977 Cardiff **Wales** 25–9
1978 Dublin **Wales** 20–16
1979 Cardiff **Wales** 24–21
1980 Dublin **Ireland** 21–7
1981 Cardiff **Wales** 9–8
1982 Dublin **Ireland** 20–12
1983 Cardiff **Wales** 23–9
1984 Dublin **Wales** 18–9
1985 Cardiff **Ireland** 21–9
1986 Dublin **Wales** 19–12
1987 Cardiff **Ireland** 15–11
1987 Wellington WC **Wales** 13–6
1988 Dublin **Wales** 12–9
1989 Cardiff **Ireland** 19–13
1990 Dublin **Ireland** 14–8
1991 Cardiff **Drawn** 21–21
1992 Dublin **Wales** 16–15
1993 Cardiff **Ireland** 19–14
1994 Dublin **Wales** 17–15
1995 Cardiff **Ireland** 16–12
1995 Johannesburg WC **Ireland** 24–23
1996 Dublin **Ireland** 30–17
1997 Cardiff **Ireland** 26–25
1998 Dublin **Wales** 30–21
1999 Wembley **Ireland** 29–23
2000 Dublin **Wales** 23–19
2001 Cardiff **Ireland** 36–6
2002 Dublin **Ireland** 54–10
2003 Cardiff **Ireland** 25–24
2003 Dublin **Ireland** 35–12
2004 Dublin **Ireland** 36–15
2005 Cardiff **Wales** 32–20
2006 Dublin **Ireland** 31–5
2007 Cardiff **Ireland** 19–9
2008 Dublin **Wales** 16–12
2009 Cardiff **Ireland** 17–15
2010 Dublin **Ireland** 27–12
2011 Cardiff **Wales** 19–13
2011 Wellington WC **Wales** 22–10

IRELAND v FRANCE

Played 89 Ireland won 29, France won 55, Drawn 5
Highest scores Ireland 31–43 in 2006, France 45–10 in 1996
Biggest wins Ireland 24–0 in 1913, France 44–5 in 2002

1909 Dublin **Ireland** 19–8
1910 Paris **Ireland** 8–3
1911 Cork **Ireland** 25–5
1912 Paris **Ireland** 11–6
1913 Cork **Ireland** 24–0
1914 Paris **Ireland** 8–6
1920 Dublin **France** 15–7
1921 Paris **France** 20–10
1922 Dublin **Ireland** 8–3
1923 Paris **France** 14–8
1924 Dublin **Ireland** 6–0
1925 Paris **Ireland** 9–3
1926 Belfast **Ireland** 11–0
1927 Paris **Ireland** 8–3
1928 Belfast **Ireland** 12–8
1929 Paris **Ireland** 6–0
1930 Belfast **France** 5–0
1931 Paris **France** 3–0
1947 Dublin **France** 12–8
1948 Paris **Ireland** 13–6
1949 Dublin **France** 16–9
1950 Paris **Drawn** 3–3
1951 Dublin **Ireland** 9–8
1952 Paris **Ireland** 11–8
1953 Belfast **Ireland** 16–3
1954 Paris **France** 8–0
1955 Dublin **France** 5–3
1956 Paris **France** 14–8
1957 Dublin **Ireland** 11–6
1958 Paris **France** 11–6
1959 Dublin **Ireland** 9–5
1960 Paris **France** 23–6
1961 Dublin **France** 15–3
1962 Paris **France** 11–0
1963 Dublin **France** 24–5
1964 Paris **France** 27–6
1965 Dublin **Drawn** 3–3
1966 Paris **France** 11–6
1967 Dublin **France** 11–6
1968 Paris **France** 16–6
1969 Dublin **Ireland** 17–9
1970 Paris **France** 8–0
1971 Dublin **Drawn** 9–9
1972 Paris **Ireland** 14–9
1972 Dublin **Ireland** 24–14
Non-championship match
1973 Dublin **Ireland** 6–4
1974 Paris **France** 9–6
1975 Dublin **Ireland** 25–6
1976 Paris **France** 26–3
1977 Dublin **France** 15–6
1978 Paris **France** 10–9
1979 Dublin **Drawn** 9–9
1980 Paris **France** 19–18
1981 Dublin **France** 19–13
1982 Paris **France** 22–9
1983 Dublin **Ireland** 22–16
1984 Paris **France** 25–12
1985 Dublin **Drawn** 15–15
1986 Paris **France** 29–9
1987 Dublin **France** 19–13
1988 Paris **France** 25–6
1989 Dublin **France** 26–21
1990 Paris **France** 31–12
1991 Dublin **France** 21–13
1992 Paris **France** 44–12
1993 Dublin **France** 21–6
1994 Paris **France** 35–15
1995 Dublin **France** 25–7
1995 Durban WC **France** 36–12
1996 Paris **France** 45–10
1997 Dublin **France** 32–15
1998 Paris **France** 18–16
1999 Dublin **France** 10–9
2000 Paris **Ireland** 27–25
2001 Dublin **Ireland** 22–15
2002 Paris **France** 44–5
2003 Dublin **Ireland** 15–12
2003 Melbourne WC **France** 43–21
2004 Paris **France** 35–17
2005 Dublin **France** 26–19
2006 Paris **France** 43–31
2007 Dublin **France** 20–17
2007 Paris WC **France** 25–3
2008 Paris **France** 26–21
2009 Dublin **Ireland** 30–21

2010	Paris **France** 33–10		Non-championship match
2011	Dublin **France** 25–22	2011	Dublin **France** 26–22
2011	Bordeaux **France** 19–12		Non-championship match

IRELAND v SOUTH AFRICA

Played 20 Ireland won 4, South Africa won 15, Drawn 1
Highest scores Ireland 32–15 in 2006, South Africa 38–0 in 1912
Biggest wins Ireland 32–15 in 2006, South Africa 38–0 in 1912

1906	Belfast **South Africa** 15–12		*2* Pretoria **South Africa** 33–0
1912	Dublin **South Africa** 38–0		South Africa won series 2–0
1931	Dublin **South Africa** 8–3	1998	Dublin **South Africa** 27–13
1951	Dublin **South Africa** 17–5	2000	Dublin **South Africa** 28–18
1960	Dublin **South Africa** 8–3	2004	*1* Bloemfontein **South Africa** 31–17
1961	Cape Town **South Africa** 24–8		*2* Cape Town **South Africa** 26–17
1965	Dublin **Ireland** 9–6		South Africa won series 2–0
1970	Dublin **Drawn** 8–8	2004	Dublin **Ireland** 17–12
1981	*1* Cape Town **South Africa** 23–15	2006	Dublin **Ireland** 32–15
	2 Durban **South Africa** 12–10	2009	Dublin **Ireland** 15–10
	South Africa won series 2–0	2010	Dublin **South Africa** 23–21
1998	*1* Bloemfontein **South Africa** 37–13		

IRELAND v NEW ZEALAND

Played 24 Ireland won 0, New Zealand won 23, Drawn 1
Highest scores Ireland 29–40 in 2001, New Zealand 66–28 in 2010
Biggest win Ireland no win, New Zealand 59–6 in 1992

1905	Dublin **New Zealand** 15–0	1997	Dublin **New Zealand** 63–15
1924	Dublin **New Zealand** 6–0	2001	Dublin **New Zealand** 40–29
1935	Dublin **New Zealand** 17–9	2002	*1* Dunedin **New Zealand** 15–6
1954	Dublin **New Zealand** 14–3		*2* Auckland **New Zealand** 40–8
1963	Dublin **New Zealand** 6–5		New Zealand won series 2–0
1973	Dublin **Drawn** 10–10	2005	Dublin **New Zealand** 45–7
1974	Dublin **New Zealand** 15–6	2006	*1* Hamilton **New Zealand** 34–23
1976	Wellington **New Zealand** 11–3		*2* Auckland **New Zealand** 27–17
1978	Dublin **New Zealand** 10–6		New Zealand won series 2–0
1989	Dublin **New Zealand** 23–6	2008	Wellington **New Zealand** 21–11
1992	*1* Dunedin **New Zealand** 24–21	2008	Dublin **New Zealand** 22–3
	2 Wellington **New Zealand** 59–6	2010	New Plymouth **New Zealand** 66–28
	New Zealand won series 2–0	2010	Dublin **New Zealand** 38–18
1995	Johannesburg WC **New Zealand** 43–19		

IRELAND v AUSTRALIA

Played 30 Ireland won 9, Australia won 20, Drawn 1
Highest scores Ireland 27–12 in 1979, Australia 46–10 in 1999
Biggest wins Ireland 27–12 in 1979 & 21–6 in 2006, Australia 46–10 in 1999

1927	Dublin **Australia** 5–3
1947	Dublin **Australia** 16–3
1958	Dublin **Ireland** 9–6
1967	Dublin **Ireland** 15–8
1967	Sydney **Ireland** 11–5
1968	Dublin **Ireland** 10–3
1976	Dublin **Australia** 20–10
1979	*1* Brisbane **Ireland** 27–12
	2 Sydney **Ireland** 9–3
	Ireland won series 2–0
1981	Dublin **Australia** 16–12
1984	Dublin **Australia** 16–9
1987	Sydney WC **Australia** 33–15
1991	Dublin WC **Australia** 19–18
1992	Dublin **Australia** 42–17
1994	*1* Brisbane **Australia** 33–13
	2 Sydney **Australia** 32–18
	Australia won series 2–0
1996	Dublin **Australia** 22–12
1999	*1* Brisbane **Australia** 46–10
	2 Perth **Australia** 32–26
	Australia won series 2–0
1999	Dublin WC **Australia** 23–3
2002	Dublin **Ireland** 18–9
2003	Perth **Australia** 45–16
2003	Melbourne WC **Australia** 17–16
2005	Dublin **Australia** 30–14
2006	Perth **Australia** 37–15
2006	Dublin **Ireland** 21–6
2008	Melbourne **Australia** 18–12
2009	Dublin **Drawn** 20–20
2010	Brisbane **Australia** 22–15
2011	Auckland WC **Ireland** 15–6

IRELAND v NEW ZEALAND NATIVES

Played 1 New Zealand Natives won 1
Highest scores Ireland 4–13 in 1888, Zew Zealand Natives 13–4 in 1888
Biggest win Ireland no win, New Zealand Natives 13–4 in 1888

1888	Dublin **New Zealand Natives** 4G 1T to 1G 1T

IRELAND v IRU PRESIDENT'S XV

Played 1 Drawn 1
Highest scores Ireland 18–18 in 1974, IRFU President's XV 18–18 in 1974

1974	Dublin **Drawn** 18–18

IRELAND v ROMANIA

Played 8 Ireland won 8
Highest scores Ireland 60–0 in 1986, Romania 35–53 in 1998
Biggest win Ireland 60–0 in 1986, Romania no win

1986	Dublin **Ireland** 60–0	2001	Bucharest **Ireland** 37–3
1993	Dublin **Ireland** 25–3	2002	Limerick **Ireland** 39–8
1998	Dublin **Ireland** 53–35	2003	Gosford WC **Ireland** 45–17
1999	Dublin WC **Ireland** 44–14	2005	Dublin **Ireland** 43–12

IRELAND v CANADA

Played 5 Ireland won 4 Drawn 1
Highest scores Ireland 55–0 in 2008, Canada 27–27 in 2000
Biggest win Ireland 55–0 in 2008, Canada no win

1987	Dunedin WC **Ireland** 46–19	2008	Limerick **Ireland** 55–0
1997	Dublin **Ireland** 33–11	2009	Vancouver **Ireland** 25–6
2000	Markham **Drawn** 27–27		

IRELAND v TONGA

Played 2 Ireland won 2
Highest scores Ireland 40–19 in 2003, Tonga 19–40 in 2003
Biggest win Ireland 32–9 in 1987, Tonga no win

1987	Brisbane WC **Ireland** 32–9	2003	Nuku'alofa **Ireland** 40–19

IRELAND v SAMOA

Played 5 Ireland won 4, Samoa won 1, Drawn 0
Highest scores Ireland 49–22 in 1988, Samoa 40–25 in 1996
Biggest wins Ireland 49–22 in 1988 and 35–8 in 2001, Samoa 40–25 in 1996

1988	Dublin **Ireland** 49–22	2003	Apia **Ireland** 40–14
1996	Dublin **Samoa** 40–25	2010	Dublin **Ireland** 20–10
2001	Dublin **Ireland** 35–8		

IRELAND v ITALY

Played 20 Ireland won 17, Italy won 3, Drawn 0
Highest scores Ireland 61–6 in 2003, Italy 37–29 in 1997 & 37–22 in 1997
Biggest wins Ireland 61–6 in 2003, Italy 37–22 in 1997

1988	Dublin **Ireland** 31–15	1997	Bologna **Italy** 37–22
1995	Treviso **Italy** 22–12	1999	Dublin **Ireland** 39–30
1997	Dublin **Italy** 37–29	2000	Dublin **Ireland** 60–13

2001	Rome **Ireland** 41–22	2007	Rome **Ireland** 51–24
2002	Dublin **Ireland** 32–17	2007	Belfast **Ireland** 23–20
2003	Rome **Ireland** 37–13		Non-championship match
2003	Limerick **Ireland** 61–6	2008	Dublin **Ireland** 16–11
	Non-championship match	2009	Rome **Ireland** 38–9
2004	Dublin **Ireland** 19–3	2010	Dublin **Ireland** 29–11
2005	Rome **Ireland** 28–17	2011	Rome **Ireland** 13–11
2006	Dublin **Ireland** 26–16	2011	Dunedin WC **Ireland** 36–6

IRELAND v ARGENTINA

Played 12 Ireland won 7 Argentina won 5
Highest scores Ireland 32–24 in 1999, Argentina 34–23 in 2000
Biggest win Ireland 29–9 in 2010, Argentina 16–0 in 2007

1990	Dublin **Ireland** 20–18	2007	*1* Santa Fé **Argentina** 22–20
1999	Dublin **Ireland** 32–24		*2* Buenos Aires **Argentina** 16–0
1999	Lens WC **Argentina** 28–24		Argentina won series 2–0
2000	Buenos Aires **Argentina** 34–23	2007	Paris WC **Argentina** 30–15
2002	Dublin **Ireland** 16–7	2008	Dublin **Ireland** 17–3
2003	Adelaide WC **Ireland** 16–15	2010	Dublin **Ireland** 29–9
2004	Dublin **Ireland** 21–19		

IRELAND v NAMIBIA

Played 4 Ireland won 2, Namibia won 2
Highest scores Ireland 64–7 in 2003, Namibia 26–15 in 1991
Biggest win Ireland 64–7 in 2003, Namibia 26–15 in 1991

1991	*1* Windhoek **Namibia** 15–6	2003	Sydney WC **Ireland** 64–7
	2 Windhoek **Namibia** 26–15	2007	Bordeaux WC **Ireland** 32–17
	Namibia won series 2–0		

IRELAND v ZIMBABWE

Played 1 Ireland won 1
Highest scores Ireland 55–11 in 1991, Zimbabwe 11–55 in 1991
Biggest win Ireland 55–11 in 1991, Zimbabwe no win

1991	Dublin WC **Ireland** 55–11

IRELAND v JAPAN

Played 5 Ireland won 5
Highest scores Ireland 78–9 in 2000, Japan 28–50 in 1995
Biggest win Ireland 78–9 in 2000, Japan no win

1991	Dublin WC **Ireland** 32–16	2005	*1* Osaka **Ireland** 44–12
1995	Bloemfontein WC **Ireland 50–28**		*2* Tokyo **Ireland** 47–18
2000	Dublin **Ireland** 78–9		Ireland won series 2–0

IRELAND v UNITED STATES

Played 7 Ireland won 7
Highest scores Ireland 83–3 in 2000, United States 18–25 in 1996
Biggest win Ireland 83–3 in 2000, United States no win

1994	Dublin **Ireland** 26–15	2004	Dublin **Ireland** 55–6
1996	Atlanta **Ireland** 25–18	2009	Santa Clara **Ireland** 27–10
1999	Dublin WC **Ireland** 53–8	2011	New Plymouth WC **Ireland** 22–10
2000	Manchester (NH) **Ireland** 83–3		

IRELAND v FIJI

Played 3 Ireland won 3
Highest scores Ireland 64–17 in 2002, Fiji 17–64 in 2002
Biggest win Ireland 64–17 in 2002, Fiji no win

1995	Dublin **Ireland** 44–8	2009	Dublin **Ireland** 41–6
2002	Dublin **Ireland** 64–17		

IRELAND v GEORGIA

Played 3 Ireland won 3
Highest scores Ireland 70–0 in 1998, Georgia 14–63 in 2002
Biggest win Ireland 70–0 in 1998, Georgia no win

1998	Dublin **Ireland** 70–0	2007	Bordeaux WC **Ireland** 14–10
2002	Dublin **Ireland** 63–14		

IRELAND v RUSSIA

Played 2 Ireland won 2
Highest scores Ireland 62–12 in 2011, Russia 12–62 in 2011
Biggest win Ireland 62–12 in 2011, Russia no win

2002	Krasnoyarsk **Ireland** 35–3	2011	Rotorua WC **Ireland** 62–12

IRELAND v PACIFIC ISLANDS

Played 1 Ireland won 1
Highest scores Ireland 61–17 in 2006, Pacific Islands 17–61 in 2006
Biggest win Ireland 61–17 in 2006, Pacific Islands no win

2006 Dublin **Ireland** 61–17

WALES v FRANCE

Played 89 Wales won 43, France won 43, Drawn 3
Highest scores Wales 49–14 in 1910, France 51–0 in 1998
Biggest wins Wales 47–5 in 1909, France 51–0 in 1998

1908 Cardiff **Wales** 36–4
1909 Paris **Wales** 47–5
1910 Swansea **Wales** 49–14
1911 Paris **Wales** 15–0
1912 Newport **Wales** 14–8
1913 Paris **Wales** 11–8
1914 Swansea **Wales** 31–0
1920 Paris **Wales** 6–5
1921 Cardiff **Wales** 12–4
1922 Paris **Wales** 11–3
1923 Swansea **Wales** 16–8
1924 Paris **Wales** 10–6
1925 Cardiff **Wales** 11–5
1926 Paris **Wales** 7–5
1927 Swansea **Wales** 25–7
1928 Paris **France** 8–3
1929 Cardiff **Wales** 8–3
1930 Paris **Wales** 11–0
1931 Swansea **Wales** 35–3
1947 Paris **Wales** 3–0
1948 Swansea **France** 11–3
1949 Paris **France** 5–3
1950 Cardiff **Wales** 21–0
1951 Paris **France** 8–3
1952 Swansea **Wales** 9–5
1953 Paris **Wales** 6–3
1954 Cardiff **Wales** 19–13
1955 Paris **Wales** 16–11
1956 Cardiff **Wales** 5–3
1957 Paris **Wales** 19–13
1958 Cardiff **France** 16–6
1959 Paris **France** 11–3
1960 Cardiff **France** 16–8
1961 Paris **France** 8–6
1962 Cardiff **Wales** 3–0
1963 Paris **France** 5–3
1964 Cardiff **Drawn** 11–11
1965 Paris **France** 22–13
1966 Cardiff **Wales** 9–8
1967 Paris **France** 20–14
1968 Cardiff **France** 14–9
1969 Paris **Drawn** 8–8
1970 Cardiff **Wales** 11–6
1971 Paris **Wales** 9–5
1972 Cardiff **Wales** 20–6
1973 Paris **France** 12–3
1974 Cardiff **Drawn** 16–16
1975 Paris **Wales** 25–10
1976 Cardiff **Wales** 19–13
1977 Paris **France** 16–9
1978 Cardiff **Wales** 16–7
1979 Paris **France** 14–13
1980 Cardiff **Wales** 18–9
1981 Paris **France** 19–15
1982 Cardiff **Wales** 22–12
1983 Paris **France** 16–9
1984 Cardiff **France** 21–16
1985 Paris **France** 14–3
1986 Cardiff **France** 23–15
1987 Paris **France** 16–9
1988 Cardiff **France** 10–9
1989 Paris **France** 31–12
1990 Cardiff **France** 29–19
1991 Paris **France** 36–3
1991 Cardiff **France** 22–9
Non-championship match
1992 Cardiff **France** 12–9
1993 Paris **France** 26–10
1994 Cardiff **Wales** 24–15
1995 Paris **France** 21–9
1996 Cardiff **Wales** 16–15

1996	Cardiff **France** 40–33	2004	Cardiff **France** 29–22
	Non-championship match	2005	Paris **Wales** 24–18
1997	Paris **France 27–22**	2006	Cardiff **France** 21–16
1998	Wembley **France** 51–0	2007	Paris **France** 32–21
1999	Paris **Wales** 34–33	2007	Cardiff **France** 34–7
1999	Cardiff **Wales** 34–23		Non-championship match
	Non-championship match	2008	Cardiff **Wales** 29–12
2000	Cardiff **France** 36–3	2009	Paris **France** 21–16
2001	Paris **Wales** 43–35	2010	Cardiff **France** 26–20
2002	Cardiff **France** 37–33	2011	Paris **France** 28–9
2003	Paris **France** 33–5	2011	Auckland WC **France** 9–8

WALES v SOUTH AFRICA

Played 26 Wales won 1, South Africa won 24, Drawn 1
Highest scores Wales 36–38 in 2004, South Africa 96–13 in 1998
Biggest win Wales 29–19 in 1999, South Africa 96–13 in 1998

1906	Swansea **South Africa** 11–0	2002	*1* Bloemfontein **South Africa** 34–19
1912	Cardiff **South Africa** 3–0		*2* Cape Town **South Africa** 19–8
1931	Swansea **South Africa** 8–3		SA won series 2–0
1951	Cardiff **South Africa** 6–3	2004	Pretoria **South Africa** 53–18
1960	Cardiff **South Africa** 3–0	2004	Cardiff **South Africa** 38–36
1964	Durban **South Africa** 24–3	2005	Cardiff **South Africa** 33–16
1970	Cardiff **Drawn** 6–6	2007	Cardiff **South Africa** 34–12
1994	Cardiff **South Africa** 20–12	2008	*1* Bloemfontein **South Africa** 43–17
1995	Johannesburg **South Africa** 40–11		*2* Pretoria **South Africa** 37–21
1996	Cardiff **South Africa** 37–20		SA won series 2–0
1998	Pretoria **South Africa** 96–13	2008	Cardiff **South Africa** 20–15
1998	Wembley **South Africa** 28–20	2010	Cardiff **South Africa** 34–31
1999	Cardiff **Wales** 29–19	2010	Cardiff **South Africa** 29–25
2000	Cardiff **South Africa** 23–13	2011	Wellington WC **South Africa** 17–16

WALES v NEW ZEALAND

Played 28 Wales won 3, New Zealand won 25, Drawn 0
Highest scores Wales 37–53 in 2003, New Zealand 55–3 in 2003
Biggest wins Wales 13–8 in 1953, New Zealand 55–3 in 2003

1905	Cardiff **Wales** 3–0	1978	Cardiff **New Zealand** 13–12
1924	Swansea **New Zealand** 19–0	1980	Cardiff **New Zealand** 23–3
1935	Cardiff **Wales** 13–12	1987	Brisbane WC **New Zealand** 49–6
1953	Cardiff **Wales** 13–8	1988	*1* Christchurch **New Zealand** 52–3
1963	Cardiff **New Zealand** 6–0		*2* Auckland **New Zealand** 54–9
1967	Cardiff **New Zealand** 13–6		New Zealand won series 2–0
1969	*1* Christchurch **New Zealand** 19–0	1989	Cardiff **New Zealand** 34–9
	2 Auckland **New Zealand** 33–12	1995	Johannesburg WC **New Zealand 34–9**
	New Zealand won series 2–0	1997	Wembley **New Zealand** 42–7
1972	Cardiff **New Zealand** 19–16	2002	Cardiff **New Zealand** 43–17

2003 Hamilton **New Zealand** 55–3
2003 Sydney WC **New Zealand** 53–37
2004 Cardiff **New Zealand** 26–25
2005 Cardiff **New Zealand** 41–3
2006 Cardiff **New Zealand** 45–10
2008 Cardiff **New Zealand** 29–9
2009 Cardiff **New Zealand** 19–12
2010 *1* Dunedin **New Zealand** 42–9
2 Hamilton **New Zealand** 29–10
New Zealand won series 2–0
2010 Cardiff **New Zealand** 37–25

WALES v AUSTRALIA

Played 31 Wales won 10, Australia won 20, Drawn 1
Highest scores Wales 29–29 in 2006, Australia 63–6 in 1991
Biggest wins Wales 28–3 in 1975, Australia 63–6 in 1991

1908 Cardiff **Wales** 9–6
1927 Cardiff **Australia** 18–8
1947 Cardiff **Wales** 6–0
1958 Cardiff **Wales** 9–3
1966 Cardiff **Australia** 14–11
1969 Sydney **Wales** 19–16
1973 Cardiff **Wales** 24–0
1975 Cardiff **Wales** 28–3
1978 *1* Brisbane **Australia** 18–8
2 Sydney **Australia** 19–17
Australia won series 2–0
1981 Cardiff **Wales** 18–13
1984 Cardiff **Australia** 28–9
1987 Rotorua WC **Wales** 22–21
1991 Brisbane **Australia** 63–6
1991 Cardiff WC **Australia** 38–3
1992 Cardiff **Australia** 23–6
1996 *1* Brisbane **Australia** 56–25
2 Sydney **Australia** 42–3
Australia won series 2–0
1996 Cardiff **Australia** 28–19
1999 Cardiff WC **Australia** 24–9
2001 Cardiff **Australia** 21–13
2003 Sydney **Australia** 30–10
2005 Cardiff **Wales** 24–22
2006 Cardiff **Drawn** 29–29
2007 *1* Sydney **Australia** 29–23
2 Brisbane **Australia** 31–0
Australia won series 2–0
2007 Cardiff WC **Australia** 32–20
2008 Cardiff **Wales** 21–18
2009 Cardiff **Australia** 33–12
2010 Cardiff **Australia** 25–16
2011 Auckland WC **Australia** 21–18

WALES v NEW ZEALAND NATIVES

Played 1 Wales won 1
Highest scores Wales 5–0 in 1888, New Zealand Natives 0–5 in 1888
Biggest win Wales 5–0 in 1888, New Zealand Natives no win

1888 Swansea **Wales** 1G 2T to 0

WALES v NEW ZEALAND ARMY

Played 1 New Zealand Army won 1
Highest scores Wales 3–6 in 1919, New Zealand Army 6–3 in 1919
Biggest win Wales no win, New Zealand Army 6–3 in 1919

1919 Swansea **New Zealand Army** 6–3

WALES v ROMANIA

Played 8 Wales won 6, Romania won 2
Highest scores Wales 81–9 in 2001, Romania 24–6 in 1983
Biggest wins Wales 81–9 in 2001, Romania 24–6 in 1983

1983	Bucharest **Romania** 24–6	2001	Cardiff **Wales** 81–9
1988	Cardiff **Romania** 15–9	2002	Wrexham **Wales** 40–3
1994	Bucharest **Wales** 16–9	2003	Wrexham **Wales** 54–8
1997	Wrexham **Wales** 70–21	2004	Cardiff **Wales** 66–7

WALES v FIJI

Played 9 Wales won 7, Fiji won 1, Drawn 1
Highest scores Wales 66–0 in 2011, Fiji 38–34 in 2007
Biggest win Wales 66–0 in 2011, Fiji 38–34 in 2007

1985	Cardiff **Wales** 40–3	2005	Cardiff **Wales** 11–10
1986	Suva **Wales** 22–15	2007	Nantes WC **Fiji** 38–34
1994	Suva **Wales** 23–8	2010	Cardiff **Drawn** 16–16
1995	Cardiff **Wales** 19–15	2011	Hamilton WC **Wales** 66–0
2002	Cardiff **Wales** 58–14		

WALES v TONGA

Played 6 Wales won 6
Highest scores Wales 51–7 in 2001, Tonga 20–27 in 2003
Biggest win Wales 51–7 in 2001, Tonga no win

1986	Nuku'Alofa **Wales** 15–7	1997	Swansea **Wales** 46–12
1987	Palmerston North WC **Wales** 29–16	2001	Cardiff **Wales** 51–7
1994	Nuku'Alofa **Wales** 18–9	2003	Canberra WC **Wales** 27–20

WALES v SAMOA

Played 8 Wales won 5, Samoa won 3, Drawn 0
Highest scores Wales 50–6 in 2000, Samoa 38–31 in 1999
Biggest wins Wales 50–6 in 2000, Samoa 34–9 in 1994

1986	Apia **Wales** 32–14	1999	Cardiff WC **Samoa** 38–31
1988	Cardiff **Wales** 28–6	2000	Cardiff **Wales** 50–6
1991	Cardiff WC **Samoa** 16–13	2009	Cardiff **Wales** 17–13
1994	Moamoa **Samoa** 34–9	2011	Hamilton WC **Wales** 17–10

WALES v CANADA

Played 12 Wales won 11, Canada won 1, Drawn 0
Highest scores Wales 61–26 in 2006, Canada 26–24 in 1993 & 26–61 in 2006
Biggest wins Wales 60–3 in 2005, Canada 26–24 in 1993

1987	Invercargill WC **Wales** 40–9	2003	Melbourne WC **Wales** 41–10
1993	Cardiff **Canada** 26–24	2005	Toronto **Wales** 60–3
1994	Toronto **Wales** 33–15	2006	Cardiff **Wales** 61–26
1997	Toronto **Wales** 28–25	2007	Nantes WC **Wales** 42–17
1999	Cardiff **Wales** 33–19	2008	Cardiff **Wales** 34–13
2002	Cardiff **Wales** 32–21	2009	Toronto **Wales** 32–23

WALES v UNITED STATES

Played 7 Wales won 7
Highest scores Wales 77–3 in 2005, United States 23–28 in 1997
Biggest win Wales 77–3 in 2005, United States no win

1987	Cardiff **Wales** 46–0		Wales won series 2–0
1997	Cardiff **Wales** 34–14	2000	Cardiff **Wales** 42–11
1997	*1* Wilmington **Wales** 30–20	2005	Hartford **Wales** 77–3
	2 San Francisco **Wales** 28–23	2009	Chicago **Wales** 48–15

WALES v NAMIBIA

Played 4 Wales won 4
Highest scores Wales 81–7 in 2011, Namibia 30–34 in 1990
Biggest win Wales 81–7 in 2011, Namibia no win

1990	*1* Windhoek **Wales** 18–9	1993	Windhoek **Wales** 38–23
	2 Windhoek **Wales** 34–30	2011	New Plymouth WC **Wales** 81–7
	Wales won series 2–0		

WALES v BARBARIANS

Played 3 Wales won 1, Barbarians won 2
Highest scores Wales 31–10 in 1996, Barbarians 31–24 in 1990 and 31–28 in 2011
Biggest wins Wales 31–10 in 1996, Barbarians 31–24 in 1990

1990	Cardiff **Barbarians** 31–24	2011	Cardiff **Barbarians** 31–28
1996	Cardiff **Wales** 31–10		

WALES v ARGENTINA

Played 13 Wales won 9, Argentina won 4
Highest scores Wales 44–50 in 2004, Argentina 50–44 in 2004
Biggest win Wales 33–16 in 2009, Argentina 45–27 in 2006

1991	Cardiff WC **Wales** 16–7
1998	Llanelli **Wales** 43–30
1999	*1* Buenos Aires **Wales** 36–26
	2 Buenos Aires **Wales** 23–16
	Wales won series 2–0
1999	Cardiff WC **Wales** 23–18
2001	Cardiff **Argentina** 30–16
2004	*1* Tucumán **Argentina** 50–44
	2 Buenos Aires **Wales** 35–20
	Series drawn 1–1
2006	*1* Puerto Madryn **Argentina** 27–25
	2 Buenos Aires **Argentina** 45–27
	Argentina won series 2–0
2007	Cardiff **Wales** 27–20
2009	Cardiff **Wales** 33–16
2011	Cardiff **Wales** 28–13

WALES v ZIMBABWE

Played 3 Wales won 3
Highest scores Wales 49–11 in 1998, Zimbabwe 14–35 in 1993
Biggest win Wales 49–11 in 1998, Zimbabwe no win

1993	*1* Bulawayo **Wales** 35–14
	2 Harare **Wales** 42–13
	Wales won series 2–0
1998	Harare **Wales** 49–11

WALES v JAPAN

Played 7 Wales won 7
Highest scores Wales 98–0 in 2004, Japan 30–53 in 2001
Biggest win Wales 98–0 in 2004, Japan no win

1993	Cardiff **Wales** 55–5
1995	Bloemfontein WC **Wales 57–10**
1999	Cardiff WC **Wales** 64–15
2001	*1* Osaka **Wales** 64–10
	2 Tokyo **Wales** 53–30
	Wales won series 2–0
2004	Cardiff **Wales** 98–0
2007	Cardiff WC **Wales** 72–18

WALES v PORTUGAL

Played 1 Wales won 1
Highest scores Wales 102–11 in 1994, Portugal 11–102 in 1994
Biggest win Wales 102–11 in 1994, Portugal no win

1994	Lisbon **Wales** 102–11

WALES v SPAIN

Played 1 Wales won 1
Highest scores Wales 54–0 in 1994, Spain 0–54 in 1994
Bigegst win Wales 54–0 in 1994, Spain no win

1994 Madrid **Wales** 54–0

WALES v ITALY

Played 18 Wales won 15, Italy won 2, Drawn 1
Highest scores Wales 60–21 in 1999, Italy 30–22 in 2003
Biggest win Wales 60–21 in 1999 and 47–8 in 2008, Italy 30–22 in 2003

1994	Cardiff **Wales** 29–19	2003	Canberra WC **Wales** 27–15
1996	Cardiff **Wales** 31–26	2004	Cardiff **Wales** 44–10
1996	Rome **Wales** 31–22	2005	Rome **Wales** 38–8
1998	Llanelli **Wales** 23–20	2006	Cardiff **Drawn** 18–18
1999	Treviso **Wales** 60–21	2007	Rome **Italy** 23–20
2000	Cardiff **Wales** 47–16	2008	Cardiff **Wales** 47–8
2001	Rome **Wales** 33–23	2009	Rome **Wales** 20–15
2002	Cardiff **Wales** 44–20	2010	Cardiff **Wales** 33–10
2003	Rome **Italy** 30–22	2011	Rome **Wales** 24–16

WALES v PACIFIC ISLANDS

Played 1 Wales won 1
Highest scores Wales 38–20 in 2006, Pacific Islands 20–38 in 2006
Biggest win Wales 38–20 in 2006, Pacific Islands no win

2006 Cardiff **Wales** 38–20

ANGLO-WELSH v NEW ZEALAND

Played 3 New Zealand won 2, Drawn 1
Highest scores Anglo Welsh 5–32 in 1908, New Zealand 32–5 in 1908
Biggest win Anglo Welsh no win, New Zealand 29–0 in 1908

1908 *1* Dunedin **New Zealand** 32–5
2 Wellington **Drawn** 3–3
3 Auckland **New Zealand** 29–0

New Zealand won series 2–0 with one drawn

BRITISH/IRISH ISLES v SOUTH AFRICA

Played 46 British/Irish won 17, South Africa won 23, Drawn 6
Highest scores: British/Irish 28–9 in 1974 & 2009, South Africa 35–16 in 1997
Biggest wins: British/Irish 28–9 in 1974 & 2009, South Africa 34–14 in 1962

1891 *1* Port Elizabeth **British/Irish** 4–0
2 Kimberley **British/Irish** 3–0
3 Cape Town **British/Irish** 4–0
British/Irish won series 3–0

1896 *1* Port Elizabeth **British/Irish** 8–0
2 Johannesburg **British/Irish** 17–8
3 Kimberley **British/Irish** 9–3
4 Cape Town **South Africa** 5–0
British/Irish won series 3–1

1903 *1* Johannesburg **Drawn** 10–10
2 Kimberley **Drawn** 0–0
3 Cape Town **South Africa** 8–0
South Africa won series 1–0 with two drawn

1910 *1* Johannesburg **South Africa** 14–10
2 Port Elizabeth **British/Irish** 8–3
3 Cape Town **South Africa** 21–5
South Africa won series 2–1

1924 *1* Durban **South Africa** 7–3
2 Johannesburg **South Africa** 17–0
3 Port Elizabeth **Drawn** 3–3
4 Cape Town **South Africa** 16–9
South Africa won series 3–0, with 1 draw

1938 *1* Johannesburg **South Africa** 26–12
2 Port Elizabeth **South Africa** 19–3
3 Cape Town **British/Irish** 21–16
South Africa won series 2–1

1955 *1* Johannesburg **British/Irish** 23–22
2 Cape Town **South Africa** 25–9
3 Pretoria **British/Irish** 9–6
4 Port Elizabeth **South Africa** 22–8
Series drawn 2–2

1962 *1* Johannesburg **Drawn** 3–3
2 Durban **South Africa** 3–0
3 Cape Town **South Africa** 8–3
4 Bloemfontein **South Africa** 34–14
South Africa won series 3–0, with 1 draw

1968 *1* Pretoria **South Africa** 25–20
2 Port Elizabeth **Drawn** 6–6
3 Cape Town **South Africa** 11–6
4 Johannesburg **South Africa** 19–6
South Africa won series 3–0, with 1 draw

1974 *1* Cape Town **British/Irish** 12–3
2 Pretoria **British/Irish** 28–9
3 Port Elizabeth **British/Irish** 26–9
4 Johannesburg **Drawn** 13–13
British/Irish won series 3–0, with 1 draw

1980 *1* Cape Town **South Africa** 26–22
2 Bloemfontein **South Africa** 26–19
3 Port Elizabeth **South Africa** 12–10
4 Pretoria **British/Irish** 17–13
South Africa won series 3–1

1997 *1* Cape Town **British/Irish** 25–16
2 Durban **British/Irish** 18–15
3 Johannesburg **South Africa** 35–16
British/Irish won series 2–1

2009 *1* Durban **South Africa** 26–21
2 Pretoria **South Africa** 28–25
3 Johannesburg **British/Irish** 28–9
South Africa won series 2–1

BRITISH/IRISH ISLES v NEW ZEALAND

Played 35 British/Irish won 6, New Zealand won 27, Drawn 2
Highest scores: British/Irish 20–7 in 1993, New Zealand 48–18 in 2005
Biggest wins: British/Irish 20–7 in 1993, New Zealand 38–6 in 1983

1904 Wellington **New Zealand** 9–3

1930 *1* Dunedin **British/Irish** 6–3
2 Christchurch **New Zealand** 13–10
3 Auckland **New Zealand** 15–10
4 Wellington **New Zealand** 22–8
New Zealand won series 3–1

1950 *1* Dunedin **Drawn** 9–9
2 Christchurch **New Zealand** 8–0
3 Wellington **New Zealand** 6–3
4 Auckland **New Zealand** 11–8

New Zealand won series 3–0, with 1 draw

1959 *1* Dunedin **New Zealand** 18–17
2 Wellington **New Zealand** 11–8
3 Christchurch **New Zealand** 22–8
4 Auckland **British/Irish** 9–6
New Zealand won series 3–1

1966 *1* Dunedin **New Zealand** 20–3
2 Wellington **New Zealand** 16–12
3 Christchurch **New Zealand** 19–6
4 Auckland **New Zealand** 24–11
New Zealand won series 4–0

1971 *1* Dunedin **British/Irish** 9–3
2 Christchurch **New Zealand** 22–12
3 Wellington **British/Irish** 13–3
4 Auckland **Drawn** 14–14
British/Irish won series 2–1, with 1 draw

1977 *1* Wellington **New Zealand** 16–12
2 Christchurch **British/Irish** 13–9
3 Dunedin **New Zealand** 19–7
4 Auckland **New Zealand** 10–9
New Zealand won series 3–1

1983 *1* Christchurch **New Zealand** 16–12
2 Wellington **New Zealand** 9–0
3 Dunedin **New Zealand** 15–8
4 Auckland **New Zealand** 38–6
New Zealand won series 4–0

1993 *1* Christchurch **New Zealand** 20–18
2 Wellington **British/Irish** 20–7
3 Auckland **New Zealand** 30–13
New Zealand won series 2–1

2005 *1* Christchurch **New Zealand** 21–3
2 Wellington **New Zealand** 48–18
3 Auckland **New Zealand** 38–19
New Zealand won series 3–0

BRITISH/IRISH ISLES v AUSTRALIA

Played 20 British/Irish won 15, Australia won 5, Drawn 0
Highest scores: British/Irish 31–0 in 1966, Australia 35–14 in 2001
Biggest wins: British/Irish 31–0 in 1966, Australia 35–14 in 2001

1899 *1* Sydney **Australia** 13–3
2 Brisbane **British/Irish** 11–0
3 Sydney **British/Irish** 11–10
4 Sydney **British/Irish** 13–0
British/Irish won series 3–1

1904 *1* Sydney **British/Irish** 17–0
2 Brisbane **British/Irish** 17–3
3 Sydney **British/Irish** 16–0
British/Irish won series 3–0

1930 Sydney **Australia** 6–5

1950 *1* Brisbane **British/Irish** 19–6
2 Sydney **British/Irish** 24–3
British/Irish won series 2–0

1959 *1* Brisbane **British/Irish** 17–6
2 Sydney **British/Irish** 24–3
British/Irish won series 2–0

1966 *1* Sydney **British/Irish** 11–8
2 Brisbane **British/Irish** 31–0
British/Irish won series 2–0

1989 *1* Sydney **Australia** 30–12
2 Brisbane **British/Irish** 19–12
3 Sydney **British/Irish** 19–18
British/Irish won series 2–1

2001 *1* Brisbane **British/Irish** 29–13
2 Melbourne **Australia** 35–14
3 Sydney **Australia** 29–23
Australia won series 2–1

BRITISH/IRISH ISLES v ARGENTINA

Played 1 British/Irish won 0, Argentina won 0, Drawn 1
Highest scores: British/Irish 25–25 in 2005, Argentina 25–25 in 2005
Biggest wins: British/Irish no win, Argentina no win

2005 Cardiff **Drawn** 25–25

FRANCE v SOUTH AFRICA

Played 38 France won 11, South Africa won 21, Drawn 6
Highest scores France 36–26 in 2006, South Africa 52–10 in 1997
Biggest wins France 30–10 in 2002, South Africa 52–10 in 1997

1913 Bordeaux **South Africa** 38–5
1952 Paris **South Africa** 25–3
1958 *1* Cape Town **Drawn** 3–3
2 Johannesburg **France** 9–5
France won series 1–0, with 1 draw
1961 Paris **Drawn** 0–0
1964 Springs (SA) **France** 8–6
1967 *1* Durban **South Africa** 26–3
2 Bloemfontein **South Africa** 16–3
3 Johannesburg **France** 19–14
4 Cape Town **Drawn** 6–6
South Africa won series 2–1, with 1 draw
1968 *1* Bordeaux **South Africa** 12–9
2 Paris **South Africa** 16–11
South Africa won series 2–0
1971 *1* Bloemfontein **South Africa** 22–9
2 Durban **Drawn** 8–8
South Africa won series 1–0, with 1 draw
1974 *1* Toulouse **South Africa** 13–4
2 Paris **South Africa** 10–8
South Africa won series 2–0
1975 *1* Bloemfontein **South Africa** 38–25
2 Pretoria **South Africa** 33–18
South Africa won series 2–0
1980 Pretoria **South Africa** 37–15
1992 *1* Lyons **South Africa** 20–15
2 Paris **France** 29–16
Series drawn 1–1
1993 *1* Durban **Drawn** 20–20
2 Johannesburg **France** 18–17
France won series 1–0, with 1 draw
1995 Durban WC **South Africa 19–15**
1996 *1* Bordeaux **South Africa** 22–12
2 Paris **South Africa** 13–12
South Africa won series 2–0
1997 *1* Lyons **South Africa** 36–32
2 Paris **South Africa** 52–10
South Africa won series 2–0
2001 *1* Johannesburg **France** 32–23
2 Durban **South Africa** 20–15
Series drawn 1–1
2001 Paris **France** 20–10
2002 Marseilles **France** 30–10
2005 *1* Durban **Drawn** 30–30
2 Port Elizabeth **South Africa** 27–13
South Africa won series 1–0, with 1 draw
2005 Paris **France** 26–20
2006 Cape Town **France** 36–26
2009 Toulouse **France** 20–13
2010 Cape Town **South Africa** 42–17

FRANCE v NEW ZEALAND

Played 51 France won 12, New Zealand won 38, Drawn 1
Highest scores France 43–31 in 1999, New Zealand 61–10 in 2007
Biggest wins France 22–8 in 1994, New Zealand 61–10 in 2007

1906 Paris **New Zealand** 38–8
1925 Toulouse **New Zealand** 30–6
1954 Paris **France** 3–0
1961 *1* Auckland **New Zealand** 13–6
2 Wellington **New Zealand** 5–3
3 Christchurch **New Zealand** 32–3
New Zealand won series 3–0
1964 Paris **New Zealand** 12–3
1967 Paris **New Zealand** 21–15
1968 *1* Christchurch **New Zealand** 12–9
2 Wellington **New Zealand** 9–3
3 Auckland **New Zealand** 19–12
New Zealand won series 3–0
1973 Paris **France** 13–6
1977 *1* Toulouse **France** 18–13
2 Paris **New Zealand** 15–3
Series drawn 1–1
1979 *1* Christchurch **New Zealand** 23–9

	2 Auckland **France** 24–19
	Series drawn 1–1
1981	*1* Toulouse **New Zealand** 13–9
	2 Paris **New Zealand** 18–6
	New Zealand won series 2–0
1984	*1* Christchurch **New Zealand** 10–9
	2 Auckland **New Zealand** 31–18
	New Zealand won series 2–0
1986	Christchurch **New Zealand** 18–9
1986	*1* Toulouse **New Zealand** 19–7
	2 Nantes **France** 16–3
	Series drawn 1–1
1987	Auckland WC **New Zealand** 29–9
1989	*1* Christchurch **New Zealand** 25–17
	2 Auckland **New Zealand** 34–20
	New Zealand won series 2–0
1990	*1* Nantes **New Zealand** 24–3
	2 Paris **New Zealand** 30–12
	New Zealand won series 2–0
1994	*1* Christchurch **France** 22–8
	2 Auckland **France** 23–20
	France won series 2–0
1995	*1* Toulouse **France** 22–15
	2 Paris **New Zealand** 37–12
	Series drawn 1–1
1999	Wellington **New Zealand** 54–7
1999	Twickenham WC **France** 43–31
2000	*1* Paris **New Zealand** 39–26
	2 Marseilles **France** 42–33
	Series drawn 1–1
2001	Wellington **New Zealand** 37–12
2002	Paris **Drawn** 20–20
2003	Christchurch **New Zealand** 31–23
2003	Sydney WC **New Zealand** 40–13
2004	Paris **New Zealand** 45–6
2006	*1* Lyons **New Zealand** 47–3
	2 Paris **New Zealand** 23–11
	New Zealand won series 2–0
2007	*1* Auckland **New Zealand** 42–11
	2 Wellington **New Zealand** 61–10
	New Zealand won series 2–0
2007	Cardiff WC **France** 20–18
2009	*1* Dunedin **France** 27–22
	2 Wellington **New Zealand** 14–10
	Series drawn 1–1
2009	Marseilles **New Zealand** 39–12
2011	Auckland WC **New Zealand** 37–17
2011	Auckland WC **New Zealand** 8–7

FRANCE v AUSTRALIA

Played 41 France won 16, Australia won 23, Drawn 2
Highest scores France 34–6 in 1976, Australia 59–16 in 2010
Biggest wins France 34–6 in 1976, Australia 59–16 in 2010

1928	Paris **Australia** 11–8
1948	Paris **France** 13–6
1958	Paris **France** 19–0
1961	Sydney **France** 15–8
1967	Paris **France** 20–14
1968	Sydney **Australia** 11–10
1971	*1* Toulouse **Australia** 13–11
	2 Paris **France** 18–9
	Series drawn 1–1
1972	*1* Sydney **Drawn** 14–14
	2 Brisbane **France** 16–15
	France won series 1–0, with 1 draw
1976	*1* Bordeaux **France** 18–15
	2 Paris **France** 34–6
	France won series 2–0
1981	*1* Brisbane **Australia** 17–15
	2 Sydney **Australia** 24–14
	Australia won series 2–0
1983	*1* Clermont-Ferrand **Drawn** 15–15
	2 Paris **France** 15–6
	France won series 1–0, with 1 draw
1986	Sydney **Australia** 27–14
1987	Sydney WC **France** 30–24
1989	*1* Strasbourg **Australia** 32–15
	2 Lille **France** 25–19
	Series drawn 1–1
1990	*1* Sydney **Australia** 21–9
	2 Brisbane **Australia** 48–31
	3 Sydney **France** 28–19
	Australia won series 2–1
1993	*1* Bordeaux **France** 16–13
	2 Paris **Australia** 24–3
	Series drawn 1–1
1997	*1* Sydney **Australia** 29–15
	2 Brisbane **Australia** 26–19
	Australia won series 2–0

1998	Paris **Australia** 32–21	2005	Brisbane **Australia** 37–31
1999	Cardiff WC **Australia** 35–12	2005	Marseilles **France** 26–16
2000	Paris **Australia** 18–13	2008	*1* Sydney **Australia** 34–13
2001	Marseilles **France** 14–13		*2* Brisbane **Australia** 40–10
2002	*1* Melbourne **Australia** 29–17		Australia won series 2–0
	2 Sydney **Australia** 31–25	2008	Paris **Australia** 18–13
	Australia won series 2–0	2009	Sydney **Australia** 22–6
2004	Paris **France** 27–14	2010	Paris **Australia** 59–16

FRANCE v UNITED STATES

Played 7 France won 6, United States won 1, Drawn 0
Highest scores France 41–9 in 1991 and 41–14 in 2003, United States 31–39 in 2004
Biggest wins France 41–9 in 1991, United States 17–3 in 1924

1920	Paris **France** 14–5		*Abandoned after 43 mins
1924	Paris **United States** 17–3		France won series 2–0
1976	Chicago **France** 33–14	2003	Wollongong WC **France** 41–14
1991	*1* Denver **France** 41–9	2004	Hartford **France** 39–31
	2 Colorado Springs **France** 10–3*		

FRANCE v ROMANIA

Played 49 France won 39, Romania won 8, Drawn 2
Highest scores France 67–20 in 2000, Romania 21–33 in 1991
Biggest wins France 59–3 in 1924, Romania 15–0 in 1980

1924	Paris **France** 59–3	1977	Clermont-Ferrand **France** 9–6
1938	Bucharest **France** 11–8	1978	Bucharest **France** 9–6
1957	Bucharest **France** 18–15	1979	Montauban **France** 30–12
1957	Bordeaux **France** 39–0	1980	Bucharest **Romania** 15–0
1960	Bucharest **Romania** 11–5	1981	Narbonne **France** 17–9
1961	Bayonne **Drawn** 5–5	1982	Bucharest **Romania** 13–9
1962	Bucharest **Romania** 3–0	1983	Toulouse **France** 26–15
1963	Toulouse **Drawn** 6–6	1984	Bucharest **France** 18–3
1964	Bucharest **France** 9–6	1986	Lille **France** 25–13
1965	Lyons **France** 8–3	1986	Bucharest **France** 20–3
1966	Bucharest **France** 9–3	1987	Wellington WC **France** 55–12
1967	Nantes **France** 11–3	1987	Agen **France** 49–3
1968	Bucharest **Romania** 15–14	1988	Bucharest **France** 16–12
1969	Tarbes **France** 14–9	1990	Auch **Romania** 12–6
1970	Bucharest **France** 14–3	1991	Bucharest **France** 33–21
1971	Béziers **France** 31–12	1991	Béziers WC **France** 30–3
1972	Constanza **France** 15–6	1992	Le Havre **France** 25–6
1973	Valence **France** 7–6	1993	Bucharest **France** 37–20
1974	Bucharest **Romania** 15–10	1993	Brive **France** 51–0
1975	Bordeaux **France** 36–12	1995	Bucharest **France** 24–15
1976	Bucharest **Romania** 15–12	1995	Tucumán LC **France 52–8**

1996 Aurillac **France** 64–12	2000 Bucharest **France** 67–20
1997 Bucharest **France** 51–20	2003 Lens **France** 56–8
1997 Lourdes LC **France 39–3**	2006 Bucharest **France** 62–14
1999 Castres **France** 62–8	

FRANCE v NEW ZEALAND MAORI

Played 1 New Zealand Maori won 1
Highest scores France 3–12 in 1926, New Zealand Maori 12–3 in 1926
Biggest win France no win, New Zealand Maori 12–3 in 1926

1926 Paris **New Zealand Maori** 12–3

FRANCE v GERMANY

Played 15 France won 13, Germany won 2, Drawn 0
Highest scores France 38–17 in 1933, Germany 17–16 in 1927 & 17–38 in 1933
Biggest wins France 34–0 in 1931, Germany 3–0 in 1938

1927 Paris **France** 30–5	1934 Hanover **France** 13–9
1927 Frankfurt **Germany** 17–16	1935 Paris **France** 18–3
1928 Hanover **France** 14–3	1936 *1* Berlin **France** 19–14
1929 Paris **France** 24–0	*2* Hanover **France** 6–3
1930 Berlin **France** 31–0	France won series 2–0
1931 Paris **France** 34–0	1937 Paris **France** 27–6
1932 Frankfurt **France** 20–4	1938 Frankfurt **Germany** 3–0
1933 Paris **France** 38–17	1938 Bucharest **France** 8–5

FRANCE v ITALY

Played 32 France won 30, Italy won 2, Drawn 0
Highest scores France 60–13 in 1967, Italy 40–32 in 1997
Biggest wins France 60–13 in 1967, Italy 40–32 in 1997

1937 Paris **France** 43–5	1964 Parma **France** 12–3
1952 Milan **France** 17–8	1965 Pau **France** 21–0
1953 Lyons **France** 22–8	1966 Naples **France** 21–0
1954 Rome **France** 39–12	1967 Toulon **France** 60–13
1955 Grenoble **France** 24–0	1995 Buenos Aires LC **France 34–22**
1956 Padua **France** 16–3	1997 Grenoble **Italy** 40–32
1957 Agen **France** 38–6	1997 Auch LC **France 30–19**
1958 Naples **France** 11–3	2000 Paris **France** 42–31
1959 Nantes **France** 22–0	2001 Rome **France** 30–19
1960 Treviso **France** 26–0	2002 Paris **France** 33–12
1961 Chambéry **France** 17–0	2003 Rome **France** 53–27
1962 Brescia **France** 6–3	2004 Paris **France** 25–0
1963 Grenoble **France** 14–12	2005 Rome **France** 56–13

2006	Paris **France** 37–12	2009	Rome **France** 50–8
2007	Rome **France** 39–3	2010	Paris **France** 46–20
2008	Paris **France** 25–13	2011	Rome **Italy** 22–21

FRANCE v BRITISH XVs

Played 5 France won 2, British XVs won 3, Drawn 0
Highest scores France 27–29 in 1989, British XV 36–3 in 1940
Biggest wins France 21–9 in 1945, British XV 36–3 in 1940

1940	Paris **British XV** 36–3	1946	Paris **France** 10–0
1945	Paris **France** 21–9	1989	Paris **British XV** 29–27
1945	Richmond **British XV** 27–6		

FRANCE v WALES XVs

Played 2 France won 1, Wales XV won 1
Highest scores France 12–0 in 1946, Wales XV 8–0 in 1945
Biggest win France 12–0 in 1946, Wales XV 8–0 in 1945

1945	Swansea **Wales XV** 8–0	1946	Paris **France** 12–0

FRANCE v IRELAND XVs

Played 1 France won 1
Highest scores France 4–3 in 1946, Ireland XV 3–4 in 1946
Biggest win France 4–3 in 1946, Ireland XV no win

1946	Dublin **France** 4–3

FRANCE v NEW ZEALAND ARMY

Played 1 New Zealand Army won 1
Highest scores France 9–14 in 1946, New Zealand Army 14–9 in 1946
Biggest win France no win, New Zealand Army 14–9 in 1946

1946	Paris **New Zealand Army** 14–9

FRANCE v ARGENTINA

Played 44 France won 32, Argentina won 11, Drawn 1
Highest scores France 47–12 in 1995 & 47–26 in 1999, Argentina 41–13 in 2010
Biggest wins France 47–12 in 1995, Argentina 41–13 in 2010

1949	*1* Buenos Aires **France** 5–0		*2* Buenos Aires **France** 30–3
	2 Buenos Aires **France** 12–3		France won series 2–0
	France won series 2–0	1960	*1* Buenos Aires **France** 37–3
1954	*1* Buenos Aires **France** 22–8		*2* Buenos Aires **France** 12–3

3 Buenos Aires **France** 29–6
France won series 3–0
1974 *1* Buenos Aires **France** 20–15
2 Buenos Aires **France** 31–27
France won series 2–0
1975 *1* Lyons **France** 29–6
2 Paris **France** 36–21
France won series 2–0
1977 *1* Buenos Aires **France** 26–3
2 Buenos Aires **Drawn** 18–18
France won series 1–0, with 1 draw
1982 *1* Toulouse **France** 25–12
2 Paris **France** 13–6
France won series 2–0
1985 *1* Buenos Aires **Argentina** 24–16
2 Buenos Aires **France** 23–15
Series drawn 1–1
1986 *1* Buenos Aires **Argentina** 15–13
2 Buenos Aires **France** 22–9
Series drawn 1–1
1988 *1* Buenos Aires **France** 18–15
2 Buenos Aires **Argentina** 18–6
Series drawn 1–1
1988 *1* Nantes **France** 29–9
2 Lille **France** 28–18
France won series 2–0
1992 *1* Buenos Aires **France** 27–12
2 Buenos Aires **France** 33–9
France won series 2–0
1992 Nantes **Argentina** 24–20
1995 Buenos Aires LC **France** 47–12
1996 *1* Buenos Aires **France** 34–27
2 Buenos Aires **France** 34–15
France won series 2–0
1997 Tarbes LC **France** 32–27
1998 *1* Buenos Aires **France** 35–18
2 Buenos Aires **France** 37–12
France won series 2–0
1998 Nantes **France** 34–14
1999 Dublin WC **France** 47–26
2002 Buenos Aires **Argentina** 28–27
2003 *1* Buenos Aires **Argentina** 10–6
2 Buenos Aires **Argentina** 33–32
Argentina won series 2–0
2004 Marseilles **Argentina** 24–14
2006 Paris **France** 27–26
2007 Paris WC **Argentina** 17–12
2007 Paris WC **Argentina** 34–10
2008 Marseilles **France** 12–6
2010 Buenos Aires **Argentina** 41–13
2010 Montpellier **France** 15–9

FRANCE v CZECHOSLOVAKIA

Played 2 France won 2
Highest scores France 28–3 in 1956, Czechoslovakia 6–19 in 1968
Biggest win France 28–3 in 1956, Czechoslovakia no win

1956 Toulouse **France** 28–3
1968 Prague **France** 19–6

FRANCE v FIJI

Played 8 France won 8
Highest scores France 77–10 in 2001, Fiji 19–28 in 1999
Biggest win France 77–10 in 2001, Fiji no win

1964 Paris **France** 21–3
1987 Auckland WC **France** 31–16
1991 Grenoble WC **France** 33–9
1998 Suva **France** 34–9
1999 Toulouse WC **France** 28–19
2001 Saint Etienne **France** 77–10
2003 Brisbane WC **France** 61–18
2010 Nantes **France** 34–12

FRANCE v JAPAN

Played 3 France won 3
Highest scores France 51–29 in 2003, Japan 29–51 in 2003
Biggest win France 51–29 in 2003, Japan no win

1973	Bordeaux **France** 30–18	2011	Albany WC **France** 47–21
2003	Townsville WC **France** 51–29		

FRANCE v ZIMBABWE

Played 1 France won 1
Highest scores France 70–12 in 1987, Zimbabwe 12–70 in 1987
Biggest win France 70–12 in 1987, Zimbabwe no win

1987	Auckland WC **France** 70–12

FRANCE v CANADA

Played 8 France won 7, Canada won 1, Drawn 0
Highest scores France 50–6 in 2005, Canada 20–33 in 1999
Biggest wins France 50–6 in 2005, Canada 18–16 in 1994

1991	Agen WC **France** 19–13	2002	Paris **France** 35–3
1994	Nepean **Canada** 18–16	2004	Toronto **France** 47–13
1994	Besançon **France** 28–9	2005	Nantes **France** 50–6
1999	Béziers WC **France** 33–20	2011	Napier WC **France** 46–19

FRANCE v TONGA

Played 4 France won 2, Tonga won 2
Highest scores France 43–8 in 2005, Tonga 20–16 in 1999
Biggest win France 43–8 in 2005, Tonga 19–14 in 2011

1995	Pretoria WC **France** 38–10	2005	Toulouse **France** 43–8
1999	Nuku'alofa **Tonga** 20–16	2011	Wellington WC **Tonga** 19–14

FRANCE v IVORY COAST

Played 1 France won 1
Highest scores France 54–18 in 1995, Ivory Coast 18–54 in 1995
Biggest win France 54–18 in 1995, Ivory Coast no win

1995	Rustenburg WC **France** 54–18

FRANCE v SAMOA

Played 2 France won 2
Highest scores France 43–5 in 2009, Samoa 22–39 in 1999
Biggest win France 43–5 in 2009, Samoa no win

1999 Apia **France** 39–22	2009 Paris **France** 43–5

FRANCE v NAMIBIA

Played 2 France won 2
Highest scores France 87–10 in 2007, Namibia 13–47 in 1999
Biggest win France 87–10 in 2007, Namibia no win

1999 Bordeaux WC **France** 47–13	2007 Toulouse WC **France** 87–10

FRANCE v GEORGIA

Played 1 France won 1
Highest scores France 64–7 in 2007, Georgia 7–64 in 2007
Biggest win France 64–7 in 2007, Georgia no win

2007 Marseilles WC **France** 64–7

FRANCE v PACIFIC ISLANDS

Played 1 Wales won 1
Highest scores France 42–17 in 2008, Pacific Islands 17–42 in 2008
Biggest win France 42–17 in 2008, Pacific Islands no win

2008 Sochaux **France** 42–17

SOUTH AFRICA v NEW ZEALAND

Played 83 New Zealand won 46, South Africa won 34, Drawn 3
Highest scores New Zealand 55–35 in 1997, South Africa 46–40 in 2000
Biggest wins New Zealand 52–16 in 2003, South Africa 17–0 in 1928

1921	*1* Dunedin **New Zealand** 13–5
	2 Auckland **South Africa** 9–5
	3 Wellington **Drawn** 0–0
	Series drawn 1–1, with 1 draw
1928	*1* Durban **South Africa** 17–0
	2 Johannesburg **New Zealand** 7–6
	3 Port Elizabeth **South Africa** 11–6
	4 Cape Town **New Zealand** 13–5
	Series drawn 2–2
1937	*1* Wellington **New Zealand** 13–7
	2 Christchurch **South Africa** 13–6
	3 Auckland **South Africa** 17–6
	South Africa won series 2–1
1949	*1* Cape Town **South Africa** 15–11
	2 Johannesburg **South Africa** 12–6
	3 Durban **South Africa** 9–3
	4 Port Elizabeth **South Africa** 11–8
	South Africa won series 4–0
1956	*1* Dunedin **New Zealand** 10–6
	2 Wellington **South Africa** 8–3

	3 Christchurch **New Zealand** 17–10
	4 Auckland **New Zealand** 11–5
	New Zealand won series 3–1
1960	*1* Johannesburg **South Africa** 13–0
	2 Cape Town **New Zealand** 11–3
	3 Bloemfontein **Drawn** 11–11
	4 Port Elizabeth **South Africa** 8–3
	South Africa won series 2–1, with 1 draw
1965	*1* Wellington **New Zealand** 6–3
	2 Dunedin **New Zealand** 13–0
	3 Christchurch **South Africa** 19–16
	4 Auckland **New Zealand** 20–3
	New Zealand won series 3–1
1970	*1* Pretoria **South Africa** 17–6
	2 Cape Town **New Zealand** 9–8
	3 Port Elizabeth **South Africa** 14–3
	4 Johannesburg **South Africa** 20–17
	South Africa won series 3–1
1976	*1* Durban **South Africa** 16–7
	2 Bloemfontein **New Zealand** 15–9
	3 Cape Town **South Africa** 15–10
	4 Johannesburg **South Africa** 15–14
	South Africa won series 3–1
1981	*1* Christchurch **New Zealand** 14–9
	2 Wellington **South Africa** 24–12
	3 Auckland **New Zealand** 25–22
	New Zealand won series 2–1
1992	Johannesburg **New Zealand** 27–24
1994	*1* Dunedin **New Zealand** 22–14
	2 Wellington **New Zealand** 13–9
	3 Auckland **Drawn** 18–18
	New Zealand won series 2–0, with 1 draw
1995	Johannesburg WC **South Africa** 15–12 (*aet*)
1996	Christchurch TN **New Zealand** 15–11
1996	Cape Town TN **New Zealand** 29–18
1996	*1* Durban **New Zealand** 23–19
	2 Pretoria **New Zealand** 33–26
	3 Johannesburg **South Africa** 32–22
	New Zealand won series 2–1
1997	Johannesburg TN **New Zealand** 35–32
1997	Auckland TN **New Zealand** 55–35
1998	Wellington TN **South Africa** 13–3
1998	Durban TN **South Africa** 24–23
1999	Dunedin TN **New Zealand** 28–0
1999	Pretoria TN **New Zealand** 34–18
1999	Cardiff WC **South Africa** 22–18
2000	Christchurch TN **New Zealand** 25–12
2000	Johannesburg TN **South Africa** 46–40
2001	Cape Town TN **New Zealand** 12–3
2001	Auckland TN **New Zealand** 26–15
2002	Wellington TN **New Zealand** 41–20
2002	Durban TN **New Zealand** 30–23
2003	Pretoria TN **New Zealand** 52–16
2003	Dunedin TN **New Zealand** 19–11
2003	Melbourne WC **New Zealand** 29–9
2004	Christchurch TN **New Zealand** 23–21
2004	Johannesburg TN **South Africa** 40–26
2005	Cape Town TN **South Africa** 22–16
2005	Dunedin TN **New Zealand** 31–27
2006	Wellington TN **New Zealand** 35–17
2006	Pretoria TN **New Zealand** 45–26
2006	Rustenburg TN **South Africa** 21–20
2007	Durban TN **New Zealand** 26–21
2007	Christchurch TN **New Zealand** 33–6
2008	Wellington TN **New Zealand** 19–8
2008	Dunedin TN **South Africa** 30–28
2008	Cape Town TN **New Zealand** 19–0
2009	Bloemfontein TN **South Africa** 28–19
2009	Durban TN **South Africa** 31–19
2009	Hamilton TN **South Africa** 32–29
2010	Auckland TN **New Zealand** 32–12
2010	Wellington TN **New Zealand** 31–17
2010	Soweto TN **New Zealand** 29–22
2011	Wellington TN **New Zealand** 40–7
2011	Port Elizabeth TN **South Africa** 18–5

SOUTH AFRICA v AUSTRALIA

Played 74 South Africa won 41, Australia won 32, Drawn 1
Highest scores South Africa 61–22 in 1997, Australia 49–0 in 2006
Biggest wins South Africa 53–8 in 2008, Australia 49–0 in 2006

1933	*1* Cape Town **South Africa** 17–3
	2 Durban **Australia** 21–6
	3 Johannesburg **South Africa** 12–3
	4 Port Elizabeth **South Africa** 11–0
	5 Bloemfontein **Australia** 15–4
	South Africa won series 3–2

1937 *1* Sydney **South Africa** 9–5
2 Sydney **South Africa** 26–17
South Africa won series 2–0
1953 *1* Johannesburg **South Africa** 25–3
2 Cape Town **Australia** 18–14
3 Durban **South Africa** 18–8
4 Port Elizabeth **South Africa** 22–9
South Africa won series 3–1
1956 *1* Sydney **South Africa** 9–0
2 Brisbane **South Africa** 9–0
South Africa won series 2–0
1961 *1* Johannesburg **South Africa** 28–3
2 Port Elizabeth **South Africa** 23–11
South Africa won series 2–0
1963 *1* Pretoria **South Africa** 14–3
2 Cape Town **Australia** 9–5
3 Johannesburg **Australia** 11–9
4 Port Elizabeth **South Africa** 22–6
Series drawn 2–2
1965 *1* Sydney **Australia** 18–11
2 Brisbane **Australia** 12–8
Australia won series 2–0
1969 *1* Johannesburg **South Africa** 30–11
2 Durban **South Africa** 16–9
3 Cape Town **South Africa** 11–3
4 Bloemfontein **South Africa** 19–8
South Africa won series 4–0
1971 *1* Sydney **South Africa** 19–11
2 Brisbane **South Africa** 14–6
3 Sydney **South Africa** 18–6
South Africa won series 3–0
1992 Cape Town **Australia** 26–3
1993 *1* Sydney **South Africa** 19–12
2 Brisbane **Australia** 28–20
3 Sydney **Australia** 19–12
Australia won series 2–1
1995 Cape Town WC **South Africa** 27–18
1996 Sydney TN **Australia** 21–16
1996 Bloemfontein TN **South Africa** 25–19
1997 Brisbane TN **Australia** 32–20
1997 Pretoria TN **South Africa** 61–22
1998 Perth TN **South Africa** 14–13
1998 Johannesburg TN **South Africa** 29–15
1999 Brisbane TN **Australia** 32–6
1999 Cape Town TN **South Africa** 10–9
1999 Twickenham WC **Australia** 27–21
2000 Melbourne **Australia** 44–23
2000 Sydney TN **Australia** 26–6
2000 Durban TN **Australia** 19–18
2001 Pretoria TN **South Africa** 20–15
2001 Perth TN **Drawn** 14–14
2002 Brisbane TN **Australia** 38–27
2002 Johannesburg TN **South Africa** 33–31
2003 Cape Town TN **South Africa** 26–22
2003 Brisbane TN **Australia** 29–9
2004 Perth TN **Australia** 30–26
2004 Durban TN **South Africa** 23–19
2005 Sydney **Australia** 30–12
2005 Johannesburg **South Africa** 33–20
2005 Pretoria TN **South Africa** 22–16
2005 Perth TN **South Africa** 22–19
2006 Brisbane TN **Australia** 49–0
2006 Sydney TN **Australia** 20–18
2006 Johannesburg TN **South Africa** 24–16
2007 Cape Town TN **South Africa** 22–19
2007 Sydney TN **Australia** 25–17
2008 Perth TN **Australia** 16–9
2008 Durban TN **Australia** 27–15
2008 Johannesburg TN **South Africa** 53–8
2009 Cape Town TN **South Africa** 29–17
2009 Perth TN **South Africa** 32–25
2009 Brisbane TN **Australia** 21–6
2010 Brisbane TN **Australia** 30–13
2010 Pretoria TN **South Africa** 44–31
2010 Bloemfontein TN **Australia** 41–39
2011 Sydney TN **Australia** 39–20
2011 Durban TN **Australia** 14–9
2011 Wellington WC **Australia** 11–9

SOUTH AFRICA v WORLD XVs

Played 3 South Africa won 3
Highest scores South Africa 45–24 in 1977, World XV 24–45 in 1977
Biggest win South Africa 45–24 in 1977, World XV no win

1977 Pretoria **South Africa** 45–24
1989 *1* Cape Town **South Africa** 20–19
2 Johannesburg **South Africa** 22–16
South Africa won series 2–0

SOUTH AFRICA v SOUTH AMERICA

Played 8 South Africa won 7, South America won 1, Drawn 0
Highest scores South Africa 50–18 in 1982, South America 21–12 in 1982
Biggest wins South Africa 50–18 in 1982, South America 21–12 in 1982

1980	*1* Johannesburg **South Africa** 24–9	1982	*1* Pretoria **South Africa** 50–18
	2 Durban **South Africa** 18–9		*2* Bloemfontein **South America** 21–12
	South Africa won series 2–0		Series drawn 1–1
1980	*1* Montevideo **South Africa** 22–13	1984	*1* Pretoria **South Africa** 32–15
	2 Santiago **South Africa** 30–16		*2* Cape Town **South Africa** 22–13
	South Africa won series 2–0		South Africa won series 2–0

SOUTH AFRICA v UNITED STATES

Played 3 South Africa won 3
Highest scores South Africa 64–10 in 2007, United States 20–43 in 2001
Biggest win South Africa 64–10 in 2007, United States no win

1981	Glenville **South Africa** 38–7	2007	Montpellier WC **South Africa** 64–10
2001	Houston **South Africa** 43–20		

SOUTH AFRICA v NEW ZEALAND CAVALIERS

Played 4 South Africa won 3, New Zealand Cavaliers won 1, Drawn 0
Highest scores South Africa 33–18 in 1986, New Zealand Cavaliers 19–18 in 1986
Biggest wins South Africa 33–18 in 1986, New Zealand Cavaliers 19–18 in 1986

1986	*1* Cape Town **South Africa** 21–15	*3* Pretoria **South Africa** 33–18
	2 Durban **New Zealand Cavaliers** 19–18	*4* Johannesburg **South Africa** 24–10
		South Africa won series 3–1

SOUTH AFRICA v ARGENTINA

Played 13 South Africa won 13
Highest scores South Africa 63–9 in 2008, Argentina 33–37 in 2000
Biggest wins South Africa 63–9 in 2008, Argentina no win

1993	*1* Buenos Aires **South Africa** 29–26		South Africa won series 2–0
	2 Buenos Aires **South Africa** 52–23	*2000*	Buenos Aires **South Africa** 37–33
	South Africa won series 2–0	2002	Springs **South Africa** 49–29
1994	*1* Port Elizabeth **South Africa** 42–22	2003	Port Elizabeth **South Africa** 26–25
	2 Johannesburg **South Africa** 46–26	2004	Buenos Aires **South Africa** 39–7
	South Africa won series 2–0	2005	Buenos Aires **South Africa** 34–23
1996	*1* Buenos Aires **South Africa** 46–15	2007	Paris WC **South Africa** 37–13
	2 Buenos Aires **South Africa** 44–21	2008	Johannesburg **South Africa** 63–9

SOUTH AFRICA v SAMOA

Played 7 South Africa won 7
Highest scores South Africa 60–8 in 1995, 60–18 in 2002 and 60–10 in 2003, Samoa 18–60 in 2002
Biggest win South Africa 60–8 in 1995 and 59–7 in 2007, Samoa no win

1995	Johannesburg **South Africa** 60–8	2007	Johannesburg **South Africa** 35–8
1995	Johannesburg WC **South Africa** 42–14	2007	Paris WC **South Africa** 59–7
2002	Pretoria **South Africa** 60–18	2011	Albany WC **South Africa** 13–5
2003	Brisbane WC **South Africa** 60–10		

SOUTH AFRICA v ROMANIA

Played 1 South Africa won 1
Highest score South Africa 21–8 in 1995, Romania 8–21 in 1995
Biggest win South Africa 21–8 in 1995, Romania no win

1995	Cape Town WC **South Africa** 21–8

SOUTH AFRICA v CANADA

Played 2 South Africa won 2
Highest scores South Africa 51–18 in 2000, Canada 18–51 in 2000
Biggest win South Africa 51–18 in 2000, Canada no win

1995	Port Elizabeth WC **South Africa** 20–0	2000	East London **South Africa** 51–18

SOUTH AFRICA v ITALY

Played 10 South Africa won 10
Highest scores South Africa 101–0 in 1999, Italy 31–62 in 1997
Biggest win South Africa 101–0 in 1999, Italy no win

1995	Rome **South Africa** 40–21	2001	Genoa **South Africa** 54–26
1997	Bologna **South Africa** 62–31	2008	Cape Town **South Africa** 26–0
1999	*1* Port Elizabeth **South Africa** 74–3	2009	Udine **South Africa** 32–10
	2 Durban **South Africa** 101–0	2010	*1* Witbank **South Africa** 29–13
	South Africa won series 2–0		*2* East London **South Africa** 55–11
2001	Port Elizabeth **South Africa** 60–14		South Africa won series 2–0

SOUTH AFRICA v FIJI

Played 3 South Africa won 3
Highest scores South Africa 49–3 in 2011, Fiji 20–37 in 2007
Biggest win South Africa 49–3 in 2011, Fiji no win

1996	Pretoria **South Africa** 43–18	2011	Wellington WC **South Africa** 49–3
2007	Marseilles WC **South Africa** 37–20		

SOUTH AFRICA v TONGA

Played 2 South Africa won 2
Highest scores South Africa 74–10 in 1997, Tonga 25–30 in 2007
Biggest win South Africa 74–10 in 1997, Tonga no win

1997	Cape Town **South Africa** 74–10	2007	Lens WC **South Africa** 30–25

SOUTH AFRICA v SPAIN

Played 1 South Africa won 1
Highest scores South Africa 47–3 in 1999, Spain 3–47 in 1999
Biggest win South Africa 47–3 in 1999, Spain no win

1999	Murrayfield WC **South Africa** 47–3

SOUTH AFRICA v URUGUAY

Played 3 South Africa won 3
Highest scores South Africa 134–3 in 2005, Uruguay 6–72 in 2003
Biggest win South Africa 134–3 in 2005, Uruguay no win

1999	Glasgow WC **South Africa** 39–3		Perth WC **South Africa** 72–6
2003	Glasgow WC **South Africa** 39–3	2005	East London **South Africa** 134–3

SOUTH AFRICA v GEORGIA

Played 1 South Africa won 1
Highest scores South Africa 46–19 in 2003, Georgia 19–46 in 2003
Biggest win South Africa 46–19 in 2003, Georgia no win

2003	Sydney WC **South Africa** 46–19

SOUTH AFRICA v PACIFIC ISLANDS

Played 1 South Africa won 1
Highest scores South Africa 38–24 in 2004, Pacific Islands 24–38 in 2004
Biggest win South Africa 38–24 in 2004, Pacific Islands no win

2004	Gosford (Aus) **South Africa** 38–24

SOUTH AFRICA v NAMIBIA

Played 2 South Africa won 2
Highest scores South Africa 105–13 in 2007, Namibia 13–105 in 2007
Biggest win South Africa 105–13 in 2007, Namibia no win

2007	Cape Town **South Africa** 105–13	2011	Albany WC **South Africa** 87–0

NEW ZEALAND v AUSTRALIA

Played 143 New Zealand won 97, Australia won 41, Drawn 5
Highest scores New Zealand 50–21 in 2003, Australia 35–39 in 2000
Biggest wins New Zealand 43–6 in 1996, Australia 28–7 in 1999

1903 Sydney **New Zealand** 22–3
1905 Dunedin **New Zealand** 14–3
1907 *1* Sydney **New Zealand** 26–6
2 Brisbane **New Zealand** 14–5
3 Sydney **Drawn** 5–5
New Zealand won series 2–0, with 1 draw
1910 *1* Sydney **New Zealand** 6–0
2 Sydney **Australia** 11–0
3 Sydney **New Zealand** 28–13
New Zealand won series 2–1
1913 *1* Wellington **New Zealand** 30–5
2 Dunedin **New Zealand** 25–13
3 Christchurch **Australia** 16–5
New Zealand won series 2–1
1914 *1* Sydney **New Zealand** 5–0
2 Brisbane **New Zealand** 17–0
3 Sydney **New Zealand** 22–7
New Zealand won series 3–0
1929 *1* Sydney **Australia** 9–8
2 Brisbane **Australia** 17–9
3 Sydney **Australia** 15–13
Australia won series 3–0
1931 Auckland **New Zealand** 20–13
1932 *1* Sydney **Australia** 22–17
2 Brisbane **New Zealand** 21–3
3 Sydney **New Zealand** 21–13
New Zealand won series 2–1
1934 *1* Sydney **Australia** 25–11
2 Sydney **Drawn** 3–3
Australia won series 1–0, with 1 draw
1936 *1* Wellington **New Zealand** 11–6
2 Dunedin **New Zealand** 38–13
New Zealand won series 2–0
1938 *1* Sydney **New Zealand** 24–9
2 Brisbane **New Zealand** 20–14
3 Sydney **New Zealand** 14–6
New Zealand won series 3–0
1946 *1* Dunedin **New Zealand** 31–8
2 Auckland **New Zealand** 14–10
New Zealand won series 2–0
1947 *1* Brisbane **New Zealand** 13–5
2 Sydney **New Zealand** 27–14
New Zealand won series 2–0
1949 *1* Wellington **Australia** 11–6
2 Auckland **Australia** 16–9
Australia won series 2–0
1951 *1* Sydney **New Zealand** 8–0
2 Sydney **New Zealand** 17–11
3 Brisbane **New Zealand** 16–6
New Zealand won series 3–0
1952 *1* Christchurch **Australia** 14–9
2 Wellington **New Zealand** 15–8
Series drawn 1–1
1955 *1* Wellington **New Zealand** 16–8
2 Dunedin **New Zealand** 8–0
3 Auckland **Australia** 8–3
New Zealand won series 2–1
1957 *1* Sydney **New Zealand** 25–11
2 Brisbane **New Zealand** 22–9
New Zealand won series 2–0
1958 *1* Wellington **New Zealand** 25–3
2 Christchurch **Australia** 6–3
3 Auckland **New Zealand** 17–8
New Zealand won series 2–1
1962 *1* Brisbane **New Zealand** 20–6
2 Sydney **New Zealand** 14–5
New Zealand won series 2–0
1962 *1* Wellington **Drawn** 9–9
2 Dunedin **New Zealand** 3–0
3 Auckland **New Zealand** 16–8
New Zealand won series 2–0, with1 draw
1964 *1* Dunedin **New Zealand** 14–9
2 Christchurch **New Zealand** 18–3
3 Wellington **Australia** 20–5
New Zealand won series 2–1
1967 Wellington **New Zealand** 29–9
1968 *1* Sydney **New Zealand** 27–11
2 Brisbane **New Zealand** 19–18
New Zealand won series 2–0
1972 *1* Wellington **New Zealand** 29–6
2 Christchurch **New Zealand** 30–17
3 Auckland **New Zealand** 38–3
New Zealand won series 3–0
1974 *1* Sydney **New Zealand** 11–6

2 Brisbane **Drawn** 16–16
3 Sydney **New Zealand** 16–6
New Zealand won series 2–0, with 1 draw
1978 1 Wellington **New Zealand** 13–12
2 Christchurch **New Zealand** 22–6
3 Auckland **Australia** 30–16
New Zealand won series 2–1
1979 Sydney **Australia** 12–6
1980 1 Sydney **Australia** 13–9
2 Brisbane **New Zealand** 12–9
3 Sydney **Australia** 26–10
Australia won series 2–1
1982 1 Christchurch **New Zealand** 23–16
2 Wellington **Australia** 19–16
3 Auckland **New Zealand** 33–18
New Zealand won series 2–1
1983 Sydney **New Zealand** 18–8
1984 1 Sydney **Australia** 16–9
2 Brisbane **New Zealand** 19–15
3 Sydney **New Zealand** 25–24
New Zealand won series 2–1
1985 Auckland **New Zealand** 10–9
1986 1 Wellington **Australia** 13–12
2 Dunedin **New Zealand** 13–12
3 Auckland **Australia** 22–9
Australia won series 2–1
1987 Sydney **New Zealand** 30–16
1988 1 Sydney **New Zealand** 32–7
2 Brisbane **Drawn** 19–19
3 Sydney **New Zealand** 30–9
New Zealand won series 2–0, with 1 draw
1989 Auckland **New Zealand** 24–12
1990 1 Christchurch **New Zealand** 21–6
2 Auckland **New Zealand** 27–17
3 Wellington **Australia** 21–9
New Zealand won series 2–1
1991 1 Sydney **Australia** 21–12
2 Auckland **New Zealand** 6–3
1991 Dublin WC **Australia** 16–6
1992 1 Sydney **Australia** 16–15
2 Brisbane **Australia** 19–17
3 Sydney **New Zealand** 26–23
Australia won series 2–1
1993 Dunedin **New Zealand** 25–10
1994 Sydney **Australia** 20–16
1995 Auckland **New Zealand** 28–16
1995 Sydney **New Zealand** 34–23
1996 Wellington TN **New Zealand** 43–6
1996 Brisbane TN **New Zealand** 32–25
New Zealand won series 2–0
1997 Christchurch **New Zealand** 30–13
1997 Melbourne TN **New Zealand** 33–18
1997 Dunedin TN **New Zealand** 36–24
New Zealand won series 3–0
1998 Melbourne TN **Australia** 24–16
1998 Christchurch TN **Australia** 27–23
1998 Sydney Australia 19–14
Australia won series 3–0
1999 Auckland TN **New Zealand** 34–15
1999 Sydney TN **Australia** 28–7
Series drawn 1–1
2000 Sydney TN **New Zealand** 39–35
2000 Wellington TN **Australia** 24–23
Series drawn 1–1
2001 Dunedin TN **Australia** 23–15
2001 Sydney TN **Australia** 29–26
Australia won series 2–0
2002 Christchurch TN **New Zealand** 12–6
2002 Sydney TN **Australia** 16–14
Series drawn 1–1
2003 Sydney TN **New Zealand** 50–21
2003 Auckland TN **New Zealand** 21–17
New Zealand won series 2–0
2003 Sydney WC **Australia** 22–10
2004 Wellington TN **New Zealand** 16–7
2004 Sydney TN **Australia** 23–18
Series drawn 1–1
2005 Sydney TN **New Zealand** 30–13
2005 Auckland TN **New Zealand** 34–24
New Zealand won series 2–0
2006 Christchurch TN **New Zealand** 32–12
2006 Brisbane TN **New Zealand** 13–9
2006 Auckland TN **New Zealand** 34–27
New Zealand won series 3–0
2007 Melbourne TN **Australia** 20–15
2007 Auckland TN **New Zealand** 26–12
Series drawn 1–1
2008 Sydney TN **Australia** 34–19
2008 Auckland TN **New Zealand** 39–10
2008 Brisbane TN **New Zealand** 28–24
2008 Hong Kong **New Zealand** 19–14
New Zealand won series 3–1
2009 Auckland TN **New Zealand** 22–16
2009 Sydney TN **New Zealand** 19–18
2009 Wellington TN **New Zealand** 33–6
2009 Tokyo **New Zealand** 32–19
New Zealand won series 4–0
2010 Melbourne TN **New Zealand** 49–28

2010	Christchurch TN **New Zealand** 20–10	2011	Auckland TN **New Zealand** 30–14
2010	Sydney TN **New Zealand** 23–22	2011	Brisbane TN **Australia** 25–20
2010	Hong Kong **Australia** 26–24	2011	Auckland WC **New Zealand** 20–6
	New Zealand won series 3–1		

NEW ZEALAND v UNITED STATES

Played 2 New Zealand won 2
Highest scores New Zealand 51–3 in 1913, United States 6–46 in 1991
Biggest win New Zealand 51–3 in 1913, United States no win

1913	Berkeley **New Zealand** 51–3	1991	Gloucester WC **New Zealand** 46–6

NEW ZEALAND v ROMANIA

Played 2 New Zealand won 2
Highest score New Zealand 85–8 in 2007, Romania 8–85 in 2007
Biggest win New Zealand 85–8 in 2007, Romania no win

1981	Bucharest **New Zealand** 14–6	2007	Toulouse WC **New Zealand** 85–8

NEW ZEALAND v ARGENTINA

Played 14 New Zealand won 13, Drawn 1
Highest scores New Zealand 93–8 in 1997, Argentina 21–21 in 1985
Biggest win New Zealand 93–8 in 1997, Argentina no win

1985	*1* Buenos Aires **New Zealand** 33–20		New Zealand won series 2–0
	2 Buenos Aires **Drawn** 21–21	1997	*1* Wellington **New Zealand** 93–8
	New Zealand won series 1–0, with 1 draw		*2* Hamilton **New Zealand** 62–10
1987	Wellington *WC* **New Zealand** 46–15		New Zealand won series 2–0
1989	*1* Dunedin **New Zealand** 60–9	2001	Christchurch **New Zealand** 67–19
	2 Wellington **New Zealand** 49–12	2001	Buenos Aires **New Zealand** 24–20
	New Zealand won series 2–0	2004	Hamilton **New Zealand** 41–7
1991	*1* Buenos Aires **New Zealand** 28–14	2006	Buenos Aires **New Zealand** 25–19
	2 Buenos Aires **New Zealand** 36–6	2011	Auckland WC **New Zealand** 33–10

NEW ZEALAND v ITALY

Played 11 New Zealand won 11
Highest scores New Zealand 101–3 in 1999, Italy 21–31 in 1991
Biggest win New Zealand 101–3 in 1999, Italy no win

1987	Auckland WC **New Zealand** 70–6	2003	Melbourne WC **New Zealand** 70–7
1991	Leicester WC **New Zealand** 31–21	2004	Rome **New Zealand** 59–10
1995	Bologna **New Zealand** 70–6	2007	Marseilles WC **New Zealand** 76–14
1999	Huddersfield WC **New Zealand** 101–3	2009	Christchurch **New Zealand** 27–6
2000	Genoa **New Zealand** 56–19	2009	Milan **New Zealand** 20–6
2002	Hamilton **New Zealand** 64–10		

NEW ZEALAND v FIJI

Played 5 New Zealand won 5
Highest scores New Zealand 91–0 in 2005, Fiji 18–68 in 2002
Biggest win New Zealand 91–0 in 2005, Fiji no win

1987	Christchurch WC **New Zealand** 74–13	2005	Albany **New Zealand** 91–0
1997	Albany **New Zealand** 71–5	2011	Dunedin **New Zealand** 60–14
2002	Wellington **New Zealand** 68–18		

NEW ZEALAND v CANADA

Played 5 New Zealand won 5
Highest scores New Zealand 79–15 in 2011, Canada 15–79 in 2011
Biggest win New Zealand 73–7 in 1995, Canada no win

1991	Lille WC **New Zealand** 29–13	2007	Hamilton **New Zealand** 64–13
1995	Auckland **New Zealand** 73–7	2011	Wellington WC **New Zealand** 79–15
2003	Melbourne WC **New Zealand** 68–6		

NEW ZEALAND v WORLD XVs

Played 3 New Zealand won 2, World XV won 1, Drawn 0
Highest scores New Zealand 54–26 in 1992, World XV 28–14 in 1992
Biggest wins New Zealand 54–26 in 1992, World XV 28–14 in 1992

1992	*1* Christchurch **World XV** 28–14	*3* Auckland **New Zealand** 26–15
	2 Wellington **New Zealand** 54–26	New Zealand won series 2–1

NEW ZEALAND v SAMOA

Played 5 New Zealand won 5
Highest scores New Zealand 101–14 in 2008, Samoa 14–101 in 2008
Biggest win New Zealand 101–14 in 2008, Samoa no win

1993	Auckland **New Zealand** 35–13	2001	Albany **New Zealand** 50–6
1996	Napier **New Zealand** 51–10	2008	New Plymouth **New Zealand** 101–14
1999	Albany **New Zealand** 71–13		

NEW ZEALAND v JAPAN

Played 2 New Zealand won 2
Highest scores New Zealand 145–17 in 1995, Japan 17–145 in 1995
Biggest win New Zealand 145–17 in 1995, Japan no win

1995	Bloemfontein WC **New Zealand** 145–17	2011	Hamilton WC **New Zealand** 83–7

NEW ZEALAND v TONGA

Played 4 New Zealand won 4
Highest scores New Zealand 102–0 in 2000, Tonga 10–41 in 2011
Biggest win New Zealand 102–0 in 2000, Tonga no win

1999	Bristol WC **New Zealand** 45–9	2003	Brisbane WC **New Zealand** 91–7
2000	Albany **New Zealand** 102–0	2011	Auckland WC **New Zealand** 41–10

NEW ZEALAND v PACIFIC ISLANDS

Played 1 New Zealand won 1
Highest scores New Zealand 41–26 in 2004, Pacific Islands 26–41 in 2004
Biggest win New Zealand 41–26 in 2004, Pacific Islands no win

2004	Albany **New Zealand** 41–26

NEW ZEALAND v PORTUGAL

Played 1 New Zealand won 1
Highest scores New Zealand 108–13 in 2007, Portugal 13–108 in 2007
Biggest win New Zealand 108–13 in 2007, Portugal no win

2007	Lyons WC **New Zealand** 108–13

AUSTRALIA v UNITED STATES

Played 7 Australia won 7
Highest scores Australia 67–9 in 1990 and 67–5 in 2011, United States 19–55 in 1999
Biggest win Australia 67–5 in 2011, United States no win

1912	Berkeley **Australia** 12–8	1990	Brisbane **Australia** 67–9
1976	Los Angeles **Australia** 24–12	1999	Limerick WC **Australia** 55–19
1983	Sydney **Australia** 49–3	2011	Wellington WC **Australia** 67–5
1987	Brisbane WC **Australia** 47–12		

AUSTRALIA v NEW ZEALAND XVs

Played 24 Australia won 6, New Zealand XVs won 18, Drawn 0
Highest scores Australia 26–20 in 1926, New Zealand XV 38–11 in 1923 and 38–8 in 1924
Biggest win Australia 17–0 in 1921, New Zealand XV 38–8 in 1924

1920	*1* Sydney **New Zealand XV** 26–15	1922	*1* Sydney **New Zealand XV** 26–19
	2 Sydney **New Zealand XV** 14–6		*2* Sydney **Australia** 14–8
	3 Sydney **New Zealand XV** 24–13		*3* Sydney **Australia** 8–6
	New Zealand XV won series 3–0		Australia won series 2–1
1921	Christchurch **Australia** 17–0	1923	*1* Dunedin **New Zealand XV** 19–9

	2 Christchurch **New Zealand XV** 34–6
	3 Wellington **New Zealand XV** 38–11
	New Zealand XV won series 3–0
1924	*1* Sydney **Australia** 20–16
	2 Sydney **New Zealand XV** 21–5
	3 Sydney **New Zealand XV** 38–8
	New Zealand XV won series 2–1
1925	*1* Sydney **New Zealand XV** 26–3
	2 Sydney **New Zealand XV** 4–0
	3 Sydney **New Zealand XV** 11–3
	New Zealand XV won series 3–0
1925	Auckland **New Zealand XV** 36–10
1926	*1* Sydney **Australia** 26–20
	2 Sydney **New Zealand XV** 11–6
	3 Sydney **New Zealand XV** 14–0
	4 Sydney **New Zealand XV** 28–21
	New Zealand XV won series 3–1
1928	*1* Wellington **New Zealand XV** 15–12
	2 Dunedin **New Zealand XV** 16–14
	3 Christchurch **Australia** 11–8
	New Zealand XV won series 2–1

AUSTRALIA v SOUTH AFRICA XVs

Played 3 South Africa XVs won 3
Highest scores Australia 11–16 in 1921, South Africa XV 28–9 in 1921
Biggest win Australia no win, South Africa XV 28–9 in 1921

1921	*1* Sydney **South Africa XV** 25–10
	2 Sydney **South Africa XV** 16–11
	3 Sydney **South Africa XV** 28–9
	South Africa XV won series 3–0

AUSTRALIA v NEW ZEALAND MAORIS

Played 16 Australia won 8, New Zealand Maoris won 6, Drawn 2
Highest scores Australia 31–6 in 1936, New Zealand Maoris 25–22 in 1922
Biggest wins Australia 31–6 in 1936, New Zealand Maoris 20–0 in 1946

1922	*1* Sydney **New Zealand Maoris** 25–22
	2 Sydney **Australia** 28–13
	3 Sydney **New Zealand Maoris** 23–22
	New Zealand Maoris won series 2–1
1923	*1* Sydney **Australia** 27–23
	2 Sydney **Australia** 21–16
	3 Sydney **Australia** 14–12
	Australia won series 3–0
1928	Wellington **New Zealand Maoris** 9–8
1931	Palmerston North **Australia** 14–3
1936	Palmerston North **Australia** 31–6
1946	Hamilton **New Zealand Maoris** 20–0
1949	*1* Sydney **New Zealand Maoris** 12–3
	2 Brisbane **Drawn** 8–8
	3 Sydney **Australia** 18–3
	Series drawn 1–1, with 1 draw
1958	*1* Brisbane **Australia** 15–14
	2 Sydney **Drawn** 3–3
	3 Melbourne **New Zealand Maoris** 13–6
	Series drawn 1–1, with 1 draw

AUSTRALIA v FIJI

Played 19 Australia won 16, Fiji won 2, Drawn 1
Highest scores Australia 66–20 in 1998, Fiji 28–52 in 1985
Biggest wins Australia 49–0 in 2007, Fiji 17–15 in 1952 & 18–16 in 1954

1952	*1* Sydney **Australia** 15–9
	2 Sydney **Fiji** 17–15
	Series drawn 1–1
1954	*1* Brisbane **Australia** 22–19
	2 Sydney **Fiji** 18–16
	Series drawn 1–1

1961	*1* Brisbane **Australia** 24–6	1980	Suva **Australia** 22–9
	2 Sydney **Australia** 20–14	1984	Suva **Australia** 16–3
	3 Melbourne **Drawn** 3–3	1985	*1* Brisbane **Australia** 52–28
	Australia won series 2–0, with 1 draw		*2* Sydney **Australia** 31–9
1972	Suva **Australia** 21–19		Australia won series 2–0
1976	*1* Sydney **Australia** 22–6	1998	Sydney **Australia** 66–20
	2 Brisbane **Australia** 21–9	2007	Perth **Australia** 49–0
	3 Sydney **Australia** 27–17	2007	Montpellier WC **Australia** 55–12
	Australia won series 3–0	2010	Canberra **Australia** 49–3

AUSTRALIA v TONGA

Played 4 Australia won 3, Tonga won 1, Drawn 0
Highest scores Australia 74–0 in 1998, Tonga 16–11 in 1973
Biggest wins Australia 74–0 in 1998, Tonga 16–11 in 1973

1973	*1* Sydney **Australia** 30–12	1993	Brisbane **Australia** 52–14
	2 Brisbane **Tonga** 16–11	1998	Canberra **Australia** 74–0
	Series drawn 1–1		

AUSTRALIA v JAPAN

Played 4 Australia won 4
Highest scores Australia 91–3 in 2007, Japan 25–50 in 1973
Biggest win Australia 91–3 in 2007, Japan no win

1975	*1* Sydney **Australia** 37–7	1987	Sydney WC **Australia** 42–23
	2 Brisbane **Australia** 50–25	2007	Lyons WC **Australia** 91–3
	Australia won series 2–0		

AUSTRALIA v ARGENTINA

Played 17 Australia won 12, Argentina won 4, Drawn 1
Highest scores Australia 53–7 in 1995 & 53–6 in 2000, Argentina 27–19 in 1987
Biggest wins Australia 53–6 in 2000, Argentina 18–3 in 1983

1979	*1* Buenos Aires **Argentina** 24–13	1991	Llanelli WC **Australia** 32–19
	2 Buenos Aires **Australia** 17–12	1995	*1* Brisbane **Australia** 53–7
	Series drawn 1–1		*2* Sydney **Australia** 30–13
1983	*1* Brisbane **Argentina** 18–3		Australia won series 2–0
	2 Sydney **Australia** 29–13	1997	*1* Buenos Aires **Australia** 23–15
	Series drawn 1–1		*2* Buenos Aires **Argentina** 18–16
1986	*1* Brisbane **Australia** 39–19		Series drawn 1–1
	2 Sydney **Australia** 26–0	2000	*1* Brisbane **Australia** 53–6
	Australia won series 2–0		*2* Canberra **Australia** 32–25
1987	*1* Buenos Aires **Drawn** 19–19		Australia won series 2–0
	2 Buenos Aires **Argentina** 27–19	2002	Buenos Aires **Australia** 17–6
	Argentina won series 1–0, with 1 draw	2003	Sydney WC **Australia** 24–8

AUSTRALIA v SAMOA

Played 5 Australia won 4, Samoa won 1
Highest scores Australia 74–7 in 2005, Samoa 32–23 in 2011
Biggest win Australia 73–3 in 1994, Samoa 32–23 in 2011

1991	Pontypool WC **Australia** 9–3	2005	Sydney **Australia** 74–7
1994	Sydney **Australia** 73–3	2011	Sydney **Samoa** 32–23
1998	Brisbane **Australia** 25–13		

AUSTRALIA v ITALY

Played 14 Australia won 14
Highest scores Australia 69–21 in 2005, Italy 21–69 in 2005
Biggest win Australia 55–6 in 1988, Italy no win

1983	Rovigo **Australia** 29–7	2005	Melbourne **Australia** 69–21
1986	Brisbane **Australia** 39–18	2006	Rome **Australia** 25–18
1988	Rome **Australia** 55–6	2008	Padua **Australia** 30–20
1994	*1* Brisbane **Australia** 23–20	2009	*1* Canberra **Australia** 31–8
	2 Melbourne **Australia** 20–7		*2* Melbourne **Australia** 34–12
	Australia won series 2–0		Australia won series 2–0
1996	Padua **Australia** 40–18	2010	Florence **Australia** 32–14
2002	Genoa **Australia** 34–3	2011	Albany WC **Australia** 32–6

AUSTRALIA v CANADA

Played 6 Australia won 6
Highest scores Australia 74–9 in 1996, Canada 16–43 in 1993
Biggest win Australia 74–9 in 1996, Canada no win

1985	*1* Sydney **Australia** 59–3	1995	Port Elizabeth WC **Australia** 27–11
	2 Brisbane **Australia** 43–15	1996	Brisbane **Australia** 74–9
	Australia won series 2–0	2007	Bordeaux WC **Australia** 37–6
1993	Calgary **Australia** 43–16		

AUSTRALIA v KOREA

Played 1 Australia won 1
Highest scores Australia 65–18 in 1987, Korea 18–65 in 1987
Biggest win Australia 65–18 in 1987, Korea no win

1987	Brisbane **Australia** 65–18

AUSTRALIA v ROMANIA

Played 3 Australia won 3
Highest scores Australia 90–8 in 2003, Romania 9–57 in 1999
Biggest win Australia 90–8 in 2003, Romania no win

1995 Stellenbosch WC **Australia** 42–3	2003 Brisbane WC **Australia** 90–8
1999 Belfast WC **Australia** 57–9	

AUSTRALIA v SPAIN

Played 1 Australia won 1
Highest scores Australia 92–10 in 2001, Spain 10–92 in 2001
Biggest win Australia 92–10 in 2001, Spain no win

2001 Madrid **Australia** 92–10

AUSTRALIA v NAMIBIA

Played 1 Australia won 1
Highest scores Australia 142–0 in 2003, Namibia 0–142 in 2003
Biggest win Australia 142–0 in 2003, Namibia no win

2003 Adelaide WC **Australia** 142–0

AUSTRALIA v PACIFIC ISLANDS

Played 1 Australia won 1
Highest scores Australia 29–14 in 2004, Pacific Islands 14–29 in 2004
Biggest win Australia 29–14 in 2004, Pacific Islands no win

2004 Adelaide **Australia** 29–14

AUSTRALIA v RUSSIA

Played 1 Australia won 1
Highest scores Australia 68–22 in 2011, Russia 22–68 in 2011
Biggest win Australia 68–22 in 2011, Russia no win

2011 Nelson WC **Australia** 68–22

WORLD TEST RUGBY RECORDS

The match and career records cover **official Test matches** *played up to 31 October 2011.*

MATCH RECORDS

MOST CONSECUTIVE TEST WINS

18 by Lithuania	2006 *Hun, Nor, Bul* 2007 *Aus, Hun, Bul* 2008 *Lat, Aus, Hun, Nor, And, Swi* 2009 *Ser, Arm, Isr, Hol, And* 2010 *Ser*
17 by N Zealand	1965 *SA* 4, 1966 *BI* 1, 2, 3, 4, 1967 *A, E, W, F, S,* 1968 *A* 1, 2, *F* 1, 2, 3, 1969 *W* 1, 2
17 by S Africa	1997 *A* 2, *It, F* 1, 2, *E, S,* 1998 *I* 1, 2, *W* 1, *E* 1, *A* 1, *NZ* 1, 2, *A* 2, *W* 2, *S, I* 3

MOST CONSECUTIVE TESTS WITHOUT DEFEAT

Matches	Wins	Draws	Period
23 by N Zealand	22	1	1987 to 1990
18 by Lithuania	18	0	2006 to 2010
17 by N Zealand	15	2	1961 to 1964
17 by N Zealand	17	0	1965 to 1969
17 by S Africa	17	0	1997 to 1998

MOST POINTS IN A MATCH

BY A TEAM

Pts	Opponents	Venue	Year
164 by Hong Kong	Singapore	Kuala Lumpur	1994
155 by Japan	Chinese Taipei	Tokyo	2002
152 by Argentina	Paraguay	Mendoza	2002
147 by Argentina	Venezuela	Santiago	2004
145 by N Zealand	Japan	Bloemfontein	1995
144 by Argentina	Paraguay	Montevideo	2003
142 by Australia	Namibia	Adelaide	2003
135 by Korea	Malaysia	Hong Kong	1992
134 by Japan	Chinese Taipei	Singapore	1998
134 by England	Romania	Twickenham	2001
134 by S Africa	Uruguay	East London	2005

BY A PLAYER

Pts	Player	Opponents	Venue	Year
60 for Japan	T Kurihara	Chinese Taipei	Tainan	2002
50 for Argentina	E Morgan	Paraguay	San Pablo	1973
50 for H Kong	A Billington	Singapore	Kuala Lumpur	1994
45 for N Zealand	S D Culhane	Japan	Bloemfontein	1995
45 for Argentina	J-M Nuñez-Piossek	Paraguay	Montevideo	2003
44 for Scotland	A G Hastings	Ivory Coast	Rustenburg	1995
44 for England	C C Hodgson	Romania	Twickenham	2001
42 for Australia	M S Rogers	Namibia	Adelaide	2003
41 for Sweden	J Hagstrom	Luxembourg	Cessange	2001
40 for Argentina	G M Jorge	Brazil	Sao Paulo	1993
40 for Japan	D Ohata	Chinese Taipei	Tokyo	2002
40 for Scotland	C D Paterson	Japan	Perth	2004

MOST TRIES IN A MATCH

BY THE TEAM

Tries	Opponents	Venue	Year
26 by Hong Kong	Singapore	Kuala Lumpur	1994
25 by Fiji	Solomon Is	Port Moresby	1969
24 by Argentina	Paraguay	Mendoza	2002
24 by Argentina	Paraguay	Montevideo	2003
23 by Japan	Chinese Taipei	Tokyo	2002
23 by Argentina	Venezuela	Santiago	2004
22 by Australia	Namibia	Adelaide	2003
21 by Fiji	Niue Island	Apia	1983
21 by N Zealand	Japan	Bloemfontein	1995
21 by S Africa	Uruguay	East London	2005

BY A PLAYER

Tries	Player	Opponents	Venue	Year
11 for Argentina	U O'Farrell	Brazil	Buenos Aires	1951
10 for H Kong	A Billington	Singapore	Kuala Lumpur	1994
9 for Argentina	J-M Nuñez-Piossek	Paraguay	Montevideo	2003
8 for Argentina	G M Jorge	Brazil	Sao Paulo	1993
8 for Japan	D Ohata	Chinese Taipei	Tokyo	2002
6 for Argentina	E Morgan	Paraguay	San Pablo	1973
6 for Fiji	T Makutu	Papua New Guinea	Suva	1979
6 for Argentina	G M Jorge	Brazil	Montevideo	1989
6 for Namibia	G Mans	Portugal	Windhoek	1990
6 for N Zealand	M C G Ellis	Japan	Bloemfontein	1995
6 for Japan	T Kurihara	Chinese Taipei	Tainan	2002
6 for S Africa	T Chavhanga	Uruguay	East London	2005
6 for Japan	D Ohata	Hong Kong	Tokyo	2005

MOST CONVERSIONS IN A MATCH

BY THE TEAM

Cons	Opponents	Venue	Year
20 by N Zealand	Japan	Bloemfontein	1995
20 by Japan	Chinese Taipei	Tokyo	2002
19 by Fiji	Solomon Islands	Port Moresby	1969
18 by Fiji	Niue Island	Apia	1983
17 by Hong Kong	Singapore	Kuala Lumpur	1994
17 by Japan	Chinese Taipei	Singapore	1998
17 by Tonga	Korea	Nuku'alofa	2003
16 by Argentina	Paraguay	Mendoza	2002
16 by Australia	Namibia	Adelaide	2003
16 by Argentina	Venezuela	Santiago	2004

BY A PLAYER

Cons	Player	Opponents	Venue	Year
20 for New Zealand	S D Culhane	Japan	Bloemfontein	1995
18 for Fiji	S Koroduadua	Niue Island	Apia	1983
17 for Hong Kong	J McKee	Singapore	Kuala Lumpur	1994
17 for Tonga	P Hola	Korea	Nuku'alofa	2003
16 for Argentina	J-L Cilley	Paraguay	Mendoza	2002
16 for Australia	M S Rogers	Namibia	Adelaide	2003
15 for England	P J Grayson	Netherlands	Huddersfield	1998
15 for Japan	T Kurihara	Chinese Taipei	Tainan	2002
14 for England	C C Hodgson	Romania	Twickenham	2001
14 for Wales	G L Henson	Japan	Cardiff	2004
14 for New Zealand	N J Evans	Portugal	Lyon	2007

MOST PENALTIES IN A MATCH

BY THE TEAM

Penalties	Opponents	Venue	Year
9 by Japan	Tonga	Tokyo	1999
9 by N Zealand	Australia	Auckland	1999
9 by Wales	France	Cardiff	1999
9 by Portugal	Georgia	Lisbon	2000
9 by N Zealand	France	Paris	2000
8 by many countries			

BY A PLAYER

Penalties	Player	Opponents	Venue	Year
9 for Japan	K Hirose	Tonga	Tokyo	1999
9 for N Zealand	A P Mehrtens	Australia	Auckland	1999
9 for Wales	N R Jenkins	France	Cardiff	1999
9 for Portugal	T Teixeira	Georgia	Lisbon	2000
9 for N Zealand	A P Mehrtens	France	Paris	2000
8 by many players				

MOST DROPPED GOALS IN A MATCH

BY THE TEAM

Drops	Opponents	Venue	Year
5 by South Africa	England	Paris	1999
4 by Romania	W Germany	Bucharest	1967
4 by Uruguay	Chile	Montevideo	2002
4 by South Africa	England	Twickenham	2006
3 by several nations			

BY A PLAYER

Drops	Player	Opponents	Venue	Year
5 for S Africa	J H de Beer	England	Paris	1999
4 for Uruguay	J Menchaca	Chile	Montevideo	2002
4 for S Africa	A S Pretorius	England	Twickenham	2006
3 for several nations				

CAREER RECORDS

MOST TEST APPEARANCES

Tests	Player	Career Span
139	G M Gregan (Australia)	1994 to 2007
123 (6)	B G O'Driscoll (Ireland/Lions)	1999 to 2011
119 (5)	J Leonard (England/Lions)	1990 to 2004
118	F Pelous (France)	1995 to 2007
118 (2)	R J R O'Gara (Ireland/Lions)	2000 to 2011
111	P Sella (France)	1982 to 1995
111	J W Smit (S Africa)	2000 to 2011
110	G B Smith (Australia)	2000 to 2009
110	V Matfield (S Africa)	2001 to 2011
110 (6)	S M Jones (Wales/Lions)	1998 to 2011
109	C D Paterson (Scotland)	1999 to 2011
107 (2)	J J Hayes (Ireland/Lions)	2000 to 2011
103 (3)	G Thomas (Wales/Lions)	1995 to 2007
103 (4)	M E Williams (Wales/Lions)	1996 to 2011
103	R H McCaw (N Zealand)	2001 to 2011
102	S J Larkham (Australia)	1996 to 2007
102	P C Montgomery (S Africa)	1997 to 2008
101	D I Campese (Australia)	1982 to 1996
101	A Troncon (Italy)	1994 to 2007
100	J M Muliaina (N Zealand)	2003 to 2011
100	N C Sharpe (Australia)	2002 to 2011
98	R Ibañez (France)	1996 to 2007
98	P A Stringer (Ireland)	2000 to 2011
97 (6)	J P Wilkinson (England/Lions)	1998 to 2011
96 (2)	C L Charvis (Wales/Lions)	1996 to 2007

The figures include Test appearances for the British/Irish Lions and South American Jaguars which are shown in brackets. Thus 119 (5) for Jason Leonard (England/Lions) indicates 114 caps for England and five Tests for the Lions.

MOST CONSECUTIVE TESTS

Tests	Player	Career Span
63	S B T Fitzpatrick (N Zealand)	1986 to 1995
62	J W C Roff (Australia)	1996 to 2001
53	G O Edwards (Wales)	1967 to 1978
52	W J McBride (Ireland)	1964 to 1975
51	C M Cullen (N Zealand)	1996 to 2000

MOST TESTS AS CAPTAIN

Tests	Captain	Career Span
83	J W Smit (S Africa)	2003 to 2011
81 (1)	B G O'Driscoll (Ireland/Lions)	2002 to 2011
66*	R H McCaw (N Zealand)	2004 to 2011
59	W D C Carling (England)	1988 to 1996
59	G M Gregan (Australia)	2001 to 2007
55	J A Eales (Australia)	1996 to 2001
51	S B T Fitzpatrick (N Zealand)	1992 to 1997
48	L Arbizu (Argentina)	1992 to 2003
46 (8)	H Porta (Argentina/Jaguars)	1971 to 1990
45 (6)	M O Johnson (England/Lions)	1997 to 2003
45	T Miuchi (Japan)	2002 to 2008

The figures include Test captaincies of the British/Irish Lions and South American Jaguars which are shown in brackets. Thus 81 (1) for Brian O'Driscoll (Ireland/Lions) indicates 80 captaincies for Ireland and one in Tests for the Lions.

** McCaw's figure includes the world record of 58 Test wins as captain. John Smit has 54 Test wins as captain of SA*

MOST POINTS IN TESTS

Points	Player	Tests	Career Span
1250	D W Carter (N Zealand)	85	2003 to 2011
1246 (67)	J P Wilkinson (England/Lions)	97 (6)	1998 to 2011
1090 (41)	N R Jenkins (Wales/Lions)	91 (4)	1991 to 2002
1075 (0)	R J R O'Gara (Ireland/Lions)	118 (2)	2000 to 2011
1010 (27)	D Dominguez (Italy/Argentina)	76 (2)	1989 to 2003
970 (53)	S M Jones (Wales/Lions)	110 (6)	1998 to 2011
967	A P Mehrtens (N Zealand)	70	1995 to 2004
911	M P Lynagh (Australia)	72	1984 to 1995
893	P C Montgomery (S Africa)	102	1997 to 2008
878	M C Burke (Australia)	81	1993 to 2004
809	C D Paterson (Scotland)	109	1999 to 2011
733 (66)	A G Hastings (Scotland/Lions)	67 (6)	1986 to 1995
684	M J Giteau (Australia)	92	2002 to 2011
670	N J Little (Fiji)	71	1996 to 2011

The figures include Test appearances for the British/Irish Lions or a second nation which are shown in brackets. Thus 1246 (67) for Jonny Wilkinson (England/Lions) indicates 1179 points for England and 67 in Tests for the Lions.

MOST TRIES IN TESTS

Tries	Player	Tests	Career Span
69	D Ohata (Japan)	58	1996 to 2006
64	D I Campese (Australia)	101	1982 to 1996
59 (2)	S M Williams (Wales/Lions)	90 (4)	2000 to 2011
50 (1)	R Underwood (England/Lions)	91 (6)	1984 to 1996
49	D C Howlett (N Zealand)	62	2000 to 2007
46	C M Cullen (N Zealand)	58	1996 to 2002
46	J T Rokocoko (N Zealand)	68	2003 to 2010
46 (1)	B G O'Driscoll (Ireland/Lions)	123 (6)	1999 to 2011
44	J W Wilson (N Zealand)	60	1993 to 2001
43	H Onozawa (Japan)	68	2001 to 2011
41 (1)	G Thomas (Wales/Lions)	103 (3)	1995 to 2007
40	C E Latham (Australia)	78	1998 to 2007
40	B G Habana (South Africa)	74	2004 to 2011

The figures include Test appearances for the British/Irish Lions which are shown in brackets. Thus 59 (2) for Shane Williams (Wales/Lions) indicates 57 tries for Wales and two in Tests for the Lions.

MOST CONVERSIONS IN TESTS

Cons	Player	Tests	Career Span
224	D W Carter (N Zealand)	85	2003 to 2011
175 (0)	R J R O'Gara (Ireland/Lions)	118 (2)	2000 to 2011
169	A P Mehrtens (N Zealand)	70	1995 to 2004
169 (7)	J P Wilkinson (England/Lions)	97 (6)	1998 to 2011
160 (7)	S M Jones (Wales/Lions)	110 (6)	1998 to 2011
153	P C Montgomery (S Africa)	102	1997 to 2008
140	M P Lynagh (Australia)	72	1984 to 1995
133 (6)	D Dominguez (Italy/Argentina)	76 (2)	1989 to 2003
131 (1)	N R Jenkins (Wales/Lions)	91 (4)	1991 to 2002
118	G J Fox (N Zealand)	46	1985 to 1993

The figures include Test appearances for the British/Irish Lions or a second nation which are shown in brackets. Thus 169 (7) for Jonny Wilkinson (England/Lions) indicates 162 conversions for England and seven in Tests for the Lions.

MOST PENALTY GOALS IN TESTS

Penalties	Player	Tests	Career Span
255 (16)	J P Wilkinson (England/Lions)	97 (6)	1998 to 2011
248 (13)	N R Jenkins (Wales/Lions)	91 (4)	1991 to 2002
215	D W Carter (N Zealand)	85	2003 to 2011
214 (5)	D Dominguez (Italy/Argentina)	76 (2)	1989 to 2003
200 (0)	R J R O'Gara (Ireland/Lions)	118 (2)	2000 to 2011
198 (12)	S M Jones (Wales/Lions)	110 (6)	1998 to 2011
188	A P Mehrtens (N Zealand)	70	1995 to 2004
177	M P Lynagh (Australia)	72	1984 to 1995
174	M C Burke (Australia)	81	1993 to 2004
170	C D Paterson (Scotland)	109	1999 to 2011
160 (20)	A G Hastings (Scotland/Lions)	67 (6)	1986 to 1995

The figures include Test appearances for the British/Irish Lions or a second nation which are shown in brackets. Thus 255 (16) for Jonny Wilkinson (England/Lions) indicates 239 penalties for England and 16 in Tests for the Lions.

MOST DROPPED GOALS IN TESTS

Drops	Player	Tests	Career Span
36 (0)	J P Wilkinson (England/Lions)	97 (6)	1998 to 2011
28 (2)	H Porta (Argentina/Jaguars)	68 (8)	1971 to 1999
23 (2)	C R Andrew (England/Lions)	76 (5)	1985 to 1997
19 (0)	D Dominguez (Italy/Argentina)	76 (2)	1989 to 2003
18	H E Botha (S Africa)	28	1980 to 1992
17	S Bettarello (Italy)	55	1979 to 1988
17	D A Parks (Scotland)	66	2004 to 2011
15	J-P Lescarboura (France)	28	1982 to 1990
15 (0)	R J R O'Gara (Ireland/Lions)	118 (2)	2000 to 2011

The figures include Test appearances for the British/Irish Lions, South American Jaguars or a second nation shown in brackets. Thus 28 (2) for Hugo Porta (Argentina/Jaguars) indicates 26 dropped goals for Argentina and two in Tests (against South Africa in the 1980s) for the South American Jaguars.

Dave Rogers/Getty Images

Jonny Wilkinson has dropped more goals in Test matches than any player in the history of the game.

The Countries

James Hook, Wales

IRB Anti-Doping Ambassador

In partnership

Tackle Doping

Join us in the fight against doping –
Keep Rugby Clean!

KEEP RUGBY CLEA

IRB ANTI-DOPING

ARGENTINA

ARGENTINA'S 2010–11 TEST RECORD

OPPONENTS	DATE	VENUE	RESULT
Italy	13 Nov	A	**Won** 22–16
France	20 Nov	A	**Lost** 9–15
Ireland	28 Nov	A	**Lost** 9–29
Chile	22 May	H	**Won** 61–6
Uruguay	25 May	H	**Won** 75–14
Wales	20 August	A	**Lost** 13–28
England	10 Sep	N	**Lost** 9–13
Romania	17 Sep	N	**Won** 43–8
Scotland	25 Sep	N	**Won** 13–12
Georgia	2 Oct	N	**Won** 25–7
New Zealand	9 Oct	A	**Lost** 10–33

PUMAS HEAD FOR A NEW ERA

By Frankie Deges

Alex Livesey/Getty Images

A thrilling win over Scotland put Argentina into the quarter-finals.

The end of an era for Argentine rugby was signalled with their quarter-final loss to the All Blacks at Eden Park. The 33–10 loss, with dignity and a promising display when looking into the future, finished a four-year post-Rugby World Cup 2007 cycle and opened the new four-year calendar that brings hope and, most of all, regular competition for Los Pumas.

Argentine rugby made huge strides in the last decade and, even if it seemed to take a step backwards after reaching the heady heights of the bronze medal at RWC 2007, it proved that the production line of players is intact. It is increasing the time that the players and coaches spend together and more matches that will make the difference.

With the substantial and welcomed assistance and support of the International Rugby Board – both in terms of finance and with the re-writing of Regulation 9 to encapsulate the new tournament Argentina will take part in from 2012 to 2015 – the future is promising for a nation that in 2011 broke through the 100,000-player barrier. That the 2011 Rugby World Cup came at the end of the southern hemisphere season means that the fruits of a captivating Puma display will be seen, as happened in early 2008, when the post-RWC season opens.

There were many that doubted the Pumas' ability to survive in the cauldron of Pool B at RWC 2011, and that they did reach the quarter-finals was down to a huge combination of heart, defence, attitude, good luck and the inability of the Scots to close down a game that seemed to go against Argentina.

Lucas González Amorosino, the 26-year-old full-back or wing, became the instant hero of Argentine rugby with a try that was scored "in 30 seconds of madness" as losing coach Andy Robinson put it after Los Pumas beat Scotland 13–12 in horrendous weather at the Wellington Regional Stadium.

Having once needed to decide whether to focus on soccer – he had been offered a professional contract – or the kind of friendship rugby has and football can't offer, González Amorosino stayed with the oval ball. A very lazy player in his own words until he realised he could be good – really good – González Amorosino is now the consummate professional.

Scotland had kicked a 71st-minute drop-goal through Dan Parks to stretch the lead to 12–6. However, straight from the kick-off, Julio Farías – at 33, a player who came from almost retiring to win his first cap and star at a Rugby World Cup in the space of a year – won the ball and after three quick rucks, and against the nature of rugby Argentina had been playing that night, the ball was spun quickly to the wing, where González Amorosino was anxiously waiting.

"When I got the ball I could see the line and knew where I wanted to go," he said after the try that saw him beat five would-be tacklers on his run to the try-line. "I knew that Chris Paterson wasn't a great tackler, so I stepped inside. The next two I just let my instincts go."

The first defender gone, it was González Amorosino's tight shirt which prevented Ally Strokosch from stopping him. This alone created doubts for the next two defenders, who were also beaten with a deft sidestep, and the wing was over the try-line.

With Argentina still trailing 12–11 with six minutes to go, it was left to captain Felipe Contepomi, who had only made it to the field thanks to his stubborn desire as he was carrying a rib cartilage injury, to kick the conversion and seal the win. "Sometimes in life, one has to take chances. I did," the Buenos Aires-born doctor said after making himself available despite a tournament-ending injury.

Strong defence and a renewed hunger were the difference between flying home and staying in contention. It was a lot better to stay in New Zealand. Having come painstakingly close to beating England in the first tournament match played at the new Otago Stadium, Los Pumas did what was expected of them against Romania. Argentina played the two games in very different styles of play, as six tries were scored in the deep south of Invercargill. Scotland came next, and then the ticket to the quarters was booked against a proud Georgian side.

Agustín Gosio, one of the try-scorers against the Lelos, was a key member of the squad. He only played 15 minutes at Rugby World Cup 2011, but his contribution was off-the-field. "He was always smiling, helping, even in the knowledge that he might never get to play," revealed Patricio Albacete. Now with London Scottish, the winger had come to the squad via the Pampas XV and their tournament-winning performance in South Africa's Vodacom Cup.

He was one of 10 past or present Pampas players in the squad. That team, first selected in 2010, is seen as the solution for those players that have not yet moved to Europe, an attempt to retain them in Argentine rugby. The best will continue to move to top clubs – but maybe if and when Super Rugby franchises start looking to Argentina for new players then the flow will be sideways and not upwards in terms of the world map.

That a third of the squad was part-time professional in either the same year or the year before the World Cup speaks volumes of the individual capacity of Argentine players. Of those, only three remain in Argentina, including flanker Farías who was first capped in November 2010 aged 32 having been lost in the wilderness of the French Second Division. After an incredible World Cup, hopes are that he has found a second wind and will be around for another couple of years.

Argentina will play in the new Four Nations for a minimum of four guaranteed seasons. This requires a number of players ready to tackle week in, week out, for six matches against the Springboks, Wallabies and All Blacks.

"Not an easy task. I would have loved to stay around, as everybody says that coaching is nothing like playing," smiled Mario Ledesma, who retired from active rugby at 38 to become forwards coach at Stade Français. One of three Pumas to have played their fourth RWC in New Zealand – with captain Contepomi and fellow retiree Martín Scelzo – he epitomised the Puma strength. "We just don't give up. Playing for the shirt and country is all we love. We might be down, we might have our issues, but when it comes to front-up we will always do that."

His last game was against the All Blacks in the quarter-final. He might have known there was no tomorrow and threw his body on the line like in that first cap against Uruguay in 1996, and the 81 in between. Being in his close friend Santiago Phelan's squad was no tokenism, Ledesma was one of the best hookers in RWC 2011. He was the best in RWC 1999 and amongst the best in RWC 2007. He retired a true hero.

He was also a crucial lieutenant in a team that had coach Phelan proving his worth. He had not had an easy run to the World Cup. Nineteen tests in four seasons, with only six wins, is not acceptable in international rugby. He stuck it out, continued to plan for RWC and he deserved the spurs. He was first to admit that sometimes his team did not play great rugby. "It is about winning," he said, almost shyly. Even against the All Blacks, the team stood its ground and went for the win – with the weapons they have: a strong defence, a strong defence and a strong defence. Lack of preparation time forced them into this pattern. Had their kicking boots travelled to New Zealand, Argentina could have made it to the semi-finals through the other side of the draw.

Phelan has been offered a two-year extension to his contract, but in the aftermath of Rugby World Cup 2011 it was unclear whether he would accept it. The new tournament will require a lot from players – either based at home or overseas.

With new opportunities opening in South Africa, the one country that has stood by Argentine rugby through thick and thin, more players will be exposed to a higher standard of rugby.

How to retain them so that they don't go to Europe is one of the keys. Maybe, the new Four Nations will generate sufficient funding for the Unión Argentina de Rugby to rethink the way players are contracted.

With the 2016 Olympic cycle coming into operation in July, the money that Sevens will generate might free other funding for bigger projects. Argentina needs to ensure that Los Pumitas (Under-20s) are more competitive in the IRB Junior World Championship so that the step up to the Test arena is less stressful.

Overall, the season that has just finished was a good one. It came within "30 seconds of madness" – 30 seconds Argentine rugby will never forget – from being a not so good season. But that is sport; the bounce of the ball can go many different ways. This time it went Argentina's way, and hopefully it will continue to bounce the same way.

ARGENTINA INTERNATIONAL STATISTICS

MATCH RECORDS UP TO 31 OCTOBER 2011

WINNING MARGIN

Date	Opponent	Result	Winning Margin
01/05/2002	Paraguay	152–0	**152**
27/04/2003	Paraguay	144–0	**144**
01/05/2004	Venezuela	147–7	**140**
02/10/1993	Brazil	114–3	**111**
09/10/1979	Brazil	109–3	**106**

MOST POINTS IN A MATCH

BY THE TEAM

Date	Opponent	Result	Points
01/05/2002	Paraguay	152–0	**152**
01/05/2004	Venezuela	147–7	**147**
27/04/2003	Paraguay	144–0	**144**
02/10/1993	Brazil	114–3	**114**
09/10/1979	Brazil	109–3	**109**

BY A PLAYER

Date	Player	Opponent	Pts
14/10/1973	Eduardo Morgan	Paraguay	**50**
27/04/2003	José María Nuñez Piossek	Paraguay	**45**
02/10/1993	Gustavo Jorge	Brazil	**40**
24/10/1977	Martin Sansot	Brazil	**36**
13/09/1951	Uriel O'Farrell	Brazil	**33**

MOST TRIES IN A MATCH

BY THE TEAM

Date	Opponent	Result	Tries
01/05/2002	Paraguay	152–0	**24**
27/04/2003	Paraguay	144–0	**24**
01/05/2004	Venezuela	147–7	**23**
08/10/1989	Brazil	103–0	**20**

BY A PLAYER

Date	Player	Opponent	Tries
13/09/1951	Uriel O'Farrell	Brazil	**11**
27/04/2003	José María Nuñez Piossek	Paraguay	**9**
02/10/1993	Gustavo Jorge	Brazil	**8**
08/10/1989	Gustavo Jorge	Brazil	**6**
14/10/1973	Eduardo Morgan	Paraguay	**6**

MOST CONVERSIONS IN A MATCH

BY THE TEAM

Date	Opponent	Result	Cons
01/05/2002	Paraguay	152–0	**16**
01/05/2004	Venezuela	147–7	**16**
09/10/1979	Brazil	109–3	**15**
21/09/1985	Paraguay	102–3	**13**
14/10/1973	Paraguay	98–3	**13**

BY A PLAYER

Date	Player	Opponent	Cons
01/05/2002	Jose Cilloy	Paraguay	**16**
21/09/1985	Hugo Porta	Paraguay	**13**
14/10/1973	Eduardo Morgan	Paraguay	**13**
25/09/1975	Eduardo de Forteza	Paraguay	**11**

MOST PENALTIES IN A MATCH

BY THE TEAM

Date	Opponent	Result	Pens
10/10/1999	Samoa	32–16	**8**
10/03/1995	Canada	29–26	**8**
17/06/2006	Wales	45–27	**8**

BY A PLAYER

Date	Player	Opponent	Pens
10/10/1999	Gonzalo Quesada	Samoa	**8**
10/03/1995	Santiago Meson	Canada	**8**
17/06/2006	Federico Todeschini	Wales	**8**

MOST DROPPED GOALS IN A MATCH

BY THE TEAM

Date	Opponent	Result	DGs
27/10/1979	Australia	24–13	**3**
02/11/1985	New Zealand	21–21	**3**
26/05/2001	Canada	20–6	**3**
21/09/1975	Uruguay	30–15	**3**
07/08/1971	SA Gazelles	12–0	**3**
30/09/2007	Ireland	30–15	**3**

BY A PLAYER

Date	Player	Opponent	DGs
27/10/1979	Hugo Porta	Australia	**3**
02/11/1985	Hugo Porta	New Zealand	**3**
07/08/1971	Tomas Harris-Smith	SA Gazelles	**3**
26/05/2001	Juan Fernández Miranda	Canada	**3**
30/09/2007	Juan Martín Hernández	Ireland	**3**

CAREER RECORDS

MOST CAPPED PLAYERS

Name	Caps
Lisandro Arbizu	**86**
Rolando Martin	**86**
Mario Ledesma	**84**
Pedro Sporleder	**78**
Felipe Contepomi	**75**

LEADING PENALTY SCORERS

Name	Penalties
Felipe Contepomi	**128**
Gonzalo Quesada	**103**
Hugo Porta	**101**
Santiago Meson	**63**
Federico Todeschini	**54**

LEADING TRY SCORERS

Name	Tries
José María Nuñez Piossek	**29**
Diego Cuesta Silva	**28**
Gustavo Jorge	**24**
Facundo Soler	**18**
Rolando Martin	**18**

LEADING DROPPED GOAL SCORERS

Name	DGs
Hugo Porta	**26**
Lisandro Arbizu	**11**
Gonzalo Quesada	**7**
Tomas Harris-Smith	**6**
Juan Martín Hernández	**6**

LEADING CONVERSIONS SCORERS

Name	Conversions
Hugo Porta	**84**
Gonzalo Quesada	**68**
Santiago Meson	**68**
Felipe Contepomi	**64**
Juan Fernández Miranda	**41**

LEADING POINTS SCORERS

Name	Points
Hugo Porta	**590**
Felipe Contepomi	**588**
Gonzalo Quesada	**486**
Santiago Meson	**370**
Federico Todeschini	**256**

ARGENTINA INTERNATIONAL PLAYERS
(UP TO 31 OCTOBER 2011)

Note: Years given for International Championship matches are for second half of season; eg 1972 means season 1971–72. Years for all other matches refer to the actual year of the match. Entries in square brackets denote matches played in RWC Finals.

A Abadie 2007 *CHL*, 2008 *Ur*, 2009 *E*, *W*, *S*
A Abella 1969 *Ur*, *CHL*
C Abud 1975 *Par*, *Bra*, *CHL*
H Achaval 1948 *OCC*
J Aguilar 1983 *CHL*, *Ur*
A Aguirre 1997 *Par*, *CHL*
ME Aguirre 1990 *E*, *S*, 1991 *Sa*
B Agulla 2009 *CHL*, *Ur*, 2010 *Ur*, *CHL*, 2011 *CHL*, *Ur*
H Agulla 2005 *Sa*, 2006 *Ur*, *E*, *It*, 2007 *It*, *F*, *Nm*, *I*, *S*, *SA*, *F*, 2008 *S*, *It*, *SA*, *F*, *It*, *I*, 2009 *E*, *E*, *E*, *W*, *S*, 2010 *Ur*, *CHL*, *S*, *S*, *F*, *I*, 2011 *W*, *E*, *R*, *S*, *Geo*, *NZ*
P Albacete 2003 *Par*, *Ur*, *F*, *SA*, *Ur*, *C*, *A*, *R*, 2004 *W*, *W*, *NZ*, *F*, *I*, 2005 *It*, *It*, 2006 *E*, *It*, *F*, 2007 *W*, *F*, *Geo*, *Nm*, *I*, *S*, *SA*, *F*, 2008 *SA*, *F*, *It*, *I*, 2009 *E*, *E*, *E*, *W*, *S*, 2010 *S*, *S*, *F*, *F*, *I*, 2011 *W*, *E*, *R*, *S*, *Geo*, *NZ*
DL Albanese 1995 *Ur*, *C*, *E*, *F*, 1996 *Ur*, *F*, *SA*, *E*, 1997 *NZ*, *Ur*, *R*, *It*, *F*, *A*, *A*, 1998 *F*, *F*, *R*, *US*, *C*, *It*, *F*, *W*, 1999 *W*, *W*, *S*, *I*, *W*, *Sa*, *J*, *I*, *F*, 2000 *I*, *A*, *A*, *SA*, 2001 *NZ*, *It*, *W*, *S*, *NZ*, 2002 *F*, *E*, *SA*, *A*, *It*, *I*, 2003 *F*, *F*, *SA*, *US*, *C*, *A*, *Nm*, *I*
F Albarracin 2007 *CHL*, 2008 *Ur*, *CHL*
M Albina 2001 *Ur*, *US*, 2003 *Par*, *Ur*, *Fj*, 2004 *CHL*, *Ven*, *W*, *W*, 2005 *J*
L Alcácer Mackinlay 2009 *CHL*, *Ur*
C Aldao 1961 *CHL*, *Bra*, *Ur*
P Alexenicer 1997 *Par*, *CHL*
H Alfonso 1936 *BI*, *CHL*
G Allen 1977 *Par*
JG Allen 1981 *C*, 1985 *F*, *F*, *Ur*, *NZ*, *NZ*, 1986 *F*, *F*, *A*, *A*, 1987 *Ur*, *Fj*, *It*, *NZ*, *Sp*, *A*, *A*, 1988 *F*, *F*, *F*, *F*, 1989 *Bra*, *CHL*, *Par*, *Ur*, *US*
L Allen 1951 *Ur*, *Bra*, *CHL*
M Allen 1990 *C*, *E*, *S*, 1991 *NZ*, *CHL*
F Allogio 2011 *CHL*, *Ur*
A Allub 1997 *Par*, *Ur*, *It*, *F*, *A*, *A*, 1998 *F*, *F*, *US*, *C*, *J*, *It*, *F*, *W*, 1999 *W*, *W*, *S*, *I*, *W*, *Sa*, *J*, *I*, *F*, 2000 *I*, *A*, *A*, *SA*, *E*, 2001 *NZ*
M Alonso 1973 *R*, *R*, *S*, 1977 *F*, *F*
A Altberg 1972 *SAG*, *SAG*, 1973 *R*, *R*, *Par*
J Altube 1998 *Par*, *CHL*, *Ur*
C Alvarez 1958 *Ur*, *Per*, *CHL*, 1959 *JSB*, *JSB*, 1960 *F*
GM Alvarez 1975 *Ur*, *Par*, *Bra*, *CHL*, 1976 *NZ*, 1977 *Bra*, *Ur*, *Par*, *CHL*
R Álvarez Kairelis 1998 *Par*, *CHL*, *Ur*, 2001 *Ur*, *US*, *C*, *W*, *S*, *NZ*, 2002 *F*, *E*, *SA*, *A*, *It*, *I*, 2003 *F*, *SA*, *Fj*, *Ur*, *C*, *Nm*, *I*, 2004 *F*, *I*, 2006 *W*, *W*, *NZ*, *CHL*, *Ur*, 2007 *I*, *It*, *W*, *F*, *Geo*, *Nm*, *I*, *S*, *SA*, *F*, 2008 *SA*, *F*, *It*, *I*, 2009 *E*
F Amelong 2007 *CHL*, 2008 *Ur*
A Amuchastegui 2002 *Ur*, *Par*, *CHL*
GP Angaut 1987 *NZ*, *Ur*, *CHL*, 1990 *S*, 1991 *NZ*, *Sa*
JJ Angelillo 1987 *Ur*, *CHL*, *A*, 1988 *F*, *F*, *F*, 1989 *It*, *Bra*, *CHL*, *Par*, *Ur*, *US*, 1990 *C*, *US*, *E*, *E*, 1994 *US*, *S*, *S*, *US*, 1995 *Par*, *CHL*, *R*, *F*
W Aniz 1960 *F*
R Annichini 1983 *CHL*, *Ur*, 1985 *F*, *CHL*, *Par*
A Anthony 1965 *OCC*, *CHL*, 1967 *Ur*, *CHL*, 1968 *W*, *W*, 1969 *S*, *S*, *Ur*, *CHL*, 1970 *I*, *I*, 1971 *SAG*, *SAG*, *OCC*, 1972 *SAG*, *SAG*, 1974 *F*, *F*
F Aranguren 2007 *CHL*, 2008 *Ur*, 2009 *CHL*, *Ur*, 2011 *CHL*, *Ur*
L Arbizu 1990 *I*, *S*, 1991 *NZ*, *NZ*, *CHL*, *A*, *W*, *Sa*, 1992 *F*, *F*, *Sp*, *Sp*, *R*, *F*, 1993 *J*, *J*, *Bra*, *CHL*, *Par*, *Ur*, *SA*, *SA*, 1995 *Ur*, *A*, *A*, *E*, *Sa*, *It*, *Par*, *CHL*, *Ur*, *R*, *It*, *F*, 1996 *Ur*, *US*, *Ur*, *C*, *SA*, *SA*, *E*, 1997 *E*, *E*, *NZ*, *NZ*, *R*, *It*, *F*, *A*, *A*, 1998 *F*, *F*, *R*, *US*, *C*, *It*, *F*, *W*, 1999 *W*, *W*, *S*, *I*, *W*, *Sa*, *J*, *I*, *F*, 2000 *A*, *A*, *SA*, *E*, 2001 *NZ*, *It*, *W*, *S*, *NZ*, 2002 *F*, *A*, *It*, *I*, 2003 *F*, *F*, *US*, *C*, 2005 *It*, *It*
F Argerich 1979 *Ur*
G Aristide 1997 *E*
J Arocena Messones 2005 *Sa*
E Arriaga 1936 *CHL*, *CHL*
S Artese 2004 *SA*
G Ascarate 2007 *CHL*, 2008 *Ur*, 2010 *CHL*
M Avellaneda 1948 *OCC*, *OCC*, 1951 *Bra*, *CHL*
M Avramovic 2005 *J*, *Sa*, 2006 *CHL*, *Ur*, *E*, *It*, 2007 *I*, 2008 *It*, *SA*, *I*, 2009 *E*
M Ayerra 1927 *GBR*
MI Ayerza 2004 *SA*, 2005 *J*, *It*, *Sa*, 2006 *W*, *W*, *CHL*, *Ur*, *E*, *It*, *F*, 2007 *I*, *I*, *Geo*, *F*, 2008 *S*, *S*, *SA*, *F*, *It*, *I*, 2009 *E*, *E*, *E*, *W*, *S*, 2010 *S*, *S*, *F*, *It*, *F*, *I*, 2011 *Geo*, *NZ*
M Azpiroz 1956 *OCC*, 1958 *Ur*, *Per*, *CHL*, 1959 *JSB*, *JSB*

J Bach 1975 *Par*, *Bra*, *CHL*
A Badano 1977 *Bra*, *Ur*, *Par*, *CHL*
J Baeck 1983 *Par*
M Baeck 1985 *Ur*, *CHL*, *Par*, 1990 *US*, *E*, *E*
DR Baetti Sabah 1980 *WXV*, *Fj*, *Fj*, 1981 *E*, *E*, *C*, 1983 *WXV*, 1987 *Ur*, *Par*, *CHL*, 1988 *F*, *F*, 1989 *It*, *NZ*, *NZ*
R Baez 2010 *CHL*, 2011 *CHL*, *Ur*
L Balfour 1977 *Bra*, *Ur*, *Par*, *CHL*
T Baravalle 2011 *Ur*
C Barrea 1996 *Ur*, *C*, *SA*
L Barrera Oro 2008 *Ur*, 2009 *Ur*
O Bartolucci 1996 *US*, *C*, *SA*, 1998 *CHL*, *Ur*, 1999 *W*, *W*, *S*, *I*, *W*, *Sa*, 2000 *I*, *A*, *A*, *SA*, *E*, 2001 *US*, *C*, 2003 *Par*, *Ur*
E Basile 1983 *CHL*, *Ur*
JL Basile 2011 *CHL*, *Ur*
L Bavio 1954 *F*
R Bazan 1951 *Ur*, *Bra*, *CHL*, 1956 *OCC*
D Beccar Varela 1975 *F*, *F*, 1976 *W*, *NZ*, 1977 *F*, *F*
M Beccar Varela 1965 *Rho*, *OCC*, *OCC*
G Begino 2007 *CHL*
J Benzi 1965 *Rho*, 1969 *S*, *Ur*, *CHL*
E Bergamaschi 2001 *US*
O Bernacchi 1954 *F*, 1956 *OCC*, *OCC*, 1958 *Ur*, *Per*, *CHL*
G Bernardi 1997 *CHL*
O Bernat 1932 *JSB*
MM Berro 1964 *Ur*, *Bra*, *CHL*
MJS Bertranou 1989 *It*, *NZ*, *NZ*, *CHL*, *Par*, 1990 *C*, *US*, *C*, *E*, *E*, *I*, *E*, *S*, 1993 *SA*
CF Betolli 2008 *Ur*, *CHL*, 2009 *Ur*
E Bianchetti 1959 *JSB*, *JSB*
G Blacksley 1971 *SAG*
T Blades 1938 *CHL*
G Bocca 1998 *J*, *Par*
C Bofelli 1997 *Ur*, 1998 *Par*, 2004 *CHL*, *Ur*, *Ven*
L Borges 2003 *Par*, *CHL*, *Ur*, 2004 *CHL*, *Ur*, *Ven*, *W*, *W*, *NZ*, *F*, *I*, *SA*, 2005 *SA*, *S*, 2006 *W*, *W*, *CHL*, *Ur*, 2007 *W*, *F*, *Geo*, *I*, *S*, *SA*, 2008 *S*, *It*, 2009 *E*, *W*, *S*, 2010 *Ur*, *S*, *I*
C Bori 1975 *F*
F Bosch 2004 *CHL*, *SA*, 2005 *J*, *Sa*
MA Bosch 1991 *A*, *Sa*, 1992 *F*, *F*
MT Bosch 2007 *It*, 2008 *It*, 2010 *F*, *I*, 2011 *W*, *E*, *R*, *S*, *Geo*, *NZ*
N Bossicovich 1995 *Ur*, *C*
CA Bottarini 1973 *Par*, *Ur*, *Bra*, *I*, 1974 *F*, 1975 *F*, *F*, 1979 *Ur*, *CHL*, *Bra*, 1983 *CHL*, *Par*, *Ur*
R Botting 1927 *GBR*, *GBR*, *GBR*
S Bottini 2011 *CHL*, *Ur*
L Bouza 1992 *Sp*

M Bouza 1966 *SAG, SAG*, 1967 *Ur, CHL*
P Bouza 1996 *Ur, F, F, E*, 1997 *E, NZ, NZ, Ur, R*, 1998 *Ur*, 2002 *Ur, Par, CHL*, 2003 *Par, CHL, Ur, US, Ur, Nm, R*, 2004 *CHL, Ur, Ven, W, NZ, SA*, 2005 *J, It, It, SA, S, It*, 2006 *CHL, Ur*, 2007 *I, I*
A Bovet 1910 *GBR*
N Bozzo 1975 *Bra*
JG Braceras 1971 *Bra, Par*, 1976 *W, NZ*, 1977 *F*
W Braddon 1927 *GBR*
EN Branca 1976 *W, NZ, NZ*, 1977 *F, F*, 1980 *Fj*, 1981 *E, E, C*, 1983 *WXV, A, A*, 1985 *F, F, Ur, CHL, Par, NZ, NZ*, 1986 *F, F, A, A*, 1987 *Ur, Fj, It, NZ, Sp, A, A*, 1988 *F, F, F, F*, 1989 *Bra, Par, Ur*, 1990 *E, E*
M Brandi 1997 *Par, CHL*, 1998 *Par, CHL, Ur*
J Bridger 1932 *JSB*
J Brolese 1998 *CHL, Ur*
E Brouchou 1975 *Ur, Par, Bra, CHL*
R Bruno 2009 *CHL, Ur*, 2010 *Ur, CHL*
F Buabse 1991 *Ur, Par, Bra*, 1992 *Sp*
PM Buabse 1989 *NZ, US*, 1991 *Sa*, 1993 *Bra*, 1995 *Ur, C, A*
E Buckley 1938 *CHL*
R Bullrich 1991 *Ur, Bra*, 1992 *R*, 1993 *Bra, CHL, SA*, 1994 *SA, SA*
S Bunader 1989 *US*, 1990 *C*
K Bush 1938 *CHL*
E Bustamante 1927 *GBR, GBR, GBR, GBR*
E Bustillo 2008 *CHL*
F Bustillo 1977 *F, F, Bra, Ur, Par, CHL*
G Bustos 2003 *Par, Ur*, 2004 *CHL, Ven*
MJ Bustos Moyano 2008 *CHL*

CJ Cáceres 2008 *Ur*, 2009 *CHL*, 2010 *Ur, CHL*
E Caffarone 1949 *F, F*, 1951 *Bra, CHL*, 1952 *I, I*, 1954 *F, F*
M Caldwell 1956 *OCC*
GO Camacho 2008 *Ur, CHL*, 2009 *E, E*, 2010 *It, F*, 2011 *W, E, R, S, NZ*
GF Camardon 1990 *E*, 1991 *NZ, CHL, A, W, Sa*, 1992 *F, F, Sp, R, F*, 1993 *J, Par, Ur, SA, SA*, 1995 *A*, 1996 *Ur, US, Ur, C, SA, E*, 1999 *W, W, Sa, J, I, F*, 2001 *US, C, NZ, It, W, S, NZ*, 2002 *F, E, SA, It, I*
PJ Camerlinckx 1989 *Bra, Par, Ur*, 1990 *C, US*, 1994 *S*, 1995 *CHL*, 1996 *Ur, F, F, US, Ur, C, SA, SA, E*, 1997 *E, E, NZ, NZ, Ur, R, It, F, A, A*, 1998 *R, US, C, F, W*, 1999 *W*
A Cameron 1936 *BI, CHL, CHL*, 1938 *CHL*
R Cameron 1927 *GBR, GBR*
J Caminotti 1987 *Ur, Par, CHL*
M Campo 1978 *E, It*, 1979 *NZ, NZ, A, A*, 1980 *WXV, Fj*, 1981 *E, E, C*, 1982 *F, F, Sp*, 1983 *WXV, A, A*, 1987 *Ur, Fj, NZ*
AT Campos 2007 *CHL*, 2008 *S, It, F, It*, 2009 *E, W, S*, 2010 *Ur, S, F*, 2011 *W, E, R, NZ*
A Canalda 1999 *S, I, F*, 2000 *A*, 2001 *Ur, US, C*
R Cano 1997 *Par*
J Capalbo 1975 *Bra*, 1977 *Bra, Ur, CHL*
AE Capelletti 1977 *F, F*, 1978 *E, It*, 1979 *NZ, NZ, A, A*, 1980 *WXV, Fj, Fj*, 1981 *E, E*
R Carballo 2006 *W, CHL, Ur*, 2008 *SA, It, I*, 2010 *S, F*
N Carbone 1969 *Ur, CHL*, 1971 *SAG*, 1973 *I, S*
PF Cardinali 2001 *US*, 2002 *Ur, Par*, 2004 *W*, 2007 *I*
M Carizza 2004 *SA*, 2005 *J, SA, S, It*, 2006 *W, CHL, Ur*, 2007 *It*, 2008 *It*, 2009 *E, E, W, S*, 2010 *S, S, F, It*, 2011 *W, E, R, S, NZ*
J Carlos Galvalisi 1983 *Par, Ur*
MA Carluccio 1973 *R, R, Ur, Bra, I*, 1975 *F, F*, 1976 *NZ*, 1977 *F, F*
M Carmona 1997 *Par, CHL*
SC Carossio 1985 *NZ*, 1987 *It, NZ*
J Carracedo 1971 *CHL, Bra, Par*, 1972 *SAG, SAG*, 1973 *R, R, Par, Ur, Bra, CHL, I, S*, 1975 *F*, 1976 *W, NZ, NZ*, 1977 *F*
M Carreras 1987 *Par*, 1991 *NZ, NZ, CHL, A, W, Sa*, 1992 *F*
M Carrique 1983 *Par, Ur*
J Casanegra 1959 *JSB, JSB*, 1960 *F, F*
GF Casas 1971 *OCC*, 1973 *Par, CHL, I*, 1975 *F, F*
DM Cash 1985 *F, F, Ur, CHL, NZ, NZ*, 1986 *F, F, A, A*, 1987 *Ur, Fj, It, NZ, Sp, A, A*, 1988 *F, F, F, F*, 1989 *It, NZ, NZ, US*, 1990 *C, US, C, E, I, E, S*, 1991 *NZ, NZ, CHL, A, Sa*, 1992 *F, F*
R Castagna 1977 *F*
A Castellina 2004 *CHL, Ur, Ven*
R Castro 1971 *CHL, Bra, Par*
J Cato 1975 *Ur, Par*
R Cazenave 1965 *Rho, JSB, OCC, CHL*, 1966 *SAG, SAG*
N Centurion 2011 *CHL, Ur*
A Cerioni 1975 *F*, 1978 *E, It*, 1979 *CHL, Bra*
G Cernegoy 1938 *CHL*
H Cespedes 1997 *Ur, CHL*
M Chesta 1966 *SAG, SAG*, 1967 *Ur, CHL*, 1968 *W, W*
W Chiswell 1949 *F*
V Christianson 1954 *F, F*, 1956 *OCC*
E Cilley 1932 *JSB, JSB*
J Cilley 1936 *BI, CHL, CHL*, 1938 *CHL*
JL Cilley 1994 *SA*, 1995 *Sa, It, Par, CHL*, 1996 *Ur, F, F, SA, SA*, 1999 *W*, 2000 *A*, 2002 *Par*
J Clement 1987 *Par*, 1989 *Bra*
R Cobelo 1987 *Ur, Par, CHL*
I Comas 1951 *Bra, CHL*, 1958 *Per, CHL*, 1960 *F*
MA Comuzzi 2008 *Ur*, 2009 *E, W*, 2011 *CHL, Ur*
A Conen 1951 *CHL*, 1952 *I, I*
J Conrard 1927 *GBR, GBR*
CA Contepomi 1964 *Bra, CHL*
F Contepomi 1998 *CHL, Ur, F, W*, 1999 *W, S, I, J, I, F*, 2000 *I, A, A, SA, E*, 2001 *Ur, US, C, NZ, It, W, S, NZ*, 2002 *F, E, SA, A, It, I*, 2003 *F, F, SA, US, C, A, Nm, I*, 2004 *W, W, F, I*, 2005 *It, It, SA, S, It*, 2006 *W, NZ, E, F*, 2007 *I, W, F, Geo, Nm, I, S, SA, F*, 2008 *S, S, SA, F, It*, 2010 *S, S, F, It, F, I*, 2011 *W, E, S, Geo, NZ*
M Contepomi 1998 *US, C, It, F, W*, 1999 *S, I, W, Sa, F*, 2003 *Ur, F, Fj, Ur, A, R*, 2004 *CHL, Ur, Ven, W, W, NZ, F, I, SA*, 2005 *SA, S*, 2006 *It, F*, 2007 *I, It, W, F, Nm, I, S, SA, F*
F Conti 1988 *F*
GEF Cooke 1927 *GBR*
KAM Cookson 1932 *JSB*
N Cooper 1936 *BI, CHL, CHL*
R Cooper 1927 *GBR, GBR, GBR, GBR*
J Copello 1975 *Ur, Bra*
C Cordeiro 1983 *Par*
J Coria 1987 *Ur, Par, CHL*, 1989 *Bra*
I Corleto 1998 *J, F, W*, 1999 *I, J, I, F*, 2000 *I, A, SA, E*, 2001 *W, S, NZ*, 2002 *F, E, SA, A, It, I*, 2003 *F, Fj, US, Ur, C, A, I*, 2006 *It, F*, 2007 *W, F, Geo, Nm, I, S, SA, F*
ME Corral 1993 *J, Bra, Par, Ur, SA, SA*, 1994 *US, S, SA, SA*, 1995 *Ur, C, A, A, E, Sa, It*
RG Cortes 2011 *CHL, Ur*
M Cortese 2005 *Sa*, 2010 *Ur, CHL*
F Cortopasso 2003 *CHL, Ur*
A Costa Repetto 2005 *Sa*
JD Costante 1971 *OCC, OCC, CHL, Bra, Par, Ur*, 1976 *W, NZ*, 1977 *F*
AF Courreges 1979 *Ur, Par, Bra*, 1982 *F, F, Sp*, 1983 *WXV, A, A*, 1987 *Sp, A, A*, 1988 *F*
PH Cox 1938 *CHL*
A Creevy 2005 *J, Sa*, 2006 *Ur*, 2009 *S*, 2010 *S, S, F, It, F, I*, 2011 *W, E, R, S, Geo, NZ*
P Cremaschi 1993 *J, J*, 1995 *Par, CHL, Ur, It*
RH Crexell 1990 *I, S*, 1991 *Par*, 1992 *Sp*, 1993 *J*, 1995 *Ur, C, A, E, Sa, It, Par, CHL, Ur*
L Criscuolo 1992 *F, F*, 1993 *Bra, SA*, 1996 *Ur, F, F*
J Cruz Legora 2002 *Par, CHL*
J Cruz Meabe 1997 *Par*
AG Cubelli 1977 *Bra, Ur, CHL*, 1978 *E, It*, 1979 *A, A*, 1980 *WXV, Fj*, 1983 *Par*, 1985 *F, F, Ur, Par, NZ, NZ*, 1990 *S*
F Cubelli 2009 *Ur*
T Cubelli 2010 *Ur, CHL*, 2011 *CHL, Ur*
D Cuesta Silva 1983 *CHL, Ur*, 1985 *F, F, Ur, CHL, NZ, NZ*, 1986 *F, F, A, A*, 1987 *Ur, Fj, It, Sp, A, A*, 1988 *F, F, F, F*, 1989 *It, NZ, NZ*, 1990 *C, E, E, I, E, S*, 1991 *NZ, NZ, CHL, A, W, Sa*, 1992 *F, F, Sp, R, F*, 1993 *J, J, Bra, Par, Ur, SA, SA*, 1994 *US, S, S, US, SA*, 1995 *Ur, C, E, Sa, It, Par, R, It, F*
J Cuesta Silva 1927 *GBR, GBR, GBR, GBR*
B Cuezzo 2007 *CHL*
M Cutler 1969 *Ur*, 1971 *CHL, Bra, Par, Ur*

A Da Milano 1964 *Bra, CHL*
F D'Agnillo 1975 *Ur, Bra*, 1977 *Bra, Ur, Par, CHL*
JL Damioli 1991 *Ur, Par, Bra*
H Dande 2001 *Ur, C*, 2004 *CHL, Ven*
J Dartiguelongue 1964 *Bra, CHL*, 1968 *W, W*
S Dassen 1983 *CHL, Par, Ur*
R de Abelleyra 1932 *JSB, JSB*
M De Achaval 2008 *CHL*, 2009 *CHL, Ur*, 2010 *It, F*
L de Chazal 2001 *Ur, C*, 2004 *SA*
E de Forteza 1975 *Ur, Par, Bra, CHL*
R de la Arena 1992 *F, Sp*

T De La Vega 2011 *CHL, Ur*
JC De Pablo 1948 *OCC*
G De Robertis 2005 *Sa*, 2006 *CHL, Ur*, 2011 *CHL*
R de Vedia 1982 *F, Sp*
T de Vedia 2007 *I, I*, 2008 *S*
R del Busto 2007 *CHL*
F del Castillo 1994 *US, SA*, 1995 *Ur, C, A*, 1996 *Ur, F*, 1997 *Par, Ur*, 1998 *Ur*
GJ del Castillo 1991 *NZ, NZ, CHL, A, W*, 1993 *J*, 1994 *S, S, US, SA*, 1995 *C, A*
L del Chazal 1983 *CHL, Par, Ur*
R Dell'Acqua 1956 *OCC*
S Dengra 1982 *F, Sp*, 1983 *WXV, A, A*, 1986 *A*, 1987 *It, NZ, Sp, A, A*, 1988 *F, F, F, F*, 1989 *It, NZ, NZ*
C Derkheim 1927 *GBR*
M Devoto 1975 *Par, Bra*, 1977 *Par*
PM Devoto 1982 *F, F, Sp*, 1983 *WXV*
R Devoto 1960 *F*
I di Santi 2009 *Ur*
M Diaz 1997 *Par, CHL*, 1998 *J, Par, CHL*
F Diaz Alberdi 1997 *Ur*, 1999 *S, I*, 2000 *A, A*
J Diez 1956 *OCC*
R Dillon 1956 *OCC*
P Dinisio 1989 *NZ*, 1990 *C, US*
M Dip 1979 *Par, Bra*
D Dominguez 1989 *CHL, Par*
E Dominguez 1949 *F, F*, 1952 *I, I*, 1954 *F, F*
A Donnelly 1910 *GBR*
L Dorado 1949 *F*
J Dumas 1973 *R, R, Ur, Bra, S*
M Dumas 1966 *SAG, SAG*
MA Durand 1997 *CHL*, 1998 *Par, CHL, Ur, It, F, W*, 2000 *SA*, 2001 *Ur, US, C, It, NZ*, 2002 *F, SA, A, It, I*, 2003 *CHL, Ur, Fj, US, Ur, C, A, Nm, R*, 2004 *CHL, Ur, Ven, W, W, NZ, F, I, SA*, 2005 *SA, S, It*, 2006 *W, NZ, CHL, Ur, It, F*, 2007 *I, I, It, W, F, Geo, I, F*, 2008 *S, S, It, SA, F, It, I*

C Echeverria 1932 *JSB*
G Ehrman 1948 *OCC*, 1949 *F, F*, 1951 *Ur, Bra, CHL*, 1952 *I, I*, 1954 *F, F*
O Elia 1954 *F*
R Elliot 1936 *BI*, 1938 *CHL*
J Escalante 1975 *Ur, Par, CHL*, 1978 *It*, 1979 *Ur, CHL, Par, Bra*
N Escary 1927 *GBR, GBR*, 1932 *JSB, JSB*
R Espagnol 1971 *SAG*
JP Estelles 2008 *CHL*
AM Etchegaray 1964 *Ur, Bra, CHL*, 1965 *Rho, JSB, CHL*, 1967 *Ur, CHL*, 1968 *W, W*, 1969 *S, S*, 1971 *SAG, OCC, OCC*, 1972 *SAG, SAG*, 1973 *Par, Bra, I*, 1974 *F, F*, 1976 *W, NZ, NZ*
R Etchegoyen 1991 *Ur, Par, Bra*
C Ezcurra 1958 *Ur, Per, CHL*
E Ezcurra 1990 *I, E, S*

JA Farias Cabello 2010 *F, I*, 2011 *W, E, S, Geo, NZ*
R Fariello 1973 *Par, Ur, CHL, S*
M Farina 1968 *W, W*, 1969 *S, S*
D Farrell 1951 *Ur*
P Felisari 1956 *OCC*
JJ Fernandez 1971 *SAG, CHL, Bra, Par, Ur*, 1972 *SAG, SAG*, 1973 *R, R, Par, Ur, CHL, I, S*, 1974 *F, F*, 1975 *F*, 1976 *W, NZ, NZ*, 1977 *F, F*
S Fernández 2008 *It, I*, 2009 *E, E, E, W, S*, 2010 *S, S, F, It, F*, 2011 *W, E, R, S, Geo, NZ*
Pablo Fernandez Bravo 1993 *SA, SA*
E Fernandez del Casal 1951 *Ur, Bra, CHL*, 1952 *I, I*, 1956 *OCC, OCC*
CI Fernandez Lobbe 1996 *US*, 1997 *E, E*, 1998 *F, F, R, US, Ur, C, J, It, F*, 1999 *W, W, S, I, W, Sa, J, I, F*, 2000 *I, A, A, SA, E*, 2001 *NZ, It, W, S, NZ*, 2002 *F, E, SA, A, It, I*, 2003 *F, F, SA, US, C, A, Nm, I*, 2004 *W, W, NZ*, 2005 *SA, S, It*, 2006 *W, W, NZ, E, F*, 2007 *It, W, F, Nm, I, S, SA*, 2008 *S, S*
JM Fernandez Lobbe 2004 *Ur, Ven*, 2005 *S, It, Sa*, 2006 *W, W, NZ, E, It, F*, 2007 *I, I, It, W, F, Geo, Nm, I, S, SA, F*, 2008 *S, S, SA, F, It, I*, 2009 *E, E, E, W, S*, 2010 *S, S, F, It, F, I*, 2011 *W, E, R, S*
JC Fernández Miranda 1997 *Ur, R, It*, 1998 *Ur, It*, 2000 *I*, 2001 *US, C*, 2002 *Ur, Par, CHL, It, I*, 2003 *Par, CHL, Ur, Fj, US, Nm, R*, 2004 *W, NZ, SA*, 2005 *J, Sa*, 2006 *CHL, Ur*, 2007 *It*
N Fernandez Miranda 1994 *US, S, S, US*, 1995 *CHL, Ur*, 1996 *F, SA, SA, E*, 1997 *E, E, NZ, NZ, Ur, R*, 1998 *R, US, C, It*, 1999 *I, F*, 2002 *Ur, CHL, It*, 2003 *CHL, Ur, F, F, SA, US, Ur, Nm, R*, 2004 *W, NZ*, 2005 *J, It, It*, 2006 *W, It*, 2007 *It, Geo, Nm*
N Ferrari 1992 *Sp, Sp*
G Fessia 2007 *I*, 2008 *Ur*, 2009 *E*, 2010 *S, S, F, It, F, I*, 2011 *R, S, Geo*
JG Figallo 2010 *F, It, I*, 2011 *W, E, R, S, Geo, NZ*
A Figuerola 2008 *It, I*, 2009 *E, W, S*, 2010 *S, S*
R Follett 1948 *OCC, OCC*, 1952 *I, I*, 1954 *F*
G Foster 1971 *CHL, Bra, Par, Ur*
R Foster 1965 *Rho, JSB, OCC, OCC, CHL*, 1966 *SAG, SAG*, 1970 *I, I*, 1971 *SAG, SAG, OCC*, 1972 *SAG, SAG*
P Franchi 1987 *Ur, Par, CHL*
JL Francombe 1932 *JSB, JSB*, 1936 *BI*
J Freixas 2003 *CHL, Ur*
R Frigerio 1948 *OCC, OCC*, 1954 *F*
J Frigoli 1936 *BI, CHL, CHL*
P Fuselli 1998 *J, Par*

E Gahan 1954 *F, F*
M Gaitán 1998 *Ur*, 2002 *Par, CHL*, 2003 *Fj, US, Nm, R*, 2004 *W*, 2007 *It, W*
MT Galarza 2010 *S, F, It, F, I*, 2011 *W, E, R, Geo*
AM Galindo 2004 *Ur, Ven*, 2008 *S, It, SA, F, It*, 2009 *E*, 2010 *Ur, It, F*
R Gallo 1964 *Bra*
P Gambarini 2006 *W, CHL, Ur*, 2007 *I, It, CHL*, 2008 *S, CHL*
E Garbarino 1992 *Sp, Sp*
FL Garcia 1994 *SA*, 1995 *A, A, Par, CHL*, 1996 *Ur, F, F*, 1997 *NZ*, 1998 *R, Ur, J*
J Garcia 1998 *Par, Ur*, 2000 *A*
PT Garcia 1948 *OCC*
E Garcia Hamilton 1993 *Bra*
P Garcia Hamilton 1998 *CHL*
HM Garcia Simon 1990 *I*, 1992 *F*
G Garcia-Orsetti 1992 *R, F*
PA Garreton 1987 *Sp, Ur, CHL, A, A*, 1988 *F, F, F, F*, 1989 *It, NZ, Bra, CHL, Ur, US*, 1990 *C, E, E, I, E, S*, 1991 *NZ, NZ, CHL, A, W, Sa*, 1992 *F, F*, 1993 *J, J*
P Garzan 2009 *CHL, Ur*
P Garzon 1990 *C*, 1991 *Par, Bra*
G Gasso 1983 *CHL, Par*
JI Gauthier 2008 *Ur, CHL*
JM Gauweloose 1975 *F, F*, 1976 *W, NZ, NZ*, 1977 *F, F*, 1981 *C*
E Gavina 1956 *OCC, OCC*, 1958 *Ur, Per, CHL*, 1959 *JSB, JSB*, 1960 *F, F*, 1961 *CHL, Bra, Ur*
OST Gebbie 1910 *GBR*
FA Genoud 2004 *CHL, Ur, Ven*, 2005 *J, It*, 2008 *Ur*
J Genoud 1952 *I, I*, 1956 *OCC, OCC*
M Gerosa 1987 *Ur, CHL*
D Giannantonio 1996 *Ur*, 1997 *Par, Ur, It, A, A*, 1998 *F, F*, 2000 *A*, 2002 *E*
MC Giargia 1973 *Par, Ur, Bra*, 1975 *Par, CHL*
R Giles 1948 *OCC*, 1949 *F, F*, 1951 *Ur*, 1952 *I, I*
C Giuliano 1959 *JSB, JSB*, 1960 *F*
L Glastra 1948 *OCC, OCC*, 1952 *I, I*
M Glastra 1979 *Ur, CHL*, 1981 *C*
FE Gomez 1985 *Ur*, 1987 *Ur, Fj, It, NZ*, 1989 *NZ*, 1990 *C, E, E*
JF Gomez 2006 *It*, 2008 *Ur, S, S, It*
N Gomez 1997 *Par, CHL*
PM Gomez Cora 2004 *NZ, SA*, 2005 *Sa*, 2006 *E*
F Gómez Kodela 2008 *Ur, CHL*, 2011 *CHL, Ur*
D Gonzalez 1987 *Par*, 1988 *F, F*
T Gonzalez 1975 *Ur, CHL*
LP Gonzalez Amorosino 2007 *CHL*, 2008 *CHL*, 2009 *E, E*, 2010 *S, S, F, It, F, I*, 2011 *R, S, Geo, NZ*
S Gonzalez Bonorino 2001 *Ur, US, C*, 2002 *Par, CHL*, 2003 *F, SA*, 2007 *I, I, It, W, F, Geo*, 2008 *S, S*
E Gonzalez del Solar 1960 *F*, 1961 *CHL, Bra, Ur*
N Gonzalez del Solar 1964 *Ur, Bra, CHL*, 1965 *Rho, JSB, OCC, OCC, CHL*
S González Iglesias 2009 *CHL, Ur*, 2011 *CHL*
AO Gosio 2011 *Geo*
H Goti 1961 *CHL, Bra, Ur*, 1964 *Ur, Bra, CHL*, 1965 *Rho*, 1966 *SAG*
LM Gradin 1965 *OCC, OCC, CHL*, 1966 *SAG, SAG*, 1969 *CHL*, 1970 *I, I*, 1973 *R, R, Par, Ur, CHL, S*
P Grande 1998 *Par, CHL, Ur*
RD Grau 1993 *J, Bra, CHL*, 1995 *Par, CHL*, 1996 *F, F, US, Ur, C, SA, SA, E*, 1997 *E, E, NZ, NZ, A, A*, 1998 *F, It, F*, 1999

W, W, S, I, W, F, 2000 A, SA, E, 2001 NZ, W, S, NZ, 2002 F, E, SA, A, It, 2003 F, SA, US, Ur, C, A, I
L Gravano 1997 CHL, 1998 CHL, Ur
LH Gribell 1910 GBR
B Grigolon 1948 OCC, 1954 F, F
V Grimoldi 1927 GBR, GBR
J Grondona 1990 C
R Grosse 1952 I, I, 1954 F, F
P Guarrochena 1977 Par
A Guastella 1956 OCC, 1959 JSB, JSB, 1960 F
J Guidi 1958 Ur, Per, CHL, 1959 JSB, 1960 F, 1961 CHL, Bra, Ur
MR Guidone 2008 CHL, 2009 CHL, Ur, 2011 CHL, Ur
E Guiñazu 2003 Par, CHL, Ur, 2004 CHL, Ur, Ven, W, W, SA, 2005 J, It, 2007 I, It, F, 2009 E
JA Guzman 2007 CHL, 2009 Ur, 2010 Ur, CHL
SN Guzmán 2010 S, I

D Halle 1989 Bra, CHL, Ur, US, 1990 US
R Handley 1966 SAG, SAG, 1968 W, W, 1969 S, S, Ur, CHL, 1970 I, I, 1971 SAG, SAG, 1972 SAG, SAG
G Hardie 1948 OCC
TA Harris-Smith 1969 S, S, 1971 SAG, OCC, OCC, 1973 Par, Ur
O Hasan Jalil 1995 Ur, 1996 Ur, C, SA, SA, 1997 E, E, NZ, R, It, F, A, 1998 F, F, R, US, C, It, F, W, 1999 W, W, S, W, Sa, J, I, 2000 SA, E, 2001 NZ, It, W, S, NZ, 2002 F, E, SA, A, It, I, 2003 US, C, A, R, 2004 W, W, NZ, F, I, 2005 It, It, SA, S, It, 2006 NZ, E, F, 2007 It, Geo, Nm, I, S, SA, F
WM Hayman 1910 GBR
BH Heatlie 1910 GBR
P Henn 2004 CHL, Ur, Ven, 2005 J, It, 2007 It
F Henrys 1910 GBR
F Heriot 1910 GBR
JM Hernández 2003 Par, Ur, F, F, SA, C, A, Nm, R, 2004 F, I, SA, 2005 SA, S, It, 2006 W, W, NZ, E, It, F, 2007 F, Geo, I, S, SA, F, 2008 It, F, It, 2009 E, E
M Hernandez 1927 GBR, GBR, GBR
L Herrera 1991 Ur, Par
A Hevia 2008 Ur
FA Higgs 2004 Ur, Ven, 2005 J
D Hine 1938 CHL
C Hirsch 1960 F
C Hirsch 1960 F
E Hirsch 1954 F, 1956 OCC
R Hogg 1958 Ur, Per, CHL, 1959 JSB, JSB, 1961 CHL, Bra, Ur
S Hogg 1956 OCC, OCC, 1958 Ur, Per, CHL, 1959 JSB, JSB
E Holmberg 1948 OCC
B Holmes 1949 F, F
E Holmgren 1958 Ur, Per, CHL, 1959 JSB, JSB, 1960 F, F
G Holmgren 1985 NZ, NZ
E Horan 1956 OCC
L Hughes 1936 CHL
M Hughes 1954 F, F
M Hughes 1949 F, F
CA Huntley Robertson 1932 JSB, JSB

A Iachetti 1975 Ur, Par, 1977 Ur, Par, CHL, 1978 E, It, 1979 NZ, NZ, A, A, 1980 WXV, Fj, Fj, 1981 E, E, 1982 F, F, Sp, 1987 Ur, Par, A, A, 1988 F, F, F, F, 1989 It, NZ, 1990 C, E, E
A Iachetti 1977 Bra, 1987 CHL
ME Iachetti 1979 NZ, NZ, A, A
M Iglesias 1973 R, 1974 F, F
G Illia 1965 Rho
JJ Imhoff 2009 CHL, Ur, 2010 CHL, 2011 W, E, R, Geo, NZ
JL Imhoff 1967 Ur, CHL
V Inchausti 1936 BI, CHL, CHL
F Insua 1971 CHL, Bra, Par, Ur, 1972 SAG, SAG, 1973 R, R, Bra, CHL, I, S, 1974 F, F, 1976 W, NZ, NZ, 1977 F, F
R Iraneta 1974 F, 1976 W, NZ
FJ Irarrazabal 1991 Sa, 1992 Sp, Sp
S Irazoqui 1993 J, CHL, Par, Ur, 1995 E, Sa, Par
A Irigoyen 1997 Par

C Jacobi 1979 CHL, Par
AG Jacobs 1927 GBR, GBR
AGW Jones 1948 OCC
GM Jorge 1989 Bra, CHL, Par, Ur, 1990 I, E, 1992 F, F, Sp, Sp, R, F, 1993 J, J, Bra, CHL, Ur, SA, SA, 1994 US, S, S, US

E Jurado 1995 A, A, E, Sa, It, Par, CHL, Ur, R, It, F, 1996 SA, E, 1997 E, E, NZ, NZ, Ur, R, It, F, A, A, 1998 F, Ur, C, It, 1999 W

E Karplus 1959 JSB, JSB, 1960 F, F, F
A Ker 1936 CHL, 1938 CHL
E Kossler 1960 F, F, F

EH Laborde 1991 A, W, Sa
G Laborde 1979 CHL, Bra
J Lacarra 1989 Par, Ur
R Lagarde 1956 OCC
JP Lagarrigue 2008 Ur, CHL
A Lalanne 2008 SA, 2009 E, E, W, S, 2010 S, I, 2011 R, Geo, NZ
M Lamas 1998 Par, CHL
M Landajo 2008 CHL, 2010 Ur, CHL
TR Landajo 1977 F, Bra, Ur, CHL, 1978 E, 1979 A, A, 1980 WXV, Fj, Fj, 1981 E, E
M Lanfranco 1991 Ur, Par, Bra
AR Lanusse 1932 JSB
M Lanusse 1951 Ur, Bra, CHL
J Lanza 1985 F, Ur, Par, NZ, NZ, 1986 F, F, A, A, 1987 Ur, Fj, It, NZ
P Lanza 1983 CHL, Par, Ur, 1985 F, F, Ur, CHL, Par, NZ, NZ, 1986 F, F, A, A, 1987 It, NZ
J Lasalle 1964 Ur
J Lavayen 1961 CHL, Bra, Ur
CG Lazcano Miranda 1998 CHL, 2004 CHL, Ur, Ven, 2005 J
RA le Fort 1990 I, E, 1991 NZ, NZ, CHL, A, W, 1992 R, F, 1993 J, SA, SA, 1995 Ur, It
F Lecot 2003 Par, Ur, 2005 J, 2007 CHL
P Ledesma 2008 It, SA
ME Ledesma Arocena 1996 Ur, C, 1997 NZ, NZ, Ur, R, It, F, A, A, 1998 F, F, Ur, C, J, Ur, F, W, 1999 W, W, Sa, J, I, F, 2000 SA, 2001 It, W, NZ, 2002 F, E, SA, A, It, I, 2003 F, SA, Fj, US, C, A, Nm, R, 2004 W, NZ, F, I, 2005 It, It, SA, S, It, 2006 W, W, NZ, CHL, Ur, E, It, F, 2007 W, F, Geo, I, S, SA, 2008 SA, F, It, I, 2009 E, E, W, 2010 S, S, F, It, F, I, 2011 W, E, R, S, Geo, NZ
J Legora 1996 F, F, US, Ur, 1997 CHL, 1998 Par
JM Leguizamón 2005 J, It, It, SA, S, It, 2006 W, NZ, CHL, Ur, E, It, F, 2007 I, I, It, W, F, Geo, Nm, S, SA, F, 2008 S, S, It, SA, I, 2009 E, E, 2010 S, S, F, 2011 W, E, R, S, Geo, NZ
GP Leiros 1973 Bra, I
C Lennon 1958 Ur, Per
TC Leonardi 2008 CHL, 2009 E, W, S
FJ Leonelli Morey 2001 Ur, 2004 Ur, Ven, 2005 J, It, SA, S, It, 2006 W, W, 2007 I, I, It, 2008 F, I, 2009 E
M Lerga 1995 Par, CHL, Ur
Lesianado 1948 OCC
I Lewis 1932 JSB
GA Llanes 1990 I, E, S, 1991 NZ, NZ, CHL, A, W, 1992 F, F, Sp, R, F, 1993 Bra, CHL, SA, SA, 1994 US, S, S, SA, SA, 1995 A, A, E, Sa, It, R, It, F, 1996 SA, SA, E, 1997 E, E, NZ, NZ, R, It, F, 1998 F, 2000 A
MA Lobato 2010 Ur, CHL
L Lobrauco 1996 US, 1997 CHL, 1998 J, CHL, Ur
MH Loffreda 1978 E, 1979 NZ, NZ, A, A, 1980 WXV, Fj, Fj, 1981 E, E, C, 1982 F, F, Sp, 1983 WXV, A, A, 1985 Ur, CHL, Par, 1987 Ur, Par, CHL, A, A, 1988 F, F, F, F, 1989 It, NZ, Bra, CHL, Par, Ur, US, 1990 C, US, E, E, 1994 US, S, S, US, SA, SA
G Logan 1936 BI
GM Longo Elía 1999 W, W, S, I, W, Sa, I, F, 2000 I, A, A, SA, E, 2001 US, NZ, It, W, S, NZ, 2002 F, E, SA, A, It, I, 2003 F, F, SA, Fj, C, A, I, 2004 W, W, NZ, F, I, 2005 It, It, SA, 2006 W, W, NZ, E, It, F, 2007 W, Nm, I, S, SA, F
L Lopez Fleming 2004 Ur, Ven, W, 2005 Sa, 2008 Ur
A Lopresti 1997 Par, CHL
J Loures 1954 F
R Loyola 1964 Ur, CHL, 1965 Rho, JSB, OCC, OCC, CHL, 1966 SAG, SAG, 1968 W, W, 1969 S, S, 1970 I, I, 1971 CHL, Bra, Par, Ur
E Lozada 2006 E, It, 2007 I, I, Geo, F, 2008 S, S, It, SA, F, It, I, 2009 E, E, E, 2010 It
F Lucioni 1927 GBR
R Lucke 1975 Ur, Par, Bra, CHL, 1981 C
FD Luna 2011 Ur
J Luna 1995 Par, CHL, Ur, R, It, F, 1997 Par, CHL

P Mac 2009 *CHL*
P Macadam 1949 *F, F*
AM Macome 1990 *I, E*, 1995 *Ur, C*
B Macome 2009 *CHL, Ur*
B Madero 2011 *CHL, Ur*
RM Madero 1978 *E, It*, 1979 *NZ, NZ, A, A*, 1980 *WXV, Fj, Fj*, 1981 *E, E, C*, 1982 *F, F, Sp*, 1983 *WXV, A, A*, 1985 *F, NZ*, 1986 *A, A*, 1987 *Ur, It, NZ, Sp, Ur, Par, CHL, A, A*, 1988 *F, F, F*, 1989 *It, NZ, NZ*, 1990 *E, E*
M Maineri 2011 *CHL, Ur*
L Makin 1927 *GBR*
A Mamanna 1991 *Par*, 1997 *Par*
J Manuel Belgrano 1956 *OCC*
A Marguery 1991 *Ur, Bra*, 1993 *CHL, Par*
R Maria 2008 *Ur*
R Martin 1938 *CHL*
RA Martin 1994 *US, S, S, US, SA, SA*, 1995 *Ur, C, A, A, E, Sa, It, CHL, Ur, R, It, F*, 1996 *Ur, F, F, Ur, C, SA, SA, E*, 1997 *E, E, NZ, NZ, It, F, A, A*, 1998 *F, F, R, US, Ur, J, Par, CHL, Ur, It, W*, 1999 *W, W, S, I, W, Sa, J, I, F*, 2000 *I, A, A, SA, E*, 2001 *Ur, US, C, NZ, It, W, S, NZ*, 2002 *Ur, Par, CHL, F, E, SA, A, It, I*, 2003 *Par, CHL, Ur, F, SA, Ur, C, A, R, I*
F Martin Aramburu 2004 *CHL, Ven, W, NZ, F, I*, 2005 *It, SA, S, It*, 2006 *NZ*, 2007 *Geo, F*, 2008 *S, SA, F, It, I*, 2009 *E, S*
J Martin Copella 1989 *CHL, Par*
C Martinez 1969 *Ur, CHL*, 1970 *I, I*
E Martinez 1971 *CHL, Bra, Ur*
O Martinez Basante 1954 *F*
M Martinez Mosquera 1971 *CHL*
M Marvaez 2009 *CHL, Ur*
RC Mastai 1975 *F*, 1976 *W, NZ, NZ*, 1977 *F, F, Bra, Ur, Par, CHL*, 1980 *WXV*
R Matarazzo 1971 *SAG, SAG, Par, Ur*, 1972 *SAG, SAG*, 1973 *R, R, Par, Ur, CHL, I, S*, 1974 *F, F*
H Maurer 1932 *JSB, JSB*
L Maurette 1948 *OCC, OCC*
C Mazzini 1977 *F, F*
CJ McCarthy 1910 *GBR*
G McCormick 1964 *Bra, CHL*, 1965 *Rho, OCC, OCC, CHL*, 1966 *SAG, SAG*
M McCormick 1927 *GBR*
A Memoli 1979 *Ur, Par, Bra*
FE Méndez 1990 *I, E*, 1991 *NZ, NZ, CHL, A, W*, 1992 *F, F, Sp, Sp, R, F*, 1994 *S, US, SA, SA*, 1995 *Ur, C, A, A, E, Sa, It, Par, CHL, Ur, R, It, F*, 1996 *SA, SA*, 1997 *E*, 1998 *F, F, R, US, Ur, C, It, F, W*, 1999 *W, W*, 2000 *I, A, A, SA, E*, 2001 *NZ, It, W, S, NZ*, 2002 *Ur, CHL, F, E, SA, A*, 2003 *F, F, SA, Fj, Ur, Nm, I*, 2004 *CHL, Ur, W, W, NZ, SA*
FJ Mendez 1991 *Ur, Par, Bra*, 1992 *Sp, Sp*
H Mendez 1967 *Ur, CHL*
L Mendez 1958 *Ur, Per, CHL*, 1959 *JSB*
CI Mendy 1987 *Ur, Par, CHL, A, A*, 1988 *F, F, F, F*, 1989 *It, NZ, NZ, US*, 1990 *C*, 1991 *Ur, Bra*
FJ Merello 2007 *CHL*, 2008 *CHL*, 2009 *Ur*, 2010 *Ur, CHL*
F Merlo 2009 *CHL*
I Merlo 1993 *Bra, CHL*
P Merlo 1985 *CHL, Par*
SE Meson 1987 *Par*, 1989 *Bra, Par, Ur, US*, 1990 *US, C, S*, 1991 *NZ, NZ, CHL, Sa*, 1992 *F, F, Sp, R, F*, 1993 *J, Bra, Par, Ur, SA, SA*, 1994 *US, S, S, US*, 1995 *Ur, C, A, A*, 1996 *US, C*, 1997 *CHL*
I Mieres 2007 *CHL*, 2008 *CHL*, 2010 *Ur, CHL*
BH Miguens 1983 *WXV, A, A*, 1985 *F, F, NZ, NZ*, 1986 *F, F, A, A*, 1987 *Sp*
E Miguens 1975 *Ur, Par, CHL*
H Miguens 1969 *S, S, Ur, CHL*, 1970 *I, I*, 1971 *OCC*, 1972 *SAG, SAG*, 1973 *R, R, Par, Ur, Bra, CHL, I, S*, 1975 *F*
J Miguens 1982 *F*, 1985 *F, F*, 1986 *F, F, A, A*
GE Milano 1982 *F, F, Sp*, 1983 *WXV, A, A*, 1985 *F, F, Ur, CHL, Par, NZ, NZ*, 1986 *F, F, A, A*, 1987 *Ur, Fj, Sp, Ur, CHL, A, A*, 1988 *F, F, F*, 1989 *It, NZ, NZ*
A Mimesi 1998 *J, Par, CHL*
B Minguez 1975 *Par, Bra, CHL*, 1979 *Ur, CHL, Par*, 1983 *WXV, A, A*, 1985 *Ur, CHL*
R Miralles 2008 *Ur*, 2011 *CHL*
B Mitchelstein 1936 *BI*
E Mitchelstein 1956 *OCC*, 1960 *F, F*
C Mold 1910 *GBR*
LE Molina 1985 *CHL*, 1987 *Ur, Fj, It, NZ*, 1989 *NZ, NZ, Bra, CHL, Par*, 1990 *C, E*, 1991 *W*
M Molina 1998 *Par, CHL, Ur*
G Montes de Oca 1961 *CHL, Bra, Ur*
E Montpelat 1948 *OCC, OCC*
G Morales Oliver 2001 *Ur, US, C*
C Morea 1951 *Ur, Bra, CHL*
FR Morel 1979 *A, A*, 1980 *WXV, Fj, Fj*, 1981 *E, E, C*, 1982 *F*, 1985 *F, F, Ur, Par, NZ, NZ*, 1986 *F, F, A*, 1987 *Ur, Fj*
A Moreno 1998 *Par, CHL, Ur*
D Morgan 1967 *CHL*, 1970 *I, I*, 1971 *SAG, SAG, OCC, OCC*, 1972 *SAG, SAG*
E Morgan 1969 *S, S*, 1972 *SAG, SAG*, 1973 *R, R, Par, Ur, Bra, CHL, I, S*, 1975 *F, F*
G Morgan 1977 *Bra, Ur, Par, CHL*, 1979 *Ur, Par, Bra*
M Morgan 1971 *SAG, OCC, OCC*
JS Morganti 1951 *Ur, Bra, CHL*
J Mostany 1987 *Ur, Fj, NZ*
R Moyano 2011 *CHL, Ur*
E Muliero 1997 *CHL*
S Muller 1927 *GBR*
R Muniz 1975 *Par, Bra, CHL*

M Nannini 2002 *Ur, Par, CHL*, 2003 *Par, CHL*
A Navajas 1932 *JSB, JSB*
E Naveyra 1998 *CHL*
G Nazassi 1997 *CHL*
ML Negri 1979 *CHL, Bra*
E Neri 1960 *F, F*, 1961 *CHL, Bra, Ur*, 1964 *Ur, Bra, CHL*, 1965 *Rho, JSB, OCC*, 1966 *SAG, SAG*
CM Neyra 1975 *F, F*, 1976 *W, NZ, NZ*, 1983 *WXV*
A Nicholson 1979 *Ur, Par, Bra*
HM Nicola 1971 *SAG, OCC, OCC, CHL, Bra, Par, Ur*, 1975 *F, F*, 1978 *E, It*, 1979 *NZ, NZ*
EP Noriega 1991 *Par*, 1992 *Sp, Sp, R, F*, 1993 *J, J, CHL, Par, Ur, SA, SA*, 1994 *US, S, S, US, SA, SA*, 1995 *Ur, C, A, A, E, Sa, It*
JM Nuñez Piossek 2001 *Ur, NZ*, 2002 *Ur, Par, CHL, A*, 2003 *Par, Ur, F, SA, Ur, C, A, R, I*, 2004 *CHL, Ur, W, W*, 2005 *It, It*, 2006 *W, W, NZ, E, F*, 2008 *S, SA*

R Ochoa 1956 *OCC*
M Odriozola 1961 *CHL, Ur*
J O'Farrell 1948 *OCC*, 1951 *Ur, Bra*, 1956 *OCC*
U O'Farrell 1951 *Ur, Bra, CHL*
C Ohanian 1998 *Par, Ur*
C Olivera 1958 *Ur, Per, CHL*, 1959 *JSB, JSB*
R Olivieri 1960 *F, F*, 1961 *CHL, Bra, Ur*
J Orengo 1996 *Ur*, 1997 *Ur, R, It*, 1998 *F, F, R, US, C, F, W*, 1999 *W*, 2000 *A, SA, E*, 2001 *Ur, US, C, NZ, W, S, NZ*, 2002 *F, E, SA, A, It, I*, 2003 *F, SA, Ur, C, A, I*, 2004 *W, W*
JP Orlandi 2008 *F, It, I*, 2009 *E, E*
C Orti 1949 *F, F*
L Ortiz 2003 *Par, CHL, Ur*
A Orzabal 1974 *F, F*
L Ostiglia 1999 *W, W, S, I, W, J, F*, 2001 *NZ, It, W, S*, 2002 *E, SA*, 2003 *Par, CHL, Ur, F, F, SA, Nm, I*, 2004 *W, W, NZ, F, I, SA*, 2007 *F, Nm, I, S, SA*
B Otaño 1960 *F, F, F*, 1961 *CHL, Bra, Ur*, 1964 *Ur, Bra, CHL*, 1965 *Rho, JSB, OCC, OCC, CHL*, 1966 *SAG, SAG*, 1968 *W, W*, 1969 *S, S, Ur, CHL*, 1970 *I, I*, 1971 *SAG, OCC, OCC*
J Otaola 1970 *I*, 1971 *CHL, Bra, Par, Ur*, 1974 *F, F*

M Pacheco 1938 *CHL*
RL Pacheco 2010 *Ur, CHL*
A Palma 1949 *F, F*, 1952 *I, I*, 1954 *F, F*
JMC Palma 1982 *F, Sp*, 1983 *WXV, A, A*
R Palma 1985 *CHL, Par*
M Palou 1996 *US, Ur*
M Parra 1975 *Ur, Bra, CHL*
A Pasalagua 1927 *GBR, GBR*
M Pascual 1965 *Rho, JSB, OCC, OCC, CHL*, 1966 *SAG, SAG*, 1967 *Ur, CHL*, 1968 *W, W*, 1969 *S, S, Ur, CHL*, 1970 *I, I*, 1971 *SAG, SAG, OCC, OCC*
HR Pascuali 1936 *BI*
H Pasman 1936 *CHL*
I Pasman 2008 *CHL*
R Passaglia 1977 *Bra, Ur, CHL*, 1978 *E, It*
G Pata Curelo 2009 *CHL, Ur*
G Paz 1979 *Ur, CHL, Par, Bra*, 1983 *CHL, Par, Ur*
JJ Paz 1991 *Ur, Bra*
S Peretti 1993 *Bra, Par, SA*
L Pereyra 2010 *Ur, CHL*
N Perez 1968 *W*

RN Perez 1992 *F, F, Sp, R, F,* 1993 *Bra, Par, Ur, SA,* 1995 *Ur, R, It, F,* 1996 *US, Ur, C, SA, SA,* 1998 *Ur,* 1999 *I*
J Perez Cobo 1979 *NZ, NZ,* 1980 *Fj,* 1981 *E, E, C*
M Peri Brusa 1998 *CHL*
R Pesce 1958 *Ur, Per, CHL*
TA Petersen 1978 *E, It,* 1979 *NZ, NZ, A, A,* 1980 *Fj, Fj,* 1981 *E, E, C,* 1982 *F,* 1983 *WXV, A, A,* 1985 *F, F, Ur, CHL, Par, NZ, NZ,* 1986 *F, F, A*
AD Petrilli 2004 *SA,* 2005 *J*
J Petrone 1949 *F, F*
R Petti 1995 *Par, CHL*
M Pfister 1994 *SA, SA,* 1996 *F,* 1998 *R, Ur, J*
S Phelan 1997 *Ur, CHL, R, It,* 1998 *F, F, R, US, C, It,* 1999 *S, I, W, Sa, J, I, F,* 2000 *I, A, A, SA, E,* 2001 *NZ, It, W, S, NZ,* 2002 *Ur, Par, CHL, F, E, SA, A, It, I,* 2003 *CHL, Ur, F, SA, Fj, C, A, R*
A Phillips 1948 *OCC,* 1949 *F, F*
S Piccaluga 2009 *CHL, Ur*
JP Piccardo 1981 *E,* 1983 *CHL, Par, Ur*
A Pichot 1995 *A, R, It, F,* 1996 *Ur, F, F,* 1997 *It, F, A, A,* 1998 *F, F, R, It, F, W,* 1999 *W, W, S, I, W, Sa, J, I, F,* 2000 *I, A, A, SA, E,* 2001 *Ur, US, C, NZ, It, W, S, NZ,* 2002 *F, E, SA, A, It, I,* 2003 *Ur, C, A, R, I,* 2004 *F, I, SA,* 2005 *It, SA, S, It,* 2006 *W, W, NZ, CHL, Ur, E, F,* 2007 *W, F, Nm, I, S, SA, F*
G Pimentel 1971 *Bra*
R Pineo 1954 *F*
E Pittinari 1991 *Ur, Par, Bra*
E Poggi 1965 *JSB, OCC, OCC, CHL,* 1966 *SAG,* 1967 *Ur,* 1969 *Ur*
C Pollano 1927 *GBR*
S Ponce 2007 *CHL*
R Pont Lezica 1951 *Ur, Bra, CHL*
H Porta 1971 *CHL, Bra, Par, Ur,* 1972 *SAG, SAG,* 1973 *R, R, Ur, Bra, CHL, I, S,* 1974 *F, F,* 1975 *F, F,* 1976 *W, NZ, NZ,* 1977 *F, F,* 1978 *E, It,* 1979 *NZ, NZ, A, A,* 1980 *WXV, Fj, Fj,* 1981 *E, E, C,* 1982 *F, F, Sp,* 1983 *A, A,* 1985 *F, F, Ur, CHL, Par, NZ, NZ,* 1986 *F, F, A,* 1987 *Fj, It, NZ, Sp, A, A,* 1990 *I, E, S*
O Portillo 1995 *Par, CHL,* 1997 *Par, CHL*
J Posse 1977 *Par*
S Posse 1991 *Par,* 1993 *Bra, CHL, Ur*
C Promanzio 1995 *C,* 1996 *Ur, F, F, E,* 1997 *E, E, NZ, Ur,* 1998 *R, J*
U Propato 1956 *OCC*
L Proto 2010 *Ur, CHL*
A Puccio 1979 *CHL, Par, Bra*
M Puigdeval 1964 *Ur, Bra*
J Pulido 1960 *F*

JC Queirolo 1964 *Ur, Bra, CHL*
G Quesada 1996 *US, Ur, C, SA, E,* 1997 *E, E, NZ, NZ,* 1998 *F, R, US, C, It,* 1999 *W, S, I, W, Sa, J, I, F,* 2000 *I, SA, E,* 2001 *NZ, It, NZ,* 2002 *F, E, SA,* 2003 *F, SA, Ur, C, Nm, R, I*
E Quetglas 1965 *CHL*
G Quinones 2004 *Ur, Ven*

R Raimundez 1959 *JSB, JSB*
C Ramallo 1979 *Ur, CHL, Par*
S Ratcliff 1936 *CHL*
F Rave 1997 *Par*
M Reggiardo 1996 *Ur, F, F, E,* 1997 *E, E, NZ, NZ, R, F, A, A,* 1998 *F, F, R, US, Ur, C, It, W,* 1999 *W, W, S, I, W, Sa, J, I, F,* 2000 *I, SA,* 2001 *NZ, It, W, S, NZ,* 2002 *F, E, SA, A, It, I,* 2003 *F, SA, Fj, US, Ur, A, Nm, I*
A Reid 1910 *GBR*
C Reyes 1927 *GBR, GBR, GBR*
M Ricci 1987 *Sp*
A Riganti 1927 *GBR, GBR, GBR*
MA Righentini 1989 *NZ*
J Rios 1960 *F, F*
I Risman 2009 *Ur*
G Rivero 1996 *Ur, US, Ur*
G Roan 2009 *CHL, Ur,* 2010 *Ur, CHL*
T Roan 2007 *CHL,* 2008 *CHL*
F Robson 1927 *GBR*
M Roby 1992 *Sp,* 1993 *J*
A Rocca 1989 *US,* 1990 *C, US, C, E,* 1991 *Ur, Bra*
O Rocha 1974 *F, F*
D Rodriguez 1998 *J, Par, CHL, Ur*
D Rodriguez 2002 *Ur, Par, CHL*
EE Rodriguez 1979 *NZ, NZ, A, A,* 1980 *WXV, Fj, Fj,* 1981 *E, E, C,* 1983 *WXV, A, A*
F Rodriguez 2007 *CHL*
M Rodríguez 2009 *E, W, S,* 2010 *S, S, F, It, F, I,* 2011 *W, E, R, S, Geo, NZ*
A Rodriguez Jurado 1927 *GBR, GBR, GBR, GBR,* 1932 *JSB, JSB,* 1936 *CHL, CHL*
M Rodriguez Jurado 1971 *SAG, OCC, CHL, Bra, Par, Ur*
A Rodriguez-Jurado 1965 *JSB, OCC, OCC, CHL,* 1966 *SAG, SAG,* 1968 *W, W,* 1969 *S, CHL,* 1970 *I,* 1971 *SAG,* 1973 *R, Par, Bra, CHL, I, S,* 1974 *F, F,* 1975 *F, F*
L Roldan 2001 *Ur, C*
AS Romagnoli 2004 *CHL, Ur, Ven*
R Roncero 1998 *J,* 2002 *Ur, Par, CHL,* 2003 *Fj, US, Nm, R,* 2004 *W, W, NZ, F, I,* 2005 *It, SA, S, It,* 2006 *W, W, NZ,* 2007 *W, F, Nm, I, S, SA, F,* 2008 *It, SA, F, It, I,* 2009 *E, E, E, W, S,* 2010 *S, S, F, It, F, I,* 2011 *W, E, R, S, NZ*
S Rondinelli 2005 *Sa*
T Rosati 2011 *CHL, Ur*
S Rosatti 1977 *Par, CHL*
M Rospide 2003 *Par, CHL, Ur*
F Rossi 1991 *Ur, Par, Bra,* 1998 *F*
D Rotondo 1997 *Par, CHL*
MA Ruiz 1997 *NZ, CHL, R, It, F, A, A,* 1998 *F, F, R, US, Ur, C, J, It, F, W,* 1999 *W, Sa, J, F,* 2002 *Ur, Par, CHL*

JE Saffery 1910 *GBR*
CMS Sainz Trapaga 1979 *Ur, Par, Bra*
A Salinas 1954 *F,* 1956 *OCC,* 1958 *Ur, CHL,* 1960 *F, F*
S Salvat 1987 *Ur, Fj, It,* 1988 *F,* 1989 *It, NZ,* 1990 *C, US, C, E, E,* 1991 *Ur, Par, Bra,* 1992 *Sp, F,* 1993 *Bra, CHL, Par, Ur, SA, SA,* 1994 *SA, SA,* 1995 *Ur, C, A, A, E, Sa, It, Par, CHL, Ur, R, It, F*
T Salzman 1936 *BI, CHL, CHL*
M Sambucetti 2001 *Ur, US, C,* 2002 *Ur, CHL,* 2003 *Par, CHL, Fj,* 2005 *It, Sa,* 2009 *W*
HA San Martin 2009 *W, S*
FN Sanchez 2010 *Ur, CHL,* 2011 *R*
T Sanderson 1932 *JSB*
D Sanes 1985 *CHL, Par,* 1986 *F, F,* 1987 *Ur, Par, CHL,* 1989 *Bra, CHL, Ur*
EJ Sanguinetti 1975 *Ur, Par, CHL,* 1978 *It,* 1979 *A,* 1982 *F, F, Sp*
G Sanguinetti 1979 *Ur, CHL, Par, Bra*
J Sansot 1948 *OCC*
M Sansot 1975 *F, F,* 1976 *W, NZ, NZ,* 1977 *Bra, CHL,* 1978 *E, It,* 1979 *NZ, NZ, A, A,* 1980 *WXV, Fj,* 1983 *WXV*
Jm Santamarina 1991 *NZ, NZ, CHL, A, W, Sa,* 1992 *F, Sp, R, F,* 1993 *J, J,* 1994 *US, S, US,* 1995 *A, A, E, Sa, It, Ur, R, It, F*
J Santiago 1948 *OCC,* 1952 *I, I*
JR Sanz 1973 *Par, Ur, Bra, CHL,* 1974 *F, F,* 1977 *F, F*
S Sanz 2003 *US,* 2004 *CHL, Ven,* 2005 *It, Sa,* 2007 *CHL*
M Sarandon 1948 *OCC, OCC,* 1949 *F, F,* 1951 *Ur, Bra, CHL,* 1952 *I, I,* 1954 *F*
J Sartori 1979 *CHL, Par, Bra*
R Sauze 1983 *Par*
FW Saywer 1910 *GBR*
MA Scelzo 1996 *US, SA,* 1997 *R, It, F, A,* 1998 *F, US, Ur, C, CHL, F,* 1999 *I, Sa, I, F,* 2000 *I, A, A,* 2003 *F, F, Fj, Ur, C, Nm, R, I,* 2005 *SA, S, It,* 2006 *W, W, NZ, CHL, Ur, E, It, F,* 2007 *W, F, Nm, I, S, SA,* 2009 *E, W, S,* 2010 *S, S, F, It, F, I,* 2011 *W, E, R, S, Geo, NZ*
F Schacht 1989 *Bra, CHL, Par, Ur, US,* 1990 *C*
E Scharemberg 1961 *CHL, Bra, Ur,* 1964 *Ur, Bra,* 1965 *Rho, JSB, OCC, OCC,* 1967 *Ur, CHL*
AM Schiavio 1983 *CHL, Ur,* 1986 *A,* 1987 *Fj, It, NZ*
E Schiavio 1936 *BI, CHL, CHL*
H Schierano 2011 *CHL, Ur*
R Schmidt 1960 *F, F, F,* 1961 *Bra,* 1964 *Ur,* 1965 *JSB*
G Schmitt 1964 *Ur, CHL*
M Schusterman 2003 *Par, Fj,* 2004 *W, W, NZ, F,* 2005 *It, It, SA, S,* 2006 *W, CHL, Ur, E,* 2007 *I, It, Geo*
AA Scolni 1983 *CHL, Par, Ur,* 1985 *F,* 1987 *Sp, A,* 1988 *F, F, F, F,* 1989 *NZ, US,* 1990 *C, US, E, E, I, E, S*
J Seaton 1968 *W, W,* 1969 *Ur, CHL*
R Seaton 1967 *Ur, CHL*
LV Senatore 2008 *Ur, CHL,* 2011 *Geo, NZ*
H Senillosa 2002 *Ur, Par, CHL,* 2003 *Par, CHL, Ur, F, SA, Fj, US, Nm, R,* 2004 *CHL, Ur, Ven, W, W, NZ, F, I,* 2005 *It, It,* 2006 *CHL, It, F,* 2007 *I, I, F, Geo, Nm, I, S, F,* 2008 *It*

R Serra 1927 *GBR, GBR, GBR*
F Serra Miras 2003 *CHL*, 2005 *J*, 2006 *W, CHL, Ur*, 2007 *I, It, W, Nm*, 2008 *S*
C Serrano 1978 *It*, 1980 *Fj*, 1983 *CHL, Par, Ur*
R Sharpe 1948 *OCC*
HL Silva 1965 *JSB, OCC*, 1967 *Ur, CHL*, 1968 *W, W*, 1969 *S, S, Ur, CHL*, 1970 *I, I*, 1971 *SAG, SAG, OCC, OCC, Ur*, 1978 *E*, 1979 *NZ, NZ, A, A*, 1980 *WXV*
R Silva 1998 *J*
F Silvestre 1988 *F*, 1989 *Bra, Par, Ur, US*, 1990 *C, US*
D Silvetti 1993 *J*
J Simes 1989 *Bra, CHL*, 1990 *C, US*, 1993 *J, J*, 1996 *Ur, F, F, US, C*
HG Simon 1991 *NZ, NZ, A, W, Sa*
E Simone 1996 *US, SA, SA, E*, 1997 *E, E, NZ, NZ, R, F, A, A*, 1998 *F, F, US, Ur, C, J, It, F, W*, 1999 *W, S, I, W, Sa, J, I, F*, 2000 *I, SA*, 2001 *Ur, US, It*, 2002 *Ur, CHL*
A Smidt 2008 *CHL*, 2010 *Ur, CHL*
A Soares-Gache 1978 *It*, 1979 *NZ, NZ*, 1981 *C*, 1982 *F, Sp*, 1983 *WXV, A, A*, 1987 *Sp, A, A*, 1988 *F*
T Solari 1996 *Ur, C, SA*, 1997 *E, E, NZ, NZ*
F Soler 1996 *Ur, F, F, SA, SA*, 1997 *E, E, NZ, NZ, Ur, R, It, F*, 1998 *F, F, R, US, C, It, W*, 2001 *Ur, US*, 2002 *Ur, Par, CHL*
JS Soler Valls 1989 *It, Bra, Par, Ur*
H Solveira 1951 *Ur*
J Sommer 1927 *GBR*
E Sorhaburu 1958 *Ur, Per*, 1960 *F*, 1961 *CHL, Ur*
E Spain 1965 *JSB, OCC, OCC, CHL*, 1967 *Ur, CHL*
PL Sporleder 1990 *I, E, S*, 1991 *NZ, NZ, CHL, A, W, Sa*, 1992 *F, F, Sp, Sp, R, F*, 1993 *J, J, Bra, CHL, Par, Ur, SA, SA*, 1994 *US, S, S, US, SA, SA*, 1995 *A, A, E, Sa, It*, 1996 *Ur, F, F, Ur, C, SA, SA, E*, 1997 *E, E, NZ, NZ, Par, Ur, R, It, F, A, A*, 1998 *F, R, US, Ur, C, Ur, It, F, W*, 1999 *W, W, J*, 2002 *Ur, Par, CHL, It, I*, 2003 *Par, CHL, Ur, F, Fj, US, Nm, R*
J Stanfield 1932 *JSB*
J Stewart 1932 *JSB, JSB*
BM Stortoni 1998 *J, Par*, 2001 *Ur, US, C, NZ, It, NZ*, 2002 *Ur, Par, CHL*, 2003 *F, Fj, US*, 2005 *It, It, S, It*, 2007 *I*, 2008 *S, S, It, SA, F, It, I*
J Stuart 2007 *CHL*, 2008 *S, It*
M Sugasti 1995 *Par, CHL*
W Sutton 1936 *CHL*
C Swain 1948 *OCC*, 1949 *F, F*, 1951 *Ur, Bra, CHL*, 1952 *I, I*

J Tagliabue 1936 *CHL, CHL*
L Tahier 1964 *Ur, CHL*
F Talbot 1936 *BI*, 1938 *CHL*
H Talbot 1936 *BI, CHL, CHL*, 1938 *CHL*
HF Talbot 1910 *GBR*
A Tejeda 2008 *S, S, It*
RE Tejerizo 2011 *CHL, Ur*
EG Teran 1977 *Bra, Ur, Par, CHL*, 1979 *CHL, Par, Bra*
G Teran 1988 *F*
MJ Teran 1991 *NZ, NZ, CHL, A, W, Sa*, 1992 *F, Sp, R, F*, 1993 *J, J, Ur, SA, SA*, 1994 *US, S, S, US, SA, SA*, 1995 *A, A, E, Sa, It, Ur, R, It, F*
FN Tetaz Chaparro 2010 *CHL*
GP Tiesi 2004 *SA*, 2005 *J, It, Sa*, 2006 *W, W, NZ, CHL, Ur, E*, 2007 *Geo, Nm, SA*, 2008 *S, S, F, It*, 2009 *E, E, E, W, S*, 2010 *S, S, F, It, F, I*, 2011 *E*
FJ Todeschini 1998 *R, Ur*, 2005 *J, It, It, S*, 2006 *W, W, NZ, CHL, Ur, E, It, F*, 2007 *I, W, Geo, Nm*, 2008 *S, S*
A Tolomei 1991 *Par, Bra*, 1993 *Bra, CHL, Par*
N Tompkins 1948 *OCC*, 1949 *F, F*, 1952 *I, I*
JA Topping 1938 *CHL*
E Torello 1983 *Par*, 1989 *CHL*
F Torino 1927 *GBR, GBR*
NC Tozer 1932 *JSB, JSB*
AA Travaglini 1967 *Ur, CHL*, 1968 *W*, 1969 *S, S*, 1970 *I, I*, 1971 *SAG, SAG, OCC, OCC*, 1972 *SAG, SAG*, 1973 *R, Par, Ur, Bra, CHL, I, S*, 1974 *F, F*, 1975 *F, F*, 1976 *W, NZ, NZ*
G Travaglini 1978 *E, It*, 1979 *NZ, NZ, A, A*, 1980 *WXV, Fj, Fj*, 1981 *E, E*, 1982 *F, F, Sp*, 1983 *WXV, A*, 1987 *Ur, Fj, It, NZ*
R Travaglini 1996 *US, Ur, C*, 1997 *NZ, R, F*, 1998 *Ur, C*
J Trucco 1977 *Bra, Ur, Par, CHL*
A Turner 1932 *JSB, JSB*
FA Turnes 1985 *F, F, Ur, NZ, NZ*, 1986 *F, F, A, A*, 1987 *Ur, Fj, NZ, Sp, A, A*, 1988 *F, F, F, F*, 1989 *It, NZ, NZ*, 1997 *Ur, F, A, A*

G Ugartemendia 1991 *Ur*, 1993 *J, CHL, Par, Ur, SA, SA*, 1994 *US, SA, SA*, 1997 *Ur*, 1998 *Par*, 2000 *E*
M Urbano 1991 *Ur, Bra*, 1995 *Par, CHL, R, It, F*
B Urdapilleta 2007 *CHL*, 2008 *Ur, SA, CHL*, 2009 *W*, 2010 *Ur*
EM Ure 1980 *WXV, Fj, Fj*, 1981 *E, E*, 1982 *F, F, Sp*, 1983 *A*, 1985 *F, F, NZ, NZ*, 1986 *F, F, A*
J Uriarte 1986 *A*, 1987 *Par*

E Valesani 1986 *A, A*
MR Valesani 1989 *It, NZ, NZ, CHL, Par, Ur, US*, 1990 *C, US, C*
T Vallejos 2011 *Geo*
GB Varela 1976 *W, NZ, NZ*, 1977 *F, F*, 1979 *Ur, CHL*
L Varela 1961 *CHL, Bra, Ur*
F Varella 1960 *F*
GM Varone 1982 *F*
C Vazquez 1927 *GBR, GBR, GBR*
F Vega 2009 *CHL, Ur*
A Velazquez 1971 *CHL, Par*
R Ventura 1975 *Ur, Bra, CHL*, 1977 *Bra, Ur*, 1978 *It*, 1979 *Ur, CHL, Par*, 1983 *CHL, Par, Ur*
E Verardo 1958 *CHL*, 1959 *JSB, JSB*, 1964 *Ur, Bra, CHL*, 1967 *Ur, CHL*
N Vergallo 2005 *Sa*, 2006 *CHL, Ur*, 2007 *I, I, CHL*, 2008 *S, S, It, SA, F, It, I*, 2009 *E*, 2010 *F, It, F, I*, 2011 *W, E, R, S, Geo, NZ*
AV Vernet Basualdo 2004 *SA*, 2005 *J*, 2006 *It*, 2007 *I, Geo, Nm, I, F*, 2008 *SA, It*, 2009 *E, E, S*
G Veron 1997 *Par*
M Viazzo 2010 *Ur, CHL*
J Vibart 1960 *F*
H Vidou 1987 *Par*, 1990 *C, US, E, E*, 1991 *NZ*
H Vidou 1960 *F*, 1961 *Bra*
C Viel Temperley 1993 *Bra, CHL, Par, Ur*, 1994 *US, S, S, US, SA, SA*, 1995 *Ur, C, A, A, E, Sa, It, Par, Ur, R, It, F*, 1996 *SA*, 1997 *E, NZ*
E Vila 1975 *Ur, Par, CHL*
JJ Villar 2001 *Ur, US, C*, 2002 *Par, CHL*
D Villen 1998 *J, Par*
M Viola 1993 *Bra*
J Virasoro 1973 *R, R, Ur, Bra, CHL, S*
JL Visca 1985 *Par*

J Walther 1971 *OCC*
M Walther 1967 *Ur, CHL*, 1968 *W, W*, 1969 *S, S, Ur, CHL*, 1970 *I, I*, 1971 *SAG, OCC, OCC*, 1973 *Bra, CHL*, 1974 *F, F*
WA Watson 1910 *GBR*
W Weiss 2011 *Ur*
F Werner 1996 *US*, 1997 *Ur*
Wessek 1960 *F*
R Wilkins 1936 *CHL, CHL*
J Wittman 1971 *SAG, SAG, OCC, OCC, Ur*, 1972 *SAG, SAG*, 1973 *R*

L Yanez 1965 *Rho, JSB, OCC, OCC, CHL*, 1966 *SAG, SAG*, 1968 *W, W*, 1969 *S, S, Ur, CHL*, 1970 *I, I*, 1971 *SAG, OCC, OCC, Ur*
EP Yanguela 1956 *OCC*
M Yanguela 1987 *It*
B Yustini 1954 *F*, 1956 *OCC*

R Zanero 1990 *C*
E Zapiola 1998 *Par*
A Zappa 1927 *GBR*

AUSTRALIA

AUSTRALIA'S 2010–11 TEST RECORD

OPPONENTS	DATE	VENUE	RESULT
New Zealand	30 Oct	N	**Won** 26–24
Wales	6 Nov	A	**Won** 25–16
England	13 Nov	A	**Lost** 18–35
Italy	20 Nov	A	**Won** 32–14
France	27 Nov	A	**Won** 59–16
Samoa	17 Jul	H	**Lost** 23–32
South Africa	23 Jul	H	**Won** 39–20
New Zealand	6 Aug	A	**Lost** 14–30
South Africa	13 Aug	A	**Won** 14–9
New Zealand	27 Aug	H	**Won** 25–20
Italy	11 Sep	N	**Won** 32–6
Ireland	17 Sep	N	**Lost** 6–15
USA	23 Sep	N	**Won** 67–5
Russia	1 Oct	N	**Won** 68–22
South Africa	9 Oct	N	**Won** 11–9
New Zealand	16 Oct	A	**Lost** 6–20
Wales	21 Oct	N	**Won** 21–8

WALLABIES HAVE TO SETTLE FOR THIRD

Hannah Johnston/Getty Images

Australia finished Rugby World Cup in grand style, picking up the bronze medal by beating Wales.

They went into the tournament as the reigning Tri-Nations champions, but Robbie Deans' exciting but erratic Australia side were unable to reach the World Cup final for what would have been a record fourth time, crashing against the rocks of a dominant and deadly All Blacks' display at the last four stage in Auckland.

The Wallabies had already flattered to deceive in the pool stages, slipping to a shock 15–6 defeat to Ireland, and when they came up against New Zealand in the semi-final at Eden Park, they were outmuscled and ultimately outplayed by the host nation in a 20–6 reverse.

The Australians had beaten their old trans-Tasman rivals at the semi-final stage in Dublin back in 1991 and in Sydney in 2003, but once Ma'a Nonu powered over the line for the All Blacks after just five minutes for what proved to be the only try of the contest, their hopes of a hat-trick of famous victories evaporated.

"The All Blacks showed tonight they are more than capable of winning the final," conceded Deans after the final whistle. "The intent is there, they are an experienced group. For the nucleus of them it is their third attempt. They are well versed, they are hungry and they have a lot of support around them. They will take a lot of stopping from here. Good luck to New Zealand in the final. They have worked hard for this opportunity.

"They made it difficult all night for us to create any momentum. We were inaccurate in the things we wanted to do, where the All Blacks were very accurate. We were still in the game at half-time, but we weren't able to get across the chalk. That was the defining element.

"There's no doubt this whole playing group will be better for the experience they've had. There will be some who may be lucky enough to get to another World Cup. There's clearly some who won't and that's what makes a World Cup what it is. A lot of very good players never get to a World Cup, and that's why players and teams and nations are so desperate to make the most of it."

The tournament began for the Australians with a potential banana skin in the shape of Italy. The Azzurri had never beaten the Wallabies in 13 previous attempts but, despite a sluggish first-half performance, Australia found a greater sense of urgency after the restart and tries from Ben Alexander, Adam Ashley-Cooper, James O'Connor and Digby Ioane wrapped up a morale-boosting 32–6 victory.

Six days later it was the Irish in Auckland for what was billed as the match to decide the winners of Pool C, but if Australia thought Ireland would buckle at Eden Park as the Italians had in the North Harbour Stadium, they were sorely mistaken.

Although the scoreline was locked at 6–6 midway through the first half courtesy of two O'Connor penalties, a belligerent Irish pack began to take control of proceedings after the break, providing the platform for three successful penalties from Jonathan Sexton and Ronan O'Gara (2) and the Wallabies were beaten 15–6.

"The Irish did well to spoil our ball, we couldn't get any momentum and we played some dumb footy," admitted second row and captain James Horwill after the game. "We weren't good enough. We didn't provide a clean enough platform for our backs and they did well to spoil us, and they played well and they deserved their win."

The result was a body blow, but Deans rallied his troops for the two remaining pool games and the team responded with a 67–5 win over the USA in Wellington followed by a 68–22 defeat of Russia in Nelson. The damage, however, had already been done by the Ireland defeat, and as Pool C runners-up Australia had to face defending champions South Africa in the quarter-finals.

The game was played in the Wellington Regional Stadium and proved to be a classic example of a smash and grab raid by the Wallabies. The Springboks comprehensively dominated both territory and possession during the match, but it was Deans' side that took their scoring opportunities. Horwill crashed over for the only try of the contest after 10 minutes, but from then on it was a battle between the boot of O'Connor and Morné Steyn for South Africa. O'Connor stretched the lead with a 16th-minute penalty, but Steyn replied with two penalties of his own either side of half-time and a subsequent drop-goal to edge the champions into a 9–8 lead.

The Australians remained under huge pressure, but the Springboks made a fatal error at the lineout late on, dragging down the jumper in the air, and O'Connor stepped forward to slot the resulting 71st-minute penalty and give the Wallabies an unlikely and dramatic 11–9 victory.

"What you saw out there was the most experienced World Cup side in the world really turn the screws on the youngest," said Deans. "Our boys came of age in terms of the way they accepted that challenge and stood up to it. We saw an epic World Cup encounter. Different, but that's what makes this game what it is.

"If you look at our experience against the Irish, I've got no doubt that if we had got through that encounter with relative ease we would have suffered against South Africa because we wouldn't have been as well prepared. They were as mentally prepared today as they could be because of the Irish defeat."

The semi-final in truth rarely threatened to become a true contest as the All Blacks got on the front foot at Eden Park almost immediately, and once Nonu had scored Australia were forced to play catch-up for the remaining 75 minutes of the contest.

A 15th-minute penalty from O'Connor after New Zealand were penalised for not releasing cut the deficit to 8–3, and a drop-goal after 31 minutes from fly-half Quade Cooper again reduced the arrears to five points, but that was as close as the Australians were to get to their old rivals. The Wallabies failed to trouble the scorers in the second half, while two penalties from Piri Weepu effortlessly stretched the All Black advantage, and at full-time the Kiwis were comfortable 20–6 winners.

"We're pretty down about losing a semi-final in a World Cup," admitted Cooper after the game. "For a lot of the boys it was their first World Cup, but I'm sure it won't be their last. Everyone's looking to the future now because we can't get this game back, but we can look forward to what's to come.

"It was a very tough night. That showed by the intensity and accuracy that they brought to the game. Right across the board they were making it a personal contest between each player and at the end of the day they came out on top."

All that remained was the Bronze Final with Wales in Auckland, and unsurprisingly Deans made wholesale changes for the clash, drafting in eight new players, including an entirely new front row contingent of James Slipper, Tatafu Polota-Nau and Salesi Ma'afu, into his starting XV.

The Wallabies had not won at Eden Park since 1986, and although the opposition was Wales rather than New Zealand they laid that ghost to rest with an entertaining 21–18 win courtesy of tries from Berrick Barnes and Ben McCalman, a conversion and two penalties from O'Connor and a Barnes drop-goal.

"We came to the tournament to win obviously, but we weren't good enough by some distance," Deans said as the Wallabies prepared to head home. "It's not easy, the blokes were pretty disappointed [after the semi-final], and the third place play-off is not the match of their preference. But it's still an opportunity to represent your country, and you saw tonight from both sides the pride they have in that."

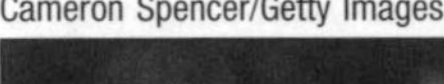

David Pocock had a great Rugby World Cup, culminating in his selection on the shortlist for IRB Player of the Year.

AUSTRALIA INTERNATIONAL STATISTICS

MATCH RECORDS UP TO 31 OCTOBER 2011

MOST CONSECUTIVE TEST WINS

10 1991 *Arg, WS, W, I, NZ, E,* 1992 *S* 1,2, *NZ* 1,2
10 1998 *NZ 3, Fj, Tg, Sm, F, E 2,* 1999 *I* 1,2, *E, SA 1*
10 1999 *NZ 2, R, I 3, US, W, SA 3, F,* 2000 *Arg 1,2,SA 1*

MOST CONSECUTIVE TESTS WITHOUT DEFEAT

Matches	Wins	Draws	Period
10	10	0	1991 to 1992
10	10	0	1998 to 1999
10	10	0	1999 to 2000

MOST POINTS IN A MATCH

BY THE TEAM

Pts	Opponents	Venue	Year
142	Namibia	Adelaide	2003
92	Spain	Madrid	2001
91	Japan	Lyons	2007
90	Romania	Brisbane	2003
76	England	Brisbane	1998
74	Canada	Brisbane	1996
74	Tonga	Canberra	1998
74	W Samoa	Sydney	2005
73	W Samoa	Sydney	1994
69	Italy	Melbourne	2005
68	Russia	Nelson	2011
67	United States	Brisbane	1990
67	United States	Wellington	2011

BY A PLAYER

Pts	Player	Opponents	Venue	Year
42	M S Rogers	Namibia	Adelaide	2003
39	M C Burke	Canada	Brisbane	1996
30	E J Flatley	Romania	Brisbane	2003
29	S A Mortlock	South Africa	Melbourne	2000
29	J D O'Connor	France	Paris	2010
28	M P Lynagh	Argentina	Brisbane	1995
27	M J Giteau	Fiji	Montpellier	2007
25	M C Burke	Scotland	Sydney	1998
25	M C Burke	France	Cardiff	1999
25	M C Burke	British/Irish Lions	Melbourne	2001
25	E J Flatley*	Ireland	Perth	2003
25	C E Latham	Namibia	Adelaide	2003
24	M P Lynagh	United States	Brisbane	1990
24	M P Lynagh	France	Brisbane	1990
24	M C Burke	New Zealand	Melbourne	1998
24	M C Burke	South Africa	Twickenham	1999

** includes a penalty try*

MOST TRIES IN A MATCH

BY THE TEAM

Tries	Opponents	Venue	Year
22	Namibia	Adelaide	2003
13	South Korea	Brisbane	1987
13	Spain	Madrid	2001
13	Romania	Brisbane	2003
13	Japan	Lyons	2007
12	United States	Brisbane	1990
12	Wales	Brisbane	1991
12	Tonga	Canberra	1998
12	Samoa	Sydney	2005
11	Western Samoa	Sydney	1994
11	England	Brisbane	1998
11	Italy	Melbourne	2005
11	United States	Wellington	2011

BY A PLAYER

Tries	Player	Opponents	Venue	Year
5	C E Latham	Namibia	Adelaide	2003
4	G Cornelsen	New Zealand	Auckland	1978
4	D I Campese	United States	Sydney	1983
4	J S Little	Tonga	Canberra	1998
4	C E Latham	Argentina	Brisbane	2000
4	L D Tuqiri	Italy	Melbourne	2005

MOST CONVERSIONS IN A MATCH

BY THE TEAM

Cons	Opponents	Venue	Year
16	Namibia	Adelaide	2003
12	Spain	Madrid	2001
11	Romania	Brisbane	2003
10	Japan	Lyons	2007
9	Canada	Brisbane	1996
9	Fiji	Parramatta	1998
9	Russia	Nelson	2011
8	Italy	Rome	1988
8	United States	Brisbane	1990
7	Canada	Sydney	1985
7	Tonga	Canberra	1998
7	Samoa	Sydney	2005
7	Italy	Melbourne	2005
7	Fiji	Canberra	2010

BY A PLAYER

Cons	Player	Opponents	Venue	Year
16	M S Rogers	Namibia	Adelaide	2003
11	E J Flatley	Romania	Brisbane	2003
10	M C Burke	Spain	Madrid	2001
9	M C Burke	Canada	Brisbane	1996
9	J A Eales	Fiji	Parramatta	1998
9	J D O'Connor	Russia	Nelson	2011
8	M P Lynagh	Italy	Rome	1988
8	M P Lynagh	United States	Brisbane	1990
7	M P Lynagh	Canada	Sydney	1985
7	S A Mortlock	Japan	Lyons	2007

MOST PENALTIES IN A MATCH

BY THE TEAM

Penalties	Opponents	Venue	Year
8	South Africa	Twickenham	1999
7	New Zealand	Sydney	1999
7	France	Cardiff	1999
7	Wales	Cardiff	2001
7	England	Twickenham	2008
6	New Zealand	Sydney	1984
6	France	Sydney	1986
6	England	Brisbane	1988
6	Argentina	Buenos Aires	1997
6	Ireland	Perth	1999
6	France	Paris	2000
6	British/Irish Lions	Melbourne	2001
6	New Zealand	Sydney	2004
6	Italy	Padua	2008
6	New Zealand	Sydney	2009
6	South Africa	Brisbane	2010
6	Italy	Florence	2010

BY A PLAYER

Penalties	Player	Opponents	Venue	Year
8	M C Burke	South Africa	Twickenham	1999
7	M C Burke	New Zealand	Sydney	1999
7	M C Burke	France	Cardiff	1999
7	M C Burke	Wales	Cardiff	2001
6	M P Lynagh	France	Sydney	1986
6	M P Lynagh	England	Brisbane	1988
6	D J Knox	Argentina	Buenos Aires	1997
6	M C Burke	France	Paris	2000
6	M C Burke	British/Irish Lions	Melbourne	2001
6	M J Giteau	England	Twickenham	2008
6	M J Giteau	New Zealand	Sydney	2009
6	B S Barnes	Italy	Florence	2010

MOST DROPPED GOALS IN A MATCH

BY THE TEAM

Drops	Opponents	Venue	Year
3	England	Twickenham	1967
3	Ireland	Dublin	1984
3	Fiji	Brisbane	1985

BY A PLAYER

Drops	Player	Opponents	Venue	Year
3	P F Hawthorne	England	Twickenham	1967
2	M G Ella	Ireland	Dublin	1984
2	D J Knox	Fiji	Brisbane	1985

MOST CAPPED PLAYERS

Caps	Player	Career Span
139	G M Gregan	1994 to 2007
110	G B Smith	2000 to 2009
102	S J Larkham	1996 to 2007
101	D I Campese	1982 to 1996
100	N C Sharpe	2002 to 2011
92	M J Giteau	2002 to 2011
86	J A Eales	1991 to 2001
86	J W C Roff	1995 to 2004
81	M C Burke	1993 to 2004
80	T J Horan	1989 to 2000
80	S A Mortlock	2000 to 2009
79	D J Wilson	1992 to 2000
79	P R Waugh	2000 to 2009
78	C E Latham	1998 to 2007
75	J S Little	1989 to 2000
75	R D Elsom	2005 to 2011
72	M P Lynagh	1984 to 1995
72	J A Paul	1998 to 2006
69	A K E Baxter	2003 to 2009
67	P N Kearns	1989 to 1999
67	D J Herbert	1994 to 2002
67	L D Tuqiri	2003 to 2008
65	S T Moore	2005 to 2011
63	N C Farr Jones	1984 to 1993
63	M J Cockbain	1997 to 2003
63	A P Ashley-Cooper	2005 to 2011
63	D J Vickerman	2002 to 2011
60	R S T Kefu	1997 to 2003
59	S P Poidevin	1980 to 1991

MOST CONSECUTIVE TESTS

Tests	Player	Span
62	J W C Roff	1996 to 2001
46	P N Kearns	1989 to 1995
44	G B Smith	2003 to 2006
42	D I Campese	1990 to 1995
37	P G Johnson	1959 to 1968

MOST TESTS AS CAPTAIN

Tests	Captain	Span
59	G M Gregan	2001 to 2007
55	J A Eales	1996 to 2001
36	N C Farr Jones	1988 to 1992
29	S A Mortlock	2006 to 2009
24	R D Elsom	2009 to 2011
19	A G Slack	1984 to 1987
16	J E Thornett	1962 to 1967
16	G V Davis	1969 to 1972

MOST POINTS IN TESTS

Points	Player	Tests	Career
911	M P Lynagh	72	1984 to 1995
878	M C Burke	81	1993 to 2004
684	M J Giteau	92	2002 to 2011
489	S A Mortlock	80	2000 to 2009
315	D I Campese	101	1982 to 1996
260	P E McLean	30	1974 to 1982
249*	J W Roff	86	1995 to 2004
200	C E Latham	78	1998 to 2007
199	J D O'Connor	36	2008 to 2011
187*	E J Flatley	38	1997 to 2005
173	J A Eales	86	1991 to 2001

** Roff and Flatley's totals include a penalty try*

MOST TRIES IN TESTS

Tries	Player	Tests	Career
64	D I Campese	101	1982 to 1996
40	C E Latham	78	1998 to 2007
31*	J W Roff	86	1995 to 2004
30	T J Horan	80	1989 to 2000
30	L D Tuqiri	67	2003 to 2008
30	D A Mitchell	58	2005 to 2011
29	M C Burke	81	1993 to 2004
29	S A Mortlock	80	2000 to 2009
29	M J Giteau	92	2002 to 2011
25	S J Larkham	102	1996 to 2007
24	B N Tune	47	1996 to 2006
22	A P Ashley-Cooper	63	2005 to 2011
21	J S Little	75	1989 to 2000

** Roff's total includes a penalty try*

MOST CONVERSIONS IN TESTS

Cons	Player	Tests	Career
140	M P Lynagh	72	1984 to 1995
104	M C Burke	81	1993 to 2004
103	M J Giteau	92	2002 to 2011
61	S A Mortlock	80	2000 to 2009
35	J D O'Connor	36	2008 to 2011
31	J A Eales	86	1991 to 2001
30	E J Flatley	38	1997 to 2005
27	P E McLean	30	1974 to 1982
27	M S Rogers	45	2002 to 2006
20	J W Roff	86	1995 to 2004
19	D J Knox	13	1985 to 1997

MOST PENALTY GOALS IN TESTS

Penalties	Player	Tests	Career
177	M P Lynagh	72	1984 to 1995
174	M C Burke	81	1993 to 2004
107	M J Giteau	92	2002 to 2011
74	S A Mortlock	80	2000 to 2009
62	P E McLean	30	1974 to 1982
34	J A Eales	86	1991 to 2001
34	E J Flatley	38	1997 to 2005
23	M C Roebuck	23	1991 to 1993
23	J D O'Connor	36	2008 to 2011

MOST DROPPED GOALS IN TESTS

Drops	Player	Tests	Career
9	P F Hawthorne	21	1962 to 1967
9	M P Lynagh	72	1984 to 1995
8	M G Ella	25	1980 to 1984
6	B S Barnes	36	2007 to 2011
4	P E McLean	30	1974 to 1982
4	M J Giteau	92	2002 to 2011

TRI-NATIONS RECORDS

RECORD	DETAIL	HOLDER	SET
Most points in season	162	in six matches	2010
Most tries in season	17	in six matches	2010
Highest score	49	49–0 v S Africa (h)	2006
Biggest win	49	49–0 v S Africa (h)	2006
Highest score conceded	61	22–61 v S Africa (a)	1997
Biggest defeat	45	8–53 v S Africa (a)	2008
Most appearances	48	G M Gregan	1996 to 2007
Most points in matches	271	M C Burke	1996 to 2004
Most points in season	72	M J Giteau	2009
Most points in match	24	M C Burke	v N Zealand (h) 1998
Most tries in matches	9	J W C Roff	1996 to 2003
	9	S A Mortlock	2000 to 2009
	9	L D Tuqiri	2003 to 2008
Most tries in season	4	S A Mortlock	2000
	4	J D O'Connor	2010
Most tries in match	2	B N Tune	v S Africa (h) 1997
	2	S J Larkham	v N Zealand (a) 1997
	2	M C Burke	v N Zealand (h) 1998
	2	J W C Roff	v S Africa (h) 1999
	2	S A Mortlock	v N Zealand (h) 2000
	2	C E Latham	v S Africa (h) 2002
	2	M J Giteau	v S Africa (h) 2006
	2	L D Tuqiri	v N Zealand (a) 2006
	2	M J Giteau	v S Africa (h) 2009
	2	J D O'Connor	v S Africa (a) 2010
Most cons in matches	36	M J Giteau	2003 to 2010
Most cons in season	12	S A Mortlock	2006
Most cons in match	5	S A Mortlock	v S Africa (h) 2006
Most pens in matches	65	M C Burke	1996 to 2004
Most pens in season	14	M C Burke	2001
	14	M J Giteau	2009
	14	M J Giteau	2010
Most pens in match	7	M C Burke	v N Zealand (h) 1999

MISCELLANEOUS RECORDS

RECORD	HOLDER	DETAIL
Longest Test Career	G M Cooke	1932–1948
Youngest Test Cap	B W Ford	18 yrs 90 days in 1957
Oldest Test Cap	A R Miller	38 yrs 113 days in 1967

CAREER RECORDS OF AUSTRALIAN INTERNATIONAL PLAYERS

(UP TO 31 OCTOBER 2011)

PLAYER BACKS :	DEBUT	CAPS	T	C	P	D	PTS
A P Ashley-Cooper	2005 v SA	63	22	0	0	0	110
B S Barnes	2007 v J	36	7	7	6	6	85
K J Beale	2009 v W	24	9	0	2	0	51
L Burgess	2008 v I	37	1	0	0	0	5
Q S Cooper	2008 v It	35	6	7	7	1	68
R W Davies	2011 v Sm	1	0	0	0	0	0
A S Fainga'a	2010 v NZ	13	2	0	0	0	10
S W Genia	2009 v NZ	33	5	0	0	0	25
M A Gerrard	2005 v It	24	9	0	0	0	45
M J Giteau	2002 v E	92	29	103	107	4	684
R G Horne	2010 v Fj	9	1	0	0	0	5
D A N Ioane	2007 v W	20	9	0	0	0	45
P J McCabe	2010 v It	11	2	0	0	0	10
D A Mitchell	2005 v SA	58	30	0	0	0	150
J D O'Connor	2008 v It	36	12	35	23	0	199
N J Phipps	2011 v Sm	3	0	0	0	0	0
L D Turner	2008 v F	14	3	0	0	0	15

FORWARDS:

B E Alexander	2008 v F	35	3	0	0	0	15
R N Brown	2008 v NZ	23	1	0	0	0	5
M D Chisholm	2004 v S	58	6	0	0	0	30
P J M Cowan	2009 v It	5	0	0	0	0	0
H Edmonds	2010 v Fj	4	0	0	0	0	0
R D Elsom	2005 v Sm	75	14	0	0	0	70
S M Fainga'a	2010 v Fj	16	0	0	0	0	0
S Higginbotham	2010 v F	10	0	0	0	0	0
M J Hodgson	2010 v Fj	6	0	0	0	0	0
J E Horwill	2007 v Fj	34	6	0	0	0	30
S M Kepu	2008 v It	14	0	0	0	0	0
R S L Ma'afu	2010 v Fj	13	1	0	0	0	5
B J McCalman	2010 v SA	20	2	0	0	0	10
S T Moore	2005 v Sm	65	5	0	0	0	25
D W Mumm	2008 v I	33	1	0	0	0	5
W L Palu	2006 v E	38	1	0	0	0	5
D W Pocock	2008 v NZ	39	4	0	0	0	20
S U T Polota-Nau	2005 v E	31	2	0	0	0	10
B A Robinson	2006 v SA	42	2	0	0	0	10
B S Robinson	2011 v Sm	1	0	0	0	0	0
U R Samo	2004 v S	15	2	0	0	0	10
N C Sharpe	2002 v F	100	7	0	0	0	35
R A Simmons	2010 v SA	15	0	0	0	0	0
J A Slipper	2010 v E	21	0	0	0	0	0
S Timani	2011 v Sm	1	0	0	0	0	0
D J Vickerman	2002 v F	63	0	0	0	0	0

AUSTRALIAN INTERNATIONAL PLAYERS (UP TO 31 OCTOBER 2011)

Note: Years given for International Championship matches are for second half of season; eg 1972 means season 1971–72. Years for all other matches refer to the actual year of the match. Entries in square brackets denote matches played in RWC Finals.

Abrahams, , A M F (NSW) 1967 NZ, 1968 NZ 1, 1969 W
Adams, N J (NSW) 1955 NZ 1
Adamson, R W (NSW) 1912 US
Alexander, B E (ACT) 2008 F1(R), 2(R), It, F3, 2009 It1(R), 2, F(R), NZ1(R), SA1(R), NZ2(t&R), SA2, 3, NZ3, 4, E, I, S, W, 2010 Fj, NZ4, W, E3, It, F, 2011 Sm, SA1, NZ1, SA2, NZ2, [It, I, US, SA, NZ, W(R)]
Allan, T (NSW) 1946 NZ 1, M, NZ 2, 1947 NZ 2, S, I, W, 1948 E, F, 1949 M 1, 2, 3, NZ 1, 2
Anderson, R P (NSW) 1925 NZ 1
Anlezark, E A (NSW) 1905 NZ
Armstrong, A R (NSW) 1923 NZ 1, 2
Ashley-Cooper, A P (ACT) 2005 SA4(R), 2007 W1, 2, Fj, SA1(R), NZ1, SA2, NZ2, [J, Fj, C, E], 2008 F1(R), 2, SA1, NZ1, 2, SA3, NZ3, 4, It, E, F3, 2009 It1(R), 2(t&R), F, NZ1, SA1, NZ2, SA2, 3, NZ3, 4, E, I, S, W, 2010 Fj, E2(R), I, SA1, NZ1, 2, SA2, 3, NZ3, NZ4, W, E3, It, F, 2011 Sm, SA1, NZ1, SA2, NZ2, [It, I, US, Ru, SA, NZ, W]
Austin, L R (NSW) 1963 E

Baker, R L (NSW) 1904 BI 1, 2
Baker, W H (NSW) 1914 NZ 1, 2, 3
Ballesty, J P (NSW) 1968 NZ 1, 2, F, I, S, 1969 W, SA 2, 3, 4,
Bannon, D P (NSW) 1946 M
Bardsley, E J (NSW) 1928 NZ 1, 3, M (R)
Barker, H S (NSW) 1952 Fj 1, 2, NZ 1, 2, 1953 SA 4, 1954 Fj 1, 2
Barnes, B S (Q, NSW) 2007 [J(R), W, Fj, E], 2008 I, F1, 2, SA1, NZ1, 2, SA2, NZ4(R), It, 2009 It1, 2, F, NZ1, SA1, NZ2, SA3, NZ3, 2010 E1, SA1(R), NZ1, SA3(R), NZ3(t&R), NZ4(R), W(R), E3(R), It, F, 2011 [US(R), Ru, SA(R), NZ(t&R), W]
Barnett, J T (NSW) 1907 NZ 1, 2, 3, 1908 W, 1909 E
Barry, M J (Q) 1971 SA 3
Bartholomeusz, M A (ACT) 2002 It (R)
Barton, R F D (NSW) 1899 BI 3
Batch, P G (Q) 1975 S, W, 1976 E, Fj 1, 2, 3, F 1, 2, 1978 W 1, 2, NZ 1, 2, 3, 1979 Arg 2
Batterham, R P (NSW) 1967 NZ, 1970 S
Battishall, B R (NSW) 1973 E
Baxter, A J (NSW) 1949 M 1, 2, 3, NZ 1, 2, 1951 NZ 1, 2, 1952 NZ 1, 2
Baxter, A K E (NSW) 2003 NZ 2(R), [Arg, R, I(R), S(R), NZ(R), E], 2004 S1, 2, E1, PI, NZ1, SA1, NZ2, SA2, S3, F, S4, E2, 2005 It, F1, SA1, 2, 3(R), NZ1, SA4, NZ2, F2, E, I(R), W(R), 2006 E1(R), 2(R), I1(R), NZ1(R), SA1(R), NZ3(R), SA3(R), W, It, I2, S(R), 2007 Fj, SA1(R), NZ1(R), SA2(R), NZ2(R), [J, W(R), C, E(R)], 2008 I(R), F1, 2, SA1, NZ1, 2, SA2(R), 3(R), NZ3, 4, E, F3, W, 2009 It1, F, NZ1, SA1, NZ2
Baxter, T J (Q) 1958 NZ 3
Beale, K J (NSW) 2009 W(R), 2010 Fj, E1(R), I(R), NZ1(R), 2, SA2, 3, NZ3, NZ4, W, E3, It, F, 2011 Sm(R), SA1, NZ1, SA2, NZ2, [It, I, US, SA, W]
Beith, B McN (NSW) 1914 NZ 3, 1920 NZ 1, 2, 3
Bell, K R (Q) 1968 S
Bell, M D NSW) 1996 C
Bennett, W G (Q) 1931 M, 1933 SA 1, 2, 3,
Bermingham, J V (Q) 1934 NZ 1, 2, 1937 SA 1
Berne, J E (NSW) 1975 S
Besomo, K S (NSW) 1979 I 2
Betts, T N (Q) 1951 NZ 2, 3, 1954 Fj 2
Biilmann, R R (NSW) 1933 SA 1, 2, 3, 4
Birt, R S W (Q) 1914 NZ 2
Black, J W (NSW) 1985 C 1, 2, NZ, Fj 1
Blackwood, J G (NSW) 1922 M 1, NZ 1, 2, 3, 1923 M 1, NZ 1, 2, 3, 1924 NZ 1, 2, 3, 1925 NZ 1, 4, 1926 NZ 1, 2, 3, 1927 I, W, S, 1928 E, F
Blades, A T (NSW) 1996 S, I, W 3, 1997 NZ 1(R), E 1(R), SA 1(R), NZ 3, SA 2, Arg 1, 2, E 2, S, 1998 E 1, S 1, 2, NZ 1, SA 1, NZ 2, SA 2, NZ 3, Fj, WS, F, E 2, 1999 I 1(R), SA 2, NZ 2, [R, I 3, W, SA 3, F]
Blades, C D (NSW) 1997 E 1
Blake, R C (Q) 2006 E1, 2, NZ2, SA2, NZ3, SA3, W
Blair, M R (NSW) 1928 F, 1931 M, NZ
Bland, G V (NSW) 1928 NZ 3, M, 1932 NZ 1, 2, 3, 1933 SA 1, 2, 4, 5
Blomley, J (NSW) 1949 M 1, 2, 3, NZ 1, 2, 1950 BI 1, 2
Boland, S B (Q) 1899 BI 3, 4, 1903 NZ
Bond, G S G (ACT) 2001 SA 2(R), Sp (R), E (R), F, W
Bond, J H (NSW) 1920 NZ 1, 2, 3, 1921 NZ
Bondfield, C (NSW) 1925 NZ 2
Bonis, E T (Q) 1929 NZ 1, 2, 3, 1930 BI, 1931 M, NZ, 1932 NZ 1, 2, 3, 1933 SA 1, 2, 3, 4, 5, 1934 NZ 1, 2, 1936 NZ 1, 2, M, 1937 SA 1, 1938 NZ 1
Bonner, J E (NSW) 1922 NZ 1, 2, 3, 1923 M 1, 2, 3, 1924 NZ 1, 2
Bosler, J M (NSW) 1953 SA 1
Bouffler, R G (NSW) 1899 BI 3
Bourke, T K (Q) 1947 NZ 2
Bowden, R (NSW) 1926 NZ 4
Bowen, S (NSW) 1993 SA 1, 2, 3, 1995 [R], NZ 1, 2, 1996 C, NZ 1, SA 2
Bowers, A J A (NSW) 1923 M 2(R), 3, NZ, 3, 1925 NZ 1, 4, 1926 NZ 1, 1927 I
Bowman, T M (NSW) 1998 E 1, S 1, 2, NZ 1, SA 1, NZ 2, SA 2, NZ 3, Fj, WS, F, E 2, 1999 I 1, 2, SA 2, [US]
Boyce, E S (NSW) 1962 NZ 1, 2, 1964 NZ 1, 2, 3, 1965 SA 1, 2, 1966 W, S, 1967 E, I 1, F, I 2
Boyce, J S (NSW) 1962 NZ 3, 4, 5, 1963 E, SA 1, 2, 3, 4, 1964 NZ 1, 3, 1965 SA 1, 2
Boyd, A (NSW) 1899 BI 3
Boyd, A F McC (Q) 1958 M 1
Brass, J E (NSW) 1966 BI 2, W, S, 1967 E, I 1, F, I 2, NZ, 1968 NZ 1, F, I, S
Breckenridge, J W (NSW) 1925 NZ 2(R), 3, 1927 I, W, S, 1928 E, F, 1929 NZ 1, 2, 3, 1930 BI
Brial, M C (NSW) 1993 F 1(R), 2, 1996 W 1(R), 2, C, NZ 1, SA 1, NZ 2, SA 2, It, I, W 3, 1997 NZ 2
Bridle, O L (V) 1931 M, 1932 NZ 1, 2, 3, 1933 SA 3, 4, 5, 1934 NZ 1, 2, 1936 NZ 1, 2, M
Broad, E G (Q) 1949 M 1
Brockhoff, J D (NSW) 1949 M 2, 3, NZ 1, 2, 1950 BI 1, 2, 1951 NZ 2, 3
Brown, B R (Q) 1972 NZ 1, 3
Brown, J V (NSW) 1956 SA 1, 2, 1957 NZ 1, 2, 1958 W, I, E, S, F
Brown, R C (NSW) 1975 E 1, 2
Brown, R N (WF) 2008 NZ3(R), 4, It, E, W, 2009 It1, F, NZ1, SA1, NZ2, SA2, S(R), 2010 Fj, E1, 2, I, SA1, NZ1, 2, SA2, 3(R), NZ3(R), E3(R)
Brown, S W (NSW) 1953 SA 2, 3, 4
Bryant, H (NSW) 1925 NZ 1, 3, 4
Buchan, A J (NSW) 1946 NZ 1, 2, 1947 NZ 1, 2, S, I, W, 1948 E, F, 1949 M 3
Buchanan, P N (NSW) 1923 M 2(R), 3
Bull, D (NSW) 1928 M
Buntine, H (NSW) 1923 NZ 1(R), 1924 NZ 2
Burdon, A (NSW) 1903 NZ, 1904 BI 1, 2, 1905 NZ
Burge, A B (NSW) 1907 NZ 3, 1908 W
Burge, P H (NSW) 1907 NZ 1, 2, 3
Burge, R (NSW) 1928 NZ 1, 2, 3(R), M (R)
Burgess, L (NSW) 2008 I, F1, 2, SA1, NZ1, 2, 4, It, E, F3, W, 2009 It1, 2, F, NZ1, SA1, NZ2, SA2, NZ3(R), S(R), W(R), 2010 Fj, E1, I, NZ1(R), SA3(R), NZ3(R), NZ4(R), W(R), E3(R), It, F(R), 2011 NZ2(R), [It(R), US(R), Ru, W(R)]
Burke, B T (NSW) 1988 S (R)

Burke, C T (NSW) 1946 NZ 2, 1947 NZ 1, 2, S, I, W, 1948 E, F, 1949 M 2, 3, NZ 1, 2, 1950 BI 1, 2, 1951 NZ 1, 2, 3, 1953 SA 2, 3, 4, 1954 Fj 1, 1955 NZ 1, 2, 3, 1956 SA 1, 2,
Burke, M C (NSW) 1993 SA 3(R), F 1, 1994 I 1, 2, It 1, 2, 1995 [C, R, E], NZ 1, 2, 1996 W 1, 2, C, NZ 1, SA 1, NZ 2, SA 2, It, S, I, W 3, 1997 E 1, NZ 2 , 1998 E 1, S 1, 2, NZ 1, SA 1, NZ 2, SA 2, NZ 3, 1999 I 2(R), E (R), SA 1, NZ 1, SA 2, NZ 2, [R, I 3, US, W, SA 3, F], 2000 F, S, E, 2001 BI 1(R), 2, 3, SA 1, NZ 1, SA 2, NZ 2, Sp, E, F, W, 2002 F 1, 2, NZ 1, SA 1, NZ 2, SA 2, Arg, I, E, It, 2003 SA 1, NZ 1, SA 2(R), NZ 2(R), [Arg, R, Nm(R), I], 2004 S1(R), PI(R), SA1(R), NZ2(t&R), SA2(R)
Burke, M P (NSW) 1984 E (R), I, 1985 C 1, 2, NZ, Fj 1, 2, 1986 It (R), F, Arg 1, 2, NZ 1, 2, 3, 1987 SK, [US, J, I, F, W], NZ, Arg 1, 2
Burnet, D R (NSW) 1972 F 1, 2, NZ 1, 2, 3, Fj
Butler, O F (NSW) 1969 SA 1, 2, 1970 S, 1971 SA 2, 3, F 1, 2

Calcraft, W J (NSW) 1985 C 1, 1986 It, Arg 2
Caldwell, B C (NSW) 1928 NZ 3
Cameron, A S (NSW) 1951 NZ 1, 2, 3, 1952 Fj 1, 2, NZ 1, 2, 1953 SA 1, 2, 3, 4, 1954 Fj 1, 2, 1955 NZ 1, 2, 3, 1956 SA 1, 2, 1957 NZ 1, 1958 I
Campbell, A M (ACT) 2005 F1(R), 2006 It(R), I2(R), S
Campbell, J D (NSW) 1910 NZ 1, 2, 3
Campbell, W A (Q) 1984 Fj, 1986 It, F, Arg 1, 2, NZ 1, 2, 3, 1987 SK, [E, US, J (R), I, F], NZ, 1988 E, 1989 BI 1, 2, 3, NZ, 1990 NZ 2, 3
Campese, D I (ACT, NSW) 1982 NZ 1, 2, 3, 1983 US, Arg 1, 2, NZ, It, F 1, 2, 1984 Fj, NZ 1, 2, 3, E, I, W, S, 1985 Fj 1, 2, 1986 It, F, Arg 1, 2, NZ 1, 2, 3, 1987 [E, US, J, I, F, W], NZ, 1988 E 1, 2, NZ 1, 2, 3, E, S, It, 1989 BI 1, 2, 3, NZ, F 1, 2, 1990 F 2, 3, US, NZ 1, 2, 3, 1991 W, E, NZ 1, 2, [Arg, WS, W, I, NZ, E], 1992 S 1, 2, NZ 1, 2, 3, SA, I, W, 1993 Tg, NZ, SA 1, 2, 3, C, F 1, 2, 1994 I 1, 2, It 1, 2, WS, NZ, 1995 Arg 1, 2, [SA, C, E], NZ 2(R), 1996 W 1, 2, C, NZ 1, SA 1, NZ 2, SA 2, It, W3
Canniffe, W D (Q) 1907 NZ 2
Cannon, B J (NSW, WF) 2001 BI 2(R), NZ 1(R), Sp (R), F (R), W (R), 2002 F 1(R), 2, SA 1(t), 2(R), I (t), It (R), 2003 I (R), W (R), E (R), SA 1, NZ 1, SA 2, NZ 2, [Arg, R, I, S, NZ, E], 2004 S1, 2, E1, PI, NZ1, 2, SA2, S3(R), 4(R), 2005 NZ1(R), SA4, NZ2, F2, E, I, W, 2006 W(R), It
Caputo, M E (ACT) 1996 W 1, 2, 1997 F 1, 2, NZ 1
Carberry, C M (NSW, Q) 1973 Tg 2, E, 1976 I, US, Fj 1, 2, 3, 1981 F 1, 2, I, W, S, 1982 E
Cardy, A M (NSW) 1966 BI 1, 2, W, S, 1967 E, I 1, F, 1968 NZ 1, 2
Carew, P J (Q) 1899 BI 1, 2, 3, 4
Carmichael, P (Q) 1904 BI 2, 1907 NZ 1, 1908 W, 1909 E
Carozza, P V (Q) 1990 F 1, 2, 3, NZ 2, 3, 1992 S 1, 2, NZ 1, 2, 3, SA, I, W, 1993 Tg, NZ
Carpenter, M G (V) 1938 NZ 1, 2,
Carr, E T A (NSW) 1913 NZ 1, 2, 3, 1914 NZ 1, 2, 3
Carr, E W (NSW) 1921 SA 1, 2, 3, NZ (R)
Carroll, D B (NSW) 1908 W, 1912 US
Carroll, J C (NSW) 1953 SA 1
Carroll, J H (NSW) 1958 M 2, 3, NZ 1, 2, 3, 1959 BI 1, 2
Carson, J (NSW) 1899 BI 1
Carson, P J (NSW) 1979 NZ, 1980 NZ 3
Carter, D G (NSW) 1988 E 1, 2, NZ 1, 1989 F 1, 2
Casey, T V (NSW) 1963 SA 2, 3, 4, 1964 NZ 1, 2, 3
Catchpole, K W (NSW) 1961 Fj 1, 2, 3, SA 1, 2, F, 1962 NZ 1, 2, 4, 1963 SA 2, 3, 4, 1964 NZ 1, 2, 3, 1965 SA 1, 2, 1966 BI 1, 2, W, S, 1967 E, I 1, F, I 2, NZ, 1968 NZ 1
Cawsey, R M (NSW) 1949 M 1, NZ 1, 2
Cerutti, W H (NSW) 1928 NZ 1, 2, 3, M, 1929 NZ 1, 2, 3, 1930 BI, 1931 M, NZ, 1932 NZ 1, 2, 3, 1933 SA 1, 2, 3, 4, 5, 1936 M, 1937 SA 1, 2
Challoner, R L (NSW) 1899 BI 2
Chambers, R (NSW) 1920 NZ 1, 3
Chapman, G A (NSW) 1962 NZ 3, 4, 5
Chisholm, M D (ACT) 2004 S3(R), 2005 Sm, It, F1, SA1, 2, 3(R), NZ1(R), 2, F2, E(t&R), I(R), W(R), 2006 E1(R), 2, I1, NZ1, SA1(R), NZ2(R), SA2(R), NZ3(t&R), SA3(R), W(R), It, I2, S(t&R), 2007 W1, 2(R), Fj, SA1(R), NZ1(R), 2(R), [W(R), Fj, C], 2008 NZ4, It, E, F3(R), W, 2009 SA2, 3, NZ3, 4, E, I, S, W(R), 2010 E1(R), 2(R), I, SA3, NZ3, 4, W, E3, It(R), F(R)
Clark, J G (Q) 1931 M, NZ, 1932 NZ 1, 2, 1933 SA 1
Clarken, J C (NSW) 1905 NZ, 1910 NZ 1, 2, 3
Cleary, M A (NSW) 1961 Fj 1, 2, 3, SA 1, 2, F
Clements, P (NSW) 1982 NZ 3
Clifford, M (NSW) 1938 NZ 3
Cobb, W G (NSW) 1899 BI 3, 4
Cockbain, M J (Q) 1997 F 2(R), NZ 1, SA 1, 2, 1998 E 1, S 1, 2, NZ 1, SA 1, NZ 2, SA 2, NZ 3, Fj, Tg (R), WS, F, E 2, 1999 I 1, 2, E, SA 1, NZ 1, SA 2, NZ 2, [US (t&R), W, SA 3, F], 2000 Arg 1, 2, SA 2(t&R), 3(t&R), F, S, E (R), 2001 BI 1(R), 2(R), 3(R), SA 1(R), NZ 1(R), SA 2(R), NZ 2(R), Sp (R), E (R), F (t+R), W, 2002 F 1(R), 2(R), NZ 1(R), SA 1(R), NZ 2(R), SA 2(R), Arg, I, E, It, 2003 [Arg(R), R(R), Nm(R), I(R), S(R), NZ(R), E(R)]
Cocks, M R (NSW, Q) 1972 F 1, 2, NZ 2, 3, Fj, 1973 Tg 1, 2, W, E, 1975 J 1
Codey, D (NSW Country, Q) 1983 Arg 1, 1984 E, W, S, 1985 C 2, NZ, 1986 F, Arg 1, 1987 [US, J, F (R), W], NZ
Cody, E W (NSW) 1913 NZ 1, 2, 3
Coker, T (Q, ACT) 1987 [E, US, F, W], 1991 NZ 2, [Arg, WS, NZ, E], 1992 NZ 1, 2, 3, W (R), 1993 Tg, NZ, 1995 Arg 2, NZ 1(R), 1997 F 1(R), 2, NZ 1, E 1, NZ 2(R), SA 1(R), NZ 3, SA 2, Arg 1, 2
Colbert, R (NSW) 1952 Fj 2, NZ 1, 2, 1953 SA 2, 3, 4
Cole, J W (NSW) 1968 NZ 1, 2, F, I, S, 1969 W, SA 1, 2, 3, 4, 1970 S, 1971 SA 1, 2, 3, F 1, 2, 1972 NZ 1, 2, 3, 1973 Tg 1, 2, 1974 NZ 1, 2, 3
Collins, P K (NSW) 1937 SA 2, 1938 NZ 2, 3
Colton, A J (Q) 1899 BI 1, 3
Colton, T (Q) 1904 BI 1, 2
Comrie-Thomson, I R (NSW) 1926 NZ 4, 1928 NZ 1, 2, 3 M
Connor, D M (Q) 1958 W, I, E, S, F, M 2, 3, NZ 1, 2, 3, 1959 BI 1, 2
Connors, M R (Q) 1999 SA 1(R), NZ 1(R), SA 2(R), NZ 2, [R (R), I 3, US, W (R), SA 3(R), F(R)], 2000 Arg 1(R), 2(R), SA 1, NZ 1, SA 2, NZ 2(t&R), SA 3, F (R), S (R), E (R)
Constable, R (Q) 1994 I 2(t & R)
Cook, M T (Q) 1986 F, 1987 SK, [J], 1988 E 1, 2, NZ 1, 2, 3, E, S, It
Cooke, B P (Q) 1979 I 1
Cooke, G M (Q) 1932 NZ 1, 2, 3, 1933 SA 1, 2, 3, 1946 NZ 2, 1947 NZ 2, S, I, W, 1948 E, F
Coolican, J E (NSW) 1982 NZ 1, 1983 It, F 1, 2
Cooney, R C (NSW) 1922 M 2
Cooper, Q S (Q) 2008 It(R), F3(R), W(R), 2009 It1(R), 2, SA2(R), 3(R), E, I, S, W, 2010 Fj, E1, 2, I, SA1, 2, 3, NZ3, NZ4, W, E3, It, F, 2011 SA1, NZ1, SA2, NZ2, [It, I, US, Ru, SA, NZ, W]
Cordingley, S J (Q, Grenoble) 2000 Arg 1(R), SA 1(R), F, S, E, 2006 E2, I1(R), NZ1(R), SA1(R), NZ2(R), SA2(R), 2007 Fj(R), [Fj(R), C], 2008 I(R), F1(R), 2(t&R), SA1(R), 2, 3, NZ3, F3(R)
Corfe, A C (Q) 1899 BI 2
Cornelsen, G (NSW) 1974 NZ 2, 3, 1975 J 2, S, W, 1976 E, F 1, 2, 1978 W 1, 2, NZ 1, 2, 3, 1979 I 1, 2, NZ, Arg 1, 2, 1980 NZ 1, 2, 3, 1981 I, W, S, 1982 E
Cornes, J R (Q) 1972 Fj
Cornforth, R G W (NSW) 1947 NZ 1, 1950 BI 2
Cornish, P (ACT) 1990 F 2, 3, NZ 1
Costello, P P S (Q) 1950 BI 2
Cottrell, N V (Q) 1949 M 1, 2, 3, NZ 1, 2, 1950 BI 1, 2, 1951 NZ 1, 2, 3, 1952 Fj 1, 2, NZ 1, 2
Cowan, P J M (WF) 2009 It2, SA3(R), NZ3(R), 2010 Fj(R), 2011 SA1(R)
Cowper, D L (V) 1931 NZ, 1932 NZ 1, 2, 3, 1933 SA 1, 2, 3, 4, 5
Cox, B P (NSW) 1952 Fj 1, 2, NZ 1, 2, 1954 Fj 2, 1955 NZ 1, 1956 SA 2, 1957 NZ 1, 2
Cox, M H (NSW) 1981 W, S
Cox, P A (NSW) 1979 Arg 1, 2, 1980 Fj, NZ 1, 2, 1981 W (R), S, 1982 S 1, 2, NZ 1, 2, 3, 1984 Fj, NZ 1, 2, 3
Craig, R R (NSW) 1908 W
Crakanthorp, J S (NSW) 1923 NZ 3
Cremin, J F (NSW) 1946 NZ 1, 2, 1947 NZ 1
Crittle, C P (NSW) 1962 NZ 4, 5, 1963 SA 2, 3, 4, 1964 NZ 1, 2, 3, 1965 SA 1, 2, 1966 BI 1, 2, S, 1967 E, I
Croft, B H D (NSW) 1928 M
Croft, D N (Q) 2002 Arg (t&R), I (R), E (t&R), It (R), 2003 [Nm]
Cross, J R (NSW) 1955 NZ 1, 2, 3
Cross, K A (NSW) 1949 M 1, NZ 1, 2, 1950 BI 1, 2, 1951 NZ 2, 3, 1952 NZ 1, 1953 SA 1, 2, 3, 4, 1954 Fj 1, 2, 1955 NZ 3, 1956 SA 1, 2, 1957 NZ 1, 2
Cross, R P (WF) 2008 F1(R), 2(R), SA1(R), NZ1, 2(R), SA2(R), 3(R), NZ3, 4, E, W, 2009 It2, F(R), NZ2(R), SA2, NZ4, E(R), S
Crossman, O C (NSW) 1923 M 1(R), 2, 3, 1924, NZ 1, 2, 3, 1925 NZ 1, 3, 4, 1926 NZ 1, 2, 3, 4, 1929 NZ 2, 1930 BI
Crowe, P J (NSW) 1976 F 2, 1978 W 1, 2, 1979 I 2, NZ, Arg 1
Crowley, D J (Q) 1989 BI 1, 2, 3, 1991 [WS], 1992 I, W, 1993 C (R), 1995 Arg 1, 2, [SA, E], NZ 1, 1996 W 2(R), C, NZ 1, SA 1, 2, I, W 3, 1998 E 1(R), S 1(R), 2(R), NZ 1(R), SA 1, NZ 2, SA 2, NZ 3, Tg, WS, 1999 I 1, 2(R), E (R), SA 1, NZ 1(R), [R (R), I 3(t&R), US, F(R)]
Curley, T G P (NSW) 1957 NZ 1, 2, 1958 W, I, E, S, F, M 1, NZ 1, 2, 3
Curran, D J (NSW) 1980 NZ 3, 1981 F 1, 2, W, 1983 Arg 1
Currie, E W (Q) 1899 BI 2
Cutler, S A G (NSW) 1982 NZ 2(R), 1984 NZ 1, 2, 3, E, I, W, S, 1985 C 1, 2, NZ, Fj 1, 2, 1986 It, F, NZ 1, 2, 3, 1987 SK, [E, J, I, F, W], NZ, Arg 1, 2, 1988 E 1, 2, NZ 1, 2, 3, E, S, It, 1989 BI 1, 2, 3, NZ, 1991 [WS]

Daley, B P (Q) 2010 E1, 2, I
Daly, A J (NSW) 1989 NZ, F 1, 2, 1990 F 1, 2, 3, US, NZ 1, 2, 3, 1991 W, E, NZ 1, 2, [Arg, W, I, NZ, E], 1992 S 1, 2, NZ 1, 2, 3, SA, 1993 Tg, NZ, SA 1, 2, 3, C, F 1, 2, 1994 I 1, 2, It 1, 2, WS, NZ, 1995 [C, R]
D'Arcy, A M (Q) 1980 Fj, NZ 3, 1981 F 1, 2, I, W, S, 1982 E, S 1, 2
Darveniza, P (NSW) 1969 W, SA 2, 3, 4
Darwin, B J (ACT) 2001 BI 1(R), SA 1(R), NZ 1(R), SA 2(R), NZ 2(t&R), Sp, E, F, W, 2002 NZ 1(R), SA 1(R), NZ 2(R), SA 2, Arg (R), I (R), E (R), It (R), 2003 I (R), W (t&R), E (R), SA 1(R), NZ 1(R), [Arg(R), R(R), Nm, I, S, NZ]
Davidson, R A L (NSW) 1952 Fj 1, 2, NZ 1, 2, 1953 SA 1, 1957 NZ 1, 2, 1958 W, I, E, S, F, M 1
Davies, R W (Q) 2011 Sm
Davis, C C (NSW) 1949 NZ 1, 1951 NZ 1, 2, 3
Davis, E H (V) 1947 S, W, 1949 M 1, 2
Davis, G V (NSW) 1963 E, SA 1, 2, 3, 4, 1964 NZ 1, 2, 3, 1965 SA 1, 1966 BI 1, 2, W, S, 1967 E, I 1, F, I 2, NZ, 1968 NZ 1, 2, F, I, S, 1969 W, SA 1, 2, 3, 4, 1970 S, 1971 SA 1, 2, 3, F 1, 2, 1972 F 1, 2, NZ 1, 2, 3
Davis, G W G (NSW) 1955 NZ 2, 3
Davis, R A (NSW) 1974 NZ 1, 2, 3
Davis, T S R (NSW) 1920 NZ 1, 2, 3, 1921 SA 1, 2, 3, NZ, 1922 M 1, 2, 3, NZ 1, 2, 3, 1923 M 3, NZ 1, 2, 3, 1924 NZ 1, 2, 1925 NZ 1
Davis, W (NSW) 1899 BI 1, 3, 4
Dawson, W L (NSW) 1946 NZ 1, 2
Diett, L J (NSW) 1959 BI 1, 2
Dix, W (NSW) 1907 NZ 1, 2, 3, 1909 E
Dixon, E J (Q) 1904 BI 3
Donald, K J (Q) 1957 NZ 1, 1958 W, I, E, S, M 2, 3, 1959 BI 1, 2
Dore, E (Q) 1904 BI 1
Dore, M J (Q) 1905 NZ
Dorr, R W (V) 1936 M, 1937 SA 1
Douglas, J A (V) 1962 NZ 3, 4, 5
Douglas, W A (NSW) 1922 NZ 3(R)
Dowse, J H (NSW) 1961 Fj 1, 2, SA 1, 2
Dunbar, A R (NSW) 1910 NZ 1, 2, 3, 1912 US
Duncan, J L (NSW) 1926 NZ 4
Dunlop, E E (V) 1932 NZ 3, 1934 NZ 1
Dunn, P K (NSW) 1958 NZ 1, 2, 3, 1959 BI 1, 2
Dunn, V A (NSW) 1920 NZ 1, 2, 3, 1921 SA 1, 2, 3, NZ
Dunning, M J (NSW, WF) 2003 [Nm, E(R)], 2004 S1(R), 2(R), E1(R), NZ1(R), SA1(R), NZ2(t&R), SA2(R), S3(R), F(R), S4(R), E2(R), 2005 Sm, It(R), F1(t&R), SA1(R), 2(R), 3, NZ1(t&R), SA4(t&R), NZ2(R), F2, E, W, 2007 W1, 2(R), Fj, SA1, NZ1, SA2, NZ2, [J, W, Fj, E], 2008 I, SA1(R), NZ1(R), SA2, 3, NZ4(R), It, 2009 E(R), W(R)
Dunworth, D A (Q) 1971 F 1, 2, 1972 F 1, 2, 1976 Fj 2
Dwyer, L J (NSW) 1910 NZ 1, 2, 3, 1912 US, 1913 NZ 3, 1914 NZ 1, 2, 3
Dyson, F J (Q) 2000 Arg 1, 2, SA 1, NZ 1, SA 2, NZ 2, SA 3, F, S, E

Eales, J A (Q) 1991 W, E, NZ 1, 2, [Arg, WS, W, I, NZ, E], 1992 S 1, 2, NZ 1, 2, 3, SA, I, 1994 I 1, 2, It 1, 2, WS, NZ, 1995 Arg 1, 2, [SA, C, R, E], NZ 1, 2, 1996 W 1, 2, C, NZ 1, SA 1, NZ 2, SA 2, It, S, I, 1997 F 1, 2, NZ 1, E 1, NZ 2, SA 1, Arg 1, 2, E 2, S, 1998 E 1, S 1, 2, NZ 1, SA 1, NZ 2, SA 2, NZ 3, Fj, Tg, WS, F, E 2, 1999 [R, I 3, W, SA 3, F], 2000 Arg 1, 2, SA 1, NZ 1, SA 2, NZ 2, SA 3, F, S, E, 2001 BI 1, 2, 3, SA 1, NZ 1, SA 2, NZ 2
Eastes, C C (NSW) 1946 NZ 1, 2, 1947 NZ 1, 2, 1949 M 1, 2
Edmonds, H (ACT) 2010 Fj, E1(R), 2(R), W(R)
Edmonds, M H M (NSW) 1998 Tg, 2001 SA 1(R)
Egerton, R H (NSW) 1991 W, E, NZ 1, 2, [Arg, W, I, NZ, E]
Ella, G A (NSW) 1982 NZ 1, 2, 1983 F 1, 2, 1988 E 2, NZ 1
Ella, G J (NSW) 1982 S 1, 1983 It, 1985 C 2(R), Fj 2
Ella, M G (NSW) 1980 NZ 1, 2, 3, 1981 F 2, S, 1982 E, S 1, NZ 1, 2, 3, 1983 US, Arg 1, 2, NZ, It, F 1, 2, 1984 Fj, NZ 1, 2, 3, E, I, W, S
Ellem, M A (NSW) 1976 Fj 3(R)
Elliott, F M (NSW) 1957 NZ 1
Elliott, R E (NSW) 1920 NZ 1, 1921 NZ, 1922 M 1, 2, NZ 1(R), 2, 3, 1923 M 1, 2, 3, NZ 1, 2, 3
Ellis, C S (NSW) 1899 BI 1, 2, 3, 4
Ellis, K J (NSW) 1958 NZ 1, 2, 3, 1959 BI 1, 2
Ellwood, B J (NSW) 1958 NZ 1, 2, 3, 1961 Fj 2, 3, SA 1, F, 1962 NZ 1, 2, 3, 4, 5, 1963 SA 1, 2, 3, 4, 1964 NZ 3, 1965 SA 1, 2, 1966 BI 1
Elsom, R D (NSW, ACT) 2005 Sm, It, F1, SA1, 2, 3(R), 4, NZ2, F2, 2006 E1, 2, I1, NZ1, SA1, NZ2, SA2, NZ3, SA3, W, It, I2, S, 2007 W1, 2, SA1, NZ1, SA2, NZ2, [J, W, Fj, E], 2008 I, F1, 2, SA1, NZ1, SA2, 3, NZ3, 2009 NZ2, SA2, 3, NZ3, 4, E, I, S, W, 2010 Fj, E1, 2, I, SA1, NZ1, 2, SA2, 3, NZ3, 4, W, E3, It, F, 2011 Sm, SA1, NZ1, SA2, NZ2, [It, I, US, Ru(R), SA, NZ]
Emanuel, D M (NSW) 1957 NZ 2, 1958 W, I, E, S, F, M 1, 2, 3
Emery, N A (NSW) 1947 NZ 2, S, I, W, 1948 E, F, 1949 M 2, 3, NZ 1, 2
Erasmus, D J (NSW) 1923 NZ 1, 2
Erby, A B (NSW) 1923 M 1, 2, NZ 2, 3, 1925 NZ 2
Evans, L J (Q) 1903 NZ, 1904 BI 1, 3
Evans, W T (Q) 1899 BI 1, 2

Fahey, E J (NSW) 1912 US, 1913 NZ 1, 2, 1914 NZ 3
Fainga'a, A S (Q) 2010 NZ1(R), 2, SA3(R), NZ3(R), 2011 SA1(R), 2(R), NZ2, [It, I, US, SA(R), NZ, W(R)]
Fainga'a, S M (Q) 2010 Fj(R), E1, 2, I, SA1, NZ1(R), 2, SA2, 3(R), NZ4(R), W, 2011 SA1(R), NZ1(R), 2(R), [Ru(R), W(R)]
Fairfax, R L (NSW) 1971 F 1, 2, 1972 F 1, 2, NZ 1, Fj, 1973 W, E
Farmer, E H (Q) 1910 NZ 1
Farquhar, C R (NSW) 1920 NZ 2
Farr-Jones, N C (NSW) 1984 E, I, W, S, 1985 C 1, 2, NZ, Fj 1, 2, 1986 It, F, Arg 1, 2, NZ 1, 2, 3, 1987 SK, [E, I, F, W (R)], NZ, Arg 2, 1988 E 1, 2, NZ 1, 2, 3, E, S, It, 1989 BI 1, 2, 3, NZ, F 1, 2, 1990 F 1, 2, 3, US, NZ 1, 2, 3, 1991 W, E, NZ 1, 2, [Arg, WS, I, NZ, E], 1992 S 1, 2, NZ 1, 2, 3, SA, 1993 NZ, SA 1, 2, 3
Fava, S G (ACT, WF) 2005 E(R), I(R), 2006 NZ1(R), SA1, NZ2
Fay, G (NSW) 1971 SA 2, 1972 NZ 1, 2, 3, 1973 Tg 1, 2, W, E, 1974 NZ 1, 2, 3, 1975 E 1, 2, J 1, S, W, 1976 I, US, 1978 W 1, 2, NZ 1, 2, 3, 1979 I 1
Fenwicke, P T (NSW) 1957 NZ 1, 1958 W, I, E, 1959 BI 1, 2
Ferguson, R T (NSW) 1922 M 3, NZ 1, 1923 M 3, NZ 3
Fihelly, J A (Q) 1907 NZ 2
Finau, S F (NSW) 1997 NZ 3
Finegan, O D A (ACT) 1996 W 1, 2, C, NZ 1, SA 1(t), S, W 3, 1997 SA 1, NZ 3, SA 2, Arg 1, 2, E 2, S, 1998 E 1(R), S 1(t + R), 2(t + R), NZ 1(R), SA 1(t), 2(R), NZ 3(R), Fj (R), Tg, WS (t + R), F (R), E 2(R), 1999 NZ 2(R), [R, I 3(R), US, W (R), SA 3(R), F (R)], 2001 BI 1, 2, 3, SA 1, NZ 1, SA 2, NZ 2, Sp, E, F, W, 2002 F 1, 2, NZ 1, SA 1, NZ 2, SA 2, I, 2003 SA 1(t&R), NZ 1(R), SA 2(R), NZ 2(R)
Finlay, A N (NSW) 1926 NZ 1, 2, 3, 1927 I, W, S, 1928 E, F, 1929 NZ 1, 2, 3, 1930 BI
Finley, F G (NSW) 1904 BI 3
Finnane, S C (NSW) 1975 E 1, J 1, 2, 1976 E, 1978 W 1, 2
Fitter, D E S (ACT) 2005 I, W
FitzSimons, P (NSW) 1989 F 1, 2, 1990 F 1, 2, 3, US, NZ 1
Flanagan, P (Q) 1907 NZ 1, 2
Flatley, E J (Q) 1997 E 2, S, 2000 S (R), 2001 BI 1(R), 2(R), 3, SA 1, NZ 1, 2(R), Sp (R), F (R), W, 2002 F 1(R), 2(R), NZ 1(t+R), SA 1(R), NZ 2(t), Arg (R), I (R), E, It, 2003 I, W, SA 1, NZ 1, SA 2, NZ 2, [Arg, R, I, S, NZ, E], 2004 S3(R), F(R), S4(R), E2, 2005 NZ1(R)
Flett, J A (NSW) 1990 US, NZ 2, 3, 1991 [WS]
Flynn, J P (Q) 1914 NZ 1, 2
Fogarty, J R (Q) 1949 M 2, 3
Foley, M A (Q) 1995 [C (R), R], 1996 W 2(R), NZ 1, SA 1, NZ 2, SA 2, It, S, I, W 3, 1997 NZ 1(R), E 1, NZ 2, SA 1, NZ 3, SA 2, Arg 1, 2, E 2, S, 1998 Tg (R), F (R), E 2(R), 1999 NZ 2(R), [US, W, SA 3, F], 2000 Arg 1, 2, SA 1, NZ 1, SA 2, NZ 2, SA 3, F, S, E, 2001 BI 1(R), 2, 3, SA 1, NZ 1, SA 2, NZ 2, Sp, E, F, W
Foote, R H (NSW) 1924 NZ 2, 3, 1926 NZ 2
Forbes, C F (Q) 1953 SA 2, 3, 4, 1954 Fj 1, 1956 SA 1, 2
Ford, B (Q) 1957 NZ 2
Ford, E E (NSW) 1927 I, W, S, 1928 E, F, 1929 NZ 1, 3
Ford, J A (NSW) 1925 NZ 4, 1926 NZ 1, 2, 1927 I, W, S, 1928 E, 1929 NZ 1, 2, 3, 1930 BI
Forman, T R (NSW) 1968 I, S, 1969 W, SA 1, 2, 3, 4
Fowles, D G (NSW) 1921 SA 1, 2, 3, 1922 M 2, 3, 1923 M 2, 3
Fox, C L (NSW) 1920 NZ 1, 2, 3, 1921 SA 1, NZ, 1922 M 1, 2, NZ 1, 1924 NZ 1, 2, 3, 1925 NZ 1, 2, 3, 1926 NZ 1, 3, 1928 F
Fox, O G (NSW) 1958 F
Francis, E (Q) 1914 NZ 1, 2
Frawley, D (Q, NSW) 1986 Arg 2(R), 1987 Arg 1, 2, 1988 E 1, 2, NZ 1, 2, 3, S, It
Freedman, J E (NSW) 1962 NZ 3, 4, 5, 1963 SA 1
Freeman, E (NSW) 1946 NZ 1(R), M
Freier, A L (NSW) 2002 Arg (R), I, E (R), It, 2003 SA 1(R), NZ 1(t), 2005 NZ2(R), 2006 E2, 2007 W1(R), 2(R), Fj, SA1(R), NZ1(R), SA2, NZ2(R), [J(R), W(R), Fj(R), C, E(R)], 2008 I(R), F1(R), 2(R), NZ3(R), W(t&R)
Freney, M E (Q) 1972 NZ 1, 2, 3, 1973 Tg 1, W, E (R)
Friend, W S (NSW) 1920 NZ 3, 1921 SA 1, 2, 3, 1922 NZ 1, 2, 3, 1923 M 1, 2, 3
Furness, D C (NSW) 1946 M
Futter, F C (NSW) 1904 BI 3

Gardner, J M (Q) 1987 Arg 2, 1988 E 1, NZ 1, E
Gardner, W C (NSW) 1950 BI 1
Garner, R L (NSW) 1949 NZ 1, 2
Gavin, K A (NSW) 1909 E

Gavin, T B (NSW) 1988 NZ 2, 3, S, It (R), 1989 NZ (R), F 1, 2, 1990 F 1, 2, 3, US, NZ 1, 2, 3, 1991 W, E, NZ 1, 1992 S 1, 2, SA, I, W, 1993 Tg, NZ, SA 1, 2, 3, C, F 1, 2, 1994 I 1, 2, It 1, 2, WS, NZ, 1995 Arg 1, 2, [SA, C, R, E], NZ 1, 2, 1996 NZ 2(R), SA 2, W 3
Gelling, A M (NSW) 1972 NZ 1, Fj
Genia, S W (Q) 2009 NZ1(R), SA1(R), NZ2(R), SA2(R), 3, NZ3, 4, E, I, S, W, 2010 E2, SA1, NZ1, 2, SA2, 3, NZ3, NZ4, W, E3, F, 2011 Sm(R), SA1, NZ1, SA2, NZ2, [It, I, US, SA, NZ, W]
George, H W (NSW) 1910 NZ 1, 2, 3, 1912 US, 1913 NZ 1, 3, 1914 NZ 1, 3
George, W G (NSW) 1923 M 1, 3, NZ 1, 2, 1924 NZ 3, 1925 NZ 2, 3, 1926 NZ 4, 1928 NZ 1, 2, 3, M
Gerrard, M A (ACT, MR) 2005 It(R), SA1(R), NZ1, 2, E, I, W, 2006 E1, 2, I1, NZ1, SA1, NZ2, SA2, NZ3(t), SA3(R), I2, S, 2007 W1, 2(R), SA2, NZ2, [J(R)], 2011 Sm
Gibbons, E de C (NSW) 1936 NZ 1, 2, M
Gibbs, P R (V) 1966 S
Giffin, D T (ACT) 1996 W 3, 1997 F 1, 2, 1999 I 1, 2, E, SA 1, NZ 1, SA 2, NZ 2, [R, I 3, US (R), W, SA 3, F], 2000 Arg 1, 2, SA 1, NZ 1, SA 2, NZ 2, SA 3, F, S, E, 2001 BI 1, 2, SA 1, NZ 2, Sp, E, F, W, 2002 Arg (R), I, E (R), It (R), 2003 I, W, E, SA 1, NZ 1, SA 2, NZ 2, [Arg, Nm(R), I, NZ(t&R), E(R)]
Gilbert, H (NSW) 1910 NZ 1, 2, 3
Girvan, B (ACT) 1988 E
Giteau, M J (ACT, WF) 2002 E (R), It (R), 2003 SA 2(R), NZ 2(R), [Arg(R), R(R), Nm, I(R), S(R), E(t)], 2004 S1, E1, PI, NZ1, SA1, NZ2, SA2, S3, F, S4, E2, 2005 Sm, It, F1, SA1, 2, 3, NZ1, SA4, F2, E(t&R), 2006 NZ1(R), SA1, NZ2, SA2, NZ3, SA3, W, It, I2, S, 2007 W1, 2, SA1, NZ1, SA2, NZ2, [J, W, Fj, E], 2008 I, F1, 2, SA1, NZ1, 2, SA2, 3, NZ3, 4, It(R), E, F3, W, 2009 It1, F, NZ1, SA1, NZ2, SA2, 3, NZ3, 4, E, I, S, W, 2010 Fj, E2, I, SA1, NZ1, 2, SA2, 3, NZ3, NZ4, W, E3, F(R), 2011 Sm
Gordon, G C (NSW) 1929 NZ 1
Gordon, K M (NSW) 1950 BI 1, 2
Gould, R G (Q) 1980 NZ 1, 2, 3, 1981 I, W, S, 1982 S 2, NZ 1, 2, 3, 1983 US, Arg 1, F 1, 2, 1984 NZ 1, 2, 3, E, I, W, S, 1985 NZ, 1986 It, 1987 SK, [E]
Gourley, S R (NSW) 1988 S, It, 1989 BI 1, 2, 3
Graham, C S (Q) 1899 BI 2
Graham, R (NSW) 1973 Tg 1, 2, W, E, 1974 NZ 2, 3, 1975 E 2, J 1, 2, S, W, 1976 I, US, Fj 1, 2, 3, F 1, 2
Gralton, A S I (Q) 1899 BI 1, 4, 1903 NZ
Grant, J C (NSW) 1988 E 1, NZ 2, 3, E
Graves, R H (NSW) 1907 NZ 1(R)
Greatorex, E N (NSW) 1923 M 3, NZ 3, 1924 NZ 1, 2, 3, 1925 NZ 1, 1928 E, F
Gregan, G M (ACT) 1994 It 1, 2, WS, NZ, 1995 Arg 1, 2, [SA, C (R), R, E], 1996 W 1, C (t), SA 1, NZ 2, SA 2, It, I, W 3, 1997 F 1, 2, NZ 1, E 1, NZ 2, SA 1, NZ 3, SA 2, Arg 1, 2, E 2, S, 1998 E 1, S 1, 2, NZ 1, SA 1, NZ 2, SA 2, NZ 3, Fj, WS, F, E 2, 1999 I 1, 2, E, SA 1, NZ 1, SA 2, NZ 2, [R, I 3, W, SA 3, F], 2000 Arg 1, 2, SA 1, NZ 1, SA 2, NZ 2, SA 3, 2001 BI 1, 2, 3, SA 1, NZ 1, SA 2, NZ 2, Sp, E, F, W, 2002 F 1, 2, NZ 1, SA 1, NZ 2, SA 2, Arg, I, E, It, 2003 I, W, E, SA 1, NZ 1, SA 2, NZ 2, [Arg, R, I, S, NZ, E], 2004 S1, 2, E1, PI, SA1, NZ2, SA2, S3, F, S4, E2, 2005 It, F1, SA1, 2, 3, NZ1, SA4, NZ2, F2, E, I, W, 2006 E1, 2(R), I1, NZ1, SA1, NZ2, SA2, NZ3, SA3, 2007 W1(R), 2(R), Fj, SA1, NZ1, SA2, NZ2, [J, W, Fj, C(R), E]
Gregory, S C (Q) 1968 NZ 3, F, I, S, 1969 SA 1, 3, 1971 SA 1, 3, F 1, 2, 1972 F 1, 2, 1973 Tg 1, 2, W, E
Grey, G O (NSW) 1972 F 2(R), NZ 1, 2, 3, Fj (R)
Grey, N P (NSW) 1998 S 2(R), SA 2(R), Fj (R), Tg (R), F, E 2, 1999 I 1(R), 2(R), E, SA 1, NZ 1, SA 2, NZ 2(t&R), [R (R), I 3(R), US, SA 3(R), F (R)], 2000 S (R), E (R), 2001 BI 1, 2, 3, SA 1, NZ 1, SA 2, NZ 2, Sp, E, F, 2003 I (R), W (R), E, [Nm, NZ(t)]
Griffin, T S (NSW) 1907 NZ 1, 3, 1908 W, 1910 NZ 1, 2, 1912 US
Grigg, P C (Q) 1980 NZ 3, 1982 S 2, NZ 1, 2, 3, 1983 Arg 2, NZ, 1984 Fj, W, S, 1985 C 1, 2, NZ, Fj 1, 2, 1986 Arg 1, 2, NZ 1, 2, 1987 SK, [E, J, I, F, W]
Grimmond, D N (NSW) 1964 NZ 2
Gudsell, K E (NSW) 1951 NZ 1, 2, 3
Guerassimoff, J (Q) 1963 SA 2, 3, 4, 1964 NZ 1, 2, 3, 1965 SA 2, 1966 BI 1, 2, 1967 E, I, F
Gunther, W J (NSW) 1957 NZ 2

Hall, D (Q) 1980 Fj, NZ 1, 2, 3, 1981 F 1, 2, 1982 S 1, 2, NZ 1, 2, 1983 US, Arg 1, 2, NZ, It
Hamalainen, H A (Q) 1929 NZ 1, 2, 3
Hamilton, B G (NSW) 1946 M
Hammand, C A (NSW) 1908 W, 1909 E
Hammon, J D C (V) 1937 SA 2
Handy, C B (Q) 1978 NZ 3, 1979 NZ, Arg 1, 2, 1980 NZ 1, 2
Hanley, R G (Q) 1983 US (R), It (R), 1985 Fj 2(R)
Hardcastle, P A (NSW) 1946 NZ 1, M, NZ 2, 1947 NZ 1, 1949 M 3
Hardcastle, W R (NSW) 1899 BI 4, 1903 NZ
Harding, M A (NSW) 1983 It
Hardman, S P (Q) 2002 F 2(R), 2006 SA1(R), 2007 SA2(t&R), [C(R)]
Hardy, M D (ACT) 1997 F 1(t), 2(R), NZ 1(R), 3(R), Arg 1(R), 2(R), 1998 Tg, WS
Harrison, J B (ACT, NSW) 2001 BI 3, NZ 1, SA 2, Sp, E, F, W (R), 2002 F 1, 2, NZ 1, SA 1, NZ 2, SA 2, Arg, I (R), E, It, 2003 [R(R), Nm, S, NZ, E], 2004 S1, 2, E1, PI, NZ1, SA1, NZ2, SA2, S3, F, S4, E2
Harry, R L L (NSW) 1996 W 1, 2, NZ 1, SA 1(t), NZ 2, It, S, 1997 F 1, 2, NZ 1, 2, SA 1, NZ 3, SA 2, Arg 1, 2, E 2, S, 1998 E 1, S 1, 2, NZ 1, Fj, 1999 SA 2, NZ 2, [R, I 3, W, SA 3, F], 2000 Arg 1, 2, SA 1, NZ 1, SA 2, NZ 2, SA 3
Hartill, M N (NSW) 1986 NZ 1, 2, 3, 1987 SK, [J], Arg 1, 1988 NZ 1, 2, E, It, 1989 BI 1(R), 2, 3, F 1, 2, 1995 Arg 1(R), 2(R), [C], NZ 1, 2
Harvey, P B (Q) 1949 M 1, 2
Harvey, R M (NSW) 1958 F, M 3
Hatherell, W I (Q) 1952 Fj 1, 2
Hauser, R G (Q) 1975 J 1(R), 2, W (R), 1976 E, I, US, Fj 1, 2, 3, F 1, 2, 1978 W 1, 2, 1979 I 1, 2
Hawker, M J (NSW) 1980 Fj, NZ 1, 2, 3, 1981 F 1, 2, I, W, 1982 E, S 1, 2, NZ 1, 2, 3, 1983 US, Arg 1, 2, NZ, It, F 1, 2, 1984 NZ 1, 2, 3, 1987 NZ
Hawthorne, P F (NSW) 1962 NZ 3, 4, 5, 1963 E, SA 1, 2, 3, 4, 1964 NZ 1, 2, 3, 1965 SA 1, 2, 1966 BI 1, 2, W, 1967 E, I 1, F, I 2, NZ
Hayes, E S (Q) 1934 NZ 1, 2, 1938 NZ 1, 2, 3
Heath, A (NSW) 1996 C, SA 1, NZ 2, SA 2, It, 1997 NZ 2, SA 1, E 2(R)
Heenan, D P (Q, ACT) 2003 W, 2006 E1
Heinrich, E L (NSW) 1961 Fj 1, 2, 3, SA 2, F, 1962 NZ 1, 2, 3, 1963 E, SA 1
Heinrich, V W (NSW) 1954 Fj 1, 2
Heming, R J (NSW) 1961 Fj 2, 3, SA 1, 2, F, 1962 NZ 2, 3, 4, 5, 1963 SA 2, 3, 4, 1964 NZ 1, 2, 3, 1965 SA 1, 2, 1966 BI 1, 2, W, 1967 F
Hemingway, W H (NSW) 1928 NZ 2, 3, 1931 M, NZ, 1932 NZ 3
Henderson, N J (ACT) 2004 PI(R), 2005 Sm(R), 2006 It(R)
Henjak, M T (ACT) 2004 E1(R), NZ1(R), 2005 Sm(R), I(R)
Henry, A R (Q) 1899 BI 2
Herbert, A G (Q) 1987 SK (R), [F (R)], 1990 F 1(R), US, NZ 2, 3, 1991 [WS], 1992 NZ 3(R), 1993 NZ (R), SA 2(R)
Herbert, D J (Q) 1994 I 2, It 1, 2, WS (R), 1995 Arg 1, 2, [SA, R], 1996 C, SA 2, It, S, I, 1997 NZ 1, 1998 E 1, S 1, 2, NZ 1, SA 1, NZ 2, SA 2, Fj, Tg, WS, F, E 2, 1999 I 1, 2, E, SA 1, NZ 1, SA 2, NZ 2, [R, I 3, W, SA 3, F], 2000 Arg 1, 2, SA 1, NZ 1, SA 2, NZ 2, SA 3, F, S, E, 2001 BI 1, 2, 3, SA 1, NZ 1, SA 2, NZ 2, Sp, E, 2002 F 1, 2, NZ 1, SA 1, NZ 2, SA 2, Arg, I, E, It
Herd, H V (NSW) 1931 M
Hickey, J (NSW) 1908 W, 1909 E
Higginbotham, S (Q) 2010 F(R), 2011 Sm(R), SA1(R), NZ1(R), SA2, NZ2(R), [It(R), I(R), Ru, W]
Hill, J (NSW) 1925 NZ 1
Hillhouse, D W (Q) 1975 S, 1976 E, Fj 1, 2, 3, F 1, 2, 1978 W 1, 2, 1983 US, Arg 1, 2, NZ, It, F 1, 2
Hills, E F (V) 1950 BI 1, 2
Hindmarsh, J A (Q) 1904 BI 1
Hindmarsh, J C (NSW) 1975 J 2, S, W, 1976 US, Fj 1, 2, 3, F 1, 2
Hipwell, J N B (NSW) 1968 NZ 1(R), 2, F, I, S, 1969 W, SA 1, 2, 3, 4, 1970 S, 1971 SA 1, 2, F 1, 2, 1972 F 1, 2, 1973 Tg 1, W, E, 1974 NZ 1, 2, 3, 1975 E 1, 2, J 1, S, W, 1978 NZ 1, 2, 3, 1981 F 1, 2, I, W, 1982 E
Hirschberg, W A (NSW) 1905 NZ
Hodgins, C H (NSW) 1910 NZ 1, 2, 3
Hodgson, A J (NSW) 1933 SA 2, 3, 4, 1934 NZ 1, 1936 NZ 1, 2, M, 1937 SA 2, 1938 NZ 1, 2, 3
Hodgson, M J (WF) 2010 Fj(R), E1(R), NZ2(R), It(R), 2011 Sm, SA1(R)
Hoiles, S A (NSW, ACT) 2004 S4(R), E2(R), 2006 W(R), 2007 W1(R), 2(R), Fj(R), SA1(R), NZ1(R), SA2, NZ2, [J(R), W(R), Fj(R), C(R), E(R)] 2006 W(R), 2007 W1(R), 2(R), Fj(R), SA1(R), NZ1(R), SA2, NZ2, [J(R), W(R), Fj(R), C(R), E(R)], 2008 F2
Holbeck, J C (ACT) 1997 NZ 1(R), E 1, NZ 2, SA 1, NZ 3, SA 2, 2001 BI 3(R)
Holdsworth, J W (NSW) 1921 SA 1, 2, 3, 1922 M 2, 3, NZ 1(R)
Holmes, G S (Q) 2005 F2(R), E(t&R), I, 2006 E1, 2, I1, NZ1, SA1, NZ2, SA2, NZ3, 2007 [Fj(R), C]
Holt, N C (Q) 1984 Fj
Honan, B D (Q) 1968 NZ 1(R), 2, F, I, S, 1969 SA 1, 2, 3, 4
Honan, R E (Q) 1964 NZ 1, 2
Horan, T J (Q) 1989 NZ, F 1, 2, 1990 F 1, NZ 1, 2, 3, 1991 W, E, NZ 1, 2, [Arg, WS, W, I, NZ, E], 1992 S 1, 2, NZ 1, 2, 3, SA, I, W, 1993 Tg, NZ, SA 1, 2, 3, C, F 1, 2, 1995 [C, R, E], NZ 1, 2, 1996 W 1, 2, C, NZ 1, SA 1, It, S, I, W 3, 1997 F 1, 2, NZ 1, E 1, NZ 2, Arg 1, 2, E 2, S, 1998 E 1, S 1, 2, NZ 1, SA 1, NZ 2, SA 2, NZ

3, Fj, Tg, WS, 1999 I 1, 2, E, SA 1, NZ 1, SA 2, NZ 2, [R, I 3, W, SA 3, F], 2000 Arg 1
Horne, R G (NSW) 2010 Fj, E1, 2, I, SA1, NZ1, 2011 [US, NZ(R), W(R)]
Horodam, D J (Q) 1913 NZ 2
Horsley, G R (Q) 1954 Fj 2
Horton, P A (NSW) 1974 NZ 1, 2, 3, 1975 E 1, 2, J 1, 2, S, W, 1976 E, F 1, 2, 1978 W 1, 2, NZ 1, 2, 3, 1979 NZ, Arg 1
Horwill, J E (Q) 2007 Fj, 2008 I, F1, 2, SA1, NZ1, 2, SA2, 3, NZ3, 2009 It1, 2, F, NZ1, SA1, NZ2, SA2, 3, NZ3, 4, E, I, S, W, 2011 SA1, NZ1, SA2, NZ2, [It, I, Ru, SA, NZ, W]
Hoskins, J E (NSW) 1924 NZ 1, 2, 3
How, R A (NSW) 1967 I 2
Howard, J (Q) 1938 NZ 1, 2
Howard, J L (NSW) 1970 S, 1971 SA 1, 1972 F 1(R), NZ 2, 1973 Tg 1, 2, W
Howard, P W (Q, ACT) 1993 NZ, 1994 WS, NZ, 1995 NZ 1(R), 2(t), 1996 W 1, 2, SA 1, NZ 2, SA 2, It, S, W 3, 1997 F 1, 2, NZ 1, Arg 1, 2, E 2, S
Howell, M L (NSW) 1946 NZ 1(R), 1947 NZ 1, S, I, W
Hughes, B D (NSW) 1913 NZ 2, 3
Hughes, J C (NSW) 1907 NZ 1, 3
Hughes, N McL (NSW) 1953 SA 1, 2, 3, 4, 1955 NZ 1, 2, 3, 1956 SA 1, 2, 1958 W, I, E, S, F
Humphreys, O W (NSW) 1920 NZ 3, 1921 NZ, 1922 M 1, 2, 3, 1925 NZ 1
Hutchinson, E E (NSW) 1937 SA 1, 2
Hutchinson, F E (NSW) 1936 NZ 1, 2, 1938 NZ 1, 3
Huxley, J L (ACT) 2007 W1, 2, Fj, SA1, NZ1, SA2, [W(R), Fj(R), C]
Hynes, P J (Q) 2008 I, F1, 2, SA1, NZ1, 2, SA2, 3, NZ3, 4, E, F3, W, 2009 It2, NZ2(R), SA2, 3(R), NZ4, E, I, S, W

Ide, W P J (Q) 1938 NZ 2, 3
Ioane, D A N (WF, Q) 2007 W2, 2008 It, F3, W, 2009 NZ4, E, I, W, 2010 Fj, E1, 2, 2011 Sm, SA1, NZ1, SA2, NZ2, [It, SA, NZ, W]
Ives, W N (NSW) 1926 NZ 1, 2, 3, 4, 1929 NZ 3

James, P M (Q) 1958 M 2, 3
James, S L (NSW) 1987 SK (R), [E (R)], NZ, Arg 1, 2, 1988 NZ 2(R)
Jamieson, A E (NSW) 1925 NZ 3(R)
Jaques, T (ACT) 2000 SA 1(R), NZ 1(R)
Jessep, E M (V) 1934 NZ 1, 2
Johansson, L D T (Q) 2005 NZ2(R), F2(R), E(R)
Johnson, A P (NSW) 1946 NZ 1, M
Johnson, B B (NSW) 1952 Fj 1, 2, NZ 1, 2, 1953 SA 2, 3, 4, 1955 NZ 1, 2
Johnson, P G (NSW) 1959 BI 1, 2, 1961 Fj 1, 2, 3, SA 1, 2, F, 1962 NZ 1, 2, 3, 4, 5, 1963 E, SA 1, 2, 3, 4, 1964 NZ 1, 2, 3, 1965 SA 1, 2, 1966 BI 1, 2, W, S, 1967 E, I 1, F, I 2, NZ, 1968 NZ 1, 2, F, I, S, 1970 S, 1971 SA 1, 2, F 1, 2
Johnstone, B (Q) 1993 Tg (R)
Jones, G G (Q) 1952 Fj 1, 2, 1953 SA 1, 2, 3, 4, 1954 Fj 1, 2, 1955 NZ 1, 2, 3, 1956 SA 1
Jones, H (NSW) 1913 NZ 1, 2, 3
Jones, P A (NSW) 1963 E, SA 1
Jorgensen, P (NSW) 1992 S 1(R), 2(R)
Joyce, J E (NSW) 1903 NZ
Judd, H A (NSW) 1903 NZ, 1904 BI 1, 2, 3, 1905 NZ
Judd, P B (NSW) 1925 NZ 4, 1926 NZ 1, 2, 3, 4, 1927 I, W, S, 1928 E, 1931 M, NZ
Junee, D K (NSW) 1989 F 1(R), 2(R), 1994 WS (R), NZ (R)

Kafer, R B (ACT) 1999 NZ 2, [R, US (R)], 2000 Arg 1(R), 2, SA 1, NZ 1(t&R), SA 2(R), 3(R), F, S, E
Kahl, P R (Q) 1992 W
Kanaar, A (NSW) 2005 NZ2(R)
Kassulke, N (Q) 1985 C 1, 2
Kay, A R (V) 1958 NZ 2, 1959 BI 2
Kay, P (NSW) 1988 E 2
Kearney, K H (NSW) 1947 NZ 1, 2, S, I, W, 1948 E, F
Kearns, P N (NSW) 1989 NZ, F 1, 2, 1990 F 1, 2, 3, US, NZ 1, 2, 3, 1991 W, E, NZ 1, 2, [Arg, WS, W, I, NZ, E], 1992 S 1, 2, NZ 1, 2, 3, SA, I, W, 1993 Tg, NZ, SA 1, 2, 3, C, F 1, 2, 1994 I 1, 2, It 1, 2, WS, NZ, 1995 Arg 1, 2, [SA, C, E], NZ 1, 2, 1998 E 1, S 1, 2, NZ 1, SA 1, NZ 2, SA 2, NZ 3, Fj, WS, F, E 2, 1999 I 2(R), SA 1(R), 2, NZ 2, [R, I 3]
Kefu, R S T (Q) 1997 SA 2(R), 1998 E 1, S 1, 2, NZ 1, SA 1, NZ 2, SA 2, NZ 3, Fj (R), Tg, WS (R), F, E 2, 1999 I 1, 2, E, SA 1, NZ 1(R), SA 2, NZ 2, [R, I 3, SA 3, F], 2000 SA 1(t&R), NZ 1(R), SA 2(R), NZ 2, SA 3(R), F, S, E, 2001 BI 1, 2, 3, SA 1, NZ 1, SA 2, NZ 2, Sp, E, F, W, 2002 F 1, NZ 1, SA 1, NZ 2, SA 2, Arg, I, E, It, 2003 I, W, E, SA 1, NZ 1, SA 2, NZ 2
Kefu, S (Q) 2001 W (R), 2003 I, W, E, SA 1, NZ 1(R)
Kelaher, J D (NSW) 1933 SA 1, 2, 3, 4, 5, 1934 NZ 1, 2, 1936 NZ 1, 2, M, 1937 SA 1, 2, 1938 NZ 3
Kelaher, T P (NSW) 1992 NZ 1, I (R), 1993 NZ
Kelleher, R J (Q) 1969 SA 2, 3
Keller, D H (NSW) 1947 NZ 1, S, I, W, 1948 E, F
Kelly, A J (NSW) 1899 BI 1
Kelly, R L F (NSW) 1936 NZ 1, 2, M, 1937 SA 1, 2, 1938 NZ 1, 2
Kent, A (Q) 1912 US
Kepu, S M (NSW) 2008 It(R), F3(R), 2009 S(R), 2011 Sm, SA1, NZ1, SA2, NZ2, [It, I, US(R), Ru, SA, NZ]
Kerr, F R (V) 1938 NZ 1
Kimlin, P J (ACT) 2009 It1(R), 2
King, S C (NSW) 1926 NZ 1, 2, 3, 4(R), 1927 W, S, 1928 E, F, 1929 NZ 1, 2, 3, 1930 BI, 1932 NZ 1, 2
Knight, M (NSW) 1978 W 1, 2, NZ 1
Knight, S O (NSW) 1969 SA 2, 4, 1970 S, 1971 SA 1, 2, 3
Knox, D J (NSW, ACT) 1985 Fj 1, 2, 1990 US (R), 1994 WS, NZ, 1996 It, S, I, 1997 SA 1, NZ 3, SA 2, Arg 1, 2
Kraefft, D F (NSW) 1947 NZ 2, S, I, W, 1948 E, F
Kreutzer, S D (Q) 1914 NZ 2

Lamb, J S (NSW) 1928 NZ 1, 2, M
Lambie, J K (NSW) 1974 NZ 1, 2, 3, 1975 W
Lane, R E (NSW) 1921 SA 1
Lane, T A (Q) 1985 C 1, 2, NZ
Lang, C W P (V) 1938 NZ 2, 3
Langford, J F (ACT) 1997 NZ 3, SA 2, E 2, S
Larkham, S J (ACT) 1996 W 2(R), 1997 F 1, 2, NZ 1, 2(R), SA 1, NZ 3, SA 2, Arg 1, 2, E 2, S, 1998 E 1, S 1, 2, NZ 1, SA 1, NZ 2, SA 2, NZ 3, Fj, Tg (t), WS, F, E 2, 1999 [I 3, US, W, SA 3, F], 2000 Arg 1, 2, SA 1, NZ 1, SA 2, NZ 2, SA 3, 2001 BI 1, 2, NZ 1, SA 2, NZ 2, Sp, E, F, W, 2002 F 1, 2, NZ 1, SA 1, NZ 2, SA 2, Arg, I, E, 2003 SA 1(R), NZ 1, SA 2, NZ 2, [Arg, R, I, S, NZ, E], 2004S1, 2, E1, PI, NZ1, SA1, NZ2, SA2, S3, F, S4, 2005 Sm(R), It, F1, SA1, 2, 3, 2006 E1, 2, I1, NZ1, SA1, NZ2, SA2, NZ3, SA3, W, It, I2, S, 2007 W2, Fj, SA1, NZ1, SA2, NZ2, [J]
Larkin, E R (NSW) 1903 NZ
Larkin, K K (Q) 1958 M 2, 3
Latham, C E (Q) 1998 F, E 2, 1999 I 1, 2, E, [US], 2000 Arg 1, 2, SA 1, NZ 1, SA 2, NZ 2, SA 3, F, S, E, 2001 BI 1, 2(R), SA 1(R), NZ 1(R), SA 2, NZ 2, Sp, E, F, W (R), 2002 F 1, 2, NZ 1, SA 1, NZ 2, SA 2, 2003 I, W, E, NZ 1(R), SA 2, NZ 2, [Nm], 2004 S1(R), 2(R), E1(R), PI(t&R), NZ1, SA1, NZ2, SA2, S3, F, S4, E2, 2005 Sm, F1, SA2, 3, F2, E, I, W, 2006 E1, 2, I1, NZ1, SA1, NZ2, SA2, NZ3, SA3, W, It, I2, S, 2007 NZ2(R), [J, W, Fj, C, E]
Latimer, N B (NSW) 1957 NZ 2
Lawton, R (Q) 1988 E 1, NZ 2(R), 3, S
Lawton, T (NSW, Q) 1920 NZ 1, 2, 1925 NZ 4, 1927 I, W, S, 1928 E, F, 1929 NZ 1, 2, 3, 1930 BI, 1932 NZ 1, 2
Lawton, T A (Q) 1983 F 1(R), 2, 1984 Fj, NZ 1, 2, 3, E, I, W, S, 1985 C 1, 2, NZ, Fj 1, 1986 It, F, Arg 1, 2, NZ 1, 2, 3, 1987 SK, [E, US, I, F, W], NZ, Arg 1, 2, 1988 E 1, 2, NZ 1, 2, 3, E, S, It, 1989 BI 1, 2, 3
Laycock, W M B (NSW) 1925 NZ 2, 3, 4, 1926 NZ 2
Leeds, A J (NSW) 1986 NZ 3, 1987 [US, W], NZ, Arg 1, 2, 1988 E 1, 2, NZ 1, 2, 3, E, S, It
Lenehan, J K (NSW) 1958 W, E, S, F, M 1, 2, 3, 1959 BI 1, 2, 1961 SA 1, 2, F, 1962 NZ 2, 3, 4, 5, 1965 SA 1, 2, 1966 W, S, 1967 E, I 1, F, I 2
L'Estrange, R D (Q) 1971 F 1, 2, 1972 NZ 1, 2, 3, 1973 Tg 1, 2, W, E, 1974 NZ 1, 2, 3, 1975 S, W, 1976 I, US
Lewis, L S (Q) 1934 NZ 1, 2, 1936 NZ 2, 1938 NZ 1
Lidbury, S (NSW) 1987 Arg 1, 1988 E 2
Lillicrap, C P (Q) 1985 Fj 2, 1987 [US, I, F, W], 1989 BI 1, 1991 [WS]
Lindsay, R T G (Q) 1932 NZ 3
Lisle, R J (NSW) 1961 Fj 1, 2, 3, SA 1
Little, J S (Q, NSW) 1989 F 1, 2, 1990 F 1, 2, 3, US, 1991 W, E, NZ 1, 2, [Arg, W, I, NZ, E], 1992 NZ 1, 2, 3, SA, I, W, 1993 Tg, NZ, SA 1, 2, 3, C, F 1, 2, 1994 WS, NZ, 1995 Arg 1, 2, [SA, C, E], NZ 1, 2, 1996 It (R), I, W 3, 1997 F 1, 2, E 1, NZ 2, SA 1, NZ 3, SA 2, 1998 E 1(R), S 2(R), NZ 2, SA 2(R), NZ 3, Fj, Tg, WS, F, E 2, 1999 I 1(R), 2, SA 2(R), NZ 2, [R, I 3(t&R), US, W (R), SA 3(t&R), F (R)], 2000 Arg 1(R), 2(R), SA 1(R), NZ 1, SA 2, NZ 2, SA 3
Livermore, A E (Q) 1946 NZ 1, M
Loane, M E (Q) 1973 Tg 1, 2, 1974 NZ 1, 1975 E 1, 2, J 1, 1976 E, I, Fj 1, 2, 3, F 1, 2, 1978 W 1, 2, 1979 I 1, 2, NZ, Arg 1, 2, 1981 F 1, 2, I, W, S, 1982 E, S 1, 2
Logan, D L (NSW) 1958 M 1
Loudon, D B (NSW) 1921 NZ, 1922 M 1, 2, 3
Loudon, R B (NSW) 1923 NZ 1(R), 2, 3, 1928 NZ 1, 2, 3, M, 1929 NZ 2, 1933 SA 2, 3, 4, 5, 1934 NZ 2
Love, E W (NSW) 1932 NZ 1, 2, 3
Lowth, D R (NSW) 1958 NZ 1
Lucas, B C (Q) 1905 NZ

Lucas, P W (NSW) 1982 NZ 1, 2, 3
Lutge, D (NSW) 1903 NZ, 1904 BI 1, 2, 3
Lynagh, M P (Q) 1984 Fj, E, I, W, S, 1985 C 1, 2, NZ, 1986 It, F, Arg 1, 2, NZ 1, 2, 3, 1987 [E, US, J, I, F, W], Arg 1, 2, 1988 E 1, 2, NZ 1, 3(R), E, S, It, 1989 BI 1, 2, 3, NZ, F 1, 2, 1990 F 1, 2, 3, US, NZ 1, 2, 3, 1991 W, E, NZ 1, 2, [Arg, WS, W, I, NZ, E], 1992 S 1, 2, NZ 1, 2, 3, SA, I, 1993 Tg, C, F 1, 2, 1994 I 1, 2, It 1, 1995 Arg 1, 2, [SA, C, E]
Lyons, D J (NSW) 2000 Arg 1(t&R), 2(R), 2001 BI 1(R), SA 1(R), 2002 F 1(R), 2, NZ 1(R), SA 1(R), NZ 2(R), SA 2(t+R), 2003 I, W, E, SA 1, [Arg, R, Nm, I, S, NZ, E], 2004 S1, 2, E1, PI, NZ1, SA1, NZ2, SA2, S3(R), F(R), S4, E2, 2005 Sm, It, F1, SA1, 2, NZ1, SA4, 2006 S, 2007 Fj, SA2(R), [C]

McArthur, M (NSW) 1909 E
McBain, M I (Q) 1983 It, F 1, 1985 Fj 2, 1986 It (R), 1987 [J], 1988 E 2(R), 1989 BI 1(R)
MacBride, J W T (NSW) 1946 NZ 1, M, NZ 2, 1947 NZ 1, 2, S, I, W, 1948 E, F
McCabe, A J M (NSW) 1909 E
McCabe, P J (ACT) 2010 It(R), 2011 Sm, SA1, NZ1, SA2, NZ2, [It, I, US(R), SA, NZ]
McCall, R J (Q) 1989 F 1, 2, 1990 F 1, 2, 3, US, NZ 1, 2, 3, 1991 W, E, NZ 1, 2, [Arg, W, I, NZ, E], 1992 S 1, 2, NZ 1, 2, 3, SA, I, W, 1993 Tg, NZ, SA 1, 2, 3, C, F 1, 2, 1994 It 2, 1995 Arg 1, 2, [SA, R, E]
McCalman, B J (WF) 2010 SA1(R), 2(R), 3, NZ3, 4, W, E3, It, F, 2011 Sm, SA1, NZ1, 2(R), [It(R), I, US, Ru, SA(R), NZ(R), W]
McCarthy, F J C (Q) 1950 BI 1
McCowan, R H (Q) 1899 BI 1, 2, 4
McCue, P A (NSW) 1907 NZ 1, 3, 1908 W, 1909 E
McDermott, L C (Q) 1962 NZ 1, 2
McDonald, B S (NSW) 1969 SA 4, 1970 S
McDonald, J C (Q) 1938 NZ 2, 3
Macdougall, D G (NSW) 1961 Fj 1, SA 1
Macdougall, S G (NSW, ACT) 1971 SA 3, 1973 E, 1974 NZ 1, 2, 3, 1975 E 1, 2, 1976 E
McGhie, G H (Q) 1929 NZ 2, 3, 1930 BI
McGill, A N (NSW) 1968 NZ 1, 2, F, 1969 W, SA 1, 2, 3, 4, 1970 S, 1971 SA 1, 2, 3, F 1, 2, 1972 F 1, 2, NZ 1, 2, 3, 1973 Tg 1, 2
McIntyre, A J (Q) 1982 NZ 1, 2, 3, 1983 F 1, 2, 1984 Fj, NZ 1, 2, 3, E, I, W, S, 1985 C 1, 2, NZ, Fj 1, 2, 1986 It, F, Arg 1, 2, 1987 [E, US, I, F, W], NZ, Arg 2, 1988 E 1, 2, NZ 1, 2, 3, E, S, It, 1989 NZ
McIsaac, T P (WF) 2006 E1, I1, NZ1, 2(R), SA2, 3(R), W, I2
McKay, G R (NSW) 1920 NZ 2, 1921 SA 2, 3, 1922 M 1, 2, 3
MacKay, L J (NSW) 2005 NZ2(R)
McKenzie, E J A (NSW, ACT) 1990 F 1, 2, 3, US, NZ 1, 2, 3, 1991 W, E, NZ 1, 2, [Arg, W, I, NZ, E], 1992 S 1, 2, NZ 1, 2, 3, SA, I, W, 1993 Tg, NZ, SA 1, 2, 3, C, F 1, 2, 1994 I 1, 2, It 1, 2, WS, NZ, 1995 Arg 1, 2, [SA, C (R), R, E], NZ 2, 1996 W 1, 2, 1997 F 1, 2, NZ 1, E 1
McKid, W A (NSW) 1976 E, Fj 1, 1978 NZ 2, 3, 1979 I 1, 2
McKinnon, A (Q) 1904 BI 2
McKivat, C H (NSW) 1907 NZ 1, 3, 1908 W, 1909 E
McLaren, S D (NSW) 1926 NZ 4
McLaughlin, R E M (NSW) 1936 NZ 1, 2
McLean, A D (Q) 1933 SA 1, 2, 3, 4, 5, 1934 NZ 1, 2, 1936 NZ 1, 2, M
McLean, J D (Q) 1904 BI 2, 3, 1905 NZ
McLean, J J (Q) 1971 SA 2, 3, F 1, 2, 1972 F 1, 2, NZ 1, 2, 3, Fj, 1973 W, E, 1974 NZ 1
McLean, P E (Q) 1974 NZ 1, 2, 3, 1975 J 1, 2, S, W, 1976 E, I, Fj 1, 2, 3, F 1, 2, 1978 W 1, 2, NZ 2, 1979 I 1, 2, NZ, Arg 1, 2, 1980 Fj, 1981 F 1, 2, I, W, S, 1982 E, S 2
McLean, P W (Q) 1978 NZ 1, 2, 3, 1979 I 1, 2, NZ, Arg 1, 2, 1980 Fj (R), NZ 3, 1981 I, W, S, 1982 E, S 1, 2
McLean, R A (NSW) 1971 SA 1, 2, 3, F 1, 2
McLean, W M (Q) 1946 NZ 1, M, NZ 2, 1947 NZ 1, 2
McMahon, M J (Q) 1913 NZ 1
McMaster, R E (Q) 1946 NZ 1, M, NZ 2, 1947 NZ 1, 2, I, W
McMeniman, H J (Q) 2005 Sm(R), It(R), F2(R), E, I, W, 2007 SA2(R), NZ2(R), [J(R), Fj(R), C, E(t&R)], 2008 F2(R), SA1(t&R), NZ2(R), SA3, NZ3(R), It, E, F3, W
MacMillan, D I (Q) 1950 BI 1, 2
McMullen, K V (NSW) 1962 NZ 3, 5, 1963 E, SA 1
McShane, J M S (NSW) 1937 SA 1, 2
Ma'afu, R S L (ACT) 2010 Fj, E1, 2, I, SA1, NZ1, 2, SA2, 3, NZ3, 2011 NZ2(R), [Ru(R), W]
Mackay, G (NSW) 1926 NZ 4
Mackney, W A R (NSW) 1933 SA 1, 5, 1934 NZ 1, 2
Magrath, E (NSW) 1961 Fj 1, SA 2, F
Maguire, D J (Q) 1989 BI 1, 2, 3
Malcolm, S J (NSW) 1927 S, 1928 E, F, NZ 1, 2, M, 1929 NZ 1, 2, 3, 1930 BI, 1931 NZ, 1932 NZ 1, 2, 3, 1933 SA 4, 5, 1934 NZ 1, 2
Malone, J H (NSW) 1936 NZ 1, 2, M, 1937 SA 2
Malouf, B P (NSW) 1982 NZ 1
Mandible, E F (NSW) 1907 NZ 2, 3, 1908 W
Manning, J (NSW) 1904 BI 2
Manning, R C S (Q) 1967 NZ
Mansfield, B W (NSW) 1975 J 2
Manu, D T (NSW) 1995 [R (t)], NZ 1, 2, 1996 W 1, 2(R), SA 1, NZ 2, It, S, I, 1997 F 1, NZ 1(t), E 1, NZ 2, SA 1
Marks, H (NSW) 1899 BI 1, 2
Marks, R J P (Q) 1962 NZ 4, 5, 1963 E, SA 2, 3, 4, 1964 NZ 1, 2, 3, 1965 SA 1, 2, 1966 W, S, 1967 E, I 1, F, I 2
Marrott, R (NSW) 1920 NZ 1, 3
Marrott, W J (NSW) 1922 NZ 2, 3, 1923 M 1, 2, 3, NZ 1, 2
Marshall, J S (NSW) 1949 M 1
Martin, G J (Q) 1989 BI 1, 2, 3, NZ, F 1, 2, 1990 F 1, 3(R), NZ 1
Martin, M C (NSW) 1980 Fj, NZ 1, 2, 1981 F 1, 2, W (R)
Massey-Westropp, M (NSW) 1914 NZ 3
Mathers, M J (NSW) 1980 Fj, NZ 2(R)
Maund, J W (NSW) 1903 NZ
Mayne, A V (NSW) 1920 NZ 1, 2, 3, 1922 M 1
Meadows, J E C (V, Q) 1974 NZ 1, 1975 S, W, 1976 I, US, Fj 1, 3, F 1, 2, 1978 NZ 1, 2, 3, 1979 I 1, 2, 1981 I, S, 1982 E, NZ 2, 3, 1983 US, Arg 2, NZ
Meadows, R W (NSW) 1958 M 1, 2, 3, NZ 1, 2, 3
Meagher, F W (NSW) 1923 NZ 3, 1924 NZ 3, 1925 NZ 4, 1926 NZ 1, 2, 3, 1927 I, W
Meibusch, J H (Q) 1904 BI 3
Meibusch, L S (Q) 1912 US
Melrose, T C (NSW) 1978 NZ 3, 1979 I 1, 2, NZ, Arg 1, 2
Merrick, S (NSW) 1995 NZ 1, 2
Messenger, H H (NSW) 1907 NZ 2, 3
Middleton, S A (NSW) 1909 E, 1910 NZ 1, 2, 3
Miller, A R (NSW) 1952 Fj 1, 2, NZ 1, 2, 1953 SA 1, 2, 3, 4, 1954 Fj 1, 2, 1955 NZ 1, 2, 3, 1956 SA 1, 2, 1957 NZ 1, 2, 1958 W, E, S, F, M 1, 2, 3, 1959 BI 1, 2, 1961 Fj 1, 2, 3, SA 2, F, 1962 NZ 1, 2, 1966 BI 1, 2, W, S, 1967 I 1, F, I 2, NZ
Miller, J M (NSW) 1962 NZ 1, 1963 E, SA 1, 1966 W, S, 1967 E
Miller, J S (Q) 1986 NZ 2, 3, 1987 SK, [US, I, F], NZ, Arg 1, 2, 1988 E 1, 2, NZ 2, 3, E, S, It, 1989 BI 1, 2, 3, NZ, 1990 F 1, 3, 1991 W, [WS, W, I]
Miller, S W J (NSW) 1899 BI 3
Mingey, N (NSW) 1920 NZ 3, 1921 SA 1, 2, 3, 1923 M 1, NZ 1, 2
Mitchell, D A (Q, WF, NSW) 2005 SA1(R), 2(R), 3(R), NZ1, SA4, NZ2, F2(R), E, I, W, 2007 W1, 2, Fj, SA1, 2(R), NZ2, [J(R), W, Fj, C, E(R)], 2008 SA1(R), NZ2(R), SA2, 3(R), NZ4, E, F3, W, 2009 It1, F, NZ1, SA1, NZ2, SA2(R), 3, NZ3, E, I, S, W, 2010 Fj(t&R), E1, 2, I, SA1, NZ1, 2, SA2, 3, NZ4, W, E3, It, F, 2011 [I(R), US, Ru]
Monaghan, L E (NSW) 1973 E, 1974 NZ 1, 2, 3, 1975 E 1, 2, S, W, 1976 E, I, US, F 1, 1978 W 1, 2, NZ 1, 1979 I 1, 2
Monti, C I A (Q) 1938 NZ 2
Moon, B J (Q) 1978 NZ 2, 3, 1979 I 1, 2, NZ, Arg 1, 2, 1980 Fj, NZ 1, 2, 3, 1981 F 1, 2, I, W, S, 1982 E, S 1, 2, 1983 US, Arg 1, 2, NZ, It, F 1, 2, 1984 Fj, NZ 1, 2, 3, E, 1986 It, F, Arg 1, 2
Mooney, T P (Q) 1954 Fj 1, 2
Moore, R C (ACT, NSW) 1999 [US], 2001 BI 2, 3, SA 1, NZ 1, SA 2, NZ 2, Sp (R), E (R), F (R), W (R), 2002 F 1(R), 2(R), SA 2(R)
Moore, S T (Q, ACT) 2005 Sm(R), It(R), F1(R), SA2(R), 3(R), F2(t&R), 2006 It(t), I2(R), S, 2007 W1, 2, Fj(R), SA1, NZ1, 2, [J, W, Fj, E], 2008 I, F1, 2, SA1, NZ1, 2, SA2, 3(R), NZ3, 4, It, E, F3, W, 2009 It1, F, NZ1, SA1, NZ2, SA2, 3(R), NZ3(R), 4, E, I, S, W, 2010 SA1(R), NZ1, SA2(t), 3, NZ3, 4, E3, It, F, 2011 Sm, SA1, NZ1, SA2, NZ2, [It, US(R), Ru, SA, NZ]
Moran, H M (NSW) 1908 W
Morgan, G (Q) 1992 NZ 1(R), 3(R), W, 1993 Tg, NZ, SA 1, 2, 3, C, F 1, 2, 1994 I 1, 2, It 1, WS, NZ, 1996 W 1, 2, C, NZ 1, SA 1, NZ 2, 1997 E 1, NZ 2
Morrissey, C V (NSW) 1925 NZ 2, 3, 4, 1926 NZ 2, 3
Morrissey, W (Q) 1914 NZ 2
Mortlock, S A (ACT) 2000 Arg 1, 2, SA 1, NZ 1, SA 2, NZ 2, SA 3, F, S, E, 2002 F 1, 2, NZ 1, SA 1, NZ 2, SA 2, Arg, I, E, It, 2003 [R(R), Nm, S, NZ, E], 2004 S2, E1, PI, NZ1, SA1, NZ2, SA2, S3, F, S4, 2005 Sm, It, F1, SA2, 3(R), NZ1, 2006 E1, 2, I1, NZ1, SA1, NZ2, SA2, NZ3, SA3, It, I2, S, 2007 W1, 2, Fj(R), SA1, NZ1, SA2, NZ2, [J, W, E], 2008 I, F1, 2, SA1, NZ2, SA2, 3, NZ3, 4, It, E, F3, W, 2009 It1, F, NZ1, SA1
Morton, A R (NSW) 1957 NZ 1, 2, 1958 F, M 1, 2, 3, NZ 1, 2, 3, 1959 BI 1, 2
Mossop, R P (NSW) 1949 NZ 1, 2, 1950 BI 1, 2, 1951 NZ 1
Moutray, I E (NSW) 1963 SA 2
Mulligan, P J (NSW) 1925 NZ 1(R)
Mumm, D W (NSW) 2008 I(t&R), F1(R), 2, SA2(R), 3(R), NZ4, It, E(R), F3, W(R), 2009 It1, 2, F, NZ1(t), SA1(R), NZ2(R), 4(R), E(R), S(R),

W, 2010 Fj, E1, 2, I, SA1, NZ1, 2, SA2, 3(R), NZ3(R), 4(R), W(R), E3(R)
Munsie, A (NSW) 1928 NZ 2
Murdoch, A R (NSW) 1993 F 1, 1996 W 1
Murphy, P J (Q) 1910 NZ 1, 2, 3, 1913 NZ 1, 2, 3, 1914 NZ 1, 2, 3
Murphy, W (Q) 1912 US

Nasser, B P (Q) 1989 F 1, 2, 1990 F 1, 2, 3, US, NZ 2, 1991 [WS]
Newman, E W (NSW) 1922 NZ 1
Nicholson, F C (Q) 1904 BI 3
Nicholson, F V (Q) 1903 NZ, 1904 BI 1
Niuqila, A S (NSW) 1988 S, It, 1989 BI 1
Noriega, E P (ACT, NSW) 1998 F, E 2, 1999 I 1, 2, E, SA 1, NZ 1, SA 2(R), NZ 2(R), 2002 F 1, 2, NZ 1, SA 1, NZ 2, Arg, I, E, It, 2003 I, W, E, SA 1, NZ 1, SA 2
Norton-Knight, S H (NSW) 2007 W1, Fj(R)
Nothling, O E (NSW) 1921 SA 1, 2, 3, NZ, 1922 M 1, 2, 3, NZ 1, 2, 3, 1923 M 1, 2, 3, NZ 1, 2, 3, 1924 NZ 1, 2, 3
Nucifora, D V (Q) 1991 [Arg (R)], 1993 C (R)

O'Brien, F W H (NSW) 1937 SA 2, 1938 NZ 3
O'Connor, J A (NSW) 1928 NZ 1, 2, 3, M
O'Connor, J D (WF) 2008 It(R), 2009 It1, 2, F(R), NZ1(R), SA1(R), NZ2, SA2, 3, NZ3, 4, I(R), S(R), W(R), 2010 E1, 2, I, SA1, NZ1, 2, SA2, 3, NZ3, NZ4, W, E3, F, 2011 SA1, NZ1, SA2, [It(R), I, Ru, SA, NZ, W]
O'Connor, M (ACT) 1994 I 1
O'Connor, M D (ACT, Q) 1979 Arg 1, 2, 1980 Fj, NZ 1, 2, 3, 1981 F 1, 2, I, 1982 E, S 1, 2
O'Donnell, C (NSW) 1913 NZ 1, 2
O'Donnell, I C (NSW) 1899 BI 3, 4
O'Donnell, J B (NSW) 1928 NZ 1, 3, M
O'Donnell, J M (NSW) 1899 BI 4
O'Gorman, J F (NSW) 1961 Fj 1, SA 1, 2, F, 1962 NZ 2, 1963 E, SA 1, 2, 3, 4, 1965 SA 1, 2, 1966 W, S, 1967 E, I 1, F, I 2
O'Neill, D J (Q) 1964 NZ 1, 2
O'Neill, J M (Q) 1952 NZ 1, 2, 1956 SA 1, 2
Ofahengaue, V (NSW) 1990 NZ 1, 2, 3, 1991 W, E, NZ 1, 2, [Arg, W, I, NZ, E], 1992 S 1, 2, SA, I, W, 1994 WS, NZ, 1995 Arg 1, 2(R), [SA, C, E], NZ 1, 2, 1997 Arg 1(t + R), 2(R), E 2, S, 1998 E 1(R), S 1(R), 2(R), NZ 1(R), SA 1(R), NZ 2(R), SA 2(R), NZ 3(R), Fj, WS, F (R)
Ormiston, I W L (NSW) 1920 NZ 1, 2, 3
Osborne, D H (V) 1975 E 1, 2, J 1
Outterside, R (NSW) 1959 BI 1, 2
Oxenham, A McE (Q) 1904 BI 2, 1907 NZ 2
Oxlade, A M (Q) 1904 BI 2, 3, 1905 NZ, 1907 NZ 2
Oxlade, B D (Q) 1938 NZ 1, 2, 3

Palfreyman, J R L (NSW) 1929 NZ 1, 1930 BI, 1931 NZ, 1932 NZ 3
Palu, W L (NSW) 2006 E2(t&R), I1(R), SA2, NZ3, SA3, W, It, I2, S(R), 2007 W1, 2, SA1, NZ1, [J, W, Fj, E], 2008 I, F1, SA1, NZ1, 2, SA2, 3, NZ3, It(R), E(R), F3, 2009 NZ1, SA1, NZ3(t&R), 4, E, I, S, W, 2011 [I(R), US]
Panoho, G M (Q) 1998 SA 2(R), NZ 3(R), Fj (R), Tg, WS (R), 1999 I 2, E, SA 1(R), NZ 1, 2000 Arg 1(R), 2(R), SA 1(R), NZ 1(R), SA 2(R), 3(R), F (R), S (R), E (R), 2001 BI 1, 2003 SA 2(R), NZ 2
Papworth, B (NSW) 1985 Fj 1, 2, 1986 It, Arg 1, 2, NZ 1, 2, 3, 1987 [E, US, J (R), I, F], NZ, Arg 1, 2
Parker, A J (Q) 1983 Arg 1(R), 2, NZ
Parkinson, C E (Q) 1907 NZ 2
Pashley, J J (NSW) 1954 Fj 1, 2, 1958 M 1, 2, 3
Paul, J A (ACT) 1998 S 1(R), NZ 1(R), SA 1(t), Fj (R), Tg, 1999 I 1, 2, E, SA 1, NZ 1, [R (R), I 3(R), W (t), F (R)], 2000 Arg 1(R), 2(R), SA 1(R), NZ 1(R), SA 2(R), NZ 2(R), SA 3(R), F (R), S (R), E (R), 2001 BI 1, 2002 F 1, NZ 1, SA 1, NZ 2, SA 2, Arg, E, 2003 I, W, E, SA 2(t&R), NZ2(R), [Arg(R), R(R), Nm, I(R), S(R), NZ(R), E(R)], 2004 S1(R), 2(R), E1(R), PI(R), NZ1(t&R), SA1, NZ2(R), SA2(R), S3, F, S4, E2, 2005 Sm, It, F1, SA1, 2, 3, NZ1, 2006 E1(R), 2(R), I1(R), NZ1(R), SA1, NZ2, SA2(R), NZ3, SA3
Pauling, T P (NSW) 1936 NZ 1, 1937 SA 1
Payne, S J (NSW) 1996 W 2, C, NZ 1, S, 1997 F 1(t), NZ 2(R), Arg 2(t)
Pearse, G K (NSW) 1975 W (R), 1976 I, US, Fj 1, 2, 3, 1978 NZ 1, 2, 3
Penman, A P (NSW) 1905 NZ
Perrin, P D (Q) 1962 NZ 1
Perrin, T D (NSW) 1931 M, NZ
Phelps, R (NSW) 1955 NZ 2, 3, 1956 SA 1, 2, 1957 NZ 1, 2, 1958 W, I, E, S, F, M 1, NZ 1, 2, 3, 1961 Fj 1, 2, 3, SA 1, 2, F, 1962 NZ 1, 2
Phipps, J A (NSW) 1953 SA 1, 2, 3, 4, 1954 Fj 1, 2, 1955 NZ 1, 2, 3, 1956 SA 1, 2
Phipps, N J (MR) 2011 Sm, SA1(R), [Ru(R)]
Phipps, W J (NSW) 1928 NZ 2
Piggott, H R (NSW) 1922 M 3(R)
Pilecki, S J (Q) 1978 W 1, 2, NZ 1, 2, 1979 I 1, 2, NZ, Arg 1, 2, 1980 Fj, NZ 1, 2, 1982 S 1, 2, 1983 US, Arg 1, 2, NZ
Pini, M (Q) 1994 I 1, It 2, WS, NZ, 1995 Arg 1, 2, [SA, R (t)]
Piper, B J C (NSW) 1946 NZ 1, M, NZ 2, 1947 NZ 1, S, I, W, 1948 E, F, 1949 M, 1, 2, 3
Pocock, D W (WF) 2008 NZ4(R), It(R), 2009 It1(R), 2, F(R), NZ1(R), SA1(R), NZ2(R), SA2(R), 3, NZ3, 4, E(R), I, W, 2010 Fj, E1, 2, I, SA1, NZ1, 2, SA2, 3, NZ3, 4, W, E3, It, F, 2011 SA1, NZ1, SA2, NZ2, [It, Ru, SA, NZ, W]
Poidevin, S P (NSW) 1980 Fj, NZ 1, 2, 3, 1981 F 1, 2, I, W, S, 1982 E, NZ 1, 2, 3, 1983 US, Arg 1, 2, NZ, It, F 1, 2, 1984 Fj, NZ 1, 2, 3, E, I, W, S, 1985 C 1, 2, NZ, Fj 1, 2, 1986 It, F, Arg 1, 2, NZ 1, 2, 3, 1987 SK, [E, J, I, F, W], Arg 1, 1988 NZ 1, 2, 3, 1989 NZ, 1991 E, NZ 1, 2, [Arg, W, I, NZ, E]
Polota-Nau, S U T (NSW) 2005 E(R), I(R), 2006 S(R), 2008 SA1(R), NZ1(R), 2(R), SA2(R), 3, It(R), E(R), 2009 It1(R), 2, F(R), SA1(R), NZ2(t&R), SA2(R), 3, NZ3, 4(R), E(R), I(R), S(R), W(R), 2010 It(R), F(R), 2011 [It(R), I, US, SA(R), NZ(R), W]
Pope, A M (Q) 1968 NZ 2(R)
Potter, R T (Q) 1961 Fj 2
Potts, J M (NSW) 1957 NZ 1, 2, 1958 W, I, 1959 BI 1
Prentice, C W (NSW) 1914 NZ 3
Prentice, W S (NSW) 1908 W, 1909 E, 1910 NZ 1, 2, 3, 1912 US
Price, R A (NSW) 1974 NZ 1, 2, 3, 1975 E 1, 2, J 1, 2, 1976 US
Primmer, C J (Q) 1951 NZ 1, 3
Proctor, I J (NSW) 1967 NZ
Prosser, R B (NSW) 1967 E, I 1, 2, NZ, 1968 NZ 1, 2, F, I, S, 1969 W, SA 1, 2, 3, 4, 1971 SA 1, 2, 3, F 1, 2, 1972 F 1, 2, NZ 1, 2, 3, Fj
Pugh, G H (NSW) 1912 US
Purcell, M P (Q) 1966 W, S, 1967 I 2
Purkis, E M (NSW) 1958 S, M 1
Pym, J E (NSW) 1923 M 1

Rainbow, A E (NSW) 1925 NZ 1
Ramalli, C (NSW) 1938 NZ 2, 3
Ramsay, K M (NSW) 1936 M, 1937 SA 1, 1938 NZ 1, 3
Rankin, R (NSW) 1936 NZ 1, 2, M, 1937 SA 1, 2, 1938 NZ 1, 2
Rathbone, C (ACT) 2004 S1, 2(R), E1, PI, NZ1, SA1, NZ2, SA2, S3, F, S4, 2005 Sm, NZ1(R), SA4, NZ2, 2006E1(R), 2(R), I1(R), SA1(R), NZ2(R), SA2(R), NZ3, SA3, W, It, I2
Rathie, D S (Q) 1972 F 1, 2
Raymond, R L (NSW) 1920 NZ 1, 2, 1921 SA 2, 3, NZ, 1922 M 1, 2, 3, NZ 1, 2, 3, 1923 M 1, 2
Redwood, C (Q) 1903 NZ, 1904 BI 1, 2, 3
Reid, E J (NSW) 1925 NZ 2, 3, 4
Reid, T W (NSW) 1961 Fj 1, 2, 3, SA 1, 1962 NZ 1
Reilly, N P (Q) 1968 NZ 1, 2, F, I, S, 1969 W, SA 1, 2, 3, 4
Reynolds, L J (NSW) 1910 NZ 2(R), 3
Reynolds, R J (NSW) 1984 Fj, NZ 1, 2, 3, 1985 Fj 1, 2, 1986 Arg 1, 2, NZ 1, 1987 [J]
Richards, E W (Q) 1904 BI 1, 3, 1905 NZ, 1907 NZ 1(R), 2
Richards, G (NSW) 1978 NZ 2(R), 3, 1981 F 1
Richards, T J (Q) 1908 W, 1909 E, 1912 US
Richards, V S (NSW) 1936 NZ 1, 2(R), M, 1937 SA 1, 1938 NZ 1
Richardson, G C (Q) 1971 SA 1, 2, 3, 1972 NZ 2, 3, Fj, 1973 Tg 1, 2, W
Rigney, W A (NSW) 1925 NZ 2, 4, 1926 NZ 4
Riley, S A (NSW) 1903 NZ
Ritchie, E V (NSW) 1924 NZ 1, 3, 1925 NZ 2, 3
Roberts, B T (NSW) 1956 SA 2
Roberts, H F (Q) 1961 Fj 1, 3, SA 2, F
Robertson, I J (NSW) 1975 J 1, 2
Robinson, B A (NSW) 2006 SA3, I2(R), S, 2007 W1(R), 2, Fj(R), 2008 I, F1, 2, SA1, NZ1, 2, SA2, 3, NZ3, 4, E, W, 2009 It1, F, NZ1, SA1, NZ2, SA2, 3, NZ3, 4, E, I, S, W, 2010 SA1, NZ1, 2, SA2, 3, NZ3, 4, W, E3, It(R), F(t&R)
Robinson, B J (ACT) 1996 It (R), S (R), I (R), 1997 F 1, 2, NZ 1, E 1, NZ 2, SA 1(R), NZ 3(R), SA 2(R), Arg 1, 2, E 2, S, 1998 Tg
Robinson, B S (Q) 2011 Sm(R)
Roche, C (Q) 1982 S 1, 2, NZ 1, 2, 3, 1983 US, Arg 1, 2, NZ, It, F 1, 2, 1984 Fj, NZ 1, 2, 3, I
Rodriguez, E E (NSW) 1984 Fj, NZ 1, 2, 3, E, I, W, S, 1985 C 1, 2, NZ, Fj 1, 1986 It, F, Arg 1, 2, NZ 1, 2, 3, 1987 SK, [E, J, W (R)], NZ, Arg 1, 2
Roe, J A (Q) 2003 [Nm(R)], 2004 E1(R), SA1(R), NZ2(R), SA2(t&R), S3, F, 2005 Sm(R), It(R), F1(R), SA1(R), 3, NZ1, SA4(t&R), NZ2(R), F2(R), E, I, W
Roebuck, M C (NSW) 1991 W, E, NZ 1, 2, [Arg, WS, W, I, NZ, E], 1992 S 1, 2, NZ 2, 3, SA, I, W, 1993 Tg, SA 1, 2, 3, C, F 2
Roff, J W (ACT) 1995 [C, R], NZ 1, 2, 1996 W 1, 2, NZ 1, SA 1, NZ

2, SA 2(R), S, I, W 3, 1997 F 1, 2, NZ 1, E 1, NZ 2, SA 1, NZ 3, SA 2, Arg 1, 2, E 2, S, 1998 E 1, S 1, 2, NZ 1, SA 1, NZ 2, SA 2, NZ 3, Fj, Tg, WS, F, E 2, 1999 I 1, 2, E, SA 1, NZ 1, SA 2, NZ 2(R), [R (R), I 3, US (R), W, SA 3, F], 2000 Arg 1, 2, SA 1, NZ 1, SA 2, NZ 2, SA 3, F, S, E, 2001 BI 1, 2, 3, SA 1, NZ 1, SA 2, NZ 2, Sp, E, F, W, 2003 I, W, E, SA 1, [Arg, R, I, S(R), NZ(t&R), E(R)], 2004 S1, 2, E1, PI

Rogers, M S (NSW) 2002 F 1(R), 2(R), NZ 1(R), SA 1(R), NZ 2(R), SA 2(t&R), Arg, 2003 E (R), SA 1, NZ 1, SA 2, NZ 2, [Arg, R, Nm, I, S, NZ, E], 2004S3(R), F(R), S4(R), E2(R), 2005 Sm(R), It, F1(R), SA1, 4, NZ2, F2, E, I, W, 2006 E1, 2, I1, NZ1, SA1(R), NZ2(R), SA2(R), NZ3(R), W, It, I2(R), S(R)

Rose, H A (NSW), 1967 I 2, NZ, 1968 NZ 1, 2, F, I, S, 1969 W, SA 1, 2, 3, 4, 1970 S

Rosenblum, M E (NSW) 1928 NZ 1, 2, 3, M

Rosenblum, R G (NSW) 1969 SA 1, 3, 1970 S

Rosewell, J S H (NSW) 1907 NZ 1, 3

Ross, A W (NSW) 1925 NZ 1, 2, 3, 1926 NZ 1, 2, 3, 1927 I, W, S, 1928 E, F, 1929 NZ 1, 1930 BI, 1931 M, NZ, 1932 NZ 2, 3, 1933 SA 5, 1934 NZ 1, 2

Ross, W S (Q) 1979 I 1, 2, Arg 2, 1980 Fj, NZ 1, 2, 3, 1982 S 1, 2, 1983 US, Arg 1, 2, NZ

Rothwell, P R (NSW) 1951 NZ 1, 2, 3, 1952 Fj 1

Row, F L (NSW) 1899 BI 1, 3, 4

Row, N E (NSW) 1907 NZ 1, 3, 1909 E, 1910 NZ 1, 2, 3

Rowles, P G (NSW) 1972 Fj, 1973 E

Roxburgh, J R (NSW) 1968 NZ 1, 2, F, 1969 W, SA 1, 2, 3, 4, 1970 S

Ruebner, G (NSW) 1966 BI 1, 2

Russell, C J (NSW) 1907 NZ 1, 2, 3, 1908 W, 1909 E

Ryan, J R (NSW) 1975 J 2, 1976 I, US, Fj 1, 2, 3

Ryan, K J (Q) 1958 E, M 1, NZ 1, 2, 3

Ryan, P F (NSW) 1963 E, SA 1, 1966 BI 1, 2

Rylance, M H (NSW) 1926 NZ 4(R)

Sailor, W J (Q) 2002 F 1, 2, Arg (R), I, E, It, 2003 I, W, E, SA 1, NZ 1, SA 2, NZ 2, [Arg, R, I, S, NZ, E], 2004 S1, 2, NZ1(R), 2(R), SA2(R), S3(R), F(R), S4(R), E2, 2005 Sm, It, F1, SA1, 2, 3, F2, I(R), W(R)

Samo, U R (ACT, Q) 2004 S1, 2, E1, PI, NZ1, S4(R), 2011 SA2(R), NZ2, [It, I, US(R), Ru, SA, NZ, W(t&R)]

Sampson, J H (NSW) 1899 BI 4

Sayle, J L (NSW) 1967 NZ

Schulte, B G (Q) 1946 NZ 1, M

Scott, P R I (NSW) 1962 NZ 1, 2

Scott-Young, S J (Q) 1990 F 2, 3(R), US, NZ 3, 1992 NZ 1, 2, 3

Shambrook, G G (Q) 1976 Fj 2, 3

Sharpe, N C (Q, WF) 2002 F 1, 2, NZ 1, SA 1, NZ 2, SA 2, 2003 I, W, E, SA 1(R), NZ 1(R), SA 2(R), [Arg, R, Nm, I, S, NZ, E], 2004 S1, 2, E1, PI, NZ1, SA1, NZ2, SA2, 2005 Sm, It, F1, SA1, 2, 3, NZ1, SA4, NZ2, F2, E, I, W, 2006 E1, 2, I1, NZ1, SA1, NZ2, SA2, NZ3, SA3, W, It, I2, S, 2007 W1, 2, SA1, NZ1, SA2, NZ2, [J, W, C, E], 2008 I, F1, SA1, NZ1, 2, 3, 4, E, F3, W, 2009 It1, F, NZ1, SA1, NZ2, 2010 Fj, E1, 2, SA1, NZ1, 2, SA2, 3, NZ3, 4, W, E3, It, F, 2011 Sm, SA1(R), 2, [US, Ru, SA(R), W]

Shaw, A A (Q) 1973 W, E, 1975 E 1, 2, J 2, S, W, 1976 E, I, US, Fj 1, 2, 3, F 1, 2, 1978 W 1, 2, NZ 1, 2, 3, 1979 I 1, 2, NZ, Arg 1, 2, 1980 Fj, NZ 1, 2, 3, 1981 F 1, 2, I, W, S, 1982 S 1, 2

Shaw, C (NSW) 1925 NZ 2, 3, 4(R)

Shaw, G A (NSW, Q) 1969 W, SA 1(R), 1970 S, 1971 SA 1, 2, 3, F 1, 2, 1973 W, E, 1974 NZ 1, 2, 3, 1975 E 1, 2, J 1, 2, W, 1976 E, I, US, Fj 1, 2, 3, F 1, 2, 1979 NZ

Sheehan, B R (ACT) 2006 SA3(R), 2008 SA2(R), 3(R)

Sheehan, W B J (NSW) 1921 SA 1, 2, 3, 1922 NZ 1, 2, 3, 1923 M 1, 2, NZ 1, 2, 3, 1924 NZ 1, 2, 1926 NZ 1, 2, 3, 1927 W, S

Shehadie, N M (NSW) 1947 NZ 2, 1948 E, F, 1949 M 1, 2, 3, NZ 1, 2, 1950 BI 1, 2, 1951 NZ 1, 2, 3, 1952 Fj 1, 2, NZ 2, 1953 SA 1, 2, 3, 4, 1954 Fj 1, 2, 1955 NZ 1, 2, 3, 1956 SA 1, 2, 1957 NZ 2, 1958 W, I

Sheil, A G R (Q) 1956 SA 1

Shepherd, C B (WF) 2006 E1(R), 2(R), I1(R), SA3, W, 2007 [C], 2008 I, F1, 2(R)

Shepherd, D J (V) 1964 NZ 3, 1965 SA 1, 2, 1966 BI 1, 2

Shepherdson, G T (ACT) 2006 I1, NZ1, SA1, NZ2(R), SA2(R), It, I2, S, 2007 W1, 2, SA1, NZ1, SA2, NZ2, [J(R), W, Fj, E]

Shute, J L (NSW) 1920 NZ 3, 1922 M 2, 3

Simmons, R A (Q) 2010 SA1(R), NZ1(R), 2(R), SA2(R), It, F, 2011 SA1, NZ1, 2(R), [It(R), I(R), US, Ru(R), NZ(t&R), W(R)]

Simpson, R J (NSW) 1913 NZ 2

Skinner, A J (NSW) 1969 W, SA 4, 1970 S

Slack, A G (Q) 1978 W 1, 2, NZ 1, 2, 1979 NZ, Arg 1, 2, 1980 Fj, 1981 I, W, S, 1982 E, S 1, NZ 3, 1983 US, Arg 1, 2 NZ, It, 1984 Fj, NZ 1, 2, 3, E, I, W, S, 1986 It, F, NZ 1, 2, 3, 1987 SK, [E, US, J, I, F, W]

Slater, S H (NSW) 1910 NZ 3

Slattery, P J (Q) 1990 US (R), 1991 W (R), E (R), [WS (R), W, I (R)], 1992 I, W, 1993 Tg, C, F 1, 2, 1994 I 1, 2, It 1(R), 1995 [C, R (R)]

Slipper, J A (Q) 2010 E1(R), 2(R), I(R), SA1(R), NZ1(R), 2(R), SA2(R), 3(R), NZ3(R), 4(R), W(R), E3(R), It, F, 2011 [It(R), I(R), US, Ru, SA(R), NZ(R), W]

Smairl, A M (NSW) 1928 NZ 1, 2, 3

Smith, B A (Q) 1987 SK, [US, J, I (R), W], Arg 1

Smith, D P (Q) 1993 SA 1, 2, 3, C, F 2, 1994 I 1, 2, It 1, 2, WS, NZ, 1995 Arg 1, 2, [SA, R, E], NZ 1, 2, 1998 SA 1(R), NZ 3(R), Fj

Smith, F B (NSW) 1905 NZ, 1907 NZ 1, 2, 3

Smith, G B (ACT) 2000 F, S, E, 2001 BI 1, 2, 3, SA 1, NZ 1, SA 2, NZ 2, Sp, E, F (R), W (R), 2002 F 1, 2, NZ 1, SA 1, NZ 2, SA 2, Arg, I, E, It, 2003 I, NZ 1, SA 2, NZ 2, [Arg, R, Nm, I, S, NZ, E], 2004 S1, 2(R), E1(t&R), PI(R), NZ1(R), SA1, NZ2, SA2, S3, F, S4, E2, 2005 Sm, It, F1, SA1, 2, 3, NZ1, SA4(R), NZ2, F2, E, I, W, 2006 E1, 2, I1, NZ1, SA1, NZ2, SA2, NZ3(t), SA3(R), It, I2(R), S, 2007 W1(R), 2, Fj(R), SA1, NZ1, SA2, NZ2, [J, W, C, E], 2008 I, F1, 2(R), SA1, NZ1, 2, SA2, 3(R), NZ3, 4, E, F3, W(R), 2009 It1, 2, F, NZ1, SA1, NZ2, SA2, 3, NZ3, 4(R), E, I(t), S, W(R)

Smith, L M (NSW) 1905 NZ

Smith, N C (NSW) 1922 NZ 2, 3, 1923 NZ 1, 1924 NZ 1, 3(R), 1925 NZ 2, 3

Smith, P V (NSW) 1967 NZ, 1968 NZ 1, 2, F, I, S, 1969 W, SA 1

Smith, R A (NSW) 1971 SA 1, 2, 1972 F 1, 2, NZ 1, 2(R), 3, Fj, 1975 E 1, 2, J 1, 2, S, W, 1976 E, I, US, Fj 1, 2, 3, F 1, 2

Smith, T S (NSW) 1921 SA 1, 2, 3, NZ, 1922 M 2, 3, NZ 1, 2, 3, 1925 NZ 1, 3, 4

Snell, H W (NSW) 1925 NZ 2, 3, 1928 NZ 3

Solomon, H J (NSW) 1949 M 3, NZ 2, 1950 BI 1, 2, 1951 NZ 1, 2, 1952 Fj 1, 2, NZ 1, 2, 1953 SA 1, 2, 3, 1955 NZ 1

Spooner, N R (Q) 1999 I 1, 2

Spragg, S A (NSW) 1899 BI 1, 2, 3, 4

Staniforth, S N G (NSW, WF) 1999 [US], 2002 I, It, 2006 SA3(R), I2(R), S, 2007 Fj, NZ1(R), SA2(R), NZ2(R), [W(R), Fj(R)]

Stanley, R G (NSW) 1921 NZ, 1922 M 1, 2, 3, NZ 1, 2, 3, 1923 M 2, 3, NZ 1, 2, 3, 1924 NZ 1, 3

Stapleton, E T (NSW) 1951 NZ 1, 2, 3, 1952 Fj 1, 2, NZ 1, 2, 1953 SA 1, 2, 3, 4, 1954 Fj 1, 1955 NZ 1, 2, 3, 1958 NZ 1

Steggall, J C (Q) 1931 M, NZ, 1932 NZ 1, 2, 3, 1933 SA 1, 2, 3, 4, 5

Stegman, T R (NSW) 1973 Tg 1, 2

Stephens, O G (NSW) 1973 Tg 1, 2, W, 1974 NZ 2, 3

Stewart, A A (NSW) 1979 NZ, Arg 1, 2

Stiles, N B (Q) 2001 BI 1, 2, 3, SA 1, NZ 1, SA 2, NZ 2, Sp, E, F, W, 2002 I

Stone, A H (NSW) 1937 SA 2, 1938 NZ 2, 3

Stone, C G (NSW) 1938 NZ 1

Stone, J M (NSW) 1946 M, NZ 2

Storey, G P (NSW) 1926 NZ 4, 1927 I, W, S, 1928 E, F, 1929 NZ 3(R), 1930 BI

Storey, K P (NSW) 1936 NZ 2

Storey, N J D (NSW) 1962 NZ 1

Strachan, D J (NSW) 1955 NZ 2, 3

Strauss, C P (NSW) 1999 I 1(R), 2(R), E (R), SA 1(R), NZ 1, SA 2(R), NZ 2(R), [R (R), I 3(R), US, W]

Street, N O (NSW) 1899 BI 2

Streeter, S F (NSW) 1978 NZ 1

Stuart, R (NSW) 1910 NZ 2, 3

Stumbles, B D (NSW) 1972 NZ 1(R), 2, 3, Fj

Sturtridge, G S (V) 1929 NZ 2, 1932 NZ 1, 2, 3, 1933 SA 1, 2, 3, 4, 5

Sullivan, P D (NSW) 1971 SA 1, 2, 3, F 1, 2, 1972 F 1, 2, NZ 1, 2, Fj, 1973 Tg 1, 2, W

Summons, A J (NSW) 1958 W, I, E, S, M 2, NZ 1, 2, 3, 1959 BI 1, 2

Suttor, D C (NSW) 1913 NZ 1, 2, 3

Swannell, B I (NSW) 1905 NZ

Sweeney, T L (Q) 1953 SA 1

Taafe, B S (NSW) 1969 SA 1, 1972 F 1, 2

Tabua, I (Q) 1993 SA 2, 3, C, F 1, 1994 I 1, 2, It 1, 2, 1995 [C, R]

Tahu, P J A (NSW) 2008 NZ1(R), SA2(R), 3, It

Tancred, A J (NSW) 1927 I, W, S

Tancred, H E (NSW) 1923 M 1, 2

Tancred, J L (NSW) 1926 NZ 3, 4, 1928 F

Tanner, W H (Q) 1899 BI 1, 2

Tarleton, K (NSW) 1925 NZ 2, 3

Tasker, W G (NSW) 1913 NZ 1, 2, 3, 1914 NZ 1, 2, 3

Tate, M J (NSW) 1951 NZ 3, 1952 Fj 1, 2, NZ 1, 2, 1953 SA 1, 1954 Fj 1, 2

Taylor, D A (Q) 1968 NZ 1, 2, F, I, S

Taylor, H C (NSW) 1923 NZ 1, 2, 3, 1924 NZ 4

Taylor, J I (NSW) 1971 SA 1, 1972 F 1, 2, Fj

Taylor, J M (NSW) 1922 M 1, 2
Teitzel, R G (Q) 1966 W, S, 1967 E, I 1, F, I 2, NZ
Telford, D G (NSW) 1926 NZ 3(R)
Thompson, C E (NSW) 1922 M 1, 1923 M 1, 2, NZ 1, 1924 NZ 2, 3
Thompson, E G (Q) 1929 NZ 1, 2, 3, 1930 BI
Thompson, F (NSW) 1913 NZ 1, 2, 3, 1914 NZ 1, 3
Thompson, J (Q) 1914 NZ 1, 2
Thompson, P D (Q) 1950 BI 1
Thompson, R J (WA) 1971 SA 3, F 2(R), 1972 Fj
Thorn, A M (NSW) 1921 SA 1, 2, 3, NZ, 1922 M 1, 3
Thorn, E J (NSW) 1922 NZ 1, 2, 3, 1923 NZ 1, 2, 3, 1924 NZ 1, 2, 3, 1925 NZ 1, 2, 1926 NZ 1, 2, 3, 4
Thornett, J E (NSW) 1955 NZ 1, 2, 3, 1956 SA 1, 2, 1958 W, I, S, F, M 2, 3, NZ 2, 3, 1959 BI 1, 2, 1961 Fj 2, 3, SA 1, 2, F, 1962 NZ 2, 3, 4, 5, 1963 E, SA 1, 2, 3, 4, 1964 NZ 1, 2, 3, 1965 SA 1, 2, 1966 BI 1, 2, 1967 F
Thornett, R N (NSW) 1961 Fj 1, 2, 3, SA 1, 2, F, 1962 NZ 1, 2, 3, 4, 5
Thorpe, A C (NSW) 1929 NZ 1(R)
Timani, S (NSW) 2011 Sm
Timbury, F R V (Q) 1910 NZ 1, 2,
Tindall, E N (NSW) 1973 Tg 2
Toby, A E (NSW) 1925 NZ 1, 4
Tolhurst, H A (NSW) 1931 M, NZ
Tombs, R C (NSW) 1992 S 1, 2, 1994 I 2, It 1, 1996 NZ 2
Tonkin, A E J (NSW) 1947 S, I, W, 1948 E, F, 1950 BI 2
Tooth, R M (NSW) 1951 NZ 1, 2, 3, 1954 Fj 1, 2, 1955 NZ 1, 2, 3, 1957 NZ 1, 2
Towers, C H T (NSW) 1926 NZ 1, 3(R), 4, 1927 I, 1928 E, F, NZ 1, 2, 3, M, 1929 NZ 1, 3, 1930 BI, 1931 M, NZ, 1934 NZ 1, 2, 1937 SA 1, 2
Trivett, R K (Q) 1966 BI 1, 2
Tune, B N (Q) 1996 W 2, C, NZ 1, SA 1, NZ 2, SA 2, 1997 F 1, 2, NZ 1, E 1, NZ 2, SA 1, NZ 3, SA 2, Arg, 1, 2, E 2, S, 1998 E 1, S 1, 2, NZ 1, SA 1, 2, NZ 3, 1999 I 1, E, SA 1, NZ 1, SA 2, NZ 2, [R, I 3, W, SA 3, F], 2000 SA 2(R), NZ 2(t&R), SA 3(R), 2001 F (R), W, 2002 NZ 1, SA 1, NZ 2, SA 2, Arg, 2006 NZ1(R)
Tuqiri, L D (NSW) 2003 I (R), W (R), E (R), SA 1(R), NZ 1, SA 2, NZ 2, [Arg(R), R(R), Nm, I(R), S, NZ, E], 2004 S1, 2, E1, PI, NZ1, SA1, NZ2, SA2, S3, F, S4, E2, 2005 It, F1, SA1, 2, 3, NZ1, SA4, NZ2, F2, E, I, W, 2006 E1, 2, I1, NZ1, SA1, NZ2, SA2, NZ3, W, It, I2, S, 2007 Fj, SA1, NZ1, [J, W, Fj, C, E], 2008 I, F1, SA1, NZ1, 2, SA2, 3, NZ3, W(R)
Turinui, M P (NSW) 2003 I, W, E, 2003 [Nm(R)], 2004 S1(R), 2, E2, 2005 Sm, It(R), F1(R), SA1, 2(t&R), 3, NZ1, SA4, NZ2, F2, E, I, W
Turnbull, A (V) 1961 Fj 3
Turnbull, R V (NSW) 1968 I
Turner, L D (NSW) 2008 F2, It, 2009 It1, 2, F, NZ1, SA1, NZ2, SA2, 3, NZ3, 2010 NZ3, It, F(R)
Tuynman, S N (NSW) 1983 F 1, 2, 1984 E, I, W, S, 1985 C 1, 2, NZ, Fj 1, 2, 1986 It, F, Arg 1, 2, NZ 1, 2, 3, 1987 SK, [E, US, J, I, W], NZ, Arg 1(R), 2, 1988 E, It, 1989 BI 1, 2, 3, NZ, 1990 NZ 1
Tweedale, E (NSW) 1946 NZ 1, 2, 1947 NZ 2, S, I, 1948 E, F, 1949 M 1, 2, 3

Valentine, J J (Q, WF) 2006 E1(R), W(R), I2(R), S(R), 2009 It2(R), F(R)
Vaughan, D (NSW) 1983 US, Arg 1, It, F 1, 2
Vaughan, G N (V) 1958 E, S, F, M 1, 2, 3
Verge, A (NSW) 1904 BI 1, 2
Vickerman, D J (ACT, NSW) 2002 F 2(R), Arg, E, It, 2003 I (R), W (R), E (R), SA 1, NZ 1, SA 2, NZ 2, [Arg(R), R, I(R), S(R)], 2004 S1(t&R), 2(R), E1(R), PI(R), NZ1(R), SA1(R), NZ2(R), SA2(R), S3, F, S4, E2, 2005 SA2(R), 3, NZ1, SA4, 2006 E1, 2, I1, NZ1, SA1, NZ2, SA2, NZ3, SA3, W, 2007 W1(R), 2, Fj, SA1, NZ1, SA2, NZ2, [J, W, Fj, E], 2008 NZ1(R), 2(t&R), SA2, 2011 Sm(R), NZ1(R), 2, [It, I, US(R), SA, NZ]

Walden, R J (NSW) 1934 NZ 2, 1936 NZ 1, 2, M
Walker, A K (NSW) 1947 NZ 1, 1948 E, F, 1950 BI 1, 2
Walker, A M (ACT) 2000 NZ 1(R), 2001 BI 1, 2, 3, SA 1, NZ 1, 2(R)
Walker, A S B (NSW) 1912 US, 1920 NZ 1, 2, 1921 SA 1, 2, 3, NZ, 1922 M 1, 3, NZ 1, 2, 3, 1923 M 2, 3, 1924 NZ 1, 2
Walker, L F (NSW) 1988 NZ 2, 3, S, It, 1989 BI 1, 2, 3, NZ
Walker, L R (NSW) 1982 NZ 2, 3
Wallace, A C (NSW) 1921 NZ, 1926 NZ 3, 4, 1927 I, W, S, 1928 E, F
Wallace, T M (NSW) 1994 It 1(R), 2
Wallach, C (NSW) 1913 NZ 1, 3, 1914 NZ 1, 2, 3
Walsh, J J (NSW) 1953 SA 1, 2, 3, 4
Walsh, P B (NSW) 1904 BI 1, 2, 3
Walsham, K P (NSW) 1962 NZ 3, 1963 E
Ward, P G (NSW) 1899 BI 1, 2, 3, 4
Ward, T (Q) 1899 BI 2
Watson, G W (Q) 1907 NZ 1
Watson, W T (NSW) 1912 US, 1913 NZ 1, 2, 3, 1914 NZ 1, 1920 NZ 1, 2, 3
Waugh, P R (NSW) 2000 E (R), 2001 NZ 1(R), SA 2(R), NZ 2(R), Sp (R), E (R), F, W, 2003 I (R), W, E, SA 1, NZ 1, SA 2, NZ2, [Arg, R, I, S, NZ, E], 2004 S1(R), 2, E1, PI, NZ1, SA1, NZ2, SA2, S3, F, S4, E2, 2005 SA1(R), 2(R), 3, NZ1(R), SA4, NZ2, F2, E, I, W, 2006 E1(R), 2(R), I1(R), NZ1(R), SA1(R), NZ2(R), SA2(R), NZ3, SA3, W, I2, S(R), 2007 W1, 2(R), Fj, SA1(R), NZ1(R), SA2(R), NZ2(R) , [W(R), Fj, C(R), E(R)], 2008 I(R), F1(R), 2, SA1(R), NZ1(R), 2, SA2(t&R), 3, NZ4(R), It, W, 2009 It2(R), F(R)
Waugh, W W (NSW, ACT) 1993 SA 1, 1995 [C], NZ 1, 2, 1996 S, I, 1997 Arg 1, 2
Weatherstone, L J (ACT) 1975 E 1, 2, J 1, 2, S (R), 1976 E, I
Webb, W (NSW) 1899 BI 3, 4
Welborn J P (NSW) 1996 SA 2, It, 1998 Tg, 1999 E, SA 1, NZ 1
Wells, B G (NSW) 1958 M 1
Westfield, R E (NSW) 1928 NZ 1, 2, 3, M, 1929 NZ 2, 3
Whitaker, C J (NSW) 1998 SA 2(R), Fj (R), Tg, 1999 NZ 2(R), [R (R), US, F (R)], 2000 S (R), 2001 Sp (R), W (R), 2002 Arg (R), It (R), 2003 I (R), W (R), SA 2(R), [Arg(R), Nm, S(R)], 2004 PI(R), NZ1, 2005 Sm, It(R), F1(R), SA1(R), 2(R), NZ1(t&R), SA4(R), NZ2(R), F2(R), E(R), W(R)
White, C J B (NSW) 1899 BI 1, 1903 NZ, 1904 BI 1
White, J M (NSW) 1904 BI 3
White, J P L (NSW) 1958 NZ 1, 2, 3, 1961 Fj 1, 2, 3, SA 1, 2, F, 1962 NZ 1, 2, 3, 4, 5, 1963 E, SA 1, 2, 3, 4, 1964 NZ 1, 2, 3, 1965 SA 1, 2
White, M C (Q) 1931 M, NZ 1932 NZ 1, 2, 1933 SA 1, 2, 3, 4, 5
White, S W (NSW) 1956 SA 1, 2, 1958 I, E, S, M 2, 3
White, W G S (Q) 1933 SA 1, 2, 3, 4, 5, 1934 NZ 1, 2, 1936 NZ 1, 2, M
White, W J (NSW) 1928 NZ 1, M, 1932 NZ 1
Wickham, S M (NSW) 1903 NZ, 1904 BI 1, 2, 3, 1905 NZ
Williams, D (Q) 1913 NZ 3, 1914 NZ 1, 2, 3
Williams, I M (NSW) 1987 Arg 1, 2, 1988 E 1, 2, NZ 1, 2, 3, 1989 BI 2, 3, NZ, F 1, 2, 1990 F 1, 2, 3, US, NZ 1
Williams, J L (NSW) 1963 SA 1, 3, 4
Williams, R W (ACT) 1999 I 1(t&R), 2(t&R), E (R), [US], 2000 Arg 1, 2, SA 1, NZ 1, SA 2, NZ 2, SA 3, F (R), S (R), E
Williams, S A (NSW) 1980 Fj, NZ 1, 2, 1981 F 1, 2, 1982 E, NZ 1, 2, 3, 1983 US, Arg 1(R), 2, NZ, It, F 1, 2, 1984 NZ 1, 2, 3, E, I, W, S, 1985 C 1, 2, NZ, Fj 1, 2
Wilson, B J (NSW) 1949 NZ 1, 2
Wilson, C R (Q) 1957 NZ 1, 1958 NZ 1, 2, 3
Wilson, D J (Q) 1992 S 1, 2, NZ 1, 2, 3, SA, I, W, 1993 Tg, NZ, SA 1, 2, 3, C, F 1, 2, 1994 I 1, 2, It 1, 2, WS, NZ, 1995 Arg 1, 2, [SA, R, E], 1996 W 1, 2, C, NZ 1, SA 1, NZ 2, SA 2, It, S, I, W 3, 1997 F 1, 2, NZ 1, E 1(t + R), NZ 2(R), SA 1, NZ 3, SA 2, E 2(R), S (R), 1998 E 1, S 1, 2, NZ 1, SA 1, NZ 2, SA 2, NZ 3, Fj, WS, F, E 2, 1999 I 1, 2, E, SA 1, NZ 1, SA 2, NZ 2, [R, I 3, W, SA 3, F], 2000 Arg 1, 2, SA 1, NZ 1, SA 2, NZ 2, SA 3
Wilson, V W (Q) 1937 SA 1, 2, 1938 NZ 1, 2, 3
Windon, C J (NSW) 1946 NZ 1, 2, 1947 NZ 1, S, I, W, 1948 E, F, 1949 M 1, 2, 3, NZ 1, 2, 1951 NZ 1, 2, 3, 1952 Fj 1, 2, NZ 1, 2
Windon, K S (NSW) 1937 SA 1, 2, 1946 M
Windsor, J C (Q) 1947 NZ 2
Winning, K C (Q) 1951 NZ 1
Wogan, L W (NSW) 1913 NZ 1, 2, 3, 1914 NZ 1, 2, 3, 1920 NZ 1, 2, 3, 1921 SA 1, 2, 3, NZ, 1922 M 3, NZ 1, 2, 3, 1923 M 1, 2, 1924 NZ 1, 2, 3
Wood, F (NSW) 1907 NZ 1, 2, 3, 1910 NZ 1, 2, 3, 1913 NZ 1, 2, 3, 1914 NZ 1, 2, 3
Wood, R N (Q) 1972 Fj
Woods, H F (NSW) 1925 NZ 4, 1926 NZ 1, 2, 3, 1927 I, W, S, 1928 E
Wright, K J (NSW) 1975 E 1, 2, J 1, 1976 US, F 1, 2, 1978 NZ 1, 2, 3
Wyld, G (NSW) 1920 NZ 2

Yanz, K (NSW) 1958 F
Young, W K (ACT, NSW) 2000 F, S, E, 2002 F 1, 2, NZ 1, SA 1, NZ 2, SA 2, Arg, E, It, 2003 I, W, E, SA 1, NZ 1, SA 2, NZ 2, [Arg, R, I, S, NZ, E], 2004 S1, 2, E1, PI, NZ1, SA1, NZ2, SA2, S3, F, S4, E2, 2005 Sm, It, F1, SA1, 2, 3, NZ1, SA4, NZ2

CANADA

CANADA'S 2010–11 TEST RECORD

OPPONENT	DATE	VENUE	RESULT
Belgium	6 Nov	A	**Won** 43–12
Spain	13 Nov	A	**Won** 60–22
Georgia	20 Nov	A	**Lost** 15–22
Portugal	27 Nov	A	**Won** 23–20
Russia	8 Jun	N	**Won** 34–18
USA	6 Aug	H	**Won** 28–22
USA	13 Aug	A	**Won** 27–7
Tonga	14 Sep	N	**Won** 25–20
France	18 Sep	N	**Lost** 19–46
Japan	27 Sep	N	**Drew** 23–23
New Zealand	2 Oct	A	**Lost** 15–79

BEARDOS INSPIRE THE CANUCKS

By Ian Gilbert

Hannah Johnston/Getty Images

Canada kick off Rugby World Cup in spectacular style with a win over Tonga.

Canada passed their first examination of Rugby World Cup 2011 with flying colours by downing Tonga 25–20 in Whangarei. Unfortunately for the Canucks, that was to be the highlight of their campaign, as despite their intention to claim third spot in Pool A it was the resurgent Tongans who snatched automatic qualification for England 2015.

While Canada sat out the opening weekend, Tonga endured a tough night against the All Blacks in the first match of the tournament, losing 41–10. Against Canada, however, Tonga were seven points clear going into the last quarter, but the Canucks managed to turn matters around to win in front of the 17,174 crowd at the Northland Events Centre.

Tries from Jebb Sinclair, Aaron Carpenter and Phil Mackenzie saw them home, but a notable feature was the direct running of Glasgow Warriors' DTH van der Merwe – as it would be throughout the tournament.

Coach Kieran Crowley was thankful of the South African-born centre's big-match temperament, as well as the return of Clermont Auvergne forward Jamie Cudmore after four years away from the national team with injury and club commitments.

Many of the Canadians are amateurs and Crowley said, "He [Cudmore] brings great experience; there is only him and DTH van der Merwe who play in the top league in the world . . . then we have three players who have played in division one in England and the rest of the guys are locals."

Cudmore, whose actor brother Daniel features in the X-Men film series, perhaps brought his own X-factor to the side, having played in Canada's 24–7 win over Tonga at RWC 2003.

"If Canadians have got one thing, they've got heart," was Crowley's verdict on the comeback. "These are some of the best professionals I've worked with, they just don't get paid. They'll run through a brick wall for you."

The team's improvement was also clear to Crowley. "Two or three years ago, we would have lost that today. It gives me confidence that they can nail it. The strength and conditioning guys have done an excellent job in that area. We'll see how their recovery technique is."

Even with the best back-up staff, the next match was always going to be tough against France, who prevailed 46–19 at Napier's McLean Park. The scoreline suggests a comfortable win for Les Bleus, but in reality it was a far closer affair, with France leading only 25–19 before a Damien Traille try and Vincent Clerc brace in the last quarter.

There were more than the usual pre-match nerves for full-back James Pritchard, whose daughter was born two hours before kick-off. "It was certainly a bit of a disruption to my usual pre-game preparations, but it was a welcome disruption," he said.

And so to Japan, a match that would pit coaches and fellow All Blacks Crowley and John Kirwan against one another. The pair were in the victorious New Zealand RWC 1987 squad together, though Crowley was understudy to full-back John Gallagher.

Canada needed to beat Japan if they were to maintain their bid for 2015 qualification, Crowley saying, "It's our tour, really."

In the event a compelling match finished 23–23 after Japan appeared set for victory at McLean Park. Fly-half Ander Monro came to Canada's rescue with a try and penalty in the final five minutes.

The feeling of anti-climax was evident, captain Pat Riordan comparing the draw to "a bit like kissing your cousin". Try-scorer Phil Mackenzie, who plays for English Championship side Esher, lamented, "Pity I didn't score another one – we would have won."

With the All Blacks strong favourites to beat Canada in the final match of the pool, this left the Canucks' ranking in the hands of Tonga, the side they had beaten, against France.

"Our main goal is to come third so we'll be watching the Tonga game and cheering for France – that's something I never thought I'd do," admitted Mackenzie.

Tonga's shock 19–14 victory over France ultimately consigned Canada to fourth in Pool A, the win taking Tonga into the top 10 of the IRB World Rankings for the first time. For Canada to usurp them in the pool they would have to pull off an even bigger surprise and beat the All Blacks on home soil.

When the sides met in the 1991 quarter-final – Canada's one foray into the knockout stages – the Canucks went down by a creditable 29–13. Their most recent RWC encounter, however, was a 68–6 reverse in 2003.

Canada's English-born scrum coach, Mike Shelley, was unequivocal about the challenge. "The pinnacle of anyone's international career is to play against the All Blacks and our boys, all 30 of them, want to play in this game."

Hooker Ryan Hamilton, who came off the bench in all four matches, added, "Obviously when you grow up you always watched the All Blacks, so it's a dream come true to play them at home in Wellington at the World Cup."

That dream became something of a nightmare at Wellington Regional Stadium, however. All Blacks winger Zac Guildford scored four tries to equal the record for a RWC debutant, and the 79–15 defeat surpassed the 2003 match as Canada's heaviest World Cup reverse.

Any speculation as to Crowley's future was a moot point, at least. "They came to me about four or five months ago and asked me if I'd sign on after the World Cup because they didn't want World Cup results to affect their decision," he said. "Thank God that [the decision] happened before today."

Conor Trainor did have the honour of touching down twice – the first Canadian to score more than eight points in their career against New Zealand – but Riordan summed up the All Blacks' scrummaging power when he said, "I think we were a bit like a deer caught in the headlights."

Off the field, the Canadians made a name for themselves with their good-humoured desire to embrace the RWC experience. With Crowley's presence good reason for any neutral Kiwis to back the Canucks, the coach said, "The support since we've been here has just been outstanding. I've got a team of humble guys who'll do anything to play, so to come out here and have people wearing beards, dressing-up and just showing their support is amazing."

The beards reference related to the forward trio of Adam Kleeberger, Hubert Buydens and Jebb Sinclair, whose luxuriant facial hair saw them dubbed "the Beardos". The craze caught on with Napier fans who showed allegiance to their North American guests by wearing fake beards in their hundreds. Kleeberger typified Canada's wholehearted approach, coming off near the end of the New Zealand games after a clash of heads with All Black Tony Woodcock.

CANADA INTERNATIONAL STATISTICS

MATCH RECORDS UP TO 31 OCTOBER 2011

WINNING MARGIN

Date	Opponent	Result	Winning Margin
24/06/2006	Barbados	69–3	**66**
14/10/1999	Namibia	72–11	**61**
12/08/2006	USA	56–7	**49**
06/07/1996	Hong Kong	57–9	**48**

MOST POINTS IN A MATCH

BY THE TEAM

Date	Opponent	Result	Points
14/10/1999	Namibia	72–11	**72**
24/06/2006	Barbados	69–3	**69**
15/07/2000	Japan	62–18	**62**
13/11/2010	Spain	60–22	**60**
06/07/1996	Hong Kong	57–9	**57**

BY A PLAYER

Date	Player	Opponent	Points
12/08/2006	James Pritchard	USA	**36**
24/06/2006	James Pritchard	Barbados	**29**
14/10/1999	Gareth Rees	Namibia	**27**
13/07/1996	Bobby Ross	Japan	**26**
25/05/1991	Mark Wyatt	Scotland	**24**

MOST TRIES IN A MATCH

BY THE TEAM

Date	Opponent	Result	Tries
24/06/2006	Barbados	69–3	**11**
14/10/1999	Namibia	72–11	**9**
11/05/1991	Japan	49–26	**8**
15/07/2000	Japan	62–18	**8**
13/11/2010	Spain	60–22	**8**

BY A PLAYER

Date	Player	Opponent	Tries
15/07/2000	Kyle Nichols	Japan	**4**
24/06/2006	James Pritchard	Barbados	**3**
12/08/2006	James Pritchard	USA	**3**
10/05/1987	Steve Gray	USA	**3**

MOST CONVERSIONS IN A MATCH

BY THE TEAM

Date	Opponent	Result	Cons
14/10/1999	Namibia	72–11	**9**
15/07/2000	Japan	62–18	**8**

BY A PLAYER

Date	Player	Opponent	Cons
14/10/1999	Gareth Rees	Namibia	**9**
15/07/2000	Jared Barker	Japan	**8**

MOST PENALTIES IN A MATCH

BY THE TEAM

Date	Opponent	Result	Pens
25/05/1991	Scotland	24–19	**8**
22/08/1998	Argentina	28–54	**7**

BY A PLAYER

Date	Player	Opponent	Pens
25/05/1991	Mark Wyatt	Scotland	**8**
22/08/1998	Gareth Rees	Argentina	**7**

MOST DROPPED GOALS IN A MATCH

BY THE TEAM

Date	Opponent	Result	DGs
08/11/1986	USA	27–16	**2**
04/07/2001	Fiji	23–52	**2**
08/06/1980	USA	16–0	**2**
24/05/1997	Hong Kong	35–27	**2**
18/09/2011	France	19–46	**2**

BY A PLAYER

Date	Player	Opponent	DGs
04/07/2001	Bobby Ross	Fiji	**2**
24/05/1997	Bobby Ross	Hong Kong	**2**
18/09/2011	Ander Monro	France	**2**

MOST CAPPED PLAYERS

Name	Caps
Al Charron	76
Winston Stanley	66
Scott Stewart	64
Rod Snow	62
Bobby Ross	57

LEADING PENALTY SCORERS

Name	Penalties
Gareth Rees	110
Bobby Ross	84
Mark Wyatt	64
James Pritchard	64
Jared Barker	55

LEADING TRY SCORERS

Name	Tries
Winston Stanley	24
Morgan Williams	13
D T H van der Merwe	12
James Pritchard	12

LEADING DROPPED GOAL SCORERS

Name	DGs
Bobby Ross	10
Gareth Rees	9
Mark Wyatt	5

LEADING CONVERSIONS SCORERS

Name	Cons
James Pritchard	74
Bobby Ross	52
Gareth Rees	51
Jared Barker	24
Mark Wyatt	24

LEADING POINTS SCORERS

Name	Points
Gareth Rees	491
Bobby Ross	421
James Pritchard	303
Mark Wyatt	263
Jared Barker	226

Chris McGrath/Getty Images

The great Al Charron is still the only Canadian with more than 70 Test caps.

CANADA INTERNATIONAL PLAYERS
(UP TO 31 OCTOBER 2011)

Note: Years given for International Championship matches are for second half of season; eg 1972 means season 1971–72. Years for all other matches refer to the actual year of the match. Entries in square brackets denote matches played in RWC Finals.

AD Abrams 2003 *US, NZ, Tg,* 2004 *US, J, EngA, US, F, It, E,* 2005 *US, J, W, EngA, US, Ar, F, R,* 2006 *S, E, US, It*
MJ Alder 1976 *Bb*
P Aldous 1971 *W*
AS Arthurs 1988 *US*
M Ashton 1971 *W*
F Asselin 1999 *Fj,* 2000 *Tg, US, SA,* 2001 *Ur, Ar, Fj,* 2002 *S, US, US, Ur, Ur, CHL, W, F*
O Atkinson 2005 *J, Ar,* 2006 *E, US, It*
S Ault 2006 *W, It,* 2008 *US, Pt,* 2009 *Geo, US, US*

JC Bain 1932 *J*
RG Banks 1999 *J, Fj, Sa, US, Tg, W, E, F, Nm,* 2000 *US, SA, I, J, It,* 2001 *US, Ur, Ar, E, Fj, J,* 2002 *S, US, US, Ur, CHL, Ur, CHL, W, F,* 2003 *EngA, US, M, M, Ur, NZ, It*
S Barber 1973 *W,* 1976 *Bb*
M Barbieri 2006 *E, US*
B Barker 1966 *BI,* 1971 *W*
J Barker 2000 *Tg, J, It,* 2002 *S, US, US, Ur, CHL, Ur, CHL, W,* 2003 *US, NZ, It,* 2004 *US, J, F, It*
T Bauer 1977 *US, E,* 1978 *US, F,* 1979 *US*
DR Baugh 1998 *J, HK, US, HK, J, Ur, Ar,* 1999 *J, Fj, Sa, US, Tg, W, E, F, Fj, Nm,* 2000 *US, SA, I, It,* 2001 *E, E,* 2002 *S, US, Ur, CHL*
A Bianco 1966 *BI*
AJ Bibby 1979 *US, F,* 1980 *W, US, NZ,* 1981 *US, Ar*
R Bice 1996 *US, A,* 1997 *US, J, HK, US, W, I,* 1998 *US, US, HK, J, Ur, US, Ar,* 1999 *J, Fj, Sa, US, Tg, W, F*
P Bickerton 2004 *US, J*
D Biddle 2006 *S, E, Bar,* 2007 *W, Fj, A*
JM Billingsley 1974 *Tg,* 1977 *US,* 1978 *F,* 1979 *US,* 1980 *W,* 1983 *US, It, It,* 1984 *US*
WG Bjarneson 1962 *Bb*
TJH Blackwell 1973 *W*
N Blevins 2009 *J, J,* 2010 *Bel, Sp, Geo, Pt*
B Bonenberg 1983 *US, It, It*
J Boone 1932 *J, J*
T Bourne 1967 *E*
CJ Braid 2010 *Bel, Geo*
R Breen 1986 *US,* 1987 *W,* 1990 *US,* 1991 *J, S, US, R,* 1993 *E, US*
R Breen 1983 *E,* 1987 *US*
R Brewer 1967 *E*
STT Brown 1989 *I, US*
N Browne 1973 *W,* 1974 *Tg*
S Bryan 1996 *Ur, US, Ar,* 1997 *HK, J, US, W,* 1998 *HK, J, US, Ar,* 1999 *Fj, Sa, US, Tg, W, E, F, Fj, Nm*
M Burak 2004 *US, J, EngA, US, F, It, E,* 2005 *EngA, US, Ar, F, R,* 2006 *US, Bar, W,* 2007 *NZ, Pt, W, Fj, J, A,* 2008 *I, W, S,* 2009 *I, W, Geo, US, US*
C Burford 1970 *Fj*
D Burgess 1962 *Bb, W23*
D Burleigh 2001 *Ur, Ar, E, E*
JB Burnham 1966 *BI,* 1967 *E,* 1970 *Fj,* 1971 *W*
HAW Buydens 2006 *E, Bar,* 2008 *US,* 2011 *Rus, US, US, Tg, F, J, NZ*

GE Cameron 1932 *J*
JWD Cannon 2001 *US, Ar, E, E, Fj, J,* 2002 *S, US, Ur, CHL, Ur, CHL, W, F,* 2003 *EngA, US, M, M, Ur, US, Ar, NZ, It,* 2004 *US, F, It, E,* 2005 *W, EngA, US, F*
R Card 1996 *US, A, Ur, US, Ar,* 1997 *US, J, HK*
ME Cardinal 1986 *US,* 1987 *US, Tg, I, US,* 1991 *S,* 1993 *A,* 1994 *US, F, E, F,* 1995 *S, Fj, NZ, R, SA,* 1996 *US, US, HK, J, A, HK, J,* 1997 *US, US, W, I,* 1998 *US, HK,* 1999 *Fj, US, W, E, Fj, Nm*
LAG Carlson 2002 *Ur, W,* 2003 *EngA*
A Carpenter 2005 *US, J, EngA, US, Ar, F, R,* 2006 *S, E, US, W, It,* 2007 *US, NZ, Pt, W, Fj, J, A,* 2008 *US, Pt, I, W, S,* 2009 *I, W, Geo, US, J, J, Rus,* 2010 *Ur, Sp, Geo, Pt,* 2011 *Rus, US, US, Tg, F, J, NZ*
NS Carr 1985 *A, A*
DJ Carson 1980 *W, US, NZ,* 1981 *US, Ar,* 1982 *J, E, US,* 1983 *It, It*
SFB Carson 1977 *E*
MP Chambers 1962 *Bb, W23,* 1966 *BI*
AJ Charron 1990 *Ar, US, Ar,* 1991 *J, S, Fj, F, NZ,* 1992 *US,* 1993 *E, E, US, A, W,* 1994 *US, F, W,* 1995 *Fj, NZ, R, A, SA, US,* 1996 *US, US, A, HK, J, Ur, US, Ar,* 1997 *US, J, HK, HK, J, US, W, I,* 1998 *US, HK, J, Ur, US, Ar,* 1999 *Fj, Sa, US, Tg, W, E, F, Fj, Nm,* 2000 *Tg, US, SA, Sa, Fj, J, It,* 2001 *Ur, Ar, E, E,* 2002 *S, US, US, Ur, CHL, Ur, CHL, F,* 2003 *W, It, Tg*
L Chung 1978 *F*
N Clapinson 1995 *US,* 1996 *US*
RM Clark 1962 *Bb*
D Clarke 1996 *A*
ME Clarkin 1985 *A, A*
B Collins 2004 *US, J*
W Collins 1977 *US, E*
GG Cooke 2000 *Tg, US,* 2001 *Fj, J,* 2003 *EngA, US, M, M, Ur, US, Ar, W, NZ, Tg,* 2004 *EngA, US, It, E,* 2005 *US, J, W, Ar, F, R,* 2006 *US*
I Cooper 1993 *W*
JA Cordle 1998 *HK, J,* 1999 *J, Fj, Sa,* 2001 *J*
GER Cox 1932 *J*
S Creagh 1988 *US*
JN Cudmore 2002 *US, CHL, W, F,* 2003 *EngA, US, W, NZ, It, Tg,* 2004 *US, F, It, E,* 2005 *W, F,* 2006 *US,* 2007 *Pt, W, Fj,* 2011 *Rus, US, US, Tg, F, J, NZ*
L Cudmore 2008 *US*
C Culpan 2006 *E,* 2007 *US, NZ, Pt, W, Fj, J*
TJ Cummings 1966 *BI,* 1973 *W*
Z Cvitak 1983 *E*

N Dala 2007 *US,* 2008 *US,* 2009 *I, W, Geo, US, US, J, J,* 2010 *Ur,* 2011 *Rus, Tg, F, NZ*
MJW Dandy 1977 *E, E*
M Danskin 2001 *J,* 2004 *EngA, F*
D Daypuck 2004 *EngA, F, It, E,* 2005 *US, J, W, EngA, Ar, F, R,* 2006 *S, US, US, W, It,* 2007 *A*
H de Goede 1974 *Tg,* 1976 *Bb,* 1977 *US, E, E,* 1978 *US,* 1979 *US, F,* 1980 *W, US, NZ,* 1981 *US,* 1982 *J, J, E, US,* 1984 *US,* 1985 *US,* 1986 *J, US,* 1987 *US, Tg, I, W*
F Deacy 1973 *W*
J Delaney 1983 *E*
P Densmore 2005 *EngA*
JD Devlin 1985 *US,* 1986 *US*
M di Girolamo 2001 *Ur, Ar,* 2002 *US, Ur, CHL, Ur, W, F,* 2003 *US, M, M, Ur, W, NZ, It, Tg,* 2004 *EngA, US, F, It, E*
GA Dixon 2000 *US, SA, I, Sa, Fj, J, It,* 2001 *US, Ar, E, E*
D Docherty 1973 *W*
TJ Dolezel 2009 *Rus,* 2010 *Ur, Bel, Sp, Geo, Pt,* 2011 *Rus*
WJ Donaldson 1978 *F,* 1979 *US, F,* 1980 *W, US, NZ,* 1981 *US,* 1982 *E, US,* 1983 *US, It, It,* 1984 *US*
A Douglas 1974 *Tg*
JT Douglas 2003 *M, M, Ur, US, Ar, NZ, It,* 2004 *US, F*
A du Temple 1932 *J, J*
SR Duke 2008 *S,* 2009 *W, Geo, J, J, Rus,* 2010 *Bel*

G Dukelow 1980 *W, US, NZ*, 1981 *US*, 1982 *J, J, E, US*, 1983 *US, It, It, E*, 1984 *US*, 1990 *US*

PJ Dunkley 1998 *J, HK, US, HK, J, US, Ar*, 1999 *J, Fj, Sa, US, Tg, E, F, Fj, Nm*, 2000 *Tg, SA, I, Sa, Fj*, 2001 *US, Ar, E, Fj, J*, 2002 *S, US, US, Ur, CHL, W, F*, 2003 *M, M, Ur, Ar*, 2005 *W*

C Dunning 2005 *EngA, US, Ar, F, R*

B Ebl 1995 *NZ*, 1998 *J, HK*

DC Eburne 1977 *US, E, E*

MA Eckardt 1974 *Tg*, 1977 *US, E, E*, 1978 *US*

IJ Edwards 1967 *E*

G Ellwand 1973 *W*

GD Ennis 1986 *J, US*, 1987 *US, Tg, I, W*, 1988 *US*, 1989 *I, US*, 1990 *Ar, US, Ar*, 1991 *J, S, US, Fj, R, F, NZ*, 1993 *E, E*, 1994 *US, W*, 1995 *Fj, NZ, R, A, SA*, 1998 *J, HK, US, US*

BW Erichsen 2009 *Rus*, 2010 *Ur, Bel*, 2011 *US, US*

EA Evans 1986 *US*, 1987 *US, Tg, I, US*, 1989 *I, US*, 1990 *Ar, Ar*, 1991 *J, S, US, Fj, R, F, NZ*, 1992 *US, E*, 1993 *E, E*, 1994 *US, F, W, E, F*, 1995 *S, Ur, Ar, Fj, NZ, R, A, SA*, 1996 *J, HK, J*, 1997 *US, J, HK, J, US, W, I*, 1998 *J, HK, US, US, US, Ar*

MC Evans 2008 *I, W, S*, 2009 *W, Geo, US, US, J, Rus*, 2010 *Ur*, 2011 *Rus, US, J, NZ*

I Exner 2005 *EngA, US*

A Fagan 2008 *Pt*

EG Fairhurst 2001 *US, Ar*, 2002 *US, Ur, CHL, Ur, CHL, W, F*, 2003 *EngA, M, M, US, NZ, Tg*, 2004 *US, J, EngA, US, F, It, E*, 2005 *US, W, EngA, US, F*, 2006 *S, E, US, Bar, US, W, It*, 2007 *US, NZ, Pt, W, A*, 2008 *US, I, W, S*, 2009 *I, W, Geo, US, US*, 2010 *Ur*, 2011 *Rus, US, Tg, F, J, NZ*

SC Fauth 2000 *Tg, US, SA, I, Sa, Fj, J, It*, 2001 *US, Ar, E, E, Fj, J*, 2002 *S, US, US, Ur, CHL, CHL, W, F*, 2003 *US, M, Ur, US, Ar, NZ, Tg*

M Felix 1985 *A, A*, 1996 *Ur, US*

P Fleck 2004 *US, J, It, E*, 2005 *US, W*, 2008 *US*

I Fleming 1976 *Bb*

AC Forbes 1932 *J, J*

F Forster 1983 *US, It, It*

AE Foster 1970 *Fj*, 1976 *Bb*, 1977 *US, E, E*

C Fowler 1988 *US*, 1990 *US*

TE Fraine 1967 *E*

RP Frame 1986 *J*, 1987 *US, Tg, I, W, US*

S Franklin 2007 *US, NZ, J*, 2008 *US, S*, 2009 *I*, 2011 *Rus, US, Tg, F, J, NZ*

G Fraser 1983 *E*

P Frize 1962 *Bb, W23*

GW Fumano 1967 *E*, 1970 *Fj*

QA Fyffe 2003 *EngA, US, NZ, It, Tg*, 2004 *US, J, EngA, US, F, It*, 2005 *US, J, W, Ar*

F Gainer 2004 *US, J, EngA, US, F, It, E*, 2005 *US, J, W, EngA, US, F, R*, 2006 *W, It*

A Godziek 1982 *J, E, US*, 1983 *US, It, It, E*, 1984 *US*

GG Gonis 1977 *US, E, E*, 1978 *US*

K Goodland 2005 *US*

I Gordon 1991 *S*, 1992 *US, E*, 1993 *US, A, W*, 1994 *F, W, E, F*, 1995 *S, R, SA, US*, 1996 *US, HK, J, A, HK*, 1997 *US, J, HK*, 1998 *J, HK, US, J, US, Ar*

JD Graf 1989 *I, US*, 1990 *Ar*, 1991 *S, R*, 1992 *US, E*, 1993 *E, E, US, A*, 1994 *US, F, W, E, F*, 1995 *S, Ur, Ar, Fj, NZ, R, A, SA, US*, 1996 *US, HK, J, A, HK, J*, 1997 *US, J, HK, HK, US, W, I*, 1998 *J, HK, US, US, HK, J, Ur, US, Ar*, 1999 *J, Fj, Sa, US, Tg, F, Nm*

W Granleese 1962 *W23*

G Grant 1977 *E, E*, 1978 *US*, 1979 *US, F*, 1980 *W*

I Grant 1983 *US, It, It, E*

PR Grantham 1962 *Bb, W23*, 1966 *BI*

SD Gray 1984 *US*, 1987 *US, W, US*, 1989 *I*, 1990 *Ar, US, Ar*, 1991 *J, S, Fj, F, NZ*, 1992 *US, E*, 1993 *E, E, US, A, W*, 1994 *US, F, W, E, F*, 1995 *S, Ar, Fj, NZ, R, A, SA, US*, 1996 *US, US, HK, J, A, HK, J, US, Ar*, 1997 *US, J, HK, J, US*

GR Greig 1973 *W*

JR Grieg 1977 *US, E*, 1978 *US*, 1979 *US, F*, 1980 *W, US, NZ*, 1981 *Ar*

J Grout 1995 *Ur*

MR Gudgeon 2010 *Bel*, 2011 *Rus*

G Gudmundseth 1973 *W*

N Hadley 1987 *US*, 1989 *I, US*, 1990 *Ar*, 1991 *S, US, Fj, R, F, NZ*, 1992 *US, E*, 1993 *E*, 1994 *E, F*

J Haley 1996 *Ur*

J Hall 1996 *US, US*, 1997 *HK*, 1998 *J, HK, J, US, Ar*

GRO Hamilton 2010 *Ur*, 2011 *Rus, US, US, Tg, F, J, NZ*

WT Handson 1985 *A, A, US*, 1986 *J, US*, 1987 *US, Tg, I, W*

JP Hawthorn 1982 *J, J, E*, 1983 *US, It, It*

A Healy 1996 *HK, J, HK, J, Ur, US, Ar*, 1997 *US, HK, HK, I*, 1998 *HK, J, Ur*, 1999 *J*

AR Heaman 1988 *US*

C Hearn 2008 *I, W, S*, 2009 *I, W, Geo, US, US, J, J*, 2010 *Ur, Bel, Sp, Geo, Pt*, 2011 *US, US, Tg, F*

B Henderson 2005 *J, F, R*

S Hendry 1996 *Ur, US, Ar*

G Henrikson 1971 *W*

L Hillier 1973 *W*

RE Hindson 1973 *W*, 1974 *Tg*, 1976 *Bb*, 1977 *US, E, E*, 1978 *US, F*, 1979 *US, F*, 1980 *W, US, NZ*, 1981 *US, Ar*, 1982 *J, J, E, US*, 1983 *US, It, It*, 1984 *US*, 1985 *A, A, US*, 1986 *J*, 1987 *US, I, W*, 1990 *Ar*

G Hirayama 1977 *E, E*, 1978 *US*, 1979 *US, F*, 1980 *W, US, NZ*, 1981 *US*, 1982 *J, E, US*

NS Hirayama 2008 *Pt, S*, 2009 *J, J, Rus*, 2010 *Bel*, 2011 *US, F, NZ*

M Holmes 1987 *US*

TN Hotson 2008 *US, Pt, I, W, S*, 2009 *I, W, Geo, US, US, J, J, Rus*, 2010 *Ur, Sp, Geo, Pt*, 2011 *Rus, US, US, Tg, F, J, NZ*

P Howlett 1974 *Tg*

BM Hunnings 1932 *J, J*

E Hunt 1966 *BI*, 1967 *E*

S Hunter 2005 *R*

J Hutchinson 1993 *E, A, W*, 1995 *S, Ar, Fj, A, SA, US*, 1996 *US, US, HK, J, A, HK, J, Ur, US, Ar*, 1997 *US, J, HK, HK, J, US, W, I*, 1998 *J, HK, US, US, HK, J, Ur, US, Ar*, 1999 *J, Fj, Sa, US, Tg, W, E, F, Fj, Nm*, 2000 *US, Sa, Fj, J*

I Hyde-Lay 1986 *J*, 1987 *US*, 1988 *US*

M Irvine 2000 *Tg, SA, I, Sa, Fj, J*, 2001 *US, Ar*

DC Jackart 1991 *J, S, US, Fj, R, F*, 1992 *US, E*, 1993 *E, E, US, A, W*, 1994 *US, F, W, E, F*, 1995 *S, Ar, Fj*

J Jackson 2003 *Ur, US, Ar, W, It, Tg*, 2004 *EngA, US, It, E*, 2005 *W, US, Ar, R*, 2006 *S*, 2007 *US, NZ, J*, 2008 *I, W, S*, 2009 *J*, 2010 *Sp, Geo*

RO Jackson 1970 *Fj*, 1971 *W*

MB James 1994 *US, F, W, E, F*, 1995 *S, Ur, Ar, Fj, NZ, R, A, US*, 1996 *US, US, HK, J, A, HK, J*, 1997 *J, US, W, I*, 1998 *US, US, Ur, US, Ar*, 1999 *Sa, W, E, F, Fj, Nm*, 2000 *It*, 2002 *S, US, US, Ur, CHL, W, F*, 2003 *M, M, Ur, US, Ar, W, Tg*, 2005 *F*, 2006 *US*, 2007 *Pt, W, Fj, J, A*

G Jennings 1981 *Ar*, 1983 *US, It, It, E*

O Johnson 1970 *Fj*

G Johnston 1978 *F*

RR Johnstone 2001 *Ur, Fj, J*, 2002 *CHL, Ur, CHL*, 2003 *EngA*

C Jones 1983 *E*

CWB Jones 1987 *US*

EL Jones 1982 *J*, 1983 *US*

TK Kariya 1967 *E*, 1970 *Fj*, 1971 *W*

A Kennedy 1985 *A, A*

I Kennedy 1993 *A, W*

ED Kettleson 1985 *US*

B Keys 2008 *US, Pt, I, W, S*, 2009 *Geo, US, J*

MMG King 2002 *US, Ur*, 2003 *M, US, Ar, NZ*, 2005 *US, J, W, EngA, US, Ar*

A Kingham 1974 *Tg*

A Kleeberger 2005 *F, R*, 2006 *S, E, US, Bar, It*, 2007 *US, NZ, Pt, J*, 2008 *US, Pt, I, W, S*, 2009 *I, W, Geo, US, US, J, J, Rus*, 2010 *Ur, Bel, Sp, Geo, Pt*, 2011 *US, US, Tg, F, J, NZ*

ERP Knaggs 2000 *Tg, US, SA, I, Sa, Fj, J*, 2001 *US, Ur, Ar, E, E, Fj, J*, 2002 *S*, 2003 *EngA, Ur, Ar, NZ*

JD Knauer 1992 *E*, 1993 *E, E, US, W*

MJ Kokan 1984 *US*, 1985 *US*

P Kyle 1984 *US*

JA Kyne 2010 *Bel*, 2011 *J*

A La Carte 2004 *US, J*

M Langley 2004 *EngA*, 2005 *Ar*

MJ Lawson 2002 *US, Ur, CHL, Ur, CHL, F*, 2003 *EngA, US, M, M, Ur, US, Ar, W, It, Tg*, 2004 *F, It, E*, 2005 *US, J, F, R*, 2006 *Bar, US, W*

P le Blanc 1994 *F*, 1995 *Ur, Fj, NZ*

CE le Fevre 1976 *Bb*

J Lecky 1962 *Bb, W23*

JL Lecky 1982 *J, US*, 1983 *US, It, It*, 1984 *US*, 1985 *A, US*, 1986 *J, US*, 1987 *I, W, US*, 1991 *J, S, Fj, R*

GB Legh 1973 *W*, 1974 *Tg*, 1976 *Bb*

LSF Leroy 1932 *J*
J Lorenz 1966 *BI*, 1970 *Fj*, 1971 *W*
DC Lougheed 1990 *Ar*, 1991 *J*, *US*, 1992 *US*, *E*, 1993 *E*, *E*, *US*, 1994 *F*, *W*, *E*, *F*, 1995 *Fj*, *NZ*, *R*, *A*, *SA*, 1996 *A*, *HK*, 1997 *J*, *W*, *I*, 1998 *US*, *Ar*, 1999 *US*, *Tg*, *W*, *E*, *F*, *Fj*, *Nm*, 2003 *W*, *It*
J Loveday 1993 *E*, *E*, *US*, *A*, 1996 *HK*, *J*, 1998 *J*, *Ur*, 1999 *Sa*, *US*
B Luke 2004 *US*, *J*
M Luke 1974 *Tg*, 1976 *Bb*, 1977 *US*, *E*, *E*, 1978 *US*, *F*, 1979 *US*, *F*, 1980 *W*, *US*, *NZ*, 1981 *US*, 1982 *J*, *US*
S Lytton 1995 *Ur*, *Ar*, *US*, 1996 *US*, *HK*, *J*, *J*, *US*, *Ar*

G MacDonald 1970 *Fj*
GDT MacDonald 1998 *HK*
P Mack 2009 *I*, *W*, *Geo*, *US*, *US*, *J*, *J*, *Rus*
I MacKay 1993 *A*, *W*
JL Mackenzie 2010 *Bel*, *Sp*, 2011 *US*
PW Mackenzie 2008 *Pt*, *I*, 2010 *Ur*, *Sp*, *Geo*, *Pt*, 2011 *Rus*, *US*, *US*, *Tg*, *F*, *J*, *NZ*
GI MacKinnon 1985 *US*, 1986 *J*, 1988 *US*, 1989 *I*, *US*, 1990 *Ar*, *Ar*, 1991 *J*, *S*, *Fj*, *R*, *F*, *NZ*, 1992 *US*, *E*, 1993 *E*, 1994 *US*, *F*, *W*, *E*, *F*, 1995 *S*, *Ur*, *Ar*, *Fj*, *NZ*, *A*, *SA*
S MacKinnon 1992 *US*, 1995 *Ur*, *Ar*, *Fj*
C MacLachlan 1981 *Ar*, 1982 *J*, *E*
P Maclean 1983 *US*, *It*, *It*, *E*
I Macmillan 1981 *Ar*, 1982 *J*, *J*, *E*, *US*
M MacSween 2009 *Rus*
B Major 2001 *Fj*, *J*
D Major 1999 *E*, *Fj*, *Nm*, 2000 *Tg*, *US*, *SA*, *I*, *Fj*, 2001 *Ur*, *E*, *E*
A Marshall 1997 *J*, 1998 *Ur*
JA Marshall 2008 *S*, 2010 *Ur*, *Bel*, *Sp*, *Geo*, *Pt*, 2011 *US*, *US*, *Tg*, *F*, *J*, *NZ*
P Mason 1974 *Tg*
B McCarthy 1996 *US*, *Ar*, 1998 *J*, *HK*, *J*
J McDonald 1974 *Tg*
RN McDonald 1966 *BI*, 1967 *E*, 1970 *Fj*
AG McGann 1985 *A*, *A*
R McGeein 1973 *W*
RI McInnes 1979 *F*, 1980 *NZ*, 1981 *US*, *Ar*, 1982 *J*, *J*, *E*, *US*, 1983 *US*, *It*, *It*, 1984 *US*, 1985 *US*
B McKee 1962 *Bb*, *W23*
B Mckee 1966 *BI*, 1970 *Fj*
SS McKeen 2004 *US*, *J*, *EngA*, *US*, *F*, *It*, *E*, 2005 *US*, *J*, *W*, *EngA*, *F*, *R*, 2006 *S*, *US*, *US*, *W*, *It*, 2007 *US*, *NZ*
JR McKellar 1985 *A*, *A*, 1986 *J*, 1987 *W*
JH McKenna 1967 *E*
C McKenzie 1992 *US*, *E*, 1993 *E*, *US*, *A*, *W*, 1994 *US*, *F*, *W*, *E*, *F*, 1995 *S*, *Ur*, *Ar*, *Fj*, *NZ*, *R*, *SA*, 1996 *US*, *HK*, *J*, *J*, 1997 *J*, *HK*, *I*
SG McTavish 1970 *Fj*, 1971 *W*, 1976 *Bb*, 1977 *US*, *E*, *E*, 1978 *US*, *F*, 1979 *US*, *F*, 1980 *W*, *US*, 1981 *US*, *Ar*, 1982 *J*, *J*, *E*, *US*, 1985 *US*, 1987 *US*, *Tg*, *I*
R McWhinney 2005 *F*, *R*
J Mensah-Coker 2006 *S*, *E*, *US*, *Bar*, *US*, *W*, *It*, 2007 *US*, *NZ*, *Pt*, *J*, *A*, 2008 *US*, *I*, *W*, *S*, 2009 *US*, *US*, *J*, *J*, *Rus*, 2010 *Ur*, *Sp*, *Geo*, *Pt*, 2011 *Rus*
C Michaluk 1995 *SA*, 1996 *US*, *J*, 1997 *US*, *HK*
N Milau 2000 *US*, *J*
DRW Milne 1966 *BI*, 1967 *E*
AB Mitchell 1932 *J*, *J*
P Monaghan 1982 *J*
AHB Monro 2006 *E*, *US*, *Bar*, *US*, *W*, *It*, 2007 *W*, *A*, 2008 *US*, *Pt*, *I*, *W*, 2009 *I*, *W*, *Geo*, *US*, *US*, *J*, *J*, *Rus*, 2010 *Ur*, *Bel*, *Pt*, 2011 *Rus*, *US*, *US*, *Tg*, *F*, *J*, *NZ*
D Moonlight 2003 *EngA*, 2004 *EngA*, *E*, 2005 *US*
JI Moonlight 2009 *Geo*
DL Moore 1962 *Bb*, *W23*
K Morgan 1997 *HK*, *HK*, *J*, *W*
VJP Moroney 1962 *Bb*
B Mosychuk 1996 *Ur*, 1997 *J*
J Moyes 1981 *Ar*, 1982 *J*, *J*, *E*, *US*
PT Murphy 2000 *Tg*, *US*, *SA*, *I*, *Sa*, *Fj*, *J*, 2001 *Fj*, *J*, 2002 *S*, *US*, *US*, *Ur*, *CHL*, *W*, *F*, 2003 *US*, *M*, *M*, 2004 *F*
WA Murray 1932 *J*
K Myhre 1970 *Fj*

J Newton 1962 *W23*
GN Niblo 1932 *J*, *J*
K Nichols 1996 *Ur*, 1998 *J*, *HK*, *US*, *US*, *Ur*, 1999 *J*, *Fj*, *Sa*, *US*, *Tg*, *Fj*, *Nm*, 2000 *Tg*, *US*, *SA*, *I*, *Sa*, *Fj*, *J*, *It*, 2001 *Ur*, *E*, *Fj*, *J*, 2002 *S*
D Nikas 1995 *Ur*, *Ar*

S O'Leary 2004 *US*, *J*, *EngA*, *E*, 2005 *US*, *J*
C O'Toole 2009 *I*, *US*, *J*, *J*, *Rus*, 2010 *Ur*, *Bel*, *Sp*, *Geo*, *Pt*, 2011 *Rus*, *US*, *US*, *Tg*, *F*, *J*, *NZ*

S Pacey 2005 *W*
C Pack 2006 *S*, *US*
J Pagano 1997 *I*, 1998 *J*, *HK*, *US*, *HK*, *J*, *US*, 1999 *J*, *Fj*, *Nm*
DV Pahl 1971 *W*
P Palmer 1983 *E*, 1984 *US*, 1985 *A*, 1986 *J*, *US*, 1987 *Tg*, *I*, *W*, 1988 *US*, 1990 *Ar*, *US*, 1991 *J*, *US*, *Fj*, *R*, *F*, 1992 *US*
K Parfrey 2005 *J*
TF Paris 2010 *Bel*, *Sp*, *Pt*
A Pasutto 2004 *US*, *J*
K Peace 1978 *F*, 1979 *US*, *F*, 1980 *W*, *US*
J Penaluna 1996 *Ur*
DN Penney 1995 *US*, 1996 *US*, *A*, *US*, *Ar*, 1997 *HK*, 1999 *E*
J Phelan 2010 *Bel*, *Sp*, *Pt*
JM Phelan 1980 *NZ*, 1981 *Ar*, 1982 *J*, *J*, 1985 *A*, *A*
M Phinney 2006 *S*, *E*
EC Pinkham 1932 *J*
C Plater 2003 *EngA*
D Pletch 2004 *US*, *J*, *EngA*, *It*, *E*, 2005 *US*, *J*, *W*, *EngA*, 2006 *S*, *E*, *US*, *Bar*, *US*, *W*, *It*, 2007 *US*, *NZ*, *Pt*, *W*, *Fj*, *J*, *A*, 2009 *US*, *US*, *J*, *J*, *Rus*, 2010 *Bel*, *Sp*, *Pt*
MT Pletch 2005 *Ar*, 2006 *S*, *E*, *US*, *Bar*, *W*, *It*, 2007 *US*, *NZ*, *Pt*, *W*, *J*, *A*, 2008 *US*, *Pt*, *I*, *W*, *S*, 2009 *W*, *Geo*, *US*, *US*, *J*, *Rus*
JG Pritchard 2003 *M*, *M*, *Ur*, *US*, *Ar*, *W*, *Tg*, 2006 *S*, *US*, *Bar*, *US*, *W*, 2007 *US*, *NZ*, *Pt*, *W*, *Fj*, *J*, *A*, 2008 *US*, *Pt*, *I*, *W*, *S*, 2009 *I*, *W*, *Geo*, *US*, *US*, *J*, *J*, *Rus*, 2010 *Ur*, *Sp*, *Geo*, *Pt*, 2011 *Rus*, *US*, *US*, *Tg*, *F*, *J*
G Puil 1962 *Bb*, *W23*
M Pyke 2004 *US*, *J*, *US*, *It*, 2005 *US*, *F*, *R*, 2006 *S*, *E*, *US*, *Bar*, *US*, *W*, *It*, 2007 *US*, *NZ*, *Pt*, *W*, *Fj*, *J*, *A*, 2008 *US*

DLJ Quigley 1976 *Bb*, 1979 *F*

RE Radu 1985 *A*, 1986 *US*, 1987 *US*, *Tg*, *I*, *US*, 1988 *US*, 1989 *I*, *US*, 1990 *Ar*, *Ar*, 1991 *US*
D Ramsey 2005 *US*
GL Rees 1986 *US*, 1987 *US*, *Tg*, *I*, *W*, *US*, 1989 *I*, *US*, 1990 *Ar*, *Ar*, 1991 *J*, *S*, *US*, *Fj*, *R*, *F*, *NZ*, 1992 *US*, *E*, 1993 *E*, *E*, *US*, *W*, 1994 *US*, *F*, *W*, *E*, *F*, 1995 *S*, *Fj*, *NZ*, *R*, *A*, *SA*, 1996 *HK*, *J*, 1997 *US*, *J*, *HK*, *J*, *US*, *W*, *I*, 1998 *US*, *US*, *Ur*, *US*, *Ar*, 1999 *Sa*, *Tg*, *W*, *E*, *F*, *Fj*, *Nm*
J Reid 2003 *M*, *US*, *Ar*, *NZ*, *Tg*
G Relph 1974 *Tg*
S Richmond 2004 *EngA*, *US*, *F*, *It*, *E*, 2005 *US*, *W*, *EngA*, *US*
PD Riordan 2003 *EngA*, 2004 *US*, *J*, *EngA*, *US*, 2006 *S*, *E*, *US*, *Bar*, *US*, *W*, *It*, 2007 *US*, *NZ*, *Pt*, *W*, *Fj*, *J*, *A*, 2008 *US*, *Pt*, *I*, *W*, 2009 *I*, *W*, *Geo*, *US*, *US*, *J*, *J*, *Rus*, 2010 *Ur*, *Bel*, *Sp*, *Geo*, *Pt*, 2011 *Rus*, *US*, *US*, *Tg*, *F*, *J*, *NZ*
JR Robertsen 1985 *A*, *A*, *US*, 1986 *US*, 1987 *US*, 1989 *I*, *US*, 1990 *Ar*, *US*, *Ar*, 1991 *Fj*, *F*
C Robertson 1997 *HK*, 1998 *US*, *US*, *HK*, *J*, *Ur*, 2001 *Ur*
AK Robinson 1998 *HK*
G Robinson 1966 *BI*
R Robson 1998 *HK*, *US*, 1999 *J*, *Tg*
S Rodgers 2005 *US*
RP Ross 1989 *I*, *US*, 1990 *US*, 1995 *Ar*, *NZ*, 1996 *US*, *US*, *HK*, *J*, *A*, *HK*, *J*, *Ur*, *US*, *Ar*, 1997 *US*, *J*, *HK*, *HK*, *J*, *US*, *W*, 1998 *J*, *HK*, *US*, *US*, *HK*, *J*, *Ur*, *US*, 1999 *J*, *Fj*, *Sa*, *US*, *W*, *E*, *F*, *Nm*, 2001 *Ur*, *E*, *E*, *Fj*, *J*, 2002 *US*, *US*, *Ur*, *CHL*, *Ur*, *CHL*, *F*, 2003 *EngA*, *US*, *M*, *Ur*, *Ar*, *W*, *Tg*
JG Rowland 1932 *J*, *J*
G Rowlands 1995 *Ar*, *NZ*, *A*, *US*, 1996 *US*, *US*
RJ Russell 1979 *US*, 1983 *E*, 1985 *A*, *A*
JB Ryan 1966 *BI*, 1967 *E*

IH Saundry 1932 *J*, *J*
MD Schiefler 1980 *US*, *NZ*, 1981 *US*, *Ar*, 1982 *J*, *E*, *US*, 1983 *US*, 1984 *US*
M Schmid 1996 *Ur*, *US*, *Ar*, 1997 *US*, *J*, *US*, *W*, *I*, 1998 *US*, *HK*, *J*, *Ur*, *Ar*, 1999 *Sa*, *US*, *W*, *E*, *F*, *Fj*, *Nm*, 2001 *US*, *Ur*, *E*, *E*
MA Scholz 2009 *Rus*, 2011 *Rus*, *US*, *US*
T Scott 1976 *Bb*
S Selkirk 1932 *J*
JD Shaw 1978 *F*
CJ Shergold 1980 *US*, *NZ*, 1981 *US*
DM Shick 1970 *Fj*, 1971 *W*
JL Sinclair 2008 *Pt*, *I*, *W*, *S*, 2009 *I*, *US*, *US*, *J*, *J*, *Rus*, 2010 *Bel*, *Sp*, *Geo*, *Pt*, 2011 *Rus*, *US*, *US*, *Tg*, *F*, *J*, *NZ*
DC Sinnott 1979 *F*, 1981 *US*, *Ar*

FG Skillings 1932 *J, J*
DM Slater 1971 *W*
C Smith 1995 *Ur, US*, 1996 *HK, J, Ur, US, Ar*, 1997 *US*, 1998 *J, HK, US, HK, Ur*, 1999 *J, Fj, Sa, US, Tg, W, E, F*
RJ Smith 2003 *EngA, M, M, Ur, US, Ar, W, NZ, Tg*, 2004 *US, J, EngA, US, F, It, E*, 2005 *US, J, W, EngA, US, Ar, F, R*, 2006 *S, Bar, US, W, It*, 2007 *US, NZ, Pt, W, Fj, J*, 2008 *US, Pt, I, W, S*, 2009 *I, W, US, US*, 2010 *Bel*, 2011 *US, US, Tg, F, J, NZ*
C Smythe 1997 *J, HK*
RGA Snow 1995 *Ar, NZ, R, A, SA, US*, 1996 *HK, J, A, HK, J*, 1997 *US, HK, J, W, I*, 1998 *US, US, US, Ar*, 1999 *J, Fj, Sa, US, W, E, F, Fj, Nm*, 2000 *I, J, It*, 2001 *US, Ar, E, E, Fj, J*, 2002 *S, US, US, Ur, CHL, Ur, CHL, W, F*, 2003 *Ur, US, Ar, W, NZ, It, Tg*, 2006 *US, Bar, US*, 2007 *Pt, W, Fj, J, A*
DA Speirs 1988 *US*, 1989 *I, US*, 1991 *Fj, NZ*
D Spicer 2004 *E*, 2005 *R*, 2006 *S, E, US, Bar, US, W*, 2007 *US, NZ, Pt, W, Fj, J*, 2008 *US*, 2009 *I, W*
WE Spofford 1981 *Ar*
W Stanley 1994 *US, F*, 1995 *S, Ur, Ar, R, A, SA, US*, 1996 *US, US, A, HK, J*, 1997 *US, J, HK, HK, US, W, I*, 1998 *US, US, HK, Ur, US, Ar*, 1999 *J, Fj, Sa, US, Tg, W, E, F, Fj, Nm*, 2000 *Tg, US, SA, I, Sa, Fj, J, It*, 2001 *E, E*, 2002 *S, US, US, Ur, CHL, Ur, CHL, W, F*, 2003 *EngA, US, M, M, Ur, US, Ar, W, It, Tg*
AI Stanton 1971 *W*, 1973 *W*, 1974 *Tg*
E Stapleton 1978 *US, F*
D Steen 1966 *BI*
SM Stephen 2005 *EngA, US*, 2006 *S, E, US, Bar, US, W*, 2007 *US, NZ, Pt, W, Fj, A*, 2008 *I, W, S*, 2009 *I, W*, 2010 *Sp, Geo, Pt*
C Stewart 1991 *S, US, Fj, R, F, NZ*, 1994 *E, F*, 1995 *S, Fj, NZ, R, A, SA*
DS Stewart 1989 *US*, 1990 *Ar*, 1991 *US, Fj, R, F, NZ*, 1992 *E*, 1993 *E, E, US, A, W*, 1994 *US, F, W, E, F*, 1995 *S, Fj, NZ, R, A, SA, US*, 1996 *US, US, A, HK, J, Ur, US, Ar*, 1997 *US, J, HK, HK, J, US, W, I* 1998 *US, J, Ur, Ar*, 1999 *Sa, US, Tg, W, E, F, Fj, Nm*, 2000 *US, SA, I, Sa, Fj, It*, 2001 *US, Ur, Ar, E, E*
R Stewart 2005 *R*
B Stoikos 2001 *Ur*
G Stover 1962 *Bb*
R Strang 1983 *E*
C Strubin 2004 *EngA, E*
IC Stuart 1984 *US*, 1985 *A, A*, 1986 *J*, 1987 *US, Tg, I, W, US*, 1988 *US*, 1989 *US*, 1990 *Ar, US, Ar*, 1992 *E*, 1993 *A, W*, 1994 *US, F, W, E*
JD Stubbs 1962 *Bb, W23*
FJ Sturrock 1971 *W*
CW Suter 1932 *J*
KF Svoboda 1985 *A, A, US*, 1986 *J, US*, 1987 *W*, 1990 *Ar, US, Ar*, 1991 *J, US, R, F*, 1992 *US, E*, 1993 *E, E, US*, 1994 *F, W, F*, 1995 *Fj, A, US*
P Szabo 1989 *I, US*, 1990 *Ar, US, Ar*, 1991 *NZ*, 1993 *US, A, W*

JN Tait 1997 *US, J, HK, HK, J, US, W, I*, 1998 *US, Ur, Ar*, 1999 *J, Fj, Sa, US, Tg, W, E, F, Fj, Nm*, 2000 *Tg, US, SA, I, Sa, Fj, J, It*, 2001 *US, Ur, Ar, E, E*, 2002 *US, W, F*
L Tait 2005 *US, J, W, EngA*, 2006 *S, E, US, Bar, US, W, It*, 2007 *US, NZ, Pt, W, Fj, A*, 2009 *I, W*, 2010 *Ur*
WG Taylor 1978 *F*, 1979 *US, F*, 1980 *W, US, NZ*, 1981 *US, Ar*, 1983 *US, It*
J Thiel 1998 *HK, J, Ur*, 1999 *J, Fj, Sa, US, Tg, W, E, F, Fj, Nm*, 2000 *SA, I, Sa, Fj, J*, 2001 *US, Ar, E, E*, 2002 *S, US, US, Ur, CHL, Ur, W, F*, 2003 *Ur, US, Ar, W, It*, 2004 *F*, 2007 *Pt, W, Fj, J, A*, 2008 *I, W*
S Thompson 2001 *Fj, J*, 2004 *US*
W Thomson 1970 *Fj*
AA Tiedemann 2009 *W, Geo, US, US*, 2010 *Ur, Bel, Geo, Pt*, 2011 *Rus, US, NZ*
K Tkachuk 2000 *Tg, US, SA, Sa, Fj, It*, 2001 *Fj, J*, 2002 *CHL, Ur, CHL, W, F*, 2003 *EngA, US, M, M, Ur, US, Ar, W, NZ, It, Tg*, 2004 *EngA, US, F, It, E*, 2005 *US, J, W, Ar, F, R*, 2006 *US, W, It*, 2007 *US, NZ*, 2008 *US, Pt, I, W, S*, 2009 *I, W, Geo, US, US, J, J, Rus*, 2010 *Sp, Geo*
H Toews 1998 *J, HK, HK, Ur*, 1999 *Tg*, 2000 *US, Sa, J, It*, 2001 *Fj, J*
R Toews 1993 *W*, 1994 *US, F, W, E*, 1995 *S, Ur, Ar, Fj*, 1996 *US, HK, J, A*, 1997 *HK, US, I*
J Tomlinson 1996 *A*, 2001 *Ur*
CA Trainor 2011 *Rus, Tg, F, J, NZ*
N Trenkel 2007 *A*
DM Tucker 1985 *A, A, US*, 1986 *US*, 1987 *US, W*
A Tyler 2005 *Ar*
A Tynan 1995 *Ur, Ar, NZ, US*, 1997 *J*
CJ Tynan 1987 *US*, 1988 *US*, 1990 *Ar, US, Ar*, 1991 *J, US, Fj, F, NZ*, 1992 *US*, 1993 *E, E, US, W*, 1996 *US, J*, 1997 *HK, J*, 1998 *US*

DN Ure 1962 *Bb, W23*

PC Vaesen 1985 *US*, 1986 *J*, 1987 *US, Tg, US*
D van Camp 2005 *J, R*, 2006 *It*, 2007 *US, NZ*, 2008 *Pt, W*, 2009 *I, Geo*
R van den Brink 1986 *US*, 1987 *Tg*, 1988 *US*, 1991 *J, US, R, F, NZ*
D Van Der Merwe 2006 *Bar, It*, 2007 *Pt, W, Fj, J, A*, 2009 *I, W, Geo, US, US*, 2010 *Ur, Sp, Geo*, 2011 *US, US, Tg, F, J, NZ*
D Van Eeuwen 1978 *F*, 1979 *US*
A van Staveren 2000 *Tg, Sa, Fj*, 2002 *US, US, Ur, CHL, Ur, CHL, W, F*, 2003 *EngA, US, M, M, Ur, US, W, NZ, Tg*
J Verstraten 2000 *US, SA, Fj, J*
J Vivian 1983 *E*, 1984 *US*

FG Walsh 2008 *I, W, S*, 2009 *US*
KC Walt 1976 *Bb*, 1977 *US, E, E*, 1978 *US, F*
JM Ward 1962 *W23*
M Webb 2004 *US, J, US, F, It*, 2005 *US, J, W, EngA, US, Ar, F*, 2006 *US, W, It*, 2007 *J, A*, 2008 *US*
M Weingart 2004 *J*, 2005 *J, EngA, US, F, R*, 2007 *Pt*
GJM Wessels 1962 *W23*
WR Wharton 1932 *J, J*
ST White 2009 *J, J, Rus*, 2010 *Ur, Bel, Sp, Geo, Pt*, 2011 *Rus, US, F, J, NZ*
K Whitley 1995 *S*
C Whittaker 1993 *US, A*, 1995 *Ur*, 1996 *A*, 1997 *J*, 1998 *J, HK, US, US, HK, J, US, Ar*, 1999 *J, Fj, US*
LW Whitty 1967 *E*
DW Whyte 1974 *Tg*, 1977 *US, E, E*
RR Wickland 1966 *BI*, 1967 *E*
JP Wiley 1977 *US, E, E*, 1978 *US, F*, 1979 *US*, 1980 *W, US, NZ*, 1981 *US*
K Wilke 1971 *W*, 1973 *W*, 1976 *Bb*, 1978 *US*
K Wilkinson 1976 *Bb*, 1978 *F*, 1979 *F*
BN Williams 1962 *W23*
J Williams 2001 *US, Ur, Ar, Fj, J*
M Williams 1999 *Tg, W, E, F, Fj, Nm*, 2000 *Tg, SA, I, Sa, Fj, J, It*, 2001 *E, E, Fj, J*, 2002 *S, US, US, Ur, CHL, W, F*, 2003 *EngA, US, M, M, Ur, US, Ar, W, It, Tg*, 2004 *EngA, US, F*, 2005 *W, Ar, F, R*, 2006 *E, US, Bar, US, W, It*, 2007 *US, NZ, W, Fj, J, A*, 2008 *Pt, W, S*
M Williams 1992 *E*, 1993 *A, W*
MH Williams 1978 *US, F*, 1980 *US*, 1982 *J*
A Wilson 2008 *US*
PG Wilson 1932 *J, J*
RS Wilson 1962 *Bb*
K Wirachowski 1992 *E*, 1993 *US*, 1996 *US, HK, Ur, US, Ar*, 1997 *US, HK*, 2000 *It*, 2001 *Ur, E, Fj, J*, 2002 *S, CHL*, 2003 *EngA, US, M*
T Wish 2004 *US, J*
K Witkowski 2005 *EngA, Ar*, 2006 *E*
N Witkowski 1998 *US, J*, 2000 *Tg, US, SA, I, Sa, Fj, J, It*, 2001 *US, E, E*, 2002 *S, US, US, Ur, CHL, Ur, CHL, W, F*, 2003 *EngA, US, M, M, Ur, Ar, W, NZ, Tg*, 2005 *EngA, US*, 2006 *E*
AH Woller 1967 *E*
S Wood 1977 *E*
TA Woods 1984 *US*, 1986 *J, US*, 1987 *US, Tg, I, W*, 1988 *US*, 1989 *I, US*, 1990 *Ar, US*, 1991 *S, F, NZ*, 1996 *US, US*, 1997 *US, J*
DP Wooldridge 2009 *I, Geo, J, J, Rus*, 2010 *Ur*
MA Wyatt 1982 *J, J, E, US*, 1983 *US, It, It, E*, 1985 *A, A, US*, 1986 *J, US*, 1987 *Tg, I, W, US*, 1988 *US*, 1989 *I, US*, 1990 *Ar, US, Ar*, 1991 *J, S, US, R, F, NZ*
H Wyndham 1973 *W*

JJ Yeganegi 1996 *US*, 1998 *J*
C Yukes 2001 *Ur, Fj, J*, 2002 *S, US, Ur, Ur*, 2003 *EngA, US, M, M, US, Ar, W, NZ, It, Tg*, 2004 *US, J, EngA, US, F, It, E*, 2005 *W, EngA, US*, 2006 *Bar, US*, 2007 *US, NZ, Pt, W, Fj, J, A*

ENGLAND

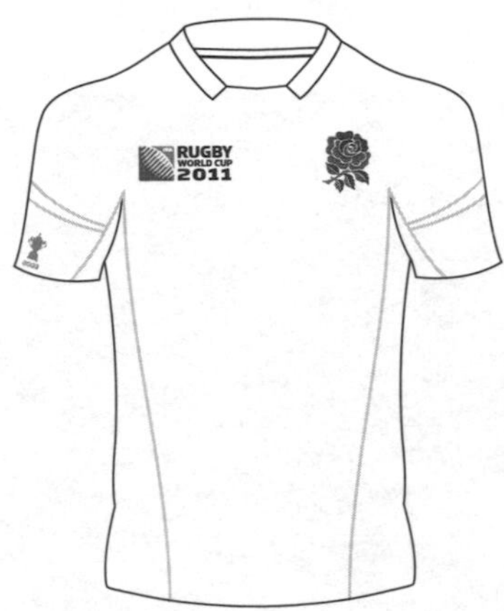

ENGLAND'S 2010–11 TEST RECORD

OPPONENTS	DATE	VENUE	RESULT
New Zealand	6 Nov	H	**Lost** 16–26
Australia	13 Nov	H	**Won** 35–18
Samoa	20 Nov	H	**Won** 26–13
South Africa	27 Nov	H	**Lost** 11–21
Wales	4 Feb	A	**Won** 26–19
Italy	12 Feb	H	**Won** 59–13
France	26 Feb	H	**Won** 17–9
Scotland	13 Mar	H	**Won** 22–16
Ireland	19 Mar	A	**Lost** 8–24
Wales	6 Aug	H	**Won** 23–19
Wales	13 Aug	A	**Lost** 9–19
Ireland	27 Aug	A	**Won** 20–9
Argentina	10 Sept	N	**Won** 13–9
Georgia	18 Sept	N	**Won** 41–10
Romania	24 Sept	N	**Won** 67–3
Scotland	1 Oct	N	**Won** 16–12
France	8 Oct	N	**Lost** 12–19

JOHNSON'S HOPES DASHED

By Paul Morgan

Ryan Pierse/Getty Images

England won a breathtaking game against Scotland but bowed out in the quarter-finals.

The deluge of questions about Martin Johnson's England future were as inevitable as they were frenzied in the wake of his side's 19–12 defeat against France in the quarter-finals of Rugby World Cup 2011 – further proof that making the transition from great player to great manager is far from a straightforward one.

Johnson famously lifted the Webb Ellis Cup in Sydney in 2003, but his dreams of becoming the first man to get his hands on the trophy as a player and subsequently as manager were dashed by Les Bleus in Auckland, bringing to a close what was a controversial, at times chaotic and ultimately unsuccessful World Cup challenge.

Sadly, England managed to generate as many headlines off the pitch as they did on it in New Zealand, but when the big test of their credentials arrived in the shape of the match at Eden Park in the last eight, they were found wanting.

The post-match press conference was predictably dominated by questions about England's failure, the off-pitch incidents and, most significantly, Johnson's chances of continuing in his role. The manager, however, was characteristically reluctant to accommodate his interrogators.

"I'm not getting into that conversation now," he insisted. "It's not the right place, the right people or the right time. I'll give it a couple of days, assess myself and how we've been.

"I'm proud of the way the guys fought back in the second half tonight. Their effort was fantastic, but we left ourselves with far too much to do. It's brutal, but France ultimately deserved to win. That's what World Cups are. One team goes home with a smile, for everyone else it ends in tears.

"I'm just disappointed for all the players, particularly the guys that won't get a chance again. These are great opportunities to get somewhere special, and we haven't taken it. I believe this team's best days are ahead of it. A lot of them are at their first World Cup, and they're better for the experience."

The omens for England's campaign should have been positive. Recently crowned Six Nations champions for the first time since 2003, Johnson was able to pick a squad high on confidence and with no major absentees through injury.

And yet from the moment they took to the field for their Pool B opener against Argentina in Dunedin, England struggled. An impassioned Pumas team made life hell for Johnson's troops in the impressive Otago Stadium from the first whistle, and for vast swathes of the match England had no answer.

The Argentineans raced into a 9–3 lead early in the second half courtesy of two penalties from full-back Martin Rodríguez and a third from skipper Felipe Contepomi, and the men in white were heavily indebted to an individual try from substitute scrum-half Ben Youngs which provided the platform for a nervy 13–9 win. England were up and running but, had the Pumas been more accurate with their goal kicking, it could have been an altogether different story.

"We were under no illusions about what Argentina can bring," insisted centre Mike Tindall, deputising as captain for Lewis Moody. "For the first 20 minutes it is hard to play rugby when you don't touch the ball or see it. We know how good their pack is, and they kept the ball really well. They squeezed and squeezed and they won their penalties. Luckily, none of their kickers could land any today.

"[Ben] Youngs came on and turned the game for us. We got our tempo going and we got a try on the back of it. The one thing I am going to give the team credit for is the way we stuck to our task. We got a win, but there is a lot to work on."

England's next two fixtures were against the outsiders of Pool B – Georgia and Romania – and for those two games England could to an extent forget about the trials and tribulations of their encounter with the Pumas.

The Georgia match in Dunedin was perhaps not as one-sided as the final 41–10 scoreline suggests, but once Johnson's team had subdued a committed Georgian pack in the first half it was one-way traffic in the second period.

Centre Shontayne Hape opened the scoring after just three minutes, and he doubled his tally 17 minutes later. England seemed set to run away it, but Georgia No. 8 Dimitri Basilaia snatched a try just before half-time and the score stood at 17–10.

If England were nervous as they emerged for the second half, it did not show and the match was effectively settled as a contest on 46 minutes when Delon Armitage raced over. Further tries from Manu Tuilagi and Chris Ashton (2) finished the job.

The clash with Romania six days later followed a far more traditional heavyweight-versus-minnow script as wings Mark Cueto and Ashton both helped themselves to hat-tricks, England scored 10 tries and the Romanians were despatched 67–3.

The final Pool B game with Scotland in Auckland was a chance for England to move through the gears, but just as they had done against Argentina, Johnson's side seemed to freeze when confronted by meaningful opposition. Three penalties and a drop-goal saw Scotland claw their way into the lead, and with three minutes left on the clock England still trailed 12–9.

It was a scoreline that would still have seen the side progress safely through to the knockout stages, but Ashton provided a degree of gloss to proceedings with the only try of the match and England emerged 16–12 winners.

"Full credit to Scotland, it was an incredibly tough day," Moody said after his side's narrow escape. "They played a tremendous game. We knew they would, and we didn't make it easy for ourselves by any stretch of the imagination with the penalty count.

"But we can only win the games in front of us, and we've done that today. We've come out on the right side of the result, but it was a tough game. We knew Scotland would come out with all their fire and they did, and in the second half we counteracted that. It's another win. That's all we're here for and that's all that matters."

The victory confirmed England as the winners of Pool B and set up the all-important clash with the French, a repeat of the RWC 2007 semi-final. Johnson made four changes from the stuttering win over Scotland, with Toby Flood, Mark Cueto, Nick Easter and Tom Palmer coming in for Tindall, Armitage, James Haskell and Courtney Lawes respectively.

France's own campaign had been plagued by reports of disharmony within the camp, but there was precious little evidence of any lack of solidarity at Eden Park as they came out in the first half and simply blew England away.

Two early penalties from scrum-half Dimitri Yachvili rocked the men in white, but the real damage was done by tries from wing Vincent Clerc and full-back Maxime Médard, and at half-time England trudged disconsolately back to the dressing room trailing 16–0.

England had to register the first score after the restart, and they did just that when Ben Foden ghosted through the French defence after 54 minutes, and when Jonny Wilkinson converted there was a glimmer of hope.

Les Bleus, however, proved obdurate in defence, despite England's increasing pressure and confidence going forward, and they stretched their lead eight minutes from the end when substitute Francois Trinh-Duc landed a drop-goal. There was still time for Cueto to wriggle over the line for England's second try of the night, but the conversion went wide and Johnson's team were unable to score the converted try they needed to take the match into extra-time.

There was to be no third successive appearance in the World Cup final for England, and as the players packed their bags for the long journey home, Johnson was left to reflect on the nature of defeat as much as the defeat itself.

"We actually started the game pretty well when we had the ball," he said as the unavoidable post-mortem began. "The key thing in the first half was probably two things – their kicking game and their aerial game. They probably reclaimed a lot more of their kicks than we did.

"We said in the week these guys will test you and be more clinical on the edge than anyone we've played before. That was the case. Our defence wasn't good enough. A couple of mistakes, two tries and it was very much uphill.

"We created two or three real chances in the first half, made some breaks and couldn't finish them off. That was the difference. They scored their two tries, we should have had two, but we didn't have any."

ENGLAND INTERNATIONAL STATISTICS

MATCH RECORDS UP TO 31 OCTOBER 2011

MOST CONSECUTIVE TEST WINS

14 2002 *W, It, Arg, NZ, A, SA,* 2003 *F1, W1, It, S, I, NZ, A, W2*
11 2000 *SA 2, A, Arg, SA3,* 2001 *W, It, S, F, C1, 2, US*
10 1882 *W,* 1883 *I, S,* 1884 *W, I, S,* 1885 *W, I,* 1886 *W, I*
10 1994 *R, C,* 1995 *I, F, W, S, Arg, It, WS, A*
10 2003 *F, Gg, SA, Sm, U, W, F, A,* 2004 *It, S*

MOST CONSECUTIVE TESTS WITHOUT DEFEAT

Matches	Wins	Draws	Period
14	14	0	2002 to 2003
12	10	2	1882 to 1887
11	10	1	1922 to 1924
11	11	0	2000 to 2001

MOST POINTS IN A MATCH

BY THE TEAM

Pts	Opponents	Venue	Year
134	Romania	Twickenham	2001
111	Uruguay	Brisbane	2003
110	Netherlands	Huddersfield	1998
106	U S A	Twickenham	1999
101	Tonga	Twickenham	1999
84	Georgia	Perth	2003
80	Italy	Twickenham	2001

BY A PLAYER

Pts	Player	Opponents	Venue	Year
44	C C Hodgson	Romania	Twickenham	2001
36	P J Grayson	Tonga	Twickenham	1999
35	J P Wilkinson	Italy	Twickenham	2001
32	J P Wilkinson	Italy	Twickenham	1999
30	C R Andrew	Canada	Twickenham	1994
30	P J Grayson	Netherlands	Huddersfield	1998
30	J P Wilkinson	Wales	Twickenham	2002
29	D J H Walder	Canada	Burnaby	2001
27	C R Andrew	South Africa	Pretoria	1994
27	J P Wilkinson	South Africa	Bloemfontein	2000
27	C C Hodgson	South Africa	Twickenham	2004
27	J P Wilkinson	Scotland	Twickenham	2007
26	J P Wilkinson	United States	Twickenham	1999

MOST TRIES IN A MATCH

BY THE TEAM

Tries	Opponents	Venue	Year
20	Romania	Twickenham	2001
17	Uruguay	Brisbane	2003
16	Netherlands	Huddersfield	1998
16	United States	Twickenham	1999
13	Wales	Blackheath	1881
13	Tonga	Twickenham	1999
12	Georgia	Perth	2003
12	Canada	Twickenham	2004
10	Japan	Sydney	1987
10	Fiji	Twickenham	1989
10	Italy	Twickenham	2001
10	Romania	Dunedin	2011

BY A PLAYER

Tries	Player	Opponents	Venue	Year
5	D Lambert	France	Richmond	1907
5	R Underwood	Fiji	Twickenham	1989
5	O J Lewsey	Uruguay	Brisbane	2003
4	G W Burton	Wales	Blackheath	1881
4	A Hudson	France	Paris	1906
4	R W Poulton	France	Paris	1914
4	C Oti	Romania	Bucharest	1989
4	J C Guscott	Netherlands	Huddersfield	1998
4	N A Back	Netherlands	Huddersfield	1998
4	J C Guscott	United States	Twickenham	1999
4	J Robinson	Romania	Twickenham	2001
4	N Easter	Wales	Twickenham	2007
4	C J Ashton	Italy	Twickenham	2011

MOST CONVERSIONS IN A MATCH

BY THE TEAM

Cons	Opponents	Venue	Year
15	Netherlands	Huddersfield	1998
14	Romania	Twickenham	2001
13	United States	Twickenham	1999
13	Uruguay	Brisbane	2003
12	Tonga	Twickenham	1999
9	Italy	Twickenham	2001
9	Georgia	Perth	2003
8	Romania	Bucharest	1989
8	Italy	Twickenham	2011
7	Wales	Blackheath	1881
7	Japan	Sydney	1987
7	Argentina	Twickenham	1990
7	Wales	Twickenham	1998
7	Wales	Twickenham	2007
7	Romania	Dunedin	2011

BY A PLAYER

Cons	Player	Opponents	Venue	Year
15	P J Grayson	Netherlands	Huddersfield	1998
14	C Hodgson	Romania	Twickenham	2001
13	J P Wilkinson	United States	Twickenham	1999
12	P J Grayson	Tonga	Twickenham	1999
11	P J Grayson	Uruguay	Brisbane	2003
9	J P Wilkinson	Italy	Twickenham	2001
8	S D Hodgkinson	Romania	Bucharest	1989
7	J M Webb	Japan	Sydney	1987
7	S D Hodgkinson	Argentina	Twickenham	1990
7	P J Grayson	Wales	Twickenham	1998
7	J P Wilkinson	Wales	Twickenham	2007

MOST PENALTIES IN A MATCH

BY THE TEAM

Penalties	Opponents	Venue	Year
8	South Africa	Bloemfontein	2000
7	Wales	Cardiff	1991
7	Scotland	Twickenham	1995
7	France	Twickenham	1999
7	Fiji	Twickenham	1999
7	South Africa	Paris	1999
7	South Africa	Twickenham	2001
7	Australia	Twickenham	2010
6	Wales	Twickenham	1986
6	Canada	Twickenham	1994
6	Argentina	Durban	1995
6	Scotland	Murrayfield	1996
6	Ireland	Twickenham	1996
6	South Africa	Twickenham	2000
6	Australia	Twickenham	2002
6	Wales	Brisbane	2003

BY A PLAYER

Penalties	Player	Opponents	Venue	Year
8	J P Wilkinson	South Africa	Bloemfontein	2000
7	S D Hodgkinson	Wales	Cardiff	1991
7	C R Andrew	Scotland	Twickenham	1995
7	J P Wilkinson	France	Twickenham	1999
7	J P Wilkinson	Fiji	Twickenham	1999
7	J P Wilkinson	South Africa	Twickenham	2001
7	T G A L Flood	Australia	Twickenham	2010
6	C R Andrew	Wales	Twickenham	1986
6	C R Andrew	Canada	Twickenham	1994
6	C R Andrew	Argentina	Durban	1995
6	P J Grayson	Scotland	Murrayfield	1996
6	P J Grayson	Ireland	Twickenham	1996
6	P J Grayson	South Africa	Paris	1999
6	J P Wilkinson	South Africa	Twickenham	2000
6	J P Wilkinson	Australia	Twickenham	2002
6	J P Wilkinson	Wales	Brisbane	2003

MOST DROPPED GOALS IN A MATCH

BY THE TEAM

Drops	Opponents	Venue	Year
3	France	Sydney	2003
2	Ireland	Twickenham	1970
2	France	Paris	1978
2	France	Paris	1980
2	Romania	Twickenham	1985
2	Fiji	Suva	1991
2	Argentina	Durban	1995
2	France	Paris	1996
2	Australia	Twickenham	2001
2	Wales	Cardiff	2003
2	Ireland	Dublin	2003
2	South Africa	Perth	2003
2	Samoa	Nantes	2007
2	Tonga	Paris	2007
2	Wales	Twickenham	2011
2	Argentina	Manchester	2009

BY A PLAYER

Drops	Player	Opponents	Venue	Year
3	J P Wilkinson	France	Sydney	2003
2	R Hiller	Ireland	Twickenham	1970
2	A G B Old	France	Paris	1978
2	J P Horton	France	Paris	1980
2	C R Andrew	Romania	Twickenham	1985
2	C R Andrew	Fiji	Suva	1991
2	C R Andrew	Argentina	Durban	1995
2	P J Grayson	France	Paris	1996
2	J P Wilkinson	Australia	Twickenham	2001
2	J P Wilkinson	Wales	Cardiff	2003
2	J P Wilkinson	Ireland	Dublin	2003
2	J P Wilkinson	South Africa	Perth	2003
2	J P Wilkinson	Samoa	Nantes	2007
2	J P Wilkinson	Tonga	Paris	2007
2	A J Goode	Argentina	Manchester	2009
2	J P Wilkinson	Wales	Twickenham	2011

CAREER RECORDS

MOST CAPPED PLAYERS

Caps	Player	Career Span
114	J Leonard	1990 to 2004
91	J P Wilkinson	1998 to 2011
85	R Underwood	1984 to 1996
85	L B N Dallaglio	1995 to 2007
84	M O Johnson	1993 to 2003
78	J P R Worsley	1999 to 2011
77	M J S Dawson	1995 to 2006
75	M J Catt	1994 to 2007
75	M J Tindall	2000 to 2011
73	P J Vickery	1998 to 2009
73	S G Thompson	2002 to 2011
72	W D C Carling	1988 to 1997
71	C R Andrew	1985 to 1997
71	R A Hill	1997 to 2004
71	L W Moody	2001 to 2011
71	S D Shaw	1996 to 2011
69	D J Grewcock	1997 to 2007
66	N A Back	1994 to 2003
65	J C Guscott	1989 to 1999
64	B C Moore	1987 to 1995
64	M E Corry	1997 to 2007
62	B J Kay	2001 to 2009
58	P J Winterbottom	1982 to 1993
57	B C Cohen	2000 to 2006
57	S W Borthwick	2001 to 2010
55	W A Dooley	1985 to 1993
55	W J H Greenwood	1997 to 2004
55	O J Lewsey	1998 to 2007
55	M J Cueto	2004 to 2011
54	G C Rowntree	1995 to 2006
51	A S Healey	1997 to 2003
51	K P P Bracken	1993 to 2003
51	J T Robinson	2001 to 2007
51	J M White	2000 to 2009

MOST CONSECUTIVE TESTS

Tests	Player	Span
44	W D C Carling	1989 to 1995
40	J Leonard	1990 to 1995
36	J V Pullin	1968 to 1975
33	W B Beaumont	1975 to 1982
30	R Underwood	1992 to 1996

MOST TESTS AS CAPTAIN

Tests	Captain	Span
59	W D C Carling	1988 to 1996
39	M O Johnson	1998 to 2003
22	L B N Dallaglio	1997 to 2004
21	W B Beaumont	1978 to 1982
21	S W Borthwick	2008 to 2010
17	M E Corry	2005 to 2007
15	P J Vickery	2002 to 2008
13	W W Wakefield	1924 to 1926
13	N M Hall	1949 to 1955
13	E Evans	1956 to 1958
13	R E G Jeeps	1960 to 1962
13	J V Pullin	1972 to 1975

MOST POINTS IN TESTS

Points	Player	Tests	Career
1179	J P Wilkinson	91	1998 to 2011
400	P J Grayson	32	1995 to 2004
396	C R Andrew	71	1985 to 1997
296	J M Webb	33	1987 to 1993
259	C C Hodgson	36	2001 to 2011
240	W H Hare	25	1974 to 1984
223	T G A L Flood	46	2006 to 2011
210	R Underwood	85	1984 to 1996

MOST TRIES IN TESTS

Tries	Player	Tests	Career
49	R Underwood	85	1984 to 1996
31	W J H Greenwood	55	1997 to 2004
31	B C Cohen	57	2000 to 2006
30	J C Guscott	65	1989 to 1999
28	J T Robinson	51	2001 to 2007
24	D D Luger	38	1998 to 2003
22	O J Lewsey	55	1998 to 2007
20	M J Cueto	55	2004 to 2011
18	C N Lowe	25	1913 to 1923
17	L B N Dallaglio	85	1995 to 2007
16	N A Back	66	1994 to 2003
16	M J S Dawson	77	1995 to 2006
15	A S Healey	51	1997 to 2003
15	C J Ashton	18	2010 to 2011
14	M J Tindall	75	2000 to 2011
13	T Underwood	27	1992 to 1998
13	I R Balshaw	35	2000 to 2008

MOST CONVERSIONS IN TESTS

Cons	Player	Tests	Career
162	J P Wilkinson	91	1998 to 2011
78	P J Grayson	32	1995 to 2004
44	C C Hodgson	36	2001 to 2011
41	J M Webb	33	1987 to 1993
35	S D Hodgkinson	14	1989 to 1991
33	C R Andrew	71	1985 to 1997
32	T G A L Flood	46	2006 to 2011
17	L Stokes	12	1875 to 1881

MOST PENALTY GOALS IN TESTS

Penalties	Player	Tests	Career
239	J P Wilkinson	91	1998 to 2011
86	C R Andrew	71	1985 to 1997
72	P J Grayson	32	1995 to 2004
67	W H Hare	25	1974 to 1984
66	J M Webb	33	1987 to 1993
47	T G A L Flood	46	2006 to 2011
44	C C Hodgson	36	2001 to 2011
43	S D Hodgkinson	14	1989 to 1991

MOST DROPPED GOALS IN TESTS

Drops	Player	Tests	Career
36	J P Wilkinson	91	1998 to 2011
21	C R Andrew	71	1985 to 1997
6	P J Grayson	32	1995 to 2004
4	J P Horton	13	1978 to 1984
4	L Cusworth	12	1979 to 1988
4	A J Goode	17	2005 to 2009

INTERNATIONAL CHAMPIONSHIP RECORDS

RECORD	DETAIL		SET
Most points in season	229	in five matches	2001
Most tries in season	29	in five matches	2001
Highest score	80	80–23 v Italy	2001
Biggest win	57	80–23 v Italy	2001
Highest score conceded	43	13–43 v Ireland	2007
Biggest defeat	30	13–43 v Ireland	2007
Most appearances	54	J Leonard	1991–2004
Most points in matches	546	J P Wilkinson	1998–2011
Most points in season	89	J P Wilkinson	2001
Most points in match	35	J P Wilkinson	v Italy, 2001
Most tries in matches	18	C N Lowe	1913–1923
	18	R Underwood	1984–1996
Most tries in season	8	C N Lowe	1914
Most tries in match	4	R W Poulton	v France, 1914
	4	C J Ashton	v Italy, 2011
Most cons in matches	89	J P Wilkinson	1998–2011
Most cons in season	24	J P Wilkinson	2001
Most cons in match	9	J P Wilkinson	v Italy, 2001
Most pens in matches	105	J P Wilkinson	1998–2011
Most pens in season	18	S D Hodgkinson	1991
	18	J P Wilkinson	2000
Most pens in match	7	S D Hodgkinson	v Wales, 1991
	7	C R Andrew	v Scotland, 1995
	7	J P Wilkinson	v France, 1999
Most drops in matches	11	J P Wilkinson	1998–2011
Most drops in season	5	J P Wilkinson	2003
Most drops in match	2	R Hiller	v Ireland, 1970
	2	A G B Old	v France, 1978
	2	J P Horton	v France, 1980
	2	P J Grayson	v France, 1996
	2	J P Wilkinson	v Wales, 2003
	2	J P Wilkinson	v Ireland, 2003

MISCELLANEOUS RECORDS

RECORD	HOLDER	DETAIL
Longest Test Career	S D Shaw	1996 to 2011
Youngest Test Cap	H C C Laird	18 yrs 134 days in 1927
Oldest Test Cap	F Gilbert	38 yrs 362 days in 1923

CAREER RECORDS OF ENGLAND INTERNATIONAL PLAYERS (UP TO 31 OCTOBER 2011)

PLAYER	DEBUT	CAPS	T	C	P	D	PTS
BACKS :							
D A Armitage	2008 v PI	26	7	0	2	1	44
C J Ashton	2010 v F	18	15	0	0	0	75
M A Banahan	2009 v Arg	16	4	0	0	0	20
O J Barkley	2001 v US	23	2	9	18	0	82
D S Care	2008 v NZ	32	3	0	0	1	18
M J Cueto	2004 v C	55	20	0	0	0	100
T G A L Flood	2006 v Arg	46	3	32	47	1	223
R J Flutey	2008 v PI	14	4	0	0	0	20
B J Foden	2009 v It	22	5	0	0	0	25
S E Hape	2010 v A	13	2	0	0	0	10
C C Hodgson	2001 v R	36	6	44	44	3	259
C D J Sharples	2011 v W	1	0	0	0	0	0
J P M Simpson	2011 v Gg	1	0	0	0	0	0
D Strettle	2007 v I	7	1	0	0	0	5
M J Tindall	2000 v I	75	14	2	0	0	74
E M Tuilagi	2011 v W	7	4	0	0	0	20
R E P Wigglesworth	2008 v It	12	1	0	0	0	5
J P Wilkinson	1998 v I	91	6	162	239	36	1179
B R Youngs	2010 v S	17	3	0	0	0	15
FORWARDS :							
D M J Attwood	2010 v NZ	2	0	0	0	0	0
M J Botha	2011 v W	1	0	0	0	0	0
D R Cole	2010 v W	23	1	0	0	0	5
A R Corbisiero	2011 v It	10	0	0	0	0	0

T R Croft	2008 v F	31	3	0	0	0	15
L P Deacon	2005 v Sm	29	0	0	0	0	0
P P L Doran-Jones	2009 v Arg	3	0	0	0	0	0
N J Easter	2007 v It	47	5	0	0	0	25
C H Fourie	2010 v NZ	8	0	0	0	0	0
D M Hartley	2008 v PI	34	1	0	0	0	5
J A W Haskell	2007 v W	42	4	0	0	0	20
C L Lawes	2009 v A	13	0	0	0	0	0
L A Mears	2005 v Sm	38	1	0	0	0	5
L W Moody	2001 v C	71	9	0	0	0	45
T P Palmer	2001 v US	33	0	0	0	0	0
S D Shaw	1996 v It	71	2	0	0	0	10
A J Sheridan	2004 v C	40	0	0	0	0	0
M J H Stevens	2004 v NZ	39	0	0	0	0	0
S G Thompson	2002 v S	73	4	0	0	0	20
D G Wilson	2009 v Arg	19	0	0	0	0	0
T A Wood	2011 v W	9	0	0	0	0	0
J P R Worsley	1999 v Tg	78	10	0	0	0	50

Dave Rogers/Getty Images

England captain Lewis Moody retired after the World Cup on 71 caps.

ENGLAND INTERNATIONAL PLAYERS (UP TO 31 OCTOBER 2011)

Note: Years given for International Championship matches are for second half of season; eg 1972 means season 1971–72. Years for all other matches refer to the actual year of the match. Entries in square brackets denote matches played in RWC Finals.

Aarvold, C D (Cambridge U, W Hartlepool, Headingley, Blackheath) 1928 A, W, I, F, S, 1929 W, I, F, 1931 W, S, F, 1932 SA, W, I, S, 1933 W
Abbott, S R (Wasps, Harlequins) 2003 W2, F3, [Sm, U, W(R)], 2004 NZ1(t&R), 2, 2006 I, A2(R)
Abendanon, N A (Bath) 2007 SA2(R), F2
Ackford, P J (Harlequins) 1988 A, 1989 S, I, F, W, R, Fj, 1990 I, F, W, S, Arg 3, 1991 W, S, I, F, A, [NZ, It, F, S, A]
Adams, A A (London Hospital) 1910 F
Adams, F R (Richmond) 1875 I, S, 1876 S, 1877 I, 1878 S, 1879 S, I
Adebayo, A A (Bath) 1996, It, 1997 Arg 1, 2, A 2, NZ 1, 1998 S
Adey, G J (Leicester) 1976 I, F
Adkins, S J (Coventry) 1950 I, F, S, 1953 W, I, F, S
Agar, A E (Harlequins) 1952 SA, W, S, I, F, 1953 W, I
Alcock, A (Guy's Hospital) 1906 SA
Alderson, F H R (Hartlepool R) 1891 W, I, S, 1892 W, S, 1893 W
Alexander, H (Richmond) 1900 I, S, 1901 W, I, S, 1902 W, I
Alexander, W (Northern) 1927 F
Allen, A O (Gloucester) 2006 NZ, Arg
Allison, D F (Coventry) 1956 W, I, S, F, 1957 W, 1958 W, S
Allport, A (Blackheath) 1892 W, 1893 I, 1894 W, I, S
Anderson, S (Rockcliff) 1899 I
Anderson, W F (Orrell) 1973 NZ 1
Anderton, C (Manchester FW) 1889 M
Andrew, C R (Cambridge U, Nottingham, Wasps, Toulouse, Newcastle) 1985 R, F, S, I, W, 1986 W, S, I, F, 1987 I, F, W, [J (R), US], 1988 S, I 1, 2, A 1, 2, Fj, A, 1989 S, I, F, W, R, Fj, 1990 I, F, W, S, Arg 3, 1991 W, S, I, F, Fj, A, [NZ, It, US, F, S, A], 1992 S, I, F, W, C, SA, 1993 F, W, NZ, 1994 S, I, F, W, SA 1, 2, R, C, 1995 I, F, W, S, [Arg, It, A, NZ, F], 1997 W (R)
Appleford, G N (London Irish) 2002 Arg
Archer, G S (Bristol, Army, Newcastle) 1996 S, I, 1997 A 2, NZ 1, SA, NZ 2, 1998 F, W, S, I, A 1, NZ 1, H, It, 1999 Tg, Fj, 2000 I, F, W, It, S
Archer, H (Bridgwater A) 1909 W, F, I
Armitage, D A (London Irish) 2008 PI, A, SA, NZ3, 2009 It, W, I, F, S, Arg 1, 2, 2010 W, It, I, S, A2(R), NZ(R), A3(R), Sm(R), 2011 W2, 3(t&R), I2(R), [Arg, Gg, R(R), S]
Armitage, S E (London Irish) 2009 It, Arg 1, 2, 2010 W(R), It(R)
Armstrong, R (Northern) 1925 W
Arthur, T G (Wasps) 1966 W, I
Ashby, R C (Wasps) 1966 I, F, 1967 A
Ashcroft, A (Waterloo) 1956 W, I, S, F, 1957 W, I, F, S, 1958 W, A, I, F, S, 1959 I, F, S
Ashcroft, A H (Birkenhead Park) 1909 A
Ashford, W (Richmond) 1897 W, I, 1898 S, W
Ashton, C J (Northampton) 2010 F, A1, 2, NZ, A3, Sm, SA, 2011 W1, It, F, S, I1, 2, [Arg, Gg, R, S, F]
Ashworth, A (Oldham) 1892 I
Askew, J G (Cambridge U) 1930 W, I, F
Aslett, A R (Richmond) 1926 W, I, F, S, 1929 S, F
Assinder, E W (O Edwardians) 1909 A, W
Aston, R L (Blackheath) 1890 S, I
Attwood, D M J (Gloucester) 2010 NZ(R), Sm(R)
Auty, J R (Headingley) 1935 S

Back, N A (Leicester) 1994 S, I, 1995 [Arg (t), It, WS], 1997 NZ 1(R), SA, NZ 2, 1998 F, W, S, I, H, It, A 2, SA 2, 1999 S, I, F, W, A, US, C, [It, NZ, Fj, SA], 2000 I, F, W, It, S, SA 1, 2, A, Arg, SA 3, 2001 W, It, S, F, I, A, R, SA, 2002 S, I, F, W, It, NZ (t + R), A, SA, 2003 F 1, W 1, S, I, NZ, A, F 3, [Gg, SA, Sm, W, F, A]
Bailey, M D (Cambridge U, Wasps) 1984 SA 1, 2, 1987 [US], 1989 Fj, 1990 I, F, S (R)
Bainbridge, S (Gosforth, Fylde) 1982 F, W, 1983 F, W, S, I, NZ, 1984 S, I, F, W, 1985 NZ 1, 2, 1987 F, W, S, [J, US]
Baker, D G S (OMTs) 1955 W, I, F, S
Baker, E M (Moseley) 1895 W, I, S, 1896 W, I, S, 1897 W
Baker, H C (Clifton) 1887 W
Balshaw, I R (Bath, Leeds, Gloucester) 2000 I (R), F (R), It (R), S (R), A (R), Arg, SA 3(R), 2001 W, It, S, F, I, 2002 S (R), I (R), 2003 F2, 3, [Sm, U, A(R)], 2004 It, S, I, 2005 It, S, 2006 A1, 2, NZ, Arg, 2007 It, SA1, 2008 W, It, F, S, I
Banahan, M A (Bath) 2009 Arg 1, 2, A, Arg 3, NZ, 2010 Sm, SA(R), 2011 It(R), F(R), S(R), I1, W2, 3, [Gg(R), S(R), F(R)]
Bance, J F (Bedford) 1954 S
Barkley, O J (Bath) 2001 US (R), 2004 It(R), I(t), W, F, NZ2(R), A1(R), 2005 W(R), F, I, It, S, A(R), Sm(R), 2006 A1, 2(R), 2007 F2, 3(R), [US, Sm, Tg], 2008 NZ1, 2(R)
Barley, B (Wakefield) 1984 I, F, W, A, 1988 A 1, 2, Fj
Barnes, S (Bristol, Bath) 1984 A, 1985 R (R), NZ 1, 2, 1986 S (R), F (R), 1987 I (R), 1988 Fj, 1993 S, I
Barr, R J (Leicester) 1932 SA, W, I
Barrett, E I M (Lennox) 1903 S
Barrington, T J M (Bristol) 1931 W, I
Barrington-Ward, L E (Edinburgh U) 1910 W, I, F, S
Barron, J H (Bingley) 1896 S, 1897 W, I
Bartlett, J T (Waterloo) 1951 W
Bartlett, R M (Harlequins) 1957 W, I, F, S, 1958 I, F, S
Barton, J (Coventry) 1967 I, F, W, 1972 F
Batchelor, T B (Oxford U) 1907 F
Bates, S M (Wasps) 1989 R
Bateson, A H (Otley) 1930 W, I, F, S
Bateson, H D (Liverpool) 1879 I
Batson, T (Blackheath) 1872 S, 1874 S, 1875 I
Batten, J M (Cambridge U) 1874 S
Baume, J L (Northern) 1950 S
Baxendell, J J N (Sale) 1998 NZ 2, SA 1
Baxter, J (Birkenhead Park) 1900 W, I, S
Bayfield, M C (Northampton) 1991 Fj, A, 1992 S, I, F, W, C, SA, 1993 F, W, S, I, 1994 S, I, SA 1, 2, R, C, 1995 I, F, W, S, [Arg, It, A, NZ, F], SA, WS, 1996 F, W
Bazley, R C (Waterloo) 1952 I, F, 1953 W, I, F, S, 1955 W, I, F, S
Beal, N D (Northampton) 1996 Arg, 1997 A 1, 1998 NZ 1, 2, SA 1, H (R), SA 2, 1999 S, F (R), A (t), C (R), [It (R), Tg (R), Fj, SA]
Beaumont, W B (Fylde) 1975 I, A 1(R), 2, 1976 A, W, S, I, F, 1977 S, I, F, W, 1978 F, W, S, I, NZ, 1979 S, I, F, W, NZ, 1980 I, F, W, S, 1981 W, S, I, F, Arg 1, 2, 1982 A, S
Bedford, H (Morley) 1889 M, 1890 S, I
Bedford, L L (Headingley) 1931 W, I
Beer, I D S (Harlequins) 1955 F, S
Beese, M C (Liverpool) 1972 W, I, F
Beim, T D (Sale) 1998 NZ 1(R), 2
Bell, D S C (Bath) 2005 It(R), S, 2009 A(R), Arg 3, NZ
Bell, F J (Northern) 1900 W
Bell, H (New Brighton) 1884 I
Bell, J L (Darlington) 1878 I
Bell, P J (Blackheath) 1968 W, I, F, S
Bell, R W (Northern) 1900 W, I, S
Bendon, G J (Wasps) 1959 W, I, F, S
Bennett, N O (St Mary's Hospital, Waterloo) 1947 W, S, F, 1948 A, W, I, S
Bennett, W N (Bedford, London Welsh) 1975 S, A1, 1976 S (R), 1979 S, I, F, W
Bennetts, B B (Penzance) 1909 A, W
Bentley, J (Sale, Newcastle) 1988 I 2, A 1, 1997 A 1, SA
Bentley, J E (Gipsies) 1871 S, 1872 S
Benton, S (Gloucester) 1998 A 1
Berridge, M J (Northampton) 1949 W, I

Berry, H (Gloucester) 1910 W, I, F, S
Berry, J (Tyldesley) 1891 W, I, S
Berry, J T W (Leicester) 1939 W, I, S
Beswick, E (Swinton) 1882 I, S
Biggs, J M (UCH) 1878 S, 1879 I
Birkett, J G G (Harlequins) 1906 S, F, SA, 1907 F, W, S, 1908 F, W, I , S, 1910 W, I, S, 1911 W, F, I , S, 1912 W, I , S, F
Birkett L (Clapham R) 1875 S, 1877 I, S
Birkett, R H (Clapham R) 1871 S, 1875 S, 1876 S, 1877 I
Bishop, C C (Blackheath) 1927 F
Black, B H (Blackheath) 1930 W, I, F, S, 1931 W, I, S, F, 1932 S, 1933 W
Blacklock, J H (Aspatria) 1898 I, 1899 I
Blakeway, P J (Gloucester) 1980 I, F, W, S, 1981 W, S, I, F, 1982 I, F, W, 1984 I, F, W, SA 1, 1985 R, F, S, I
Blakiston, A F (Northampton) 1920 S, 1921 W, I, S, F, 1922 W, 1923 S, F, 1924 W, I, F, S, 1925 NZ, W, I, S, F
Blatherwick, T (Manchester) 1878 I
Body, J A (Gipsies) 1872 S, 1873 S
Bolton, C A (United Services) 1909 F
Bolton, R (Harlequins) 1933 W, 1936 S, 1937 S, 1938 W, I
Bolton, W N (Blackheath) 1882 I, S, 1883 W, I, S, 1884 W, I, S, 1885 I, 1887 I, S
Bonaventura, M S (Blackheath) 1931 W
Bond, A M (Sale) 1978 NZ, 1979 S, I, NZ, 1980 I, 1982 I
Bonham-Carter, E (Oxford U) 1891 S
Bonsor, F (Bradford) 1886 W, I, S, 1887 W, S, 1889 M
Boobbyer, B (Rosslyn Park) 1950 W, I, F, S, 1951 W, F, 1952 S, I, F
Booth, L A (Headingley) 1933 W, I, S, 1934 S, 1935 W, I, S
Borthwick, S W (Bath, Saracens) 2001 F, C 1, 2(R), US, R, 2003 A(t), W 2(t), F 2, 2004 I, F(R), NZ1(R), 2, A1, C, SA, A2, 2005 W(R), It(R), S(R), A, NZ, Sm, 2006 W, It, S, F, I, 2007 W2, F3, [SA1(t&R), Sm(R), Tg], 2008 W, It, F, S, I, NZ1, 2, PI, A, SA, NZ3, 2009 It, W, I, F, S, Arg 1, 2, A, Arg 3, NZ, 2010 W, It, I, S
Botha, M J (Saracens) 2011 W2(R)
Botting, I J (Oxford U) 1950 W, I
Boughton, H J (Gloucester) 1935 W, I, S
Boyle, C W (Oxford U) 1873 S
Boyle, S B (Gloucester) 1983 W, S, I
Boylen, F (Hartlepool R) 1908 F, W, I, S
Bracken, K P P (Bristol, Saracens) 1993 NZ, 1994 S, I, C, 1995 I, F, W, S, [It, WS (t)], SA, 1996 It (R), 1997 Arg 1, 2, A 2, NZ 1, 2, 1998 F, W, 1999 S(R), I, F, A, 2000 SA 1, 2, A, 2001 It (R), S (R), F (R), C 1, 2, US, I (R), A, R (R), SA, 2002 S, I, F, W, It, 2003 W 1, It(R), I(t), NZ, A, F3, [SA, U(R), W(R), F(t&R)]
Bradby, M S (United Services) 1922 I, F
Bradley, R (W Hartlepool) 1903 W
Bradshaw, H (Bramley) 1892 S, 1893 W, I, S, 1894 W, I, S
Brain, S E (Coventry) 1984 SA 2, A (R), 1985 R, F, S, I, W, NZ 1, 2, 1986 W, S, I, F
Braithwaite, J (Leicester) 1905 NZ
Braithwaite-Exley, B (Headingley) 1949 W
Brettargh, A T (Liverpool OB) 1900 W, 1903 I, S, 1904 W, I, S, 1905 I, S
Brewer, J (Gipsies) 1876 I
Briggs, A (Bradford) 1892 W, I, S
Brinn, A (Gloucester) 1972 W, I, S
Broadley, T (Bingley) 1893 W, S, 1894 W, I, S, 1896 S
Bromet, W E (Richmond) 1891 W, I, 1892 W, I, S, 1893 W, I, S, 1895 W, I, S, 1896 I
Brook, P W P (Harlequins) 1930 S, 1931 F, 1936 S
Brooke, T J (Richmond) 1968 F, S
Brooks, F G (Bedford) 1906 SA
Brooks, M J (Oxford U) 1874 S
Brophy, T J (Liverpool) 1964 I, F, S, 1965 W, I, 1966 W, I, F
Brough, J W (Silloth) 1925 NZ, W
Brougham, H (Harlequins) 1912 W, I, S, F
Brown, A A (Exeter) 1938 S
Brown A T (Gloucester) 2006 A1, 2007 SA1, 2
Brown, L G (Oxford U, Blackheath) 1911 W, F, I, S, 1913 SA, W, F, I, S, 1914 W, I, S, F, 1921 W, I, S, F, 1922 W
Brown, M N (Harlequins) 2007 SA1, 2, 2008 NZ1
Brown S P (Richmond) 1998 A 1, SA 1
Brown, T W (Bristol) 1928 S, 1929 W, I, S, F, 1932 S, 1933 W, I, S
Brunton, J (N Durham) 1914 W, I, S
Brutton, E B (Cambridge U) 1886 S
Bryden, C C (Clapham R) 1876 I, 1877 S
Bryden, H A (Clapham R) 1874 S
Buckingham, R A (Leicester) 1927 F
Bucknall, A L (Richmond) 1969 SA, 1970 I, W, S, F, 1971 W, I, F, S (2[1C])
Buckton, J R D (Saracens) 1988 A (R), ,1990 Arg 1, 2
Budd, A J (Blackheath) 1878 I, 1879 S, I, 1881 W, S
Budworth, R T D (Blackheath) 1890 W, 1891 W, S
Bull, A G (Northampton) 1914 W
Bullough, E (Wigan) 1892 W, I, S
Bulpitt, M P (Blackheath) 1970 S
Bulteel, A J (Manchester) 1876 I
Bunting, W L (Moseley) 1897 I, S, 1898 I, S, W, 1899 S, 1900 S, 1901 I, S
Burland, D W (Bristol) 1931 W, I, F, 1932 I, S, 1933 W, I, S
Burns, B H (Blackheath) 1871 S
Burton, G W (Blackheath) 1879 S, I, 1880 S, 1881 I, W, S
Burton, H C (Richmond) 1926 W
Burton, M A (Gloucester) 1972 W, I, F, S, SA, 1974 F, W, 1975 S, A 1, 2, 1976 A, W, S, I, F, 1978 F, W
Bush, J A (Clifton) 1872 S, 1873 S, 1875 S, 1876 I, S
Butcher, C J S (Harlequins) 1984 SA 1, 2, A
Butcher, W V (Streatham) 1903 S, 1904 W, I, S, 1905 W, I, S
Butler, A G (Harlequins) 1937 W, I
Butler, P E (Gloucester) 1975 A 1, 1976 F
Butterfield, J (Northampton) 1953 F, S, 1954 W, NZ, I, S, F, 1955 W, I, F, S, 1956 W, I, S, F, 1957 W, I, F, S, 1958 W, A, I, F, S, 1959 W, I, F, S
Byrne, F A (Moseley) 1897 W
Byrne, J F (Moseley) 1894 W, I, S, 1895 I, S, 1896 I, 1897 W, I, S, 1898 I, S, W, 1899 I

Cain, J J (Waterloo) 1950 W
Cairns, M I (Saracens) 2007 SA1(R)
Callard, J E B (Bath) 1993 NZ, 1994 S, I, 1995 [WS], SA
Campbell, D A (Cambridge U) 1937 W, I
Candler, P L (St Bart's Hospital) 1935 W, 1936 NZ, W, I, S, 1937 W, I, S, 1938 W, S
Cannell, L B (Oxford U, St Mary's Hospital) 1948 F, 1949 W, I, F, S, 1950 W, I, F, S, 1952 SA, W, 1953 W, I, F, 1956 I, S, F, 1957 W, I
Caplan, D W N (Headingley) 1978 S, I
Cardus, R M (Roundhay) 1979 F, W
Care, D S (Harlequins) 2008 NZ1(R), 2, PI, A, SA, NZ3, 2009 I(R), F(R), S(R), Arg 1, 2, A, Arg 3(R), NZ(R), 2010 W, It, I, S, F, A1, 2(R), NZ(R), A3(R), Sm(R), SA(R), 2011 W1(R), It(R), F(R), S(R), I1(R), W2, 3(R)
Carey, G M (Blackheath) 1895 W, I, S, 1896 W, I
Carleton, J (Orrell) 1979 NZ, 1980 I, F, W, S, 1981 W, S, I, F, Arg 1, 2, 1982 A, S, I, F, W, 1983 F, W, S, I, NZ, 1984 S, I, F, W, A
Carling, W D C (Durham U, Harlequins) 1988 F, W, S, I 1, 2, A2, Fj, A, 1989 S, I, F, W, Fj, 1990 I, F, W, S, Arg 1, 2, 3, 1991 W, S, I, F, Fj, A, [NZ, It, US, F, S, A], 1992 S, I, F, W, C, SA, 1993 F, W, S, I, NZ, 1994 S, I, F, W, SA 1, 2, R, C, 1995 I, F, W, S, [Arg, WS, A, NZ, F], SA, WS, 1996 F, W, S, I, It, Arg, 1997 S, I, F, W
Carpenter, A D (Gloucester) 1932 SA
Carr, R S L (Manchester) 1939 W, I, S
Cartwright, V H (Nottingham) 1903 W, I, S, 1904 W, S, 1905 W, I, S, NZ, 1906 W, I, S, F, SA
Catcheside, H C (Percy Park) 1924 W, I, F, S, 1926 W, I, 1927 I, S
Catt, M J (Bath, London Irish) 1994 W (R), C (R), 1995 I, F, W, S, [Arg, It, WS, A, NZ, F], SA, WS, 1996 F, W, S, I, It, Arg, 1997 W, Arg 1, A 1, 2, NZ 1, SA, 1998 F, W (R), I, A 2(R), SA 2, 1999 S, F, W, A, C (R), [Tg (R), Fj, SA (R)], 2000 I, F, W, It, S, SA 1, 2, A, Arg, 2001 W, It, S, F, I, A, R (R), SA, 2003 [Sm(R), U, W(R), F, A(R)], 2004 W(R), F(R), NZ1, A1, 2006 A1, 2, 2007 F1, W1, F2, [US, SA1, A, F, SA2]
Cattell, R H B (Blackheath) 1895 W, I, S, 1896 W, I, S, 1900 W
Cave, J W (Richmond) 1889 M
Cave, W T C (Blackheath) 1905 W
Challis, R (Bristol) 1957 I, F, S
Chambers, E L (Bedford) 1908 F, 1910 W, I
Chantrill, B S (Bristol) 1924 W, I, F, S
Chapman, C E (Cambridge U) 1884 W
Chapman D E (Richmond) 1998 A 1(R)
Chapman, F E (Hartlepool) 1910 W, I, F, S, 1912 W, 1914 W, I
Cheesman, W I (OMTs) 1913 SA, W, F, I
Cheston, E C (Richmond) 1873 S, 1874 S, 1875 I, S, 1876 S
Chilcott, G J (Bath) 1984 A, 1986 I, F, 1987 F (R), W, [J, US, W (R)], 1988 I 2(R), Fj, 1989 I (R), F, W, R
Christophers, P D (Bristol) 2002 Arg, SA, 2003 W 1 (R)
Christopherson, P (Blackheath) 1891 W, S
Chuter, G S (Leicester) 2006 A1(R), 2, NZ, Arg, SA1, 2(R), 2007 S, It, I, F1, W1, 2(R), [US(R), SA1(R), Sm, Tg, A(R), F(R), SA2(R)], 2008 S(R), I(R), 2009 Arg 2(R), 2010 A1(R), 2(R)
Cipriani, D J (Wasps) 2008 W(R), It(R), I, PI, A, SA, NZ3(R)
Clark, C W H (Liverpool) 1876 I
Clarke, A J (Coventry) 1935 W, I, S, 1936 NZ, W, I

Clarke, B B (Bath, Richmond) 1992 SA, 1993 F, W, S, I, NZ, 1994 S, F, W, SA 1, 2, R, C, 1995 I, F, W, S, [Arg, It, A, NZ, F], SA, WS, 1996 F, W, S, I, Arg (R), 1997 W, Arg 1, 2, A 1(R), 1998 A 1(t), NZ 1, 2, SA 1, H, It, 1999 A (R)
Clarke, S J S (Cambridge U, Blackheath) 1963 W, I, F, S, NZ 1, 2, A, 1964 NZ, W, I, 1965 I, F, S
Clayton, J H (Liverpool) 1871 S
Clements, J W (O Cranleighans) 1959 I, F, S
Cleveland, C R (Blackheath) 1887 W, S
Clibborn, W G (Richmond) 1886 W, I, S, 1887 W, I, S
Clough, F J (Cambridge U, Orrell) 1986 I, F, 1987 [J (R), US]
Coates, C H (Yorkshire W) 1880 S, 1881 S, 1882 S
Coates, V H M (Bath) 1913 SA, W, F, I, S
Cobby, W (Hull) 1900 W
Cockerham, A (Bradford Olicana) 1900 W
Cockerill, R (Leicester) 1997 Arg 1(R), 2, A 2(t+R), NZ 1, SA, NZ 2, 1998 W, S, I, A 1, NZ 1, 2, SA 1, H, It, A 2, SA 2, 1999 S, I, F, W, A, C (R), [It, NZ, Tg (R), Fj (R)]
Codling, A J (Harlequins) 2002 Arg
Cohen, B C (Northampton) 2000 I, F, W, It, S, SA 2, Arg, SA 3, 2001 W, It, S, F, R, 2002 S, I, F, W, It, NZ, A, SA, 2003 F 1, W 1, S, I, NZ, A, F2, 3, [Gg, SA, Sm, W, F, A], 2004 It, S, I, W, F, NZ1, 2, A1, C(R), A2(R), 2005 F(R), A, NZ, 2006 W, It, S, F, I, NZ, Arg, SA1, 2
Colclough, M J (Angoulême, Wasps, Swansea) 1978 S, I, 1979 NZ, 1980 F, W, S, 1981 W, S, I, F, 1982 A, S, I, F, W, 1983 F, NZ, 1984 S, I, F, W, 1986 W, S, I, F
Cole, D R (Leicester) 2010 W(R), It, I, S, F, A1, 2, NZ, A3, Sm(R), SA, 2011 W1, It, F, S, I1, W3, I2, [Arg, Gg, R, S, F]
Coley, E (Northampton) 1929 F, 1932 W
Collins, P J (Camborne) 1952 S, I, F
Collins, W E (O Cheltonians) 1874 S, 1875 I, S, 1876 I, S
Considine, S G U (Bath) 1925 F
Conway, G S (Cambridge U, Rugby, Manchester) 1920 F, I, S, 1921 F, 1922 W, I, F, S, 1923 W, I, S, F, 1924 W, I, F, S, 1925 NZ, 1927 W
Cook, J G (Bedford) 1937 S
Cook, P W (Richmond) 1965 I, F
Cooke, D A (Harlequins) 1976 W, S, I, F
Cooke, D H (Harlequins) 1981 W, S, I, F, 1984 I, 1985 R, F, S, I, W, NZ 1, 2
Cooke, P (Richmond) 1939 W, I
Coop, T (Leigh) 1892 S
Cooper, J G (Moseley) 1909 A, W
Cooper, M J (Moseley) 1973 F, S, NZ 2(R), 1975 F, W, 1976 A, W, 1977 S, I, F, W
Coopper, S F (Blackheath) 1900 W, 1902 W, I, 1905 W, I, S, 1907 W
Corbett, L J (Bristol) 1921 F, 1923 W, I, 1924 W, I, F, S, 1925 NZ, W, I, S, F, 1927 W, I, S, F
Corbisiero, A R (London Irish) 2011 It, F(R), S, I1, W2, 3, [Gg(R), R, S(R), F(R)]
Corless, B J (Coventry, Moseley) 1976 A, I (R), 1977 S, I, F, W, 1978 F, W, S, I
Corry, M E (Bristol, Leicester) 1997 Arg 1, 2, 1998 H, It, SA 2(t), 1999 F(R), A, C (t), [It (R), NZ (t+R), SA (R)], 2000 I (R), F (R), W (R), It (R), S (R), Arg (R), SA 3(t), 2001 W (R), It (R), F (t), C 1, I, 2002 F (t+R), W (t), 2003 W 2, F 2, 3, [U], 2004 A1(R), C, SA, A2, 2005 F, I, It, S, A, NZ, Sm, 2006 W, It, S, F, I, NZ, Arg, SA1, 2, 2007 S, It, I, F1, W1, 2, F2(R), 3, [US(R), SA1, Sm, Tg, A, F, SA2]
Cotton, F E (Loughborough Colls, Coventry, Sale) 1971 S (2[1C]), P, 1973 W, I, F, S, NZ 2, A, 1974 S, I, 1975 I, F, W, 1976 A, W, S, I, F, 1977 S, I, F, W, 1978 S, I, 1979 NZ, 1980 I, F, W, S, 1981 W
Coulman, M J (Moseley) 1967 A, I, F, S, W, 1968 W, I, F, S
Coulson, T J (Coventry) 1927 W, 1928 A, W
Court, E D (Blackheath) 1885 W
Coverdale, H (Blackheath) 1910 F, 1912 I, F, 1920 W
Cove-Smith, R (OMTs) 1921 S, F, 1922 I, F, S, 1923 W, I, S, F, 1924 W, I, S, F, 1925 NZ, W, I, S, F, 1927 W, I, S, F, 1928 A, W, I, F, S, 1929 W, I
Cowling, R J (Leicester) 1977 S, I, F, W, 1978 F, NZ, 1979 S, I
Cowman, A R (Loughborough Colls, Coventry) 1971 S (2[1C]), P, 1973 W, I
Cox, N S (Sunderland) 1901 S
Crane, J S (Leicester) 2008 SA(R), 2009 Arg 1(R), A
Cranmer, P (Richmond, Moseley) 1934 W, I, S, 1935 W, I, S, 1936 NZ, W, I, S, 1937 W, I, S, 1938 W, I, S
Creed, R N (Coventry) 1971 P
Cridlan, A G (Blackheath) 1935 W, I, S
Croft, T R (Leicester) 2008 F(R), S, I, NZ2(R), PI, A, SA(R), NZ3(R), 2009 It(R), W(R), I(R), F, S, A, Arg 3, NZ(R), 2010 A1, 2, NZ, A3, Sm(R), SA, 2011 S(R), I1(R), W2, I2, [Arg, Gg(R), R, S, F]
Crompton, C A (Blackheath) 1871 S
Crompton, D E (Bristol) 2007 SA1(R)
Crosse, C W (Oxford U) 1874 S, 1875 I
Cueto, M J (Sale) 2004 C, SA, A2, 2005 W, F, I, It, S, A, NZ, Sm, 2006 W, It, S, F, I, SA1, 2, 2007 W1, F3, [US, Sm, Tg, SA2], 2009 It, W, I, F, S, Arg 1, 2, A, Arg 3, NZ, 2010 W, It, I, S, F, A1, 2, NZ, A3, Sm, SA, 2011 W1, It, F, S, I1, W2, 3, I2, [R, F]
Cumberlege, B S (Blackheath) 1920 W, I, S, 1921 W, I, S, F, 1922 W
Cumming, D C (Blackheath) 1925 S, F
Cunliffe, F L (RMA) 1874 S
Currey, F I (Marlborough N) 1872 S
Currie, J D (Oxford U, Harlequins, Bristol) 1956 W, I, S, F, 1957 W, I, F, S, 1958 W, A, I, F, S, 1959 W, I, F, S, 1960 W, I, F, S, 1961 SA, 1962 W, I, F
Cusani, D A (Orrell) 1987 I
Cusworth, L (Leicester) 1979 NZ, 1982 F, W, 1983 F, W, NZ, 1984 S, I, F, W, 1988 F, W

D'Aguilar, F B G (Royal Engineers) 1872 S
Dallaglio, L B N (Wasps) 1995 SA (R), WS, 1996 F, W, S, I, It, Arg, 1997 S, I, F, A 1, 2, NZ 1, SA, NZ 2, 1998 F, W, S, I, A 2, SA 2, 1999 S, I, F, W, US, C, [It, NZ, Tg, Fj, SA], 2000 I, F, W, It, S, SA 1, 2, A, Arg, SA 3, 2001 W, It, S, F, 2002 It (R), NZ, A (t), SA(R), 2003 F 1 (R), W 1, It, S, I, NZ, A, [Gg, SA, Sm, U, W, F, A], 2004 It, S, I, W, F, NZ1, 2, A1, 2006 W(t&R), It(R), S(R), F(R), 2007 W2(R), F2, 3(R), [US, Tg(R), A(R), F(R), SA2(R)]
Dalton, T J (Coventry) 1969 S(R)
Danby, T (Harlequins) 1949 W
Daniell, J (Richmond) 1899 W, 1900 I, S, 1902 I, S, 1904 I, S
Darby, A J L (Birkenhead Park) 1899 I
Davenport, A (Ravenscourt Park) 1871 S
Davey, J (Redruth) 1908 S, 1909 W
Davey, R F (Teignmouth) 1931 W
Davidson, Jas (Aspatria) 1897 S, 1898 S, W, 1899 I, S
Davidson, Jos (Aspatria) 1899 W, S
Davies, G H (Cambridge U, Coventry, Wasps) 1981 S, I, F, Arg 1, 2, 1982 A, S, I, 1983 F, W, S, 1984 S, SA 1, 2, 1985 R (R), NZ 1, 2, 1986 W, S, I, F
Davies, P H (Sale) 1927 I
Davies, V G (Harlequins) 1922 W, 1925 NZ
Davies, W J A (United Services, RN) 1913 SA, W, F, I, S, 1914 I, S, F, 1920 F, I, S, 1921 W, I, S, F, 1922 I, F, S, 1923 W, I, S, F
Davies, W P C (Harlequins) 1953 S, 1954 NZ, I, 1955 W, I, F, S, 1956 W, 1957 F, S, 1958 W
Davis, A M (Torquay Ath, Harlequins) 1963 W, I, S, NZ 1, 2, 1964 NZ, W, I, F, S, 1966 W, 1967 A, 1969 SA, 1970 I, W, S
Dawe, R G R (Bath) 1987 I, F, W, [US], 1995 [WS]
Dawson, E F (RIEC) 1878 I
Dawson, M J S (Northampton, Wasps) 1995 WS, 1996 F, W, S, I, 1997 A 1, SA, NZ 2(R), 1998 W (R), S, I, NZ 1, 2, SA 1, H, It, A 2, SA 2, 1999 S, F(R), W, A(R), US, C, [It, NZ, Tg, Fj (R), SA], 2000 I, F, W, It, S, A (R), Arg, SA 3, 2001 W, It, S, F, I, 2002 W (R), It (R), NZ, A, SA, 2003 It, S, I, A(R), F3(R), [Gg, Sm, W, F, A], 2004 It(R), S(R), I, W, F, NZ1, 2(R), A1(R), 2005 W, F(R), I(R), It(R), S(R), A, NZ, 2006 W(R), It(R), S(t&R), F, I(R)
Day, H L V (Leicester) 1920 W, 1922 W, F, 1926 S
Deacon, L P (Leicester) 2005 Sm, 2006 A1, 2(R), 2007 S, It, I, F1(R), W1(R), 2009 Arg 1, 2, A, Arg 3, NZ(R), 2010 W(R), It(R), I(R), S, F, 2011 W1, It, F, S, I1, W3, I2, [Arg, R, S, F]
Dean, G J (Harlequins) 1931 I
Dee, J M (Hartlepool R) 1962 S, 1963 NZ 1
Devitt, Sir T G (Blackheath) 1926 I, F, 1928 A, W
Dewhurst, J H (Richmond) 1887 W, I, S, 1890 W
De Glanville, P R (Bath) 1992 SA (R), 1993 W (R), NZ, 1994 S, I, F, W, SA 1, 2, C (R), 1995 [Arg (R), It, WS], SA (R), 1996 W (R), I (R), It, 1997 S, I, F, W, Arg 1, 2, A 1, 2, NZ 1, 2, 1998 W (R), S (R), I (R), A 2, SA 2, 1999 A (R), US, [It, NZ, Fj (R), SA]
De Winton, R F C (Marlborough N) 1893 W
Dibble, R (Bridgwater A) 1906 S, F, SA, 1908 F, W, I, S, 1909 A, W, F, I, S, 1910 S, 1911 W, F, S, 1912 W, I, S
Dicks, J (Northampton) 1934 W, I, S, 1935 W, I, S, 1936 S, 1937 I
Dillon, E W (Blackheath) 1904 W, I, S, 1905 W
Dingle, A J (Hartlepool R) 1913 I, 1914 S, F
Diprose, A J (Saracens) 1997 Arg 1, 2, A 2, NZ 1, 1998 W (R), S (R), I, A 1, NZ 2, SA 1
Dixon, P J (Harlequins, Gosforth) 1971 P, 1972 W, I, F, S, 1973 I, F, S, 1974 S, I, F, W, 1975 I, 1976 F, 1977 S, I, F, W, 1978 F, S, I, NZ
Dobbs, G E B (Devonport A) 1906 W, I
Doble, S A (Moseley) 1972 SA, 1973 NZ 1, W
Dobson, D D (Newton Abbot) 1902 W, I, S, 1903 W, I, S
Dobson, T H (Bradford) 1895 S
Dodge, P W (Leicester) 1978 W, S, I, NZ, 1979 S, I, F, W, 1980 W,

S, 1981 W, S, I, F, Arg 1, 2, 1982 A, S, F, W, 1983 F, W, S, I, NZ, 1985 R, F, S, I, W, NZ 1, 2
Donnelly, M P (Oxford U) 1947 I
Dooley, W A (Preston Grasshoppers, Fylde) 1985 R, F, S, I, W, NZ 2(R), 1986 W, S, I, F, 1987 F, W, [A, US, W], 1988 F, W, S, I 1, 2, A 1, 2, Fj, A, 1989 S, I, F, W, R, Fj, 1990 I, F, W, S, Arg 1, 2, 3, 1991 W, S, I, F, [NZ, US, F, S, A], 1992 S, I, F, W, C, SA, 1993 W, S, I
Doran-Jones, P P L (Gloucester) 2009 Arg 3(R), 2011 S(R), I1(R)
Dovey, B A (Rosslyn Park) 1963 W, I
Down, P J (Bristol) 1909 A
Dowson, A O (Moseley) 1899 S
Drake-Lee, N J (Cambridge U, Leicester) 1963 W, I, F, S, 1964 NZ, W, I, 1965 W
Duckett, H (Bradford) 1893 I, S
Duckham, D J (Coventry) 1969 I, F, S, W, SA, 1970 I, W, S, F, 1971 W, I, F, S (2[1C]), P, 1972 W, I, F, S, 1973 NZ 1, W, I, F, S, NZ 2, A, 1974 S, I, F, W, 1975 I, F, W, 1976 A, W, S
Dudgeon, H W (Richmond) 1897 S, 1898 I, S, W, 1899 W, I, S
Dugdale, J M (Ravenscourt Park) 1871 S
Dun, A F (Wasps) 1984 W
Duncan, R F H (Guy's Hospital) 1922 I, F, S
Duncombe, N S (Harlequins) 2002 S (R), I (R)
Dunkley, P E (Harlequins) 1931 I, S, 1936 NZ, W, I, S
Duthie, J (W Hartlepool) 1903 W
Dyson, J W (Huddersfield) 1890 S, 1892 S, 1893 I, S

Easter, N J (Harlequins) 2007 It, F1, SA1, 2, W2, F3, [SA1, Sm, Tg, A, F, SA2], 2008 It, F, S, I, Pl, A, SA, NZ3, 2009 It, W, I, F, S, Arg 1, 2, 2010 W, It, I, S, F, A1, 2, NZ, A3, Sm, SA, 2011 W1, It, F, S, I1, W3, [Arg, S(t&R), F]
Ebdon, P J (Wellington) 1897 W, I
Eddison, J H (Headingley) 1912 W, I, S, F
Edgar, C S (Birkenhead Park) 1901 S
Edwards, R (Newport) 1921 W, I, S, F, 1922 W, F, 1923 W, 1924 W, F, S, 1925 NZ
Egerton, D W (Bath) 1988 I 2, A 1, Fj (R), A, 1989 Fj, 1990 I, Arg 2(R)
Elliot, C H (Sunderland) 1886 W
Elliot, E W (Sunderland) 1901 W, I, S, 1904 W
Elliot, W (United Services, RN) 1932 I, S, 1933 W, I, S, 1934 W, I
Elliott, A E (St Thomas's Hospital) 1894 S
Ellis, H A (Leicester) 2004 SA(R), A2(R), 2005 W(R), F, I, It, S, Sm, 2006 W, It, S, F(R), I, 2007 S, It, I, F1, W1, 2008 Pl(R), A(R), SA(R), NZ3(R), 2009 It, W, I, F, S
Ellis, J (Wakefield) 1939 S
Ellis, S S (Queen's House) 1880 I
Emmott, C (Bradford) 1892 W
Enthoven, H J (Richmond) 1878 I
Erinle, A O (Biarritz) 2009 A(R), NZ
Estcourt, N S D (Blackheath) 1955 S
Evans, B J (Leicester) 1988 A 2, Fj
Evans, E (Sale) 1948 A, 1950 W, 1951 I, F, S, 1952 SA, W, S, I, F, 1953 I, F, S, 1954 W, NZ, I, F, 1956 W, I, S, F, 1957 W, I, F, S, 1958 W, A, I, F, S
Evans, G W (Coventry) 1972 S, 1973 W (R), F, S, NZ 2, 1974 S, I, F, W
Evans, N L (RNEC) 1932 W, I, S, 1933 W, I
Evanson, A M (Richmond) 1883 W, I, S, 1884 S
Evanson, W A D (Richmond) 1875 S, 1877 S, 1878 S, 1879 S, I
Evershed, F (Blackheath) 1889 M, 1890 W, S, I, 1892 W, I, S, 1893 W, I, S
Eyres, W C T (Richmond) 1927 I

Fagan, A R St L (Richmond) 1887 I
Fairbrother, K E (Coventry) 1969 I, F, S, W, SA, 1970 I, W, S, F, 1971 W, I, F
Faithfull, C K T (Harlequins) 1924 I, 1926 F, S
Fallas, H (Wakefield T) 1884 I
Farrell, A D (Saracens) 2007 S, It, I, W2, F3, [US(R), SA1, Tg(R)]
Fegan, J H C (Blackheath) 1895 W, I, S
Fernandes, C W L (Leeds) 1881 I, W, S
Fidler, J H (Gloucester) 1981 Arg 1, 2, 1984 SA 1, 2
Fidler, R J (Gloucester) 1998 NZ 2, SA 1
Field, E (Middlesex W) 1893 W, I
Fielding, K J (Moseley, Loughborough Colls) 1969 I, F, S, SA, 1970 I, F, 1972 W, I, F, S
Finch, R T (Cambridge U) 1880 S
Finlan, J F (Moseley) 1967 I, F, S, W, NZ, 1968 W, I, 1969 I, F, S, W, 1970 F, 1973 NZ 1
Finlinson, H W (Blackheath) 1895 W, I, S
Finney, S (RIE Coll) 1872 S, 1873 S
Firth, F (Halifax) 1894 W, I, S
Flatman, D L (Saracens) 2000 SA 1(t), 2(t+R), A (t), Arg (t+R), 2001 F (t), C 2(t+R), US (t+R), 2002 Arg
Fletcher, N C (OMTs) 1901 W, I, S, 1903 S
Fletcher, T (Seaton) 1897 W
Fletcher, W R B (Marlborough N) 1873 S, 1875 S
Flood, T G A L (Newcastle, Leicester) 2006 Arg(R), SA2(R), 2007 S(R), It(R), F1, W1, SA1, 2, W2(t), [A(R), F(R), SA2(R)], 2008 W, It, F, S, I, NZ2, Pl(R), A(R), SA(R), NZ3, 2009 W(R), I, F, S, 2010 W, S(R), F, A1, 2, NZ, A3, Sm, SA, 2011 W1, It, F, S, I1, W3, I2(R), [Gg, R(R), S(R), F]
Flutey, R J (Wasps, Brive) 2008 Pl, A, SA, NZ3, 2009 It, W, I, F, S, 2010 It, I, S, F, 2011 W2
Foden, B J (Northampton) 2009 It(R), 2010 I(R), S(R), F, A1, 2, NZ, A3, Sm, SA, 2011 W1, It, F, S, I1, W3, I2, [Arg, Gg, R, S, F]
Fookes, E F (Sowerby Bridge) 1896 W, I, S, 1897 W, I, S, 1898 I, W, 1899 I, S
Ford, P J (Gloucester) 1964 W, I, F, S
Forrest, J W (United Services, RN) 1930 W, I, F, S, 1931 W, I, S, F, 1934 I, S
Forrest, R (Wellington) 1899 W, 1900 S, 1902 I, S, 1903 I, S
Forrester, J (Gloucester) 2005 W(t), Sm(t&R)
Foulds, R T (Waterloo) 1929 W, I
Fourie, C H (Leeds, Sale) 2010 NZ(R), A3(R), Sm, SA(R), 2011 It(R), F(R), W3, I2
Fowler, F D (Manchester) 1878 S, 1879 S
Fowler, H (Oxford U) 1878 S, 1881 W, S
Fowler, R H (Leeds) 1877 I
Fox, F H (Wellington) 1890 W, S
Francis, T E S (Cambridge U) 1926 W, I, F, S
Frankcom, G P (Cambridge U, Bedford) 1965 W, I, F, S
Fraser, E C (Blackheath) 1875 I
Fraser, G (Richmond) 1902 W, I, S, 1903 W, I
Freakes, H D (Oxford U) 1938 W, 1939 W, I
Freeman, H (Marlborough N) 1872 S, 1873 S, 1874 S
French, R J (St Helens) 1961 W, I, F, S
Freshwater, P T (Perpignan) 2005 v Sm(R), 2006 S(t&R), I(R), Arg, 2007 S, It, I, F3, [SA1(R), Sm(R)]
Fry, H A (Liverpool) 1934 W, I, S
Fry, T W (Queen's House) 1880 I, S, 1881 W
Fuller, H G (Cambridge U) 1882 I, S, 1883 W, I, S, 1884 W

Gadney, B C (Leicester, Headingley) 1932 I, S, 1933 I, S, 1934 W, I, S, 1935 S, 1936 NZ, W, I, S, 1937 S, 1938 W
Gamlin, H T (Blackheath) 1899 W, S, 1900 W, I, S, 1901 S, 1902 W, I, S, 1903 W, I, S, 1904 W, I, S
Gardner, E R (Devonport Services) 1921 W, I, S, 1922 W, I, F, 1923 W, I, S, F
Gardner, H P (Richmond) 1878 I
Garforth, D J (Leicester) 1997 W (R), Arg 1, 2, A 1, NZ 1, SA, NZ 2, 1998 F, W (R), S, I, H, It, A 2, SA 2, 1999 S, I, F, W, A, C (R), [It (R), NZ (R), Fj], 2000 It
Garnett, H W T (Bradford) 1877 S
Gavins, M N (Leicester) 1961 W
Gay, D J (Bath) 1968 W, I, F, S
Gent, D R (Gloucester) 1905 NZ, 1906 W, I, 1910 W, I
Genth, J S M (Manchester) 1874 S, 1875 S
George, J T (Falmouth) 1947 S, F, 1949 I
Geraghty, S J J (London Irish, Northampton) 2007 F1(R), W1(R), 2009 It(R), A, Arg 3, NZ(R)
Gerrard, R A (Bath) 1932 SA, W, I, S, 1933 W, I, S, 1934 W, I, S, 1936 NZ, W, I, S
Gibbs, G A (Bristol) 1947 F, 1948 I
Gibbs, J C (Harlequins) 1925 NZ, W, 1926 F, 1927 W, I, S, F
Gibbs, N (Harlequins) 1954 S, F
Giblin, L F (Blackheath) 1896 W, I, 1897 S
Gibson, A S (Manchester) 1871 S
Gibson, C O P (Northern) 1901 W
Gibson, G R (Northern) 1899 W, 1901 S
Gibson, T A (Northern) 1905 W, S
Gilbert, F G (Devonport Services) 1923 W, I
Gilbert, R (Devonport A) 1908 W, I, S
Giles, J L (Coventry) 1935 W, I, 1937 W, I, 1938 I, S
Gittings, W J (Coventry) 1967 NZ
Glover, P B (Bath) 1967 A, 1971 F, P
Godfray, R E (Richmond) 1905 NZ
Godwin, H O (Coventry) 1959 F, S, 1963 S, NZ 1, 2, A, 1964 NZ, I, F, S, 1967 NZ
Gomarsall, A C T (Wasps, Bedford, Gloucester, Harlequins) 1996 It, Arg, 1997 S, I, F, Arg 2(R) 2000 It (R), 2002 Arg, SA(R), 2003 F 1, W 1(R), 2, F2(R), [Gg(R), U], 2004 It, S, NZ1(R), 2, A1, C, SA, A2, 2007 SA1, 2, F2(R), 3(R), [SA1(R), Sm, Tg, A, F, SA2], 2008 W, It
Goode, A J (Leicester, Brive) 2005 It(R), S(R), 2006 W(R), F(R), I, A1(R), 2, SA1(R), 2, 2009 It, W, I(R), F(R), S(R), Arg1, 2, 3(R)
Gordon-Smith, G W (Blackheath) 1900 W, I, S

ENGLAND

Gotley, A L H (Oxford U) 1910 F, S, 1911 W, F, I, S
Graham, D (Aspatria) 1901 W
Graham, H J (Wimbledon H) 1875 I, S, 1876 I, S
Graham, J D G (Wimbledon H) 1876 I
Gray, A (Otley) 1947 W, I, S
Grayson, P J (Northampton) 1995 WS, 1996 F, W, S, I, 1997 S, I, F, A 2(t), SA (R), NZ 2, 1998 F, W, S, I, H, It, A 2, 1999 I, [NZ (R), Tg, Fj (R), SA], 2003 S(R), I(t), F2, 3(R), [Gg(R), U], 2004 It, S, I
Green, J (Skipton) 1905 I, 1906 S, F, SA, 1907 F, W, I, S
Green, J F (West Kent) 1871 S
Green, W R (Wasps) 1997 A 2, 1998 NZ 1(t+R), 1999 US (R), 2003 W 2(R)
Greening, P B T (Gloucester, Wasps) 1996 It (R), 1997 W (R), Arg 1 1998 NZ 1(R), 2(R), 1999 A (R), US, C, [It (R), NZ (R), Tg, Fj, SA], 2000 I, F, W, It, S, SA 1, 2, A, SA 3, 2001 F, I
Greenstock, N J J (Wasps) 1997 Arg 1, 2, A 1, SA
Greenwell, J H (Rockcliff) 1893 W, I
Greenwood, J E (Cambridge U, Leicester) 1912 F, 1913 SA, W, F, I, S, 1914 W, S, F, 1920 W, F, I, S
Greenwood, J R H (Waterloo) 1966 I, F, S, 1967 A, 1969 I
Greenwood, W J H (Leicester, Harlequins) 1997 A 2, NZ 1, SA, NZ 2, 1998 F, W, S, I, H, It, 1999 C, [It, Tg, Fj, SA], 2000 Arg (R), SA 3, 2001 W, It, S, F, I, A, R, SA, 2002 S, I, F, W, It, NZ, A, SA, 2003 F 1, W 1, It, S, I, NZ, A, F3, [Gg, SA, U(R), W, F, A], 2004 It, S, I, W, F, C(R), SA(R), A2(R)
Greg, W (Manchester) 1876 I, S
Gregory, G G (Bristol) 1931 I, S, F, 1932 SA, W, I, S, 1933 W, I, S, 1934 W, I, S
Gregory, J A (Blackheath) 1949 W
Grewcock, D J (Coventry, Saracens, Bath) 1997 Arg 2, SA, 1998 W (R), S (R), I (R), A 1, NZ 1, SA 2(R), 1999 S (R), A (R), US, C, [It, NZ, Tg (R), SA], 2000 SA 1, 2, A, Arg, SA 3, 2001 W, It, S, I, A, R (R), SA, 2002 S (R), I (R), F (R), W, It, NZ, SA (R), 2003 F 1 (R), W 1 (R), It, S (R), I (t), W 2, F 2, [U], 2004 It, S, W, F, NZ1, 2(R), C, SA, A2, 2005 W, F, I, It, S, A, NZ, 2006 W, It, S, F, I(R), NZ, Arg, 2007 S, It, I
Grylls, W M (Redruth) 1905 I
Guest, R H (Waterloo) 1939 W, I, S, 1947 W, I, S, F, 1948 A, W, I, S, 1949 F, S
Guillemard, A G (West Kent) 1871 S, 1872 S
Gummer, C H A (Plymouth A) 1929 F
Gunner, C R (Marlborough N) 1876 I
Gurdon, C (Richmond) 1880 I, S, 1881 I, W, S, 1882 I, S, 1883 S, 1884 W, S, 1885 I, 1886 W, I, S
Gurdon, E T (Richmond) 1878 S, 1879 I, 1880 S, 1881 I, W, S, 1882 S, 1883 W, I, S, 1884 W, I, S, 1885 W, I, 1886 S
Guscott, J C (Bath) 1989 R, Fj, 1990 I, F, W, S, Arg 3, 1991 W, S, I, F, Fj, A, [NZ, It, F, S, A], 1992 S, I, F, W, C, SA, 1993 F, W, S, I, 1994 R, C, 1995 I, F, W, S, [Arg, It, A, NZ, F], SA, WS, 1996 F, W, S, I, Arg, 1997 I (R), W (R), 1998 F, W, S, I, H, It, A 2, SA 2, 1999 S, I, F, A, US, C, [It (R), NZ, Tg]

Haag, M (Bath) 1997 Arg 1, 2
Haigh, L (Manchester) 1910 W, I, S, 1911 W, F, I, S
Hale, P M (Moseley) 1969 SA, 1970 I, W
Hall, C (Gloucester) 1901 I, S
Hall, J (N Durham) 1894 W, I, S
Hall, J P (Bath) 1984 S (R), I, F, SA 1, 2, A, 1985 R, F, S, I, W, NZ 1, 2, 1986 W, S, 1987 I, F, W, S, 1990 Arg 3, 1994 S
Hall, N M (Richmond) 1947 W, I, S, F, 1949 W, I, 1952 SA, W, S, I, F, 1953 W, I, F, S, 1955 W, I
Halliday, S J (Bath, Harlequins) 1986 W, S, 1987 S, 1988 S, I 1, 2, A 1, A, 1989 S, I, F, W, R, Fj (R), 1990 W, S, 1991 [US, S, A], 1992 S, I, F, W
Hamersley, A St G (Marlborough N) 1871 S, 1872 S, 1873 S, 1874 S
Hamilton-Hill, E A (Harlequins) 1936 NZ, W, I
Hamilton-Wickes, R H (Cambridge U) 1924 I, 1925 NZ, W, I, S, F, 1926 W, I, S, 1927 W
Hammett, E D G (Newport) 1920 W, F, S, 1921 W, I, S, F, 1922 W
Hammond, C E L (Harlequins) 1905 S, NZ, 1906 W, I, S, F, 1908 W, I
Hancock, A W (Northampton) 1965 F, S, 1966 F
Hancock, G E (Birkenhead Park) 1939 W, I, S
Hancock, J H (Newport) 1955 W, I
Hancock, P F (Blackheath) 1886 W, I, 1890 W
Hancock, P S (Richmond) 1904 W, I, S
Handford, F G (Manchester) 1909 W, F, I, S
Hands, R H M (Blackheath) 1910 F, S
Hanley, J (Plymouth A) 1927 W, S, F, 1928 W, I, F, S
Hanley, S M (Sale) 1999 W
Hannaford, R C (Bristol) 1971 W, I, F
Hanvey, R J (Aspatria) 1926 W, I, F, S
Hape, S E (Bath, London Irish) 2010 A1, 2, NZ, A3, Sm, SA, 2011 W1, It, F, S, I1, W3, [Gg]
Harding, E H (Devonport Services) 1931 I
Harding, R M (Bristol) 1985 R, F, S, 1987 S, [A, J, W], 1988 I 1(R), 2, A 1, 2, Fj
Harding, V S J (Saracens) 1961 F, S, 1962 W, I, F, S
Hardwick, P F (Percy Park) 1902 I, S, 1903 W, I, S, 1904 W, I, S
Hardwick, R J K (Coventry) 1996 It (R)
Hardy, E M P (Blackheath) 1951 I, F, S
Hare, W H (Nottingham, Leicester) 1974 W, 1978 F, NZ, 1979 NZ, 1980 I, F, W, S, 1981 W, S, Arg 1, 2, 1982 F, W, 1983 F, W, S, I, NZ, 1984 S, I, F, W, SA 1, 2
Harper, C H (Exeter) 1899 W
Harriman, A T (Harlequins) 1988 A
Harris, S W (Blackheath) 1920 I, S
Harris, T W (Northampton) 1929 S, 1932 I
Harrison, A C (Hartlepool R) 1931 I, S
Harrison, A L (United Services, RN) 1914 I, F
Harrison, G (Hull) 1877 I, S, 1879 S, I, 1880 S, 1885 W, I
Harrison, H C (United Services, RN) 1909 S, 1914 I, S, F
Harrison, M E (Wakefield) 1985 NZ 1, 2, 1986 S, I, F, 1987 I, F, W, S, [A, J, US, W], 1988 F, W
Hartley, B C (Blackheath) 1901 S, 1902 S
Hartley, D M (Northampton) 2008 PI(R), A(R), SA(R), NZ3(R), 2009 It(R), W(R), I(R), F(R), S(R), Arg 1, 2, A(R), Arg 3, NZ, 2010 W, It, I, S, F, NZ(R), A3, Sm, SA, 2011 W1, It, F, S, I1, W2, I2(R), [Arg(R), Gg, S(R), F(R)]
Haskell, J A W (Wasps, Stade Français, Ricoh Black Rams) 2007 W1, F2, 2008 W, It, F, I(R), NZ1, 2, PI(t&R), A(R), SA, NZ3, 2009 It, W, I, F(R), S(R), Arg 1, 2(R), A(R), Arg 3, NZ, 2010 W, It, I, S, F(R), A1(R), Sm, 2011 W1, It, F, S, I1, W2, 3(R), I2, [Arg, Gg, R, S, F(R)]
Haslett, L W (Birkenhead Park) 1926 I, F
Hastings, G W D (Gloucester) 1955 W, I, F, S, 1957 W, I, F, S, 1958 W, A, I, F, S
Havelock, H (Hartlepool R) 1908 F, W, I
Hawcridge, J J (Bradford) 1885 W, I
Hayward, L W (Cheltenham) 1910 I
Hazell, A R (Gloucester) 2004 C, SA(t&R), 2005 W, F(t), It(R), S(R), 2007 SA1
Hazell, D St G (Leicester) 1955 W, I, F, S
Healey, A S (Leicester) 1997 I (R), W, A 1(R), 2(R), NZ 1(R), SA (R), NZ 2, 1998 F, W, S, I, A 1, NZ 1, 2, H, It, A 2, SA 2(R), 1999 US, C, [It, NZ, Tg, Fj, SA (R)], 2000 I, F, W, It, S, SA 1, 2, A, SA 3(R), 2001 W (R), It, S, F, I (R), A, R, SA, 2002 S, I, F, W, It (R), NZ (R), A (R), SA(R), 2003 F2
Hearn, R D (Bedford) 1966 F, S, 1967 I, F, S, W
Heath, A H (Oxford U) 1876 S
Heaton, J (Waterloo) 1935 W, I, S, 1939 W, I, S, 1947 I, S, F
Henderson, A P (Edinburgh Wands) 1947 W, I, S, F, 1948 I, S, F, 1949 W, I
Henderson, R S F (Blackheath) 1883 W, S, 1884 W, S, 1885 W
Heppell, W G (Devonport A) 1903 I
Herbert, A J (Wasps) 1958 F, S, 1959 W, I, F, S
Hesford, R (Bristol) 1981 S (R), 1982 A, S, F (R), 1983 F (R), 1985 R, F, S, I, W
Heslop, N J (Orrell) 1990 Arg 1, 2, 3, 1991 W, S, I, F, [US, F], 1992 W (R)
Hetherington, J G G (Northampton) 1958 A, I, 1959 W, I, F, S
Hewitt, E N (Coventry) 1951 W, I, F
Hewitt, W W (Queen's House) 1881 I, W, S, 1882 I
Hickson, J L (Bradford) 1887 W, I, S, 1890 W, S, I
Higgins, R (Liverpool) 1954 W, NZ, I, S, 1955 W, I, F, S, 1957 W, I, F, S, 1959 W
Hignell, A J (Cambridge U, Bristol) 1975 A 2, 1976 A, W, S, I, 1977 S, I, F, W, 1978 W, 1979 S, I, F, W
Hill, B A (Blackheath) 1903 I, S, 1904 W, I, 1905 W, NZ, 1906 SA, 1907 F, W
Hill, R A (Saracens) 1997 S, I, F, W, A 1, 2, NZ 1, SA, NZ 2, 1998 F, W, H (R), It (R), A 2, SA 2, 1999 S, I, F, W, A, US, C, [It, NZ, Tg, Fj (R), SA], 2000 I, F, W, It, S, SA 1, 2, A, Arg, SA 3, 2001 W, It, S, F, I, A, SA, 2002 S, I, F, W, It, NZ, A, SA, 2003 F 1, W 1, It, S, I, NZ, A, F 3, [Gg, F, A], 2004 It, S, I, W, F, NZ1, 2, A1
Hill, R J (Bath) 1984 SA 1, 2, 1985 I (R), NZ 2(R), 1986 F (R), 1987 I, F, W, [US], 1989 Fj, 1990 I, F, W, S, Arg 1, 2, 3, 1991 W, S, I, F, Fj, A, [NZ, It, US, F, S, A]
Hillard, R J (Oxford U) 1925 NZ
Hiller, R (Harlequins) 1968 W, I, F, S, 1969 I, F, S, W, SA, 1970 I, W, S, 1971 I, F, S (2[1C]), P, 1972 W, I
Hind, A E (Leicester) 1905 NZ, 1906 W
Hind, G R (Blackheath) 1910 S, 1911 I
Hipkiss, D J (Leicester) 2007 W2, F3, [Sm(R), Tg(R), F(R), SA2(R)], 2008 NZ3(R), 2009 Arg 1, 2, A, Arg 3, NZ, 2010 W(R)
Hobbs, R F A (Blackheath) 1899 S, 1903 W
Hobbs, R G S (Richmond) 1932 SA, W, I, S
Hobson, J D (Bristol) 2008 NZ2(R)

Hodges, H A (Nottingham) 1906 W, I
Hodgkinson, S D (Nottingham) 1989 R, Fj, 1990 I, F, W, S, Arg 1, 2, 3, 1991 W, S, I, F, [US]
Hodgson, C C (Sale, Saracens) 2001 R, 2002 S (R), I (R), It (R), Arg, 2003 F 1, W 1, It (R), 2004 NZ1, 2, A1, C, SA, A2, 2005 W, F, I, It, S, A, NZ, Sm, 2006 W, It, S, F, NZ, Arg, SA1, 2008 S(R), NZ1, 2010 A3(R), Sm(R), SA(R), 2011 W2(R), 3(R)
Hodgson, J McD (Northern) 1932 SA, W, I, S, 1934 W, I, 1936 I
Hodgson, P K (London Irish) 2008 I(R), 2009 Arg 1(R), 2(R), A(R), Arg 3, NZ, 2010 W(R), It(R), I(R)
Hodgson, S A M (Durham City) 1960 W, I, F, S, 1961 SA, W, 1962 W, I, F, S, 1964 W
Hofmeyr, M B (Oxford U) 1950 W, F, S
Hogarth, T B (Hartlepool R) 1906 F
Holford, G (Gloucester) 1920 W, F
Holland, D (Devonport A) 1912 W, I, S
Holliday, T E (Aspatria) 1923 S, F, 1925 I, S, F, 1926 F, S
Holmes, C B (Manchester) 1947 S, 1948 I, F
Holmes, E (Manningham) 1890 S, I
Holmes, W A (Nuneaton) 1950 W, I, F, S, 1951 W, I, F, S, 1952 SA, S, I, F, 1953 W, I, F, S
Holmes, W B (Cambridge U) 1949 W, I, F, S
Hook, W G (Gloucester) 1951 S, 1952 SA, W
Hooper, C A (Middlesex W) 1894 W, I, S
Hopley, D P (Wasps) 1995 [WS (R)], SA, WS
Hopley, F J V (Blackheath) 1907 F, W, 1908 I
Horak, M J (London Irish) 2002 Arg
Hordern, P C (Gloucester) 1931 I, S, F, 1934 W
Horley, C H (Swinton) 1885 I
Hornby, A N (Manchester) 1877 I, S, 1878 S, I, 1880 I, 1881 I, S, 1882 I, S
Horrocks-Taylor, J P (Cambridge U, Leicester, Middlesbrough) 1958 W, A, 1961 S, 1962 S, 1963 NZ 1, 2, A, 1964 NZ, W
Horsfall, E L (Harlequins) 1949 W
Horton, A L (Blackheath) 1965 W, I, F, S, 1966 F, S, 1967 NZ
Horton, J P (Bath) 1978 W, S, I, NZ, 1980 I, F, W, S, 1981 W, 1983 S, I, 1984 SA 1, 2
Horton, N E (Moseley, Toulouse) 1969 I, F, S, W, 1971 I, F, S, 1974 S, 1975 W, 1977 S, I, F, W, 1978 F, W, 1979 S, I, F, W, 1980 I
Hosen, R W (Bristol, Northampton) 1963 NZ 1, 2, A, 1964 F, S, 1967 A, I, F, S, W
Hosking, G R d'A (Devonport Services) 1949 W, I, F, S, 1950 W
Houghton, S (Runcorn) 1892 I, 1896 W
Howard, P D (O Millhillians) 1930 W, I, F, S, 1931 W, I, S, F
Hubbard, G C (Blackheath) 1892 W, I
Hubbard, J C (Harlequins) 1930 S
Hudson, A (Gloucester) 1906 W, I, F, 1908 F, W, I, S, 1910 F
Hughes, G E (Barrow) 1896 S
Hull, P A (Bristol, RAF) 1994 SA 1, 2, R, C
Hulme, F C (Birkenhead Park) 1903 W, I, 1905 W, I
Hunt, J T (Manchester) 1882 I, S, 1884 W
Hunt, R (Manchester) 1880 I, 1881 W, S, 1882 I
Hunt, W H (Manchester) 1876 S, 1877 I, S, 1878 I
Hunter, I (Northampton) 1992 C, 1993 F, W, 1994 F, W, 1995 [WS, F]
Huntsman, R P (Headingley) 1985 NZ 1, 2
Hurst, A C B (Wasps) 1962 S
Huskisson, T F (OMTs) 1937 W, I, S, 1938 W, I, 1939 W, I, S
Hutchinson, F (Headingley) 1909 F, I, S
Hutchinson, J E (Durham City) 1906 I
Hutchinson, W C (RIE Coll) 1876 S, 1877 I
Hutchinson, W H H (Hull) 1875 I, 1876 I
Huth, H (Huddersfield) 1879 S
Hyde, J P (Northampton) 1950 F, S
Hynes, W B (United Services, RN) 1912 F

Ibbitson, E D (Headingley) 1909 W, F, I, S
Imrie, H M (Durham City) 1906 NZ, 1907 I
Inglis, R E (Blackheath) 1886 W, I, S
Irvin, S H (Devonport A) 1905 W
Isherwood, F W (Ravenscourt Park) 1872 S

Jackett, E J (Leicester, Falmouth) 1905 NZ, 1906 W, I, S, F, SA, 1907 W, I, S, 1909 W, F, I, S
Jackson, A H (Blackheath) 1878 I, 1880 I
Jackson, B S (Broughton Park) 1970 S (R), F
Jackson, P B (Coventry) 1956 W, I, F, 1957 W, I, F, S, 1958 W, A, F, S, 1959 W, I, F, S, 1961 S, 1963 W, I, F, S
Jackson, W J (Halifax) 1894 S
Jacob, F (Cambridge U) 1897 W, I, S, 1898 I, S, W, 1899 W, I
Jacob, H P (Blackheath) 1924 W, I, F, S, 1930 F
Jacob, P G (Blackheath) 1898 I
Jacobs, C R (Northampton) 1956 W, I, S, F, 1957 W, I, F, S, 1958 W, A, I, F, S, 1960 W, I, F, S, 1961 SA, W, I, F, S, 1963 NZ 1, 2, A, 1964 W, I, F, S
Jago, R A (Devonport A) 1906 W, I, SA, 1907 W, I
Janion, J P A G (Bedford) 1971 W, I, F, S (2[1C]), P, 1972 W, S, SA, 1973 A, 1975 A 1, 2
Jarman, J W (Bristol) 1900 W
Jeavons, N C (Moseley) 1981 S, I, F, Arg 1, 2, 1982 A, S, I, F, W, 1983 F, W, S, I
Jeeps, R E G (Northampton) 1956 W, 1957 W, I, F, S, 1958 W, A, I, F, S, 1959 I, 1960 W, I, F, S, 1961 SA, W, I, F, S, 1962 W, I, F, S
Jeffery, G L (Blackheath) 1886 W, I, S, 1887 W, I, S
Jennins, C R (Waterloo) 1967 A, I, F
Jewitt, J (Hartlepool R) 1902 W
Johns, W A (Gloucester) 1909 W, F, I, S, 1910 W, I, F
Johnson, M O (Leicester) 1993 F, NZ, 1994 S, I, F, W, R, C, 1995 I, F, W, S, [Arg, It, WS, A, NZ, F], SA, WS, 1996 F, W, S, I, It, Arg, 1997 S, I, F, W, A 2, NZ 1, 2, 1998 F, W, S, I, H, It, A 2, SA 2, 1999 S, I, F, W, A, US, C, [It, NZ, Tg, Fj, SA], 2000 SA 1, 2, A, Arg, SA 3, 2001 W, It, S, F, SA, 2002 S, I, F, It (t+R), NZ, A, SA, 2003 F 1, W 1, S, I, NZ, A, F 3, [Gg, SA, Sm, U(R), W, F, A]
Johnston, J B (Saracens) 2002 Arg, NZ (R)
Johnston, W R (Bristol) 1910 W, I, S, 1912 W, I, S, F, 1913 SA, W, F, I, S, 1914 W, I, S, F
Jones, C M (Sale) 2004 It(R), S, I(R), W, NZ1, 2005 W, 2006 A1(R), 2, SA1(R), 2, 2007 SA1, 2(R)
Jones, F P (New Brighton) 1893 S
Jones, H A (Barnstaple) 1950 W, I, F
Jorden, A M (Cambridge U, Blackheath, Bedford) 1970 F, 1973 I, F, S, 1974 F, 1975 W, S
Jowett, D (Heckmondwike) 1889 M, 1890 S, I, 1891 W, I, S
Judd, P E (Coventry) 1962 W, I, F, S, 1963 S, NZ 1, 2, A, 1964 NZ, 1965 I, F, S, 1966 W, I, F, S, 1967 A, I, F, S, W, NZ

Kay, B J (Leicester) 2001 C 1, 2, A, R, SA (t+R), 2002 S, I, F, W, It, Arg, NZ (R), A, SA, 2003 F 1, W 1, It, S, I, NZ, A, F 3, [Gg, SA, Sm, W, F, A], 2004 It, S, I, W, F, C(R), SA(R), 2005 W, F, I, It, S, 2006 A2, NZ, Arg, SA1, 2(R), 2007 F2, [US, SA1, Sm, Tg, A, F, SA2], 2008 W(R), It(R), F(R), S(R), I(R), NZ1(R), 2(R), 2009 Arg 1(R), 2(t&R)
Kayll, H E (Sunderland) 1878 S
Keeling, J H (Guy's Hospital) 1948 A, W
Keen, B W (Newcastle U) 1968 W, I, F, S
Keeton, G H (Leicester) 1904 W, I, S
Kelly, G A (Bedford) 1947 W, I, S, 1948 W
Kelly, T S (London Devonians) 1906 W, I, S, F, SA, 1907 F, W, I, S, 1908 F, I, S
Kemble, A T (Liverpool) 1885 W, I, 1887 I
Kemp, D T (Blackheath) 1935 W
Kemp, T A (Richmond) 1937 W, I, 1939 S, 1948 A, W
Kendall, P D (Birkenhead Park) 1901 S, 1902 W, 1903 S
Kendall-Carpenter, J MacG K (Oxford U, Bath) 1949 I, F, S, 1950 W, I, F, S, 1951 I, F, S, 1952 SA, W, S, I, F, 1953 W, I, F, S, 1954 W, NZ, I, F
Kendrew, D A (Leicester) 1930 W, I, 1933 I, S, 1934 S, 1935 W, I, 1936 NZ, W, I
Kennedy, N J (London Irish) 2008 PI, NZ3, 2009 It, W, I, F(R), S(R)
Kennedy, R D (Camborne S of M) 1949 I, F, S
Kent, C P (Rosslyn Park) 1977 S, I, F, W, 1978 F (R)
Kent, T (Salford) 1891 W, I, S, 1892 W, I, S
Kershaw, C A (United Services, RN) 1920 W, F, I, S, 1921 W, I, S, F, 1922 W, I, F, S, 1923 W, I, S, F
Kewley, E (Liverpool) 1874 S, 1875 S, 1876 I, S, 1877 I, S, 1878 S
Kewney, A L (Leicester) 1906 W, I, S, F, 1909 A, W, F, I, S, 1911 W, F, I, S, 1912 I, S, 1913 SA
Key, A (O Cranleighans) 1930 I, 1933 W
Keyworth, M (Swansea) 1976 A, W, S, I
Kilner, B (Wakefield T) 1880 I
Kindersley, R S (Exeter) 1883 W, 1884 S, 1885 W
King, A D (Wasps) 1997 Arg 2(R), 1998 SA 2(R), 2000 It (R), 2001 C 2(R), 2003 W2
King, I (Harrogate) 1954 W, NZ, I
King, J A (Headingley) 1911 W, F, I, S, 1912 W, I, S, 1913 SA, W, F, I, S
King, Q E M A (Army) 1921 S
Kingston, P (Gloucester) 1975 A 1, 2, 1979 I, F, W
Kitching, A E (Blackheath) 1913 I
Kittermaster, H J (Harlequins) 1925 NZ, W, I, 1926 W, I, F, S
Knight, F (Plymouth) 1909 A
Knight, P M (Bristol) 1972 F, S, SA
Knowles, E (Millom) 1896 S, 1897 S
Knowles, T C (Birkenhead Park) 1931 S
Krige, J A (Guy's Hospital) 1920 W

Labuschagne, N A (Harlequins, Guy's Hospital) 1953 W, 1955 W,

I, F, S
Lagden, R O (Richmond) 1911 S
Laird, H C C (Harlequins) 1927 W, I, S, 1928 A, W, I, F, S, 1929 W, I
Lambert, D (Harlequins) 1907 F, 1908 F, W, S, 1911 W, F, I
Lampkowski, M S (Headingley) 1976 A, W, S, I
Lapage, W N (United Services, RN) 1908 F, W, I, S
Larter, P J (Northampton, RAF) 1967 A, NZ, 1968 W, I, F, S, 1969 I, F, S, W, SA, 1970 I, W, F, S, 1971 W, I, F, S (2[1C]), P, 1972 SA, 1973 NZ 1, W
Law, A F (Richmond) 1877 S
Law, D E (Birkenhead Park) 1927 I
Lawes, C L (Northampton) 2009 A(R), 2010 S(R), A1(R), 2, NZ, A3, Sm, SA, 2011 W3, I2, [Arg, S, F(R)]
Lawrence, Hon H A (Richmond) 1873 S, 1874 S, 1875 I, S
Lawrie, P W (Leicester) 1910 S, 1911 S
Lawson, R G (Workington) 1925 I
Lawson, T M (Workington) 1928 A, W
Leadbetter, M M (Broughton Park) 1970 F
Leadbetter, V H (Edinburgh Wands) 1954 S, F
Leake, W R M (Harlequins) 1891 W, I, S
Leather, G (Liverpool) 1907 I
Lee, F H (Marlborough N) 1876 S, 1877 I
Lee, H (Blackheath) 1907 F
Le Fleming, J (Blackheath) 1887 W
Leonard, J (Saracens, Harlequins) 1990 Arg 1, 2, 3, 1991 W, S, I, F, Fj, A, [NZ, It, US, F, S, A], 1992 S, I, F, W, C, SA, 1993 F, W, S, I, NZ, 1994 S, I, F, W, SA 1, 2, R, C, 1995 I, F, W, S, [Arg, It, A, NZ, F], SA, WS, 1996 F, W, S, I, It, Arg, 1997 S, I, F, W, A 2, NZ 1, SA, NZ 2, 1998 F, W, S, I, H, It, A 2 SA 2, 1999 S, I, F, W, A, C (R), [It, NZ, Fj, SA], 2000 I, F, W, It, S, SA 1, 2, A, Arg, SA 3, 2001 W, It, S, F, I, R, 2002 S (R), I (R), F (R), It (R), A, SA, 2003 F 1, S, I, NZ, W 2, F 2(t+R), 3(R), [Gg(t&R), SA(R), Sm, U, W, F(t&R), A(R)], 2004 It(R)
Leslie-Jones, F A (Richmond) 1895 W, I
Lewis, A O (Bath) 1952 SA, W, S, I, F, 1953 W, I, F, S, 1954 F
Lewsey, O J (Wasps) 1998 NZ 1, 2, SA 1, 2001 C 1, 2, US, 2003 It, S, I, NZ, A, F2, 3(t+R), [Gg, SA, U, F, A], 2004 It, S, I, W, F, NZ1, 2, A1, C, SA, A2, 2005 W, F, I, It, S, A, NZ, Sm, 2006 W, S, F, Arg(R), SA1, 2, 2007 S, It, I, F1, 2, 3, [US, SA1, Sm, Tg, A, F]
Leyland, R (Waterloo) 1935 W, I, S
Linnett, M S (Moseley) 1989 Fj
Lipman, M R (Bath) 2004 NZ2(R), A1(R), 2006 A2, 2008 It, F, S, I, Pl(R), A(R), NZ3
Livesay, R O'H (Blackheath) 1898 W, 1899 W
Lloyd, L D (Leicester) 2000 SA 1(R), 2(R), 2001 C 1, 2, US
Lloyd, R H (Harlequins) 1967 NZ, 1968 W, I, F, S
Locke, H M (Birkenhead Park) 1923 S, F, 1924 W, F, S, 1925 W, I, S, F, 1927 W, I, S
Lockwood, R E (Heckmondwike) 1887 W, I, S, 1889 M, 1891 W, I, S, 1892 W, I, S, 1893 W, I, 1894 W, I
Login, S H M (RN Coll) 1876 I
Lohden, F C (Blackheath) 1893 W
Long, A E (Bath) 1997 A 2, 2001 US (R)
Longland, R J (Northampton) 1932 S, 1933 W, S, 1934 W, I, S, 1935 W, I, S, 1936 NZ, W, I, S, 1937 W, I, S, 1938 W, I, S
Lowe, C N (Cambridge U, Blackheath) 1913 SA, W, F, I, S, 1914 W, I, S, F, 1920 W, F, I, S, 1921 W, I, S, F, 1922 W, I, F, S, 1923 W, I, S, F
Lowrie, F W (Wakefield T) 1889 M, 1890 W
Lowry, W M (Birkenhead Park) 1920 F
Lozowski, R A P (Wasps) 1984 A
Luddington, W G E (Devonport Services) 1923 W, I, S, F, 1924 W, I, F, S, 1925 W, I, S, F, 1926 W
Luger, D D (Harlequins, Saracens) 1990 I I, It, SA 2, 1999 S, I, F, W, A, US, C, [It, NZ, Tg, Fj, SA], 2000 SA 1, A, Arg, SA 3, 2001 W, I, A, R, SA, 2002 F (R), W, It, 2003 F 1, W 1, It, S (R), I (R), NZ(R), W 2, [Gg(R), SA(R), U, W]
Lund, M B (Sale) 2006 A1, 2(R), NZ(R), Arg(t&R), 2007 S, It, I, F1(R), W1(R), SA2
Luscombe, F (Gipsies) 1872 S, 1873 S, 1875 I, S, 1876 I, S
Luscombe, J H (Gipsies) 1871 S
Luxmoore, A F C C (Richmond) 1900 S, 1901 W
Luya, H F (Waterloo, Headingley) 1948 W, I, S, F, 1949 W
Lyon, A (Liverpool) 1871 S
Lyon, G H d'O (United Services, RN) 1908 S, 1909 A

McCanlis, M A (Gloucester) 1931 W, I
McCarthy, N (Gloucester) 1999 I (t), US (R), 2000 It (R)
McFadyean, C W (Moseley) 1966 I, F, S, 1967 A, I, F, S, W, NZ, 1968 W, I
MacIlwaine, A H (United Services, Hull & E Riding) 1912 W, I, S, F, 1920 I
Mackie, O G (Wakefield T, Cambridge U) 1897 S, 1898 I
Mackinlay, J E H (St George's Hospital) 1872 S, 1873 S, 1875 I
MacLaren, W (Manchester) 1871 S
MacLennan, R R F (OMTs) 1925 I, S, F
McLeod, N F (RIE Coll) 1879 S, I
Madge, R J P (Exeter) 1948 A, W, I, S
Malir, F W S (Otley) 1930 W, I, S
Mallett, J A (Bath) 1995 [WS (R)]
Mallinder, J (Sale) 1997 Arg 1, 2
Mangles, R H (Richmond) 1897 W, I
Manley, D C (Exeter) 1963 W, I, F, S
Mann, W E (United Services, Army) 1911 W, F, I
Mantell, N D (Rosslyn Park) 1975 A 1
Mapletoft, M S (Gloucester) 1997 Arg 2
Markendale, E T (Manchester R) 1880 I
Marques, R W D (Cambridge U, Harlequins) 1956 W, I, S, F, 1957 W, I, F, S, 1958 W, A, I, F, S, 1959 W, I, F, S, 1960 W, I, F, S, 1961 SA, W
Marquis, J C (Birkenhead Park) 1900 I, S
Marriott, C J B (Blackheath) 1884 W, I, S, 1886 W, I, S, 1887 I
Marriott, E E (Manchester) 1876 I
Marriott, V R (Harlequins) 1963 NZ 1, 2, A, 1964 NZ
Marsden, G H (Morley) 1900 W, I, S
Marsh, H (RIE Coll) 1873 S
Marsh, J (Swinton) 1892 I
Marshall, H (Blackheath) 1893 W
Marshall, M W (Blackheath) 1873 S, 1874 S, 1875 I, S, 1876 I, S, 1877 I, S, 1878 S, I
Marshall, R M (Oxford U) 1938 I, S, 1939 W, I, S
Martin, C R (Bath) 1985 F, S, I, W
Martin, N O (Harlequins) 1972 F (R)
Martindale, S A (Kendal) 1929 F
Massey, E J (Leicester) 1925 W, I, S
Mather, B-J (Sale) 1999 W
Mathias, J L (Bristol) 1905 W, I, S, NZ
Matters, J C (RNE Coll) 1899 S
Matthews, J R C (Harlequins) 1949 F, S, 1950 I, F, S, 1952 SA, W, S, I, F
Maud, P (Blackheath) 1893 W, I
Maxwell, A W (New Brighton, Headingley) 1975 A 1, 1976 A, W, S, I, F, 1978 F
Maxwell-Hyslop, J E (Oxford U) 1922 I, F, S
May, T A (Newcastle) 2009 Arg 1, 2
Maynard, A F (Cambridge U) 1914 W, I, S
Mears, L A (Bath) 2005 Sm(R), 2006 W(R), It(R), F(R), I, A1, 2(R), NZ(R), Arg(R), SA1(R), 2, 2007 S(R), It(R), I(R), W1(R), F2(R), 3(R), [Tg(R)], 2008 W(R), It(R), F(R), S, I, NZ1, 2, Pl, A, SA, NZ3, 2009 It, W, I, F, S, 2010 I(R), 2011 W2(R), 3(R), [R(R)]
Meikle, G W C (Waterloo) 1934 W, I, S
Meikle, S S C (Waterloo) 1929 S
Mellish, F W (Blackheath) 1920 W, F, I, S, 1921 W, I
Melville, N D (Wasps) 1984 A, 1985 I, W, NZ 1, 2, 1986 W, S, I, F, 1988 F, W, S, I 1
Merriam, L P B (Blackheath) 1920 W, F
Michell, A T (Oxford U) 1875 I, S, 1876 I
Middleton, B B (Birkenhead Park) 1882 I, 1883 I
Middleton, J A (Richmond) 1922 S
Miles, J H (Leicester) 1903 W
Millett, H (Richmond) 1920 F
Mills, F W (Marlborough N) 1872 S, 1873 S
Mills, S G F (Gloucester) 1981 Arg 1, 2, 1983 W, 1984 SA 1, A
Mills, W A (Devonport A) 1906 W, I, S, F, SA, 1907 F, W, I, S, 1908 F, W
Milman, D L K (Bedford) 1937 W, 1938 W, I, S
Milton, C H (Camborne S of M) 1906 I
Milton, J G (Camborne S of M) 1904 W, I, S, 1905 S, 1907 I
Milton, W H (Marlborough N) 1874 S, 1875 I
Mitchell, F (Blackheath) 1895 W, I, S, 1896 W, I, S
Mitchell, W G (Richmond) 1890 W, S, I, 1891 W, I, S, 1893 S
Mobbs, E R (Northampton) 1909 A, W, F, I, S, 1910 I, F
Moberley, W O (Ravenscourt Park) 1872 S
Monye, Y C C (Harlequins) 2008 Pl, A, SA, NZ3, 2009 F, S, A, Arg 3, NZ, 2010 W, It, I, S
Moody, L W (Leicester, Bath) 2001 C 1, 2, US, I (R), R, SA (R), 2002 I (R), W, It, Arg, NZ, A, SA, 2003 F 1, W 2, F 2, 3(R), [Gg(R), SA, Sm(R), U, W, F(R), A(R)], 2004 C, SA, A2, 2005 F, I, It, S, A, NZ, Sm, 2006 W, It, S, F, I, A1, NZ, Arg, SA1(R), 2(R), W2(R), 2007 [US(R), SA1(R), Sm(R), Tg, A, F, SA2], 2008 W, 2009 A, Arg 3, NZ, 2010 W, It, I, S(R), F, A1, 2, NZ, A3, SA, 2011 W2, [Gg, R, S, F]
Moore, B C (Nottingham, Harlequins) 1987 S, [A, J, W], 1988 F, W, S, I 1, 2, A 1, 2, Fj, A, 1989 S, I, F, W, R, Fj, 1990 I, F, W, S, Arg 1, 2, 1991 W, S, I, F, Fj, A, [NZ, It, F, S, A], 1992 S, I, F, W, SA, 1993 F, W, S, I, NZ, 1994 S, I, F, W, SA 1, 2, R, C, 1995 I, F, W, S, [Arg, It, WS (R), A, NZ, F]
Moore, E J (Blackheath) 1883 I, S

THE COUNTRIES

Moore, N J N H (Bristol) 1904 W, I, S
Moore, P B C (Blackheath) 1951 W
Moore, W K T (Leicester) 1947 W, I, 1949 F, S, 1950 I, F, S
Mordell, R J (Rosslyn Park) 1978 W
Morfitt, S (W Hartlepool) 1894 W, I, S, 1896 W, I, S
Morgan, J R (Hawick) 1920 W
Morgan, O C (Gloucester) 2007 S, I
Morgan, W G D (Medicals, Newcastle) 1960 W, I, F, S, 1961 SA, W, I, F, S
Morley, A J (Bristol) 1972 SA, 1973 NZ 1, W, I, 1975 S, A 1, 2
Morris, A D W (United Services, RN) 1909 A, W, F
Morris, C D (Liverpool St Helens, Orrell) 1988 A, 1989 S, I, F, W, 1992 S, I, F, W, C, SA, 1993 F, W, S, I, 1994 F, W, SA 1, 2, R, 1995 S (t), [Arg, WS, A, NZ, F]
Morris, R (Northampton) 2003 W 1, It
Morrison, P H (Cambridge U) 1890 W, S, I, 1891 I
Morse, S (Marlborough N) 1873 S, 1874 S, 1875 S
Mortimer, W (Marlborough N) 1899 W
Morton, H J S (Blackheath) 1909 I, S, 1910 W, I
Moss, F (Broughton) 1885 W, I, 1886 W
Mullan, M J (Worcester) 2010 It(R)
Mullins, A R (Harlequins) 1989 Fj
Mycock, J (Sale) 1947 W, I, S, F, 1948 A
Myers, E (Bradford) 1920 I, S, 1921 W, I, 1922 W, I, F, S, 1923 W, I, S, F, 1924 W, I, F, S, 1925 S, F
Myers, H (Keighley) 1898 I

Nanson, W M B (Carlisle) 1907 F, W
Narraway, L J W (Gloucester) 2008 W, It(R), S(R), NZ1, 2, 2009 W(R), I(R)
Nash, E H (Richmond) 1875 I
Neale, B A (Rosslyn Park) 1951 I, F, S
Neale, M E (Blackheath) 1912 F
Neame, S (O Cheltonians) 1879 S, I, 1880 I, S
Neary, A (Broughton Park) 1971 W, I, F, S (2[1C]), P, 1972 W, I, F, S, SA, 1973 NZ 1, W, I, F, S, NZ 2, A, 1974 S, I, F, W, 1975 I, F, W, S, A 1, 1976 A, W, S, I, F, 1977 I, 1978 F (R), 1979 S, I, F, W, NZ, 1980 I, F, W, S
Nelmes, B G (Cardiff) 1975 A 1, 2, 1978 W, S, I, NZ
Newbold, C J (Blackheath) 1904 W, I, S, 1905 W, I, S
Newman, S C (Oxford U) 1947 F, 1948 A, W
Newton, A W (Blackheath) 1907 S
Newton, P A (Blackheath) 1882 S
Newton-Thompson, J O (Oxford U) 1947 S, F
Nichol, W (Brighouse R) 1892 W, S
Nicholas, P L (Exeter) 1902 W
Nicholson, B E (Harlequins) 1938 W, I
Nicholson, E S (Leicester) 1935 W, I, S, 1936 NZ, W
Nicholson, E T (Birkenhead Park) 1900 W, I
Nicholson, T (Rockcliff) 1893 I
Ninnes, B F (Coventry) 1971 W
Noon, J D (Newcastle) 2001 C 1, 2, US, 2003 W 2, F 2(t+R), 2005 W, F, I, It, S, A, NZ, 2006 W, It, S, F, I, 2006 A1(R), 2, NZ, Arg, SA1, 2, 2007 SA2, F2, [US, SA1], 2008 It, F, S, I, NZ1(R), 2, PI, A, SA, NZ3, 2009 It
Norman, D J (Leicester) 1932 SA, W
North, E H G (Blackheath) 1891 W, I, S
Northmore, S (Millom) 1897 I
Novak, M J (Harlequins) 1970 W, S, F
Novis, A L (Blackheath) 1929 S, F, 1930 W, I, F, 1933 I, S

Oakeley, F E (United Services, RN) 1913 S, 1914 I, S, F
Oakes, R F (Hartlepool R) 1897 W, I, S, 1898 I, S, W, 1899 W, S
Oakley, L F L (Bedford) 1951 W
Obolensky, A (Oxford U) 1936 NZ, W, I, S
Ojo, T O (London Irish) 2008 NZ1, 2
Ojomoh, S O (Bath, Gloucester) 1994 I, F, SA 1(R), 2, R, 1995 S (R), [Arg, WS, A (t), F], 1996 F, 1998 NZ 1
Old, A G B (Middlesbrough, Leicester, Sheffield) 1972 W, I, F, S, SA, 1973 NZ 2, A, 1974 S, I, F, W, 1975 I, A 2, 1976 S, I, 1978 F
Oldham, W L (Coventry) 1908 S, 1909 A
Olver, C J (Northampton) 1990 Arg 3, 1991 [US], 1992 C
O'Neill, A (Teignmouth, Torquay A) 1901 W, I, S
Openshaw, W E (Manchester) 1879 I
Orwin, J (Gloucester, RAF, Bedford) 1985 R, F, S, I, W, NZ 1, 2, 1988 F, W, S, I 1, 2, A 1, 2
Osborne, R R (Manchester) 1871 S
Osborne, S H (Oxford U) 1905 S
Oti, C (Cambridge U, Nottingham, Wasps) 1988 S, I 1, 1989 S, I, F, W, R, 1990 Arg 1, 2, 1991 Fj, A, [NZ, It]
Oughtred, B (Hartlepool R) 1901 S, 1902 W, I, S, 1903 W, I
Owen, J E (Coventry) 1963 W, I, F, S, A, 1964 NZ, 1965 W, I, F, S, 1966 I, F, S, 1967 NZ
Owen-Smith, H G O (St Mary's Hospital) 1934 W, I, S, 1936 NZ, W, I, S, 1937 W, I, S

Page, J J (Bedford, Northampton) 1971 W, I, F, S, 1975 S
Paice, D J (London Irish) 2008 NZ1(R), 2(R)
Pallant, J N (Notts) 1967 I, F, S
Palmer, A C (London Hospital) 1909 I, S
Palmer, F H (Richmond) 1905 W
Palmer, G V (Richmond) 1928 I, F, S
Palmer, J A (Bath) 1984 SA 1, 2, 1986 I (R)
Palmer, T P (Leeds, Wasps, Stade Français) 2001 US (R), 2006 Arg(R), SA1, 2, 2007 It(R), I(R), F1, W1, 2008 NZ1, 2, PI(R), A, SA, 2010 F(R), A1, 2, NZ, A3, Sm, SA, 2011 W1, It, F, S, I1, W2, 3(R), I2(R), [Arg(R), Gg, R, S(R), F]
Pargetter, T A (Coventry) 1962 S, 1963 F, NZ 1
Parker, G W (Gloucester) 1938 I, S
Parker, Hon S (Liverpool) 1874 S, 1875 S
Parsons, E I (RAF) 1939 S
Parsons, M J (Northampton) 1968 W, I, F, S
Patterson, W M (Sale) 1961 SA, S
Pattisson, R M (Blackheath) 1883 I, S
Paul, H R (Gloucester) 2002 F(R), 2004 It(t&R), S(R), C, SA, A2
Paul, J E (RIE Coll) 1875 S
Payne, A T (Bristol) 1935 I, S
Payne, C M (Harlequins) 1964 I, F, S, 1965 I, F, S, 1966 W, I, F, S
Payne, J H (Broughton) 1882 S, 1883 W, I, S, 1884 I, 1885 W, I
Payne, T A N (Wasps) 2004 A1, 2006 A1(R), 2(R), 2007 F1, W1, 2008 It, NZ1(R), 2, SA, NZ3, 2009 Arg 1, 2, A, Arg 3, NZ, 2010 W, It, I, S, F, A1, 2
Pearce, G S (Northampton) 1979 S, I, F, W, 1981 Arg 1, 2, 1982 A, S, 1983 F, W, S, I, NZ, 1984 S, SA 2, A, 1985 R, F, S, I, W, NZ 1, 2, 1986 W, S, I, F, 1987 I, F, W, S, [A, US, W], 1988 Fj, 1991 [US]
Pears, D (Harlequins) 1990 Arg 1, 2, 1992 F (R), 1994 F
Pearson, A W (Blackheath) 1875 I, S, 1876 I, S, 1877 S, 1878 S, I
Peart, T G A H (Hartlepool R) 1964 F, S
Pease, F E (Hartlepool R) 1887 I
Penny, S H (Leicester) 1909 A
Penny, W J (United Hospitals) 1878 I, 1879 S, I
Percival, L J (Rugby) 1891 I, 1892 I, 1893 S
Periton, H G (Waterloo) 1925 W, 1926 W, I, F, S, 1927 W, I, S, F, 1928 A, I, F, S, 1929 W, I, S, F, 1930 W, I, F, S
Perrott, E S (O Cheltonians) 1875 I
Perry, D G (Bedford) 1963 F, S, NZ 1, 2, A 1964 NZ, W, I, 1965 W, I, F, S, 1966 W, I, F
Perry, M B (Bath) 1997 A 2, NZ 1, SA, NZ 2, 1998 W, S, I, A 1, NZ 1, 2, SA 1, H, It, A 2, 1999 I, F, W, A US, C, [It, NZ, Tg, Fj, SA], 2000 I, F, W, It, S, SA 1, 2, A, SA 3, 2001 W (R), F (R)
Perry, S A (Bristol) 2006 NZ, Arg, SA1(R), 2(R), 2007 I(R), F1(R), W1(R), SA1(R), 2(R), W2, F2, 3, [US, SA1]
Perry, S V (Cambridge U, Waterloo) 1947 W, I, 1948 A, W, I, S, F
Peters, J (Plymouth) 1906 S, F, 1907 I, S, 1908 W
Phillips, C (Birkenhead Park) 1880 S, 1881 I, S
Phillips, M S (Fylde) 1958 A, I, F, S, 1959 W, I, F, S, 1960 W, I, F, S, 1961 W, 1963 W, I, F, S, NZ 1, 2, A, 1964 NZ, W, I, F, S
Pickering, A S (Harrogate) 1907 I
Pickering, R D A (Bradford) 1967 I, F, S, W, 1968 F, S
Pickles, R C W (Bristol) 1922 I, F
Pierce, R (Liverpool) 1898 I, 1903 S
Pilkington, W N (Cambridge U) 1898 S
Pillman, C H (Blackheath) 1910 W, I, F, S, 1911 W, F, I, S, 1912 W, F, 1913 SA, W, F, I, S, 1914 W, I, S
Pillman, R L (Blackheath) 1914 F
Pinch, J (Lancaster) 1896 W, I, 1897 S
Pinching, W W (Guy's Hospital) 1872 S
Pitman, I J (Oxford U) 1922 S
Plummer, K C (Bristol) 1969 W, 1976 S, I, F
Pool-Jones, R J (Stade Francais) 1998 A 1
Poole, F O (Oxford U) 1895 W, I, S
Poole, R W (Hartlepool R) 1896 S
Pope, E B (Blackheath) 1931 W, S, F
Portus, G V (Blackheath) 1908 F, I
Potter, S (Leicester) 1998 A 1(t)
Poulton, R W (later Poulton Palmer) (Oxford U, Harlequins, Liverpool) 1909 F, I, S, 1910 W, 1911 S, 1912 W, I, S, 1913 SA, W, F, I, S, 1914 W, I, S, F
Powell, D L (Northampton) 1966 W, I, 1969 I, F, S, W, 1971 W, I, F, S (2[1C])
Pratten, W E (Blackheath) 1927 S, F
Preece, I (Coventry) 1948 I, S, F, 1949 F, S, 1950 W, I, F, S, 1951 W, I, F
Preece, P S (Coventry) 1972 SA, 1973 NZ 1, W, I, F, S, NZ 2, 1975 I, F, W, A 2, 1976 W (R)
Preedy, M (Gloucester) 1984 SA 1
Prentice, F D (Leicester) 1928 I, F, S

Prescott, R E (Harlequins) 1937 W, I, 1938 I, 1939 W, I, S
Preston, N J (Richmond) 1979 NZ, 1980 I, F
Price, H L (Harlequins) 1922 I, S, 1923 W, I
Price, J (Coventry) 1961 I
Price, P L A (RIE Coll) 1877 I, S, 1878 S
Price, T W (Cheltenham) 1948 S, F, 1949 W, I, F, S
Probyn, J A (Wasps, Askeans) 1988 F, W, S, I 1, 2, A 1, 2, A, 1989 S, I, R (R), 1990 I, F, W, S, Arg 1, 2, 3, 1991 W, S, I, F, Fj, A, [NZ, It, F, S, A], 1992 S, I, F, W, 1993 F, W, S, I
Prout, D H (Northampton) 1968 W, I
Pullin, J V (Bristol) 1966 W, 1968 W, I, F, S, 1969 I, F, S, W, SA, 1970 I, W, S, F, 1971 W, I, F, S (2[1C]), P, 1972 W, I, F, S, SA, 1973 NZ 1, W, I, F, S, NZ 2, A, 1974 S, I, F, W, 1975 I, W (R), S, A 1, 2, 1976 F
Purdy, S J (Rugby) 1962 S
Pyke, J (St Helens Recreation) 1892 W
Pym, J A (Blackheath) 1912 W, I, S, F

Quinn, J P (New Brighton) 1954 W, NZ, I, S, F

Rafter, M (Bristol) 1977 S, F, W, 1978 F, W, S, I, NZ, 1979 S, I, F, W, NZ, 1980 W(R), 1981 W, Arg 1, 2
Ralston, C W (Richmond) 1971 S (C), P, 1972 W, I, F, S, SA, 1973 NZ 1, W, I, F, S, NZ 2, A, 1974 S, I, F, W, 1975 I, F, W, S
Ramsden, H E (Bingley) 1898 S, W
Ranson, J M (Rosslyn Park) 1963 NZ 1, 2, A, 1964 W, I, F, S
Raphael, J E (OMTs) 1902 W, I, S, 1905 W, S, NZ, 1906 W, S, F
Ravenscroft, J (Birkenhead Park) 1881 I
Ravenscroft, S C W (Saracens) 1998 A 1, NZ 2(R)
Rawlinson, W C W (Blackheath) 1876 S
Redfern, S P (Leicester) 1984 I (R)
Redman, N C (Bath) 1984 A, 1986 S (R), 1987 I, S, [A, J, W], 1988 Fj, 1990 Arg 1, 2, 1991 Fj, [It, US], 1993 NZ, 1994 F, W, SA 1, 2, 1997 Arg 1, A 1
Redmond, G F (Cambridge U) 1970 F
Redwood, B W (Bristol) 1968 W, I
Rees, D L (Sale) 1997 A 2, NZ 1, SA, NZ 2, 1998 F, W, SA 2(R), 1999 S, I, F, A
Rees, G W (Nottingham) 1984 SA 2(R), A, 1986 I, F, 1987 F, W, S, [A, J, US, W], 1988 S (R), I 1, 2, A 1, 2, Fj, 1989 W (R), R (R), Fj (R), 1990 Arg 3(R), 1991 Fj, [US]
Rees, T (Wasps) 2007 S(R), It(R), I(R), F1, W1, F3, [US, SA1], 2008 W(R), NZ1, 2, PI, A, SA, NZ3(R)
Reeve, J S R (Harlequins) 1929 F, 1930 W, I, F, S, 1931 W, I, S
Regan, M (Liverpool) 1953 W, I, F, S, 1954 W, NZ, I, S, F, 1956 I, S, F
Regan, M P (Bristol, Bath, Leeds) 1995 SA, WS, 1996 F, W, S, I, It, Arg, 1997 S, I, F, W, A 1, NZ 2(R), 1998 F, 2000 SA 1(t), A(R), Arg, SA 3(t), 2001 It(R), S(R), C 2(R), R, 2003 F 1(t), It(R), W 2, [Gg(R), Sm], 2004 It(R), I(R), NZ1(R), 2, A1, 2007 SA1, 2, W2, F2, 3, [US, SA1, A, F, SA2], 2008 W, It, F
Rendall, P A G (Wasps, Askeans) 1984 W, SA 2, 1986 W, S, 1987 I, F, S, [A, J, W], 1988 F, W, S, I 1, 2, A 1, 2, A, 1989 S, I, F, W, R, 1990 I, F, W, S, 1991 [It (R)]
Rew, H (Blackheath) 1929 S, F, 1930 F, S, 1931 W, S, F, 1934 W, I, S
Reynolds, F J (O Cranleighans) 1937 S, 1938 I, S
Reynolds, S (Richmond) 1900 W, I, S, 1901 I
Rhodes, J (Castleford) 1896 W, I, S
Richards, D (Leicester) 1986 I, F, 1987 S, [A, J, US, W], 1988 F, W, S, I 1, A 1, 2, Fj, A, 1989 S, I, F, W, R, 1990 Arg 3, 1991 W, S, I, F, Fj, A, [NZ, It, US], 1992 S (R), F, W, C, 1993 NZ, 1994 W, SA 1, C, 1995 I, F, W, S, [WS, A, NZ], 1996 F (t), S, I
Richards, E E (Plymouth A) 1929 S, F
Richards, J (Bradford) 1891 W, I, S
Richards, P C (Gloucester, London Irish) 2006 A1, 2, NZ(R), Arg(R), SA1, 2, 2007 [US(R), SA1(R), Tg(R), A(t), F(R), SA2(R)], 2008 NZ2(R)
Richards, S B (Richmond) 1965 W, I, F, S, 1967 A, I, F, S, W
Richardson, J V (Birkenhead Park) 1928 A, W, I, F, S
Richardson, W R (Manchester) 1881 I
Rickards, C H (Gipsies) 1873 S
Rimmer, G (Waterloo) 1949 W, I, 1950 W, 1951 W, I, F, 1952 SA, W, 1954 W, NZ, I, S
Rimmer, L I (Bath) 1961 SA, W, I, F, S
Ripley, A G (Rosslyn Park) 1972 W, I, F, S, SA, 1973 NZ 1, W, I, F, S, NZ 2, A, 1974 S, I, F, W, 1975 I, F, S, A 1, 2, 1976 A, W, S
Risman, A B W (Loughborough Coll) 1959 W, I, F, S, 1961 SA, W, I, F
Ritson, J A S (Northern) 1910 F, S, 1912 F, 1913 SA, W, F, I, S
Rittson-Thomas, G C (Oxford U) 1951 W, I, F
Robbins, G L (Coventry) 1986 W, S
Robbins, P G D (Oxford U, Moseley, Coventry) 1956 W, I, S, F, 1957 W, I, F, S, 1958 W, A, I, S, 1960 W, I, F, S, 1961 SA, W, 1962 S
Roberts, A D (Northern) 1911 W, F, I, S, 1912 I, S, F, 1914 I
Roberts, E W (RNE Coll) 1901 W, I, 1905 NZ, 1906 W, I, 1907 S
Roberts, G D (Harlequins) 1907 S, 1908 F, W
Roberts, J (Sale) 1960 W, I, F, S, 1961 SA, W, I, F, S, 1962 W, I, F, S, 1963 W, I, F, S, 1964 NZ
Roberts, R S (Coventry) 1932 I
Roberts, S (Swinton) 1887 W, I
Roberts, V G (Penryn, Harlequins) 1947 F, 1949 W, I, F, S, 1950 I, F, S, 1951 W, I, F, S, 1956 W, I, S, F
Robertshaw, A R (Bradford) 1886 W, I, S, 1887 W, S
Robinson, A (Blackheath) 1889 M, 1890 W, S, I
Robinson, E T (Coventry) 1954 S, 1961 I, F, S
Robinson, G C (Percy Park) 1897 I, S, 1898 I, 1899 W, 1900 I, S, 1901 I, S
Robinson, J T (Sale) 2001 It (R), S (R), F (R), I, A, R, SA, 2002 S, I, F, It, NZ, A, SA, 2003 F 1, W 1, S, I, NZ, A, F 3, [Gg, SA, Sm, U(R), W, F, A], 2004 It, S, I, W, F, C, SA, A2, 2005 W, F, I, 2007 S, It, F1, W1, SA1, W2, F3, [US, SA1, A, F, SA2]
Robinson, J J (Headingley) 1893 S, 1902 W, I, S
Robinson, R A (Bath) 1988 A 2, Fj, A, 1989 S, I, F, W, 1995 SA
Robshaw, C D C (Harlequins) 2009 Arg 2
Robson, A (Northern) 1924 W, I, F, S, 1926 W
Robson, M (Oxford U) 1930 W, I, F, S
Rodber, T A K (Army, Northampton) 1992 S, I, 1993 NZ, 1994 I, F, W, SA 1, 2, R, C, 1995 I, F, W, S, [Arg, It, WS (R), A, NZ, F], SA, WS, 1996 W, S (R), I (t), It, Arg, 1997 S, I, F, W, A 1, 1998 H (R), It (R), A 2, SA 2, 1999 S, I, F, W, A, US (R), [NZ (R), Fj (R)]
Rogers, D P (Bedford) 1961 I, F, S, 1962 W, I, F, 1963 W, I, F, S, NZ 1, 2, A, 1964 NZ, W, I, F, S, 1965 W, I, F, S, 1966 W, I, F, S, 1967 A, S, W, NZ, 1969 I, F, S, W
Rogers, J H (Moseley) 1890 W, S, I, 1891 S
Rogers, W L Y (Blackheath) 1905 W, I
Rollitt, D M (Bristol) 1967 I, F, S, W, 1969 I, F, S, W, 1975 S, A 1, 2
Roncoroni, A D S (West Herts, Richmond) 1933 W, I, S
Rose, W M H (Cambridge U, Coventry, Harlequins) 1981 I, F, 1982 A, S, I, 1987 I, F, W, S, [A]
Rossborough, P A (Coventry) 1971 W, 1973 NZ 2, A, 1974 S, I, 1975 I, F
Rosser, D W A (Wasps) 1965 W, I, F, S, 1966 W
Rotherham, Alan (Richmond) 1883 W, S, 1884 W, S, 1885 W, I, 1886 W, I, S, 1887 W, I, S
Rotherham, Arthur (Richmond) 1898 S, W, 1899 W, I, S
Roughley, D (Liverpool) 1973 A, 1974 S, I
Rowell, R E (Leicester) 1964 W, 1965 W
Rowley, A J (Coventry) 1932 SA
Rowley, H C (Manchester) 1879 S, I, 1880 I, S, 1881 I, W, S, 1882 I, S
Rowntree, G C (Leicester) 1995 S (t), [It, WS], WS, 1996 F, W, S, I, It, Arg, 1997 S, I, F, W, A 1, 1998 A 1, NZ 1, 2, SA 1, H (R), It (R), 1999 US, C, [It (R), Tg, Fj (R)], 2001 C 1, 2, US, I(R), A, R, SA, 2002 S, I, F, W, It, 2003 F 1(R), W 1, It, S, I, NZ, F 2, 2004 C, SA, A2, 2005 W, F, I, It, 2006 A1, 2
Royds, P M R (Blackheath) 1898 S, W, 1899 W
Royle, A V (Broughton R) 1889 M
Rudd, E L (Liverpool) 1965 W, I, S, 1966 W, I, S
Russell, R F (Leicester) 1905 NZ
Rutherford, D (Percy Park, Gloucester) 1960 W, I, F, S, 1961 SA, 1965 W, I, F, S, 1966 W, I, F, S, 1967 NZ
Ryalls, H J (New Brighton) 1885 W, I
Ryan, D (Wasps, Newcastle) 1990 Arg 1, 2, 1992 C, 1998 S
Ryan, P H (Richmond) 1955 W, I

Sackey, P H (Wasps) 2006 NZ, Arg, 2007 F2, 3(R), [SA1, Sm, Tg, A, F, SA2], 2008 W, It, F, S, I, PI, A, SA, NZ3, 2009 It, W, I
Sadler, E H (Army) 1933 I, S
Sagar, J W (Cambridge U) 1901 W, I
Salmon, J L B (Harlequins) 1985 NZ 1, 2, 1986 W, S, 1987 I, F, W, S, [A, J, US, W]
Sample, C H (Cambridge U) 1884 I, 1885 I, 1886 S
Sampson, P C (Wasps) 1998 SA 1, 2001 C 1, 2
Sanders, D L (Harlequins) 1954 W, NZ, I, S, F, 1956 W, I, S, F
Sanders, F W (Plymouth A) 1923 I, S, F
Sanderson, A (Sale) 2001 R (R), 2002 Arg, 2003 It(t + R), W 2(R), F 2
Sanderson, P H (Sale, Harlequins, Worcester) 1998 NZ 1, 2, SA 1, 2001 C 1(R), 2(R), US(t+R), 2005 A, NZ, Sm, 2006 A1, 2, NZ, Arg, SA1, 2, 2007 SA1(R)
Sandford, J R P (Marlborough N) 1906 I
Sangwin, R D (Hull and E Riding) 1964 NZ, W
Sargent, G A F (Gloucester) 1981 I (R)
Savage, K F (Northampton) 1966 W, I, F, S, 1967 A, I, F, S, W, NZ,

1968 W, F, S
Sawyer, C M (Broughton) 1880 S, 1881 I
Saxby, L E (Gloucester) 1932 SA, W
Scarbrough, D G R (Leeds, Saracens) 2003 W 2, 2007 SA2
Schofield, D F (Sale) 2007 SA1, 2(R)
Schofield, J W (Manchester) 1880 I
Scholfield, J A (Preston Grasshoppers) 1911 W
Schwarz, R O (Richmond) 1899 S, 1901 W, I
Scorfield, E S (Percy Park) 1910 F
Scott, C T (Blackheath) 1900 W, I, 1901 W, I
Scott, E K (St Mary's Hospital, Redruth) 1947 W, 1948 A, W, I, S
Scott, F S (Bristol) 1907 W
Scott, H (Manchester) 1955 F
Scott, J P (Rosslyn Park, Cardiff) 1978 F, W, S, I, NZ, 1979 S (R), I, F, W, NZ, 1980 I, F, W, S, 1981 W, S, I, F, Arg 1, 2, 1982 I, F, W, 1983 F, W, S, I, NZ, 1984 S, I, F, W, SA 1, 2
Scott, J S M (Oxford U) 1958 F
Scott, M T (Cambridge U) 1887 I, 1890 S, I
Scott, W M (Cambridge U) 1889 M
Seddon, R L (Broughton R) 1887 W, I, S
Sellar, K A (United Services, RN) 1927 W, I, S, 1928 A, W, I, F
Sever, H S (Sale) 1936 NZ, W, I, S, 1937 W, I, S, 1938 W, I, S
Shackleton, I R (Cambridge U) 1969 SA, 1970 I, W, S
Sharp, R A W (Oxford U, Wasps, Redruth) 1960 W, I, F, S, 1961 I, F, 1962 W, I, F, 1963 W, I, F, S, 1967 A
Sharples, C D J (Gloucester) 2011 W2(R)
Shaw, C H (Moseley) 1906 S, SA, 1907 F, W, I, S
Shaw, F (Cleckheaton) 1898 I
Shaw, J F (RNE Coll) 1898 S, W
Shaw, S D (Bristol, Wasps) 1996 It, Arg, 1997 S, I, F, W, A 1, SA (R), 2000 I, F, W, It, S, SA 1(R), 2(R), 2001 C 1(R), 2, US, I, 2003 It (R), W 2, F 2(R), 3(R), 2004 It(t&R), S(R), NZ1, 2, A1, 2005 Sm(R), 2006 W(R), It(R), S(R), F(R), I, 2007 W2, F2, 3, [US, SA1, Sm, A, F, SA2], 2008 W, It, F, S, I, A(R), SA(R), 2009 F, S, NZ, 2010 W, It, I, F, A1, 2(R), 3(R), SA(R), 2011 W1(R), It(R), F(R), S(R), I1(R), W2, I2(R), [Gg, R(R), F(R)]
Sheasby, C M A (Wasps) 1996 It, Arg, 1997 W (R), Arg 1(R), 2(R), SA (R), NZ 2(t)
Sheppard, A (Bristol) 1981 W (R), 1985 W
Sheridan, A J (Sale) 2004 C(R), 2005 A, NZ, Sm, 2006 W, It, S, F(R), I, NZ, SA1, 2007 W2, F2, [US, SA1, Sm, Tg, A, F, SA2], 2008 W, F, S, I, NZ1, PI, A, 2009 It, W, I, F, S, 2010 NZ, A3, Sm, SA, 2011 W1, F, I2, [Arg]
Sherrard, C W (Blackheath) 1871 S, 1872 S
Sherriff, G A (Saracens) 1966 S, 1967 A, NZ
Shewring, H E (Bristol) 1905 I, NZ, 1906 W, S, F, SA, 1907 F, W, I, S
Shooter, J H (Morley) 1899 I, S, 1900 I, S
Shuttleworth, D W (Headingley) 1951 S, 1953 S
Sibree, H J H (Harlequins) 1908 F, 1909 I, S
Silk, N (Harlequins) 1965 W, I, F, S
Simms, K G (Cambridge U, Liverpool, Wasps) 1985 R, F, S, I, W, 1986 I, F, 1987 I, F, W, [A, J, W], 1988 F, W
Simpson, C P (Harlequins) 1965 W
Simpson, J P M (Wasps) 2011 [Gg(R)]
Simpson, P D (Bath) 1983 NZ, 1984 S, 1987 I
Simpson, T (Rockcliff) 1902 S, 1903 W, I, S, 1904 I, S, 1905 I, S, 1906 S, SA, 1909 F
Simpson-Daniel, J D (Gloucester) 2002 NZ, A, 2003 W 1(t + R), It, W 2, 2004 I(R), NZ1, 2005 Sm, 2006 It(R), 2007 SA1(R)
Sims, D (Gloucester) 1998 NZ 1(R), 2, SA 1
Skinner, M G (Harlequins) 1988 F, W, S, I 1, 2, 1989 Fj, 1990 I, F, W, S, Arg 1, 2, 1991 Fj (R), [US, F, S, A], 1992 S, I, F, W
Skirving, B D (Saracens) 2007 SA2
Sladen, G M (United Services, RN) 1929 W, I, S
Sleightholme, J M (Bath) 1996 F, W, S, I, It, Arg, 1997 S, I, F, W, Arg 1, 2
Slemen, M A C (Liverpool) 1976 I, F, 1977 S, I, F, W, 1978 F, W, S, I, NZ, 1979 S, I, F, W, NZ, 1980 I, F, W, S, 1981 W, S, I, F, 1982 A, S, I, F, W, 1983 NZ, 1984 S
Slocock, L A N (Liverpool) 1907 F, W, I, S, 1908 F, W, I, S
Slow, C F (Leicester) 1934 S
Small, H D (Oxford U) 1950 W, I, F, S
Smallwood, A M (Leicester) 1920 F, I, 1921 W, I, S, F, 1922 I, S, 1923 W, I, S, F, 1925 I, S
Smart, C E (Newport) 1979 F, W, NZ, 1981 S, I, F, Arg 1, 2, 1982 A, S, I, F, W, 1983 F, W, S, I
Smart, S E J (Gloucester) 1913 SA, W, F, I, S, 1914 W, I, S, F, 1920 W, I, S
Smeddle, R W (Cambridge U) 1929 W, I, S, 1931 F
Smith, C C (Gloucester) 1901 W
Smith, D F (Richmond) 1910 W, I
Smith, J V (Cambridge U, Rosslyn Park) 1950 W, I, F, S
Smith, K (Roundhay) 1974 F, W, 1975 W, S
Smith, M J K (Oxford U) 1956 W
Smith, O J (Leicester) 2003 It (R), W 2(R), F 2, 2005 It(R), S(R)
Smith, S J (Sale) 1973 I, F, S, A, 1974 I, F, 1975 W (R), 1976 F, 1977 F (R), 1979 NZ, 1980 I, F, W, S, 1981 W, S, I, F, Arg 1, 2, 1982 A, S, I, F, W, 1983 F, W, S
Smith, S R (Richmond) 1959 W, F, S, 1964 F, S
Smith, S T (Wasps) 1985 R, F, S, I, W, NZ 1, 2, 1986 W, S
Smith, T H (Northampton) 1951 W
Soane, F (Bath) 1893 S, 1894 W, I, S
Sobey, W H (O Millhillians) 1930 W, F, S, 1932 SA, W
Solomon, B (Redruth) 1910 W
Sparks, R H W (Plymouth A) 1928 I, F, S, 1929 W, I, S, 1931 I, S, F
Speed, H (Castleford) 1894 W, I, S, 1896 S
Spence, F W (Birkenhead Park) 1890 I
Spencer, J (Harlequins) 1966 W
Spencer, J S (Cambridge U, Headingley) 1969 I, F, S, W, SA, 1970 I, W, S, F, 1971 W, I, S (2[1C]), P
Spong, R S (O Millhillians) 1929 F, 1930 W, I, F, S, 1931 F, 1932 SA, W
Spooner, R H (Liverpool) 1903 W
Springman, H H (Liverpool) 1879 S, 1887 S
Spurling, A (Blackheath) 1882 I
Spurling, N (Blackheath) 1886 I, S, 1887 W
Squires, P J (Harrogate) 1973 F, S, NZ 2, A, 1974 S, I, F, W, 1975 I, F, W, S, A 1, 2, 1976 A, W, 1977 S, I, F, W, 1978 F, W, S, I, NZ, 1979 S, I, F, W
Stafford R C (Bedford) 1912 W, I, S, F
Stafford, W F H (RE) 1874 S
Stanbury, E (Plymouth A) 1926 W, I, S, 1927 W, I, S, F, 1928 A, W, I, F, S, 1929 W, I, S, F
Standing, G (Blackheath) 1883 W, I
Stanger-Leathes, C F (Northern) 1905 I
Stark, K J (O Alleynians) 1927 W, I, S, F, 1928 A, W, I, F, S
Starks, A (Castleford) 1896 W, I
Starmer-Smith, N C (Harlequins) 1969 SA, 1970 I, W, S, F, 1971 S (C), P
Start, S P (United Services, RN) 1907 S
Steeds, J H (Saracens) 1949 F, S, 1950 I, F, S
Steele-Bodger, M R (Cambridge U) 1947 W, I, S, F, 1948 A, W, I, S, F
Steinthal, F E (Ilkley) 1913 W, F
Stephenson, M (Newcastle) 2001 C 1, 2, US
Stevens, C B (Penzance-Newlyn, Harlequins) 1969 SA, 1970 I, W, S, 1971 P, 1972 W, I, F, S, SA, 1973 NZ 1, W, I, F, S, NZ 2, A, 1974 S, I, F, W, 1975 I, F, W, S
Stevens, M J H (Bath, Saracens) 2004 NZ1(R), 2(t), 2005 I, It, S, NZ(R), Sm, 2006 W, It, F, 2007 SA2, W2(R), F2, 3(R), [US(R), SA1, Sm, Tg, A(R), F(R), SA2(R)], 2008 W(R), It, F(R), S(R), I(R), NZ1, 2, PI, A(t&R), SA(R), NZ3(R), 2011 W2, 3(R), I2(R), [Arg(R), Gg, S, F]
Still, E R (Oxford U, Ravenscourt P) 1873 S
Stimpson, T R G (Newcastle, Leicester) 1996 It, 1997 S, I, F, W, A 1, NZ 2(t+R), 1998 A 1, NZ 1, 2(R), SA 1(R), 1999 US (R), C (R), 2000 SA 1, 2001 C 1(t), 2(R), 2002 W (R), Arg, SA (R)
Stirling, R V (Leicester, RAF, Wasps) 1951 W, I, F, S, 1952 SA, W, S, I, F, 1953 W, I, F, S, 1954 W, NZ, I, S, F
Stoddart, A E (Blackheath) 1885 W, I, 1886 W, I, S, 1889 M, 1890 W, I, 1893 W, S
Stoddart, W B (Liverpool) 1897 W, I, S
Stokes, F (Blackheath) 1871 S, 1872 S, 1873 S
Stokes, L (Blackheath) 1875 I, 1876 S, 1877 I, S, 1878 S, 1879 S, I, 1880 I, S, 1881 I, W, S
Stone, F le S (Blackheath) 1914 F
Stoop, A D (Harlequins) 1905 S, 1906 S, F, SA, 1907 F, W, 1910 W, I, S, 1911 W, F, I, S, 1912 W, S
Stoop, F M (Harlequins) 1910 S, 1911 F, I, 1913 SA
Stout, F M (Richmond) 1897 W, I, 1898 I, S, W, 1899 I, S, 1903 S, 1904 W, I, S, 1905 W, I, S
Stout, P W (Richmond) 1898 S, W, 1899 W, I, S
Strettle, D (Harlequins, Saracens) 2007 I, F1, W1, 2, 2008 W, NZ1, 2011 I1(R)
Stringer, N C (Wasps) 1982 A (R), 1983 NZ (R), 1984 SA 1(R), A, 1985 R
Strong, E L (Oxford U) 1884 W, I, S
Sturnham B (Saracens) 1998 A 1, NZ 1(t), 2(t)
Summerscales, G E (Durham City) 1905 NZ
Sutcliffe, J W (Heckmondwike) 1889 M
Swarbrick, D W (Oxford U) 1947 W, I, F, 1948 A, W, 1949 I
Swayne, D H (Oxford U) 1931 W
Swayne, J W R (Bridgwater) 1929 W
Swift, A H (Swansea) 1981 Arg 1, 2, 1983 F, W, S, 1984 SA 2
Syddall, J P (Waterloo) 1982 I, 1984 A
Sykes, A R V (Blackheath) 1914 F
Sykes, F D (Northampton) 1955 F, S, 1963 NZ 2, A

Sykes, P W (Wasps) 1948 F, 1952 S, I, F, 1953 W, I, F
Syrett, R E (Wasps) 1958 W, A, I, F, 1960 W, I, F, S, 1962 W, I, F

Tait, M J M (Newcastle, Sale) 2005 W, 2006 A1, 2, SA1, 2, 2007 It(R), I(R), F1(R), W1, SA1, 2, W2, [US(R), SA1(R), Sm, Tg, A, F, SA2], 2008 It(t), F(R), S(R), I(t&R), NZ2, 2009 It(R), W(R), I(R), F(R), S(R), Arg 1(R), 2(R), NZ(R), 2010 W, It, I, S, F(R), A1(R)
Tallent, J A (Cambridge U, Blackheath) 1931 S, F, 1932 SA, W, 1935 I
Tanner, C C (Cambridge U, Gloucester) 1930 S, 1932 SA, W, I, S
Tarr, F N (Leicester) 1909 A, W, F, 1913 S
Tatham, W M (Oxford U) 1882 S, 1883 W, I, S, 1884 W, I, S
Taylor, A S (Blackheath) 1883 W, I, 1886 W, I
Taylor, E W (Rockcliff) 1892 I, 1893 I, 1894 W, I, S, 1895 W, I, S, 1896 W, I, 1897 W, I, S, 1899 I
Taylor, F (Leicester) 1920 F, I
Taylor, F M (Leicester) 1914 W
Taylor, H H (Blackheath) 1879 S, 1880 S, 1881 I, W, 1882 S
Taylor, J T (W Hartlepool) 1897 I, 1899 I, 1900 I, 1901 W, I, 1902 W, I, S, 1903 W, I, 1905 S
Taylor, P J (Northampton) 1955 W, I, 1962 W, I, F, S
Taylor, R B (Northampton) 1966 W, 1967 I, F, S, W, NZ, 1969 F, S, W, SA, 1970 I, W, S, F, 1971 S (2[1C])
Taylor, W J (Blackheath) 1928 A, W, I, F, S
Teague, M C (Gloucester, Moseley) 1985 F (R), NZ 1, 2, 1989 S, I, F, W, R, 1990 F, W, S, 1991 W, S, I, F, Fj, A, [NZ, It, F, S, A], 1992 SA, 1993 F, W, S, I
Teden, D E (Richmond) 1939 W, I, S
Teggin, A (Broughton R) 1884 I, 1885 W, 1886 I, S, 1887 I, S
Tetley, T S (Bradford) 1876 S
Thomas, C (Barnstaple) 1895 W, I, S, 1899 I
Thompson, P H (Headingley, Waterloo) 1956 W, I, S, F, 1957 W, I, F, S, 1958 W, A, I, F, S, 1959 W, I, F, S
Thompson, S G (Northampton, Brive, Leeds, Wasps) 2002 S, I, F, W, It, Arg, NZ, A, SA, 2003 F 1, W 1, It, S, I, NZ, A, F 2(R), 3, [Gg, SA, Sm(R), W, F, A], 2004 It, S, I, W, F, NZ1, A1(R), C, SA, A2, 2005 W, F, I, It, S, A, NZ, Sm, 2006 W, It, S, F, I(R), 2009 Arg 1(R), A, Arg 3(R), NZ(R), 2010 W(R), It(R), S(R), F(R), A1, 2, NZ, A3(R), Sm(R), SA(R), 2011 W1(R), It(R), F(R), S(R), I1(R), W3, I2, [Arg, Gg(t&R), R, S, F]
Thomson, G T (Halifax) 1878 S, 1882 I, S, 1883 W, I, S, 1884 I, S, 1885 I
Thomson, W B (Blackheath) 1892 W, 1895 W, I, S
Thorne, J D (Bristol) 1963 W, I, F
Tindall, M J (Bath, Gloucester) 2000 I, F, W, It, S, SA 1, 2, A, Arg, SA 3, 2001 W (R), R, SA (R), 2002 S, I, F, W, It, NZ, A, SA, 2003 It, S, I, NZ, A, F 2, [Gg, SA, Sm, W, F(R), A], 2004 W, F, NZ1, 2, A1, C, SA, A2, 2005 A, NZ, Sm, 2006 W, It, S, F, I(t&R), 2007 S, It, I, F1, 2008 W, NZ1, 2, 2009 W, I, F, S, 2010 F, A1, 2, NZ, A3, SA, 2011 W1, It, F, S, W3, I2, [Arg, R, S]
Tindall, V R (Liverpool U) 1951 W, I, F, S
Titterrell, A J (Sale) 2004 NZ2(R), C(R), 2005 It(R), S(R), 2007 SA2(R)
Tobin, F (Liverpool) 1871 S
Todd, A F (Blackheath) 1900 I, S
Todd, R (Manchester) 1877 S
Toft, H B (Waterloo) 1936 S, 1937 W, I, S, 1938 W, I, S, 1939 W, I, S
Toothill, J T (Bradford) 1890 S, I, 1891 W, I, 1892 W, I, S, 1893 W, I, S, 1894 W, I
Tosswill, L R (Exeter) 1902 W, I, S
Touzel, C J C (Liverpool) 1877 I, S
Towell, A C (Bedford) 1948 F, 1951 S
Travers, B H (Harlequins) 1947 W, I, 1948 A, W, 1949 F, S
Treadwell, W T (Wasps) 1966 I, F, S
Trick, D M (Bath) 1983 I, 1984 SA 1
Tristram, H B (Oxford U) 1883 S, 1884 W, S, 1885 W, 1887 S
Troop, C L (Aldershot S) 1933 I, S
Tucker, J S (Bristol) 1922 W, 1925 NZ, W, I, S, F, 1926 W, I, F, S, 1927 W, I, S, F, 1928 A, W, I, F, S, 1929 W, I, F, 1930 W, I, F, S, 1931 W
Tucker, W E (Blackheath) 1894 W, I, 1895 W, I, S
Tucker, W E (Blackheath) 1926 I, 1930 W, I
Tuilagi, E M (Leicester) 2011 W2, I2, [Arg, Gg, R, S, F]
Turner, D P (Richmond) 1871 S, 1872 S, 1873 S, 1874 S, 1875 I, S
Turner, E B (St George's Hospital) 1876 I, 1877 I, 1878 I
Turner, G R (St George's Hospital) 1876 S
Turner, H J C (Manchester) 1871 S
Turner, M F (Blackheath) 1948 S, F
Turner, S C (Sale) 2007 W1(R), SA1, 2(R)
Turquand-Young, D (Richmond) 1928 A, W, 1929 I, S, F
Twynam, H T (Richmond) 1879 I, 1880 I, 1881 W, 1882 I, 1883 I, 1884 W, I, S

Ubogu, V E (Bath) 1992 C, SA, 1993 NZ, 1994 S, I, F, W, SA 1, 2, R, C, 1995 I, F, W, S, [Arg, WS, A, NZ, F], SA, 1999 F (R), W (R), A (R)
Underwood, A M (Exeter) 1962 W, I, F, S, 1964 I
Underwood, R (Leicester, RAF) 1984 I, F, W, A, 1985 R, F, S, I, W, 1986 W, I, F, 1987 I, F, W, S, [A, J, W], 1988 F, W, S, I 1, 2, A 1, 2, Fj, A, 1989 S, I, F, W, R, Fj, 1990 I, F, W, S, Arg 3, 1991 W, S, I, F, Fj, A, [NZ, It, US, F, S, A], 1992 S, I, F, W, SA, 1993 F, W, S, I, NZ, 1994 S, I, F, W, SA 1, 2, R, C, 1995 I, F, W, S, [Arg, It, WS, A, NZ, F], SA, WS, 1996 F, W, S, I
Underwood, T (Leicester, Newcastle) 1992 C, SA, 1993 S, I, NZ, 1994 S, I, W, SA 1, 2, R, C, 1995 I, F, W, S, [Arg, It, A, NZ], 1996 Arg, 1997 S, I, F, W, 1998 A 2, SA 2
Unwin, E J (Rosslyn Park, Army) 1937 S, 1938 W, I, S
Unwin, G T (Blackheath) 1898 S
Uren, R (Waterloo) 1948 I, S, F, 1950 I
Uttley, R M (Gosforth) 1973 I, F, S, NZ 2, A, 1974 I, F, W, 1975 F, W, S, A 1, 2, 1977 S, I, F, W, 1978 NZ 1979 S, 1980 I, F, W, S

Vainikolo, L P I (Gloucester) 2008 W(R), It, F, S, I
Valentine J (Swinton) 1890 W, 1896 W, I, S
Vanderspar, C H R (Richmond) 1873 S
Van Gisbergen, M C (Wasps) 2005 A(t)
Van Ryneveld, C B (Oxford U) 1949 W, I, F, S
Varley, H (Liversedge) 1892 S
Varndell, T W (Leicester) 2005 Sm(R), 2006 A1, 2, 2008 NZ2
Vassall, H (Blackheath) 1881 W, S, 1882 I, S, 1883 W
Vassall, H H (Blackheath) 1908 I
Vaughan, D B (Headingley) 1948 A, W, I, S, 1949 I, F, S, 1950 W
Vaughan-Jones, A (Army) 1932 I, S, 1933 W
Verelst, C L (Liverpool) 1876 I, 1878 I
Vernon, G F (Blackheath) 1878 S, I, 1880 I, S, 1881 I
Vesty, S B (Leicester) 2009 Arg 1(R), 2(R)
Vickery, G (Aberavon) 1905 I
Vickery, P J (Gloucester, Wasps) 1998 W, A 1, NZ 1, 2, SA 1, 1999 US, C, [It, NZ, Tg, SA], 2000 I, F, W, S, A, Arg (R), SA 3(R), 2001 W, It, S, A, SA, 2002 I, F, Arg, NZ, A, SA, 2003 NZ(R), A, [Gg, SA, Sm(R), U, W, F, A], 2004 It, S, I, W, F, 2005 W(R), F, A, NZ, 2006 SA1(R), 2, 2007 S, It, I, W2, F2(R), 3, [US, Tg(R), A, F, SA2], 2008 W, F, S, I, PI(R), A, SA, NZ3, 2009 It, W, I, F, S
Vivyan, E J (Devonport A) 1901 W, 1904 W, I, S
Voyce, A T (Gloucester) 1920 I, S, 1921 W, I, S, F, 1922 W, I, F, S, 1923 W, I, S, F, 1924 W, I, F, S, 1925 NZ, W, I, S, F, 1926 W, I, F, S
Voyce, T M D (Bath, Wasps) 2001 US (R), 2004 NZ2, A1, 2005 Sm, 2006 W(R), It, F(R), I, A1
Vyvyan, H D (Saracens) 2004 C(R)

Wackett, J A S (Rosslyn Park) 1959 W, I
Wade, C G (Richmond) 1883 W, I, S, 1884 W, S, 1885 W, 1886 W, I
Wade, M R (Cambridge U) 1962 W, I, F
Wakefield, W W (Harlequins) 1920 W, F, I, S, 1921 W, I, S, F, 1922 W, I, F, S, 1923 W, I, S, F, 1924 W, I, F, S, 1925 NZ, W, I, S, F, 1926 W, I, F, S, 1927 S, F
Walder, D J H (Newcastle) 2001 C 1, 2, US, 2003 W 2(R)
Walker, G A (Blackheath) 1939 W, I
Walker, H W (Coventry) 1947 W, I, S, F, 1948 A, W, I, S, F
Walker, R (Manchester) 1874 S, 1875 I, 1876 S, 1879 S, 1880 S
Wallens, J N S (Waterloo) 1927 F
Walshe, N P J (Bath) 2006 A1(R), 2(R)
Walton, E J (Castleford) 1901 W, I, 1902 I, S
Walton, W (Castleford) 1894 S
Ward, G (Leicester) 1913 W, F, S, 1914 W, I, S
Ward, H (Bradford) 1895 W
Ward, J I (Richmond) 1881 I, 1882 I
Ward, J W (Castleford) 1896 W, I, S
Wardlow, C S (Northampton) 1969 SA (R), 1971 W, I, F, S (2[1C])
Warfield, P J (Rosslyn Park, Durham U) 1973 NZ 1, W, I, 1975 I, F, S
Warr, A L (Oxford U) 1934 W, I
Waters, F H H (Wasps) 2001 US, 2004 NZ2(R), A1(R)
Watkins, J A (Gloucester) 1972 SA, 1973 NZ 1, W, NZ 2, A, 1975 F, W
Watkins, J K (United Services, RN) 1939 W, I, S
Watson, F B (United Services, RN) 1908 S, 1909 S
Watson, J H D (Blackheath) 1914 W, S, F
Watt, D E J (Bristol) 1967 I, F, S, W
Webb, C S H (Devonport Services, RN) 1932 SA, W, I, S, 1933 W, I, S, 1935 S, 1936 NZ, W, I, S
Webb, J M (Bristol, Bath) 1987 [A (R), J, US, W], 1988 F, W, S, I 1, 2, A 1, 2, A, 1989 S, I, F, W, 1991 Fj, A, [NZ, It, F, S, A], 1992 S, I, F, W, C, SA, 1993 F, W, S, I
Webb, J W G (Northampton) 1926 F, S, 1929 S
Webb, R E (Coventry) 1967 S, W, NZ, 1968 I, F, S, 1969 I, F, S, W,

1972 I, F
Webb, St L H (Bedford) 1959 W, I, F, S
Webster, J G (Moseley) 1972 W, I, SA, 1973 NZ 1, W, NZ 2, 1974 S, W, 1975 I, F, W
Wedge, T G (St Ives) 1907 F, 1909 W
Weighill, R H G (RAF, Harlequins) 1947 S, F, 1948 S, F
Wells, C M (Cambridge U, Harlequins) 1893 S, 1894 W, S, 1896 S, 1897 W, S
West, B R (Loughborough Colls, Northampton) 1968 W, I, F, S, 1969 SA, 1970 I, W, S
West, D E (Leicester) 1998 F (R), S (R), 2000 Arg (R), 2001 W, It, S, F (t), C 1, 2, US, I (R), A, SA, 2002 F (R), W (R), It (R), 2003 W 2(R), F 2, 3(t+R), [U, F(R)]
West, R (Gloucester) 1995 [WS]
Weston, H T F (Northampton) 1901 S
Weston, L E (W of Scotland) 1972 F, S
Weston, M P (Richmond, Durham City) 1960 W, I, F, S, 1961 SA, W, I, F, S, 1962 W, I, F, 1963 W, I, F, S, NZ 1, 2, A, 1964 NZ, W, I, F, S, 1965 F, S, 1966 S, 1968 F, S
Weston, W H (Northampton) 1933 I, S, 1934 I, S, 1935 W, I, S, 1936 NZ, W, S, 1937 W, I, S, 1938 W, I, S
Wheatley, A A (Coventry) 1937 W, I, S, 1938 W, S
Wheatley, H F (Coventry) 1936 I, 1937 S, 1938 W, S, 1939 W, I, S
Wheeler, P J (Leicester) 1975 F, W, 1976 A, W, S, I, 1977 S, I, F, W, 1978 F, W, S, I, NZ, 1979 S, I, F, W, NZ, 1980 I, F, W, S, 1981 W, S, I, F, 1982 A, S, I, F, W, 1983 F, S, I, NZ, 1984 S, I, F, W
White, C (Gosforth) 1983 NZ, 1984 S, I, F
White, D F (Northampton) 1947 W, I, S, 1948 I, F, 1951 S, 1952 SA, W, S, I, F, 1953 W, I, S
White, J M (Saracens, Bristol, Leicester) 2000 SA 1, 2, Arg, SA 3, 2001 F, C 1, 2, US, I, R (R), 2002 S, W, It, 2003 F 1(R), W 2, F 2, 3, [Sm, U(R)], 2004 W(R), F(R), NZ1, 2, A1, C, SA, A2, 2005 W, 2006 W(R), It(R), S, F, I, A1, 2, NZ, Arg, SA1, 2, 2007 S(R), It(R), I(R), F1, W1, 2009 It(R), W(R), I(t&R), F(t&R), S(R), Arg 1(R), 2
White-Cooper, W R S (Harlequins) 2001 C 2, US
Whiteley, E C P (O Alleynians) 1931 S, F
Whiteley, W (Bramley) 1896 W
Whitely, H (Northern) 1929 W
Wightman, B J (Moseley, Coventry) 1959 W, 1963 W, I, NZ 2, A
Wigglesworth, H J (Thornes) 1884 I
Wigglesworth, R E P (Sale, Saracens) 2008 It(R), F, S, I, NZ1, 2011 W2(R), 3, I2, [Arg, R(R), S(R), F(R)]
Wilkins, D T (United Services, RN, Roundhay) 1951 W, I, F, S, 1952 SA, W, S, I, F, 1953 W, I, F, S
Wilkinson, E (Bradford) 1886 W, I, S, 1887 W, S
Wilkinson, H (Halifax) 1929 W, I, S, 1930 F
Wilkinson, H J (Halifax) 1889 M
Wilkinson, J P (Newcastle, Toulon) 1998 I (R), A 1, NZ 1, 1999 S, I, F, W, A, US, C, [It, NZ, Fj, SA (R)], 2000 I, F, W, It, S, SA 2, A, Arg, SA 3, 2001 W, It, S, F, I, A, SA, 2002 S, I, F, W, It, NZ, A, SA, 2003 F 1, W 1, It, S, I, NZ, A, F 3, [Gg, SA, Sm, W, F, A], 2007 S, It, I, SA1, 2, W2, F2(R), F3, [Sm, Tg, A, F, SA2], 2008 W, It, F, S, I(R), 2009 A, Arg 3, NZ, 2010 W, It, I, S, F(R), A1(R), 2(R), 2011 W1(R), It(R), F(R), S(R), I1(R), W2, I2, [Arg, R, S, F]
Wilkinson, P (Law Club) 1872 S
Wilkinson, R M (Bedford) 1975 A 2, 1976 A, W, S, I, F
Willcocks, T J (Plymouth) 1902 W
Willcox, J G (Oxford U, Harlequins) 1961 I, F, S, 1962 W, I, F, S, 1963 W, I, F, S, 1964 NZ, W, I, F, S
William-Powlett, P B R W (United Services, RN) 1922 S
Williams, C G (Gloucester, RAF) 1976 F
Williams, C S (Manchester) 1910 F
Williams, J E (O Millhillians, Sale) 1954 F, 1955 W, I, F, S, 1956 I, S, F, 1965 W
Williams, J M (Penzance-Newlyn) 1951 I, S
Williams, P N (Orrell) 1987 S, [A, J, W]
Williams, S G (Devonport A) 1902 W, I, S, 1903 I, S, 1907 I, S
Williams, S H (Newport) 1911 W, F, I, S
Williamson, R H (Oxford U) 1908 W, I, S, 1909 A, F
Wilson, A J (Camborne S of M) 1909 I
Wilson, C E (Blackheath) 1898 I
Wilson, C P (Cambridge U, Marlborough N) 1881 W
Wilson, D G (Newcastle, Bath) 2009 Arg 1, 2(R), A, NZ(R), 2010 W, It(R), I(R), S(R), F(R), A1(R), 2(t&R), NZ(R), A3(R), Sm, SA(R), 2011 W1(R), It(R), W2(R), [R(R)]
Wilson, D S (Met Police, Harlequins) 1953 F, 1954 W, NZ, I, S, F, 1955 F, S
Wilson, G S (Tyldesley) 1929 W, I
Wilson, K J (Gloucester) 1963 F
Wilson, R P (Liverpool OB) 1891 W, I, S
Wilson, W C (Richmond) 1907 I, S
Winn, C E (Rosslyn Park) 1952 SA, W, S, I, F, 1954 W, S, F
Winterbottom, P J (Headingley, Harlequins) 1982 A, S, I, F, W, 1983 F, W, S, I, NZ, 1984 S, F, W, SA 1, 2, 1986 W, S, I, F, 1987 I, F, W, [A, J, US, W], 1988 F, W, S, 1989 R, Fj, 1990 I, F, W, S, Arg 1, 2, 3, 1991 W, S, I, F, A, [NZ, It, F, S, A], 1992 S, I, F, W, C, SA, 1993 F, W, S, I
Winters, R A (Bristol) 2007 SA1(R), 2
Wintle, T C (Northampton) 1966 S, 1969 I, F, S, W
Wodehouse, N A (United Services, RN) 1910 F, 1911 W, F, I, S, 1912 W, I, S, F, 1913 SA, W, F, I, S
Wood, A (Halifax) 1884 I
Wood, A E (Gloucester, Cheltenham) 1908 F, W, I
Wood, G W (Leicester) 1914 W
Wood, M B (Wasps) 2001 C 2(R), US (R)
Wood, R (Liversedge) 1894 I
Wood, R D (Liverpool OB) 1901 I, 1903 W, I
Wood, T A (Northampton) 2011 W1, It, F, S, I1, W2(R), 3, [Gg, R(R)]
Woodgate, E E (Paignton) 1952 W
Woodhead, E (Huddersfield) 1880 I
Woodman, T J (Gloucester) 1999 US (R), 2000 I (R), It (R), 2001 W (R), It (R), 2002 NZ, 2003 S (R), I(t + R), A, F 3, [Gg, SA, W(R), F, A], 2004 It, S, I, W, F, NZ1, 2
Woodruff, C G (Harlequins) 1951 W, I, F, S
Woods, S M J (Cambridge U, Wellington) 1890 W, S, I, 1891 W, I, S, 1892 I, S, 1893 W, I, 1895 W, I, S
Woods, T (Bridgwater) 1908 S
Woods, T (United Services, RN) 1920 S, 1921 W, I, S, F
Woodward, C R (Leicester) 1980 I (R), F, W, S, 1981 W, S, I, F, Arg 1, 2, 1982 A, S, I, F, W, 1983 I, NZ, 1984 S, I, F, W
Woodward, J E (Wasps) 1952 SA, W, S, 1953 W, I, F, S, 1954 W, NZ, I, S, F, 1955 W, I, 1956 S
Wooldridge, C S (Oxford U, Blackheath) 1883 W, I, S, 1884 W, I, S, 1885 I
Wordsworth, A J (Cambridge U) 1975 A 1(R)
Worsley, J P R (Wasps) 1999 [Tg, Fj], 2000 It (R), S (R), SA 1(R), 2(R), 2001 It (R), S (R), F (R), C 1, 2, US, A, R, SA, 2002 S, I, F, W (t+R), Arg, 2003 W 1(R), It, S(R), I(t), NZ(R), A(R), W 2, [SA(t), Sm, U], 2004 It, I, W(R), F, NZ1(R), 2, A1, SA, A2, 2005 W, F, I, It, S, 2006 W, It, S, F, I, A1(R), 2, SA1, 2, 2007 S, I, F1, W1, 2, F2, 3(R), [US, Sm, A(R), F(R), SA2(R)], 2008 NZ1(R), 2(R), 2009 It(R), W, I, F, S, Arg 3(R), NZ, 2010 I(R), S, F, 2011 W1(R)
Worsley, M A (London Irish, Harlequins) 2003 It(R), 2004 A1(R), 2005 S(R)
Worton, J R B (Harlequins, Army) 1926 W, 1927 W
Wrench, D F B (Harlequins) 1964 F, S
Wright, C C G (Cambridge U, Blackheath) 1909 I, S
Wright, F T (Edinburgh Acady, Manchester) 1881 S
Wright, I D (Northampton) 1971 W, I, F, S (R)
Wright. J C (Met Police) 1934 W
Wright, J F (Bradford) 1890 W
Wright, T P (Blackheath) 1960 W, I, F, S, 1961 SA, W, I, F, S, 1962 W, I, F, S
Wright, W H G (Plymouth) 1920 W, F
Wyatt, D M (Bedford) 1976 S (R)

Yarranton, P G (RAF, Wasps) 1954 W, NZ, I, 1955 F, S
Yates, K P (Bath, Saracens) 1997 Arg 1, 2, 2007 SA1, 2
Yiend, W (Hartlepool R, Gloucester) 1889 M, 1892 W, I, S, 1893 I, S
Young, A T (Cambridge U, Blackheath, Army) 1924 W, I, F, S, 1925 NZ, F, 1926 I, F, S, 1927 I, S, F, 1928 A, W, I, F, S, 1929 I
Young, J R C (Oxford U, Harlequins) 1958 I, 1960 W, I, F, S, 1961 SA, W, I, F
Young, M (Gosforth) 1977 S, I, F, W, 1978 F, W, S, I, NZ, 1979 S
Young, P D (Dublin Wands) 1954 W, NZ, I, S, F, 1955 W, I, F, S
Youngs, N G (Leicester) 1983 I, NZ, 1984 S, I, F, W
Youngs, B R (Leicester) 2010 S(R), A1(R), 2, NZ, A3, Sm, SA, 2011 W1, It, F, S, I1, [Arg(R), Gg, R, S, F]

David Rogers/Getty Images

Brad Barritt and Chris Wyles of Saracens tackle Alesana Tuilagi of Leicester Tigers during the AVIVA Premiership final on 28 May 2011.

AVIVA PREMIERSHIP RUGBY

SARACENS FINALLY GET OVER THE LINE

By Iain Spragg

Getty Images

Saracens go wild at the end of the Aviva Premiership final.

Saracens' prolonged and frequently frustrating wait to be crowned champions of England finally came to an end after they toppled Leicester in the Aviva Premiership final in front of an 80,000-strong crowd at Twickenham, avenging their dramatic and heartbreaking defeat to the Tigers 12 months earlier.

Despite lofty ambitions and generous investment from owner Nigel Wray over the 16 years he had been involved with the club, the Londoners had never previously claimed the league title but were finally able to lay that ghost to rest at HQ after a nerve-jangling 22–18 victory

Scott Heavey/Getty Images

James Short scores the only try in the final.

over the defending champions that remained in doubt until the final whistle.

The closest Sarries had come to lifting the trophy had been a year earlier only to be cruelly denied by a Dan Hipkiss try three minutes from time that sealed a famous 33–27 triumph for Leicester, but Saracens made no mistake against the same opposition at the second time of asking, surviving a characteristically abrasive late Tigers onslaught.

In fact, in the dying minutes of the Twickenham clash, Leicester produced 32 phases of play as they desperately searched for the try that would have snatched victory, but crucially this time Sarries' defence held firm and the Londoners were champions.

"We hope today is the start of something, not the end of something," said Mark McCall, who became the Saracens director of rugby in January after Brendan Venter moved to the role of technical director. "We're a club that's growing and had we conceded a try in the last minute we would still have been going places.

"In a sick sort of way maybe it was fitting it ended that way. It tells you a lot about Leicester as a club, the way they never give up and don't lose easily. But it also says a lot about our character, our spirit, how we fought for each other, that we refused to yield during that period. We want to be here every year and do what Leicester have done as a club."

It was certainly fitting that it was Leicester and Saracens who met at Twickenham. Both were the standout sides over the 22 games of the regular season and although it was the Tigers who finished top of the final table, two points ahead of their London rivals, Saracens triumphed both times the two clubs met – winning 26–20 at Vicarage Road in October and then 15–14 at Welford Road in April. They were joined in the play-offs by third-placed Gloucester and Northampton in fourth.

The first semi-final saw the Tigers entertain the Saints and it was a typically attritional game between two old rivals. The first-half will be remembered for Manu Tuilagi's vicious off-the-ball attack on Chris Ashton, which inexplicably led to both players being shown a yellow card, while it was the older Tuilagi brother Alesana who lit up the second with the only try of the match in the 71st minute.

The score, coupled with two penalties from Toby Flood, was enough to wrap up a 11–3 win at Welford Road and Richard Cockerill's side were heading to HQ for the Premiership final for a seventh consecutive season. "It was a good performance against a really good side," Cockerill said. "Our attitude to defend and not let them get any cheap points and our tenacity at the breakdown was very good. We controlled the gain-line really well, and that was our best all-round performance for a long time. We wanted to put them under pressure. You stop them from getting on the front foot and they are not as effective as they can be."

A day later Saracens and Gloucester crossed swords at Vicarage Road and the second semi-final proved as close and claustrophobic as the first. Three penalties in blustery conditions from young fly-half Owen Farrell edged Sarries into a 9–3 lead late in the second-half, but when his opposite number, Cherry and Whites number 10 Nicky Robinson, raced over a try after 68 minutes and then landed the conversion, McCall's side suddenly found themselves 10–9 down.

Farrell, however, was presented with one more chance when Gloucester were penalised for not rolling away and although he had squandered four of his previous seven attempts, he held his nerve when it mattered most and Saracens held firm for the remaining eight minutes to claim a 12–10 win.

"It says everything about Owen Farrell that he missed a couple of kicks at goal and he is the guy who wants to put his hand up to kick the winning penalty," McCall said. "He has been incredible for us over a six-month period. He has guided the team to this run of victories we have had and he did that again today. We felt we were in control in the first half, but it wasn't evident on the scoreboard. We left some chances out there. It was tight and nervy."

Two weeks later both clubs headed to Twickenham to renew rivalries in the final and although the eagerly-anticipated showdown was to produce just one try, it was a game that was constantly poised on a knife edge and gripping until the very end.

The first major incident at HQ came in the fifth minute when Sarries came within inches of the Tigers line but failed to get quick ball from the resulting ruck. Referee Wayne Barnes decided Ben Youngs had killed the ball, and the scrum-half spent 10 minutes in the sin bin.

Farrell made no mistake with the resulting penalty but, despite being a man down, Leicester clawed their way back with a Flood penalty on 10 minutes. The pattern for the game was now established and although Sarries got their try on 29 minutes when James Short burst past Scott Hamilton to score in the corner, the furthest they could pull away from the Tigers was on 35 minutes when Farrell's third penalty of the afternoon made it 16–6 to the Londoners.

There were to be only 15 more points scored in the second half. Flood and Farrell traded early penalties, but the pivotal moments came later on. Farrell landed his fifth three-pointer to make it 22–15 to Saracens and, although he landed his sixth moments later to make it 22–18, there was no way back for Leicester despite their enthralling late assault.

Saracens were finally champions and safely in possession of their first piece of silverware since they lifted the Tetley's Bitter Cup back in 1998.

"After last year, revenge feels very sweet," admitted Man of the Match Schalk Brits. "The Leicester boys came out and had an amazing second half, they are an amazing side with a never-say-die attitude. I'm over the moon."

AVIVA PREMIERSHIP 2010–11 RESULTS

3 September 2010: **Sale** 35 **Newcastle** 18. 4 September: **London Irish** 33 **Saracens** 16, **Exeter** 20 **Gloucester** 10, **Wasps** 29 **Harlequins** 29. 5 September: **Leeds** 16 **Bath** 32, **Northampton** 27 **Leicester** 19. 10 September: **Newcastle** 29 **Wasps** 17. 11 September: **Harlequins** 16 **Northampton** 20, **Bath** 20 **London Irish** 13, **Gloucester** 22 **Leeds** 21, **Leicester** 37 **Exeter** 27. 12 September: **Saracens** 28 **Sale** 13. 17 September: **Northampton** 31 **Bath** 10, **Sale** 21 **Harlequins** 17. 18 September: **Exeter** 22 **Newcastle** 17, **Wasps** 37 **Leicester** 30. 19 September: **London Irish** 23 **Gloucester** 16, **Leeds** 14 **Saracens** 26. 25 September: **Bath** 31 **Sale** 16, **Gloucester** 22 **Wasps** 20, **Harlequins** 40 **Exeter** 13, **Leicester** 48 **Leeds** 6, **Newcastle** 12 **London Irish** 46. 26 September: **Saracens** 24 **Northampton** 17. 1 October: **Sale** 24 **Wasps** 25, **Bath** 3 **Gloucester** 18. 2 October: **Harlequins** 23 **Newcastle** 12, **London Irish** 40 **Leeds** 24, **Northampton** 27 **Exeter** 21. 3 October: **Saracens** 26 **Leicester** 20. 22 October: **Leeds** 3 **Sale** 6, **Newcastle** 13 **Saracens** 15. 23 October: **Leicester** 21 **Bath** 15, **Gloucester** 33 **Harlequins** 26, **Exeter** 9 **London Irish** 12. 24 October: **Wasps** 10 **Northampton** 37. 30 October: **Northampton** 34 **Newcastle** 13, **Saracens** 9 **Exeter** 23, **Gloucester** 19 **Leicester** 12. 31 October: **Harlequins** 6 **Bath** 6, **Leeds** 8 **Wasps** 17, **London Irish** 39 **Sale** 26. 19 November: **Leicester** 18 **Harlequins** 13, **Sale** 10 **Northampton** 19. 20 November: **Exeter** 15 **Leeds** 9. 21 November: **Wasps** 33 **London Irish** 25, **Newcastle** 12 **Gloucester** 6, **Bath** 13 **Saracens** 17. 26 November: **Northampton** 35 **London Irish** 23. 27 November: **Exeter** 24 **Sale** 19, **Leicester** 44 **Newcastle** 19, **Gloucester** 19 **Saracens** 13, **Bath** 6 **Wasps** 11. 28 November: **Harlequins** 51 **Leeds** 18. 4 December: **London Irish** 14 **Leicester** 23. 5 December: **Saracens** 26 **Harlequins** 14, **Wasps** 24 **Exeter** 12. 26 December: **Saracens** 13 **Wasps** 6. 27 December: **Leicester** 54 **Sale** 21, **Harlequins** 28 **London Irish** 18. 1 January 2011: **Leeds** 15 **Gloucester** 13, **Northampton** 13 **Harlequins** 16, **London Irish** 24 **Bath** 25. 2 January: **Sale** 28 **Saracens** 22, **Wasps** 33 **Newcastle** 16, **Exeter** 15 **Leicester** 22. 7 January: **Newcastle** 19 **Sale** 19. 8 January: **Bath** 16 **Leeds** 13, **Harlequins** 17 **Wasps** 10, **Gloucester** 37 **Exeter** 23, **Leicester** 27 **Northampton** 16. 9 January: **Saracens** 12 **London Irish** 6. 11 February: **Sale** 7 **Bath** 19. 12 February: **London Irish** 23 **Newcastle** 14, **Northampton** 15 **Saracens** 29, **Exeter** 20 **Harlequins** 6. 13 February: **Leeds** 9 **Leicester** 15, **Wasps** 9 **Gloucester** 10. 18 February: **Gloucester** 23 **London Irish** 9, **Newcastle** 13 **Exeter** 23. 19 February: **Bath** 38 **Northampton** 8, **Harlequins** 21 **Sale** 9, **Leicester** 21 **Wasps** 12. 20 February: **Saracens** 39 **Leeds** 0. 25 February: **Sale** 16 **Leicester** 18. 26 February: **London Irish** 15 **Harlequins** 9, **Northampton** 16 **Gloucester** 18, **Exeter** 9 **Bath** 12. 27 February: **Wasps** 15 **Saracens** 26, **Leeds** 5 **Newcastle** 22. 4 March: **Newcastle** 33 **Harlequins** 18. 5 March: **Gloucester** 34 **Bath** 22, **Leicester** 14 **Saracens** 15. 6 March: **Exeter** 30 **Northampton** 9, **Leeds** 27 **London Irish** 19, **Wasps** 33 **Sale** 26. 12 March: **Leeds** 13 **Northampton** 23. 25 March: **Sale** 15 **Leeds** 12. 26 March: **Harlequins** 53 **Gloucester** 15, **London Irish** 39 **Exeter** 17, **Bath** 6 **Leicester** 37. 27 March: **Northampton** 39 **Wasps** 3, **Saracens** 24 **Newcastle** 9. 2 April: **Northampton** 53 **Sale** 24, **Gloucester** 34 **Newcastle** 9, **Harlequins** 13 **Leicester** 17. 3 April: **Saracens** 20 **Bath** 9, **Leeds** 27 **Exeter** 22, **London Irish** 25 **Wasps** 12. 8 April: **Sale** 36 **Gloucester** 31. 9 April: **Bath** 26 **Exeter** 18, **Newcastle** 29 **Leeds** 30. 15 April: **Newcastle** 15 **Northampton** 22. 16 April: **Bath** 19 **Harlequins** 15, **Exeter** 12 **Saracens** 33, **Leicester** 41 **Gloucester** 41, **Sale** 20 **London Irish** 34. 17 April: **Wasps** 51 **Leeds** 18. 19 April: **Gloucester** 27 **Northampton** 15. 22 April: **Sale** 24 **Exeter** 30, **Newcastle** 13 **Leicester** 24. 23 April: **London Irish** 20 **Northampton** 26, **Wasps** 10 **Bath** 43. 24 April: **Saracens** 35 **Gloucester** 12, **Leeds** 3 **Harlequins** 38. 30 April: **Newcastle** 11 **Bath** 14. 7 May: **Bath** 42 **Newcastle** 12, **Exeter** 21 **Wasps** 8, **Gloucester** 68 **Sale** 17, **Harlequins** 13 **Saracens** 16, **Leicester** 32 **London Irish** 23, **Northampton** 31 **Leeds** 24.

FINAL TABLE

	P	W	D	L	F	A	BP	PTS
Leicester	22	16	1	5	594	403	12	**78**
Saracens	22	18	0	4	484	318	4	**76**
Gloucester	22	14	1	7	528	452	9	**67**
Northampton	22	14	0	8	533	430	9	**65**
Bath	22	13	1	8	427	367	8	**62**
London Irish	22	11	0	11	523	459	10	**54**
Harlequins	22	9	2	11	482	384	12	**52**
Exeter	22	10	0	12	428	460	5	**43**
Wasps	22	9	1	12	425	497	5	**43**
Sale	22	6	1	15	432	618	6	**32**
Newcastle	22	4	1	17	360	553	5	**23**
Leeds	22	4	0	18	315	590	7	**23**

Scott Heavey/Getty Images

The Aviva Premiership said goodbye to Neil Back and Leeds Carnegie at the end of 2011.

SEMI-FINALS

14 May, Welford Road, Leicester

LEICESTER TIGERS 11 (2PG, 1T)
NORTHAMPTON SAINTS 3 (1PG)

LEICESTER: S Hamilton; M Smith, M Tuilagi, A Allen, A Tuilagi; T Flood, B Youngs; M Ayerza, G Chuter, M Castrogiovanni, S Mafi, G Skivington, T Croft, C Newby (captain), J Crane *Substitutions:* H Agulla for Smith (49 mins); D Cole for Castrogiovanni (55 mins); T Waldron for Crane (65 mins); E Slater for Mafi (69 mins); J Grindal for Youngs (77 mins)

SCORERS: *Try:* A Tuilagi *Penalty Goals:* Flood (2)

NORTHAMPTON: B Foden, C Ashton, J Clarke, J Downey, B Reihana; S Myler, L Dickson; S Tonga'uiha, D Hartley (captain), B Mujati, C Lawes, C Day, C Clark, P Dowson, R Wilson *Substitutions:* M Sorensen for Day (69 mins); M Easter for Lawes (73 mins); S Geraghty for Myler (77 mins)

SCORERS: *Penalty Goal:* Myler

YELLOW CARDS: M Tuilagi (32 mins), Ashton (32 mins)

REFEREE: W Barnes (England)

15 May, Vicarage Road, Watford

SARACENS 12 (4PG) GLOUCESTER 10 (1G, 1PG)

SARACENS: A Goode; D Strettle, C Wyles, B Barritt, J Short; O Farrell, R Wigglesworth; M Stevens, S Brits, C Nieto, S Borthwick (captain), M Botha, K Brown, J Burger, E Joubert *Substitutions:* H Vyvyan for Botha (50 mins); N De Kock for Wigglesworth (temp 50–56 mins); R Gill for Stevens (50 mins); N Cato for Short (52 mins); De Kock for Wigglesworth (61 mins); A Saull for Brown (64 mins); P Du Plessis for Nieto (75 mins); Stevens for Gill (81 mins)

SCORERS: *Penalty Goals:* Farrell (4)

GLOUCESTER: F Burns; C Sharples, T Molenaar, E Fuimaono-Sapolu, J Simpson-Daniel; N Robinson, R Lawson; N Wood, S Lawson, P Doran-Jones, J Hamilton, A Brown, A Strokosch, A Qera, L Narraway (captain) *Substitutions:* D Attwood for Hamilton (52 mins); D Lewis for Lawson (64 mins); H Trinder for Molenaar (68 mins); A Dickinson for Wood (71 mins); B Deacon for Qera (75 mins); T Voyce for Burns (82 mins); D Dawidiuk for Lawson (82 mins)

SCORERS: *Try:* Robinson *Conversion:* Robinson *Penalty Goal:* Robinson

REFEREE: A Small (London)

FINAL

28 MAY, Twickenham, London

LEICESTER TIGERS 18 (6PG)
SARACENS 22 (1G, 5PG)

LEICESTER: S Hamilton; H Agulla, M Smith, A Allen, A Tuilagi; T Flood, B Youngs; M Ayerza, G Chuter, M Castrogiovanni, S Mafi, G Skivington, T Croft, C Newby (captain), J Crane *Substitutions:* T Waldrom for Crane (50); D Cole for Castrogiovanni (53 mins); R Hawkins for Chuter (68 mins); E Slater for Mafi (71 mins); B Twelvetrees for Hamilton (75 mins); B Stankovich for Ayerza (78 mins)

SCORERS: *Penalty Goals:* Flood (6)

SARACENS: A Goode; D Strettle, C Wyles, B Barritt, J Short; O Farrell, N De Kock; M Stevens, S Brits, C Nieto, S Borthwick (captain), M Botha, K Brown, J Burger, E Joubert *Substitutions:* R Wigglesworth for de Kock (50 mins); H Vyvyan for Botha (57 mins); P Du Plessis for Nieto (60 mins); R Gill for Stevens (62 mins)

SCORERS: *Try:* Short *Conversion:* Farrell *Penalty Goals:* Farrell (5)

YELLOW CARD: Youngs (5 mins)

REFEREE: Wayne Barnes (England)

Scott Heavey/Getty Images

Toby Flood's six penalties weren't enough to get Leicester home in the final.

FIJI'S 2010–11 TEST RECORD

OPPONENT	DATE	VENUE	RESULT
France	13 Nov	A	**Lost** 12–34
Wales	19 Nov	A	**Drew** 16–16
Italy	27 Nov	A	**Lost** 16–24
Tonga	2 Jul	H	**Lost** 21–45
Samoa	9 Jul	H	**Won** 36–18
Japan	13 Nov	H	**Lost** 13–24
New Zealand	22 Jul	A	**Lost** 14–60
Tonga	13 Aug	H	**Won** 27–12
Tonga	19 Aug	H	**Lost** 20–32
Namibia	10 Sep	N	**Won** 49–25
South Africa	17 Sep	N	**Lost** 3–49
Samoa	25 Sep	N	**Lost** 7–27
Wales	2 Oct	N	**Lost** 0–66

YOUNG STARS START NEW ERA FOR FIJI

By Ian Gilbert

Sandra Mu/Getty Images

Viliame Veikoso is tackled during the Rugby World Cup 2011 match between Wales and Fiji at Waikato Stadium.

As pre-match entertainment goes, one of the more exhilarating sights of Rugby World Cup 2011 was the call to arms when Pool D rivals and Pacific Island neighbours Fiji and Samoa met.

As Samoa performed their pre-match war dance, the *siva tau*, the Fijians advanced forward with their *cibi*. "There was a lot of passion and a lot of emotion going around in those first 10 to 15 minutes," admitted Fiji captain Deacon Manu.

Given the number of Aucklanders hailing from these proud rugby nations, it was a scheduling masterstroke to stage the match – Fiji's third fixture of the tournament – at Eden Park; the 60,327 turnout suggested the game could have been in Suva or Apia. However, anyone expecting the usual flowing Islander rugby would be disappointed as Fiji were thwarted by the Samoans 27–7.

Samoa showed they could play pragmatic rugby in the key matches by initially accumulating points through the boot of Tusi Pisi, but it wasn't until after the break that scrum-half Kahn Fotuali'i scored the first try.

The Samoans acknowledged that the flying Fijians were dangerous with ball in hand, so set out to starve them of possession up front, successfully so. For the first time in a Rugby World Cup match Fiji failed to score in the first half.

That reverse meant the end of Fiji's quarter-final hopes as their final match was against a resurgent Wales side. Nonetheless, a gracious Manu lent his support to the Samoans for their final match, against South Africa.

"Samoa have got a big ask in front of them, but anything is possible in this tournament," he said. "They've certainly proved that they're capable of putting a performance on for the full 80 minutes."

The tournament had started well enough for Fiji, with a 49–25 win against Pool D underdogs Namibia in Rotorua. Fiji are renowned for their attacking flair, but backs coach Shannon Fraser only hinted at the excitement to come: "It's part of our style, but it's not the only thing we've got. There'll be a fair bit of ball spread wide, but we won't be pinning everything on that."

The star was wing Vereniki Goneva with four tries but skipper Manu's focus turned immediately to their next fixture, against South Africa in Wellington. "We have to make sure the guys keep expressing themselves on the field and play the rugby that we want to play," he said. "If that's the free-flowing rugby we're accustomed to, then so be it."

Fiji gave South Africa an almighty scare in their 2007 quarter-final in Marseille before the Springboks pulled away to win 37–20 en route to the title. This time there was little joy for the Fijians as the outstanding Springbok forwards helped conjure six tries for a 49–3 win.

Then came the Samoan match, a must-win if the Fijians were to entertain any thoughts of advancing from the pool. They were also without back-row Dominiko Waqaniburotu, whose suspension for a dangerous tackle in the match against South Africa effectively ended his World Cup.

No. 8 Sisa Koyamaibole explained the allure of the fixture: "It is Pacific rivalry and Samoa is the best team in the Pacific so we always look forward to playing them."

The match also divided the Tagicakibau household, brothers Michael and Sailosi were in the Fiji and Samoa squads respectively, although they didn't line up against each other in the fixture. The two both play in the Aviva Premiership, Michael with Saracens and Sailosi with London Irish, and Michael admitted he would avoid too much banter with his big brother. "I don't like to say too much to him to wind him up," he said. "Being the younger brother, I like to keep it quiet and humble."

Nonetheless, the Auckland-born brothers could count on plenty of family support. "The whole family is coming up," said Michael. "They have T-shirts, half and half. Half-Fiji and half-Samoa. I don't think they will mind too much which team wins."

Talking of brothers, Australian fans would have noticed the presence of Sydney-born prop Campese Ma'afu in the Fiji squad, not only for the intriguing name (Ma'afu senior was so in awe of the legendary Wallaby winger David's feats he named his son after him) but also as the brother of Wallabies front-rower Salesi.

Veteran fly-half Nicky Little was restored to the starting side for the Samoa game, reaching the milestone of 70 caps. The total is a record, not just for Fiji but for any of the Pacific Islands, and Little is the first Fijian to compete in four Rugby World Cups.

There was a certain symmetry about his intervention from the replacements' bench for the last quarter against South Africa, against whom he won his first cap in 1996. But there was to be no fairytale chapter for Little against Samoa, and Fiji moved on for their final game against Wales – a match that has particular resonance for Manu, who plays his club rugby in the principality for the Llanelli-based Scarlets.

Fiji beat Wales at the last World Cup to advance to that quarter-final against the Springboks.

On that day in Nantes the Welsh played a loose game that played into the hands of the strong-running Fijians; this time it was the Welsh who prospered at Hamilton's Waikato Stadium as relentless attacking created nine tries to consign the Islanders to a 66–0 defeat.

The Welsh ran up a 31–0 half-time lead then responded to coach Warren Gatland's urgings not to ease off the pressure. "We knew we would have to try to play our hand to get in their face physically. To their credit, Wales took advantage of our mistakes," admitted Fiji assistant coach Greg Mumm.

Fiji's tournament record of won one, lost three could be seen only as disappointing after their exploits at France 2007, and Mumm acknowledged that, "there's a number of areas in which we've failed at this World Cup. It's very disappointing for the players and the people of Fiji."

Off the pitch, the Fijians acknowledged the warmth of their reception, team manager Pio Tikoisuva commenting, "We are very traditional and cultural people. We really respect the Maori community and what they have done. It's almost like back home and the way we offer visitors a traditional welcome."

Looking ahead, coach Samu Domoni expects lessons learned at this tournament to stand Fiji in good stead for England 2015 – for which Fiji must qualify after finishing fourth in Pool D. "It's a very young side and it's a good investment for us, so we can plan for the next World Cup," he said.

FIJI INTERNATIONAL STATISTICS

MATCH RECORDS UP TO 31 OCTOBER 2011

WINNING MARGIN

Date	Opponent	Result	Winning Margin
10/09/1983	Niue Island	120–4	**116**
21/08/1969	Solomon Islands	113–13	**100**
08/09/1983	Solomon Islands	86–0	**86**
30/08/1979	Papua New Guinea	86–0	**86**
23/08/1969	Papua New Guinea	88–3	**85**

MOST POINTS IN A MATCH

BY THE TEAM

Date	Opponent	Result	Points
10/09/1983	Niue Island	120–4	**120**
21/08/1969	Solomon Islands	113–13	**113**
23/08/1969	Papua New Guinea	88–3	**88**
08/09/1983	Solomon Islands	86–0	**86**
30/08/1979	Papua New Guinea	86–0	**86**

BY A PLAYER

Date	Player	Opponent	Points
10/09/1983	Severo Koroduadua	Niue Island	**36**
21/08/1969	Semesa Sikivou	Solomon Islands	**27**
28/08/1999	Nicky Little	Italy	**25**

MOST TRIES IN A MATCH

BY THE TEAM

Date	Opponent	Result	Tries
21/08/1969	Solomon Islands	113–13	**25**
10/09/1983	Niue Island	120–4	**21**
23/08/1969	Papua New Guinea	88–3	**20**
18/08/1969	Papua New Guinea	79–0	**19**
30/08/1979	Papua New Guinea	86–0	**18**

BY A PLAYER

Date	Player	Opponent	Tries
30/08/1979	Tevita Makutu	Papua New Guinea	**6**
18/08/1969	George Sailosi	Papua New Guinea	**5**

MOST CONVERSIONS IN A MATCH

BY THE TEAM

Date	Opponent	Result	Cons
21/08/1969	Solomon Islands	113–13	**19**
10/09/1983	Niue Island	120–4	**18**

BY A PLAYER

Date	Player	Opponent	Cons
10/09/1983	Severo Koroduadua	Niue Island	**18**
21/08/1969	Semesa Sikivou	Solomon Islands	**12**
07/10/1989	Severo Koroduadua	Belgium	**10**

MOST PENALTIES IN A MATCH

BY THE TEAM

Date	Opponent	Result	Pens
08/07/2001	Samoa	28–17	**7**

BY A PLAYER

Date	Player	Opponent	Pens
08/07/2001	Nicky Little	Samoa	**7**
26/05/2000	Nicky Little	Tonga	**6**
25/05/2001	Nicky Little	Tonga	**6**
05/10/1996	Nicky Little	Hong Kong	**6**
08/07/1967	Inoke Tabualevu	Tonga	**6**

MOST DROPPED GOALS IN A MATCH

BY THE TEAM

Date	Opponent	Result	DGs
02/07/1994	Samoa	20–13	**3**
12/10/1991	Romania	15–17	**3**

BY A PLAYER

Date	Player	Opponent	Pens
02/07/1994	Opeti Turuva	Samoa	**3**
12/10/1991	Tomasi Rabaka	Romania	**2**

MOST CAPPED PLAYERS

Name	Caps
Nicky Little	71
Jacob Rauluni	50
Joeli Veitayaki	49
Emori Katalau	47
Norman Ligairi	47

LEADING TRY SCORERS

Name	Tries
Senivalati Laulau	18
Norman Ligairi	16
Viliame Satala	16
Fero Lasagavibau	16

LEADING CONVERSIONS SCORERS

Name	Cons
Nicky Little	117
Severo Koroduadua	56
Waisale Serevi	40

LEADING PENALTY SCORERS

Name	Pens
Nicky Little	140
Severo Koroduadua	47
Seremaia Bai	42
Waisale Serevi	27

LEADING DROPPED GOAL SCORERS

Name	DGs
Opeti Turuva	5
Severo Koroduadua	5
Waisale Serevi	3

LEADING POINTS SCORERS

Name	Points
Nicky Little	670
Severo Koroduadua	268
Seremaia Bai	223
Waisale Serevi	221

Phillipe Lopez/AFP/Getty Images

Nicky Little has now won more caps and scored more points in Tests than any other Fijian.

FRANCE

FRANCE'S 2010–11 TEST RECORD

OPPONENTS	DATE	VENUE	RESULT
Fiji	13 Nov	H	**Won** 34–12
Argentina	20 Nov	H	**Won** 15–9
Australia	27 Nov	H	**Lost** 16–59
Scotland	5 Feb	H	**Won** 34–21
Ireland	13 Feb	A	**Won** 25–22
England	26 Feb	A	**Lost** 9–17
Italy	12 Mar	A	**Lost** 21–22
Wales	19 Mar	H	**Won** 28–9
Ireland	13 Aug	H	**Won** 19–12
Ireland	20 Aug	A	**Won** 26–22
Japan	10 Sep	N	**Won** 47–21
Canada	18 Sep	N	**Won** 46–19
New Zealand	24 Sep	A	**Lost** 17–37
Tonga	1 Oct	N	**Lost** 19–14
England	8 Oct	N	**Won** 19–12
Wales	15 Oct	N	**Won** 9–8
New Zealand	23 Oct	A	**Lost** 7–8

FRANCE LOSE THIRD FINAL

By Iain Spragg

Stu Forster/Getty Images

Thierry Dusautoir proved to be an inspirational leader for Marc Lievremont's team as they made it to the final.

To describe France's progress to the final of Rugby World Cup 2011 as both troubled and at times tortuous would be an understatement and, although they produced their best performance of the tournament in the title decider against the All Blacks, Marc Lièvremont's unpredictable side fell just short of making history in Auckland as the hosts emerged 8–7 winners.

France had lost the inaugural World Cup final to New Zealand in 1987 and were also defeated by Australia in Cardiff at the same stage 12 years later and, despite defying pre-match predictions of a New Zealand rout at Eden Park, they were unable to avoid an unwelcome hat-trick of defeats in their ongoing quest to lift the Webb Ellis Cup.

That France even reached the final was something of a minor miracle after reports of a fundamental breakdown of the relationship between Lièvremont and his players, and Les Bleus certainly defied expectations by battling through to face New Zealand.

A fairytale end to the dramatic story did not materialise, though, despite a converted try from captain and IRB Player of the Year Thierry Dusautoir, and a third French side were condemned to finish as World Cup runners-up rather than champions.

"We are very disappointed with the result, we didn't do enough," Dusautoir said after the final. "We've been lucky in previous rounds of this tournament but we weren't lucky tonight. We did everything we set out to do except get the points and win the game.

"I was very happy when I scored that try because I knew it was close to the poles, and it would mean the scoreline would be closer. But that was the last time I was happy as, while we continued to put pressure on the All Blacks, we just couldn't convert that into points.

"I'm very proud of my boys for what they did during the World Cup. We lost two games in the pool and we came to the final so I'm really proud of them. We read a lot of stuff this week. I hope we showed that we were able to play rugby and play the final of the Rugby World Cup.

"It was very difficult against this All Blacks team, and we needed just a little bit more tonight. Rugby is also about the mental aspect, but perhaps we needed more skill on this occasion."

France began the tournament at North Harbour Stadium against Japan looking to make a statement of intent, but although their final winning margin of 47–21 appeared comprehensive enough, the victory was not without a degree of anxiety.

First-half tries from Julien Pierre, Francois Trinh-Duc and Vincent Clerc saw the French race into a 25–8 lead, but when James Arlidge went over for his second try of the match in the 49th minute and then landed a penalty nine minutes later, the score was only 25–21 to Les Bleus and the result remained in the balance. It was only in the final ten minutes that Lièvremont's men finally pulled clear with scores from Lionel Nallet, Pascal Pape and Morgan Parra, but there was no disguising the deficiencies in the French performance.

It was a similar story in Les Bleus' next Pool A match against Canada in Napier eight days later. For the first hour, the Canucks were very much in the game and France were heavily indebted to a hat-trick from Clerc, two of his three tries coming in the final two minutes of the contest, as they recorded a 46–19 win.

It was now time for the real test of France's mettle in the shape of hosts New Zealand, and Lièvremont found himself in the cross hairs of the media after making five changes to his side, most notably selecting scrum-half Parra to play at 10 despite having just 35 minutes of Test match experience in the position. With the runners-up in Pool A likely to avoid either South Africa or Australia in the quarter-finals, the coach was accused of fielding a deliberately weakened side against the All Blacks and in effect accepting defeat before kick-off.

The game in Auckland, however, was certainly not as one-sided as some of Lièvremont's critics had predicted. New Zealand were ultimately comfortable 37–17 winners, but France twice breached the All Black defence through Maxime Mermoz and Trinh-Duc to earn a degree of respectability.

"We made too many mistakes," said Dusautoir after the match. "We came back at the end of the second half. We need to work hard again, and we took away a good lesson in this game. Unfortunately, in the first half our scrum was not so good, but it was better in the second half. Thanks to all the supporters who have come to support us. We will do better next time and be ready for the quarter-finals."

The final pool match was against Tonga and, although France did progress to the last eight as Dusautoir had predicted, the match produced arguably the greatest upset in Rugby World Cup history as Les Bleus crashed to a shock 19–14 defeat in Wellington. The final scoreline would have been even more humiliating had Clerc not scored in the 80th minute, and from the outside France appeared to be in total disarray.

"I don't think we can be happy with this qualification," Lièvremont conceded after the final whistle. "It's a bitter qualification, but we have qualified. The next week will be very important. We've had two defeats from four pool matches. I think it will be the first time a team has qualified with two defeats.

"I don't think we need to dwell or analyse the technical aspects of the match now. I want the players to react and refocus on those values I've already talked about. We have no choice. We're still alive. We're still part of this adventure, and I still want to fight and I think my players still want to fight too, even though they are disappointed after tonight's performance."

Rumours of splits within the squad and a player revolt against the coach were now rife as Les Bleus prepared to face England in the quarter-finals, but adhering to the adage that adversity can often breed unity and cohesion France suddenly produced their best display of the tournament to date to record a famous 19–12 win.

Les Bleus, playing with an intensity and desire not previously in evidence in New Zealand, blew England away in the first half of the clash with tries from Clerc and Maxime Médard and, although their cross-Channel rivals rallied after the break, there was no way back and France finally had their revenge for their World Cup defeats to the English in 1991, 1995 and on home soil in 2007.

"It was a very emotional evening," admitted Lièvremont. "I got the feeling that in a way tonight the players have really done their part of the contract. They've played as well as past generations. Now in the past we've seen very often French teams transcend themselves when faced with a strong opposition and they've given their best. Sometimes after that they've failed. Now we'll see whether this group, this particular team, just want to do the same as past generations or we'll see whether this team wants to write its own story."

Wales now stood between France and a third appearance in a World Cup final. Les Bleus had comfortably beaten the Welsh in the Six Nations in Paris in March, but their encounter in Auckland was to prove altogether closer and more controversial.

Wales drew first blood after seven minutes through James Hook, but the defining moment of the match came 10 minutes later when referee Alain Rolland showed a red card to Wales captain Sam Warburton for what he ruled a dangerous tip tackle on Clerc. A contentious decision in the eyes of many, but whatever the rights and wrongs it meant France would play the final hour of the match with an extra man.

Three subsequent penalties from Parra edged France into the lead, but Wales battled on valiantly and, when Mike Phillips scored the only try of the match on 58 minutes, it seemed Lièvremont's men were poised to throw away their golden chance of reaching the final. Wales continued to press and strung together a desperate 26 phases in the dying minutes at Eden Park but could find no way through and France clung on for an ugly, but all-important, 9–8 victory.

"I don't care at all whether it was a good match or not, whether the Welsh deserve to be in the final," Lièvremont said. "We have qualified for the final and that's all that counts. We didn't start the match very well, so we lost our confidence and very quickly we started to play with 15 against 14 and we remained very inhibited. However, we have won and that's the only thing that counts for me.

"Four months ago we had quite a lot of injured players and yet they have all played and we are now in the final, so I'm not going to brood or be unhappy just because the match was not the best match of all. I think we have to pay tribute to the Welsh team that played virtually all the match with 14 men against 15.

"They have been amazingly brave, but the French team might have a guardian angel. I'm not really superstitious, but we have had a very narrow escape. We're still here and we are in the final, although we have not played the best and most spectacular rugby."

Any hope, however, that victory over Wales and a place in the final would help heal the divisions in the French camp were quickly dispelled when the players defied Lièvremont's orders not to go out and celebrate after the match, and the following day the coach decided to publicly chastise his squad.

"I told them they are a bunch of spoiled brats," he said. "Undisciplined, disobedient, sometimes selfish. Always complaining, always moaning. It has been like this for four years. We are in the final, but it is a shame they don't look after themselves. The problem is, we are not world champions yet, we're only in the final. Does it really surprise you, my attitude? In 1999 we spent four days celebrating our semi-final win. We didn't prepare properly, and I don't want us to relive this same thing."

The coach's anger, however, did not extend to wielding the selectoral axe and he named the same XV that overcame Wales to face New Zealand, insisting he would make no apologies if his side abandoned their traditional expansive, attacking game in favour of a more pragmatic approach in an effort to beat the All Blacks.

What the coach got in the final was a performance of pure passion from his side, and although New Zealand drew first blood with a 15th-minute try from Tony Woodcock from a lineout the French refused to buckle and continued to match their hosts in every department.

The All Blacks stretched their lead to 8–0 on 45 minutes when Stephen Donald landed a penalty, but France got their just rewards two minutes later when Dusautoir went over after Yachvili had gone close, and when Trinh-Duc landed the conversion Les Bleus were just one point adrift.

France laid siege to the New Zealand line in the closing minutes of the clash, but another score of any description to win the match proved a bridge too far and the All Blacks clung on to claim the World Cup for a second time.

"I feel immensely sad and immensely proud at the same time," Lièvremont said after his final game as coach and the imminent arrival of Philippe Saint-André as his successor. "People have always said and thought that the All Blacks were the greatest team of all time, but tonight I think it's the France team that was great and even immense. It's tough to take, but we needed a little bit more."

FRANCE INTERNATIONAL STATISTICS

MATCH RECORDS UP TO 31 OCTOBER 2011

MOST CONSECUTIVE TEST WINS

10 1931 *E,G*, 1932 *G*, 1933 *G*, 1934 *G*, 1935 *G*, 1936 *G1,2*, 1937 *G,It*
8 1998 *E, S, I, W, Arg 1,2, Fj, Arg 3*
8 2001 *SA 3, A, Fj* 2002 *It, W, E, S, I*
8 2004 *I, It, W, S, E, US, C, A*

MOST CONSECUTIVE TESTS WITHOUT DEFEAT

Matches	Wins	Draws	Period
10	10	0	1931 to 1938
10	8	2	1958 to 1959
10	9	1	1986 to 1987

MOST POINTS IN A MATCH

BY THE TEAM

Pts	Opponents	Venue	Year
87	Namibia	Toulouse	2007
77	Fiji	Saint Etienne	2001
70	Zimbabwe	Auckland	1987
67	Romania	Bucharest	2000
64	Romania	Aurillac	1996
64	Georgia	Marseilles	2007
62	Romania	Castres	1999
62	Romania	Bucharest	2006
61	Fiji	Brisbane	2003
60	Italy	Toulon	1967
59	Romania	Paris	1924
56	Romania	Lens	2003
56	Italy	Rome	2005

BY A PLAYER

Pts	Player	Opponents	Venue	Year
30	D Camberabero	Zimbabwe	Auckland	1987
28	C Lamaison	New Zealand	Twickenham	1999
28	F Michalak	Scotland	Sydney	2003
27	G Camberabero	Italy	Toulon	1967
27	C Lamaison	New Zealand	Marseilles	2000
27	G Merceron	South Africa	Johannesburg	2001
27	J-B Elissalde	Namibia	Toulouse	2007
26	T Lacroix	Ireland	Durban	1995
26	F Michalak	Fiji	Brisbane	2003
25	J-P Romeu	United States	Chicago	1976
25	P Berot	Romania	Agen	1987
25	T Lacroix	Tonga	Pretoria	1995

MOST TRIES IN A MATCH

BY THE TEAM

Tries	Opponents	Venue	Year
13	Romania	Paris	1924
13	Zimbabwe	Auckland	1987
13	Namibia	Toulouse	2007
12	Fiji	Saint Etienne	2001
11	Italy	Toulon	1967
10	Romania	Aurillac	1996
10	Romania	Bucharest	2000

BY A PLAYER

Tries	Player	Opponents	Venue	Year
4	A Jauréguy	Romania	Paris	1924
4	M Celhay	Italy	Paris	1937

MOST CONVERSIONS IN A MATCH

BY THE TEAM

Cons	Opponents	Venue	Year
11	Namibia	Toulouse	2007
9	Italy	Toulon	1967
9	Zimbabwe	Auckland	1987
8	Romania	Wellington	1987
8	Romania	Lens	2003

BY A PLAYER

Cons	Player	Opponents	Venue	Year
11	J-B Elissalde	Namibia	Toulouse	2007
9	G Camberabero	Italy	Toulon	1967
9	D Camberabero	Zimbabwe	Auckland	1987
8	G Laporte	Romania	Wellington	1987

MOST PENALTIES IN A MATCH

BY THE TEAM

Penalties	Opponents	Venue	Year
8	Ireland	Durban	1995
7	Wales	Paris	2001
7	Italy	Paris	2002
6	Argentina	Buenos Aires	1977
6	Scotland	Paris	1997
6	Italy	Auch	1997
6	Ireland	Paris	2000
6	South Africa	Johannesburg	2001
6	Argentina	Buenos Aires	2003
6	Fiji	Brisbane	2003
6	England	Twickenham	2005
6	Wales	Paris	2007
6	England	Twickenham	2007
6	Ireland	Dublin	2011

BY A PLAYER

Penalties	Player	Opponents	Venue	Year
8	T Lacroix	Ireland	Durban	1995
7	G Merceron	Italy	Paris	2002
6	J-M Aguirre	Argentina	Buenos Aires	1977
6	C Lamaison	Scotland	Paris	1997
6	C Lamaison	Italy	Auch	1997
6	G Merceron	Ireland	Paris	2000
6	G Merceron	South Africa	Johannesburg	2001
6	F Michalak	Fiji	Brisbane	2003
6	D Yachvili	England	Twickenham	2005

MOST DROPPED GOALS IN A MATCH

BY THE TEAM

Drops	Opponents	Venue	Year
3	Ireland	Paris	1960
3	England	Twickenham	1985
3	New Zealand	Christchurch	1986
3	Australia	Sydney	1990
3	Scotland	Paris	1991
3	New Zealand	Christchurch	1994

BY A PLAYER

Drops	Player	Opponents	Venue	Year
3	P Albaladejo	Ireland	Paris	1960
3	J-P Lescarboura	England	Twickenham	1985
3	J-P Lescarboura	New Zealand	Christchurch	1986
3	D Camberabero	Australia	Sydney	1990

CAREER RECORDS

MOST CAPPED PLAYERS

Caps	Player	Career Span
118	F Pelous	1995 to 2007
111	P Sella	1982 to 1995
98	R Ibañez	1996 to 2007
93	S Blanco	1980 to 1991
89	O Magne	1997 to 2007
86	D Traille	2001 to 2011
84	S Marconnet	1998 to 2011
78	A Benazzi	1990 to 2001
77	I Harinordoquy	2002 to 2011
73	Y Jauzion	2001 to 2011
71	J-L Sadourny	1991 to 2001
71	O Brouzet	1994 to 2003
71	C Califano	1994 to 2007
71	A Rougerie	2001 to 2011
70	J Bonnaire	2004 to 2011
70	L Nallet	2000 to 2011
69	R Bertranne	1971 to 1981
69	P Saint-André	1990 to 1997
69	P de Villiers	1999 to 2007
67	C Dominici	1998 to 2007
64	F Galthié	1991 to 2003
63	M Crauste	1957 to 1966
63	B Dauga	1964 to 1972
63	S Betsen	1997 to 2007

MOST CONSECUTIVE TESTS

Tests	Player	Span
46	R Bertranne	1973 to 1979
45	P Sella	1982 to 1987
44	M Crauste	1960 to 1966
35	B Dauga	1964 to 1968

MOST TESTS AS CAPTAIN

Tests	Captain	Span
42	F Pelous	1997 to 2006
41	R Ibanez	1998 to 2007
34	J-P Rives	1978 to 1984
34	P Saint-André	1994 to 1997
26	T Dusautoir	2009 to 2011
25	D Dubroca	1986 to 1988
25	F Galthié	1999 to 2003
24	G Basquet	1948 to 1952
22	M Crauste	1961 to 1966

MOST POINTS IN TESTS

Points	Player	Tests	Career
380	C Lamaison	37	1996 to 2001
367	T Lacroix	43	1989 to 1997
357	D Yachvili	59	2002 to 2011
354	D Camberabero	36	1982 to 1993
267	G Merceron	32	1999 to 2003
265	J-P Romeu	34	1972 to 1977
252	F Michalak	54	2001 to 2010
247	T Castaignède	54	1995 to 2007
233	S Blanco	93	1980 to 1991
232	M Parra	36	2008 to 2011
214	J-B Elissalde	35	2000 to 2008
200	J-P Lescarboura	28	1982 to 1990

MOST TRIES IN TESTS

Tries	Player	Tests	Career
38	S Blanco	93	1980 to 1991
33*	P Saint-André	69	1990 to 1997
31	V Clerc	57	2002 to 2011
30	P Sella	111	1982 to 1995
26	E Ntamack	46	1994 to 2000
26	P Bernat Salles	41	1992 to 2001
25	C Dominici	67	1998 to 2007
23	C Darrouy	40	1957 to 1967

* Saint-André's total includes a penalty try against Romania in 1992

MOST CONVERSIONS IN TESTS

Cons	Player	Tests	Career
59	C Lamaison	37	1996 to 2001
49	D Yachvili	59	2002 to 2011
48	D Camberabero	36	1982 to 1993
45	M Vannier	43	1953 to 1961
42	T Castaignède	54	1995 to 2007
40	J-B Elissalde	35	2000 to 2008
36	R Dourthe	31	1995 to 2001
36	G Merceron	32	1999 to 2003
36	F Michalak	54	2001 to 2010
33	M Parra	36	2008 to 2011
32	T Lacroix	43	1989 to 1997
29	P Villepreux	34	1967 to 1972

MOST PENALTY GOALS IN TESTS

Penalties	Player	Tests	Career
89	T Lacroix	43	1989 to 1997
81	D Yachvili	59	2002 to 2011
78	C Lamaison	37	1996 to 2001
59	D Camberabero	36	1982 to 1993
57	G Merceron	32	1999 to 2003
56	J-P Romeu	34	1972 to 1977
51	M Parra	36	2008 to 2011
39	F Michalak	54	2001 to 2010
38	J-B Elissalde	35	2000 to 2008
33	P Villepreux	34	1967 to 1972
33	P Bérot	19	1986 to 1989

MOST DROPPED GOALS IN TESTS

Drops	Player	Tests	Career
15	J-P Lescarboura	28	1982 to 1990
12	P Albaladejo	30	1954 to 1964
11	G Camberabero	14	1961 to 1968
11	D Camberabero	36	1982 to 1993
9	J-P Romeu	34	1972 to 1977

INTERNATIONAL CHAMPIONSHIP RECORDS

RECORD	DETAIL	SET	
Most points in season	156	in five matches	2002
Most tries in season	18	in four matches	1998
	18	in five matches	2006
Highest score	56	56–13 v Italy	2005
Biggest win	51	51–0 v Wales	1998
Highest score conceded	49	14–49 v Wales	1910
Biggest defeat	37	0–37 v England	1911
Most appearances	50	P Sella	1983–1995
Most points in matches	201	D Yachvili	2003–2011
Most points in season	80	G Merceron	2002
Most points in match	24	S Viars	v Ireland, 1992
	24	C Lamaison	v Scotland, 1997
	24	J-B Elissalde	v Wales, 2004
Most tries in matches	14	S Blanco	1981–1991
	14	P Sella	1983–1995
Most tries in season	5	P Estève	1983
	5	E Bonneval	1987
	5	E Ntamack	1999
	5	P Bernat Salles	2001
	5	V Clerc	2008
Most tries in match	3	M Crauste	v England, 1962
	3	C Darrouy	v Ireland, 1963
	3	E Bonneval	v Scotland, 1987
	3	D Venditti	v Ireland, 1997
	3	E Ntamack	v Wales, 1999
	3	V Clerc	v Ireland, 2008
Most cons in matches	28	D Yachvili	2003–2011
Most cons in season	11	M Parra	2010
Most cons in match	6	D Yachvili	v Italy, 2003
Most pens in matches	45	D Yachvili	2003–2011
Most pens in season	18	G Merceron	2002
Most pens in match	7	G Merceron	v Italy, 2002
Most drops in matches	9	J-P Lescarboura	1982–1988
Most drops in season	5	G Camberabero	1967
Most drops in match	3	P Albaladejo	v Ireland, 1960
	3	J-P Lescarboura	v England, 1985

MISCELLANEOUS RECORDS

RECORD	HOLDER	DETAIL
Longest Test Career	F Haget	1974 to 1987
	C Califano	1994 to 2007
	S Marconnet	1998 to 2011
Youngest Test Cap	C Dourthe	18 yrs 7 days in 1966
Oldest Test Cap	A Roques	37 yrs 329 days in 1963

CAREER RECORDS OF FRANCE INTERNATIONAL PLAYERS

(UP TO 31 OCTOBER 2011)

PLAYER BACKS :	DEBUT	CAPS	T	C	P	D	PTS
M Andreu	2010 v W	6	2	0	0	0	10
J Arias	2009 v A	2	0	0	0	0	0
M Bastareaud	2009 v W	9	2	0	0	0	10
L Beauxis	2007 v It	15	1	18	21	2	110
V Clerc	2002 SA	57	31	0	0	0	155
J-M Doussain	2011 v NZ	1	0	0	0	0	0
J Dupuy	2009 v NZ	6	0	4	9	0	35
F Estebanez	2010 v Fj	8	0	0	0	0	0
B Fall	2009 v Sm	2	1	0	0	0	5
C Heymans	2000 v It	59	16	0	0	0	80
Y Huget	2010 v Arg	7	0	0	0	0	0
Y Jauzion	2001 v SA	73	20	0	0	1	103
J Malzieu	2008 v S	16	4	0	0	0	20
D Marty	2005 v It	37	11	0	0	0	55
M Médard	2008 v Arg	28	9	0	0	1	48
M Mermoz	2008 v A	15	1	0	0	0	5
A Palisson	2008 v A	20	2	0	0	0	10
M Parra	2008 v S	36	2	33	51	1	232
C Poitrenaud	2001 v SA	44	7	0	0	0	35
J Porical	2010 v Arg	4	0	0	1	0	3
A Rougerie	2001 v SA	71	22	0	0	0	110
D Skrela	2001 v NZ	23	0	14	27	1	112
J Tomas	2008 v It	3	0	0	0	0	0
D Traille	2001 v SA	86	14	8	12	2	128
F Trinh-Duc	2008 v S	35	9	2	1	6	70
D Yachvili	2002 v C	59	2	49	81	2	357

FORWARDS :							
F Barcella	2008 v It	20	0	0	0	0	0
J Bonnaire	2004 v S	70	6	0	0	0	30
S Chabal	2000 v S	62	6	0	0	0	30
T Domingo	2009 v W	17	1	0	0	0	5
L Ducalcon	2010 v S	10	0	0	0	0	0
T Dusautoir	2006 v R	49	6	0	0	0	30
G Guirado	2008 v It	15	0	0	0	0	0
I Harinordoquy	2002 v W	77	13	0	0	0	65
R Lakafia	2011 v I	3	0	0	0	0	0
A Lapandry	2009 v Sm	6	1	0	0	0	5
W Lauret	2010 v SA	1	0	0	0	0	0
S Marconnet	1998 v Arg	84	3	0	0	0	15
N Mas	2003 v NZ	49	0	0	0	0	0
R Millo-Chluski	2005 v SA	18	0	0	0	0	0
L Nallet	2000 v R	70	9	0	0	0	45
B Noirot	2010 v Fj	1	0	0	0	0	0
F Ouedraogo	2007 v NZ	25	1	0	0	0	5
P Papé	2004 v I	35	3	0	0	0	15
L Picamoles	2008 v I	21	1	0	0	0	5
J Pierre	2007 v NZ	26	1	0	0	0	5
J-B Poux	2001 v Fj	37	3	0	0	0	15
J Schuster	2010 v Fj	2	0	0	0	0	0
W Servat	2004 v I	44	2	0	0	0	10
D Szarzewski	2004 v C	56	6	0	0	0	30
J Thion	2003 v Arg	54	1	0	0	0	5

FRENCH INTERNATIONAL PLAYERS (UP TO 31 OCTOBER 2011)

Note: Years given for International Championship matches are for second half of season; eg 1972 means season 1971–72. Years for all other matches refer to the actual year of the match. Entries in square brackets denote matches played in RWC Finals.

Abadie, A (Pau) 1964 I
Abadie, A (Graulhet) 1965 R, 1967 SA 1, 3, 4, NZ, 1968 S, I
Abadie, L (Tarbes) 1963 R
Accoceberry, G (Bègles) 1994 NZ 1, 2, C 2, 1995 W, E, S, I, R 1, [Iv, S], It, 1996 I, W 1, R, Arg 1, W 2(R), SA 2, 1997 S, It 1
Aguerre, R (Biarritz O) 1979 S
Aguilar, D (Pau) 1937 G
Aguirre, J-M (Bagnères) 1971 A 2, 1972 S, 1973 W, I, J, R, 1974 I, W, Arg 2, R, SA 1, 1976 W (R), E, US, A 2, R, 1977 W, E, S, I, Arg 1, 2, NZ 1, 2, R, 1978 E, S, I, W, R, 1979 I, W, E, S, NZ 1, 2, R, 1980 W, I
Ainciart, E (Bayonne) 1933 G, 1934 G, 1935 G, 1937 G, It, 1938 G 1
Albaladéjo, P (Dax) 1954 E, It, 1960 W, I, It, R, 1961 S, SA, E, W, I, NZ 1, 2, A, 1962 S, E, W, I, 1963 S, I, E, W, It, 1964 S, NZ, W, It, I, SA, Fj
Albouy, A (Castres) 2002 It (R)
Alvarez, A-J (Tyrosse) 1945 B2, 1946 B, I, K, W, 1947 S, I, W, E, 1948 I, A, S, W, E, 1949 I, E, W, 1951 S, E, W
Amand, H (SF) 1906 NZ
Ambert, A (Toulouse) 1930 S, I, E, G, W
Amestoy, J-B (Mont-de-Marsan) 1964 NZ, E
André, G (RCF) 1913 SA, E, W, I, 1914 I, W, E
Andreu, M (Castres) 2010 W(R), It, E, SA(R), Arg2, A(R)
Andrieu, M (Nîmes) 1986 Arg 2, NZ 1, R 2, NZ 2, 1987 [R, Z], R, 1988 E, S, I, W, Arg 1, 2, 3, 4, R, 1989 I, W, E, S, NZ 2, B, A 2, 1990 W, E, I (R)
Anduran, J (SCUF) 1910 W
Aqua, J-L (Toulon) 1999 R, Tg, NZ 1(R)
Araou, R (Narbonne) 1924 R
Arcalis, R (Brive) 1950 S, I, 1951 I, E, W
Arias, J (SF) 2009 A(R), 2010 Fj
Arino, M (Agen) 1962 R
Aristouy, P (Pau) 1948 S, 1949 Arg 2, 1950 S, I, E, W
Arlettaz, P (Perpignan) 1995 R 2
Armary, L (Lourdes) 1987 [R], R, 1988 S, I, W, Arg 3, 4, R, 1989 W, S, A 1, 2, 1990 W, E, S, I, A 1, 2, 3, NZ 1, 1991 W 2, 1992 S, I, R, Arg 1, 2, SA 1, 2, Arg, 1993 E, S, I, W, SA 1, 2, R 2, A 1, 2, 1994 I, W, NZ 1(t), 2(t), 1995 I, R 1 [Tg, I, SA]
Arnal, J-M (RCF) 1914 I, W
Arnaudet, M (Lourdes) 1964 I, 1967 It, W
Arotca, R (Bayonne) 1938 R
Arrieta, J (SF) 1953 E, W
Arthapignet, P (see Harislur-Arthapignet)
Artiguste, E (Castres) 1999 WS
Astre, R (Béziers) 1971 R, 1972 I 1, 1973 E (R), 1975 E, S, I, SA 1, 2, Arg 2, 1976 A 2, R
Attoub, D (Castres) 2006 R
Aucagne, D (Pau) 1997 W (R), S, It 1, R 1(R), A 1, R 2(R), SA 2(R), 1998 S (R), W (R), Arg 2(R), Fj (R), Arg 3, A, 1999 W 1(R), S (R)
Audebert, A (Montferrand) 2000 R, 2002 W (R)
Aué, J-M (Castres) 1998 W (R)
Augé, J (Dax) 1929 S, W
Augras-Fabre, L (Agen) 1931 I, S, W
August, B (Biarritz) 2007 W1(R)
Auradou, D (SF) 1999 E (R), S (R), WS (R), Tg, NZ 1, W 2(R), [Arg (R)], 2000 A (R), NZ 1, 2, 2001 S, I, It, W, E (R), SA 1, 2, NZ (R), SA 3, A, Fj, 2002 It, E, I (R), C (R), 2003 S (R), It (R), W (R), Arg, 1, 2, NZ (R), R (R), E 2(R), 3, [J(R), US, NZ] , 2004 I(R), It(R), S(R), E(R)
Averous, J-L (La Voulte) 1975 S, I, SA 1, 2, 1976 I, W, E, US, A 1, 2, R, 1977 W, E, S, I, Arg 1, R, 1978 E, S, I, 1979 NZ 1, 2, 1980 E, S, 1981 A 2
Avril, D (Biarritz) 2005 A1
Azam, O (Montferrand, Gloucester) 1995 R 2, Arg (R), 2000 A (R), NZ 2(R), 2001 SA 2(R), NZ, 2002 E (R), I (R), Arg (R), A 1
Azarete, J-L (Dax, St Jean-de-Luz) 1969 W, R, 1970 S, I, W, R, 1971 S, I, E, SA 1, 2, A 1, 1972 E, W, I 2, A 1, R, 1973 NZ, W, I, R, 1974 I, R, SA 1, 2, 1975 W

Baby, B (Toulouse, Clermont-Auvergne) 2005 I, SA2(R), A1, 2008 Arg, PI, A3, 2009 I(R), S, W
Bacqué, N (Pau) 1997 R 2
Bader, E (Primevères) 1926 M, 1927 I, S
Badin, C (Chalon) 1973 W, I, 1975 Arg 1
Baillette, M (Perpignan) 1925 I, NZ, S, 1926 W, M, 1927 I, W, G 2, 1929 G, 1930 S, I, E, G, 1931 I, S, E, 1932 G
Baladie, G (Agen) 1945 B 1, 2, W, 1946 B, I, K
Ballarin, J (Tarbes) 1924 E, 1925 NZ, S
Baquey, J (Toulouse) 1921 I
Barbazanges, A (Roanne) 1932 G, 1933 G
Barcella, F (Auch, Biarritz) 2008 It, W, Arg, 2009 S, W, It, NZ1, 2, A, SA, NZ3, 2010 Arg1, 2011 I3(R), [J, C(t&R), NZ1(R), Tg(R), E(R), W(R), NZ2(R)]
Barrau, M (Beaumont, Toulouse) 1971 S, E, W, 1972 E, W, A 1, 2, 1973 S, NZ, E, I, J, R, 1974 I, S
Barrau, M (Agen) 2004 US, C(R), NZ(R)
Barrère, P (Toulon) 1929 G, 1931 W
Barrière, R (Béziers) 1960 R
Barthe, F (SBUC) 1925 W, E
Barthe, J (Lourdes) 1954 Arg 1, 2, 1955 S, 1956 I, W, It, E, Cz, 1957 S, I, E, W, R 1, 2, 1958 S, E, A, W, It, I, SA 1, 2, 1959 S, E, It, W
Basauri, R (Albi) 1954 Arg 1
Bascou, P (Bayonne) 1914 E
Basquet, G (Agen) 1945 W, 1946 B, I, K, W, 1947 S, I, W, E, 1948 I, A, S, W, E, 1949 S, I, E, W, Arg 1, 1950 S, I, E, W, 1951 S, I, E, W, 1952 S, I, SA, W, E, It
Bastareaud, M (SF) 2009 W, E, It(R), NZ1, 2010 S, I, W, It(R), E
Bastiat, J-P (Dax) 1969 R, 1970 S, I, W, 1971 S, I, SA 2, 1972 S, A 1, 1973 E, 1974 Arg 1, 2, SA 2, 1975 W, Arg 1, 2, R, 1976 S, I, W, E, A 1, 2, R, 1977 W, E, S, I, 1978 E, S, I, W
Baudry, N (Montferrand) 1949 S, I, W, Arg 1, 2
Baulon, R (Vienne, Bayonne) 1954 S, NZ, W, E, It, 1955 I, E, W, It, 1956 S, I, W, It, E, Cz, 1957 S, I, It
Baux, J-P (Lannemezan) 1968 NZ 1, 2, SA 1, 2
Bavozet, J (Lyon) 1911 S, E, W
Bayard, J (Toulouse) 1923 S, W, E, 1924 W, R, US
Bayardon, J (Chalon) 1964 S, NZ, E
Beaurin-Gressier, C (SF) 1907 E, 1908 E
Beauxis, L (SF) 2007 It(R), I(R), W1(R), E1(R), S, W2, [Nm(R), I(R), Gg, NZ, E, Arg 2(R)], 2009 I, S, A
Bégu, J (Dax) 1982 Arg 2(R), 1984 E, S

Béguerie, C (Agen) 1979 NZ 1
Béguet, L (RCF) 1922 I, 1923 S, W, E, I, 1924 S, I, E, R, US
Béhotéguy, A (Bayonne, Cognac) 1923 E, 1924 S, I, E, W, R, US, 1926 E, 1927 E, G 1, 2, 1928 A, I, E, G, W, 1929 S, W, E
Béhotéguy, H (RCF, Cognac) 1923 W, 1928 A, I, E, G, W
Bélascain, C (Bayonne) 1977 R, 1978 E, S, I, W, R, 1979 I, W, E, S, 1982 W, E, S, I, 1983 E, S, I, W
Belletante, G (Nantes) 1951 I, E, W
Belot, F (Toulouse) 2000 I (R)
Benazzi, A (Agen) 1990 A 1, 2, 3, NZ 1, 2, 1991 E, US 1(R), 2, [R, Fj, C], 1992 SA 1(R), 2, Arg, 1993 E, S, I, W, A 1, 2, 1994 I, W, E, S, C 1, NZ 1, 2, C 2, 1995 W, E, S, I, [Tg, Iv, S, I, SA, E], NZ 1, 2, 1996 E, S, I, W 1, Arg 1, 2, W 2, SA 1, 2, 1997 I, W, E, S, R 1, A 1, 2, It 2, R 2(R), Arg, SA 1, 2, 1999 R, WS, W 2, [C, Nm (R), Fj, Arg, NZ 2, A], 2000 W, E, I, It (R), R, 2001 S (R), I (t&R), E
Bénésis, R (Narbonne) 1969 W, R, 1970 S, I, W, E, R, 1971 S, I, E, W, A 2, R, 1972 S, I 1, E, W, I 2, A 1, R, 1973 NZ, E, W, I, J, R, 1974 I, W, E, S
Benetière, J (Roanne) 1954 It, Arg 1
Benetton, P (Agen) 1989 B, 1990 NZ 2, 1991 US 2, 1992 Arg 1, 2(R), SA 1(R), 2, Arg, 1993 E, S, I, W, SA 1, 2, R 2, A 1, 2, 1994 I, W, E, S, C 1, NZ 1, 2, C 2, 1995 W, E, S, I, [Tg, Iv (R), S], It, R 2(R), Arg, NZ 1, 2, 1996 Arg 1, 2, W 2, SA 1, 2, 1997 I, It 1, 2(R), R 2, Arg, SA 1, 2 1998 E, S (R), I (R), W (R), Arg 1(R), 2(R), Fj (R), 1999 I, W 1, S (R)
Benezech, L (RCF) 1994 E, S, C 1, NZ 1, 2, C 2, 1995 W, E, [Iv, S, E], R 2, Arg, NZ 1, 2
Berbizier, P (Lourdes, Agen) 1981 S, I, W, E, NZ 1, 2, 1982 I, R, 1983 S, I, 1984 S (R), NZ 1, 2, 1985 Arg 1, 2, 1986 S, I, W, E, R 1, Arg 1, A, NZ 1, R 2, NZ 2, 3, 1987 W, E, S, I, [S, R, Fj, A, NZ], R, 1988 E, S, I, W, Arg 1, 2, 1989 I, W, E, S, NZ 1, 2, B, A 1, 1990 W, E, 1991 S, I, W 1, E
Berejnoï, J-C (Tulle) 1963 R, 1964 S, W, It, I, SA, Fj, R, 1965 S, I, E, W, It, R, 1966 S, I, E, W, It, R, 1967 S, A, E, It, W, I, R
Bergès, B (Toulouse) 1926 I
Berges-Cau, R (Lourdes) 1976 E (R)
Bergese, F (Bayonne) 1936 G 2, 1937 G, It, 1938 G 1, R, G 2
Bergougnan, Y (Toulouse) 1945 B 1, W, 1946 B, I, K, W, 1947 S, I, W, E, 1948 S, W, E, 1949 S, E, Arg 1, 2
Bernard, R (Bergerac) 1951 S, I, E, W
Bernat-Salles, P (Pau, Bègles-Bordeaux, Biarritz) 1992 Arg, 1993 R 1, SA 1, 2, R 2, A 1, 2, 1994 I, 1995 E, S, 1996 E (R), 1997 R 1, A 1, 2, 1998 E, S, I, W, Arg 1, 2, Fj, Arg 3(R), A 1999 I, W 1, R, Tg, [Nm, Fj, Arg, NZ 2, A], 2000 I, It, NZ 1(R), 2, 2001 S, I, It, W, E
Bernon, J (Lourdes) 1922 I, 1923 S
Bérot, J-L (Toulouse) 1968 NZ 3, A, 1969 S, I, 1970 E, R, 1971 S, I, E, W, SA 1, 2, A 1, 2, R, 1972 S, I 1, E, W, A 1, 1974 I
Bérot, P (Agen) 1986 R 2, NZ 2, 3, 1987 W, E, S, I, R, 1988 E, S, I, Arg 1, 2, 3, 4, R, 1989 S, NZ 1, 2
Bertrand, P (Bourg) 1951 I, E, W, 1953 S, I, E, W, It
Bertranne, R (Bagnères) 1971 E, W, SA 2, A 1, 2, 1972 S, I 1, 1973 NZ, E, J, R, 1974 I, W, E, S, Arg 1, 2, R, SA 1, 2, 1975 W, E, S, I, SA 1, 2, Arg 1, 2, R, 1976 S, I, W, E, US, A 1, 2, R, 1977 W, E, S, I, Arg 1, 2, NZ 1, 2, R, 1978 E, S, I, W, R, 1979 I, W, E, S, R, 1980 W, E, S, I, SA, R, 1981 S, I, W, E, R, NZ 1, 2
Berty, D (Toulouse) 1990 NZ 2, 1992 R (R), 1993 R 2, 1995 NZ 1(R), 1996 W 2(R), SA 1
Besset, E (Grenoble) 1924 S
Besset, L (SCUF) 1914 W, E
Besson, M (CASG) 1924 I, 1925 I, E, 1926 S, W, 1927 I
Besson, P (Brive) 1963 S, I, E, 1965 R, 1968 SA 1
Betsen, S (Biarritz) 1997 It 1(R), 2000 W (R), E (R), A (R), NZ 1(R), 2(R), 2001 S (R), I (R), It (R), W (R), SA 3(R), A, Fj, 2002 It, W, E, S, I, Arg, A 1, 2, SA, NZ, C, 2003 E 1, S, I, It, W, R, E 2, [Fj, J, S, I, E], 2004 I, It, W, S, E, A, Arg, NZ, 2005 E, W, I, It, 2006 SA, NZ2(R), Arg(R), 2007 It, I, W1, E1, S, E2, W2, [Arg 1, I, Gg, NZ, E]
Bianchi, J (Toulon) 1986 Arg 1
Bichindaritz, J (Biarritz O) 1954 It, Arg 1, 2
Bidabé, P (Biarritz) 2004 C, 2006 R
Bidart, L (La Rochelle) 1953 W
Biémouret, P (Agen) 1969 E, W, 1970 I, W, E, 1971 W, SA 1, 2, A 1, 1972 E, W, I 2, A 2, R, 1973 S, NZ, E, W, I
Biénès, R (Cognac) 1950 S, I, E, W, 1951 S, I, E, W, 1952 S, I, SA, W, E, It, 1953 S, I, E, 1954 S, I, NZ, W, E, Arg 1, 2, 1956 S, I, W, It, E
Bigot, C (Quillan) 1930 S, E, 1931 I, S
Bilbao, L (St Jean-de-Luz) 1978 I, 1979 I
Billac, E (Bayonne) 1920 S, E, W, I, US, 1921 S, W, 1922 W, 1923 E
Billière, M (Toulouse) 1968 NZ 3
Bioussa, A (Toulouse) 1924 W, US, 1925 I, NZ, S, E, 1926 S, I, E, 1928 E, G, W, 1929 I, S, W, E, 1930 S, I, E, G, W
Bioussa, C (Toulouse) 1913 W, I, 1914 I
Biraben, M (Dax) 1920 W, I, US, 1921 S, W, E, I, 1922 S, E, I
Blain, A (Carcassonne) 1934 G
Blanco, S (Biarritz O) 1980 SA, R, 1981 S, W, E, A 1, 2, R, NZ 1, 2, 1982 W, E, S, I, R, Arg 1, 2, 1983 E, S, I, W, 1984 I, W, E, S, NZ 1, 2, R, 1985 E, S, I, W, Arg 1, 2, 1986 S, I, W, E, R 1, Arg 2, A, NZ 1, R 2, NZ 2, 3, 1987 W, E, S, I, [S, R, Fj, A, NZ], R, 1988 E, S, I, W, Arg 1, 2, 3, 4, R, 1989 I, W, E, S, NZ 1, 2, B, A 1, 1990 E, S, I, R, A 1, 2, 3, NZ 1, 2, 1991 S, I, W 1, E, R, US 1, 2, W 2, [R, Fj, C, E]
Blond, J (SF) 1935 G, 1936 G 2, 1937 G, 1938 G 1, R, G 2
Blond, X (RCF) 1990 A 3, 1991 S, I, W 1, E, 1994 NZ 2(R)
Boffelli, V (Aurillac) 1971 A 2, R, 1972 S, I 1, 1973 J, R, 1974 I, W, E, S, Arg 1, 2, R, SA 1, 2, 1975 W, S, I
Bonal, J-M (Toulouse) 1968 E, W, Cz, NZ 2, 3, SA 1, 2, R, 1969 S, I, E, R, 1970 W, E
Bonamy, R (SB) 1928 A, I
Bondouy, P (Narbonne, Toulouse) 1997 S (R), It 1, A 2(R), R 2, 2000 R (R)
Bonetti, S (Biarritz) 2001 It, W, NZ (R)
Boniface, A (Mont-de-Marsan) 1954 I, NZ, W, E, It, Arg 1, 2, 1955 S, I, 1956 S, I, W, It, Cz, 1957 S, I, W, R 2, 1958 S, E, 1959 E, 1961 NZ 1, 3, A, R, 1962 E, W, I, It, R, 1963 S, I, E, W, It, R, 1964 S, NZ, E, W, It, 1965 W, It, R, 1966 S, I, E, W
Boniface, G (Mont-de-Marsan) 1960 W, I, It, R, Arg 1, 2, 3, 1961 S, SA, E, W, It, I, NZ 1, 2, 3, R, 1962 R, 1963 S, I, E, W, It, R, 1964 S, 1965 S, I, E, W, It, R, 1966 S, I, E, W
Bonnaire, J (Bourgoin, Clermont-Auvergne) 2004 S(t&R), A(R), NZ(R), 2005 S, E, W, I, It, SA1, 2, A1, C, Tg, SA3, 2006 S, I, It(R), E(R), W, R, SA(R), NZ1, 2, Arg, 2007 It, I(R), W1, E1, S, E2, 3(R), [Arg1(R), Nm, I, Gg, NZ, E], 2008 S(R), I, E, It(R), W, 2009 E(R), It, SA(R), Sm, NZ3, 2010 S(R), I(R), W, It, E, SA, Arg1, Arg2, A(R), 2011 S, I1, E(R), It, W, I2(R), 3, [J(R), C, NZ1, Tg, E, W, NZ2]
Bonnes, E (Narbonne) 1924 W, R, US
Bonneval, E (Toulouse) 1984 NZ 2(R), 1985 W, Arg 1, 1986 W, E, R 1, Arg 1, 2, A, R 2, NZ 2, 3, 1987 W, E, S, I, [Z], 1988 E
Bonnus, F (Toulon) 1950 S, I, E, W
Bonnus, M (Toulon) 1937 It, 1938 G 1, R, G 2, 1940 B
Bontemps, D (La Rochelle) 1968 SA 2
Borchard, G (RCF) 1908 E, 1909 E, W, I, 1911 I
Borde, F (RCF) 1920 I, US, 1921 S, W, E, 1922 S, W, 1923 S, I, 1924 E, 1925 I, 1926 E
Bordenave, L (Toulon) 1948 A, S, W, E, 1949 S
Bory, D (Montferrand) 2000 I, It, A, NZ 1, 2001 S, I, SA 1, 2, 3, A, Fj, 2002 It, E, S, I, C, 2003 [US, NZ]
Boubée, J (Tarbes) 1921 S, E, I, 1922 E, W, 1923 E, I, 1925 NZ, S
Boudreaux, R (SCUF) 1910 W, S
Bouet, D (Dax) 1989 NZ 1, 2, B, A 2, 1990 A 3
Bouguyon, G (Grenoble) 1961 SA, E, W, It, I, NZ 1, 2, 3, A
Bouic, G (Agen) 1996 SA 1
Bouilhou, J (Toulouse) 2001 NZ, 2003 Arg 1
Boujet, C (Grenoble) 1968 NZ 2, A (R), SA 1
Bouquet, J (Bourgoin, Vienne) 1954 S, 1955 E, 1956 S, I, W, It, E, Cz, 1957 S, E, W, R 2, 1958 S, E, 1959 S, It, W, I, 1960 S, E, W, I, R, 1961 S, SA, E, W, It, I, R, 1962 S, E, W, I
Bourdeu, J R (Lourdes) 1952 S, I, SA, W, E, It, 1953 S, I, E
Bourgarel, R (Toulouse) 1969 R, 1970 S, I, E, R, 1971 W, SA 1, 2, 1973 S
Bourguignon, G (Narbonne) 1988 Arg 3, 1989 I, E, B, A 1, 1990 R

THE IRB/EMIRATES AIRLINE RUGBY PHOTOGRAPH OF THE YEAR 2011

Now in its sixth year, the IRB/Emirates Airline Rugby Photograph of the Year, celebrating superb rugby pictures which capture the 'Spirit of Rugby', continues to flourish.

This year more than 300 entries were received, with the shortlist containing images from some of the remotest outposts of the rugby world to the glamour and glory of Rugby World Cup 2011. Tasked with finding the photograph which best illustrates the 'Spirit of Rugby', this year's judging panel – which convened just days after the Rugby World Cup final in Auckland, New Zealand – had quite a challenge to select the six images you see here which make up the shortlist and, of course, the one winner.

This year's judging panel was: Paul Morgan, editor of the IRB Yearbook and Rugby World magazine; world renowned sports photographer Dave Rogers from Getty Images, Samantha Dunn, sponsorship controller, Emirates Airline, and Dominic Rumbles, head of communications, IRB.

The prize for the winner is a trip for two to the Emirates Airline Dubai Rugby Sevens, courtesy of Emirates Airline.

THE RUNNERS-UP: IN NO PARTICULAR ORDER

◀ Blind Determination
Carl Fourie (Gallo)
Plaatjies Fundiswa of Border stretches for the line during the SARU Interprovincial Sevens women's final between Eastern Province and Border on 6 November 2010 in Cape Town.

"I like the image as it shows women's rugby at its best. Plaatjies did not expect the tackle and her face was a mixture of surprise and then determination to get to the tryline."
Carl Fourie

▲ Rallying Cry
James Crombie (Inpho)
The King's Hospital School team's Jonathan Molloy rallies his troops before a Father Godfrey Cup first round game against The High School. The Father Godfrey Cup is a Leinster-based schools tournament in Ireland.

"I really like how this image shows the special bond between the team. It shows the intensity of rugby at any level of the game."
James Crombie

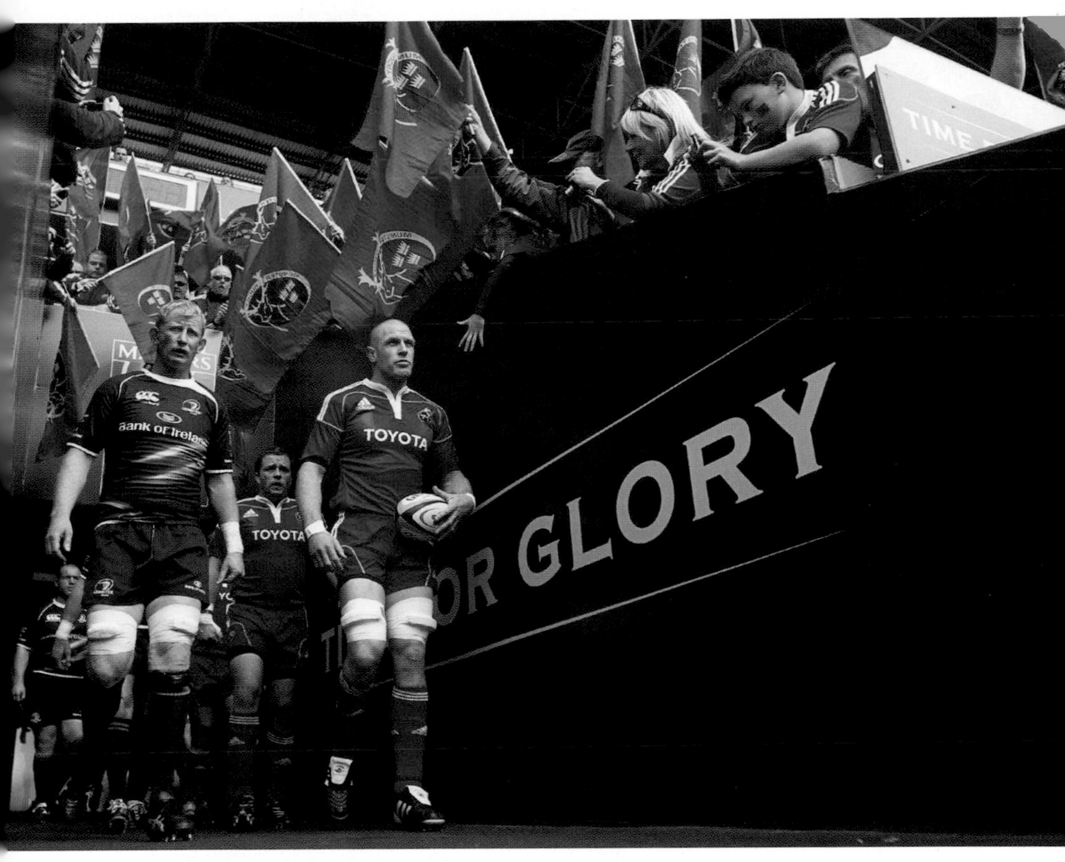

▲ Clash of the Titans

Colm O'Neill (O'Neillfoto)

Leinster captain Leo Cullen (left) and Munster captain Paul O'Connell lead their teams out ahead of one of rugby's most intensely contested derby matches.

"I had to get in and under the TV cameraman to get that low angle. The result, for me, was the perfect shot. There is a sense of perspective that almost draws the players towards the viewer and the sense of occasion from the home fans willing their team on. The icing on the cake shows both captains leading their team to 'Glory'."

Colm O'Neill

▲ It's a Try!
Stefan Wermuth (Reuters)
France's Vincent Clerc celebrates scoring the opening try against England in the quarter final of Rugby World Cup 2011 at Eden Park, Auckland, on 8 October.

"I was in the corner and Vicent Clerc scored a try right in front of me. The expression on his face and the body language for me tell the story of that game and the passion for rugby."
Stefan Wermuth

"For me this picture perfectly reflects the efforts, commitment and dedication 'against all odds' of Indonesian players, and by extension all those in 'under-developed' rugby countries."
Anne-Laure Mousteou

▲ Against all Odds

Anne-Laure Mousteou

Players from Matano Miners and Sumbawa Bagas play on in horrendous conditions in the Makassar Tournament in Sulawesi, Indonesia. Torrential rain had threatened the first ever rugby tournament on the island but the players had insisted on playing on whatever the conditions.

AND THE WINNER IS...

The Helping Hand

Andrew Cornaga (Photosport)
All Blacks lock Brad Thorn offers a hand of support to dejected Argentina player Santiago Fernandez after the New Zealand v Argentina quarter final match of Rugby World Cup 2011.

"Argentina had taken New Zealand on in the forwards and scored the first try of the match. But at the end of the game the All Blacks were triumphant 33–10 and Argentina were left to rue what might have been.

Santiago Fernandez fell down on the ground in the goal area at the final whistle and Brad Thorn walked over from the 22 line to offer him a hand up. It showed the camaraderie between the two teams.

Although there are several frames of Brad helping Santiago up off the turf, I guess this shot of Brad's hand being offered, as Santiago has his hands over his face disappointed, is the one that stood out. Thorn has always been such a gladiator and great sportsman.

The IRB/Emirates Rugby Photograph of the Year is one of the best prizes in the world of photojournalism and a competition every rugby photographer would like to win. Thank you very much to the IRB and Emirates – it's great to have your support."

Andrew Cornaga

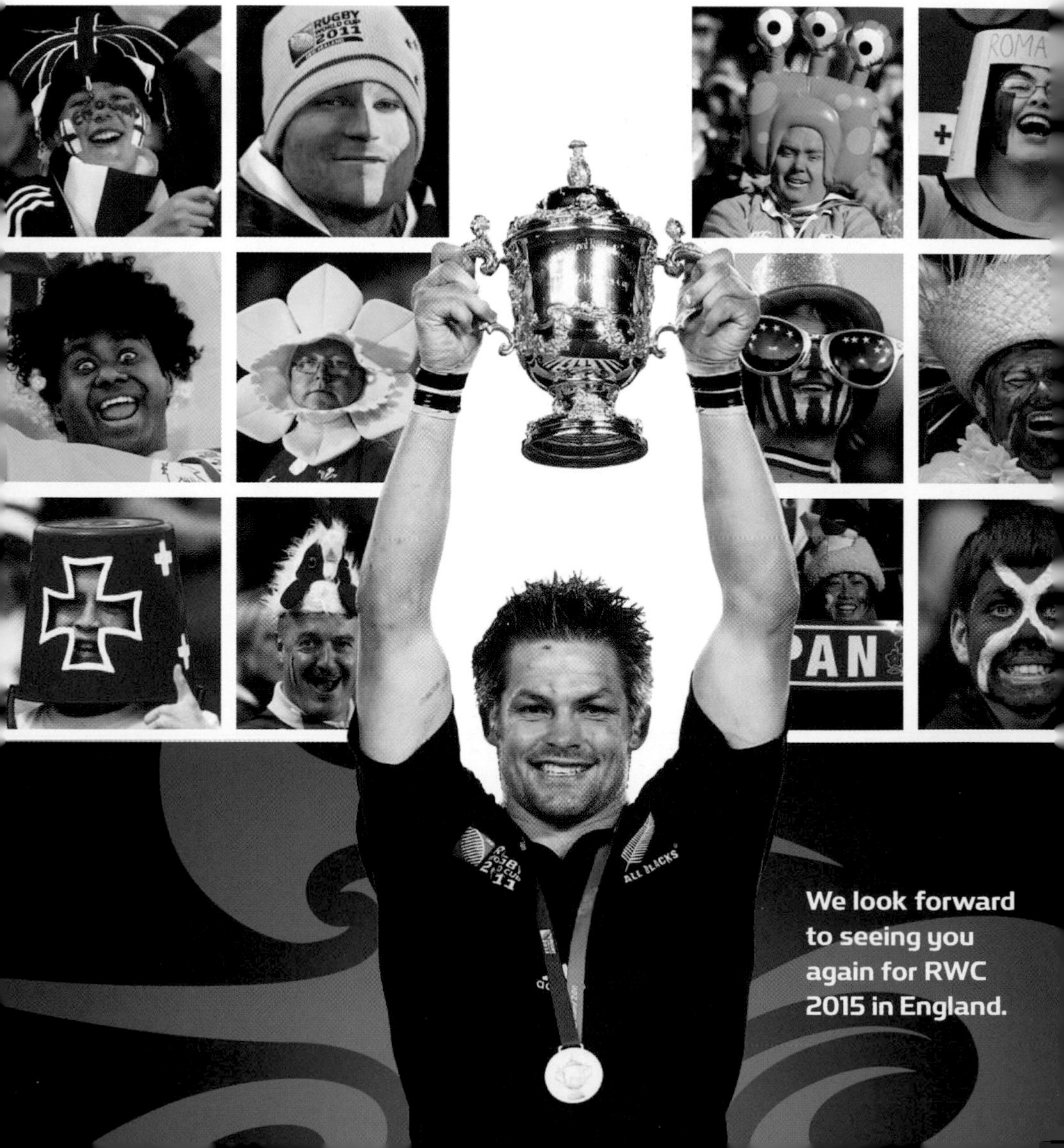

Bousquet, A (Béziers) 1921 E, I, 1924 R
Bousquet, R (Albi) 1926 M, 1927 I, S, W, E, G 1, 1929 W, E, 1930 W
Bousses, G (Bourgoin) 2006 S(R)
Boyau, M (SBUC) 1912 I, S, W, E, 1913 W, I
Boyer, P (Toulon) 1935 G
Boyet, B (Bourgoin) 2006 I(R), 2007 NZ1, 2, 2008 A1, 2(R)
Boyoud, R (Dax) 2008 A1(R), 2, 2009 S(R)
Branca, G (SF) 1928 S, 1929 I, S
Branlat, A (RCF) 1906 NZ, E, 1908 W
Bréjassou, R (Tarbes) 1952 S, I, SA, W, E, 1953 W, E, 1954 S, I, NZ, 1955 S, I, E, W, It
Brèthes, R (St Séver) 1960 Arg 2
Bringeon, A (Biarritz O) 1925 W
Brouzet, O (Grenoble, Bègles, Northampton, Montferrand) 1994 S, NZ 2(R), 1995 E, S, I, R 1, [Tg, Iv, E (t)], It, Arg (R), 1996 W 1(R), 1997 R 1, A 1, 2, It 2, Arg, SA 1, 2, 1998 E, S, I, W, Arg 1, 2, Fj, Arg 3, A, 1999 I, W 1, E, S, R, [C (R), Nm, Fj (R), Arg, NZ 2(R), A (R)], 2000 W, E, S, I, It, A, NZ 1(R), 2(R), 2001 SA 1, 2, NZ, 2002 W, E, S, I, Arg, A 1(R), 2, SA, NZ, C, 2003 E 1, S, I, It, W, E 3, [Fj(R), J, S(R), US, I(R)]
Bru, Y (Toulouse) 2001 A (R), Fj (R), 2002 It, 2003 Arg 2, NZ, R, E 2, 3(R), [J, S(R), US, I(t&R), NZ], 2004 I(R), It(R), W(R), S(R), E(R)
Brugnaut, J (Dax) 2008 S, I(R)
Brun, G (Vienne) 1950 E, W, 1951 S, E, W, 1952 S, I, SA, W, E, It, 1953 E, W, It
Bruneau, M (SBUC) 1910 W, E, 1913 SA, E
Brunet, Y (Perpignan) 1975 SA 1, 1977 Arg 1
Bruno, S (Béziers, Sale) 2002 W (R), 2004 A(R), NZ(t&R), 2005 S(R), E, W, I, It, SA1, 2(R), A1(R), 2(R), C, SA3(R), 2006 S(R), I(R), 2007 I(R), E1(R), NZ1, 2, E3(R), W2(R), [Gg, Arg 2(t&R)], 2008 A1, 2
Brusque, N (Pau, Biarritz) 1997 R 2(R), 2002 W, E, S, I, Arg, A 2, SA, NZ, C, 2003 E 2, [Fj, S, I, E, NZ(R)], 2004 I, It, W, S, E, A, Arg, 2005 SA1(R), 2, A1, 2006 S
Buchet, E (Nice) 1980 R, 1982 E, R (R), Arg 1, 2
Buisson, H (see Empereur-Buisson)
Buonomo, Y (Béziers) 1971 A 2, R, 1972 I 1
Burgun, M (RCF) 1909 I, 1910 W, S, I, 1911 S, E, 1912 I, S, 1913 S, E, 1914 E
Bustaffa, D (Carcassonne) 1977 Arg 1, 2, NZ 1, 2, 1978 W, R, 1980 W, E, S, SA, R
Buzy, C-E (Lourdes) 1946 K, W, 1947 S, I, W, E, 1948 I, A, S, W, E, 1949 S, I, E, W, Arg 1, 2

Caballero, Y (Montauban) 2008 A2(R)
Cabanier, J-M (Montauban) 1963 R, 1964 S, Fj, 1965 S, I, W, It, R, 1966 S, I, E, W, It, R, 1967 S, A, E, It, W, I, SA 1, 3, NZ, R, 1968 S, I
Cabannes, L (RCF, Harlequins) 1990 NZ 2(R), 1991 S, I, W 1, E, US 2, W 2, [R, Fj, C, E], 1992 W, E, S, I, R, Arg 2, SA 1, 2, 1993 E, S, I, W, R 1, SA 1, 2, 1994 E, S, C 1, NZ 1, 2, 1995 W, E, S, R 1, [Tg (R), Iv, S, I, SA, E], 1996 E, S, I, W 1, 1997 It 2, Arg, SA 1, 2
Cabrol, H (Béziers) 1972 A 1(R), 2, 1973 J, 1974 SA 2
Cadenat, J (SCUF) 1910 S, E, 1911 W, I, 1912 W, E, 1913 I
Cadieu, J-M (Toulouse) 1991 R, US 1, [R, Fj, C, E], 1992 W, I, R, Arg 1, 2, SA 1
Cahuc, F (St Girons) 1922 S
Califano, C (Toulouse, Saracens, Gloucester) 1994 NZ 1, 2, C 2, 1995 W, E, S, I, [Iv, S, I, SA, E], It, Arg, NZ 1, 2, 1996 E, S, I, W 1, R, Arg 1, 2, SA 1, 2, 1997 I, W, E, A 1, 2, It 2, R 2(R), Arg, SA 1, 2, 1998 E, S, I, W, 1999 I, W 1, E (R), S, WS, Tg (R), NZ 1, W 2, [C, Nm, Fj], 2000 W, E, S, I, It, R, A, NZ 1, 2(R), 2001 S (R), I (R), It, W, SA 1(R), 2(R), NZ, 2003 E 1, S (R), I (R), 2007 NZ1, 2
Cals, R (RCF) 1938 G 1
Calvo, G (Lourdes) 1961 NZ 1, 3
Camberabero, D (La Voulte, Béziers) 1982 R, Arg 1, 2, 1983 E, W, 1987 [R (R), Z, Fj (R), A, NZ], 1988 I, 1989 B, A 1, 1990 W, S, I, R, A 1, 2, 3, NZ 1, 2, 1991 S, I, W 1, E, R, US 1, 2, W 2, [R, Fj, C], 1993 E, S, I
Camberabero, G (La Voulte) 1961 NZ 3, 1962 R, 1964 R, 1967 A, E, It, W, I, SA 1, 3, 4, 1968 S, E, W
Camberabero, L (La Voulte) 1964 R, 1965 S, I, 1966 E, W, 1967 A, E, It, W, I, 1968 S, E, W
Cambré, T (Oloron) 1920 E, W, I, US
Camel, A (Toulouse) 1928 S, A, I, E, G, W, 1929 W, E, G, 1930 S, I, E, G, W, 1935 G
Camel, M (Toulouse) 1929 S, W, E
Camicas, F (Tarbes) 1927 G 2, 1928 S, I, E, G, W, 1929 I, S, W, E
Camo, E (Villeneuve) 1931 I, S, W, E, G, 1932 G
Campaès, A (Lourdes) 1965 W, 1967 NZ, 1968 S, I, E, W, Cz, NZ 1, 2, A, 1969 S, W, 1972 R, 1973 NZ
Campan, O (Agen) 1993 SA 1(R), 2(R), R 2(R), 1996 I, W 1, R
Candelon, J (Narbonne) 2005 SA1, A1(R)
Cantoni, J (Béziers) 1970 W, R, 1971 S, I, E, W, SA 1, 2, R, 1972 S, I 1, 1973 S, NZ, W, I, 1975 W (R)
Capdouze, J (Pau) 1964 SA, Fj, R, 1965 S, I, E
Capendeguy, J-M (Bègles) 1967 NZ, R
Capitani, P (Toulon) 1954 Arg 1, 2
Capmau, J-L (Toulouse) 1914 E
Carabignac, G (Agen) 1951 S, I, 1952 SA, W, E, 1953 S, I
Carbonne, J (Perpignan) 1927 W
Carbonneau, P (Toulouse, Brive, Pau) 1995 R 2, Arg, NZ 1, 2, 1996 E, S, R (R), Arg 2, W 2, SA 1, 1997 I (R), W, E, S (R), R 1(R), A 1, 2, 1998 E, S, I, W, Arg 1, 2, Fj, Arg 3, A, 1999 I, W 1, E, S, 2000 NZ 2(R), 2001 I
Carminati, A (Béziers, Brive) 1986 R 2, NZ 2, 1987 [R, Z], 1988 I, W, Arg 1, 2, 1989 I, W, S, NZ 1(R), 2, A 2, 1990 S, 1995 It, R 2, Arg, NZ 1, 2
Caron, L (Lyon O, Castres) 1947 E, 1948 I, A, W, E, 1949 S, I, E, W, Arg 1
Carpentier, M (Lourdes) 1980 E, SA, R, 1981 S, I, A 1, 1982 E, S
Carrère, C (Toulon) 1966 R, 1967 S, A, E, W, I, SA 1, 3, 4, NZ, R, 1968 S, I, E, W, Cz, NZ 3, A, R, 1969 S, I, 1970 S, I, W, E, 1971 E, W
Carrère, J (Vichy, Toulon) 1956 S, 1957 E, W, R 2, 1958 S, SA 1, 2, 1959 I
Carrère, R (Mont-de-Marsan) 1953 E, It
Casadei, D (Brive) 1997 S, R 1, SA 2(R)
Casaux, L (Tarbes) 1959 I, It, 1962 S
Cassagne, P (Pau) 1957 It
Cassayet-Armagnac, A (Tarbes, Narbonne) 1920 S, E, W, US, 1921 W, E, I, 1922 S, E, W, 1923 S, W, E, I, 1924 S, E, W, R, US, 1925 I, NZ, S, W, 1926 S, I, E, W, M, 1927 I, S, W
Cassiède, M (Dax) 1961 NZ 3, A, R
Castaignède, S (Mont-de-Marsan) 1999 W 2, [C (R), Nm (R), Fj, Arg (R), NZ 2(R), A (R)]
Castaignède, T (Toulouse, Castres, Saracens) 1995 R 2, Arg, NZ 1, 2, 1996 E, S, I, W 1, Arg 1, 2, 1997 I, A 1, 2, It 2, 1998 E, S, I, W, Arg 1, 2, Fj, 1999 I, W 1, E, S, R, WS, Tg (R), NZ 1, W 2, [C], 2000 W, E, S, It, 2002 SA, NZ, C, 2003 E 1(R), S (R), It, W, Arg 1, 2005 A2(R), C, Tg, SA3, 2006 It, E, W, R, SA(R), 2007 NZ1, 2
Castel, R (Toulouse, Béziers) 1996 I, W 1, W 2, SA 1(R), 2, 1997 I (R), W, E (R), S (R), A 1(R), 1998 Arg 3(R), A (R), 1999 W 1(R), E, S
Castets, J (Toulon) 1923 W, E, I
Caujolle, J (Tarbes) 1909 E, 1913 SA, E, 1914 W, E
Caunègre, R (SB) 1938 R, G 2
Caussade, A (Lourdes) 1978 R, 1979 I, W, E, NZ 1, 2, R, 1980 W, E, S, 1981 S (R), I
Caussarieu, G (Pau) 1929 I
Cayrefourcq, E (Tarbes) 1921 E
Cazalbou, J (Toulouse) 1997 It 2(R), R 2, Arg, SA 2(R)
Cazals, P (Mont-de-Marsan) 1961 NZ 1, A, R
Cazenave, A (Pau) 1927 E, G 1, 1928 S, A, G
Cazenave, F (RCF) 1950 E, 1952 S, 1954 I, NZ, W, E
Cécillon, M (Bourgoin) 1988 I, W, Arg 2, 3, 4, R, 1989 I, E, NZ 1, 2, A 1, 1991 S, I, E (R), R, US 1, W 2, [E], 1992 W, E, S, I, R, Arg 1, 2, SA 1, 2, 1993 E, S, I, W, R 1, SA 1, 2, R 2, A 1, 2, 1994 I, W, NZ 1(R), 1995 I, R 1, [Tg, S (R), I, SA]
Celaya, M (Biarritz O, SBUC) 1953 E, W, It, 1954 I, E, It, Arg 1, 2, 1955 S, I, E, W, It, 1956 S, I, W, It, E, Cz 1957 S, I, E, W, R 2, 1958 S, E, A, W, It, 1959 S, E, 1960 S, E, W, I, R, Arg 1, 2, 3, 1961 S, SA, E, W, It, I, NZ 1, 2, 3, A, R
Celhay, M (Bayonne) 1935 G, 1936 G 1, 1937 G, It, 1938 G 1, 1940 B

Cermeno, F (Perpignan) 2000 R
Cessieux, N (Lyon) 1906 NZ
Cester, E (TOEC, Valence) 1966 S, I, E, 1967 W, 1968 S, I, E, W, Cz, NZ 1, 3, A, SA 1, 2, R, 1969 S, I, E, W, 1970 S, I, W, E, 1971 A 1, 1972 R, 1973 S, NZ, W, I, J, R, 1974 I, W, E, S
Chabal, S (Bourgoin, Sale, Racing-Metro) 2000 S, 2001 SA 1, 2, NZ (R), Fj (R), 2002 Arg (R), A 2, SA (R), NZ (t), C (R), 2003 E 1(R), S (R), I (R), Arg 2, NZ (R), E 2(R), 3, [J(R), US, NZ], 2005 S, E, A2(R), Tg, 2007 It, I, E1, NZ1, 2, E2(R), W2, [Arg1(R), Nm, I, NZ(R), E(R), Arg 2(R)], 2008 A1, 2, Arg(R), PI(R), A3, 2009 I, S(R), W, E, It, NZ1(R), 2, SA(R), Sm, NZ3, 2010 W(R), It(R), E(R), Fj(R), Arg2, A, 2011 S(R), I1(R), E, It
Chaban-Delmas, J (CASG) 1945 B 2
Chabowski, H (Nice, Bourgoin) 1985 Arg 2, 1986 R 2, NZ 2, 1989 B (R)
Chadebech, P (Brive) 1982 R, Arg 1, 2, 1986 S, I
Champ, E (Toulon) 1985 Arg 1, 2, 1986 I, W, E, R 1, Arg 1, 2, A, NZ 1, R 2, NZ 2, 3, 1987 W, E, S, I, [S, R, Fj, A, NZ], R, 1988 E, S, Arg 1, 3, 4, R, 1989 W, S, A 1, 2, 1990 W, E, NZ 1, 1991 R, US 1, [R, Fj, C, E]
Chapuy, L (SF) 1926 S
Charpentier, G (SF) 1911 E, 1912 W, E
Charton, P (Montferrand) 1940 B
Charvet, D (Toulouse) 1986 W, E, R 1, Arg 1, A, NZ 1, 3, 1987 W, E, S, I, [S, R, Z, Fj, A, NZ], R, 1989 E (R), 1990 W, E, 1991 S, I
Chassagne, J (Montferrand) 1938 G 1
Chatau, A (Bayonne) 1913 SA
Chaud, E (Toulon) 1932 G, 1934 G, 1935 G
Chazalet, A (Bourgoin) 1999 Tg
Chenevay, C (Grenoble) 1968 SA 1
Chevallier, B (Montferrand) 1952 S, I, SA, W, E, It, 1953 E, W, It, 1954 S, I, NZ, W, Arg 1, 1955 S, I, E, W, It, 1956 S, I, W, It, E, Cz, 1957 S
Chiberry, J (Chambéry) 1955 It
Chilo, A (RCF) 1920 S, W, 1925 I, NZ
Cholley, G (Castres) 1975 E, S, I, SA 1, 2, Arg 1, 2, R, 1976 S, I, W, E, A 1, 2, R, 1977 W, E, S, I, Arg 1, 2, NZ 1, 2, R, 1978 E, S, I, W, R, 1979 I, S
Chouly, D (Brive, Perpignan) 2007 NZ1(R), 2, 2009 NZ2(R), A(R)
Choy J (Narbonne) 1930 S, I, E, G, W, 1931 I, 1933 G, 1934 G, 1935 G, 1936 G 2
Cigagna, A (Toulouse) 1995 [E]
Cimarosti, J (Castres) 1976 US (R)
Cistacq, J-C (Agen) 2000 R (R)
Clady, A (Lezignan) 1929 G, 1931 I, S, E, G
Clarac, H (St Girons) 1938 G 1
Claudel, R (Lyon) 1932 G, 1934 G
Clauzel, F (Béziers) 1924 E, W, 1925 W
Clavé, J (Agen) 1936 G 2, 1938 R, G 2
Claverie, H (Lourdes) 1954 NZ, W
Cléda, T (Pau) 1998 E (R), S (R), I (R), W (R), Arg 1(R), Fj (R), Arg 3(R), 1999 I (R), S
Clément, G (RCF) 1931 W
Clément, J (RCF) 1921 S, W, E, 1922 S, E, W, I, 1923 S, W, I
Clemente, M (Oloron) 1978 R, 1980 S, I
Clerc, V (Toulouse) 2002 SA, NZ, C, 2003 E 1, S, I, It (R), W (R), Arg 2, NZ, 2004 I, It, W, 2005 SA2, Tg, 2006 SA, 2007 I, W1, E1, S, E2, W2, [Nm, I, Gg(R), NZ, E, Arg 2(R)], 2008 S, I, E, It(t), W, 2009 NZ1, 2, A(R), SA, Sm, NZ3, 2010 S(R), I, SA, Arg1, 2011 S(R), I1(R), E, It, W, I2, 3(R), [J, C, NZ1, Tg, E, W, NZ2]
Cluchague, L (Biarritz O) 1924 S, 1925 E
Coderc, J (Chalon) 1932 G, 1933 G, 1934 G, 1935 G, 1936 G 1
Codorniou, D (Narbonne) 1979 NZ 1, 2, R, 1980 W, E, S, I, 1981 S, W, E, A 2, 1983 E, S, I, W, A 1, 2, R, 1984 I, W, E, S, NZ 1, 2, R, 1985 E, S, I, W, Arg 1, 2
Coeurveille, C (Agen) 1992 Arg 1(R), 2
Cognet, L (Montferrand) 1932 G, 1936 G 1, 2, 1937 G, It
Collazo, P (Bègles) 2000 R
Colombier, J (St Junien) 1952 SA, W, E
Colomine, G (Narbonne) 1979 NZ 1
Comba, F (SF) 1998 Arg 1, 2, Fj, Arg 3, 1999 I, W 1, E, S, 2000 A, NZ 1, 2, 2001 S, I
Combe, J (SF) 1910 S, E, I, 1911 S
Combes, G (Fumel) 1945 B 2
Communeau, M (SF) 1906 NZ, E, 1907 E, 1908 E, W, 1909 E, W, I, 1910 S, E, I, 1911 S, E, I, 1912 I, S, W, E, 1913 SA, E, W
Condom, J (Boucau, Biarritz O) 1982 R, 1983 E, S, I, W, A 1, 2, R, 1984 I, W, E, S, NZ 1, 2, R, 1985 E, S, I, W, Arg 1, 2, 1986 S, I, W, E, R 1, Arg 1, 2, NZ 1, R 2, NZ 2, 3, 1987 W, E, S, I, [S, R, Z, A, NZ], R, 1988 E, S, W, Arg 1, 2, 3, 4, R, 1989 I, W, E, S, NZ 1, 2, A 1, 1990 I, R, A 2, 3(R)
Conilh de Beyssac, J-J (SBUC) 1912 I, S, 1914 I, W, E
Constant, G (Perpignan) 1920 W
Correia, P (Albi) 2008 A2
Coscolla, G (Béziers) 1921 S, W
Costantino, J (Montferrand) 1973 R
Costes, A (Montferrand) 1994 C 2, 1995 R 1, [Iv], 1997 It 1, 1999 WS, Tg (R), NZ 1, [Nm (R), Fj (R), Arg (R), NZ 2(R), A (t&R)], 2000 S (R), I
Costes, F (Montferrand) 1979 E, S, NZ 1, 2, R, 1980 W, I
Couffignal, H (Colomiers) 1993 R 1
Coulon, E (Grenoble) 1928 S
Courtiols, M (Bègles) 1991 R, US 1, W 2
Coux, J-F (Bourgoin) 2007 NZ1, 2
Couzinet, D (Biarritz) 2004 US, C(R), 2008 A1(R)
Crabos, R (RCF) 1920 S, E, W, I, US, 1921 S, W, E, I, 1922 S, E, W, I, 1923 S, I, 1924 S, I
Crampagne, J (Bègles) 1967 SA 4
Crancée, R (Lourdes) 1960 Arg 3, 1961 S
Crauste, M (RCF, Lourdes) 1957 R 1, 2, 1958 S, E, A, W, It, I, 1959 E, It, W, I, 1960 S, E, W, I, It, R, Arg 1, 3, 1961 S, SA, E, W, It, I, NZ 1, 2, 3, A, R, 1962 S, E, W, I, It, R, 1963 S, I, E, W, It, R, 1964 S, NZ, E, W, It, I, SA, Fj, R, 1965 S, I, E, W, It, R, 1966 S, I, E, W, It
Cremaschi, M (Lourdes) 1980 R, 1981 R, NZ 1, 2, 1982 W, S, 1983 A 1, 2, R, 1984 I, W
Crenca, J-J (Agen) 1996 SA 2(R), 1999 R, Tg, WS (R), NZ 1(R), 2001 SA 1, 2, NZ (R), SA 3, A, Fj, 2002 It, W, E, S, I, Arg, A 2, SA, NZ, C, 2003 E 1, S, I, It, W, R, E 2, [Fj, J(t&R), S, I, E, NZ(R)], 2004 I(R), It(R), W(R), S(R), E(R)
Crichton, W H (Le Havre) 1906 NZ, E
Cristina, J (Montferrand) 1979 R
Cussac, P (Biarritz O) 1934 G
Cutzach, A (Quillan) 1929 G

Daguerre, F (Biarritz O) 1936 G 1
Daguerre, J (CASG) 1933 G
Dal Maso, M (Mont-de-Marsan, Agen, Colomiers) 1988 R (R), 1990 NZ 2, 1996 SA 1(R), 2, 1997 I, W, E, S, It 1, R 1(R), A 1, 2, It 2, Arg, SA 1, 2, 1998 W (R), Arg 1(t), Fj (R), 1999 R (R), WS (R), Tg, NZ 1(R), W 2(R), [Nm (R), Fj (R), Arg (R), A (R)], 2000 W, E, S, I, It
Danion, J (Toulon) 1924 I
Danos, P (Toulon, Béziers) 1954 Arg 1, 2, 1957 R 2, 1958 S, E, W, It, I, SA 1, 2, 1959 S, E, It, W, I, 1960 S, E
Dantiacq, D (Pau) 1997 R 1
Darbos, P (Dax) 1969 R
Darracq, R (Dax) 1957 It
Darrieussecq, A (Biarritz O) 1973 E
Darrieussecq, J (Mont-de-Marsan) 1953 It
Darrouy, C (Mont-de-Marsan) 1957 I, E, W, It, R 1, 1959 E, 1961 R, 1963 S, I, E, W, It, 1964 NZ, E, W, It, I, SA, Fj, R, 1965 S, I, E, It, R, 1966 S, I, E, W, It, R, 1967 S, A, E, It, W, I, SA 1, 2, 4
Daudé, J (Bourgoin) 2000 S
Daudignon, G (SF) 1928 S
Dauga, B (Mont-de-Marsan) 1964 S, NZ, E, W, It, I, SA, Fj, R, 1965 S, I, E, W, It, R, 1966 S, I, E, W, It, R, 1967 S, A, E, It, W, I, SA 1, 2, 3, 4, NZ, R, 1968 S, I, NZ 1, 2, 3, A, SA 1, 2, R, 1969 S, I, E, R, 1970 S, I, W, E, R, 1971 S, I, E, W, SA 1, 2, A 1, 2, R, 1972 S, I 1, W
Dauger, J (Bayonne) 1945 B 1, 2, 1953 S
Daulouède, P (Tyrosse) 1937 G, It, 1938 G 1, 1940 B
David, Y (Bourgoin, Toulouse) 2008 It, 2009 SA, Sm(R), NZ3(R)
Debaty, V (Perpignan) 2006 R(R)
De Besombes, S (Perpignan) 1998 Arg 1(R), Fj (R)
Decamps, P (RCF) 1911 S
Dedet, J (SF) 1910 S, E, I, 1911 W, I, 1912 S, 1913 E, I

Dedeyn, P (RCF) 1906 NZ
Dedieu, P (Béziers) 1963 E, It, 1964 W, It, I, SA, Fj, R, 1965 S, I, E, W
De Gregorio, J (Grenoble) 1960 S, E, W, I, It, R, Arg 1, 2, 1961 S, SA, E, W, It, I, 1962 S, E, W, 1963 S, W, It, 1964 NZ, E
Dehez, J-L (Agen) 1967 SA 2, 1969 R
De Jouvencel, E (SF) 1909 W, I
De Laborderie, M (RCF) 1921 I, 1922 I, 1925 W, E
Delage, C (Agen) 1983 S, I
De Malherbe, H (CASG) 1932 G, 1933 G
De Malmann, R (RCF) 1908 E, W, 1909 E, W, I, 1910 E, I
De Muizon, J J (SF) 1910 I
Delaigue, G (Toulon) 1973 J, R
Delaigue, Y (Toulon, Toulouse, Castres) 1994 S, NZ 2(R), C 2, 1995 I, R 1, [Tg, Iv], It, R 2(R), 1997 It 1, 2003 Arg 1, 2, 2005 S, E, W, I, It, A2(R), Tg, SA3(R)
Delmotte, G (Toulon) 1999 R, Tg
Delque, A (Toulouse) 1937 It, 1938 G 1, R, G 2
De Rougemont, M (Toulon) 1995 E (t), R 1(t), [Iv], NZ 1, 2, 1996 I (R), Arg 1, 2, W 2, SA 1, 1997 E (R), S (R), It 1
Desbrosse, C (Toulouse) 1999 [Nm (R)], 2000 I
Descamps, P (SB) 1927 G 2
Desclaux, F (RCF) 1949 Arg 1, 2, 1953 It
Desclaux, J (Perpignan) 1934 G, 1935 G, 1936 G 1, 2, 1937 G, It, 1938 G 1, R, G 2, 1945 B 1
Deslandes, C (RCF) 1990 A 1, NZ 2, 1991 W 1, 1992 R, Arg 1, 2
Desnoyer, L (Brive) 1974 R
Destarac, L (Tarbes) 1926 S, I, E, W, M, 1927 W, E, G 1, 2
Desvouges, R (SF) 1914 W
Detrez, P-E (Nîmes) 1983 A 2(R), 1986 Arg 1(R), 2, A (R), NZ1
Devergie, T (Nîmes) 1988 R, 1989 NZ 1, 2, B, A 2, 1990 W, E, S, I, R, A 1, 2, 3, 1991 US 2, W 2, 1992 R (R), Arg 2(R)
De Villiers, P (SF) 1999 W 2, [Arg (R), NZ 2(R), A (R)], 2000 W (R), E (R), S (R), I (R), It (R), NZ 1(R), 2, 2001 S, I, It, W, E, SA 1, 2, NZ (R), SA 3, A, Fj, 2002 It, W, E, I, SA, NZ, C, 2003 Arg 1, 2, NZ (R), 2004 I, It, W, S, E, US, C, NZ, 2005 S, I(R), It(R), SA1(R), 2, A1(R), 2, C, Tg(R), SA3, 2006 S, I, It, E, W, SA, NZ1, 2, Arg, 2007 It, I, E1, S, W2, [Arg1, Nm, I, NZ, E]
Deygas, M (Vienne) 1937 It
Deylaud, C (Toulouse) 1992 R, Arg 1, 2, SA 1, 1994 C 1, NZ 1, 2, 1995 W, E, S, [Iv (R), S, I, SA], It, Arg
Diarra, I (Montauban) 2008 It
Dintrans, P (Tarbes) 1979 NZ 1, 2, R, 1980 E, S, I, SA, R, 1981 S, I, W, E, A 1, 2, R, NZ 1, 2, 1982 W, E, S, I, R, Arg 1, 2, 1983 E, W, A 1, 2, R, 1984 I, W, E, S, NZ 1, 2, R, 1985 E, S, I, W, Arg 1, 2, 1987 [R], 1988 Arg 1, 2, 3, 1989 W, E, S, 1990 R
Dispagne, S (Toulouse) 1996 I (R), W 1
Dizabo, P (Tyrosse) 1948 A, S, E, 1949 S, I, E, W, Arg 2, 1950 S, I, 1960 Arg 1, 2, 3
Domec, A (Carcassonne) 1929 W
Domec, H (Lourdes) 1953 W, It, 1954 S, I, NZ, W, E, It, 1955 S, I, E, W, 1956 I, W, It, 1958 E, A, W, It, I
Domenech, A (Vichy, Brive) 1954 W, E, It, 1955 S, I, E, W, 1956 S, I, W, It, E, Cz, 1957 S, I, E, W, It, R 1, 2, 1958 S, E, It, 1959 It, 1960 S, E, W, I, It, R, Arg 1, 2, 3, 1961 S, SA, E, W, It, I, NZ 1, 2, 3, A, R, 1962 S, E, W, I, It, R, 1963 W, It
Domercq, J (Bayonne) 1912 I, S
Domingo, T (Clermont-Auvergne) 2009 W(R), E(R), It(R), NZ2(R), Sm, 2010 S, I, W, It, E, SA, Arg2, A, 2011 S, I1, E, W
Dominici, C (SF) 1998 E, S, Arg 1, 2, 1999 E, S, WS, NZ 1, W 2, [C, Fj, Arg, NZ 2, A], 2000 W, E, S, R, 2001 I (R), It, W, E, SA 1, 2, NZ, Fj, 2003 Arg 1, R, E 2, 3, [Fj, J, S, I, E], 2004 I, It, W, S, E, A(R), NZ(R), 2005 S, E, W, I, It, 2006 S, I, It, E, W, NZ1, 2(R), Arg, 2007 It, I, W1, E1, S(R), E3, W2(R), [Arg 1, Gg, NZ(R), E(R), Arg 2]
Dorot, J (RCF) 1935 G
Dospital, P (Bayonne) 1977 R, 1980 I, 1981 S, I, W, E, 1982 I, R, Arg 1, 2, 1983 E, S, I, W, 1984 E, S, NZ 1, 2, R, 1985 E, S, I, W, Arg 1
Dourthe, C (Dax) 1966 R, 1967 S, A, E, W, I, SA 1, 2, 3, NZ, 1968 W, NZ 3, SA 1, 2, 1969 W, 1971 SA 2(R), R, 1972 I 1, 2, A 1, 2, R, 1973 S, NZ, E, 1974 I, Arg 1, 2, SA 1, 2, 1975 W, E, S
Dourthe, M (Dax) 2000 NZ 2(t)
Dourthe, R (Dax, SF, Béziers) 1995 R 2, Arg, NZ 1, 2, 1996 E, R, 1996 Arg 1, 2, W 2, SA 1, 2, 1997 W, A 1, 1999 I, W 1, 2, [C, Nm, Fj, Arg, NZ 2, A], 2000 W, E, It, R, A, NZ 1, 2, 2001 S, I
Doussain, J-M (Toulouse) 2011 [NZ2(R)]
Doussau, E (Angoulême) 1938 R
Droitecourt, M (Montferrand) 1972 R, 1973 NZ (R), E, 1974 E, S, Arg 1, SA 2, 1975 SA 1, 2, Arg 1, 2, R, 1976 S, I, W, A 1, 1977 Arg 2
Dubertrand, A (Montferrand) 1971 A 1, 2, R, 1972 I 2, 1974 I, W, E, SA 2, 1975 Arg 1, 2, R, 1976 S, US
Dubois, D (Bègles) 1971 S
Dubroca, D (Agen) 1979 NZ 2, 1981 NZ 2(R), 1982 E, S, 1984 W, E, S, 1985 Arg 2, 1986 S, I, W, E, R 1, Arg 2, A, NZ 1, R 2, NZ 2, 3, 1987 W, E, S, I, [S, Z, Fj, A, NZ], R, 1988 E, S, I, W
Ducalcon, L (Castres) 2010 S(R), Fj, Arg2(R), 2011 S(R), It(R), W(R), I2, [C, NZ1, Tg]
Duché, A (Limoges) 1929 G
Duclos, A (Lourdes) 1931 S
Ducousso, J (Tarbes) 1925 S, W, E
Dufau, G (RCF) 1948 I, A, 1949 I, W, 1950 S, E, W, 1951 S, I, E, W, 1952 SA, W, 1953 S, I, E, W, 1954 S, I, NZ, W, E, It, 1955 S, I, E, W, It, 1956 S, I, W, It, 1957 S, I, E, W, It, R 1
Dufau, J (Biarritz) 1912 I, S, W, E
Duffaut, Y (Agen) 1954 Arg 1, 2
Duffour, R (Tarbes) 1911 W
Dufourcq, J (SBUC) 1906 NZ, E, 1907 E, 1908 W
Duhard, Y (Bagnères) 1980 E
Duhau, J (SF) 1928 I, 1930 I, G, 1931 I, S, W, 1933 G
Dulaurens, C (Toulouse) 1926 I, 1928 S, 1929 W
Duluc, A (Béziers) 1934 G
Du Manoir, Y le P (RCF) 1925 I, NZ, S, W, E, 1926 S, 1927 I, S
Dupont, C (Lourdes) 1923 S, W, I, 1924 S, I, W, R, US, 1925 S, 1927 E, G 1, 2, 1928 A, G, W, 1929 I
Dupont, J-L (Agen) 1983 S
Dupont, L (RCF) 1934 G, 1935 G, 1936 G 1, 2, 1938 R, G 2
Dupouy, A (SB) 1924 W, R
Duprat, B (Bayonne) 1966 E, W, It, R, 1967 S, A, E, SA 2, 3, 1968 S, I, 1972 E, W, I 2, A 1
Dupré, P (RCF) 1909 W
Dupuy, J (Leicester, SF) 2009 NZ1, 2, A(R), SA, Sm(R), NZ3
Dupuy, J-V (Tarbes) 1956 S, I, W, It, E, Cz, 1957 S, I, E, W, It, R 2, 1958 S, E, SA 1, 2, 1959 S, E, It, W, I, 1960 W, I, It, Arg 1, 3, 1961 S, SA, E, NZ 2, R, 1962 S, E, W, I, It, 1963 W, It, R, 1964 S
Durand, N (Perpignan) 2007 NZ1, 2
Dusautoir, T (Biarritz, Toulouse) 2006 R, SA, NZ1, 2007 E3, W2(R), [Nm, I, NZ, E, Arg 2], 2008 S, I, E, W, Arg, PI, A3, 2009 I, S, W, E, It, NZ1, 2, A, SA, Sm, NZ3, 2010 S, I, W, It, E, SA, Arg1, 2, A, 2011 S, I1, E, It, W, I2, [J, NZ1, Tg, E, W, NZ2]
Du Souich, C J (see Judas du Souich)
Dutin, B (Mont-de-Marsan) 1968 NZ 2, A, SA 2, R
Dutour, F X (Toulouse) 1911 E, I, 1912 S, W, E, 1913 S
Dutrain, H (Toulouse) 1945 W, 1946 B, I, 1947 E, 1949 I, E, W, Arg 1
Dutrey, J (Lourdes) 1940 B
Duval, R (SF) 1908 E, W, 1909 E, 1911 E, W, I

Echavé, L (Agen) 1961 S
Elhorga, P (Agen) 2001 NZ, 2002 A 1, 2, 2003 Arg 2, NZ (R), R, [Fj(R), US, I(R), NZ], 2004 I(R), It(R), S, E, 2005 S, E, 2006 NZ2, Arg, 2008 A1
Elissalde, E (Bayonne) 1936 G 2, 1940 B
Elissalde, J-B (La Rochelle, Toulouse) 2000 S (R), R (R), 2003 It (R), W (R), 2004 I, It, W, A, Arg, 2005 SA1, 2(R), A1, 2, SA3, 2006 S, I, It, W(R), NZ1(R), 2, 2007 E2(R), 3, W2(R), [Arg 1(R), Nm, I, Gg(R), NZ, E, Arg 2], 2008 S, I, W, Arg, PI
Elissalde, J-P (La Rochelle) 1980 SA, R, 1981 A 1, 2, R
Empereur-Buisson, H (Béziers) 1931 E, G

Erbani, D (Agen) 1981 A 1, 2, NZ 1, 2, 1982 Arg 1, 2, 1983 S (R), I, W, A 1, 2, R, 1984 W, E, R, 1985 E, W (R), Arg 2, 1986 S, I, W, E, R 1, Arg 2, NZ 1, 2(R), 3, 1987 W, E, S, I, [S, R, Fj, A, NZ], 1988 E, S, 1989 I (R), W, E, S, NZ 1, A 2, 1990 W, E
Escaffre, P (Narbonne) 1933 G, 1934 G
Escommier, M (Montelimar) 1955 It
Esponda, J-M (RCF) 1967 SA 1, 2, R, 1968 NZ 1, 2, SA 2, R, 1969 S, I (R), E
Estebanez, F (Brive, Racing Metro) 2010 Fj, Arg2(R), A(R), 2011 W(R), I3, [J, NZ1(R), Tg(R)]
Estève, A (Béziers) 1971 SA 1, 1972 I 1, E, W, I 2, A 2, R, 1973 S, NZ, E, I, 1974 I, W, E, S, R, SA 1, 2, 1975 W, E
Estève, P (Narbonne, Lavelanet) 1982 R, Arg 1, 2, 1983 E, S, I, W, A 1, 2, R, 1984 I, W, E, S, NZ 1, 2, R, 1985 E, S, I, W, 1986 S, I, 1987 [S, Z]
Etcheberry, J (Rochefort, Cognac) 1923 W, I, 1924 S, I, E, W, R, US, 1926 S, I, E, M, 1927 I, S, W, G 2
Etchenique, J-M (Biarritz O) 1974 R, SA 1, 1975 E, Arg 2
Etchepare, A (Bayonne) 1922 I
Etcheverry, M (Pau) 1971 S, I
Eutrope, A (SCUF) 1913 I

Fabre, E (Toulouse) 1937 It, 1938 G 1, 2
Fabre, J (Toulouse) 1963 S, I, E, W, It, 1964 S, NZ, E
Fabre, L (Lezignan) 1930 G
Fabre, M (Béziers) 1981 A 1, R, NZ 1, 2, 1982 I, R
Failliot, P (RCF) 1911 S, W, I, 1912 I, S, E, 1913 E, W
Fall, B (Bayonne) 2009 Sm, 2010 S
Fargues, G (Dax) 1923 I
Fauré, F (Tarbes) 1914 I, W, E
Faure, L (Sale) 2008 S, I, E, A1, PI, A3, 2009 I, E
Fauvel, J-P (Tulle) 1980 R
Favre, M (Lyon) 1913 E, W
Ferrand, L (Chalon) 1940 B
Ferrien, R (Tarbes) 1950 S, I, E, W
Finat, R (CASG) 1932 G, 1933 G
Fite, R (Brive) 1963 W, It
Floch, A (Clermont-Auvergne) 2008 E(R), It, W
Forest, M (Bourgoin) 2007 NZ1(R), 2(R)
Forestier, J (SCUF) 1912 W
Forgues, F (Bayonne) 1911 S, E, W, 1912 I, W, E, 1913 S, SA, W, 1914 I, E
Fort, J (Agen) 1967 It, W, I, SA 1, 2, 3, 4
Fourcade, G (BEC) 1909 E, W
Foures, H (Toulouse) 1951 S, I, E, W
Fournet, F (Montferrand) 1950 W
Fouroux, J (La Voulte) 1972 I 2, R, 1974 W, E, Arg 1, 2, R, SA 1, 2, 1975 W, Arg 1, R, 1976 S, I, W, E, US, A 1, 1977 W, E, S, I, Arg 1, 2, NZ 1, 2, R
Francquenelle, A (Vaugirard) 1911 S, 1913 W, I
Fritz, F (Toulouse) 2005 SA1, A2, SA3, 2006 S, I, It, E, W, SA, NZ1, 2, Arg, 2007 It, 2009 I, E(R), It, NZ2(R), A, 2010 Arg1
Froment, R (Castres) 2004 US(R)
Furcade, R (Perpignan) 1952 S

Gabernet, S (Toulouse) 1980 E, S, 1981 S, I, W, E, A 1, 2, R, NZ 1, 2, 1982 I, 1983 A 2, R
Gachassin, J (Lourdes) 1961 S, I, 1963 R, 1964 S, NZ, E, W, It, I, SA, Fj, R, 1965 S, I, E, W, It, R, 1966 S, I, E, W, 1967 S, A, It, W, I, NZ, 1968 I, E, 1969 S, I
Galasso, A (Toulon, Montferrand) 2000 R (R), 2001 E (R)
Galau, H (Toulouse) 1924 S, I, E, W, US
Galia, J (Quillan) 1927 E, G 1, 2, 1928 S, A, I, E, W, 1929 I, E, G, 1930 S, I, E, G, W, 1931 S, W, E, G
Gallart, P (Béziers) 1990 R, A 1, 2(R), 3, 1992 S, I, R, Arg 1, 2, SA 1, 2, Arg, 1994 I, W, E, 1995 I (t), R 1, [Tg]
Gallion, J (Toulon) 1978 E, S, I, W, 1979 I, W, E, S, NZ 2, R, 1980 W, E, S, I, 1983 A 1, 2, R, 1984 I, W, E, S, R, 1985 E, S, I, W, 1986 Arg 2
Galthié, F (Colomiers, SF) 1991 R, US 1, [R, Fj, C, E], 1992 W, E, S, R, Arg, 1994 I, W, E, 1995 [SA, E], 1996 W 1(R), 1997 I, It 2, SA 1, 2, 1998 W (R), Fj (R), 1999 R, WS (R), Tg, NZ 1(R), [Fj (R), Arg, NZ 2, A], 2000 W, E, A, NZ 1, 2, 2001 S, It, W, E, SA 1, 2, NZ, SA 3, A, Fj, 2002 E, S, I, SA, NZ, C, 2003 E 1, S, Arg 1, 2, NZ, R, E 2, [Fj, J, S, I, E]
Galy, J (Perpignan) 1953 W
Garbajosa, X (Toulouse) 1998 I, W, Arg 2(R), Fj, 1999 W 1(R), E, S, WS, NZ 1, W 2, [C, Nm (R), Fj (R), Arg, NZ 2, A], 2000 A, NZ 1, 2, 2001 S, I, E, 2002 It (R), W, SA (R), C (R), 2003 E 1, S, I, It, W, E 3
Garuet-Lempirou, J-P (Lourdes) 1983 A 1, 2, R, 1984 I, NZ 1, 2, R, 1985 E, S, I, W, Arg 1, 1986 S, I, W, E, R 1, Arg 1, NZ 1, R 2, NZ 2, 3, 1987 W, E, S, I, [S, R, Fj, A, NZ], 1988 E, S, Arg 1, 2, R, 1989 E (R), S, NZ 1, 2, 1990 W, E
Gasc, J (Graulhet) 1977 NZ 2
Gasparotto, G (Montferrand) 1976 A 2, R
Gauby, G (Perpignan) 1956 Cz
Gaudermen, P (RCF) 1906 E
Gayraud, W (Toulouse) 1920 I
Gelez, F (Agen) 2001 SA 3, 2002 I (R), A 1, SA, NZ, C (R), 2003 S, I
Geneste, R (BEC) 1945 B 1, 1949 Arg 2
Genet, J-P (RCF) 1992 S, I, R
Gensane, R (Béziers) 1962 S, E, W, I, It, R, 1963 S
Gérald, G (RCF) 1927 E, G 2, 1928 S, 1929 I, S, W, E, G, 1930 S, I, E, G, W, 1931 I, S, E, G
Gérard, D (Bègles) 1999 Tg
Gérintes, G (CASG) 1924 R, 1925 I, 1926 W
Geschwind, P (RCF) 1936 G 1, 2
Giacardy, M (SBUC) 1907 E
Gimbert, P (Bègles) 1991 R, US 1, 1992 W, E
Giordani, P (Dax) 1999 E, S
Glas, S (Bourgoin) 1996 S (t), I (R), W 1, R, Arg 2(R), W 2, SA 1, 2, 1997 I, W, E, S, It 2(R), R 2, Arg, SA 1, 2, 1998 E, S, I, W, Arg 1, 2, Fj, Arg 3, A, 1999 W 2, [C, Nm, Arg (R), NZ 2(R), A (t&R)], 2000 I, 2001 E, SA 1, 2, NZ
Gomès, A (SF) 1998 Arg 1, 2, Fj, Arg 3, A, 1999 I (R)
Gommes, J (RCF) 1909 I
Gonnet, C-A (Albi) 1921 E, I, 1922 E, W, 1924 S, E, 1926 S, I, E, W, M, 1927 I, S, W, E, G 1
Gonzalez, J-M (Bayonne) 1992 Arg 1, 2, SA 1, 2, Arg, 1993 R 1, SA 1, 2, R 2, A 1, 2, 1994 I, W, E, S, C 1, NZ 1, 2, C 2, 1995 W, E, S, I, R 1, [Tg, S, I, SA, E], It, Arg, 1996 E, S, I, W 1
Got, R (Perpignan) 1920 I, US, 1921 S, W, 1922 S, E, W, I, 1924 I, E, W, R, US
Gourdon, J-F (RCF, Bagnères) 1974 S, Arg 1, 2, R, SA 1, 2, 1975 W, E, S, I, R, 1976 S, I, W, E, 1978 E, S, 1979 W, E, S, R, 1980 I
Gourragne, J-F (Béziers) 1990 NZ 2, 1991 W 1
Goutta, B (Perpignan) 2004 C
Goyard, A (Lyon U) 1936 G 1, 2, 1937 G, It, 1938 G 1, R, G 2
Graciet, R (SBUC) 1926 I, W, 1927 S, G 1, 1929 E, 1930 W
Grandclaude, J-P (Perpignan) 2005 E(R), W(R), 2007 NZ1
Graou, S (Auch, Colomiers) 1992 Arg (R), 1993 SA 1, 2, R 2, A 2(R), 1995 R 2, Arg (t), NZ 2(R)
Gratton, J (Agen) 1984 NZ 2, R, 1985 E, S, I, W, Arg 1, 2, 1986 S, NZ 1
Graule, V (Arl Perpignan) 1926 I, E, W, 1927 S, W, 1931 G
Greffe, M (Grenoble) 1968 W, Cz, NZ 1, 2, SA 1
Griffard, J (Lyon U) 1932 G, 1933 G, 1934 G
Gruarin, A (Toulon) 1964 W, It, I, SA, Fj, R, 1965 S, I, E, W, It, 1966 S, I, E, W, It, R, 1967 S, A, E, It, W, I, NZ, 1968 S, I
Guélorget, P (RCF) 1931 E, G
Guichemerre, A (Dax) 1920 E, 1921 E, I, 1923 S
Guilbert, A (Toulon) 1975 E, S, I, SA 1, 2, 1976 A 1, 1977 Arg 1, 2, NZ 1, 2, R, 1979 I, W, E
Guillemin, P (RCF) 1908 E, W, 1909 E, I, 1910 W, S, E, I, 1911 S, E, W
Guilleux, P (Agen) 1952 SA, It
Guirado, G (Perpignan) 2008 It(R), 2009 A(R), Sm(R), 2010 SA(R), Arg1(R), Fj, Arg2(R), A(R), 2011 S(R), E(R), It(R), W(R), I2(R), 3(R), [C(R)]
Guiral, M (Agen) 1931 G, 1932 G, 1933 G
Guiraud, H (Nîmes) 1996 R

Haget, A (PUC) 1953 E, 1954 I, NZ, E, Arg 2, 1955 E, W, It, 1957 I, E, It, R 1, 1958 It, SA 2
Haget, F (Agen, Biarritz O) 1974 Arg 1, 2, 1975 SA 2, Arg 1, 2, R, 1976 S, 1978 S, I, W, R, 1979 I, W, E, S, NZ 1, 2, R, 1980 W, S, I, 1984 S, NZ 1, 2, R, 1985 E, S, I, 1986 S, I, W, E, R 1, Arg 1, A, NZ 1, 1987 S, I, [R, Fj]

Haget, H (CASG) 1928 S, 1930 G
Halet, R (Strasbourg) 1925 NZ, S, W
Hall, S (Béziers) 2002 It, W
Harinordoquy, I (Pau, Biarritz) 2002 W, E, S, I, A 1, 2, SA, NZ, C, 2003 E 1, S, I, It, W, Arg 1(R), 2, NZ, R, E 2, 3(R), [Fj, S, I, E], 2004 I, It, W, E, A, Arg, NZ, 2005 W(R), 2006 R(R), SA, 2007 It(R), I, W1(R), E1(R), S, E3, W2, [Arg 1, Nm(R), NZ(R), E(R), Arg 2], 2008 A1, 2, Arg, PI, A3, 2009 I, S, W, E, It, SA, 2010 S, I, W, It, E, Fj, Arg2(R), 2011 S, I1, E, It(R), W, I2, [J, C(R), NZ1(R), Tg(R), E, W, NZ2]
Harislur-Arthapignet, P (Tarbes) 1988 Arg 4(R)
Harize, D (Cahors, Toulouse) 1975 SA 1, 2, 1976 A 1, 2, R, 1977 W, E, S, I
Hauc, J (Toulon) 1928 E, G, 1929 I, S, G
Hauser, M (Lourdes) 1969 E
Hedembaigt, M (Bayonne) 1913 S, SA, 1914 W
Hericé, D (Bègles) 1950 I
Herrero, A (Toulon) 1963 R, 1964 NZ, E, W, It, I, SA, Fj, R, 1965 S, I, E, W, 1966 W, It, R, 1967 S, A, E, It, I, R
Herrero, B (Nice) 1983 I, 1986 Arg 1
Heyer, F (Montferrand) 1990 A 2
Heymans, C (Agen, Toulouse, Bayonne) 2000 It (R) R, 2002 A 2(R), SA, NZ, 2004 W(R), US, C(R), A, Arg, NZ, 2005 I, It, SA1, 2, A1, 2, C, SA3, 2006 S, I, W(R), R, SA, NZ2, Arg, 2007 It, I(R), E1(R), S, E3, W2, [Arg 1, Nm, I, NZ, E], 2008 S, I, E, W(R), Arg, PI, A3, 2009 I(R), S, W, E, It, NZ1, 2, A, SA, NZ3(R), 2011 I3, [J, NZ1(R), Tg(R), E(R)]
Hiquet, J-C (Agen) 1964 E
Hoche, M (PUC) 1957 I, E, W, It, R 1
Hondagné-Monge, M (Tarbes) 1988 Arg 2(R)
Hontas, P (Biarritz) 1990 S, I, R, 1991 R, 1992 Arg, 1993 E, S, I, W
Hortoland, J-P (Béziers) 1971 A 2
Houblain, H (SCUF) 1909 E, 1910 W
Houdet, R (SF) 1927 S, W, G 1, 1928 G, W, 1929 I, S, E, 1930 S, E
Hourdebaigt, A (SBUC) 1909 I, 1910 W, S, E, I
Hubert, A (ASF) 1906 E, 1907 E, 1908 E, W, 1909 E, W, I
Hueber, A (Lourdes, Toulon) 1990 A 3, NZ 1, 1991 US 2, 1992 I, Arg 1, 2, SA 1, 2, 1993 E, S, I, W, R 1, SA 1, 2, R 2, A 1, 2, 1995 [Tg, S (R), I], 2000 It, R
Huget, Y (Bayonne) 2010 Arg2, A, 2011 S, I1, E, It, W(R)
Hutin, R (CASG) 1927 I, S, W
Hyardet, A (Castres) 1995 It, Arg (R)

Ibañez, R (Dax, Perpignan, Castres, Saracens, Wasps) 1996 W 1(R), 1997 It 1(R), R 1, It 2(R), R 2, SA 2(R), 1998 E, S, I, W, Arg 1, 2, Fj, Arg 3, A, 1999 I, W 1, E, S, R, WS, Tg (R), NZ 1, W 2, [C, Nm, Fj, Arg, NZ 2, A], 2000 W (R), E (R), S (R), I (R), It (R), R, 2001 S, I, It, W, E, SA 1, 2, NZ (R), SA 3, A, Fj, 2002 It (R), W, E, S, I, Arg, A 1(R), 2, SA, NZ, C, 2003 E 1, S, I, It, W, R (R), E 2(R), 3, [Fj, J(R), S, I, E, NZ(R)], 2005 C(R), Tg, 2006 I, It, E, W, R, SA(R), NZ1(R), 2, Arg, 2007 It, I, W1, E1, S, NZ1(R), 2(R), E2, 3, [Arg 1, Nm(R), I, NZ, E, Arg 2]
Icard, J (SF) 1909 E, W
Iguiniz, E (Bayonne) 1914 E
Ihingoué, D (BEC) 1912 I, S
Imbernon, J-F (Perpignan) 1976 I, W, E, US, A 1, 1977 W, E, S, I, Arg 1, 2, NZ 1, 2, 1978 E, R, 1979 I, 1981 S, I, W, E, 1982 I, 1983 I, W
Iraçabal, J (Bayonne) 1968 NZ 1, 2, SA 1, 1969 S, I, W, R, 1970 S, I, W, E, R, 1971 W, SA 1, 2, A 1, 1972 E, W, I 2, A 2, R, 1973 S, NZ, E, W, I, J, 1974 I, W, E, S, Arg 1, 2, SA 2(R)
Isaac, H (RCF) 1907 E, 1908 E
Ithurra, E (Biarritz O) 1936 G 1, 2, 1937 G

Jacquet, L (Clermont-Auvergne) 2006 NZ2(R), Arg, 2008 S, I(t&R)
Janeczek, T (Tarbes) 1982 Arg 1, 2, 1990 R
Janik, K (Toulouse) 1987 R
Janin, D (Bourgoin) 2008 A1(R), 2
Jarasse, A (Brive) 1945 B 1
Jardel, J (SB) 1928 I, E
Jauréguy, A (RCF, Toulouse, SF) 1920 S, E, W, I, US, 1922 S, W, 1923 S, W, E, I, 1924 S, W, R, US, 1925 I, NZ, 1926 S, E, W, M, 1927 I, E, 1928 S, A, E, G, W, 1929 I, S, E
Jauréguy, P (Toulouse) 1913 S, SA, W, I
Jauzion, Y (Colomiers, Toulouse) 2001 SA 1, 2, NZ, 2002 A 1(R), 2(R), 2003 Arg 2, NZ, R, E 2, 3, [Fj, S, I, E], 2004 I, It, W, S, E, A, Arg, NZ(t), 2005 W, I, It, SA1, 2, A1, 2, C, Tg(R), SA3, 2006 R, SA, NZ1, 2, Arg, 2007 It, I, W1, E1, S, E3, W2, [Arg 1, Nm(R), I(R), Gg, NZ, E], 2008 It, W, Arg, PI, A3, 2009 I, S, W, E, It, NZ1(R), Sm, NZ3, 2010 S, I, W, It, E, Arg2, A, 2011 I1(R), E, It
Jeangrand, M-H (Tarbes) 1921 I
Jeanjean, N (Toulouse) 2001 SA 1, 2, NZ, SA 3(R), A (R), Fj (R), 2002 It, Arg, A 1
Jeanjean, P (Toulon) 1948 I
Jérôme, G (SF) 1906 NZ, E
Joinel, J-L (Brive) 1977 NZ 1, 1978 R, 1979 I, W, E, S, NZ 1, 2, R, 1980 W, E, S, I, SA, 1981 S, I, W, E, R, NZ 1, 2, 1982 E, S, I, R, 1983 E, S, I, W, A 1, 2, R, 1984 I, W, E, S, NZ 1, 2, 1985 S, I, W, Arg 1, 1986 S, I, W, E, R 1, Arg 1, 2, A, 1987 [Z]
Jol, M (Biarritz O) 1947 S, I, W, E, 1949 S, I, E, W, Arg 1, 2
Jordana, J-L (Pau, Toulouse) 1996 R (R), Arg 1(t), 2, W 2, 1997 I (t), W, S (R)
Judas du Souich, C (SCUF) 1911 W, I
Juillet, C (Montferrand, SF) 1995 R 2, Arg, 1999 E, S, WS, NZ 1, [C, Fj, Arg, NZ 2, A], 2000 A, NZ 1, 2, 2001 S, I, It, W
Junquas, L (Tyrosse) 1945 B 1, 2, W, 1946 B, I, K, W, 1947 S, I, W, E, 1948 S, W

Kaczorowski, D (Le Creusot) 1974 I (R)
Kaempf, A (St Jean-de-Luz) 1946 B
Kayser, B (Leicester) 2008 A1(R), 2(R), Arg(R), PI(R), A3(R), 2009 I(R), S(R), W(R), E(R)

Labadie, P (Bayonne) 1952 S, I, SA, W, E, It, 1953 S, I, It, 1954 S, I, NZ, W, E, Arg 2, 1955 S, I, E, W, 1956 I, 1957 I
Labarthète, R (Pau) 1952 S
Labazuy, A (Lourdes) 1952 I, 1954 S, W, 1956 E, 1958 A, W, I, 1959 S, E, It, W
Labit, C (Toulouse) 1999 S, R (R), WS (R), Tg, 2000 R (R), 2002 Arg, A 1(R), 2003 Arg 1, 2, NZ (R), R (R), E 3, [Fj(R), J, US, E(R), NZ]
Laborde, C (RCF) 1962 It, R, 1963 R, 1964 SA, 1965 E
Labrousse, T (Brive) 1996 R, SA 1
Lacans, P (Béziers) 1980 SA, 1981 W, E, A 2, R, 1982 W
Lacassagne, H (SBUC) 1906 NZ, 1907 E
Lacaussade, R (Bègles) 1948 A, S
Lacaze, C (Lourdes, Angoulême) 1961 NZ 2, 3, A, R, 1962 E, W, I, It, 1963 W, R, 1964 S, NZ, E, 1965 It, R, 1966 S, I, E, W, It, R, 1967 S, E, SA 1, 3, 4, R, 1968 S, E, W, Cz, NZ 1, 1969 E
Lacaze, H (Périgueux) 1928 I, G, W, 1929 I, W
Lacaze, P (Lourdes) 1958 SA 1, 2, 1959 S, E, It, W, I
Lacazedieu, C (Dax) 1923 W, I, 1928 A, I, 1929 S
Lacombe, B (Agen) 1989 B, 1990 A 2
Lacome, M (Pau) 1960 Arg 2
Lacoste, R (Tarbes) 1914 I, W, E
Lacrampe, F (Béziers) 1949 Arg 2
Lacroix, P (Mont-de-Marsan, Agen) 1958 A, 1960 W, I, It, R, Arg 1, 2, 3, 1961 S, SA, E, W, I, NZ 1, 2, 3, A, R, 1962 S, E, W, I, R, 1963 S, I, E, W
Lacroix, T (Dax, Harlequins) 1989 A 1(R), 2, 1991 W 1(R), 2(R), [R, C (R), E], 1992 SA 2, 1993 E, S, I, W, SA 1, 2, R 2, A 1, 2, 1994 I, W, E, S, C 1, NZ 1, 2, C 2, 1995 W, E, S, R 1, [Tg, Iv, S, I, SA, E], 1996 E, S, I, 1997 It 2, R 2, Arg, SA 1, 2
Lacroix, T (Albi) 2008 A1(R), 2
Lafarge, Y (Montferrand) 1978 R, 1979 NZ 1, 1981 I (R)
Laffitte, R (SCUF) 1910 W, S
Laffont, H (Narbonne) 1926 W
Lafond, A (Bayonne) 1922 E
Lafond, J-B (RCF) 1983 A 1, 1985 Arg 1, 2 1986 S, I, W, E, R 1, 1987 I (R), 1988 W, 1989 I, W, E, 1990 W, A 3(R), NZ 2, 1991 S, I, W 1, E, R, US 1, W 2, [R (R), Fj, C, E], 1992 W, E, S, I (R), SA 2, 1993 E, S, I, W
Lagisquet, P (Bayonne) 1983 A 1, 2, R, 1984 I, W, NZ 1, 2, 1986 R 1(R), Arg 1, 2, A, NZ 1, 1987 [S, R, Fj, A, NZ], R, 1988 S, I, W, Arg 1, 2, 3, 4, R, 1989 I, W, E, S, NZ 1, 2, B, A 1, 2, 1990 W, E, S, I, A 1, 2, 3, 1991 S, I, US 2, [R]

Lagrange, J-C (RCF) 1966 It
Laharrague, J (Brive, Perpignan, Sale) 2005 W, I, It, SA1, A1, 2, C(R), Tg, 2006 R(R), SA, NZ1, 2007 NZ2
Laharrague, N (Perpignan) 2007 NZ1(R), 2(R)
Lakafia, R (Biarritz) 2011 I2, [J, Tg]
Lalande, M (RCF) 1923 S, W, I
Lalanne, F (Mont-de-Marsan) 2000 R
Lamaison, C (Brive, Agen) 1996 SA 1(R), 2, 1997 W, E, S, R 1, A 2, It 2, R 2, Arg, SA 1, 2, 1998 E, S, I, W, Arg 3(R), A, 1999 R, WS (R), Tg, NZ 1(R), W 2(R), [C (R), Nm, Fj, Arg, NZ 2, A], 2000 W, A, NZ 1, 2, 2001 S, I, It, W (R)
Lamboley, G (Toulouse) 2005 S(R), E(R), W(R), I(R), It(R), SA1(R), 2(R), A1, 2(R), C(R), Tg, SA3(R), 2007 W1(R), 2010 Arg1(R)
Landreau, F (SF) 2000 A, NZ 1, 2, 2001 E (R)
Lane, G (RCF) 1906 NZ, E, 1907 E, 1908 E, W, 1909 E, W, I, 1910 W, E, 1911 S, W, 1912 I, W, E, 1913 S
Langlade, J-C (Hyères) 1990 R, A 1, NZ 1
Lapandry, A (Clermont-Auvergne) 2009 Sm, 2010 W(R), It(R), E(R), Fj, 2011 W(R)
Laperne, D (Dax) 1997 R 1(R)
Laporte, G (Graulhet) 1981 I, W, E, R, NZ 1, 2, 1986 S, I, W, E, R 1, Arg 1, A (R), 1987 [R, Z (R), Fj]
Larreguy, G (Bayonne) 1954 It
Larribau, J (Périgueux) 1912 I, S, W, E, 1913 S, 1914 I, E
Larrieu, J (Tarbes) 1920 I, US, 1921 W, 1923 S, W, E, I
Larrieux, M (SBUC) 1927 G 2
Larrue, H (Carmaux) 1960 W, I, It, R, Arg 1, 2, 3
Lasaosa, P (Dax) 1950 I, 1952 S, I, E, It, 1955 It
Lascubé, G (Agen) 1991 S, I, W 1, E, US 2, W 2, [R, Fj, C, E], 1992 W, E
Lassegue, J-B (Toulouse) 1946 W, 1947 S, I, W, 1948 W, 1949 I, E, W, Arg 1
Lasserre, F (René) (Bayonne, Cognac, Grenoble) 1914 I, 1920 S, 1921 S, W, I, 1922 S, E, W, I, 1923 W, E, 1924 S, I, R, US
Lasserre, J-C (Dax) 1963 It, 1964 S, NZ, E, W, It, I, Fj, 1965 W, It, R, 1966 R, 1967 S
Lasserre, M (Agen) 1967 SA 2, 3, 1968 E, W, Cz, NZ 3, A, SA 1, 2, 1969 S, I, E, 1970 E, 1971 E, W
Laterrade, G (Tarbes) 1910 E, I, 1911 S, E, I
Laudouar, J (Soustons, SBUC) 1961 NZ 1, 2, R, 1962 I, R
Lauga, P (Vichy) 1950 S, I, E, W
Laurent, A (Biarritz O) 1925 NZ, S, W, E, 1926 W
Laurent, J (Bayonne) 1920 S, E, W
Laurent, M (Auch) 1932 G, 1933 G, 1934 G, 1935 G, 1936 G 1
Lauret, W (Biarritz) 2010 SA
Laussucq, C (SF) 1999 S (R), 2000 W (R), S, I
Lavail, G (Perpignan) 1937 G, 1940 B
Lavaud, R (Carcassonne) 1914 I, W
Lavergne, P (Limoges) 1950 S
Lavigne, B (Agen) 1984 R, 1985 E
Lavigne, J (Dax) 1920 E, W
Laziès, H (Auch) 1954 Arg 2, 1955 It, 1956 E, 1957 S
Le Bourhis, R (La Rochelle) 1961 R
Lecointre, M (Nantes) 1952 It
Le Corvec, G (Perpignan) 2007 NZ1
Lecouls, B (Biarritz) 2008 A1, 2(R), Arg, PI(R), A3(R), 2009 I
Le Droff, J (Auch) 1963 It, R, 1964 S, NZ, E, 1970 E, R, 1971 S, I
Lefèvre, R (Brive) 1961 NZ 2
Leflamand, L (Bourgoin) 1996 SA 2, 1997 W, E, S, It 2, Arg, SA 1, 2(R)
Lefort, J-B (Biarritz O) 1938 G 1
Le Goff, R (Métro) 1938 R, G 2
Legrain, M (SF) 1909 I, 1910 I, 1911 S, E, W, I, 1913 S, SA, E, I, 1914 I, W
Lemeur, Y (RCF) 1993 R 1
Lenient, J-J (Vichy) 1967 R
Lepatey, J (Mazamet) 1954 It, 1955 S, I, E, W
Lepatey, L (Mazamet) 1924 S, I, E
Lescarboura, J-P (Dax) 1982 W, E, S, I, 1983 A 1, 2, R, 1984 I, W, E, S, NZ 1, 2, R, 1985 E, S, I, W, Arg 1, 2, 1986 Arg 2, A, NZ 1, R 2, NZ 2, 1988 S, W, 1990 R
Lesieur, E (SF) 1906 E, 1908 E, W, 1909 E, W, I, 1910 S, E, I, 1911 E, I, 1912 W
Leuvielle, M (SBUC) 1908 W, 1913 S, SA, E, W, 1914 W, E
Levasseur, R (SF) 1925 W, E
Levée, H (RCF) 1906 NZ
Lewis, E W (Le Havre) 1906 E
Lhermet, J-M (Montferrand) 1990 S, I, 1993 R 1
Libaros, G (Tarbes) 1936 G 1, 1940 B
Liebenberg, B (SF) 2003 R (R), E 2(R), 3, [US, I(R), NZ(R)], 2004 I(R), US, C, NZ, 2005 S, E
Lièvremont, M (Perpignan, SF) 1995 It, R 2, Arg (R), NZ 2(R), 1996 R, Arg 1(R), SA 2(R), 1997 R 1, A 2(R), 1998 E (R), S, I, W, Arg 1, 2, Fj, Arg 3, A, 1999 W 2, [C, Nm, Fj, Arg, NZ 2, A]
Lièvremont, M (Dax) 2008 A1(R), 2
Lièvremont, T (Perpignan, SF, Biarritz) 1996 W 2(R), 1998 E, S, I, W, Arg 1, 2, Fj, Arg 3, A, 1999 I, W 1, E, W 2, [Nm], 2000 W (R), E (R), S (R), I, It, 2001 E (R), 2004 I(R), It(R), W, S, US, C, 2005 A2, C, Tg(t&R), SA3(R), 2006 S(R), It, E, W
Lira, M (La Voulte) 1962 R, 1963 I, E, W, It, R, 1964 W, It, I, SA, 1965 S, I, R
Llari, R (Carcassonne) 1926 S
Lobies, J (RCF) 1921 S, W, E
Lombard, F (Narbonne) 1934 G, 1937 It
Lombard, T (SF) 1998 Arg 3, A, 1999 I, W 1, S (R), 2000 W, E, S, A, NZ 1, 2001 It, W
Lombarteix, R (Montferrand) 1938 R, G 2
Londios, J (Montauban) 1967 SA 3
Loppy, L (Toulon) 1993 R 2
Lorieux, A (Grenoble, Aix) 1981 A 1, R, NZ 1, 2, 1982 W, 1983 A 2, R, 1984 I, W, E, 1985 Arg 1, 2(R), 1986 R 2, NZ 2, 3, 1987 W, E, [S, Z, Fj, A, NZ], 1988 S, I, W, Arg 1, 2, 4, 1989 W, A 2
Loury, A (RCF) 1927 E, G 1, 2, 1928 S, A, I
Loustau, L (Perpignan) 2004 C
Loustau, M (Dax) 1923 E
Lubin-Lebrère, M-F (Toulouse) 1914 I, W, E, 1920 S, E, W, I, US, 1921 S, 1922 S, E, W, 1924 W, US, 1925 I
Lubrano, A (Béziers) 1972 A 2, 1973 S
Lux, J-P (Tyrosse, Dax) 1967 E, It, W, I, SA 1, 2, 4, R, 1968 I, E, Cz, NZ 3, A, SA 1, 2, 1969 S, I, E, 1970 S, I, W, E, R, 1971 S, I, E, W, A 1, 2, 1972 S, I 1, E, W, I 2, A 1, 2, R, 1973 S, NZ, E, 1974 I, W, E, S, Arg 1, 2, 1975 W

Macabiau, A (Perpignan) 1994 S, C 1
Maclos, P (SF) 1906 E, 1907 E
Magne, O (Dax, Brive, Montferrand, Clermont-Auvergne, London Irish) 1997 W (R), E, S, R 1(R), A 1, 2, It 2(R), R 2, Arg (R), 1998 E, S, I, W, Arg 1, 2, Fj, Arg 3, A, 1999 I, R, WS, NZ 1, W 2, [C, Nm, Fj, Arg, NZ 2, A], 2000 W, E, S, It, R, A, NZ 1, 2, 2001 S, I, It, W, E, SA 1, 2, NZ, SA 3, A, Fj, 2002 It, E, S, I, Arg, A 1, 2(R), SA, NZ, C, 2003 E 1, S, I, It, W, R, E 2, 3(R), [Fj, J, S, I, E, NZ(R)], 2004 I, It, W(R), S, E, A, Arg, NZ, 2005 SA1, 2(R), A1, 2006 I, It, E, W(R), 2007 NZ1, 2
Magnanou, C (RCF) 1923 E, 1925 W, E, 1926 S, 1929 S, W, 1930 S, I, E, W
Magnol, L (Toulouse) 1928 S, 1929 S, W, E
Magois, H (La Rochelle) 1968 SA 1, 2, R
Majérus, R (SF) 1928 W, 1929 I, S, 1930 S, I, E, G, W
Malbet, J-C (Agen) 1967 SA 2, 4
Maleig, A (Oloron) 1979 W, E, NZ 2, 1980 W, E, SA, R
Mallier, L (Brive) 1999 R, W 2(R), [C (R)], 2000 I (R), It
Malquier, Y (Narbonne) 1979 S
Malzieu, J (Clermont-Auvergne) 2008 S, It, W, Arg, PI, A3, 2009 I, S(R), W, E, It(R), 2010 I(R), W, It(R), E(R), Arg1
Manterola, T (Lourdes) 1955 It, 1957 R 1
Mantoulan, C (Pau) 1959 I
Marcet, J (Albi) 1925 I, NZ, S, W, E, 1926 I, E
Marchal, J-F (Lourdes) 1979 S, R, 1980 W, S, I
Marconnet, S (SF, Biarritz) 1998 Arg 3, A, 1999 I (R), W 1(R), E, S (R), R, Tg, 2000 A, NZ 1, 2, 2001 S, I, It (R), W (R), E, 2002 S (R), Arg (R), A 1, 2, SA (R), C (R), 2003 E1(R), S, I, It, W, Arg 1(t+R), 2, NZ, R, E 2, 3(t+R), [S, US(R), I, E, NZ], 2004 I, It, W, S, E, A, Arg, NZ, 2005 S, E, W, I, It, SA1, 2, A1(R), 2(R), C, Tg, SA3(R), 2006 S, I(R), It(R), E, W, R, SA, NZ1, 2(R), Arg(R), 2007 It(R), I, W1(R), 2009 W, E, It, NZ1, A, SA(R), Sm, NZ3, 2010 I(R), 2011 I1(R), E(R), It, I2
Marchand, R (Poitiers) 1920 S, W

Marfaing, M (Toulouse) 1992 R, Arg 1
Marlu, J (Montferrand, Biarritz) 1998 Fj (R), 2002 S (R), I (R), 2005 E
Marocco, P (Montferrand) 1968 S, I, W, E, R 1, Arg 1, 2, A, 1988 Arg 4, 1989 I, 1990 E (R), NZ 1(R), 1991 S, I, W 1, E, US 2, [R, Fj, C, E]
Marot, A (Brive) 1969 R, 1970 S, I, W, 1971 SA 1, 1972 I 2, 1976 A 1
Marquesuzaa, A (RCF) 1958 It, SA 1, 2, 1959 S, E, It, W, 1960 S, E, Arg 1
Marracq, H (Pau) 1961 R
Marsh, T (Montferrand) 2001 SA 3, A, Fj, 2002 It, W, E, S, I, Arg, A 1, 2, 2003 [Fj, J, S, I, E, NZ], 2004 C, A, Arg, NZ
Martin, C (Lyon) 1909 I, 1910 W, S
Martin, H (SBUC) 1907 E, 1908 W
Martin, J-L (Béziers) 1971 A 2, R, 1972 S, I 1
Martin, L (Pau) 1948 I, A, S, W, E, 1950 S
Martin, R (SF, Bayonne) 2002 E (t+R), S (R), I (R), 2005 SA1(t&R), 2, A1, 2, C, SA3, 2006 S, I(t&R), R, SA(R), NZ1(R), 2, Arg, 2007 E2, W2, [Arg 1, Gg(R), Arg 2(R)], 2009 NZ2(R), A(R)
Martine, R (Lourdes) 1952 S, I, It, 1953 It, 1954 S, I, NZ, W, E, It, Arg 2, 1955 S, I, W, 1958 A, W, It, I, SA 1, 2, 1960 S, E, Arg 3, 1961 S, It
Martinez, A (Narbonne) 2002 A 1, 2004 C
Martinez, G (Toulouse) 1982 W, E, S, Arg 1, 2, 1983 E, W
Marty, D (Perpignan) 2005 It, C, Tg, 2006 I, It(R), R(R), NZ1(R), Arg(R), 2007 I, W1, E1, S, E2, [Nm, I, Gg, NZ, E, Arg 2], 2008 S, I, E, 2009 SA(R), Sm, NZ3, 2010 S(R), I(R), W(R), It, E(R), SA, Fj, 2011 W, I2, [J(R), C, E(R)]
Mas, F (Béziers) 1962 R, 1963 S, I, E, W
Mas, N (Perpignan) 2003 NZ, 2005 E, W, I, It, 2007 W1, NZ1, 2(R), E2(R), 3(R), W2, [Nm(R), Gg(R), Arg 2], 2008 S(R), I, E, It, W, Arg(R), PI, A3, 2009 I(R), S, NZ1(R), 2, A(R), SA, Sm(R), NZ3(R), 2010 S, I, W, It, E, SA, Arg1, 2, A, 2011 S, I1, E, It, W, I3, [J, E, W, NZ2]
Maso, J (Perpignan, Narbonne) 1966 It, R, 1967 S, R, 1968 S, W, Cz, NZ 1, 2, 3, A, R, 1969 S, I, W, 1971 SA 1, 2, R, 1972 E, W, A 2, 1973 W, I, J, R
Massare, J (PUC) 1945 B 1, 2, W, 1946 B, I, W
Massé, A (SBUC) 1908 W, 1909 E, W, 1910 W, S, E, I
Masse, H (Grenoble) 1937 G
Matheu-Cambas, J (Agen) 1945 W, 1946 B, I, K, W, 1947 S, I, W, E, 1948 I, A, S, W, E, 1949 S, I, E, W, Arg 1, 2, 1950 E, W, 1951 S, I
Matiu, L (Biarritz) 2000 W, E
Mauduy, G (Périgueux) 1957 It, R 1, 2, 1958 S, E, 1961 W, It
Mauran, J (Castres) 1952 SA, W, E, It, 1953 I, E
Mauriat, P (Lyon) 1907 E, 1908 E, W, 1909 W, I, 1910 W, S, E, I, 1911 S, E, W, I, 1912 I, S, 1913 S, SA, W, I
Maurin, G (ASF) 1906 E
Maury, A (Toulouse) 1925 I, NZ, S, W, E, 1926 S, I, E
Mayssonnié, A (Toulouse) 1908 E, W, 1910 W
Mazars, L (Narbonne, Bayonne) 2007 NZ2, 2010 Arg1
Mazas, L (Colomiers, Biarritz) 1992 Arg, 1996 SA 1
Médard, M (Toulouse) 2008 Arg, PI, A3, 2009 I, S, W, E, It, NZ1, 2, A, SA(R), Sm, NZ3, 2010 Fj, 2011 S, I1, It, W, I2(R), 3, [J, C(R), NZ1, Tg, E, W, NZ2]
Mela, A (Albi) 2008 S(R), I, It(R), W(R)
Melville, E (Toulon) 1990 I (R), A 1, 2, 3, NZ 1, 1991 US 2
Menrath, R (SCUF) 1910 W
Menthiller, Y (Romans) 1964 W, It, SA, R, 1965 E
Merceron, G (Montferrand) 1999 R (R), Tg, 2000 S, I, R, 2001 S (R), W, E, SA 1, 2, NZ (R), Fj, 2002 It, W, E, S, I, Arg, A 2, C, 2003 E 1, It (R), W (R), NZ (t+R), R (R), E 3, [Fj(R), J(R), S(R), US, E(R), NZ]
Meret, F (Tarbes) 1940 B
Mericq, S (Agen) 1959 I, 1960 S, E, W, 1961 I
Merle, O (Grenoble, Montferrand) 1993 SA 1, 2, R 2, A 1, 2, 1994 I, W, E, S, C 1, NZ 1, 2, C 2, 1995 W, I, R 1, [Tg, S, I, SA, E], It, R 2, Arg, NZ 1, 2, 1996 E, S, R, Arg 1, 2, W 2, SA 2, 1997 I, W, E, S, It 1, R 1, A 1, 2, It 2, R 2, SA 1(R), 2
Mermoz, M (Toulouse, Perpignan) 2008 A2, 2009 S(R), NZ2, A, SA, 2010 SA, Arg1(R), 2011 S, I2, [C, NZ1, Tg, E, W, NZ2]
Merquey, J (Toulon) 1950 S, I, E, W
Mesnel, F (RCF) 1986 NZ 2(R), 3, 1987 W, E, S, I, [S, Z, Fj, A, NZ], R, 1988 E, Arg 1, 2, 3, 4, R, 1989 I, W, E, S, NZ 1, A 1, 2, 1990 E, S, I, A 2, 3, NZ 1, 2, 1991 S, I, W 1, E, R, US 1, 2, W 2, [R, Fj, C, E], 1992 W, E, S, I, SA 1, 2, 1993 E (R), W, 1995 I, R 1, [Iv, E]
Mesny, P (RCF, Grenoble) 1979 NZ 1, 2, 1980 SA, R, 1981 I, W (R), A 1, 2, R, NZ 1, 2, 1982 I, Arg 1, 2
Meyer, G-S (Périgueux) 1960 S, E, It, R, Arg 2
Meynard, J (Cognac) 1954 Arg 1, 1956 Cz
Mias, L (Mazamet) 1951 S, I, E, W, 1952 I, SA, W, E, It, 1953 S, I, W, It, 1954 S, I, NZ, W, 1957 R 2, 1958 S, E, A, W, I, SA 1, 2, 1959 S, It, W, I
Michalak, F (Toulouse) 2001 SA 3(R), A, Fj (R), 2002 It, A 1, 2, 2003 It, W, Arg 2(R), NZ, R, E 2, [Fj, J, S, I, E, NZ(R)], 2004 I, W, S, E, A, Arg, NZ, 2005 S(R), E(R), W(R), I(R), It(R), SA1, 2, A1, 2, C, Tg(R), SA3, 2006 S, I, It, E, W, 2007 E2(R), 3, [Arg1(t&R), Nm, I, NZ(R), E(R), Arg 2], 2009 It(R), 2010 S(R), I(R), W(R)
Mignardi, A (Agen) 2007 NZ1, 2
Mignoni, P (Béziers, Clermont-Auvergne) 1997 R 2(R), Arg (t), 1999 R (R), WS, NZ 1, W 2(R), [C, Nm], 2002 W, E (R), I (R), Arg, A 2(R), 2005 S, It(R), C(R), 2006 R, 2007 It, I, W1, E1(R), S, E2, 3(R), W2, [Arg 1, Gg, Arg 2(R)]
Milhères, C (Biarritz) 2001 E
Milliand, P (Grenoble) 1936 G 2, 1937 G, It
Millo-Chluski, R (Toulouse) 2005 SA1, 2008 Arg, PI, A3(R), 2009 I(R), S, W(R), NZ1, 2, A, SA, Sm(R), NZ3, 2010 SA, Fj, A(R), 2011 I2, [C]
Milloud, O (Bourgoin) 2000 R (R), 2001 NZ, 2002 W (R), E (R), 2003 It (R), W (R), Arg 1, R (R), E 2(t+R), 3, [J, S(R), US, I(R), E(R)], 2004 US, C(R), A, Arg, NZ(R), 2005 S(R), E(R), W(R), SA1, 2(R), A1, 2, C(R), Tg, SA3, 2006 S(R), I, It, E(R), W(R), NZ1(R), 2, Arg, 2007 It, I(R), W1, E1, S, E2, 3, [Arg 1, I, Gg, NZ, E]
Minjat, R (Lyon) 1945 B 1
Miorin, H (Toulouse) 1996 R, SA 1, 1997 I, W, E, S, It 1, 2000 It (R), R (R)
Mir, J-H (Lourdes) 1967 R, 1968 I
Mir, J-P (Lourdes) 1967 A
Modin, R (Brive) 1987 [Z]
Moga, A-M-A (Bègles) 1945 B 1, 2, W, 1946 B, I, K, W, 1947 S, I, W, E, 1948 I, A, S, W, E, 1949 S, I, E, W, Arg 1, 2
Mola, U (Dax, Castres) 1997 S (R), 1999 R (R), WS, Tg (R), NZ 1, W 2, [C, Nm, Fj, Arg (R), NZ 2(R), A (R)]
Amméjat, B (Cahors, Albi) 1958 It, I, SA 1, 2, 1959 S, E, It, W, I, 1960 S, E, I, R, 1962 S, E, W, I, It, R, 1963 S, I, W
Moncla, F (RCF, Pau) 1956 Cz, 1957 I, E, W, It, R 1, 1958 SA 1, 2, 1959 S, E, It, W, I, 1960 S, E, W, I, It, R, Arg 1, 2, 3, 1961 S, SA, E, W, It, I, NZ 1, 2, 3
Moni, C (Nice, SF) 1996 R, 2000 A, NZ 1, 2, 2001 S, I, It, W
Monié, R (Perpignan) 1956 Cz, 1957 E
Monier, R (SBUC) 1911 I, 1912 S
Monniot, M (RCF) 1912 W, E
Montade, A (Perpignan) 1925 I, NZ, S, W, 1926 W
Montanella, F (Auch) 2007 NZ1(R)
Montlaur, P (Agen) 1992 E (R), 1994 S (R)
Moraitis, B (Toulon) 1969 E, W
Morel, A (Grenoble) 1954 Arg 2
Morère, J (Toulouse) 1927 E, G 1, 1928 S, A
Moscato, V (Bègles) 1991 R, US 1, 1992 W, E
Mougeot, C (Bègles) 1992 W, E, Arg
Mouniq, P (Toulouse) 1911 S, E, W, I, 1912 I, E, 1913 S, SA, E
Moure, H (SCUF) 1908 E
Moureu, P (Béziers) 1920 I, US, 1921 W, E, I, 1922 S, W, I, 1923 S, W, E, I, 1924 S, I, E, W, 1925 E
Mournet, A (Bagnères) 1981 A 1(R)
Mouronval, F (SF) 1909 I
Muhr, A H (RCF) 1906 NZ, E, 1907 E
Murillo, G (Dijon) 1954 It, Arg 1

Nallet, L (Bourgoin, Castres, Racing-Metro) 2000 R, 2001 E, SA 1(R), 2(R), NZ, SA3(R), A (R), Fj (R), 2003 NZ, 2005 A2(R), C, Tg(R), SA3, 2006 I(R), It(R), E(R), W(R), R, SA(R), NZ1(R), 2, Arg, 2007 It, I, W1, E1, S, E3(R), [Nm, I(R), Gg, Arg 2], 2008 S, I, E, It, W, A1, 2, Arg, PI, A3, 2009 I, S, W, E, It, SA, NZ3(R), 2010 S, I, W, It, E, SA, Arg1, 2, 2011 S, I1, E, It, W, I2(R), 3, [J, NZ1, Tg, E, W, NZ2]

Namur, R (Toulon) 1931 E, G
Noble, J-C (La Voulte) 1968 E, W, Cz, NZ 3, A, R
Noirot, B (Racing Metro) 2010 Fj(R)
Normand, A (Toulouse) 1957 R 1
Novès, G (Toulouse) 1977 NZ 1, 2, R, 1978 W, R, 1979 I, W
Ntamack, E (Toulouse) 1994 W, C 1, NZ 1, 2, C 2, 1995 W, I, R 1, [Tg, S, I, SA, E], It, R 2, Arg, NZ 1, 2, 1996 E, S, I, W 1, R (R), Arg 1, 2, W 2, 1997 I, 1998 Arg 3, 1999 I, W 1, E, S, WS, NZ 1, W 2(R), [C (R), Nm, Fj, Arg, NZ 2, A], 2000 W, E, S, I, It
Ntamack F (Colomiers) 2001 SA 3
Nyanga, Y (Béziers, Toulouse) 2004 US, C, 2005 S(R), E(R), W, I, It, SA1, 2, A1(R), 2, C(t&R), Tg, SA3, 2006 S, I, It, E, W, 2007 E2(R), 3, [Nm, I(R), Gg, Arg 2]

Olibeau, O (Perpignan) 2007 NZ1(R), 2(R)
Olive, D (Montferrand) 1951 I, 1952 I
Ondarts, P (Biarritz O) 1986 NZ 3, 1987 W, E, S, I, [S, Z, Fj, A, NZ], R, 1988 E, I, W, Arg 1, 2, 3, 4, R, 1989 I, W, E, NZ 1, 2, A 2, 1990 W, E, S, I, R (R), NZ 1, 2, 1991 S, I, W 1, E, US 2, W 2, [R, Fj, C, E]
Orso, J-C (Nice, Toulon) 1982 Arg 1, 2, 1983 E, S, A 1, 1984 E (R), S, NZ 1, 1985 I (R), W, 1988 I
Othats, J (Dax) 1960 Arg 2, 3
Ouedraogo, F (Montpellier) 2007 NZ2(R), 2008 S, I, E(R), It, W, A1, 2, Arg(R), PI, A3, 2009 I, S, W, NZ1, 2, A, NZ3, 2010 S, I, Fj, A, 2011 I3, [C, W(R)]
Ougier, S (Toulouse) 1992 R, Arg 1, 1993 E (R), 1997 It 1

Paco, A (Béziers) 1974 Arg 1, 2, R, SA 1, 2, 1975 W, E, Arg 1, 2, R, 1976 S, I, W, E, US, A 1, 2, R, 1977 W, E, S, I, NZ 1, 2, R, 1978 E, S, I, W, R, 1979 I, W, E, S, 1980 W
Palat, J (Perpignan) 1938 G 2
Palisson, A (Brive) 2008 A1, 2, Arg(R), PI(R), A3(R), 2010 I, W, It, E, Fj(R), Arg2, A, 2011 E(R), W, I2, 3, [Tg, E, W, NZ2]
Palmié, M (Béziers) 1975 SA 1, 2, Arg 1, 2, R, 1976 S, I, W, E, US, 1977 W, E, S, I, Arg 1, 2, NZ 1, 2, R, 1978 E, S, I, W
Paoli, R (see Simonpaoli)
Paparemborde, R (Pau) 1975 SA 1, 2, Arg 1, 2, R, 1976 S, I, W, E, US, A 1, 2, R, 1977 W, E, S, I, Arg 1, NZ 1, 2, 1978 E, S, I, W, R, 1979 I, W, E, S, NZ 1, 2, R, 1980 W, E, S, SA, R, 1981 S, I, W, E, A 1, 2, R, NZ 1, 2, 1982 W, I, R, Arg 1, 2 1983 E, S, I, W
Papé, P (Bourgoin, Castres, SF) 2004 I, It, W, S, E, C, NZ(R), 2005 I(R), It(R), SA1, 2, A1, 2006 NZ1, 2, 2007 It(R), I, S(R), NZ1, 2, 2008 E, 2009 NZ1, A, Sm, 2010 S, I, Arg1, 2011 W(R), I3, [J(R), C, NZ1, Tg, E, W, NZ2]
Pardo, L (Hendaye) 1924 I, E
Pardo, L (Bayonne) 1980 SA, R, 1981 S, I, W, E, A 1, 1982 W, E, S, 1983 A 1(R), 1985 S, I, Arg 2
Pargade, J-H (Lyon U) 1953 It
Pariès, L (Biarritz O) 1968 SA 2, R, 1970 S, I, W, 1975 E, S, I
Parra, M (Bourgoin, Clermont-Auvergne) 2008 S(R), I(R), E, Arg(R), 2009 I(R), S(R), W, E, It, SA(R), Sm, NZ3(R), 2010 S, I, W, It, E, SA, Arg1, Fj(R), Arg2, A, 2011 S, I1, E(R), It, W, I2(R), 3, [J(R), C, NZ1, Tg, E, W, NZ2]
Pascalin, P (Mont-de-Marsan) 1950 I, E, W, 1951 S, I, E, W
Pascarel, J-R (TOEC) 1912 W, E, 1913 S, SA, E, I
Pascot, J (Perpignan) 1922 S, E, I, 1923 S, 1926 I, 1927 G 2
Paul, R (Montferrand) 1940 B
Pauthe, G (Graulhet) 1956 E
Pebeyre, E-J (Fumel, Brive) 1945 W, 1946 I, K, W, 1947 S, I, W, E
Pebeyre, M (Vichy, Montferrand) 1970 E, R, 1971 I, SA 1, 2, A 1, 1973 W
Péclier, A (Bourgoin) 2004 US, C
Pécune, J (Tarbes) 1974 W, E, S, 1975 Arg 1, 2, R, 1976 I, W, E, US
Pédeutour, P (Bègles) 1980 I
Pellissier, L (RCF) 1928 A, I, E, G, W
Pelous, F (Dax, Toulouse) 1995 R 2, Arg, NZ 1, 2, 1996 E, S, I, R (R), Arg 1, 2, W 2, SA 1, 2, 1997 I, W, E, S, It 1, R 1, A 1, 2, It 2, R 2, Arg, SA 1, 2(R), 1998 E, S, I, W, Arg 1, 2, Fj, Arg 3, A, 1999 I, W 1, E, R (R), WS, Tg (R), NZ 1, W 2, [C, Nm, Fj, NZ 2, A], 2000 W, E, S, I, It, A, NZ 1, 2, 2001 S, I, It, W, E, 2002 It (R), W (R), E (R), S, I, Arg, A 1, 2, SA, NZ, C, 2003 E 1, S, I, It, W, R, E 2, 3(R), [Fj, J, S, I, E, NZ(R)], 2004 I, It, W, S, E, US, C, A, Arg, NZ, 2005 S, E, W, I, It, A2, 2006 S, I, It, E, W, R, SA, NZ1, 2007 E2, 3, W2(R), [Arg1, Nm(R), Gg(R), NZ, E]
Penaud, A (Brive, Toulouse) 1992 W, E, S, I, R, Arg 1, 2, SA 1, 2, Arg, 1993 R 1, SA 1, 2, R 2, A 1, 2, 1994 I, W, E, 1995 NZ 1, 2, 1996 S, R, Arg 1, 2, W 2, 1997 I, E, R 1, A 2, 2000 W (R), It
Périé, M (Toulon) 1996 E, S, I (R)
Péron, P (RCF) 1975 SA 1, 2
Perrier, P (Bayonne) 1982 W, E, S, I (R)
Pesteil, J-P (Béziers) 1975 SA 1, 1976 A 2, R
Petit, C (Lorrain) 1931 W
Peyras, J-B (Bayonne) 2008 A2(R)
Peyrelade, H (Tarbes) 1940 B
Peyrelongue, J (Biarritz) 2004 It, S(R), C(R), A(R), Arg(R), NZ
Peyroutou, G (Périgueux) 1911 S, E
Phliponeau, J-F (Montferrand) 1973 W, I
Piazza, A (Montauban) 1968 NZ 1, A
Picamoles, L (Montpellier, Toulouse) 2008 I(R), E, It, A1, 2(t&R), Arg, PI(R), A3(R), 2009 I(R), S(R), E(R), It(R), NZ1, 2, SA, 2010 SA(R), Arg1, 2011 I3, [C, NZ1, E(R)]
Picard, T (Montferrand) 1985 Arg 2, 1986 R 1(R), Arg 2
Pierre, J (Bourgoin, Clermont-Auvergne) 2007 NZ1, 2, 2010 S(R), I(R), W, It, E, SA(R), Arg1(R), Fj(R), Arg2, A, 2011 S, I1, E, It, W, I2, 3(R), [J, C(R), NZ1(R), Tg(R), E(R), W(R), NZ2(R)]
Pierrot, G (Pau) 1914 I, W, E
Pilon, J (Périgueux) 1949 E, 1950 E
Piqué, J (Pau) 1961 NZ 2, 3, A, 1962 S, It, 1964 NZ, E, W, It, I, SA, Fj, R, 1965 S, I, E, W, It
Piquemal, M (Tarbes) 1927 I, S, 1929 I, G, 1930 S, I, E, G, W
Piquiral, E (RCF) 1924 S, I, E, W, R, US, 1925 E, 1926 S, I, E, W, M, 1927 I, S, W, E, G 1, 2, 1928 E
Piteu, R (Pau) 1921 S, W, E, I, 1922 S, E, W, I, 1923 E, 1924 E, 1925 I, NZ, W, E, 1926 E
Plantefol, A (RCF) 1967 SA 2, 3, 4, NZ, R, 1968 E, W, Cz, NZ 2, 1969 E, W
Plantey, S (RCF) 1961 A, 1962 It
Podevin, G (SF) 1913 W, I
Poeydebasque, F (Bayonne) 1914 I, W
Poirier, A (SCUF) 1907 E
Poitrenaud, C (Toulouse) 2001 SA 3, A, Fj, 2003 E 1, S, I, It, W, Arg 1, NZ, E 3, [J, US, E(R), NZ], 2004 E(R), US, C, Arg(R), NZ, 2006 R, 2007 It, I, W1, E1, S, E2, 3, [Nm, I, Gg, Arg 2], 2009 I, S, 2010 S, I, W, It, E, SA, Arg1(R), 2011 S(R), I1, E
Pomathios, M (Agen, Lyon U, Bourg) 1948 I, A, S, W, E, 1949 S, I, E, W, Arg 1, 2, 1950 S, I, W, 1951 S, I, E, W, 1952 W, E, 1953 S, I, W, 1954 S
Pons, P (Toulouse) 1920 S, E, W, 1921 S, W, 1922 S
Porcu, C (Agen) 2002 Arg (R), A 1, 2(R)
Porical, J (Perpignan) 2010 Arg1, Fj, Arg2(R), A
Porra, M (Lyon) 1931 I
Porthault, A (RCF) 1951 S, E, W, 1952 I, 1953 S, I, It
Portolan, C (Toulouse) 1986 A, 1989 I, E
Potel, A (Begles) 1932 G
Poux, J-B (Narbonne, Toulouse) 2001 Fj (R), 2002 S, I (R), Arg, A 1(R), 2(R), 2003 E 3, [Fj, J, US, NZ], 2007 E2, 3, W2(R), [Nm, I(R), Gg, NZ(R), E(R), Arg 2], 2008 E(R), It(R), W(R), 2010 W(R), It(R), E(R), SA(R), Arg1(R), 2011 I2(R), 3, [J(R), C, NZ1, Tg, E, W, NZ2]
Prat, J (Lourdes) 1945 B 1, 2, W, 1946 B, I, K, W, 1947 S, I, W, E, 1948 I, A, S, W, E, 1949 S, I, E, W, Arg 1, 2, 1950 S, I, E, W, 1951 S, E, W, 1952 S, I, SA, W, E, It, 1953 S, I, E, W, It, 1954 S, I, NZ, W, E, It, 1955 S, I, E, W, It
Prat, M (Lourdes) 1951 I, 1952 S, I, SA, W, E, 1953 S, I, E, 1954 I, NZ, W, E, It, 1955 S, I, E, W, It, 1956 I, W, It, Cz, 1957 S, I, W, It, R 1, 1958 A, W, I
Prévost, A (Albi) 1926 M, 1927 I, S, W
Prin-Clary, J (Cavaillon, Brive) 1945 B 1, 2, W, 1946 B, I, K, W, 1947 S, I, W
Privat, T (Béziers, Clermont-Auvergne) 2001 SA 3, A, Fj, 2002 It, W, S (R), SA (R), 2003 [NZ], 2005 SA2, A1(R)
Puech, L (Toulouse) 1920 S, E, I, 1921 E, I
Puget, M (Toulouse) 1961 It, 1966 S, I, It, 1967 SA 1, 3, 4, NZ, 1968 Cz, NZ 1, 2, SA 1, 2, R, 1969 E, R, 1970 W

Puig, A (Perpignan) 1926 S, E
Pujol, A (SOE Toulouse) 1906 NZ
Pujolle, M (Nice) 1989 B, A 1, 1990 S, I, R, A 1, 2, NZ 2
Puricelli, J (Bayonne) 2009 NZ1(R), A, Sm(R), NZ3(R)

Quaglio, A (Mazamet) 1957 R 2, 1958 S, E, A, W, I, SA 1, 2, 1959 S, E, It, W, I
Quilis, A (Narbonne) 1967 SA 1, 4, NZ, 1970 R, 1971 I

Rabadan, P (SF) 2004 US(R), C(R)
Ramis, R (Perpignan) 1922 E, I, 1923 W
Rancoule, H (Lourdes, Toulon, Tarbes) 1955 E, W, It, 1958 A, W, It, I, SA 1, 1959 S, It, W, 1960 I, It, R, Arg 1, 2, 1961 SA, E, W, It, NZ 1, 2, 1962 S, E, W, I, It
Rapin, A (SBUC) 1938 R
Raymond, F (Toulouse) 1925 S, 1927 W, 1928 I
Raynal, F (Perpignan) 1935 G, 1936 G 1, 2, 1937 G, It
Raynaud, F (Carcassonne) 1933 G
Raynaud, M (Narbonne) 1999 W 1, E (R)
Razat, J-P (Agen) 1962 R, 1963 S, I, R
Rebujent, R (RCF) 1963 E
Revailler, D (Graulhet) 1981 S, I, W, E, A 1, 2, R, NZ 1, 2, 1982 W, S, I, R, Arg 1
Revillon, J (RCF) 1926 I, E, 1927 S
Ribère, E (Perpignan, Quillan) 1924 I, 1925, I, NZ, S, 1926 S, I, W, M, 1927 I, S, W, E, G 1, 2, 1928 S, A, I, E, G, W, 1929 I, E, G, 1930 S, I, E, W, 1931 I, S, W, E, G, 1932 G, 1933 G
Rives, J-P (Toulouse, RCF) 1975 E, S, I, Arg 1, 2, R, 1976 S, I, W, E, US, A 1, 2, R, 1977 W, E, S, I, Arg 1, 2, R, 1978 E, S, I, W, R, 1979 I, W, E, S, NZ 1, 2, R, 1980 W, E, S, I, SA, 1981 S, I, W, E, A 2, 1982 W, E, S, I, R, 1983 E, S, I, W, A 1, 2, R, 1984 I, W, E, S
Rochon, A (Montferrand) 1936 G 1
Rodrigo, M (Mauléon) 1931 I, W
Rodriguez, L (Mont-de-Marsan, Montferrand, Dax) 1981 A 1, 2, R, NZ 1, 2, 1982 W, E, S, I, R, 1983 E, S, 1984 I, NZ 1, 2, R, 1985 E, S, I, W, 1986 Arg 1, A, R 2, NZ 2, 3, 1987 W, E, S, I, [S, Z, Fj, A, NZ], R, 1988 E, S, I, W, Arg 1, 2, 3, 4, R, 1989 I, E, S, NZ 1, 2, B, A 1, 1990 W, E, S, I, NZ 1
Rogé, L (Béziers) 1952 It, 1953 E, W, It, 1954 S, Arg 1, 2, 1955 S, I, 1956 W, It, E, 1957 S, 1960 S, E
Rollet, J (Bayonne) 1960 Arg 3, 1961 NZ 3, A, 1962 It, 1963 I
Romero, H (Montauban) 1962 S, E, W, I, It, R, 1963 E
Romeu, J-P (Montferrand) 1972 R, 1973 S, NZ, E, W, I, R, 1974 W, E, S, Arg 1, 2, R, SA 1, 2(R), 1975 W, SA 2, Arg 1, 2, R, 1976 S, I, W, E, US, 1977 W, E, S, I, Arg 1, 2, NZ 1, 2, R
Roques, A (Cahors) 1958 A, W, It, I, SA 1, 2, 1959 S, E, W, I, 1960 S, E, W, I, It, Arg 1, 2, 3, 1961 S, SA, E, W, It, I, 1962 S, E, W, I, It, 1963 S
Roques, J-C (Brive) 1966 S, I, It, R
Rossignol, J-C (Brive) 1972 A 2
Rouan, J (Narbonne) 1953 S, I
Roucariès, G (Perpignan) 1956 S
Rouffia, L (Narbonne) 1945 B 2, W, 1946 W, 1948 I
Rougerie, A (Montferrand, Clermont-Auvergne) 2001 SA 3, A, Fj (R), 2002 It, W, E, S, I, Arg, A 1, 2, 2003 E 1, S, I, It, W, Arg 1, 2, NZ, R, E 2, 3(R), [Fj, J, S, I, E], 2004 US, C, A, Arg, NZ, 2005 S, W, A2, C, Tg, SA3, 2006 I, It, E, W, NZ1, 2, 2007 E2, W2, [Arg1, Nm(R), I(R), Gg, Arg 2], 2008 S(R), I, E, It, 2010 S, SA, Arg2, A, 2011 S, I1, E, It, I3, [J, C, NZ1, Tg, E, W, NZ2]
Rougerie, J (Montferrand) 1973 J
Rougé-Thomas, P (Toulouse) 1989 NZ 1, 2
Roujas, F (Tarbes) 1910 I
Roumat, O (Dax) 1989 NZ 2(R), B, 1990 W, E, S, I, R, A 1, 2, 3, NZ 1, 2, 1991 S, I, W 1, E, R, US 1, W 2, [R, Fj, C, E], 1992 W (R), E (R), S, I, SA 1, 2, Arg, 1993 E, S, I, W, R 1, SA 1, 2, R 2, A 1, 2, 1994 I, W, E, C 1, NZ 1, 2, C 2, 1995 W, E, S, [Iv, S, I, SA, E], 1996 E, S, I, W 1, Arg 1, 2
Rousie, M (Villeneuve) 1931 S, G, 1932 G, 1933 G
Rousset, G (Béziers) 1975 SA 1, 1976 US
Rué, J-B (Agen) 2002 SA (R), C (R), 2003 E 1(R), S (R), It (R), W (R), Arg 1, 2(R)
Ruiz, A (Tarbes) 1968 SA 2, R
Rupert, J-J (Tyrosse) 1963 R, 1964 S, Fj, 1965 E, W, It, 1966 S, I, E, W, It, 1967 It, R, 1968 S

Sadourny, J-L (Colomiers) 1991 W 2(R), [C (R)], 1992 E (R), S, I, Arg 1(R), 2, SA 1, 2, 1993 R 1, SA 1, 2, R 2, A 1, 2, 1994 I, W, E, S, C 1, NZ 1, 2, C 2, 1995 W, E, S, I, R 1, [Tg, S, I, SA, E], It, R 2, Arg, NZ 1, 2, 1996 E, S, I, W 1, Arg 1, 2, W 2, SA 1, 2, 1997 I, W, E, S, It 1, R 1, A 1, 2, It 2, R 2, Arg, SA 1, 2, 1998 E, S, I, W, 1999 R, Tg, NZ 1(R), 2000 NZ 2, 2001 It, W, E
Sagot, P (SF) 1906 NZ, 1908 E, 1909 W
Sahuc, A (Métro) 1945 B 1, 2
Sahuc, F (Toulouse) 1936 G 2
Saint-André, P (Montferrand, Gloucester) 1990 R, A 3, NZ 1, 2, 1991 I (R), W 1, E, US 1, 2, W 2, [R, Fj, C, E], 1992 W, E, S, I, R, Arg 1, 2, SA 1, 2, 1993 E, S, I, W, SA 1, 2, A 1, 2, 1994 I, W, E, S, C 1, NZ 1, 2, C 2, 1995 W, E, S, I, R 1, [Tg, Iv, S, I, SA, E], It, R 2, Arg, NZ 1, 2, 1996 E, S, I, W 1, R, Arg 1, 2, W 2, 1997 It 1, 2, R 2, Arg, SA 1, 2
Saisset, O (Béziers) 1971 R, 1972 S, I 1, A 1, 2, 1973 S, NZ, E, W, I, J, R, 1974 I, Arg 2, SA 1, 2, 1975 W
Salas, P (Narbonne) 1979 NZ 1, 2, R, 1980 W, E, 1981 A 1, 1982 Arg 2
Salinié, R (Perpignan) 1923 E
Sallefranque, M (Dax) 1981 A 2, 1982 W, E, S
Salut, J (TOEC) 1966 R, 1967 S, 1968 I, E, Cz, NZ 1, 1969 I
Samatan, R (Agen) 1930 S, I, E, G, W, 1931 I, S, W, E, G
Sanac, A (Perpignan) 1952 It, 1953 S, I, 1954 E, 1956 Cz, 1957 S, I, E, W, It
Sangalli, F (Narbonne) 1975 I, SA 1, 2, 1976 S, A 1, 2, R, 1977 W, E, S, I, Arg 1, 2, NZ 1, 2
Sanz, H (Narbonne) 1988 Arg 3, 4, R, 1989 A 2, 1990 S, I, R, A 1, 2, NZ 2, 1991 W 2
Sappa, M (Nice) 1973 J, R, 1977 R
Sarrade, R (Pau) 1929 I
Sarraméa, O (Castres) 1999 R, WS (R), Tg, NZ 1
Saux, J-P (Pau) 1960 W, It, Arg 1, 2, 1961 SA, E, W, It, I, NZ 1, 2, 3, A, 1962 S, E, W, I, It, 1963 S, I, E, It
Savitsky, M (La Voulte) 1969 R
Savy, M (Montferrand) 1931 I, S, W, E, 1936 G 1
Sayrou, J (Perpignan) 1926 W, M, 1928 E, G, W, 1929 S, W, E, G
Schuster, J (Perpignan) 2010 Fj, A(R)
Scohy, R (BEC) 1931 S, W, E, G
Sébedio, J (Tarbes) 1913 S, E, 1914 I, 1920 S, I, US, 1922 S, E, 1923 S
Séguier, R (Béziers) 1973 J, R
Seigne, L (Agen, Merignac) 1989 B, A 1, 1990 NZ 1, 1993 E, S, I, W, R 1, A 1, 2, 1994 S, C 1, 1995 E (R), S
Sella, P (Agen) 1982 R, Arg 1, 2, 1983 E, S, I, W, A 1, 2, R, 1984 I, W, E, S, NZ 1, 2, R, 1985 E, S, I, W, Arg 1, 2, 1986 S, I, W, E, R 1, Arg 1, 2, A, NZ 1, R 2, NZ 2, 3, 1987 W, E, S, I, [S, R, Z (R), Fj, A, NZ], 1988 E, S, I, W, Arg 1, 2, 3, 4, R, 1989 I, W, E, S, NZ 1, 2, B, A 1, 2, 1990 W, E, S, I, A 1, 2, 3, 1991 W 1, E, R, US 1, 2, W 2, [Fj, C, E], 1992 W, E, S, I, Arg, 1993 E, S, I, W, R 1, SA 1, 2, R 2, A 1, 2, 1994 I, W, E, S, C 1, NZ 1, 2, C 2, 1995 W, E, S, I, [Tg, S, I, SA, E]
Semmartin, J (SCUF) 1913 W, I
Sénal, G (Béziers) 1974 Arg 1, 2, R, SA 1, 2, 1975 W
Sentilles, J (Tarbes) 1912 W, E, 1913 S, SA
Serin, L (Béziers) 1928 E, 1929 W, E, G, 1930 S, I, E, G, W, 1931 I, W, E
Serre, P (Perpignan) 1920 S, E
Serrière, P (RCF) 1986 A, 1987 R, 1988 E
Servat, W (Toulouse) 2004 I, It, W, S, E, US, C, A, Arg, NZ 2005 S, E(R), W(R), It(R), SA1(R), 2, 2008 S, I(R), E(R), W(R), 2009 It(R), NZ1, 2, SA, NZ3, 2010 S, I, W, It, E, Arg2, A, 2011 S, I1, E, It, W, [J, C, NZ1(R), Tg, E, W, NZ2]
Servole, L (Toulon) 1931 I, S, W, E, G, 1934 G, 1935 G
Sicart, N (Perpignan) 1922 I
Sillières, J (Tarbes) 1968 R, 1970 S, I, 1971 S, I, E, 1972 E, W
Siman, M (Montferrand) 1948 E, 1949 S, 1950 S, I, E, W
Simon, S (Bègles) 1991 R, US 1
Simonpaoli, R (SF) 1911 I, 1912 I, S
Sitjar, M (Agen) 1964 W, It, I, R, 1965 It, R, 1967 A, E, It, W, I, SA 1, 2

Skrela, D (Colomiers, SF, Toulouse) 2001 NZ, 2007 It, I, W1, E1, 2, 3(R), W2, [Arg 1, Gg(R), Arg 2], 2008 S(R), I, E(R), W, Arg, PI, A3, 2010 SA(R), Fj(R), 2011 I2(R), 3, [J(R)]
Skrela, J-C (Toulouse) 1971 SA 2, A 1, 2, 1972 I 1(R), E, W, I 2, A 1, 1973 W, J, R, 1974 W, E, S, Arg 1, R, 1975 W (R), E, S, I, SA 1, 2, Arg 1, 2, R, 1976 S, I, W, E, US, A 1, 2, R, 1977 W, E, S, I, Arg 1, 2, NZ 1, 2, R, 1978 E, S, I, W
Soler, M (Quillan) 1929 G
Soro, R (Lourdes, Romans) 1945 B 1, 2, W, 1946 B, I, K, 1947 S, I, W, E, 1948 I, A, S, W, E, 1949 S, I, E, W, Arg 1, 2
Sorondo, L-M (Montauban) 1946 K, 1947 S, I, W, E, 1948 I
Soulette, C (Béziers, Toulouse) 1997 R 2, 1998 S (R), I (R), W (R), Arg 1, 2, Fj, 1999 W 2(R), [C (R), Nm (R), Arg, NZ 2, A]
Soulié, E (CASG) 1920 E, I, US, 1921 S, E, I, 1922 E, W, I
Sourgens, J (Bègles) 1926 M
Sourgens, O (Bourgoin) 2007 NZ2
Souverbie, J-M (Bègles) 2000 R
Spanghero, C (Narbonne) 1971 E, W, SA 1, 2, A 1, 2, R, 1972 S, E, W, I 2, A 1, 2, 1974 I, W, E, S, R, SA 1, 1975 E, S, I
Spanghero, W (Narbonne) 1964 SA, Fj, R, 1965 S, I, E, W, It, R, 1966 S, I, E, W, It, R, 1967 S, A, E, SA 1, 2, 3, 4, NZ, 1968 S, I, E, W, NZ 1, 2, 3, A, SA 1, 2, R, 1969 S, I, W, 1970 R, 1971 E, W, SA 1, 1972 E, I 2, A 1, 2, R, 1973 S, NZ, E, W, I
Stener, G (PUC) 1956 S, I, E, 1958 SA 1, 2
Struxiano, P (Toulouse) 1913 W, I, 1920 S, E, W, I, US
Sutra, G (Narbonne) 1967 SA 2, 1969 W, 1970 S, I
Swierczinski, C (Bègles) 1969 E, 1977 Arg 2
Szarzewski, D (Béziers, SF) 2004 C(R), 2005 I(R), A1, 2, SA3, 2006 S, E(R), W(t&R), R(R), SA, NZ1, 2(R), Arg(R), 2007 It(R), E2(R), W2, [Arg1(R), Nm, I(R), Gg(R), NZ(R), E(R)], 2008 S(R), I, E, It, W, Arg, PI, A3, 2009 I, S, W, E, It, NZ1(R), 2(R), A, SA(R), Sm, NZ3(R), 2010 S(R), I(R), W(R), It(R), E(R), SA, Arg1, 2011 I2, 3, [J(R), NZ1, Tg(R), E(R), W(R), NZ2(R)]

Tabacco, P (SF) 2001 SA 1, 2, NZ, SA 3, A, Fj, 2003 It (R), W (R), Arg 1, NZ, E 2(R), 3, [S(R), US, I(R), NZ], 2004 US, 2005 S
Tachdjian, M (RCF) 1991 S, I, E
Taffary, M (RCF) 1975 W, E, S, I
Taillantou, J (Pau) 1930 I, G, W
Tarricq, P (Lourdes) 1958 A, W, It, I
Tavernier, H (Toulouse) 1913 I
Téchoueyres, W (SBUC) 1994 E, S, 1995 [Iv]
Terreau, M-M (Bourg) 1945 W, 1946 B, I, K, W, 1947 S, I, W, E, 1948 I, A, W, E, 1949 S, Arg 1, 2, 1951 S
Theuriet, A (SCUF) 1909 E, W, 1910 S, 1911 W, 1913 E
Thevenot, M (SCUF) 1910 W, E, I
Thierry, R (RCF) 1920 S, E, W, US
Thiers, P (Montferrand) 1936 G 1, 2, 1937 G, It, 1938 G 1, 2, 1940 B, 1945 B, 1, 2
Thiéry, B (Bayonne, Biarritz) 2007 NZ1, 2(R), 2008 A1, 2
Thion, J (Perpignan, Biarritz) 2003 Arg 1, 2, NZ, R, E 2, [Fj, S, I, E], 2004 A, Arg, NZ 2005 S, E, W, I, It, A2, C, Tg, SA3, 2006 S, I, It, E, W, R(R), SA, 2007 It, I(R), W1, E1, S, E2, 3, W2, [Arg 1, I, Gg, NZ, E, Arg 2], 2008 E(R), It, W, 2009 E, It(R), 2010 Fj, Arg2(R), A, 2011 S(R), I1(R), E(R), It(R)
Tignol, P (Toulouse) 1953 S, I
Tilh, H (Nantes) 1912 W, E, 1913 S, SA, E, W
Tillous-Borde, S (Castres) 2008 A1(R), 2, PI(R), A3, 2009 I, S, W(R), E(R)
Tolot, J-L (Agen) 1987 [Z]
Tomas, J (Clermont-Auvergne, Montpellier) 2008 It(R), A3(R), 2011 W(R)
Tordo, J-F (Nice) 1991 US 1(R), 1992 W, E, S, I, R, Arg 1, 2, SA 1, Arg, 1993 E, S, I, W, R 1
Torossian, F (Pau) 1997 R 1
Torreilles, S (Perpignan) 1956 S
Tournaire, F (Narbonne, Toulouse) 1995 It, 1996 I, W 1, R, Arg 1, 2(R), W 2, SA 1, 2, 1997 I, E, S, It 1, R 1, A 1, 2, It 2, R 2, Arg, SA 1, 2, 1998 E, S, I, W, Arg 1, 2, Fj, Arg 3, A, 1999 I, W 1, E, S, R (R), WS, NZ 1, [C, Nm, Fj, Arg, NZ 2, A], 2000 W, E, S, I, It, A (R)
Tourte, R (St Girons) 1940 B
Traille, D (Pau, Biarritz) 2001 SA 3, A, Fj, 2002 It, W, E, S, I, Arg, A 1, 2, SA, NZ, C, 2003 E 1, S, I, It, W, Arg, 1, 2, NZ, R, E 2, [Fj(R), J, S(R), US, NZ], 2004 I, It, W, S, E, 2005 S, E, W, It(R), SA1(R), 2, A1(R), 2006 It, E, W, R, SA, NZ1, 2, Arg, 2007 S(R), E2, 3, W2(R), [Arg 1, Nm, I, NZ, E], 2008 S, I, E, It(R), W, A1, PI(R), A3(R), 2009 E(R), It, NZ1, 2, A, SA, Sm(R), NZ3, 2010 Fj, Arg2, A, 2011 S, I1, E(R), It(R), W, I2, [C, NZ1, 2(R)]
Trillo, J (Bègles) 1967 SA 3, 4, NZ, R, 1968 S, I, NZ 1, 2, 3, A, 1969 I, E, W, R, 1970 E, R, 1971 S, I, SA 1, 2, A 1, 2, 1972 S, A 1, 2, R, 1973 S, E
Trinh-Duc, F (Montpellier) 2008 S, I(R), E, It, W(R), A1, 2, 2009 W(R), E, It, NZ1, 2, SA, Sm, NZ3, 2010 S, I, W, It, E, SA, Arg1, 2011 S, I1, E, It, W, I2, 3(R), [J, C, NZ1(R), Tg(R), E(R), NZ2(t&R)]
Triviaux, R (Cognac) 1931 E, G
Tucco-Chala, M (PUC) 1940 B

Ugartemendia, J-L (St Jean-de-Luz) 1975 S, I

Vaills, G (Perpignan) 1928 A, 1929 G
Valbon, L (Brive) 2004 US, 2005 S(R), 2006 S, E(R), 2007 NZ1(R)
Vallot, C (SCUF) 1912 S
Van Heerden, A (Tarbes) 1992 E, S
Vannier, M (RCF, Chalon) 1953 W, 1954 S, I, Arg 1, 2, 1955 S, I, E, W, It, 1956 S, I, W, It, E, 1957 S, I, E, W, It, R 1, 2, 1958 S, E, A, W, It, I, 1960 S, E, W, I, It, R, Arg 1, 3, 1961 SA, E, W, It, I, NZ 1, A
Vaquer, F (Perpignan) 1921 S, W, 1922 W
Vaquerin, A (Béziers) 1971 R, 1972 S, I 1, A 1, 1973 S, 1974 W, E, S, Arg 1, 2, R, SA 1, 2, 1975 W, E, S, I, 1976 US, A 1(R), 2, R, 1977 Arg 2, 1979 W, E, 1980 S, I
Vareilles, C (SF) 1907 E, 1908 E, W, 1910 S, E
Varenne, F (RCF) 1952 S
Varvier, T (RCF) 1906 E, 1909 E, W, 1911 E, W, 1912 I
Vassal, G (Carcassonne) 1938 R, G 2
Vaysse, J (Albi) 1924 US, 1926 M
Vellat, E (Grenoble) 1927 I, E, G 1, 2, 1928 A
Venditti, D (Bourgoin, Brive) 1996 R, SA 1(R), 2, 1997 I, W, E, S, R 1, A 1, SA 2, 2000 W (R), E, S, It (R)
Vergé, L (Bègles) 1993 R 1(R)
Verger, A (SF) 1927 W, E, G 1, 1928 I, E, G, W
Verges, S-A (SF) 1906 NZ, E, 1907 E
Vermeulen, E (Brive, Montferrand, Clermont-Auvergne) 2001 SA 1(R), 2(R), 2003 NZ, 2006 NZ1, 2, Arg, 2007 W1, S(R), 2008 S, W(R)
Viard, G (Narbonne) 1969 W, 1970 S, R, 1971 S, I
Viars, S (Brive) 1992 W, E, I, R, Arg 1, 2, SA 1, 2(R), Arg, 1993 R 1, 1994 C 1(R), NZ 1(t), 1995 E (R), [Iv], 1997 R 1(R), A 1(R), 2
Vigerie, M (Agen) 1931 W
Vigier, R (Montferrand) 1956 S, W, It, E, Cz, 1957 S, E, W, It, R 1, 2, 1958 S, E, A, W, It, I, SA 1, 2, 1959 S, E, It, W, I
Vigneau, A (Bayonne) 1935 G
Vignes, C (RCF) 1957 R 1, 2, 1958 S, E
Vila, E (Tarbes) 1926 M
Vilagra, J (Vienne) 1945 B 2
Villepreux, P (Toulouse) 1967 It, I, SA 2, NZ, 1968 I, Cz, NZ 1, 2, 3, A, 1969 S, I, E, W, R, 1970 S, I, W, E, R, 1971 S, I, E, W, A 1, 2, R, 1972 S, I 1, E, W, I 2, A 1, 2
Viviès, B (Agen) 1978 E, S, I, W, 1980 SA, R, 1981 S, A 1, 1983 A 1(R)
Volot, M (SF) 1945 W, 1946 B, I, K, W

Weller, S (Grenoble) 1989 A 1, 2, 1990 A 1, NZ 1
Wolf, J-P (Béziers) 1980 SA, R, 1981 A 2, 1982 E

Yachvili, D (Biarritz) 2002 C (R), 2003 S (R), I, It, W, R (R), E 3, [US, NZ], 2004 I(R), It(R), W(R), S, E, 2005 S(R), E, W, I, It, SA1(R), 2, C, Tg, 2006 S(R), I(R), It(R), E, W, SA, NZ1, 2(R), Arg, 2007 E1, 2008 E(R), It, W(R), A1, 2(R), 2009 NZ1(R), 2(R), A, 2010 It(R), SA(R), Arg1(R), Fj, Arg2(R), A(R), 2011 S(R), I1(R), E, I2, 3(R), [J, C(R), NZ1, Tg, E, W, NZ2]
Yachvili, M (Tulle, Brive) 1968 E, W, Cz, NZ 3, A, R, 1969 S, I, R, 1971 E, SA 1, 2 A 1, 1972 R, 1975 SA 2

Zago, F (Montauban) 1963 I, E

GEORGIA

GEORGIA'S 2010–11 TEST RECORD

OPPONENTS	DATE	VENUE	RESULT
Canada	20 Nov	H	**Won** 22–15
USA	27 Nov	H	**Won** 19–17
Ukraine	5 Feb	H	**Won** 62–3
Spain	12 Feb	H	**Won** 60–0
Portugal	26 Feb	A	**Won** 13–12
Romania	12 Mar	H	**Won** 18–11
Namibia	19 Jun	N	**Won** 23–18
Scotland	14 Sep	N	**Lost** 6–15
England	18 Sep	N	**Lost** 10–41
Romania	28 Sep	N	**Won** 25–9
Argentina	2 Oct	N	**Lost** 7–25

GEORGIA PROVE THEIR STAR QUALITY

By Karen Bond

Stu Forster/Getty Images

Georgia's reward for a great campaign was beating Romania in Palmerston North.

Four years ago Georgia had gone close to causing one of the biggest upsets in Rugby World Cup history with their battling display against Ireland in a 14–10 loss in Lens, ultimately returning home with just the small matter of a first-ever win on the game's biggest stage of all, against Namibia. This time the Lelos arrived in New Zealand not merely targeting victory over their familiar foes Romania in Pool B, but also determined to give Argentina, England and Scotland a real run for their money.

This confidence was understandable given the evolution of Georgian rugby since RWC 2007, the Lelos' exploits in France resulting in a boom in popularity, so much so that rugby is now the country's national sport. A driving force behind this momentum has been Georgian Rugby Union President George Nijaradze, while unprecedented financial support from the country's government has also been priceless, along with the

IRB-funded state-of-the-art National Academy which opened its doors in late 2010.

Georgia arrived at RWC 2011 as the best European side outside the Six Nations, regular winners of the European Nations Cup and with just one defeat in 21 matches in this competition since France 2007. That solitary defeat came against Romania after qualification was already secured, but the Lelos were in no mood for a repeat on rugby's greatest stage. First, though, there was the small matter of matches against Scotland and England to prepare for.

With Georgia's head coach being Richie Dixon, a proud Scot and former national team coach, it was perhaps fitting they would open their RWC 2011 campaign against Scotland in Invercargill on 14 September. Dixon, who had taken over unexpectedly in 2010, insisted he "would have preferred not to be playing Scotland" but he was also quick to admit that "Scotland is a game where we can really give a good account of ourselves"

That was exactly what the Lelos did in a 15–6 loss to Scotland on a rain-soaked evening at Rugby Park when neither side was able to cross the try-line, the points instead coming from the boots of Dan Parks and Merab Kvirikashvili. Scotland, unfortunately for Georgia, had been given an almighty scare by Romania in their opening match four days earlier and were in no mood for a repeat performance, having worked hard in training to counter the Lelos' forward pack.

Georgia did not help themselves by conceding more than double the number of penalties as Scotland in the driving rain, a statistic which left Dixon "bitterly disappointed" as it "let Scotland off the hook at times" and "kept us on the back foot". There were positive signs, though, in their first-ever international match against Scotland, with Georgia carrying the ball powerfully in the first half and keeping their opponents at bay with a committed defensive effort.

"It was a very difficult game for Georgia, but it was a very big experience to play against Scotland," admitted centre David Kacharava. "In a couple of years we can play against teams like Scotland and Ireland and we will match them."

The difference between Georgia and their next opponents, former champions England, was not lost on his team-mate David Zirakashvili when he said "look at them and look at us. Some of us are playing in the third division, and they are all stars and play in big clubs. All of them are dangerous, but we will give all that we have. Even if we fall, I want us to fall like warriors."

Georgia did fall, but Zirakashvili got his wish as they left Otago Stadium with the plaudits of fans and commentators ringing in their ears, England captain Lewis Moody acknowledging "they have come a long way" since an 84–6 defeat at RWC 2003. The 41–10 scoreline this time around flattered England, and it was only three tries in the final quarter against a stretched Georgian defence that made it appear convincing on paper.

In reality it was anything but, Georgia's ferocity at the breakdown "surprised" England according to Dixon as they forced them into conceding 11 penalties and surrendering 75 per cent territory in the first half. Georgia trailed only 17–10 at the break, the biggest cheer of the night in Dunedin reserved for when their impressive No. 8 Dimitri Basilaia bulldozed his way over the line for the Lelos' first try of RWC 2011.

The try was no more than Georgia deserved, wing Irakli Machkhaneli – winning his 50th cap along with Giorgi Chkhaidze – unlucky not to have scored earlier, just being knocked into touch as he dived for the corner. The final margin could have been even closer had Kvirikashvili had his kicking boots on, the fly-half missing five of his six attempts at goal, but there was no prouder man than Dixon. "We are pleased; we certainly demonstrated we can play this game. We gained a lot of respect from the people we played against and the people who were watching us around the world."

Georgia had the luxury of 10 days before their next match against Romania and took the opportunity of getting out to meet the locals in their new base of Masterton, 105km from Arena Manawatu – the venue for the Lelos' final two matches – and home to 22,000 people. Former All Blacks coach Sir Brian Lochore and more than a dozen families invited the entire Georgian delegation into their homes for dinner.

Touched by the generosity of their hosts, the Georgians returned the favour the following day when Nijaradze donned an apron and prepared all the traditional dishes for a banquet. The whole team had dressed in chokha, the men's national costume, and after all the dishes had been cleared away they serenaded their guests with a rendition of *O Sole Mio* and the traditional Georgian song *Chemo Kargo Kvekana*.

"We really wanted to return the favour to the wonderful people who have welcomed us to New Zealand," Nijaradze explained. "This is rugby – it brought us to New Zealand and it has brought us together today. If we can give them just a small feeling of what it's like in Georgia – through our food, through our wine, through our music – then we are very happy."

Refreshed from the break, Georgia duly realised their primary target of beating Romania 25–9 with Kvirikashvili kicking five penalties and the conversion to Mamuka Gorgodze's second-half try for a personal haul of 17 points, a RWC record for the Lelos. A safety-first approach meant both sides took the option to kick for points, and while there was plenty of attacking endeavour, it was matched by defensive commitment, leaving Dixon to admit that "sadly the two teams know each other so well they almost forgot to play tonight."

Buoyed by only their second RWC victory, Georgia took on an Argentina side needing only a bonus point to confirm a quarter-final with New Zealand and gave as good as they got, threatening to throw a cat among the pigeons by leading 7–5 at half-time after Lasha Khmaladze's first Test try cancelled out Juan Jose Imhoff's effort for Los Pumas.

Argentina had edged ahead going into the final quarter before making certain of victory with two tries, one of them by captain Felipe Contepomi, who admitted afterwards that Georgia "did a really good game, they put us to the limit." Dixon echoed the sentiment, feeling that "we didn't get as much out of the game as what we put into it."

Georgia returned home with their heads high, having left a mark on RWC 2011 with their performances, passion and determination. The future looks bright, especially with Dixon admitting that he has "learned to love these boys and respect the way they want to play rugby. I don't envision giving up on these boys lightly. At the moment I have no desire to stop this. Since the last Rugby World Cup everyone has moved forward, and Georgia has done so too."

Martin Bureau/AFP

Richie Dixon offered Georgia a guiding hand at this Rugby World Cup.

GEORGIA INTERNATIONAL STATISTICS

MATCH RECORDS UP TO 31 OCTOBER 2011

WINNING MARGIN

Date	Opponent	Result	Winning Margin
07/04/2007	Czech Republic	98–3	95
03/02/2002	Netherlands	88–0	88
06/02/2010	Germany	77–3	74
26/02/2005	Ukraine	65–0	65
12/06/2005	Czech Republic	75–10	65

MOST POINTS IN A MATCH

BY THE TEAM

Date	Opponent	Result	Points
07/04/2007	Czech Republic	98–3	98
03/02/2002	Netherlands	88–0	88
06/02/2010	Germany	77–3	77
12/06/2005	Czech Republic	75–10	75

BY A PLAYER

Date	Player	Opponent	Points
06/02/2010	Merab Kvirikashvili	Germany	32
08/03/2003	Pavle Jimsheladze	Russia	23
07/04/2007	Merab Kvirikashvili	Czech Republic	23
12/06/2005	Malkhaz Urjukashvili	Czech Republic	20
28/02/2009	Lasha Malaguradze	Spain	20

MOST TRIES IN A MATCH

BY THE TEAM

Date	Opponent	Result	Tries
07/04/2007	Czech Republic	98–3	16
03/02/2002	Netherlands	88–0	14
23/03/1995	Bulgaria	70–8	11
26/02/2005	Ukraine	65–0	11
12/06/2005	Czech Republic	75–10	11
06/02/2010	Germany	77–3	11

BY A PLAYER

Date	Player	Opponent	Tries
23/03/1995	Pavle Jimsheladze	Bulgaria	3
23/03/1995	Archil Kavtarashvili	Bulgaria	3
12/06/2005	Mamuka Gorgodze	Czech Republic	3
07/04/2007	David Dadunashvili	Czech Republic	3
07/04/2007	Malkhaz Urjukashvili	Czech Republic	3
26/04/2008	Mamuka Gorgodze	Spain	3

MOST CONVERSIONS IN A MATCH

BY THE TEAM

Date	Opponent	Result	Cons
06/02/2010	Germany	77–3	11
03/02/2002	Netherlands	88–0	9
07/04/2007	Czech Republic	98–3	9
12/06/2005	Czech Republic	75–10	7

BY A PLAYER

Date	Player	Opponent	Cons
06/02/2010	Merab Kvirikashvili	Germany	11
03/02/2002	Pavle Jimsheladze	Netherlands	9
07/04/2007	Merab Kvirikashvili	Czech Republic	9
12/06/2005	Malkhaz Urjukashvili	Czech Republic	7

MOST PENALTIES IN A MATCH

BY THE TEAM

Date	Opponent	Result	Pens
08/03/2003	Russia	23–17	6
28/09/2011	Romania	25–9	6

BY A PLAYER

Date	Player	Opponent	Pens
08/03/2003	Pavle Jimsheladze	Russia	6

MOST DROPPED GOALS IN A MATCH

BY THE TEAM

Date	Opponent	Result	DGs
20/10/1996	Russia	29–20	2
21/11/1991	Ukraine	19–15	2
15/07/1992	Ukraine	15–0	2
04/06/1994	Switzerland	22–21	2

BY A PLAYER

Date	Player	Opponent	DGs
15/07/1992	Davit Chavleishvili	Ukraine	2

MOST CAPPED PLAYERS

Player	Caps
Irakli Abuseridze	76
Malkhaz Urjukashvili	69
Gia Labadze	65
Ilia Zedginidze	64

LEADING PENALTY SCORERS

Player	Pens
Pavle Jimsheladze	48
Malkhaz Urjukashvili	45
Merab Kvirikashvili	41

LEADING TRY SCORERS

Player	Tries
Mamuka Gorgodze	19
Malkhaz Urjukashvili	18
Irakli Machkhaneli	16
Tedo Zibzibadze	15

LEADING DROPPED GOAL SCORERS

Player	DGs
Kakha Machitidze	4
Nugzar Dzagnidze	3
Pavle Jimsheladze	3
Lasha Malaguradze	3

LEADING CONVERSIONS SCORERS

Player	Cons
Merab Kvirikashvili	67
Pavle Jimsheladze	61
Malkhaz Urjukashvili	45

LEADING POINTS SCORERS

Player	Points
Pavle Jimsheladze	320
Malkhaz Urjukashvili	318
Merab Kvirikashvili	288
Nugzar Dzagnidze	105

Mike Hewitt/Getty Images

The man mountain Mamuka Gorgodze is now Georgia's leading try-scorer.

GEORGIA INTERNATIONAL PLAYERS (UP TO 31 OCTOBER 2011)

Note: Years given for International Championship matches are for second half of season; eg 1972 means season 1971–72. Years for all other matches refer to the actual year of the match. Entries in square brackets denote matches played in RWC Finals.

V Abashidze 1998 *It, Ukr, I,* 1999 *Tg, Tg,* 2000 *It, Mor, Sp,* 2001 *H, Pt, Rus, Sp, R,* 2006 *J*
N Abdaladze 1997 *Cro, De*
I Abuseridze 2000 *It, Pt, Mor, Sp, H, R,* 2001 *H, Pt, Rus, Sp, R,* 2002 *Pt, Rus, Sp, R, I, Rus,* 2003 *Pt, Rus, CZR, R, It, E, Sa, SA,* 2004 *Rus,* 2005 *Pt, Ukr, R,* 2006 *Rus, R, Pt, Ukr, J, R, Sp, Pt, Pt,* 2007 *R, Rus, CZR, Nm, ESp, ItA, Ar, I, Nm, F,* 2008 *Pt, R, Pt, Rus, Sp, S,* 2009 *Ger, Pt, Sp, R, Rus, ArJ, ItA,* 2010 *Pt, Sp, R, Rus, C, US,* 2011 *Ukr, Sp, Pt, R, Rus, S, E, R, Ar*
V Akhvlediani 2007 *CZR*
K Alania 1993 *Lux,* 1994 *Swi,* 1996 *CZR, CZR, Rus,* 1997 *Pt, Pol, Cro, De,* 1998 *It,* 2001 *H, Pt, Sp, F, SA,* 2002 *H, Pt, Rus, Sp, R, I, Rus,* 2003 *Rus,* 2004 *Pt, Sp*
N Andghuladze 1997 *Pol,* 2000 *It, Pt, Mor, Sp, H, R,* 2004 *Sp, Rus, CZR, R*
D Ashvetia 1998 *Ukr,* 2005 *Pt,* 2006 *R,* 2007 *Sp*
K Asieshvili 2008 *ItA,* 2010 *S, ItA, Nm*

G Babunashvili 1992 *Ukr, Ukr, Lat,* 1993 *Rus, Pol, Lux,* 1996 *CZR*
Z Bakuradze 1989 *Z,* 1990 *Z,* 1991 *Ukr, Ukr,* 1993 *Rus, Pol*
D Baramidze 2000 *H*
O Barkalaia 2002 *I,* 2004 *Sp, Rus, CZR, R, Ur, CHL, Rus,* 2005 *Pt, Ukr, R, CZR, CHL,* 2006 *Rus, R, Pt, Ukr, J, Bb, R, Sp,* 2007 *Nm, ItA, I, F,* 2008 *Pt, R, Pt, Rus, Sp, ESp, Ur, ItA, S,* 2009 *Ger, Sp, R*
D Basilaia 2008 *Pt, R, Pt, CZR, Rus, Sp, S,* 2009 *Ger, Sp, R, C, US, ItA,* 2011 *Nm, S, E, R*
R Belkania 2004 *Sp,* 2005 *CHL,* 2007 *Sp, Rus*
G Beriashvili 1993 *Rus, Pol,* 1995 *Ger*
G Berishvili 2011 *Nm, E, R*
M Besselia 1991 *Ukr,* 1993 *Rus, Pol,* 1996 *Rus,* 1997 *Pt*
D Bolgashvili 2000 *It, Pt, H, R,* 2001 *H, Pt, Rus, Sp, R, F, SA,* 2002 *H, Pt, Rus, I,* 2003 *Pt, Sp, Rus, CZR, R, E, Sa, SA,* 2004 *Rus, Ur, CHL, Rus,* 2005 *CZR,* 2007 *Sp,* 2010 *ItA*
J Bregvadze 2008 *ESp, ItA,* 2009 *C, IrA,* 2010 *Sp, R, S, Nm,* 2011 *Ukr, Sp, R, Rus, Nm, S, E, R, Ar*
G Buguianishvili 1996 *CZR, Rus,* 1997 *Pol,* 1998 *It, Rus, I, R,* 2000 *Sp, H, R,* 2001 *H, F, SA,* 2002 *Rus*

D Chavleishvili 1990 *Z, Z,* 1992 *Ukr, Ukr, Lat,* 1993 *Pol, Lux*
D Chichua 2008 *CZR*
I Chikava 1993 *Pol, Lux,* 1994 *Swi,* 1995 *Bul, Mol, H,* 1996 *CZR, CZR,* 1997 *Pol,* 1998 *I*
R Chikvaidze 2004 *Ur, CHL*
L Chikvinidze 1994 *Swi,* 1995 *Bul, Mol, Ger, H,* 1996 *CZR, Rus*
G Chkhaidze 2002 *H, R, I, Rus,* 2003 *Pt, CZR, It, E, SA, Ur,* 2004 *CZR, R,* 2006 *Pt, Ukr,* 2007 *R, Rus, CZR, Nm, ESp, ItA, Ar, I, Nm, F,* 2008 *R, Pt, CZR, Rus, Sp,* 2009 *Ger, Pt, Sp, R, Rus, ArJ, ItA,* 2010 *Ger, Pt, Sp, R, Rus, C, US,* 2011 *Ukr, Sp, Pt, R, Rus, S, E, R, Ar*
S Chkhenkeli 1997 *Pol*
I Chkhikvadze 2005 *CHL,* 2007 *Sp,* 2008 *Pt, R, Pt, CZR, Rus, ESp, Ur, ItA, S,* 2009 *Ger, Sp, ItA,* 2010 *Sp, Rus, S, ItA, Nm, C, US,* 2011 *Pt, Nm, R*
I Chkonia 2007 *ESp, ItA*

D Dadunashvili 2003 *It, E, SA, Ur,* 2004 *Sp, Rus, CZR, R,* 2005 *CHL,* 2007 *Sp, Rus, CZR, Nm, ItA,* 2008 *Pt, R, Pt, CZR, Rus, Sp, S,* 2009 *C, IrA, US, ItA,* 2010 *Sp, S, ItA, Nm*
L Datunashvili 2004 *Sp,* 2005 *Pt, Ukr, R, CZR,* 2006 *Rus, R, Pt, Ukr, J, Bb, CZR, Pt, Pt,* 2007 *R, Rus, Nm, ESp, ItA, I, Nm, F,* 2008 *Pt, Pt,* 2009 *Sp, R, Rus, C, US, ArJ,* 2010 *Ger, Pt, Sp, R, Rus, C, US,* 2011 *Ukr, Sp, Pt, R, Rus, S, E, R, Ar*
V Didebulidze 1991 *Ukr,* 1994 *Kaz,* 1995 *Bul, Mol,* 1996 *CZR,* 1997 *De,* 1999 *Tg,* 2000 *H,* 2001 *H, Pt, Rus, Sp, R, F, SA,* 2002 *H, Pt, Rus, Sp, R, I, Rus,* 2003 *Pt, Sp, Rus, CZR, R, It, E, Sa, SA,* 2004 *Rus,* 2005 *Pt,* 2006 *R, R,* 2007 *R, Sp, Rus, CZR, Nm, ESp, ItA, Ar, Nm, F*
E Dzagnidze 1992 *Ukr, Ukr, Lat,* 1993 *Rus, Pol,* 1995 *Bul, Mol, Ger, H,* 1998 *I*
N Dzagnidze 1989 *Z,* 1990 *Z, Z,* 1991 *Ukr,* 1992 *Ukr, Ukr, Lat,* 1993 *Rus, Pol,* 1994 *Swi,* 1995 *Ger, H*
T Dzagnidze 2008 *ESp*
D Dzneladze 1992 *Ukr, Lat,* 1993 *Lux,* 1994 *Kaz*
P Dzotsenidze 1995 *Ger, H,* 1997 *Pt, Pol*

G Elizbarashvili 2002 *Rus,* 2003 *Sp,* 2004 *CHL,* 2005 *CZR,* 2006 *Pt, Ukr, J, Bb, CZR, Sp, Pt,* 2007 *R, Sp, Rus, I, F,* 2009 *C, IrA*
O Eloshvili 2002 *H,* 2003 *SA,* 2006 *Bb, CZR,* 2007 *Sp, CZR, Nm, ESp, ItA, I, F*
S Essakia 1999 *Tg, Tg,* 2000 *It, Mor, Sp, H,* 2004 *CZR, R*

M Gagnidze 1991 *Ukr, Ukr*
D Gasviani 2004 *Sp, Rus,* 2005 *CZR, CHL,* 2006 *Ukr, J,* 2007 *Rus, CZR,* 2008 *ESp, Ur, ItA, S*
A Ghibradze 1992 *Ukr, Ukr, Lat,* 1994 *Swi,* 1995 *Bul, Mol, Ger,* 1996 *CZR*
D Ghudushauri 1989 *Z,* 1991 *Ukr, Ukr*
L Ghvaberidze 2004 *Pt*
R Gigauri 2006 *Ukr, J, Bb, CZR, Sp, Pt, Pt,* 2007 *R, Nm, ESp, ItA, Ar, Nm, F,* 2008 *Pt, R, Pt, Rus, Sp, ESp, Ur,* 2009 *C, IrA, US, ArJ, ItA,* 2010 *S, ItA, Nm,* 2011 *Nm, S, E, R*
A Giorgadze 1996 *CZR,* 1998 *It, Ukr, Rus, R,* 1999 *Tg, Tg,* 2000 *It, Pt, Mor, H, R,* 2001 *H, Pt, Rus, Sp, R, F, SA,* 2002 *H, Pt, Rus, Sp, R, I, Rus,* 2003 *Pt, Sp, Rus, R, It, E, Sa, SA, Ur,* 2005 *Pt, Ukr, R, CZR,* 2006 *Rus, R, Pt, Bb, CZR, Sp, Pt,* 2007 *R, Ar, I, Nm, F,* 2009 *Ger, Pt, Sp, ArJ,* 2010 *Ger, Pt, C, US,* 2011 *Pt, S, Ar*
I Giorgadze 2001 *F, SA,* 2003 *Pt, Sp, Rus, R, It, E, Sa, Ur,* 2004 *Rus,* 2005 *Pt, R, CZR,* 2006 *Rus, R, Pt, Bb, CZR, R, Sp, Pt, Pt,* 2007 *R, Sp, Rus, CZR, Ar, Nm, F,* 2008 *R,* 2009 *Ger, Pt, Sp, Rus,* 2010 *Ger, Sp, R, Rus,* 2011 *Ukr*
M Gorgodze 2003 *Sp, Rus,* 2004 *Pt, Sp, Rus, CZR, R, Ur, CHL, Rus,* 2005 *Pt, Ukr, R, CZR, CHL,* 2006 *Rus, Pt, Bb, CZR, R, Sp, Pt, Pt,* 2007 *Ar, I, Nm,* 2008 *R, Rus, Sp,* 2009 *Ger, Pt, Sp, R, Rus, ArJ,* 2011 *R, Rus, S, E, R, Ar*
E Gueguchadze 1990 *Z, Z*
L Gugava 2004 *Sp, Rus, CZR, Ur, CHL, Rus,* 2005 *Pt, Ukr,* 2006 *Bb, CZR,* 2009 *C, IrA, US,* 2010 *C, US,* 2011 *Ukr, Sp, Pt, R, Rus, Nm, Ar*
I Guiorkhelidze 1998 *R,* 1999 *Tg, Tg*
G Guiunashvili 1989 *Z,* 1990 *Z,* 1991 *Ukr, Ukr,* 1992 *Ukr, Ukr, Lat,* 1993 *Rus, Pol, Lux,* 1994 *Swi,* 1996 *Rus,* 1997 *Pt*
K Guiunashvili 1990 *Z, Z,* 1991 *Ukr, Ukr,* 1992 *Ukr, Ukr, Lat*
B Gujaraidze 2008 *ESp*
S Gujaraidze 2003 *SA, Ur*
I Gundishvili 2002 *I,* 2003 *Pt, Sp, Rus, CZR,* 2008 *ESp, Ur, ItA,* 2009 *C, US*
D Gurgenidze 2007 *Sp, ItA*
A Gusharashvili 1998 *Ukr*

D Iobidze 1993 *Rus, Pol*
E Iovadze 1993 *Lux,* 1994 *Kaz,* 1995 *Bul, Mol, Ger, H,* 2001 *Sp, F, SA,* 2002 *H, Rus, Sp, R, I*

A Issakadze 1989 *Z*
N Iurini 1991 *Ukr*, 1994 *Swi*, 1995 *Ger*, *H*, 1996 *CZR*, *CZR*, *Rus*, 1997 *Pt*, *Pol*, *Cro*, *De*, 1998 *Ukr*, *Rus*, 2000 *It*, *Sp*, *H*, *R*

S Janelidze 1991 *Ukr*, *Ukr*, 1993 *Rus*, 1994 *Kaz*, 1995 *Ger*, 1997 *Pt*, 1998 *Ukr*, *I*, *R*, 1999 *Tg*, 2000 *R*
R Japarashvili 1992 *Ukr*, *Ukr*, *Lat*, 1993 *Pol*, *Lux*, 1996 *CZR*, 1997 *Pt*
L Javelidze 1997 *Cro*, 1998 *I*, 2001 *H*, *R*, *F*, *SA*, 2002 *H*, *R*, 2004 *R*, 2005 *Ukr*, 2007 *Sp*
G Jgenti 2004 *Ur*, 2005 *CHL*, 2007 *Sp*, *CZR*, *Nm*, *ESp*, *ItA*, 2009 *C*, *IrA*, *US*, 2011 *R*
D Jghenti 2004 *CZR*, *R*
D Jhamutashvili 2005 *CHL*
P Jimsheladze 1995 *Bul*, *Mol*, *H*, 1996 *CZR*, *CZR*, *Rus*, 1997 *De*, 1998 *It*, *Ukr*, *Rus*, *I*, *R*, 1999 *Tg*, *Tg*, 2000 *Pt*, *Mor*, *Sp*, *H*, *R*, 2001 *H*, *Pt*, *Rus*, *Sp*, *R*, *F*, *SA*, 2002 *H*, *Pt*, *Rus*, *Sp*, *I*, *Rus*, 2003 *Pt*, *Sp*, *Rus*, *CZR*, *R*, *It*, *E*, *Sa*, *SA*, *Ur*, 2004 *Rus*, 2005 *R*, 2006 *Rus*, *R*, *Pt*, *Ukr*, *J*, *Bb*, *CZR*, *Pt*, *Pt*, 2007 *R*, *Rus*, *CZR*, *Ar*
K Jintcharadze 1993 *Rus*, *Pol*, 2000 *It*, *Mor*

D Kacharava 2006 *Ukr*, *J*, *R*, *Sp*, *Pt*, 2007 *R*, *Sp*, *Rus*, *CZR*, *Nm*, *ESp*, *ItA*, *I*, *Nm*, 2008 *Pt*, *R*, *Pt*, *CZR*, *Rus*, *Sp*, *S*, 2009 *Ger*, *Pt*, *Sp*, *R*, *Rus*, *C*, *IrA*, *US*, *ArJ*, *ItA*, 2010 *Ger*, *Pt*, *Sp*, *R*, *Rus*, *C*, *US*, 2011 *Ukr*, *Sp*, *Pt*, *R*, *Rus*, *S*, *E*, *R*, *Ar*
G Kacharava 2005 *Ukr*, 2006 *J*, *Bb*, *CZR*, *R*, 2007 *Sp*, 2008 *CZR*
G Kakhiani 1995 *Bul*, *Mol*
V Kakovin 2008 *S*, 2009 *C*, *IrA*, *US*, *ItA*, 2010 *S*, *ItA*, *Nm*, 2011 *Ukr*, *Sp*, *Pt*, *Rus*, *Nm*, *R*, *Ar*
V Katsadze 1997 *Pol*, 1998 *It*, *Ukr*, *Rus*, *I*, *R*, 1999 *Tg*, *Tg*, 2000 *Pt*, *Mor*, *Sp*, *H*, *R*, 2001 *H*, *Pt*, *Rus*, *Sp*, *R*, 2002 *Pt*, *Rus*, *Sp*, *R*, *I*, *Rus*, 2003 *Pt*, *Sp*, *CZR*, *R*, *E*, *Sa*, *SA*, *Ur*, 2004 *Sp*, 2005 *Ukr*
A Kavtarashvili 1994 *Swi*, 1995 *Bul*, *Mol*, *Ger*, 1996 *CZR*, *Rus*, 1997 *Pt*, *Cro*, *De*, 1998 *It*, *Rus*, *I*, *R*, 1999 *Tg*, *Tg*, 2000 *It*, *H*, *R*, 2001 *H*, 2003 *SA*, *Ur*
G Kavtidze 2008 *S*
I Kerauli 1991 *Ukr*, *Ukr*, 1992 *Ukr*, *Ukr*
L Khachirashvili 2005 *Ukr*
T Khakhaleishili 1994 *Kaz*
B Khamashuridze 1998 *It*, *Ukr*, *Rus*, *I*, *R*, 1999 *Tg*, *Tg*, 2000 *It*, *Pt*, *Sp*, *H*, *R*, 2001 *Pt*, *Rus*, *Sp*, *R*, *F*, *SA*, 2002 *H*, *Pt*, *Rus*, *Sp*, *R*, *I*, *Rus*, 2003 *Pt*, *CZR*, *R*, *It*, *E*, *Sa*, *SA*, *Ur*, 2004 *Pt*, *Rus*, *Rus*, 2005 *Pt*, *Ukr*, *CHL*, 2006 *Rus*, *R*, *Pt*, *R*, *Sp*, *Pt*, *Pt*, 2007 *Rus*, *CZR*, *ESp*, *Ar*, *Nm*, *F*, 2008 *Pt*, 2010 *US*, 2011 *Ukr*, *Sp*, *R*, *Rus*, *Nm*
B Khamashuridze 1989 *Z*
M Kharshiladze 1991 *Ukr*
R Khekhelashvili 1999 *Tg*, *Tg*, 2000 *It*, *Pt*, *Mor*, *Sp*, *H*, *R*, 2001 *H*, *Pt*, *R*, *F*, *SA*, 2002 *H*, *Pt*, *Rus*, *Sp*, *R*, *I*, 2003 *Sp*, *Rus*, *CZR*, *R*, *E*, *Sa*, 2004 *Sp*
D Khinchagishvili 2003 *Sp*, *CZR*, 2004 *Pt*, *Sp*, *Rus*, 2006 *Bb*, *CZR*, *Sp*, *Pt*, *Pt*, 2007 *R*, *Rus*, *Nm*, *ESp*, *ItA*, *Ar*, *I*, *Nm*, 2009 *Ger*, *Pt*, *Sp*, *R*, *Rus*, *ArJ*, *ItA*, 2010 *Ger*, *Pt*, *R*, *Rus*, *C*, 2011 *Ukr*, *Pt*, *R*, *Rus*, *S*, *E*, *R*
L Khmaladze 2008 *ESp*, *ItA*, 2009 *ItA*, 2010 *S*, *ItA*, *Nm*, 2011 *Nm*, *E*, *R*, *Ar*
G Khonelidze 2003 *SA*
G Khositashvili 2008 *ESp*, *Ur*, *ItA*
N Khuade 1989 *Z*, 1990 *Z*, *Z*, 1991 *Ukr*, *Ukr*, 1993 *Rus*, *Pol*, *Lux*, 1994 *Swi*, 1995 *Ger*
Z Khutsishvili 1993 *Lux*, 1994 *Kaz*, *Swi*, 1995 *Bul*, 1996 *CZR*
A Khvedelidze 1989 *Z*, 1990 *Z*, *Z*, 1991 *Ukr*, *Ukr*, 1992 *Ukr*, *Ukr*, *Lat*, 1993 *Rus*, *Pol*
I Kiasashvili 2008 *Pt*, *CZR*, *Ur*, 2010 *S*, *Nm*
D Kiknadze 2004 *Rus*, 2005 *Pt*, *Ukr*
A Kobakhidze 1997 *Cro*, 1998 *I*
K Kobakhidze 1995 *Ger*, *H*, 1996 *Rus*, 1997 *Pt*, 1998 *It*, *Ukr*, *Rus*, *I*, *R*, 1999 *Tg*, 2000 *It*
Z Koberidze 2004 *Ur*
V Kolelishvili 2008 *ItA*, 2010 *S*, *ItA*, *Nm*, *US*, 2011 *Pt*, *Rus*, *Nm*, *S*, *Ar*
A Kopaleishvili 2004 *Ur*
A Kopaliani 2003 *It*, *SA*, *Ur*, 2004 *Pt*, 2005 *Ukr*, *R*, 2006 *Rus*, *R*, *Ukr*, *J*, *Bb*, *CZR*, *R*, *Sp*, *Pt*, 2007 *R*, *Sp*, *Rus*, *CZR*, *Ar*, *I*, *Nm*, *F*
G Korkelia 2010 *S*, *ItA*
D Kubriashvili 2008 *Pt*, *R*, *Pt*, *Rus*, *Sp*, 2009 *Pt*, *Sp*, *R*, *Rus*, *ArJ*, *ItA*, 2010 *Ger*, *Pt*, *Sp*, *US*, 2011 *Nm*, *S*, *E*, *Ar*
E Kuparadze 2007 *ESp*
G Kutarashvili 2004 *Pt*, *Sp*, *CZR*, *R*, 2005 *CHL*, 2006 *Rus*, *R*, *Pt*, *Ukr*, *J*, *R*
B Kvinikhidze 2002 *R*, 2004 *Pt*, *Sp*, *CZR*, *R*, 2005 *CHL*
M Kvirikashvili 2003 *Pt*, *Sp*, *CZR*, *E*, *Sa*, *SA*, *Ur*, 2004 *Rus*, *CZR*, *R*, *CHL*, 2005 *CZR*, *CHL*, 2007 *R*, *Sp*, *Rus*, *CZR*, *Nm*, *ESp*, *ItA*, *Ar*, *I*, *Nm*, *F*, 2008 *Pt*, *CZR*, *Rus*, *Sp*, *S*, 2009 *Ger*, *Pt*, *R*, *Rus*, *C*, *IrA*, *US*, *ArJ*, *ItA*, 2010 *Ger*, *Pt*, *Sp*, *R*, *Rus*, *ItA*, *Nm*, *C*, *US*, 2011 *Ukr*, *Sp*, *Pt*, *R*, *Rus*, *S*, *E*, *R*, *Ar*

G Labadze 1996 *CZR*, *Rus*, 1997 *Pt*, *Pol*, *Cro*, *De*, 1998 *It*, *Ukr*, *Rus*, *I*, *R*, 1999 *Tg*, *Tg*, 2000 *It*, *Pt*, *Sp*, *H*, *R*, 2001 *H*, *Pt*, *Rus*, *Sp*, *F*, *SA*, 2002 *Pt*, *Rus*, *Sp*, *R*, *Rus*, 2003 *Rus*, *CZR*, *R*, *It*, *E*, *Sa*, 2004 *Rus*, 2005 *R*, 2006 *Rus*, *R*, *Pt*, *J*, *R*, *Pt*, *Pt*, 2007 *Rus*, *Ar*, *Nm*, 2009 *Ger*, *Pt*, *Sp*, *R*, *Rus*, *C*, *IrA*, *US*, *ArJ*, 2010 *Ger*, *Pt*, *Sp*, *R*, *Rus*, *C*, 2011 *Ukr*, *Sp*, *R*
I Lezhava 1991 *Ukr*, *Ukr*, 1992 *Ukr*, 1995 *Bul*
Z Lezhava 1991 *Ukr*, 1995 *Ger*, 1996 *CZR*, *CZR*, *Rus*, 1997 *Pt*, *Cro*, *De*, 1998 *It*, *Rus*, *R*, 1999 *Tg*
L Liluashvili 1997 *Pt*
V Liluashvili 1989 *Z*, 1990 *Z*, *Z*
O Liparteliani 1989 *Z*, 1990 *Z*, *Z*
S Liparteliani 1991 *Ukr*, 1994 *Kaz*, *Swi*, 1996 *CZR*
Z Liparteliani 1994 *Kaz*, *Swi*, 1995 *Bul*, *Mol*, *Ger*, *H*
G Lomgadze 2009 *US*
D Losaberidze 2009 *IrA*
M Lossaberidze 1989 *Z*

K Machitidze 1989 *Z*, 1993 *Rus*, 1995 *Bul*, *Mol*, *Ger*, *H*, 1996 *CZR*, *CZR*, *Rus*, 1997 *Pt*, *Pol*, *Cro*, *De*, 1998 *It*, *Ukr*, *Rus*, *R*, 1999 *Tg*
I Machkhaneli 2002 *H*, *R*, 2003 *It*, *E*, *Sa*, *SA*, *Ur*, 2004 *Pt*, *Ur*, *CHL*, *Rus*, 2005 *Pt*, *Ukr*, *R*, *CZR*, *CHL*, 2006 *Rus*, *R*, *Pt*, *Bb*, *CZR*, *R*, *Pt*, 2007 *R*, *Ar*, *I*, *Nm*, 2008 *S*, 2009 *Ger*, *Pt*, *Sp*, *R*, *Rus*, *US*, *ArJ*, *ItA*, 2010 *Ger*, *Pt*, *Sp*, *R*, *Rus*, *C*, *US*, 2011 *Ukr*, *Sp*, *Pt*, *R*, *Rus*, *S*, *E*
M Magrakvelidze 1998 *Ukr*, 2000 *Mor*, 2001 *F*, 2002 *Pt*, *Sp*, *R*, 2004 *Rus*, 2005 *Pt*, *R*, 2006 *Bb*, *CZR*, *Pt*, *Pt*, 2007 *R*, *CZR*, *Nm*, *ESp*, *ItA*, *I*, *F*
I Maisuradze 1997 *Cro*, 1998 *It*, *Ukr*, 1999 *Tg*, *Tg*, 2004 *Rus*, *R*, 2005 *CZR*, 2006 *Bb*, *CZR*, *R*, *Pt*, *Pt*, 2007 *R*, *Sp*, *Rus*, *CZR*, *ESp*, *ItA*, *I*, *F*
S Maisuradze 2008 *Pt*, *CZR*, *Rus*, *Sp*, *ESp*, *Ur*, *ItA*, *S*, 2009 *IrA*, *US*, *ItA*, 2010 *S*, *Nm*, *C*, *US*, 2011 *Pt*
V Maisuradze 2011 *Ukr*, *Sp*, *Pt*, *R*, *Rus*, *Nm*, *S*, *E*, *R*, *Ar*
Z Maisuradze 2004 *Pt*, *Sp*, *CZR*, *Ur*, *CHL*, *Rus*, 2005 *Ukr*, *R*, 2006 *Rus*, *R*, *Pt*, *Ukr*, *J*, *Bb*, *CZR*, *Sp*, 2007 *Nm*, *ESp*, *ItA*, *Ar*, *I*, *F*, 2008 *Pt*, 2009 *C*, *IrA*, *US*, 2011 *Ukr*, *Sp*, *Nm*
L Malaguradze 2008 *Pt*, *R*, *Pt*, *CZR*, *Rus*, *Sp*, *ESp*, *Ur*, *ItA*, *S*, 2009 *Ger*, *Pt*, *Sp*, *R*, *Rus*, *C*, *IrA*, *US*, *ArJ*, *ItA*, 2010 *Ger*, *Pt*, *Sp*, *R*, *Rus*, *C*, *US*, 2011 *Ukr*, *Sp*, *Pt*, *Rus*, *Ar*
K Margvelashvili 2003 *It*, *E*, *Sa*, *SA*
M Marjanishvili 1990 *Z*, *Z*, 1992 *Ukr*, *Ukr*, *Lat*, 1993 *Rus*, *Pol*, *Lux*
A Matchutadze 1993 *Lux*, 1994 *Kaz*, 1995 *Bul*, *Mol*, 1997 *Pt*, *Pol*, *Cro*, *De*
Z Matiashvili 2003 *Sp*, 2005 *CHL*
G Mchedlishvili 2008 *CZR*
S Melikidze 2008 *CZR*, *Sp*, *ESp*, *ItA*
L Mgueladze 1992 *Ukr*, *Ukr*
N Mgueladze 1995 *Bul*, *Mol*, *H*, 1997 *Pol*
K Mikautadze 2010 *S*, *ItA*, *Nm*
I Modebadze 2003 *SA*, *Ur*, 2004 *Sp*
S Modebadze 1994 *Kaz*, 1995 *Mol*, 1996 *CZR*, *CZR*, *Rus*, 1997 *Pt*, *Pol*, *Cro*, *De*, 1998 *It*, *Ukr*, *Rus*, 1999 *Tg*, 2000 *It*, *Pt*, 2001 *Sp*, *F*, *SA*, 2002 *H*, *Pt*, *Rus*, *Sp*, *R*
A Mtchedlishvili 2004 *Ur*, *CHL*, 2008 *CZR*
S Mtchedlishvili 2000 *It*, 2007 *Sp*
Z Mtchedlishvili 1995 *Mol*, 1996 *CZR*, 1997 *Cro*, *De*, 1998 *It*, *Ukr*, *Rus*, *I*, *R*, 1999 *Tg*, *Tg*, 2000 *Pt*, *Mor*, *Sp*, *H*, *R*, 2001 *Rus*, *Sp*, *R*, *F*, *SA*, 2002 *H*, *Pt*, *Rus*, *I*, *Rus*, 2003 *Pt*, *Sp*, *Rus*, *CZR*, *R*, *It*, *E*, *Sa*, *Ur*, 2004 *Pt*, *Rus*, 2005 *Pt*, 2006 *J*, 2007 *Rus*, *CZR*, *Nm*, *ESp*, *ItA*, *F*
M Mtiulishvili 1991 *Ukr*, 1994 *Kaz*, 1996 *CZR*, *CZR*, *Rus*, 1997 *Pt*, *Pol*, *Cro*, *De*, 1998 *It*, *Ukr*, *Rus*, *R*, 2001 *H*, *Pt*, *Rus*, *Sp*, *R*, 2002 *H*, *Pt*, *Rus*, *Sp*, *R*, *I*, 2003 *Rus*, *CZR*, *R*, 2004 *Rus*, *CZR*, *R*

V Nadiradze 1994 *Kaz*, *Swi*, 1995 *H*, 1996 *Rus*, 1997 *Pt*, *De*, 1998 *I*, *R*, 1999 *Tg*, 2000 *Pt*, *Mor*, *Sp*, *H*, *R*, 2001 *H*, *Pt*, *Rus*, *Sp*, *R*, *F*, *SA*, 2002 *H*, *Pt*, *Rus*, *Sp*, *R*, *I*, *Rus*, 2003 *Rus*, *CZR*, *R*, *It*, *E*, *Sa*

A **Natchqebia** 1990 *Z, Z*
Y **Natriashvili** 2006 *Ukr, J*, 2007 *ItA*, 2008 *Pt, R, Pt, Rus, Sp, ESp, Ur, ItA, S*, 2009 *Ger, Pt, Sp, R, Rus, C, IrA, US, ArJ, ItA*, 2010 *Ger, R, Rus, ItA, Nm, US*, 2011 *Ukr, Sp, Pt, R*
N **Natroshvili** 1992 *Ukr, Ukr, Lat*
G **Nemsadze** 2005 *CHL*, 2006 *Ukr*, 2007 *Sp*, 2008 *CZR, Sp, ESp, Ur, ItA*, 2009 *IrA, US, ArJ, ItA*, 2010 *Ger, Pt, R, Rus, US*, 2011 *R, Rus, Nm, Ar*
A **Nijaradze** 2008 *CZR*
I **Nikolaenko** 1999 *Tg, Tg*, 2000 *It, Mor, Sp, H, R*, 2001 *R, F*, 2003 *Pt, Sp, E, Sa, SA, Ur*
I **Ninidze** 2004 *Ur, CHL*
M **Ninidze** 2010 *S, Nm*

D **Oboladze** 1993 *Rus, Pol, Lux*, 1994 *Swi*, 1995 *Bul, Mol, Ger, H*, 1996 *CZR, CZR, Rus*, 1997 *Pt, Pol*, 1998 *It, Ukr*
T **Odisharia** 1989 *Z*, 1994 *Kaz*

S **Papashvili** 2001 *SA*, 2004 *CZR, R*, 2006 *Bb, CZR*, 2007 *Sp*
S **Partsikanashvili** 1994 *Kaz*, 1996 *CZR, Rus*, 1997 *Pol*, 1999 *Tg, Tg*, 2000 *It, Pt, Mor*
A **Peikrishvili** 2008 *Pt, Pt*, 2009 *R*, 2010 *Pt, R, Rus*, 2011 *Sp*
G **Peradze** 1991 *Ukr*
Z **Peradze** 1997 *Pol*, 1998 *Rus*
Z **Petriashvili** 2009 *C*
D **Pinchukovi** 2004 *CZR*
L **Pirpilashvili** 2004 *Rus, CZR, R, Ur, CHL*, 2005 *Ukr, R, CZR*
G **Pirtskhalava** 1989 *Z*, 1995 *Ger*, 1996 *CZR, Rus*, 1997 *Pt, Pol*
T **Pkhakadze** 1989 *Z*, 1990 *Z, Z*, 1993 *Rus, Pol, Lux*, 1994 *Kaz*, 1996 *CZR*

G **Rapava-Ruskini** 1990 *Z*, 1992 *Ukr, Lat*, 1994 *Kaz*, 1996 *Rus*, 1997 *Pt, Cro, De*, 1998 *It, Ukr, Rus, R*, 1999 *Tg*
T **Ratianidze** 2000 *It*, 2001 *H, Pt, Sp, R, SA*, 2002 *Pt, Rus, Sp, R, I, Rus*, 2003 *Pt, Sp, Rus, CZR, R*
Z **Rekhviashvili** 1995 *H*, 1997 *Pt, Pol*
G **Rokhvadze** 2008 *ItA*, 2009 *C, IrA, US*, 2010 *S, ItA*

S **Sakandelidze** 1996 *CZR*, 1998 *Ukr*
S **Sakvarelidze** 2010 *S, ItA*
B **Samkharadze** 2004 *Pt, Sp, Rus, CZR, R, Ur, CHL*, 2005 *CZR, CHL*, 2006 *Rus, R, Pt, Ukr, Bb, CZR, R, Sp, Pt, Pt*, 2007 *R, Sp, Rus, CZR, Nm, ESp, Ar, I, Nm, F*, 2008 *Pt, R, Pt, Sp, ESp, Ur, ItA, S*, 2009 *Ger, Sp, R, ArJ, ItA*, 2010 *Ger, Pt, Sp, R, S, ItA, Nm, C*, 2011 *Ukr, Sp, Pt, Nm, E, R, Ar*
A **Sanadze** 2004 *CHL*
P **Saneblidze** 1994 *Kaz*
G **Sanikidze** 2004 *Ur, CHL*
B **Sardanashvili** 2004 *CHL*
V **Satseradze** 1989 *Z*, 1990 *Z*, 1991 *Ukr*, 1992 *Ukr, Ukr, Lat*
E **Shanidze** 1994 *Swi*
B **Sheklashvili** 2010 *S, ItA, Nm*, 2011 *Sp*
G **Shkinin** 2004 *CZR, R, CHL*, 2005 *CHL*, 2006 *Rus, R, Ukr, J, R, Sp, Pt, Pt*, 2007 *R, Sp, Rus, CZR, Nm, ESp, ItA, Ar, I, Nm*, 2008 *R, Pt, CZR, Rus, Sp, ESp, Ur, ItA, S*, 2009 *Pt*
B **Shvanguiradze** 1990 *Z, Z*, 1992 *Ukr, Ukr, Lat*, 1993 *Rus, Pol, Lux*
G **Shvelidze** 1998 *I, R*, 1999 *Tg, Tg*, 2000 *It, Pt, Sp, H, R*, 2001 *H, Pt, Sp, F, SA*, 2002 *H, Rus, I, Rus*, 2003 *Pt, Sp, Rus, CZR, R, It, E, Sa, Ur*, 2004 *Rus*, 2005 *Pt, CZR*, 2006 *Rus, R, Pt, R, Sp, Pt, Pt*, 2007 *Ar, I, Nm, F*, 2008 *Pt, R, Pt, CZR, Rus*, 2009 *Ger, Pt, Sp, R, Rus, ArJ*, 2010 *Sp, R, Rus, C, US*, 2011 *Pt, Nm, E, R, Ar*
I **Sikharulidze** 1994 *Kaz*
T **Sokhadze** 2005 *CZR*, 2006 *Rus, R, Pt, Ukr, J, Pt, Pt*, 2009 *C, IrA*
M **Sujashvili** 2004 *Pt, Rus*, 2005 *Pt, Ukr, R, CZR*, 2006 *Pt, Ukr, J, Bb, CZR*
S **Sultanishvili** 1998 *Ukr*
S **Sutiashvili** 2005 *CHL*, 2006 *Ukr*, 2007 *CZR, Nm, ESp*, 2008 *Pt, R, CZR, Rus, S*, 2010 *S, ItA, Nm, C, US*, 2011 *Ukr, Sp, Pt, R, Rus, S, E*
P **Svanidze** 1992 *Ukr*

T **Tavadze** 1991 *Ukr, Ukr*
L **Tavartkiladze** 2009 *ItA*, 2010 *Ger, Sp, R, Rus, S, ItA, Nm*, 2011 *Sp*
N **Tchavtchavadze** 1998 *It, Ukr*, 2004 *CZR, R, Ur, CHL*
M **Tcheishvili** 1989 *Z*, 1990 *Z, Z*, 1995 *H*
B **Tepnadze** 1995 *H*, 1996 *CZR*, 1997 *Cro*, 1998 *I, R*, 1999 *Tg*
A **Todua** 2008 *CZR, Rus, Sp, ESp, Ur, ItA, S*, 2009 *Sp, R, C, IrA, US, ArJ, ItA*, 2010 *Ger, Pt, R, Rus, S, ItA, Nm*, 2011 *Nm, S, E, R, Ar*
P **Tqabladze** 1993 *Lux*, 1995 *Bul*
L **Tsabadze** 1994 *Kaz, Swi*, 1995 *Bul, Ger, H*, 1996 *CZR, Rus*, 1997 *Cro, De*, 1998 *It, Rus, I, R*, 1999 *Tg, Tg*, 2000 *Pt, Mor, Sp, R*, 2001 *H, Pt, Rus, Sp, R, F, SA*, 2002 *H, Pt, Rus, Sp, R, I, Rus*
B **Tsiklauri** 2008 *ItA*
G **Tsiklauri** 2003 *SA, Ur*
D **Tskhvediani** 1998 *Ukr*
V **Tskitishvili** 1994 *Swi*, 1995 *Bul, Mol*
T **Turdzeladze** 1989 *Z*, 1990 *Z, Z*, 1991 *Ukr*, 1995 *Ger, H*

K **Uchava** 2002 *Sp*, 2004 *Sp*, 2008 *Pt, R, Pt, Rus, Sp, ESp, Ur, ItA, S*, 2009 *Ger, Pt, R, C, IrA*, 2010 *S, ItA, Nm*
B **Udesiani** 2001 *Sp, F*, 2002 *H*, 2004 *Pt, Sp, CZR, R, Rus*, 2005 *Pt, Ukr, R, CZR, CHL*, 2006 *Rus, R, Ukr, J, Bb, CZR, R, Sp, Pt, Pt*, 2007 *R, Rus, CZR, Ar, Nm*, 2008 *CZR, Sp, ESp, Ur, ItA, S*, 2010 *Ger, Pt, Sp, R, Rus, C, US*, 2011 *Ukr*
B **Urjukashvili** 2011 *Ukr, Sp, Pt, Rus, Nm*
M **Urjukashvili** 1997 *Cro, De*, 1998 *Ukr, Rus, R*, 1999 *Tg, Tg*, 2000 *It, Pt, Mor, Sp*, 2001 *Pt, Rus, Sp, R, F, SA*, 2002 *H, Pt, Sp, R, I, Rus*, 2003 *Pt, Sp, Rus, R, It, E, Sa, Ur*, 2004 *Pt, Rus, Ur, CHL, Rus*, 2005 *Pt, R, CZR*, 2006 *Rus, R, Pt, Ukr, J, R, Sp*, 2007 *Rus, CZR, Nm, ESp, ItA, Ar, I, Nm, F*, 2008 *Sp*, 2009 *R, Rus*, 2010 *Ger, Sp, R, Rus, ItA, Nm, C*, 2011 *Nm, S, R, Ar*
R **Urushadze** 1997 *Pol*, 2002 *R*, 2004 *Pt, Rus, Rus*, 2005 *Pt, Ukr, R, CZR, CHL*, 2006 *Rus, R, Pt, Bb, CZR, R, Sp, Pt, Pt*, 2007 *Nm, ESp, ItA, I, Nm, F*, 2008 *Pt, R, Pt, Rus, Sp, S*, 2009 *Ger, Pt, Sp, R, Rus, C, IrA, US, ArJ, ItA*

Z **Valishvili** 2004 *CHL*
D **Vartaniani** 1991 *Ukr, Ukr*, 1992 *Ukr, Ukr, Lat*, 1997 *Pol*, 2000 *Sp, H, R*
L **Vashadze** 1991 *Ukr*, 1992 *Ukr, Ukr, Lat*

G **Yachvili** 2001 *H, Pt, R*, 2003 *Pt, Sp, Rus, CZR, R, It, E, Sa, Ur*

I **Zedginidze** 1998 *I*, 2000 *It, Pt, Mor, Sp, H, R*, 2001 *H, Pt, Rus, Sp, R*, 2002 *H, Rus, Sp, I, Rus*, 2003 *Pt, Sp, Rus, CZR, R, It, Sa, SA, Ur*, 2004 *Pt, Sp, Rus, CZR, R, Rus*, 2005 *Pt, Ukr, R, CZR*, 2006 *Rus, R, Pt, Ukr, CZR, R, Sp, Pt, Pt*, 2007 *R, Ar, I*, 2008 *S*, 2009 *Ger, Pt, Sp, Rus, ArJ, ItA*, 2010 *Ger, Pt, Sp, R, Rus*, 2011 *Nm, E, R, Ar*
T **Zibzibadze** 2000 *It, Pt, Mor, Sp*, 2001 *H, Pt, Rus, Sp, R, F, SA*, 2002 *H, Pt, Rus, Sp, R, I, Rus*, 2003 *Pt, Sp, Rus, CZR, R, It, E, Sa, Ur*, 2004 *Pt, Sp, Rus, CZR, R, Rus*, 2005 *Pt, Ukr, R, CZR*, 2009 *Ger, Pt, Sp, R, ArJ*, 2010 *Ger, Pt, Sp, R, Rus, S, ItA, Nm, C, US*, 2011 *Sp, Pt, R, Rus, S, E, R, Ar*
D **Zirakashvili** 2004 *Ur, CHL, Rus*, 2005 *Ukr, R, CZR*, 2006 *Rus, R, Pt, R, Sp, Pt*, 2007 *R, Ar, Nm, F*, 2008 *R*, 2009 *Ger*, 2010 *Ger, Pt, Sp, Rus, C, US*, 2011 *Ukr, Pt, R, Rus, S, E, R*

THE COUNTRIES

IRELAND

IRELAND'S 2010–11 TEST RECORD

OPPONENTS	DATE	VENUE	RESULT
South Africa	6 Nov	H	**Lost** 21–23
Samoa	13 Nov	H	**Won** 20–10
New Zealand	20 Nov	H	**Lost** 18–38
Argentina	28 Nov	H	**Won** 29–9
Italy	5 Feb	A	**Won** 13–11
France	13 Feb	H	**Lost** 22–25
Scotland	27 Feb	A	**Won** 21–18
Wales	12 Mar	A	**Lost** 13–19
England	19 Mar	H	**Won** 24–8
Scotland	6 Aug	A	**Lost** 6–10
France	13 Aug	A	**Lost** 12–19
France	20 Aug	H	**Lost** 22–26
England	27 Aug	H	**Lost** 9–20
USA	11 Sept	N	**Won** 22–10
Australia	17 Sept	N	**Won** 15–6
Russia	25 Sept	N	**Won** 62–12
Italy	2 Oct	N	**Won** 36–6
Wales	8 Oct	N	**Lost** 10–22

GOLDEN GENERATION FALL SHORT

By Iain Spragg

Sandra Mu/Getty Images

The win over Australia at Eden Park was the highlight of Ireland's campaign.

Ireland's dreams of reaching the Rugby World Cup semi-finals for the first time in their history were shattered by a resurgent Wales side in Wellington, the fifth time in seven attempts the men in green had experienced a heartbreaking defeat at the last eight stage of the tournament.

Irish hopes of a best-ever showing in the competition were sky high after Declan Kidney's side recorded a famous victory over Australia in the pool stages, but hope quickly turned to despair in the Wellington Regional Stadium as the team were unable to counter Wales' attacking instincts, succumbing to a 22–10 defeat.

The result not only signalled a depressingly familiar quarter-final exit but, in all probability, the end of the World Cup careers of some of the leading lights of Ireland's "golden generation" of players, most notably veterans Brian O'Driscoll, Paul O'Connell and Ronan O'Gara.

"It's disappointing, collectively and personally," admitted captain O'Driscoll, who was featuring in his fourth World Cup campaign. "I won't get this opportunity again, and that really sucks.

"We got outplayed in the second half, they scored two good tries. Maybe there was some weak defence, but we are very disappointed to be going home. It was a great opportunity after winning the group, but they proved worthy semi-finalists and good luck to them.

"We needed to deliver a performance similar to against Australia, but we didn't. We knocked on too much ball, and when you turn too much ball over against quality opposition they make you pay, and we are the ones left disappointed.

"We had high hopes going into the game. We thought we were in good form, and we just got outplayed on the day. We just felt we could keep the pressure on, and the boys backed themselves to drive over. That cost us a bit."

The Irish kicked off their Rugby World Cup 2011 campaign in New Plymouth against the USA and, despite playing four warm-up games before boarding the plane to New Zealand, they looked distinctly rusty against the Eagles at Stadium Taranaki.

A first-half try from Tommy Bowe put Ireland in the ascendency, but it was not until the second half that Kidney's team established any real supremacy, and a second score from Bowe and a try from Rory Best eventually wrapped up a 22–10 victory.

Six days later the tournament began in earnest for the Irish in the formidable shape of the Wallabies in Auckland. The four previous encounters between the two teams in the World Cup had all resulted in Australian victories, but Ireland finally managed to turn the tables on the reigning Tri-Nations champions courtesy of a dominant display from their front five.

It was a game which was ultimately decided by the kickers rather than tries, and it was Ireland's Jonathan Sexton and O'Gara with two penalties apiece, plus a Sexton drop-goal, who combined to land 15 points while James O'Connor could only reply with two penalties for the Australians. Ireland had produced the shock of the tournament to date, and were now favourites to top Pool C.

"It's a performance we knew we had in us," said O'Driscoll, a veteran of the defeat to the Wallabies in 2003. "With the crowd here tonight it felt like we were in Dublin. I'm just delighted that we were able to give them something to shout about.

"It is difficult to win games when your pack are second best, but there was no doubt today our pack laid the platform for the victory – that is unquestionable. The tight five needed to front-up, and our front row was immense and just gave us an opportunity to play territory and get ourselves into situations where we could kick points, and there were some phenomenal turnovers as well.

"They were definitely the ones who put us in the position to win the game, and I have no problem giving them the credit they deserve."

Next up was Russia and, despite fielding a largely second-string side in Rotorua, the Irish were in no mood to surrender the momentum gained from the Australia game, running in nine tries in a comprehensive 62–12 victory.

The pool climaxed with the clash with the Italians in Dunedin. Despite having toppled the Wallabies, Pool C was still sufficiently tight to dictate that Ireland had to beat the Azzurri to progress and, having only just escaped from Rome with a 13–11 victory in the Six Nations in February, Kidney could afford to take nothing for granted.

The early exchanges suggested another close encounter. O'Gara and Mirco Bergamasco exchanged penalties throughout the first half, and when the whistle sounded for the break Ireland had edged into a welcome but hardly conclusive 9–6 lead.

The second period was a different beast altogether, and after seven minutes' play a break from Bowe gave O'Driscoll the chance to score his 45th Test try for his country. Ireland never looked back. Italy failed to trouble the scorers again, and a brace of tries from Keith Earls supplied the icing on the cake as the men in green cantered to a 36–6 triumph and a place in the quarter-finals.

"This was an all-or-nothing game for us, and we just wanted to get out of the pool," Kidney said as Ireland left the Otago Stadium and he began to focus on the quarter-final showdown with Wales. "The first half was nip-and-tuck, as it always is in matches between Ireland and Italy, but the tries early in the second half gave us a bit of daylight.

"It was a case of taking the breaks when they came and now we're looking forward to the challenge of facing Wales. It will be like a Six Nations game because the players know each other so well; space will be cut down. It will be like a cup final. That's what this competition is all about. Today was a cup final, and thankfully we've qualified for another one."

Once Best was passed fit after a shoulder injury scare, Kidney opted to put his faith in the same XV that had overcome the Italians, hoping to record a fifth win over the side from the Principality in the last seven meetings between the Celtic rivals.

The match, however, could not have started in worse fashion for

Kidney's troops when wing Shane Williams scampered over the line as early as the third minute, and when Rhys Priestland landed a testing conversion from near the right touchline Ireland suddenly found themselves trailing 7–0.

To their credit, the Irish steadied themselves despite the initial onslaught, and after Leigh Halfpenny and O'Gara had exchanged successful penalties they appeared to have found a way back into the match when Earls plunged over in the corner four minutes after the restart. O'Gara added the conversion and the score stood at 10–10.

It was as close as Ireland came to overhauling Wales. Just six minutes after Earls' morale-boosting score, scrum-half Mike Phillips darted towards and over the line before the cover defence could get to him and Priestland extended the lead to seven points with the conversion.

Ireland remained in the hunt until the 63rd minute but only had themselves to blame when lacklustre tackling allowed centre Jonathan Davies to barrel his way through the defence for Wales' third try. Ireland were beaten and heading home.

"It will be a hard one to take – there'll be a few long days," admitted Kidney after the game. "But they're good men, they'll rise again and that's all that you can ever do in life. It's all or nothing – we knew that going in last week, and we knew it this week.

"We've had both experiences now and obviously today's one was a bitter one to take, but all credit to Wales – they outscored us three tries to one, and when you're beaten like that you can have no complaints and just wish them well for future matches.

"We felt that once we kept the pace on the game that we would get the score and that's the way it transpired. Just before half-time we put a bit of pace on it, we put pace on it for the first five or ten minutes of the second half. Then Wales came down, managed to get a score which gave them that little bit of impetus, and they managed to pin us back from there on in."

IRELAND INTERNATIONAL STATISTICS

MATCH RECORDS UP TO 31 OCTOBER 2011

MOST CONSECUTIVE TEST WINS

10 2002 *R, Ru, Gg, A, Fj, Arg,* 2003 *S1, It1, F, W1*
8 2003 *Tg, Sm, W2, It2, S2, R, Nm, Arg*
8 2008 *Arg,* 2009 *F, It, E, S, W, C, US*
6 1968 *S, W, A,* 1969 *F, E, S*
6 2004 *SA, US, Arg,* 2005 *It, S, E*

MOST CONSECUTIVE TESTS WITHOUT DEFEAT

Matches	Wins	Draws	Period
12	11	1	2008 to 2010
10	10	0	2002 to 2003
8	8	0	2003
7	6	1	1968 to 1969
6	6	0	2004 to 2005

MOST POINTS IN A MATCH

BY THE TEAM

Pts	Opponents	Venue	Year
83	United States	Manchester (NH)	2000
78	Japan	Dublin	2000
70	Georgia	Dublin	1998
64	Fiji	Dublin	2002
64	Namibia	Sydney	2003
63	Georgia	Dublin	2002
62	Russia	Rotorua	2011
61	Italy	Limerick	2003
61	Pacific Islands	Dublin	2006
60	Romania	Dublin	1986
60	Italy	Dublin	2000
55	Zimbabwe	Dublin	1991
55	United States	Dublin	2004
55	Canada	Limerick	2008
54	Wales	Dublin	2002
53	Romania	Dublin	1998
53	United States	Dublin	1999
51	Italy	Rome	2007
50	Japan	Bloemfontein	1995

BY A PLAYER

Pts	Player	Opponents	Venue	Year
32	R J R O'Gara	Samoa	Apia	2003
30	R J R O'Gara	Italy	Dublin	2000
26	D G Humphreys	Scotland	Murrayfield	2003
26	D G Humphreys	Italy	Limerick	2003
26	P Wallace	Pacific Islands	Dublin	2006
24	P A Burke	Italy	Dublin	1997
24	D G Humphreys	Argentina	Lens	1999
23	R P Keyes	Zimbabwe	Dublin	1991
23	R J R O'Gara	Japan	Dublin	2000
22	D G Humphreys	Wales	Dublin	2002
21	S O Campbell	Scotland	Dublin	1982
21	S O Campbell	England	Dublin	1983
21	R J R O'Gara	Italy	Rome	2001
21	R J R O'Gara	Argentina	Dublin	2004
21	R J R O'Gara	England	Dublin	2007
20	M J Kiernan	Romania	Dublin	1986
20	E P Elwood	Romania	Dublin	1993
20	S J P Mason	Samoa	Dublin	1996
20	E P Elwood	Georgia	Dublin	1998
20	K G M Wood	United States	Dublin	1999
20	D A Hickie	Italy	Limerick	2003
20	D G Humphreys	United States	Dublin	2004

MOST TRIES IN A MATCH

BY THE TEAM

Tries	Opponents	Venue	Year
13	United States	Manchester (NH)	2000
11	Japan	Dublin	2000
10	Romania	Dublin	1986
10	Georgia	Dublin	1998
10	Namibia	Sydney	2003
9	Fiji	Dublin	2003
9	Russia	Rotorua	2011
8	Western Samoa	Dublin	1988
8	Zimbabwe	Dublin	1991
8	Georgia	Dublin	2002
8	Italy	Limerick	2003
8	Pacific Islands	Dublin	2006
8	Italy	Rome	2007
8	Canada	Limerick	2008
7	Japan	Bloemfontein	1995
7	Romania	Dublin	1998
7	United States	Dublin	1999
7	United States	Dublin	2004
7	Japan	Tokyo	2005

BY A PLAYER

Tries	Player	Opponents	Venue	Year
4	B F Robinson	Zimbabwe	Dublin	1991
4	K G M Wood	United States	Dublin	1999
4	D A Hickie	Italy	Limerick	2003
3	R Montgomery	Wales	Birkenhead	1887
3	J P Quinn	France	Cork	1913
3	E O'D Davy	Scotland	Murrayfield	1930
3	S J Byrne	Scotland	Murrayfield	1953
3	K D Crossan	Romania	Dublin	1986
3	B J Mullin	Tonga	Brisbane	1987
3	M R Mostyn	Argentina	Dublin	1999
3	B G O'Driscoll	France	Paris	2000
3	M J Mullins	United States	Manchester (NH)	2000
3	D A Hickie	Japan	Dublin	2000
3	R A J Henderson	Italy	Rome	2001
3	B G O'Driscoll	Scotland	Dublin	2002
3	K M Maggs	Fiji	Dublin	2002

MOST CONVERSIONS IN A MATCH

BY THE TEAM

Cons	Opponents	Venue	Year
10	Georgia	Dublin	1998
10	Japan	Dublin	2000
9	United States	Manchester (NH)	2000
7	Romania	Dublin	1986
7	Georgia	Dublin	2002
7	Namibia	Sydney	2003
7	United States	Dublin	2004
7	Russia	Rotorua	2011
6	Japan	Bloemfontein	1995
6	Romania	Dublin	1998
6	United States	Dublin	1999
6	Italy	Dublin	2000
6	Italy	Limerick	2003
6	Japan	Tokyo	2005
6	Pacific Islands	Dublin	2006
6	Canada	Limerick	2008

BY A PLAYER

Cons	Player	Opponents	Venue	Year
10	E P Elwood	Georgia	Dublin	1998
10	R J R O'Gara	Japan	Dublin	2000
8	R J R O'Gara	United States	Manchester (NH)	2000
7	M J Kiernan	Romania	Dublin	1986
7	R J R O'Gara	Namibia	Sydney	2003
7	D G Humphreys	United States	Dublin	2004
6	P A Burke	Japan	Bloemfontein	1995
6	R J R O'Gara	Italy	Dublin	2000
6	D G Humphreys	Italy	Limerick	2003
6	D G Humphreys	Japan	Tokyo	2005
6	P Wallace	Pacific Islands	Dublin	2006
6	R J R O'Gara	Russia	Rotorua	2011
5	M J Kiernan	Canada	Dunedin	1987
5	E P Elwood	Romania	Dublin	1999
5	R J R O'Gara	Georgia	Dublin	2002
5	D G Humphreys	Fiji	Dublin	2002
5	D G Humphreys	Romania	Dublin	2005
5	R J R O'Gara	Canada	Limerick	2008
5	J Sexton	Fiji	Dublin	2009

MOST PENALTIES IN A MATCH

BY THE TEAM

Penalties	Opponents	Venue	Year
8	Italy	Dublin	1997
7	Argentina	Lens	1999
6	Scotland	Dublin	1982
6	Romania	Dublin	1993
6	United States	Atlanta	1996
6	Western Samoa	Dublin	1996
6	Italy	Dublin	2000
6	Wales	Dublin	2002
6	Australia	Dublin	2002
6	Samoa	Apia	2003
6	Japan	Osaka	2005

BY A PLAYER

Penalties	Player	Opponents	Venue	Year
8	P A Burke	Italy	Dublin	1997
7	D G Humphreys	Argentina	Lens	1999
6	S O Campbell	Scotland	Dublin	1982
6	E P Elwood	Romania	Dublin	1993
6	S J P Mason	Western Samoa	Dublin	1996
6	R J R O'Gara	Italy	Dublin	2000
6	D G Humphreys	Wales	Dublin	2002
6	R J R O'Gara	Australia	Dublin	2002

MOST DROPPED GOALS IN A MATCH

BY THE TEAM

Drops	Opponents	Venue	Year
2	Australia	Dublin	1967
2	France	Dublin	1975
2	Australia	Sydney	1979
2	England	Dublin	1981
2	Canada	Dunedin	1987
2	England	Dublin	1993
2	Wales	Wembley	1999
2	New Zealand	Dublin	2001
2	Argentina	Dublin	2004
2	England	Dublin	2005

BY A PLAYER

Drops	Player	Opponents	Venue	Year
2	C M H Gibson	Australia	Dublin	1967
2	W M McCombe	France	Dublin	1975
2	S O Campbell	Australia	Sydney	1979
2	E P Elwood	England	Dublin	1993
2	D G Humphreys	Wales	Wembley	1999
2	D G Humphreys	New Zealand	Dublin	2001
2	R J R O'Gara	Argentina	Dublin	2004
2	R J R O'Gara	England	Dublin	2005

CAREER RECORDS

MOST CAPPED PLAYERS

Caps	Player	Career Span
117	B G O'Driscoll	1999 to 2011
116	R J R O'Gara	2000 to 2011
105	J J Hayes	2000 to 2011
98	P A Stringer	2000 to 2011
92	M E O'Kelly	1997 to 2009
82	G T Dempsey	1998 to 2008
82	P J O'Connell	2002 to 2011
80	D P O'Callaghan	2003 to 2011
72	D G Humphreys	1996 to 2005
72	D P Wallace	2000 to 2011
72	G E A Murphy	2000 to 2011
70	K M Maggs	1997 to 2005
69	C M H Gibson	1964 to 1979
67	M J Horan	2000 to 2011
65	S H Easterby	2000 to 2008
65	S P Horgan	2000 to 2009
63	W J McBride	1962 to 1975
63	G W D'Arcy	1999 to 2011
62	A G Foley	1995 to 2005
62	D A Hickie	1997 to 2007
61	J F Slattery	1970 to 1984
59	P S Johns	1990 to 2000
58	P A Orr	1976 to 1987
58	K G M Wood	1994 to 2003
57	D P Leamy	2004 to 2011
55	B J Mullin	1984 to 1995
54	T J Kiernan	1960 to 1973
54	P M Clohessy	1993 to 2002
54	R D Best	2005 to 2011
52	D G Lenihan	1981 to 1992
51	M I Keane	1974 to 1984

MOST CONSECUTIVE TESTS

Tests	Player	Span
52	W J McBride	1964 to 1975
49	P A Orr	1976 to 1986
43	D G Lenihan	1981 to 1989
39	M I Keane	1974 to 1981
38	P A Stringer	2003 to 2007
37	G V Stephenson	1920 to 1929

MOST TESTS AS CAPTAIN

Tests	Captain	Span
80	B G O'Driscoll	2002 to 2011
36	K G M Wood	1996 to 2003
24	T J Kiernan	1963 to 1973
19	C F Fitzgerald	1982 to 1986
17	J F Slattery	1979 to 1981
17	D G Lenihan	1986 to 1990

MOST POINTS IN TESTS

Points	Player	Tests	Career
1075	R J R O'Gara	116	2000 to 2011
565*	D G Humphreys	72	1996 to 2005
308	M J Kiernan	43	1982 to 1991
296	E P Elwood	35	1993 to 1999
240	B G O'Driscoll	117	1999 to 2011
217	S O Campbell	22	1976 to 1984
161	J J Sexton	24	2009 to 2011
158	T J Kiernan	54	1960 to 1973
145	D A Hickie	62	1997 to 2007
113	A J P Ward	19	1978 to 1987

* Humphreys's total includes a penalty try against Scotland in 1999

MOST TRIES IN TESTS

Tries	Player	Tests	Career
45	B G O'Driscoll	117	1999 to 2011
29	D A Hickie	62	1997 to 2007
21	S P Horgan	65	2000 to 2009
19	G T Dempsey	82	1998 to 2008
19	T J Bowe	44	2004 to 2011
18	G E A Murphy	72	2000 to 2011
17	B J Mullin	55	1984 to 1995
16	R J R O'Gara	116	2000 to 2011
15	K G M Wood	58	1994 to 2003
15	K M Maggs	70	1997 to 2005
14	G V Stephenson	42	1920 to 1930
12	K D Crossan	41	1982 to 1992
12	D P Wallace	72	2000 to 2011
11	A T A Duggan	25	1963 to 1972
11	S P Geoghegan	37	1991 to 1996
11	K G Earls	26	2008 to 2011

MOST CONVERSIONS IN TESTS

Cons	Player	Tests	Career
175	R J R O'Gara	116	2000 to 2011
88	D G Humphreys	72	1996 to 2005
43	E P Elwood	35	1993 to 1999
40	M J Kiernan	43	1982 to 1991
26	T J Kiernan	54	1960 to 1973
16	R A Lloyd	19	1910 to 1920
15	S O Campbell	22	1976 to 1984
15	J J Sexton	24	2009 to 2011

MOST PENALTY GOALS IN TESTS

Penalties	Player	Tests	Career
200	R J R O'Gara	116	2000 to 2011
110	D G Humphreys	72	1996 to 2005
68	E P Elwood	35	1993 to 1999
62	M J Kiernan	43	1982 to 1991
54	S O Campbell	22	1976 to 1984
40	J J Sexton	24	2009 to 2011
31	T J Kiernan	54	1960 to 1973
29	A J P Ward	19	1978 to 1987

MOST DROPPED GOALS IN TESTS

Drops	Player	Tests	Career
15	R J R O'Gara	116	2000 to 2011
8	D G Humphreys	72	1996 to 2005
7	R A Lloyd	19	1910 to 1920
7	S O Campbell	22	1976 to 1984
6	C M H Gibson	69	1964 to 1979
6	B J McGann	25	1969 to 1976
6	M J Kiernan	43	1982 to 1991

INTERNATIONAL CHAMPIONSHIP RECORDS

RECORD	DETAIL		SET
Most points in season	168	in five matches	2000
Most tries in season	17	in five matches	2000
	17	in five matches	2004
	17	in five matches	2007
Highest score	60	60–13 v Italy	2000
Biggest win	47	60–13 v Italy	2000
Highest score conceded	50	18–50 v England	2000
Biggest defeat	40	6–46 v England	1997
Most appearances	56	C M H Gibson	1964–1979
	56	R J R O'Gara	2000–2011
Most points in matches	551	R J R O'Gara	2000–2011
Most points in season	82	R J R O'Gara	2007
Most points in match	30	R J R O'Gara	v Italy, 2000
Most tries in matches	25	B G O'Driscoll	2000–2011
Most tries in season	5	J E Arigho	1928
	5	B G O'Driscoll	2000
Most tries in match	3	R Montgomery	v Wales, 1887
	3	J P Quinn	v France, 1913
	3	E O'D Davy	v Scotland, 1930
	3	S J Byrne	v Scotland, 1953
	3	B G O'Driscoll	v France, 2000
	3	R A J Henderson	v Italy, 2001
	3	B G O'Driscoll	v Scotland, 2002
Most cons in matches	81	R J R O'Gara	2000–2011
Most cons in season	11	R J R O'Gara	2000
	11	R J R O'Gara	2004
Most cons in match	6	R J R O'Gara	v Italy, 2000
Most pens in matches	107	R J R O'Gara	2000–2011
Most pens in season	17	R J R O'Gara	2006
Most pens in match	6	S O Campbell	v Scotland, 1982
	6	R J R O'Gara	v Italy, 2000
	6	D G Humphreys	v Wales, 2002
Most drops in matches	7	R A Lloyd	1910–1920
Most drops in season	2	on several occasions	
Most drops in match	2	W M McCombe	v France, 1975
	2	E P Elwood	v England, 1993
	2	D G Humphreys	v Wales, 1999
	2	R J R O'Gara	v England, 2005

MISCELLANEOUS RECORDS

RECORD	HOLDER	DETAIL
Longest Test Career	A J F O'Reilly	1955 to 1970
	C M H Gibson	1964 to 1979
Youngest Test Cap	F S Hewitt	17 yrs 157 days in 1924
Oldest Test Cap	J J Hayes	37 yrs 277 days in 2011

CAREER RECORDS OF IRELAND INTERNATIONAL PLAYERS

(UP TO 31 OCTOBER 2011)

PLAYER BACKS :	DEBUT	CAPS	T	C	P	D	PTS
I J Boss	2006 v NZ	15	3	0	0	0	15
T J Bowe	2004 v US	44	19	0	0	0	95
G W D'Arcy	1999 v R	63	7	0	0	0	35
K G Earls	2008 v C	26	11	0	0	0	55
L M Fitzgerald	2006 v PI	23	2	0	0	0	10
F A Jones	2011 v S	3	0	0	0	0	0
R D J Kearney	2007 v Arg	33	7	1	0	0	37
F L McFadden	2011 v It	6	2	0	0	0	10
G E A Murphy	2000 v US	72	18	1	1	1	98
C Murray	2011 v F	6	0	0	0	0	0
B G O'Driscoll	1999 v A	117	45	0	0	5	240
R J R O'Gara	2000 v S	116	16	175	200	15	1075
T G O'Leary	2007 v Arg	22	3	0	0	0	15
E G Reddan	2006 F	37	1	0	0	0	5
J J Sexton	2009 v Fj	24	1	15	40	2	161
P A Stringer	2000 v S	98	6	0	0	0	30
A D Trimble	2005 v A	41	9	0	0	0	45
P R Wallace	2006 v SA	29	2	11	7	0	53

FORWARDS :

R D Best	2005 v NZ	54	5	0	0	0	25
T D Buckley	2007 v Arg	25	2	0	0	0	10
T G Court	2009 v It	24	0	0	0	0	0
S M Cronin	2009 v Fj	15	0	0	0	0	0
L F M Cullen	2002 v NZ	32	0	0	0	0	0
S Ferris	2006 v PI	30	2	0	0	0	10
J P Flannery	2005 v R	41	3	0	0	0	15
J J Hayes	2000 v S	105	2	0	0	0	10
C E Healy	2009 v A	25	1	0	0	0	5
J P R Heaslip	2006 v PI	43	7	0	0	0	35
M R Horan	2000 v US	67	6	0	0	0	30
S Jennings	2007 v Arg	12	1	0	0	0	5
D P Leamy	2004 v US	57	2	0	0	0	10
M P McCarthy	2011 v S	2	0	0	0	0	0
K R McLaughlin	2010 v It	2	0	0	0	0	0
S K O'Brien	2009 v Fj	15	2	0	0	0	10
D P O'Callaghan	2003 v W	80	1	0	0	0	5
P J O'Connell	2002 v W	82	6	0	0	0	30
M R O'Driscoll	2001 v R	23	0	0	0	0	0
N Ronan	2009 v C	4	0	0	0	0	0
M R Ross	2009 v C	15	0	0	0	0	0
R J Ruddock	2010 v A	1	0	0	0	0	0
D C Ryan	2008 v Arg	13	0	0	0	0	0
D Toner	2010 v Sm	3	0	0	0	0	0
D M Tuohy	2010 v NZ	2	1	0	0	0	5
D A Varley	2010 v A	2	0	0	0	0	0
D P Wallace	2000 v Arg	72	12	0	0	0	60

Shaun Botterill/Getty Images

Paul O'Connell won his 82nd cap at the Rugby World Cup.

IRELAND INTERNATIONAL PLAYERS (UP TO 31 OCTOBER 2011)

Note: Years given for International Championship matches are for second half of season; eg 1972 means season 1971–72. Years for all other matches refer to the actual year of the match. Entries in square brackets denote matches played in RWC Finals.

Abraham, M (Bective Rangers) 1912 E, S, W, SA, 1914 W
Adams, C (Old Wesley), 1908 E, 1909 E, F, 1910 F, 1911 E, S, W, F, 1912 S, W, SA, 1913 W, F, 1914 F, E, S
Agar, R D (Malone) 1947 F, E, S, W, 1948 F, 1949 S, W, 1950 F, E, W
Agnew, P J (CIYMS) 1974 F (R), 1976 A
Ahearne, T (Queen's Coll, Cork) 1899 E
Aherne, L F P (Dolphin, Lansdowne) 1988 E 2, WS, It, 1989 F, W, E, S, NZ, 1990 E, S, F, W (R), 1992 E, S, F, A
Alexander, R (NIFC, Police Union) 1936 E, S, W, 1937 E, S, W, 1938 E, S, 1939 E, S, W
Allen, C E (Derry, Liverpool) 1900 E, S, W, 1901 E, S, W, 1903 S, W, 1904 E, S, W, 1905 E, S, W, NZ, 1906 E, S, W, SA, 1907 S, W
Allen, G G (Derry, Liverpool) 1896 E, S, W, 1897 E, S, 1898 E, S, 1899 E, W
Allen, T C (NIFC) 1885 E, S 1
Allen, W S (Wanderers) 1875 E
Allison, J B (Edinburgh U) 1899 E, S, 1900 E, S, W, 1901 E, S, W, 1902 E, S, W, 1903 S
Anderson, F E (Queen's U, Belfast, NIFC) 1953 F, E, S, W, 1954 NZ, F, E, S, W, 1955 F, E, S, W
Anderson, H J (Old Wesley) 1903 E, S, 1906 E, S
Anderson, W A (Dungannon) 1984 A, 1985 S, F, W, E, 1986 F, S, R, 1987 E, S, F, W, [W, C, Tg, A], 1988 S, F, W, E 1, 2, 1989 F, W, E, NZ, 1990 E, S
Andrews, G (NIFC) 1875 E, 1876 E
Andrews, H W (NIFC) 1888 M, 1889 S, W
Archer, A M (Dublin U, NIFC) 1879 S
Arigho, J E (Lansdowne) 1928 F, E, W, 1929 F, E, S, W, 1930 F, E, S, W, 1931 F, E, S, W, SA
Armstrong, W K (NIFC) 1960 SA, 1961 E
Arnott, D T (Lansdowne) 1876 E
Ash, W H (NIFC) 1875 E, 1876 E, 1877 S
Aston, H R (Dublin U) 1908 E, W
Atkins, A P (Bective Rangers) 1924 F
Atkinson, J M (NIFC) 1927 F, A
Atkinson, J R (Dublin U) 1882 W, S

Bagot, J C (Dublin U, Lansdowne) 1879 S, E, 1880 E, S, 1881 S
Bailey, A H (UC Dublin, Lansdowne) 1934 W, 1935 E, S, W, NZ, 1936 E, S, W, 1937 E, S, W, 1938 E, S
Bailey, N (Northampton) 1952 E
Bardon, M E (Bohemians) 1934 E
Barlow, M (Wanderers) 1875 E
Barnes, R J (Dublin U, Armagh) 1933 W
Barr, A (Belfast Collegians) 1898 W, 1899 S, 1901 E, S
Barry, N J (Garryowen) 1991 Nm 2(R)
Beamish, C E St J (RAF, Leicester) 1933 W, S, 1934 S, W, 1935 E, S, W, NZ, 1936 E, S, W, 1938 W
Beamish, G R (RAF, Leicester) 1925 E, S, W, 1928 F, E, S, W, 1929 F, E, S, W, 1930 F, S, W, 1931 F, E, S, W, SA, 1932 E, S, W, 1933 E, W, S
Beatty, W J (NIFC, Richmond) 1910 F, 1912 F, W
Becker, V A (Lansdowne) 1974 F, W
Beckett, G G P (Dublin U) 1908 E, S, W
Bell, J C (Ballymena, Northampton, Dungannon) 1994 A 1, 2, US, 1995 S, It, [NZ, W, F], Fj, 1996 US, S, F, W, E, WS, A, 1997 It 1, F, W, E, S, 1998 Gg, R, SA 3, 1999 F, W, S It (R), A 2, [US (R), A 3(R), R], 2001 R (R), 2003 Tg, Sm, It 2(R)
Bell, R J (NIFC) 1875 E, 1876 E
Bell, W E (Belfast Collegians) 1953 F, E, S, W
Bennett, F (Belfast Collegians) 1913 S
Bent, G C (Dublin U) 1882 W, E
Berkery, P J (Lansdowne) 1954 W, 1955 W, 1956 S, W, 1957 F, E, S, W, 1958 A, E, S
Bermingham, J J C (Blackrock Coll) 1921 E, S, W, F
Best, N A (Ulster) 2005 NZ(R), R, 2006 NZ1, 2, A1, SA, A2, 2007 F(R), E(R), S1(R), Arg1, 2(R), S2, It2, [Nm(R), Gg(R), F(R), Arg(t&R)]
Best, R D (Ulster) 2005 NZ(R), A(t), 2006 W(R), A1(R), SA, A2, PI(R), 2007 W, F, E, S1, It1, S2(R), It2, [Nm, Gg, Arg(R)], 2008 It, F(R), S(R), W, E, NZ1(R), A, C(R), NZ2, Arg(R), 2009 F(R), It(R), E(R), S, W(R), C, US, 2010 It(R), F(R), E, W, S, SA, Sm(R), NZ2, 2011 It, F1, S1, W, E1, F2, 3, E2(R), [US, A, It, W]
Best, S J (Belfast Harlequins, Ulster) 2003 Tg (R), W 2, S 2(R), 2003 [Nm(R)], 2004 W(R), US(R), 2005 J1, 2, NZ(R), R, 2006 F(R), W(R), PI(R), 2007 E(R), S1, It1(R), Arg1, 2, S2, It2(R), [Nm(R), Gg(R), F(R)]
Bishop, J P (London Irish) 1998 SA, 1, 2, Gg, R, SA 3, 1999 F, W, E, S, It, A 1, 2, Arg 1, [US, A 3, Arg 2], 2000 E, Arg, C, 2002 NZ 1, 2, Fj, Arg, 2003 W 1, E
Blackham, J C (Queen's Coll, Cork) 1909 S, W, F, 1910 E, S, W
Blake-Knox, S E F (NIFC) 1976 E, S, 1977 F (R)
Blayney, J J (Wanderers) 1950 S
Bond, A T W (Derry) 1894 S, W
Bornemann, W W (Wanderers) 1960 E, S, W, SA
Boss, I J (Ulster, Leinster) 2006 NZ2(R), A1(R), SA(R), A2, PI(R), 2007 F, E(R), Arg1, S2, It2(R), [Gg(R), Arg(R)], 2010 Sm(R), 2011 S2(R), [Ru]
Bowe, T J (Ulster, Ospreys) 2004 US, 2005 J1, 2, NZ, A, R, 2006 It, F, 2007 Arg1, S2, 2008 S, W, E, NZ1, A, C, NZ2, Arg, 2009 F, It, E, S, W, A, SA, 2010 It, F, E, W, S, NZ1, A, SA, Sm, NZ2, Arg, 2011 S1, W, E1, 2, [US, A, It, W]
Bowen, D St J (Cork Const) 1977 W, E, S
Boyd, C A (Dublin U) 1900 S, 1901 S, W
Boyle, C V (Dublin U) 1935 NZ, 1936 E, S, W, 1937 E, S, W, 1938 W, 1939 W
Brabazon, H M (Dublin U) 1884 E, 1885 S 1, 1886 E
Bradley, M J (Dolphin) 1920 W, F, 1922 E, S, W, F, 1923 E, S, W, F, 1925 F, S, W, 1926 F, E, S, W, 1927 F, W
Bradley, M T (Cork Constitution) 1984 A, 1985 S, F, W, E, 1986 F, W, E, S, R, 1987 E, S, F, W, [W, C, Tg, A], 1988 S, F, W, E 1, 1990 W, 1992 NZ 1, 2, 1993 S, F, W, E, R, 1994 F, W, E, S, A 1, 2, US, 1995 S, F, [NZ]
Bradshaw, G (Belfast Collegians) 1903 W
Bradshaw, R M (Wanderers) 1885 E, S 1, 2
Brady, A M (UC Dublin, Malone) 1966 S, 1968 E, S, W
Brady, J A (Wanderers) 1976 E, S
Brady, J R (CIYMS) 1951 S, W, 1953 F, E, S, W, 1954 W, 1956 W, 1957 F, E, S, W
Bramwell, T (NIFC) 1928 F
Brand, T N (NIFC) 1924 NZ
Brennan, J I (CIYMS) 1957 S, W
Brennan, T (St Mary's Coll, Barnhall) 1998 SA 1(R), 2(R), 1999 F (R), S (R), It, A 2, Arg 1, [US, A 3], 2000 E (R), 2001 W (R), E (R), Sm (R)
Bresnihan, F P K (UC Dublin, Lansdowne, London Irish) 1966 E, W, 1967 A 1, E, S, W, F, 1968 F, E, S, W, A, 1969 F, E, S, W, 1970 SA, F, E, S, W, 1971 F, E, S, W
Brett, J T (Monkstown) 1914 W
Bristow, J R (NIFC) 1879 E
Brophy, N H (Blackrock Coll, UC Dublin, London Irish) 1957 F, E, 1959 E, S, W, F, 1960 F, SA, 1961 S, W, 1962 E, S, W, 1963 E, W, 1967 E, S, W, F, A 2
Brown, E L (Instonians) 1958 F
Brown, G S (Monkstown, United Services) 1912 S, W, SA
Brown, H (Windsor) 1877 E
Brown, T (Windsor) 1877 E, S
Brown, W H (Dublin U) 1899 E
Brown, W J (Malone) 1970 SA, F, S, W
Brown, W S (Dublin U) 1893 S, W, 1894 E, S, W

Browne, A W (Dublin U) 1951 SA
Browne, D (Blackrock Coll) 1920 F
Browne, H C (United Services and RN) 1929 E, S, W
Browne, W F (United Services and Army) 1925 E, S, W, 1926 S, W, 1927 F, E, S, W, A, 1928 E, S
Browning, D R (Wanderers) 1881 E, S
Bruce, S A M (NIFC) 1883 E, S, 1884 E
Brunker, A A (Lansdowne) 1895 E, W
Bryant, C H (Cardiff) 1920 E, S
Buchanan, A McM (Dublin U) 1926 E, S, W, 1927 S, W, A
Buchanan, J W B (Dublin U) 1882 S, 1884 E, S
Buckley, J H (Sunday's Well) 1973 E, S
Buckley, T D (Munster, Sale) 2007 Arg1(R), 2(R), 2008 It(R), F(R), S(R), W(R), E(R), NZ1(R), A(R), C, NZ2(R), 2009 C, US, Fj(R), 2010 E(R), W(R), S(R), NZ1, A, SA, Arg, 2011 S2, F2(R), [US(R), Ru]
Bulger, L Q (Lansdowne) 1896 E, S, W, 1897 E, S, 1898 E, S, W
Bulger, M J (Dublin U) 1888 M
Burges, J H (Rosslyn Park) 1950 F, E
Burgess, R B (Dublin U) 1912 SA
Burke, P A (Cork Constitution, Bristol, Harlequins) 1995 E, S, W (R), It, [J], Fj, 1996 US (R), A, 1997 It 1, S (R), 2001 R (R), 2003 S 1(R), Sm (R)
Burkitt, J C S (Queen's Coll, Cork) 1881 E
Burns, I J (Wanderers) 1980 E (R)
Butler, L G (Blackrock Coll) 1960 W
Butler, N (Bective Rangers) 1920 E
Byers, R M (NIFC) 1928 S, W, 1929 E, S, W
Byrne, E (St Mary's Coll) 2001 It (R), F (R), S (R), W (R), E (R), Sm, NZ (R), 2003 A (R), Sm (R)
Byrne, E M J (Blackrock Coll) 1977 S, F, 1978 F, W, E, NZ
Byrne, J S (Blackrock Coll, Leinster, Saracens) 2001 R (R), 2002 W (R), E (R), S (R), It, NZ 2(R), R, Ru (R), Gg, A, Arg, 2003 S 1, It 1, F, W 1, E, A, Tg, Sm, W 2(R), It 2, S2(R), [R(R), Nm(R)], 2004 F, W, E, It, S, SA1, 2, 3, Arg, 2005 It, S, E, F, W, NZ, A, R
Byrne, N F (UC Dublin) 1962 F
Byrne, S J (UC Dublin, Lansdowne) 1953 S, W, 1955 F
Byron, W G (NIFC) 1896 E, S, W, 1897 E, S, 1898 E, S, W, 1899 E, S, W

Caddell, E D (Dublin U, Wanderers) 1904 S, 1905 E, S, W, NZ, 1906 E, S, W, SA, 1907 E, S, 1908 S, W
Cagney, S J (London Irish) 1925 W, 1926 F, E, S, W, 1927 F, 1928 E, S, W, 1929 F, E, S, W
Caldwell, R (Ulster) 2009 C(R), US(R)
Callan, C P (Lansdowne) 1947 F, E, S, W, 1948 F, E, S, W, 1949 F, E
Cameron, E D (Bective Rangers) 1891 S, W
Campbell, C E (Old Wesley) 1970 SA
Campbell, E F (Monkstown) 1899 S, W, 1900 E, W
Campbell, K P (Ulster) 2005 J1(R), 2(R), R
Campbell, S B B (Derry) 1911 E, S, W, F, 1912 F, E, S, W, SA, 1913 E, S, F
Campbell, S O (Old Belvedere) 1976 A, 1979 A 1, 2, 1980 E, S, F, W, 1981 F, W, E, S, SA 1, 1982 W, E, S, F, 1983 S, F, W, E, 1984 F, W
Canniffe, D M (Lansdowne) 1976 W, E
Cantrell, J L (UC Dublin, Blackrock Coll) 1976 A, F, W, E, S, 1981 S, SA 1, 2, A
Carey, R W (Dungannon) 1992 NZ 1, 2
Carney, B B (Munster) 2007 Arg1, 2, S2, It2(R)
Carpendale, M J (Monkstown) 1886 S, 1887 W, 1888 W, S
Carr, N J (Ards) 1985 S, F, W, E, 1986 W, E, S, R, 1987 E, S, W
Carroll, C (Bective Rangers) 1930 F
Carroll, R (Lansdowne) 1947 F, 1950 S, W
Casement, B N (Dublin U) 1875 E, 1876 E, 1879 E
Casement, F (Dublin U) 1906 E, S, W
Casey, J C (Young Munster) 1930 S, 1932 E
Casey, P J (UC Dublin, Lansdowne) 1963 F, E, S, W, NZ, 1964 E, S, W, F, 1965 F, E, S
Casey, R E (Blackrock Coll, London Irish) 1999 [A 3(t), Arg 2(R)], 2000 E, US (R), C (R), 2009 C, US
Cave, D M (Ulster) 2009 C, US
Chambers, J (Dublin U) 1886 E, S, 1887 E, S, W
Chambers, R R (Instonians) 1951 F, E, S, W, 1952 F, W
Clancy, T P J (Lansdowne) 1988 W, E 1, 2, WS, It, 1989 F, W, E, S
Clarke, A T H (Northampton, Dungannon) 1995 Fj (R), 1996 W, E, WS, 1997 F (R), It 2(R), 1998 Gg (R), R
Clarke, C P (Terenure Coll) 1993 F, W, E, 1998 W, E
Clarke, D J (Dolphin) 1991 W, Nm 1, 2, [J, A], 1992 NZ 2(R)
Clarke, J A B (Bective Rangers) 1922 S, W, F, 1923 F, 1924 E, S, W
Clegg, R J (Bangor) 1973 F, 1975 E, S, F, W
Clifford, J T (Young Munster) 1949 F, E, S, W, 1950 F, E, S, W, 1951 F, E, SA, 1952 F, S, W

Clinch, A D (Dublin U, Wanderers) 1892 S, 1893 W, 1895 E, S, W, 1896 E, S, W, 1897 E, S
Clinch, J D (Wanderers, Dublin U) 1923 W, 1924 F, E, S, W, NZ, 1925 F, E, S, 1926 E, S, W, 1927 F, 1928 F, E, S, W, 1929 F, E, S, W, 1930 F, E, S, W, 1931 F, E, S, W, SA
Clohessy, P M (Young Munster) 1993 F, W, E, 1994 F, W, E, S, A 1, 2, US, 1995 E, S, F, W, 1996 S, F, 1997 It 2, 1998 F (R), W (R), SA 2(R), Gg, R, SA 3, 1999 F, W, E, S, It, A 1, 2 Arg 1, [US, A 3(R)], 2000 E, S, It, F, W, Arg, J, SA, 2001 It, F, R, S, W, E, Sm (R), NZ, 2002 W, E, S, It, F
Clune, J J (Blackrock Coll) 1912 SA, 1913 W, F, 1914 F, E, W
Coffey, J J (Lansdowne) 1900 E, 1901 W, 1902 E, S, W, 1903 E, S, W, 1905 E, S, W, NZ, 1906 E, S, W, SA, 1907 E, 1908 W, 1910 F
Cogan, W St J (Queen's Coll, Cork) 1907 E, S
Collier, S R (Queen's Coll, Belfast) 1883 S
Collins, P C (Lansdowne, London Irish) 1987 [C], 1990 S (R)
Collis, W R F (KCH, Harlequins) 1924 F, W, NZ, 1925 F, E, S, 1926 F
Collis, W S (Wanderers) 1884 W
Collopy, G (Bective Rangers) 1891 S, 1892 S
Collopy, R (Bective Rangers) 1923 E, S, W, F, 1924 F, E, S, W, NZ, 1925 F, E, S, W
Collopy, W P (Bective Rangers) 1914 F, E, S, W, 1921 E, S, W, F, 1922 E, S, W, F, 1923 S, W, F, 1924 F, E, S, W
Combe, A (NIFC) 1875 E
Condon, H C (London Irish) 1984 S (R)
Cook, H G (Lansdowne) 1884 W
Coote, P B (RAF, Leicester) 1933 S
Corcoran, J C (London Irish) 1947 A, 1948 F
Corken, T S (Belfast Collegians) 1937 E, S, W
Corkery, D S (Cork Constitution, Bristol) 1994 A 1, 2, US, 1995 E, [NZ, J, W, F], Fj, 1996 US, S, F, W, E, WS, A, 1997 It 1, F, W, E, S, 1998 S, F, W, E, 1999 A 1(R), 2(R)
Corley, H H (Dublin U, Wanderers) 1902 E, S, W, 1903 E, S, W, 1904 E, S
Cormac, H S T (Clontarf) 1921 E, S, W
Corrigan, R (Greystones, Lansdowne, Leinster) 1997 C (R), It 2, 1998 S, F, W, E, SA 3(R), 1999 A 1(R), 2(R), [Arg 2], 2002 NZ 1, 2, R, Ru, Gg, A, Fj (R), Arg, 2003 S 1, It 1, A, Tg, Sm, W 2, It 2, S 2, [R, Arg, A, F], 2004 F, W, E, It, S, SA1, 2, 3, Arg, 2005 It, S, E, F, W, J1(R), 2(R), 2006 F
Costello, P (Bective Rangers) 1960 F
Costello, R A (Garryowen) 1993 S
Costello, V C P (St Mary's Coll, London Irish) 1996 US, F, W, E. WS (R), 1997 C, It 2(R), 1998 S (R), F, W, E, SA 1, 2, Gg, R, SA 3, 1999 F, W (R), E, S (R), It, A 1, 2002 R (R), A, Arg, 2003 S 1, It 1, F, E, A, It 2, S 2, [R, Arg, F], 2004 F(R), W(R), It(R), S(R)
Cotton, J (Wanderers) 1889 W
Coulter, H H (Queen's U, Belfast) 1920 E, S, W
Court, T G (Ulster) 2009 It(R), W(t), C, US(R), Fj, 2010 It(R), F(t&R), NZ1(R), A(R), SA(R), Sm, NZ2, Arg(R), 2011 It(R), F1(R), S1(R), W(R), E1(R), S2, F3(R), E2(R), [US, A(R), It(R)]
Courtney, A W (UC Dublin) 1920 S, W, F, 1921 E, S, W, F
Cox, H L (Dublin U) 1875 E, 1876 E, 1877 E, S
Craig, R G (Queen's U, Belfast) 1938 S, W
Crawford, E C (Dublin U) 1885 E, S 1
Crawford, W E (Lansdowne) 1920 E, S, W, F, 1921 E, S, W, F, 1922 E, S, 1923 E, S, W, F, 1924 F, E, W, NZ, 1925 F, E, S, W, 1926 F, E, S, W, 1927 F, E, S, W
Crean, T J (Wanderers) 1894 E, S, W, 1895 E, S, W, 1896 E, S, W
Crichton, R Y (Dublin U) 1920 E, S, W, F, 1921 F, 1922 E, 1923 W, F, 1924 F, E, S, W, NZ, 1925 E, S
Croker, E W D (Limerick) 1878 E
Cromey, G E (Queen's U, Belfast) 1937 E, S, W, 1938 E, S, W, 1939 E, S, W
Cronin, B M (Garryowen) 1995 S, 1997 S
Cronin, S M (Connacht, Leinster) 2009 Fj(R), 2010 W(R), NZ1, A, Sm, NZ2(R), Arg, 2011 It(R), F1(R), S1(R), W(R), E1(R), S2, [Ru, It(R)]
Cronyn, A P (Dublin U, Lansdowne) 1875 E, 1876 E, 1880 S
Crossan, K D (Instonians) 1982 S, 1984 F, W, E, S, 1985 S, F, W, E, 1986 E, S, R, 1987 E, S, F, W, [W, C, Tg, A], 1988 S, F, W, E 1, WS, It, 1989 W, S, NZ, 1990 E, S, F, W, Arg, 1991 E, S, Nm 2 [Z, J, S], 1992 W
Crotty, D J (Garryowen) 1996 A, 1997 It 1, F, W, 2000 C
Crowe, J F (UC Dublin) 1974 NZ
Crowe, L (Old Belvedere) 1950 E, S, W
Crowe, M P (Lansdowne) 1929 W, 1930 E, S, W, 1931 F, S, W, SA, 1932 S, W, 1933 W, S, 1934 E
Crowe, P M (Blackrock Coll) 1935 E, 1938 E
Cullen, L F M (Blackrock Coll, Leinster, Leicester) 2002 NZ 2(R), R (R), Ru (R), Gg (R), A (R), Fj, Arg (R), 2003 S 1(R), It 1(R), F (R), W 1, Tg, Sm, It 2, 2004 US(R), 2005 J1, 2, R, 2007 Arg2,

THE COUNTRIES

2009 Fj, 2010 It, F, E(R), W(R), 2011 It(R), F1(R), S1(R), W(R), E1(R), S2, F2, [Ru]
Cullen, T J (UC Dublin) 1949 F
Cullen, W J (Monkstown and Manchester) 1920 E
Culliton, M G (Wanderers) 1959 E, S, W, F, 1960 E, S, W, F, SA, 1961 E, S, W, F, 1962 S, F, 1964 E, S, W, F
Cummins, W E A (Queen's Coll, Cork) 1879 S, 1881 E, 1882 E
Cunningham, D McC (NIFC) 1923 E, S, W, 1925 F, E, W
Cunningham, M J (UC Cork) 1955 F, E, S, W, 1956 F, S, W
Cunningham, V J G (St Mary's Coll) 1988 E 2, It, 1990 Arg (R), 1991 Nm 1, 2, [Z, J(R)], 1992 NZ 1, 2, A, 1993 S, F, W, E, R, 1994 F
Cunningham, W A (Lansdowne) 1920 W, 1921 E, S, W, F, 1922 E, 1923 S, W
Cuppaidge, J L (Dublin U) 1879 E, 1880 E, S
Currell, J (NIFC) 1877 S
Curtis, A B (Oxford U) 1950 F, E, S
Curtis, D M (London Irish) 1991 W, E, S, Nm 1, 2, [Z, J, S, A], 1992 W, E, S (R), F
Cuscaden, W A (Dublin U, Bray) 1876 E
Cussen, D J (Dublin U) 1921 E, S, W, F, 1922 E, 1923 E, S, W, F, 1926 F, E, S, W, 1927 F, E

Daly, J C (London Irish) 1947 F, E, S, W, 1948 E, S, W
Daly, M J (Harlequins) 1938 E
Danaher, P P A (Lansdowne, Garryowen) 1988 S, F, W, WS, It, 1989 F, NZ (R), 1990 F, 1992 S, F, NZ 1, A, 1993 S, F, W, E, R, 1994 F, W, E, S, A 1, 2, US, 1995 E, S, F, W
D'Arcy, G W (Lansdowne, Leinster) 1999 [R (R)], 2002 Fj (R), 2003 Tg (R), Sm (R), W 2(R), 2004 F, W, E, It, S, SA1, 2005 It, NZ, A, R, 2006 It, F, W, S, E, NZ1, 2, A1, SA, A2, PI(R), 2007 W, F, E, S1, It1, 2, [Nm, Gg, F, Arg], 2008 It, 2009 F(t&R), It(R), S, W, Fj, SA(R), 2010 It, F, E, W, S, NZ1, SA, NZ2, Arg, 2011 It, F1, S1, W, E1, F3, E2, [US, A, It, W]
Dargan, M J (Old Belvedere) 1952 S, W
Davidson, C T (NIFC) 1921 F
Davidson, I G (NIFC) 1899 E, 1900 S, W, 1901 E, S, W, 1902 E, S, W
Davidson, J C (Dungannon) 1969 F, E, S, W, 1973 NZ, 1976 NZ
Davidson, J W (Dungannon, London Irish, Castres) 1995 Fj, 1996 S, F, W, E, WS, A, 1997 It 1, F, W, E, S, 1998 Gg (R), R (R), SA 3(R), 1999 F, W, E, S, It, A 1, 2(R), Arg 1, [US, R (R), Arg 2], 2000 S (R), W (R), US, C, 2001 It (R), S
Davies, F E (Lansdowne) 1892 S, W, 1893 E, S, W
Davis, J L (Monkstown) 1898 E, S
Davis, W J N (Edinburgh U, Bessbrook) 1890 S, W, E, 1891 E, S, W, 1892 E, S, 1895 S
Davison, W (Belfast Academy) 1887 W
Davy, E O'D (UC Dublin, Lansdowne) 1925 W, 1926 F, E, S, W, 1927 F, E, S, W, A, 1928 F, E, S, W, 1929 F, E, S, W, 1930 F, E, S, W, 1931 F, E, S, W, SA, 1932 E, S, W, 1933 E, W, S, 1934 E
Dawson, A R (Wanderers) 1958 A, E, S, W, F, 1959 E, S, W, F, 1960 F, SA, 1961 E, S, W, F, SA, 1962 S, F, W, 1963 F, E, S, W, NZ, 1964 E, S, F
Dawson, K (London Irish) 1997 NZ, C, 1998 S, 1999 [R, Arg 2], 2000 E, S, It, F, W, J, SA, 2001 R, S, W (R), E (R), Sm, 2002 Fj, 2003 Tg, It 2(R), S 2(R)
Dean, P M (St Mary's Coll) 1981 SA 1, 2, A, 1982 W, E, S, F, 1984 A, 1985 S, F, W, E, 1986 F, W, R, 1987 E, S, F, W, [W, A], 1988 S, F, W, E 1, 2, WS, It, 1989 F, W, E, S
Deane, E C (Monkstown) 1909 E
Deering, M J (Bective Rangers) 1929 W
Deering, S J (Bective Rangers) 1935 E, S, W, NZ, 1936 E, S, W, 1937 E, S
Deering, S M (Garryowen, St Mary's Coll) 1974 W, 1976 F, W, E, S, 1977 W, E, 1978 NZ
De Lacy, H (Harlequins) 1948 E, S
Delany, M G (Bective Rangers) 1895 W
Dempsey, G T (Terenure Coll, Leinster) 1998 Gg (R). SA 3, 1999 F, E, S, It, A 2, 2000 E (R), S, It, F, W, SA, 2001 It, F, S, W, E, NZ, 2002 W, E, S, It, F, NZ 1, 2, R, Ru, Gg, A, Arg, 2003 S 1, E (R), A, Sm, W 2(R), It 2, S 2(R), [R, Nm, Arg, A, F], 2004 F, W, E, It, S, SA1, 2, 3, US(R), Arg, 2005 It(R), S, E, F, W, J1, 2, NZ(R), R(R), 2006 E(R), NZ1(R), 2(t&R), A1, SA, A2(R), PI, 2007 W, F, E, S1, It1, 2, [Nm, Gg, F], 2008 It, F, A(R), NZ2
Dennison, S P (Garryowen) 1973 F, 1975 E, S
Dick, C J (Ballymena) 1961 W, F, SA, 1962 W, 1963 F, E, S, W
Dick, J S (Queen's U, Belfast) 1962 E
Dick, J S (Queen's U, Cork) 1887 E, S, W
Dickson, J A N (Dublin U) 1920 E, W, F
Doherty, A E (Old Wesley) 1974 P (R)
Doherty, W D (Guy's Hospital) 1920 E, S, W, 1921 E, S, W, F
Donaldson, J A (Belfast Collegians) 1958 A, E, S, W
Donovan, T M (Queen's Coll, Cork) 1889 S
Dooley, J F (Galwegians) 1959 E, S, W
Doran, B R W (Lansdowne) 1900 S, W, 1901 E, S, W, 1902 E, S, W
Doran, E F (Lansdowne) 1890 S, W
Doran, G P (Lansdowne) 1899 S, W, 1900 E, S, 1902 S, W, 1903 W, 1904 E
Douglas, A C (Instonians) 1923 F, 1924 E, S, 1927 A, 1928 S
Dowling, I (Munster) 2009 C, US
Downing, A J (Dublin U) 1882 W
Dowse, J C A (Monkstown) 1914 F, S, W
Doyle, J A P (Greystones) 1984 E, S
Doyle, J T (Bective Rangers) 1935 W
Doyle, M G (Blackrock Coll, UC Dublin, Cambridge U, Edinburgh Wands) 1965 F, E, S, W, SA, 1966 F, E, S, W, 1967 A 1, E, S, W, F, A 2, 1968 F, E, S, W, A
Doyle, T J (Wanderers) 1968 E, S, W
Duffy, G W (Harlequins, Connacht) 2004 SA 2(R), 2005 S(R), J1, 2, 2007 Arg1, 2, S2, [Arg(R)], 2009 C, US
Duggan, A T A (Lansdowne) 1963 NZ, 1964 F, 1966 W, 1967 A 1, S, W, A 2, 1968 F, E, S, W, 1969 F, E, S, W, 1970 SA, F, E, S, W, 1971 F, E, S, W, 1972 F 2
Duggan, W (UC Cork) 1920 S, W
Duggan, W P (Blackrock Coll) 1975 E, S, F, W, 1976 A, F, W, S, NZ, 1977 W, E, S, F, 1978 S, F, W, E, NZ, 1979 E, S, A 1, 2, 1980 E, 1981 F, W, E, S, SA 1, 2, A, 1982 W, E, S, 1983 S, F, W, E, 1984 F, W, E, S
Duignan, P (Galwegians) 1998 Gg, R
Duncan, W R (Malone) 1984 W, E
Dunlea, F J (Lansdowne) 1989 W, E, S
Dunlop, R (Dublin U) 1889 W, 1890 S, W, E, 1891 E, S, W, 1892 E, S, 1893 W, 1894 W
Dunn, P E F (Bective Rangers) 1923 S
Dunn, T B (NIFC) 1935 NZ
Dunne, M J (Lansdowne) 1929 F, E, S, 1930 F, E, S, W, 1932 E, S, W, 1933 E, W, S, 1934 E, S, W
Dwyer, P J (UC Dublin) 1962 W, 1963 F, NZ, 1964 S, W

Earls, K G (Munster) 2008 C, NZ2(R), 2009 A(R), Fj, SA, 2010 It(R), F, E, W, S, SA(R), NZ2(R), Arg(R), 2011 It, F1, S1, W, E1, F2, 3, E2, [US, A, Ru, It, W]
Easterby, S H (Llanelli Scarlets) 2000 S, It, F, W, Arg, US, C, 2001 S, Sm (R), 2002 W, E (R), S (R), It, F, NZ 1, 2, R, Ru, Gg, 2003 Tg, Sm, It 2, S 2(t+R), [Nm, Arg, A, F], 2004 F, W, E, It, S, SA1, 2, 3, US, Arg, 2005 It, S, E, F, W, NZ, A, 2006 It, F, W, S, E, SA(R), A2(R), PI, 2007 W, F, E, S1, It1, 2, [Nm, Gg, F, Arg], 2008 It, S(R), E(R)
Easterby, W G (Ebbw Vale, Ballynahinch, Llanelli, Leinster) 2000 US, C (R), 2001 R (R), S, W (R), Sm (R), 2002 W (R), S (R), R (R), Ru (R), Gg (R), Fj, 2003 S 1(R), It 1(R), Tg, Sm, W 2(R), It 2, S 2(R), [R(R), Nm(R), F(R)], 2004 W(R), It(R), S(R), SA2(R), US, 2005 S(R)
Edwards, H G (Dublin U) 1877 E, 1878 E
Edwards, R W (Malone) 1904 W
Edwards, T (Lansdowne) 1888 M, 1890 S, W, E, 1892 W, 1893 E
Edwards, W V (Malone) 1912 F, E
Egan, J D (Bective Rangers) 1922 S
Egan, J T (Cork Constitution) 1931 F, E, SA
Egan, M S (Garryowen) 1893 E, 1895 S
Ekin, W (Queen's Coll, Belfast) 1888 W, S
Elliott, W R J (Bangor) 1979 S
Elwood, E P (Lansdowne, Galwegians) 1993 W, E, R, 1994 F, W, E, S, A 1, 2, 1995 F, W, [NZ, W, F], 1996 US, S, 1997 F, W, E, NZ, C, It 2(R), 1998 F, W, E, SA 1, 2, Gg, R, SA 3, 1999 It, Arg 1(R), [US (R), A 3(R), R]
English, M A F (Lansdowne, Limerick Bohemians) 1958 W, F, 1959 E, S, F, 1960 E, S, 1961 S, W, F, 1962 F, W, 1963 E, S, W, NZ
Ennis, F N G (Wanderers) 1979 A 1(R)
Ensor, A H (Wanderers) 1973 W, F, 1974 F, W, E, S, P, NZ, 1975 E, S, F, W, 1976 A, F, W, E, NZ, 1977 E, 1978 S, F, W, E
Entrican, J C (Queen's U, Belfast) 1931 S
Erskine, D J (Sale) 1997 NZ (R), C, It 2

Fagan, G L (Kingstown School) 1878 E
Fagan, W B C (Wanderers) 1956 F, E, S
Farrell, J L (Bective Rangers) 1926 F, E, S, W, 1927 F, E, S, W, A, 1928 F, E, S, W, 1929 F, E, S, W, 1930 F, E, S, W, 1931 F, E, S, W, SA, 1932 E, S, W
Feddis, N (Lansdowne) 1956 E
Feighery, C F P (Lansdowne) 1972 F 1, E, F 2
Feighery, T A O (St Mary's Coll) 1977 W, E
Ferris, H H (Queen's Coll, Belfast) 1901 W
Ferris, J H (Queen's Coll, Belfast) 1900 E, S, W
Ferris, S (Ulster) 2006 PI, 2007 Arg1(R), 2, S2, 2008 A(R), C, NZ2(R),

Arg, 2009 F, It, E, S, W, A, Fj, SA, 2010 F, E, W, S, SA, Sm(R), NZ2, Arg, 2011 F3(R), E2, [US, A, It, W]

Field, M J (Malone) 1994 E, S, A 1(R), 1995 F (R), W (t), It (R), [NZ(t + R), J], Fj, 1996 F (R), W, E, A (R), 1997 F, W, E, S

Finlay, J E (Queen's Coll, Belfast) 1913 E, S, W, 1920 E, S, W

Finlay, W (NIFC) 1876 E, 1877 E, S, 1878 E, 1879 S, E, 1880 S, 1882 S

Finn, M C (UC Cork, Cork Constitution) 1979 E, 1982 W, E, S, F, 1983 S, F, W, E, 1984 E, S, A, 1986 F, W

Finn, R G A (UC Dublin) 1977 F

Fitzgerald, C C (Glasgow U, Dungannon) 1902 E, 1903 E, S

Fitzgerald, C F (St Mary's Coll) 1979 A 1, 2, 1980 E, S, F, W, 1982 W, E, S, F, 1983 S, F, W, E, 1984 F, W, A, 1985 S, F, W, E, 1986 F, W, E, S

Fitzgerald, D C (Lansdowne, De La Salle Palmerston) 1984 E, S, 1986 W, E, S, R, 1987 E, S, F, W, [W, C, A], 1988 S, F, W, E 1, 1989 NZ (R), 1990 E, S, F, W, Arg, 1991 F, W, E, S, Nm 1, 2, [Z, S, A], 1992 W, S (R)

Fitzgerald, J (Wanderers) 1884 W

Fitzgerald, J J (Young Munster) 1988 S, F, 1990 S, F, W, 1991 F, W, E, S, [J], 1994 A 1, 2

Fitzgerald, L M (Leinster) 2006 PI, 2007 Arg2(R), 2008 W(R), E(R), C, NZ2, Arg, 2009 F, It, E, S, W, A, 2010 SA, Sm, NZ2, 2011 It, F1, S1, W, S2, F2, 3(R)

Fitzgibbon, M J J (Shannon) 1992 W, E, S, F, NZ 1, 2

Fitzpatrick, J M (Dungannon) 1998 SA 1, 2 Gg (R), R (R), SA 3, 1999 F (R), W (R), E (R), It, Arg 1(R), [US (R), A 3, R, Arg 2(t&R)], 2000 S (R), It (R), Arg (R), US, C, SA (t&R), 2001 R (R), 2003 W 1(R), E (R), Tg, W 2(R), It 2(R)

Fitzpatrick, M P (Wanderers) 1978 S, 1980 S, F, W, 1981 F, W, E, S, A, 1985 F (R)

Flannery, J P (Munster) 2005 R(R), 2006 It, F, W, S, E, NZ1, 2, A1, 2007 W(R), F(R), E(R), S1(R), It1(R), Arg1, S2, It2(R), [Nm(R), Gg(R), F, Arg], 2008 NZ1, A(R), C, NZ2(R), Arg, 2009 F, It, E, S(R), W, A, Fj, SA, 2010 It, F, 2011 S2(R), F2(R), 3(R), E2, [US(R)]

Flavin, P (Blackrock Coll) 1997 F (R), S

Fletcher, W W (Kingstown) 1882 W, S, 1883 E

Flood, R S (Dublin U) 1925 W

Flynn, M K (Wanderers) 1959 F, 1960 F, 1962 E, S, F, W, 1964 E, S, W, F, 1965 F, E, S, W, SA, 1966 F, E, S, 1972 F 1, E, F 2, 1973 NZ

Fogarty, J (Leinster) 2010 NZ1(R)

Fogarty, T (Garryowen) 1891 W

Foley, A G (Shannon, Munster) 1995 E, S, F, W, It, [J(t + R)], 1996 A, 1997 It 1, E (R), 2000 E, S, It, F, W, Arg, C, J, SA, 2001 It, F, R, S, W, E, Sm, NZ, 2002 W, E, S, It, F, NZ 1, 2, R, Ru, Gg, A, Fj, Arg, 2003 S 1, It 1, F, W 1, E, W 2, [R, A], 2004 F, W, E, It, S, SA1, 2, 3, US(R), Arg, 2005 It, S, E, F, W

Foley, B O (Shannon) 1976 F, E, 1977 W (R), 1980 F, W, 1981 F, E, S, SA 1, 2, A

Forbes, R E (Malone) 1907 E

Forrest, A J (Wanderers) 1880 E, S, 1881 E, S, 1882 W, E, 1883 E, 1885 S 2

Forrest, E G (Wanderers) 1888 M, 1889 S, W, 1890 S, E, 1891 E, 1893 S, W, 1894 E, S, W, 1895 W, 1897 E, S

Forrest, H (Wanderers) 1893 S, W

Fortune, J J (Clontarf) 1963 NZ, 1964 E

Foster, A R (Derry) 1910 E, S, F, 1911 E, S, W, F, 1912 F, E, S, W, 1914 E, S, W, 1921 E, S, W

Francis, N P J (Blackrock Coll, London Irish, Old Belvedere) 1987 [Tg, A], 1988 WS, It, 1989 S, 1990 E, F, W, 1991 E, S, Nm 1, 2, [Z, J, S, A], 1992 W, E, S, 1993 F, R, 1994 F, W, E, S, A 1, 2, US, 1995 E, [NZ, J, W, F], Fj, 1996 US, S

Franks, J G (Dublin U) 1898 E, S, W

Frazer, E F (Bective Rangers) 1891 S, 1892 S

Freer, A E (Lansdowne) 1901 E, S, W

Fulcher, G M (Cork Constitution, London Irish) 1994 A 2, US, 1995 E (R), S, F, W, It, [NZ, W, F], Fj, 1996 US, S, F, W, E, A, 1997 It 1, W (R), 1998 SA 1(R)

Fulton, J (NIFC) 1895 S, W, 1896 E, 1897 E, 1898 W, 1899 E, 1900 W, 1901 E, 1902 E, S, W, 1903 E, S, W, 1904 E, S

Furlong, J N (UC Galway) 1992 NZ 1, 2

Gaffikin, W (Windsor) 1875 E

Gage, J H (Queen's U, Belfast) 1926 S, W, 1927 S, W

Galbraith, E (Dublin U) 1875 E

Galbraith, H T (Belfast Acad) 1890 W

Galbraith, R (Dublin U) 1875 E, 1876 E, 1877 E

Galwey, M J (Shannon) 1991 F, W, Nm 2(R), [J], 1992 E, S, F, NZ 1, 2, A, 1993 F, W, E, R, 1994 F, W, E, S, A 1, US (R), 1995 E, 1996 WS, 1998 F (R), 1999 W (R), 2000 E (R), S, It, F, W, Arg, C, 2001 It, F, R, W, E, Sm, NZ, 2002 W, E, S

Ganly, J B (Monkstown) 1927 F, E, S, W, A, 1928 F, E, S, W, 1929 F, S, 1930 F

Gardiner, F (NIFC) 1900 E, S, 1901 E, W, 1902 E, S, W, 1903 E, W, 1904 E, S, W, 1906 E, S, W, 1907 S, W, 1908 S, W, 1909 E, S, F

Gardiner, J B (NIFC) 1923 E, S, W, F, 1924 F, E, S, W, NZ, 1925 F, E, S, W

Gardiner, S (Belfast Albion) 1893 E, S

Gardiner, W (NIFC) 1892 E, S, 1893 E, S, W, 1894 E, S, W, 1895 E, S, W, 1896 E, S, W, 1897 E, S, 1898 W

Garry, M G (Bective Rangers) 1909 E, S, W, F, 1911 E, S, W

Gaston, J T (Dublin U) 1954 NZ, F, E, S, W, 1955 W 1956 F, E

Gavin, T J (Moseley, London Irish) 1949 F, E

Geoghegan, S P (London Irish, Bath) 1991 F, W, E, S, Nm 1, [Z, S, A], 1992 E, S, F, A, 1993 S, F, W, E, R, 1994 F, W, E, S, A 1, 2, US, 1995 E, S, F, W, [NZ, J, W, F], Fj, 1996 US, S, W, E

Gibson, C M H (Cambridge U, NIFC) 1964 E, S, W, F, 1965 F, E, S, W, SA, 1966 F, E, S, W, 1967 A 1, E, S, W, F, A 2, 1968 E, S, W, A, 1969 E, S, W, 1970 SA, F, E, S, W, 1971 F, E, S, W, 1972 F 1, E, F 2, 1973 NZ, E, S, W, F, 1974 F, W, E, S, P, 1975 E, S, F, W, 1976 A, F, W, E, S, NZ, 1977 W, E, S, F, 1978 F, W, E, NZ, 1979 S, A 1, 2

Gibson, M E (Lansdowne, London Irish) 1979 F, W, E, S, 1981 W (R), 1986 R, 1988 S, F, W, E 2

Gifford, H P (Wanderers) 1890 S

Gillespie, J C (Dublin U) 1922 W, F

Gilpin, F G (Queen's U, Belfast) 1962 E, S, F

Glass, D C (Belfast Collegians) 1958 F, 1960 W, 1961 W, SA

Gleeson, K D (St Mary's Coll, Leinster) 2002 W (R), F (R), NZ 1, 2, R, Ru, Gg, A, Arg, 2003 S 1, It 1, F, W 1, E, A, W 2, [R, A, F], 2004 F, W, E, It, 2006 NZ1(R), A1(R), 2007 Arg1, S2(R)

Glennon, B T (Lansdowne) 1993 F (R)

Glennon, J J (Skerries) 1980 E, S, 1987 E, S, F, [W (R)]

Godfrey, R P (UC Dublin) 1954 S, W

Goodall, K G (City of Derry, Newcastle U) 1967 A 1, E, S, W, F, A 2, 1968 F, E, S, W, A, 1969 F, E, S, 1970 SA, F, E, S, W

Gordon, A (Dublin U) 1884 S

Gordon, T G (NIFC) 1877 E, S, 1878 E

Gotto, R P C (NIFC) 1906 SA

Goulding, W J (Cork) 1879 S

Grace, T O (UC Dublin, St Mary's Coll) 1972 F 1, E, 1973 NZ, E, S, W, 1974 E, S, P, NZ, 1975 E, S, F, W, 1976 A, F, W, E, S, NZ, 1977 W, E, S, F, 1978 S

Graham, R I (Dublin U) 1911 F

Grant, E L (CIYMS) 1971 F, E, S, W

Grant, P J (Bective Rangers) 1894 S, W

Graves, C R A (Wanderers) 1934 E, S, W, 1935 E, S, W, NZ, 1936 E, S, W, 1937 E, S, 1938 E, S, W

Gray, R D (Old Wesley) 1923 E, S, 1925 F, 1926 F

Greene, E H (Dublin U, Kingstown) 1882 W, 1884 W, 1885 E, S 2, 1886 E

Greer, R (Kingstown) 1876 E

Greeves, T J (NIFC) 1907 E, S, W, 1909 W, F

Gregg, R J (Queen's U, Belfast) 1953 F, E, S, W, 1954 F, E, S

Griffin, C S (London Irish) 1951 F, E

Griffin, J L (Wanderers) 1949 S, W

Griffiths, W (Limerick) 1878 E

Grimshaw, C (Queen's U, Belfast) 1969 E (R)

Guerin, B N (Galwegians) 1956 S

Gwynn, A P (Dublin U) 1895 W

Gwynn, L H (Dublin U) 1893 S, 1894 E, S, W, 1897 S, 1898 E, S

Hakin, R F (CIYMS) 1976 W, S, NZ, 1977 W, E, F

Hall, R O N (Dublin U) 1884 W

Hall, W H (Instonians) 1923 E, S, W, F, 1924 F, S

Hallaran, C F G T (Royal Navy) 1921 E, S, W, 1922 E, S, W, 1923 E, F, 1924 F, E, S, W, 1925 F, 1926 F, E

Halpin, G F (Wanderers, London Irish) 1990 E, 1991 [J], 1992 E, S, F, 1993 R, 1994 F (R), 1995 It, [NZ, W, F]

Halpin, T (Garryowen) 1909 S, W, F, 1910 E, S, W, 1911 E, S, W, F, 1912 F, E, S

Halvey, E O (Shannon) 1995 F, W, It, [J, W (t), F (R)], 1997 NZ, C (R)

Hamilton, A J (Lansdowne) 1884 W

Hamilton, G F (NIFC) 1991 F, W, E, S, Nm 2, [Z, J, S, A], 1992 A

Hamilton, R L (NIFC) 1926 F

Hamilton, R W (Wanderers) 1893 W

Hamilton, W J (Dublin U) 1877 E

Hamlet, G T (Old Wesley) 1902 E, S, W, 1903 E, S, W, 1904 S, W, 1905 E, S, W, NZ, 1906 SA, 1907 E, S, W, 1908 E, S, W, 1909 E, S, W, F, 1910 E, S, F, 1911 E, S, W, F

Hanrahan, C J (Dolphin) 1926 S, W, 1927 E, S, W, A, 1928 F, E, S, 1929 F, E, S, W, 1930 F, E, S, W, 1931 F, 1932 S, W

Harbison, H T (Bective Rangers) 1984 W (R), E, S, 1986 R, 1987 E, S, F, W

Hardy, G G (Bective Rangers) 1962 S

Harman, G R A (Dublin U) 1899 E, W
Harper, J (Instonians) 1947 F, E, S
Harpur, T G (Dublin U) 1908 E, S, W
Harrison, T (Cork) 1879 S, 1880 S, 1881 E
Harvey, F M W (Wanderers) 1907 W, 1911 F
Harvey, G A D (Wanderers) 1903 E, S, 1904 W, 1905 E, S
Harvey, T A (Dublin U) 1900 W, 1901 S, W, 1902 E, S, W, 1903 E, W
Haycock, P P (Terenure Coll) 1989 E
Hayes, J J (Shannon, Munster) 2000 S, It, F, W, Arg, C, J, SA, 2001 It, F, R, S, W, E, Sm, NZ, 2002 W, E, S, It, F, NZ 1, 2, R, Ru, Gg, A, Fj, Arg, 2003 S 1, It 1, F, W 1, E, [R(R), Nm, Arg, A, F], 2004 F, W, E, It, S, SA1, 2, 3, US, Arg, 2005 It, S, E, F, W, NZ, A, R(R), 2006 It, F, W, S, E, NZ1, 2, A1, SA, A2, PI, 2007 W, F, E, S1, It1, S2(R), It2, [Nm, Gg, F, Arg], 2008 It, F, S, W, E, NZ1, A, C(R), NZ2, Arg, 2009 F, It, E, S, W, A, Fj, SA, 2010 It, F, E, W, S, Sm, NZ2(R), 2011 S2(R)
Headon, T A (UC Dublin) 1939 S, W
Healey, P (Limerick) 1901 E, S, W, 1902 E, S, W, 1903 E, S, W, 1904 S
Healy, C E (Leinster) 2009 A, SA, 2010 It, F, E, W, S, NZ1, A, SA, Sm(R), NZ2, Arg, 2011 It, F1, S1, W, E1, F2, 3, E2, [A, Ru, It, W]
Heaslip, J P R (Leinster) 2006 PI, 2007 Arg1, S2, 2008 It(R), F, S, W, E, NZ1, A, C, NZ2, Arg, 2009 F, It, E, S(R), W, A, Fj, SA, 2010 It, F, E, W, S, NZ1, SA, Sm, NZ2, Arg, 2011 F1, S1, W, E1, F2(R), 3, E2, [US, A, Ru, It, W]
Heffernan, M R (Cork Constitution) 1911 E, S, W, F
Hemphill, R (Dublin U) 1912 F, E, S, W
Henderson, N J (Queen's U, Belfast, NIFC) 1949 S, W, 1950 F, 1951 F, E, S, W, SA, 1952 F, S, W, E, 1953 F, E, S, W, 1954 NZ, F, E, S, W, 1955 F, E, S, W, 1956 S, W, 1957 F, E, S, W, 1958 A, E, S, W, F, 1959 E, S, W, F
Henderson R A J (London Irish, Wasps, Young Munster) 1996 WS, 1997 NZ, C, 1998 F, W, SA 1(R), 2(R), 1999 F (R), E, S (R), It, 2000 S (R), It (R), F, W, Arg, US, J (R), SA, 2001 It, F, 2002 W (R), E (R), F, R (R), Ru (t), Gg (R), 2003 It 1(R), 2
Henebrey, G J (Garryowen) 1906 E, S, W, SA, 1909 W, F
Henry, C G (Ulster) 2010 A
Heron, A G (Queen's Coll, Belfast) 1901 E
Heron, J (NIFC) 1877 S, 1879 E
Heron, W T (NIFC) 1880 E, S
Herrick, R W (Dublin U) 1886 S
Heuston, F S (Kingstown) 1882 W, 1883 E, S
Hewitt, D (Queen's U, Belfast, Instonians) 1958 A, E, S, F, 1959 S, W, F, 1960 E, S, W, F, 1961 E, S, W, F, 1962 S, F, 1965 W
Hewitt, F S (Instonians) 1924 W, NZ, 1925 F, E, S, 1926 E, 1927 E, S, W
Hewitt, J A (NIFC) 1981 SA 1(R), 2(R)
Hewitt, T R (Queen's U, Belfast) 1924 W, NZ, 1925 F, E, S, 1926 F, E, S, W
Hewitt, V A (Instonians) 1935 S, W, NZ, 1936 E, S, W
Hewitt, W J (Instonians) 1954 E, 1956 S, 1959 W, 1961 SA
Hewson, F T (Wanderers) 1875 E
Hickie, D A (St Mary's Coll, Leinster) 1997 W, E, S, NZ, C, It 2, 1998 S, F, W, E, SA 1, 2, 2000 S, It, F, W, J, SA, 2001 F, R, S, W, E, NZ, 2002 W, E, S, It, F, R, Ru, Gg, A, 2003 S 1, It 1, F, W 1, E, It 2, S 2, [R, Nm, Arg, A], 2004 SA3, Arg, 2005 It, S, E, F, W, 2006 A2, PI, 2007 W, F, E, S1, It1, 2, [Nm, Gg, Arg]
Hickie, D J (St Mary's Coll) 1971 F, E, S, W, 1972 F 1, E
Higgins, J A D (Civil Service) 1947 S, W, A, 1948 F, S, W
Higgins, W W (NIFC) 1884 E, S
Hillary, M F (UC Dublin) 1952 E
Hingerty, D J (UC Dublin) 1947 F, E, S, W
Hinton, W P (Old Wesley) 1907 W, 1908 E, S, W, 1909 E, S, 1910 E, S, W, F, 1911 E, S, W, 1912 F, E, W
Hipwell, M L (Terenure Coll) 1962 E, S, 1968 F, A, 1969 F (R), S (R), W, 1971 F, E, S, W, 1972 F 2
Hobbs, T H M (Dublin U) 1884 S, 1885 E
Hobson, E W (Dublin U) 1876 E
Hogan, N A (Terenure Coll, London Irish) 1995 E, W, [J, W, F], 1996 F, W, E, WS, 1997 F, W, E, It 2
Hogan, P (Garryowen) 1992 F
Hogan, T (Munster, Leinster) 2005 J1(R), 2(R), 2007 It1(R), Arg1
Hogg, W (Dublin U) 1885 S 2
Holland, J J (Wanderers) 1981 SA 1, 2, 1986 W
Holmes, G W (Dublin U) 1912 SA, 1913 E, S
Holmes, L J (Lisburn) 1889 S, W
Hooks, K J (Queen's U, Belfast, Ards, Bangor) 1981 S, 1989 NZ, 1990 F, W, Arg, 1991 F
Horan, A K (Blackheath) 1920 E, W
Horan, M J (Shannon, Munster) 2000 US (R), 2002 Fj, Arg (R), 2003 S 1(R), It 1(R), F, W 1, E, A, Sm, It 2, S 2, [R, Nm, Arg(t&R), A(R), F(R)], 2004 It(R), S(R), SA1(R), 2(t&R), 3(R), US, 2005 It(R), S(R), E(R), F(R), W(R), J1, 2, NZ, A, R, 2006 It, W, S, E, NZ1, 2, A1, SA, A2(R), 2007 W, F, E, It1, 2, [Nm, Gg, F, Arg], 2008 It, F, S, W, E, NZ1, A, C, NZ2, Arg, 2009 F, It, E, S, W, 2011 S2(R)
Horgan, A P (Cork Const, Munster) 2003 Sm, W 2, S 2, 2004 F(R), 2005 J1, 2, NZ
Horgan, S P (Lansdowne, Leinster) 2000 S, It, W, Arg, C, J, SA (R), 2001 It, S, W, E, NZ, 2002 S, It, F, A, Fj, Arg, 2003 S 1, [R, Nm, Arg, A, F], 2004 F, W, E, It, S, SA1, 2, 3, US, Arg, 2005 It, S, E, NZ, A, R, 2006 It, F, W, S, E, NZ1, 2, A1, SA, A2, PI, 2007 F, E, S1, It1, [Gg, F, Arg], 2008 S(R), W, E, NZ1, A, C(R), 2009 Fj
Houston, K J (Oxford U, London Irish) 1961 SA, 1964 S, W, 1965 F, E, SA
Howe, T G (Dungannon, Ballymena, Ulster) 2000 US, J, SA, 2001 It, F, R, Sm, 2002 It (R), 2003 Tg, W 2, 2004 F, W, E, SA2
Hughes, R W (NIFC) 1878 E, 1880 E, S, 1881 S, 1882 E, S, 1883 E, S, 1884 E, S, 1885 E, 1886 E
Humphreys, D G (London Irish, Dungannon, Ulster) 1996 F, W, E, WS, 1997 E (R), S, It 2, 1998 S, E (R), SA 2(t + R), R (R), 1999 F, W, E, S, A 1, 2, Arg 1, [US, A 3, Arg 2], 2000 E, S (R), F (t&R), W (R), Arg, US (R), C, J (R), SA (R), 2001 It (R), R, S (R), W, E, NZ, 2002 W, E, S, It, F, NZ 1(R), 2(R), R (t+R), Ru (R), Gg (R), Fj, 2003 S 1, It 1, F, W 1, E, A, W 2, It 2, S 2(R), [R, Arg, A(R), F(R)], 2004W(R), It(R), S(R), SA2(R), US, 2005 S(R), W(R), J1, 2, NZ(R), A(R), R
Hunt, E W F de Vere (Army, Rosslyn Park) 1930 F, 1932 E, S, W, 1933 E
Hunter, D V (Dublin U) 1885 S 2
Hunter, L M (Civil Service) 1968 W, A
Hunter, W R (CIYMS) 1962 E, S, W, F, 1963 F, E, S, 1966 F, E, S
Hurley, D (Munster) 2009 US(t&R)
Hurley, H D (Old Wesley, Moseley) 1995 Fj (t), 1996 WS
Hutton, S A (Malone) 1967 S, W, F, A 2

Ireland J (Windsor) 1876 E, 1877 E
Irvine, H A S (Collegians) 1901 S
Irwin, D G (Queen's U, Belfast, Instonians) 1980 F, W, 1981 F, W, E, S, SA 1, 2, A, 1982 W, 1983 S, F, W, E, 1984 F, W, 1987 [Tg, A (R)], 1989 F, W, E, S, NZ, 1990 E, S
Irwin, J W S (NIFC) 1938 E, S, 1939 E, S, W
Irwin, S T (Queen's Coll, Belfast) 1900 E, S, W, 1901 E, W, 1902 E, S, W, 1903 S

Jack, H W (UC Cork) 1914 S, W, 1921 W
Jackman, B J (Leinster) 2005 J1(R), 2(R), 2007 Arg1(R), 2(R), 2008 It(R), F, S, W(R), E(R)
Jackson, A R V (Wanderers) 1911 E, S, W, F, 1913 W, F, 1914 F, E, S, W
Jackson, F (NIFC) 1923 E
Jackson, H W (Dublin U) 1877 E
Jameson, J S (Lansdowne) 1888 M, 1889 S, W, 1891 W, 1892 E, W, 1893 S
Jeffares, E W (Wanderers) 1913 E, S
Jennings, S (Leicester, Leinster) 2007 Arg 2, 2008 NZ1(R), A, C, NZ2(R), 2010 E(R), W(R), NZ1(R), A, 2011 F3, [US, Ru(R)]
Johns, P S (Dublin U, Dungannon, Saracens) 1990 Arg, 1992 NZ 1, 2, A, 1993 S, F, W, E, R, 1994 F, W, E, S, A 1, 2, US, 1995 E, S, W, It, [NZ, J, W, F], Fj, 1996 US, S, F, WS, 1997 It 1(R), F, W, E, S, NZ, C, It 2, 1998 S, F, W, E, SA 1, 2, Gg, R, SA 3, 1999 F, W, E, S, It, A 1, 2, Arg 1, [US, A 3, R], 2000 F (R), J
Johnston, J (Belfast Acad) 1881 S, 1882 S, 1884 S, 1885 S 1, 2, 1886 E, 1887 E, S, W
Johnston, M (Dublin U) 1880 E, S, 1881 E, S, 1882 E, 1884 E, S, 1886 E
Johnston, R (Wanderers) 1893 E, W
Johnston, R W (Dublin U) 1890 S, W, E
Johnston, T J (Queen's Coll, Belfast) 1892 E, S, W, 1893 E, S, 1895 E
Johnstone, W E (Dublin U) 1884 W
Johnstone-Smyth, T R (Lansdowne) 1882 E
Jones, F A (Munster) 2011 S2(R), F2(R), 3

Kavanagh, J R (UC Dublin, Wanderers) 1953 F, E, S, W, 1954 NZ, S, W, 1955 F, E, 1956 E, S, W, 1957 F, E, S, W, 1958 A, E, S, W, 1959 E, S, W, F, 1960 E, S, W, F, SA, 1961 E, S, W, F, SA, 1962 F
Kavanagh, P J (UC Dublin, Wanderers) 1952 E, 1955 W
Keane, K P (Garryowen) 1998 E (R)
Keane, M I (Lansdowne) 1974 F, W, E, S, P, NZ, 1975 E, S, F, W, 1976 A, F, W, E, S, NZ, 1977 W, E, S, F, 1978 S, F, W, E, NZ, 1979 F, W, E, S, A 1, 2, 1980 E, S, F, W, 1981 F, W, E, S, 1982 W, E, S, F, 1983 S, F, W, E, 1984 F, W, E, S
Kearney, R D J (Leinster) 2007 Arg 2, 2008 It(R), F, S, W, E, NZ1, A, C, NZ2, Arg, 2009 F, It, E, S, W, A, Fj, SA, 2010 It, F, W(R), S(R), NZ1, A, SA, NZ2, 2011 S2, F2, [A, Ru, It, W]

Kearney, R K (Wanderers) 1982 F, 1984 A, 1986 F, W
Keatley, I J (Connacht) 2009 C, US
Keeffe, E (Sunday's Well) 1947 F, E, S, W, A, 1948 F
Kelly, H C (NIFC) 1877 E, S, 1878 E, 1879 S, 1880 E, S
Kelly, J C (UC Dublin) 1962 F, W, 1963 F, E, S, W, NZ, 1964 E, S, W, F
Kelly, J P (Cork Constitution) 2002 It, NZ 1, 2, R, Ru, Gg, A (R), 2003 It 1, F, A, Tg, Sm, It 2, [R(R), Nm(R), A(R), F]
Kelly, S (Lansdowne) 1954 S, W, 1955 S, 1960 W, F
Kelly, W (Wanderers) 1884 S
Kennedy, A G (Belfast Collegians) 1956 F
Kennedy, A P (London Irish) 1986 W, E
Kennedy, F (Wanderers) 1880 E, 1881 E, 1882 W
Kennedy, F A (Wanderers) 1904 E, W
Kennedy, H (Bradford) 1938 S, W
Kennedy, J M (Wanderers) 1882 W, 1884 W
Kennedy, K W (Queen's U, Belfast, London Irish) 1965 F, E, S, W, SA, 1966 F, E, W, 1967 A 1, E, S, W, F, A 2, 1968 F, A, 1969 F, E, S, W, 1970 SA, F, E, S, W, 1971 F, E, S, W, 1972 F 1, E, F 2, 1973 NZ, E, S, W, F, 1974 F, W, E, S, P, NZ, 1975 F, W
Kennedy, T J (St Mary's Coll) 1978 NZ, 1979 F, W, E (R), A 1, 2, 1980 E, S, F, W, 1981 SA 1, 2, A
Kenny, P (Wanderers) 1992 NZ 2(R)
Keogh, F S (Bective Rangers) 1964 W, F
Keon, J J (Limerick) 1879 E
Keyes, R P (Cork Constitution) 1986 E, 1991 [Z, J, S, A], 1992 W, E, S
Kidd, F W (Dublin U, Lansdowne) 1877 E, S, 1878 E
Kiely, M D (Lansdowne) 1962 W, 1963 F, E, S, W
Kiernan, M J (Dolphin, Lansdowne) 1982 W (R), E, S, F, 1983 S, F, W, E, 1984 E, S, A, 1985 S, F, W, E, 1986 F, W, E, S, R, 1987 E, S, F, W, [W, C, A], 1988 S, F, W, E 1, 2, WS, 1989 F, W, E, S, 1990 E, S, F, W, Arg, 1991 F
Kiernan, T J (UC Cork, Cork Const) 1960 E, S, W, F, SA, 1961 E, S, W, F, SA, 1962 E, W, 1963 F, S, W, NZ, 1964 E, S, 1965 F, E, S, W, SA, 1966 F, E, S, W, 1967 A 1, E, S, W, F, A 2, 1968 F, E, S, W, A, 1969 F, E, S, W, 1970 SA, F, E, S, W, 1971 F, 1972 F 1, E, F 2, 1973 NZ, E, S
Killeen, G V (Garryowen) 1912 E, S, W, 1913 E, S, W, F, 1914 E, S, W
King, H (Dublin U) 1883 E, S
Kingston, T J (Dolphin) 1987 [W, Tg, A], 1988 S, F, W, E 1, 1990 F, W, 1991 [J], 1993 F, W, E, R, 1994 F, W, E, S, 1995 F, W, It, [NZ, J (R), W, F], Fj, 1996 US, S, F
Knox, J H (Dublin U, Lansdowne) 1904 W, 1905 E, S, W, NZ, 1906 E, S, W, 1907 W, 1908 S
Kyle, J W (Queen's U, Belfast, NIFC) 1947 F, E, S, W, A, 1948 F, E, S, W, 1949 F, E, S, W, 1950 F, E, S, W, 1951 F, E, S, W, SA, 1952 F, S, W, E, 1953 F, E, S, W, 1954 NZ, F, 1955 F, E, W, 1956 F, E, S, W, 1957 F, E, S, W, 1958 A, E, S

Lambert, N H (Lansdowne) 1934 S, W
Lamont, R A (Instonians) 1965 F, E, SA, 1966 F, E, S, W, 1970 SA, F, E, S, W
Landers, M F (Cork Const) 1904 W, 1905 E, S, W, NZ
Lane, D J (UC Cork) 1934 S, W, 1935 E, S
Lane, M F (UC Cork) 1947 W, 1949 F, E, S, W, 1950 F, E, S, W, 1951 F, S, W, SA, 1952 F, S, 1953 F, E
Lane, P (Old Crescent) 1964 W
Langan, D J (Clontarf) 1934 W
Langbroek, J A (Blackrock Coll) 1987 [Tg]
Lavery, P (London Irish) 1974 W, 1976 W
Lawlor, P J (Clontarf) 1951 S, SA, 1952 F, S, W, E, 1953 F, 1954 NZ, E, S, 1956 F, E
Lawlor, P J (Bective Rangers) 1935 E, S, W, 1937 E, S, W
Lawlor, P J (Bective Rangers) 1990 Arg, 1992 A, 1993 S
Leahy, K T (Wanderers) 1992 NZ 1
Leahy, M W (UC Cork) 1964 W
Leamy, D P (Munster) 2004 US, 2005 It, J2, NZ, A, R, 2006 It, F, W, S, E, NZ1, 2, A1, SA, A2, PI(R), 2007 W, F, E, S1, It1, 2, [Nm, Gg, F, Arg], 2008 It, F, S, W, E, NZ1, A, 2009 F(R), It(t&R), E(R), S, W(R), C, US, A(t&R), Fj, 2010 Sm, NZ2(R), Arg(R) , 2011 It, S1(R), W(R), E1(R), S2, F2, E2(R), [US(R), Ru(R), It(R), W(R)]
Lee, S (NIFC) 1891 E, S, W, 1892 E, S, W, 1893 E, S, W, 1894 E, S, W, 1895 E, W, 1896 E, S, W, 1897 E, 1898 E
Le Fanu, V C (Cambridge U, Lansdowne) 1886 E, S, 1887 E, W, 1888 S, 1889 W, 1890 E, 1891 E, 1892 E, S, W
Lenihan, D G (UC Cork, Cork Const) 1981 A, 1982 W, E, S, F, 1983 S, F, W, E, 1984 F, W, E, S, A, 1985 S, F, W, E, 1986 F, W, E, S, R, 1987 E, S, F, W, [W, C, Tg, A], 1988 S, F, W, E 1, 2, WS, It, 1989 F, W, E, S, NZ, 1990 S, F, W, Arg, 1991 Nm 2, [Z, S, A], 1992 W
L'Estrange, L P F (Dublin U) 1962 E
Levis, F H (Wanderers) 1884 E
Lewis, K P (Leinster) 2005 J2(R), 2007 Arg1, 2(R)
Lightfoot, E J (Lansdowne) 1931 F, E, S, W, SA, 1932 E, S, W, 1933 E, W, S
Lindsay, H (Dublin U, Armagh) 1893 E, S, W, 1894 E, S, W, 1895 E, 1896 E, S, W, 1898 E, S, W
Little, T J (Bective Rangers) 1898 W, 1899 S, W, 1900 S, W, 1901 E, S
Lloyd, R A (Dublin U, Liverpool) 1910 E, S, 1911 E, S, W, F, 1912 F, E, S, W, SA, 1913 E, S, W, F, 1914 F, E, 1920 E, F
Longwell, G W (Ballymena) 2000 J (R), SA, 2001 F (R), R, S (R), Sm, NZ (R), 2002 W (R), E (R), S (R), It, F, NZ 1, 2, R, Ru, Gg, A, Arg, 2003 S 1, It 1, F, E, A, It 2, 2004 It(R)
Lydon, C T J (Galwegians) 1956 S
Lyle, R K (Dublin U) 1910 W, F
Lyle, T R (Dublin U) 1885 E, S 1, 2, 1886 E, 1887 E, S
Lynch, J F (St Mary's Coll) 1971 F, E, S, W, 1972 F 1, E, F 2, 1973 NZ, E, S, W, 1974 F, W, E, S, P, NZ
Lynch, L M (Lansdowne) 1956 S
Lytle, J H (NIFC) 1894 E, S, W, 1895 W, 1896 E, S, W, 1897 E, S, 1898 E, S, 1899 S
Lytle, J N (NIFC) 1888 M, 1889 W, 1890 E, 1891 E, S, 1894 E, S, W
Lyttle, V J (Collegians, Bedford) 1938 E, 1939 E, S

McAleese, D R (Ballymena) 1992 F
McAllan, G H (Dungannon) 1896 S, W
Macauley, J (Limerick) 1887 E, S
McBride, W D (Malone) 1988 W, E 1, WS, It, 1989 S, 1990 F, W, Arg, 1993 S, F, W, E, R, 1994 W, E, S, A 1(R), 1995 S, F, [NZ, W, F], Fj (R), 1996 W, E, WS, A, 1997 It 1(R), F, W, E, S
McBride, W J (Ballymena) 1962 E, S, F, W, 1963 F, E, S, W, NZ, 1964 E, S, F, 1965 F, E, S, W, SA, 1966 F, E, S, W, 1967 A 1, E, S, W, F, A 2, 1968 F, E, S, W, A, 1969 F, E, S, W, 1970 SA, F, E, S, W, 1971 F, E, S, W, 1972 F 1, E, F 2, 1973 NZ, E, S, W, F, 1974 F, W, E, S, P, NZ, 1975 E, S, F, W
McCahill, S A (Sunday's Well) 1995 Fj (t)
McCall, B W (London Irish) 1985 F (R), 1986 E, S
McCall, M C (Bangor, Dungannon, London Irish) 1992 NZ 1(R), 2, 1994 W, 1996 E (R), A, 1997 It 1, NZ, C, It 2, 1998 S, E, SA 1, 2
McCallan, B (Ballymena) 1960 E, S
McCarten, R J (London Irish) 1961 E, W, F
McCarthy, E A (Kingstown) 1882 W
McCarthy, J S (Dolphin) 1948 F, E, S, W, 1949 F, E, S, W, 1950 W, 1951 F, E, S, W, SA, 1952 F, S, W, E, 1953 F, E, S, 1954 NZ, F, E, S, W, 1955 F, E
McCarthy, M P (Connacht) 2011 S2, F3(R)
McCarthy, P D (Cork Const) 1992 NZ 1, 2, A, 1993 S, R (R)
MacCarthy, St G (Dublin U) 1882 W
McCarthy, T (Cork) 1898 W
McClelland, T A (Queen's U, Belfast) 1921 E, S, W, F, 1922 E, W, F, 1923 E, S, W, F, 1924 F, E, S, W, NZ
McClenahan, R O (Instonians) 1923 E, S, W
McClinton, A N (NIFC) 1910 W, F
McCombe, W McM (Dublin U, Bangor) 1968 F, 1975 E, S, F, W
McConnell, A A (Collegians) 1947 A, 1948 F, E, S, W, 1949 F, E
McConnell, G (Derry, Edinburgh U) 1912 F, E, 1913 W, F
McConnell, J W (Lansdowne) 1913 S
McCormac, F M (Wanderers) 1909 W, 1910 W, F
McCormick, W J (Wanderers) 1930 E
McCoull, H C (Belfast Albion) 1895 E, S, W, 1899 E
McCourt, D (Queen's U, Belfast) 1947 A
McCoy, J J (Dungannon, Bangor, Ballymena) 1984 W, A, 1985 S, F, W, E, 1986 F, 1987 [Tg], 1988 E 2, WS, It, 1989 F, W, E, S, NZ
McCracken, H (NIFC) 1954 W
McCullen, A (Lansdowne) 2003 Sm
McCullough, M T (Ulster) 2005 J1, 2, NZ(R), A(R)
McDermott, S J (London Irish) 1955 S, W
Macdonald, J A (Methodist Coll, Belfast) 1875 E, 1876 E, 1877 S, 1878 E, 1879 S, 1880 E, 1881 S, 1882 E, S, 1883 E, S, 1884 E, S
McDonald, J P (Malone) 1987 [C], 1990 E (R), S, Arg
McDonnell, A C (Dublin U) 1889 W, 1890 S, W, 1891 E
McDowell, J C (Instonians) 1924 F, NZ
McFadden, F L (Leinster) 2011 It, F1, S2, F2(R), E2(R), [Ru]
McFarland, B A T (Derry) 1920 S, W, F, 1922 W
McGann, B J (Lansdowne) 1969 F, E, S, W, 1970 SA, F, E, S, W, 1971 F, E, S, W, 1972 F 1, E, F 2, 1973 NZ, E, S, W, 1976 F, W, E, S, NZ
McGowan, A N (Blackrock Coll) 1994 US
McGown, T M W (NIFC) 1899 E, S, 1901 S
McGrath, D G (UC Dublin, Cork Const) 1984 S, 1987 [W, C, Tg, A]

McGrath, N F (Oxford U, London Irish) 1934 W
McGrath, P J (UC Cork) 1965 E, S, W, SA, 1966 F, E, S, W, 1967 A 1, A 2
McGrath, R J M (Wanderers) 1977 W, E, F (R), 1981 SA 1, 2, A, 1982 W, E, S, F, 1983 S, F, W, E, 1984 F, W
McGrath, T (Garryowen) 1956 W, 1958 F, 1960 E, S, W, F, 1961 SA
McGuinness, C D (St Mary's Coll) 1997 NZ, C, 1998 F, W, E, SA 1, 2, Gg, R (R), SA 3, 1999 F, W, E, S
McGuire, E P (UC Galway) 1963 E, S, W, NZ, 1964 E, S, W, F
MacHale, S (Lansdowne) 1965 F, E, S, W, SA, 1966 F, E, S, W, 1967 S, W, F
McHugh, M (St Mary's Coll) 2003 Tg
McIldowie, G (Malone) 1906 SA, 1910 E, S, W
McIlrath, J A (Ballymena) 1976 A, F, NZ, 1977 W, E
McIlwaine, E H (NIFC) 1895 S, W
McIlwaine, E N (NIFC) 1875 E, 1876 E
McIlwaine, J E (NIFC) 1897 E, S, 1898 E, S, W, 1899 E, W
McIntosh, L M (Dublin U) 1884 S
MacIvor, C V (Dublin U) 1912 F, E, S, W, 1913 E, S, F
McIvor, S C (Garryowen) 1996 A, 1997 It 1, S (R)
McKay, J W (Queen's U, Belfast) 1947 F, E, S, W, A, 1948 F, E, S, W, 1949 F, E, S, W, 1950 F, E, S, W, 1951 F, E, S, W, SA, 1952 F
McKee, W D (NIFC) 1947 A, 1948 F, E, S, W, 1949 F, E, S, W, 1950 F, E, 1951 SA
McKeen, A J W (Lansdowne) 1999 [R (R)]
McKelvey, J M (Queen's U, Belfast) 1956 F, E
McKenna, P (St Mary's Coll) 2000 Arg
McKibbin, A R (Instonians, London Irish) 1977 W, E, S, 1978 S, F, W, E, NZ, 1979 F, W, E, S, 1980 E, S
McKibbin, C H (Instonians) 1976 S (R)
McKibbin, D (Instonians) 1950 F, E, S, W, 1951 F, E, S, W
McKibbin, H R (Queen's U, Belfast) 1938 W, 1939 E, S, W
McKinney, S A (Dungannon) 1972 F 1, E, F 2, 1973 W, F, 1974 F, E, S, P, NZ, 1975 E, S, 1976 A, F, W, E, S, NZ, 1977 W, E, S, 1978 S (R), F, W, E
McLaughlin, J H (Derry) 1887 E, S, 1888 W, S
McLaughlin, K R (Leinster) 2010 It, 2011 S2(R)
McLean, R E (Dublin U) 1881 S, 1882 W, E, S, 1883 E, S, 1884 E, S, 1885 E, S 1
Maclear, B (Cork County, Monkstown) 1905 E, S, W, NZ, 1906 E, S, W, SA, 1907 E, S, W
McLennan, A C (Wanderers) 1977 F, 1978 S, F, W, E, NZ, 1979 F, W, E, S, 1980 E, F, 1981 F, W, E, S, SA 1, 2
McLoughlin, F M (Northern) 1976 A
McLoughlin, G A J (Shannon) 1979 F, W, E, S, A 1, 2, 1980 E, 1981 SA 1, 2, 1982 W, E, S, F, 1983 S, F, W, E, 1984 F
McLoughlin, R J (UC Dublin, Blackrock Coll, Gosforth) 1962 E, S, F, 1963 E, S, W, NZ, 1964 E, S, 1965 F, E, S, W, SA, 1966 F, E, S, W, 1971 F, E, S, W, 1972 F 1, E, F 2, 1973 NZ, E, S, W, F, 1974 F, W, E, S, P, NZ, 1975 E, S, F, W
McMahon, L B (Blackrock Coll, UC Dublin) 1931 E, SA, 1933 E, 1934 E, 1936 E, S, W, 1937 E, S, W, 1938 E, S
McMaster, A W (Ballymena) 1972 F 1, E, F 2, 1973 NZ, E, S, W, F, 1974 F, E, S, P, 1975 F, W, 1976 A, F, W, NZ
McMordie, J (Queen's Coll, Belfast) 1886 S
McMorrow, A (Garryowen) 1951 W
McMullen, A R (Cork) 1881 E, S
McNamara, V (UC Cork) 1914 E, S, W
McNaughton, P P (Greystones) 1978 S, F, W, E, 1979 F, W, E, S, A 1, 2, 1980 E, S, F, W, 1981 F
MacNeill, H P (Dublin U, Oxford U, Blackrock Coll, London Irish) 1981 F, W, E, S, A, 1982 W, E, S, F, 1983 S, F, W, E, 1984 F, W, E, A, 1985 S, F, W, E, 1986 F, W, E, S, R, 1987 E, S, F, W, [W, C, Tg, A], 1988 S (R), E 1, 2
McQuilkin, K P (Bective Rangers, Lansdowne) 1996 US, S, F, 1997 F (t & R), S
MacSweeney, D A (Blackrock Coll) 1955 S
McVicker, H (Army, Richmond) 1927 E, S, W, A, 1928 F
McVicker, J (Collegians) 1924 F, E, S, W, NZ, 1925 F, E, S, W, 1926 F, E, S, W, 1927 F, E, S, W, A, 1928 W, 1930 F
McVicker, S (Queen's U, Belfast) 1922 E, S, W, F
McWeeney, J P J (St Mary's Coll) 1997 NZ
Madden, M N (Sunday's Well) 1955 E, S, W
Magee, A M (Louis) (Bective Rangers, London Irish) 1895 E, S, W, 1896 E, S, W, 1897 E, S, 1898 E, S, W, 1899 E, S, W, 1900 E, S, W, 1901 E, S, W, 1902 E, S, W, 1903 E, S, W, 1904 W
Magee, J T (Bective Rangers) 1895 E, S
Maggs, K M (Bristol, Bath, Ulster) 1997 NZ (R), C, It 2, 1998 S, F, W, E, SA 1, 2, Gg, R (R), SA 3, 1999 F, W, E, S, It, A 1, 2, Arg 1, [US, A 3, Arg 2], 2000 E, F, Arg, US (R), C, 2001 It (R), F (R), R, S (R), W, E, Sm, NZ, 2002 W, E, S, R, Ru, Gg, A, Fj, Arg, 2003 S 1, It 1, F, W 1, E, A, W 2, S 2, [R, Nm, Arg, A, F], 2004 F, W(R), E(R), It(R), S(R), SA1(R), 2, US, 2005 S, F, W, J1
Maginiss, R M (Dublin U) 1875 E, 1876 E
Magrath, R M (Cork Constitution) 1909 S
Maguire, J F (Cork) 1884 S
Mahoney, J (Dolphin) 1923 E
Malcolmson, G L (RAF, NIFC) 1935 NZ, 1936 E, S, W, 1937 E, S, W
Malone, N G (Oxford U, Leicester) 1993 S, F, 1994 US (R)
Mannion, N P (Corinthians, Lansdowne, Wanderers) 1988 WS, It, 1989 F, W, E, S, NZ, 1990 E, S, F, W, Arg, 1991 Nm 1(R), 2, [J], 1993 S
Marshall, B D E (Queen's U, Belfast) 1963 E
Mason, S J P (Orrell, Richmond) 1996 W, E, WS
Massey-Westropp, R H (Limerick, Monkstown) 1886 E
Matier, R N (NIFC) 1878 E, 1879 S
Matthews, P M (Ards, Wanderers) 1984 A, 1985 S, F, W, E, 1986 R, 1987 E, S, F, W, [W, Tg, A], 1988 S, F, W, E 1, 2, WS, It, 1989 F, W, E, S, NZ, 1990 E, S, 1991 F, W, E, S, Nm 1 [Z, S, A], 1992 W, E, S
Mattsson, J (Wanderers) 1948 E
Mayne, R B (Queen's U, Belfast) 1937 W, 1938 E, W, 1939 E, S, W
Mayne, R H (Belfast Academy) 1888 W, S
Mayne, T (NIFC) 1921 E, S, F
Mays, K M A (UC Dublin) 1973 NZ, E, S, W
Meares, A W D (Dublin U) 1899 S, W, 1900 E, W
Megaw, J (Richmond, Instonians) 1934 W, 1938 E
Millar, A (Kingstown) 1880 E, S, 1883 E
Millar, H J (Monkstown) 1904 W, 1905 E, S, W
Millar, S (Ballymena) 1958 F, 1959 E, S, W, F, 1960 E, S, W, F, SA, 1961 E, S, W, F, SA, 1962 E, S, F, 1963 F, E, S, W, 1964 F, 1968 F, E, S, W, A, 1969 F, E, S, W, 1970 SA, F, E, S, W
Millar, W H J (Queen's U, Belfast) 1951 E, S, W, 1952 S, W
Miller, E R P (Leicester, Terenure Coll, Leinster) 1997 It 1, F, W, E, NZ, It 2, 1998 S, W (R), Gg, R, 1999 F, W, E (R), S, Arg 1(R), [US (R), A 3(t&R), Arg 2(R)], 2000 US, C (R), SA, 2001 R, W, E, Sm, NZ, 2002 E, S, It (R), Fj (R), 2003 W 1(t+R), Tg, Sm, It 2, S 2, [Nm, Arg(R), A(t&R), F(R)], 2004 SA3(R), US, Arg(R), 2005 It(R), S(R), F(R), W(R), J1(R), 2
Miller, F H (Wanderers) 1886 S
Milliken, R A (Bangor) 1973 E, S, W, F, 1974 F, W, E, S, P, NZ, 1975 E, S, F, W
Millin, T J (Dublin U) 1925 W
Minch, J B (Bective Rangers) 1912 SA, 1913 E, S, 1914 E, S
Moffat, J (Belfast Academy) 1888 W, S, M, 1889 S, 1890 S, W, 1891 S
Moffatt, J E (Old Wesley) 1904 S, 1905 E, S, W
Moffett, J W (Ballymena) 1961 E, S
Molloy, M G (UC Galway, London Irish) 1966 F, E, 1967 A 1, E, S, W, F, A 2, 1968 F, E, S, W, A, 1969 F, E, S, W, 1970 F, E, S, W, 1971 F, E, S, W, 1973 F, 1976 A
Moloney, J J (St Mary's Coll) 1972 F 1, E, F 2, 1973 NZ, E, S, W, F, 1974 F, W, E, S, P, NZ, 1975 E, S, F, W, 1976 S, 1978 S, F, W, E, 1979 A 1, 2, 1980 S, W
Moloney, L A (Garryowen) 1976 W (R), S, 1978 S (R), NZ
Molony, J U (UC Dublin) 1950 S
Monteith, J D E (Queen's U, Belfast) 1947 E, S, W
Montgomery, A (NIFC) 1895 S
Montgomery, F P (Queen's U, Belfast) 1914 E, S, W
Montgomery, R (Cambridge U) 1887 E, S, W, 1891 E, 1892 W
Moore, C M (Dublin U) 1887 S, 1888 W, S
Moore, D F (Wanderers) 1883 E, S, 1884 E, W
Moore, F W (Wanderers) 1884 W, 1885 E, S 2, 1886 S
Moore, H (Windsor) 1876 E, 1877 S
Moore, H (Queen's U, Belfast) 1910 S, 1911 W, F, 1912 F, E, S, W, SA
Moore, T A P (Highfield) 1967 A 2, 1973 NZ, E, S, W, F, 1974 F, W, E, S, P, NZ
Moore, W D (Queen's Coll, Belfast) 1878 E
Moran, F G (Clontarf) 1936 E, 1937 E, S, W, 1938 S, W, 1939 E, S, W
Morell, H B (Dublin U) 1881 E, S, 1882 W, E
Morgan, G J (Clontarf) 1934 E, S, W, 1935 E, S, W, NZ, 1936 E, S, W, 1937 E, S, W, 1938 E, S, W, 1939 E, S, W
Moriarty, C C H (Monkstown) 1899 W
Moroney, J C M (Garryowen) 1968 W, A, 1969 F, E, S, W
Moroney, R J M (Lansdowne) 1984 F, W, 1985 F
Moroney, T A (UC Dublin) 1964 W, 1967 A 1, E
Morphy, E McG (Dublin U) 1908 E
Morris, D P (Bective Rangers) 1931 W, 1932 E, 1935 E, S, W, NZ
Morrow, J W R (Queen's Coll, Belfast) 1882 S, 1883 E, S, 1884 E, W, 1885 S 1, 2, 1886 E, S, 1888 S
Morrow, R D (Bangor) 1986 F, E, S
Mortell, M (Bective Rangers, Dolphin) 1953 F, E, S, W, 1954 NZ, F, E, S, W
Morton, W A (Dublin U) 1888 S

Mostyn, M R (Galwegians) 1999 A 1, Arg 1, [US, A 3, R, Arg 2]
Moyers, L W (Dublin U) 1884 W
Moylett, M M F (Shannon) 1988 E 1
Mulcahy, W A (UC Dublin, Bective Rangers, Bohemians) 1958 A, E, S, W, F, 1959 E, S, W, F, 1960 E, S, W, SA, 1961 E, S, W, SA, 1962 E, S, F, W, 1963 F, E, S, W, NZ, 1964 E, S, W, F, 1965 F, E, S, W, SA
Muldoon, J (Connacht) 2009 C, US, 2010 NZ1
Mullan, B (Clontarf) 1947 F, E, S, W, 1948 F, E, S, W
Mullane, J P (Limerick Bohemians) 1928 W, 1929 F
Mullen, K D (Old Belvedere) 1947 F, E, S, W, A, 1948 F, E, S, W, 1949 F, E, S, W, 1950 F, E, S, W, 1951 F, E, S, W, SA, 1952 F, S, W
Mulligan, A A (Wanderers) 1956 F, E, 1957 F, E, S, W, 1958 A, E, S, F, 1959 E, S, W, F, 1960 E, S, W, F, SA, 1961 W, F, SA
Mullin, B J (Dublin U, Oxford U, Blackrock Coll, London Irish) 1984 A, 1985 S, W, E, 1986 F, W, E, S, R, 1987 E, S, F, W, [W, C, Tg, A], 1988 S, F, W, E 1, 2, WS, It, 1989 F, W, E, S, NZ, 1990 E, S, W, Arg, 1991 F, W, E, S, Nm 1, 2, [J, S, A], 1992 W, E, S, 1994 US, 1995 E, S, F, W, It, [NZ, J, W, F]
Mullins, M J (Young Munster, Old Crescent) 1999 Arg 1(R), [R], 2000 E, S, It, Arg (t&R), US, C, 2001 It, R, W (R), E (R), Sm (R), NZ (R), 2003 Tg, Sm
Murphy, B J (Munster) 2007 Arg 1(R), 2, 2009 C, US
Murphy, C J (Lansdowne) 1939 E, S, W, 1947 F, E
Murphy, G E A (Leicester) 2000 US, C (R), J, 2001 R, S, Sm, 2002 W, E, NZ 1, 2, Fj, 2003 S 1(R), It 1, F, W 1, E, A, W 2, It 2(R), S 2, 2004 It, S, SA1, 3, US, Arg, 2005 It, S, E, F, W, NZ, A, R, 2006 It, F, W, S, E, NZ1, 2, A1(R), SA(R), A2, 2007 W(t&R), F, Arg1(t&R), 2, S2, It2, [Nm(R), Arg], 2008 It, F, S, E, NZ1(R), A(R), Arg, 2009 F(R), It(R), S(R), W(R), 2010 E, W, S, NZ1(R), A(R), Arg, 2011 E2, [US, Ru(R)]
Murphy, J G M W (London Irish) 1951 SA, 1952 S, W, E, 1954 NZ, 1958 W
Murphy, J J (Greystones) 1981 SA 1, 1982 W (R), 1984 S
Murphy, J N (Greystones) 1992 A
Murphy, K J (Cork Constitution) 1990 E, S, F, W, Arg, 1991 F, W (R), S (R), 1992 S, F, NZ 2(R)
Murphy, N A A (Cork Constitution) 1958 A, E, S, W, F, 1959 E, S, W, F, 1960 E, S, W, F, SA, 1961 E, S, W, 1962 E, 1963 NZ, 1964 E, S, W, F, 1965 F, E, S, W, SA, 1966 F, E, S, W, 1967 A 1, E, S, W, F, 1969 F, E, S, W
Murphy, N F (Cork Constitution) 1930 E, W, 1931 F, E, S, W, SA, 1932 E, S, W, 1933 E
Murphy-O'Connor, J (Bective Rangers) 1954 E
Murray, C (Munster) 2011 F2(R), E2(R), [US, A(R), It, W]
Murray, H W (Dublin U) 1877 S, 1878 E, 1879 E
Murray, J B (UC Dublin) 1963 F
Murray, P F (Wanderers) 1927 F, 1929 F, E, S, 1930 F, E, S, W, 1931 F, E, S, W, SA, 1932 E, S, W, 1933 E, W, S
Murtagh, C W (Portadown) 1977 S
Myles, J (Dublin U) 1875 E

Nash, L C (Queen's Coll, Cork) 1889 S, 1890 W, E, 1891 E, S, W
Neely, M R (Collegians) 1947 F, E, S, W
Neill, H J (NIFC) 1885 E, S 1, 2, 1886 S, 1887 E, S, W, 1888 W, S
Neill, J McF (Instonians) 1926 F
Nelson, J E (Malone) 1947 A, 1948 E, S, W, 1949 F, E, S, W, 1950 F, E, S, W, 1951 F, E, W, 1954 F
Nelson, R (Queen's Coll, Belfast) 1882 E, S, 1883 S, 1886 S
Nesdale, R P (Newcastle) 1997 W, E, S, NZ (R), C, 1998 F (R), W (R), Gg, SA 3(R), 1999 It, A 2(R), [US (R), R]
Nesdale, T J (Garryowen) 1961 F
Neville, W C (Dublin U) 1879 S, E
Nicholson, P C (Dublin U) 1900 E, S, W
Norton, G W (Bective Rangers) 1949 F, E, S, W, 1950 F, E, S, W, 1951 F, E, S
Notley, J R (Wanderers) 1952 F, S
Nowlan, K W (St Mary's Coll) 1997 NZ, C, It 2

O'Brien, B (Derry) 1893 S, W
O'Brien, B A P (Shannon) 1968 F, E, S
O'Brien, D J (London Irish, Cardiff, Old Belvedere) 1948 E, S, W, 1949 F, E, S, W, 1950 F, E, S, W, 1951 F, E, S, W, SA, 1952 F, S, W, E
O'Brien, K A (Broughton Park) 1980 E, 1981 SA 1(R), 2
O'Brien, S K (Leinster) 2009 Fj(R), SA(R), 2010 It(R), Sm, 2011 It, F1, S1, W, E1, F2, 3, [A, Ru, It, W]
O'Brien-Butler, P E (Monkstown) 1897 S, 1898 E, S, 1899 S, W, 1900 E
O'Callaghan, C T (Carlow) 1910 W, F, 1911 E, S, W, F, 1912 F
O'Callaghan, D P (Cork Const, Munster) 2003 W 1(R), Tg (R), Sm (R), W 2(R), It2(R), [R(R), A(t&R)], 2004 F(t&R), W, It, S(t&R), SA2(R), US, 2005 It(R), S(R), W(R), NZ, A, R, 2006 It(R), F(R), W, S(R), E(R), NZ1, 2, A1, SA, A2, PI(R), 2007 W, F, E, S1, It1, 2, [Nm, Gg, F, Arg], 2008 It, F, S, W, E, NZ1, A, C, NZ2, Arg, 2009 F, It, E, S, W, A, Fj(R), SA, 2010 E, W, S, NZ1, A, SA, Sm, NZ2, Arg, 2011 It, F1, S1, W, E1, F2, 3, E2, [US, A, Ru, It, W]
O'Callaghan, M P (Sunday's Well) 1962 W, 1964 E, F
O'Callaghan, P (Dolphin) 1967 A 1, E, A 2, 1968 F, E, S, W, 1969 F, E, S, W, 1970 SA, F, E, S, W, 1976 F, W, E, S, NZ
O'Connell, K D (Sunday's Well) 1994 F, E (t)
O'Connell, P (Bective Rangers) 1913 W, F, 1914 F, E, S, W
O'Connell, P J (Young Munster, Munster) 2002 W, It (R), F (R), NZ 1, 2003 E (R), A (R), Tg, Sm, W 2, S 2, [R, Nm, Arg, A, F], 2004 F, W, E, S, SA1, 2, 3, US, Arg, 2005 It, S, E, F, W, 2006 It, F, S, E, NZ1, 2, A1, SA, A2, PI, 2007 W, F, E, S1, 2, It2, [Nm, Gg, F, Arg], 2008 S(R), W, E, NZ1, A, C, NZ2, Arg, 2009 F, It, E, S, W, A, Fj, SA, 2010 It, F, E, W, S, 2011 It, F1, S1, W, E1, F2(R), 3, E2, [US, A, It, W]
O'Connell, W J (Lansdowne) 1955 F
O'Connor, H S (Dublin U) 1957 F, E, S, W
O'Connor, J (Garryowen) 1895 S
O'Connor, J H (Bective Rangers) 1888 M, 1890 S, W, E, 1891 E, S, 1892 E, W, 1893 E, S, 1894 E, S, W, 1895 E, 1896 E, S, W
O'Connor, J H (Wasps) 2004 SA3, Arg, 2005 S, E, F, W, J1, NZ, A, R, 2006 W(R), E(t&R)
O'Connor, J J (Garryowen) 1909 F
O'Connor, J J (UC Cork) 1933 S, 1934 E, S, W, 1935 E, S, W, NZ, 1936 S, W, 1938 S
O'Connor, P J (Lansdowne) 1887 W
O'Cuinneagain, D (Sale, Ballymena) 1998 SA 1, 2, Gg (R), R (R), SA 3, 1999 F, W, E, S, It, A 1, 2, Arg 1, [US, A 3, R, Arg 2], 2000 E, It (R)
Odbert, R V M (RAF) 1928 F
O'Donnell, R C (St Mary's Coll) 1979 A 1, 2, 1980 S, F, W
O'Donoghue, P J (Bective Rangers) 1955 F, E, S, W, 1956 W, 1957 F, E, 1958 A, E, S, W
O'Driscoll, B G (Blackrock Coll, Leinster) 1999 A 1, 2, Arg 1, [US, A 3, R (R), Arg 2], 2000 E, S, It, F, W, J, SA, 2001 F, S, W, E, Sm, NZ, 2002 W, E, S, It, F, NZ 1, 2, R, Ru, Gg, A, Fj, Arg, 2003 S 1, It 1, F, W 1, E, W 2, It 2, S 2, [R, Nm, Arg, A, F], 2004 W, E, It, S, SA1, 2, 3, US, Arg, 2005 It, E, F, W, 2006 It, F, W, S, E, NZ1, 2, A1, SA, A2, PI, 2007 W, E, S1, It1, S2, [Nm, Gg, F, Arg], 2008 It, F, S, W, NZ1, A, C, NZ2, Arg, 2009 F, It, E, S, W, A, Fj, SA, 2010 It, F, E, W, S, NZ1, A, SA, Sm, NZ2, Arg, 2011 It, F1, S1, W, E1, F3, [US, A, It, W]
O'Driscoll, B J (Manchester) 1971 F (R), E, S, W
O'Driscoll, J B (London Irish, Manchester) 1978 S, 1979 A 1, 2, 1980 E, S, F, W, 1981 F, W, E, S, SA 1, 2, A, 1982 W, E, S, F, 1983 S, F, W, E, 1984 F, W, E, S
O'Driscoll, M R (Cork Const, Munster) 2001 R (R), 2002 Fj (R), 2005 R(R), 2006 W(R), NZ1(R), 2(R), A1(R), 2007 E(R), It1, Arg1(t&R), 2, 2008 It(R), F(R), S, E(R), 2009 C, US, 2010 NZ1, A, SA, NZ2, Arg, 2011 S2(R)
O'Flanagan, K P (London Irish) 1947 A
O'Flanagan, M (Lansdowne) 1948 S
O'Gara, R J R (Cork Const, Munster) 2000 S, It, F, W, Arg (R), US, C (R), J, SA, 2001 It, F, S, W (R), E (R), Sm, 2002 W (R), E (R), S (R), It (t), F (R), NZ 1, 2, R, Ru, Gg, A, Arg, 2003 W 1(R), E (R), A (t+R), Tg, Sm, S 2, [R(R), Nm, Arg(R), A, F], 2004 F, W, E, It, S, SA1, 2, 3, Arg, 2005 It, S, E, F, W, NZ, A, R(R), 2006 It, F, W, S, E, NZ1, 2, A1, SA, A2, PI(R), 2007 W, F, E, S1, It1, S2(R), It2, [Nm, Gg, F, Arg], 2008 It, F, S, W, E, NZ1, A, C, NZ2, Arg, 2009 F, It, E, S, W, A, 2010 It, F, E(R), W(R), S(R), NZ1, SA(R), Sm, NZ2(R), Arg(R), 2011 It(R), F1(R), S1, W, E1(R), F2, 3(R), E2, [US(R), A(R), Ru, It, W]
O'Grady, D (Sale) 1997 It 2
O'Hanlon, B (Dolphin) 1947 E, S, W, 1948 F, E, S, W, 1949 F, E, S, W, 1950 F
O'Hara, P T J (Sunday's Well, Cork Const) 1988 WS (R), 1989 F, W, E, NZ, 1990 E, S, F, W, 1991 Nm 1, [J], 1993 F, W, E, 1994 US
O'Kelly, M E (London Irish, St Mary's Coll, Leinster) 1997 NZ, C, It 2, 1998 S, F, W, E, SA 1, 2, Gg, R, SA 3, 1999 A 1(R), 2, Arg 1(R), [US (R), A 3, R, Arg 2], 2000 E, S, It, F, W, Arg, US, J, SA, 2001 It, F, S, W, E, NZ, 2002 E, S, It, F, NZ 1(R), 2, R, Ru, Gg, A, Fj, Arg, 2003 S 1, It 1, F, W 1, E, A, W 2, S 2, [R, Nm, Arg, A, F], 2004 F, W(R), E, It, S, SA1, 2, 3, Arg, 2005 It, S, E, F, W, NZ, A, 2006 It, F, W, S, E, SA(R), A2(R), PI, 2007 Arg1, 2(R), S2, It2(R), [F(R), Arg(R)], 2008 It, F, 2009 It(R)
O'Leary, A (Cork Constitution) 1952 S, W, E
O'Leary, T G (Munster) 2007 Arg1(R), 2008 NZ2, Arg, 2009 F, It, E, S(R), W, A, Fj(R), SA, 2010 It, F, E, W, S, NZ1, A, 2011 It, F1, S2, F3
O'Loughlin, D B (UC Cork) 1938 E, S, W, 1939 E, S, W
O'Mahony, D W (UC Dublin, Moseley, Bedford) 1995 It, [F], 1997 It 2, 1998 R

O'Mahony, David (Cork Constitution) 1995 It
O'Meara, B T (Cork Constitution) 1997 E (R), S, NZ (R), 1998 S, 1999 [US (R), R (R)], 2001 It (R), 2003 Sm (R), It 2(R)
O'Meara, J A (UC Cork, Dolphin) 1951 F, E, S, W, SA, 1952 F, S, W, E, 1953 F, E, S, W, 1954 NZ, F, E, S, 1955 F, E, 1956 S, W, 1958 W
O'Neill, H O'H (Queen's U, Belfast, UC Cork) 1930 E, S, W, 1933 E, S, W
O'Neill, J B (Queen's U, Belfast) 1920 S
O'Neill, W A (UC Dublin, Wanderers) 1952 E, 1953 F, E, S, W, 1954 NZ
O'Reilly, A J F (Old Belvedere, Leicester) 1955 F, E, S, W, 1956 F, E, S, W, 1957 F, E, S, W, 1958 A, E, S, W, F, 1959 E, S, W, F, 1960 E, 1961 E, F, SA, 1963 F, S, W, 1970 E
Orr, P A (Old Wesley) 1976 F, W, E, S, NZ, 1977 W, E, S, F, 1978 S, F, W, E, NZ, 1979 F, W, E, S, A 1, 2, 1980 E, S, F, W, 1981 F, W, E, S, SA 1, 2, A, 1982 W, E, S, F, 1983 S, F, W, E, 1984 F, W, E, S, A, 1985 S, F, W, E, 1986 F, S, R, 1987 E, S, F, W, [W, C, A]
O'Shea, C M P (Lansdowne, London Irish) 1993 R, 1994 F, W, E, S, A 1, 2, US, 1995 E, S, [J, W, F], 1997 It 1, F, S (R), 1998 S, F, SA 1, 2, Gg, R, SA 3, 1999 F, W, E, S, It, A 1, Arg 1, [US, A 3, R, Arg 2], 2000 E
O'Sullivan, A C (Dublin U) 1882 S
O'Sullivan, J M (Limerick) 1884 S, 1887 S
O'Sullivan, P J A (Galwegians) 1957 F, E, S, W, 1959 E, S, W, F, 1960 SA, 1961 E, S, 1962 F, W, 1963 F, NZ
O'Sullivan, W (Queen's Coll, Cork) 1895 S
Owens, R H (Dublin U) 1922 E, S

Parfrey, P (UC Cork) 1974 NZ
Parke, J C (Monkstown) 1903 W, 1904 E, S, W, 1905 W, NZ, 1906 E, S, W, SA, 1907 E, S, W, 1908 E, S, W, 1909 E, S, W, F
Parr, J S (Wanderers) 1914 F, E, S, W
Patterson, C S (Instonians) 1978 NZ, 1979 F, W, E, S, A 1, 2, 1980 E, S, F, W
Patterson, R d'A (Wanderers) 1912 F, S, W, SA, 1913 E, S, W, F
Payne, C T (NIFC) 1926 E, 1927 F, E, S, A, 1928 F, E, S, W, 1929 F, E, W, 1930 F, E, S, W
Pedlow, A C (CIYMS) 1953 W, 1954 NZ, F, E, 1955 F, E, S, W, 1956 F, E, S, W, 1957 F, E, S, W, 1958 A, E, S, W, F, 1959 E, 1960 E, S, W, F, SA, 1961 S, 1962 W, 1963 F
Pedlow, J (Bessbrook) 1882 S, 1884 W
Pedlow, R (Bessbrook) 1891 W
Pedlow, T B (Queen's Coll, Belfast) 1889 S, W
Peel, T (Limerick) 1892 E, S, W
Peirce, W (Cork) 1881 E
Phipps, G C (Army) 1950 E, W, 1952 F, W, E
Pike, T O (Lansdowne) 1927 E, S, W, A, 1928 F, E, S, W
Pike, V J (Lansdowne) 1931 E, S, W, SA, 1932 E, S, W, 1933 E, W, S, 1934 E, S, W
Pike, W W (Kingstown) 1879 E, 1881 E, S, 1882 E, 1883 S
Pinion, G (Belfast Collegians) 1909 E, S, W, F
Piper, O J S (Cork Constitution) 1909 E, S, W, F, 1910 E, S, W, F
Polden, S E (Clontarf) 1913 W, F, 1914 F, 1920 F
Popham, I (Cork Constitution) 1922 S, W, F, 1923 F
Popplewell, N J (Greystones, Wasps, Newcastle) 1989 NZ, 1990 Arg, 1991 Nm 1, 2, [Z, S, A], 1992 W, E, S, F, NZ 1, 2, A, 1993 S, F, W, E, R, 1994 F, W, E, S, US, 1995 E, S, F, W, It, [NZ, J, W, F], Fj, 1996 US, S, F, W, E, A, 1997 It 1, F, W, E, NZ, C, 1998 S (t), F (R)
Potterton, H N (Wanderers) 1920 W
Pratt, R H (Dublin U) 1933 E, W, S, 1934 E, S
Price, A H (Dublin U) 1920 S, F
Pringle, J C (NIFC) 1902 S, W
Purcell, N M (Lansdowne) 1921 E, S, W, F
Purdon, H (NIFC) 1879 S, E, 1880 E, 1881 E, S
Purdon, W B (Queen's Coll, Belfast) 1906 E, S, W
Purser, F C (Dublin U) 1898 E, S, W

Quinlan, A N (Shannon, Munster) 1999 [R (R)], 2001 It, F, 2002 NZ 2(R), Ru (R), Gg (R), A (R), Fj, Arg (R), 2003 S 1(R), It 1(R), F (R), W 1, E (R), A, W 2, [R(R), Nm, Arg], 2004 SA1(R), 2(R), 2005 J1, 2(t&R), 2007 Arg2, S2(t&R), 2008 C(R), NZ2
Quinlan, D P (Northampton) 2005 J1(R), 2
Quinlan, S V J (Blackrock Coll) 1956 F, E, W, 1958 W
Quinn, B T (Old Belvedere) 1947 F
Quinn, F P (Old Belvedere) 1981 F, W, E
Quinn, J P (Dublin U) 1910 E, S, 1911 E, S, W, F, 1912 E, S, W, 1913 E, W, F, 1914 F, E, S
Quinn, K (Old Belvedere) 1947 F, A, 1953 F, E, S
Quinn, M A M (Lansdowne) 1973 F, 1974 F, W, E, S, P, NZ, 1977 S, F, 1981 SA 2
Quirke, J M T (Blackrock Coll) 1962 E, S, 1968 S

Rainey, P I (Ballymena) 1989 NZ
Rambaut, D F (Dublin U) 1887 E, S, W, 1888 W
Rea, H H (Edinburgh U) 1967 A 1, 1969 F
Read, H M (Dublin U) 1910 E, S, 1911 E, S, W, F, 1912 F, E, S, W, SA, 1913 E, S
Reardon, J V (Cork Constitution) 1934 E, S
Reddan, E G (Wasps, Leinster) 2006 F(R), 2007 Arg2, S2(R), [F, Arg], 2008 It, F, S, W, E, NZ1, A(R), C, NZ2(R), 2009 C(R), US(R), Fj, 2010 It(R), F(R), W(R), NZ1(R), SA, NZ2, Arg(R), 2011 It(R), F1(R), S1, W, E1, F2, 3(R), E2, [US(R), A, Ru(R), It(R), W(R)]
Reid, C (NIFC) 1899 S, W, 1900 E, 1903 W
Reid, J L (Richmond) 1934 S, W
Reid, P J (Garryowen) 1947 A, 1948 F, E, W
Reid, T E (Garryowen) 1953 E, S, W, 1954 NZ, F, 1955 E, S, 1956 F, E, 1957 F, E, S, W
Reidy, C J (London Irish) 1937 W
Reidy, G F (Dolphin, Lansdowne) 1953 W, 1954 F, E, S, W
Richey, H A (Dublin U) 1889 W, 1890 S
Ridgeway, E C (Wanderers) 1932 S, W, 1935 E, S, W
Rigney, B J (Greystones) 1991 F, W, E, S, Nm 1, 1992 F, NZ 1(R), 2
Ringland, T M (Queen's U, Belfast, Ballymena) 1981 A, 1982 W, E, F, 1983 S, F, W, E, 1984 F, W, E, S, A, 1985 S, F, W, E, 1986 F, W, E, S, R, 1987 E, S, F, W, [W, C, Tg, A], 1988 S, F, W, E 1
Riordan, W F (Cork Constitution) 1910 E
Ritchie, J S (London Irish) 1956 F, E
Robb, C G (Queen's Coll, Belfast) 1904 E, S, W, 1905 NZ, 1906 S
Robbie, J C (Dublin U, Greystones) 1976 A, F, NZ, 1977 S, F, 1981 F, W, E, S
Robinson, B F (Ballymena, London Irish) 1991 F, W, E, S, Nm 1, 2, [Z, S, A], 1992 W, E, S, F, NZ 1, 2, A, 1993 W, E, R, 1994 F, W, E, S, A 1, 2
Robinson, T T H (Wanderers) 1904 E, S, 1905 E, S, W, NZ, 1906 SA, 1907 E, S, W
Roche, J (Wanderers) 1890 S, W, E, 1891 E, S, W, 1892 W
Roche, R E (UC Galway) 1955 E, S, 1957 S, W
Roche, W J (UC Cork) 1920 E, S, F
Roddy, P J (Bective Rangers) 1920 S, F
Roe, R (Lansdowne) 1952 E, 1953 F, E, S, W, 1954 F, E, S, W, 1955 F, E, S, W, 1956 F, E, S, W, 1957 F, E, S, W
Rolland, A C (Blackrock Coll) 1990 Arg, 1994 US (R), 1995 It (R)
Ronan, N (Munster) 2009 C, US, 2010 A, 2011 S2
Rooke, C V (Dublin U) 1891 E, W, 1892 E, S, W, 1893 E, S, W, 1894 E, S, W, 1895 E, S, W, 1896 E, S, W, 1897 E, S
Ross, D J (Belfast Academy) 1884 E, 1885 S 1, 2, 1886 E, S
Ross, G R P (CIYMS) 1955 W
Ross, J F (NIFC) 1886 S
Ross, J P (Lansdowne) 1885 E, S 1, 2, 1886 E, S
Ross, M R (Harlequins, Leinster) 2009 C(R), US, 2011 It, F1, S1, W, E1, F2, 3, E2, [US, A, Ru(R), It, W]
Ross, N G (Malone) 1927 F, E
Ross, W McC (Queen's U, Belfast) 1932 E, S, W, 1933 E, W, S, 1934 E, S, 1935 NZ
Ruddock, R J (Leinster) 2010 A(R)
Russell, J (UC Cork) 1931 F, E, S, W, SA, 1933 E, W, S, 1934 E, S, W, 1935 E, S, W, 1936 E, S, W, 1937 E, S
Russell, P (Instonians) 1990 E, 1992 NZ 1, 2, A
Rutherford, W G (Tipperary) 1884 E, S, 1885 E, S 1, 1886 E, 1888 W
Ryan, D C (Munster) 2008 Arg(R), 2009 C(R), US(R), 2010 It(R), F(R), SA(R), Sm(R), 2011 S2, F2, E2(R), [Ru, It(R), W(R)]
Ryan, E (Dolphin) 1937 W, 1938 E, S
Ryan, J (Rockwell Coll) 1897 E, 1898 E, S, W, 1899 E, S, W, 1900 S, W, 1901 E, S, W, 1902 E, 1904 E
Ryan, J G (UC Dublin) 1939 E, S, W
Ryan, M (Rockwell Coll) 1897 E, S, 1898 E, S, W, 1899 E, S, W, 1900 E, S, W, 1901 E, S, W, 1903 E, 1904 E, S

Saunders, R (London Irish) 1991 F, W, E, S, Nm 1, 2, [Z, J, S, A], 1992 W, 1994 F (t)
Saverimutto, C (Sale) 1995 Fj, 1996 US, S
Sayers, H J M (Lansdowne) 1935 E, S, W, 1936 E, S, W, 1938 W, 1939 E, S, W
Scally, C J (U C Dublin) 1998 Gg (R), R, 1999 S (R), It
Schute, F (Wanderers) 1878 E, 1879 E
Schute, F G (Dublin U) 1912 SA, 1913 E, S
Scott, D (Malone) 1961 F, SA, 1962 S
Scott, R D (Queen's U, Belfast) 1967 E, F, 1968 F, E, S
Scovell, R H (Kingstown) 1883 E, 1884 E
Scriven, G (Dublin U) 1879 S, E, 1880 E, S, 1881 E, 1882 S, 1883 E, S
Sealy, J (Dublin U) 1896 E, S, W, 1897 S, 1899 E, S, W, 1900 E, S
Sexton, J J (Leinster) 2009 Fj, SA, 2010 F(R), E, W, S, NZ1(R), A,

SA, NZ2, Arg, 2011 It, F1, S1(R), W(R), E1, S2, F3, E2(R), [US, A, Ru(R), It(R), W(R)]
Sexton, J F (Dublin U, Lansdowne) 1988 E 2, WS, It, 1989 F
Sexton, W J (Garryowen) 1984 A, 1988 S, E 2
Shanahan, T (Lansdowne) 1885 E, S 1, 2, 1886 E, 1888 S, W
Shaw, G M (Windsor) 1877 S
Sheahan, F J (Cork Const, Munster) 2000 US (R), 2001 It (R), R, W (R), Sm, 2002 W, E, S, Gg (R), A (t+R), Fj, 2003 S 1(R), It 1(R), 2004 F(R), W(R), It(R), S(R), SA1(R), US, 2005 It(R), S(R), W(R), J1, 2, 2006 SA(R), A2(R), PI, 2007 Arg2, [F(t&R)]
Sheehan, M D (London Irish) 1932 E
Sherry, B F (Terenure Coll) 1967 A 1, E, S, A 2, 1968 F, E
Sherry, M J A (Lansdowne) 1975 F, W
Shields, P M (Ballymena) 2003 Sm (R), It 2(R)
Siggins, J A E (Belfast Collegians) 1931 F, E, S, W, SA, 1932 E, S, W, 1933 E, W, S, 1934 E, S, W, 1935 E, S, W, NZ, 1936 E, S, W, 1937 E, S, W
Slattery, J F (UC Dublin, Blackrock Coll) 1970 SA, F, E, S, W, 1971 F, E, S, W, 1972 F 1, E, F 2, 1973 NZ, E, S, W, F, 1974 F, W, E, S, P, NZ, 1975 E, S, F, W, 1976 A, 1977 S, F, 1978 S, F, W, E, NZ, 1979 F, W, E, S, A 1, 2, 1980 E, S, F, W, 1981 F, W, E, S, SA 1, 2, A, 1982 W, E, S, F, 1983 S, F, W, E, 1984 F
Smartt, F N B (Dublin U) 1908 E, S, 1909 E
Smith, B A (Oxford U, Leicester) 1989 NZ, 1990 S, F, W, Arg, 1991 F, W, E, S
Smith, J H (London Irish) 1951 F, E, S, W, SA, 1952 F, S, W, E, 1954 NZ, W, F
Smith, R E (Lansdowne) 1892 E
Smith, S J (Ballymena) 1988 E 2, WS, It, 1989 F, W, E, S, NZ, 1990 E, 1991 F, W, E, S, Nm 1, 2, [Z, S, A], 1992 W, E, S, F, NZ 1, 2, 1993 S
Smithwick, F F S (Monkstown) 1898 S, W
Smyth, J T (Queen's U, Belfast) 1920 F
Smyth, P J (Belfast Collegians) 1911 E, S, F
Smyth, R S (Dublin U) 1903 E, S, 1904 E
Smyth, T (Malone, Newport) 1908 E, S, W, 1909 E, S, W, 1910 E, S, W, F, 1911 E, S, W, 1912 E
Smyth, W S (Belfast Collegians) 1910 W, F, 1920 E
Solomons, B A H (Dublin U) 1908 E, S, W, 1909 E, S, W, F, 1910 E, S, W
Spain, A W (UC Dublin) 1924 NZ
Sparrow, W (Dublin U) 1893 W, 1894 E
Spillane, B J (Bohemians) 1985 S, F, W, E, 1986 F, W, E, 1987 F, W, [W, C, A (R)], 1989 E (R)
Spring, D E (Dublin U) 1978 S, NZ, 1979 S, 1980 S, F, W, 1981 W
Spring, R M (Lansdowne) 1979 F, W, E
Spunner, H F (Wanderers) 1881 E, S, 1884 W
Stack, C R R (Dublin U) 1889 S
Stack, G H (Dublin U) 1875 E
Staples, J E (London Irish, Harlequins) 1991 W, E, S, Nm 1, 2, [Z, J, S, A], 1992 W, E, NZ 1, 2, A, 1995 F, W, It, [NZ], Fj, 1996 US, S, F, A, 1997 W, E, S
Staunton, J W (Garryowen, Wasps) 2001 Sm, 2005 J1(R), 2(R), 2006 A1(R), 2007 Arg2
Steele, H W (Ballymena) 1976 E, 1977 F, 1978 F, W, E, 1979 F, W, E, A 1, 2
Stephenson, G V (Queen's U, Belfast, London Hosp) 1920 F, 1921 E, S, W, F, 1922 E, S, W, F, 1923 E, S, W, F, 1924 F, E, S, W, NZ, 1925 F, E, S, W, 1926 F, E, S, W, 1927 F, E, S, W, A, 1928 F, E, S, W, 1929 F, E, W, 1930 F, E, S, W
Stephenson, H W V (United Services) 1922 S, W, F, 1924 F, E, S, W, NZ, 1925 F, E, S, W, 1927 A, 1928 E
Stevenson, J (Dungannon) 1888 M, 1889 S
Stevenson, J B (Instonians) 1958 A, E, S, W, F
Stevenson, R (Dungannon) 1887 E, S, W, 1888 M, 1889 S, W, 1890 S, W, E, 1891 W, 1892 W, 1893 E, S, W
Stevenson, T H (Belfast Acad) 1895 E, W, 1896 E, S, W, 1897 E, S
Stewart, A L (NIFC) 1913 W, F, 1914 F
Stewart, J W (Queen's U, Belfast, NIFC) 1922 F, 1924 S, 1928 F, E, S, W, 1929 F, E, S, W
Stoker, E W (Wanderers) 1888 W, S
Stoker, F O (Wanderers) 1886 S, 1888 W, M, 1889 S, 1891 W
Stokes, O S (Cork Bankers) 1882 E, 1884 E
Stokes, P (Garryowen) 1913 E, S, 1914 F, 1920 E, S, W, F, 1921 E, S, F, 1922 W, F
Stokes, R D (Queen's Coll, Cork) 1891 S, W
Strathdee, E (Queen's U, Belfast) 1947 E, S, W, A, 1948 W, F, 1949 E, S, W
Stringer, P A (Shannon, Munster) 2000 S, It, F, W, Arg, C, J, SA, 2001 It, F, R, S (R), W, E, Sm, NZ, 2002 W, E, S, It, F, NZ 1, 2, R, Ru, Gg, A, Arg, 2003 S 1, It 1, F, W 1, E, A, W 2, S 2, [R, Nm, Arg, A, F], 2004 F, W, E, It, S, SA1, 2, 3, US(R), Arg, 2005 It, S, E, F, W, J1, 2, NZ, A, R(R), 2006 It, F, W, S, E, NZ1, 2, A1, SA, A2(R), PI, 2007 W, E, S1, It1, 2, [Nm, Gg], 2008 It(R), S(R), E(R), NZ1(R), A, C(R), 2009 It(t&R), E(R), S, W(R), C, US, 2010 SA(R), Sm, NZ2(R), Arg, 2011 S1(R), W(R), E1(R)
Stuart, C P (Clontarf) 1912 SA
Stuart, I M B (Dublin U) 1924 E, S
Sugars, H S (Dublin U) 1905 NZ, 1906 SA, 1907 S
Sugden, M (Wanderers) 1925 F, E, S, W, 1926 F, E, S, W, 1927 E, S, W, A, 1928 F, E, S, W, 1929 F, E, S, W, 1930 F, E, S, W, 1931 F, E, S, W
Sullivan, D B (UC Dublin) 1922 E, S, W, F
Sweeney, J A (Blackrock Coll) 1907 E, S, W
Symes, G R (Monkstown) 1895 E
Synge, J S (Lansdowne) 1929 S

Taggart, T (Dublin U) 1887 W
Taylor, A S (Queen's Coll, Belfast) 1910 E, S, W, 1912 F
Taylor, D R (Queen's Coll, Belfast) 1903 E
Taylor, J (Belfast Collegians) 1914 E, S, W
Taylor, J W (NIFC) 1879 S, 1880 E, S, 1881 S, 1882 E, S, 1883 E, S
Tector, W R (Wanderers) 1955 F, E, S
Tedford, A (Malone) 1902 E, S, W, 1903 E, S, W, 1904 E, S, W, 1905 E, S, W, NZ, 1906 E, S, W, SA, 1907 E, S, W, 1908 E, S, W
Teehan, C (UC Cork) 1939 E, S, W
Thompson, C (Belfast Collegians) 1907 E, S, 1908 E, S, W, 1909 E, S, W, F, 1910 E, S, W, F
Thompson, J A (Queen's Coll, Belfast) 1885 S 1, 2
Thompson, J K S (Dublin U) 1921 W, 1922 E, S, F, 1923 E, S, W, F
Thompson, R G (Lansdowne) 1882 W
Thompson, R H (Instonians) 1951 SA, 1952 F, 1954 NZ, F, E, S, W, 1955 F, S, W, 1956 W
Thornhill, T (Wanderers) 1892 E, S, W, 1893 E
Thrift, H (Dublin U) 1904 W, 1905 E, S, W, NZ, 1906 E, W, SA, 1907 E, S, W, 1908 E, S, W, 1909 E, S, W, F
Tierney, D (UC Cork) 1938 S, W, 1939 E
Tierney, T A (Garryowen) 1999 A 1, 2, Arg 1, [US, A 3, R, Arg 2], 2000 E
Tillie, C R (Dublin U) 1887 E, S, 1888 W, S
Todd, A W P (Dublin U) 1913 W, F, 1914 F
Toner, D (Leinster) 2010 Sm, NZ2(R), Arg(R)
Topping, J A (Ballymena) 1996 WS, A, 1997 It 1, F, E, 1999 [R], 2000 US, 2003 A
Torrens, J D (Bohemians) 1938 W, 1939 E, S, W
Trimble, A D (Ulster) 2005 A, R, 2006 F(R), W, S, E, NZ1, 2, A1, SA, 2007 W, F(R), E(R), It1(R), Arg1, S2(R), It2, [Nm, F], 2008 It, F, S, W, E, 2009 Fj(R), 2010 It, E(R), NZ1, A, Sm, Arg, 2011 E1, S2, F2, 3, E2, [US(R), A(t&R), Ru, It(R), W(R)]
Tucker, C C (Shannon) 1979 F, W, 1980 F (R)
Tuke, B B (Bective Rangers) 1890 E, 1891 E, S, 1892 E, 1894 E, S, W, 1895 E, S
Tuohy, D M (Ulster) 2010 NZ1(R), A(t&R)
Turley, N (Blackrock Coll) 1962 E
Tweed, D A (Ballymena) 1995 F, W, It, [J]
Tydings, J J (Young Munster) 1968 A
Tyrrell, W (Queen's U, Belfast) 1910 F, 1913 E, S, W, F, 1914 F, E, S, W

Uprichard, R J H (Harlequins, RAF) 1950 S, W

Varley, D A (Munster) 2010 A(R), Arg(R)

Waide, S L (Oxford U, NIFC) 1932 E, S, W, 1933 E, W
Waites, J (Bective Rangers) 1886 S, 1888 M, 1889 W, 1890 S, W, E, 1891 E
Waldron, O C (Oxford U, London Irish) 1966 S, W, 1968 A
Walker, S (Instonians) 1934 E, S, 1935 E, S, W, NZ, 1936 E, S, W, 1937 E, S, W, 1938 E, S, W
Walkington, D B (NIFC) 1887 E, W, 1888 W, 1890 W, E, 1891 E, S, W
Walkington, R B (NIFC) 1875 E, 1876 E, 1877 E, S, 1878 E, 1879 S, 1880 E, S, 1882 E, S
Wall, H (Dolphin) 1965 S, W
Wallace, D P (Garryowen, Munster) 2000 Arg, US, 2001 It, F, R (R), S (R), W, E, NZ, 2002 W, E, S, It, F, 2003 Tg (R), Sm (R), W 2(t+R), S 2, 2004 S, SA1, 2, 2005 J2, 2006 It, F, W, S, E, NZ1, 2, A1, SA, A2, 2007 W, F, E, S1, It1, [Nm, Gg, F, Arg], 2008 It, F, S, W, E, NZ1, C(R), NZ2, Arg, 2009 F, It, E, S, W, A, SA, 2010 It, F, E, W, S, NZ1, SA, NZ2, Arg, 2011 It, F1, S1, W, E1, 2
Wallace, Jas (Wanderers) 1904 E, S
Wallace, Jos (Wanderers) 1903 S, W, 1904 E, S, W, 1905 E, S, W, NZ, 1906 W
Wallace, P R (Ulster) 2006 SA(R), PI, 2007 E(R), Arg1, S2, [Nm(R)], 2008 S(R), E(R), NZ1, A, C(R), NZ2(R), 2009 F, It, E, W(R), A, Fj(R), SA, 2010 It(R), F(t&R), A, Sm, 2011 It(R), W(R), E1(R), S2, F2, [Ru]

Wallace, P S (Blackrock Coll, Saracens) 1995 [J], Fj, 1996 US, W, E, WS, A, 1997 It 1, F, W, E, S, NZ, C, 1998 S, F, W, E, SA 1, 2, Gg, R, 1999 F, W, E, S, It (R), 1999 A 1, 2, Arg 1, [US, A 3, R, Arg 2], 2000 E, US, C (R), 2002 W (R), E (R), S (R), It (R), F (R), NZ 2(R), Ru (R), Gg (R)
Wallace, R M (Garryowen, Saracens) 1991 Nm 1(R), 1992 W, E, S, F, A, 1993 S, F, W, E, R, 1994 F, W, E, S, 1995 W, It, [NZ, J, W], Fj, 1996 US, S, F, WS, 1998 S, F, W, E
Wallace, T H (Cardiff) 1920 E, S, W
Wallis, A K (Wanderers) 1892 E, S, W, 1893 E, W
Wallis, C O'N (Old Cranleighans, Wanderers) 1935 NZ
Wallis, T G (Wanderers) 1921 F, 1922 E, S, W, F
Wallis, W A (Wanderers) 1880 S, 1881 E, S, 1882 W, 1883 S
Walmsley, G (Bective Rangers) 1894 E
Walpole, A (Dublin U) 1888 S, M
Walsh, E J (Lansdowne) 1887 E, S, W, 1892 E, S, W, 1893 E
Walsh, H D (Dublin U) 1875 E, 1876 E
Walsh, J C (UC Cork, Sunday's Well) 1960 S, SA, 1961 E, S, F, SA, 1963 E, S, W, NZ, 1964 E, S, W, F, 1965 F, S, W, SA, 1966 F, S, W, 1967 E, S, W, F, A 2
Ward, A J (Ballynahinch) 1998 F, W, E, SA 1, 2, Gg, R, SA 3, 1999 W, E, S, It (R), A 1, 2, Arg 1, [US, A 3, R, Arg 2], 2000 F (R), W (t&R), Arg (R), US (R), C, J, SA (R), 2001 It (R), F (R)
Ward, A J P (Garryowen, St Mary's Coll, Greystones) 1978 S, F, W, E, NZ, 1979 F, W, E, S, 1981 W, E, S, A, 1983 E (R), 1984 E, S, 1986 S, 1987 [C, Tg]
Warren, J P (Kingstown) 1883 E
Warren, R G (Lansdowne) 1884 W, 1885 E, S 1, 2, 1886 E, 1887 E, S, W, 1888 W, S, M, 1889 S, W, 1890 S, W, E
Watson, R (Wanderers) 1912 SA
Wells, H G (Bective Rangers) 1891 S, W, 1894 E, S
Westby, A J (Dublin U) 1876 E
Wheeler, G H (Queen's Coll, Belfast) 1884 S, 1885 E
Wheeler, J R (Queen's U, Belfast) 1922 E, S, W, F, 1924 E
Whelan, P C (Garryowen) 1975 E, S, 1976 NZ, 1977 W, E, S, F, 1978 S, F, W, E, NZ, 1979 F, W, E, S, 1981 F, W, E
White, M (Queen's Coll, Cork) 1906 E, S, W, SA, 1907 E, W
Whitestone, A M (Dublin U) 1877 E, 1879 S, E, 1880 E, 1883 S
Whitten, I W (Ulster) 2009 C, US
Whittle, D (Bangor) 1988 F
Wilkinson, C R (Malone) 1993 S
Wilkinson, R W (Wanderers) 1947 A
Williamson, F W (Dolphin) 1930 E, S, W
Willis, W J (Lansdowne) 1879 E
Wilson, F (CIYMS) 1977 W, E, S
Wilson, H G (Glasgow U, Malone) 1905 E, S, W, NZ, 1906 E, S, W, SA, 1907 E, S, W, 1908 E, S, W, 1909 E, S, W, 1910 W
Wilson, R G (Ulster) 2005 J1
Wilson, W H (Bray) 1877 E, S
Withers, H H C (Army, Blackheath) 1931 F, E, S, W, SA
Wolfe, E J (Armagh) 1882 E
Wood, G H (Dublin U) 1913 W, 1914 F
Wood, B G M (Garryowen) 1954 E, S, 1956 F, E, S, W, 1957 F, E, S, W, 1958 A, E, S, W, F, 1959 E, S, W, F, 1960 E, S, W, F, SA, 1961 E, S, W, F, SA
Wood, K G M (Garryowen, Harlequins) 1994 A 1, 2, US, 1995 E, S, [J], 1996 A, 1997 It 1, F, 1997 NZ, It 2, 1998 S, F, W, E, SA 1, 2, R (R), SA 3, 1999 F, W, E, S, It (R), A 1, 2, Arg 1, [US, A 3, R (R), Arg 2], 2000 E, S, It, F, W, Arg, US, C, J, SA, 2001 It, F, S, W, E, NZ, 2002 F, NZ 1, 2, Ru, 2003 W 2, S 2, [R, Nm, Arg, A, F]
Woods, D C (Bessbrook) 1888 M, 1889 S
Woods, N K P J (Blackrock Coll, London Irish) 1994 A 1, 2, 1995 E, F, 1996 F, W, E, 1999 W
Wright, R A (Monkstown) 1912 S

Yeates, R A (Dublin U) 1889 S, W
Young, B G (Ulster) 2006 NZ2(R), A1(R), SA(R), A2, Pl, 2007 Arg1, 2, S2
Young, G (UC Cork) 1913 E
Young, R M (Collegians) 1965 F, E, S, W, SA, 1966 F, E, S, W, 1967 W, F, 1968 W, A, 1969 F, E, S, W, 1970 SA, F, E, S, W, 1971 F, E, S, W

BELVO MAKE HISTORY

Promoted sides often harbour modest ambitions when they are first elevated a division, but no-one obviously told Old Belvedere to aim low in their first season back in the Ulster Bank League Division One as the Leinstermen claimed Ireland's top flight title for the first time since the club was founded in 1930.

Belvo were undisputed outsiders going into the final against defending champions Cork Constitution at Donnybrook but, watched by Ireland head coach Declan Kidney, the home side produced a pulsating and determined display to defy the odds and become the first Leinster side to lift the trophy since St Mary's College 11 years earlier.

Cork Con had beaten Old Belvedere home and away during the regular season to finish top of the table, but once wing David Mongan raced over after just eight minutes Phil Werahiko's side sensed an upset was on the cards and a subsequent brace from Man of the Match John Kennedy sealed an historic, albeit narrow, 20–17 triumph.

"We're relieved," said Werahiko after the final whistle. "We knew from the first half, when we spent a lot of time scrambling, that we would have to push on and run it a lot more. We knew we had to get our hands on the ball and concentrate on the basics. We got a bit more ball to run with and we felt we had as many good attacking players as Con. Happily we managed to finish off enough chances to get the result."

It was certainly fitting that Cork Con and Old Belvedere were the two sides to contest the final. Cork Constitution had topped the league table in the regular season with just two defeats in their 14 games, while Belvo finished second, just three adrift of Brian Walsh's side, and both teams enjoyed home advantage in the play-off semi-finals.

The first saw Belvo entertain Clontarf at Anglesea Road, and it was a classic case of better late than never as the home side stole a 22–20 victory in injury-time courtesy of an audacious chip and successful chase from wing Eddie Devitt.

The second semi-final saw Young Munster travel to Temple Hill and, with the home forwards the dominant force, it was Cork Con who grabbed the only try of the match through second row Brian Hayes to secure a 19–9 win.

Belvo drew first blood in the final courtesy of Mongan's try, but three penalties from scrum-half Gerry Hurley gave Cork Con a 9–7 lead at the break, and when full-back Sean Scanlon raced over just before the hour mark, after the first try from Kennedy, Cork Con found themselves 14–12 in front.

The result briefly hung in the balance as both teams searched for a knockout blow, and it was Kennedy who eventually supplied it with his second try of the afternoon to wrap up an historic win for Old Belvedere.

"We had our chances in the first half," said Cork Con coach Walsh. "We were very close to scoring a couple of tries, and then we had a late penalty miss. Some things go for you, some things don't. It was disappointing, but credit to Belvedere for taking their opportunities."

In the cup, the Irish Rugby Football Union reintroduced the old Bateman Cup format in which the four provincial cup winners contested the semi-finals and finals and, just as the league produced an unexpected result, so did the new-look knockout competition as Bruff and Dungannon – two sides outside Division 1A – battled their way through to the final at Templeville Road.

Bruff in particular showed no respect for reputations en route to the final as the Limerick club claimed the scalps of Shannon, Cork and finally Garryowen to win the Munster Senior Cup, while Dungannon were crowned Ulster Senior Cup champions.

Bruff reached the final after beating Leinster champions UCD 24–22 in the last four, while Dungannon narrowly overcame Corinthians of Connacht 16–13 to set up an intriguing clash.

The final began in explosive style for Bruff when prop David Horan burrowed over after just two minutes of play, but a try before half-time from centre Paul Magee pulled Dungannon back into contention, and after 40 minutes the Munstermen enjoyed a slender 11–10 advantage.

The second half saw veteran Bruff player-coach Peter Malone crash over to stretch the lead, but young full-back Conor Gaston hit back with Dungannon's second try of the match, and ultimately it was the steady boot of Bruff fly-half Tony Cahill that proved decisive as the number 10 kicked a conversion and four penalties for a famous 24–18 victory.

"To beat a club like Dungannon, a club with a great history who have won the All-Ireland League, and to stand toe to toe with them is a great mark for ourselves," admitted Malone. "It's a great bunch of guys with a great club structure behind us, so hopefully it's just reward for everyone involved. A lot of these guys have been with us since junior level, so they've come full circle from junior to senior All-Ireland champions.

"It was an epic cup run; we have no problem getting up for cup rugby. So with cup games it's so easy to motivate guys. It's our league form that's been the problem this year, but with cup days like this there's never a problem – we love taking big scalps."

ULSTER BANK DIVISION ONE A 2010–11 RESULTS

1 October 2010: **Garryowen** 14 **Young Munster** 20. 2 October: **Blackrock** 23 **Cork Constitution** 31, **Dolphin** 16 **Shannon** 9, **St Mary's** 9 **Old Belvedere** 17. 8 October: **Shannon** 16 **Garryowen** 9. 9 October: **Dolphin** 16 **Blackrock** 21, **Young Munster** 15 **St Mary's** 9, **Old Belvedere** 9 **Cork Constitution** 12. 23 October: **Blackrock** 20 **Old Belvedere** 29, **Cork Constitution** 32 **Young Munster** 19, **Garryowen** 45 **Dolphin** 27, **St Mary's** 53 **Shannon** 0. 30 October: **Blackrock** 16 **Garryowen** 11, **Dolphin** 9 **St Mary's** 10, **Shannon** 20 **Cork Constitution** 26, **Young Munster** 0 **Old Belvedere** 31. 13 November: **Cork Constitution** 9 **Dolphin** 19, **Young Munster** 14 **Blackrock** 15, **Old Belvedere** 38 **Shannon** 16, **St Mary's** 29 **Garryowen** 6. 26 November: **Shannon** 18 **Young Munster** 17. 27 November: **Blackrock** 18 **St Mary's** 21, **Dolphin** 15 **Old Belvedere** 18, **Garryowen** 11 **Cork Constitution** 11. 8 January 2011: **Cork Constitution** 22 **St Mary's** 17, **Old Belvedere** 24 **Garryowen** 3, **Shannon** 38 **Blackrock** 22, **Young Munster** 35 **Dolphin** 0. 28 January: **Garryowen** 25 **Shannon** 13. 29 January: **Blackrock** 16 **Dolphin** 32, **Cork Constitution** 23 **Old Belvedere** 12, **St Mary's** 13 **Young Munster** 11. 5 February: **Dolphin** 14 **Garryowen** 3, **Shannon** 20 **St Mary's** 15, **Young Munster** 6 **Cork Constitution** 3, **Old Belvedere** 10 **Blackrock** 9. 12 February: **Cork Constitution** 17 **Shannon** 0, **Garryowen** 20 **Blackrock** 21, **Old Belvedere** 17 **Young Munster** 19, **St Mary's** 29 **Dolphin** 10. 19 February: **Blackrock** 11 **Young Munster** 13, **Dolphin** 16 **Cork Constitution** 23, **Garryowen** 15 **St Mary's** 39, **Shannon** 23 **Old Belvedere** 30. 26 February: **Cork Constitution** 11 **Garryowen** 11, **Old Belvedere** 16 **Dolphin** 16, **St Mary's** 15 **Blackrock** 34, **Young Munster** 16 **Shannon** 3. 26 March: **Blackrock** 25 **Shannon** 21, **Garryowen** 13 **Old Belvedere** 3, **St Mary's** 0 **Cork Constitution** 22. 27 March: **Dolphin** 13 **Young Munster** 12. 2 April: **Cork Constitution** 33 **Blackrock** 16, **Old Belvedere** 25 **St Mary's** 19, **Shannon** 28 **Dolphin** 18, **Young Munster** 23 **Garryowen** 18.

FINAL TABLE

	P	W	D	L	F	A	BP	Pts
Cork Constitution	14	10	2	2	275	179	3	**47**
Old Belvedere	14	9	1	4	279	197	6	**44**
Young Munster	14	8	0	6	220	197	5	**37**
St Mary's	14	7	0	7	278	224	7	**35**
Blackrock	14	6	0	8	267	304	4	**28**
Dolphin	14	5	1	8	221	274	4	**26**
Shannon	14	5	0	9	225	327	6	**26**
Garryowen	14	3	2	9	204	267	6	**22**

SEMI-FINALS

16 April, 2011

Old Belvedere 22 **Clontarf** 20

17 April, 2011

Cork Constitution 19 **Young Munster** 9

FINAL

1 May 2011, Donnybrook, Dublin

CORK CONSTITUTION 17 (1T, 4PG)
OLD BELVEDERE 20 (1G, 2T, 1PG)

CORK CONSTITUTION: S Scanlon; R Lane, C Jouve, I Dineen, S Zebo; S Deasy, G Hurley; M Gately, D Fogarty, S Archer, B Hayes, I Nagle, B Cuttriss, B Holland, F Cogan (captain)
SUBSTITUTIONS: R Quinn for Fogarty (temp 30–40 mins); D Williams for Jouve (43 mins); Quinn for Fogarty (43 mins); P O'Mahony for Cuttriss (45 mins)
SCORERS: *Try*: Scanlon *Penalty Goals:* Hurley (4)

OLD BELVEDERE: D Riordan; E Devitt, J Kennedy, B Woods, D Mongan; A Dunne (captain), S Keogh; V Soden, D Gilchrist, S Maguire, R Leyden, B Marshall, J Slattery, J Risdon, L Auva'a
SUBSTITUTIONS: Chris Keane for Woods (temp 25–34 mins); B Diaper for Slattery (temp 33–40 mins); Conal Keane for Dunne (59 mins); Chris Keane for Keogh (59 mins); K Buckley for Gilchrist (59 mins); D Moore for Marshall (63 mins)
SCORERS: *Tries:* Mongan, Kennedy (2) *Conversion:* Dunne *Penalty Goal:* Conal Keane
REFEREE: D Phillips (IRFU)

ULSTER BANK DIVISION ONE B: Winners: Clontarf
ULSTER BANK DIVISION TWO: Winners: Ballynahinch
ULSTER BANK DIVISION THREE: Winners: City Of Derry

BATEMAN ALL-IRELAND CUP 2010–11 RESULTS

SEMI-FINALS: 23 January, 2011: **Bruff** 24 **UCD** 22. 12 March, 2011: **Dungannon** 16 **Galway Corinthians** 13

FINAL

9 April 2011, Templeville Road, Dublin

BRUFF 24 (1G, 1T, 4PG)
DUNGANNON 18 (1G, 1T, 2PG)

BRUFF: B Deady; T O'Callaghan, T Carroll, E Cahill, J Malone; T Cahill, E Maher; D Horan, C O'Regan (captain), G Ryan, A Laffan, M O'Connell, A Bourke, J Shine, P Malone **SUBSTITUTIONS:** D Murnane for Laffan (63 mins); Ger Collins for Ryan (74 mins)
SCORERS: *Tries*: Horan, Malone *Conversion:* Cahill *Penalty Goals:* Cahill (4)

DUNGANNON: C Gaston; M Lawton, P Magee (captain), G Telford, C Cochrane; P Jackson, M Kirkwood; P Whyte, A Duhig, G Sinnamon, A Fry, M Rainey, T Anderson, R Halsall, A Birch **SUBSTITUTIONS:** C Threlfall for Rainey (48 mins); M Farquhar for Whyte (57 mins); K Campbell for Kirkwood (63 mins): S McKenzie for Fry (74 mins)
SCORERS: *Tries:* Magee, Gaston *Conversion:* Lawton *Penalty Goals:* Lawton (2)

ITALY

ITALY'S 2010–11 TEST RECORD

OPPONENTS	DATE	VENUE	RESULT
Argentina	13 Nov	H	**Lost** 16–22
Australia	20 Nov	H	**Lost** 14–32
Fiji	27 Nov	H	**Won** 24–16
Ireland	5 Feb	H	**Lost** 11–13
England	12 Feb	A	**Lost** 13–59
Wales	26 Feb	H	**Lost** 16–24
France	12 Mar	H	**Won** 22–21
Scotland	19 Mar	A	**Lost** 8–21
Japan	13 Aug	H	**Won** 31–24
Scotland	20 Aug	A	**Lost** 12–23
Australia	11 Sep	N	**Lost** 6–32
Russia	20 Sep	N	**Won** 53–17
USA	27 Sep	N	**Won** 27–10
Ireland	2 Oct	N	**Lost** 6–36

LAST-EIGHT FINISH SLIPS FROM ITALIANS' GRASP

By Ian Gilbert

Teaukura Moetaua/Getty Images

Nick Mallett led Italy to wins over USA and Russia before departing from the job as Italy coach.

With coach Nick Mallett's tenure coming to an end after the 2011 Rugby World Cup, Italy were desperate to deliver a last-eight finish for the man who has done so much to strengthen the country's rugby.

The Azzurri's bid to make the knockout stages for the first time proved ultimately unsuccessful, but along the way there was plenty of evidence of their ability to execute clinical, cool-headed rugby.

Italy came into the tournament with good grounds for optimism. They had posted their first Six Nations win over France earlier in the year, winning 22–21 in Rome on the penultimate weekend, and ended their warm-up matches with a win against Japan and a defeat by Scotland.

With the powerhouses of Australia and Ireland lurking, along with less-vaunted opposition in Russia and USA, Italy were under no illusions about the challenge of making it out of Pool C.

Their opener could scarcely have come any harder with twice world champions Australia in Auckland. As Mallett said beforehand, "Italy doesn't go into any match in the World Cup, or Six Nations or tour Down Under confident of a win. But we are confident we can give Australia a really good game."

Italy are no strangers to tough openers: the last time the Rugby World Cup was played in New Zealand, they were on the end of a 70–6 masterclass by the All Blacks, and a certain John Kirwan – who would go on to coach Italy – scored one of the tries of the tournament.

Back to 2011, and Italy were very much in the reckoning at half-time at North Harbour Stadium, poised at 6–6 after Wallaby fly-half Quade Cooper had traded penalties with winger Mirco Bergamasco. However, the enigmatic James O'Connor came off the bench to spark Australia into life, and the rejuvenated Wallabies sank Italian hopes with four second-half tries to win 32–6.

"I'm very proud of them," reflected Mallett afterwards. "I do feel sorry that we didn't keep up the pace in the second half."

The result meant Italy's campaign became a sudden-death affair. Convincing victories had to be registered against Russia and USA to set up a showdown with Ireland in the final match of the pool stages on 2 October.

The surprise that Italy hadn't banked on came when Australia took on Ireland at Eden Park in the match of the second weekend. Ireland's 15–6 victory shook up the form book and left Italy very much in control of their own destiny.

In fact, it rather left Italy in control of everyone else's, too, provided the Azzurri could take bonus points against both Russia and USA – and this was where the permutations began to exercise the mathematicians.

Italy responded to Mallett's demands for a victory – with at least four tries – in resounding fashion, recording a 53–17 win over Russia in Nelson. Captain and No. 8 Sergio Parisse crashed over for the first try, but it was the backs who claimed the glory that night, with young centre Tommaso Benvenuti and wing Giulio Toniolatti claiming a brace each among the Azzurri's nine tries.

Parisse, ever the statesman, said of the nine-try finish, "We didn't want to disrespect Russia, and they put us in trouble on occasions. Even so, we were having fun out there."

One man with little to celebrate after that win, however, was hooker Tommaso D'Apice, who injured ligaments in his left knee and returned home. He was replaced in the squad by Franco Sbaraglini.

It was back to Trafalgar Park for the next match, against USA, but this time it was the turn of Parisse and the pack to star, with the Stade Français man going over after just three minutes. The forwards ground down their opponents to such effect that the bonus point came with a penalty try, awarded when the Eagles dropped a scrum.

With tighthead prop Martin Castrogiovanni voted Man of the Match, Italy proved their traditional forward strength remains potent. "It was important that we dominated, and it is important to keep working on it as it will be tougher against Ireland," Castrogiovanni said of the Azzurri's set piece.

They were prophetic words from the Leicester Tigers man. A restaurateur away from the pitch – in partnership with club team-mate, Ireland's Geordan Murphy – the forward feast against the Eagles turned to famine against the better-drilled Irish.

Ireland, who had lost all four of their warm-up matches against France (twice), Scotland and England, had seemed vulnerable before the tournament. Italy knew they were within reach, having lost only 13–11 in Rome in the 2011 Six Nations. But the Irish had really hit form in this tournament, with wise old heads such as Paul O'Connell and Brian O'Driscoll determined to make what will probably be their last World Cup a memorable one.

The match was played at Otago Stadium in Dunedin, and on a night when most of the 28,027 crowd appeared to be wearing green, the relentless Irish ran out 36–6 winners. "It was like Lansdowne Road – in fact, I have played in Dublin before when it hasn't been that good," captain O'Driscoll said of the support.

The first half saw the Irish edge ahead 9–6 at the break, but the loss of Castrogiovanni just before the interval was a key turning point. Leinster flanker Sean O'Brien, just 24 but already a crucial member of the Irish eight, was Man of the Match with another of the indefatigable displays that made him European Player of the Year.

Mallett was phlegmatic after his last match in charge. "Their front five played well, and the backs played well and didn't give us the chance to play much rugby," he said.

The South African, who isn't one for misty-eyed nostalgia, added, "I don't want to talk about my legacy because only history will tell if I was a good Italy coach or not.

"I was extremely touched by [Ireland coach] Declan Kidney, who came up to me and said some fantastic things to me. Rugby is really fortunate to have a man like Declan Kidney involved in it."

So for Italy the curtain fell on another World Cup campaign, the seventh time they have failed to get out of the pool stages. But if evidence were needed of their improvement, they can take satisfaction from several areas.

Castrogiovanni and Parisse would make many observers' World XV; Benvenuti's versatility at wing and centre is an asset, and in 27-year-old Alessandro Zanni they have a flanker who will be at the height of his powers come RWC 2015. Fly-half Craig Gower's failure to recover from injury before the tournament was a blow, but 23-year-old Riccardo Bocchino gained valuable experience as understudy to veteran Luciano Orquera in the number-10 jersey. The Italians can already start planning for England 2015, with their third-place finish in Pool C guaranteeing qualification. Although hooker Leonardo Ghiraldini's 15-week ban for foul play (making contact with the eye or the eye area of Irish prop Cian Healy) was a sour footnote, the Italians generally competed with aplomb. Off the field, they were welcomed in style, and there cannot be too many international captains who inspire someone to design a jacket for them. The 196cm-tall Parisse was presented with a tailored jacket by Otago Polytechnic School of Design graduate Kathryn Corry to wear on the streets of Paris, where he plays his club rugby.

While in Nelson, the squad impressed with their amiable approach by throwing open a closed practice session to allow youngsters from Papanui High School, who were competing in a Special Olympics New Zealand Regional Games event, to take photos.

Of the Rugby World Cup experience as a whole, Parisse said, "For the young players it will be an important experience for them and help with their development."

However, the back-row forward, a veteran of Heineken Cup campaigns for his club against some of the best players in the world, is a realist. "We have to be proud of what we have done, and there are always positives and negatives, but ultimately we didn't achieve our goal," he said.

With Mallett's time up, former Perpignan coach Jacques Brunel is charged with taking the Azzurri forward to the 2012 Six Nations and beyond. He can count on the pride and polish of Parisse at the helm; the loose forward will turn 32 during the next global gathering in 2015 and will arguably be in his prime as a forward – a year younger than England's Martin Johnson was in 2003, for instance.

The presence of Treviso and Aironi in the RaboDirect Pro12 will further the standards of the national XV, and the Azzurri remain the team most likely to "do an Argentina" by shaking out one of the usual suspects from the quarter-finals in 2015. But first, the Six Nations. With the formidable challenge of France in Paris their first encounter, what better yardstick for Italy's new coach to measure how far his side have come – or how far there is still to go.

ITALY INTERNATIONAL STATISTICS

MATCH RECORDS UP TO 31 OCTOBER 2011

WINNING MARGIN

Date	Opponent	Result	Winning Margin
18/05/1994	Czech Republic	104–8	**96**
07/10/2006	Portugal	83–0	**83**
17/06/1993	Croatia	76–11	**65**
19/06/1993	Morocco	70–9	**61**
02/03/1996	Portugal	64–3	**61**

MOST POINTS IN A MATCH

BY THE TEAM

Date	Opponent	Result	Points
18/05/1994	Czech Republic	104–8	**104**
07/10/2006	Portugal	83–0	**83**
17/06/1993	Croatia	76–11	**76**
19/06/1993	Morocco	70–9	**70**

BY A PLAYER

Date	Player	Opponent	Points
10/11/2001	Diego Dominguez	Fiji	**29**
05/02/2000	Diego Dominguez	Scotland	**29**
01/07/1983	Stefano Bettarello	Canada	**29**
21/05/1994	Diego Dominguez	Netherlands	**28**
20/12/1997	Diego Dominguez	Ireland	**27**
28/02/2009	Lasha Malaguradze	Spain	**20**

MOST TRIES IN A MATCH

BY THE TEAM

Date	Opponent	Result	Tries
18/05/1994	Czech Republic	104–8	**16**
07/10/2006	Portugal	83–0	**13**
18/11/1998	Netherlands	67–7	**11**
17/06/1993	Croatia	76–11	**11**

BY A PLAYER

Date	Player	Opponent	Tries
19/06/1993	Ivan Francescato	Morocco	**4**
10/10/1937	Renzo Cova	Belgium	**4**

MOST CONVERSIONS IN A MATCH

BY THE TEAM

Date	Opponent	Result	Cons
18/05/1994	Czech Republic	104–8	**12**
19/06/1993	Morocco	70–9	**10**
17/06/1993	Croatia	76–11	**9**
07/10/2006	Portugal	83–0	**9**

BY A PLAYER

Date	Player	Opponent	Cons
18/05/1994	Luigi Troiani	Czech Republic	**12**
19/06/1993	Gabriel Filizzola	Morocco	**10**
17/06/1993	Luigi Troiani	Croatia	**9**

MOST PENALTIES IN A MATCH

BY THE TEAM

Date	Opponent	Result	Pens
01/10/1994	Romania	24–6	**8**
27/11/2010	Fiji	24–16	**8**
10/11/2001	Fiji	66–10	**7**

BY A PLAYER

Date	Player	Opponent	Pens
01/10/1994	Diego Dominguez	Romania	**8**
27/11/2010	Mirco Bergamasco	Fiji	**8**
10/11/2001	Diego Dominguez	Fiji	**7**

MOST DROPPED GOALS IN A MATCH

BY THE TEAM

Date	Opponent	Result	DGs
07/10/1990	Romania	29–21	**3**
05/02/2000	Scotland	34–20	**3**
11/07/1973	Transvaal	24–28	**3**

BY A PLAYER

Date	Player	Opponent	DGs
05/02/2000	Diego Dominguez	Scotland	**3**
11/07/1973	Rocco Caligiuri	Transvaal	**3**

MOST CAPPED PLAYERS

Player	Caps
Alessandro Troncon	101
Andrea Lo Cicero	91
Marco Bortolami	88
Mauro Bergamasco	88
Mirco Bergamasco	85

LEADING PENALTY SCORERS

Player	Pens
Diego Dominguez	209
Stefano Bettarello	106
Luigi Troiani	57
Ramiro Pez	52
Mirco Bergamasco	47

LEADING TRY SCORERS

Player	Tries
Marcello Cuttitta	25
Paolo Vaccari	22
Manrico Marchetto	21
Carlo Checchinato	21
Alessandro Troncon	19

LEADING DROPPED GOAL SCORERS

Player	DGs
Diego Dominguez	19
Stefano Bettarello	15
Ramiro Pez	6
Massimo Bonomi	5
Oscar Collodo	5

LEADING CONVERSIONS SCORERS

Player	Cons
Diego Dominguez	127
Luigi Troiani	57
Stefano Bettarello	46
David Bortolussi	35
Ramiro Pez	33

LEADING POINTS SCORERS

Player	Points
Diego Dominguez	983
Stefano Bettarello	483
Luigi Troiani	294
Ramiro Pez	260
Mirco Bergamasco	250

Warren Little/Getty Images

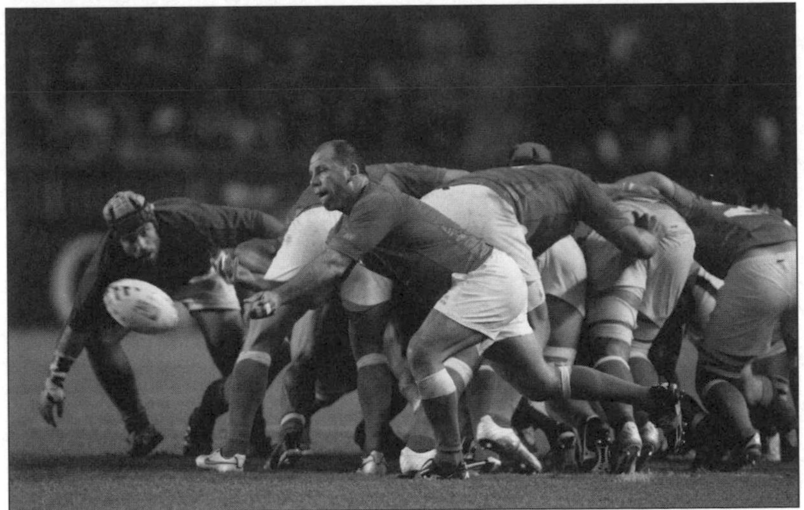

Alessandro Troncon is still the only Italian to win 100 Test caps.

ITALY INTERNATIONAL PLAYERS (UP TO 31 OCTOBER 2011)

Note: Years given for International Championship matches are for second half of season; eg 1972 means season 1971–72. Years for all other matches refer to the actual year of the match. Entries in square brackets denote matches played in RWC Finals.

E Abbiati 1968 *WGe*, 1970 *R*, 1971 *Mor*, *F*, 1972 *Pt*, *Sp*, *Sp*, *Yug*, 1973 *Pt*, *ETv*, 1974 *Leo*
A Agosti 1933 *Cze*
M Aguero 2005 *Tg*, *Ar*, *Fj*, 2006 *Fj*, 2007 *Ur*, *Ar*, *I*, *Pt*, 2008 *A*, *Ar*, *Pl*, 2009 *A*, 2010 *I*, *E*, *S*, *F*, *W*
A Agujari 1967 *Pt*
E Aio 1974 *WGe*
G Aiolfi 1952 *Sp*, *Ger*, *F*, 1953 *F*, 1955 *Ger*, *F*
A Alacevich 1939 *R*
A Albonico 1934 *R*, 1935 *F*, 1936 *Ger*, *R*, 1937 *Ger*, *R*, *Bel*, *Ger*, *F*, 1938 *Ger*
N Aldorvandi 1994 *Sp*, *CZR*, *H*
M Alfonsetti 1994 *F*
E Allevi 1929 *Sp*, 1933 *Cze*
I Aloisio 1933 *Cze*, *Cze*, 1934 *Cat*, *R*, 1935 *Cat*, 1936 *Ger*, *R*
A Altigeri 1973 *Rho*, *WTv*, *Bor*, *NEC*, *Nat*, *Leo*, *FS*, *Tva*, *Cze*, *Yug*, *A*, 1974 *Pt*, *WGe*, 1975 *F*, *E*, *Pol*, *H*, *Sp*, 1976 *F*, *R*, *J*, 1978 *Ar*, *USS*, *Sp*, 1979 *F*, *Pol*, *R*
T Altissimi 1929 *Sp*
V Ambron 1962 *Ger*, *R*, 1963 *F*, 1964 *Ger*, *F*, 1965 *F*, *Cze*, 1966 *F*, *Ger*, *R*, 1967 *Pt*, *R*, 1968 *Pt*, *WGe*, *Yug*, 1969 *Bul*, *Sp*, *Bel*, 1970 *Mad*, *Mad*, *R*, 1971 *Mor*, 1972 *Sp*, *Sp*
R Ambrosio 1987 *NZ*, *USS*, *Sp*, 1988 *F*, *R*, *A*, *I*, 1989 *R*, *Sp*, *Ar*, *Z*, *USS*
B Ancillotti 1978 *Sp*, 1979 *F*, *Pol*, *R*
E Andina 1952 *F*, 1955 *F*
C Angelozzi 1979 *E*, *Mor*, 1980 *Coo*
A Angioli 1960 *Ger*, *F*, 1961 *Ger*, *F*, 1962 *F*, *Ger*, *R*, 1963 *F*
A Angrisiani 1979 *Mor*, *F*, *Pol*, *USS*, *Mor*, 1980 *Coo*, 1984 *Tun*
S Annibal 1980 *Fj*, *Coo*, *Pol*, *Sp*, 1981 *F*, *WGe*, 1982 *R*, *E*, *WGe*, 1983 *F*, *USS*, *Sp*, *Mor*, *F*, *A*, 1984 *F*, 1985 *F*, *Z*, *Z*, 1986 *Tun*, *F*, *Pt*, 1990 *F*
JM Antoni 2001 *Nm*, *SA*
C Appiani 1976 *Sp*, 1977 *Mor*, *Pol*, *Sp*, 1978 *USS*
S Appiani 1985 *R*, 1986 *Pt*, 1988 *A*, 1989 *F*
O Arancio 1993 *Rus*, 1994 *CZR*, *H*, *A*, *A*, *R*, *W*, *F*, 1995 *S*, *I*, *Sa*, *E*, *Ar*, *F*, *R*, *NZ*, *SA*, 1996 *W*, *Pt*, *W*, *A*, *E*, *S*, 1997 *I*, *I*, 1998 *S*, *Ar*, *E*, 1999 *F*, *W*, *I*, *SA*, *E*, *NZ*
D Armellin 1965 *Cze*, 1966 *Ger*, 1968 *Pt*, *WGe*, *Yug*, 1969 *Bul*, *Sp*, *Bel*, *F*
A Arrigoni 1949 *Cze*
G Artuso 1977 *Pol*, *R*, 1978 *Sp*, 1979 *F*, *E*, *NZ*, *Mor*, 1980 *F*, *R*, *JAB*, 1981 *F*, 1982 *F*, *E*, *Mor*, 1983 *F*, *R*, *USS*, *C*, *C*, 1984 *USS*, 1985 *R*, *EngB*, *USS*, *R*, 1986 *Tun*, *F*, *Tun*, 1987 *Pt*, *F*, *R*, *NZ*
E Augeri 1962 *F*, *Ger*, *R*, 1963 *F*
A Autore 1961 *Ger*, *F*, 1962 *F*, 1964 *Ger*, 1966 *Ger*, 1968 *Pt*, *WGe*, *Yug*, 1969 *Bul*, *Sp*, *Bel*, *F*
L Avigo 1959 *F*, 1962 *F*, *Ger*, *R*, 1963 *F*, 1964 *Ger*, *F*, 1965 *F*, *Cze*, 1966 *Ger*, *R*
R Aymonod 1933 *Cze*, 1934 *Cat*, *R*, 1935 *F*
A Azzali 1981 *WGe*, 1982 *F*, *R*, *WGe*, 1983 *F*, *R*, *USS*, *Sp*, *Mor*, *F*, 1984 *F*, *Mor*, *R*, 1985 *R*, *EngB*, *Sp*

S Babbo 1996 *Pt*
A Bacchetti 2009 *I*, *S*
A Balducci 1929 *Sp*
F Baraldi 1973 *Cze*, *Yug*, 1974 *Mid*, *Sus*, *Oxo*, 1975 *E*, *Pol*, *H*, *Sp*, 1976 *F*, *R*, *A*, 1977 *F*, *Mor*, *Cze*
R Baraldi 1971 *R*
A Barattin 1996 *A*, *E*
S Barba 1985 *R*, *EngB*, 1986 *E*, *A*, 1987 *Pt*, *F*, *R*, *Ar*, *Fj*, 1988 *R*, *USS*, *A*, 1990 *F*, *Pol*, *Sp*, *H*, *R*, *USS*, 1991 *F*, *R*, *Nm*, *Nm*, *US*, *E*, *USS*, 1992 *Sp*, *F*, *R*, *R*, *S*, 1993 *Sp*, *F*, *Cro*, *Mor*, *Sp*
RJ Barbieri 2006 *J*, *Fj*, *Pt*, 2007 *Ur*, *Ar*, *I*, 2008 *SA*, 2010 *Ar*, *A*, *Fj*, 2011 *E*, *W*, *F*, *S*, *S*, *A*
G Barbini 1978 *USS*
M Barbini 2002 *NZ*, *Sp*, *Ar*, *A*, 2003 *I*, *NZ*, 2004 *F*, *I*, *R*, *J*, *NZ*, *US*, 2005 *W*, *E*, 2007 *I*
N Barbini 1953 *Ger*, *R*, 1954 *Sp*, *F*, 1955 *Ger*, *F*, *Sp*, *Cze*, 1956 *Ger*, 1957 *Ger*, 1958 *R*, 1960 *Ger*, *F*
F Bargelli 1979 *E*, *Sp*, *Mor*, *F*, *Pol*, *USS*, *NZ*, *Mor*, 1980 *F*, *R*, *Fj*, *Sp*, 1981 *F*, *R*
S Barilari 1948 *Cze*, 1953 *Ger*, *R*
M Baroni 1999 *F*, *W*, *I*, *SA*, *SA*, 2000 *C*
V Barzaghi 1929 *Sp*, 1930 *Sp*, 1933 *Cze*
JL Basei 1979 *E*, *Sp*, *Mor*, *F*, *Pol*, *USS*, *NZ*, *Mor*, 1980 *F*, *R*, *Fj*, *JAB*, *Coo*, *USS*, 1981 *R*
A Battagion 1948 *F*, *Cze*
F Battaglini 1948 *F*
M Battaglini 1940 *R*, *Ger*, 1951 *Sp*, 1953 *F*, *R*
A Becca 1937 *R*, 1938 *Ger*, 1939 *R*, 1940 *Ger*
E Bellinazzo 1958 *R*, 1959 *F*, 1960 *Ger*, *F*, 1961 *Ger*, *F*, 1962 *F*, *Ger*, 1964 *Ger*, *F*, 1966 *F*, *Ger*, *R*, 1967 *F*
A Benatti 2001 *Fj*, *SA*, *Sa*, 2002 *W*, 2003 *NZ*
C Bentivoglio 1977 *Pol*
T Benvenuti 2010 *Ar*, *A*, *Fj*, 2011 *W*, *F*, *S*, *J*, *S*, *A*, *Rus*, *US*, *I*
D Beretta 1993 *S*
A Bergamasco 1973 *Bor*, *Tva*, 1977 *Pol*, 1978 *USS*
M Bergamasco 1998 *H*, *E*, 1999 *SA*, *E*, 2000 *S*, *W*, *I*, *E*, *F*, *C*, 2001 *I*, *E*, *F*, *S*, *W*, *Fj*, *SA*, *Sa*, 2002 *F*, *S*, *W*, *I*, *E*, *NZ*, *Sp*, *R*, *A*, 2003 *W*, *I*, *S*, *I*, *Geo*, *NZ*, *Tg*, *W*, 2004 *J*, *C*, *NZ*, 2005 *I*, *W*, *Ar*, *A*, *Ar*, *Fj*, 2006 *I*, *E*, *F*, *J*, *Fj*, *Pt*, *Rus*, *A*, *Ar*, *C*, 2007 *F*, *S*, *W*, *J*, *NZ*, *R*, *Pt*, *S*, 2008 *I*, *E*, *W*, *Ar*, *A*, *Ar*, *Pl*, 2009 *E*, *I*, *S*, *W*, *F*, *A*, *NZ*, *NZ*, *SA*, *Sa*, 2010 *I*, *E*, *S*, *F*, *W*, 2011 *J*, *Rus*, *US*, *I*
M Bergamasco 2002 *F*, *S*, *W*, *Ar*, *A*, 2003 *W*, *I*, *E*, *F*, *S*, *S*, *Geo*, *NZ*, *C*, 2004 *E*, *F*, *S*, *I*, *W*, 2005 *I*, *W*, *S*, *Tg*, *Ar*, *Fj*, 2006 *I*, *E*, *F*, *W*, *S*, *J*, *Fj*, *Pt*, *Rus*, *A*, *Ar*, *C*, 2007 *F*, *E*, *S*, *W*, *I*, *J*, *I*, *NZ*, *R*, *S*, 2008 *I*, *E*, *W*, *F*, *S*, *Ar*, *A*, *Ar*, *Pl*, 2009 *E*, *I*, *S*, *W*, *F*, *A*, *NZ*, *NZ*, *SA*, *Sa*, 2010 *I*, *E*, *S*, *F*, *W*, *SA*, *SA*, *Ar*, *A*, *Fj*, 2011 *I*, *E*, *W*, *F*, *S*, *S*, *A*, *US*, *I*
L Bernabo 1970 *Mad*, *Mad*, *R*, 1972 *Sp*, *Sp*
V Bernabò 2004 *US*, 2005 *Tg*, *Fj*, 2007 *E*, *S*, *W*, *I*, *Ur*, *Ar*, *J*, *I*, *NZ*, *R*, 2010 *W*, *SA*, 2011 *I*, *E*, *W*, *S*
F Berni 1985 *R*, *Sp*, *Z*, *Z*, 1986 *E*, *A*, 1987 *R*, *NZ*, 1988 *A*, 1989 *F*
D Bertoli 1967 *R*
V Bertolotto 1936 *Ger*, *R*, 1937 *Ger*, *R*, 1942 *R*, 1948 *F*
O Bettarello 1958 *F*, 1959 *F*, 1961 *Ger*
R Bettarello 1953 *Ger*, *R*
S Bettarello 1979 *Pol*, *E*, *Sp*, *F*, *NZ*, *Mor*, 1980 *F*, *R*, *Fj*, *JAB*, *Coo*, *Pol*, *USS*, *Sp*, 1981 *F*, *R*, *USS*, *WGe*, 1982 *F*, *R*, *E*, *WGe*, *Mor*, 1983 *F*, *R*, *USS*, *C*, *Sp*, *Mor*, *F*, *A*, 1984 *F*, *Mor*, *R*, *Tun*, *USS*, 1985 *F*, *R*, *EngB*, *Sp*, *Z*, *USS*, *R*, 1986 *Tun*, *F*, *Pt*, *E*, *A*, *Tun*, *USS*, 1987 *R*, *USS*, *Sp*, 1988 *USS*, *A*
L Bettella 1969 *Sp*, *Bel*, *F*
R Bevilacqua 1937 *Bel*, *Ger*, *F*, 1938 *Ger*, 1939 *Ger*, *R*, 1940 *R*, *Ger*, 1942 *R*
C Bezzi 2003 *W*, *I*, *E*, *F*, *S*, *I*, *NZ*, *W*, 2004 *US*, 2005 *Ar*, *A*
G Biadene 1958 *R*, 1959 *F*
G Bigi 1930 *Sp*, 1933 *Cze*
M Bimbati 1989 *Z*
M Birtig 1998 *H*, 1999 *F*

F Blessano 1975 *F, R, Pol, H, Sp*, 1976 *F, R, J*, 1977 *F, Mor, Pol, R, Cze, R, Sp*, 1978 *F, Ar, Sp*, 1979 *F, Pol, R*
L Boccaletto 1969 *Bul, Bel, F*, 1970 *Cze, Mad, Mad, R*, 1971 *F, R*, 1972 *Pt, Sp, Sp*, 1975 *E*
S Boccazzi 1985 *Z*, 1988 *USS*
R Bocchino 2010 *I, F, W, SA, A, Fj*, 2011 *J, S, A, Rus, US, I*
M Bocconelli 1967 *R*
M Bollesan 1963 *F*, 1964 *F*, 1965 *F*, 1966 *F, Ger*, 1967 *F, Pt*, 1968 *Pt, WGe, Yug*, 1969 *Bul, Sp, Bel, F*, 1970 *Cze, Mad, Mad, R*, 1971 *Mor, F, R*, 1972 *Pt, Pt, Sp, Sp, Yug*, 1973 *Pt, Rho, WTv, Bor, NEC, Nat, ETv, Leo, FS, Tva, Yug, A*, 1974 *Pt, Mid, Sus, Oxo, WGe, Leo*, 1975 *F, Sp, Cze*
A Bona 1972 *Sp, Yug*, 1973 *Rho, WTv, Bor, NEC, Nat, ETv, Leo, FS, Tva, Cze, Yug, A*, 1974 *Pt, WGe, Leo*, 1975 *F, Sp, R, Cze, E, Pol, H, Sp*, 1976 *F, R, J, A, Sp*, 1977 *F, Mor*, 1978 *Ar, USS, Sp*, 1979 *F, Sp, Mor, F, Pol, USS, NZ, Mor*, 1980 *F, R, Fj, JAB, Pol, Sp*, 1981 *F*
L Bonaiti 1979 *R*, 1980 *Pol*
G Bonati 1939 *Ger, R*
S Bonetti 1972 *Yug*, 1973 *Rho, WTv, Bor, NEC, Nat, ETv, Leo, FS, Tva*, 1974 *Pt, Mid, Sus, Oxo, Leo*, 1975 *F, Sp, R, Cze, E, Pol, H, Sp*, 1976 *R, J, A, Sp*, 1977 *F, Mor, R, Sp*, 1978 *F*, 1979 *F*, 1980 *USS*
S Bonfante 1936 *Ger, R*
G Bonino 1949 *F*
M Bonomi 1988 *F, R*, 1990 *Sp, H, R, USS*, 1991 *F, R, Nm, Nm, E, NZ, USS*, 1992 *R, R*, 1993 *Cro, Mor, Sp, F, S*, 1994 *Sp, R, H, A, A, W*, 1995 *S, I, Sa, F, Ar, R, NZ*, 1996 *W*
S Bordon 1990 *R, USS*, 1991 *Nm, USS*, 1992 *F, R*, 1993 *Sp, F, Pt, Rus, F*, 1994 *R, A, A, R, W, F*, 1995 *I, E, Ar, F, Ar, NZ, SA*, 1996 *W, A, E*, 1997 *I, F*
L Borsetto 1977 *Pol*
V Borsetto 1948 *F, Cze*
M Bortolami 2001 *Nm, SA, Fj, SA, Sa*, 2002 *F, S, W, I, E, NZ, Sp, R, Ar, A*, 2003 *W, I, E, S, Geo, Tg, C*, 2004 *E, F, S, I, W, R, J, C, NZ*, 2005 *I, W, S, E, F, Ar, Ar, A, Tg, Ar, Fj*, 2006 *I, E, F, W, S, J, Fj, Pt, Rus, A, Ar, C*, 2007 *F, E, S, W, I, J, I, NZ, R, Pt*, 2008 *W, F, S, A, Ar, Pl*, 2009 *E, S, W, F, A, A, NZ*, 2010 *I, E, S, F, W, SA, SA*, 2011 *J, A, Rus, I*
G Bortolini 1933 *Cze*, 1934 *Cat*
D Bortolussi 2006 *J, Fj, Pt, Rus, Ar, C*, 2007 *Ur, Ar, J, I, NZ, R, Pt, S*, 2008 *I, E*
L Boscaino 1967 *Pt*
L Bossi 1940 *R, Ger*
A Bottacchiara 1991 *NZ, USS*, 1992 *Sp, F, R, R*
G Bottacin 1956 *Cze*
O Bottonelli 1929 *Sp*, 1934 *R*, 1935 *Cat, F*, 1937 *Ger*, 1939 *Ger*
L Bove 1948 *Cze*, 1949 *F, Cze*
O Bracaglia 1939 *R*
M Braga 1958 *R*
L Bricchi 1929 *Sp*, 1930 *Sp*, 1933 *Cze*
L Brighetti 1934 *Cat*
A Brunelli 1969 *Bel*, 1970 *Mad*, 1971 *F*
M Brunello 1988 *I*, 1989 *F*, 1990 *F, Sp, H, R, USS*, 1993 *Pt*
S Brusin 1957 *Ger*
KS Burton 2007 *Ur, Ar*, 2009 *A, NZ*, 2011 *I, E, W, F, S*
P Buso 2008 *W*
G Busson 1957 *Ger*, 1958 *R*, 1959 *F*, 1960 *Ger, F*, 1961 *Ger, F*, 1962 *F, Ger*, 1963 *F*

F Caccia-Dominioni 1935 *F*, 1937 *Ger*
C Caione 1995 *R*, 1996 *Pt*, 1997 *F, R*, 1998 *Rus, Ar, H, E*, 1999 *F, S, SA, Ur, Sp, Fj, Tg, NZ*, 2000 *Sa, Fj, C, R, NZ*, 2001 *I, E, S, Fj*
R Caligiuri 1969 *F*, 1973 *Pt, Rho, WTv, NEC, Nat, ETv, Leo, FS, Tva*, 1975 *E, Pol, H, Sp*, 1976 *F, R, J, A, Sp*, 1978 *F, Ar, USS, Sp*, 1979 *F, Pol, R*
A Caluzzi 1970 *R*, 1971 *Mor, F*, 1972 *Pt, Pt, Sp, Sp*, 1973 *Pt*, 1974 *Oxo, WGe, Leo*
P Camiscioni 1975 *E*, 1976 *R, J, A, Sp*, 1977 *F*, 1978 *F*
M Campagna 1933 *Cze*, 1934 *Cat*, 1936 *Ger, R*, 1937 *Ger, R, Bel*, 1938 *Ger*
GJ Canale 2003 *S, Geo, NZ, Tg, C, W*, 2004 *S, I, W, R, J, C*, 2005 *I, Ar, Ar, A, Tg, Ar, Fj*, 2006 *I, E, F, W, S, A, Ar, C*, 2007 *F, E, S, W, J, I, R, Pt, S*, 2008 *I, E, W, F, S, A*, 2009 *E, I, S, W, F, A, NZ, NZ, Sa*, 2010 *I, E, S, F, W, SA, SA, Ar, A, Fj*, 2011 *I, E, W, F, S, J, S, A, Rus, US, I*
PL Canavosio 2005 *A, Tg, Fj*, 2006 *I, E, F, W, S, Fj, Pt, Rus, A, Ar*, 2007 *Ar, J, I, Pt*, 2008 *I, SA, Ar, A, Ar*, 2009 *S, W, F, A*, 2010 *E, S, F, W, Ar, A*, 2011 *I, E, W, S, J, Rus*
C Cantoni 1956 *Ger, F, Cze*, 1957 *Ger*
L Capitani 1989 *F, R, Sp, Ar, Z, USS*
M Capuzzoni 1993 *Cro*, 1995 *I*
A Caranci 1989 *R*
M Carli 1955 *Sp, Cze*
C Carloni 1935 *F*
D Carpente 2004 *R, J*
T Carraro 1937 *R*
T Casagrande 1977 *R*
U Cassellato 1990 *Sp*, 1992 *R, S*, 1993 *Sp, F, Pt, Cro, Mor, F, S*
R Cassina 1992 *R, S*
A Castellani 1994 *CZR*, 1995 *Ar, R*, 1996 *W, S*, 1997 *Ar, R, I*, 1998 *S, W, Rus, H, E*, 1999 *F, W, Ur, Sp, Fj, Tg, NZ*
ML Castrogiovanni 2002 *NZ, Sp, R, Ar, A*, 2003 *I, E, F, S, I, Geo, NZ, Tg, C, W*, 2004 *E, F, S, I, W, J*, 2005 *I, W, S, E, F, Ar, A, Ar, Fj*, 2006 *I, E, F, W, S, Pt, Rus, A, Ar, C*, 2007 *F, E, S, J, I, NZ, R, Pt, S*, 2008 *I, E, W, F, S*, 2009 *E, I, S, W, F, NZ, SA, Sa*, 2010 *I, E, S, F, W, SA, Ar, A, Fj*, 2011 *I, E, W, F, S, J, S, A, Rus, US, I*
L Catotti 1979 *Pol, E*
A Cazzini 1933 *Cze, Cze*, 1934 *Cat, R*, 1935 *Cat, F*, 1936 *Ger, R*, 1937 *Ger, R, Bel, Ger, F*, 1939 *R*, 1942 *R*
G Cecchetto 1955 *F*
A Cecchetto-Milani 1952 *Sp, Ger, F*
G Cecchin 1970 *Cze, R*, 1971 *F, R*, 1972 *Pt*
G Ceccotti 1972 *Pt, Sp*
A Centinari 1930 *Sp*
R Centinari 1935 *F*, 1936 *Ger, R*, 1937 *Bel, F*, 1939 *Ger*
A Cepolino 1999 *Ur, Sp, Fj, Tg, NZ*
L Cesani 1929 *Sp*, 1930 *Sp*, 1935 *Cat, F*
F Ceselin 1989 *F, R*
C Checchinato 1990 *Sp*, 1991 *Nm, Nm, US, NZ, USS*, 1992 *Sp, F, R, S*, 1993 *Pt, Cro, Sp, F, Rus, F, S*, 1994 *Sp, R, CZR, A, A, R, W, F*, 1995 *Sa, F, Ar, R, NZ*, 1996 *W, E*, 1997 *I, F, Ar, R, SA, I*, 1998 *Rus, Ar, H, E*, 1999 *F, S, SA, SA, Ur, Fj, E, Tg, NZ*, 2000 *S, W, I, E, F, Sa, Fj*, 2001 *I, E, F, S, W, Nm, SA, Ur, Ar, Fj, SA, Sa*, 2002 *F, S, W, Sp, R*, 2003 *Geo, NZ, Tg, C, W*, 2004 *E, F, I*
G Chechinato 1973 *Cze, Yug, A*, 1974 *WGe, Leo*
G Cherubini 1949 *Cze*, 1951 *Sp*
T Ciccio 1992 *R*, 1993 *Sp, F, Mor, F*
E Cicognani 1940 *Ger*
R Cinelli 1968 *Pt*, 1969 *Sp*
G Cinti 1973 *Rho, WTv, ETv*
F Cioni 1967 *Pt, R*, 1968 *Pt*, 1969 *Bul, Sp, Bel*, 1970 *Cze, Mad, Mad, R*
L Cittadini 2008 *I*, 2010 *SA, SA, A*, 2011 *J, S, A, Rus*
L Clerici 1939 *Ger*
A Colella 1983 *R, USS, C, C, Sp, Mor, F, A, USS*, 1984 *R, Tun, USS*, 1985 *F, R, EngB, Sp, Z, Z, USS, R*, 1986 *Tun, F, Pt, E, A, Tun, USS*, 1987 *Pt, F, Ar, Fj, USS, Sp*, 1988 *F, R, USS*, 1989 *R, Sp, Ar*, 1990 *Pol, R*
O Collodo 1977 *Pol, Cze, R, Sp*, 1978 *F*, 1986 *Pt, E, A, USS*, 1987 *Pt, F, R, NZ, Ar, Fj*
S Colombini 1971 *R*
F Colombo 1933 *Cze*
G Colussi 1957 *F*, 1958 *F*, 1964 *Ger, F*, 1965 *F, Cze*, 1968 *Pt*
C Colusso 1982 *F*
A Comin 1955 *Ger, F, Sp, F, Cze*, 1956 *F, Cze*, 1958 *F*
U Conforto 1965 *Cze*, 1966 *Ger, R*, 1967 *F, R*, 1968 *Pt, WGe, Yug*, 1969 *Bul, Sp, Bel, F*, 1970 *Cze*, 1971 *Mor, F*, 1972 *Yug*, 1973 *Pt*
F Coppio 1993 *F, Pt, Cro, Mor, Sp*
L Cornella 1999 *Sp*
R Corvo 1985 *F, Sp, Z*
U Cossara 1971 *Mor, F, R*, 1972 *Pt, Sp*, 1973 *Pt, Rho, NEC, Nat, Leo, FS, Tva, Cze*, 1975 *F, Sp, R, Cze, E, Pol, H*, 1976 *F, J, A*, 1977 *Pol*
A Costa 1940 *R, Ger*, 1942 *R*
S Costanzo 2004 *R, C, NZ, US*
E Cottafava 1973 *Pt*
R Cova 1937 *Bel, Ger, F*, 1938 *Ger*, 1939 *Ger, R*, 1942 *R*
C Covi 1988 *F, R, USS, A, I*, 1989 *F, R, Sp, Ar, Z, USS*, 1990 *F, Pol, R*, 1991 *F, R, Nm, Nm*, 1996 *E*
F Crepaz 1972 *Pt*
M Crescenzo 1984 *R*
U Crespi 1933 *Cze, Cze*, 1934 *Cat, R*, 1935 *Cat*, 1937 *Ger*
W Cristofoletto 1992 *R*, 1993 *Mor, Sp, F*, 1996 *Pt, A, E, S*, 1997 *I, F, F, Ar, SA, I*, 1998 *S, W, Rus, Ar, E*, 1999 *F, S, W, I, SA, SA, Sp, Fj, E, NZ*, 2000 *E, F*

G Croci 1990 *Sp, H, R, USS,* 1991 *F, R, Nm, US, E, NZ, USS,* 1992 *Sp, F,* 1993 *S,* 1996 *S,* 1997 *I, F, F, Ar, R, SA, I,* 1998 *S, W*
R Crotti 1993 *S,* 1995 *SA*
L Cuccharelli 1966 *R,* 1967 *R*
G Cucchiella 1973 *A,* 1974 *Sus,* 1979 *Sp, F, Pol, USS, NZ, Mor,* 1980 *F, R, Fj, JAB, Coo,* 1985 *USS, R,* 1986 *Tun, F, Pt, E,* 1987 *Pt, F, Fj*
M Cuttitta 1990 *Pol, R, Sp, H, R, USS,* 1991 *F, Nm, Nm, US, E, NZ, USS,* 1992 *Sp, F, R, R, S,* 1993 *Sp, F, Pt, Cro, Mor, Sp, F, Rus, F, S,* 1994 *Sp, R, CZR, H, A, A, W, F,* 1995 *S, I, Sa, E, Ar, F, Ar, R, NZ, SA,* 1996 *W, Pt, W, E, S,* 1997 *I, F, F, Ar, SA, I,* 1998 *W, Rus, Ar, H, E,* 1999 *F, S, W,* 2000 *S, W, I, E*
M Cuttitta 1987 *Pt, F, R, NZ, Ar, Fj, USS, Sp,* 1988 *F, R,* 1989 *Z, USS,* 1990 *Pol, R,* 1991 *F, R, Nm, US, E, NZ, USS,* 1992 *Sp, F, R, R, S,* 1993 *Sp, F, Mor, Sp, F, F,* 1994 *Sp, R, H, A, A, F,* 1995 *S, I, Sa,* 1996 *S,* 1997 *I, F, F, Ar, R, SA, I,* 1998 *S, W, Rus, Ar,* 1999 *F*

G Dagnini 1949 *F*
D Dal Maso 2000 *Sa, Fj,* 2001 *I, E,* 2004 *J, C, NZ, US,* 2005 *I, W, S, E, F, A*
M Dal Sie 1993 *Pt,* 1994 *R, W, F,* 1995 *F, Ar,* 1996 *A*
A D'Alberton 1966 *F, Ger, R,* 1967 *F, R*
D Daldoss 1979 *Pol, R, E, Sp, Mor*
C D'Alessio 1937 *R, Bel, F,* 1938 *Ger,* 1939 *Ger*
D Dallan 1999 *F, S, W,* 2000 *S, W, I, E, F, C, R, NZ,* 2001 *I, E, F, W, Fj, SA, Sa,* 2002 *F, S, I, E, NZ, Sp, R,* 2003 *W, I, E, F, S, Tg, C, W,* 2004 *E, F, S, I, W, C,* 2006 *J,* 2007 *F, E*
M Dallan 1997 *Ar, R, I,* 1998 *Ar, H, E,* 1999 *SA, SA,* 2000 *S, Sa, C,* 2001 *F, S,* 2003 *Tg, C,* 2004 *E, F, S*
A Danieli 1955 *Ger, F, Sp, F, Cze*
V D'Anna 1993 *Rus*
T D'Apice 2011 *J, S, Rus*
P Dari 1951 *Sp,* 1952 *Sp, Ger, F,* 1953 *Ger, R,* 1954 *Sp, F*
G De Angelis 1934 *Cat, R,* 1935 *Cat, F,* 1937 *R*
E De Anna 1972 *Yug,* 1973 *Cze, A,* 1975 *F, Sp, R, Cze, E, Pol, H, Sp,* 1976 *F, R,* 1978 *Ar, USS, Sp,* 1979 *F, R, Sp, Mor, F, USS, NZ,* 1980 *F, R, Fj, JAB*
R De Bernardo 1980 *USS, Sp,* 1981 *F, R, USS, WGe,* 1982 *R, E,* 1983 *R, USS, C, C, Sp, Mor, F, A, USS,* 1984 *F, USS,* 1985 *R, EngB,* 1988 *I,* 1989 *Ar, Z*
CF De Biase 1987 *Sp,* 1988 *F, A*
G De Carli 1996 *W,* 1997 *R,* 1998 *S, Rus, Ar, H, E,* 1999 *F, I, SA, SA, Ur, Fj,* 2000 *S, Sa, Fj,* 2001 *I, E, W, SA, Ur, Fj, SA, Sa,* 2002 *F, S, W, I, E,* 2003 *W, I, E*
B de Jager 2006 *J*
L De Joanni 1983 *C, Mor, F, A, USS,* 1984 *R, Tun, USS,* 1985 *F, R, EngB, Sp, Z,* 1986 *A, Tun,* 1989 *F, R, Sp, Ar, Z,* 1990 *R*
R De Marchis 1935 *F*
H De Marco 1993 *Pt*
JR de Marigny 2004 *E, F, S, I, W, US,* 2005 *I, W, S,* 2007 *F, E, S, W, I, Ur, J, I, NZ, Pt*
A de Rossi 1999 *Ur, Sp, E,* 2000 *I, E, F, Sa, C, R, NZ,* 2001 *SA, Ur, Ar,* 2002 *I, E, NZ, Sp, R,* 2003 *W, I, E, F, S, I, Geo, Tg, C, W,* 2004 *E, F, S, I, W, R*
C De Rossi 1994 *Sp, H, R*
L De Santis 1952 *Sp*
M De Stefani 1989 *Z*
C De Vecchi 1948 *F*
G Degli Antoni 1963 *F,* 1965 *F,* 1966 *F, Ger, R,* 1967 *F*
G Del Bono 1951 *Sp*
M Del Bono 1960 *Ger, F,* 1961 *Ger, F,* 1962 *F, Ger, R,* 1963 *F,* 1964 *Ger, F*
CA Del Fava 2004 *W, R, J,* 2005 *I, W, S, E, F, Tg, Ar, Fj,* 2006 *I, E, F, W, S, J, Fj, Pt,* 2007 *Ur, Ar, Pt, S,* 2008 *I, E, W, F, S, SA, Ar, A, Ar,* 2009 *I, S, W, F, A, NZ, NZ, SA, Sa,* 2010 *I, S, F, SA, Ar, A, Fj,* 2011 *I, E, F, S, S, A*
C Della Valle 1968 *WGe, Yug,* 1969 *F,* 1970 *Mad, Mad,* 1971 *F*
S Dellapè 2002 *F, S, I, E, NZ, Sp, Ar,* 2003 *F, S, S, Geo, Tg, C, W,* 2004 *E, F, S, I, W, C, NZ,* 2005 *I, W, S, E, F, Ar,* 2006 *I, E, W, S, J, Fj, Pt, Rus, A, Ar, C,* 2007 *F, E, S, W, I, J, NZ, R, S,* 2008 *I, E, W, SA, Ar,* 2009 *E, I, S, W, F,* 2010 *Ar, A, Fj,* 2011 *I, E, W, F*
G Delli Ficorilli 1969 *F*
PE Derbyshire 2009 *A,* 2010 *E, F, SA, SA, Ar, A, Fj,* 2011 *F, S, J, S, A, Rus, US, I*
A Di Bello 1930 *Sp,* 1933 *Cze, Cze,* 1934 *Cat*
F Di Carlo 1975 *Sp, R, Cze, Sp,* 1976 *F, Sp,* 1977 *Pol, R, Pol,* 1978 *Ar, USS*
B Di Cola 1973 *A*
G Di Cola 1972 *Sp, Sp,* 1973 *A*
F Di Maura 1971 *Mor*
A Di Zitti 1958 *R,* 1960 *Ger,* 1961 *Ger, F,* 1962 *F, Ger, R,* 1964 *Ger, F,* 1965 *F, Cze,* 1966 *F, Ger, R,* 1967 *F, Pt, R,* 1969 *Bul, Sp, Bel,* 1972 *Pt, Sp*
R Dolfato 1985 *F,* 1986 *A,* 1987 *Pt, Fj, USS, Sp,* 1988 *F, R, USS*
D Dominguez 1991 *F, R, Nm, Nm, US, E, NZ, USS,* 1992 *Sp, F, R, S,* 1993 *Sp, F, Rus, F, S,* 1994 *R, H, R, W,* 1995 *S, I, Sa, E, Ar, SA,* 1996 *W, Pt, W, A, E, S,* 1997 *I, F, F, Ar, R, SA, I,* 1998 *S, W, Rus, Ar, H, E,* 1999 *F, S, W, I, Ur, Sp, Fj, E, Tg, NZ,* 2000 *S, W, I, E, F,* 2001 *F, S, W, Fj, SA, Sa,* 2002 *F, S, I, E, Ar,* 2003 *W, I*
D Dondana 1929 *Sp,* 1930 *Sp*
G Dora 1929 *Sp*
R D'Orazio 1969 *Bul*
M Dotti IV 1939 *R,* 1940 *R, Ger*
F Dotto 1971 *Mor, F,* 1972 *Pt, Pt, Sp*
P Dotto 1993 *Sp, Cro,* 1994 *Sp, R*

J Erasmus 2008 *F, S, SA*

U Faccioli 1948 *F*
A Falancia 1975 *E, Pol*
G Faliva 1999 *SA,* 2002 *NZ, Ar, A*
G Faltiba 1993 *Pt*
G Fanton 1979 *Pol*
P Farina 1987 *F, NZ, Fj*
P Farinelli 1940 *R,* 1949 *F, Cze,* 1951 *Sp,* 1952 *Sp*
T Fattori 1936 *Ger, R,* 1937 *R, Ger, F,* 1938 *Ger,* 1939 *Ger, R,* 1940 *R, Ger*
E Fava 1948 *F, Cze*
P Favaretto 1951 *Sp*
R Favaro 1988 *F, USS, A, I,* 1989 *F, R, Sp, Ar, Z, USS,* 1990 *F, Pol, R, H, R, USS,* 1991 *F, R, Nm, Nm, US, E, NZ, USS,* 1992 *Sp, F, R,* 1993 *Sp, F, Cro, Sp, F,* 1994 *CZR, A, A, R, W, F,* 1995 *S, I, Sa,* 1996 *Pt*
S Favaro 2009 *A, NZ, NZ, SA, Sa,* 2010 *SA*
G Favretto 1948 *Cze,* 1949 *Cze*
A Fedrigo 1972 *Yug,* 1973 *Pt, Rho, WTv, Bor, NEC, Nat, ETv, Leo, FS, Cze, Yug, A,* 1974 *Pt, Mid, Sus, Oxo, WGe, Leo,* 1975 *F, Sp, R, Cze, E, Pol, H, Sp,* 1976 *F, J, A, Sp,* 1977 *F, Pol, R, Cze, R, Sp,* 1978 *F, Ar,* 1979 *Pol, R*
P Fedrigo 1973 *Pt*
I Fernandez- Rouyet 2008 *SA, Ar,* 2009 *A, NZ, NZ, SA, Sa*
P Ferracin 1975 *R, Cze, E, Pol, H, Sp,* 1976 *F,* 1977 *Mor, Pol,* 1978 *USS*
C Festuccia 2003 *W, I, E, F, S, S, I, Geo, NZ, Tg, C, W,* 2004 *E, F, S, I,* 2005 *F, Ar, Ar, A, Tg, Ar,* 2006 *E, F, W, S, Pt, Rus, A, Ar, C,* 2007 *F, E, S, W, I, Ur, Ar, J, NZ, R, S,* 2008 *I, E, W,* 2009 *E, I,* 2010 *A, Fj,* 2011 *F, S*
G Figari 1940 *R, Ger,* 1942 *R*
EG Filizzola 1993 *Pt, Mor, Sp, F, Rus, F, S,* 1994 *Sp, CZR, A,* 1995 *R, NZ*
M Finocchi 1968 *Yug,* 1969 *F,* 1970 *Cze, Mad, Mad, R,* 1971 *Mor, R*
G Fornari 1952 *Sp, Ger, F,* 1953 *F, Ger, R,* 1954 *Sp, F,* 1955 *Ger, F, Sp, F, Cze,* 1956 *Ger, F, Cze*
B Francescato 1977 *Cze, R, Sp,* 1978 *F, Sp,* 1979 *F,* 1981 *R*
I Francescato 1990 *R, USS,* 1991 *F, R, US, E, NZ, USS,* 1992 *R, S,* 1993 *Mor, F,* 1994 *Sp, H, R, W, F,* 1995 *S, I, Sa, E, Ar, F, Ar, R, NZ, SA,* 1996 *W, Pt, W, A, E, S,* 1997 *F, F, Ar, R, SA*
N Francescato 1972 *Yug,* 1973 *Rho, WTv, Bor, NEC, Nat, ETv, Leo,* 1974 *Pt,* 1976 *J, A, Sp,* 1977 *F, Mor, Pol, R, R, Sp,* 1978 *F, Ar, USS, Sp,* 1979 *F, R, E, Sp, Mor, F, Pol, USS, NZ,* 1980 *F, R, Fj, JAB, Coo, Pol, USS, Sp,* 1981 *F, R,* 1982 *Mor*
R Francescato 1976 *Sp,* 1978 *Ar, USS,* 1979 *Sp, F, Pol, USS, NZ, Mor,* 1980 *F, R, Fj, JAB, Coo, Pol, USS, Sp,* 1981 *F, R,* 1982 *WGe,* 1983 *F, R, USS, C, C, Sp, Mor, F, A,* 1984 *Mor, R, Tun,* 1985 *F, Sp, Z, USS,* 1986 *Tun, F*
G Franceschini 1975 *H, Sp,* 1976 *F, J,* 1977 *F, Pol, Pol, Cze, R, Sp*
A Francese 1939 *R,* 1940 *R*
J Francesio 2000 *W, I, Sa,* 2001 *Ur*
F Frati 2000 *C, NZ,* 2001 *I, S*
F Frelich 1955 *Cze,* 1957 *F, Ger,* 1958 *F, R*
M Fumei 1984 *F*

J Furno 2011 *S*
A Fusco 1982 *E*, 1985 *R*, 1986 *Tun*, *F*, *Tun*
E Fusco 1960 *Ger*, *F*, 1961 *F*, 1962 *F*, *Ger*, *R*, 1963 *F*, 1964 *Ger*, *F*, 1965 *F*, 1966 *F*

R Gabanella 1951 *Sp*, 1952 *Sp*
P Gabrielli 1948 *Cze*, 1949 *F*, *Cze*, 1951 *Sp*, 1954 *F*
F Gaetaniello 1975 *H*, 1976 *R*, *A*, *Sp*, 1977 *F*, *Pol*, *R*, *Pol*, *R*, *Sp*, 1978 *Sp*, 1979 *Pol*, *R*, *E*, *Sp*, *Mor*, *F*, *Pol*, *USS*, *NZ*, *Mor*, 1980 *Fj*, *JAB*, *Sp*, 1981 *F*, *R*, *USS*, *WGe*, 1982 *F*, *R*, *E*, *WGe*, *Mor*, 1983 *F*, *R*, *USS*, *C*, *C*, *Sp*
F Gaetaniello 1980 *Sp*, 1982 *E*, 1984 *USS*, 1985 *R*, *Sp*, *Z*, *Z*, *USS*, *R*, 1986 *Pt*, *E*, *A*, *Tun*, *USS*, 1987 *Pt*, *F*, *NZ*, *Ar*, *Fj*, *USS*, *Sp*, 1988 *F*, 1990 *F*, *R*, *Sp*, *H*, 1991 *Nm*, *US*, *E*, *NZ*
A Galante 2007 *Ur*, *Ar*
A Galeazzo 1985 *Sp*, 1987 *Pt*, *R*, *Ar*, *USS*
M Galletto 1972 *Pt*, *Sp*, *Yug*
E Galon 2001 *I*, 2005 *Tg*, *Ar*, *Fj*, 2006 *W*, *S*, *Rus*, 2007 *I*, *Ur*, *Ar*, *I*, *NZ*, *R*, *S*, 2008 *I*, *E*, *W*, *F*, *S*
R Ganzerla 1973 *Bor*, *NEC*
G Garcia 2008 *SA*, *Ar*, *A*, *Ar*, *PI*, 2009 *E*, *I*, *S*, *A*, *NZ*, *NZ*, *SA*, *Sa*, 2010 *I*, *E*, *S*, *F*, *W*, 2011 *I*, *E*, *F*, *S*, *A*, *US*, *I*
M Gardin 1981 *USS*, *WGe*, 1982 *Mor*, 1983 *F*, *R*, 1984 *Mor*, *R*, *USS*, 1985 *EngB*, *USS*, *R*, 1986 *Tun*, *F*, *Pt*, *Tun*, *USS*, 1987 *Pt*, *F*, *R*, *NZ*, *Ar*, *Fj*, *USS*, *Sp*, 1988 *R*
JM Gardner 1992 *R*, *S*, 1993 *Rus*, *F*, 1994 *Sp*, *R*, *H*, *F*, 1995 *S*, *I*, *Sa*, *E*, *Ar*, 1996 *W*, 1997 *I*, *F*, *SA*, *I*, 1998 *S*, *W*
P Gargiullo 1973 *FS*, 1974 *Mid*, *Sus*, *Oxo*
F Garguillo 1972 *Yug*
F Garguilo 1967 *F*, *Pt*, 1968 *Yug*, 1974 *Sus*
S Garozzo 2001 *Ur*, *Ar*, 2002 *Ar*
M Gatto 1967 *Pt*, *R*
G Gattoni 1933 *Cze*, *Cze*
Q Geldenhuys 2009 *A*, *A*, *NZ*, *NZ*, *SA*, *Sa*, 2010 *I*, *E*, *S*, *F*, *W*, *SA*, *SA*, *Ar*, *A*, *Fj*, 2011 *I*, *E*, *W*, *F*, *S*, *J*, *Rus*, *US*, *I*
A Gerardo 1968 *Yug*, 1969 *Sp*, 1970 *Cze*, *Mad*, 1971 *R*, 1972 *Sp*
F Geremia 1980 *JAB*, *Pol*
G Geremia 1956 *Cze*
E Gerosa 1952 *Sp*, *Ger*, *F*, 1953 *F*, *Ger*, *R*, 1954 *Sp*
M Gerosa 1994 *CZR*, *A*, *A*, *R*, *W*, 1995 *E*, *Ar*
C Ghezzi 1938 *Ger*, 1939 *Ger*, *R*, 1940 *R*, *Ger*
A Ghini 1981 *USS*, *WGe*, 1982 *F*, *R*, *E*, *Mor*, 1983 *F*, *R*, *C*, *Mor*, *F*, *A*, *USS*, 1984 *F*, *Mor*, *R*, *USS*, 1985 *F*, *R*, *EngB*, *Z*, *Z*, *USS*, 1987 *Fj*, 1988 *R*, *USS*
L Ghiraldini 2006 *J*, *Fj*, 2007 *I*, *J*, *Pt*, 2008 *I*, *E*, *W*, *F*, *S*, *SA*, *Ar*, *A*, *Ar*, *PI*, 2009 *S*, *W*, *F*, *A*, *A*, *NZ*, *NZ*, *SA*, *Sa*, 2010 *I*, *E*, *S*, *F*, *W*, *SA*, *SA*, *Ar*, 2011 *I*, *E*, *W*, *F*, *S*, *J*, *A*, *US*, *I*
S Ghizzoni 1977 *F*, *Mor*, *Pol*, *R*, *Pol*, *Cze*, *R*, *Sp*, 1978 *F*, *Ar*, *USS*, 1979 *F*, *Pol*, *Sp*, *Mor*, *F*, *Pol*, 1980 *R*, *Fj*, *JAB*, *Coo*, *Pol*, *USS*, *Sp*, 1981 *F*, 1982 *F*, *R*, *E*, *WGe*, *Mor*, 1983 *F*, *USS*, *C*, *C*, *Sp*, *Mor*, *F*, *A*, *USS*, 1984 *F*, *Mor*, *R*, *Tun*, *USS*, 1985 *F*, *R*, *EngB*, *Z*, *Z*, *USS*, *R*, 1986 *F*, *E*, *A*, *Tun*, *USS*, 1987 *Pt*, *F*, *R*, *NZ*
M Giacheri 1992 *R*, 1993 *Sp*, *F*, *Pt*, *Rus*, *F*, *S*, 1994 *Sp*, *R*, *CZR*, *H*, *A*, *A*, *F*, 1995 *S*, *I*, *E*, *Ar*, *F*, *Ar*, *R*, *NZ*, *SA*, 1996 *W*, 1999 *S*, *W*, *I*, *Ur*, *Fj*, *E*, *Tg*, *NZ*, 2001 *Nm*, *SA*, *Ur*, *Ar*, *SA*, 2002 *F*, *S*, *W*, *I*, *E*, *NZ*, *A*, 2003 *E*, *F*, *S*, *I*
G Giani 1966 *Ger*, *R*, 1967 *F*, *Pt*, *R*
G Gini 1968 *Pt*, *WGe*, *Yug*, 1969 *Bul*, *Sp*, *Bel*, *F*, 1970 *Cze*, *Mad*, *Mad*, *R*, 1971 *Mor*, *F*, 1972 *Pt*, *Pt*, 1974 *Mid*, *Oxo*
G Giorgio 1968 *Pt*, *WGe*
M Giovanelli 1989 *Z*, *USS*, 1990 *Pol*, *Sp*, *H*, *R*, *USS*, 1991 *F*, *R*, *Nm*, *E*, *NZ*, *USS*, 1992 *Sp*, *F*, *S*, 1993 *Sp*, *F*, *Pt*, *Cro*, *Mor*, *Sp*, *F*, 1994 *R*, *CZR*, *H*, *A*, *A*, 1995 *F*, *Ar*, *R*, *NZ*, *SA*, 1996 *A*, *E*, *S*, 1997 *F*, *F*, *Ar*, *R*, *SA*, *I*, 1998 *S*, *W*, *Rus*, *Ar*, *H*, *E*, 1999 *S*, *W*, *I*, *SA*, *SA*, *Ur*, *Sp*, *Fj*, *E*, *Tg*, *NZ*, 2000 *S*
E Giugovaz 1965 *Cze*, 1966 *F*
R Giuliani 1951 *Sp*
E Gori 2010 *A*, *Fj*, 2011 *I*, *J*, *S*, *A*, *Rus*, *US*, *I*
M Gorni 1939 *R*, 1940 *R*, *Ger*
M Goti 1990 *H*
C Gower 2009 *A*, *A*, *NZ*, *NZ*, *SA*, *Sa*, 2010 *I*, *E*, *S*, *F*, *W*, *SA*, *SA*, *Ar*
G Grasselli 1952 *Ger*
G Grespan 1989 *F*, *Sp*, *USS*, 1990 *F*, *R*, 1991 *R*, *NZ*, *USS*, 1992 *R*, *S*, 1993 *Sp*, *F*, *Cro*, *Sp*, *F*, *Rus*, 1994 *Sp*, *CZR*, *R*, *W*
PR Griffen 2004 *E*, *F*, *S*, *I*, *W*, *R*, *J*, *C*, *NZ*, *US*, 2005 *W*, *S*, *F*, *Ar*, *Ar*, *A*, *Tg*, *Ar*, *Fj*, 2006 *I*, *E*, *F*, *W*, *S*, *J*, *Fj*, *Rus*, *A*, *Ar*, *C*, 2007 *F*, *I*, *Ur*, *Ar*, *I*, *NZ*, *R*, *Pt*, 2009 *I*, *S*, *W*, *F*
A Gritti 1996 *Pt*, 2000 *S*, *W*, *I*, *E*, *F*, *Sa*, *Fj*, *C*, *R*, *NZ*, 2001 *E*, *F*, *S*, *W*
G Guidi 1996 *Pt*, *E*, 1997 *F*, *Ar*, *R*

M Innocenti 1981 *WGe*, 1982 *F*, *R*, *E*, *WGe*, *Mor*, 1983 *F*, *USS*, *C*, *C*, *Mor*, *F*, *A*, *USS*, 1984 *F*, *Mor*, *Tun*, *USS*, 1985 *F*, *R*, *EngB*, *Sp*, *USS*, *R*, 1986 *Tun*, *F*, *Pt*, *E*, *A*, *Tun*, *USS*, 1987 *Pt*, *F*, *R*, *NZ*, *Ar*, *Fj*, *USS*, *Sp*, 1988 *F*, *R*, *A*
G Intoppa 2004 *R*, *J*, *C*, *NZ*, 2005 *I*, *W*, *E*

C Jannone 1981 *USS*, 1982 *F*, *R*

S Lanfranchi 1949 *F*, *Cze*, 1953 *F*, *Ger*, *R*, 1954 *Sp*, *F*, 1955 *F*, 1956 *Ger*, *Cze*, 1957 *F*, 1958 *F*, 1959 *F*, 1960 *F*, 1961 *F*, 1962 *F*, *Ger*, *R*, 1963 *F*, 1964 *Ger*, *F*
G Lanzi 1998 *Ar*, *H*, *E*, 1999 *Sp*, 2000 *S*, *W*, *I*, 2001 *I*
G Lari 1972 *Yug*, 1973 *Yug*, *A*, 1974 *Pt*, *Mid*, *Sus*, *Oxo*, *Leo*
E Lazzarini 1970 *Cze*, 1971 *Mor*, *F*, *R*, 1972 *Pt*, *Pt*, *Sp*, *Sp*, 1973 *Pt*, *Rho*, *WTv*, *Bor*, *NEC*, *Leo*, *FS*, *Tva*, *Cze*, *Yug*, *A*, 1974 *Pt*, *Mid*, *Sus*, *Oxo*, *WGe*
U Levorato 1956 *Ger*, *F*, 1957 *F*, 1958 *F*, *R*, 1959 *F*, 1961 *Ger*, *F*, 1962 *F*, *Ger*, *R*, 1963 *F*, 1964 *Ger*, *F*, 1965 *F*
A Lijoi 1977 *Pol*, *R*, 1978 *Sp*, 1979 *R*, *Mor*
G Limone 1979 *E*, *Mor*, *USS*, *Mor*, 1980 *JAB*, *Sp*, 1981 *USS*, *WGe*, 1982 *E*, 1983 *USS*
A Lo Cicero 2000 *E*, *F*, *Sa*, *Fj*, *C*, *R*, *NZ*, 2001 *I*, *E*, *F*, *S*, *W*, *Fj*, *SA*, *Sa*, 2002 *F*, *S*, *W*, *Sp*, *R*, *A*, 2003 *F*, *S*, *S*, *I*, *Geo*, *Tg*, *C*, *W*, 2004 *E*, *F*, *S*, *I*, *W*, *R*, *J*, *C*, *NZ*, *US*, 2005 *I*, *W*, *S*, *E*, *F*, *Ar*, *Ar*, *A*, *Tg*, *Ar*, 2006 *E*, *F*, *W*, *S*, *J*, *Fj*, *Pt*, *Rus*, *A*, *Ar*, *C*, 2007 *F*, *E*, *S*, *W*, *Ur*, *Ar*, *J*, *NZ*, *R*, *Pt*, *S*, 2008 *I*, *E*, *W*, *F*, *S*, *Ar*, *PI*, 2010 *Ar*, *A*, *Fj*, 2011 *I*, *E*, *W*, *F*, *S*, *J*, *S*, *A*, *US*, *I*
C Loranzi 1973 *Nat*, *ETv*, *Leo*, *FS*, *Tva*
F Lorigiola 1979 *Sp*, *F*, *Pol*, *USS*, *NZ*, *Mor*, 1980 *F*, *R*, *Fj*, *JAB*, *Pol*, *USS*, *Sp*, 1981 *F*, *R*, *USS*, 1982 *WGe*, 1983 *R*, *USS*, *C*, *Sp*, 1984 *Tun*, 1985 *Sp*, 1986 *Pt*, *E*, *A*, *Tun*, *USS*, 1987 *Pt*, *F*, *R*, *NZ*, *Ar*, 1988 *F*
G Luchini 1973 *Rho*, *Nat*
L Luise 1955 *Ger*, *F*, *Sp*, *F*, *Cze*, 1956 *Ger*, *F*, *Cze*, 1957 *Ger*, 1958 *F*
R Luise III 1959 *F*, 1960 *Ger*, *F*, 1961 *Ger*, *F*, 1962 *F*, *Ger*, *R*, 1965 *F*, *Cze*, 1966 *F*, 1971 *R*, 1972 *Pt*, *Sp*, *Sp*
T Lupini 1987 *R*, *NZ*, *Ar*, *Fj*, *USS*, *Sp*, 1988 *F*, *R*, *USS*, *A*, 1989 *R*

O Maestri 1935 *Cat*, *F*, 1937 *Ger*
R Maffioli 1933 *Cze*, *Cze*, 1934 *Cat*, *R*, 1935 *Cat*, 1936 *Ger*, *R*, 1937 *Ger*, *R*, *Bel*, *Ger*
R Maini 1948 *F*, *Cze*
G Malosti 1953 *F*, 1954 *Sp*, 1955 *F*, 1956 *Ger*, *F*, 1957 *F*, 1958 *F*
G Mancini 1952 *Ger*, *F*, 1953 *F*, *Ger*, *R*, 1954 *Sp*, *F*, 1955 *Cze*, 1956 *Ger*, *F*, *Cze*, 1957 *F*
R Mandelli 2004 *I*, *W*, *R*, *J*, *US*, 2007 *F*, *E*, *Ur*, *Ar*
A Mannato 2004 *US*, 2005 *Ar*, *A*
E Manni 1976 *J*, *A*, *Sp*, 1977 *Mor*
L Manteri 1996 *W*, *A*, *E*, *S*
A Marcato 2006 *J*, *Pt*, 2008 *I*, *E*, *W*, *F*, *S*, *SA*, *Ar*, *A*, *Ar*, *PI*, 2009 *E*, *S*, *W*, *F*
M Marchetto 1972 *Yug*, 1973 *Pt*, *Cze*, *Yug*, 1974 *Pt*, *Mid*, *Sus*, *WGe*, *Leo*, 1975 *F*, *Sp*, *R*, *Cze*, *E*, *Pol*, *H*, *Sp*, 1976 *F*, *R*, *J*, *A*, *Sp*, 1977 *F*, *Mor*, *Pol*, *R*, *Cze*, *R*, *Sp*, 1978 *F*, *USS*, *Sp*, 1979 *F*, *Pol*, *R*, *E*, *Pol*, *USS*, *NZ*, *Mor*, 1980 *F*, *Coo*, 1981 *USS*
A Marescalchi 1933 *Cze*, 1935 *F*, 1937 *R*
P Mariani 1976 *R*, *A*, *Sp*, 1977 *F*, *Pol*, 1978 *F*, *Ar*, *USS*, *Sp*, 1979 *F*, *Pol*, *R*, *Sp*, *F*, *Pol*, *USS*, *NZ*, *Mor*, 1980 *F*, *R*, *Fj*, *JAB*
P Marini 1949 *F*, *Cze*, 1951 *Sp*, 1953 *F*, *Ger*, *R*, 1955 *Ger*
L Martin 1997 *F*, *R*, 1998 *S*, *W*, *Rus*, *H*, *E*, 1999 *F*, *S*, *W*, *I*, *SA*, *SA*, *Ur*, *Sp*, *Fj*, *E*, 2000 *S*, *W*, *I*, *E*, *F*, *Sa*, *Fj*, *C*, *R*, *NZ*, 2001 *I*, *E*, *S*, *W*, *SA*, *Ar*, *Fj*, *SA*, *Sa*, 2002 *F*, *S*
F Martinenghi 1952 *Sp*, *Ger*
R Martinez-Frugoni 2002 *NZ*, *Sp*, *R*, 2003 *W*, *I*, *E*, *F*, *S*, *S*, *NZ*
G Martini 1965 *F*, 1967 *F*, 1968 *Pt*
R Martini 1959 *F*, 1960 *Ger*, *F*, 1961 *Ger*, *F*, 1964 *Ger*, *F*, 1965 *F*, 1968 *WGe*, *Yug*
P Masci 1948 *Cze*, 1949 *F*, *Cze*, 1952 *Sp*, *Ger*, *F*, 1953 *F*, 1954 *Sp*, 1955 *F*
M Mascioletti 1977 *Mor*, *Pol*, 1978 *Ar*, *USS*, *Sp*, 1979 *Pol*, *E*, *Sp*, *Mor*, *F*, *Pol*, *USS*, *NZ*, *Mor*, 1980 *F*, *R*, *Fj*, 1981 *WGe*, 1982 *F*, *R*, *WGe*, 1983 *F*, *R*, *USS*, *C*, *C*, *Sp*, *Mor*, *F*, *A*, *USS*, 1984 *F*, *Mor*, *Tun*, 1985 *F*, *R*, *Z*, *Z*, *USS*, *R*, 1986 *Tun*, *F*,

Pt, E, Tun, USS, 1987 *NZ, Ar, Fj,* 1989 *Sp, Ar, Z, USS,* 1990 *Pol*
A Masi 1999 *Sp,* 2003 *E, F, S, S, I, NZ, Tg, C, W,* 2004 *E, I, W, R, J, C,* 2005 *I, W, S, E, F, Ar, Ar, A,* 2006 *J, Fj, Pt, Rus,* 2007 *F, S, J, NZ, R, Pt, S,* 2008 *I, E, W, F, S, SA, A, Ar, Pl,* 2009 *E, I,* 2010 *I, E, S, F, SA, SA, Ar, A, Fj,* 2011 *I, E, W, F, S, S, A, Rus, I*
L Mastrodomenico 2000 *Sa, C, NZ,* 2001 *Nm, Ar*
I Matacchini 1948 *F, Cze,* 1949 *F, Cze,* 1954 *Sp,* 1955 *Ger, F, Sp, F*
L Mattarolo 1973 *Bor, Nat, ETv, Leo, FS, Tva, Cze*
M Mattei 1967 *R*
R Mattei 1978 *F, USS*
F Mazzantini 1965 *Cze,* 1966 *F,* 1967 *F*
M Mazzantini 2000 *S,* 2001 *S, W,* 2002 *E, NZ,* 2003 *E, F, Geo, NZ, C*
F Mazzariol 1995 *F, Ar, R, NZ,* 1996 *Pt,* 1997 *F, R, SA,* 1998 *Ar, H,* 1999 *F, SA, SA, Sp, E, NZ,* 2000 *Fj, C,* 2001 *Nm, SA, Ur, Ar, Fj, SA,* 2002 *W, NZ, Sp,* 2003 *S, I, NZ, C, W,* 2004 *R*
G Mazzi 1998 *H,* 1999 *SA, SA, Ur, Sp*
N Mazzucato 1995 *SA,* 1996 *Pt, S,* 1997 *I,* 1999 *Sp, E, Tg, NZ,* 2000 *F, Sa, Fj, R,* 2001 *Nm, SA, Ur, Ar,* 2002 *W, I, E, NZ, Sp, R, Ar, A,* 2003 *E, F, S, I, NZ, Tg, W,* 2004 *E, F, S, I, W, R, J*
I Mazzucchelli 1965 *F, Cze,* 1966 *F, Ger, R,* 1967 *F,* 1968 *Pt, WGe,* 1969 *Bul, F,* 1971 *F,* 1972 *Pt, Sp,* 1974 *WGe,* 1975 *F, R, Cze, Pol,* 1976 *F, R*
LJ McLean 2008 *SA, Ar, Pl,* 2009 *E, I, S, W, F, A, A, NZ, NZ, SA, Sa,* 2010 *I, E, S, F, W, SA, SA, Ar, A, Fj,* 2011 *I, E, W, S, J, A, Rus, US, I*
P Menapace 1996 *Pt*
E Michelon 1969 *Bel, F,* 1970 *Cze, Mad, Mad, R,* 1971 *R*
A Miele 1968 *Yug,* 1970 *Mad,* 1971 *R,* 1972 *Pt, Sp*
GE Milano 1990 *USS*
A Mioni 1955 *Ger, F, F,* 1957 *F*
A Modonesi 1929 *Sp*
L Modonesi 1966 *Ger, R,* 1967 *F, Pt, R,* 1968 *Pt, WGe,* 1970 *Cze, Mad, Mad, R,* 1971 *F,* 1974 *Leo,* 1975 *F, Sp, R, Cze*
N Molari 1957 *F,* 1958 *R*
F Molinari 1973 *NEC*
G Molinari 1948 *F*
P Monfeli 1970 *R,* 1971 *Mor, F,* 1972 *Pt,* 1976 *J, A, Sp,* 1977 *F, R, Cze, R, Sp,* 1978 *F*
JF Montauriol 2009 *E, A*
G Morelli 1988 *I,* 1989 *F, R*
G Morelli 1976 *F,* 1982 *F, R, Mor,* 1983 *R, C, Sp, A, USS,* 1984 *Mor, R, USS,* 1985 *R, EngB, Z, Z, USS, R,* 1986 *Tun, F, E, A, Tun, USS,* 1987 *F, NZ*
G Morelli 1981 *WGe,* 1982 *R, E, Mor,* 1983 *USS,* 1984 *F*
A Moreno 1999 *Tg, NZ,* 2002 *F, S,* 2008 *Ar*
A Moretti 1997 *R,* 1998 *Rus,* 1999 *Ur, Sp, Tg, NZ,* 2002 *E, NZ, Sp, R, Ar, A,* 2005 *Ar*
U Moretti 1933 *Cze,* 1934 *R,* 1935 *Cat,* 1937 *R, Ger, F,* 1942 *R*
A Morimondi 1930 *Sp,* 1933 *Cze,* 1934 *Cat,* 1935 *Cat*
A Moscardi 1993 *Pt,* 1995 *R,* 1996 *S,* 1998 *Ar, H, E,* 1999 *F, S, W, I, SA, SA, Ur, Fj, E, Tg, NZ,* 2000 *S, W, I, E, F, Sa, Fj, C, R, NZ,* 2001 *I, E, F, S, W, Nm, SA, Ur, Ar, Fj, SA, Sa,* 2002 *F, S, W, I, E*
A Muraro 2000 *C, R, NZ,* 2001 *I, E, Nm, SA, Ur, Ar, Fj, SA, Sa,* 2002 *F*

E Nathan 1930 *Sp*
G Navarini 1957 *Ger,* 1958 *R*
M Nicolosi 1982 *R*
C Nieto 2002 *E,* 2005 *Ar, Ar, A, Tg, Ar, Fj,* 2006 *I, E, F, W, J, Fj, A, Ar, C,* 2007 *F, S, W, I, Ar,* 2008 *E, F, S, SA, Ar, A, Ar, Pl,* 2009 *E, I, S, W, F*
A Nisti 1929 *Sp,* 1930 *Sp*
L Nitoglia 2004 *C, NZ, US,* 2005 *I, W, S, E, F, Ar, Tg, Ar, Fj,* 2006 *I, E, F, W, S*

F Ongaro 2000 *C,* 2001 *Nm, SA, Ur, Ar,* 2002 *Ar, A,* 2003 *E, F, S, I, Geo, NZ, Tg, C, W,* 2004 *E, F, S, I, W, R, J, C, NZ, US,* 2005 *I, W, S, E, F, Tg, Ar, Fj,* 2006 *I, E, F, W, S, J, Fj, Pt, Rus, Ar, C,* 2007 *F, S, Ur, Ar, I, NZ, S,* 2008 *F, S, SA, Ar, A, Ar, Pl,* 2009 *E, I, NZ, SA, Sa,* 2010 *I, E, S, F, W, SA, SA, Ar, A, Fj,* 2011 *I, E, S, Rus, US, I*
C Orlandi 1992 *S,* 1993 *Sp, F, Mor, F, Rus, F, S,* 1994 *Sp, CZR, H, A, A, R, W,* 1995 *S, I, Sa, E, Ar, F, Ar, R, NZ, SA,* 1996 *W, Pt, W, A, E, S,* 1997 *I, F, F, Ar, R, SA, I,* 1998 *S, W,* 2000 *W, F*
S Orlando 2004 *E, S, W, C, NZ, US,* 2005 *E, F, Ar, A,* 2006 *J,* 2007 *Ur, Ar, Pt*
L Orquera 2004 *C, NZ, US,* 2005 *I, W, S, E, F, Ar, Tg,* 2008 *A, Ar,* 2009 *W, F,* 2010 *Ar, A, Fj,* 2011 *I, E, W, F, S, J, S, A, US, I*
A Osti 1981 *F, R, USS,* 1982 *E, Mor,* 1983 *R, C, A, USS,* 1984 *R, USS,* 1985 *F,* 1986 *Tun,* 1988 *R*

S Pace 2001 *SA, Sa,* 2005 *Fj*
S Pace 1977 *Mor,* 1984 *R, Tun*
P Pacifici 1969 *Bul, Sp, F,* 1970 *Cze, Mad, Mad, R,* 1971 *Mor, F*
R Paciucci 1937 *R, Ger, F*
F Paganelli 1972 *Sp*
S Palmer 2002 *Ar, A,* 2003 *I, E, F, S, S, NZ, C, W,* 2004 *I, R*
P Paoletti 1972 *Pt, Sp, Yug,* 1973 *Pt, Rho, WTv, Bor, NEC, Nat, ETv, Leo, FS, Tva,* 1974 *Mid, Oxo, WGe, Leo,* 1975 *F, Sp,* 1976 *R*
T Paoletti 2000 *S, W, I, E, F, Sa, C, R, NZ,* 2001 *F, Nm, Ur, Ar, Fj, SA*
G Paolin 1929 *Sp*
S Parisse 2002 *NZ, Sp, R, Ar, A,* 2003 *S, I, Geo, NZ, Tg, C, W,* 2004 *E, F, S,* 2005 *I, W, S, E, F, Ar, Ar, A, Tg, Ar, Fj,* 2006 *I, E, F, W, S, Fj, Pt, Rus, A, Ar, C,* 2007 *F, E, S, W, I, J, I, NZ, R, Pt, S,* 2008 *I, E, W, F, S, Ar, A, Ar, Pl,* 2009 *E, I, S, W, F, A, A, NZ, NZ, SA,* 2010 *SA, SA, Ar, A, Fj,* 2011 *I, E, W, F, S, J, S, A, Rus, US, I*
E Parmiggiani 1942 *R,* 1948 *Cze*
P Paselli 1929 *Sp,* 1930 *Sp,* 1933 *Cze*
E Passarotto 1975 *Sp*
E Patrizio 2007 *Ur,* 2008 *F, S, SA*
R Pavan 2008 *SA*
A Pavanello 2007 *Ar,* 2009 *SA, Sa*
E Pavanello 2002 *R, Ar, A,* 2004 *R, J, C, NZ, US,* 2005 *Ar, A*
P Pavesi 1977 *Pol,* 1979 *Mor,* 1980 *USS*
M Pavin 1980 *USS,* 1986 *F, Pt, E, A, Tun, USS,* 1987 *Ar*
R Pedrazzi 2001 *Nm, Ar,* 2002 *F, S, W,* 2005 *S, E, F*
P Pedroni 1989 *Z, USS,* 1990 *F, Pol, R,* 1991 *F, R, Nm,* 1993 *Rus, F,* 1994 *Sp, R, CZR, H,* 1995 *I, Sa, E, Ar, F, Ar, R, NZ, SA,* 1996 *W, W*
G Peens 2002 *W, I, E, NZ, Sp, R, Ar, A,* 2003 *E, F, S, S, I, Geo, NZ,* 2004 *NZ,* 2005 *E, F, Ar, Ar, A,* 2006 *Pt, A*
L Pelliccione 1983 *Sp, Mor, F*
L Pelliccione 1977 *Pol*
M Percudani 1952 *F,* 1954 *F,* 1955 *Ger, Sp, F, Cze,* 1956 *Cze,* 1957 *F,* 1958 *R*
F Perrini 1955 *Sp, F, Cze,* 1956 *Ger, F, Cze,* 1957 *F,* 1958 *F,* 1959 *F,* 1962 *R,* 1963 *F*
F Perrone 1951 *Sp*
AR Persico 2000 *S, W, E, F, Sa, Fj,* 2001 *F, S, W, Nm, SA, Ur, Ar, Fj, SA, Sa,* 2002 *F, S, W, I, E, NZ, Sp, R, Ar, A,* 2003 *W, I, E, F, S, I, Geo, Tg, C, W,* 2004 *E, F, S, I, W, R, J, C, NZ,* 2005 *I, W, S, E, F, Ar, Ar, Tg, Ar,* 2006 *I, E*
J Pertile 1994 *R,* 1995 *Ar,* 1996 *W, A, E, S,* 1997 *I, F, SA,* 1998 *Rus,* 1999 *S, W, I, SA, SA*
S Perugini 2000 *I, F, Sa, Fj,* 2001 *S, W, Nm, SA, Ur, Ar,* 2002 *W, I,* 2003 *W, S, Geo, NZ, Tg, W,* 2004 *E, F, I, W, C, NZ, US,* 2005 *I, W, S, E, F,* 2006 *I, E, F, W, S, Pt, Rus,* 2007 *F, E, S, W, I, J, I, NZ, Pt, S,* 2008 *I, E, W, F, S, A, Ar, Pl,* 2009 *E, I, S, W, F, A, A, NZ, NZ, SA, Sa,* 2010 *I, E, S, F, W, SA, SA, Ar, Fj,* 2011 *I, E, W, F, S, Rus, US, I*
L Perziano 1993 *Pt*
M Perziano 2000 *NZ,* 2001 *F, S, W, Nm, SA, Ur, Ar, Fj, SA*
V Pesce 1988 *I,* 1989 *R*
P Pescetto 1956 *Ger, Cze,* 1957 *F*
G Petralia 1984 *F*
R Pez 2000 *Sa, Fj, C, R, NZ,* 2001 *I,* 2002 *S, W, E, A,* 2003 *I, E, F, S, S, Geo,* 2005 *Ar, A, Tg, Ar, Fj,* 2006 *I, E, F, W, S, J, Fj, Pt, Rus, A, Ar,* 2007 *F, E, S, W, I, J, R, S*
M Phillips 2002 *F, S, W, I, E,* 2003 *W, I, E, F, S, S, I, NZ, W*
G Pianna 1934 *R,* 1935 *Cat, F,* 1936 *Ger, R,* 1938 *Ger*
A Piazza 1990 *USS*
F Piccini 1963 *F,* 1964 *Ger,* 1966 *F*
S Picone 2004 *I, W,* 2005 *F,* 2006 *E, F, S, J, Pt, Rus, Ar, C,* 2008 *E, W, F, S, SA, Ar,* 2009 *NZ, SA, Sa,* 2010 *I, SA, SA*
F Pietroscanti 1987 *USS, Sp,* 1988 *A, I,* 1989 *F, R, Sp, Ar, Z, USS,* 1990 *F, Pol, R, H,* 1991 *Nm, Nm,* 1992 *Sp, F, R,* 1993 *Sp, Mor, Sp, F, Rus, F*
F Pignotti 1968 *WGe, Yug,* 1969 *Bul, Sp, Bel*
C Pilat 1997 *I,* 1998 *S, W,* 2000 *E, Sa,* 2001 *I, W*
MJ Pini 1998 *H, E,* 1999 *F, Ur, Fj, E, Tg, NZ,* 2000 *S, W, I, F*

THE COUNTRIES

M Piovan 1973 Pt, 1974 Pt, Mid, Sus, Oxo, 1976 A, 1977 F, Mor, R, 1979 F
R Piovan 1996 Pt, 1997 R, 2000 R, NZ
M Piovene 1995 NZ
E Piras 1971 R
M Pisaneschi 1948 Cze, 1949 Cze, 1953 F, Ger, R, 1954 Sp, F, 1955 Ger, F, Sp, F, Cze
F Pitorri 1948 Cze, 1949 F
M Pitorri 1973 NEC
G Pivetta 1979 R, E, Mor, 1980 Coo, USS, 1981 R, USS, WGe, 1982 F, R, WGe, Mor, 1983 F, USS, C, Sp, Mor, F, USS, 1984 F, Mor, R, Tun, 1985 F, R, Sp, Z, Z, 1986 Pt, 1987 Sp, 1989 R, Sp, 1990 F, Pol, R, Sp, R, USS, 1991 F, R, Nm, Nm, US, E, NZ, USS, 1992 Sp, F, R, R, 1993 Cro, Mor, Sp
M Platania 1994 F, 1995 F, R, 1996 Pt
I Ponchia 1955 F, Sp, F, Cze, 1956 F, 1957 Ger, 1958 F
E Ponzi 1973 Cze, A, 1974 WGe, 1975 F, Sp, R, Cze, E, Pol, H, Sp, 1976 F, R, J, A, Sp, 1977 F, Mor, Pol, R
G Porcellato 1989 R
G Porzio 1970 Cze, Mad, Mad
C Possamai 1970 Cze, Mad, Mad
W Pozzebon 2001 I, E, F, S, W, Nm, SA, Ur, Ar, Fj, SA, Sa, 2002 NZ, Sp, 2004 R, J, C, NZ, US, 2005 W, E, 2006 C
C Pratichetti 1988 R, 1990 Pol
M Pratichetti 2004 NZ, 2007 E, W, I, Ur, Ar, I, Pt, 2008 SA, Ar, Ar, PI, 2009 E, I, S, W, F, A, NZ, SA, 2010 W, SA, 2011 J, Rus
G Preo 1999 I, 2000 I, E, Sa, Fj, R, NZ
P Presutti 1974 Mid, Sus, Oxo, 1977 Pol, Cze, R, Sp, 1978 F
FP Properzi-Curti 1990 Pol, Sp, H, R, 1991 F, Nm, Nm, US, E, NZ, 1992 Sp, F, R, 1993 Cro, Mor, F, Rus, F, S, 1994 Sp, R, H, A, A, 1995 S, I, Sa, E, Ar, NZ, SA, 1996 W, Pt, W, A, E, 1997 I, F, F, Ar, SA, 1998 Ar, 1999 S, W, I, SA, SA, Ur, E, Tg, NZ, 2001 F, S, W
C Prosperini 1966 R, 1967 F, Pt, R
F Pucciarello 1999 Sp, Fj, E, 2002 S, W, I, E, Ar
G Puglisi 1971 F, 1972 Yug, 1973 Cze
M Pulli 1968 Pt, 1972 Pt, Pt
A Puppo 1972 Pt, Pt, Sp, Sp, 1973 Pt, Rho, WTv, Bor, NEC, Nat, ETv, Leo, FS, Tva, 1974 Mid, Sus, Oxo, WGe, Leo, 1977 R

I Quaglio 1970 R, 1971 R, 1972 Pt, Sp, 1973 WTv, Bor, NEC, Nat, Leo, FS, Tva, 1975 H, Sp, 1976 F, R
M Quaglio 1984 Tun, 1988 F, R
R Quartaroli 2009 W, F, A
JM Queirolo 2000 Sa, Fj, 2001 E, F, Fj, 2002 NZ, Sp, A, 2003 Geo
P Quintavala 1958 R

C Raffo 1929 Sp, 1930 Sp, 1933 Cze, Cze, 1937 R, Bel
G Raineri 1998 H, 2000 Fj, R, NZ, 2001 I, E, S, W, Nm, SA, Ur, Ar, 2002 W, I, E, NZ, 2003 W, I, E, F, S, Geo
G Raisi 1956 Ger, F, 1957 F, Ger, 1960 Ger, 1964 Ger, F
R Rampazzo 1996 W, 1999 I
M Ravazzolo 1993 Cro, Sp, F, F, S, 1994 Sp, R, CZR, H, 1995 S, I, Sa, F, Ar, NZ, 1996 W, Pt, W, A, 1997 F, Ar, R, SA
A Re Garbagnati 1936 Ger, R, 1937 Ger, Bel, Ger, F, 1938 Ger, 1939 Ger, R, 1940 R, Ger, 1942 R
P Reale 1987 USS, Sp, 1988 USS, A, I, 1989 Z, 1992 S
T Reato 2008 I, SA, Ar, A, Ar, PI, 2009 E, I, A
G Riccardi 1955 Ger, F, Sp, F, Cze, 1956 F, Cze
G Ricci 1967 Pt, 1969 Bul, Sp, Bel, F
G Ricciarelli 1962 Ger
L Riccioni 1951 Sp, 1952 Sp, Ger, F, 1953 F, Ger, 1954 F
S Rigo 1992 S, 1993 Sp, F, Pt
A Rinaldo 1977 Mor, Pol, R, Cze
W Rista 1968 Yug, 1969 Bul, Sp, Bel, F
M Rivaro 2000 S, W, I, 2001 E
M Rizzo 2005 A, 2008 SA
G Rizzoli 1935 F, 1936 Ger, R
C Robazza 1978 Ar, Sp, 1979 F, Pol, R, E, Sp, F, Pol, USS, NZ, Mor, 1980 F, R, Fj, JAB, Coo, Pol, Sp, 1981 F, R, USS, WGe, 1982 E, WGe, 1983 F, USS, C, Mor, F, 1984 F, Tun, 1985 F
KP Robertson 2004 R, J, C, NZ, US, 2005 I, W, S, F, Ar, Ar, A, 2006 Pt, Rus, 2007 F, E, S, W, I, Ur, Ar, J, I, NZ, R, S, 2008 I, E, F, S, SA, Ar, A, Ar, PI, 2009 E, I, A, NZ, NZ, Sa, 2010 I, E, S, F, W, SA
A Rocca 1973 WTv, Bor, NEC, 1977 R
G Romagnoli 1965 F, Cze, 1967 Pt, R
S Romagnoli 1982 Mor, 1984 R, Tun, USS, 1985 F, Z, Z, 1986 Tun, Pt, A, Tun, USS, 1987 Pt, F, Fj
G Romano 1942 R
P Romano 1942 R
F Roselli 1995 F, R, 1996 W, 1998 Rus, Ar, H, E, 1999 F, S, W, I, SA, SA, Ur, Fj, Tg
P Rosi 1948 F, Cze, 1949 F, Cze, 1951 Sp, 1952 Ger, F, 1953 F, Ger, R, 1954 Sp, F
G Rossi 1981 USS, WGe, 1982 E, WGe, Mor, 1983 F, R, USS, C, C, Mor, F, A, USS, 1984 Mor, 1985 F, R, EngB, Sp, Z, USS, R, 1986 Tun, F, E, A, Tun, USS, 1987 R, NZ, Ar, USS, Sp, 1988 USS, A, I, 1989 F, R, Sp, Ar, Z, USS, 1990 F, R, 1991 R
N Rossi 1973 Yug, 1974 Pt, Mid, Sus, Oxo, WGe, Leo, 1975 Sp, Cze, E, H, 1976 J, A, Sp, 1977 Cze, 1980 USS
Z Rossi 1959 F, 1961 Ger, F, 1962 F, Ger, R
E Rossini 1948 F, Cze, 1949 F, Cze, 1951 Sp, 1952 Ger
B Rovelli 1960 Ger, F, 1961 Ger, F
G Rubini 2009 S, W, F, A
A Russo 1986 E

D Sacca 2003 I
R Saetti 1988 USS, I, 1989 F, R, Sp, Ar, Z, USS, 1990 F, Sp, H, R, USS, 1991 R, Nm, Nm, US, E, 1992 R
R Saetti 1957 Ger, 1958 F, R, 1959 F, 1960 F, 1961 Ger, F, 1964 Ger, F
A Sagramora 1970 Mad, Mad, 1971 R
E Saibene 1957 F, Ger
C Salmasco 1965 F, 1967 F
L Salsi 1971 Mor, 1972 Pt, Sp, Yug, 1973 Pt, Rho, WTv, Nat, ETv, Leo, FS, Tva, Cze, Yug, A, 1974 Pt, Oxo, WGe, Leo, 1975 Sp, R, Sp, 1977 R, Pol, Cze, R, Sp, 1978 F
F Salvadego 1985 Z
R Salvan 1973 Yug, 1974 Pt
L Salvati 1987 USS, 1988 USS, I
R Santofadre 1952 Sp, Ger, F, 1954 Sp, F
F Sartorato 1956 Ger, F, 1957 F
M Savi 2004 R, J, 2005 E
S Saviozzi 1998 Rus, H, 1999 W, I, SA, SA, Ur, Fj, Tg, NZ, 2000 C, NZ, 2002 NZ, Sp
F Sbaraglini 2009 S, F, A, NZ, 2010 SA
D Scaglia 1994 R, W, 1995 S, 1996 W, A, 1999 W
E Scalzotto 1974 Mid, Sus, Oxo
A Scanavacca 1999 Ur, 2001 E, 2002 Sp, R, 2004 US, 2006 Ar, C, 2007 F, E, S, I
R Sciacol 1965 Cze
I Scodavolpe 1954 Sp
F Screnci 1977 Cze, R, Sp, 1978 F, 1979 Pol, R, E, 1982 F, 1984 Mor
A Selvaggio 1973 Rho, WTv, ETv, Leo, FS, Tva
F Semenzato 2011 E, W, F, S, S, A, US, I
M Sepe 2006 J, Fj, 2010 SA
D Sesenna 1992 R, 1993 Cro, Mor, F, 1994 R
G Sessa 1930 Sp
G Sessi 1942 R
A Sgarbi 2008 E, W, 2009 A, A, SA, 2010 Ar, A, Fj, 2011 I, E, W, S, J, Rus
E Sgorbati 1968 WGe, Yug
E Sgorbati 1933 Cze, 1934 Cat, R, 1935 Cat, F, 1936 Ger, 1937 Ger, 1938 Ger, 1939 Ger, 1940 R, Ger, 1942 R
A Sgorlon 1993 Pt, Mor, Sp, F, Rus, F, S, 1994 CZR, R, W, 1995 S, E, Ar, F, Ar, R, NZ, SA, 1996 W, Pt, W, A, E, S, 1997 I, F, F, Ar, R, SA, I, 1998 S, W, Rus, 1999 F, S, W
P Sguario 1958 R, 1959 F, 1960 Ger, F, 1961 Ger, 1962 R
M Silini 1955 Ger, Sp, F, Cze, 1956 Cze, 1957 Ger, 1958 F, 1959 F
S Silvestri 1954 F
U Silvestri 1967 Pt, R, 1968 Pt, WGe
U Silvestri 1949 F, Cze
L Simonelli 1956 Ger, F, Cze, 1958 F, 1960 Ger, F
F Sinitich 1980 Fj, Coo, Pol, Sp, 1981 R, 1983 USS
JW Sole 2005 Ar, Tg, Ar, 2006 I, E, F, W, S, J, Fj, Rus, A, Ar, C, 2007 F, E, I, Ur, Ar, J, I, R, S, 2008 I, E, W, F, S, SA, Ar, A, Ar, PI, 2009 E, I, S, W, F, NZ, SA, Sa, 2010 I, E, S, F, W, 2011 I
F Soro 1965 Cze, 1966 F, Ger, R
A Spagnoli 1973 Rho
E Speziali 1965 Cze
W Spragg 2006 C
F Staibano 2006 J, Fj, 2007 W, I, Ur, Ar, 2009 A, A, NZ
MP Stanojevic 2006 Pt, Rus, A, Ar, C, 2007 J, NZ
U Stenta 1937 Bel, Ger, F, 1938 Ger, 1939 Ger, R, 1940 R, Ger, 1942 R

P Stievano 1948 *F*, 1952 *F*, 1953 *F*, *Ger*, *R*, 1954 *Sp*, *F*, 1955 *Ger*
S Stocco 1998 *H*, 1999 *S*, *I*, 2000 *Fj*
CA Stoica 1997 *I*, *F*, *SA*, *I*, 1998 *S*, *W*, *Rus*, *Ar*, *H*, *E*, 1999 *S*, *W*, *SA*, *SA*, *Ur*, *Sp*, *Fj*, *E*, *Tg*, *NZ*, 2000 *S*, *W*, *I*, *E*, *F*, *Sa*, *Fj*, *C*, *R*, *NZ*, 2001 *I*, *E*, *F*, *S*, *W*, *Fj*, *SA*, *Sa*, 2002 *F*, *S*, *W*, *I*, *E*, *Sp*, *R*, *Ar*, *A*, 2003 *W*, *I*, *S*, *I*, *Geo*, *Tg*, *C*, *W*, 2004 *E*, *F*, *S*, *I*, *W*, *US*, 2005 *S*, *Tg*, *Ar*, 2006 *I*, *E*, *F*, *W*, *S*, 2007 *Ur*, *Ar*

L Tagliabue 1930 *Sp*, 1933 *Cze*, *Cze*, 1934 *Cat*, *R*, 1935 *F*, 1937 *Ger*
S Tartaglini 1948 *Cze*, 1949 *F*, *Cze*, 1951 *Sp*, 1952 *Sp*, *Ger*, *F*, 1953 *F*
A Tassin 1973 *A*
A Taveggia 1954 *F*, 1955 *Ger*, *F*, *Sp*, *F*, 1956 *Ger*, *F*, *Cze*, 1957 *F*, *Ger*, 1958 *F*, *R*, 1959 *F*, 1960 *Ger*, *F*, 1967 *Pt*
D Tebaldi 1985 *Z*, *Z*, 1987 *R*, *Ar*, *Fj*, *USS*, *Sp*, 1988 *F*, *A*, *I*, 1989 *F*, 1990 *F*, *Pol*, *R*, 1991 *Nm*
T Tebaldi 2009 *A*, *A*, *NZ*, *NZ*, *SA*, *Sa*, 2010 *I*, *E*, *S*, *F*, *W*, *SA*, *SA*, *Ar*
T Tedeschi 1948 *F*
G Testoni 1937 *Bel*, 1938 *Ger*, 1942 *R*
C Tinari 1980 *JAB*, *Coo*, *Pol*, *USS*, *Sp*, 1981 *USS*, *WGe*, 1982 *F*, *WGe*, 1983 *R*, *USS*, *C*, *C*, *Sp*, *Mor*, *A*, *USS*, 1984 *Mor*, *R*
M Tommasi 1990 *Pol*, 1992 *R*, *S*, 1993 *Pt*, *Cro*, *Sp*, *F*
G Toniolatti 2008 *A*, 2009 *E*, *I*, *A*, *NZ*, 2011 *J*, *Rus*, *US*
C Torresan 1980 *F*, *R*, *Fj*, *Coo*, *Pol*, *USS*, 1981 *R*, *USS*, 1982 *R*, *Mor*, 1983 *C*, *F*, *A*, *USS*, 1984 *F*, *Mor*, *Tun*, *USS*, 1985 *Z*, *Z*, *USS*
F Tozzi 1933 *Cze*
P Travagli 2004 *C*, *NZ*, 2008 *I*, *E*, *W*, *F*, *S*, *Ar*, *Pl*
L Travini 1999 *SA*, *Ur*, *Sp*, *Fj*, 2000 *I*
F Trebbi 1933 *Cze*, *Cze*
F Trentin 1979 *Mor*, *F*, *Pol*, *USS*, 1981 *R*
M Trevisiol 1988 *F*, *USS*, *A*, *I*, 1989 *F*, *Ar*, *USS*, 1994 *R*
M Trippiteli 1979 *Pol*, 1980 *Pol*, *Sp*, 1981 *F*, *R*, 1982 *F*, *E*, *WGe*, 1984 *Tun*
LR Troiani 1985 *R*, 1986 *Tun*, *F*, *Pt*, *A*, *USS*, 1987 *Pt*, *F*, 1988 *R*, *USS*, *A*, *I*, 1989 *Sp*, *Ar*, *Z*, *USS*, 1990 *F*, *Pol*, *R*, *Sp*, *H*, *R*, *USS*, 1991 *F*, *R*, *Nm*, *Nm*, *US*, *E*, 1992 *Sp*, *F*, *R*, *R*, *S*, 1993 *Sp*, *F*, *Cro*, *Rus*, *F*, 1994 *Sp*, *CZR*, *A*, *A*, *F*, 1995 *S*, *E*, *Ar*
A Troncon 1994 *Sp*, *R*, *CZR*, *H*, *A*, *A*, *R*, *W*, *F*, 1995 *S*, *I*, *Sa*, *E*, *Ar*, *F*, *Ar*, *R*, *NZ*, *SA*, 1996 *W*, *W*, *A*, *E*, *S*, 1997 *I*, *F*, *F*, *Ar*, *SA*, *I*, 1998 *S*, *W*, *Rus*, *Ar*, *H*, *E*, 1999 *F*, *S*, *W*, *I*, *Ur*, *Sp*, *Fj*, *E*, *Tg*, *NZ*, 2000 *S*, *W*, *I*, *E*, *F*, *R*, *NZ*, 2001 *I*, *F*, *Nm*, *SA*, *Ur*, *Ar*, *Fj*, *SA*, *Sa*, 2002 *F*, *S*, *W*, *I*, *E*, *Sp*, *R*, *Ar*, *A*, 2003 *W*, *I*, *E*, *F*, *S*, *S*, *I*, *Geo*, *NZ*, *Tg*, *C*, *W*, 2004 *R*, *J*, 2005 *I*, *W*, *S*, *E*, *F*, 2007 *F*, *E*, *S*, *W*, *I*, *J*, *I*, *NZ*, *R*, *Pt*, *S*
G Troncon 1962 *F*, *Ger*, *R*, 1963 *F*, 1964 *Ger*, *F*, 1965 *Cze*, 1966 *F*, *R*, 1967 *F*, 1968 *Yug*, 1972 *Pt*
L Turcato 1952 *Sp*, *Ger*, *F*, 1953 *Ger*, *R*
M Turcato 1949 *F*, 1951 *Sp*

P Vaccari 1991 *Nm*, *Nm*, *US*, *E*, *NZ*, *USS*, 1992 *Sp*, *F*, *R*, *R*, *S*, 1993 *Mor*, *Sp*, *F*, *Rus*, *F*, *S*, 1994 *Sp*, *R*, *CZR*, *H*, *A*, *A*, *R*, *W*, *F*, 1995 *I*, *Sa*, *E*, *Ar*, *F*, *Ar*, *R*, *NZ*, *SA*, 1996 *W*, *W*, *E*, *S*, 1997 *I*, *F*, *F*, *Ar*, *R*, *SA*, *I*, 1998 *S*, *W*, *Ar*, 1999 *Ur*, *Sp*, *E*, *Tg*, *NZ*, 2001 *Fj*, 2002 *F*, *S*, *Ar*, *A*, 2003 *W*, *I*, *E*, *F*, *S*
V Vagnetti 1939 *R*, 1940 *R*
F Valier 1968 *Yug*, 1969 *F*, 1970 *Cze*, *R*, 1971 *Mor*, *R*, 1972 *Pt*
L Valtorta 1957 *Ger*, 1958 *F*
C Van Zyl 2011 *J*, *S*, *A*, *Rus*, *US*, *I*
O Vene 1966 *F*
E Venturi 1983 *C*, 1985 *EngB*, *Sp*, 1986 *Tun*, *Pt*, 1988 *USS*, *A*, 1989 *F*, *R*, *Sp*, *Ar*, *USS*, 1990 *F*, *Pol*, *R*, *Sp*, *H*, *R*, *USS*, 1991 *F*, *R*, *NZ*, *USS*, 1992 *Sp*, *F*, *R*, 1993 *Sp*, *F*
P Vezzani 1973 *Yug*, 1975 *F*, *Sp*, *R*, *Cze*, *E*, *Pol*, *H*, *Sp*, 1976 *F*
F Vialetto 1972 *Yug*
V Viccariotto 1948 *F*
S Vigliano 1937 *R*, *Bel*, *Ger*, *F*, 1939 *R*, 1942 *R*
L Villagra 2000 *Sa*, *Fj*
E Vinci I 1929 *Sp*
P Vinci II 1929 *Sp*, 1930 *Sp*, 1933 *Cze*
F Vinci III 1929 *Sp*, 1930 *Sp*, 1934 *Cat*, *R*, 1935 *Cat*, *F*, 1936 *Ger*, *R*, 1937 *Ger*, *R*, *Ger*, *F*, 1939 *Ger*, *R*, 1940 *Ger*
P Vinci IV 1929 *Sp*, 1930 *Sp*, 1933 *Cze*, *Cze*, 1934 *Cat*, *R*, 1935 *Cat*, *F*, 1937 *Ger*, *Bel*, *Ger*, *F*, 1939 *Ger*
A Visentin 1970 *R*, 1972 *Pt*, *Sp*, 1973 *Rho*, *WTv*, *Bor*, *NEC*, *Nat*, *ETv*, *Leo*, *FS*, *Tva*, *Cze*, *Yug*, *A*, 1974 *Pt*, *Leo*, 1975 *F*, *Sp*, *R*, *Cze*, 1976 *R*, 1978 *Ar*
G Visentin 1935 *Cat*, *F*, 1936 *R*, 1937 *Ger*, *Bel*, *Ger*, *F*, 1938 *Ger*, 1939 *Ger*
T Visentin 1996 *W*
W Visser 1999 *I*, *SA*, *SA*, 2000 *S*, *W*, *I*, *F*, *C*, *R*, *NZ*, 2001 *I*, *E*, *F*, *S*, *W*, *Nm*, *SA*, *Ur*, *Ar*, *Fj*, *SA*, *Sa*
F Vitadello 1985 *Sp*, 1987 *Pt*
C Vitelli 1973 *Cze*, *Yug*, 1974 *Pt*, *Sus*
I Vittorini 1969 *Sp*
RMS Vosawai 2007 *J*, *I*, *NZ*, *R*, *Pt*, 2010 *W*, *SA*, 2011 *W*

RS Wakarua 2003 *Tg*, *C*, *W*, 2004 *E*, *F*, *S*, *W*, *J*, *C*, *NZ*, 2005 *Fj*
F Williams 1995 *SA*

M Zaffiri 2000 *Fj*, *R*, *NZ*, 2001 *W*, 2003 *S*, 2005 *Tg*, *Fj*, 2006 *W*, *S*, *C*, 2007 *E*, *S*, *W*, *I*
R Zanatta 1954 *Sp*, *F*
G Zanchi 1953 *Ger*, *R*, 1955 *Sp*, *Cze*, 1957 *Ger*
A Zanella 1977 *Mor*
M Zanella 1976 *J*, *Sp*, 1977 *R*, *Pol*, *Cze*, 1978 *Ar*, 1980 *Pol*, *USS*
E Zanetti 1942 *R*
F Zani 1960 *Ger*, *F*, 1961 *Ger*, *F*, 1962 *F*, *R*, 1963 *F*, 1964 *F*, 1965 *F*, 1966 *Ger*, *R*
G Zani 1934 *R*
A Zanni 2005 *Tg*, *Ar*, *Fj*, 2006 *F*, *W*, *S*, *Pt*, *Rus*, *A*, *Ar*, *C*, 2007 *S*, *W*, *I*, *Ur*, *I*, *NZ*, 2008 *I*, *E*, *W*, *F*, *S*, *SA*, *Ar*, *A*, *Pl*, 2009 *E*, *I*, *S*, *W*, *F*, *A*, *A*, *NZ*, *NZ*, *SA*, *Sa*, 2010 *I*, *E*, *S*, *F*, *W*, *SA*, *SA*, *Ar*, *A*, *Fj*, 2011 *I*, *E*, *W*, *F*, *S*, *J*, *S*, *A*, *Rus*, *US*, *I*
C Zanoletti 2001 *Sa*, 2002 *E*, *NZ*, *R*, *Ar*, *A*, 2005 *A*
G Zanon 1981 *F*, *R*, *USS*, *WGe*, 1982 *R*, *E*, *WGe*, *Mor*, 1983 *F*, *R*, *USS*, *C*, *C*, *Sp*, *Mor*, *F*, *A*, *USS*, 1984 *F*, *Mor*, *R*, *USS*, 1985 *F*, *R*, *EngB*, *Sp*, *Z*, *Z*, *USS*, 1986 *USS*, 1987 *R*, *Ar*, *USS*, 1989 *Sp*, *Ar*, 1990 *F*, *Pol*, *R*, *Sp*, *H*, *R*, *USS*, 1991 *Nm*, *US*, *E*
M Zingarelli 1973 *A*
N Zisti 1999 *E*, *NZ*, 2000 *E*, *F*
G Zoffoli 1936 *Ger*, *R*, 1937 *Ger*, *R*, *Ger*, 1938 *Ger*, 1939 *R*
S Zorzi 1985 *R*, 1986 *Tun*, *F*, 1988 *F*, *R*, *USS*, 1992 *R*
A Zucchelo 1956 *Ger*, *F*
C Zucchi 1952 *Sp*, 1953 *F*
L Zuin 1977 *Cze*, 1978 *Ar*, *USS*, *Sp*, 1979 *F*, *Pol*, *R*

JAPAN

JAPAN'S 2010–11 TEST RECORD

OPPONENTS	DATE	VENUE	RESULT
Samoa	30 Oc	H	**Lost** 13–10
Russia	6 Nov	H	**Won** 75–3
Hong Kong	30 April	A	**Won** 45–22
Kazakhstan	7 May	A	**Won** 61–0
UAE	13 May	A	**Won** 111–0
Sri Lanka	21 May	A	**Won** 90–13
Samoa	2 July	H	**Lost** 34–15
Tonga	9 July	N	**Won** 28–27
Fiji	13 July	A	**Won** 24–13
Italy	13 Aug	A	**Lost** 31–24
United States	21 Aug	H	**Won** 20–14
France	10 Sept	N	**Lost** 47–21
New Zealand	16 Sept	A	**Lost** 83–7
Tonga	21 Sept	N	**Lost** 31–8
Canada	27 Sept	N	**Drew** 23–23

KIRWAN DEPARTS ON SAD NOTE

By Rich Freeman

Phil Walter/Getty Images

John Kirwan achieved a huge amount in his time with Japan.

Japan's Rugby World Cup 2011 campaign was supposed to be the dawn of a new era – a chance to show the world that the Land of the Rising Sun was capable of competing with the big boys.

But in the end, it was a case of "been there, done that," as once again the Brave Blossoms returned home empty handed.

A tournament that started so well ended in tears as Japan failed to pick up the two wins they had targeted, their sole points coming from a draw with Canada, the second time they have shared the honours with their oldest international rival at rugby's flagship event.

"England, France, the All Blacks are coming to win it. Others are coming to make the quarter-finals. Our goal is to win at least two games and to show the world how far we've come," was the message from coach John Kirwan as the Brave Blossoms were welcomed to the tournament.

The optimism was based on a good performance in the IRB Pacific Nations Cup, which Japan had won for the first time.

And for 60 minutes against France it looked as if Japan really were in New Zealand to compete with the best.

James Arlidge put in a masterful performance at fly-half, scoring 21 points, as Japan closed to within four points midway through the second half.

But an inability to turn pressure into points allowed the French to regroup and three late tries flattered Les Bleus as they ran out 47–21 winners.

"We look at this game as if we are equals. We will wake up tomorrow disappointed. We will work hard and move forward," said Kirwan, who admitted his team had failed to make the most of the window of opportunity that had presented itself to win the game.

To make matters worse, No. 8 Ryu Koliniasi Holani was forced to return home after damaging his knee – a blow that Kirwan described as having a huge impact on the squad.

Japan's second game was against New Zealand and with Kirwan mindful of the "winnable" games against Tonga and Canada, the former All Black decided to rest most of his first-choice players.

The decision was accepted by most overseas observers, particularly as Japan picked up a couple more serious injuries. But in Japan the news was given a mixed reception, and the 83–7 loss did nothing to quieten the growing number of dissenters.

"Obviously we are disappointed with the scoreline," Kirwan said after the game that saw Hirotoki Onozawa join an elite band of players to score in three different World Cups. "I think in the first half we missed 13 tackles, and if you miss one tackle against the All Blacks you could lose the game."

With little time to recover, the squad travelled from Hamilton to Whangarei to take on Tonga, a team Japan had not lost to with Kirwan at the helm.

Sadly, a mistake by the otherwise impressive Takashi Kikutani in the first minute set the tone for the game as Japan lost 31–18.

"It's very disappointing for us – I don't think we played particularly well, and it makes the last game important to win. We haven't won a [RWC] game in 20 years," said Kirwan.

And that unwanted record will continue for another four years after Japan drew the final game 23–23, having led by eight points with six minutes remaining.

The Japan Rugby Football Union weren't happy, saying the team had failed to improve, and Kirwan decided not to renew his contract when it expired on 31 December.

It seems the dawn must wait a further four years at least.

JAPAN INTERNATIONAL STATISTICS

MATCH RECORDS UP TO 31 OCTOBER 2011

WINNING MARGIN

Date	Opponent	Result	Winning Margin
06/07/2002	Chinese Taipei	155–3	**152**
27/10/1998	Chinese Taipei	134–6	**128**
21/07/2002	Chinese Taipei	120–3	**117**
13/05/2011	United Arab Emirates	111–0	**111**
03/05/2008	Arabian Gulf	114–6	**108**

MOST POINTS IN A MATCH

BY THE TEAM

Date	Opponent	Result	Points
06/07/2002	Chinese Taipei	155–3	**155**
27/10/1998	Chinese Taipei	134–6	**134**
21/07/2002	Chinese Taipei	120–3	**120**
03/05/2008	Arabian Gulf	114–6	**114**
13/05/2011	United Arab Emirates	111–0	**111**

BY A PLAYER

Date	Player	Opponent	Points
21/07/2002	Toru Kurihara	Chinese Taipei	**60**
06/07/2002	Daisuke Ohata	Chinese Taipei	**40**
16/06/2002	Toru Kurihara	Korea	**35**
08/05/1999	Keiji Hirose	Tonga	**34**
08/05/2005	Keiji Hirose	Hong Kong	**31**

MOST TRIES IN A MATCH

BY THE TEAM

Date	Opponent	Result	Tries
06/07/2002	Chinese Taipei	155–3	**23**
27/10/1998	Chinese Taipei	134–6	**20**
21/07/2002	Chinese Taipei	120–3	**18**
03/05/2008	Arabian Gulf	114–6	**18**
13/05/2011	United Arab Emirates	111–0	**17**

BY A PLAYER

Date	Player	Opponent	Tries
06/07/2002	Daisuke Ohata	Chinese Taipei	**8**
21/07/2002	Toru Kurihara	Chinese Taipei	**6**
08/05/2005	Daisuke Ohata	Hong Kong	**6**

MOST CONVERSIONS IN A MATCH

BY THE TEAM

Date	Opponent	Result	Cons
06/07/2002	Chinese Taipei	155–3	**20**
27/10/1998	Chinese Taipei	134–6	**17**
21/07/2002	Chinese Taipei	120–3	**15**

BY A PLAYER

Date	Player	Opponent	Cons
21/07/2002	Toru Kurihara	Chinese Taipei	**15**
06/07/2002	Andy Miller	Chinese Taipei	**12**
13/05/2011	James Arlidge	United Arab Emirates	**12**

MOST PENALTIES IN A MATCH

BY THE TEAM

Date	Opponent	Result	Pens
08/05/1999	Tonga	44–17	**9**
08/04/1990	Tonga	28–16	**6**

BY A PLAYER

Date	Player	Opponent	Pens
08/05/1999	Keiji Hirose	Tonga	**9**
08/04/1990	Takahiro Hosokawa	Tonga	**6**

MOST DROPPED GOALS IN A MATCH

BY THE TEAM

Date	Opponent	Result	DGs
15/09/1998	Argentina	44–29	**2**

BY A PLAYER

Date	Player	Opponent	DGs
15/09/1998	Kensuke Iwabuchi	Argentina	**2**

MOST CAPPED PLAYERS

Name	Caps
Yukio Motoki	**79**
Hirotoki Onozawa	**68**
Takeomi Ito	**61**
Daisuke Ohata	**58**
Hitoshi Ono	**54**

LEADING TRY SCORERS

Name	Tries
Daisuke Ohata	**69**
Hirotoki Onozawa	**43**
Terunori Masuho	**28**
Takashi Kikutani	**23**

LEADING CONVERSIONS SCORERS

Name	Cons
James Arlidge	**78**
Keiji Hirose	**77**
Toru Kurihara	**71**
Ryan Nicholas	**53**

LEADING PENALTY SCORERS

Name	Pens
Keiji Hirose	**76**
Toru Kurihara	**35**
James Arlidge	**28**
Takahiro Hosokawa	**24**

LEADING DROPPED GOAL SCORERS

Name	DGs
Kyohei Morita	**5**

LEADING POINTS SCORERS

Name	Points
Keiji Hirose	**413**
Toru Kurihara	**347**
Daisuke Ohata	**345**
James Arlidge	**286**
Hirotoki Onozawa	**215**

MN Chan/Getty Images

The incredible Daisuke Ohata, who scored a stunning 69 Test tries for Japan.

JAPAN INTERNATIONAL PLAYERS (UP TO 31 OCTOBER 2011)

Note: Years given for International Championship matches are for second half of season; eg 1972 means season 1971–72. Years for all other matches refer to the actual year of the match. Entries in square brackets denote matches played in RWC Finals.

T Adachi 1932 *C, C*
M Aizawa 1984 *Kor*, 1986 *US, C, S, E, Kor*, 1987 *A, NZ, NZ*, 1988 *OU, Kor*
H Akama 1973 *F*, 1975 *A, W*, 1976 *S, E, It, Kor*, 1977 *S*
T Akatsuka 1994 *Fj*, 1995 *Tg, NZ*, 2005 *Sp*, 2006 *HK, Kor*
J Akune 2001 *W, C*
M Amino 2000 *Kor, C*, 2003 *Rus, AuA, Kor, E, E, S, Fj, US*
E Ando 2006 *AG, Kor, Geo, Tg, Sa, JAB, Fj*, 2007 *HK, Fj, Tg, Sa, JAB, It*
D Anglesey 2002 *Tg, Tai, Tai*
T Aoi 1959 *BCo, BCo, OCC*, 1963 *BCo*
S Aoki 1989 *S*, 1990 *Fj*, 1991 *US, C*, 1993 *W*
Y Aoki 2007 *Kor, AuA, JAB*, 2008 *Kor, Kaz, HK, AuA, Tg, Fj, Sa, US, US*, 2009 *Kaz, Sin, Sa, JAB, Tg, Fj*, 2011 *Sa, Tg, US, NZ*
S Arai 1959 *BCo, BCo*
JA Arlidge 2007 *Kor*, 2008 *Kor, AG, Kaz, HK, AuA, Tg, Fj, M, Sa*, 2009 *Sa, JAB, Tg, Fj, C, C*, 2010 *Kor, AG, Kaz, HK, Fj, Sa, Tg, Sa, Rus*, 2011 *Kaz, ARE, Tg, It, F, Tg, C*
G Aruga 2006 *HK, Kor*, 2007 *Kor, HK, AuA, Sa, JAB, It, Fj, C*, 2008 *Kor, HK*, 2009 *C, C*, 2011 *ARE, Fj*
K Aruga 1974 *NZU*, 1975 *A, A, W, W*, 1976 *S, E, It, Kor*
R Asano 2003 *AuA, AuA, F, Fj*, 2005 *Ar, HK, Kor, R, C, I, I, Sp*, 2006 *Kor, Geo, Tg, It, HK, Kor*, 2007 *Kor, It, W*
M Atokawa 1969 *HK*, 1970 *Tha, BCo*, 1971 *E, E*
H Atou 1976 *BCo*

T Baba 1932 *C*
GTM Bachop 1999 *C, Tg, Sa, Fj, Sp, Sa, W, Ar*
I Basiyalo 1997 *HK, US, US, C, HK*
D Bickle 1996 *HK, HK, C, US, US, C*

KCC Chang 1930 *BCo*, 1932 *C, C*
T Chiba 1930 *BCo*
M Chida 1980 *Kor*, 1982 *HK, C, C, Kor*, 1983 *W*, 1984 *F, F, Kor*, 1985 *US, I, I, F, F*, 1986 *US, C, S, E, Kor*, 1987 *US, E*

H Daimon 2004 *S, W*

K Endo 2004 *It*, 2006 *AG, Kor, Geo, Tg, It, JAB, Fj*, 2007 *HK, Fj, Tg, AuA, Sa, It, Fj, W, C*, 2008 *AuA, Tg, Fj, M, US, US*, 2009 *C, C*, 2010 *Kor, AG, Kaz, HK, Fj, Sa, Tg, Sa, Rus*, 2011 *ARE, Sa, Tg, It, F, Tg, C*
J Enomoto 2005 *Sp*
R Enomoto 1959 *BCo, BCo*

B Ferguson 1993 *W*, 1994 *Fj, Fj, HK, Kor*, 1995 *Tg, Tg, R, W, I, NZ*, 1996 *HK, HK, C, US, US, C*
K Fijii 2000 *Sa*
S Fuchigami 2000 *I*, 2002 *Rus, Tai*, 2003 *US, Rus*
A Fuji 1959 *BCo, BCo*
A Fujii 1956 *AuUn*
M Fujii 1930 *BCo*
M Fujikake 1993 *W*, 1994 *HK*, 1995 *Tg*
T Fujimoto-Kamohara 1969 *HK*, 1970 *BCo*, 1971 *E, E*, 1972 *HK*, 1973 *W*
N Fujita 2010 *Kor, AG, Kaz, Rus*, 2011 *HK, ARE, SL, Fj, It, US, F, NZ, Tg, C*
T Fujita 1980 *H, F*, 1983 *W*, 1984 *F, F, Kor*, 1985 *US, I, I, F, F*, 1986 *US, C, S, E*, 1987 *US, E, A, NZ, NZ*, 1989 *S*, 1990 *Fj, Tg, Kor, Sa*, 1991 *US, US, I*
M Fujiwara 1973 *W*, 1974 *NZU*, 1975 *A, A, W, W*, 1976 *S, E, It*, 1977 *S*, 1978 *F, Kor*, 1979 *HK, E*, 1980 *H, F*
K Fukumuro 1990 *Kor*
K Fukuoka 2000 *Fj*
S Fukuoka 1990 *Kor*
R Fukurodate 1976 *BCo, Kor*, 1979 *E, E*, 1980 *H, F, Kor*
T Fumihara 2000 *I*

T Goda 1990 *Fj, Tg, Kor, Sa, US, Kor*, 1991 *US*, 1995 *Tg*
WR Gordon 1997 *HK, C, US, US*, 1998 *C, US, HK, HK, US, C*, 1999 *C, Sa, Fj, Sp, Sa, W, Ar*
A Goromaru 2005 *Ur, R, C, I*, 2009 *Kaz, HK, Kor, Sin, JAB, C*, 2010 *Sa*
S Goto 2005 *Ur, Ar, Kor, R, C, I, I*, 2006 *HK*

M Hagimoto 1987 *E*
T Hagiwara-Maekawa 1930 *BCo*
K Hamabe 1996 *C, US, US, C, Kor*, 1997 *HK, C, US, US, C*, 2001 *Sa, C*
T Haneda 1995 *Tg*
S Hara 1970 *BCo*, 1971 *E, E*, 1973 *W, F*, 1974 *NZU, SL*, 1975 *A, W*, 1976 *E*
T Harada 1959 *BCo*
S Hasegawa 1997 *HK*, 1998 *C, US, HK, HK, US, C, Ar, Kor, Tai, HK, Kor*, 1999 *C, Tg, Sa, Fj, US, Sa, W*, 2000 *Fj, US, Tg, Sa, C*, 2001 *W, W, Sa, C*, 2002 *Tg, Kor, Tai, Kor*, 2003 *US, AuA, E, S, F, Fj, US*
S Hashimoto 1953 *OCC*
K Hatakeyama 2008 *US, US*, 2009 *HK, Sin, Sa, JAB, Tg, Fj, C, C*, 2010 *Kor, Kaz, Sa, Tg, Sa*, 2011 *Kaz, ARE, SL, Sa, Tg, Fj, It, US, F, NZ, Tg, C*
T Hatakeyama 1976 *It, Kor*, 1977 *S*, 1978 *F, Kor*, 1979 *HK, E, E*
T Hayashi 1980 *F*, 1982 *C, C, Kor*, 1983 *W*, 1984 *F, F*, 1985 *US, I, I, F, F*, 1986 *US, C, S, E, Kor*, 1987 *US, E, A, IrSt, NZ, NZ*, 1990 *Tg, Sa*, 1991 *US, C, HK, S, I, Z*, 1992 *HK*
T Hayashi 1989 *S*
T Higashida 1983 *W*
T Hirai 1980 *Kor*, 1982 *HK*
S Hirao 1983 *W*, 1984 *F, F*, 1985 *US, I, I*, 1986 *US, C, S, E*, 1987 *US, E, A, NZ, NZ*, 1988 *Kor*, 1989 *S*, 1990 *Fj, Tg, Kor, US, Kor*, 1991 *US, C, HK, S, I, Z*, 1995 *R, W, I*
S Hirao 1932 *C, C*
T Hirao 1998 *Kor*, 1999 *Tg, Sa, W*, 2001 *Tai, Sa, C*, 2004 *Kor, Rus, C, It*
H Hirashima 2008 *US, US*, 2009 *Kaz, Kor, Sa, JAB, Tg, Fj, C, C*, 2010 *Kor, AG, Kaz, HK, Fj, Sa, Tg, Sa, Rus*, 2011 *Kaz, ARE, Sa, Tg, It, F, Tg, C*
T Hirata 2000 *US, C*
J Hiratsuka 1999 *US*
K Hirose 1994 *Kor*, 1995 *Tg, NZ*, 1996 *HK, HK, C, US, US, Kor*, 1998 *HK, HK, US, C, Kor, Tai, HK, Kor*, 1999 *C, Tg, Sa, Fj, US, Sp, Sa, W, Ar*, 2000 *Fj, US, Kor, C, I*, 2003 *AuA, AuA, Kor, E, E, S*, 2005 *HK, I, Sp*
T Hirose 1988 *Kor*
T Hirose 2007 *HK*
E Hirotsu 1995 *Tg*
Y Hisadomi 2002 *Rus*, 2003 *Rus, AuA, Kor, E*, 2004 *Kor, C,*

It, S, R, 2005 Sp, 2006 AG, Kor, Geo, Tg, It, Sa, JAB, Fj, HK, Kor
A Hiwasa 2011 *HK, ARE, Sa, Fj, It, US, F, NZ, Tg, C*
M Hohokabe 1978 *F, Kor*
RK Holani 2008 *Kaz, HK, AuA, Fj, M, Sa, US, US*, 2010 *HK, Fj, Sa, Tg, Sa, Rus*, 2011 *HK, ARE, Sa, Tg, It, F*
K Honjo 1982 *C, C*, 1985 *US, I, F*
K Horaguchi 1979 *E, E*, 1980 *F*, 1982 *HK, C, C, Kor*, 1983 *W*, 1984 *F*, 1985 *US, I, I, F, F*, 1987 *US, E*
H Hori 1956 *AuUn*
S Horie 2009 *C, C*, 2010 *Kor, Kaz, HK, Fj, Sa, Tg, Sa, Rus*, 2011 *Tg, Fj, It, US, F, Tg, C*
M Horikoshi 1988 *Kor*, 1989 *S*, 1990 *Fj, Tg, Kor, US, Kor*, 1991 *US, C, HK, I, Z*, 1992 *HK*, 1993 *Ar, Ar*, 1994 *Kor*, 1995 *Tg, R, W, I*, 1997 *C*, 1998 *C, US, Tai, HK, Kor*
S Hoshino 1975 *W*, 1976 *S*, 1978 *Kor*, 1979 *HK*
T Hosokawa 1990 *Tg, Kor, Sa, US*, 1991 *US, S, I, Z*, 1993 *Ar, Ar*

S Iburi 1972 *HK*
M Iguchi 1973 *F*, 1974 *NZU*, 1975 *A, A, W*
H Ijyuin 1932 *C, C*
W Ikeda 2004 *Kor, Rus, C, It, S, R, W*, 2005 *Sp*, 2006 *AG, Geo, Tg, It, JAB, Fj*
Y Ikeda 1980 *Kor*, 1983 *W*, 1984 *F, F*
Y Ikegaya 2008 *AG, HK, M*
H Ikuta 1987 *US, A, NZ*
K Imaizumi 1988 *Kor*, 1994 *Fj, HK*, 1996 *US*, 1997 *C, US, US, C*
k Imakoma 1988 *Kor*
K Imamura 1959 *BCo, BCo*
R Imamura 1959 *BCo, BCo*
Y Imamura 2006 *AG, Geo, It, Sa, Fj*, 2007 *HK, Fj, Tg, AuA, Sa, JAB, It, Fj, W, C*, 2008 *AG, Kaz, HK, AuA, M*, 2009 *Kaz, Kor, Sin, Sa, JAB, Tg, Fj*, 2010 *Rus*, 2011 *Kaz, SL, Sa, Fj, NZ*
R Imazato 1969 *HK*, 1970 *Tha, BCo*, 1971 *E, E*, 1972 *HK*, 1973 *W, F*, 1974 *JAB*, 1975 *CU, A, A, W, W*, 1976 *S, E, It*
T Inokuchi 2007 *It, A, W*, 2008 *AG, HK, AuA, M*
Y Inose 2008 *AG, Kaz, AuA, Tg, M, Sa*
M Inoue 1982 *C, C, Kor*
M Irie 2008 *US*
R Ishi 1999 *Sp*
K Ishii 1986 *S*
J Ishiyama 1980 *H, F, Kor*, 1982 *HK, C, Kor*, 1983 *W*, 1985 *US, I, I, F, F*
K Ishizuka 1963 *BCo*
T Ishizuka 1974 *NZU, SL*, 1975 *A, W, W*, 1978 *F, Kor*, 1979 *HK, E, E*, 1980 *H, F, Kor*, 1982 *HK, C, C, NZU, NZU, EnSt, NZU, Kor*
H Ito 2004 *Kor, Rus*
M Ito 2000 *Tg, Sa, Kor, C, I*, 2004 *Kor, C*, 2005 *Sp*, 2006 *AG, Kor, Geo, Tg, Sa, Fj, HK, Kor*
M Ito 1969 *HK*
T Ito 1996 *HK, HK, C, US, US, C, Kor*, 1997 *HK, C, US, US*, 1998 *C, US, HK, HK, US, C, Ar, Kor, Tai, HK, Kor*, 1999 *Tg, Sa, Fj, US, Sp, Sa, W, Ar*, 2000 *I*, 2001 *Kor, W, Sa, C*, 2002 *Rus, Tg, Kor, Tai, Kor, Tai*, 2003 *US, Rus, AuA, AuA, Kor, E, E, S, F, Fj, US*, 2004 *Kor, Rus, C, It*, 2005 *Ur, Ar, R, C, I*
T Ito 1963 *BCo*, 1969 *HK*, 1970 *Tha, BCo*, 1971 *E*, 1972 *HK*, 1973 *W, F*, 1974 *NZU*
T Ito 1980 *H, F*, 1982 *HK, C, Kor*
JT Ives 2011 *HK, Kaz, ARE, SL, Sa, Tg, Fj, It*
K Iwabuchi 1997 *HK, C, US, US, C, HK*, 1998 *C, US, Ar, Tai, HK*, 1999 *C*, 2001 *Tai, W, W, Sa*, 2002 *Tg, Kor, Tai, Kor*
Y Iwama 2000 *US, Tg, Sa, Kor, C*, 2001 *Tai*
H Iwashita 1930 *BCo*
Y Izawa 1970 *Tha, BCo*, 1971 *E, E*, 1972 *HK*, 1973 *W, F*, 1974 *NZU*, 1975 *A, A, W*, 1976 *S, E, It*
K Izawa-Nakamura 1995 *Tg, Tg, I, NZ*, 1996 *US, Kor*, 1997 *HK, C, US, US, C, HK*, 1998 *Ar, Kor, Tai, HK, Kor*

JW Joseph 1999 *C, Tg, Sa, Fj, US, Sp, Sa, W, Ar*

S Ka 1934 *AuUn*
H Kajihara 1989 *S*, 1990 *Fj, Tg, Kor, Sa, US, Kor*, 1991 *US, HK, S, I, Z*, 1993 *Ar, Ar*, 1994 *Fj, Fj, Kor*, 1995 *Tg, R, W, I, NZ*, 1996 *HK, HK, C, US, US, C, Kor*, 1997 *C*
S Kaleta 1992 *HK*, 1993 *Ar, Ar, W*
K Kamata 1970 *BCo*
T Kanai 2009 *Kaz, HK, Sin, JAB*
F Kanaya 1980 *F*, 1982 *HK, C, C*, 1983 *W*, 1984 *F, F, Kor*, 1985 *US*
R Kanazawa 2010 *AG, Sa, Tg*
Kanbara 1971 *E*
H Kaneshiro 1993 *Ar*
H Kano 1974 *SL*, 1982 *Kor*
T Kasahara 1932 *C, C*
K Kasai 1999 *C*, 2005 *Ar, HK, Kor, R, C, I, I*, 2006 *AG, Tg*
Y Kasai 1985 *F, F*
Y Katakura 1959 *BCo*
A Kato 2001 *Tai*
H Kato 1993 *Ar, Ar*
D Katsuno 2002 *Kor*
T Katsuraguchi 1970 *Tha*
H Kawachi 1980 *H, Kor*, 1982 *C*, 1983 *W*, 1984 *F, F, Kor*
K Kawachi 1984 *Kor*
R Kawai 2000 *I*
N Kawamata 2008 *US*, 2009 *HK, Kor, C, C*, 2010 *HK, Fj, Sa, Tg, Sa, Rus*, 2011 *HK, Kaz, SL, Tg, Fj, US, NZ*
K Kawasaki 1963 *BCo*
M Kawasaki 1970 *Tha*
T Kawasaki 2000 *US, Tg*
Y Kawase 1983 *W*, 1985 *US, I, I, F*, 1986 *Kor*, 1987 *A*
T Kikutani 2005 *Sp*, 2006 *AG, Kor, Geo, Tg, It, Sa, JAB, Fj, Kor*, 2008 *Kor, AG, AuA, Tg, Fj, Sa, US, US*, 2009 *Kaz, HK, Kor, Sin, Sa, JAB, Tg, Fj, C, C*, 2010 *Kor, AG, Fj, Sa, Tg, Sa, Rus*, 2011 *HK, Kaz, ARE, SL, Sa, Tg, Fj, It, US, F, NZ, Tg, C*
CW Kim 2007 *W, C*
K Kimura 1996 *C*
T Kimura 1984 *F, F, Kor*, 1985 *US*, 1986 *E, Kor*, 1987 *E, A, NZ*
T Kinashita 2002 *Tg, Kor*
T Kinoshita 1932 *C, C*
H Kiso 2001 *Kor, Tai*, 2003 *AuA, AuA, Kor, E, E, S, Fj, US*, 2004 *S, R, W*, 2005 *HK, I, Sp*, 2006 *AG, Kor, Geo, It, Sa, JAB, Fj, HK, Kor*, 2007 *Kor, Fj, AuA, A, W, C*, 2008 *US*
T Kitagawa 2005 *Sp*, 2006 *AG, Kor, Tg, Sa, JAB*, 2008 *Kor, AG, Kaz, HK, AuA, Tg, Fj, M, Sa, US, US*, 2009 *Kaz, Kor, Sa, JAB, Tg, Fj, C, C*, 2010 *Kor, AG, HK, Fj, Sa, Tg, Sa, Rus*, 2011 *HK, Sa, Fj, It, F, NZ, Tg, C*
T Kitagawa 2006 *HK*, 2007 *HK, A*
Y Kitagawa 2007 *Kor*, 2009 *HK, Kor, Sin, JAB*, 2011 *NZ*
T Kitahara 1978 *Kor*, 1979 *HK*
H Kitajima 1963 *BCo*
T Kitano 1930 *BCo*, 1932 *C, C*
S Kitaoka 1959 *BCo*
T Kizu 2009 *C*, 2010 *AG*, 2011 *HK, Kaz, ARE, Sa, Fj*
H Kobayashi 1983 *W*, 1984 *F, Kor*, 1985 *I, F*, 1986 *Kor*
I Kobayashi 1975 *A, A, W, W*, 1976 *BCo, S, E, It, Kor*, 1977 *S*, 1978 *F, Kor*, 1979 *HK, E, E*
K Kobayashi 1959 *BCo, BCo*
K Koizumi 1997 *US, C, HK*, 2000 *Fj, US, Tg, Sa, C*, 2001 *W, C*, 2002 *Tg, Tai*
J Komura 1992 *HK*, 1998 *Kor*, 2000 *Kor, C*
GN Konia 2003 *US, AuA, AuA, F, Fj, US*
K Konishi 1986 *US, Kor*
Y Konishi 1980 *F, Kor*, 1982 *HK, Kor*, 1983 *W*, 1984 *F, F, Kor*, 1985 *US, I, I, F, F*, 1986 *US, C, S, E, Kor*, 1987 *NZ*
M Koshiyama 1984 *F, F, Kor*, 1985 *US, I, I*, 1986 *C, Kor*, 1987 *NZ, NZ*
T Kouda 1988 *Kor*
O Koyabu 1974 *SL*
K Kubo 2000 *I*, 2001 *Kor, W, Sa, C*, 2002 *Rus, Kor, Tai, Kor, Kor*, 2003 *US, Rus, E, F, Fj*, 2004 *Kor, C, It*
K Kubota 2004 *S, R, W*
T Kudo-Nakayama 1979 *E*
T Kumagae 2004 *Kor, Rus, C, It, S, R, W*, 2005 *Ur, Ar, Kor, R, C, I, I, Sp*, 2006 *AG, Kor, Geo, It, Sa, Fj*, 2007 *HK, Fj, AuA, Sa, A*
N Kumagai 1977 *S*, 1978 *F*, 1979 *HK*
M Kunda 1990 *Sa, US, Kor*, 1991 *C, HK, S, I, Z*, 1992 *HK*, 1993 *Ar, Ar, W*, 1994 *Fj, Fj, HK, Kor*, 1995 *Tg, R, W, I, NZ*,

1996 *HK, HK, C,* 1997 *HK, C, US, US,* 1998 *C, HK, HK, US, C, Ar, Kor, HK, Kor,* 1999 *Sa, Fj, US, Sp, Sa, W, Ar*

S Kurihara 1986 *S, E,* 1987 *E*

S Kurihara 1974 *SL*

T Kurihara 2000 *Fj, US, Tg, Sa, Kor, C,* 2001 *Kor, W, W, Sa, C,* 2002 *Rus, Tg, Kor, Tai, Kor, Tai,* 2003 *US, Rus, AuA, AuA, E, E, S, F, Fj, US*

M Kurokawa 1998 *Tai, HK, Kor,* 2000 *Fj, Tg, Sa, Kor, C*

T Kurosaka 1970 *BCo,* 1974 *SL,* 1975 *A, A, W, W*

M Kusatsu 1963 *BCo*

T Kusumi 2007 *A, W,* 2008 *Kor*

E Kutsuki 1985 *F,* 1986 *US, C, S, E,* 1987 *US, E, A, NZ, NZ,* 1989 *S,* 1990 *Fj, Tg, Kor, Sa, US, Kor,* 1991 *US, US, C, HK, S, I, Z,* 1992 *HK,* 1993 *W,* 1994 *Fj, Fj, HK*

S Latu 1987 *US, A, NZ, NZ,* 1989 *S,* 1990 *Fj, Tg, Kor, Sa, US, Kor,* 1991 *US, C, HK, S, I, Z,* 1992 *HK,* 1993 *Ar, Ar,* 1994 *Fj, Fj, HK, Kor,* 1995 *Tg, Tg, R, W, I, NZ*

ST Latu 1993 *W,* 1994 *Fj, Fj, HK, Kor,* 1995 *Tg, R, W, I*

MG Leitch 2008 *US, US,* 2009 *Kaz, HK, Kor, Sa, JAB, C, C,* 2010 *HK, Fj, Tg, Rus,* 2011 *HK, ARE, Tg, Fj, It, F, NZ, Tg, C*

CED Loamanu 2005 *Ur, HK,* 2007 *Kor, Fj, Tg, Sa, JAB, It, Fj, W, C,* 2008 *AuA, Tg, Fj, M, Sa*

ET Luaiufi 1990 *Fj, Kor, US, Kor,* 1991 *US, US, C, HK, S, I, Z*

T Madea 1991 *US, C, HK,* 1995 *Tg*

P Mafileo 2008 *US*

S Makabe 2009 *C,* 2010 *Kaz*

HAW Makiri 2005 *Ur, Ar, HK, Kor, R, I, I,* 2006 *AG, Tg, Sa, JAB,* 2007 *Kor, Tg, AuA, Sa, JAB, It, A, Fj, W, C,* 2008 *AuA, Tg, Fj, M, Sa*

M Mantani 1969 *HK,* 1970 *Tha, BCo,* 1971 *E, E,* 1972 *HK*

G Marsh 2007 *AuA, Sa, JAB*

T Masuho 1991 *US, C, HK, S, I, Z,* 1993 *Ar, Ar,* 1994 *Fj, Fj, Kor,* 1995 *Tg, W,* 1996 *HK, C, US, US, C,* 1997 *HK, C, US, C, HK,* 1998 *C, US, HK, HK, US, C, Ar, Kor, Tai, HK,* 1999 *C, US, Sp, Sa,* 2000 *Fj, US, Tg, Sa, Kor, C,* 2001 *Kor, W, Sa, C*

Y Masutome 1986 *Kor*

K Matsubara 1930 *BCo*

T Matsubara 1932 *C, C*

Y Matsubara 2004 *Kor, Rus, C, It,* 2005 *Sp,* 2006 *AG, Kor, Geo, Tg, It, Sa, JAB, Fj, Kor,* 2007 *Kor, Fj, Tg, Sa, JAB, It, Fj, W, C*

T Matsuda 1992 *HK,* 1993 *W,* 1994 *Fj, HK, Kor,* 1995 *Tg, R, W, I, NZ,* 1996 *HK, HK, C, US, US, C, Kor,* 1998 *US, HK, HK, US, C, Ar, Kor, Tai, HK, Kor,* 1999 *C, Fj, US, Sp, Sa, Ar,* 2001 *Kor, Tai, W,* 2003 *US, AuA, Kor, E, S, Fj, US*

J Matsumoto 1977 *S,* 1978 *F,* 1980 *H,* 1982 *C, C*

T Matsunaga 1985 *F, F*

Y Matsunobu 1963 *BCo*

H Matsuo 2003 *AuA, AuA, Kor, E, E*

K Matsuo 1986 *US, C, S, E, Kor,* 1987 *E, NZ,* 1988 *Kor,* 1990 *Tg, Kor, Sa, US,* 1991 *US, HK, S, I, Z,* 1993 *Ar, Ar,* 1994 *Fj, Fj, HK,* 1995 *Tg*

Y Matsuo 1974 *SL,* 1976 *BCo, E, It, Kor,* 1977 *S,* 1979 *HK, E, E,* 1982 *HK, C, C,* 1983 *OCC, W,* 1984 *F, F, Kor*

S Matsuoka 1963 *BCo,* 1970 *Tha*

K Matsushita 2008 *US, US,* 2010 *AG, HK, Fj, Sa, Tg*

F Mau 2004 *Rus, C, It, S, R, W*

AF McCormick 1996 *HK, HK, US,* 1997 *HK, C, US, US, C, HK,* 1998 *C, US, HK, Ar, Kor, Tai, HK,* 1999 *C, Tg, Sa, Fj, US, Sp, Sa, W, Ar*

R Miki 1999 *Sp,* 2002 *Tg, Tai, Kor, Tai, Kor,* 2004 *S, R, W*

A Miller 2002 *Rus, Kor, Tai, Kor, Tai,* 2003 *Kor, S, F, Fj, US*

S Miln 1998 *C, US, HK, HK, US*

Y Minamikawa 1976 *BCo,* 1978 *F, Kor,* 1979 *HK, E, E,* 1980 *H, F, Kor,* 1982 *HK, C, C, Kor*

M Mishima 1930 *BCo,* 1932 *C, C*

T Miuchi 2002 *Rus, Kor, Kor, Tai, Kor,* 2003 *US, Rus, AuA, Kor, E, E, S, F, Fj, US,* 2004 *Rus, C, It, S, R, W,* 2005 *Ur, Ar, HK, Kor, R, C, I, I,* 2006 *HK, Kor,* 2007 *Kor, HK, Fj, Tg, Sa, It, Fj, W, C,* 2008 *Kor, AG, Kaz, HK, AuA, Tg, Fj, Sa*

S Miura 1963 *BCo*

K Miyai 1959 *BCo, BCo,* 1963 *BCo*

K Miyaji 1969 *HK*

K Miyajima 1959 *BCo, BCo*

H Miyaji-Yoshizawa 1930 *BCo*

T Miyake 2005 *Sp,* 2006 *Sa, JAB, Fj*

K Miyamoto 1986 *S, E,* 1987 *US, E, A,* 1988 *Kor,* 1991 *I*

K Miyata 1971 *E, E,* 1972 *HK*

M Miyauchi 1975 *W,* 1976 *It, Kor*

K Mizobe 1997 *C*

K Mizoguchi 1997 *C*

K Mizube 1997 *HK*

H Mizuno 2004 *R,* 2005 *HK, Kor, R, C, I,* 2006 *AG, Geo, Tg, It, Sa, JAB*

M Mizutani 1970 *Tha,* 1971 *E*

N Mizuyama 2008 *Tg, M, Sa, US*

S Mori 1974 *NZU, SL,* 1975 *A, A, W, W,* 1976 *BCo, S, E, It, Kor,* 1977 *S,* 1978 *F,* 1979 *HK, E, E, CU,* 1980 *NZU, H, F, Kor,* 1981 *AuUn*

K Morioka 1982 *Kor*

K Morita 2004 *C, It,* 2005 *Ur, Ar, Kor, R, C, I*

A Moriya 2006 *Tg, It, Sa, JAB, Fj,* 2008 *AG, Kaz*

Y Motoki 1991 *US, US, C,* 1992 *HK,* 1993 *Ar, Ar,* 1994 *Fj, Fj, Kor,* 1995 *Tg, Tg, R, W, I, NZ,* 1996 *HK, HK, C, US, US, C, Kor,* 1997 *HK, C, US, US, C, HK,* 1998 *C, US, HK, HK, US, C, Ar, Kor, HK, Kor,* 1999 *C, Tg, Sa, Fj, US, Sp, Sa, W, Ar,* 2001 *W, W, Sa, C,* 2002 *Rus, Tg, Kor, Tai, Kor, Tai, Kor,* 2003 *Kor, E, E, S, Fj, US,* 2004 *Kor, Rus, C, It, S, R, W,* 2005 *Ur, Ar, HK, Kor, R, C, I, I*

K Motoyoshi 2001 *Tai*

S Mukai 1985 *I, I, F,* 1986 *US, C, E, Kor,* 1987 *US, A, NZ, NZ*

M Mukoyama 2004 *Kor, C, It, S, R, W*

K Muraguchi 1976 *S, Kor*

D Murai 1985 *I, I, F, F,* 1987 *E*

K Murata 1963 *BCo*

W Murata 1991 *US, S,* 1995 *Tg, NZ,* 1996 *HK, HK, C, US, US, C, Kor,* 1997 *HK, C, US, US, HK,* 1998 *HK, HK, US, C, Ar, Kor, Kor,* 1999 *US, W,* 2001 *W, W, Sa,* 2002 *Rus, Tg, Kor, Tai, Kor, Tai,* 2003 *US, AuA, E,* 2005 *Ur, Ar, Kor, I, I*

Y Murata 1971 *E, E,* 1972 *HK,* 1973 *W,* 1974 *NZU, SL*

M Nagai 1988 *Kor*

Y Nagatomo 1993 *W,* 1994 *Fj, HK,* 1995 *Tg,* 1996 *US, US,* 1997 *C*

Y Nagatomo 2010 *Kor, AG, Kaz*

T Naito 1934 *AuUn*

M Nakabayashi 2005 *HK, Kor, R, I*

T Nakai 2005 *Ur, HK, C, I, I, Sp,* 2006 *AG, Kor, Geo, Tg, It, Fj*

T Nakamichi 1996 *HK, HK, US, US, C,* 1998 *Ar, Kor,* 1999 *C, Sa, Fj, Sp, W, Ar,* 2000 *Fj, US, Tg*

N Nakamura 1998 *C, US, HK, HK, US, C, Ar, Kor, Tai, HK, Kor,* 1999 *C, Tg, Sa, Fj, US, Sp, W, Ar,* 2000 *I*

S Nakamura 2009 *Kaz, Sin,* 2010 *AG, Kaz, HK, Fj*

S Nakashima 1989 *S,* 1990 *Fj, Tg, Kor, Sa, US,* 1991 *US, US, C, HK, S*

T Nakayama 1976 *BCo,* 1978 *F,* 1979 *E,* 1980 *H,* 1982 *C, C*

Y Nakayama 2008 *Kor, AG, Kaz, HK, Tg, M,* 2009 *HK, Kor, Sin, Tg, Fj*

H Namba 2000 *Fj, US, Tg, Sa, Kor, C, I,* 2001 *Tai, W, W, C,* 2002 *Rus, Tg, Kor, Tai, Kor,* 2003 *US, Rus, AuA, AuA, Kor, E, E, F*

RT Nicholas 2008 *Kor, Kaz, HK, AuA, Tg, Fj, Sa, US, US,* 2009 *HK, Kor, Sa, JAB, Tg, Fj, C, C,* 2010 *Kor, Kaz, HK, Fj, Sa, Tg, Sa, Rus,* 2011 *HK, ARE, Sa, Tg, Fj, It, US, F, Tg, C*

H Nishida 1994 *Fj*

S Nishigaki 1932 *C, C*

T Nishihara 2011 *Sa, It, US*

T Nishiura 2004 *W,* 2006 *HK, Kor,* 2007 *Kor, Fj, Tg, Sa, It, Fj, W, C,* 2008 *Kor, HK, AuA, Tg, Fj, Sa*

H Nishizumi 1963 *BCo*

M Niwa 1932 *C*

I Nogami 1932 *C,* 1936 *NZU*

T Nozawa 2000 *Tg, Sa, Kor, C*

M Oda 2000 *US, Tg, Sa, Kor, I*

H Ogasawara 1969 *HK,* 1970 *Tha, BCo,* 1971 *E, E,* 1973 *F,* 1974 *NZU,* 1975 *A, A, W, W,* 1976 *NZU,* 1977 *S*

K Oguchi 1997 *US, C, HK*, 1998 *Tai*, 1999 *Sa, Ar*, 2000 *Fj, Tg, Sa, Kor*
K Ohara 1998 *Kor, Tai*, 2000 *Kor, C, I*
D Ohata 1996 *Kor*, 1997 *HK, C, US*, 1998 *HK, C, Ar, Kor, HK*, 1999 *C, Tg, Sa, Fj, US, Sp, Sa, W, Ar*, 2000 *Fj, US, Kor, C, I*, 2002 *Rus, Kor, Tai, Kor, Tai, Kor*, 2003 *US, Rus, AuA, AuA, Kor, E, E, S, F, Fj, US*, 2004 *Kor, Rus, C, It*, 2005 *Ur, Ar, HK, Kor, R, C, I, I*, 2006 *AG, Kor, Geo, Tg, HK, Kor*
K Ohigashi 1973 *W, F*, 1974 *NZU, SL*
K Ohigashi 2004 *Kor, Rus, C*, 2007 *Kor, HK, AuA, JAB*
K Ohotsuka 1959 *BCo*
S Oikawa 1980 *H*
E Okabe 1963 *BCo*, 1967 *NZU*
Y Okada 1932 *C, C*
M Okidoi 1987 *A, NZ, NZ*
N Okubo 1999 *Tg, Sa, Fj, US, Sp, Sa, W, Ar*, 2000 *Fj, US, Tg, Sa, Kor, C*, 2002 *Rus, Tg, Kor, Tai, Kor, Tai*, 2003 *US, Rus, S, F, Fj, US*, 2004 *S, R, W*
T Omata 1970 *NZU, BCo, NZU*
S Onishi 2000 *Fj, US, Tg, Sa, Kor, C*, 2001 *Kor, Tai, W, C*, 2005 *Sp*, 2006 *AG, Kor, Geo, Tg, It, JAB, HK, Kor*, 2007 *HK, Tg, AuA, Sa, JAB, It, Fj, W, C*, 2008 *Kor, AG, HK, M, Sa*
H Ono 2004 *Kor, Rus, C, S*, 2005 *Ar, Kor, I*, 2006 *Kor, Geo, It, Sa, JAB, Fj, HK, Kor*, 2007 *Kor, Fj, Tg, Sa, JAB, It, Fj, W, C*, 2008 *Kor, AG, AuA, Tg, Fj, US*, 2009 *HK, Sin, Sa, JAB, Tg, C, C*, 2010 *Kor, Kaz, HK, Fj, Sa, Tg, Sa, Rus*, 2011 *Kaz, ARE, SL, Tg, Fj, US, NZ, Tg, C*
K Ono 2007 *Kor, AuA, JAB, It, A*
S Ono 1932 *C, C*
H Onozawa 2001 *W, Sa, C*, 2002 *Rus, Kor, Tai, Kor*, 2003 *Rus, AuA, AuA, Kor, E, E, S, F, Fj, US*, 2004 *Kor, Rus, C, It*, 2005 *Ur, Ar, HK, Kor, R, C, I, Sp*, 2006 *HK, Kor*, 2007 *Kor, Tg, AuA, JAB, A, Fj, W, C*, 2008 *Kor, AG, Kaz, HK, AuA, Tg, Fj, Sa*, 2009 *Kaz, HK, Kor, Sa, Tg, C, C*, 2010 *Fj, Sa, Tg, Sa*, 2011 *HK, SL, Sa, Tg, Fj, US, F, NZ, Tg, C*
S Onuki 1984 *F, F, Kor*, 1985 *US, I, I, F, F*, 1986 *US, C, S, E, Kor*, 1987 *US, E*
PD O'Reilly 2005 *Kor*, 2006 *JAB, Fj, HK, Kor*, 2007 *It, Fj, C*, 2009 *Kaz, C, C*
G Ota 1930 *BCo*
O Ota 1986 *US, S*, 1989 *S*, 1990 *Fj, Tg, Kor, Sa, US, Kor*, 1991 *US, C, HK, S, I, Z*, 1992 *HK*, 1993 *Ar, Ar, W*, 1994 *Fj, HK, Kor*, 1995 *Tg, R, W, I, NZ*
T Otao 2004 *W*, 2009 *Kaz, HK, Kor, Sin, JAB, Tg*
L Oto 1992 *HK*, 1995 *R, W, I, NZ*, 1996 *C*, 1997 *C, HK*
M Oto 1972 *HK*
N Oto 2001 *Kor, Tai, W, Sa*, 2005 *Sp*, 2006 *Kor, Tg, It, Sa, JAB, Fj*, 2007 *A*
K Otukolo 2005 *HK, Kor, C*
F Ouchi 1991 *US*
H Ouchi 1990 *Kor*, 1993 *Ar, W*, 1994 *HK*
N Owashi 1992 *HK*
M Oyabu 1998 *Kor*
A Oyagi 1983 *W*, 1984 *F, F, Kor*, 1985 *US, I, I, F, F*, 1986 *US, C*, 1987 *US, E, NZ, NZ*, 1988 *Kor*, 1989 *S*, 1990 *Fj, Tg, Kor, Sa, US, Kor*, 1991 *US, C, I, Z*
J Oyamada 1997 *HK, US*
A Ozaki 2008 *Kor, AG, HK*
M Ozaki 1963 *BCo*, 1967 *NZU*, 1968 *JAB, NZU*, 1969 *HK*
H Ozeki 1996 *HK, HK, US, C, Kor*

A Parker 2002 *Rus, Tg, Kor, Tai, Kor, Tai*, 2003 *US, Rus, AuA, AuA, Kor, E, E, S, F, Fj, US*, 2004 *It*
R Parkinson 2003 *Rus, AuA, E, S, Fj*, 2005 *Ur, Ar, HK, I, I*

D Quate 2009 *C*

BB Robins 2007 *Kor, Fj, Tg, AuA, Sa, JAB, It, Fj, W, C*, 2008 *Kor, AG, Kaz, HK, AuA, Tg, Fj, M, Sa, US, US*, 2009 *Kaz*, 2010 *Sa, Rus*, 2011 *C*

K Sagawa 1977 *S*
R Saito 1952 *OU*, 1953 *OCC*
Y Saito 2001 *Tai, W, W, Sa, C*, 2002 *Rus, Kor, Tai, Kor*, 2003 *Kor, E, E, US*, 2004 *Kor*
M Sakamoto 1978 *F, Kor*, 1980 *Kor*
M Sakata 1996 *C, US, US, C, Kor*, 1997 *US, US, C, HK*, 1998 *US, HK, Tai*, 1999 *C, Tg, US, Sp, Sa, W, Ar*, 2001 *W, W, Sa, C*, 2002 *Rus, Tg, Kor, Tai, Kor*, 2003 *US, Rus, AuA, S, F, Fj*
Y Sakata 1969 *HK*, 1970 *Tha, BCo*, 1971 *E, E*, 1972 *HK*
Y Sakuraba 1986 *S, E*, 1987 *A, NZ, NZ*, 1988 *Kor*, 1992 *HK*, 1993 *Ar, Ar, W*, 1994 *Fj, HK, Kor*, 1995 *Tg, R, W, I, NZ*, 1996 *HK, Kor*, 1997 *C, US, C, HK*, 1998 *C, US, HK, HK, US, C, Ar, Kor, Tai, HK, Kor*, 1999 *C, Tg, Sa, Fj, W, Ar*
L Samurai Vatuvei 2001 *Kor, Tai, W, W, Sa, C*, 2002 *Rus, Tg, Kor, Kor, Tai*, 2003 *US, Rus, AuA*, 2004 *Kor, Rus, C, It*, 2006 *HK, Kor*, 2007 *It, A, C*
T Saruta 1969 *HK*
M Sasada 1976 *BCo, E, It, Kor*, 1977 *S*, 1979 *HK, E*
Y Sasada 1973 *W, F*
T Sasaki 2007 *HK, Fj, Tg, AuA, JAB, A*
K Sato 1996 *US, US, C*, 1997 *C*
T Sato 2005 *Sp*, 2006 *AG, Kor, Geo, Tg, Sa, Fj*, 2007 *Kor, AuA*
T Sato 2008 *Kor, AG, Kaz, HK*
T Sato 2008 *AG, Kaz, HK*
Y Sato 1994 *Fj*, 1995 *Tg*, 1996 *C*
T Sawaguchi 2002 *Kor*
K Sawaki 1998 *Ar, Tai, Kor*, 1999 *Sa*, 2004 *S*, 2006 *HK, Kor*
K Segawa 1982 *HK*
K Sejimo 1980 *H, F*, 1982 *HK, C, C, Kor*
K Shibata 1972 *HK*, 1973 *W*, 1974 *SL*, 1975 *A*, 1976 *BCo, S, E*
M Shichinohe 2002 *Tai, Kor*
S Shiga 1959 *BCo, BCo*
F Shimazaki 1970 *Tha, BCo*, 1971 *E, E*, 1972 *HK*, 1973 *W, F*
S Shimizu 1996 *Kor*
S Shimizu 1930 *BCo*
M Shimoji 1979 *HK*
S Shimomura 2004 *S, R*, 2007 *HK*
M Shimosono 1970 *Tha*, 1971 *E, E*, 1972 *HK*, 1973 *F*
Y Shinomiya 2003 *US, AuA, Kor*
K Shinozuka 2008 *Kor, AG, Kaz, HK, M*
K Shomen 2002 *Kor*, 2006 *Kor*
G Smith 1998 *C, US, HK, HK, US, C, Ar, Kor, HK*, 1999 *C, Tg, Sa, Fj, US, Sa, W, Ar*
T Soma 2005 *Sp*, 2006 *AG, Kor, Geo, Tg, It*, 2007 *Kor, HK, Fj, Tg, AuA, Sa, JAB, It, Fj, W, C*, 2008 *Kor, Kaz, AuA, Tg, Fj, M, Sa*
Y Sonoda 2000 *Fj, US, Tg*, 2001 *Tai, W, C*, 2002 *Rus, Kor*, 2003 *US, Rus, AuA, Kor, E, E, S, F, Fj, US*
H Sugarwara 2000 *Fj, US, Tg, I*, 2001 *Tai, W*
T Sugata 1998 *Kor*
H Suzuki 1930 *BCo*

G Tachikawa 1999 *C, Tg*, 2005 *Ur, Ar, Kor, R, C, I, I, Sp*, 2007 *Kor, Fj, Tg*, 2010 *Kor, Kaz, HK*, 2011 *Kaz, ARE, SL, Sa*
H Taione 1986 *US, C, S*, 1988 *Kor*
K Taira 2007 *Kor, Fj, AuA, A, Fj, W, C*, 2008 *Tg, Fj, Sa, US*, 2009 *HK, Sin, Sa, JAB, Tg, Fj, C*, 2010 *Kor, Kaz, HK, Fj, Sa, Rus*, 2011 *HK, Kaz, Tg, Fj, It, US, F, NZ*
H Takafumi 1999 *Fj*
S Takagi 2005 *Ur, HK, R, I, I*
H Takahashi 2005 *Ur, Ar, Kor, C, I*
K Takahashi 1990 *Fj, Sa, Kor*, 1991 *US, US, C*, 1992 *HK*, 1993 *Ar, Ar, W*, 1994 *Fj, HK*, 1995 *Tg, W, NZ*, 1996 *HK, HK, C*, 1997 *US, C, HK*
Y Takahashi 1952 *OU*
T Takata 1974 *NZU*, 1975 *A, A, W, W*, 1976 *BCo, S, WaCl, E, It, Kor*, 1977 *OU, S*
K Takayangi 2001 *Kor, Tai*
K Takei 2004 *It*, 2006 *AG, Kor, Geo, It, Fj*
T Takeyama 1994 *Kor*, 1995 *Tg*
M Takura 1989 *S*, 1990 *Fj, Tg, Kor, Sa, US*, 1991 *US, HK, S, I, Z*, 1994 *Fj, Kor*, 1995 *Tg, R, I*
H Tamura 1998 *HK, US, C, Ar, Kor, Tai, HK, Kor*, 1999 *C*
A Tanabe 2010 *Rus*, 2011 *Kaz, SL*
F Tanaka 2008 *AG, HK, AuA, Tg, Fj, Sa, US, US*, 2009 *Kaz, HK, Sin, Sa, Tg, Fj*, 2010 *Kor, Kaz, HK, Fj, Sa, Tg, Sa, Rus*, 2011 *Kaz, ARE, SL, Sa, Tg, It, F, Tg, C*

K Tanaka 2004 *S, R, W*
N Tanaka 1974 *SL*, 1975 *A, W*, 1976 *BCo, S, E*, 1977 *S*, 1980 *F, Kor*, 1982 *HK, Kor*
S Tanaka 1959 *BCo, BCo*
N Tanifuji 1979 *HK, E, E*, 1982 *C, C*, 1983 *W*, 1984 *F, Kor*, 1985 *US*
Y Tanigawa 1969 *HK*
I Taniguchi 2010 *Rus*, 2011 *Kaz, SL, Sa, Tg, Fj, US, F, NZ, Tg*
T Taniguchi 2006 *Tg, It, JAB*, 2008 *Kor, Kaz, HK, AuA, Tg, Fj, M, Sa, US*
H Tanuma 1996 *Kor*, 1997 *HK, C, US, US, HK*, 1998 *C, US, HK*, 1999 *Sa, Fj, US, Sp, Sa, W, Ar*, 2000 *Fj, US, Tg, Sa, Kor, C, I*, 2001 *Kor, Tai, W, W, Sa, C*, 2002 *Kor*, 2003 *AuA, E, F*
J Tarrant 2009 *Kaz, HK, Kor, Sa, JAB, Tg, Fj*
M Tatsukawa 2000 *Sa*
T Taufa 2009 *Kaz, Kor, Sin, Sa, JAB, Tg, Fj, C, C*, 2010 *Kor, AG, Kaz, HK, Fj, Sa, Tg, Sa*, 2011 *HK, Kaz, ARE, SL, C*
N Taumoefolau 1985 *F, F*, 1986 *US, C, S, E, Kor*, 1987 *US, E, A, NZ*, 1988 *Kor*, 1989 *S*, 1990 *Fj*
T Terai 1969 *HK*, 1970 *Tha*, 1971 *E, E*, 1972 *HK*, 1973 *W, F*, 1974 *NZU*, 1975 *A, W, W*, 1976 *S, E, It, Kor*
S Teramura 1930 *BCo*
LM Thompson 2007 *HK, Fj, Tg, Sa, JAB, It, Fj, W, C*, 2008 *M, Sa, US, US*, 2009 *Kaz, Kor, Sa, Tg, Fj*, 2010 *Kor, AG, Kaz, HK, Fj, Sa, Tg, Sa, Rus*, 2011 *HK, Kaz, SL, Sa, Tg, It, US, F, Tg, C*
R Thompson 1998 *C, US, HK, HK, US, C*
Z Toba-Nakajima 1930 *BCo*, 1932 *C*
K Todd 2000 *Fj, Sa, I*
H Tominaga 1959 *BCo, BCo*
K Tomioka 2008 *US, US*, 2009 *Kor, Sin, Sa, JAB*
T Tomioka 2005 *I, I*
T Toshi 1932 *C, C*
H Toshima 1980 *H, F*, 1982 *HK, C, C*, 1984 *F, F, Kor*
M Toyoda 2008 *US*
N Toyoda 1982 *HK*
S Toyoda 1974 *SL*
T Toyoda 1978 *Kor*
M Toyota 2009 *Sin, Sa, Tg, Fj*, 2010 *Kor, AG, Kaz, HK*
K Toyoyama 1976 *BCo*, 1979 *E, E*, 1980 *H*
M Toyoyama 2000 *Fj, US, Sa, C*, 2001 *Kor, W, W, Sa, C*, 2002 *Rus, Kor, Tai, Kor, Tai*, 2003 *US, Rus, AuA, Kor, E, E, S, Fj, US*
M Tsuchida 1985 *F*
T Tsuchiya 1956 *AuUn*, 1959 *BCo, BCo*
E Tsuji 1980 *Kor*, 1982 *Kor*
T Tsuji 2003 *S, Fj, US*, 2005 *HK, R, C*, 2006 *Kor*
Y Tsujimoto 2001 *Kor*
K Tsukagoshi 2002 *Kor*, 2005 *Ur, Ar, HK, Kor, R, C, I, I*
S Tsukda 2001 *Kor, C*, 2002 *Tg, Tai, Kor, Tai, Kor*, 2003 *AuA, E*
T Tsuyama 1976 *BCo, Kor*
P Tuidraki 1997 *HK, C*, 1998 *C, US, HK, HK, US, C, Tai*, 1999 *Tg, Sa, Fj, Sa, W, Ar*, 2000 *I*, 2001 *Tai, W, W*
A Tupuailai 2009 *C, C*, 2010 *Kor, AG, Kaz, HK, Fj, Sa, Tg, Sa, Rus*, 2011 *HK, Kaz, SL, It, US, F, NZ, Tg, C*

M Uchida 1969 *HK*
A Ueda 1975 *W*, 1978 *Kor*, 1979 *E, E*
T Ueda 2011 *HK, Kaz, ARE, SL, US, NZ*
S Ueki 1963 *BCo*
R Ueno 2011 *SL*
N Ueyama 1973 *F*, 1974 *NZU, SL*, 1975 *A, A, W, W*, 1976 *BCo, E, It, Kor*, 1978 *F*, 1980 *Kor*
H Ujino 1976 *BCo*, 1977 *S*, 1978 *F, Kor*, 1979 *HK, E, E*, 1980 *H, Kor*, 1982 *HK, Kor*
R Umei 1958 *NZ23, NZ23, NZ23*
Y Uryu 2000 *Sa*, 2001 *Kor*
T Usuzuki 2011 *ARE, SL, Sa, Fj, It, US, NZ*

S Vatuvei 2010 *Kor, AG, Kaz, Sa*, 2011 *US, NZ, Tg, C*

K Wada 1997 *HK, US, US, C, HK*
K Wada 2010 *AG, Kaz, Fj, Tg, Rus*
S Wada 1930 *BCo*
T Wada 1975 *A*, 1976 *S*, 1979 *E, E*
J Washington 2005 *Ur, Ar, HK, Kor, R, C, I*
M Washiya 2000 *Kor, C*
H Watanabe 1990 *Sa*
T Watanabe 2002 *Kor*
Y Watanabe 1996 *HK, HK*, 1998 *C, US, HK, Ar, Kor, Tai, HK*, 1999 *C, Tg, US, Sp, Sa*, 2000 *Fj, US*, 2003 *Rus, AuA, AuA, E, S*, 2004 *Kor*, 2005 *HK, R, C*, 2007 *HK, Fj, Tg, Sa, JAB, A, W*
SJ Webb 2008 *AG, Kaz, HK, AuA, Tg, Fj, M, US, US*, 2009 *Kaz, Kor, Sa, Tg, Fj, C, C*, 2010 *Kor, Kaz, HK, Fj, Sa, Tg*, 2011 *HK, Kaz, ARE, SL, Sa, Tg, Fj, It, US, F, NZ, Tg, C*
IM Williams 1993 *W*
MC Williams 2011 *Sa, Fj, US, F, NZ, C*

T Yagai 1930 *BCo*
T Yajima 1978 *Kor*, 1979 *E*
K Yamada 1963 *BCo*
K Yamaguchi 1936 *NZU*
T Yamaguchi 2004 *S, R, W*
Y Yamaguchi 1970 *Tha, BCo*, 1971 *E, E*, 1972 *HK*
E Yamamoto 2001 *Kor, W*, 2002 *Tg, Kor*
I Yamamoto 1973 *W*
M Yamamoto 2002 *Rus, Kor, Tai, Kor*, 2003 *Rus, AuA, AuA, Kor, E, E, Fj, US*, 2004 *Kor, Rus, C, S, R, W*, 2006 *Sa, JAB, Fj*, 2007 *HK, Fj, AuA, JAB, A*
M Yamamoto 2004 *C, S, W*, 2006 *HK, Kor*, 2007 *HK, Fj, Tg, AuA, Sa*
T Yamamoto 1988 *Kor*, 1989 *S*, 1990 *Fj*
R Yamamura 2002 *Tg, Tai, Tai*, 2003 *AuA, F*, 2004 *Kor, Rus, C, It, S, R, W*, 2005 *Ur, Ar, HK, Kor, R, C, I, I, Sp*, 2006 *Kor, Geo, It, Sa, JAB, Fj, HK, Kor*, 2007 *Kor, Tg, AuA, Sa, JAB, It, A, Fj, W, C*
R Yamanaka 2010 *AG*
T Yamaoka 2004 *It, S, R, W*, 2005 *Sp*, 2006 *AG, Kor, Geo, Tg, It, Sa, JAB, Fj*
H Yamashita 2009 *Kaz, HK, Kor, Sin, Sa, JAB, Tg, Fj*
O Yamashita 1974 *SL*
M Yasuda 1984 *F*
N Yasuda 2000 *Kor, I*
Y Yasue 2009 *HK, Kor*
T Yasui 1976 *S, E*, 1977 *S*, 1978 *F, Kor*, 1979 *HK, E*
K Yasumi 1986 *C*, 1987 *US, NZ*
Y Yatomi 2006 *Kor*, 2007 *HK, Fj, Tg, AuA, Sa, JAB, A, Fj*, 2009 *Kaz, Kor, JAB, C*
O Yatsuhashi 1996 *US, C*, 1998 *US, HK, HK, US, C, Ar, Tai, Kor*, 2000 *Kor, C*
A Yokoi 1969 *HK*, 1970 *Tha, NZU, BCo*, 1971 *E*, 1972 *AuUn, AuUn, HK*, 1973 *W, E, F*, 1974 *NZU*
A Yoshida 1995 *R, W, I, NZ*, 1996 *C, US, C, Kor*, 1997 *US, HK*, 1999 *Sa*, 2000 *Fj, US, Tg, Sa, Kor, C*
H Yoshida 2001 *Sa, C*, 2002 *Tg, Tai*, 2004 *R, W*, 2006 *AG, Kor, Geo, Tg, Sa, JAB, Fj, HK, Kor*
H Yoshida 2008 *Kor, AG, Kaz, M*, 2009 *Kaz, HK, Sin*
J Yoshida 1973 *W, F*
M Yoshida 1974 *NZU*, 1975 *A, A, W*, 1976 *BCo, S, E, It, Kor*, 1977 *S*, 1978 *F, Kor*
T Yoshida 2002 *Tg, Tai, Kor*, 2003 *E*
T Yoshida 2007 *Kor, Fj, Tg, Sa, It, Fj, W, C*, 2008 *Kor, Kaz, AuA, Tg, M, Sa, US*, 2009 *Kor, Sa, JAB, C, C*, 2010 *AG, HK, Sa*, 2011 *US, NZ*
Y Yoshida 1988 *Kor*, 1989 *S*, 1990 *Fj, Tg, Kor, Sa, US, Kor*, 1991 *US, US, C, HK, S, I, Z*, 1992 *HK*, 1993 *Ar, Ar, W*, 1994 *Fj, Fj, HK, Kor*, 1995 *Tg, Tg, R, I, NZ*, 1996 *HK*
K Yoshinaga 1986 *Kor*, 1987 *US, A, NZ*, 1990 *Sa*
K Yoshino 1973 *W*
T Yoshino 1985 *US, I, I, F, F*, 1986 *Kor*, 1987 *NZ*
H Yuhara 2010 *Kor, AG, HK, Fj, Rus*, 2011 *HK, ARE, SL, NZ*

NAMIBIA

NAMIBIA'S 2010–11 TEST RECORD

OPPONENT	DATE	VENUE	RESULT
Portugal	20 Nov	A	**Lost** 12–24
Spain	27 Nov	A	**Lost** 20–33
Romania	10 Jun	A	**Lost** 11–13
Portugal	15 Jun	N	**Won** 29–23
Georgia	19 Jun	N	**Lost** 18–23
Fiji	10 Sep	N	**Lost** 25–49
Samoa	14 Sep	N	**Lost** 12–49
South Africa	22 Sep	N	**Lost** 0–87
Wales	26 Sep	N	**Lost** 7–81

TOE-TO-TOE WITH THE PROS

By Ian Gilbert

Alex Livesey/Getty images

Jacques Burger led Namibia with distinction, pride and passion.

Prop Jané du Toit put it perfectly when he illustrated what Namibia were up against at Rugby World Cup 2011: "I'm an accounts manager in the day; I have to get up at 5am to train before work."

Du Toit's rugby CV includes a stint with South African Currie Cup side Boland, and captain Jacques Burger was a key part of Saracens' march to the Aviva Premiership title last season, but for the most part the Namibians are committed amateurs.

Notwithstanding their wholehearted commitment, the Namibians' fitness wilted in the latter stages of matches as scores ran out to unflattering proportions against Pool D opponents South Africa, Wales, Samoa and Fiji.

Still, several players caught the eye: Burger's indomitable approach, whether with ball in hand or in defence, was always in evidence. So too was his good grace at post-match press conferences, despite having to front as a defeated captain each time, and a feel for a one-liner. After the 49–12 loss to Samoa, when Alesana Tuilagi ran in a hat-trick, Burger commented, "We have to hit around their legs, they're big boys. I'd like to see what they ate growing up."

The Namibians had opened their Rugby World Cup 2011 campaign against Fiji and were determined not to be fazed by opponents who began the tournament five places higher than them in the IRB World Rankings. With more than half the squad playing in their first World Cup, coach Johan Diergaardt didn't hesitate in naming wing Danie Dames and prop Raoul Larson to win their first caps.

Before the match Eugene Jantjies showed a typical scrum-half's confidence in declaring, "We're going to surprise everybody." Unfortunately for his side, the surprises were short-lived. Namibia led 12–7 after 15 minutes through the kicking of fly-half Theuns Kotze but Fiji, quarter-finalists four years ago, found their rhythm as wing Vereniki Goneva crossed for four tries in the 49–25 victory.

Off the pitch Namibia, who played all their matches in the North Island, made sure they soaked up the Kiwi welcome. Former New Zealand centre Andy Jefferd, who was at the reception for Namibia, had no doubt about the important role of the Rugby World Cup in helping the smaller nations grow.

"It's not just about the All Blacks and South Africa and Australia," he said. "It's about all the minor unions, too. It's wonderful hosting a team like Namibia here in Gisborne. You need [smaller] sides to promote the game around the world."

With the hard-hitting Samoans next up on the Namibian schedule – the match to be played, like the first, in Rotorua – wing Conrad Marais said, "We are going to show them that as much as the islanders like to play tough, the guys from Africa are pretty hard as well."

Hardness was not enough, though, as Samoa matched Fiji's near-half-century of points, but centre Danie van Wyk took only positive memories. "It was quite tough," he said. "What a pleasure to get out there, though. How fortunate we are to play a world-class team."

Namibia faced the physical Pacific Island sides in the space of five days, but there were no complaints about the schedule. Full-back Chrysander Botha insisted "we had a good recovery. We can't use that as an excuse. Everyone was well-rested."

The next match, against South Africa, pitted neighbour against neighbour, the first all-African affair on the Rugby World Cup stage. Namibia used to be known as South West Africa, under which name it competed in the Currie Cup.

"Of course, we want to do our nation proud, but we also respect them very much because we are the same people and have the same culture," explained Danie van Wyk.

There was a note of irony when South Africa went through their warm-up at Auckland's North Harbour Stadium as kicking coach and

Springbok legend Percy Montgomery was actually born in Namibia. The skills he and the other trainers have imbued in the Springboks were too much for Namibia as the defending champions ran in 12 tries to win 87–0. "You cannot play rugby without the ball, and you cannot tackle for 80 minutes without getting tired," was coach Diergaardt's verdict.

The experienced Du Toit knows what the top sides are capable of, saying, "Although I'm a former full-time player, for the amateur guys it's a huge eye-opener to see what the full-timers can do. They punish you."

The Welwitchias, as Namibia are known, wound up their campaign against Wales, who had narrowly lost to South Africa and would go on to make the semi-finals of the tournament. The 81–7 defeat at New Plymouth's Stadium Taranaki was as comprehensive as that by the Springboks, but Namibia did at least have the consolation of fielding the Man of the Match, flanker Tinus du Plessis.

Du Plessis was one of the players who hoped an eye-catching tournament might improve his chances of landing a professional contract – which will only benefit the standard of his country's rugby. "In Europe or in South Africa, you play week in week out, so we as a team need more players playing full-time rugby in order for Namibian rugby to move forward," he said.

There are just 1,000 registered players in the country, most of them – such as No. 8 PJ van Lill, a dentist – juggling training with a regular job. Jacques Burger would love to see some way to forge a professional set-up to improve the long-term prospects of Namibian rugby. "Someone really needs to invest in those guys and get them in a professional set-up," he said. "Obviously, it's tough to say that, but if they were in a professional set-up, a lot of these guys would really wow someone and become really good rugby players."

In the meantime, Namibia's Rugby World Cup 2011 total of 266 points conceded was the second-highest for any team at a RWC, exceeded only by the Welwitchias in 2003. In fairness, the Namibians were unlucky to be in a pool comprising defending champions South Africa, plus sides such as Fiji, Samoa and Wales whose games are based on wide movement, skewing the scorelines somewhat.

Namibia have now lost all 15 RWC matches they have played, but on the other hand, their points total of 44 and five tries was their best tournament showing.

The last word should go to Du Toit on what it really means to compete in the blue and white of his nation. "In 2007 I enjoyed the World Cup in France so much that I told myself, 'well, I've got three or four years left in me, if I can make the team for the 2011 World Cup that will be my swansong.'"

NAMIBIA INTERNATIONAL STATISTICS

MATCH RECORDS UP TO 31 OCTOBER 2011

WINNING MARGIN

Date	Opponent	Result	Winning Margin
15/06/2002	Madagascar	112–0	**112**
21/04/1990	Portugal	86–9	**77**
27/05/2006	Kenya	82–12	**70**
26/05/2007	Zambia	80–10	**70**

MOST POINTS IN A MATCH

BY THE TEAM

Date	Opponent	Result	Points
15/06/2002	Madagascar	112–0	**112**
21/04/1990	Portugal	86–9	**86**
31/08/2003	Uganda	82–13	**82**
27/05/2006	Kenya	82–12	**82**

BY A PLAYER

Date	Player	Opponent	Points
06/07/1993	Jaco Coetzee	Kenya	**35**
26/05/2007	Justinus van der Westhuizen	Zambia	**33**
27/06/2009	Chrysander Botha	Cote D'Ivoire	**29**
21/04/1990	Moolman Olivier	Portugal	**26**
15/06/2002	Riaan van Wyk	Madagascar	**25**

MOST TRIES IN A MATCH

BY THE TEAM

Date	Opponent	Result	Tries
15/06/2002	Madagascar	112–0	**18**
21/04/1990	Portugal	86–9	**16**
17/10/1999	Germany	79–13	**13**

BY A PLAYER

Date	Player	Opponent	Tries
21/04/1990	Gerhard Mans	Portugal	**6**
15/06/2002	Riaan van Wyk	Madagascar	**5**
16/05/1992	Eden Meyer	Zimbabwe	**4**
16/08/2003	Melrick Africa	Kenya	**4**

MOST CONVERSIONS IN A MATCH

BY THE TEAM

Date	Opponent	Result	Cons
15/06/2002	Madagascar	112–0	**11**
21/04/1990	Portugal	86–9	**11**
31/08/2003	Uganda	82–13	**11**
27/05/2006	Kenya	82–12	**11**

BY A PLAYER

Date	Player	Opponent	Cons
21/04/1990	Moolman Olivier	Portugal	**11**
27/05/2006	Morne Schreuder	Kenya	**11**
26/05/2007	Justinus van der Westhuizen	Zambia	**9**
31/08/2003	Rudi van Vuuren	Uganda	**8**
04/07/1993	Jaco Coetzee	Arabian Gulf	**8**

MOST PENALTIES IN A MATCH

BY THE TEAM

Date	Opponent	Result	Pens
22/06/1991	Italy	33–19	**5**
23/01/1998	Portugal	36–19	**5**
30/06/1990	France A	20–25	**5**
28/11/2009	Tunisia	22–10	**5**
15/06/2011	Portugal	29–23	**5**

BY A PLAYER

Date	Player	Opponent	Pens
22/06/1991	Jaco Coetzee	Italy	**5**
23/01/1998	Rudi van Vuuren	Portugal	**5**
30/06/1990	Shaun McCulley	France A	**5**
28/11/2009	Emile Wessels	Tunisia	**5**
15/06/2011	Theuns Kotze	Portugal	**5**

MOST DROPPED GOALS IN A MATCH

BY THE TEAM

Date	Opponent	Result	DGs
10/09/2011	Fiji	25–49	**3**

BY A PLAYER

Date	Player	Opponent	Pens
10/09/2011	Theuns Kotze	Fiji	**3**

MOST CAPPED PLAYERS

Name	Caps
Hugo Horn	35
Herman Lindvelt	33
Eugene Jantjies	32
Johnnie Redelinghuys	30
Nico Esterhuyse	30

LEADING TRY SCORERS

Name	Tries
Gerhard Mans	27
Eden Meyer	21
Melrick Africa	12

LEADING CONVERSIONS SCORERS

Name	Cons
Jaco Coetzee	82
Morne Schreuder	36
Rudi van Vuuren	26

LEADING PENALTY SCORERS

Name	Pens
Jaco Coetzee	46
Emile Wessels	21
Morne Schreuder	18
Rudi van Vuuren	14

LEADING DROPPED GOAL SCORERS

Name	DGs
Jaco Coetzee	3
Theuns Kotze	3

LEADING POINTS SCORERS

Name	Points
Jaco Coetzee	340
Morne Schreuder	146
Gerhard Mans	118
Rudi van Vuuren	109
Chrysander Botha	102

Alex Livesey/Getty Images

Namibian star Chrysander Botha went through the 100-point barrier for Tests this year.

NAMIBIA INTERNATIONAL PLAYERS

(UP TO 31 OCTOBER 2011)

Note: Years given for International Championship matches are for second half of season; eg 1972 means season 1971–72. Years for all other matches refer to the actual year of the match. Entries in square brackets denote matches played in RWC Finals.

MJ Africa 2003 *Sa, Ken, Uga, Ar, I, A,* 2005 *Mad, Mor,* 2006 *Ken, Tun, Ken, Tun, Mor, Mor,* 2007 *Za, Geo, R, Uga, SA, I, F, Ar, Geo*
W Alberts 1991 *Sp, Pt, It, It, Z, Z, I, I, Z, Z, Z,* 1995 *Z,* 1996 *Z, Z*
H Amakali 2005 *Mad*
J Augustyn 1991 *Z,* 1998 *Iv, Mor, Z*

RS Bardenhorst 2007 *Geo, R*
J Barnard 1990 *Z, Pt, W, W, F, F,* 1991 *Sp, Pt, It, It, Z, Z, I, I, Z, Z, Z,* 1992 *Z, Z*
D Beukes 2000 *Z, Ur,* 2001 *Z, Z*
E Beukes 1990 *Z, F, WGe*
J Beukes 1994 *Z, Mor,* 1995 *Z*
AJ Blaauw 1996 *Z, Z,* 1997 *Tg,* 1998 *Pt, Tun, Z, Iv, Mor, Z,* 1999 *Z, Fj, F, C, Ger,* 2000 *Z, Z, Ur,* 2001 *It,* 2003 *Ar, I, A, R,* 2004 *Mor*
ML Blom 2010 *Sp,* 2011 *Pt, Geo*
J Bock 2005 *Mad, Mor,* 2009 *Iv, Iv,* 2010 *R, Geo, Pt*
JH Bock 2005 *Mad, Mor,* 2006 *Ken, Tun, Ken, Tun, Mor, Mor,* 2007 *Za, R, SA, I, F, Ar, Geo,* 2009 *Pt, Tun,* 2010 *R, Geo,* 2011 *R, Pt, Geo, SA*
J Booysen 2003 *Sa, Ken, Ar, A,* 2007 *Uga*
M Booysen 1993 *W, AG, Z,* 1994 *Rus, Z, HK,* 1996 *Z, Z*
LW Botes 2006 *Ken, Mor,* 2007 *Za, Geo, R, Uga, SA, F*
CA Botha 2008 *Z,* 2009 *Iv, Iv, Pt, Tun, Tun,* 2010 *Rus, R, Geo, Pt, Sp,* 2011 *R, Pt, Geo, Fj, Sa, SA, W*
HP Botha 2000 *Z, Z, Ur*
H Breedt 1998 *Tun, Z*
H Brink 1992 *Z, Z,* 1993 *W, Ken, Z,* 1994 *Rus, Z, Iv, Mor, HK*
J Britz 1996 *Z*
E Buitenbag 2010 *Rus*
B Buitendag 1990 *W, W, F, F, WGe,* 1991 *Sp, Pt, It, It, Z, Z, I, I, Z, Z, Z,* 1992 *Z, Z,* 1993 *W, AG, Ken, Z*
J Burger 2004 *Za, Ken, Z, Mor,* 2006 *Tun, Tun, Mor, Mor,* 2007 *Za, Geo, R, SA, I, F, Ar, Geo,* 2008 *Z,* 2009 *Iv, Iv, Pt, Tun, Tun,* 2010 *R, Geo, Pt,* 2011 *Fj, Sa, SA, W*

B Calitz 1995 *Z*
C Campbell 2008 *Z*
DJ Coetzee 1990 *Pt, W, F, F, WGe,* 1991 *Sp, Pt, It, It, Z, Z, I, I, Z, Z, Z,* 1992 *Z, Z,* 1993 *W, AG, Ken, Z,* 1994 *Z, Iv, Mor, HK,* 1995 *Z, Z*
JC Coetzee 1990 *W*
M Couw 2006 *Ken*
B Cronjé 1994 *Rus*

HDP Dames 2011 *Fj, Sa, SA, W*
J Dames 1998 *Tun, Z*
D de Beer 2000 *Z*
S de Beer 1995 *Z,* 1997 *Tg,* 1998 *Tun, Z, Iv, Mor, Z,* 1999 *Ger*
AD de Klerk 2009 *Iv, Iv*
CJ De Koe 2010 *Geo, Pt, Sp*
DP De La Harpe 2010 *Rus, R, Geo, Pt, Sp,* 2011 *R, Pt, Geo, Fj, Sa, SA, W*
RCA De La Harpe 2011 *R, Pt, Geo, Fj, SA, W*
SC De La Harpe 2010 *Sp*
H de Waal 1990 *Z, Pt*
N de Wet 2000 *Ur*
R Dedig 2004 *Mor, Za, Ken, Z, Mor*
CJH Derks 1990 *Z, Pt, W, W, F, F, WGe,* 1991 *Sp, Pt, It, It, Z, Z, I, I, Z, Z, Z,* 1992 *Z, Z,* 1993 *W, AG, Z,* 1994 *Rus, Z, Iv, Mor, HK*
J Deysel 1990 *Z, Pt, W, W,* 1991 *Sp, Pt, It, It, Z, Z, I, I, Z, Z, Z,* 1992 *Z*
V Dreyer 2002 *Z,* 2003 *Ar, I*
J Drotsky 2006 *Ken,* 2008 *Sen*
AJ Du Plessis 2010 *Pt, Sp*
I du Plessis 2005 *Mor,* 2009 *Tun*
M du Plessis 2001 *Z,* 2005 *Mor*
N du Plessis 1993 *Ken,* 1994 *Rus,* 1995 *Z*
O Du Plessis 2008 *Sen*
T Du Plessis 2006 *Ken, Tun, Mor, Mor,* 2007 *Geo, R, Uga, SA, I, F, Ar, Geo,* 2008 *Sen, Z,* 2009 *Iv, Iv, Pt, Tun, Tun,* 2010 *R, Geo, Pt, Sp,* 2011 *R, Pt, Geo, Fj, SA, W*
P du Plooy 1992 *Z, Z,* 1994 *Z, Mor, HK*
S du Rand 2007 *Geo, R, Uga*
JA Du Toit 2007 *Za, Geo, R, Uga, SA, I, F, Geo,* 2008 *Sen, Z,* 2009 *Pt, Tun, Tun,* 2010 *Rus, R, Geo, Pt, Sp,* 2011 *R, Pt, Geo, Sa, SA, W*
N du Toit 2002 *Tun,* 2003 *Sa, Ar, I, A, R*
V du Toit 1990 *Pt, W, W, F*
JH Duvenhage 2000 *Z, Z,* 2001 *It, Z, Z,* 2002 *Mad,* 2003 *Sa, Uga, Ar, I, R,* 2007 *Za, R, Uga*

A Engelbrecht 2000 *Z*
J Engelbrecht 1990 *WGe,* 1994 *Rus, Z, Iv, Mor, HK,* 1995 *Z, Z*
N Engelbrecht 1996 *Z*
H Engels 1990 *F, WGe*
E Erasmus 1997 *Tg*
G Esterhuizen 2008 *Sen, Z*
SF Esterhuizen 2008 *Z,* 2009 *Iv, Iv, Pt, Tun, Tun,* 2010 *Rus, R, Geo, Pt, Sp,* 2011 *R, Pt*
N Esterhuyse 2006 *Ken, Tun, Mor,* 2007 *Za, Geo, R, Uga, SA, I, F, Ar, Geo,* 2008 *Z,* 2009 *Iv, Iv, Pt, Tun, Tun,* 2010 *Rus, R, Geo, Pt, Sp,* 2011 *R, Pt, Geo, Fj, Sa, SA, W*

D Farmer 1997 *Tg,* 1998 *Pt, Iv, Mor, Z,* 1999 *Z, Fj, Ger*
F Fisch 1999 *Z, Ger*
TR Forbes 2010 *Rus*
HH Franken 2011 *Sa*
S Furter 1999 *Z, Fj, F, C, Ger,* 2001 *It,* 2002 *Mad, Z, Tun, Tun,* 2003 *Sa, Ken, Uga, Ar, I, A, R,* 2004 *Mor,* 2006 *Ken, Tun, Ken*

E Gaoab 2005 *Mad, Mor*
I Gaya 2004 *Za, Ken*
J Genis 2000 *Z, Z, Ur,* 2001 *Z*
N Genis 2006 *Mor*
R Gentz 2001 *It*
R Glundeung 2006 *Ken*
CJ Goosen 1991 *Sp, Pt, It, It,* 1993 *W*
D Gouws 2000 *Z, Z, Ur,* 2001 *It, Z, Z*
T Gouws 2003 *Ken, Uga,* 2004 *Za, Ken,* 2006 *Ken, Tun*
A Graham 2001 *It, Z, Z,* 2002 *Mad, Tun,* 2003 *Ken, Uga, I,* 2004 *Mor*
A Greeff 1997 *Tg*
D Grobelaar 2008 *Z*

DP Grobler 2001 *Z*, 2002 *Mad*, *Tun*, *Tun*, 2003 *Sa*, *Ken*, *Uga*, *Ar*, *I*, *A*, *R*, 2004 *Mor*, *Za*, *Ken*, *Z*, *Mor*, 2006 *Ken*, *Tun*, *Ken*, 2007 *Za*, *Geo*, *R*, *SA*, *Ar*
HJ Grobler 1990 *Z*, *Pt*, *W*, *W*, *F*, *F*, *WGe*, 1991 *Sp*, *Pt*, *It*, *It*, *Z*, *Z*, *I*, *I*, *Z*, *Z*, *Z*, 1992 *Z*, *Z*
T Grünewald 1990 *Z*
D Grunschloss 2003 *A*, *R*

F Hartung 1996 *Z*, *Z*
RJ Herridge 2009 *Pt*, *Tun*, *Tun*
L Holtzhausen 1997 *Tg*, 1998 *Pt*, *Tun*, *Z*, *Iv*, *Mor*, *Z*, 1999 *Ger*
F Horn 2005 *Mad*, *Mor*, 2006 *Ken*
H Horn 1997 *Tg*, 1998 *Pt*, *Iv*, *Mor*, *Z*, 1999 *Z*, *Fj*, *F*, *C*, *Ger*, 2001 *It*, 2002 *Mad*, *Z*, *Tun*, 2003 *Sa*, 2007 *Za*, *Geo*, *R*, *Uga*, *SA*, *I*, *F*, *Ar*, *Geo*, 2008 *Sen*, *Z*, 2009 *Iv*, *Iv*, *Tun*, *Tun*, 2010 *Rus*, 2011 *Fj*, *Sa*, *SA*, *W*
K Horn 1997 *Tg*, 1998 *Pt*
Q Hough 1995 *Z*, *Z*, 1998 *Pt*, *Tun*, *Z*, *Iv*, *Mor*, *Z*, 1999 *Z*, *Fj*, *F*, *C*
D Husselman 1993 *AG*, 1994 *Z*, *Mor*, 2002 *Mad*, *Z*, *Tun*, 2003 *Sa*, *Ar*, *I*, *A*
JJ Husselman 2004 *Za*, *Ken*

E Isaacs 1993 *Ken*, 1994 *Iv*
P Isaacs 2000 *Z*, *Z*, *Ur*, 2001 *Z*, *Z*, 2003 *A*, 2005 *Mad*, *Mor*
E Izaacs 1998 *Pt*, 1999 *Z*, *Ger*, 2000 *Z*, *Z*, *Ur*, 2001 *It*, *Z*, *Z*, 2002 *Mad*, *Z*, *Tun*, *Tun*, 2003 *Sa*, *Ken*, *Ar*, *A*, *R*

M Jacobs 1999 *Z*, *Fj*, *F*, *Ger*
E Jansen 2006 *Ken*
EA Jantjies 2006 *Ken*, *Tun*, *Ken*, *Tun*, 2007 *Za*, *Geo*, *R*, *Uga*, *SA*, *I*, *F*, *Ar*, *Geo*, 2008 *Sen*, *Z*, 2009 *Iv*, *Iv*, *Pt*, *Tun*, *Tun*, 2010 *Rus*, *R*, *Geo*, *Pt*, *Sp*, 2011 *R*, *Pt*, *Geo*, *Fj*, *Sa*, *SA*, *W*
R Jantjies 1994 *HK*, 1995 *Z*, *Z*, 1996 *Z*, 1998 *Pt*, *Tun*, *Iv*, *Mor*, *Z*, 1999 *Z*, *Fj*, *F*, *C*, 2000 *Z*, *Z*
M Jeary 2003 *Uga*, 2004 *Ken*, *Z*, *Mor*
R Jeary 2000 *Z*, *Ur*
D Jeffrey 1990 *F*
J Jenkins 2002 *Mad*, *Tun*, 2003 *Ken*

D Kamonga 2004 *Mor*, *Za*, *Ken*, *Z*, *Mor*, 2007 *Uga*, *Geo*
M Kapitako 2000 *Z*, *Z*, 2001 *It*, *Z*, *Z*, 2003 *Uga*, 2004 *Za*, 2006 *Tun*
M Katjiuanjo 2005 *Mad*, *Mor*
M Kazombiaze 2006 *Ken*, *Tun*
U Kazombiaze 2006 *Ken*, *Tun*, *Mor*, *Mor*, 2007 *Za*, *Uga*, *SA*, *I*, *F*, *Ar*, *Geo*, 2008 *Sen*, *Z*, 2009 *Iv*, *Iv*, *Pt*, *Tun*, *Tun*, 2010 *Rus*, *Geo*, 2011 *W*
R Kitshoff 2010 *Pt*, *Sp*, 2011 *R*, *Pt*, *Geo*, *Fj*, *Sa*, *SA*, *W*
DPW Koen 2006 *Tun*
HVW Koll 2009 *Pt*, *Tun*, 2010 *Rus*, *R*, *Geo*, *Pt*, *Sp*, 2011 *R*, *Pt*, *Geo*, *Fj*, *Sa*, *SA*, *W*
A Kotze 1991 *Sp*, *Z*, *Z*, *I*, *I*, 1993 *W*, *AG*, *Z*
D Kotze 1993 *W*, *AG*, *Ken*, *Z*, 1994 *Rus*, *HK*
J Kotze 1995 *Z*, *Z*, 1996 *Z*, *Z*, 2000 *Z*, *Z*, 2001 *It*, *Z*, *Z*, 2002 *Mad*, *Z*, *Tun*, *Tun*, 2004 *Za*, *Ken*, *Z*, *Mor*
P Kotze 2001 *It*
P Kotze 1996 *Z*
TAW Kotze 2011 *Pt*, *Fj*, *Sa*, *SA*, *W*
L Kotzee 2008 *Z*
JL Kruger 2001 *It*, *Z*, *Z*
R Kruger 2003 *Ken*, *Uga*, 2005 *Mad*, *Mor*
R Kruger 2004 *Mor*, *Za*, *Ken*, *Mor*

SO Lambert 2000 *Z*, *Ur*, 2001 *It*, *Z*, *Z*, 2003 *Ken*, *Uga*, 2004 *Mor*, 2005 *Mad*, 2006 *Ken*, *Tun*, *Ken*
B Langenhoven 2007 *SA*, *I*, *F*, *Ar*, *Geo*, 2008 *Sen*, *Z*, 2009 *Pt*, *Tun*, *Tun*, 2010 *Rus*
R Larson 2011 *Fj*, *Sa*, *W*
G Lensing 2002 *Mad*, *Z*, *Tun*, *Tun*, 2003 *Sa*, *Ar*, *I*, *A*, *R*, 2004 *Mor*, 2006 *Ken*, *Mor*, *Mor*, 2007 *R*, *SA*, *I*, *F*, *Ar*, *Geo*, 2009 *Iv*, *Iv*, *Tun*, *Tun*
C Lesch 2005 *Mad*, *Mor*
HD Lindvelt 1998 *Iv*, *Z*, 1999 *F*, *C*, *Ger*, 2001 *It*, *Z*, *Z*, 2002 *Mad*, *Z*, *Tun*, *Tun*, 2003 *Sa*, *Ken*, *Uga*, *Ar*, *I*, *A*, 2004 *Mor*, *Za*, *Ken*, *Z*, *Mor*, 2006 *Ken*, *Tun*, *Ken*, *Mor*, *Mor*, 2007 *Za*, *Geo*, *SA*, *F*, *Ar*

J Lombaard 1996 *Z*
H Loots 1990 *Z*
J Losper 2005 *Mor*
SJ Losper 1990 *Z*, *Pt*, *W*, *W*, *F*, *F*, *WGe*, 1991 *Sp*, *Pt*, *It*, *It*, *Z*, *Z*, *I*, *I*, *Z*, *Z*, *Z*
TC Losper 2007 *Za*, *Geo*, *R*, *Uga*, *SA*, *I*, *F*, 2008 *Sen*, 2011 *Geo*, *W*
W Lötter 1990 *Z*
RC Loubser 1999 *F*, 2005 *Mad*, *Mor*
O Louw 1993 *Ken*, *Z*, 1994 *Z*, *Iv*, 1996 *Z*

M MacKenzie 2004 *Mor*, 2006 *Ken*, *Tun*, 2007 *Uga*, *I*, *F*, *Ar*
B Malgas 1991 *Z*, *Z*, *Z*, 1993 *W*, *AG*, *Ken*, *Z*, 1994 *Rus*, *Z*, *Iv*, *Mor*, *HK*, 1995 *Z*, *Z*, 1996 *Z*
G Mans 1990 *Z*, *Pt*, *W*, *W*, *F*, 1991 *Sp*, *Pt*, *It*, *It*, *Z*, *Z*, *I*, *I*, *Z*, *Z*, *Z*, 1992 *Z*, *Z*, 1993 *W*, *AG*, *Ken*, *Z*, 1994 *Rus*, *Z*, *Iv*, *Mor*, *HK*
C Marais 2010 *Pt*, *Sp*, 2011 *Fj*, *SA*
M Marais 1992 *Z*, 1993 *W*, *AG*, *Z*
W Maritz 1990 *Z*, 1991 *Z*, *Z*, *I*, *I*, *Z*, *Z*, *Z*
S McCulley 1990 *W*, *W*, *F*, *WGe*
E Meyer 1991 *Sp*, *Pt*, *It*, *It*, *Z*, *Z*, *I*, *I*, *Z*, *Z*, *Z*, 1992 *Z*, *Z*, 1993 *W*, 1994 *Z*, *Iv*, *Mor*, *HK*, 1995 *Z*, *Z*, 1996 *Z*
H Meyer 2004 *Za*, *Ken*, *Z*, *Mor*
JM Meyer 2003 *Ken*, *Uga*, *Ar*, *I*, *R*, 2006 *Ken*, *Tun*, *Tun*, *Mor*, *Mor*, 2007 *Uga*, *SA*, *I*, *F*, *Ar*, *Geo*
P Meyer 2005 *Mad*
DA Mouton 1999 *Z*, *Fj*, *Ger*, 2000 *Z*, *Z*, *Ur*, 2002 *Mad*, *Z*, *Tun*, 2003 *Sa*, *Ken*, *Uga*, *Ar*, *I*, *A*, *R*, 2004 *Mor*, 2005 *Mad*, *Mor*, 2006 *Tun*, *Ken*, *Tun*, *Mor*, 2007 *Ar*, 2008 *Sen*
H Mouton 2000 *Z*
P Mouton 2005 *Mad*, *Mor*

H Neethling 1993 *Ken*
G Nel 2006 *Mor*, *Mor*
S Nell 2000 *Z*, *Z*
J Nienaber 1998 *Pt*, *Tun*, *Z*, *Mor*, *Z*
J Nieuwenhuis 2007 *Za*, *Geo*, *R*, *Uga*, *SA*, *I*, *F*, *Geo*, 2008 *Sen*, *Z*, 2009 *Iv*, *Iv*, *Tun*, *Tun*, 2010 *R*, *Geo*, *Sp*, 2011 *R*, *Pt*, *Geo*, *Fj*, *SA*, *W*

EB O'Callaghan 2010 *R*, *Geo*, *Pt*, *Sp*, 2011 *R*, *Pt*, *Geo*, *Fj*, *Sa*, *SA*, *W*
J Olivier 1999 *Z*, *Fj*, *Ger*, 2000 *Z*, *Z*, *Ur*
M Olivier 1990 *Pt*, *F*
LT Oosthuizen 1990 *Z*, *Pt*, *W*, *W*, *F*, *F*, *WGe*
J Opperman 1999 *Z*, *Fj*, *F*, *C*, *Ger*
T Opperman 2002 *Mad*, *Z*
WJ Otto 1993 *AG*, *Z*, 1994 *Rus*

R Pedro 1998 *Z*, 1999 *Ger*, 2000 *Ur*, 2001 *It*, *Z*, *Z*, 2003 *Sa*, *Ken*, *Uga*, *Ar*, *I*, *A*, *R*, 2004 *Mor*
DG Philander 2008 *Sen*, 2009 *Iv*, *Iv*, *Pt*, *Tun*, *Tun*, 2010 *Rus*, 2011 *R*, *Pt*, *Geo*, *W*
F Pienaar 2006 *Ken*
D Pieters 2008 *Sen*
L Plaath 2001 *It*, *Z*, *Z*
CJ Powell 2001 *It*, *Z*, *Z*, 2002 *Mad*, *Z*, *Tun*, *Tun*, 2003 *Sa*, *Ken*, *Uga*, *Ar*, *I*, *R*, 2004 *Mor*, *Ken*, *Z*, *Mor*, 2006 *Ken*, *Tun*, *Tun*, *Mor*, *Mor*, 2007 *Za*, *Geo*, *R*, *Ar*, *Geo*

JH Redelinghuys 2006 *Ken*, *Tun*, *Mor*, 2007 *Za*, *Geo*, *R*, *Uga*, *SA*, *I*, *F*, *Ar*, *Geo*, 2008 *Sen*, *Z*, 2009 *Iv*, *Pt*, *Tun*, 2010 *Rus*, *R*, *Geo*, *Pt*, *Sp*, 2011 *R*, *Pt*, *Geo*, *Fj*, *Sa*, *SA*, *W*
C Redlinghaus 2001 *It*
H Reinders 1996 *Z*
G Rich 1993 *W*
C Roets 1995 *Z*
P Rossouw 2004 *Za*, *Ken*, *Z*, *Mor*, 2005 *Mad*, *Mor*, 2006 *Mor*, *Mor*, 2007 *Za*, *Geo*, *R*

A Samuelson 1995 *Z*, 1996 *Z*, *Z*, 1997 *Tg*, 1998 *Pt*, *Tun*, *Z*, *Iv*, *Mor*, *Z*, 1999 *Z*, *Fj*, *F*, *C*, *Ger*
M Schreuder 2002 *Mad*, *Z*, *Tun*, *Tun*, 2003 *Sa*, *Ken*, *Uga*, *I*, *A*, *R*, 2004 *Mor*, *Za*, *Ken*, *Z*, *Mor*, 2006 *Ken*, *Ken*, 2007 *Ar*, *Geo*
C Schumacher 1995 *Z*
JH Senekal 1998 *Iv*, *Mor*, *Z*, 1999 *Z*, *Fj*, *F*, *C*, *Ger*, 2002

Mad, *Z*, 2003 *Sa*, *Ken*, *Uga*, *Ar*, *I*, *A*, *R*, 2005 *Mad*, 2006 *Ken*, *Mor*, *Mor*, 2007 *Geo*, *R*, *Uga*, *I*, *Ar*, *Geo*
A Skinner 1990 *Z*, *Pt*, *W*, *W*, *F*, *F*, *WGe*
G Smit 1990 *F*
E Smith 1998 *Tun*, *Iv*, *Mor*, *Z*, 1999 *Fj*, *F*, *C*, 2002 *Mad*
P Smith 1993 *Ken*, 1994 *Iv*, 1995 *Z*, *Z*
S Smith 1990 *Pt*, *W*, *W*, *F*, 1992 *Z*, *Z*, 1993 *W*, *AG*, *Ken*, *Z*, 1994 *Rus*, *Z*, *Iv*, *Mor*, *HK*, 1996 *Z*
W Smith 2002 *Mad*, *Z*, *Tun*
D Snyders 2003 *Uga*, 2005 *Mad*
H Snyman 1990 *F*, *F*, 1991 *Sp*, *Pt*, *It*, *It*, *Z*, *Z*, *I*, *I*, *Z*, *Z*, *Z*, 1992 *Z*, *Z*, 1993 *W*, *AG*, *Ken*, *Z*, 1994 *Z*, *Iv*, *Mor*, *HK*, 1995 *Z*, *Z*, 1996 *Z*, *Z*
M Snyman 1994 *Rus*, *Z*, *Iv*, *Mor*, *HK*
D Spangenberg 2005 *Mad*, *Mor*
A Steenkamp 1994 *Iv*, *Mor*
C Steenkamp 2007 *Uga*
T Steenkamp 1992 *Z*, *Z*, 1993 *Ken*, 1994 *Rus*, *Iv*, 1995 *Z*, 1996 *Z*, 1998 *Pt*, *Tun*, *Z*
P Steyn 1996 *Z*, *Z*, 1997 *Tg*, 1998 *Pt*, *Tun*, *Z*, *Iv*, *Mor*, 1999 *Z*, *Fj*, *F*, *C*
A Stoop 1990 *Z*, *Pt*, *W*, 1991 *Sp*, *Pt*, *It*, *It*, *Z*, *I*, *I*, *Z*
L Stoop 1994 *Iv*
G Suze 2005 *Mad*
N Swanepoel 2003 *Ken*, *Ar*, *I*, *A*, *R*, 2004 *Mor*, *Za*, *Ken*, *Z*, *Mor*
H Swart 1995 *Z*, 1996 *Z*, 1997 *Tg*, 1998 *Pt*, *Tun*, *Z*
JL Swart 1990 *F*, *WGe*
BM Swartz 1990 *W*, *W*, *F*, *F*, *WGe*

R Theart 1998 *Pt*
J Theron 1998 *Iv*, *Mor*, *Z*, 1999 *Fj*, *F*, *C*, *Ger*, 2004 *Mor*
RHR Thompson 2004 *Za*, *Ken*, *Mor*, 2005 *Mad*, 2006 *Ken*, *Tun*, *Ken*, *Tun*, *Mor*, *Mor*
D Tredoux 2001 *Z*

L van Coller 1993 *AG*, *Ken*, 1994 *Rus*, *Iv*
GE van der Berg 2005 *Mor*, 2006 *Ken*, *Tun*, *Tun*, *Mor*
L van der Linde 2006 *Tun*
A van der Merwe 1990 *Pt*, *W*, *W*, *F*, *F*, *WGe*, 1991 *Sp*, *Pt*, *It*, *It*, *Z*, *Z*, *I*, *I*, *Z*, *Z*, *Z*, 1992 *Z*, *Z*
D van der Merwe 1990 *WGe*
S van der Merwe 1997 *Tg*, 1998 *Iv*, *Mor*, *Z*, 1999 *Z*, *Fj*, *F*, *C*, 2002 *Z*, *Tun*, *Tun*, 2003 *Sa*, *Ken*, *Ar*, *I*, *A*, *R*, 2004 *Za*, *Ken*, *Z*, *Mor*, 2006 *Tun*, *Mor*
J van der Westhuizen 2007 *Za*, *Geo*
L van Dyk 1998 *Tun*, *Z*, *Iv*, *Mor*, *Z*, 1999 *Fj*, *F*, *C*, *Ger*, 2002 *Mad*
JA van Lill 2002 *Mad*, *Tun*, *Tun*, 2003 *Sa*, *Ar*, *I*, *A*, *R*, 2004 *Mor*, 2006 *Tun*, 2007 *Za*
PJ Van Lill 2006 *Ken*, 2008 *Sen*, *Z*, 2009 *Iv*, *Pt*, *Tun*, *Tun*, 2010 *Rus*, *R*, *Geo*, *Pt*, *Sp*, 2011 *R*, *Pt*, *Geo*, *Fj*, *Sa*, *SA*
RE Van Neel 2010 *Rus*, 2011 *Sa*
F van Rensburg 1995 *Z*, 1996 *Z*, *Z*, 1997 *Tg*, 1998 *Tun*, *Z*, 1999 *Z*, *Fj*, *F*, *C*, *Ger*, 2000 *Z*, 2001 *It*, *Z*, *Z*
SJ van Rensburg 1998 *Z*, *Iv*, *Mor*, *Z*, 1999 *Z*, *Fj*, *F*, *Ger*, 2000 *Z*, *Ur*
SL Van Rooi 2003 *Uga*, *A*, 2004 *Mor*, 2005 *Mor*
A van Rooyen 1991 *Sp*, *Pt*, *It*, *It*, *I*, 1992 *Z*, *Z*
M van Rooyen 1996 *Z*, 1998 *Pt*, *Tun*, *Z*, *Mor*, *Z*, 1999 *Z*, *F*, *C*
C van Schalkwyk 1993 *AG*, *Z*
A Van Tonder 1995 *Z*
CJ van Tonder 2002 *Tun*, 2003 *Sa*, *Ken*, *Uga*, *I*, *A*, *R*, 2004 *Mor*, *Za*, *Ken*, *Z*, *Mor*, 2006 *Ken*, *Ken*, 2007 *Za*
JH Van Tonder 2004 *Mor*, *Ken*, *Z*, *Mor*, 2006 *Ken*, *Tun*, 2007 *Uga*, *SA*, *I*, *F*, *Ar*, *Geo*, 2008 *Z*, 2009 *Iv*, *Iv*, *Pt*, *Tun*
N van Vuuren 1993 *AG*
RJ van Vuuren 1997 *Tg*, 1998 *Pt*, *Tun*, *Z*, 1999 *Z*, *Ger*, 2000 *Z*, *Z*, *Ur*, 2002 *Mad*, *Z*, 2003 *Ken*, *Uga*, *R*
A van Wyk 1993 *W*, *Ken*, 1994 *Iv*, *HK*
D Van Wyk 2011 *R*, *Pt*, *Geo*, *Fj*, *Sa*, *SA*, *W*
G van Wyk 1999 *Z*, *Fj*, *F*, *C*, 2000 *Z*, *Z*, *Ur*, 2001 *It*
L van Wyk 2004 *Mor*
M Van Wyk 2009 *Iv*, *Iv*, *Pt*, 2010 *Rus*, *Geo*, *Pt*, 2011 *R*, *Pt*, *Geo*
R van Wyk 2002 *Mad*, *Z*, *Tun*, *Tun*, 2003 *Sa*, 2004 *Mor*, *Za*, *Ken*, *Z*, *Mor*
R van Wyk 2004 *Za*, *Ken*, *Z*, *Mor*
J van Zyl 2008 *Sen*
R van Zyl 1997 *Tg*, 1998 *Tun*, *Z*, *Iv*, *Mor*, *Z*
WP Van Zyl 2007 *SA*, *I*, *F*, *Ar*, *Geo*, 2008 *Z*, 2009 *Iv*, *Iv*, *Pt*, *Tun*, *Tun*, 2010 *R*, *Geo*, *Pt*, *Sp*, 2011 *Fj*, *Sa*, *SA*, *W*
M Venter 2003 *Uga*, 2004 *Mor*, 2008 *Z*, 2009 *Iv*, *Iv*, *Pt*, *Tun*, *Tun*, 2010 *Rus*
D Vermaak 1998 *Z*
JJ Vermaak 1990 *Pt*, 1994 *Rus*, 1996 *Z*
A Vermeulen 2010 *Rus*
B Vermeulen 1995 *Z*
D Vermeulen 1996 *Z*, *Z*, 1997 *Tg*, 1998 *Pt*
G Vermeulen 1991 *Z*
M Visser 2007 *Za*, *Geo*, *R*, *Uga*, *SA*, *Ar*, *Geo*, 2009 *Iv*, *Iv*, *Pt*, *Tun*, *Tun*, 2010 *Rus*, *R*, *Geo*, *Pt*, *Sp*, 2011 *SA*
CW Viviers 2010 *Sp*, 2011 *R*, *Pt*, *Geo*
P von Wielligh 1991 *It*, *Z*, 1992 *Z*, 1993 *AG*, *Z*, 1994 *Iv*, *Mor*, 1995 *Z*, 1996 *Z*

B Walters 2009 *Pt*
GAE Walters 2008 *Z*, 2009 *Iv*, 2010 *R*, *Geo*, *Pt*, *Sp*
W Wentzel 1991 *Sp*, *Z*, *Z*
E Wessels 2002 *Tun*, *Tun*, 2003 *Sa*, *Ar*, *I*, *A*, *R*, 2006 *Tun*, *Mor*, *Mor*, 2007 *SA*, *I*, *F*, 2009 *Iv*, *Pt*, *Tun*, *Tun*, 2010 *Rus*
LP Winkler 2008 *Z*, 2009 *Iv*, *Iv*, 2010 *Rus*, *R*, *Geo*, 2011 *R*, *Pt*, *Geo*, *Fj*, *Sa*
RC Witbooi 2004 *Za*, *Z*, 2005 *Mor*, 2006 *Ken*, *Tun*, *Ken*, 2007 *Za*, *Geo*, *R*, *Uga*, *I*, *F*, *Geo*, 2008 *Sen*
J Wohler 2005 *Mad*, *Mor*

J Zaayman 1997 *Tg*, 1998 *Pt*, *Tun*, *Z*, *Iv*, *Mor*, *Z*, 1999 *Z*, *Fj*, *F*, *C*, *Ger*

NEW ZEALAND

NEW ZEALAND'S 2010–11 TEST RECORD

OPPONENTS	DATE	VENUE	RESULT
Australia	30 Oct	N	**Lost** 24–26
England	6 Nov	A	**Won** 26–16
Scotland	13 Nov	A	**Won** 49–3
Ireland	20 Nov	A	**Won** 38–13
Wales	27 Nov	A	**Won** 37–25
Fiji	22 Jul	H	**Won** 60–14
South Africa	30 Jul	H	**Won** 40–7
Australia	6 Aug	H	**Won** 30–14
South Africa	20 Aug	A	**Lost** 5–18
Australia	27 Aug	A	**Lost** 20–25
Tonga	9 Sep	H	**Won** 41–10
Japan	16 Sep	H	**Won** 83–7
France	24 Sep	H	**Won** 37–17
Canada	2 Oct	H	**Won** 79–15
Argentina	9 Oct	H	**Won** 33–10
Australia	16 Oct	H	**Won** 20–6
France	23 Oct	H	**Won** 8–7

ON TOP OF THE WORLD

By Iain Spragg

Cameron Spencer/Getty Images

This was the moment when prop Tony Woodcock became an unlikely hero with New Zealand's only try in the final.

It was nearly a quarter of a century in the making but after 24 years of heartbreak, recrimination and soul searching, New Zealand were finally crowned world champions, winning the Rugby World Cup for the first time since the inaugural tournament in 1987 after an epic 8–7 victory over France in Auckland.

The first ever World Cup final saw the All Blacks overcome Les Bleus 29–9 at Eden Park and, although the 2011 renewal of the rivalry at the same ground was an altogether closer, more dramatic encounter, it was the Kiwis who once again emerged victorious courtesy of an early try from Tony Woodcock and a penalty from fourth-choice fly-half Stephen Donald.

The French had beaten New Zealand in the semi-finals of the competition at Twickenham in 1999 and in the quarter-finals of the 2007 tournament at the Millennium Stadium but, despite a heroic display in Auckland, they could not complete the hat-trick and the All Blacks joined Australia and South Africa as two-time champions.

For the All Blacks, victory represented both national and individual redemption after so many near misses and failures at previous tournaments, while for Graham Henry it was a magnificent send-off in his final game as New Zealand coach after an eight-year reign.

"I'm so proud to be a New Zealander standing here," Henry said after masterminding the All Blacks' long-awaited anointment as world champions. "Richie [McCaw] and the boys just hanging in there right through the 80 minutes to win this thing is superb. This is something we've dreamed of for a while and now we can rest in peace. I've got so much respect for what the boys have done over eight years. It's been outstanding."

The All Blacks' journey to their first final since they were ambushed by the Springboks at Ellis Park in 1995 began against Tonga in Auckland, and a first-half brace of tries apiece from Israel Dagg and Richard Kahui saw New Zealand storm into a 29–0 lead at the break. Jerome Kaino and Ma'a Nonu added further scores in the second period and New Zealand were up and running with a 41–10 victory.

There were no alarms a week later when they played Japan in Hamilton, running in 13 tries against the Brave Blossoms in a one-sided 83–7 romp, and Henry's side prepared for their Pool A showdown with France brimming with confidence.

The game was billed as the first genuine examination of the All Blacks' title credentials, but the match failed to ignite as a genuine contest. Adam Thomson, Cory Jane and Dagg all went over the whitewash in the opening quarter, and from that point onwards New Zealand were comfortably able to keep Les Bleus at arm's reach and they cantered to a 37–17 win that confirmed their place in the quarter-finals.

"We realised we had to take a step up this week," said McCaw, who became the first All Black to reach the milestone of 100 Tests for his country, against France. "We had to absorb a fair bit early on, and I was proud of the way the boys did that. When we got the opportunity, we put the points on the board. We have a fair way to go yet in the World Cup, but I'm looking forward to the next four or five weeks. Hopefully we can do something special."

The final Pool A clash against Canada also marked another New Zealand milestone, but this time it was Henry who was making history with his 100th game in charge of the All Blacks, and his team ensured the party did not fall flat with a resounding 79–15 victory over the Canucks which included a four-try salvo from wing Zac Guildford. It was Henry's 85th win as coach since his appointment in 2004.

It was not, however, all good news for the Kiwis. The day before the Canada game, talismanic fly-half Dan Carter picked up a serious groin injury in training and New Zealand looked ahead to the knockout stages of the tournament knowing they could not call on the services of their prolific playmaker.

The loss of Carter may have been a body blow, but the All Blacks showed no hangover from the news when they faced Argentina in the quarter-final at Eden Park. The Pumas had battled through to the semi-finals in Rugby World Cup 2007 in France, but there was to be no repeat of those heroics four years later as New Zealand overcame the South Americans' early, stubborn resistance.

Argentina briefly led 7–6 after half an hour following a try from Julio Faras Cabello, but New Zealand hauled in the Pumas courtesy of seven penalties from Piri Weepu and they went for the kill in the closing quarter of the match, crossing the whitewash through Kieran Read and Brad Thorn to record a 33–10 win and set-up a semi-final showdown with old rivals Australia.

"I've never been to a semi-final before," Henry said after the final whistle. "It's amazing, great. I was pleased with the game. I thought it was a tough old game of football, and I thought both sides played particularly well. I was pleased with the composure of our fellas. They were under a lot of pressure at times and kept their heads. Quarter-finals are always tough games, and I'm sure we'll be better for that particular game."

New Zealand went into the semi-final against Australia smarting from their 25–20 Tri-Nations defeat to the Wallabies in Brisbane two months earlier and, having uncharacteristically lost two of their last three games against the men in gold, a sense of nervous anticipation dominated with the final so tantalisingly close.

Henry was forced to make another change at 10 when Colin Slade, Carter's initial replacement, was himself ruled out with a groin injury and Chiefs fly-half Aaron Cruden was drafted into the starting XV for the Eden Park clash.

Wallaby fly-half Quade Cooper got the match started, but his kick-off went straight into touch and the early mistake proved a bad omen for Australia as the New Zealanders took the match by the scruff of the neck, scoring a fifth-minute try through Nonu after a superb break from Dagg.

It was a score from which the Wallabies never fully recovered. Charged once again with the kicking duties, Weepu landed four penalties while Cruden chipped in with a drop-goal. Australia could only muster a James O'Connor drop-goal and Cooper penalty, and after a 20–6 win the All Blacks' serene progress to the final continued.

"It was awesome, we realised we had to front up and be on the job for 80 minutes," McCaw said. "Every single man did their bit, and that's what you've got to do in knockout rugby. We've got the job to do next week, but I'm pleased with how the guys fronted up. The intensity of the ball-carriers and at the breakdown was the key. One to five have been around a long time, that's been building, and it was a pretty good performance tonight."

Injuries were kind to Henry as he considered his options for the final and he named the same starting line-up to face the French. Back-rower Thomson recovered from an ankle knock to replace Victor Vito on the New Zealand bench and the stage was set for the All Blacks' date with destiny.

The final may have been a low-scoring affair, but what it lacked in terms of points it more than compensated for with drama and suspense in Auckland.

The big talking point before kick-off was which French team would turn up for the game, but the early exchanges at Eden Park left no one in doubt that Marc Lièvremont's side were ready for the battle and the two teams began what was to be an epic arm wrestle.

New Zealand scored first. An attacking lineout in the French 22 saw Keven Mealamu find Kaino with the throw and the flanker deftly fed Woodcock, who barrelled over untouched. Weepu missed the conversion, but the Kiwis were ahead and, despite immense French pressure, it was a lead they refused to relinquish.

The All Blacks went 8–0 up after 45 minutes when Donald, New Zealand's fourth-choice 10 behind Carter, Slade and Cruden, slotted an easy penalty chance and, although France scored a converted try from captain Thierry Dusautoir just two minutes later, they clung on to their advantage for dear life and the mantle of world champions was finally theirs once again.

"You just have to keep getting up and believing in the mate beside you and trust in him and make sure you do your job," McCaw said after he lifted the trophy. "Everyone around New Zealand has given this team so much over the past six weeks and now we've repaid them. I think at some stage some team was going to do it, and this group of 30 had the opportunity. There's going to be a lot of stories told as we get older, but no one here can take it away from this group. They're tough men, and I think the whole country should be very proud of every single one of them."

NEW ZEALAND INTERNATIONAL STATISTICS

MATCH RECORDS UP TO 31 OCTOBER 2011

MOST CONSECUTIVE TEST WINS

17 1965 *SA* 4, 1966 *BI* 1, 2, 3, 4, 1967 *A, E, W, F, S,* 1968 *A* 1, 2, *F* 1, 2, 3, 1969 *W* 1, 2
15 2005 *A* 1, *SA* 2, *A* 2, *W, I, E, S,* 2006 *I* 1, 2, *Arg, A* 1, *SA* 1, *A* 2, 3, *SA* 2
15 2009 *A* 3, 4, *W, It, E, F* 3, 2010 *I* 1, *W* 1, 2, *SA* 1, 2, *A* 1, 2, *SA* 3, *A* 3
12 1988 *A* 3, 1989 *F* 1, 2, *Arg* 1, 2, *A, W, I,* 1990 *S* 1, 2, *A* 1, 2

MOST CONSECUTIVE TESTS WITHOUT DEFEAT

Matches	Wins	Draws	Period
23	22	1	1987 to 1990
17	17	0	1965 to 1969
17	15	2	1961 to 1964
15	15	0	2005 to 2006
15	15	0	2009 to 2010

MOST POINTS IN A MATCH

BY THE TEAM

Pts	Opponents	Venue	Year
145	Japan	Bloemfontein	1995
108	Portugal	Lyons	2007
102	Tonga	Albany	2000
101	Italy	Huddersfield	1999
101	Samoa	N Plymouth	2008
93	Argentina	Wellington	1997
91	Tonga	Brisbane	2003
91	Fiji	Albany	2005
85	Romania	Toulouse	2007
83	Japan	Hamilton	2011
79	Canada	Wellington	2011
76	Italy	Marseilles	2007
74	Fiji	Christchurch	1987
73	Canada	Auckland	1995
71	Fiji	Albany	1997
71	Samoa	Albany	1999

BY A PLAYER

Pts	Player	Opponents	Venue	Year
45	S D Culhane	Japan	Bloemfontein	1995
36	T E Brown	Italy	Huddersfield	1999
33	C J Spencer	Argentina	Wellington	1997
33	A P Mehrtens	Ireland	Dublin	1997
33	D W Carter	British/Irish	Wellington	2005
33	N J Evans	Portugal	Lyons	2007
32	T E Brown	Tonga	Albany	2000
30	M C G Ellis	Japan	Bloemfontein	1995
30	T E Brown	Samoa	Albany	2001
29	A P Mehrtens	Australia	Auckland	1999
29	A P Mehrtens	France	Paris	2000
29	L R MacDonald	Tonga	Brisbane	2003
29	D W Carter	Canada	Hamilton	2007

MOST TRIES IN A MATCH

BY THE TEAM

Tries	Opponents	Venue	Year
21	Japan	Bloemfontein	1995
16	Portugal	Lyons	2007
15	Tonga	Albany	2000
15	Fiji	Albany	2005
15	Samoa	N Plymouth	2008
14	Argentina	Wellington	1997
14	Italy	Huddersfield	1999
13	U S A	Berkeley	1913
13	Tonga	Brisbane	2003
13	Romania	Toulouse	2007
13	Japan	Hamilton	2011
12	Italy	Auckland	1987
12	Fiji	Christchurch	1987
12	Canada	Wellington	2011

BY A PLAYER

Tries	Player	Opponents	Venue	Year
6	M C G Ellis	Japan	Bloemfontein	1995
5	J W Wilson	Fiji	Albany	1997
4	D McGregor	England	Crystal Palace	1905
4	C I Green	Fiji	Christchurch	1987
4	J A Gallagher	Fiji	Christchurch	1987
4	J J Kirwan	Wales	Christchurch	1988
4	J T Lomu	England	Cape Town	1995
4	C M Cullen	Scotland	Dunedin	1996
4	J W Wilson	Samoa	Albany	1999
4	J M Muliaina	Canada	Melbourne	2003
4	S W Sivivatu	Fiji	Albany	2005
4	Z R Guildford	Canada	Wellington	2011

MOST CONVERSIONS IN A MATCH

BY THE TEAM

Cons	Opponents	Venue	Year
20	Japan	Bloemfontein	1995
14	Portugal	Lyons	2007
13	Tonga	Brisbane	2003
13	Samoa	N Plymouth	2008
12	Tonga	Albany	2000
11	Italy	Huddersfield	1999
10	Fiji	Christchurch	1987
10	Argentina	Wellington	1997
10	Romania	Toulouse	2007
9	Canada	Melbourne	2003
9	Italy	Marseilles	2007
9	Ireland	N Plymouth	2010
9	Japan	Hamilton	2011
8	Italy	Auckland	1987
8	Wales	Auckland	1988
8	Fiji	Albany	1997
8	Italy	Hamilton	2003
8	Fiji	Albany	2005
8	Canada	Wellington	2011

BY A PLAYER

Cons	Player	Opponents	Venue	Year
20	S D Culhane	Japan	Bloemfontein	1995
14	N J Evans	Portugal	Lyons	2007
12	T E Brown	Tonga	Albany	2000
12	L R MacDonald	Tonga	Brisbane	2003
11	T E Brown	Italy	Huddersfield	1999
10	G J Fox	Fiji	Christchurch	1987
10	C J Spencer	Argentina	Wellington	1997
9	D W Carter	Canada	Melbourne	2003
9	C R Slade	Japan	Hamilton	2011
8	G J Fox	Italy	Auckland	1987
8	G J Fox	Wales	Auckland	1988
8	A P Mehrtens	Italy	Hamilton	2002

MOST DROPPED GOALS IN A MATCH

BY THE TEAM

Drops	Opponents	Venue	Year
3	France	Christchurch	1986

BY A PLAYER

Drops	Player	Opponents	Venue	Year
2	O D Bruce	Ireland	Dublin	1978
2	F M Botica	France	Christchurch	1986
2	A P Mehrtens	Australia	Auckland	1995

MOST PENALTIES IN A MATCH

BY THE TEAM

Penalties	Opponents	Venue	Year
9	Australia	Auckland	1999
9	France	Paris	2000
7	Western Samoa	Auckland	1993
7	South Africa	Pretoria	1999
7	South Africa	Wellington	2006
7	Australia	Auckland	2007
7	Argentina	Auckland	2011
6	British/Irish Lions	Dunedin	1959
6	England	Christchurch	1985
6	Argentina	Wellington	1987
6	Scotland	Christchurch	1987
6	France	Paris	1990
6	South Africa	Auckland	1994
6	Australia	Brisbane	1996
6	Ireland	Dublin	1997
6	South Africa	Cardiff	1999
6	Scotland	Murrayfield	2001
6	South Africa	Christchurch	2004
6	Australia	Sydney	2004
6	South Africa	Dunedin	2008
6	Australia	Tokyo	2009

BY A PLAYER

Penalties	Player	Opponents	Venue	Year
9	A P Mehrtens	Australia	Auckland	1999
9	A P Mehrtens	France	Paris	2000
7	G J Fox	Western Samoa	Auckland	1993
7	A P Mehrtens	South Africa	Pretoria	1999
7	D W Carter	South Africa	Wellington	2006
7	D W Carter	Australia	Auckland	2007
7	P A T Weepu	Argentina	Auckland	2011
6	D B Clarke	British/Irish Lions	Dunedin	1959
6	K J Crowley	England	Christchurch	1985
6	G J Fox	Argentina	Wellington	1987
6	G J Fox	Scotland	Christchurch	1987
6	G J Fox	France	Paris	1990
6	S P Howarth	South Africa	Auckland	1994
6	A P Mehrtens	Australia	Brisbane	1996
6	A P Mehrtens	Ireland	Dublin	1997
6	A P Mehrtens	South Africa	Cardiff	1999
6	A P Mehrtens	Scotland	Murrayfield	2001
6	D W Carter	South Africa	Dunedin	2008
6	D W Carter	Australia	Tokyo	2009

CAREER RECORDS

MOST CAPPED PLAYERS

Caps	Player	Career Span
103	R H McCaw	2001 to 2011
100	J M Muliaina	2003 to 2011
92	S B T Fitzpatrick	1986 to 1997
92	K F Mealamu	2002 to 2011
85	D W Carter	2003 to 2011
83	T D Woodcock	2002 to 2011
81	J W Marshall	1995 to 2005
79	I D Jones	1990 to 1999
74	J F Umaga	1997 to 2005
73	A J Williams	2002 to 2011
70	A P Mehrtens	1995 to 2004
68	J T Rokocoko	2003 to 2010
67	C R Jack	2001 to 2007
66	G M Somerville	2000 to 2008
66	M A Nonu	2003 to 2011
63	J J Kirwan	1984 to 1994
63	J T Lomu	1994 to 2002
62	R M Brooke	1992 to 1999
62	D C Howlett	2000 to 2007
62	R So'oialo	2002 to 2009
62	A K Hore	2002 to 2011
60	C W Dowd	1993 to 2000
60	J W Wilson	1993 to 2001
59	A D Oliver	1997 to 2007
59	B C Thorn	2003 to 2011
58	G W Whetton	1981 to 1991
58	Z V Brooke	1987 to 1997
58	C M Cullen	1996 to 2002
57	B T Kelleher	1999 to 2007
56	O M Brown	1992 to 1998
56	L R MacDonald	2000 to 2008
56	P A T Weepu	2004 to 2011
55	C E Meads	1957 to 1971
55	F E Bunce	1992 to 1997
55	M N Jones	1987 to 1998
55	C G Smith	2004 to 2011

MOST CONSECUTIVE TESTS

Tests	Player	Span
63	S B T Fitzpatrick	1986 to 1995
51	C M Cullen	1996 to 2000
49	R M Brooke	1995 to 1999
41	J W Wilson	1996 to 1999
40	G W Whetton	1986 to 1991

MOST TESTS AS CAPTAIN

Tests	Captain	Span
66	R H McCaw	2004 to 2011
51	S B T Fitzpatrick	1992 to 1997
30	W J Whineray	1958 to 1965
23	R D Thorne	2002 to 2007
22	T C Randell	1998 to 2002
21	J F Umaga	2004 to 2005
19	G N K Mourie	1977 to 1982
18	B J Lochore	1966 to 1970
17	A G Dalton	1981 to 1985

MOST POINTS IN TESTS

Points	Player	Tests	Career
1250	D W Carter	85	2003 to 2011
967	A P Mehrtens	70	1995 to 2004
645	G J Fox	46	1985 to 1993
291	C J Spencer	35	1997 to 2004
245	D C Howlett	62	2000 to 2007
236	C M Cullen	58	1996 to 2002
234	J W Wilson	60	1993 to 2001
230	J T Rokocoko	68	2003 to 2010
207	D B Clarke	31	1956 to 1964
201	A R Hewson	19	1981 to 1984
185	J T Lomu	63	1994 to 2002
185*	J F Umaga	74	1997 to 2005

** Umaga's haul includes a penalty try*

MOST TRIES IN TESTS

Tries	Player	Tests	Career
49	D C Howlett	62	2000 to 2007
46	C M Cullen	58	1996 to 2002
46	J T Rokocoko	68	2003 to 2010
44	J W Wilson	60	1993 to 2001
37	J T Lomu	63	1994 to 2002
37*	J F Umaga	74	1997 to 2005
35	J J Kirwan	63	1984 to 1994
34	J M Muliaina	100	2003 to 2011
29	D W Carter	85	2003 to 2011
29	S W Sivivatu	45	2005 to 2011
24	J W Marshall	81	1995 to 2005
22	M A Nonu	66	2003 to 2011
21	C G Smith	55	2004 to 2011
20	F E Bunce	55	1992 to 1997
20*	R H McCaw	103	2001 to 2011

** Umaga and McCaw's hauls each include a penalty try*

MOST CONVERSIONS IN TESTS

Cons	Player	Tests	Career
224	D W Carter	85	2003 to 2011
169	A P Mehrtens	70	1995 to 2004
118	G J Fox	46	1985 to 1993
49	C J Spencer	35	1997 to 2004
43	T E Brown	18	1999 to 2001
33	D B Clarke	31	1956 to 1964
32	S D Culhane	6	1995 to 1996

MOST PENALTY GOALS IN TESTS

Penalties	Player	Tests	Career
215	D W Carter	85	2003 to 2011
188	A P Mehrtens	70	1995 to 2004
128	G J Fox	46	1985 to 1993
43	A R Hewson	19	1981 to 1984
41	C J Spencer	35	1997 to 2004
38	D B Clarke	31	1956 to 1964
24	W F McCormick	16	1965 to 1971

MOST DROPPED GOALS IN TESTS

Drops	Player	Tests	Career
10	A P Mehrtens	70	1995 to 2004
7	G J Fox	46	1985 to 1993
5	D B Clarke	31	1956 to 1964
5	M A Herewini	10	1962 to 1967
5	O D Bruce	14	1976 to 1978

TRI-NATIONS RECORDS

RECORD	DETAIL	HOLDER	SET
Most points in season	184	in six matches	2010
Most tries in season	22	in six matches	2010
Highest score	55	55–35 v S Africa (h)	1997
Biggest win	37	43–6 v Australia (h)	1996
Highest score conceded	46	40–46 v S Africa (a)	2000
Biggest defeat	21	7–28 v Australia (a)	1999
Most appearances	43	J M Muliaina	2003 to 2011
Most points in matches	461	D W Carter	2003 to 2011
Most points in season	99	D W Carter	2006
Most points in match	29	A P Mehrtens	v Australia (h) 1999
Most tries in matches	16	C M Cullen	1996 to 2002
Most tries in season	7	C M Cullen	2000
Most tries in match	3	J T Rokocoko	v Australia (a) 2003
	3	D C Howlett	v Australia (h) 2005
Most cons in matches	61	D W Carter	2003 to 2011
Most cons in season	14	D W Carter	2006
Most cons in match	4	C J Spencer	v S Africa (h) 1997
	4	A P Mehrtens	v Australia (a) 2000
	4	A P Mehrtens	v S Africa (a) 2000
	4	C J Spencer	v S Africa (a) 2003
	4	D W Carter	v S Africa (a) 2006
	4	D W Carter	v Australia (a) 2008
	4	D W Carter	v Australia (a) 2010
Most pens in matches	100	D W Carter	2003 to 2011
Most pens in season	21	D W Carter	2006
Most pens in match	9	A P Mehrtens	v Australia (h) 1999

MISCELLANEOUS RECORDS

RECORD	HOLDER	DETAIL
Longest Test Career	E Hughes/C E Meads	1907–21/1957–71
Youngest Test Cap	J T Lomu	19 yrs 45 days in 1994
Oldest Test Cap	E Hughes	40 yrs 123 days in 1921

CAREER RECORDS OF NEW ZEALAND INTERNATIONAL PLAYERS (UP TO 31 OCTOBER 2011)

PLAYER BACKS :	DEBUT:	CAPS	T	C	P	D	PTS
D W Carter	2003 v W	85	29	224	215	4	1250
Q J Cowan	2004 v It	51	7	0	0	0	35
A W Cruden	2010 v I	9	1	1	0	1	10
I J A Dagg	2010 v I	12	7	0	0	0	35
M P Delany	2009 v It	1	0	0	0	0	0
S R Donald	2008 v E	23	1	15	21	0	98
A M Ellis	2006 v E	26	4	0	0	0	20
T E Ellison	2009 v It	1	0	0	0	0	0
H E Gear	2008 v A	8	5	0	0	0	25
Z R Guildford	2009 v W	8	6	0	0	0	30
C S Jane	2008 v A	32	9	0	0	0	45
R D Kahui	2008 v E	17	10	0	0	0	50
L T C Masaga	2009 v It	1	0	0	0	0	0
A S Mathewson	2010 v A	4	0	0	0	0	0
J M Muliaina	2003 v E	100	34	0	0	0	170
M A Nonu	2003 v E	66	22	0	0	0	110
R M N Ranger	2010 v W	3	1	0	0	0	5
J T Rokocoko	2003 v E	68	46	0	0	0	230
S W Sivivatu	2005 v Fj	45	29	0	0	0	145
C R Slade	2010 v A	10	3	18	3	0	60
B R Smith	2009 v It	2	0	0	0	0	0
C G Smith	2004 v It	55	21	0	0	0	105
B J Stanley	2010 v I	3	0	0	0	0	0
I Toeava	2005 v S	36	8	0	0	0	40
P A T Weepu	2004 v W	56	7	10	16	0	103
S Williams	2010 v E	14	4	0	0	0	20

FORWARDS :							
I F "John" Afoa	2005 v I	36	1	0	0	0	5
A F Boric	2008 v E	24	2	0	0	0	10
D J Braid	2002 v W	6	1	0	0	0	5
W W V Crockett	2009 v It	6	1	0	0	0	5
A P de Malmanche	2009 v It	5	0	0	0	0	0
T J S Donnelly	2009 v A	15	0	0	0	0	0
J J Eaton	2005 v I	15	1	0	0	0	5
H T P Elliot	2010 v S	2	0	0	0	0	0
C R Flynn	2003 v C	15	3	0	0	0	15
B J Franks	2010 v I	15	1	0	0	0	5
O T Franks	2009 v It	31	0	0	0	0	0
J M R A Hoeata	2011 v Fj	3	0	0	0	0	0
A K Hore	2002 v E	62	7	0	0	0	35
J Kaino	2006 v I	48	8	0	0	0	40
T D Latimer	2009 v F	5	0	0	0	0	0
R H McCaw	2001 v I	103	20*	0	0	0	100
J L Mackintosh	2008 v S	1	0	0	0	0	0
K F Mealamu	2002 v W	92	12	0	0	0	60
L J Messam	2008 v S	9	1	0	0	0	5
K J O'Neill	2008 v SA	1	0	0	0	0	0
K J Read	2008 v S	36	7	0	0	0	35
I B Ross	2009 v F	8	2	0	0	0	10
A J Thomson	2008 v I	24	4	0	0	0	20
B C Thorn	2003 v W	59	4	0	0	0	20
N S Tialata	2005 v W	43	2	0	0	0	10
V V J Vito	2010 v I	13	2	0	0	0	10
G B Whitelock	2009 v It	1	1	0	0	0	5
S L Whitelock	2010 v I	25	3	0	0	0	15
A J Williams	2002 v E	73	7	0	0	0	35
T D Woodcock	2002 v W	83	8	0	0	0	40

NB McCaw's figures include a penalty try awarded against Ireland in 2008.

NEW ZEALAND INTERNATIONAL PLAYERS
(UP TO 31 OCTOBER 2011)

Note: Years given for International Championship matches are for second half of season; eg 1972 means season 1971–72. Years for all other matches refer to the actual year of the match. Entries in square brackets denote matches played in RWC Finals.

Abbott, H L (Taranaki) 1906 F
Afoa, I F (Auckland) 2005 I, S, 2006 E(R), 2008 I1, SA2, A1(R), 2(R), SA3(R), A3(R), S, I2(t&R), W(R), E3(R), 2009 F1(R), 2(R), It1, SA2(R), A2(R), SA3(R), A3(R), 4(R), It2(R), E(R), 2010 SA3(R), A3(R), 4(R), E(R), S(R), I2(R), W3(R), 2011 Fj(R), SA1(R), 2, A2(R), [J(R), Arg(R)]
Aitken, G G (Wellington) 1921 SA 1, 2
Alatini, P F (Otago) 1999 F 1(R), [It, SA 3(R)], 2000 Tg, S 1, A 1, SA 1, A 2, SA 2, It, 2001 Sm, Arg 1, F, SA 1, A 1, SA 2, A 2
Allen, F R (Auckland) 1946 A 1, 2, 1947 A 1, 2, 1949 SA 1, 2
Allen, M R (Taranaki, Manawatu) 1993 WS (t), 1996 S 2 (t), 1997 Arg 1(R), 2(R), SA 2(R), A 3(R), E 2, W (R)
Allen, N H (Counties) 1980 A 3, W
Alley, G T (Canterbury) 1928 SA 1, 2, 3
Anderson, A (Canterbury) 1983 S, E, 1984 A 1, 2, 3, 1987 [Fj]
Anderson, B L (Wairarapa-Bush) 1986 A 1
Anesi, S R (Waikato) 2005 Fj(R)
Archer, W R (Otago, Southland) 1955 A 1, 2, 1956 SA 1, 3
Argus, W G (Canterbury) 1946 A 1, 2, 1947 A 1, 2
Arnold, D A (Canterbury) 1963 I, W, 1964 E, F
Arnold, K D (Waikato) 1947 A 1, 2
Ashby, D L (Southland) 1958 A 2
Asher, A A (Auckland) 1903 A
Ashworth, B G (Auckland) 1978 A 1, 2
Ashworth, J C (Canterbury, Hawke's Bay) 1978 A 1, 2, 3, 1980 A 1, 2, 3, 1981 SA 1, 2, 3, 1982 A 1, 2, 1983 BI 1, 2, 3, 4, A, 1984 F 1, 2, A 1, 2, 3, 1985 E 1, 2, A
Atiga, B A C (Auckland) 2003 [Tg(R)]
Atkinson, H (West Coast) 1913 A 1
Avery, H E (Wellington) 1910 A 1, 2, 3

Bachop, G T M (Canterbury) 1989 W, I, 1990 S 1, 2, A 1, 2, 3, F 1, 2, 1991 Arg 1, 2, A 1, 2, [E, US, C, A, S], 1992 Wld 1, 1994 SA 1, 2, 3, A, 1995 C, [I, W, S, E, SA], A 1, 2
Bachop, S J (Otago) 1994 F 2, SA 1, 2, 3, A
Badeley, C E O (Auckland) 1921 SA 1, 2
Baird, J A S (Otago) 1913 A 2
Ball, N (Wellington) 1931 A, 1932 A 2, 3, 1935 W, 1936 E
Barrett, J (Auckland) 1913 A 2, 3
Barry, E F (Wellington) 1934 A 2
Barry, L J (North Harbour) 1995 F 2
Bates, S P (Waikato) 2004 It(R)
Batty, G B (Wellington, Bay of Plenty) 1972 W, S, 1973 E 1, I, F, E 2, 1974 A 1, 3, I, 1975 S, 1976 SA 1, 2, 3, 4, 1977 BI 1
Batty, W (Auckland) 1930 BI 1, 3, 4, 1931 A
Beatty, G E (Taranaki) 1950 BI 1
Bell, R H (Otago) 1951 A 3, 1952 A 1, 2
Bellis, E A (Wanganui) 1921 SA 1, 2, 3
Bennet, R (Otago) 1905 A
Berghan, T (Otago) 1938 A 1, 2, 3
Berry, M J (Wairarapa-Bush) 1986 A 3(R)
Berryman, N R (Northland) 1998 SA 2(R)
Bevan, V D (Wellington) 1949 A 1, 2, 1950 BI 1, 2, 3, 4
Birtwistle, W M (Canterbury) 1965 SA 1, 2, 3, 4, 1967 E, W, S
Black, J E (Canterbury) 1977 F 1, 1979 A, 1980 A 3
Black, N W (Auckland) 1949 SA 3
Black, R S (Otago) 1914 A 1
Blackadder, T J (Canterbury) 1998 E 1(R), 2, 2000 Tg, S 1, 2, A 1, SA 1, A 2, SA 2, F 1, 2, It
Blair, B A (Canterbury) 2001 S (R), Arg 2, 2002 E, W
Blake, A W (Wairarapa) 1949 A 1
Blowers, A F (Auckland) 1996 SA 2(R), 4(R), 1997 I, E 1(R), W (R), 1999 F 1(R), SA 1, A 1(R), SA 2, A 2(R), [It]
Boggs, E G (Auckland) 1946 A 2, 1949 SA 1
Bond, J G (Canterbury) 1949 A 2
Booth, E E (Otago) 1906 F, 1907 A 1, 3
Boric, A F (North Harbour) 2008 E1(R), 2(R), SA2, A2(R), SA3(R), Sm, A3(R), 4(R), S, E3(R), 2009 It2, E(R), F3(R), 2010 I1, W1, A3(R), E(R), S(R), I2, W3(R), 2011 [Tg(R), J(R), F1(R), C(R)]
Boroevich, K G (Wellington) 1986 F 1, A 1, F 3(R)
Botica, F M (North Harbour) 1986 F 1, A 1, 2, 3, F 2, 3, 1989 Arg 1(R)
Bowden, N J G (Taranaki) 1952 A 2
Bowers, R G (Wellington) 1954 I, F
Bowman, A W (Hawke's Bay) 1938 A 1, 2, 3
Braid, D J (Auckland) 2002 W, 2003 [C(R), Tg], 2008 A1, 2010 S(R), W3(R)
Braid, G J (Bay of Plenty) 1983 S, E
Bremner, S G (Auckland, Canterbury) 1952 A 2, 1956 SA 2
Brewer, M R (Otago, Canterbury) 1986 F 1, A 1, 2, 3, F 2, 3, 1988 A 1, 1989 A, W, I, 1990 S 1, 2, A 1, 2, 3, F 1, 2, 1992 I 2, A 1, 1994 F 1, 2, SA 1, 2, 3, A, 1995 C, [I, W, E, SA], A 1, 2
Briscoe, K C (Taranaki) 1959 BI 2, 1960 SA 1, 2, 3, 4, 1963 I, W, 1964 E, S
Brooke, R M (Auckland) 1992 I 2, A 1, 2, 3, SA, 1993 BI 1, 2, 3, A, WS, 1994 SA 2, 3, 1995 C, [J, S, E, SA], A 1, 2, It, F 1, 2, 1996 WS, S 1, 2, A 1, SA 1, A 2, SA 2, 3, 4, 5, 1997 Fj, Arg 1, 2, A 1, SA 1, A 2, SA 2, A 3, I, E 1, W, E 2, 1998 E 1, 2, A 1, SA 1, A 2, SA 2, A 3, 1999 WS, F 1, SA 1, A 1, SA 2, A 2, [Tg, E, It (R), S, F 2]
Brooke, Z V (Auckland) 1987 [Arg], 1989 Arg 2(R), 1990 A 1, 2, 3, F 1(R), 1991 Arg 2, A 1, 2, [E, It, C, A, S], 1992 A 2, 3, SA, 1993 BI 1, 2, 3(R), WS (R), S, E, 1994 F 2, SA 1, 2, 3, A, 1995 [J, S, E, SA], A 1, 2, It, F 1, 2, 1996 WS, S 1, 2, A 1, SA 1, A 2, SA 2, 3, 4, 5, 1997 Arg 1, 2, A 1, SA 1, A 2, SA 2, A 3, I, E 1, W, E 2
Brooke-Cowden, M (Auckland) 1986 F 1, A 1, 1987 [W]
Broomhall, S R (Canterbury) 2002 SA 1(R), 2(R), E, F
Brown, C (Taranaki) 1913 A 2, 3
Brown, O M (Auckland) 1992 I 2, A 1, 2, 3, SA, 1993 BI 1, 2, 3, A, S, E, 1994 F 1, 2, SA 1, 2, 3, A, 1995 C, [I, W, S, E, SA], A 1, 2, It, F 1, 2, 1996 WS, S 1, 2, A 1, SA 1, A 2, SA 2, 3, 4, 5, 1997 Fj, Arg 1, 2, A 1, SA 1, A 2, SA 2, A 3, I, E 1, W, E 2, 1998 E 1, 2, A 1, SA 1, A 2, SA 2
Brown, R H (Taranaki) 1955 A 3, 1956 SA 1, 2, 3, 4, 1957 A 1, 2, 1958 A 1, 2, 3, 1959 BI 1, 3, 1961 F 1, 2, 3, 1962 A 1
Brown, T E (Otago) 1999 WS, F 1(R), SA 1(R), A 1(R), 2(R), [E (R), It, S (R)], 2000 Tg, S 2(R), A 1(R), SA 1(R), A 2(R), 2001 Sm, Arg 1(R), F, SA 1, A 1
Brownlie, C J (Hawke's Bay) 1924 W, 1925 E, F
Brownlie, M J (Hawke's Bay) 1924 I, W, 1925 E, F, 1928 SA 1, 2, 3, 4
Bruce, J A (Auckland) 1914 A 1, 2
Bruce, O D (Canterbury) 1976 SA 1, 2, 4, 1977 BI 2, 3, 4, F 1, 2, 1978 A 1, 2, I, W, E, S
Bryers, R F (King Country) 1949 A 1
Budd, T A (Southland) 1946 A 2, 1949 A 2
Bullock-Douglas, G A H (Wanganui) 1932 A 1, 2, 3, 1934 A 1, 2
Bunce, F E (North Harbour) 1992 Wld 1, 2, 3, I 1, 2, A 1, 2, 3, SA, 1993 BI 1, 2, 3, A, WS, S, E, 1994 F 1, 2, SA 1, 2, 3, A, 1995 C, [I, W, S, E, SA], A 1, 2, It, F 1, 2, 1996 WS, S 1, 2, A1, SA 1, A 2, SA 2, 3, 4, 5, 1997 Fj, Arg 1, 2, A 1, SA 1, A 2, SA 2, A 3, I, E 1, W, E 2
Burgess, G A J (Auckland) 1981 SA 2
Burgess, G F (Southland) 1905 A
Burgess, R E (Manawatu) 1971 BI 1, 2, 3, 1972 A 3, W, 1973 I, F

Burke, P S (Taranaki) 1955 A 1, 1957 A 1, 2
Burns, P J (Canterbury) 1908 AW 2, 1910 A 1, 2, 3, 1913 A 3
Bush, R G (Otago) 1931 A
Bush, W K (Canterbury) 1974 A 1, 2, 1975 S, 1976 I, SA, 2, 4, 1977 BI 2, 3, 4(R), 1978 I, W, 1979 A
Buxton, J B (Canterbury) 1955 A 3, 1956 SA 1

Cain, M J (Taranaki) 1913 US, 1914 A 1, 2, 3
Callesen, J A (Manawatu) 1974 A 1, 2, 3, 1975 S
Cameron, D (Taranaki) 1908 AW 1, 2, 3
Cameron, L M (Manawatu) 1980 A 3, 1981 SA 1(R), 2, 3, R
Carleton, S R (Canterbury) 1928 SA 1, 2, 3, 1929 A 1, 2, 3
Carrington, K R (Auckland) 1971 BI 1, 3, 4
Carter, D W (Canterbury) 2003 W, F, A 1(R), [It, C, Tg, SA(R), F(R)], 2004 E1, 2, PI, A1, SA1, A2, It, W, F, 2005 Fj, BI1, 2, SA1, A1, W, E, 2006 Arg, A1, SA1, A2, 3, SA2, 3, E, F1, 2, W, 2007 F1, C, SA1, A1, SA2, A2, [It, S, F], 2008 I1, E1, 2, SA1, 2, A1, 2, SA3, Sm, A3, 4, S(R), I2, W, E3, 2009 A2, SA3, A3, 4, W, E, F3, 2010 I1, W1, 2, SA1, 2, A1, 2, SA3, A4, E, S, I2, W3, 2011 Fj(R), SA1, A1, 2, [Tg, F1]
Carter, M P (Auckland) 1991 A 2, [It, A], 1997 Fj (R), A 1(R), 1998 E 2(R), A 2
Casey, S T (Otago) 1905 S, I, E, W, 1907 A 1, 2, 3, 1908 AW 1
Cashmore, A R (Auckland) 1996 S 2(R), 1997 A 2(R)
Catley, E H (Waikato) 1946 A 1, 1947 A 1, 2, 1949 SA 1, 2, 3, 4
Caughey, T H C (Auckland) 1932 A 1, 3, 1934 A 1, 2, 1935 S, I, 1936 E, A 1, 1937 SA 3
Caulton, R W (Wellington) 1959 BI 2, 3, 4, 1960 SA 1, 4, 1961 F 2, 1963 E 1, 2, I, W, 1964 E, S, F, A 1, 2, 3
Cherrington, N P (North Auckland) 1950 BI 1
Christian, D L (Auckland) 1949 SA 4
Clamp, M (Wellington) 1984 A 2, 3
Clark, D W (Otago) 1964 A 1, 2
Clark, W H (Wellington) 1953 W, 1954 I, E, S, 1955 A 1, 2, 1956 SA 2, 3, 4
Clarke, A H (Auckland) 1958 A 3, 1959 BI 4, 1960 SA 1
Clarke, D B (Waikato) 1956 SA 3, 4, 1957 A 1, 2, 1958 A 1, 3, 1959 BI 1, 2, 3, 4, 1960 SA 1, 2, 3, 4, 1961 F 1, 2, 3, 1962 A 1, 2, 3, 4, 5, 1963 E 1, 2, I, W, 1964 E, S, F, A 2, 3
Clarke, E (Auckland) 1992 Wld 2, 3, I 1, 2, 1993 BI 1, 2, S (R), E, 1998 SA 2, A 3
Clarke, I J (Waikato) 1953 W, 1955 A 1, 2, 3, 1956 SA 1, 2, 3, 4, 1957 A 1, 2, 1958 A 1, 3, 1959 BI 1, 2, 1960 SA 2, 4, 1961 F 1, 2, 3, 1962 A 1, 2, 3, 1963 E 1, 2
Clarke, R L (Taranaki) 1932 A 2, 3
Cobden, D G (Canterbury) 1937 SA 1
Cockerill, M S (Taranaki) 1951 A 1, 2, 3
Cockroft, E A P (South Canterbury) 1913 A 3, 1914 A 2, 3
Codlin, B W (Counties) 1980 A 1, 2, 3
Collins, A H (Taranaki) 1932 A 2, 3, 1934 A 1
Collins, J (Wellington) 2001 Arg 1, 2003 E (R), W, F, SA 1, A 1, SA 2, A 2, [It, W, SA, A, F], 2004 E2(R), Arg, PI(R), A1(R), SA1, It, F, 2005 Fj, BI1, 2, 3, SA1, A1, SA2, W, E, 2006 Arg, A1, 2, 3, SA2(R), 3, F1, 2, W, 2007 F2, C, SA1, A1, SA2(R), A2, [It, Pt, R, F]
Collins, J L (Poverty Bay) 1964 A 1, 1965 SA 1, 4
Colman, J T H (Taranaki) 1907 A 1, 2, 1908 AW 1, 3
Connor, D M (Auckland) 1961 F 1, 2, 3, 1962 A 1, 2, 3, 4, 5, 1963 E 1, 2, 1964 A 2, 3
Conway, R J (Otago, Bay of Plenty) 1959 BI 2, 3, 4, 1960 SA 1, 3, 4, 1965 SA 1, 2, 3, 4
Cooke, A E (Auckland, Wellington) 1924 I, W, 1925 E, F, 1930 BI 1, 2, 3, 4
Cooke, R J (Canterbury) 1903 A
Cooksley, M S B (Counties, Waikato) 1992 Wld 1, 1993 BI 2, 3(R), A, 1994 F 1, 2, SA 1, 2, A, 2001 A 1(R), SA 2(t&R)
Cooper, G J L (Auckland, Otago) 1986 F 1, A 1, 2, 1992 Wld 1, 2, 3, I 1
Cooper, M J A (Waikato) 1992 I 2, SA (R), 1993 BI 1(R), 3(t), WS (t), S, 1994 F 1, 2
Corner, M M N (Auckland) 1930 BI 2, 3, 4, 1931 A, 1934 A 1, 1936 E
Cossey, R R (Counties) 1958 A 1
Cottrell, A I (Canterbury) 1929 A 1, 2, 3, 1930 BI 1, 2, 3, 4, 1931 A, 1932 A 1, 2, 3
Cottrell, W D (Canterbury) 1968 A 1, 2, F 2, 3, 1970 SA 1, 1971 BI 1, 2, 3, 4
Couch, M B R (Wairarapa) 1947 A 1, 1949 A 1, 2
Coughlan, T D (South Canterbury) 1958 A 1
Cowan, Q J (Southland) 2004 It(R), 2005 W(R), I(R), S(R), 2006 I1(R), SA1(R), A2(R), SA2(R), 3, 2008 E1(R), 2(R), SA1(R), A1(t&R), 2, SA3, Sm, A3, 4, I2, W, E3, 2009 F1, 2, A1, SA2, A2, SA3, A3, 4, W(R), It2(R), E, F3, 2010 I1, W1, 2, SA1, 2(R), A1, SA3, A3(R), 4, S, W3, 2011 Fj, SA1, 2, [Tg, J(R), C, Arg(R)]
Creighton, J N (Canterbury) 1962 A 4
Cribb, R T (North Harbour) 2000 S 1, 2, A 1, SA 1, A 2, SA 2, F 1, 2, It, 2001 Sm, F, SA 1, A 1, SA 2, A 2
Crichton, S (Wellington) 1983 S, E
Crockett, W W V (Canterbury) 2009 It1, W, It2, 2011 Fj, SA1, A1
Cross, T (Canterbury) 1904 BI, 1905 A
Crowley, K J (Taranaki) 1985 E 1, 2, A, Arg 1, 2, 1986 A 3, F 2, 3, 1987 [Arg], 1990 S 1, 2, A 1, 2, 3, F 1, 2, 1991 Arg 1, 2, [A]
Crowley, P J B (Auckland) 1949 SA 3, 4, 1950 BI 1, 2, 3, 4
Cruden, A W (Manawatu) 2010 I1(R), W1(R), 2(R), SA2(R), A1(R), 3, 2011 [Arg(R), A, F2]
Culhane, S D (Southland) 1995 [J], It, F 1, 2, 1996 SA 3, 4
Cullen C M (Manawatu, Central Vikings, Wellington) 1996 WS, S 1, 2, A 1, SA 1, A 2, SA 2, 3, 4, 5, 1997 Fj, Arg 1, 2, A 1, SA 1, A 2, SA 2, A 3, I, E 1, W, E 2, 1998 E 1, 2, A 1, SA 1, A 2, SA 2, A 3, 1999 WS, F 1, SA 1, A 1, SA 2, A 2, [Tg, E, It (R), S, F 2, SA 3], 2000 Tg, S 1, 2, A 1, SA 1, A 2, SA 2, F 1, 2, It, 2001 A 2(R), 2002 It, Fj, A 1, SA 1, A 2, F
Cummings, W (Canterbury) 1913 A 2, 3
Cundy, R T (Wairarapa) 1929 A 2(R)
Cunningham, G R (Auckland) 1979 A, S, E, 1980 A 1, 2
Cunningham, W (Auckland) 1905 S, I, 1906 F, 1907 A 1, 2, 3, 1908 AW 1, 2, 3
Cupples, L F (Bay of Plenty) 1924 I, W
Currie, C J (Canterbury) 1978 I, W
Cuthill, J E (Otago) 1913 A 1, US

Dagg, I J A (Hawke's Bay) 2010 I1, W1, SA2(R), A1(R), SA3(R), A3, 2011 SA2, [Tg, F1, C, A, F2]
Dalley, W C (Canterbury) 1924 I, 1928 SA 1, 2, 3, 4
Dalton, A G (Counties) 1977 F 2, 1978 A 1, 2, 3, I, W, E, S, 1979 F 1, 2, S, 1981 S 1, 2, SA 1, 2, 3, R, F 1, 2, 1982 A 1, 2, 3, 1983 BI 1, 2, 3, 4, A, 1984 F 1, 2, A 1, 2, 3, 1985 E 1, 2, A
Dalton, D (Hawke's Bay) 1935 I, W, 1936 A 1, 2, 1937 SA 1, 2, 3, 1938 A 1, 2
Dalton, R A (Wellington) 1947 A 1, 2
Dalzell, G N (Canterbury) 1953 W, 1954 I, E, S, F
Davie, M G (Canterbury) 1983 E (R)
Davies, W A (Auckland, Otago) 1960 SA 4, 1962 A 4, 5
Davis, K (Auckland) 1952 A 2, 1953 W, 1954 I, E, S, F, 1955 A 2, 1958 A 1, 2, 3
Davis, L J (Canterbury) 1976 I, 1977 BI 3, 4
Davis, W L (Hawke's Bay) 1967 A, E, W, F, S, 1968 A 1, 2, F 1, 1969 W 1, 2, 1970 SA 2
Deans, I B (Canterbury) 1988 W 1, 2, A 1, 2, 3, 1989 F 1, 2, Arg 1, 2, A
Deans, R G (Canterbury) 1905 S, I, E, W, 1908 AW 3
Deans, R M (Canterbury) 1983 S, E, 1984 A 1(R), 2, 3
Delamore, G W (Wellington) 1949 SA 4
Delany, M P (Bay of Plenty) 2009 It 2
De Malmanche, A P (Waikato) 2009 It1(R), A3(R), 2010 I1(R), W1(R), 2(R)
Dermody, C (Southland) 2006 I1, 2, E(R)
Devine, S J (Auckland) 2002 E, W 2003 E (R), W, F, SA 1, A 1(R), [C, SA(R), F]
Dewar, H (Taranaki) 1913 A 1, US
Diack, E S (Otago) 1959 BI 2
Dick, J (Auckland) 1937 SA 1, 2, 1938 A 3
Dick, M J (Auckland) 1963 I, W, 1964 E, S, F, 1965 SA 3, 1966 BI 4, 1967 A, E, W, F, 1969 W 1, 2, 1970 SA 1, 4
Dixon, M J (Canterbury) 1954 I, E, S, F, 1956 SA 1, 2, 3, 4, 1957 A 1, 2
Dobson, R L (Auckland) 1949 A 1
Dodd, E H (Wellington) 1905 A
Donald, A J (Wanganui) 1983 S, E, 1984 F 1, 2, A 1, 2, 3
Donald, J G (Wairarapa) 1921 SA 1, 2
Donald, Q (Wairarapa) 1924 I, W, 1925 E, F
Donald, S R (Waikato) 2008 E1(R), 2(R), A2(R), SA3(R), Sm(R), A3(R), 4, S, I2(R), 2009 F1, 2, A1, SA1, 2, A2(R), SA3, A4(R), It2(R), F3(R), 2010 A4(R), S(R), W3(R), 2011[F2(R)]
Donaldson, M W (Manawatu) 1977 F 1, 2, 1978 A 1, 2, 3, I, E, S, 1979 F 1, 2, A, S (R), 1981 SA 3(R)
Donnelly, T J S (Otago) 2009 A3, 4, W(R), It2, E, F3, 2010 W2, SA1, 2, A1, 2, SA3, A3, 4, I2
Dougan, J P (Wellington) 1972 A 1, 1973 E 2
Dowd, C W (Auckland) 1993 BI 1, 2, 3, A, WS, S, E, 1994 SA 1(R), 1995 C, [I, W, J, E, SA], A 1, 2, It, F 1, 2, 1996 WS, S 1, 2, A 1, SA 1, A 2, SA 2, 3, 4, 5, 1997 Fj, Arg 1, 2, A 1, SA 1, A 2, SA 2, A 3, I, E 1, W, 1998 E 1, 2, A 1, SA 1, A 2, 3(R),

1999 SA 2(R), A 2(R), [Tg (R), E, It, S, F 2, SA 3], 2000 Tg, S 1(R), 2(R), A 1(R), SA 1(R), A 2(R)
Dowd, G W (North Harbour) 1992 I 1(R)
Downing, A J (Auckland) 1913 A 1, US, 1914 A 1, 2, 3
Drake, J A (Auckland) 1986 F 2, 3, 1987 [Fj, Arg, S, W, F], A
Duff, R H (Canterbury) 1951 A 1, 2, 3, 1952 A 1, 2, 1955 A 2, 3, 1956 SA 1, 2, 3, 4
Duggan, R J L (Waikato) 1999 [It (R)]
Duncan, J (Otago) 1903 A
Duncan, M G (Hawke's Bay) 1971 BI 3(R), 4
Duncan, W D (Otago) 1921 SA 1, 2, 3
Dunn, E J (North Auckland) 1979 S, 1981 S 1
Dunn, I T W (North Auckland) 1983 BI 1, 4, A
Dunn, J M (Auckland) 1946 A 1

Earl, A T (Canterbury) 1986 F 1, A 1, F 3(R), 1987 [Arg], 1989 W, I, 1991 Arg 1(R), 2, A 1, [E (R), US, S], 1992 A 2, 3(R)
Eastgate, B P (Canterbury) 1952 A 1, 2, 1954 S
Eaton, J J (Taranaki) 2005 I, E(t), S(R), 2006 Arg, A1, 2(R), 3, SA3(R), F1(R), 2(R), 2009 A1(R), SA1(R), A3(R), 4(R), W
Elliot, H T P (Hawke's Bay) 2010 S, I2
Elliott, K G (Wellington) 1946 A 1, 2
Ellis, A M (Canterbury) 2006 E(R), F2(R), 2007 [Pt(R), R], 2008 I1, E1, 2, SA1, 2, A1, S(R), 2009 It2, E(R), F3(R), 2010 E(R), S(R), I2, W3(R), 2011 A1(R), SA2(R), A2(R), [J, F1(R), C(R), A(R), F2(R)]
Ellis, M C G (Otago) 1993 S, E, 1995 C, [I (R), W, J, S, SA (R)]
Ellison, T E (Wellington) 2009 It 2
Elsom, A E G (Canterbury) 1952 A 1, 2, 1953 W, 1955 A 1, 2, 3
Elvidge, R R (Otago) 1946 A 1, 2, 1949 SA 1, 2, 3, 4, 1950 BI 1, 2, 3
Erceg, C P (Auckland) 1951 A 1, 2, 3, 1952 A 1
Evans, B R (Hawke's Bay) 2009 F1(R), 2(R)
Evans, D A (Hawke's Bay) 1910 A 2
Evans, N J (North Harbour, Otago) 2004 E1(R), 2, Arg, PI(R), 2005 I, S, 2006 F2(R), W(R), 2007 F1(R), 2, SA2(R), A2(R), [Pt, S(R), R, F(R)]
Eveleigh, K A (Manawatu) 1976 SA 2, 4, 1977 BI 1, 2

Fanning, A H N (Canterbury) 1913 A 3
Fanning, B J (Canterbury) 1903 A, 1904 BI
Farrell, C P (Auckland) 1977 BI 1, 2
Fawcett, C L (Auckland) 1976 SA 2, 3
Fea, W R (Otago) 1921 SA 3
Feek, G E (Canterbury) 1999 WS (R), A 1(R), SA 2, [E (t), It], 2000 F 1, 2, It, 2001 I, S
Filipo, R A (Wellington) 2007 C, SA1(R), A1(R), 2008 S(R)
Finlay, B E L (Manawatu) 1959 BI 1
Finlay, J (Manawatu) 1946 A 1
Finlayson, I (North Auckland) 1928 SA 1, 2, 3, 4, 1930 BI 1, 2
Fitzgerald, J T (Wellington) 1952 A 1
Fitzpatrick, B B J (Wellington) 1953 W, 1954 I, F
Fitzpatrick, S B T (Auckland) 1986 F 1, A 1, F 2, 3, 1987 [It, Fj, Arg, S, W, F], A, 1988 W 1, 2, A 1, 2, 3, 1989 F 1, 2, Arg 1, 2, A, W, I, 1990 S 1, 2, A 1, 2, 3, F 1, 2, 1991 Arg 1, 2, A 1, 2, [E, US, It, C, A, S], 1992 Wld 1, 2, 3, I 1, 2, A 1, 2, 3, SA, 1993 BI 1, 2, 3, A, WS, S, E, 1994 F 1, 2, SA 1, 2, 3, A, 1995 C, [I, W, S, E, SA], A 1, 2, It, F 1, 2, 1996 WS, S 1, 2, A 1, SA 1, A 2, SA 2, 3, 4, 5, 1997 Fj, Arg 1, 2, A 1, SA 1, A 2, SA 2, A 3, W (R)
Flavell, T V (North Harbour, Auckland) 2000 Tg, S 1(R), A 1(R), SA 1, 2(t), F 1(R), 2(R), It, 2001 Sm, Arg 1, F, SA 1, A 1, SA 2, A 2, 2006 I1(R), 2, 2007 F1(R), 2(R), C, SA1, A1
Fleming, J K (Wellington) 1979 S, E, 1980 A 1, 2, 3
Fletcher, C J C (North Auckland) 1921 SA 3
Flynn, C R (Canterbury) 2003 [C(R), Tg], 2004 It(R), 2008 S(R), I2(R), 2009 It2, F3(R), 2010 SA1(R), 2(R), A1(R), 2(R), 3(R), 2011 Fj(R), SA1(R), [Tg(R)]
Fogarty, R (Taranaki) 1921 SA 1, 3
Ford, B R (Marlborough) 1977 BI 3, 4, 1978 I, 1979 E
Forster, S T (Otago) 1993 S, E, 1994 F 1, 2, 1995 It, F 1
Fox, G J (Auckland) 1985 Arg 1, 1987 [It, Fj, Arg, S, W, F], A, 1988 W 1, 2, A 1, 2, 3, 1989 F 1, 2, Arg 1, 2, A, W, I, 1990 S 1, 2, A 1, 2, 3, F 1, 2, 1991 Arg 1, 2, A 1, 2, [E, It, C, A], 1992 Wld 1, 2(R), A 1, 2, 3, SA, 1993 BI 1, 2, 3, A, WS
Francis, A R H (Auckland) 1905 A, 1907 A 1, 2, 3, 1908 AW 1, 2, 3, 1910 A 1, 2, 3
Francis, W C (Wellington) 1913 A 2, 3, 1914 A 1, 2, 3
Franks, B J (Tasman) 2010 I1, W1, SA1(R), 2(R), A1(R), 2(R), SA3, 2011 Fj, SA1, A1(R), SA2(R), [Tg(R), F1(R), C(R), A(R)]
Franks, O T (Canterbury) 2009 It1(R), A1(R), SA1(R), 2, A2, SA3, W(R), E, F3(R) , 2010 I1, W1, 2(t&R), SA1, 2, A1, 2, 3, 4, E, S, I2, W3, 2011 A1, 2, [Tg, J, F1, C, Arg, A, F2]
Fraser, B G (Wellington) 1979 S, E, 1980 A 3, W, 1981 S 1, 2, SA 1, 2, 3, R, F 1, 2, 1982 A 1, 2, 3, 1983 BI 1, 2, 3, 4, A, S, E, 1984 A 1
Frazer, H F (Hawke's Bay) 1946 A 1, 2, 1947 A 1, 2, 1949 SA 2
Fryer, F C (Canterbury) 1907 A 1, 2, 3, 1908 AW 2
Fuller, W B (Canterbury) 1910 A 1, 2
Furlong, B D M (Hawke's Bay) 1970 SA 4

Gallagher, J A (Wellington) 1987 [It, Fj, S, W, F], A, 1988 W 1, 2, A 1, 2, 3, 1989 F 1, 2, Arg 1, 2, A, W, I
Gallaher, D (Auckland) 1903 A, 1904 BI, 1905 S, E, W, 1906 F
Gard, P C (North Otago) 1971 BI 4
Gardiner, A J (Taranaki) 1974 A 3
Gear, H E (Wellington) 2008 A4, 2009 A3(R), 2010 E, S, I2, W3, 2011 A1, SA2
Gear, R L (North Harbour, Nelson Bays, Tasman) 2004 PI, It, 2005 BI1(R), 2, 3, SA1, A1, SA2, W, S, 2006 Arg, A1, 2, SA2, 3(R), E, W, 2007 C(R), A1
Geddes, J H (Southland) 1929 A 1
Geddes, W McK (Auckland) 1913 A 2
Gemmell, B McL (Auckland) 1974 A 1, 2
George, V L (Southland) 1938 A 1, 2, 3
Gibbes, J B (Waikato) 2004 E1, 2, Arg(R), PI, A1, 2, SA2, 2005 BI2(R)
Gibson, D P E (Canterbury) 1999 WS, F 1, SA 1, A 1, SA 2, A 2, [Tg (R), E (R), It, S (R), F 2(R)], 2000 F 1, 2, 2002 It, I 1(R), 2(R), Fj, A 2(R), SA 2(R)
Gilbert, G D M (West Coast) 1935 S, I, W, 1936 E
Gillespie, C T (Wellington) 1913 A 2
Gillespie, W D (Otago) 1958 A 3
Gillett, G A (Canterbury, Auckland) 1905 S, I, E, W, 1907 A 2, 3, 1908 AW 1, 3
Gillies, C C (Otago) 1936 A 2
Gilray, C M (Otago) 1905 A
Glasgow, F T (Taranaki, Southland) 1905 S, I, E, W, 1906 F, 1908 AW 3
Glenn, W S (Taranaki) 1904 BI, 1906 F
Goddard, M P (South Canterbury) 1946 A 2, 1947 A 1, 2, 1949 SA 3, 4
Going, S M (North Auckland) 1967 A, F, 1968 F 3, 1969 W 1, 2, 1970 SA 1(R), 4, 1971 BI 1, 2, 3, 4, 1972 A 1, 2, 3, W, S, 1973 E 1, I, F, E 2, 1974 I, 1975 S, 1976 I (R), SA 1, 2, 3, 4, 1977 BI 1, 2
Gordon, S B (Waikato) 1993 S, E
Graham, D J (Canterbury) 1958 A 1, 2, 1960 SA 2, 3, 1961 F 1, 2, 3, 1962 A 1, 2, 3, 4, 5, 1963 E 1, 2, I, W, 1964 E, S, F, A 1, 2, 3
Graham, J B (Otago) 1913 US, 1914 A 1, 3
Graham, W G (Otago) 1979 F 1(R)
Grant, L A (South Canterbury) 1947 A 1, 2, 1949 SA 1, 2
Gray, G D (Canterbury) 1908 AW 2, 1913 A 1, US
Gray, K F (Wellington) 1963 I, W, 1964 E, S, F, A 1, 2, 3, 1965 SA 1, 2, 3, 4, 1966 BI 1, 2, 3, 4, 1967 W, F, S, 1968 A 1, F 2, 3, 1969 W 1, 2
Gray, W N (Bay of Plenty) 1955 A 2, 3, 1956 SA 1, 2, 3, 4
Green, C I (Canterbury) 1983 S (R), E, 1984 A 1, 2, 3, 1985 E 1, 2, A, Arg 1, 2, 1986 A 2, 3, F 2, 3, 1987 [It, Fj, S, W, F], A
Grenside, B A (Hawke's Bay) 1928 SA 1, 2, 3, 4, 1929 A 2, 3
Griffiths, J L (Wellington) 1934 A 2, 1935 S, I, W, 1936 A 1, 2, 1938 A 3
Guildford, Z R (Hawke's Bay) 2009 W, E, 2010 I1(R), W2, 2011 Fj, SA1, A2, [C]
Guy, R A (North Auckland) 1971 BI 1, 2, 3, 4

Haden, A M (Auckland) 1977 BI 1, 2, 3, 4, F 1, 2, 1978 A 1, 2, 3, I, W, E, S, 1979 F 1, 2, A, S, E, 1980 A 1, 2, 3, W, 1981 S 2, SA 1, 2, 3, R, F 1, 2, 1982 A 1, 2, 3, 1983 BI 1, 2, 3, 4, A, 1984 F 1, 2, 1985 Arg 1, 2
Hadley, S (Auckland) 1928 SA 1, 2, 3, 4
Hadley, W E (Auckland) 1934 A 1, 2, 1935 S, I, W, 1936 E, A 1, 2
Haig, J S (Otago) 1946 A 1, 2
Haig, L S (Otago) 1950 BI 2, 3, 4, 1951 A 1, 2, 3, 1953 W, 1954 E, S
Hales, D A (Canterbury) 1972 A 1, 2, 3, W
Hamilton, D C (Southland) 1908 AW 2
Hamilton, S E (Canterbury) 2006 Arg, SA1
Hammett, M G (Canterbury) 1999 F 1(R), SA 2(R), [It, S (R), SA 3], 2000 Tg, S 1(R), 2(t&R), A 1(R), SA 1(R), A 2(R), SA 2(R), F 2(R), It (R), 2001 Arg 1(t), 2002 It (R), I 1, 2, A 1, SA 1, 2(R), 2003 SA 1(R), A 1(R), SA 2, [It(R), C, W(R), SA(R), F(R)]
Hammond, I A (Marlborough) 1952 A 2
Harper, E T (Canterbury) 1904 BI, 1906 F

Harding, S (Otago) 2002 Fj
Harris, P C (Manawatu) 1976 SA 3
Hart, A H (Taranaki) 1924 I
Hart, G F (Canterbury) 1930 BI 1, 2, 3, 4, 1931 A, 1934 A 1, 1935 S, I, W, 1936 A 1, 2
Harvey, B A (Wairarapa-Bush) 1986 F 1
Harvey, I H (Wairarapa) 1928 SA 4
Harvey, L R (Otago) 1949 SA 1, 2, 3, 4, 1950 BI 1, 2, 3, 4
Harvey, P (Canterbury) 1904 BI
Hasell, E W (Canterbury) 1913 A 2, 3
Hayman, C J (Otago) 2001 Sm (R), Arg 1, F (R), A 1(R), SA 2(R), A 2(R), 2002 F (t), W, 2004 E1, 2, PI, A1, 2, SA2, It, W(R), F, 2005 BI1, SA1, A1, SA2, A2, W, E, 2006 I1, 2, A1, SA1, A2, 3, SA3, E, F1, 2, W, 2007 F1, 2, SA1, A1, SA2, A2, [It, Pt(R), S, F]
Hayward, H O (Auckland) 1908 AW 3
Hazlett, E J (Southland) 1966 BI 1, 2, 3, 4, 1967 A, E
Hazlett, W E (Southland) 1928 SA 1, 2, 3, 4, 1930 BI 1, 2, 3, 4
Heeps, T R (Wellington) 1962 A 1, 2, 3, 4, 5
Heke, W R (North Auckland) 1929 A 1, 2, 3
Hemi, R C (Waikato) 1953 W, 1954 I, E, S, F, 1955 A 1, 2, 3, 1956 SA 1, 3, 4, 1957 A 1, 2, 1959 BI 1, 3, 4
Henderson, P (Wanganui) 1949 SA 1, 2, 3, 4, 1950 BI 2, 3, 4
Henderson, P W (Otago) 1991 Arg 1, [C], 1992 Wld 1, 2, 3, I 1, 1995 [J]
Herewini, M A (Auckland) 1962 A 5, 1963 I, 1964 S, F, 1965 SA 4, 1966 BI 1, 2, 3, 4, 1967 A
Hewett, D N (Canterbury) 2001 I (R), S (R), Arg 2, 2002 It (R), I 1, 2, A 1, SA 1, A 2, SA 2, 2003 E, F, SA 1, A 1, SA 2, A 2, [It, Tg(R), W, SA, A, F]
Hewett, J A (Auckland) 1991 [It]
Hewitt, N J (Southland) 1995 [I (t), J], 1996 A 1(R), 1997 SA 1(R), I, E 1, W, E 2, 1998 E 2(t + R)
Hewson, A R (Wellington) 1981 S 1, 2, SA 1, 2, 3, R, F 1, 2, 1982 A 1, 2, 3, 1983 BI 1, 2, 3, 4, A, 1984 F 1, 2, A 1
Higginson, G (Canterbury, Hawke's Bay) 1980 W, 1981 S 1, SA 1, 1982 A 1, 2, 1983 A
Hill, D W (Waikato) 2006 I2(R)
Hill, S F (Canterbury) 1955 A 3, 1956 SA 1, 3, 4, 1957 A 1, 2, 1958 A 3, 1959 BI 1, 2, 3, 4
Hines, G R (Waikato) 1980 A 3
Hobbs, M J B (Canterbury) 1983 BI 1, 2, 3, 4, A, S, E, 1984 F 1, 2, A 1, 2, 3, 1985 E 1, 2, A, Arg 1, 2, 1986 A 2, 3, F 2, 3
Hoeata, J M R A (Taranaki) 2011 Fj, SA1(R), 2(R)
Hoeft, C H (Otago) 1998 E 2(t + R), A 2(R), SA 2, A 3, 1999 WS, F 1, SA 1, A 1, 2, [Tg, E, S, F 2, SA 3(R)], 2000 S 1, 2, A 1, SA 1, A 2, SA 2, 2001 Sm, Arg 1, F, SA 1, A 1, SA 2, A 2, 2003 W, [C, F(R)]
Holah, M R (Waikato) 2001 Sm, Arg 1(t&R), F (R), SA 1(R), A 1(R), SA 2(R), A 2(R), 2002 It, I 2(R), A 2(t), E, F, W (R), 2003 W, F (R), A 1(R), SA 2, [It(R), C, Tg(R), W(R), SA(t&R), A(R), F(t&R)], 2004 E1(R), 2, Arg(R), PI, A1, SA1, A2, SA2, 2005 BI3(R), A1(R), 2006 I1, SA3(t)
Holder, E C (Buller) 1934 A 2
Hook, L S (Auckland) 1929 A 1, 2, 3
Hooper, J A (Canterbury) 1937 SA 1, 2, 3
Hopkinson, A E (Canterbury) 1967 S, 1968 A 2, F 1, 2, 3, 1969 W 2, 1970 SA 1, 2, 3
Hore, A K (Taranaki) 2002 E, F, 2004 E1(t), 2(R), Arg, A1(t), 2005 W(R), I(R), S(R), 2006 I2(R), Arg(R), A1(R), SA1(R), A2(R), SA3, E(R), F2(R), W(R), 2007 F1(R), C, SA2(R), [Pt, S(R), R(R), F(R)], 2008 I1, E1, 2, SA1, 2, A1, 2, SA3, Sm, A3, 4, 2009 F1, A1, SA1, 2, A2, SA3, A3, 4, W, E, F3, 2010 S(R), I2(R), W3(R), 2011 Fj, SA1, A1(R), SA2(R), A2(R), [Tg, J(R), F1(R), C, Arg(R), A(R), F2(R)]
Hore, J (Otago) 1930 BI 2, 3, 4, 1932 A 1, 2, 3, 1934 A 1, 2, 1935 S, 1936 E
Horsley, R H (Wellington) 1960 SA 2, 3, 4
Hotop, J (Canterbury) 1952 A 1, 2, 1955 A 3
Howarth, S P (Auckland) 1994 SA 1, 2, 3, A
Howlett, D C (Auckland) 2000 Tg (R), F 1, 2, It, 2001 Sm, Arg 1(R), F (R), SA 1, A 1, 2, I, S, Arg 2, 2002 It, I 1, 2(R), Fj, A 1, SA 1, A 2, SA 2, E, F, W, 2003 E, W, F, SA 1, A 1, SA 2, A 2, [It, C(R), Tg, W, SA, A, F], 2004 E1, A1, SA1, A2, SA2, W, F, 2005 Fj, BI1, A2, I, E, 2006 I1, 2, SA1, A3, SA3, 2007 F2(R), C, SA2, A2, [It, S, R(R)]
Hughes, A M (Auckland) 1949 A 1, 2, 1950 BI 1, 2, 3, 4
Hughes, E (Southland, Wellington) 1907 A 1, 2, 3, 1908 AW 1, 1921 SA 1, 2
Hunter, B A (Otago) 1971 BI 1, 2, 3
Hunter, J (Taranaki) 1905 S, I, E, W, 1906 F, 1907 A 1, 2, 3, 1908 AW 1, 2, 3
Hurst, I A (Canterbury) 1973 I, F, E 2, 1974 A 1, 2

Ieremia, A (Wellington) 1994 SA 1, 2, 3, 1995 [J], 1996 SA 2(R), 5(R), 1997 A 1(R), SA 1(R), A 2, SA 2, A 3, I, E 1, 1999 WS, F 1, SA 1, A 1, SA 2, A 2, [Tg, E, S, F 2, SA 3], 2000 Tg, S 1, 2, A 1, 2, SA 2
Ifwersen, K D (Auckland) 1921 SA 3
Innes, C R (Auckland) 1989 W, I, 1990 A 1, 2, 3, F 1, 2, 1991 Arg 1, 2, A 1, 2, [E, US, It, C, A, S]
Innes, G D (Canterbury) 1932 A 2
Irvine, I B (North Auckland) 1952 A 1
Irvine, J G (Otago) 1914 A 1, 2, 3
Irvine, W R (Hawke's Bay, Wairarapa) 1924 I, W, 1925 E, F, 1930 BI 1
Irwin, M W (Otago) 1955 A 1, 2, 1956 SA 1, 1958 A 2, 1959 BI 3, 4, 1960 SA 1

Jack, C R (Canterbury, Tasman) 2001 Arg 1(R), SA 1(R), 2, A 2, I, S, Arg 2, 2002 I 1, 2, A 1, SA 1, A 2, SA 2, 2003 E, W, F, SA 1, A 1, SA 2(R), A 2, [It, C, SA, A, F], 2004 E1, 2, Arg, PI, A1, SA1, A2, SA2, It, W, F, 2005 Fj(R), BI1, 2, 3, SA1, A1, SA2, A2, W, E, S, 2006 I1, 2, A1, SA1, A2, 3, SA2(R), 3, E, F2, 2007 F1, 2, A1, SA2, A2, [It, Pt, S(R), R(R), F(R)]
Jackson, E S (Hawke's Bay) 1936 A 1, 2, 1937 SA 1, 2, 3, 1938 A 3
Jaffray, J L (Otago, South Canterbury) 1972 A 2, 1975 S, 1976 I, SA 1, 1977 BI 2, 1979 F 1, 2
Jane, C S (Wellington) 2008 A4(R), S(R), 2009 F1, 2, It1(R), A1, SA3(R), A3, 4, W, It2, F3, 2010 I1, W1, 2, SA1, 2, A1, 2, SA3, A3, 4, I2, 2011 SA1, 2(R), A2, [Tg(R), J, F1, Arg, A, F2]
Jarden, R A (Wellington) 1951 A 1, 2, 1952 A 1, 2, 1953 W, 1954 I, E, S, F, 1955 A 1, 2, 3, 1956 SA 1, 2, 3, 4
Jefferd, A C R (East Coast) 1981 S 1, 2, SA 1
Jessep, E M (Wellington) 1931 A, 1932 A 1
Johnson, L M (Wellington) 1928 SA 1, 2, 3, 4
Johnston, W (Otago) 1907 A 1, 2, 3
Johnstone, B R (Auckland) 1976 SA 2, 1977 BI 1, 2, F 1, 2, 1978 I, W, E, S, 1979 F 1, 2, S, E
Johnstone, C R (Canterbury) 2005 Fj(R), BI2(R), 3(R)
Johnstone, P (Otago) 1949 SA 2, 4, 1950 BI 1, 2, 3, 4, 1951 A 1, 2, 3
Jones, I D (North Auckland, North Harbour) 1990 S 1, 2, A 1, 2, 3, F 1, 2, 1991 Arg 1, 2, A 1, 2, [E, US, It, C, A, S], 1992 Wld 1, 2, 3, I 1, 2, A 1, 2, 3, SA, 1993 BI 1, 2(R), 3, WS, S, E, 1994 F 1, 2, SA 1, 3, A, 1995 C, [I, W, S, E, SA], A 1, 2, It, F 1, 2, 1996 WS, S 1, 2, A 1, SA 1, A 2, SA 2, 3, 4, 5, 1997 Fj, Arg 1, 2, A 1, SA 1, A 2, SA 2, A 3, I, E 1, W, E 2, 1998 E 1, 2, A 1, SA 1, A 2, 3(R), 1999 F 1(R), [It, S (R)]
Jones, M G (North Auckland) 1973 E 2
Jones, M N (Auckland) 1987 [It, Fj, S, F], A, 1988 W 1, 2, A 2, 3, 1989 F 1, 2, Arg 1, 2, 1990 F 1, 2, 1991 Arg 1, 2, A 1, 2, [E, US, S], 1992 Wld 1, 3, I 2, A 1, 3, SA, 1993 BI 1, 2, 3, A, WS, 1994 SA 3(R), A, 1995 A 1(R), 2, It, F 1, 2, 1996 WS, S 1, 2, A 1, SA 1, A 2, SA 2, 3, 4, 5, 1997 Fj, 1998 E 1, A 1, SA 1, A 2
Jones, P F H (North Auckland) 1954 E, S, 1955 A 1, 2, 1956 SA 3, 4, 1958 A 1, 2, 3, 1959 BI 1, 1960 SA 1
Joseph, H T (Canterbury) 1971 BI 2, 3
Joseph, J W (Otago) 1992 Wld 2, 3(R), I 1, A 1(R), 3, SA, 1993 BI 1, 2, 3, A, WS, S, E, 1994 SA 2(t), 1995 C, [I, W, J (R), S, SA (R)]

Kahui, R D (Waikato) 2008 E2, A1, 2, SA3, Sm, A3, S, W, 2010 W1(R), 2, SA1(R), 2011 SA2, [Tg, J, F1, A, F2]
Kaino, J (Auckland) 2006 I1(R), 2, 2008 I1, E1, SA1, 2, A1, 2, SA3, Sm, A3, 4, I2, W, E3, 2009 F2, It1, A1, SA1, 2, A2, SA3, W, E(R), F3, 2010 I1, W2, SA1, 2, A1, 2, SA3, A3(R), 4, E, I2, W3, 2011 Fj(R), SA1, A1, SA2, [Tg, J, F1, C, Arg, A, F2]
Karam, J F (Wellington, Horowhenua) 1972 W, S, 1973 E 1, I, F, 1974 A 1, 2, 3, I, 1975 S
Katene, T (Wellington) 1955 A 2
Kearney, J C (Otago) 1947 A 2, 1949 SA 1, 2, 3
Kelleher, B T (Otago, Waikato) 1999 WS (R), SA 1(R), A 2(R), [Tg (R), E (R), It, F 2], 2000 S 1, A 1(R), 2(R), It (R), 2001 Sm, F (R), A 1(R), SA 2, A 2, I, S, 2002 It, I 2(R), Fj, SA 1(R), 2(R), 2003 F (R), [A(R)], 2004 Arg, PI(R), SA1(R), 2(R), It, W(R), F, 2005 Fj, BI1(R), 2, 3, SA1, W, E, 2006 I1, 2, A1, 2, 3, SA3(R), E, F1(R), 2, W, 2007 F2, C, SA1, A1, 2, [It, S, F]
Kelly, J W (Auckland) 1949 A 1, 2
Kember, G F (Wellington) 1970 SA 4
Ketels, R C (Counties) 1980 W, 1981 S 1, 2, R, F 1
Kiernan, H A D (Auckland) 1903 A
Kilby, F D (Wellington) 1932 A 1, 2, 3, 1934 A 2
Killeen, B A (Auckland) 1936 A 1
King, R M (Waikato) 2002 W
King, R R (West Coast) 1934 A 2, 1935 S, I, W, 1936 E, A 1, 2, 1937 SA 1, 2, 3, 1938 A 1, 2, 3

Kingstone, C N (Taranaki) 1921 SA 1, 2, 3
Kirk, D E (Auckland) 1985 E 1, 2, A, Arg 1, 1986 F 1, A 1, 2, 3, F 2, 3, 1987 [It, Fj, Arg, S, W, F], A
Kirkpatrick, I A (Canterbury, Poverty Bay) 1967 F, 1968 A 1(R), 2, F 1, 2, 3, 1969 W 1, 2, 1970 SA 1, 2, 3, 4, 1971 BI 1, 2, 3, 4, 1972 A 1, 2, 3, W, S, 1973 E 1, I, F, E 2, 1974 A 1, 2, 3, I 1975 S, 1976 I, SA 1, 2, 3, 4, 1977 BI 1, 2, 3, 4
Kirton, E W (Otago) 1967 E, W, F, S, 1968 A 1, 2, F 1, 2, 3, 1969 W 1, 2, 1970 SA 2, 3
Kirwan, J J (Auckland) 1984 F 1, 2, 1985 E 1, 2, A, Arg 1, 2, 1986 F 1, A 1, 2, 3, F 2, 3, 1987 [It, Fj, Arg, S, W, F], A, 1988 W 1, 2, A 1, 2, 3, 1989 F 1, 2, Arg 1, 2, A, 1990 S 1, 2, A 1, 2, 3, F 1, 2, 1991 Arg 2, A 1, 2, [E, It, C, A, S], 1992 Wld 1, 2(R), 3, I 1, 2, A 1, 2, 3, SA, 1993 BI 2, 3, A, WS, 1994 F 1, 2, SA 1, 2, 3
Kivell, A L (Taranaki) 1929 A 2, 3
Knight, A (Auckland) 1934 A 1
Knight, G A (Manawatu) 1977 F 1, 2, 1978 A 1, 2, 3, E, S, 1979 F 1, 2, A, 1980 A 1, 2, 3, W, 1981 S 1, 2, SA 1, 3, 1982 A 1, 2, 3, 1983 BI 1, 2, 3, 4, A, 1984 F 1, 2, A 1, 2, 3, 1985 E 1, 2, A, 1986 A 2, 3
Knight, L G (Poverty Bay) 1977 BI 1, 2, 3, 4, F 1, 2
Koteka, T T (Waikato) 1981 F 2, 1982 A 3
Kreft, A J (Otago) 1968 A 2
Kronfeld, J A (Otago) 1995 C, [I, W, S, E, SA], A 1, 2(R) 1996 WS, S 1, 2, A 1, SA 1, A 2, SA 2, 3, 4, 5, 1997 Fj, Arg 1, 2, A 1, SA 1, A 2, SA 2, A 3, I (R), E 1, W, E 2, 1998 E 1, 2, A 1, SA 1, 2 A 3, 1999 WS, F 1, SA 1, A 1, SA 2, A 2, [Tg, E, S, F 2, SA 3], 2000 Tg, S 1(R), 2, A 1(R), SA 1, A 2, SA 2

Laidlaw, C R (Otago, Canterbury) 1964 F, A 1, 1965 SA 1, 2, 3, 4, 1966 BI 1, 2, 3, 4, 1967 E, W, S, 1968 A 1, 2, F 1, 2, 1970 SA 1, 2, 3
Laidlaw, K F (Southland) 1960 SA 2, 3, 4
Lambert, K K (Manawatu) 1972 S (R), 1973 E 1, I, F, E 2, 1974 I, 1976 SA 1, 3, 4, 1977 BI 1, 4
Lambourn, A (Wellington) 1934 A 1, 2, 1935 S, I, W, 1936 E, 1937 SA 1, 2, 3, 1938 A 3
Larsen, B P (North Harbour) 1992 Wld 2, 3, I 1, 1994 F 1, 2, SA 1, 2, 3, A (t), 1995 [I, W, J, E(R)], It, F 1, 1996 S 2(t), SA 4(R)
Latimer, T D (Bay of Plenty) 2009 F1(R), 2, It1, 2, F3(R)
Lauaki, S T (Waikato) 2005 Fj(R), BI1(R), 2(R), 3, A2, I, S, 2007 [It(R), Pt, S(R), R], 2008 E1(R), 2(R), SA1(R), 2(R), A1(R), Sm(R)
Laulala, C D E (Canterbury) 2004 W, 2006 I2
Le Lievre, J M (Canterbury) 1962 A 4
Lee, D D (Otago) 2002 E (R), F
Lendrum, R N (Counties) 1973 E 2
Leonard, B G (Waikato) 2007 F1(R), 2(R), SA2(R), A2(R), [It(R), Pt, S(R), R(R), F(R)], 2009 It1, SA1, A3(R), W
Leslie, A R (Wellington) 1974 A 1, 2, 3, I, 1975 S, 1976 I, SA 1, 2, 3, 4
Leys, E T (Wellington) 1929 A 3
Lilburne, H T (Canterbury, Wellington) 1928 SA 3, 4, 1929 A 1, 2, 3, 1930 BI 1, 4, 1931 A, 1932 A 1, 1934 A 2
Lindsay, D F (Otago) 1928 SA 1, 2, 3
Lineen, T R (Auckland) 1957 A 1, 2, 1958 A 1, 2, 3, 1959 BI 1, 2, 3, 4, 1960 SA 1, 2, 3
Lister, T N (South Canterbury) 1968 A 1, 2, F 1, 1969 W 1, 2, 1970 SA 1, 4, 1971 BI 4
Little, P F (Auckland) 1961 F 2, 3, 1962 A 2, 3, 5, 1963 I, W, 1964 E, S, F
Little, W K (North Harbour) 1990 S 1, 2, A 1, 2, 3, F 1, 2, 1991 Arg 1, 2, A 1, [It, S], 1992 Wld 1, 2, 3, I 1, 2, A 1, 2, 3, SA, 1993 BI 1, WS (R), 1994 SA 2(R), A, 1995 C, [I, W, S, E, SA], A 1, 2, It, F 1, 2, 1996 S 2, A 1, SA 1, A 2, SA 2, 3, 4, 5, 1997 W, E 2, 1998 E 1, A 1, SA 1, A 2
Loader, C J (Wellington) 1954 I, E, S, F
Lochore, B J (Wairarapa) 1964 E, S, 1965 SA 1, 2, 3, 4, 1966 BI 1, 2, 3, 4, 1967 A, E, W, F, S, 1968 A 1, F 2, 3, 1969 W 1, 2, 1970 SA 1, 2, 3, 4, 1971 BI 3
Loe, R W (Waikato, Canterbury) 1987 [It, Arg], 1988 W 1, 2, A 1, 2, 3, 1989 F 1, 2, Arg 1, 2, A, W, I, 1990 S 1, 2, A 1, 2, 3, F 1, 2, 1991 Arg 1, 2, A 1, 2, [E, It, C, A, S], 1992 Wld 1, 2, 3, I 1, A 1, 2, 3, SA, 1994 F 1, 2, SA 1, 2, 3, A, 1995 [J, S, SA (R)], A 2(t), F 2(R)
Lomu, J T (Counties Manukau, Wellington) 1994 F 1, 2, 1995 [I, W, S, E, SA], A 1, 2, It, F 1, 2, 1996 WS, S 1, A 1, SA 1, A 2, 1997 E 1, W, E 2, 1998 E 1, 2, A 1(R), SA 1, A 2, SA 2, A 3, 1999 WS (R), SA 1(R), A 1(R), SA 2(R), A 2(R), [Tg, E, It, S, F 2, SA 3], 2000 Tg, S 1, 2, A 1, SA 1, A 2, SA 2, F 1, 2001 Arg 1, F, SA 1, A 1, SA 2, A 2, I, S, Arg 2, 2002 It (R), I 1(R), 2, Fj, SA 1(R), E, F, W
Long, A J (Auckland) 1903 A

Loveridge, D S (Taranaki) 1978 W, 1979 S, E, 1980 A 1, 2, 3, W, 1981 S 1, 2, SA 1, 2, 3, R, F 1, 2, 1982 A 1, 2, 3, 1983 BI 1, 2, 3, 4, A, 1985 Arg 2
Lowen, K R (Waikato) 2002 E
Lucas, F W (Auckland) 1924 I, 1925 F, 1928 SA 4, 1930 BI 1, 2, 3, 4
Lunn, W A (Otago) 1949 A 1, 2
Lynch, T W (South Canterbury) 1913 A 1, 1914 A 1, 2, 3
Lynch, T W (Canterbury) 1951 A 1, 2, 3

McAlister, C L (North Harbour) 2005 BI3, SA1(R), A1(R), SA2(R), A2(R), 2006 I1, 2, SA1(R), A3, SA2, F1, W, 2007 F2, C, SA1(R), A1, SA2, A2, [It, S, R, F], 2009 F1(R), 2(R), It1, SA1(R), 2(R), A2, It2, F3(R)
McAtamney, F S (Otago) 1956 SA 2
McCahill, B J (Auckland) 1987 [Arg, S (R), W (R)], 1989 Arg 1(R), 2(R), 1991 A 2, [E, US, C, A]
McCaw, R H (Canterbury) 2001 I, S, Arg 2, 2002 I 1, 2, A 1, SA 1, A 2, SA 2, 2003 E, F, SA 1, A 1, 2, [It, C(R), Tg(R), W, SA, A, F], 2004 E1, Arg, It, W, F, 2005 Fj, BI1, 2, SA1, A1, SA2, A2, W(R), I, S, 2006 I1, 2, A1, SA1, A2, 3, SA2, 3, E, F1, 2, W, 2007 F1, 2, C(R), SA1, A1, SA2, A2, [It, S, R(R), F], 2008 I1, E1, 2, A2, SA3, A3, 4, S(R), I2, W, E3, 2009 A1, SA1, 2, A2, SA3, A3, 4, W, E, F3, 2010 I1, W1, 2, SA1, 2, A1, 2, SA3, A3, 4, E, S, I2, W3, 2011 Fj, SA1, A1, 2, [Tg, F1, Arg, A, F2]
McCaw, W A (Southland) 1951 A 1, 2, 3, 1953 W, 1954 F
McCool, M J (Wairarapa-Bush) 1979 A
McCormick, W F (Canterbury) 1965 SA 4, 1967 E, W, F, S, 1968 A 1, 2, F 1, 2, 3, 1969 W 1, 2, 1970 SA 1, 2, 3, 1971 BI 1
McCullough, J F (Taranaki) 1959 BI 2, 3, 4
McDonald, A (Otago) 1905 S, I, E, W, 1907 A 1, 1908 AW 1, 1913 A 1, US
Macdonald, A J (Auckland) 2005 W(R), S
Macdonald, H H (Canterbury, North Auckland) 1972 W, S, 1973 E 1, I, F, E 2, 1974 I, 1975 S, 1976 I, SA 1, 2, 3
MacDonald, L R (Canterbury) 2000 S 1(R), 2(R), SA 1(t), 2(R), 2001 Sm, Arg 1, F, SA 1(R), A 1(R), SA 2, A 2, I, S, 2002 I 1, 2, Fj (R), A 2(R), SA 2, 2003 A 2(R), [It(R), C, Tg, W, SA, A, F], 2005 BI1, 2(R), SA1, 2, A2, W(R), I, E(R), S(R), 2006 Arg, A1, SA1, A2, 3(R), SA2, F1, 2, 2007 F1, 2, C(R), SA1(R), [It, Pt(R), S, F], 2008 I1(R), E1(R), 2, SA1(R), 2(R)
McDonnell, J M (Otago) 2002 It, I 1(R), 2(R), Fj, SA 1(R), A 2(R), E, F
McDowell, S C (Auckland, Bay of Plenty) 1985 Arg 1, 2, 1986 A 2, 3, F 2, 3, 1987 [It, Fj, S, W, F], A, 1988 W 1, 2, A 1, 2, 3, 1989 F 1, 2, Arg 1, 2, A, W, I, 1990 S 1, 2, A 1, 2, 3, F 1, 2, 1991 Arg 1, 2, A 1, 2, [E, US, It, C, A, S], 1992 Wld 1, 2, 3, I 1, 2
McEldowney, J T (Taranaki) 1977 BI 3, 4
MacEwan, I N (Wellington) 1956 SA 2, 1957 A 1, 2, 1958 A 1, 2, 3, 1959 BI 1, 2, 3, 1960 SA 1, 2, 3, 4, 1961 F 1, 2, 3, 1962 A 1, 2, 3, 4
McGrattan, B (Wellington) 1983 S, E, 1985 Arg 1, 2, 1986 F 1, A 1
McGregor, A J (Auckland) 1913 A 1, US
McGregor, D (Canterbury, Southland) 1903 A, 1904 BI, 1905 E, W
McGregor, N P (Canterbury) 1924 W, 1925 E
McGregor, R W (Auckland) 1903 A, 1904 BI
McHugh, M J (Auckland) 1946 A 1, 2, 1949 SA 3
McIntosh, D N (Wellington) 1956 SA 1, 2, 1957 A 1, 2
McKay, D W (Auckland) 1961 F 1, 2, 3, 1963 E 1, 2
McKechnie, B J (Southland) 1977 F 1, 2, 1978 A 2(R), 3, W (R), E, S, 1979 A, 1981 SA 1(R), F 1
McKellar, G F (Wellington) 1910 A 1, 2, 3
McKenzie, R J (Wellington) 1913 A 1, US, 1914 A 2, 3
McKenzie, R McC (Manawatu) 1934 A 1, 1935 S, 1936 A 1, 1937 SA 1, 2, 3, 1938 A 1, 2, 3
McLachlan, J S (Auckland) 1974 A 2
McLaren, H C (Waikato) 1952 A 1
McLean, A L (Bay of Plenty) 1921 SA 2, 3
McLean, H F (Wellington, Auckland) 1930 BI 3, 4, 1932 A 1, 2, 3, 1934 A 1, 1935 I, W, 1936 E
McLean, J K (King Country, Auckland) 1947 A 1, 1949 A 2
McLeod, B E (Counties) 1964 A 1, 2, 3, 1965 SA 1, 2, 3, 4, 1966 BI 1, 2, 3, 4, 1967 E, W, F, S, 1968 A 1, 2, F 1, 2, 3, 1969 W 1, 2, 1970 SA 1, 2
McLeod, S J (Waikato) 1996 WS, S 1, 1997 Fj (R), Arg 2(t + R), I (R), E 1(R), W (t), E 2(R), 1998 A 1, SA 1(R)
McMinn, A F (Wairarapa, Manawatu) 1903 A, 1905 A
McMinn, F A (Manawatu) 1904 BI
McMullen, R F (Auckland) 1957 A 1, 2, 1958 A 1, 2, 3, 1959 BI 1, 2, 3, 1960 SA 2, 3, 4
McNab, J R (Otago) 1949 SA 1, 2, 3, 1950 BI 1, 2, 3

McNaughton, A M (Bay of Plenty) 1971 BI 1, 2, 3
McNeece, J (Southland) 1913 A 2, 3, 1914 A 1, 2, 3
McPhail, B E (Canterbury) 1959 BI 1, 4
Macpherson, D G (Otago) 1905 A
MacPherson, G L (Otago) 1986 F 1
MacRae, I R (Hawke's Bay) 1966 BI 1, 2, 3, 4, 1967 A, E, W, F, S, 1968 F 1, 2, 1969 W 1, 2, 1970 SA 1, 2, 3, 4
McRae, J A (Southland) 1946 A 1(R), 2
McWilliams, R G (Auckland) 1928 SA 2, 3, 4, 1929 A 1, 2, 3, 1930 BI 1, 2, 3, 4
Mackintosh, J L (Southland) 2008 S
Mackrell, W H C (Auckland) 1906 F
Macky, J V (Auckland) 1913 A 2
Maguire, J R (Auckland) 1910 A 1, 2, 3
Mahoney, A (Bush) 1935 S, I, W, 1936 E
Mains, L W (Otago) 1971 BI 2, 3, 4, 1976 I
Major, J (Taranaki) 1967 A
Maka, I (Otago) 1998 E 2(R), A 1(R), SA 1(R), 2
Maling, T S (Otago) 2002 It, I 2(R), Fj, A 1, SA 1, A 2, SA 2, 2004 Arg, A1, SA1, 2
Manchester, J E (Canterbury) 1932 A 1, 2, 3, 1934 A 1, 2, 1935 S, I, W, 1936 E
Mannix, S J (Wellington) 1994 F 1
Marshall, J W (Southland, Canterbury) 1995 F 2, 1996 WS, S 1, 2, A 1, SA 1, A 2, SA 2, 3, 4, 5, 1997 Fj, Arg 1, 2, A 1, SA 1, A 2, SA 2, A 3, I, E 1, W, E 2, 1998 A 1, SA 1, A 2, SA 2, A 3, 1999 WS, F 1, SA 1, A 1, SA 2, A 2, [Tg, E, S, F 2(R), SA 3], 2000 Tg, S 2, A 1, SA 1, A 2, SA 2, F 1, 2, It, 2001 Arg 1, F, SA 1, A 1, 2(R), 2002 I 1, 2, Fj (R), A 1, SA 1, A 2, SA 2, 2003 E, SA 1(R), A 1, SA 2, A 2, [It, Tg, W, SA, A], 2004 E1, 2, PI, A1, SA1, A2, SA2, 2005 Fj(R), BI1, 2(R), 3(R)
Masaga, L T C (Counties Manukau) 2009 It1
Masoe, M C (Taranaki, Wellington) 2005 W, E, 2006Arg, A1(R), SA1(R), A2(R), 3(R), SA2, E, F2(R), 2007 F1, 2(R), C, A1(R), SA2(R), [It(R), Pt, S, R, F(R)]
Mason, D F (Wellington) 1947 A 2(R)
Masters, R R (Canterbury) 1924 I, W, 1925 E, F
Mataira, H K (Hawke's Bay) 1934 A 2
Matheson, J D (Otago) 1972 A 1, 2, 3, W, S
Mathewson, A S (Wellington) 2010 A2(R), 4(R), E, I2(R)
Mauger, A J D (Canterbury) 2001 I, S, Arg 2, 2002 It (R), I 1, 2, Fj, A 1, SA 1, A 2, SA 2, 2003 SA 1, A 1, SA 2, A 2, [W, SA, A, F], 2004 SA2(R), It(R), W, F(R), 2005 Fj, BI1, 2, SA1, A1, SA2, A2, I, E, 2006 I1, 2, A1, 2, SA3, E, 2007 F1, C, SA1, A1, [It(R), Pt, R]
Max, D S (Nelson) 1931 A, 1934 A 1, 2
Maxwell, N M C (Canterbury) 1999 WS, F 1, SA 1, A 1, SA 2, A 2, [Tg, E, S, F 2, SA 3], 2000 S 1, 2, A 1, SA 1(R), A 2, SA 2, F 1, 2, It (R), 2001 Sm, Arg 1, F, SA 1, A 1, SA 2, A2, I, S, Arg 2, 2002 It, I 1, 2, Fj, 2004 It, F
Mayerhofler, M A (Canterbury) 1998 E 1, 2, SA 1, A 2, SA 2, A 3
Meads, C E (King Country) 1957 A 1, 2, 1958 A 1, 2, 3, 1959 BI 2, 3, 4, 1960 SA 1, 2, 3, 4, 1961 F 1, 2, 3, 1962 A 1, 2, 3, 5, 1963 E 1, 2, I, W, 1964 E, S, F, A 1, 2, 3, 1965 SA 1, 2, 3, 4, 1966 BI 1, 2, 3, 4, 1967 A, E, W, F, S, 1968 A 1, 2, F 1, 2, 3, 1969 W 1, 2, 1970 SA 3, 4, 1971 BI 1, 2, 3, 4
Meads, S T (King Country) 1961 F 1, 1962 A 4, 5, 1963 I, 1964 A 1, 2, 3, 1965 SA 1, 2, 3, 4, 1966 BI 1, 2, 3, 4
Mealamu, K F (Auckland) 2002 W, 2003 E (R), W, F (R), SA 1, A 1, SA 2(R), A 2, [It, W, SA, A, F], 2004 E1, 2, PI, A1, SA1, A2, SA2, W, F(R), 2005 Fj(R), BI1, 2, 3, SA1, A1, SA2, A2, I, E, 2006 I1, 2, A1, 2, 3, SA2(R), E, F1(R), 2, 2007 F1, 2(R), SA1(R), A1(R), SA2, A2(R), [It, Pt(R), R], 2008 I1(R), E1(t&R), 2(t&R), SA1(R), 2(R), A1(R), 2(R), SA3(R), Sm(R), A3(R), 4(R), S, I2, W, E3, 2009 F1(R), 2, It1, A1(R), SA1(R), 2(R), 2010 I1, W1, 2, SA1, 2, A1, 2, SA3, A3, 4, E, W3, 2011 A1, SA2, A2, [J, F1, C(R), Arg, A, F2]
Meates, K F (Canterbury) 1952 A 1, 2
Meates, W A (Otago) 1949 SA 2, 3, 4, 1950 BI 1, 2, 3, 4
Meeuws, K J (Otago, Auckland) 1998 A 3, 1999 WS, F 1, SA 1, A 1, SA 2, A 2, [Tg, It (R), S (R), F 2(R), SA 3], 2000 Tg (R), S 2, A 1, SA 1, A 2, SA 2, 2001 Arg 2, 2002 It, Fj, E, F, W (R), 2003 W, F (R), SA 1(R), A 1(R), SA 2, [It(R), C, Tg, W(R), SA(R), A(R)], 2004 E1, 2, PI, A1, SA1, A2, SA2
Mehrtens, A P (Canterbury) 1995 C, [I, W, S, E, SA], A 1, 2, 1996 WS, S 1, 2, A 1, SA 1, A 2, SA 2, 5, 1997 Fj, SA 2(R), I, E 1, W, E 2, 1998 E 1, 2, A 1, SA 1(R), A 2, SA 2, A 3, 1999 F 1, SA 1, A 1, SA 2, A 2, [Tg, E, S, F 2, SA 3], 2000 S 1, 2, A 1, SA 1, A 2, SA 2, F 1, 2, It (R), 2001 Arg 1, A 1(R), SA 2, A 2, I, S, Arg 2, 2002 It, I 1, 2, Fj (R), A 1, SA 1, A 2, SA 2, E (R), F, W, 2004 E2(R), Arg, A2(R), SA2
Messam, L J (Waikato) 2008 S, 2009 F1, It2, 2010 SA1(R), 2(R), S, 2011 Fj, SA1(R), 2
Metcalfe, T C (Southland) 1931 A, 1932 A 1
Mexted, G G (Wellington) 1950 BI 4
Mexted, M G (Wellington) 1979 S, E, 1980 A 1, 2, 3, W, 1981 S 1, 2, SA 1, 2, 3, R, F 1, 2, 1982 A 1, 2, 3, 1983 BI 1, 2, 3, 4, A, S, E, 1984 F 1, 2, A 1, 2, 3, 1985 E 1, 2, A, Arg 1, 2
Mika, B M (Auckland) 2002 E (R), F, W (R)
Mika, D G (Auckland) 1999 WS, F 1, SA 1(R), A 1, 2, [It, SA 3(R)]
Mill, J J (Hawke's Bay, Wairarapa) 1924 W, 1925 E, F, 1930 BI 1
Milliken, H M (Canterbury) 1938 A 1, 2, 3
Milner, H P (Wanganui) 1970 SA 3
Mitchell, N A (Southland, Otago) 1935 S, I, W, 1936 E, A 2, 1937 SA 3, 1938 A 1, 2
Mitchell, T W (Canterbury) 1976 SA 4(R)
Mitchell, W J (Canterbury) 1910 A 2, 3
Mitchinson, F E (Wellington) 1907 A 1, 2, 3, 1908 AW 1, 2, 3, 1910 A 1, 2, 3, 1913 A 1(R), US
Moffitt, J E (Wellington) 1921 SA 1, 2, 3
Moore, G J T (Otago) 1949 A 1
Moreton, R C (Canterbury) 1962 A 3, 4, 1964 A 1, 2, 3, 1965 SA 2, 3
Morgan, J E (North Auckland) 1974 A 3, I, 1976 SA 2, 3, 4
Morris, T J (Nelson Bays) 1972 A 1, 2, 3
Morrison, T C (South Canterbury) 1938 A 1, 2, 3
Morrison, T G (Otago) 1973 E 2(R)
Morrissey, P J (Canterbury) 1962 A 3, 4, 5
Mourie, G N K (Taranaki) 1977 BI 3, 4, F 1, 2, 1978 I, W, E, S, 1979 F 1, 2, A, S, E, 1980 W, 1981 S 1, 2, F 1, 2, 1982 A 1, 2, 3
Muliaina, J M (Auckland, Waikato) 2003 E (R), W, F, SA 1, A 1, SA 2, A 2, [It, C, Tg, W, SA, A, F], 2004 E1, 2, Arg, PI, A1, SA1, A2, SA2, It, W, F, 2005 Fj, BI1(R), 2, 3, SA1, A1, SA2, A2, W, E, 2006 I1, 2, A1, SA1, A2, 3, SA2, 3, E, F1(R), 2, W, 2007 C, SA1, A1, SA2, A2, [It, Pt, F], 2008 I1, E1, 2(t), SA1, 2, A1, 2, SA3, Sm, A3, I2, W, E3, 2009 F1, 2, It1, A1, SA1, 2, A2, SA3, A3, 4, W, It2(R), E, F3, 2010 W2, SA1, 2, A1, 2, SA3, A3, 4, E, S, I2, W3, 2011 Fj, SA1, A1, 2, [C, Arg]
Muller, B L (Taranaki) 1967 A, E, W, F, 1968 A 1, F 1, 1969 W 1, 1970 SA 1, 2, 4, 1971 BI 1, 2, 3, 4
Mumm, W J (Buller) 1949 A 1
Murdoch, K (Otago) 1970 SA 4, 1972 A 3, W
Murdoch, P H (Auckland) 1964 A 2, 3, 1965 SA 1, 2, 3
Murray, H V (Canterbury) 1913 A 1, US, 1914 A 2, 3
Murray, P C (Wanganui) 1908 AW 2
Myers, R G (Waikato) 1978 A 3
Mynott, H J (Taranaki) 1905 I, W, 1906 F, 1907 A 1, 2, 3, 1910 A 1, 3

Nathan, W J (Auckland) 1962 A 1, 2, 3, 4, 5, 1963 E 1, 2, W, 1964 F, 1966 BI 1, 2, 3, 4, 1967 A
Nelson, K A (Otago) 1962 A 4, 5
Nepia, G (Hawke's Bay, East Coast) 1924 I, W, 1925 E, F, 1929 A 1, 1930 BI 1, 2, 3, 4
Nesbit, S R (Auckland) 1960 SA 2, 3
Newby, C A (North Harbour) 2004 E2(t), SA2(R), 2006 I2(R)
Newton, F (Canterbury) 1905 E, W, 1906 F
Nicholls, H E (Wellington) 1921 SA 1
Nicholls, M F (Wellington) 1921 SA 1, 2, 3, 1924 I, W, 1925 E, F, 1928 SA 4, 1930 BI 2, 3
Nicholson, G W (Auckland) 1903 A, 1904 BI, 1907 A 2, 3
Nonu, M A (Wellington) 2003 E, [It(R), C, Tg(R)], 2004 It(R), W(R), F(R), 2005 BI2(R), W(R), I, S(R), 2006 I1, E, F1(R), 2, W(R), 2007 F1(R), 2(R), 2008 I1, E1, 2, SA1, 2, A1, 2, SA3, Sm, A3, 4(R), S, I2, W, E3, 2009 F1, 2, It1, A1, SA1, 2, A2(t&R), SA3, A3, 4, W, E, F3, 2010 SA1, 2, A1, 2, SA3, A3, 4, E, I2, W3(R), 2011 Fj, SA1, A1, 2, [Tg, J, F1, Arg, A, F2]
Norton, R W (Canterbury) 1971 BI 1, 2, 3, 4, 1972 A 1, 2, 3, W, S, 1973 E 1, I, F, E 2, 1974 A 1, 2, 3, I, 1975 S, 1976 I, SA 1, 2, 3, 4, 1977 BI 1, 2, 3, 4

O'Brien, J G (Auckland) 1914 A 1
O'Callaghan, M W (Manawatu) 1968 F 1, 2, 3
O'Callaghan, T R (Wellington) 1949 A 2
O'Donnell, D H (Wellington) 1949 A 2
O'Halloran, J D (Wellington) 2000 It (R)
Old, G H (Manawatu) 1981 SA 3, R (R), 1982 A 1(R)
O'Leary, M J (Auckland) 1910 A 1, 3, 1913 A 2, 3
Oliver, A D (Otago) 1997 Fj (t), 1998 E 1, 2, A 1, SA 1, A 2, SA 2, A 3, 1999 WS, F 1, SA 1, A 1, SA 2, A 2, [Tg, E, S, F 2, SA 3(R)], 2000 Tg (R), S 1, 2, A 1, SA 1, A 2, SA 2, F 1, 2, It, 2001 Sm, Arg 1, F, SA 1, A 1, SA 2, A 2, I, S, Arg 2, 2003 E, F, 2004 It, F, 2005 W, S, 2006 Arg, SA1, 2, 3(R), F1, W, 2007 F2, SA1, A1, 2, [It(R), Pt(R), S, F]

Oliver, C J (Canterbury) 1929 A 1, 2, 1934 A 1, 1935 S, I, W, 1936 E
Oliver, D J (Wellington) 1930 BI 1, 2
Oliver, D O (Otago) 1954 I, F
Oliver, F J (Southland, Otago, Manawatu) 1976 SA 4, 1977 BI 1, 2, 3, 4, F 1, 2, 1978 A 1, 2, 3, I, W, E, S, 1979 F 1, 2, 1981 SA 2
O'Neill, K J (Canterbury) 2008 SA2(R)
Orr, R W (Otago) 1949 A 1
Osborne, G M (North Harbour) 1995 C, [I, W, J, E, SA], A 1, 2, F 1(R), 2, 1996 SA 2, 3, 4, 5, 1997 Arg 1(R), A 2, 3, I, 1999 [It]
Osborne, W M (Wanganui) 1975 S, 1976 SA 2(R), 4(R), 1977 BI 1, 2, 3, 4, F 1(R), 2, 1978 I, W, E, S, 1980 W, 1982 A 1, 3
O'Sullivan, J M (Taranaki) 1905 S, I, E, W, 1907 A 3
O'Sullivan, T P A (Taranaki) 1960 SA 1, 1961 F 1, 1962 A 1, 2

Page, J R (Wellington) 1931 A, 1932 A 1, 2, 3, 1934 A 1, 2
Palmer, B P (Auckland) 1929 A 2, 1932 A 2, 3
Parker, J H (Canterbury) 1924 I, W, 1925 E
Parkhill, A A (Otago) 1937 SA 1, 2, 3, 1938 A 1, 2, 3
Parkinson, R M (Poverty Bay) 1972 A 1, 2, 3, W, S, 1973 E 1, 2
Paterson, A M (Otago) 1908 AW 2, 3, 1910 A 1, 2, 3
Paton, H (Otago) 1910 A 1, 3
Pene, A R B (Otago) 1992 Wld 1(R), 2, 3, I 1, 2, A 1, 2(R), 1993 BI 3, A, WS, S, E, 1994 F 1, 2(R), SA 1(R)
Phillips, W J (King Country) 1937 SA 2, 1938 A 1, 2
Philpott, S (Canterbury) 1991 [It (R), S (R)]
Pickering, E A R (Waikato) 1958 A 2, 1959 BI 1, 4
Pierce, M J (Wellington) 1985 E 1, 2, A, Arg 1, 1986 A 2, 3, F 2, 3, 1987 [It, Arg, S, W, F], A, 1988 W 1, 2, A 1, 2, 3, 1989 F 1, 2, Arg 1, 2, A, W, I
Pokere, S T (Southland, Auckland) 1981 SA 3, 1982 A 1, 2, 3, 1983 BI 1, 2, 3, 4, A, S, E, 1984 F 1, 2, A 2, 3, 1985 E 1, 2, A
Pollock, H R (Wellington) 1932 A 1, 2, 3, 1936 A 1, 2
Porter, C G (Wellington) 1925 F, 1929 A 2, 3, 1930 BI 1, 2, 3, 4
Preston, J P (Canterbury, Wellington) 1991 [US, S], 1992 SA (R), 1993 BI 2, 3, A, WS, 1996 SA 4(R), 1997 I (R), E 1(R)
Procter, A C (Otago) 1932 A 1
Purdue, C A (Southland) 1905 A
Purdue, E (Southland) 1905 A
Purdue, G B (Southland) 1931 A, 1932 A 1, 2, 3
Purvis, G H (Waikato) 1991 [US], 1993 WS
Purvis, N A (Otago) 1976 I

Quaid, C E (Otago) 1938 A 1, 2

Ralph, C S (Auckland, Canterbury) 1998 E 2, 2002 It, I 1, 2, A 1, SA 1, A 2, SA 2, 2003 E, A 1(R), [C, Tg, SA(R), F(t&R)]
Ranby, R M (Waikato) 2001 Sm (R)
Randell, T C (Otago) 1997 Fj, Arg 1, 2, A 1, SA 1, A 2, SA 2, A 3, I, E 1, W, E 2, 1998 E 1, 2, A 1, SA 1, A 2, SA 2, A 3, 1999 WS, F 1, SA 1, A 1, SA 2, A 2, [Tg, E, It, S, F 2, SA 3], 2000 Tg, S 1, 2(R), A 1, SA 1, A 2, SA 2, F 2(R), It (R), 2001 Arg 1, F, SA 1, A 1, SA 2, A 2, 2002 It, Fj, E, F, W
Ranger, R M N (Northland) 2010 W2(R), SA2, A3(R)
Rangi, R E (Auckland) 1964 A 2, 3, 1965 SA 1, 2, 3, 4, 1966 BI 1, 2, 3, 4
Rankin, J G (Canterbury) 1936 A 1, 2, 1937 SA 2
Rawlinson, G P (North Harbour) 2006 I1, 2(R), SA2, 2007 SA1
Read, K J (Canterbury) 2008 S, I2(R), E3(R), 2009 F1, 2, It1, A1(R), SA1(R), 2(R), A2, SA3, A3, 4(R), W, E, F3, 2010 I1, W1, 2, SA1, 2, A1, 2, SA3, A3, 4, E, S, I2, W3, 2011 A1, 2, [C, Arg, A, F2]
Reedy, W J (Wellington) 1908 AW 2, 3
Reid, A R (Waikato) 1952 A 1, 1956 SA 3, 4, 1957 A 1, 2
Reid, H R (Bay of Plenty) 1980 A 1, 2, W, 1983 S, E, 1985 Arg 1, 2, 1986 A 2, 3
Reid, K H (Wairarapa) 1929 A 1, 3
Reid, S T (Hawke's Bay) 1935 S, I, W, 1936 E, A 1, 2, 1937 SA 1, 2, 3
Reihana, B T (Waikato) 2000 F 2, It
Reside, W B (Wairarapa) 1929 A 1
Rhind, P K (Canterbury) 1946 A 1, 2
Richardson, J (Otago, Southland) 1921 SA 1, 2, 3, 1924 I, W, 1925 E, F
Rickit, H (Waikato) 1981 S 1, 2
Riechelmann, C C (Auckland) 1997 Fj (R), Arg 1(R), A 1(R), SA 2(t), I (R), E 2(t)
Ridland, A J (Southland) 1910 A 1, 2, 3
Roberts, E J (Wellington) 1914 A 1, 2, 3, 1921 SA 2, 3
Roberts, F (Wellington) 1905 S, I, E, W, 1907 A 1, 2, 3, 1908 AW 1, 3, 1910 A 1, 2, 3
Roberts, R W (Taranaki) 1913 A 1, US, 1914 A 1, 2, 3
Robertson, B J (Counties) 1972 A 1, 3, S, 1973 E 1, I, F, 1974 A 1, 2, 3, I, 1976 I, SA 1, 2, 3, 4, 1977 BI 1, 3, 4, F 1, 2, 1978 A 1, 2, 3, W, E, S, 1979 F 1, 2, A, 1980 A 2, 3, W, 1981 S 1, 2
Robertson, D J (Otago) 1974 A 1, 2, 3, I, 1975 S, 1976 I, SA 1, 3, 4, 1977 BI 1
Robertson, S M (Canterbury) 1998 A 2(R), SA 2(R), A 3(R), 1999 [It (R)], 2000 Tg (R), S 1, 2(R), A 1, SA 1(R), 2(R), F 1, 2, It, 2001 I, S, Arg 2, 2002 I 1, 2, Fj (R), A 1, SA 1, A 2, SA 2
Robilliard, A C C (Canterbury) 1928 SA 1, 2, 3, 4
Robinson, C E (Southland) 1951 A 1, 2, 3, 1952 A 1, 2
Robinson, K J (Waikato) 2002 E, F (R), W, 2004 E1, 2, PI, 2006 E, W, 2007 SA2, A2, [R, F]
Robinson, M D (North Harbour) 1998 E 1(R), 2001 S (R), Arg 2
Robinson, M P (Canterbury) 2000 S 2, SA 1, 2002 It, I 2, A 1, SA 1, E (t&R), F, W (R)
Rokocoko, J T (Auckland) 2003 E, W, F, SA 1, A 1, SA 2, A 2, [It, W, SA, A, F], 2004 E1, 2, Arg, PI, A1, SA1, A2, SA2, It, W, F, 2005 SA1(R), A1, SA2, A2, W, E(R), S, 2006 I1, 2, A1, 2, 3, SA3, E, F1, 2, 2007 F1, 2, SA1, A1, SA2, A2, [Pt, R, F], 2008 S, I2, W, E3, 2009 F1, 2, It1, SA1, 2, A2, SA3, A3, 2010 I1, W1, SA1, A1, 2, SA3, A4, E
Rollerson, D L (Manawatu) 1980 W, 1981 S 2, SA 1, 2, 3, R, F 1(R), 2
Roper, R A (Taranaki) 1949 A 2, 1950 BI 1, 2, 3, 4
Ross, I B (Canterbury) 2009 F1, 2, It1, A1, SA1, 2, A2, SA3
Rowley, H C B (Wanganui) 1949 A 2
Rush, E J (North Harbour) 1995 [W (R), J], It, F 1, 2, 1996 S 1(R), 2, A 1(t), SA 1(R)
Rush, X J (Auckland) 1998 A 3, 2004 E1, 2, PI, A1, SA1, A2, SA2
Rutledge, L M (Southland) 1978 A 1, 2, 3, I, W, E, S, 1979 F 1, 2, A, 1980 A 1, 2, 3
Ryan, J (Wellington) 1910 A 2, 1914 A 1, 2, 3
Ryan, J A C (Otago) 2005 Fj, BI3(R), A1(R), SA2(R), A2(R), W, S, 2006 F1, W(R)

Sadler, B S (Wellington) 1935 S, I, W, 1936 A 1, 2
Salmon, J L B (Wellington) 1981 R, F 1, 2(R)
Savage, L T (Canterbury) 1949 SA 1, 2, 4
Saxton, C K (South Canterbury) 1938 A 1, 2, 3
Schuler, K J (Manawatu, North Harbour) 1990 A 2(R), 1992 A 2, 1995 [I (R), J]
Schuster, N J (Wellington) 1988 A 1, 2, 3, 1989 F 1, 2, Arg 1, 2, A, W, I
Schwalger, J E (Wellington) 2007 C, 2008 I1(R)
Scott, R W H (Auckland) 1946 A 1, 2, 1947 A 1, 2, 1949 SA 1, 2, 3, 4, 1950 BI 1, 2, 3, 4, 1953 W, 1954 I, E, S, F
Scown, A I (Taranaki) 1972 A 1, 2, 3, W (R), S
Scrimshaw, G (Canterbury) 1928 SA 1
Seear, G A (Otago) 1977 F 1, 2, 1978 A 1, 2, 3, I, W, E, S, 1979 F 1, 2, A
Seeling, C E (Auckland) 1904 BI, 1905 S, I, E, W, 1906 F, 1907 A 1, 2, 1908 AW 1, 2, 3
Sellars, G M V (Auckland) 1913 A 1, US
Senio, K (Bay of Plenty) 2005 A2(R)
Shaw, M W (Manawatu, Hawke's Bay) 1980 A 1, 2, 3(R), W, 1981 S 1, 2, SA 1, 2, R, F 1, 2, 1982 A 1, 2, 3, 1983 BI 1, 2, 3, 4, A, S, E, 1984 F 1, 2, A 1, 1985 E 1, 2, A, Arg 1, 2, 1986 A 3
Shelford, F N K (Bay of Plenty) 1981 SA 3, R, 1984 A 2, 3
Shelford, W T (North Harbour) 1986 F 2, 3, 1987 [It, Fj, S, W, F], A, 1988 W 1, 2, A 1, 2, 3, 1989 F 1, 2, Arg 1, 2, A, W, I, 1990 S 1, 2
Siddells, S K (Wellington) 1921 SA 3
Simon, H J (Otago) 1937 SA 1, 2, 3
Simpson, J G (Auckland) 1947 A 1, 2, 1949 SA 1, 2, 3, 4, 1950 BI 1, 2, 3
Simpson, V L J (Canterbury) 1985 Arg 1, 2
Sims, G S (Otago) 1972 A 2
Sivivatu, S W (Waikato) 2005 Fj, BI1, 2, 3, I, E, 2006 SA2, 3, E(R), F1, 2, W, 2007 F1, 2, C, SA1, A1(R), [It, S, R, F], 2008 I1, E1, 2, SA1, 2, A1, 2, SA3, A3, 4, I2, W, E3, 2009 A1, SA1, 2, A2, SA3, A4, It2, E, F3, 2011 Fj, A1
Skeen, J R (Auckland) 1952 A 2
Skinner, K L (Otago, Counties) 1949 SA 1, 2, 3, 4, 1950 BI 1, 2, 3, 4, 1951 A 1, 2, 3, 1952 A 1, 2, 1953 W, 1954 I, E, S, F, 1956 SA 3, 4
Skudder, G R (Waikato) 1969 W 2
Slade, C R (Canterbury) 2010 A3(R), 2011 Fj, SA1(R), A1(R), SA2, [Tg(R), J, F1(R), C, Arg]
Slater, G L (Taranaki) 2000 F 1(R), 2(R), It (R)
Sloane, P H (North Auckland) 1979 E

Smith, A E (Taranaki) 1969 W 1, 2, 1970 SA 1
Smith, B R (Otago) 2009 It 2, 2011 Fj(R)
Smith, B W (Waikato) 1984 F 1, 2, A 1
Smith, C G (Wellington) 2004 It, F, 2005 Fj(R), BI3, W, S, 2006 F1, W, 2007 SA2(R), [Pt, S, R(R)], 2008 I1, E1, SA1, 2, A1(R), 2, SA3, Sm, A3, 4, I2, E3, 2009 F2, A1, SA1, 2, A2, 4, W, E, F3, 2010 I1, W1, SA1, 2, A1, 2, SA3, A3, 4, S, I2, W3, 2011 Fj, SA1, A1, 2, [J, F1, C, Arg, A, F2]
Smith, G W (Auckland) 1905 S, I
Smith, I S T (Otago, North Otago) 1964 A 1, 2, 3, 1965 SA 1, 2, 4, 1966 BI 1, 2, 3
Smith, J B (North Auckland) 1946 A 1, 1947 A 2, 1949 A 1, 2
Smith, R M (Canterbury) 1955 A 1
Smith, W E (Nelson) 1905 A
Smith, W R (Canterbury) 1980 A 1, 1982 A 1, 2, 3, 1983 BI 2, 3, S, E, 1984 F 1, 2, A 1, 2, 3, 1985 E 1, 2, A, Arg 2
Snow, E M (Nelson) 1929 A 1, 2, 3
Solomon, F (Auckland) 1931 A, 1932 A 2, 3
Somerville, G M (Canterbury) 2000 Tg, S 1, SA 2(R), F 1, 2, It, 2001 Sm, Arg 1(R), F, SA 1, A 1, SA 2, A 2, I, S, Arg 2(t+R), 2002 I 1, 2, A 1, SA 1, A 2, SA 2, 2003 E, F, SA 1, A 1, SA 2(R), A 2, [It, Tg, W, SA, A, F], 2004 Arg, SA1, A2(R), SA2(R), It(R), W, F(R), 2005 Fj, BI1(R)2, 3, SA1(R), A1(R), SA2(R), A2(R), 2006 Arg, A1(R), SA1(R), A2(R), 3(R), SA2, 2007 [Pt, R], 2008 E1, 2, SA1, A1, 2, SA3, Sm, A3, 4(R)
Sonntag, W T C (Otago) 1929 A 1, 2, 3
So'oialo, R (Wellington) 2002 W, 2003 E, SA 1(R), [It(R), C, Tg, W(t)], 2004 W, F, 2005 Fj, BI1, 2, 3, SA1, A1, SA2, A2, W, I(R), E, 2006 I1, 2, A1, SA1, A2, 3, SA3, E(R), F1, 2, W, 2007 F1(R), 2, SA1, A1, SA2, A2, [It, Pt(R), S, F], 2008 I1, E1, 2, SA1, 2, A1, 2, SA3, Sm, A3, 4, I2, W, E3, 2009 A1, SA1, 2, A2(R), 3(R), 4, It2
Speight, M W (Waikato) 1986 A 1
Spencer, C J (Auckland) 1997 Arg 1, 2, A 1, SA 1, A 2, SA 2, A 3, E 2(R), 1998 E 2(R), A 1(R), SA 1, A 3(R), 2000 F 1(t&R), It, 2002 E, 2003 E, W, F, SA 1, A 1, SA 2, A 2, [It, C, Tg, W, SA, A, F], 2004 E1, 2, PI, A1, SA1, A2
Spencer, J C (Wellington) 1905 A, 1907 A 1(R)
Spiers, J E (Counties) 1979 S, E, 1981 R, F 1, 2
Spillane, A P (South Canterbury) 1913 A 2, 3
Stanley, B J (Auckland) 2010 I1, W1, 2
Stanley, J T (Auckland) 1986 F 1, A 1, 2, 3, F 2, 3, 1987 [It, Fj, Arg, S, W, F], A, 1988 W 1, 2, A 1, 2, 3, 1989 F 1, 2, Arg 1, 2, A, W, I, 1990 S 1, 2
Stead, J W (Southland) 1904 BI, 1905 S, I, E, 1906 F, 1908 AW 1, 3
Steel, A G (Canterbury) 1966 BI 1, 2, 3, 4, 1967 A, F, S, 1968 A 1, 2
Steel, J (West Coast) 1921 SA 1, 2, 3, 1924 W, 1925 E, F
Steele, L B (Wellington) 1951 A 1, 2, 3
Steere, E R G (Hawke's Bay) 1930 BI 1, 2, 3, 4, 1931 A, 1932 A 1
Steinmetz, P C (Wellington) 2002 W (R)
Stensness, L (Auckland) 1993 BI 3, A, WS, 1997 Fj, Arg 1, 2, A 1, SA 1
Stephens, O G (Wellington) 1968 F 3
Stevens, I N (Wellington) 1972 S, 1973 E 1, 1974 A 3
Stewart, A J (Canterbury, South Canterbury) 1963 E 1, 2, I, W, 1964 E, S, F, A 3
Stewart, J D (Auckland) 1913 A 2, 3
Stewart, K W (Southland) 1973 E 2, 1974 A 1, 2, 3, I, 1975 S, 1976 I, SA 1, 3, 1979 S, E, 1981 SA 1, 2
Stewart, R T (South Canterbury, Canterbury) 1928 SA 1, 2, 3, 4, 1930 BI 2
Stohr, L B (Taranaki) 1910 A 1, 2, 3
Stone, A M (Waikato, Bay of Plenty) 1981 F 1, 2, 1983 BI 3(R), 1984 A 3, 1986 F 1, A 1, 3, F 2, 3
Storey, P W (South Canterbury) 1921 SA 1, 2
Strachan, A D (Auckland, North Harbour) 1992 Wld 2, 3, I 1, 2, A 1, 2, 3, SA, 1993 BI 1, 1995 [J, SA (t)]
Strahan, S C (Manawatu) 1967 A, E, W, F, S, 1968 A 1, 2, F 1, 2, 3, 1970 SA 1, 2, 3, 1972 A 1, 2, 3, 1973 E 2
Strang, W A (South Canterbury) 1928 SA 1, 2, 1930 BI 3, 4, 1931 A
Stringfellow, J C (Wairarapa) 1929 A 1(R), 3
Stuart, K C (Canterbury) 1955 A 1
Stuart, R C (Canterbury) 1949 A 1, 2, 1953 W, 1954 I, E, S, F
Stuart, R L (Hawke's Bay) 1977 F 1(R)
Sullivan, J L (Taranaki) 1937 SA 1, 2, 3, 1938 A 1, 2, 3
Sutherland, A R (Marlborough) 1970 SA 2, 4, 1971 BI 1, 1972 A 1, 2, 3, W, 1973 E 1, I, F
Svenson, K S (Wellington) 1924 I, W, 1925 E, F
Swain, J P (Hawke's Bay) 1928 SA 1, 2, 3, 4

Tanner, J M (Auckland) 1950 BI 4, 1951 A 1, 2, 3, 1953 W
Tanner, K J (Canterbury) 1974 A 1, 2, 3, I, 1975 S, 1976 I, SA 1
Taumoepeau, S (Auckland) 2004 It, 2005 I(R), S
Taylor, G L (Northland) 1996 SA 5(R)
Taylor, H M (Canterbury) 1913 A 1, US, 1914 A 1, 2, 3
Taylor, J M (Otago) 1937 SA 1, 2, 3, 1938 A 1, 2, 3
Taylor, M B (Waikato) 1979 F 1, 2, A, S, E, 1980 A 1, 2
Taylor, N M (Bay of Plenty, Hawke's Bay) 1977 BI 2, 4(R), F 1, 2, 1978 A 1, 2, 3, I, 1982 A 2
Taylor, R (Taranaki) 1913 A 2, 3
Taylor, W T (Canterbury) 1983 BI 1, 2, 3, 4, A, S, 1984 F 1, 2, A 1, 2, 1985 E 1, 2, A, Arg 1, 2, 1986 A 2, 1987 [It, Fj, S, W, F], A, 1988 W 1, 2
Tetzlaff, P L (Auckland) 1947 A 1, 2
Thimbleby, N W (Hawke's Bay) 1970 SA 3
Thomas, B T (Auckland, Wellington) 1962 A 5, 1964 A 1, 2, 3
Thomson, A J (Otago) 2008 I1(t&R), E2, SA1, 2, A2(R), SA3(R), Sm, A4(t&R), S, 2009 F1, SA3(R), A3, 4, W(R), E, 2010 W1(R), 2(R), 2011 Fj, SA1, A1(R), SA2, A2, [J, F1]
Thomson, H D (Wellington) 1908 AW 1
Thorn, B C (Canterbury, Tasman) 2003 W (R), F (R), SA 1(R), A 1(R), SA 2, [It, C, Tg, W, SA(R), A(R), F(R)], 2008 I1, E1, 2, SA1, A1, 2, SA3, A3, 4, I2, W, E3, 2009 F1, 2, It1, A1, SA1, 2, A2, SA3, A3, 4, W, E, F3, 2010 I1, W1, 2, SA1, 2, A1, 2, SA3, A3, 4, E, S, W3, 2011 A1, 2, [Tg, J, F1, C(R), Arg, A, F2]
Thorne, G S (Auckland) 1968 A 1, 2, F 1, 2, 3, 1969 W 1, 1970 SA 1, 2, 3, 4
Thorne, R D (Canterbury) 1999 SA 2(R), [Tg, E, S, F 2, SA 3], 2000 Tg, S 2, A 2(R), F 1, 2, 2001 Sm, Arg 1, F, SA 1, A 1, I, S, Arg 2, 2002 It, I 1, 2, Fj, A 1, SA 1, A2, SA 2, 2003 E, W, F, SA 1, A 1, SA 2, A 2, [It, C, Tg, W, SA, A, F], 2006 SA1, 2, E, W(R), 2007 F1, C, SA2, [S, R]
Thornton, N H (Auckland) 1947 A 1, 2, 1949 SA 1
Tialata, N S (Wellington) 2005 W, E(t), S(R), 2006 I1(R), 2(R), Arg(R), SA1, 2, 3(R), F1(R), 2(R), W, 2007 F1(R), 2(R), C, A1(R), SA2(R), [It(t&R), Pt, S(R), R], 2008 I1, E1, 2, SA1(R), 2(R), Sm(R), A4, S(R), I2, W, E3, 2009 F1, 2, A1, SA1, A3, 4, W, It2, F3, 2010 I1(R), W2
Tiatia, F I (Wellington) 2000 Tg (R), It
Tilyard, J T (Wellington) 1913 A 3
Timu, J K R (Otago) 1991 Arg 1, A 1, 2, [E, US, C, A], 1992 Wld 2, I 2, A 1, 2, 3, SA, 1993 BI 1, 2, 3, A, WS, S, E, 1994 F 1, 2, SA 1, 2, 3, A
Tindill, E W T (Wellington) 1936 E
Toeava, I (Auckland) 2005 S, 2006 Arg, A1(t&R), A3, SA2(R), 2007 F1, 2, SA1, 2, A2, [It(R), Pt, S(R), R, F(R)], 2008 SA3(R), Sm(R), A4, S, I2(R), E3(R), 2009 F1, 2(R), It1, SA3(R), A3, 2010 A4(R), E(R), S, W3, 2011 SA2, A2(R), [Tg, J, C(R), Arg(R)]
Tonu'u, O F J (Auckland) 1997 Fj (R), A 3(R), 1998 E 1, 2, SA 1(R)
Townsend, L J (Otago) 1955 A 1, 3
Tremain, K R (Canterbury, Hawke's Bay) 1959 BI 2, 3, 4, 1960 SA 1, 2, 3, 4, 1961 F 2, 3 1962 A 1, 2, 3, 1963 E 1, 2, I, W, 1964 E, S, F, A 1, 2, 3, 1965 SA 1, 2, 3, 4, 1966 BI 1, 2, 3, 4, 1967 A, E, W, S, 1968 A 1, F 1, 2, 3
Trevathan, D (Otago) 1937 SA 1, 2, 3
Tuck, J M (Waikato) 1929 A 1, 2, 3
Tuiali'i, M M (Auckland) 2004 Arg, A2(R), SA2(R), It, W, 2005 I, E(R), S(R), 2006 Arg
Tuigamala, V L (Auckland) 1991 [US, It, C, S], 1992 Wld 1, 2, 3, I 1, A 1, 2, 3, SA, 1993 BI 1, 2, 3, A, WS, S, E
Tuitavake, A S M (North Harbour) 2008 I1, E1, A1, 2(R), Sm, S
Tuitupou, S (Auckland) 2004 E1(R), 2(R), Arg, SA1(R), A2(R), SA2, 2006 Arg, SA1, 2(R)
Turner, R S (North Harbour) 1992 Wld 1, 2(R)
Turtill, H S (Canterbury) 1905 A
Twigden, T M (Auckland) 1980 A 2, 3
Tyler, G A (Auckland) 1903 A, 1904 BI, 1905 S, I, E, W, 1906 F

Udy, D K (Wairarapa) 1903 A
Umaga, J F (Wellington) 1997 Fj, Arg 1, 2, A 1, SA 1, 2, 1999 WS, F 1, SA 1, A 1, SA 2, A 2, [Tg, E, S, F 2, SA 3], 2000 Tg, S 1, 2, A 1, SA 1, A 2, SA 2, F 1, 2, It, 2001 Sm, Arg 1, F, SA 1, A 1, SA 2, A 2, I, S, Arg 2, 2002 I 1, Fj, SA 1(R), A 2, SA 2, E, F, W, 2003 E, W, F, SA 1, A 1, SA 2, A 2, [It], 2004 E1, 2, Arg, PI, A1, SA1, A2, SA2, It, F, 2005 Fj, BI1, 2, 3, SA1, A1, SA2, A2, W, E, S
Urbahn, R J (Taranaki) 1959 BI 1, 3, 4
Urlich, R A (Auckland) 1970 SA 3, 4
Uttley, I N (Wellington) 1963 E 1, 2

Vidiri, J (Counties Manukau) 1998 E 2(R), A 1
Vincent, P B (Canterbury) 1956 SA 1, 2
Vito, V V J (Wellington) 2010 I1(R), W1, A1(R), 2(R), SA3(R), A3, 2011 SA2(R), A2(R), [Tg, J, C, Arg(R), A(R)]
Vodanovich, I M H (Wellington) 1955 A 1, 2, 3

Wallace, W J (Wellington) 1903 A, 1904 BI, 1905 S, I, E, W, 1906 F, 1907 A 1, 2, 3, 1908 AW 2
Waller, D A G (Wellington) 2001 Arg 2(t)
Walsh, P T (Counties) 1955 A 1, 2, 3, 1956 SA 1, 2, 4, 1957 A 1, 2, 1958 A 1, 2, 3, 1959 BI 1, 1963 E 2
Ward, R H (Southland) 1936 A 2, 1937 SA 1, 3
Waterman, A C (North Auckland) 1929 A 1, 2
Watkins, E L (Wellington) 1905 A
Watt, B A (Canterbury) 1962 A 1, 4, 1963 E 1, 2, W, 1964 E, S, A 1
Watt, J M (Otago) 1936 A 1, 2
Watt, J R (Wellington) 1958 A 2, 1960 SA 1, 2, 3, 4, 1961 F 1, 3, 1962 A 1, 2
Watts, M G (Taranaki) 1979 F 1, 2, 1980 A 1, 2, 3(R)
Webb, D S (North Auckland) 1959 BI 2
Weepu, P A T (Wellington) 2004 W, 2005 SA1(R), A1, SA2, A2, I, E(R), S, 2006 Arg, A1(R), SA1, A3(R), SA2, F1, W(R), 2007 F1, C(R), SA1(R), A1(R), SA2, 2008 A2(R), SA3(R), Sm(R), A3(R), 4(R), S, I2(R), W(R), E3(R), 2009 F1(R), 2(R), It1(R), A1(R), SA1(R), 2(R), 2010 I1(R), W1(R), 2(R), SA1(R), 2, A1(R), 2, SA3(R), A3, 2011 Fj(R), SA1(R), A1, SA2(R), A2, [Tg(R), J(R), F1, C(R), Arg, A, F2]
Wells, J (Wellington) 1936 A 1, 2
West, A H (Taranaki) 1921 SA 2, 3
Whetton, A J (Auckland) 1984 A 1(R), 3(R), 1985 A (R), Arg 1(R), 1986 A 2, 1987 [It, Fj, Arg, S, W, F], A, 1988 W 1, 2, A 1, 2, 3, 1989 F 1, 2, Arg 1, 2, A, 1990 S 1, 2, A 1, 2, 3, F 1, 2, 1991 Arg 1, [E, US, It, C, A]
Whetton, G W (Auckland) 1981 SA 3, R, F 1, 2, 1982 A 3, 1983 BI 1, 2, 3, 4, 1984 F 1, 2, A 1, 2, 3, 1985 E 1, 2, A, Arg 2, 1986 A 2, 3, F 2, 3, 1987 [It, Fj, Arg, S, W, F], A, 1988 W 1, 2, A 1, 2, 3, 1989 F 1, 2, Arg 1, 2, A, W, I, 1990 S 1, 2, A 1, 2, 3, F 1, 2, 1991 Arg 1, 2, A 1, 2, [E, US, It, C, A, S]
Whineray, W J (Canterbury, Waikato, Auckland) 1957 A 1, 2, 1958 A 1, 2, 3, 1959 BI 1, 2, 3, 4, 1960 SA 1, 2, 3, 4, 1961 F 1, 2, 3, 1962 A 1, 2, 3, 4, 5, 1963 E 1, 2, I, W, 1964 E, S, F, 1965 SA 1, 2, 3, 4
White, A (Southland) 1921 SA 1, 1924 I, 1925 E, F
White, H L (Auckland) 1954 I, E, F, 1955 A 3
White, R A (Poverty Bay) 1949 A 1, 2, 1950 BI 1, 2, 3, 4, 1951 A 1, 2, 3, 1952 A 1, 2, 1953 W, 1954 I, E, S, F, 1955 A 1, 2, 3, 1956 SA 1, 2, 3, 4
White, R M (Wellington) 1946 A 1, 2, 1947 A 1, 2
Whitelock, G B (Canterbury) 2009 It1(R)
Whitelock, S L (Canterbury) 2010 I1(R), W1(R), 2(R), SA1(R), 2(R), A1(R), 2(R), SA3(R), A4(R), E, S, I2(R), W3, 2011 Fj(R), SA1, A1(R), SA2, A2, [Tg(R), J, F1, C, Arg, A, F2]
Whiting, G J (King Country) 1972 A 1, 2, S, 1973 E 1, I, F
Whiting, P J (Auckland) 1971 BI 1, 2, 4, 1972 A 1, 2, 3, W, S, 1973 E 1, I, F, 1974 A 1, 2, 3, I, 1976 I, SA 1, 2, 3, 4
Williams, A J (Auckland, Tasman) 2002 E, F, W, 2003 E, W, F, SA 1, A 1, SA 2, A 2, [Tg, W, SA, A, F], 2004 SA1(R), A2, It(R), W, F(R), 2005 Fj, BI1, 2, 3, SA1, A1, SA2, A2, I, E, 2006 Arg, A1(R), SA1, A2, 3(R), SA2, 3, F1, 2, W, 2007 F1, 2, [It, Pt, S, F], 2008 I1, E1, 2, SA1, 2, A1, 2, SA3, Sm, A3, 4, S, I2, W, E3, 2011 Fj, SA1, A1, SA2, A2(R), [Tg, J(R), F1(R), C, Arg(R), A(R), F2(R)]
Williams, B G (Auckland) 1970 SA 1, 2, 3, 4, 1971 BI 1, 2, 4, 1972 A 1, 2, 3, W, S, 1973 E 1, I, F, E 2, 1974 A 1, 2, 3, I, 1975 S, 1976 I, SA 1, 2, 3, 4, 1977 BI 1, 2, 3, 4, F 1, 1978 A 1, 2, 3, I (R), W, E, S
Williams, G C (Wellington) 1967 E, W, F, S, 1968 A 2
Williams, P (Otago) 1913 A 1
Williams, S (Canterbury) 2010 E, S, I2(R), W3, 2011 SA1(R), A1(R), SA2, [Tg, J(R), F1(R), C, Arg, A(R), F2(R)]
Williment, M (Wellington) 1964 A 1, 1965 SA 1, 2, 3, 1966 BI 1, 2, 3, 4, 1967 A
Willis, R K (Waikato) 1998 SA 2, A 3, 1999 SA 1(R), A 1(R), SA 2(R), A 2(R), [Tg (R), E (R), It, F 2(R), SA 3], 2002 SA 1(R)
Willis, T E (Otago) 2002 It, Fj, SA 2(R), A 2, SA 2
Willocks, C (Otago) 1946 A 1, 2, 1949 SA 1, 3, 4
Wilson, B W (Otago) 1977 BI 3, 4, 1978 A 1, 2, 3, 1979 F 1, 2, A
Wilson, D D (Canterbury) 1954 E, S
Wilson, H W (Otago) 1949 A 1, 1950 BI 4, 1951 A 1, 2, 3
Wilson, J W (Otago) 1993 S, E, 1994 A, 1995 C, [I, J, S, E, SA], A 1, 2, It, F 1, 1996 WS, S 1, 2, A 1, SA 1, A 2, SA 2, 3, 4, 5, 1997 Fj, Arg 1, 2, A 1, SA 1, A 2, SA 2, A 3, I, E 1, W, E 2, 1998 E 1, 2, A 1, SA 1, A 2, SA 2, A 3, 1999 WS, F 1, SA 1, A 1, SA 2, A 2, [Tg, E, It, S, F 2, SA 3], 2001 Sm, Arg 1, F, SA 1, A 1, SA 2
Wilson, N A (Wellington) 1908 AW 1, 2, 1910 A 1, 2, 3, 1913 A 2, 3, 1914 A 1, 2, 3
Wilson, N L (Otago) 1951 A 1, 2, 3
Wilson, R G (Canterbury) 1979 S, E
Wilson, S S (Wellington) 1977 F 1, 2, 1978 A 1, 2, 3, I, W, E, S, 1979 F 1, 2, A, S, E, 1980 A 1, W, 1981 S 1, 2, SA 1, 2, 3, R, F 1, 2, 1982 A 1, 2, 3, 1983 BI 1, 2, 3, 4, A, S, E
Witcombe, D J C (Auckland) 2005 Fj, BI1(R), 2(R), SA1(R), A1(R)
Wolfe, T N (Wellington, Taranaki) 1961 F 1, 2, 3, 1962 A 2, 3, 1963 E 1
Wood, M E (Canterbury, Auckland) 1903 A, 1904 BI
Woodcock, T D (North Harbour) 2002 W, 2004 E1(t&R), 2(t&R), Arg, W, F, 2005 Fj, BI1, 2, 3, SA1, A1, SA2, A2, W(R), I, E, 2006 Arg, A1, 2, 3, SA2(R), 3, E, F1, 2, W(R), 2007 F1, 2, SA1, A1, SA2, A2, [It, Pt(R), S, F], 2008 E2(R), SA1, 2, A1, 2, SA3, Sm, A3, 4, I2, W, E3, 2009 F1, 2, It1(R), A1, SA1, 2, A2, SA3, A3, 4, E, F3, 2010 W1(R), 2, SA1, 2, A1, 2, SA3, A3, 4, E, S, I2, W3, 2011 SA2, A2, [Tg, J, F1, C, Arg, A, F2]
Woodman, F A (North Auckland) 1981 SA 1, 2, F 2
Wrigley, E (Wairarapa) 1905 A
Wright, T J (Auckland) 1986 F 1, A 1, 1987 [Arg], 1988 W 1, 2, A 1, 2, 3, 1989 F 1, 2, Arg 1, 2, A, W, I, 1990 S 1, 2, A 1, 2, 3, F 1, 2, 1991 Arg 1, 2, A 1, 2, [E, US, It, S]
Wulf, R N (North Harbour) 2008 E2, SA1, 2, Sm(R)
Wylie, J T (Auckland) 1913 A 1, US
Wyllie, A J (Canterbury) 1970 SA 2, 3, 1971 BI 2, 3, 4, 1972 W, S, 1973 E 1, I, F, E 2

Yates, V M (North Auckland) 1961 F 1, 2, 3
Young, D (Canterbury) 1956 SA 2, 1958 A 1, 2, 3, 1960 SA 1, 2, 3, 4, 1961 F 1, 2, 3, 1962 A 1, 2, 3, 5, 1963 E 1, 2, I, W, 1964 E, S, F

FOUR IN A ROW FOR CANTABRIANS

Sandra Mu/Getty Images

Canterbury can't contain their joy at winning this year's ITM Cup Premiership Final.

It was almost exactly a year after the first earthquake which shook Christchurch that Canterbury found themselves in the ITM Cup Premiership Final, and it was perhaps fitting that after a troubled 12 months for the region it was Rob Penney's side who emerged as provincial champions after a 12–3 victory over Waikato.

That first earthquake was tragically followed by a far more devastating one in February, and as the area continued with the laborious rebuilding process, one which denied the city the chance to host any of its seven scheduled Rugby World Cup games in the AMI Stadium, it was a rare ray of light as Canterbury reaffirmed their status as the dominant force in New Zealand provincial rugby.

Their hero on the day was substitute fly-half Tom Taylor, the son of former All Black Warwick, who came off the bench after just 20 minutes at Waikato Stadium to replace the injured Tyler Bleyendaal and then kicked four successful penalties to hand the Cantabs the silverware yet again.

The result was Canterbury's fourth successive triumph in the final, and in the process they became only the second team to achieve four titles in a row since the inception of the National Provincial Championship in New Zealand, emulating the success of the dominant Auckland sides of 1987–90 and 1993–96.

But it was the aftermath of the earthquake rather than rewriting rugby history that was in the thoughts of Canterbury captain George Whitelock, a veteran of the three previous final triumphs, as he collected the trophy in the Waikato Stadium.

"That was pretty special after what happened in the region and that was motivating for us," Whitelock admitted on the anniversary of the first quake. "Our performance tonight was really pleasing. We improved a hell of a lot every game. Our win ratio wasn't great, but we scored bonus-point tries and that kept us up there."

The league campaign began in the middle of July and, although it was eventually to be Waikato who were top of the table and Canterbury in second after 10 games, finishing two points clear of Bay of Plenty and Taranaki in third and fourth respectively, both finalists made relatively poor starts to the season.

The Mooloos began with a 19–9 win against Southland in Invercargill in Week One, but surprisingly then went down to back-to-back defeats against Taranaki and Bay of Plenty in Weeks Three and Four and had it not been for their strong second-half rally, winning six of the last seven matches, they would have not progressed to the final.

They turned the corner in Week Five at the end of July with a thumping 35–6 rout of Tasman and, once they had narrowly scraped past Counties in Pukekohe a week later, they had successfully steadied the ship.

The Cantabs were also slow out of the blocks. A high-scoring 40–33 victory over Auckland on the opening day was encouraging enough, but successive reverses to Southland and Wellington in Weeks Three and Four nullified that momentum, and ultimately it was the nine bonus points they garnered over the 10 games that earned the side a place in the final.

Bay of Plenty and Taranki finished the campaign strongly but ultimately left their bids to reach the final too late. Both sides won their last two games to apply the pressure on the top two, but Waikato's 26–19 victory over Auckland in Hamilton, followed by Canterbury's 29–16 triumph against Otago in Dunedin on the final weekend of the regular season, ensured it was ultimately a futile effort.

The final in early September was an eagerly anticipated repeat of the 2010 final. That had ended in a 33–13 victory for Canterbury and yielded six tries in total in the AMI Stadium, but the 2011 version at the Waikato Stadium failed to produce a single five-point score. It was the first time the tournament's showpiece fixture finished without anyone crossing the line.

Waikato enjoyed the better of the early exchanges but spurned arguably the best scoring chance of the entire contest when experienced number 10 Stephen Donald spilled the ball with the line looming large after a break from prop Toby Smith.

Donald, playing in his last game for the Mooloos before joining English Premiership side Bath, redeemed himself to a degree minutes later with a penalty after a high tackle by Wyatt Crockett, but the kick was to be Waikato's only points of the match.

The Canterbury pack now began to exert control, and after Waikato infringed at a lineout Taylor stepped forward to land the subsequent penalty and level the scores at 3–3. On 31 minutes, the Mooloos were penalised for collapsing a scrum, and Taylor accepted the three points on offer. A third penalty moments before the break merely underlined the Cantabs' superiority, and Penney's team headed to the dressing room 9–3 to the good.

The pattern of the second half was slightly different to the first in that Waikato enjoyed a greater share of the possession, but each time they probed the Canterbury defence they could find no way through, and when Taylor landed a superb long-range penalty with just six minutes left on the clock the Mooloos' hopes of a famous comeback were dashed and the Cantabs were champions once again.

"We're extremely proud, both as players and as a management group," said coach Penney after the game. "For some of the players it is their first title, but we have a few who have been involved in all four titles. The win means different things to different people, but any championship win is very special.

"Tom [Taylor] was a cool player today who has a big future. He had been a prospect to play last year but physically wasn't ready. That disappointed him, but he went away and worked on his physique and had the benefits this year. He has some great years in front of him. We are blessed with the quality of 10s who have emerged in the country now.

"We wanted to nullify Stephen Donald's running, especially down the inside channel, and to monopolise possession and take control at the breakdown. It was a gutsy performance. We knew if we could keep it close, in the later stages Waikato would try to play as individuals and that would enhance our defensive capability.

For Donald, the game was his 57th and final appearance for Waikato before heading to the northern hemisphere, and defeat a bitter pill to swallow after a seven-year association with the province.

"Obviously it would have been nice to have gone out with a win and got another title for this great rugby public, but it wasn't to be and we had the life sucked out of us by Canterbury and that was it," he said.

"I thought in the first 20 minutes we probably had them but just couldn't finish off. I guess it was just a typical Canterbury performance in a big game, and we then had to force the issue and, once we got outside the range of a converted try with 10 minutes to go, it was always going to be tough once they had possession.

"We thought we were creating it but, whether it be a last pass or an interpretation of the ruck, it just wasn't happening for us. It was the story of the season. You could probably name four or five opportunities that we would have liked to have capitalised on, but it just didn't happen."

Meanwhile, in the final of the ITM Cup Championship, Hawke's Bay earned themselves promotion to the Premiership after a thrilling 35–30 victory over Manawatu in Palmerston North.

Despite having seven players on World Cup duty and trio Hika Elliot, Mike Coman and Tu Umaga-Marshall all out injured, the Magpies outscored the home side by four tries to three through Tua Saseve, Richard Buckman, Tino Nemani and Sinoti Sinoti which, coupled with 15 points from the boot of Andrew Horrell, was enough to give Hawke's Bay a famous victory at the FMG Stadium.

Manawatu replied with tries from Doug Tietjens, Francis Bryant and Mike Fitzgerald, as well as 15 points from fly-half Aaron Cruden, in what proved to be a classic encounter, but they left their fightback too late and Hawke's Bay hung on.

"I couldn't have asked for a better farewell present," said former All Black lock Bryn Evans, captaining the Magpies for the last time before joining English club London Irish. "I have no doubt I'm leaving this team in good hands. There are a lot of young guys with a lot to offer.

"This team has a good future and we proved this tonight. We played without a lot of our first-stringers and beat the form team from both ITM Cup competitions. We came down to play and got the rewards we wanted. We didn't want to die wondering."

ROMANIA

ROMANIA'S 2010–11 TEST RECORD

OPPONENT	DATE	VENUE	RESULT
Uruguay	13 Nov	A	**Drew** 21–21
Uruguay	27 Nov	H	**Won** 39–12
Portugal	5 Feb	A	**Lost** 17–24
Russia	26 Feb	H	**Won** 33–3
Georgia	12 Mar	A	**Lost** 11–18
Spain	19 Mar	H	**Won** 64–8
Namibia	10 Jun	H	**Won** 13–11
Argentina Jaguars	19 Jun	H	**Lost** 13–37
Ukraine	20 Aug	A	**Won** 16–41
Scotland	10 Sep	N	**Lost** 24–34
Argentina	17 Sep	N	**Lost** 8–43
England	24 Sep	N	**Lost** 3–67
Georgia	28 Sep	N	**Lost** 9–25

THE OAKS MAKE SOLID PROGRESS

By Ian Gilbert

Getty Images

Marius Tincu, a world-class operator in the Romania pack.

Several of Romania's squad ply their trade in the uncompromising arena of French club rugby, and in captain and hooker Marius Tincu they have a competitor respected throughout the game. Add to this the recruitment of assistant coach Steve McDowall, New Zealand's 1987 World Cup-winning prop, now fine-tuning Romania's scrum, and the Oaks had several elements needed to stir up the Pool B mix.

Romania faced a tough trio of matches against Scotland, Argentina and England before a final battle for bragging rights with Georgia. That last match offered Romania's best chance of a win, a fixture talked about as "their final". However, with two wins against the Scots – they had never beaten England or Argentina – the first match seemed their best chance of a high-profile scalp.

McDowall said beforehand that they planned to take the game to Scotland. "Romania have a lot of big guys and they do play a very physical game. Scotland do as well. They play fast, they play hard and it's something that we have been looking at. We've been trying to prepare a game that's competitive, upfront."

When No 8 Daniel Carpo crashed over, with the conversion putting Romania 24–21 ahead with 13 minutes left, the first upset of Rugby World Cup 2011 appeared well on the cards at Rugby Park in Invercargill. However, a penalty from the reliable Chris Paterson and two late tries from wing Simon Danielli got Scotland out of jail 34–24.

"The team you saw today is not the same one that lost [42–0] to Scotland in 2007," captain Tincu said, referring to the previous World Cup. "That team played with their hearts in their boots. Today we actually had fun playing."

Rather than bask in the glory of a near-miss, McDowall was already looking ahead to the Argentina match. "Physically, in the forwards, I know we can match them but their pace in the backs really has the potential to dazzle us," he said.

His words proved all-too prophetic. Rather than the expected forwards arm wrestle, the Pumas chose to adopt an expansive style to run in six tries and leave Romania on the wrong end of a 43–8 reverse.

While these two sides were at a similar stage of development when they first met in the 1970s, Argentina has kicked on to make the knockout stages at three of the past four Rugby World Cups, including 2011. Romania remain without a win against the Pumas.

"You can't be proud when you only defend. You have to be proud when you have the ball," was head coach Romeo Gontineac's post-match reflection.

Unfortunately things continued in a similar vein against England, who turned in probably their best performance of the tournament to win 67–3 at Otago Stadium with wings Mark Cueto and Chris Ashton each scoring hat-tricks in the ten-try performance.

England manager Martin Johnson, though, praised Romania after the match in Dunedin, saying: "They came and had a real dig, they played their hearts out and we wish them well in the rest of the tournament."

Gontineac always knew the Six Nations champions were a formidable hurdle, and was clear where his side's focus was. "Georgia is our final," he said. "They are our priority, because they play at our level."

For Cristian Petre, Romania's most capped player with 85 appearances by the end of the tournament, it was an improvement of sorts on the sides' previous fixture, in November 2001. On that occasion – Petre's debut – England won 134–0.

The second row and vice-captain was, like his coach, gearing up for Georgia. "We play every year," he said. "We win, we lose, it is our level. England, we never expected to win. Georgia is our level. It is our priority."

Even the well wishes of a rugby legend such as Johnson didn't help Romania. It was the Georgians, having won four of the sides' past five encounters, who emerged victorious from the clash of the European Nations Cup rivals at Arena Manawatu with a 25–9 victory.

Georgia fly-half Merab Kvirikashvili contributed a match-winning 17 points, while the lone try came from the Man of the Match Mamuka Gorgodze, the flanker who plays his club rugby for Montpellier in France's Top 14.

While the territory and possession was fairly evenly split, Romania made 110 tackles to Georgia's 60. It was only Georgia's second Rugby World Cup victory, having beaten Namibia in the 2007 tournament, and left Romania propping up a pool for only the second time in seven tournaments.

McDowall, though, was quick to underline the value of the Rugby World Cup to countries such as Romania for developing the sport domestically. "We have a lot of young players. It's a big step up for them, so I think the people back home in Romania have a certain amount of expectation, like New Zealand does for their team."

One player who stood out throughout Romania's campaign was their captain and hooker Tincu, who his England counterpart Steve Thompson labelled "one of the outstanding players of the tournament so far" after their battle. Tincu's inspirational ability is in no doubt. "On the field I try to work, to show everyone to do the same things as me – or better – and, when I speak, I speak with my heart," he said. "I say, 'I do this just for you, not for me'."

Gontineac is well qualified to comment on the state of Romanian rugby, featuring in his fifth World Cup after four as a player. "We thought we had improved our rugby, but when we play at this level we can see we have a lot of work to do," he said. "Only with high-level games can you improve. There is still a big difference between us and the teams of the Six Nations."

Mark Egan, the IRB Head of Development and Performance, felt that Romania's first game showed the investment in the Tier 2 nations was heading in the right direction. "We knew this improved competitiveness was going to come, but I guess some teams have surprised us," he said. "Romania's performance against Scotland in their opening game, to only lose by ten points and at one stage to be ahead with only seven or eight minutes to go, that was a great performance and they were the last team to qualify for the Rugby World Cup."

The New Zealand public took the Pool B underdogs to their hearts, too, with one Queenstown primary school painting Romanian flags on their faces and enjoying a kickabout with the team.

ROMANIA INTERNATIONAL STATISTICS

MATCH RECORDS UP TO 31 OCTOBER 2011

WINNING MARGIN

Date	Opponent	Result	Winning Margin
21/09/1976	Bulgaria	100–0	**100**
19/03/2005	Ukraine	97–0	**97**
13/04/1996	Portugal	92–0	**92**
17/11/1976	Morocco	89–0	**89**
19/04/1996	Belgium	83–5	**78**

MOST POINTS IN A MATCH

BY THE TEAM

Date	Opponent	Result	Points
21/09/1976	Bulgaria	100–0	**100**
19/03/2005	Ukraine	97–0	**97**
13/04/1996	Portugal	92–0	**92**
17/11/1976	Morocco	89–0	**89**

BY A PLAYER

Date	Player	Opponent	Points
05/10/2002	Ionut Tofan	Spain	**30**
13/04/1996	Virgil Popisteanu	Portugal	**27**
04/02/2001	Petre Mitu	Portugal	**27**
13/04/1996	Ionel Rotaru	Portugal	**25**

MOST TRIES IN A MATCH

BY THE TEAM

Date	Opponent	Result	Tries
17/11/1976	Morocco	89–0	**17**
21/10/1951	East Germany	64–26	**16**
19/03/2005	Ukraine	97–0	**15**
16/04/1978	Spain	74–3	**14**

BY A PLAYER

Date	Player	Opponent	Tries
30/04/1972	Gheorghe Rascanu	Morocco	**5**
18/10/1986	Cornel Popescu	Portugal	**5**
13/04/1996	Ionel Rotaru	Portugal	**5**

MOST CONVERSIONS IN A MATCH

BY THE TEAM

Date	Opponent	Result	Cons
13/04/1996	Portugal	92–0	**12**
19/03/2005	Ukraine	97–0	**11**
04/10/1997	Belgium	83–13	**10**

BY A PLAYER

Date	Player	Opponent	Cons
13/04/1996	Virgil Popisteanu	Portugal	**12**
04/10/1997	Serban Guranescu	Belgium	**10**
19/03/2005	Marin Danut Dumbrava	Ukraine	**8**
22/03/2008	Florin Adrian Vlaicu	Czech Republic	**8**

MOST PENALTIES IN A MATCH

BY THE TEAM

Date	Opponent	Result	Pens
15/06/2010	Argentina Jaguars	24–8	**7**
14/05/1994	Italy	26–12	**6**
04/02/2001	Portugal	47–0	**6**

BY A PLAYER

Date	Player	Opponent	Pens
14/05/1994	Neculai Nichitean	Italy	**6**
04/02/2001	Petre Mitu	Portugal	**6**

MOST DROPPED GOALS IN A MATCH

BY THE TEAM

Date	Opponent	Result	DGs
29/10/1967	West Germany	27–5	**4**
14/11/1965	West Germany	9–8	**3**
17/10/1976	Poland	38–8	**3**
03/10/1990	Spain	19–6	**3**

BY A PLAYER

Date	Player	Opponent	DGs
29/10/1967	Valeriu Irimescu	West Germany	**3**
17/10/1976	Alexandru Dumitru	Poland	**3**

MOST CAPPED PLAYERS

Player	Caps
Cristian Constantin Petre	86
Adrian Lungu	77
Romeo Stefan Gontineac	77
Lucian Mihai Sirbu	77
Gabriel Brezoianu	72

LEADING TRY SCORERS

Player	Tries
Petre Motrescu	33
Gabriel Brezoianu	28
Florica Murariu	27

LEADING CONVERSIONS SCORERS

Player	Cons
Marin Danut Dumbrava	69
Petre Mitu	53
Florin Adrian Vlaicu	53
Ionut Tofan	52

LEADING PENALTY SCORERS

Player	Pens
Marin Danut Dumbrava	70
Neculai Nichitean	53
Petre Mitu	53
Ionut Tofan	46

LEADING DROPPED GOAL SCORERS

Player	DGs
Alexandru Dumitru	14
Neculai Nichitean	10
Valeriu Irimescu	10
Gelu Ignat	8

LEADING POINTS SCORERS

Player	Points
Marin Danut Dumbrava	369
Petre Mitu	335
Ionut Tofan	322
Neculai Nichitean	257
Florin Adrian Vlaicu	252

Teaukura Moetaua/Getty Images

Marin Danut Dumbrava has now forged ahead of Petre Mitu in the Romania scoring charts.

ROMANIA INTERNATIONAL PLAYERS (UP TO 31 OCTOBER 2011)

Note: Years given for International Championship matches are for second half of season; eg 1972 means season 1971–72. Years for all other matches refer to the actual year of the match. Entries in square brackets denote matches played in RWC Finals.

A Achim 1974 *Pol*, 1976 *Pol*, *Mor*
M Adascalitei 2007 *Rus*, 2009 *Pt*, *Ur*, *F*, *ItA*
M Aldea 1979 *USS*, *W*, *Pol*, *F*, 1980 *It*, *USS*, *I*, *F*, 1981 *It*, *Sp*, *USS*, *S*, *NZ*, *F*, 1982 *WGe*, *It*, *USS*, *Z*, *Z*, *F*, 1983 *Mor*, *WGe*, *It*, *USS*, *Pol*, *W*, *USS*, *F*, 1984 *It*, *S*, *F*, 1985 *E*, *USS*
C Alexandrescu 1934 *It*
N Anastasiade 1927 *Cze*, 1934 *It*
V Anastasiade 1939 *It*
I Andrei 2003 *W*, *I*, *Ar*, *Nm*, 2004 *CZR*, *Pt*, *Sp*, *Rus*, *Geo*, *It*, *W*, *J*, *CZR*, 2005 *Rus*, *US*, *S*, *Pt*, 2006 *CZR*, 2007 *Pt*, 2008 *Sp*, *Pt*, *Rus*
I Andriesi 1937 *It*, *H*, *Ger*, 1938 *F*, *Ger*, 1939 *It*, 1940 *It*
E Apjoc 1996 *Bel*, 2000 *It*, 2001 *Pt*
A Apostol 2011 *Nm*, *E*
D Armasel 1924 *F*, *US*
A Atanasiu 1970 *It*, *F*, 1971 *It*, *Mor*, *F*, 1972 *Mor*, *Cze*, *WGe*, 1973 *Sp*, *Mor*, *Ar*, *Ar*, *WGe*, 1974 *Pol*

I Bacioiu 1976 *USS*, *Bul*, *Pol*, *F*, *Mor*
N Baciu 1964 *Cze*, *EGe*, 1967 *It*, *F*, 1968 *Cze*, *Cze*, *F*, 1969 *Pol*, *WGe*, *F*, 1970 *It*, 1971 *It*, *Mor*, *F*, 1972 *Mor*, *Cze*, *WGe*, 1973 *Ar*, *Ar*, 1974 *Cze*, *EGe*
B Balan 2003 *Pt*, *Sp*, *Geo*, 2004 *W*, 2005 *Rus*, *Ukr*, *J*, *US*, *S*, *Pt*, 2006 *Geo*, *Pt*, *Ukr*, *Rus*, *F*, *Geo*, *Sp*, *S*, 2007 *Sp*, *ESp*, *ItA*, *Nm*, *It*, *S*, *Pt*, *NZ*, 2009 *Fj*, 2010 *Ger*, *Rus*, *Ur*, *Ur*, 2011 *Pt*
D Balan 1983 *F*
PV Balan 1998 *H*, *Pol*, *Ukr*, *Ar*, *Geo*, *I*, 1999 *F*, *S*, *A*, *US*, *I*, 2000 *Mor*, *H*, *Pt*, *Sp*, *Geo*, *F*, *It*, 2001 *Pt*, *Sp*, *H*, *Rus*, *Geo*, *I*, *E*, 2002 *Pt*, *Sp*, *H*, *Rus*, *Geo*, *Sp*, *S*, *S*, 2003 *CZR*, *F*, *W*, *I*, *Nm*, 2004 *It*, *W*, *J*, *CZR*, 2005 *Geo*, *C*, *I*, 2006 *Geo*, *Pt*, *F*, *Geo*, *Sp*, *S*, 2007 *Geo*, 2009 *Ur*, *F*
L Balcan 1963 *Bul*, *EGe*, *Cze*
F Balmus 2000 *Mor*, *H*, *Pt*
S Bals 1927 *F*, *Ger*, *Cze*
G Baltaretu 1965 *WGe*, *F*
C Barascu 1957 *F*
M Baraulea 2004 *CZR*, *Pt*, *Geo*
A Barbu 1958 *WGe*, *It*, 1959 *EGe*, *Pol*, *Cze*, *EGe*, 1960 *F*
A Barbuliceanu 2008 *Rus*, *ESp*, 2009 *Sp*, *Ger*, *Rus*, *Geo*, *Pt*
S Bargaunas 1971 *It*, *Mor*, 1972 *F*, 1974 *Cze*, 1975 *It*
S Barsan 1934 *It*, 1936 *F*, *It*, 1937 *It*, *H*, *F*, *Ger*, 1938 *F*, *Ger*, 1939 *It*, 1940 *It*, 1942 *It*
RC Basalau 2007 *Pt*, 2008 *Geo*, *Pt*, *Rus*, *CZR*, *Ur*, *Rus*, *ESp*, 2010 *ItA*, *Tun*
CD Beca 2009 *Sp*, *Ger*, *Rus*, *Geo*, *Pt*, 2011 *Pt*
E Beches 1979 *It*, *Sp*, *USS*, 1982 *WGe*, *It*, 1983 *Pol*
M Bejan 2001 *I*, *W*, 2002 *Pt*, 2003 *Geo*, *CZR*, 2004 *It*
C Beju 1936 *F*, *It*, *Ger*
G Bentia 1919 *US*, *F*, 1924 *F*, *US*
V Bezarau 1995 *Ar*, *F*, *It*
R Bezuscu 1985 *It*, 1987 *F*
G Bigiu 2007 *Pt*, 2008 *Geo*, *Sp*, *Pt*, *Rus*, *CZR*, *Ur*, *Rus*
M Blagescu 1952 *EGe*, *EGe*, 1953 *It*, 1955 *Cze*, 1957 *F*, *Cze*, *Bel*, *F*
G Blasek 1937 *It*, *H*, *F*, *Ger*, 1940 *It*, 1942 *It*
A Bogheanu 1980 *Mor*
D Boldor 1988 *It*, *Sp*, *US*, *USS*, *USS*, *W*, 1989 *It*, *E*, *Sp*, *Z*
A Boroi 1975 *Sp*
P Bors 1975 *JAB*, 1976 *Sp*, 1977 *It*, 1980 *It*, *USS*, *I*, *Pol*, *F*, 1981 *It*, *Sp*, *USS*, *S*, *NZ*, *F*, 1982 *WGe*, 1983 *Mor*, *WGe*, *It*, *USS*, 1984 *It*
IC Botezatu 2009 *Ger*, *Rus*, *Geo*, *ItA*, 2010 *Ger*, *Rus*, *Ukr*, *Ukr*, *Nm*, *ArJ*, 2011 *Pt*
D Bozian 1997 *Bel*, 1998 *H*, *Pol*, *Ukr*
V Brabateanu 1919 *US*, *F*
M Braga 1970 *It*, *F*
C Branescu 1994 *It*, *E*, 1997 *F*
I Bratulescu 1927 *Ger*, *Cze*
G Brezoianu 1996 *Bel*, 1997 *F*, 1998 *H*, *Pol*, *Ukr*, *Ar*, *Geo*, *I*, 1999 *F*, *S*, *A*, *US*, *I*, 2000 *H*, *Pt*, *Sp*, *Geo*, *F*, *It*, 2001 *Sp*, *Rus*, *Geo*, *I*, *W*, *E*, 2002 *Pt*, *Sp*, *H*, *Rus*, *Geo*, *I*, *It*, *Sp*, *W*, *S*, *S*, 2003 *Pt*, *Sp*, *Rus*, *Geo*, *CZR*, *F*, *W*, *I*, *A*, *Ar*, *Nm*, 2005 *Rus*, *Ukr*, *J*, *US*, *S*, *Pt*, *C*, *I*, 2006 *CZR*, *Pt*, *Ukr*, *Rus*, *F*, *Geo*, *Sp*, *S*, 2007 *Geo*, *Sp*, *CZR*, *ESp*, *ItA*, *Nm*, *It*, *S*, *NZ*
V Brici 1991 *NZ*, 1992 *USS*, *F*, *It*, 1993 *Tun*, *F*, *Sp*, *I*, 1994 *Sp*, *Ger*, *Rus*, *It*, *W*, *It*, *E*, 1995 *F*, *S*, *J*, *J*, *SA*, *A*, 1996 *Pt*, *F*, 1997 *WalA*, *F*
TE Brinza 1990 *It*, *USS*, 1991 *C*, 1992 *It*, *Ar*, 1993 *Pt*, *Tun*, *F*, *F*, *I*, 1994 *Sp*, *Ger*, *It*, *W*, *It*, *E*, 1995 *F*, *S*, *J*, *J*, *SA*, *A*, 1996 *Pt*, *F*, *Pol*, 1997 *WalA*, *F*, *W*, *Ar*, *F*, *It*, 1998 *Ukr*, 1999 *A*, *US*, *I*, 2000 *H*, *Geo*, 2002 *H*
I Bucan 1976 *Bul*, 1977 *Sp*, 1978 *Cze*, 1979 *F*, 1980 *It*, *USS*, *I*, *Pol*, *F*, 1981 *It*, *Sp*, *USS*, *S*, *NZ*, *F*, 1982 *WGe*, *It*, *USS*, *Z*, *Z*, *F*, 1983 *Mor*, *WGe*, *It*, *USS*, *Pol*, *W*, *USS*, *F*, 1984 *It*, *S*, *F*, *Sp*, 1985 *E*, *Tun*, *USS*, *USS*, *It*, 1986 *Pt*, *S*, *F*, *Pt*, 1987 *It*, *USS*, *Z*, *S*, *USS*, *F*
M Bucos 1972 *Mor*, *Cze*, *WGe*, 1973 *Sp*, 1975 *JAB*, *Pol*, *F*, 1976 *H*, *It*, *Sp*, *USS*, *Bul*, *Pol*, *F*, *Mor*, 1977 *Sp*, *It*, *F*, *Pol*, *It*, *F*, 1978 *Pol*, *F*, 1979 *W*, 1980 *It*, *Mor*
P Buda 1953 *It*, 1955 *Cze*, 1957 *F*, *Cze*
C Budica 1974 *Cze*, *EGe*, *Cze*
SS Burcea 2006 *F*, 2007 *ESp*, *ItA*, *Nm*, *Rus*, *Pt*, 2008 *Geo*, *Pt*, *CZR*, *Ur*, *Rus*, *ESp*, 2009 *Sp*, *Ger*, *Rus*, *Geo*, *Pt*, *ItA*, *Fj*, 2010 *Ger*, *Rus*, *Geo*, *Pt*, *Ukr*, *Ukr*, *Nm*, *ArJ*, *ItA*, *Tun*, *Ur*, *Ur*, 2011 *Rus*, *ArJ*, *Ukr*, *S*, *E*
M Burghelea 1974 *Cze*, *EGe*, *F*, 1975 *It*
S Burlescu 1936 *F*, *It*, *Ger*, 1938 *F*, *Ger*, 1939 *It*
M Butugan 2003 *Pt*

VN Calafeteanu 2004 *J*, 2005 *Ukr*, 2006 *CZR*, *Pt*, *Ukr*, *F*, *Sp*, *S*, 2007 *Geo*, *Sp*, *CZR*, *ESp*, *ItA*, *Nm*, *It*, *S*, *Pt*, *NZ*, 2008 *Geo*, *Sp*, *Pt*, *CZR*, 2009 *Ger*, *Geo*, *Pt*, *Ur*, *F*, *ItA*, *ItA*, *Fj*, 2010 *Ger*, *Rus*, *Tun*, *Ur*, *Ur*, 2011 *Pt*, *Geo*, *Sp*, *Nm*, *ArJ*, *Ar*, *E*, *Geo*
A Caligari 1951 *EGe*, 1953 *It*
S Caliman 1958 *EGe*, 1960 *Pol*, *EGe*, *Cze*
P Calistrat 1940 *It*, 1942 *It*
ION Camenita 1939 *It*
CF Caplescu 2007 *Sp*, *CZR*, *Rus*, *Pt*, 2008 *Rus*, *CZR*, *Ur*
C Capmare 1983 *Pol*, 1984 *It*
N Capusan 1960 *F*, 1961 *Pol*, *Cze*, *EGe*, *F*, 1962 *Cze*, *EGe*, *Pol*, *It*
R Capusan 1963 *Bul*, *EGe*, *Cze*
G Caracostea 1919 *US*, *F*
G Caragea 1980 *I*, *Pol*, *F*, 1981 *It*, *Sp*, *USS*, *S*, *NZ*, *F*, 1982 *WGe*, *It*, *USS*, *Z*, *Z*, *F*, 1983 *Mor*, *WGe*, *It*, *USS*, *Pol*, *W*, *F*, 1984 *F*, *Sp*, 1985 *E*, *Tun*, 1986 *S*, *F*, *Tun*, *Tun*, *Pt*, *F*, *I*, 1988 *It*, *Sp*, *US*, *USS*, 1989 *E*
C Carp 1989 *Z*, *Sa*, *USS*
D Carpo 2008 *Sp*, *Pt*, *Rus*, *CZR*, *Ur*, *Rus*, *ESp*, 2009 *Sp*, *Ger*, *Rus*, *Geo*, *Pt*, *Ur*, *F*, 2010 *Ger*, *Rus*, *Geo*, *Pt*, *Sp*, *ArJ*, *ItA*, *Tun*, *Ur*, *Ur*, 2011 *Pt*, *Rus*, *Geo*, *Sp*, *Nm*, *ArJ*, *Ukr*, *S*, *Ar*, *Geo*
GA Catuna 2009 *ItA*
I Cazan 2010 *ItA*, *Tun*, *Ur*, 2011 *Pt*, *Rus*, *Geo*, *Sp*, *Nm*, *ArJ*, *S*, *Ar*, *E*
G Celea 1963 *EGe*
D Chiriac 1999 *S*, *A*, *I*, 2001 *H*
G Chiriac 1996 *Bel*, 2001 *Pt*, *Rus*, 2002 *Sp*, *H*, *Rus*, *Geo*, *I*, *Sp*, *W*, *S*, *S*, 2003 *Sp*, *Rus*, *Geo*, *F*, *W*, *I*, *A*, *Ar*, *Nm*
R Chiriac 1952 *EGe*, 1955 *Cze*, 1957 *F*, *Bel*, *F*, 1958 *Sp*, *WGe*, 1960 *F*, 1961 *Pol*, *EGe*, *Cze*, *EGe*, *F*, 1962 *Cze*, *EGe*, *Pol*, *It*, *F*, 1963 *Bul*, *EGe*, *Cze*, *F*, 1964 *Cze*, *EGe*, *WGe*, *F*
M Chiricencu 1980 *It*, *Pol*
S Chirila 1989 *Sp*, *S*, 1990 *F*, *H*, *Sp*, *It*, *USS*, 1991 *It*
V Chirita 1999 *S*
G Cilinca 1993 *Pt*
N Cioarec 1974 *Pol*, 1976 *It*, 1979 *Pol*
P Ciobanel 1961 *Pol*, *EGe*, *Cze*, *EGe*, *F*, 1962 *Cze*, *EGe*, *Pol*, *It*, *F*,

1963 *F*, 1964 *Cze*, *EGe*, *WGe*, *F*, 1965 *WGe*, *F*, 1966 *Cze*, *It*, *F*, 1967 *F*, 1968 *Cze*, *Cze*, *F*, 1969 *Pol*, *WGe*, *Cze*, *F*, 1970 *F*, 1971 *F*
I Ciobanu 1952 *EGe*
M Ciobanu 1949 *Cze*, 1951 *EGe*
R Cioca 1994 *Sp*, *Ger*, *Rus*, *It*, *It*, *E*, 1995 *S*, 1996 *Bel*
I Ciofu 2000 *It*, 2003 *Pt*
ML Ciolacu 1998 *Ukr*, *Ar*, *Geo*, *I*, 1999 *F*, 2001 *Sp*, *H*, *Rus*, *Geo*, *W*, *E*
S Ciorascu 1988 *US*, *USS*, *USS*, *F*, *W*, 1989 *It*, *E*, *Sp*, *Z*, *Sa*, *USS*, *S*, 1990 *It*, *F*, *H*, *Sp*, *USS*, 1991 *It*, *NZ*, *S*, *F*, *C*, *Fj*, 1992 *Sp*, *It*, *It*, *Ar*, 1994 *Ger*, *Rus*, *It*, *W*, 1995 *F*, *S*, *J*, *C*, *SA*, *A*, 1996 *F*, 1997 *F*, *It*, 1999 *F*
M Ciornei 1972 *WGe*, *F*, 1973 *Ar*, *Ar*, *WGe*, *F*, 1974 *Mor*, *Pol*, *EGe*, *F*, *Cze*, 1975 *It*, *Sp*
SE Ciuntu 2007 *NZ*, *Rus*, *Pt*, 2008 *Geo*, *Sp*, *Pt*, *Rus*, *CZR*, *Ur*, *ESp*, 2009 *Sp*, *Ger*, *Rus*, *Geo*, *Pt*, *Ur*, *F*, *ItA*, *Fj*, 2010 *Ger*, *Rus*, *Geo*, *Pt*, *Sp*, *Ukr*, *Ukr*, *Nm*, *ArJ*, *ItA*, *Tun*, 2011 *Ukr*, *S*, *E*, *Geo*
C Cocor 1940 *It*, 1949 *Cze*
M Codea 1998 *Ukr*, 2001 *E*
L Codoi 1980 *I*, *Pol*, 1984 *F*, 1985 *Tun*, *USS*
C Cojocariu 1990 *It*, *F*, *H*, *Sp*, *It*, *USS*, 1991 *It*, *NZ*, *F*, *S*, *F*, *C*, *Fj*, 1992 *Sp*, *It*, *USS*, *F*, *Ar*, 1993 *Pt*, *F*, *F*, *I*, 1994 *Sp*, *Ger*, *Rus*, *It*, *W*, *It*, *E*, 1995 *F*, *S*, *J*, *J*, *C*, *SA*, *A*, *Ar*, *F*, *It*, 1996 *F*
L Colceriu 1991 *S*, *Fj*, 1992 *Sp*, *It*, *It*, 1993 *I*, 1994 *Sp*, *Ger*, *Rus*, *It*, *W*, *It*, 1995 *F*, *J*, *J*, *C*, *SA*, *A*, 1997 *WalA*, *F*, *W*, *Bel*, *Ar*, *F*, *It*, 1998 *Pol*, *Ukr*
D Coliba 1987 *USS*, *F*
M Coltuneac 2002 *Sp*, *W*, *S*
T Coman 1984 *Sp*, 1986 *F*, *Tun*, *Tun*, *I*, 1988 *Sp*, *US*, *USS*, *USS*, 1989 *It*, 1992 *F*
C Constantin 2001 *Pt*, 2002 *Geo*, *W*
F Constantin 1972 *Mor*, *Cze*, *WGe*, 1973 *Ar*, *Ar*, *WGe*, 1980 *Mor*, 1982 *It*
I Constantin 1971 *Mor*, 1972 *WGe*, 1973 *Ar*, *Ar*, *WGe*, *F*, 1974 *Mor*, *Pol*, *Sp*, *F*, *Cze*, 1975 *It*, *Sp*, *JAB*, *Pol*, *F*, 1976 *H*, *It*, *Sp*, *USS*, *Bul*, *Pol*, 1977 *It*, *F*, 1978 *Pol*, *F*, 1979 *It*, *Sp*, *USS*, *W*, *Pol*, *F*, 1980 *It*, *USS*, *I*, *Pol*, *F*, 1981 *It*, *Sp*, *USS*, *S*, *NZ*, *F*, 1982 *WGe*, *It*, *USS*, *Z*, *Z*, 1983 *WGe*, *USS*, 1985 *It*
L Constantin 1983 *USS*, *F*, 1984 *It*, *S*, *F*, *Sp*, 1985 *E*, *It*, *Tun*, *USS*, *USS*, *It*, 1986 *Pt*, *S*, *F*, *Tun*, *Tun*, *Pt*, *F*, *I*, 1987 *It*, *USS*, *Z*, *F*, *S*, *USS*, *F*, 1991 *It*, *NZ*, *F*
LT Constantin 1985 *USS*
S Constantin 1980 *Mor*, 1982 *Z*, *Z*, 1983 *Pol*, *W*, *USS*, *F*, 1984 *S*, *F*, 1985 *USS*, 1986 *Pt*, *S*, *F*, *Tun*, 1987 *It*, *Z*, *S*
T Constantin 1992 *USS*, *F*, *It*, 1993 *Pt*, *F*, *Sp*, 1996 *Pt*, 1997 *It*, 1999 *F*, *US*, *I*, 2000 *Pt*, *Sp*, *Geo*, *F*, 2002 *Rus*, *Geo*
T Constantin 1985 *USS*
N Copil 1985 *USS*, *It*, 1986 *S*
D Coravu 1968 *F*
N Cordos 1958 *EGe*, 1961 *EGe*, 1963 *Bul*, *Cze*, 1964 *Cze*, *EGe*
V Cornel 1977 *F*, 1978 *Cze*, *Sp*
G Corneliu 1980 *Mor*, *USS*, 1982 *WGe*, *It*, *Z*, *Z*, 1986 *Tun*, *Pt*, *F*, 1993 *I*, 1994 *W*
G Corneliu 1976 *USS*, *Bul*, 1977 *F*, 1979 *It*, 1981 *S*, 1982 *Z*
M Corneliu 1979 *USS*
F Corodeanu 1997 *WalA*, *F*, *W*, 1998 *H*, *Pol*, *Ar*, *Geo*, 1999 *F*, *S*, *A*, *US*, *I*, 2000 *H*, *Sp*, *Geo*, *F*, *It*, 2001 *Pt*, *Sp*, *H*, *Rus*, *Geo*, *I*, *E*, 2002 *Pt*, *Sp*, *Rus*, *Geo*, *It*, *Sp*, *W*, *S*, *S*, 2003 *Sp*, 2005 *Geo*, *J*, *US*, *S*, *Pt*, *C*, *I*, 2006 *Geo*, *CZR*, *Pt*, *Geo*, *Sp*, *S*, 2007 *Geo*, *ESp*, *ItA*, *Nm*, *It*, *S*, *Pt*, *NZ*, 2008 *Ur*, *Rus*, *ESp*, 2009 *Sp*, *Ger*, *Rus*, *Pt*
Coste 2007 *Pt*, 2008 *Geo*, *Sp*, *Pt*, *Rus*, *CZR*, *Ur*, 2009 *Sp*, *Rus*, *Geo*, *Pt*, *F*, 2010 *Ukr*
L Costea 1994 *E*, 1995 *S*, *J*, *J*, *Ar*, *F*, 1997 *WalA*, *F*
L Cotor 1957 *F*, *Cze*, 1959 *EGe*, *Pol*, *Cze*, 1960 *F*
F Covaci 1936 *Ger*, 1937 *H*, *F*, *Ger*, 1940 *It*, 1942 *It*
C Cratunescu 1919 *US*, *F*
N Crissoveloni 1936 *F*, *It*, 1937 *H*, *F*, *Ger*, 1938 *F*, *Ger*
S Cristea 1973 *Mor*
C Cristoloveanu 1952 *EGe*
G Crivat 1938 *F*, *Ger*
V Csoma 1983 *WGe*
D Curea 2005 *Rus*, *Ukr*, *J*, *US*, *S*, *Pt*

V Daiciulescu 1966 *Cze*, *F*, 1967 *It*, *Pol*, 1968 *F*, 1969 *Pol*
A Damian 1934 *It*, 1936 *F*, *It*, *Ger*, 1937 *It*, 1938 *F*, *Ger*, 1939 *It*, 1949 *Cze*
G Daraban 1969 *Cze*, 1972 *Mor*, *Cze*, *WGe*, *F*, 1973 *Sp*, *Mor*, *Ar*, *Ar*, 1974 *Cze*, *EGe*, *F*, *Cze*, 1975 *It*, *Sp*, *JAB*, *Pol*, *F*, 1976 *H*, *It*, *Sp*, *USS*, *Bul*, *Pol*, *F*, *Mor*, 1977 *Sp*, *It*, *F*, 1978 *Cze*, *Sp*, *Pol*, *F*, 1982 *F*, 1983 *Mor*, *WGe*, *It*, *USS*, *W*
CR Dascalu 2006 *Ukr*, *F*, *Geo*, *Sp*, *S*, 2007 *Sp*, *CZR*, *ESp*, *NZ*, *Rus*, *Pt*, 2008 *Geo*, *Rus*, *Ur*, *Rus*, *ESp*, 2009 *Sp*, *Rus*, *Geo*, *Ur*, *ItA*, *ItA*, 2010 *Ger*, *Rus*, *Geo*, *Sp*, *Ukr*, *Ukr*, *Nm*, 2011 *Pt*, *Rus*, *Geo*
V David 1984 *Sp*, 1986 *Pt*, *S*, *F*, *Tun*, 1987 *USS*, *Z*, *F*, 1992 *USS*
S Demci 1998 *Ar*, 2001 *H*, *Rus*, *Geo*, *I*, *W*
R Demian 1959 *EGe*, 1960 *F*, 1961 *Pol*, *EGe*, *Cze*, *EGe*, *F*, 1962 *Cze*, *Pol*, *It*, *F*, 1963 *Bul*, *EGe*, *Cze*, *F*, 1964 *WGe*, *F*, 1965 *WGe*, *F*, 1966 *Cze*, *It*, *F*, 1967 *It*, *Pt*, *Pol*, *WGe*, *F*, 1968 *Cze*, *F*, 1969 *Pol*, *WGe*, *F*, 1971 *It*, *Mor*
E Denischi 1949 *Cze*, 1952 *EGe*, *EGe*
I Diaconu 1942 *It*
C Diamandi-Telu 1938 *Ger*, 1939 *It*
ND Dima 1999 *A*, *US*, *I*, 2000 *H*, *Pt*, *Geo*, *F*, *It*, 2001 *Sp*, *H*, *Rus*, *Geo*, *W*, *E*, 2002 *Pt*, *Sp*, *Rus*, *W*, *S*, *S*, 2004 *CZR*, *Pt*, *Sp*, *Rus*, *Geo*, 2009 *ItA*, *ItA*, 2010 *Ger*, *Geo*, *Pt*, *Sp*, *Nm*, *ArJ*, *Ur*, *Ur*, 2011 *Geo*, *Sp*, *Nm*, *Ukr*
TI Dimofte 2004 *It*, *W*, *CZR*, 2005 *C*, *I*, 2006 *Geo*, *CZR*, *Pt*, *Ukr*, *Rus*, *F*, *Geo*, *Sp*, *S*, 2007 *ESp*, *ItA*, *Nm*, *It*, *S*, *Pt*, *NZ*, *Rus*, *Pt*, 2008 *Geo*, *Sp*, *Pt*, *Rus*, *CZR*, *Ur*, *Rus*, *ESp*, 2009 *Sp*, *Ger*, *Rus*, *Geo*, *Pt*, *Ur*, *F*, *ItA*, *Fj*, 2010 *Ger*, *Rus*, *Geo*, *Pt*, *Sp*, *Ukr*, *Ukr*, *Nm*, *ItA*, *Tun*, *Ur*, *Ur*, 2011 *Sp*, *Nm*, *ArJ*, *Ukr*, *S*, *Ar*, *Geo*
C Dinescu 1934 *It*, 1936 *F*, *It*, *Ger*, 1937 *It*, *H*, *F*, *Ger*, 1938 *F*, *Ger*, 1940 *It*, 1942 *It*
C Dinu 1965 *WGe*, *F*, 1966 *Cze*, *It*, *F*, 1967 *It*, *Pt*, *Pol*, *WGe*, 1968 *F*, 1969 *Pol*, *WGe*, *Cze*, *F*, 1970 *It*, *F*, 1971 *Mor*, *F*, 1972 *Mor*, *Cze*, *WGe*, *F*, 1973 *Sp*, *Mor*, *Ar*, *Ar*, *WGe*, *F*, 1974 *Mor*, *Pol*, *Sp*, *Cze*, *F*, *Cze*, 1975 *It*, *Sp*, 1976 *H*, *It*, *Sp*, *Pol*, *F*, *Mor*, 1977 *Sp*, *It*, *F*, *Pol*, *It*, *F*, 1978 *Sp*, *Pol*, *F*, 1979 *Sp*, *USS*, *W*, *Pol*, 1980 *I*, *Pol*, *F*, 1981 *It*, *Sp*, *USS*, *NZ*, *F*, 1982 *F*, 1983 *Mor*, *WGe*, *It*, *USS*
F Dinu 2000 *Mor*, *H*
G Dinu 1990 *It*, *F*, *H*, *Sp*, *It*, *USS*, 1991 *It*, *S*, *F*, *C*, *Fj*, 1992 *Sp*, *It*, *USS*, *F*, *It*, 1993 *F*
G Dinu 1975 *Pol*, 1979 *It*, *Sp*, 1983 *Pol*, *USS*
F Dobre 2001 *E*, 2004 *W*, *CZR*, 2007 *Pt*, 2008 *CZR*
I Dobre 1951 *EGe*, 1952 *EGe*, 1953 *It*, 1955 *Cze*, 1957 *Cze*, *Bel*, *F*, 1958 *Sp*
I Doja 1986 *Tun*, *Pt*, *F*, *I*, 1988 *F*, *W*, 1989 *Sp*, *Z*, *Sa*, *S*, 1990 *It*, 1991 *It*, *NZ*, *F*, *C*, 1992 *Sp*
V Doja 1997 *Bel*, 1998 *Pol*, *Geo*, *I*
A Domocos 1989 *Z*, *Sa*, *USS*
I Dorutiu 1957 *Cze*, *Bel*, *F*, 1958 *Sp*, *WGe*
A Draghici 1919 *US*
C Dragnea 1995 *F*, 1996 *Pol*, 1997 *WalA*, *F*, *Bel*, *Ar*, *F*, *It*, 1998 *H*, *Pol*, 1999 *F*, 2000 *F*
I Dragnea 1985 *Tun*
S Dragnea 2002 *S*
M Dragomir 1996 *Bel*, 1997 *Bel*, 1998 *H*, *Pol*, *Ukr*, *Geo*, *I*, 2001 *I*, *W*, *E*
M Dragomir 2001 *H*, *Geo*, 2002 *I*
V Dragomir 1964 *Cze*, *EGe*, 1966 *It*, 1967 *Pol*, *WGe*
G Dragomirescu 1919 *F*
G Dragomirescu-Rahtopol 1963 *Bul*, *EGe*, *Cze*, *F*, 1964 *Cze*, *EGe*, *WGe*, *F*, 1965 *WGe*, *F*, 1966 *Cze*, 1967 *It*, *Pt*, *Pol*, *WGe*, *F*, 1968 *Cze*, *Cze*, *F*, 1969 *Pol*, *WGe*, *Cze*, *F*, 1970 *It*, *F*, 1971 *It*, *Mor*, 1972 *Mor*, *Cze*, *WGe*, *F*, 1973 *WGe*, *F*
N Dragos 1995 *Ar*, *It*, 1997 *WalA*, *F*, *Ar*, *F*, *It*, 1998 *H*, *Pol*, *Ukr*, *Ar*, *Geo*, *I*, 1999 *F*, *S*, 2000 *Sp*, *Geo*, *F*
CS Draguceanu 1994 *Sp*, *Ger*, *Rus*, *It*, *W*, *It*, *E*, 1995 *S*, *J*, *Ar*, *F*, *It*, 1996 *Bel*, 1997 *W*, *Bel*, *Ar*, *F*, *It*, 1998 *H*, *Pol*, *Ukr*, *Ar*, *Geo*, *I*, 1999 *S*, *A*, *US*, *I*, 2000 *Mor*, *H*, *Pt*, *Sp*, *Geo*, *F*, *It*
C Dragulescu 1969 *Cze*, 1970 *F*, 1971 *It*, 1972 *Cze*
G Drobota 1960 *Pol*, *Cze*, 1961 *EGe*, *EGe*, *F*, 1962 *Cze*, *EGe*, *Pol*, *F*, 1964 *Cze*, *EGe*, *F*
D Dumbrava 2002 *W*, *S*, 2003 *Sp*, *Rus*, *Geo*, *CZR*, *F*, *W*, *I*, *A*, *Nm*, 2004 *CZR*, *Pt*, *Sp*, *Rus*, *Geo*, *It*, *J*, *CZR*, 2005 *Rus*, *Geo*, *Ukr*, *J*, *US*, *S*, *Pt*, *C*, 2006 *Geo*, *Pt*, *Rus*, 2007 *Sp*, *CZR*, *Pt*, *Rus*, *Pt*, 2008 *Sp*, *Pt*, *Rus*, *CZR*, *Ur*, *Rus*, *ESp*, 2009 *Fj*, 2010 *Geo*, *Pt*, *Sp*, *Ukr*, *Ukr*, *Nm*, *ArJ*, *ItA*, *Tun*, *Ur*, *Ur*, 2011 *Pt*, *Rus*, *Geo*, *Sp*, *Nm*, *Ukr*, *S*, *E*, *Geo*
H Dumitras 1984 *It*, 1985 *E*, *It*, *USS*, 1986 *Pt*, *F*, *I*, 1987 *It*, *USS*, *Z*, *S*, *USS*, *F*, 1988 *It*, *Sp*, *US*, *USS*, *USS*, *F*, *W*, 1989 *It*, *E*, *Z*, *Sa*, *USS*, *S*, 1990 *It*, *F*, *H*, *Sp*, *USS*, 1991 *It*, *NZ*, *F*, *S*, *F*, *C*, *Fj*, 1992 *Sp*, *USS*, *F*, *Ar*, 1993 *Pt*, *Tun*, *F*, *Sp*, *F*, *I*
I Dumitras 2002 *H*, 2006 *Geo*, *CZR*, *Ukr*, *Rus*, *F*, 2007 *Geo*, *Sp*, *CZR*, *ESp*, *ItA*, *Nm*, *It*, *S*, *Pt*, *NZ*, 2009 *Ur*, *F*, *ItA*, *ItA*, *Fj*, 2010 *Ger*, *Rus*, *Geo*, *Pt*, *Sp*, *Ur*, *Ur*, 2011 *Pt*, *Rus*, *Geo*, *Sp*, *ArJ*, *Ukr*, *S*, *Ar*, *E*, *Geo*
E Dumitrescu 1953 *It*, 1958 *Sp*, *WGe*
G Dumitrescu 1988 *It*, *Sp*, *F*, *W*, 1989 *It*, *E*, *Sp*, *Z*, *Sa*, *USS*, *S*, 1990 *It*, *F*, *H*, *Sp*, *It*, *USS*, 1991 *It*, *NZ*, *F*, 1997 *It*
L Dumitrescu 1997 *Bel*, *Ar*, 2001 *W*
G Dumitriu 1937 *H*, *F*, *Ger*
A Dumitru 1974 *Pol*, 1975 *Sp*, *JAB*, 1976 *Sp*, *USS*, *Bul*, *Pol*, *F*, *Mor*, 1977 *Sp*, *It*, *F*, *Pol*, *F*, 1978 *Cze*, *Sp*, 1979 *It*, *Sp*, *USS*, *W*, *F*, 1980 *It*, *I*, *Pol*, *F*, 1981 *Sp*, *USS*, *S*, *NZ*, *F*, 1982 *Z*, 1983 *It*, *USS*, *Pol*, *W*, 1984 *It*, *S*, *F*, *Sp*, 1985 *E*, 1987 *It*, *USS*, *Z*, *S*, *USS*, *F*, 1988 *USS*
D Dumitru 2002 *S*, 2009 *Ur*, *F*, *ItA*, *ItA*, *Fj*
G Dumitru 1973 *Sp*, *Mor*, *Ar*, *Ar*, *WGe*, *F*, 1974 *Mor*, *Sp*, *Cze*, *EGe*,

F, 1975 JAB, Pol, F, 1976 H, It, Sp, 1977 Sp, Pol, F, 1978 Cze, Sp, Pol, F, 1979 It, Sp, USS, W, Pol, F, 1980 It, Mor, USS, I, Pol, F, 1981 It, Sp, USS, S, NZ, F, 1982 WGe, It, USS, Z, Z, F, 1983 Mor, WGe, It, USS, Pol, USS, F, 1984 It, S, F, 1985 E, It, Tun, USS, 1986 F, I, 1987 USS, F, S, USS, F
M Dumitru 1990 F, H, Sp, It, USS, 1991 NZ, F, F, C, 1992 F, 1993 F, Sp, F
M Dumitru 1997 WalA, 1998 Ar, 1999 F, 2000 Mor, H, Pt, Sp, Geo, F, 2002 H, 2003 Sp
M Dumitru 2002 Pt, Sp, H, I
S Dumitru 2004 It, 2005 Rus, Ukr, US, S, Pt
R Durbac 1968 Cze, 1969 WGe, Cze, 1970 It, F, 1971 It, Mor, F, 1972 WGe, F, 1973 Ar, Ar, WGe, F, 1974 Mor, Pol, Sp, Cze, EGe, F, Cze, 1975 It, Sp, JAB, Pol, F
A Duta 1973 Ar

R Eckert 1927 F, Ger, Cze
I Enache 1977 It
M Ezaru 2000 Pt, Geo, F

V Falcusanu 1974 Sp, Cze
G Fantaneanu 1934 It, 1936 F, It, Ger, 1937 It, H, F, Ger
C Fercu 2005 C, I, 2006 Geo, CZR, Pt, Ukr, Rus, F, Geo, Sp, 2007 Geo, Sp, CZR, ESp, ItA, Nm, It, S, Pt, 2008 Geo, Sp, Pt, Rus, CZR, Ur, Rus, ESp, 2009 Sp, Ger, Rus, Pt, Ur, F, 2010 Ger, Rus, Geo, Pt, Sp, Ukr, Nm, ArJ, ItA, Tun, Ur, Ur, 2011 Rus, Geo, Sp, Nm, ArJ, Ukr
C Florea 1937 It, F, Ger
G Florea 1981 S, NZ, F, 1982 WGe, It, USS, Z, Z, 1984 Sp, 1985 USS, 1986 Pt, F
S Florea 2000 It, 2001 Sp, Geo, I, E, 2002 It, Sp, W, 2003 Sp, Rus, Geo, CZR, A, Ar, Nm, 2007 Sp, CZR, S, NZ, 2009 Sp, Ger, 2010 Rus, Ukr, Ukr, Nm, 2011 S, Ar, E, Geo
I Florescu 1957 F, Cze
M Florescu 1995 F
P Florescu 1967 It, Pt, Pol, WGe, F, 1968 Cze, Cze, F, 1969 Pol, WGe, Cze, F, 1971 Mor, 1973 Sp, Mor, Ar, Ar, 1974 Cze, EGe, F
P Florian 1927 F, 1934 It
T Florian 1927 F, Ger
V Flutur 1994 Ger, 1995 J, J, C, SA, A, Ar, F, It, 1996 Bel, Pol, 1997 WalA, F
M Foca 1992 It, USS, It, Ar, 1993 Pt, Tun, F
C Fugigi 1964 Cze, 1969 Cze, 1972 Mor, Cze, WGe, F, 1973 Sp, Ar, Ar, WGe, F, 1974 Mor, Sp, Cze, EGe, 1975 It, Sp, JAB
C Fugigi 1992 Ar
R Fugigi 1995 It, 1996 Pt, F, Pol, 1998 Ukr, Ar, I, 1999 S, I
S Fuicu 1976 H, 1980 USS, I, Pol, F, 1981 It, Sp, USS, S, NZ, F, 1982 Z, Z, F, 1983 Mor, WGe, It, USS, W, 1984 It
N Fulina 1988 F, W, 1989 It, E, Sp, Sa, USS, 1990 It, F, H, Sp, USS, 1991 NZ, C, Fj, 1992 It, It, 1993 Pt, F, Sp, F, I, 1994 Sp, Ger, Rus, It, W, It

CM Gal 2005 I, 2006 Geo, CZR, Pt, S, 2007 Geo, CZR, ESp, ItA, Nm, It, S, NZ, Rus, Pt, 2008 Geo, Sp, Pt, Rus, 2009 Ger, Pt, ItA, ItA, Fj, 2010 Geo, Pt, Sp, Ukr, Ukr, Nm, ArJ, ItA, Tun, Ur, Ur, 2011 Pt, Geo, Sp, Nm, ArJ, S, Ar, E, Geo
S Galan 1985 It, It
I Garlesteanu 1924 F, US, 1927 F, Cze
A Gealapu 1994 It, E, 1995 F, S, J, J, C, SA, A, Ar, F, It, 1996 Pt, F, Pol
C Gheara 2004 CZR, Sp, Rus, Geo, 2010 Ger, 2011 Rus, Ukr, Ar, Geo
C Gheorghe 1992 It, 1993 Tun, F, Sp, 1994 Sp, Ger, E
D Gherasim 1959 Cze
V Ghiata 1951 EGe
S Ghica 1937 H, F, 1942 It
V Ghioc 2000 It, 2001 Pt, Sp, Rus, Geo, I, W, E, 2002 Pt, Sp, H, W, S, S, 2003 CZR, Ar, 2004 It, W, CZR, 2005 Ukr, J, S, 2008 Pt
N Ghiondea 1949 Cze, 1951 EGe
D Ghiuzelea 1951 EGe, 1952 EGe, EGe, 1953 It, 1955 Cze, 1957 Cze
A Girbu 1992 Ar, 1993 Tun, Sp, F, I, 1994 Sp, 1995 Ar, F, It, 1996 Pt, F, Pol, 1997 WalA, F, Ar, F, It, 1998 H, Pol, Geo, I
L Giucal 2009 Sp, Ger
M Giucal 1985 It, Tun, USS, It, 1986 Pt, F, Tun
A Giugiuc 1963 Bul, EGe, Cze, 1964 Cze, EGe, 1966 Cze
V Giuglea 1986 S, Tun
I Glavan 1942 It
RS Gontineac 1995 F, S, J, J, C, SA, A, 1996 Pt, F, Pol, 1997 F, W, Ar, F, It, 1998 H, Pol, Ukr, Ar, Geo, I, 1999 F, S, A, US, I, 2000 H, Sp, Geo, F, 2001 Rus, Geo, 2002 Pt, Sp, Rus, Geo, I, It, Sp, W, S, S, 2003 Pt, Sp, Geo, CZR, F, W, I, A, Ar, Nm, 2004 CZR, Pt, Rus, Geo, It, W, J, CZR, 2005 Geo, C, 2006 Geo, Pt, Ukr, Rus, F, Geo, Sp, S, 2007 Geo, Sp, It, S, Pt, NZ, 2008 ESp
A Gorcioaia 2009 Ger
G Graur 1958 It, 1959 EGe, Pol, Cze, EGe, 1960 Pol, EGe, Cze, 1961 EGe, 1962 EGe, It
E Grigore 1982 WGe, 1984 Sp, 1985 E, Tun, 1987 It, USS, Z, F, S
V Grigorescu 1936 F, It, Ger, 1939 It
M Guramare 1982 WGe, It, 1983 Mor, WGe, 1988 Sp
A Guranescu 1991 S, F, 1992 USS, It, 1993 Pt, Tun, I, 1994 Ger, Rus, It, W, E, 1995 SA, A, Ar, F, It
S Guranescu 1997 W, Bel, Ar, 2001 Sp, H, Rus, I

A Hariton 1973 Mor, Ar, Ar, 1978 Cze, Sp
T Hell 1958 EGe
CN Hildan 1998 H, Pol, Geo, 1999 S
L Hodorca 1984 It, 1985 Tun, 1986 Pt, S, F, Tun, Tun, I, 1987 It, Z, 1988 F
M Holban 1980 Mor, 1982 F, 1985 It, USS, 1986 Pt, I
J Hussar 1919 US

D Iacob 1996 Bel, 2001 Pt, Sp, H, Geo, W
ML Iacob 1997 W, Bel, Ar, F, It, 1999 S
DG Ianus 2009 Sp, 2010 Ukr, Nm, ItA, Tun, 2011 Rus, Geo, Sp, Nm, Ar, E, Geo
P Ianusevici 1974 Pol, Cze, EGe, Cze, 1975 It, 1976 USS, Bul, Pol, F, Mor, 1977 Sp, Pol, It, F, 1978 F
I Iconomu 1919 US, F
M Iconomu 1919 US, F
N Ifrim 1937 F, Ger
G Ignat 1986 Pt, S, F, Tun, 1988 It, Sp, US, USS, USS, F, W, 1989 It, E, Sp, S, 1990 It, F, H, Sp, 1991 It, NZ, 1992 Sp, It, USS, F
V Ilca 1987 F
I Ilie 1952 EGe, EGe, 1953 It, 1955 Cze, 1957 F, Cze, Bel, F, 1958 It, 1959 EGe
M Iliescu 1961 EGe, 1963 Bul, EGe, Cze, F, 1965 WGe, F, 1967 WGe
T Ioan 1937 H, F, Ger
V Ioan 1927 Ger, Cze, 1937 It
F Ion 1991 S, 1992 Sp, 1993 F
G Ion 1984 Sp, 1986 F, I, 1988 USS, F, W, 1989 It, E, Sp, Sa, USS, S, 1990 It, F, H, Sp, It, USS, 1991 It, NZ, F, S, F, C, Fj, 1992 Sp, It, USS, F, Ar, 1993 Pt, F, Sp, F, 1994 Sp, Rus, It, W, It, 1997 WalA
P Ion 2003 Ar, 2004 It, 2005 Rus, Ukr, J, US, S, 2006 Geo, CZR, Pt, Ukr, Rus, F, Geo, S, 2007 Geo, Sp, CZR, ESp, ItA, Pt, NZ, Rus, 2008 Geo, Sp, Rus, Ur, Rus, ESp, 2009 Sp, Ger, Rus, Geo, Pt, Ur, F, ItA, ItA, Fj, 2010 Ger, Rus, Geo, Pt, 2011 ArJ, Ukr, S, Ar, E, Geo
V Ion 1980 Mor, USS, 1982 Z, Z, F, 1983 Mor, It, USS, W, USS, F, 1984 S, 1985 It, 1987 It, USS, Z, F, S
A Ionescu 1958 EGe, It, 1959 EGe, Pol, Cze, 1960 Pol, EGe, Cze, 1961 Pol, Cze, EGe, F, 1962 EGe, It, F, 1963 F, 1964 Cze, EGe, F, 1965 WGe, 1966 Cze, It, F
D Ionescu 1949 Cze, 1951 EGe, 1952 EGe, EGe, 1953 It, 1955 Cze, 1957 F, Cze, F, 1958 Sp, It
G Ionescu 1934 It, 1936 F, It, Ger, 1937 It, F, 1938 F, Ger, 1940 It, 1942 It
G Ionescu 1949 Cze
M Ionescu 1972 Mor, 1976 USS, Bul, Pol, F, 1977 It, F, Pol, It, F, 1978 Cze, Sp, Pol, F, 1979 It, Sp, USS, W, Pol, F, 1980 I, 1981 NZ, 1983 USS
R Ionescu 1968 Cze, Cze, 1971 F
S Ionescu 1936 It, Ger, 1937 It
V Ionescu 1993 Tun, F, 1994 Ger, Rus, 1998 Ukr
V Ionescu 1992 It
F Ionita 1974 Sp, 1978 Pol, F
P Iordachescu 1957 F, Cze, Bel, F, 1958 Sp, WGe, EGe, It, 1959 EGe, Pol, Cze, EGe, 1960 Pol, EGe, Cze, 1961 EGe, 1963 F, 1964 Cze, EGe, WGe, 1965 WGe, F, 1966 Cze
M Iordan 1980 Mor
P Iordanescu 1949 Cze
V Iorgulescu 1967 WGe, 1968 Cze, F, 1969 Pol, WGe, Cze, 1970 It, F, 1971 F, 1973 Ar, Ar
V Irimescu 1960 F, 1961 Pol, Cze, EGe, F, 1962 Cze, EGe, Pol, It, F, 1963 F, 1964 F, 1965 WGe, F, 1966 Cze, It, F, 1967 It, Pt, Pol, WGe, F, 1968 Cze, Cze, F, 1969 Pol, WGe, Cze, F, 1970 It, F, 1971 F
I Irimia 1936 F, It, Ger, 1937 It, H, Ger, 1938 F, Ger, 1939 It, 1940 It
G Irisescu 1993 Sp
A Iulian 2003 CZR
VM Ivan 2010 Geo, Pt, Sp, Ukr, Ukr, Tun
I Ivanciuc 1991 Fj, 1994 E, 1995 J, C, SA, A

I Jipescu 1927 F

C Kramer 1955 Cze, 1958 Sp, WGe, It, 1960 Pol, EGe, Cze
T Krantz 1940 It, 1942 It
C Kurtzbauer 1939 It

C Lapusneanu 1934 *It*
MA Lazar 2008 *CZR, Ur, Rus, ESp*, 2009 *Geo*, 2010 *Geo, Pt, Sp, Tun, Ur, Ur*, 2011 *Rus, Sp, Nm, ArJ, Ukr, S, Ar, Geo*
MV Lemnaru 2009 *Sp, Rus*, 2010 *Ur, Ur*, 2011 *Rus, Geo, Sp, ArJ, S, Ar, Geo*
G Leonte 1984 *S, F*, 1985 *E, It, USS*, 1987 *It, USS, Z, S, USS, F*, 1988 *It, Sp, US, USS, USS, F, W*, 1989 *It, E, Sp, Z, Sa, USS, S*, 1990 *It, F, H, Sp, It*, 1991 *It, NZ, F, S, F, C*, 1992 *USS, F, It, Ar*, 1993 *Tun, F, Sp, F, I*, 1994 *Sp, Ger, Rus, It, W, It*, 1995 *F, S, J, J, C, SA, A*
M Leuciuc 1987 *F*
T Luca 1995 *Ar, F, It*, 1996 *F*
V Lucaci 1996 *Bel*
V Lucaci 2009 *Fj*, 2010 *Sp, Ukr*, 2011 *Pt, Sp*
A Lungu 1980 *It, USS*, 1981 *It, Sp, USS, S, NZ, F*, 1982 *WGe, It, USS, Z, Z, F*, 1983 *Mor, WGe, It, USS, Pol, W, USS, F*, 1984 *It, S, F, Sp*, 1985 *E, It, Tun, USS, USS, It*, 1986 *Pt, S, F, Tun, Tun, Pt, F, I*, 1987 *It, USS, Z, F, S, USS, F*, 1988 *It, Sp, US, USS, USS, F, W*, 1989 *It, E, Sp, Z, Sa, USS, S*, 1990 *It, F, It*, 1991 *It, NZ, F, S, F, C, Fj*, 1992 *Sp, It, USS, F, Ar*, 1995 *A*
R Lungu 2002 *Pt, H, It, Sp, W, S*, 2003 *Pt*
A Lupu 2006 *S*
C Lupu 1998 *Pol, I*, 1999 *F*, 2000 *Mor, It*, 2001 *Pt, H, Rus, W*, 2002 *H, Rus*
S Luric 1951 *EGe*, 1952 *EGe, EGe*, 1953 *It*, 1955 *Cze*
V Luscal 1958 *Sp, WGe, EGe*

F Macaneata 1983 *USS*
M Macovei 2006 *Ukr, Rus*, 2007 *Geo, Rus, Pt*, 2008 *Geo, Rus, CZR, Ur, Rus, ESp*, 2009 *Rus, Geo, ItA*, 2010 *Ger, Geo, Sp, Ukr*, 2011 *Pt, Geo, Nm, Ukr, S, Ar, E, Geo*
V Maftei 1995 *Ar, F, It*, 1996 *Bel*, 1997 *WalA, W, F*, 1998 *Ar*, 2001 *Pt, Sp, H, Geo, I*, 2002 *Pt, Sp, Rus, Geo, I, It, Sp, S*, 2003 *Pt, Geo, CZR, F, W, I, A, Ar, Nm*, 2004 *Pt, Sp, Rus, Geo, W, J, CZR*, 2005 *Rus, Geo, Ukr, C, I*, 2006 *CZR*
G Malancu 1976 *H, It, USS, Bul*
A Man 1988 *US*
V Man 1988 *USS, USS*
D Manoileanu 1949 *Cze*
DG Manole 2009 *Ger*
G Manole 1959 *Pol*, 1960 *Pol, EGe, Cze*
AV Manta 1996 *Bel*, 1997 *F*, 1998 *Ar, Geo, I*, 2000 *F*, 2001 *Pt, Sp, Rus, Geo*, 2002 *Sp, H, Rus, I, It, Sp*, 2003 *Pt, Rus*, 2005 *C, I*, 2006 *Geo, CZR, Pt, Geo*, 2007 *It, S, NZ*, 2009 *Pt, Ur, F, ItA*, 2010 *Rus, Pt, Ukr, Tun, Ur, Ur*
H Manu 1919 *US, F*, 1927 *F, Ger*
N Marascu 1919 *F*, 1924 *F, US*, 1927 *F, Cze*
A Marasescu 1927 *F, Ger*, 1936 *It, Ger*
E Marculescu 1936 *F, It, Ger*, 1937 *It*, 1939 *It*, 1940 *It*
A Marghescu 1980 *Pol*, 1981 *It*, 1983 *W, USS, F*, 1984 *S, F, Sp*, 1985 *E*
I Marica 1972 *WGe, F*, 1973 *Sp, Mor, WGe, F*, 1974 *Mor, Sp, Cze, EGe, F, Cze*, 1975 *It, Sp*
A Marin 1978 *Cze, Sp, Pol*, 1979 *F*, 1980 *Pol*, 1982 *USS*, 1983 *Pol*, 1984 *Sp*, 1985 *USS, It*, 1986 *Pt*, 1987 *USS, Z*
A Marin 2008 *CZR*
N Marin 1991 *Fj*, 1992 *Sp, It*, 1993 *F, I*, 1995 *Ar, F, It*
A Marinache 1949 *Cze*, 1951 *EGe*, 1952 *EGe, EGe*, 1955 *Cze*, 1957 *F, Bel, F*, 1960 *F*, 1961 *Pol, EGe, Cze, EGe, F*, 1962 *Cze, Pol*
V Marinescu 1967 *Pt, WGe*, 1968 *Cze*, 1969 *Cze, F*
F Marioara 1994 *E*, 1996 *Pol*, 1998 *Geo, I*
S Maris 2010 *Ukr, Ukr, Nm, ArJ, ItA, Tun*
V Mariscaru 2011 *Rus, Geo*
A Mateescu 1959 *EGe, Pol, Cze, EGe*, 1960 *Pol, EGe, Cze*, 1962 *EGe, Pol*, 1963 *Bul, EGe, Cze*, 1964 *Cze, EGe*, 1965 *WGe, F*, 1966 *F*, 1970 *It, F*, 1973 *Sp, WGe, F*, 1974 *Mor, Pol, Sp*
A Mateiescu 1934 *It*, 1936 *F, Ger*
R Mavrodin 1998 *Geo, I*, 1999 *F, A, US, I*, 2000 *H, Pt, Sp, Geo, F, It*, 2002 *Pt, Sp, H, I, It, Sp, W*, 2003 *I, A, Ar, Nm*, 2004 *Pt, Sp, Rus, Geo, W, J, CZR*, 2005 *Rus, J, US, S, Pt*, 2006 *Ukr, Rus, F, Geo, Sp, S*, 2007 *Geo, ESp, ItA, Nm, It, S, Pt, NZ*, 2009 *Ur*
F Maxim 2007 *Rus*
G Mazilu 1958 *Sp, WGe*, 1959 *EGe, Pol, Cze*
S Mehedinti 1951 *EGe*, 1953 *It*
G Melinte 1958 *EGe, It*
P Mergisescu 1960 *Pol, EGe, Cze*
C Mersoiu 2000 *Mor, Pt*, 2001 *I*, 2002 *S, S*, 2003 *Pt, Sp, Geo, CZR, F, W*, 2004 *CZR, Pt, Sp, Rus, It, W, J, CZR*, 2005 *Rus, Geo, Ukr, I*, 2006 *CZR, Pt, Geo, Sp*, 2007 *Geo, Sp, CZR, Rus, Pt*, 2008 *Geo, Sp, Pt, Rus, CZR, Ur, Rus, ESp*, 2009 *Geo*
A Miclescu 1971 *Mor*
S Mihailescu 1919 *F*, 1924 *F, US*, 1927 *F*
D Mihalache 1973 *Mor*
M Mihalache 2007 *Pt*, 2008 *Geo, Sp, Rus*
V Mihalascu 1967 *Pol, WGe*
A Mitocaru 1992 *Ar*, 1993 *Pt, Sp, F*
P Mitu 1996 *Bel, Pol*, 1997 *W, Bel, Ar, It*, 1998 *H, Pol, Ukr, Ar, Geo, I*, 1999 *F, S, A, US, I*, 2000 *H, Pt, Sp, Geo, It*, 2001 *Pt, Sp, H, Rus*, 2002 *Pt, Sp, H, Rus, Geo, Sp, W, S, S*, 2003 *Geo*, 2005 *I*, 2006 *Geo*, 2009 *Sp, Ger, Rus, Pt*
M Miu 2003 *Pt, Sp*
V Mladin 1955 *Cze*, 1957 *Bel, F*, 1958 *Sp, WGe, It*, 1959 *EGe*, 1960 *F*
S Mocanu 1996 *Bel*, 1998 *H, Pol, Ukr*, 2000 *Mor, Pt*
T Moldoveanu 1937 *F, Ger*, 1938 *F, Ger*, 1939 *It*, 1940 *It*
O Morariu 1984 *Sp*, 1985 *Tun*
V Morariu 1952 *EGe, EGe*, 1953 *It*, 1955 *Cze*, 1957 *F, Cze, Bel, F*, 1959 *EGe*, 1960 *F*, 1961 *Pol, Cze, EGe, F*, 1962 *Cze, EGe, Pol, It, F*, 1963 *F*, 1964 *WGe, F*
C Moscu 1934 *It*, 1937 *It*
M Mot 1980 *Mor*, 1982 *It, USS, Z*, 1985 *It, It*, 1986 *F, Tun*, 1988 *US, USS*
M Motoc 1988 *US*, 1989 *S*
P Motrescu 1973 *Mor, Ar, Ar*, 1974 *Mor, Pol, Sp, Cze*, 1975 *JAB, Pol, F*, 1976 *H, It, Sp, Bul, Pol, F, Mor*, 1977 *Sp, It, F, Pol, It, F*, 1978 *Cze, Sp, Pol, F*, 1979 *It, Sp, USS, W, Pol*, 1980 *It, Mor*
B Munteanu 2000 *It*
IC Munteanu 1940 *It*, 1942 *It*
M Munteanu 1973 *WGe, F*, 1974 *Mor, Sp, Cze, EGe, F, Cze*, 1975 *It, Sp, JAB, Pol, F*, 1976 *H, It, Sp, Pol, Mor*, 1978 *Pol, F*, 1979 *It, Sp, W, Pol*, 1980 *It, I, Pol, F*, 1981 *It, Sp, USS, S, NZ, F*, 1982 *F*, 1983 *Mor, WGe, It, USS, Pol, W, USS, F*, 1984 *It, S, F*, 1985 *USS*, 1986 *S, Tun, Pt, F*, 1988 *It, Sp*
T Munteanu 2003 *CZR*, 2004 *CZR*
F Murariu 1976 *H, USS, Bul, Pol, F, Mor*, 1977 *Sp, It, F, Pol, It, F*, 1978 *Cze, Sp, Pol, F*, 1979 *It, Sp, USS, W, Pol, F*, 1980 *It, I, Pol, F*, 1981 *USS, NZ*, 1982 *USS, Z, Z, F*, 1983 *Mor, WGe, It, USS, Pol, W, F*, 1984 *It, S, F, Sp*, 1985 *E, It, Tun, USS, USS, It*, 1986 *Pt, S, F, Tun*, 1987 *It, USS, Z, S, USS, F*, 1988 *It, Sp, US, USS, USS, F, W*, 1989 *It, E, Sp, Z*
D Musat 1974 *Sp, Cze, EGe, Cze*, 1975 *It, JAB, Pol, F*, 1976 *Mor*, 1980 *Mor*

M Nache 1980 *Mor*
M Nagel 1958 *EGe*, 1960 *Pol, EGe, Cze*
R Nanu 1952 *EGe, EGe*, 1953 *It*, 1955 *Cze*, 1957 *F, Bel, F*
V Nastase 1985 *Tun, USS*, 1986 *Tun, Pt, F, I*
D Neaga 1988 *It, Sp, USS, F, W*, 1989 *It, E, Sp, Z, Sa, USS, S*, 1990 *It, F, H, Sp, USS*, 1991 *It, F, S, F, C, Fj*, 1993 *Tun, F, Sp, I*, 1994 *Sp, Ger, Rus, It, W, It, E*, 1995 *F, S, J, J, C*, 1996 *Pt, F*
I Neagu 1972 *Mor, Cze*
E Necula 1987 *It, F*
P Nedelcovici 1924 *F*
C Nedelcu 1964 *Cze, EGe*
M Nedelcu 1993 *Pt, Tun, F*, 1994 *Sp, It*, 1995 *Ar, F, It*
V Nedelcu 1996 *Pol*, 1997 *WalA, F, W, Ar, F*, 1998 *H, Pol, Ukr, Ar*, 2000 *H*, 2001 *I, W, E*, 2002 *Rus, Geo*
I Negreci 1994 *E*, 1995 *F, J, C, SA, A, Ar, F, It*
I Nemes 1924 *F, US*, 1927 *Ger, Cze*
N Nere 2006 *CZR*, 2007 *CZR, Rus, Pt*, 2008 *Sp, Pt, Rus*, 2009 *Sp, Ger, Rus, Geo, Pt*, 2011 *Pt, Rus, Geo, Sp, Nm, E*
G Nica 1964 *Cze, EGe, WGe*, 1966 *It, F*, 1967 *Pol, F*, 1969 *Pol, WGe, Cze, F*, 1970 *It, F*, 1971 *It, Mor, F*, 1972 *Mor, Cze, WGe, F*, 1973 *Sp, Mor, Ar, Ar, WGe, F*, 1974 *Mor, Pol, Sp, Cze, EGe, F, Cze*, 1975 *It, Sp, JAB, Pol, F*, 1976 *H, It, Sp, USS, Bul, Pol, F, Mor*, 1977 *Sp, It, F, Pol, It, F*, 1978 *Pol, F*
N Nichitean 1990 *It, Sp, It, USS*, 1991 *It, F, F, C, Fj*, 1992 *USS, It, Ar*, 1993 *Pt, Tun, F, Sp*, 1994 *Sp, Ger, Rus, It, W, It*, 1995 *F, S, J, J, C*, 1997 *WalA, F*
G Nicola 1927 *F, Ger, Cze*
C Nicolae 2003 *Pt, Rus*, 2006 *Sp*, 2007 *ItA, Nm, Pt, Rus*, 2009 *Geo, Pt, Ur, F, ItA, Fj*, 2010 *Pt, Ukr, Nm, ArJ, Tun, Ur*, 2011 *Pt, Nm, ArJ, Ukr, E*
M Nicolae 2003 *I, A*
N Nicolau 1940 *It*
M Nicolescu 1969 *Pol, WGe, Cze, F*, 1971 *It, Mor, F*, 1972 *Mor, Cze, WGe, F*, 1973 *Sp, Mor, Ar, Ar, WGe, F*, 1974 *Mor, Cze, EGe, F, Cze*, 1975 *It, Sp, Pol, F*
P Niculescu 1958 *It*, 1959 *EGe, Cze*
V Niculescu 1938 *F, Ger*
F Nistor 1986 *Tun*
V Nistor 1959 *EGe, Pol, EGe*

M Oblomenco 1967 *It, Pt, WGe, F*
G Olarasu 2000 *Mor, H*
M Olarasu 2000 *Mor*
V Onutu 1967 *It, Pt, Pol, WGe, F*, 1968 *Cze*, 1969 *F*, 1971 *It, Mor*
N Oprea 2000 *It*, 2001 *Pt, Sp, H, Rus, Geo, I, W, E*

F Opris 1986 *F, Tun, Tun, Pt, F, I,* 1987 *F*
G Oprisor 2004 *W, J, CZR,* 2005 *Rus, Ukr, J, US, S, Pt*
T Oroian 1988 *F, W,* 1989 *It, E, Sp, Z, USS,* 1990 *Sp, It,* 1993 *Pt, Tun, F, Sp, I,* 1994 *Sp, Ger, Rus, It, W, It, E,* 1995 *F, S, J, J, C*
M Ortelecan 1972 *Mor, Cze, WGe, F,* 1974 *Pol,* 1976 *It, Sp, USS, Bul, F,* 1977 *Sp, It, F, Pol, It, F,* 1978 *Cze, Sp,* 1979 *F,* 1980 *USS*

A Palosanu 1952 *EGe, EGe,* 1955 *Cze,* 1957 *F, Cze*
E Pana 1937 *F, Ger*
M Paraschiv 1975 *Sp, JAB, Pol, F,* 1976 *H, It, Sp, USS, Bul, F, Mor,* 1977 *Sp, It, Pol, F,* 1978 *Cze, Sp, Pol, F,* 1979 *It, Sp, W,* 1980 *It, I, F,* 1981 *It, USS, S, NZ, F,* 1982 *WGe, It, USS, Z, Z, F,* 1983 *Mor, WGe, It, USS, Pol, W, USS, F,* 1984 *It, S, F,* 1985 *E, It, Tun, USS, USS, It,* 1986 *Pt, S, Tun,* 1987 *It, USS, Z, F, S, USS, F*
G Parcalabescu 1940 *It,* 1942 *It,* 1949 *Cze,* 1951 *EGe,* 1952 *EGe, EGe,* 1953 *It,* 1955 *Cze,* 1957 *Cze, Bel, F,* 1958 *It,* 1959 *EGe, Pol, Cze,* 1960 *Pol, EGe, Cze*
G Pasache 2001 *E*
V Pascu 1983 *It, Pol, W, USS, F,* 1984 *It,* 1985 *USS,* 1986 *Pt, S, F, Tun, I,* 1987 *F,* 1988 *It*
C Patrichi 1993 *Pt, Tun*
A Pavlovici 1972 *Mor, Cze*
A Penciu 1955 *Cze,* 1957 *F, Cze, Bel, F,* 1958 *Sp, WGe, EGe, It,* 1959 *EGe, Pol, Cze, EGe,* 1960 *F,* 1961 *Pol, EGe, Cze, EGe, F,* 1962 *Cze, EGe, Pol, It, F,* 1963 *Bul, Cze, F,* 1964 *WGe, F,* 1965 *WGe, F,* 1966 *It, F,* 1967 *F*
I Peter 1973 *Sp, Mor*
AA Petrache 1998 *H, Pol,* 1999 *F, S, A, US, I,* 2000 *Mor, H, Pt, Sp, Geo, F,* 2001 *W, E,* 2002 *Pt, Sp, H, Rus, I, It, Sp, W, S, S,* 2003 *Pt, Sp, Rus,* 2004 *It, W, J, CZR*
CC Petre 2001 *E,* 2002 *Pt, Sp, H, Rus, Geo, I, It, Sp, W, S, S,* 2003 *Pt, Rus, Geo, CZR, F, W, I, A, Ar, Nm,* 2004 *CZR, Pt, Sp, Rus, Geo, It, W, J, CZR,* 2005 *Rus, Geo, Ukr, J, US, S, Pt, C, I,* 2006 *Geo, CZR, Pt, Ukr, Rus, F, Geo, Sp, S,* 2007 *Geo, Sp, CZR, ESp, ItA, Nm, It, S, Pt, NZ,* 2008 *Sp, Rus,* 2009 *Ger, Pt, Ur, F, ItA, ItA,* 2010 *Ger, Rus, Geo, Pt, Sp, Tun, Ur, Ur,* 2011 *Pt, Rus, Geo, Sp, Nm, ArJ, Ukr, S, Ar, E, Geo*
SA Petrichei 2002 *I, S, S,* 2003 *Sp, Rus, Geo, CZR, F, W, I, Ar, Nm,* 2004 *Pt, Sp, Rus, Geo,* 2007 *ESp, Nm,* 2009 *Ur, ItA, ItA, Fj*
P Petrisor 1985 *It,* 1987 *USS*
H Peuciulescu 1927 *F*
M Picoiu 2001 *Pt, H,* 2002 *Pt, Sp, H, Rus, I, It, Sp, W*
A Pilotschi 1985 *It, Tun,* 1987 *S*
C Pinghert 1996 *Bel*
I Pintea 1974 *Pol,* 1976 *Pol, F, Mor,* 1977 *Sp, It, F, Pol, It, F,* 1979 *It, Sp, USS, W, Pol, F,* 1980 *It, USS*
D Piti 1987 *USS, F,* 1988 *It, Sp, US,* 1991 *S*
T Pllotschi 2011 *Sp*
Plumea 1927 *Ger*
S Podarescu 1979 *Pol, F,* 1980 *USS,* 1982 *WGe, It, USS, F,* 1983 *Mor, WGe, USS, F,* 1984 *It,* 1985 *E, It*
C Podea 2001 *Geo, I,* 2002 *I, It, Sp, W, S,* 2003 *Pt, Sp, Rus, F, A*
R Polizu 1919 *US*
A Pop 1970 *It,* 1971 *It, Mor,* 1972 *Mor, Cze, F,* 1973 *WGe, F,* 1974 *Mor, Pol, Sp, EGe, F, Cze,* 1975 *It, Sp, JAB, Pol, F*
D Popa 1993 *Tun, F, Sp*
I Popa 1934 *It,* 1936 *F, It, Ger,* 1937 *H, F,* 1938 *F, Ger,* 1939 *It,* 1940 *It,* 1942 *It*
M Popa 1962 *EGe*
N Popa 1952 *EGe*
V Poparlan 2007 *Nm, Pt,* 2008 *Geo, Sp, Pt, Ur, Rus, ESp,* 2009 *Sp, Ger, Rus, Geo,* 2011 *Pt, Rus, Geo, Sp, ArJ, Ukr, S, Ar, E, Geo*
A Popean 1999 *S,* 2001 *Pt, H*
C Popescu 1986 *Tun, Pt, F*
CD Popescu 1997 *Bel,* 2003 *CZR, F, W, I, A, Ar, Nm,* 2004 *CZR, Pt, Sp, Rus, Geo, J, CZR,* 2005 *Rus, S, Pt, C,* 2006 *CZR, Ukr, Rus, F, Geo, Sp, S,* 2007 *Geo, Sp, CZR, ESp, ItA, Nm, It, Pt,* 2009 *Ur, F, ItA,* 2010 *Geo, Pt, Sp, Ukr, Ukr, ArJ, ItA, Tun, Ur, Ur,* 2011 *Pt, Rus, ArJ*
I Popescu 1958 *EGe*
I Popescu 2001 *Pt, Sp, H, Rus, Geo*
C Popescu-Colibasi 1934 *It*
V Popisteanu 1996 *Pt, F, Pol*
F Popovici 1973 *Sp, Mor*
N Postolache 1972 *WGe, F,* 1973 *Sp, Mor, WGe, F,* 1974 *Mor, Pol, Sp, EGe, F, Cze,* 1975 *It, Sp, Pol, F,* 1976 *H, It*
C Preda 1961 *Pol, Cze,* 1962 *EGe, F,* 1963 *Bul, EGe, Cze, F,* 1964 *Cze, EGe, WGe, F*

NF Racean 1988 *USS, USS, F, W,* 1989 *It, E, Z, Sa, USS,* 1990 *H, Sp, It, USS,* 1991 *NZ, F, F, C, Fj,* 1992 *Sp, It, USS, F, It, Ar,* 1993 *Pt, Tun, F, Sp,* 1994 *Ger, Rus, It, W,* 1995 *F, S, J, J, C, SA, A*
A Radoi 2008 *CZR,* 2009 *ItA, Fj,* 2010 *Sp, Ukr, Ukr, Nm, ArJ, ItA, Tun,* 2011 *Geo, Sp, ArJ, Ukr*
M Radoi 1995 *F,* 1996 *Pt, Pol,* 1997 *WalA, F, W, Bel, Ar, F, It,* 1998 *H, Pol, Ukr*
P Radoi 1980 *Mor*
T Radu 1991 *NZ*
C Raducanu 1985 *It,* 1987 *It, USS, Z, F, S,* 1989 *It, E, Sp, Z*
A Radulescu 1980 *USS, Pol,* 1981 *It, Sp, USS, S, F,* 1982 *WGe, It, USS, Z, Z,* 1983 *Pol, W, USS, F,* 1984 *It, S, F, Sp,* 1985 *E, USS,* 1988 *It, Sp, US, USS, USS, F, W,* 1989 *It, E, Sa, USS,* 1990 *It, F, H, Sp, It, USS*
T Radulescu 1958 *Sp, WGe,* 1959 *EGe, Pol, Cze, EGe,* 1963 *Bul, EGe, Cze,* 1964 *F,* 1965 *WGe, F,* 1966 *Cze*
D Rascanu 1972 *WGe, F*
G Rascanu 1966 *It, F,* 1967 *It, Pt, Pol, WGe, F,* 1968 *Cze, Cze, F,* 1969 *Pol, WGe, Cze, F,* 1970 *It, F,* 1971 *It, Mor, F,* 1972 *Mor, Cze, WGe, F,* 1974 *Sp*
C Ratiu 2003 *CZR,* 2005 *J, US, S, Pt, C, I,* 2006 *CZR, Pt, Ukr, Rus, F, Geo, Sp, S,* 2007 *Sp, CZR, ESp, It, S, Pt, NZ, Rus, Pt,* 2009 *Geo, Pt,* 2010 *Sp,* 2011 *Nm, ArJ, Ukr, E*
I Ratiu 1992 *It*
S Rentea 2000 *Mor*
I Roman 1976 *Bul*
C Rosu 1993 *I*
I Rotaru 1995 *J, J, C, Ar, It,* 1996 *Pt, F, Pol,* 1997 *W, Bel, Ar, F*
L Rotaru 1999 *F, A, I*
N Rus 2007 *Rus*
VS Rus 2007 *Rus, Pt,* 2008 *Geo, Pt, Rus,* 2009 *F, ItA, Fj*
M Rusu 1959 *EGe,* 1960 *F,* 1961 *Pol, Cze,* 1962 *Cze, EGe, Pol, It, F,* 1963 *Bul, EGe, Cze, F,* 1964 *WGe, F,* 1965 *WGe, F,* 1966 *Cze, It, F,* 1967 *It, Pt, Pol*
V Rusu 1960 *Pol, EGe, Cze,* 1961 *EGe, F,* 1962 *Cze, EGe, Pol, It, F,* 1964 *Cze, EGe, WGe, F,* 1965 *WGe,* 1966 *It, F,* 1967 *WGe,* 1968 *Cze*

I Sadoveanu 1939 *It,* 1942 *It*
AA Salageanu 1995 *Ar, F, It,* 1996 *Pt, F, Pol,* 1997 *W, Bel, F*
V Samuil 2000 *It,* 2001 *Pt, E,* 2002 *Pt, Sp, Geo*
C Sasu 1989 *Z,* 1991 *It, NZ, F, S, F, C, Fj,* 1993 *I*
C Sauan 1999 *S, A, US, I,* 2000 *It,* 2002 *Geo, I, It, Sp,* 2003 *Pt, Rus, Geo, CZR, F, W, I, A, Ar, Nm,* 2004 *CZR, Pt, Sp, Rus, Geo, It, W, J, CZR,* 2005 *Rus, Geo, Ukr, J, US, S, Pt,* 2006 *Rus,* 2007 *Geo*
G Sava 1989 *Z, S,* 1990 *H, Sp, It, USS,* 1991 *It, F, S, F, C,* 1992 *Sp*
I Sava 1959 *EGe, Pol, Cze, EGe,* 1960 *F,* 1961 *Pol, EGe, Cze, EGe, F,* 1962 *Cze, Pol, It, F*
C Scarlat 1976 *H, Sp,* 1977 *F,* 1978 *Cze, Sp,* 1979 *It, Sp, USS, W, Pol, F,* 1980 *It, USS,* 1982 *USS*
R Schmettau 1919 *US, F*
V Sebe 1960 *Pol, EGe, Cze*
I Seceleanu 1992 *It, USS, F, It, Ar,* 1993 *Pt, Tun, F, Sp, F*
S Seceleanu 1986 *Pt, F, I,* 1990 *It*
E Septar 1996 *Bel, Pol,* 1997 *WalA, W,* 1998 *Pol, Ukr, I,* 1999 *F, S, A, US, I,* 2000 *It*
B Serban 1989 *Sa, USS, S,* 1990 *It,* 1992 *It, USS*
C Serban 1964 *Cze, EGe, WGe,* 1967 *Pol,* 1968 *Cze, F,* 1969 *Pol, WGe, Cze, F,* 1970 *It, F,* 1971 *It, Mor, F,* 1972 *F,* 1973 *WGe, F,* 1974 *Mor*
M Serbu 1967 *It*
E Sfetescu 1924 *F, US,* 1927 *Cze*
E Sfetescu 1934 *It,* 1936 *F, Ger,* 1937 *It*
G Sfetescu 1927 *F, Ger*
M Sfetescu 1924 *F, US,* 1927 *Ger, Cze*
N Sfetescu 1927 *F, Ger, Cze*
G Simion 1998 *H*
G Simion 1919 *US*
I Simion 1976 *H, It, Sp,* 1979 *Pol, F,* 1980 *F*
ML Sirbe 2008 *CZR,* 2010 *Ukr, Ukr, Nm, ArJ, Tun,* 2011 *Pt, Nm*
L Sirbu 1996 *Pt,* 2000 *Mor, H, Pt, Geo, F,* 2001 *H, Rus, Geo, I, W, E,* 2002 *Pt, Sp, H, Rus, I, It, S, S,* 2003 *Pt, Sp, CZR, F, W, I, A, Ar, Nm,* 2004 *Pt, Sp, Rus, Geo, It, W, CZR,* 2005 *Rus, Geo, Ukr, J, US, S, Pt, C,* 2006 *Geo, Pt, Ukr, Rus, F, Geo, Sp,* 2007 *Geo, ItA, It, S, Pt, NZ,* 2009 *Ur, F, ItA, ItA, Fj,* 2010 *Ger, Rus, Geo, Pt, Sp, Nm, ArJ, ItA, Ur, Ur,* 2011 *Rus, Nm, Ukr, S, E*
M Slobozeanu 1936 *F,* 1937 *H, F, Ger,* 1938 *F, Ger*
OS Slusariuc 1993 *Tun,* 1995 *J, J, C,* 1996 *Pt, F,* 1997 *Bel, Ar, F,* 1998 *H, Ar, Geo, I,* 1999 *F, S, A*
S Soare 2001 *I, W,* 2002 *Geo*
S Soare 1924 *F, US*
M Socaciu 2000 *It,* 2001 *I, W, E,* 2002 *It, W, S, S,* 2003 *Pt, Sp, Rus, Geo, CZR, F, W, I, A, Nm,* 2004 *CZR, Pt, Sp, Rus, Geo, It, W, J, CZR,* 2005 *Rus, Geo, Ukr, J, US, Pt, C, I,* 2006 *CZR*
S Socol 2001 *Sp, H, Rus, Geo,* 2002 *Pt, It, Sp, W,* 2003 *Sp, Rus, Geo, F, W, I, A, Ar, Nm,* 2004 *CZR, Pt, Sp, Rus, Geo,* 2005 *Rus, Geo, Ukr, C, I,* 2006 *Geo, CZR, Pt, Ukr, Rus, F, Geo, Sp, S,* 2007 *Geo, Sp, CZR, It, S, Pt, NZ,* 2009 *Ur, F, ItA, Fj,* 2010 *Ger, Rus, Geo, Pt, Sp, Ukr, Ukr, Nm, ArJ, ItA, Ur, Ur,* 2011 *Rus, Geo*

N Soculescu 1949 *Cze*, 1951 *EGe*, 1952 *EGe*, *EGe*, 1953 *It*, 1955 *Cze*
N Soculescu 1927 *Ger*
V Soculescu 1927 *Cze*
GL Solomie 1992 *Sp*, *F*, *It*, *Ar*, 1993 *Pt*, *Tun*, *F*, *Sp*, *F*, *I*, 1994 *Sp*, *Ger*, *W*, *It*, *E*, 1995 *F*, *S*, *J*, *J*, *C*, *SA*, *A*, *Ar*, *F*, *It*, 1996 *Pt*, *F*, *Pol*, 1997 *WalA*, *F*, *W*, *Bel*, *Ar*, *F*, *It*, 1998 *H*, *Pol*, *Ukr*, *Ar*, *Geo*, *I*, 1999 *S*, *A*, *US*, *I*, 2000 *Sp*, *F*, *It*, 2001 *Sp*, *H*, *Rus*
C Stan 1990 *H*, *USS*, 1991 *It*, *F*, *S*, *F*, *C*, *Fj*, 1992 *Sp*, *It*, *It*, *Ar*, 1996 *Pt*, *Bel*, *F*, *Pol*, 1997 *WalA*, *F*, *W*, *Bel*, 1998 *Ar*, *Geo*, 1999 *F*, *S*, *A*, *US*, *I*
A Stanca 1996 *Pt*, *Pol*
R Stanca 1997 *F*, 2003 *Sp*, *Rus*, 2009 *Geo*, *Pt*
A Stanciu 1958 *EGe*, *It*
G Stanciu 1958 *EGe*, *It*
C Stanescu 1957 *Bel*, 1958 *WGe*, 1959 *EGe*, 1960 *F*, 1961 *Pol*, *EGe*, *Cze*, 1962 *Cze*, *It*, *F*, 1963 *Bul*, *EGe*, *Cze*, *F*, 1964 *WGe*, *F*, 1966 *Cze*, *It*
C Stefan 1951 *EGe*, 1952 *EGe*
E Stoian 1927 *Cze*
E Stoica 1973 *Ar*, *Ar*, 1974 *Cze*, 1975 *Sp*, *Pol*, *F*, 1976 *Sp*, *USS*, *Bul*, *F*, *Mor*, 1977 *Sp*, *It*, *F*, *Pol*, *It*, *F*, 1978 *Cze*, *Sp*, *Pol*, *F*, 1979 *It*, *Sp*, *USS*, *W*, *Pol*, *F*, 1980 *It*, *USS*, *I*, *Pol*, *F*, 1981 *It*, *Sp*, *USS*, *S*, *NZ*, *F*, 1982 *WGe*, *It*, *USS*, *Z*, *Z*, *F*
G Stoica 1963 *Bul*, *Cze*, 1964 *WGe*, 1966 *It*, *F*, 1967 *Pt*, *F*, 1968 *Cze*, *Cze*, *F*, 1969 *Pol*
I Stroe 1986 *Pt*
E Suciu 1976 *Bul*, *Pol*, 1977 *It*, *F*, *It*, 1979 *USS*, *Pol*, *F*, 1981 *Sp*
M Suciu 1968 *F*, 1969 *Pol*, *WGe*, *Cze*, 1970 *It*, *F*, 1971 *It*, *Mor*, *F*, 1972 *Mor*, *F*
O Sugar 1983 *It*, 1989 *Z*, *Sa*, *USS*, *S*, 1991 *NZ*, *F*
K Suiogan 1996 *Bel*
F Surugiu 2008 *Ur*, *Rus*, *ESp*, 2010 *Ukr*, *Ukr*, *Nm*, *ArJ*, *ItA*, 2011 *Pt*, *Rus*, *Geo*, *Sp*, *ArJ*, *Ukr*, *S*, *Ar*, *Geo*

D Talaba 1996 *Bel*, 1997 *F*, *It*
C Tanase 1938 *F*, *Ger*, 1939 *It*, 1940 *It*
A Tanasescu 1919 *F*, 1924 *F*, *US*
N Tanoviceanu 1937 *It*, *H*, *F*, 1939 *It*
I Tarabega 1934 *It*, 1936 *It*
F Tasca 2008 *Ur*, *Rus*, *ESp*, 2009 *Sp*, *Ger*, *Rus*, *Geo*, *Pt*
V Tata 1971 *F*, 1973 *Ar*, *Ar*
CF Tatu 2003 *Ar*, 2004 *CZR*, *Pt*, *Sp*, *Rus*, *Geo*, *It*, *W*, 2005 *Ukr*, *J*
I Tatucu 1973 *Sp*, *Mor*, 1974 *Cze*, *F*
D Teleasa 1971 *It*, 1973 *Sp*, *Ar*, *Ar*
D Tenescu 1951 *EGe*
I Teodorescu 2001 *I*, *W*, *E*, 2002 *Pt*, *Sp*, *S*, *S*, 2003 *Pt*, *Sp*, *Rus*, *W*, *I*, *A*, *Ar*, *Nm*, 2004 *CZR*, *Pt*, *Sp*, *Rus*, *Geo*, *W*, *J*, *CZR*, 2005 *Rus*, *Geo*, *Ukr*, *J*, *US*, *S*, *Pt*, *C*, *I*, 2006 *Geo*, *CZR*, *Pt*, *Ukr*, *F*, *Geo*, *S*, 2007 *ESp*, *ItA*
I Teodorescu 1958 *Sp*, *WGe*, *EGe*, *It*, 1960 *Pol*, *EGe*, *Cze*, 1963 *Bul*, *EGe*, *Cze*, 1965 *WGe*, *F*
A Teofilovici 1957 *F*, *Cze*, *Bel*, *F*, 1958 *Sp*, *WGe*, 1959 *EGe*, 1960 *F*, 1961 *Pol*, *EGe*, *Cze*, *EGe*, *F*, 1962 *Cze*, *Pol*, *It*, *F*, 1963 *Bul*, *EGe*, *Cze*, *F*, 1964 *WGe*
O Tepurica 1985 *USS*
M Tibuleac 1957 *Bel*, *F*, 1959 *Pol*, *Cze*, 1966 *Cze*, 1967 *It*, *Pt*, *Pol*, *WGe*, 1968 *Cze*, *Cze*
G Ticlean 1919 *F*
M Tigora 2004 *CZR*
A Tinca 1987 *USS*, *F*
VM Tincu 2002 *Pt*, *Sp*, *H*, *Rus*, *Geo*, *I*, *It*, *Sp*, *S*, *S*, 2003 *Pt*, *Sp*, *Rus*, *Geo*, *F*, *W*, 2004 *Sp*, 2005 *Geo*, *Ukr*, *C*, *I*, 2006 *Geo*, *CZR*, *F*, *S*, 2007 *Geo*, *Sp*, *CZR*, *ESp*, *ItA*, *Nm*, *It*, *S*, *Pt*, *NZ*, 2008 *Geo*, 2009 *F*, *ItA*, *ItA*, 2010 *Ger*, *Rus*, *Geo*, *Pt*, *Ur*, *Ur*, 2011 *Nm*, *S*, *Ar*, *F*, *Geo*
M Toader 1982 *WGe*, 1984 *Sp*, 1985 *E*, *It*, *Tun*, *USS*, 1986 *S*, *F*, *Tun*, *Tun*, *Pt*, *F*, *I*, 1987 *It*, *USS*, *Z*, *F*, *S*, *USS*, *F*, 1988 *F*, *W*, 1989 *It*, *E*, *Sp*, *Sa*, *USS*, *S*, 1990 *It*, *F*, *It*
P Toderasc 2000 *It*, 2001 *Pt*, *Rus*, *Geo*, *W*, *E*, 2002 *H*, *Rus*, *Geo*, *I*, *It*, *Sp*, *W*, *S*, *S*, 2003 *Sp*, *Rus*, *Geo*, *CZR*, *F*, *W*, *I*, *A*, *Ar*, *Nm*, 2004 *CZR*, *Pt*, *Sp*, *Rus*, *Geo*, *It*, *J*, *CZR*, 2005 *J*, *US*, *S*, *Pt*, *C*, *I*, 2006 *Geo*, *Pt*, *Ukr*, *Sp*, 2007 *Geo*, *ESp*, *ItA*, *Nm*, *It*, *S*, 2009 *ItA*, *Fj*
IR Tofan 1997 *Bel*, *Ar*, *F*, *It*, 1998 *H*, *Ar*, 1999 *I*, 2000 *Mor*, *Sp*, *Geo*, 2001 *Pt*, *Sp*, *H*, *Geo*, *I*, *W*, *E*, 2002 *Pt*, *Sp*, *H*, *Rus*, *Geo*, *I*, *It*, *Sp*, *W*, *S*, *S*, 2003 *Pt*, *Sp*, *Rus*, *Geo*, *CZR*, *F*, *W*, *I*, *A*, *Ar*, *Nm*, 2004 *Sp*, *Geo*, *It*, *W*, *J*, 2005 *Rus*, *Geo*, *Ukr*, *J*, *US*, *I*, 2006 *Geo*, *CZR*, *Pt*, *Geo*, *Sp*, *S*, 2007 *Geo*, *ESp*, *ItA*, *Nm*, *S*
S Tofan 1985 *USS*, *It*, 1986 *Tun*, *Pt*, *F*, *I*, 1987 *It*, *USS*, *Z*, *F*, *S*, *USS*, *F*, 1988 *It*, *Sp*, *US*, *USS*, 1991 *NZ*, 1992 *Ar*, 1993 *Pt*, 1994 *It*, *E*
O Tonita 2000 *Mor*, *H*, *Pt*, *Sp*, *Geo*, *F*, 2001 *Pt*, *Sp*, *H*, *Rus*, *Geo*, *I*, 2002 *Sp*, *It*, *Sp*, *W*, 2003 *Rus*, *Geo*, *F*, *W*, *I*, *A*, *Ar*, *Nm*, 2004 *Sp*, *Rus*, *Geo*, *It*, 2005 *Rus*, *Pt*, *C*, *I*, 2006 *Geo*, *Pt*, *Geo*, *Sp*, *S*, 2007 *Sp*, *CZR*, *It*, *S*, *Pt*, *NZ*, 2009 *Ur*, *F*, *ItA*, *ItA*, *Fj*, 2010 *Ger*, *Rus*, *Geo*, *Pt*, *Nm*, *ArJ*, *ItA*, *Ur*, *Ur*, 2011 *Pt*, *Rus*, *ArJ*, *Ukr*, *S*, *Ar*, *E*, *Geo*
Traian 1942 *It*
N Tranca 1992 *Sp*
B Tudor 2003 *CZR*, *A*
F Tudor 1924 *F*, *US*
M Tudor 1924 *F*, *US*
AM Tudori 2003 *F*, *W*, *I*, *A*, *Ar*, *Nm*, 2004 *Sp*, *Rus*, *Geo*, *W*, *J*, *CZR*, 2005 *Rus*, *Geo*, *Ukr*, *J*, *US*, *S*, *Pt*, 2006 *Geo*, *CZR*, *Ukr*, *Rus*, *F*, 2007 *Sp*, *CZR*, *ESp*, *ItA*, *Nm*, *It*, *S*, *Pt*, 2009 *Geo*, *Ur*, *ItA*
D Tudosa 1999 *S*, 2002 *Geo*, *I*, *It*, 2003 *Pt*, *W*
T Tudose 1977 *It*, 1978 *Cze*, *Sp*, *Pol*, *F*, 1979 *It*, *Sp*, *USS*, 1980 *USS*
V Tufa 1985 *USS*, 1986 *Pt*, *S*, 1990 *It*, 1991 *F*, 1995 *F*, *S*, *J*, *J*, *SA*, *A*, 1996 *Pt*, *F*, *Pol*
D Tunaru 1985 *It*
V Turlea 1974 *Sp*, 1975 *JAB*, *Pol*, *F*, 1977 *Pol*
C Turut 1937 *H*, 1938 *F*
I Tutuianu 1960 *Pol*, *EGe*, 1963 *Bul*, *EGe*, *Cze*, 1964 *Cze*, *EGe*, *WGe*, 1965 *WGe*, *F*, 1966 *Cze*, *It*, *F*, 1967 *Pt*, *Pol*, *WGe*, *F*, 1968 *Cze*, *Cze*, *F*, 1969 *Pol*, *WGe*, *Cze*, *F*, 1970 *It*, *F*, 1971 *F*
G Tutunea 1992 *Sp*

M Ungur 1996 *Bel*
V Ungureanu 1979 *It*
V Urdea 1979 *F*
SF Ursache 2009 *ItA*, 2010 *Ukr*, *Nm*
V Ursache 2004 *It*, *W*, *CZR*, 2005 *S*, *C*, 2006 *Geo*, *Ukr*, *Rus*, *F*, *S*, 2007 *Geo*, *Sp*, *CZR*, *ESp*, *ItA*, *Nm*, *Pt*, *NZ*, *Rus*, 2008 *Pt*, *Rus*, *CZR*, *Rus*, 2009 *ItA*, *Fj*, 2010 *Ger*, *Rus*, *Geo*, *Pt*, *Sp*, *Ukr*, *Ukr*, *Nm*, *ArJ*, *ItA*, *Tun*, *Ur*, *Ur*, 2011 *Geo*, *Sp*, *Nm*, *ArJ*, *S*, *Ar*, *Geo*

R Vacioiu 1977 *It*, *F*, *It*
E Valeriu 1949 *Cze*, 1952 *EGe*
M Vardala 1924 *F*, *US*
N Vardela 1927 *F*, *Ger*
G Varga 1976 *It*, *USS*, *Bul*, *Pol*, *F*, *Mor*, 1977 *Sp*, *It*, *F*, *Pol*, 1978 *Sp*
N Varta 1958 *EGe*
G Varzaru 1980 *Mor*, *I*, *Pol*, *F*, 1981 *It*, *Sp*, *USS*, *F*, 1983 *Mor*, *WGe*, *It*, *USS*, *F*, 1984 *S*, *F*, 1985 *Tun*, *USS*, 1986 *F*, 1988 *It*, *Sp*, *US*, *USS*, *USS*
Z Vasluianu 1989 *Sp*, *Z*, *Sa*
P Veluda 1967 *It*, *Pt*, *Pol*, *WGe*, *F*, 1968 *Cze*, *Cze*
R Veluda 1949 *Cze*, 1952 *EGe*
N Veres 1986 *Tun*, *Pt*, 1987 *F*, *USS*, *F*, 1988 *It*, *Sp*, *USS*
M Vidrascu 1919 *US*, *F*
P Vidrascu 1919 *US*, 1924 *F*, *US*, 1927 *Cze*
M Vioreanu 1994 *E*, 1998 *H*, *Pol*, *Ukr*, *Ar*, *Geo*, *I*, 1999 *F*, *S*, *A*, *US*, *I*, 2000 *Mor*, *Pt*, *Sp*, *Geo*, *F*, 2001 *Geo*, 2002 *Rus*, *Geo*, *I*, *It*, *Sp*, 2003 *Sp*, *Rus*, *F*, *I*, *A*, *Ar*, *Nm*
A Visan 1949 *Cze*
D Vlad 2005 *US*, *S*, *C*, *I*, 2006 *Rus*, 2007 *Sp*, *CZR*, *It*, *Rus*, *Pt*, 2008 *Sp*, *CZR*
G Vlad 1991 *C*, *Fj*, 1992 *Sp*, *It*, *USS*, *F*, *It*, *Ar*, 1993 *Pt*, *F*, *I*, 1994 *Sp*, *Ger*, *Rus*, *It*, *W*, *It*, *E*, 1995 *F*, *C*, *SA*, *A*, *Ar*, *It*, 1996 *Pt*, *F*, 1997 *W*, *Ar*, *F*, *It*, 1998 *Ar*
V Vlad 1980 *Mor*
FA Vlaicu 2006 *Ukr*, *F*, *Geo*, *Sp*, *S*, 2007 *Geo*, *Sp*, *CZR*, *ESp*, *ItA*, *Nm*, *S*, *NZ*, *Pt*, 2008 *Geo*, *Pt*, *Rus*, *CZR*, *Ur*, 2009 *Sp*, *Ger*, *Rus*, *Geo*, *Pt*, *Ur*, *F*, *ItA*, *ItA*, *Fj*, 2010 *Ger*, *Rus*, *Geo*, *Sp*, *Ukr*, *Ukr*, *ArJ*, *ItA*, *Tun*, *Ur*, 2011 *Pt*, *Rus*, *Geo*, *Sp*, *Nm*, *ArJ*, *Ukr*, *S*, *Ar*, *E*, *Geo*
C Vlasceanu 2000 *Mor*, *Pt*, *Sp*, *Geo*, *F*
B Voicu 2003 *CZR*, 2004 *CZR*, *Pt*, *Sp*, *Rus*, *It*, *J*, 2005 *J*, *Pt*
M Voicu 1979 *Pol*
M Voicu 2002 *Pt*
V Voicu 1951 *EGe*, 1952 *EGe*, *EGe*, 1953 *It*, 1955 *Cze*
R Voinov 1985 *It*, 1986 *Pt*, *S*, *F*, *Tun*
P Volvoreanu 1924 *US*
G Vraca 1919 *US*, *F*
M Vusec 1959 *EGe*, *Pol*, *Cze*, *EGe*, 1960 *F*, 1961 *Pol*, *EGe*, *Cze*, *EGe*, *F*, 1962 *Cze*, *EGe*, *Pol*, *It*, *F*, 1963 *Bul*, *EGe*, *Cze*, *F*, 1964 *WGe*, *F*, 1965 *WGe*, *F*, 1966 *It*, *F*, 1967 *It*, *Pt*, *Pol*, *WGe*, *F*, 1968 *Cze*, *Cze*, *F*, 1969 *Pol*, *F*
RL Vusec 1998 *Geo*, *I*, 1999 *F*, *S*, *A*, *US*, *I*, 2000 *Mor*, *H*, *Pt*, *Sp*, *F*, 2002 *H*, *Rus*, *I*

F Wirth 1934 *It*

I Zafiescu 1979 *W*, *Pol*, *F*
M Zafiescu 1980 *Mor*, 1986 *I*
D Zamfir 1949 *Cze*
B Zebega Suman 2004 *CZR*, *Pt*, *Rus*, *Geo*, *It*, *W*, *CZR*, 2005 *Rus*, *Ukr*, *US*, *S*, 2006 *Ukr*, *Sp*, 2007 *Rus*, *Pt*, 2008 *Geo*, *Pt*, *Rus*, *CZR*, *Ur*, 2010 *Ger*, *Sp*, *Ukr*, *Ukr*, *Nm*, *ArJ*, 2011 *Pt*, *Rus*, *Geo*, *Sp*, *Nm*, *ArJ*, *Ukr*, *S*, *E*
D Zlatoianu 1958 *Sp*, *WGe*, *EGe*, *It*, 1959 *EGe*, 1960 *Pol*, *EGe*, *Cze*, 1961 *EGe*, *EGe*, *F*, 1964 *Cze*, *EGe*, 1966 *Cze*

RUSSIA

RUSSIA'S 2010–11 TEST RECORD

OPPONENT	DATE	VENUE	RESULT
Argentina Jaguars	23 Oct	H	**Lost** 20–40
Argentina Jaguars	30 Oct	H	**Lost** 6–32
Japan	6 Nov	A	**Lost** 3–75
Spain	5 Feb	A	**Won** 28–24
Portugal	12 Feb	H	**Lost** 19–21
Romania	26 Feb	A	**Lost** 3–33
Ukraine	12 Mar	A	**Lost** 5–41
Georgia	19 Mar	H	**Lost** 9–15
Canada	8 Jun	N	**Lost** 18–34
Italy A	12 Jun	N	**Lost** 19–24
USA	18 Jun	N	**Lost** 25–32
USA	15 Sep	N	**Lost** 6–13
Italy	20 Sep	N	**Lost** 17–53
Ireland	25 Sep	N	**Lost** 12–62
Australia	1 Oct	N	**Lost** 22–68

FUTURE IS BRIGHT FOR THE RUSSIANS

By Karen Bond

Mark Kolbe/Getty Images

Vladislav Korshunov led his side superbly in New Zealand.

While many nations arrived in New Zealand with the intention of returning home with the Webb Ellis Cup, the Russian squad could have been forgiven for feeling as though they had already won it simply by being at Rugby World Cup 2011.

They had had 18 months to prepare for their debut on the sport's greatest stage since qualification was confirmed following a 21–21 draw with Romania in the European Nations Cup in February 2010, but it was perhaps only on arrival in the Land of the Long White Cloud that the significance for Russian rugby, not just for the present but also the long-term, truly hit home.

"We are shocked by the attention that is given to rugby in New Zealand," admitted coach Nikolay Nerush in the days leading up to Russia's first RWC match against the USA in New Plymouth on 15 September. "We seem to be more popular here in Blenheim than we are in our country. However, looking at the sport's development in New Zealand is encouraging as it gives us new impetus to carry on our efforts."

His captain Vladislav Korshunov echoed this sentiment, hopeful that "our presence here at the World Cup should let other Russian players know that they can also achieve that and hopefully do even better."

The excitement continued to build in the Russian ranks as they watched the opening weekend of the tournament unfold with smaller nations giving the Tier 1 teams a few scares, counting down the days until they became the final team to begin their RWC 2011 campaign.

The Pool C encounter with the Eagles had been dubbed "the clash of the superpowers" and banners proclaiming "we won the space race" could be seen in the stands at Stadium Taranaki as fans braved the freezing rain to create a lively atmosphere on the night.

There was to be no fairytale debut victory for Russia, though, with the USA running out 13–6 winners to end a six-match losing streak dating back to RWC 2003. It was not for want of trying and the Eagles had to man a rearguard action in the final 10 minutes to keep their try-line intact, but the set piece let Russia down with six lineouts lost on their own throw.

Yury Kushnarev will go down in the history books as Russia's first RWC point scorer with his third-minute penalty, but the fly-half and USA full-back Chris Wyles did not have the best of nights with the boot, making Mike Petri's try the difference between the two sides at the final whistle.

"Certain errors cost us the game," admitted Russia team director Kingsley Jones. "We didn't use our opportunities. Unfortunately, the lineouts didn't function, but the team have come a long way to be competing right until the end of the game."

The chance of a victory in their debut tournament had gone with Italy, Ireland and Australia to come, but Russia were still determined to leave their mark, starting against the Azzurri five days later, with centre Konstantin Rachkov admitting "we have not come to the World Cup to play just one game."

Before the Italy match came round, though, there was cause for No. 8 Victor Gresev to celebrate after his wife gave birth to a daughter back home. "It is really weird that a few of the greatest events in my life have coincided at the time when I am that far from my home in Russia. All my thoughts are with my family right now, but I wouldn't say that they distract me much from my performance. On the contrary, it gives me extra emotions. I should definitely double my efforts since I will play for my whole family, and especially for its new member."

Gresev was drafted into the starting line-up to face Italy at Trafalgar Park, but the Bears were overwhelmed in the first half as the Azzurri wrapped up the bonus point in just 23 minutes en route to a 38–7 lead at half-time. Russia had, though, scored their first RWC try through Alexander Yanyushkin, the diminutive scrum-half touching down within minutes of replacing Alexander Shakirov after 27 minutes in Nelson.

The explosive Yanyushkin was a standout player for Russia, providing the spark which led to two more tries being scored, through Vladimir Ostroushko and Alexey Makovetskiy, in what turned out to be a 53–17 defeat.

That Yanyushkin, the smallest player in the tournament at only 1.65m, was even at RWC 2011 was in itself a miracle after he tore his right Achilles in April and had surgery the following month. "Only four months have passed since that time, so I am really happy about being invited to the World Cup at all," admitted Yanyushkin. "It's not sunk in yet that my try has created a piece of Russian rugby history, but I am rather disappointed that we did not manage to turn the game into a better result."

The lively Yanyushkin was promoted to the starting line-up to face Ireland five days later, a task made even harder by the fact the Irish were in buoyant mood after upsetting Australia in their previous match. Three tries late in the first half allowed Ireland to go in with a commanding 36–0 lead, but Russia did have their moments at Rotorua International Stadium.

Their breakthrough finally came when Yanyushkin's well-timed pass unleashed Vasily Artemyev, the Russian who speaks English with an Irish twang after his time at Blackrock College in Dublin. A second try followed through replacement Denis Simplikevich, the wing touching down in the corner before being mobbed by his team-mates. The 20-year-old had been playing for Russia's Under-20s at the IRB Junior World Rugby Trophy in Georgia earlier in the year, but his try ensured he will never forget his Test debut despite the margin of defeat growing to 62–12 by the final whistle.

"It's probably something new for our guys to have 30,000 people around," admitted Nerush after the match. "We felt psychological pressure, so we made simple mistakes, conceded penalties, conceded three tries in three minutes at the end of the first half. Then we got used to the atmosphere and started playing better."

Russia returned to Nelson for their final match of RWC 2011 against Australia, hoping to bow out with another spirited performance against a side ranked 18 places above them in the IRB World Rankings. The signs were not good when Australia had the try bonus point in the bag after just 15 minutes, but just when the Wallabies were threatening to run up a cricket score the Russians found new resolve and were rewarded when Ostroushko scored out wide.

Australia picked up where they left off with tries either side of half-time, but the introduction of Rachkov gave the Russians another boost and again they were rewarded when Simplikevich anticipated a Quade Cooper pass and raced 50 metres to score his second try of the tournament. As Australia rang the changes they lost shape and sloppy errors crept into their game, something Russia seized upon with Rachkov adding a third try. Russia lost the match 68–22 but they could hold their heads high after becoming the first team to score three tries against Australia in a RWC match since Wales in the 1987 Bronze Final.

Russia bid farewell not only to the tournament but also Nerush, who announced after the match that he was stepping down as head coach. "I took this decision a long time ago. Even if we won the Webb Ellis Cup I would not have changed my mind. When I took up the team in 2009 our main target was to qualify for the Rugby World Cup. We have accomplished this goal, so I deem my job to be done. Now it's time to step aside as new people should come to the team to bring new emotions and energy. Our team should move forward."

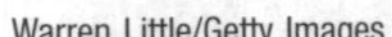

Warren Little/Getty Images

Konstantin Rachkov led Russia's scoring with 19 points at Rugby World Cup.

RUSSIA INTERNATIONAL STATISTICS

MATCH RECORDS UP TO 31 OCTOBER 2011

WINNING MARGIN

Date	Opponent	Result	Winning Margin
13/05/2000	Denmark	104–7	**97**
16/04/2000	Germany	89–6	**83**
11/06/2005	Ukraine	72–0	**72**
25/05/1995	Norway	66–0	**66**
18/09/1999	Ukraine	71–5	**66**

MOST POINTS IN A MATCH

BY THE TEAM

Date	Opponent	Result	Points
13/05/2000	Denmark	104–7	**104**
16/04/2000	Germany	89–6	**89**
17/02/2002	Netherlands	73–10	**73**
15/05/1999	Poland	72–13	**72**
11/06/2005	Ukraine	72–0	**72**

BY A PLAYER

Date	Player	Opponent	Points
16/04/2000	Konstantin Rachkov	Germany	**29**
15/05/1999	Konstantin Rachkov	Poland	**27**
16/02/2003	Konstantin Rachkov	Spain	**27**
02/06/2002	Werner Pieterse	Netherlands	**25**
19/07/2003	Konstantin Rachkov	USA A	**25**

MOST TRIES IN A MATCH

BY THE TEAM

Date	Opponent	Result	Tries
13/05/2000	Denmark	104–7	**17**
16/04/2000	Germany	89–6	**15**
02/10/1997	Poland	70–26	**12**

BY A PLAYER

Date	Player	Opponent	Tries
18/09/1999	Sergey Sergeev	Ukraine	**4**
13/05/2000	Andrey Kuzin	Denmark	**4**
21/04/2007	Igor Galinovskiy	Czech Republic	**4**

MOST CONVERSIONS IN A MATCH

BY THE TEAM

Date	Opponent	Result	Cons
18/09/1999	Ukraine	71–5	**8**
15/05/1999	Poland	72–13	**8**
13/05/2000	Denmark	104–7	**8**

BY A PLAYER

Date	Player	Opponent	Cons
15/05/1999	Konstantin Rachkov	Poland	**8**
13/05/2000	Konstantin Rachkov	Denmark	**7**
16/04/2000	Konstantin Rachkov	Germany	**7**

MOST PENALTIES IN A MATCH

BY THE TEAM

Date	Opponent	Result	Pens
16/02/2003	Spain	52–19	**6**
19/07/2003	USA A	30–21	**6**
08/03/2008	Spain	42–16	**6**

BY A PLAYER

Date	Player	Opponent	Pens
16/02/2003	Konstantin Rachkov	Spain	**6**
19/07/2003	Konstantin Rachkov	USA A	**6**
20/10/1996	Sergey Boldakov	Georgia	**5**
25/05/1993	Viktor Yakovlev	Georgia	**5**

MOST DROPPED GOALS IN A MATCH

BY THE TEAM

Date	Opponent	Result	DGs
08/03/2003	Georgia	17–23	**2**

BY A PLAYER

Date	Player	Opponent	DGs
08/03/2003	Konstantin Rachkov	Georgia	**2**

MOST CAPPED PLAYERS

Name	Caps
Andrey Kuzin	78
Alexander Khrokin	75
Vyacheslav Grachev	73
Vladislav Korshunov	58

LEADING TRY SCORERS

Name	Tries
Vyacheslav Grachev	31
Andrey Kuzin	25
Konstantin Rachkov	16
Alexander Gvozdovsky	15
Alexander Zakarlyuk	14

LEADING CONVERSIONS SCORERS

Name	Cons
Konstantin Rachkov	54
Yury Kushnarev	38
Vladimir Simonov	25
Victor Motorin	24

LEADING PENALTY SCORERS

Name	Pens
Yury Kushnarev	70
Konstantin Rachkov	47
Vladimir Simonov	21

LEADING DROPPED GOAL SCORERS

Name	DGs
Konstantin Rachkov	6
Werner Pieterse	2

LEADING POINTS SCORERS

Name	Points
Konstantin Rachkov	347
Yury Kushnarev	316
Vladimir Simonov	178
Vyacheslav Grachev	155
Andrey Kuzin	125

Mike Hewitt/Getty Images

Vyacheslav Grachev is a world-class operator in the Russian back row, with a remarkable 31 Test tries.

Stephane de Sakutin/AFP/Getty Images

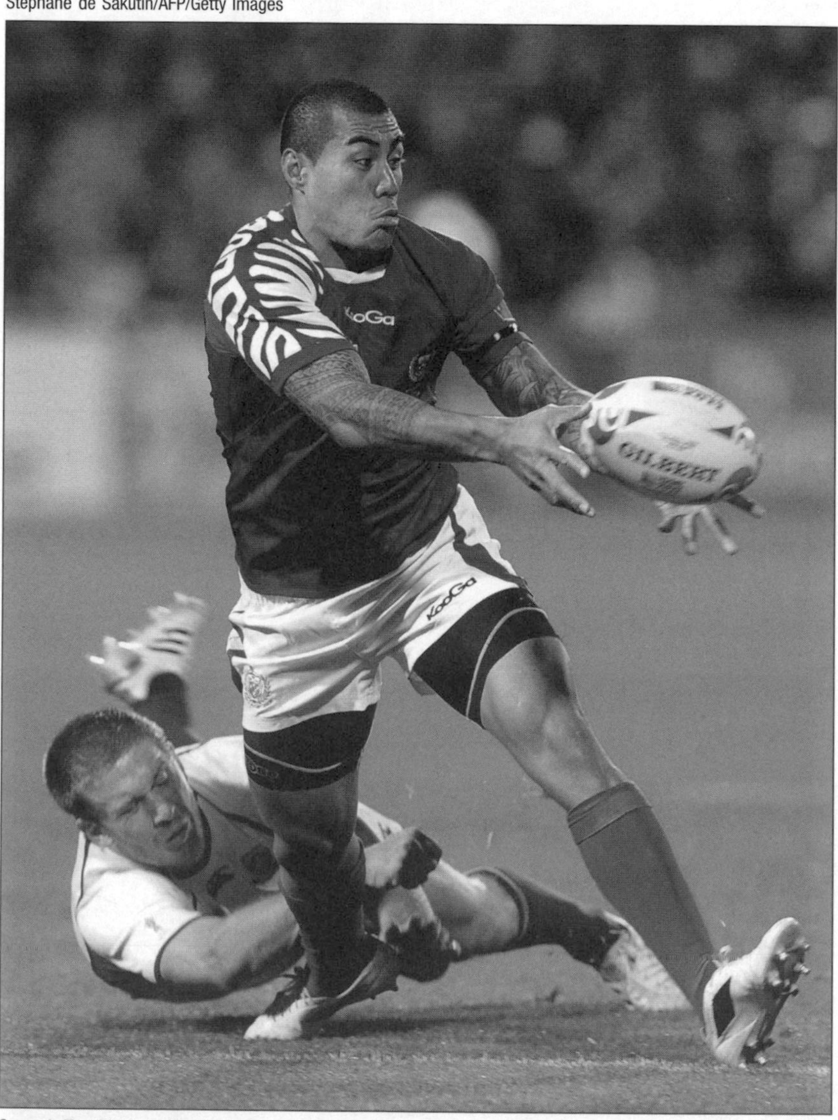

Samoa's Tusi Pisi is tackled by South African Springbok centre Francois Steyn during the Rugby World Cup 2011 Pool D match at the North Harbour stadium in Auckland.

SAMOA

SAMOA'S 2010–11 TEST RECORD

OPPONENT	DATE	VENUE	RESULT
Japan	30 Oct	A	**Won** 13–10
Ireland	13 Nov	A	**Lost** 10–20
England	20 Nov	A	**Lost** 13–26
Scotland	27 Nov	A	**Lost** 16–19
Japan	2 Jul	A	**Won** 34–15
Fiji	9 Jul	A	**Lost** 18–36
Tonga	13 Jul	N	**Lost** 19–29
Australia	17 Jul	A	**Won** 32–23
Namibia	14 Sep	N	**Won** 49–12
Wales	18 Sep	N	**Lost** 10–17
Fiji	25 Sep	N	**Won** 27–7
South Africa	30 Sep	N	**Lost** 5–13

SAMOA LAY BLOCKS FOR THE FUTURE

By Ian Gilbert

It's a sure measure of Samoa's Rugby World Cup progress that South Africa and Wales took the Islanders' challenge anything but lightly at New Zealand 2011.

In their first appearance at a RWC in 1991, playing as Western Samoa, they defeated Wales and Argentina and got within six points of Australia.

These days, sides are in no doubt as to Samoa's ability to spring an upset and there would have been some concern in Wales when the countries were drawn together in Pool D – along with South Africa, Fiji and Namibia – given Samoa's two previous RWC victories over the Welsh.

Furthermore, given their strong cultural ties with New Zealand, the Samoans could be pretty sure of some strong crowd support.

Samoa's run-up to the tournament received a huge boost back in July when, after consecutive defeats by Fiji and Tonga in the IRB Pacific Nations Cup, they stunned Australia 32–23 in Sydney. The Wallabies were without a few first-choice players that day, but 11 of the starting side made their country's World Cup squad.

With Fiji also possessing the free-running game allied to power to make life difficult for opponents, there were four sides in Pool D with realistic hopes of taking a quarter-final spot.

Alesana Tuilagi got Samoa off to a dream start, running in a hat-trick as they comprehensively accounted for Namibia 49–12 in their first match.

The second Sunday of the tournament thus shaped as D-Day for Samoa and Wales, edged out by South Africa in their first game, at Waikato Stadium, Hamilton.

Anthony Perenise crossed late in the first half for a try, converted by Paul Williams, to put Samoa 10–6 ahead and on the scent of another Welsh scalp.

But two Rhys Priestland penalties calmed Welsh nerves before veteran Shane Williams jinked across to make it 17–10. Try as they might, Samoa just could not fashion a score in the closing moments of the match.

The tackle count – 142 to 98 – told its own story as a tremendous Welsh rearguard action snuffed out opposition attacks. Samoa captain and hooker Mahonri Schwalger was upbeat despite the loss. "I've got belief in my team. We'll make the quarter-finals if we win the next two games. So it's not over for us."

With Fiji next up, there was little time for Samoa to lick their wounds. With the tradition in both these countries of inventive open rugby, it promised to be a delight for the purists. However, Samoa were wary of the wide running of the flying Fijians, and a 36–18 defeat in Suva back in July was still fresh in the memory.

Barnstorming winger Tuilagi hinted as much when asked about the physicality of fixtures between the two teams. "It's not always going to have to be physical, sometimes you have to be smart."

Fiji had also beaten the outgunned Namibians 49–25 to set up the encounter nicely. After the emotion-charged prelude of each side performing their cultural challenges – Samoa with their *siva tau* and Fiji's *cibi* – it was Samoa who showed the cool heads to stifle their opponents' possession for a 27–7 victory in front of the 60,327 Eden Park crowd.

"We always knew that their backs are dangerous so we really had to smash their forwards," said prop Census Johnston.

Tusi Pisi kicked all Samoa's first-half points – three penalties and a drop-goal – and Fiji were always battling to get back on terms after being 12–0 astray at the turnaround. Samoa found their try-scoring touch after the break, first through scrum-half Kahn Fotuali'i then Ospreys No. 8 George Stowers.

With that mission accomplished, Samoan thoughts could turn to the challenge of South Africa, whom they had met in the 1995, 2003 and 2007 World Cups, losing all three and conceding an average of almost 54 points in the process. They had never beaten the Springboks in any Test, but were nonetheless bullish about their chances.

"We've come into this tournament with a goal and we knew we had to beat either one of South Africa or Wales. We failed with the first one so we'll be doing everything in our powers to try and beat South Africa," admitted assistant coach Brian 'Aussie' McLean.

Come match day at North Harbour Stadium, the majority of the crowd support – given Auckland's large Samoan community – was a given. Whether they could prise open the Springboks' defence – the meanest in the tournament, having conceded only one try to that point – was another thing.

The match also had special significance as it was two years on from the fatal 2009 tsunami that hit Samoa and the surrounding area, forcing a total evacuation of the capital, Apia.

The Boks led 13–0 at half-time thanks to a Bryan Habana try and the boot of Morné Steyn, but Samoa were unfazed.

Stowers dragged them back into contention with a 51st-minute try, but try as they might the Samoans just couldn't force another score against the defending champions, and when Paul Williams was dismissed for striking Heinrich Brüssow in the 70th minute, it was too great a mountain to climb.

South Africa Springbok John Smit followed him off the field a minute later when he was issued with a yellow card so both sides finished with 14 men.

As with the Wales game, Samoa's opponents had to make a phenomenal number of tackles – 152 to 77 – to keep them out as players such as Seilala Mapusua, Tuilagi and Eliota Fuimaono Sapolu tried again and again to crash through.

As Samoa departed the tournament, Schwalger was a sombre but proud man. "The boys are pretty disappointed," he said. "I think this is the end of the road for us, but this team is going to do well in the next couple of years. If we get the chance to play these big teams we'll give them a good go."

McLean added: "We might be a small country but we play like a big team. We're pretty happy with our performance in the tournament."

Johnston, who plays his club rugby for French giants Toulouse, reflected on a stirring few months for Samoa. "We've got to take a lot of positives out of this game," he said. "Beating Australia earlier in the year, coming close to beating Wales, we are getting better."

Many of the Samoan players have prospered at overseas clubs, with players such as midfield general Mapusua – now playing in Japan – showing the tactical nous acquired in the high-pressure arena of the Heineken Cup and English Premiership with London Irish.

However, the IRB is also committed to developing the game in Samoa through moves such as the High Performance Facility in Faleata, Apia, which officially opened just before the tournament and was used by the team for their preparations.

The state-of-the-art centre comprises a gym, recovery and rehabilitation centre, two training pitches, accommodation for up to 90 athletes and a dedicated Samoa Rugby Union administration centre.

The IRB, working in partnership with the Samoan Government, has contributed more than £1 million to the project, and Chairman Bernard Lapasset said, "The IRB is committed to the development of rugby throughout Oceania in order to increase competitiveness and is investing £17 million in the region between 2009 and 2012."

Wing David Lemi sees a bright future for his country's national game. "They have got good facilities now, so hopefully that will help us improve," he said. "I am confident that Samoa will be in top-tier rugby fighting the top nations soon."

With more than half the squad born in New Zealand, Samoa didn't forget the strong ties between their island nation and their Pacific neighbour.

When the side trained at Auckland Grammar School, it was in familiar surrounds for old boys Daniel Leo, Taiasina Tuifua and Fuimaono Sapolu.

The squad's welcoming ceremony in Rotorua, meanwhile, drew hordes of well-wishers and the visitors responded with two songs to express their gratitude. "[The songs are] about being proud of where we come from, but still being humble," second row Filipo Levi said.

And that was just the support in New Zealand. When the squad left for RWC 2011, the route to the airport was so crowded with supporters that a 45-minute drive took more than two hours.

Whether at the matches or back home, the fans' contribution wasn't forgotten by the players and Schwalger made sure he paid tribute to them. "Our supporters have been great, they have been behind us, especially the people back home in the whole month towards the World Cup. I'm so proud of our people."

While they couldn't grab a last-eight spot as was their intended ambition, there was some consolation for Samoa with third spot in the pool and with it automatic qualification for RWC 2015 – meaning regional bragging rights over Fiji, who will have to qualify.

SAMOA INTERNATIONAL STATISTICS

MATCH RECORDS UP TO 31 OCTOBER 2011

WINNING MARGIN

Date	Opponent	Result	Winning Margin
11/07/2009	PNG	115–7	**108**
08/04/1990	Korea	74–7	**67**
18/07/2009	PNG	73–12	**61**
10/06/2000	Japan	68–9	**59**
29/06/1997	Tonga	62–13	**49**

MOST POINTS IN A MATCH

BY THE TEAM

Date	Opponent	Result	Points
11/07/2009	PNG	115–7	**115**
08/04/1990	Korea	74–7	**74**
18/07/2009	PNG	73–12	**73**
10/06/2000	Japan	68–9	**68**
29/06/1997	Tonga	62–13	**62**

BY A PLAYER

Date	Player	Opponent	Points
11/07/2009	Gavin Williams	PNG	**30**
29/05/2004	Roger Warren	Tonga	**24**
03/10/1999	Silao Leaega	Japan	**23**
08/04/1990	Andy Aiolupo	Korea	**23**
08/07/2000	Toa Samania	Italy	**23**

MOST TRIES IN A MATCH

BY THE TEAM

Date	Opponent	Result	Tries
11/07/2009	PNG	115–7	**17**
08/04/1990	Korea	74–7	**13**
18/07/2009	PNG	73–12	**11**

BY A PLAYER

Date	Player	Opponent	Tries
28/05/1991	Tupo Fa'amasino	Tonga	**4**
10/06/2000	Elvis Seveali'l	Japan	**4**
02/07/2005	Alesana Tuilagi	Tonga	**4**
11/07/2009	Esera Lauina	PNG	**4**

MOST CONVERSIONS IN A MATCH

BY THE TEAM

Date	Opponent	Result	Cons
11/07/2009	PNG	115–7	**15**
18/07/2009	PNG	73–12	**9**
08/04/1990	Korea	74–7	**8**

BY A PLAYER

Date	Player	Opponent	Cons
11/07/2009	Gavin Williams	PNG	**10**
18/07/2009	Titi Jnr Esau	PNG	**9**
08/04/1990	Andy Aiolupo	Korea	**8**

MOST PENALTIES IN A MATCH

BY THE TEAM

Date	Opponent	Result	Pens
29/05/2004	Tonga	24–14	**8**

BY A PLAYER

Date	Player	Opponent	Pens
29/05/2004	Roger Warren	Tonga	**8**

MOST DROPPED GOALS IN A MATCH

BY THE TEAM

1 on 10 Occasions

BY A PLAYER

1 on 10 Occasions

MOST CAPPED PLAYERS

Name	Caps
Brian Lima	**65**
To'o Vaega	**60**
Semo Sititi	**59**
Opeta Palepoi	**42**
Mahonri Schwalger	**40**

LEADING TRY SCORERS

Name	Tries
Brian Lima	**31**
Semo Sititi	**17**
Afato So'oialo	**15**
To'o Vaega	**15**
Alesana Tuilagi	**15**

LEADING CONVERSIONS SCORERS

Name	Cons
Andy Aiolupo	**35**
Earl Va'a	**33**
Silao Leaega	**26**
Tanner Vili	**21**
Gavin Williams	**18**

LEADING PENALTY SCORERS

Name	Pens
Darren Kellett	**35**
Earl Va'a	**31**
Silao Leaega	**31**
Roger Warren	**29**
Andy Aiolupo	**24**

LEADING DROPPED GOAL SCORERS

Name	DGs
Darren Kellet	**2**
Roger Warren	**2**
Steve Bachop	**2**

LEADING POINTS SCORERS

Name	Points
Earl Va'a	**184**
Andy Aiolupo	**172**
Silao Leaega	**160**
Darren Kellett	**155**
Brian Lima	**150**

SAMOA INTERNATIONAL PLAYERS (UP TO 31 OCTOBER 2011)

Note: Years given for International Championship matches are for second half of season; eg 1972 means season 1971–72. Years for all other matches refer to the actual year of the match. Entries in square brackets denote matches played in RWC Finals.

A'ati 1932 *Tg*
JT Afoa 2010 *Tg, J*
Agnew 1924 *Fj, Fj*
S Ah Fook 1947 *Tg*
F Ah Long 1955 *Fj*
Ah Mu 1932 *Tg*
T Aialupo 1986 *W*
F Aima'asu 1981 *Fj*, 1982 *Fj, Fj, Fj, Tg*, 1988 *Tg, Fj*
AA Aiolupo 1983 *Tg*, 1984 *Fj, Tg*, 1985 *Fj, Tg, Tg*, 1986 *Fj, Tg*, 1987 *Fj, Tg*, 1988 *Tg, Fj, I, W*, 1989 *Fj, WGe, Bel, R*, 1990 *Kor, Tg, J, Tg, Fj*, 1991 *W, A, Ar, S*, 1992 *Tg, Fj*, 1993 *Tg, Fj, NZ*, 1994 *Tg, W, A*
A Aiono 2009 *PNG*, 2010 *J, I, E, S*, 2011 *Tg*
Aitofele 1924 *Fj, Fj*
P Alalatoa 1986 *W*
V Alalatoa 1988 *I, W*, 1989 *Fj*, 1991 *Tg, W, A, Ar, S*, 1992 *Tg, Fj*
P Alauni 2009 *PNG*
R Ale 1997 *Tg, Fj*, 1999 *J, Ar, W, S*
A Alelupo 1994 *Fj*
T Aleni 1982 *Tg*, 1983 *Tg*, 1985 *Tg*, 1986 *W, Fj, Tg*, 1987 *Fj*
S Alesana 1979 *Tg, Fj*, 1980 *Tg*, 1981 *Fj, Fj*, 1982 *Fj, Tg*, 1983 *Tg, Fj*, 1984 *Fj, Tg*, 1985 *Fj, Tg*
T Allen 1924 *Fj, Fj*
K Anufe 2009 *Tg*
L Aoelua 2008 *NZ*
T Aoese 1981 *Fj, Fj*, 1982 *Fj, Fj, Fj, Tg*, 1983 *Tg*
J Apelu 1985 *Tg*
F Asi 1963 *Fj, Fj, Tg*
F Asi 1975 *Tg*
L Asi 2010 *J*
SP Asi 1999 *S*, 2000 *Fj, J, Tg, C, It, US, W, S*, 2001 *Tg, Fj, NZ, Fj, Tg, Fj*
Atiga 1924 *Fj*
S Ati'ifale 1979 *Tg*, 1980 *Tg*, 1981 *Fj, Fj*
J Atoa 1975 *Tg*, 1981 *Fj*
O Avei 2011 *J, Tg, SA*

SJ Bachop 1991 *Tg, Fj, W, A, Ar, S*, 1998 *Tg, Fj*, 1999 *J, C, F, NZ, US, Fj, J, Ar, W, S*
C Betham 1955 *Fj*
ML Birtwistle 1991 *Fj, W, A, Ar, S*, 1993 *Fj, NZ*, 1994 *Tg, W, Fj, A*, 1996 *I*
W Brame 2009 *J, Fj*
FE Bunce 1991 *W, A, Ar, S*

CH Capper 1924 *Fj*
J Cavanagh 1955 *Fj, Fj, Fj*
J Clarke 1997 *Tg*, 1998 *A*, 1999 *US, Fj, J*
A Collins 2005 *S, Ar*
A Cortz 2007 *Fj*
G Cowley 2005 *S, Ar*, 2006 *J, Tg*
T Cowley 2000 *J, C, It*
L Crichton 2006 *Fj, Tg*, 2007 *Fj, SA, J, Tg, SA, Tg, E, US*
O Crichton 1988 *Tg*
O Crichton 1955 *Fj, Fj, Fj*, 1957 *Tg, Tg*
T Curtis 2000 *Fj, J, Tg, C, It, US*

H Ekeroma 1972 *Tg, Tg*
G Elisara 2003 *I, Nm*
S Enari 1975 *Tg*
S Epati 1972 *Tg*
T Esau 2009 *PNG, PNG, F, It*
K Ese 1947 *Tg*
S Esera 1981 *Fj*
L Eves 1957 *Tg, Tg*

H Fa'afili 2008 *Fj, Tg, J*, 2009 *J, Tg, Fj, PNG, W, F, It*
T Fa'afou 2007 *Fj*
P Fa'alogo 1963 *Fj*
Fa'amaile 1947 *Tg*
T Fa'amasino 1988 *W*, 1989 *Bel, R*, 1990 *Kor, Tg, J, Tg, Fj*, 1991 *Tg, Fj, A*, 1995 *It, Ar, E, SA, Fj, Tg*, 1996 *NZ, Tg, Fj*
JS Fa'amatuainu 2005 *S, Ar*, 2008 *Fj, J*, 2009 *J, Tg, Fj, PNG, W, F, It*, 2011 *Tg*
S Fa'aofo 1990 *Tg*
Fa'asalele 1957 *Tg, Tg*
F Fa'asau 1963 *Fj, Tg*
M Faasavalu 2002 *SA*, 2003 *I, Nm, Ur, Geo, E, SA*, 2011 *J, Fj, A, Nm, W, Fj, SA*
V Faasua 1987 *Fj*, 1988 *Tg, Fj, W*
S Fa'asua 2000 *W*
F Fa'asuaga 1947 *Tg*
L Fa'atau 2000 *Fj, Tg, C, US*, 2001 *I, It*, 2002 *Fj, Tg, Fj, Tg, SA*, 2003 *I, Ur, E, SA*, 2004 *Tg, S, Fj*, 2005 *A, Tg, Tg, Fj, S, E, Ar*, 2006 *J, Fj, Tg*, 2007 *Fj, SA, J, Tg, SA, US*
F Fagasoaia 2010 *J*
K Faiva'ai 1998 *Tg, Fj, A*, 1999 *J, C, Tg, NZ, US, Fj*
L Falaniko 1990 *Tg, Fj*, 1991 *Tg*, 1993 *Tg, Fj, NZ*, 1995 *SA, It, Ar, E, SA, Fj, Tg, S, E*, 1996 *NZ*, 1999 *US, Fj, W, S*
E Fale 2008 *Tg*
S Fale 1955 *Fj*
S Fanolua 1990 *Tg, Fj*, 1991 *Tg, Fj*
TL Fanolua 1996 *NZ, Fj*, 1997 *Tg*, 1998 *Tg, Fj, A*, 1999 *W, S*, 2000 *J, Tg, C, It, US*, 2001 *Tg, Fj, NZ, Fj, Tg, J, Fj*, 2002 *Fj*, 2003 *Nm, Ur, Geo, E*, 2005 *A, Tg, Fj, Fj*
R Fanuatanu 2003 *I, Geo*
M Faoagali 1999 *J, C*
A Faosiliva 2006 *J, Tg*, 2008 *Tg, NZ*, 2010 *Tg, J, Fj*
DS Farani 2005 *Tg, Fj, S, E, Ar*, 2006 *J, Fj, Tg*
J Fatialofa 2009 *F*
M Fatialofa 1996 *Tg*
PM Fatialofa 1988 *I, W*, 1989 *Bel, R*, 1990 *Kor, Tg, J*, 1991 *Tg, Fj, W, A, Ar, S*, 1992 *Tg, Fj*, 1993 *Tg, Fj, NZ*, 1994 *Tg, W, Fj, A*, 1995 *SA, It, Ar, E, SA, Fj, Tg, S, E*, 1996 *NZ, Fj*
Fatu 1947 *Tg*
E Feagai 1963 *Fj, Tg*
S Feagai 1963 *Fj, Fj*
D Feaunati 2003 *Nm, Ur, Geo, E, SA*
I Fea'unati 1996 *I*, 1997 *Tg*, 1999 *Tg, NZ, Fj, Ar*, 2000 *Fj, J, Tg, C, It, US*, 2006 *Fj, Tg*
M Fepuleai 1957 *Tg*
V Fepuleai 1988 *W*, 1989 *Fj, WGe, R*
I Fesuiai'i 1985 *Fj, Tg*
JA Filemu 1995 *S, E*, 1996 *NZ, Tg, Fj, I*, 1997 *Fj*, 1999 *J, C, Tg, F, NZ*, 2000 *Fj, J, Tg, C, It, US*, 2001 *Tg, Fj, Tg, J*
F Fili 2003 *I, Nm*, 2009 *W, F*, 2011 *Tg*
F Filisoa 2005 *Tg*
T Fong 1983 *Tg, Fj*, 1984 *Fj, Tg*, 1986 *W, Fj, Tg*, 1987 *Fj, Tg*
K Fotuali'i 2010 *J, I, E, S*, 2011 *A, Nm, W, Fj, SA*
S Fretton 1947 *Tg*
Fruean 1932 *Tg*
J Fruean 1972 *Tg*, 1975 *Tg*
S Fruean 1955 *Fj, Fj*
P Fuatai 1988 *Tg, Fj*, 1989 *Fj, WGe, R*
S Fuatai 1972 *Tg*
T Fuga 1999 *F, NZ, US*, 2000 *Fj, J, Tg, C, It, US*, 2007 *SA, Tg*
ES Fuimaono Sapolu 2005 *S, E, Ar*, 2006 *Fj, Tg*, 2007 *SA, E, US*, 2008 *Fj, Tg, J*, 2009 *J, Fj, PNG, PNG, F, It*, 2011 *Fj, A, Nm, W, Fj, SA*

T Galuvao 1972 *Tg*
N George 2004 *Tg, Fj*
C Glendinning 1999 *J, C, Tg, F, NZ, US, Fj, J, W, S*, 2000 *Fj, J, Tg, C, It, US*, 2001 *Tg, Fj, NZ, Fj, Tg, Fj*
A Grey 1957 *Tg, Tg*
I Grey 1985 *Fj, Tg*
P Grey 1975 *Tg*, 1979 *Tg, Fj*, 1980 *Tg*

G Harder 1995 *SA, It, Ar, SA*
Hellesoe 1932 *Tg*
B Helleur 2011 *Tg, A*
J Helleur 2010 *Tg, J, Fj, J*
M Hewitt 1955 *Fj, Fj*
J Huch 1982 *Fj, Fj*, 1986 *Fj, Tg*
J Hunt 1957 *Tg, Tg*

A Ieremia 1992 *Tg, Fj*, 1993 *Tg, Fj, NZ*
I Imo 1924 *Fj*
T Imo 1955 *Fj, Fj, Fj*, 1957 *Tg, Tg*
A Ioane 1957 *Tg, Tg, Tg*
E Ioane 1990 *Tg, Fj*, 1991 *Tg, Fj, S*
T Iona 1975 *Tg*
T Iosua 2006 *J*, 2011 *J, Fj, Tg*
Iupati 1924 *Fj*
M Iupeli 1988 *Tg, Fj, I, W*, 1989 *Fj, WGe, R*, 1993 *Tg, NZ*, 1994 *Tg, W, Fj, A*, 1995 *SA, E*
S Iuta 1947 *Tg*

T Jensen 1987 *Tg*, 1989 *Bel*
CAI Johnston 2005 *A, Tg, Fj, S, E, Ar*, 2006 *Fj, Tg*, 2007 *SA, J, Tg, SA, Tg, E, US*, 2008 *Fj, J*, 2009 *J, Tg, Fj, PNG, W, F, It*, 2010 *J, Fj, E, S*, 2011 *Tg, A, Nm, W, Fj, SA*
J Johnston 2008 *Tg, J*, 2011 *Tg*
MN Jones 1986 *W*

S Kalapu 1957 *Tg*
D Kaleopa 1990 *Kor, Tg, J*, 1991 *A*, 1992 *Fj*, 1993 *Tg, Fj*
S Kaleta 1994 *Tg, W*, 1995 *S, E*, 1996 *NZ*, 1997 *Tg, Fj*
T Kali 1975 *Tg*
L Kamu 1955 *Fj, Fj, Fj*
MG Keenan 1991 *W, A, Ar*, 1992 *Tg, Fj*, 1993 *NZ*, 1994 *Tg, W, Fj, A*
JR Keil 2010 *J, J*
F Kelemete 1984 *Fj, Tg*, 1985 *Tg*, 1986 *W*
DK Kellet 1993 *Tg, Fj, NZ*, 1994 *Tg, W, Fj, A*, 1995 *It, Ar, Fj, Tg, S, E*
DA Kerslake 2005 *Tg, Fj, Tg, Fj*, 2006 *J, Tg*, 2007 *Fj, SA, J, Tg*
A Koko 1999 *J*
R Koko 1983 *Tg, Fj, Fj*, 1984 *Fj, Tg*, 1985 *Fj, Tg, Tg*, 1986 *W, Fj, Tg*, 1987 *Fj, Tg*, 1988 *Tg, Fj, I, W*, 1989 *WGe, R*, 1993 *Tg, NZ*, 1994 *Tg*
M Krause 1984 *Tg*, 1986 *W*
H Kruse 1963 *Fj, Fj, Tg*
JA Kuoi 1987 *Fj, Tg*, 1988 *I, W*, 1990 *Kor, Tg*

B Laban 1955 *Fj*, 1957 *Tg, Tg*
SL Lafaiali'I 2001 *Tg, Fj, NZ, Tg*, 2002 *Fj, Tg, Fj, Tg, SA*, 2003 *I, Nm, Ur, Geo, E, SA*, 2004 *Tg, S, Fj*, 2005 *A, S, E*, 2007 *Fj, J, Tg, Tg, US*
I Laga'aia 1975 *Tg*, 1979 *Tg, Fj*
F Lalomilo 2001 *I, It*
PR Lam 1991 *W, Ar, S*, 1994 *W, Fj, A*, 1995 *SA, Ar, E, SA, Fj, Tg, S, E*, 1996 *NZ, Tg, Fj, I*, 1997 *Tg, Fj*, 1998 *Tg, Fj, A*, 1999 *J, C, Tg, F, NZ, US, Fj, J, Ar, W, S*
F Lameta 1990 *Tg, Fj*
S Lameta 1982 *Fj*
G Latu 1994 *Tg, W, Fj, A*, 1995 *SA, Ar, E, SA, Fj, Tg*
E Lauina 2008 *Fj, Tg, J, NZ*, 2009 *J, Tg, Fj, PNG, PNG*
M Lautau 1985 *Fj*
T Lavea 2010 *I, E, S*, 2011 *J, Fj, Nm, W*
FH Lavea Levi 2007 *Fj, SA, J, Tg*, 2008 *Fj, J, NZ*, 2009 *J, Tg, Fj, PNG, W, F, It*, 2010 *Tg, J, Fj, I, E, S*, 2011 *J, Fj, Tg, A, Fj*
S Leaega 1997 *Tg, Fj*, 1999 *J, J, Ar, W, S*, 2001 *Tg, Fj, NZ, Fj, Tg, Fj, I, It*, 2002 *Fj, Tg, SA*
K Lealamanua 2000 *Fj, J, Tg, C, It*, 2001 *NZ, Fj, Tg, J, Fj*, 2002 *Fj, Tg, Fj, Tg, SA*, 2003 *I, Nm, Ur, Geo, E, SA*, 2004 *Tg, S, Fj*, 2005 *S, E*, 2007 *SA, Tg, E, US*
GE Leaupepe 1995 *SA, Ar, E, Fj, Tg, S, E*, 1996 *NZ, Tg, Fj, I*, 1997 *Tg, Fj*, 1998 *Tg, A*, 1999 *J, C, Tg, F, NZ, US, Fj, J, Ar, W*, 2005 *A*
S Leaupepe 1979 *Tg, Fj*, 1980 *Tg*
P Leavai 1990 *J*
A Leavasa 1979 *Tg, Fj*, 1980 *Tg*
P Leavasa 1955 *Fj, Fj, Fj*, 1957 *Tg, Tg, Tg*
PL Leavasa 1993 *Tg, Fj*, 1995 *It, Ar, E, S, E*, 1996 *NZ, Tg, Fj, I*, 1997 *Tg, Fj*, 2002 *Tg, Fj, Tg, SA*
S Leavasa 1955 *Fj, Fj, Fj*, 1957 *Tg*
T Leiasamaivao 1993 *Tg, NZ*, 1994 *Tg, W, Fj*, 1995 *SA, It, Ar, E, SA, S, E*, 1996 *NZ, Tg, Fj, I*, 1997 *Tg, Fj*
N Leleimalefaga 2007 *Fj, US*
S Lemalu 2003 *Ur, Geo, E*, 2004 *Tg, S, Fj*, 2008 *Tg, J, NZ*, 2010 *J, I*, 2011 *Fj, Tg*
S Lemamea 1988 *I, W*, 1989 *Fj, WGe, Bel, R*, 1990 *J*, 1992 *Tg, Fj*, 1995 *E, SA, Fj, Tg*
D Lemi 2004 *Tg, S, Fj*, 2005 *Tg, Fj, Tg, Fj*, 2007 *Fj, SA, J, Tg, SA, Tg, E, US*, 2008 *Fj, Tg, J*, 2009 *W, F, It*, 2010 *Tg, J, Fj, I, E, S*, 2011 *Fj, Tg, SA*
DA Leo 2005 *A, Tg, Fj, Tg, Fj, S, E, Ar*, 2006 *J, Fj, Tg*, 2007 *SA, J, Tg, SA, Tg, E*, 2008 *Tg, J*, 2009 *J, Fj, PNG*, 2010 *S*, 2011 *J, Fj, A, Nm, W, Fj, SA*
J Leota 2011 *Fj, Tg*
M Leota 2000 *Fj, Tg, C*
P Leota 1990 *Kor, Tg, J*
T Leota 1997 *Tg, Fj*, 1998 *Tg, Fj, A*, 1999 *J, C, Tg, F, Fj, J, Ar, W, S*, 2000 *Fj, J*, 2001 *Tg, Fj, NZ, Fj, J, Fj*, 2002 *Fj, Tg, Fj, Tg, SA*, 2003 *I*, 2005 *A*
A Le'u 1987 *Fj, Tg*, 1989 *WGe, R*, 1990 *Kor, J, Tg, Fj*, 1993 *Tg, Fj, NZ*, 1996 *I*
T Leupolu 2001 *I, It*, 2002 *Fj, Tg, Fj, Tg, SA*, 2003 *I, Nm, SA*, 2004 *Tg, S, Fj*, 2005 *Ar*
R Levasa 2008 *NZ*, 2009 *J, PNG*, 2010 *J, Fj*
A Liaina 1963 *Fj, Fj, Tg*
S Liaina 1963 *Fj, Fj, Tg*
P Lilomaiava 1993 *NZ*
BP Lima 1991 *Tg, Fj, W, A, Ar, S*, 1992 *Tg, Fj*, 1993 *Fj, NZ*, 1994 *Tg, W, Fj, A*, 1995 *SA, It, Ar, E, SA, Fj, Tg, S, E*, 1996 *NZ, Tg, Fj*, 1997 *Fj*, 1998 *Tg, Fj, A*, 1999 *Tg, F, NZ, US, J, Ar, W, S*, 2000 *C, It, US*, 2001 *Fj, Tg, Fj, I, It*, 2002 *Fj, Tg*, 2003 *I, Nm, Ur, Geo, E, SA*, 2004 *Tg, S, Fj*, 2005 *A, Fj*, 2006 *J, Fj*, 2007 *Fj, Tg, SA, E*
F Lima 1981 *Fj*
M Lima 1982 *Fj, Fj*
M Lome 1957 *Tg, Tg, Tg*, 1963 *Fj*
M Luafalealo 1999 *J*, 2000 *It, US*, 2001 *Tg, Fj, NZ, Fj, J, Fj*
E Lua'iufi 1987 *Fj, Tg*, 1988 *Tg, Fj*
Lui 1932 *Tg*
L Lui 2004 *Fj*, 2005 *Tg, Fj, Ar*, 2006 *J, Tg*, 2007 *Tg, Tg, E, US*, 2009 *J, Tg, Fj, PNG, PNG, W, F*, 2010 *Tg, J, Fj, J*
M Lupeli 1993 *Fj*

A Macdonald 1924 *Fj, Fj*, 1932 *Tg*
M Magele 2009 *PNG*
T Magele 1988 *Tg*
U Mai 2008 *Tg, J, NZ*, 2009 *J, Fj, PNG, PNG, W, F, It*, 2010 *Tg, J, Fj*, 2011 *J, Fj, Tg*
F Mailei 1963 *Fj, Tg*
F Malele 1979 *Tg, Fj*, 1980 *Tg*
J Maligi 2000 *W, S*
P Maligi 1982 *Fj, Tg*, 1983 *Tg, Fj*, 1984 *Fj, Tg*, 1985 *Fj, Tg, Tg*, 1986 *Fj, Tg*
L Malo 1979 *Fj*
J Mamea 2000 *W, S*
L Mano 1988 *Fj, I, W*
C Manu 2002 *Fj, Tg, Tg, SA*
S Mapusua 2006 *J, Fj, Tg*, 2007 *SA, J, Tg, Tg, E, US*, 2009 *Tg, Fj, W, F, It*, 2010 *I, E, S*, 2011 *J, A, Nm, W, Fj, SA*
P Mareko 1979 *Fj*
K Mariner 2005 *Ar*
M Mata'afa 1947 *Tg*
P Matailina 1957 *Tg, Tg, Tg*
O Matauiau 1996 *Tg, Fj*, 1999 *Ar, W, S*, 2000 *It, W, S*
K Mavaega 1985 *Tg*
M McFadyen 1957 *Tg*
K McFall 1983 *Fj*
J Meafou 2007 *Tg, SA, E*, 2008 *NZ*
L Mealamu 2000 *W, S*
I Melei 1972 *Tg*
C Meredith 1932 *Tg*
J Meredith 2001 *I, It*, 2002 *Fj, Tg, Fj, Tg, SA*, 2003 *I, Nm, Ur, Geo, E, SA*, 2004 *Tg, S, Fj*, 2005 *A, Tg, Fj, Fj*
J Meredith 1963 *Fj, Fj, Tg*
O Meredith 1947 *Tg*
A Mika 2000 *S*
D Mika 1994 *W, A*
MAN Mika 1995 *SA, It, Ar, E, SA, S, E*, 1997 *Tg, Fj*, 1999 *Tg, F, NZ, J, Ar, W*
S Mika 2004 *Fj*, 2005 *A, Tg, Fj, Tg, Fj*

S Mikaele 2008 *NZ*, 2009 *PNG*, *PNG*, 2010 *J*
P Misa 2000 *W*, *S*
S Moala 2008 *Fj*
F Moamanu 1989 *WGe*
S Moamanu 1985 *Fj*, 1986 *Fj*, *Tg*
M Moke 1990 *Kor*, *Tg*, *J*, *Tg*, *Fj*
P Momoisea 1972 *Tg*, *Tg*
H Moors 1924 *Fj*, *Fj*
R Moors 1994 *Tg*
Mose 1932 *Tg*
S Motoi 1984 *Tg*
F Motusagu 2000 *Tg*, *It*, 2005 *A*
R Muagututia 2010 *J*
L Mulipola 2009 *PNG*, 2010 *J*, 2011 *J*, *Fj*, *Tg*, *SA*
L Mulipola 2009 *F*, *It*

P Neenee 1987 *Fj*, *Tg*, 1991 *Tg*, *Fj*
O Nelson 1955 *Fj*, *Fj*, *Fj*, 1957 *Tg*, *Tg*
N Ngapaku 2000 *J*, *C*, *US*
F Nickel 1957 *Tg*
N Nifo 2009 *PNG*
Nimmo 1957 *Tg*
T Nu'uali'itia 1994 *Tg*, *A*, 1995 *SA*, *It*, *Ar*, *E*, *SA*, 1996 *NZ*

R Ofisa 2011 *Tg*
A Olive 2008 *Tg*
F Otto 2010 *Tg*, *Fj*, *E*, *S*, 2011 *Tg*

FJP Palaamo 1998 *Tg*, *Fj*, *A*, 1999 *J*, *C*, *F*, *NZ*, *US*, *Fj*, 2007 *Fj*, *E*, 2009 *Fj*, *PNG*, *PNG*
S Pala'amo 1955 *Fj*, *Fj*, *Fj*, 1957 *Tg*
A Palamo 1979 *Tg*, *Fj*, 1980 *Tg*, 1981 *Fj*, *Fj*, 1982 *Fj*, *Fj*, *Fj*, *Tg*
LN Palamo 1979 *Tg*, *Fj*, 1981 *Fj*, *Fj*, 1982 *Fj*, *Fj*, *Fj*, *Tg*, 1984 *Fj*, *Tg*, 1985 *Tg*, 1986 *W*, *Fj*, *Tg*
T Palamo 1972 *Tg*
O Palepoi 1998 *Tg*, *Fj*, *A*, 1999 *J*, *F*, *NZ*, *US*, *Fj*, *J*, *Ar*, 2000 *J*, *C*, *It*, *US*, *W*, 2001 *Tg*, *Fj*, *NZ*, *Fj*, *Tg*, *J*, *Fj*, *I*, *It*, 2002 *Fj*, *Tg*, *Fj*, *Tg*, *SA*, 2003 *I*, *Nm*, *Ur*, *Geo*, *E*, *SA*, 2004 *Tg*, *S*, 2005 *A*, *Tg*, *Fj*, *Tg*, *Fj*
Panapa 1932 *Tg*
M Papali'I 1955 *Fj*, *Fj*
P Papali'I 1924 *Fj*, *Fj*
PJ Paramore 1991 *Tg*, *Fj*, *A*, 1992 *Fj*, 1994 *Tg*, 1995 *SA*, *It*, *Ar*, *SA*, *Fj*, *Tg*, 1996 *I*, 1997 *Tg*, *Fj*, 1998 *Tg*, *Fj*, *A*, 1999 *J*, *Ar*, *W*, 2001 *Tg*, *Fj*, *NZ*, *Fj*, *Tg*, *J*, *Fj*
J Parkinson 2005 *A*, *Tg*
T Pati 1997 *Tg*
M Patolo 1986 *W*, *Fj*, *Tg*
HV Patu 1995 *S*, *E*, 1996 *I*, 2000 *W*, *S*
O Patu 1980 *Tg*
T Patu 1979 *Tg*, *Fj*, 1980 *Tg*, 1981 *Fj*, *Fj*
P Paul 1955 *Fj*, *Fj*, *Fj*
M Paulino 2008 *NZ*, 2010 *J*
P Paulo 1989 *Bel*, 1990 *Tg*, *Fj*
T Paulo 2010 *E*, *S*, 2011 *J*, *Fj*, *Tg*, *A*, *Nm*, *W*, *Fj*
A Perelini 1991 *Tg*, *Fj*, *W*, *A*, *Ar*, *S*, 1992 *Tg*, *Fj*, 1993 *NZ*
AI Perenise 2010 *Tg*, *J*, *Fj*, *J*, *I*, *E*, *S*, 2011 *J*, *Fj*, *A*, *Nm*, *W*, *Fj*, *SA*
S Perez 1963 *Fj*, *Fj*, *Tg*
MS Pesamino 2009 *PNG*, *PNG*, 2010 *Tg*, *J*, *Fj*, *J*
N Petaia 1963 *Fj*
Petelo 1932 *Tg*
T Petelo 1985 *Fj*
P Petia 2003 *Nm*
O Pifeleti 1987 *Fj*
T Pisi 2011 *J*, *Fj*, *A*, *Nm*, *Fj*, *SA*
TG Pisi 2010 *Tg*, *Fj*, *I*, *E*, *S*, 2011 *J*, *A*, *Nm*, *W*, *Fj*
S Po Ching 1990 *Kor*, *Tg*, 1991 *Tg*
S Poching 2000 *W*, *S*, 2001 *Tg*
AJ Poluleuligaga 2007 *SA*, *J*, *Tg*, *SA*, *Tg*, *E*, *US*, 2008 *NZ*, 2009 *J*, *Tg*, *Fj*, *W*, *F*, *It*, 2010 *Tg*, *J*, *I*, *E*, 2011 *Nm*
HA Porter 2011 *Tg*
P Poulos 2003 *Ur*, *Geo*, *E*, *SA*
E Puleitu 1995 *SA*, *E*
S Punivalu 1981 *Fj*, *Fj*, 1982 *Fj*, *Fj*, *Fj*, 1983 *Tg*, *Fj*
JEP Purdie 2007 *Fj*, *SA*, *J*, *Tg*, *SA*, *Tg*, *E*, *US*

I Railey 1924 *Fj*, *Fj*
D Rasmussen 2003 *I*, *Ur*, *Geo*, *E*, *SA*, 2004 *Tg*, *S*, *Fj*
R Rasmussen 1997 *Tg*
B Reidy 1995 *SA*, *Fj*, *Tg*, 1996 *NZ*, *Tg*, *Fj*, *I*, 1998 *Fj*, *A*, 1999 *Tg*, *F*, *NZ*, *US*, *Fj*, *J*, *Ar*, *W*, *S*
K Roberts 1972 *Tg*
F Ropati 1982 *Fj*, *Fj*, *Fj*, 1984 *Fj*, *Tg*
R Ropati 2003 *SA*, 2008 *NZ*
W Ryan 1983 *Fj*, 1985 *Tg*

E Sa'aga 1924 *Fj*, *Fj*, 1932 *Tg*
PD Saena 1988 *Tg*, *Fj*, *I*, 1989 *Fj*, *Bel*, *R*, 1990 *Kor*, *Tg*, *J*, *Tg*, *Fj*, 1991 *Tg*, *Fj*, 1992 *Tg*, *Fj*, 1993 *Tg*, *Fj*
L Sagaga 1963 *Fj*, *Tg*
K Saifoloi 1979 *Tg*, *Fj*, 1980 *Tg*, 1982 *Fj*, *Fj*, 1984 *Fj*, *Tg*
P Saili 1957 *Tg*, *Tg*, *Tg*
M Salanoa 2005 *Tg*, *Fj*, 2006 *J*, *Fj*, *Tg*, 2007 *Fj*, *SA*, *J*, *Tg*, *Tg*
M Salavea 2010 *Tg*, *Fj*, *I*, *E*, *S*, 2011 *J*, *Tg*, *A*, *W*, *Fj*
T Salesa 1979 *Tg*, *Fj*, 1980 *Tg*, 1981 *Fj*, *Fj*, 1982 *Fj*, *Fj*, *Fj*, *Tg*, 1983 *Tg*, *Fj*, *Fj*, 1984 *Fj*, *Tg*, 1985 *Fj*, *Tg*, *Tg*, 1986 *Fj*, *Tg*, 1987 *Fj*, *Tg*, 1988 *Tg*, *Fj*, *I*, 1989 *Fj*, *WGe*, *R*
G Salima 2008 *Fj*
T Samania 1994 *W*, *Fj*, *A*, 1996 *NZ*, 2000 *Fj*, *J*, *C*, *It*, 2001 *Tg*
D Sanft 2006 *J*
Q Sanft 2000 *W*, *S*
L Sasi 1982 *Fj*, *Tg*, 1983 *Tg*, *Fj*, 1984 *Fj*, *Tg*, 1985 *Tg*, 1986 *W*, *Fj*, *Tg*, 1987 *Fj*, *Tg*, 1988 *Tg*, *Fj*
B Sasulu 2008 *Fj*
S Sauila 1989 *Bel*
L Savai'inaea 1957 *Tg*, *Tg*
J Schaafhausen 1947 *Tg*
W Schaafhausen 1947 *Tg*
P Schmidt 1989 *Fj*, *WGe*
P Schmidt 1980 *Tg*, 1985 *Tg*
R Schmidt 1979 *Tg*, 1980 *Tg*
D Schuster 1982 *Tg*, 1983 *Tg*, *Fj*, *Fj*
H Schuster 1989 *Fj*, 1990 *Kor*, *Tg*, *J*
J Schuster 1985 *Fj*, *Tg*, *Tg*
M Schuster 2000 *S*, 2004 *Tg*, *S*, *Fj*
NSJ Schuster 1999 *Tg*, *F*, *US*
P Schuster 1975 *Tg*
M Schwalger 2000 *W*, *S*, 2001 *It*, 2003 *Nm*, *Ur*, *Geo*, *E*, 2005 *S*, *E*, *Ar*, 2006 *J*, *Fj*, *Tg*, 2007 *Fj*, *SA*, *Tg*, *SA*, *Tg*, *E*, *US*, 2008 *Fj*, 2009 *J*, *Tg*, *Fj*, *PNG*, *W*, *F*, *It*, 2010 *Tg*, *J*, *Fj*, *I*, *E*, *S*, 2011 *Fj*, *A*, *Nm*, *W*, *Fj*, *SA*
Sefo 1932 *Tg*
E Sefo 1984 *Fj*
T Sefo 1987 *Tg*, 1988 *I*
P Segi 2001 *Fj*, *NZ*, *Fj*, *Tg*, *J*, *I*, *It*, 2002 *Fj*, *Tg*, *Fj*, *Tg*
K Seinafo 1992 *Tg*
F Selesele 2010 *Tg*, *J*, *J*
S Semeane 2009 *It*
J Senio 2004 *Tg*, *S*, *Fj*, 2005 *Tg*, *Fj*, *Tg*, *Fj*, 2006 *J*, *Fj*, *Tg*
U Setu 2010 *Tg*, *J*
T Seumanutafa 1981 *Fj*
E Seveali'I 2000 *Fj*, *J*, *Tg*, *C*, 2001 *Tg*, *NZ*, *J*, *Fj*, *It*, 2002 *Fj*, *Tg*, *Fj*, *Tg*, *SA*, 2005 *E*, 2007 *SA*, *J*, *Tg*, *SA*, *Tg*, *US*
F Sililoto 1980 *Tg*, 1981 *Fj*, *Fj*, 1982 *Fj*, *Fj*, *Fj*
Simanu 1932 *Tg*
A Simanu 1975 *Tg*, 1981 *Fj*
Sinaumea 1924 *Fj*
F Sini 1995 *SA*, *Ar*, *E*, *SA*
S Sinoti 2010 *J*
K Sio 1988 *Tg*, *Fj*, *I*, *W*, 1989 *Fj*, *WGe*, *R*, 1990 *J*, *Tg*, *Fj*, 1992 *Tg*, *Fj*, 1993 *NZ*, 1994 *Tg*
T Sio 1990 *Tg*, 1992 *Fj*
P Sioa 1981 *Fj*, *Fj*
S Sititi 1999 *J*, *C*, *F*, *J*, *W*, *S*, 2000 *Fj*, *J*, *Tg*, *C*, *US*, 2001 *Tg*, *Fj*, *NZ*, *Fj*, *Tg*, *J*, *Fj*, *I*, *It*, 2002 *Fj*, *Tg*, *Fj*, *Tg*, *SA*, 2003 *I*, *Nm*, *Ur*, *Geo*, *E*, *SA*, 2004 *Tg*, *S*, *Fj*, 2005 *A*, *Fj*, *Tg*, *Fj*, *S*, *E*, *Ar*, 2006 *J*, *Fj*, *Tg*, 2007 *Fj*, *SA*, *J*, *Tg*, *SA*, *Tg*, *E*, *US*, 2008 *Fj*, *Tg*, *J*, *NZ*, 2009 *J*, *PNG*, *PNG*
F Siu 1975 *Tg*
P Siu 1963 *Fj*, *Fj*, *Tg*
E Skelton 2009 *J*, *Tg*, *PNG*, *PNG*
S Skelton 1982 *Fj*
C Slade 2006 *J*, *Fj*, *Tg*, 2008 *Fj*, *Tg*, *NZ*
R Slade 1972 *Tg*
S Smith 1995 *S*, *E*, 1996 *Tg*, *Fj*, 1999 *C*, *Tg*, *F*, *NZ*
P Solia 1955 *Fj*, *Fj*
I Solipo 1981 *Fj*
F Solomona 1985 *Tg*
J Sooialo 2011 *J*, *Fj*, *Tg*, *W*
A So'oialo 1996 *I*, 1997 *Tg*, *Fj*, 1998 *Tg*, 1999 *Tg*, *F*, *NZ*, *US*, *Fj*, *J*, *Ar*, 2000 *Tg*, *It*, 2001 *Tg*, *Fj*, *NZ*, *Fj*, *Tg*, *J*, *I*
S So'oialo 1998 *Tg*, *Fj*, 1999 *NZ*, *US*, *Fj*, *J*, *Ar*, *W*, *S*, 2000 *W*, *S*, 2001 *Tg*, *Fj*, *NZ*, *Fj*, *J*, *Fj*, *I*, 2002 *Tg*, *Fj*, *Tg*, *SA*, 2003 *I*, *Nm*, *Ur*, *Geo*, *E*, *SA*, 2004 *Tg*, *S*, *Fj*, 2005 *E*, 2007 *Fj*, *SA*, *J*, *Tg*, *E*, *US*
F So'olefai 1999 *C*, *Tg*, 2000 *W*, *S*, 2001 *Tg*, *Fj*, *NZ*, *Fj*, *J*
V Stet 1963 *Fj*

A Stewart 2005 *A, Tg*
G Stowers 2001 *I*, 2008 *Fj, Tg, J, NZ*, 2009 *J, Tg, Fj, PNG, W, It*, 2010 *Tg, J, Fj, I, E, S*, 2011 *Fj, A, Nm, W, Fj, SA*
R Stowers 2008 *Fj*
F Sua 1982 *Fj, Fj, Fj, Tg*, 1983 *Tg, Fj*, 1984 *Fj*, 1985 *Fj, Tg, Tg*, 1986 *Fj, Tg*, 1987 *Fj*
JI Sua 2011 *W, Fj*
P Swepson 1957 *Tg*

S Ta'ala 1996 *Tg, Fj, I*, 1997 *Tg, Fj*, 1998 *Tg, Fj, A*, 1999 *J, C, Tg, US, Fj, J, Ar, W, S*, 2001 *J*
T Taega 1997 *Fj*
PI Taele 2005 *Tg, Fj, E, Ar*, 2006 *J, Fj, Tg*, 2010 *J*
D Tafeamalii 2000 *W, S*
T Tafua 1981 *Fj, Fj*, 1982 *Fj, Fj, Fj, Tg*, 1983 *Tg, Fj*, 1985 *Fj, Tg, Tg*, 1986 *W, Fj, Tg*, 1987 *Tg*, 1989 *Fj, WGe, R*
L Tafunai 2004 *Tg, Fj*, 2005 *Tg, Fj, Tg, Fj, S, Ar*, 2008 *Tg, J, NZ*
TDL Tagaloa 1990 *Kor, Tg, J, Tg, Fj*, 1991 *W, A, Ar, S*
S Tagicakibau 2003 *Nm, Ur, Geo, E, SA*, 2004 *Tg, S, Fj*, 2005 *S, E, Ar*, 2007 *Tg*, 2009 *J, Tg, Fj*, 2011 *J, Fj, A, Nm, W, Fj*
Tagimanu 1924 *Fj*
I Taina 2005 *Tg, Fj, Tg, Fj, S*
F Taiomaivao 1989 *Bel*
F Talapusi 1979 *Tg, Fj*, 1980 *Tg*
F Talapusi 2005 *A, Fj, Tg, Fj*
Tamalua 1932 *Tg*
F Tanoa'i 1996 *Tg, Fj*
S Tanuko 1987 *Tg*
P Tapelu 2002 *SA*
V Tasi 1981 *Fj*, 1982 *Fj, Fj, Fj, Tg*, 1983 *Tg, Fj*, 1984 *Fj, Tg*
J Tatupu 2010 *J*
S Tatupu 1990 *Tg*, 1993 *Tg, Fj, NZ*, 1995 *It, Ar, E, SA, Fj, Tg*
N Tauafao 2005 *A, Tg, Fj, Tg, Fj, S, Ar*, 2007 *Fj*, 2008 *Fj, Tg, J, NZ*, 2009 *J, Fj, PNG, PNG*
S Taulafo 2009 *W, F, It*, 2010 *Tg, Fj, I, E, S*, 2011 *J, A, Nm, W, Fj, SA*
I Tautau 1985 *Fj, Tg*, 1986 *W*
T Tavita 1984 *Fj, Tg*
E Taylor 2011 *J, Fj*
H Tea 2008 *Fj, Tg, J, NZ*, 2009 *PNG*
I Tekori 2007 *SA, J, SA, Tg, E, US*, 2009 *Tg, Fj, W, F*, 2010 *Tg, J, Fj, I, E, S*, 2011 *J, Nm, W, SA*
AT Telea 1995 *S, E*, 1996 *NZ, Tg, Fj*
E Telea 2008 *Fj*
S Telea 1989 *Bel*
A Teo 1947 *Tg*
F Teo 1955 *Fj*
V Teo 1957 *Tg, Tg*
K Thompson 2007 *Fj, SA, Tg, SA, Tg, E, US*, 2008 *Tg, J*, 2009 *W, F, It*, 2010 *Tg, Fj, I, E, S*, 2011 *A, Nm, W, Fj, SA*
H Thomson 1947 *Tg*
A Tiatia 2001 *Tg, Fj, NZ, Fj, Tg, J, Fj*
R Tiatia 1972 *Tg*
S Tilialo 1972 *Tg*
M Timoteo 2009 *Tg, F, It*
F Tipi 1998 *Fj, A*, 1999 *J, C, F, NZ, Fj*
F Toala 1998 *Fj*, 1999 *J, C, S*, 2000 *W, S*
L Toelupe 1979 *Fj*
P Toelupe 2008 *Fj, J, NZ*
T Tofaeono 1989 *Fj, Bel*
A Toleafoa 2000 *W, S*, 2002 *Tg, SA*
K Toleafoa 1955 *Fj, Fj*
PL Toleafoa 2006 *J, Fj*
K Tole'afoa 1998 *Tg, A*, 1999 *Ar*
F Toloa 1979 *Tg*, 1980 *Tg*
R Tolufale 2008 *NZ*, 2009 *PNG*
J Tomuli 2001 *I, It*, 2002 *Fj, Tg, Fj, Tg, SA*, 2003 *I, Nm, Ur, Geo, E, SA*, 2006 *J*
L Tone 1998 *Tg, Fj, A*, 1999 *J, C, Tg, F, NZ, US, J, Ar, W, S*, 2000 *Fj, J, Tg, C, It, US, S*, 2001 *NZ, Fj, Tg, J, Fj*
S Tone 2000 *W*
Toni 1924 *Fj*
OFJ Tonu'u 1992 *Tg*, 1993 *Tg, Fj, NZ*
F To'omalatai 1989 *Bel*
PS To'omalatai 1985 *Fj, Tg*, 1986 *W, Fj, Tg*, 1988 *Tg, Fj, I, W*, 1989 *Fj, WGe, Bel, R*, 1990 *Kor, Tg, J, Tg, Fj*, 1991 *Tg, Fj, W, A, Ar, S*, 1992 *Tg, Fj*, 1993 *Fj*, 1994 *A*, 1995 *Fj*
O Treviranus 2009 *J, Tg, Fj, PNG, PNG, W, F, It*, 2010 *J, Fj, J, I, E, S*, 2011 *Fj, Tg, Nm, W, SA*
Tualai 1924 *Fj, Fj*
I Tualaulelei 1963 *Fj, Fj, Tg*
F Tuatagaloa 1957 *Tg*
K Tuatagaloa 1963 *Fj, Fj, Tg*, 1972 *Tg*
V Tuatagaloa 1963 *Fj, Tg*
Tufele 1924 *Fj*
D Tuiavi'I 2003 *I, Nm, Ur, E, SA*
T Tuifua 2011 *J, Fj, A, Nm, Fj, SA*
VL Tuigamala 1996 *Fj, I*, 1997 *Tg, Fj*, 1998 *Tg, Fj, A*, 1999 *F, NZ, US, Fj, J, Ar, W, S*, 2000 *Fj, J, Tg, US*, 2001 *J, Fj, I, It*
AF Tuilagi 2005 *Tg, Fj, Tg, Fj, S, Ar*, 2006 *J, Tg*, 2007 *Fj, SA, J*, 2008 *Tg, J*, 2009 *W*
AT Tuilagi 2002 *Fj, Tg, SA*, 2005 *A, Tg, Fj, Tg, Fj, S, E*, 2007 *SA, J, Tg, SA, Tg, E, US*, 2010 *I, E, S*, 2011 *J, A, Nm, W, Fj, SA*
F Tuilagi 1992 *Tg*, 1994 *W, Fj, A*, 1995 *SA, SA, Fj*, 2000 *W, S*, 2001 *Fj, NZ, Tg*, 2002 *Fj, Tg, Fj, Tg, SA*
H Tuilagi 2002 *Fj, Tg, Fj, Tg*, 2007 *SA, E*, 2008 *J*, 2009 *W, F, It*
T Tuisaula 1947 *Tg*
R Tuivaiti 2004 *Fj*
A Tunupopo 1963 *Fj*
P Tupa'i 2005 *A, Tg, S, E, Ar*
A Tupou 2008 *NZ*, 2009 *PNG*
S Tupuola 1982 *Fj, Fj, Fj, Tg*, 1983 *Tg, Fj*, 1985 *Tg*, 1986 *Fj, Tg*, 1987 *Fj, Tg*, 1988 *W*, 1989 *R*
P Tu'uau 1972 *Tg, Tg*, 1975 *Tg*
D Tyrrell 2000 *Fj, J, C*, 2001 *It*, 2002 *Fj, Tg, SA*, 2003 *I, Nm, Ur, Geo, E, SA*

S Uati 1988 *Tg, Fj*
T Ugapo 1988 *Tg, Fj, I, W*, 1989 *Fj, WGe, Bel*
U Ulia 2004 *Tg, S, Fj*, 2005 *Ar*, 2006 *J, Fj, Tg*, 2007 *Fj, Tg, Tg, US*
J Ulugia 1985 *Fj, Tg*
M Umaga 1995 *SA, It, Ar, E, SA*, 1998 *Tg, Fj, A*, 1999 *Tg, F, NZ, US, Fj*
A Utu'utu 1979 *Tg, Fj*
L Utu'utu 1975 *Tg*

E Va'a 1996 *I*, 1997 *Fj*, 1998 *A*, 1999 *Tg, NZ, Fj, J, W, S*, 2001 *Tg, Fj, NZ, Fj, Tg, J, Fj, I*, 2002 *Fj, Tg, Fj, Tg, SA*, 2003 *I, Nm, Ur, Geo, E, SA*
JH Va'a 2005 *A, Fj, Tg, Fj, S, E, Ar*, 2006 *Fj, Tg*, 2007 *SA, J, Tg, SA*, 2009 *J, Tg, Fj, W, It*
M Vaea 1991 *Tg, Fj, W, A, Ar, S*, 1992 *Fj*, 1995 *S*
K Vaega 1982 *Fj, Tg*, 1983 *Fj*
TM Vaega 1986 *W*, 1989 *WGe, Bel, R*, 1990 *Kor, Tg, J, Tg, Fj*, 1991 *Tg, Fj, W, A, Ar, S*, 1992 *Tg, Fj*, 1993 *Tg, Fj, NZ*, 1994 *Tg, W, Fj, A*, 1995 *SA, It, Ar, E, SA, Fj, Tg, S, E*, 1996 *NZ, Tg, Fj, I*, 1997 *Tg*, 1998 *Fj, A*, 1999 *J, C, F, NZ, Fj, J, Ar, W, S*, 2000 *Fj, J, Tg, C, It, US*, 2001 *Fj, Tg, J, Fj, I*
A Vaeluaga 2000 *W, S*, 2001 *Tg, Fj, Tg, J, Fj, I*, 2007 *SA, J, SA, E, US*
F Vagaia 1972 *Tg*
K Vai 1987 *Fj, Tg*, 1989 *Bel*
S Vaifale 1989 *R*, 1990 *Kor, Tg, J, Tg, Fj*, 1991 *Tg, Fj, W, Ar, S*, 1992 *Tg, Fj*, 1993 *NZ*, 1994 *Tg, W, Fj, A*, 1995 *SA, It, SA, Fj, S, E*, 1996 *NZ, Tg*, 1997 *Tg, Fj*
S Vaili 2001 *I, It*, 2002 *Fj, Tg, Fj, Tg*, 2003 *Geo*, 2004 *Tg, S, Fj*
L Vailoaloa 2005 *A*, 2011 *J, Fj, Tg*
S Vaisola Sefo 2007 *US*
T Veiru 2000 *W, S*
M Vili 1957 *Tg*
M Vili 1975 *Tg*
T Vili 1999 *C, Tg, US, Ar*, 2000 *Fj, J, Tg, C, It, US*, 2001 *Tg, Fj, J, Fj, I, It*, 2003 *Ur, Geo, E, SA*, 2004 *Tg, S, Fj*, 2005 *A, Tg, Fj, S, E*, 2006 *J, Fj, Tg*
K Viliamu 2001 *I, It*, 2002 *Fj, SA*, 2003 *I, Ur, Geo, E, SA*, 2004 *S*
T Viliamu 1947 *Tg*
Visesio 1932 *Tg*
FV Vitale 1994 *W, Fj, A*, 1995 *Fj, Tg*
F Vito 1972 *Tg*, 1975 *Tg*
M von Dincklage 2004 *S*

R Warren 2004 *Tg, S*, 2005 *Tg, Fj, Tg, Fj, S, Ar*, 2008 *Fj, Tg, J, NZ*
S Wendt 1955 *Fj, Fj, Fj*
AF Williams 2009 *J, Fj, PNG, PNG, F, It*, 2010 *J, J*
DR Williams 1988 *I, W*, 1995 *SA, It, E*
G Williams 2007 *Fj, SA, SA, Tg*, 2008 *Tg, J*, 2009 *J, Tg, Fj, PNG, PNG, W, It*, 2010 *J, I, E*
H Williams 2001 *Tg, Tg, J*
PB Williams 2010 *Tg, J, Fj, I, E, S*, 2011 *A, Nm, W, Fj, SA*

P Young 1988 *I*, 1989 *Bel*

SCOTLAND

SCOTLAND'S 2010–11 TEST RECORD

OPPONENTS	DATE	VENUE	RESULT
New Zealand	13 Nov	H	**Lost** 3–49
South Africa	20 Nov	H	**Won** 21–17
Samoa	27 Nov	H	**Won** 19–16
France	5 Feb	A	**Lost** 21–34
Wales	12 Feb	H	**Lost** 6–24
Ireland	27 Feb	H	**Lost** 18–21
England	13 Mar	A	**Lost** 16–22
Italy	19 Mar	A	**Won** 21–8
Ireland	6 Aug	H	**Won** 10–6
Italy	20 Aug	H	**Won** 23–12
Romania	10 Sept	N	**Won** 34–24
Georgia	14 Sept	N	**Won** 15–6
Argentina	25 Sept	N	**Lost** 12–13
England	1 Oct	N	**Lost** 12–16

SCOTS SUFFER EARLY EXIT

By Iain Spragg

Dave Rogers/Getty Images

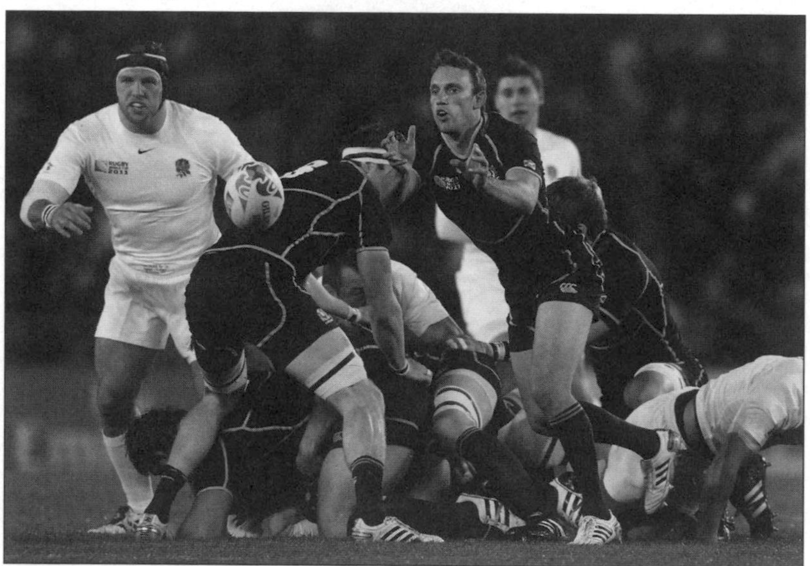

Scotland suffered agonisingly close defeats to Argentina and England to go out in the pool stages.

A fatal inability to protect a lead was to prove the agonising difference between progress to the knockout stages and an uncharacteristically premature flight home as Andy Robinson's side failed to reach the Rugby World Cup quarter-finals for the first time in Scotland's history after narrow defeats to Argentina and England in the pool phase.

Scotland had reached the last eight in all six previous incarnations of the tournament, but that record finally came to an abrupt end in New Zealand as the Scots failed to close out winning positions against both the Pumas in their penultimate Pool B fixture and then against the English as the pool came to a climax.

After victories over Romania and Georgia, a heartbreaking 13–12 defeat to the Argentineans in Wellington left Scottish hopes of qualification on a knife edge. A week later they were beaten 16–12 by the Auld Enemy in Auckland and, with Argentina duly despatching the Georgians the following day, Scotland's third-place finish in the pool was confirmed and their fate sealed.

On both occasions, the Scots headed into the final 10 minutes of the game in the lead, but both times they failed to finish the job.

"Winning and losing is about small margins, it's about the inches," said Robinson after his side's reverse against England. "That's what Test rugby is about. You've got to be able to finish teams off. We weren't able to do that. It's a hard lesson. Sometimes sport can be cruel, but it's about how you can bounce back and get yourselves ready for your next challenge.

"We're hugely disappointed to lose the game, as we were last week [against Argentina]. In both cases, where it's come to winning games, we've lost out. But I've got to give every credit to my side. The way they have carried themselves throughout the World Cup, the friends they've made, I think they've been an outstanding group of people. I've been delighted to be their head coach.

"Obviously everybody's hugely disappointed with the way that we ended the tournament and with not qualifying for the quarter-final stages. But there's a lot of positives I'm going to take out of the tournament, and for the squad it's important now we're able to start the planning for the Six Nations.

"I have a contract to 2015, and I have the desire to still coach Scotland. The way the players have gone about this tournament, the enthusiasm that they've had, has fuelled my desire even more to create a successful Scotland team."

Robinson earned that long-term contract, announced on the eve of the Six Nations campaign, after masterminding Scotland's 21–17 victory over world champions South Africa at Murrayfield in November and, despite disappointing results in the Championship itself, warm-up victories over Ireland and Italy sent the Scots to the World Cup in good heart and harbouring a quiet sense of confidence.

The head coach named lock Alastair Kellock as his captain for the tournament and, despite surprisingly overlooking Glasgow No. 8 Johnnie Beattie, it was a familiar-looking 30-man squad that boarded the plane to New Zealand.

Scotland's tournament opener saw them tackle Romania in Invercargill's Rugby Park Stadium. Mike Blair's seventh-minute try followed by Joe Ansbro's 20th-minute score initially hinted at the comfortable victory all sides crave at the beginning of a World Cup campaign, but the Oaks rallied with tries either side of half-time to take the advantage and Scotland were ultimately indebted to two late scores from Simon Danielli as they ran out stuttering 34–24 winners.

"We had the ability after the first 15 minutes to really push on and keep going," Kellock said after the game. "The errors that we made and the mistakes that let Romania get into that lead were basic, simple things – a clear out at a ruck, urgency, accuracy at the breakdown. Things we can fix and will fix. I'm gutted we put ourselves in that position, but I'm delighted we managed to drag ourselves out of it."

Four days later Scotland were in action again in Invercargill against Georgia, but Robinson's team were no more convincing in a 15–6 victory over the Lelos than they had been against the Romanians.

The blustery, wet conditions did not lend themselves to a feast of running rugby, but Scotland rarely threatened the Georgian line and were forced to rely on the boot of Dan Parks as their sole source of points, the Cardiff Blues fly-half landing four penalties and a drop-goal.

"We came up against a big old Georgian side who were really determined, really physical, and ultimately it was a workmanlike performance to put them away today," admitted scrum-half and stand-in skipper Rory Lawson. "We just kept plugging away in the right areas and then took the points when they were on offer.

"We came here looking to get two wins, and it's tough with a four-day turnaround, but we got what we came for. Now we prepare for the next challenge."

At this stage, Scotland topped the pool with nine points, but the acid test of the team's credentials lay ahead, and they decamped to Wellington for the pivotal clash with the Pumas.

The result in the Wellington Regional Stadium hung by a thread throughout, but at half-time the Scots had edged into a 6–3 lead courtesy of penalties from Chris Paterson and Ruaridh Jackson. Successful drop-goals from Jackson and Parks in six second-half minutes left Robinson's team needing to defend a 12–6 scoreline with nine minutes to play, but they were unable to hang on, substitute Lucas Gonzalez Amorosino crashing over for Argentina for the only try of the game and victory.

"We got to 12–6, and I felt we were in control of the game," said a disappointed Robinson after the final whistle. "The reason why we lost this game was just a moment of dropping off concentration. That team is grieving in the dressing room. It really is. It felt it got into an outstanding position.

"You've got to take your hat off to Argentina, to find a way of being able to win a game when in that second half I thought they were outplayed. They were able to find an answer, which is disappointing from our side, but their never-say-die attitude got them through."

Scotland now prepared for the England game in Auckland – the first time in 129 matches and 140 years the two teams had played on neutral soil – knowing that they needed to beat the Auld Enemy by eight points for the bonus point win which would guarantee themselves a quarter-final place irrespective of what happened to Argentina against Georgia 24 hours later.

Robinson made six changes from the XV beaten by Argentina, recalling Kellock, Euan Murray and Richie Vernon in the pack while Mike Blair, Danielli and Ansbro were restored to the back-line.

As they had in only one of their previous three games in the pool, it was Scotland who drew first blood at Eden Park when Paterson landed an eighth-minute penalty after an infringement at the scrum, and when Parks doubled the advantage eight minutes later the Scots began dreaming of a famous victory and a route to the last eight.

England replied with a Jonny Wilkinson penalty, but when Parks landed a drop-goal moments before the break Scotland headed to the dressing room with a 9–3 lead and the momentum.

The men in blue still needed an eight-point winning margin and they got it, albeit temporarily, when Paterson kicked his second penalty on 55 minutes, and if the match had ended then Scotland would have qualified for the knockout stages.

There were, of course, 25 minutes to play, and England clawed their way back into the match with a Wilkinson drop-goal and second penalty, and with three minutes remaining Robinson's team held a slender 12–9 lead that collectively they knew would be unlikely to take them through.

In the end, it was to prove hypothetical as England scored the only try of the match through wing Chris Ashton, converted by substitute Toby Flood, to secure a 16–12 triumph that confirmed the English as pool winners.

In theory, Scotland could have stayed in the tournament had Georgia ambushed Argentina in Palmerston North the next day, but the Pumas were not in a generous mood, winning 25–7 to reach the quarter-finals for a second successive World Cup. Scotland were going home early.

"The difference was Argentina and England maybe had one or two chances and were very clinical when they had those chances," Kellock reflected after the last-gasp defeat to England. "We created opportunities to score tries, but we didn't take them. We should have kept building the pressure. There's never a doubt about our commitment. To a man, we left ourselves out there."

SCOTLAND INTERNATIONAL STATISTICS

MATCH RECORDS UP TO 31 OCTOBER 2011

MOST CONSECUTIVE TEST WINS

6 1925 *F, W, I, E,* 1926 *F, W*
6 1989 *Fj, R,* 1990 *I, F, W, E*

MOST CONSECUTIVE TESTS WITHOUT DEFEAT

Matches	Wins	Draws	Period
9	6*	3	1885 to 1887
6	6	0	1925 to 1926
6	6	0	1989 to 1990
6	4	2	1877 to 1880
6	5	1	1983 to 1984

** includes an abandoned match*

MOST POINTS IN A MATCH

BY THE TEAM

Pts	Opponents	Venue	Year
100	Japan	Perth	2004
89	Ivory Coast	Rustenburg	1995
65	United States	San Francisco	2002
60	Zimbabwe	Wellington	1987
60	Romania	Hampden Park	1999
56	Portugal	Saint Etienne	2007
55	Romania	Dunedin	1987
53	United States	Murrayfield	2000
51	Zimbabwe	Murrayfield	1991
49	Argentina	Murrayfield	1990
49	Romania	Murrayfield	1995

BY A PLAYER

Pts	Player	Opponents	Venue	Year
44	A G Hastings	Ivory Coast	Rustenburg	1995
40	C D Paterson	Japan	Perth	2004
33	G P J Townsend	United States	Murrayfield	2000
31	A G Hastings	Tonga	Pretoria	1995
27	A G Hastings	Romania	Dunedin	1987
26	K M Logan	Romania	Hampden Park	1999
24	B J Laney	Italy	Rome	2002
24	D A Parks	Argentina	Tucumán	2010
23	G Ross	Tonga	Murrayfield	2001
21	A G Hastings	England	Murrayfield	1986
21	A G Hastings	Romania	Bucharest	1986
21	C D Paterson	Wales	Murrayfield	2007
21	D A Parks	South Africa	Murrayfield	2010

MOST TRIES IN A MATCH

BY THE TEAM

Tries	Opponents	Venue	Year
15	Japan	Perth	2004
13	Ivory Coast	Rustenburg	1995
12	Wales	Raeburn Place	1887
11	Zimbabwe	Wellington	1987
10	United States	San Francisco	2002
9	Romania	Dunedin	1987
9	Argentina	Murrayfield	1990

BY A PLAYER

Tries	Player	Opponents	Venue	Year
5	G C Lindsay	Wales	Raeburn Place	1887
4	W A Stewart	Ireland	Inverleith	1913
4	I S Smith	France	Inverleith	1925
4	I S Smith	Wales	Swansea	1925
4	A G Hastings	Ivory Coast	Rustenburg	1995

MOST CONVERSIONS IN A MATCH

BY THE TEAM

Cons	Opponents	Venue	Year
11	Japan	Perth	2004
9	Ivory Coast	Rustenburg	1995
8	Zimbabwe	Wellington	1987
8	Romania	Dunedin	1987
8	Portugal	Saint Etienne	2007

BY A PLAYER

Cons	Player	Opponents	Venue	Year
11	C D Paterson	Japan	Perth	2004
9	A G Hastings	Ivory Coast	Rustenburg	1995
8	A G Hastings	Zimbabwe	Wellington	1987
8	A G Hastings	Romania	Dunedin	1987

MOST PENALTIES IN A MATCH

BY THE TEAM

Penalties	Opponents	Venue	Year
8	Tonga	Pretoria	1995
7	Wales	Murrayfield	2007
6	France	Murrayfield	1986
6	Italy	Murrayfield	2005
6	Ireland	Murrayfield	2007
6	Italy	Saint Etienne	2007
6	Argentina	Tucumán	2010
6	South Africa	Murrayfield	2010

BY A PLAYER

Pens	Player	Opponents	Venue	Year
8	A G Hastings	Tonga	Pretoria	1995
7	C D Paterson	Wales	Murrayfield	2007
6	A G Hastings	France	Murrayfield	1986
6	C D Paterson	Italy	Murrayfield	2005
6	C D Paterson	Ireland	Murrayfield	2007
6	C D Paterson	Italy	Saint Etienne	2007
6	D A Parks	Argentina	Tucumán	2010
6	D A Parks	South Africa	Murrayfield	2010

MOST DROPPED GOALS IN A MATCH

BY THE TEAM

Drops	Opponents	Venue	Year
3	Ireland	Murrayfield	1973
2	on several occasions		

BY A PLAYER

Drops	Player	Opponents	Venue	Year
2	R C MacKenzie	Ireland	Belfast	1877
2	N J Finlay	Ireland	Glasgow	1880
2	B M Simmers	Wales	Murrayfield	1965
2	D W Morgan	Ireland	Murrayfield	1973
2	B M Gossman	France	Parc des Princes	1983
2	J Y Rutherford	New Zealand	Murrayfield	1983
2	J Y Rutherford	Wales	Murrayfield	1985
2	J Y Rutherford	Ireland	Murrayfield	1987
2	C M Chalmers	England	Twickenham	1995
2	D A Parks	Wales	Cardiff	2010
2	D A Parks	Argentina	Tucumán	2010

CAREER RECORDS

MOST CAPPED PLAYERS

Caps	Player	Career Span
109	C D Paterson	1999 to 2011
87	S Murray	1997 to 2007
82	G P J Townsend	1993 to 2003
77	J P R White	2000 to 2009
77	N J Hines	2000 to 2011
75	G C Bulloch	1997 to 2005
75	M R L Blair	2002 to 2011
71	S B Grimes	1997 to 2005
70	K M Logan	1992 to 2003
66	S M Taylor	2000 to 2009
66	D A Parks	2004 to 2011
65	S Hastings	1986 to 1997
61	A G Hastings	1986 to 1995
61	G W Weir	1990 to 2000
61	T J Smith	1997 to 2005
60	C M Chalmers	1989 to 1999
60	B W Redpath	1993 to 2003
60	S F Lamont	2004 to 2011
60	A F Jacobsen	2002 to 2011
59	H F G Southwell	2004 to 2011
55	C P Cusiter	2004 to 2011
53	A R Henderson	2001 to 2008
53	R W Ford	2004 to 2011
52	J M Renwick	1972 to 1984
52	C T Deans	1978 to 1987
52	A G Stanger	1989 to 1998
52	A P Burnell	1989 to 1999
51	A R Irvine	1972 to 1982
51	G Armstrong	1988 to 1999

MOST CONSECUTIVE TESTS

Tests	Player	Span
49	A B Carmichael	1967 to 1978
44	C D Paterson	2004 to 2008
40	H F McLeod	1954 to 1962
37	J M Bannerman	1921 to 1929
35	A G Stanger	1989 to 1994

MOST TESTS AS CAPTAIN

Tests	Captain	Span
25	D M B Sole	1989 to 1992
21	B W Redpath	1998 to 2003
20	A G Hastings	1993 to 1995
19	J McLauchlan	1973 to 1979
19	J P R White	2005 to 2008
16	R I Wainwright	1995 to 1998
15	M C Morrison	1899 to 1904
15	A R Smith	1957 to 1962
15	A R Irvine	1980 to 1982

MOST POINTS IN TESTS

Points	Player	Tests	Career
809	C D Paterson	109	1999 to 2011
667	A G Hastings	61	1986 to 1995
273	A R Irvine	51	1972 to 1982
260	D A Parks	66	2004 to 2011
220	K M Logan	70	1992 to 2003
210	P W Dods	23	1983 to 1991
166	C M Chalmers	60	1989 to 1999
164	G P J Townsend	82	1993 to 2003
141	B J Laney	20	2001 to 2004
123	D W Hodge	26	1997 to 2002
106	A G Stanger	52	1989 to 1998

MOST TRIES IN TESTS

Tries	Player	Tests	Career
24	I S Smith	32	1924 to 1933
24	A G Stanger	52	1989 to 1998
22	C D Paterson	109	1999 to 2011
17	A G Hastings	61	1986 to 1995
17	A V Tait	27	1987 to 1999
17	G P J Townsend	82	1993 to 2003
15	I Tukalo	37	1985 to 1992
13	K M Logan	70	1992 to 2003
12	A R Smith	33	1955 to 1962

MOST CONVERSIONS IN TESTS

Cons	Player	Tests	Career
90	C D Paterson	109	1999 to 2011
86	A G Hastings	61	1986 to 1995
34	K M Logan	70	1992 to 2003
26	P W Dods	23	1983 to 1991
25	A R Irvine	51	1972 to 1982
19	D Drysdale	26	1923 to 1929
17	B J Laney	20	2001 to 2004
15	D W Hodge	26	1997 to 2002
15	D A Parks	66	2004 to 2011
14	F H Turner	15	1911 to 1914
14	R J S Shepherd	20	1995 to 1998

MOST PENALTY GOALS IN TESTS

Penalties	Player	Tests	Career
170	C D Paterson	109	1999 to 2011
140	A G Hastings	61	1986 to 1995
61	A R Irvine	51	1972 to 1982
53	D A Parks	66	2004 to 2011
50	P W Dods	23	1983 to 1991
32	C M Chalmers	60	1989 to 1999
29	K M Logan	70	1992 to 2003
29	B J Laney	20	2001 to 2004
21	M Dods	8	1994 to 1996
21	R J S Shepherd	20	1995 to 1998

MOST DROPPED GOALS IN TESTS

Drops	Player	Tests	Career
17	D A Parks	66	2004 to 2011
12	J Y Rutherford	42	1979 to 1987
9	C M Chalmers	60	1989 to 1999
7	I R McGeechan	32	1972 to 1979
7	G P J Townsend	82	1993 to 2003
6	D W Morgan	21	1973 to 1978
5	H Waddell	15	1924 to 1930

Dave Rogers/Getty Images

Dan Parks is still Scotland's dropped goal king with 17 in Test matches.

INTERNATIONAL CHAMPIONSHIP RECORDS

RECORD	DETAIL	HOLDER	SET
Most points in season	120	in four matches	1999
Most tries in season	17	in four matches	1925
Highest score	38	38–10 v Ireland	1997
Biggest win	28	31–3 v France	1912
	28	38–10 v Ireland	1997
Highest score conceded	51	16–51 v France	1998
Biggest defeat	40	3–43 v England	2001
Most appearances	53	C D Paterson	2000–2011
Most points in matches	403	C D Paterson	2000–2011
Most points in season	65	C D Paterson	2007
Most points in match	24	B J Laney	v Italy, 2002
Most tries in matches	24	I S Smith	1924–1933
Most tries in season	8	I S Smith	1925
Most tries in match	5	G C Lindsay	v Wales, 1887
Most cons in matches	34	C D Paterson	2000–2011
Most cons in season	11	K M Logan	1999
Most cons in match	5	F H Turner	v France, 1912
	5	J W Allan	v England, 1931
	5	R J S Shepherd	v Ireland, 1997
Most pens in matches	99	C D Paterson	2000–2011
Most pens in season	16	C D Paterson	2007
Most pens in match	7	C D Paterson	v Wales, 2007
Most drops in matches	9	D A Parks	2004–2011
Most drops in season	5	D A Parks	2010
Most drops in match	2	on several occasions	

MISCELLANEOUS RECORDS

RECORD	HOLDER	DETAIL
Longest Test Career	W C W Murdoch	1935 to 1948
Youngest Test Cap	N J Finlay	17 yrs 36 days in 1875*
Oldest Test Cap	J McLauchlan	37 yrs 210 days in 1979

* C Reid, also 17 yrs 36 days on debut in 1881, was a day older than Finlay, having lived through an extra leap-year day.

CAREER RECORDS OF SCOTLAND INTERNATIONAL PLAYERS (UP TO 31 OCTOBER 2011)

PLAYER BACKS :	DEBUT	CAPS	T	C	P	D	PTS
J A Ansbro	2010 v SA	9	2	0	0	0	10
M R L Blair	2002 v C	75	7	0	0	0	35
C P Cusiter	2004 v W	55	3	0	0	0	15
J E Cuthbert	2011 v I	1	0	0	0	0	0
S C J Danielli	2003 v It	32	8	0	0	0	40
N J de Luca	2008 v F	29	1	0	0	0	5
M B Evans	2008 v C	24	3	0	0	0	15
R J H Jackson	2010 v NZ	11	0	2	2	2	16
G D Laidlaw	2010 v NZ	2	0	0	0	0	0
R P Lamont	2005 v W	26	6	0	0	0	30
S F Lamont	2004 v Sm	60	8	0	0	0	40
R G M Lawson	2006 v A	30	0	0	0	0	0
G A Morrison	2004 v A	32	3	0	0	0	15
D A Parks	2004 v W	66	4	15	53	17	260
C D Paterson	1999 v Sp	109	22	90	170	3	809
H F G Southwell	2004 v Sm	59	8	0	0	0	40
N Walker	2002 v R	24	6	0	0	0	30
FORWARDS :							
J A Barclay	2007 v NZ	32	2	0	0	0	10
J W Beattie	2006 v R	16	3	0	0	0	15
K D R Brown	2005 v R	49	4	0	0	0	20
G D S Cross	2009 v W	8	0	0	0	0	0

D K Denton	2011 v I	1	0	0	0	0	0
A G Dickinson	2007 v NZ	24	1	0	0	0	5
R W Ford	2004 v A	53	2	0	0	0	10
R J Gray	2010 v F	16	0	0	0	0	0
D W H Hall	2003 v W	37	1	0	0	0	5
J L Hamilton	2006 v R	34	1	0	0	0	5
N J Hines	2000 v NZ	77	2	0	0	0	10
A F Jacobsen	2002 v C	60	0	0	0	0	0
A D Kellock	2004 v A	36	1	0	0	0	5
S Lawson	2005 v R	29	2	0	0	0	10
M J Low	2009 v F	15	0	0	0	0	0
S J MacLeod	2004 v A	24	0	0	0	0	0
E A Murray	2005 v R	41	2	0	0	0	10
R M Rennie	2008 v I	11	0	0	0	0	0
A K Strokosch	2006 v A	23	1	0	0	0	5
R J Vernon	2009 v Fj	15	0	0	0	0	0

Phil Walter/Getty Images

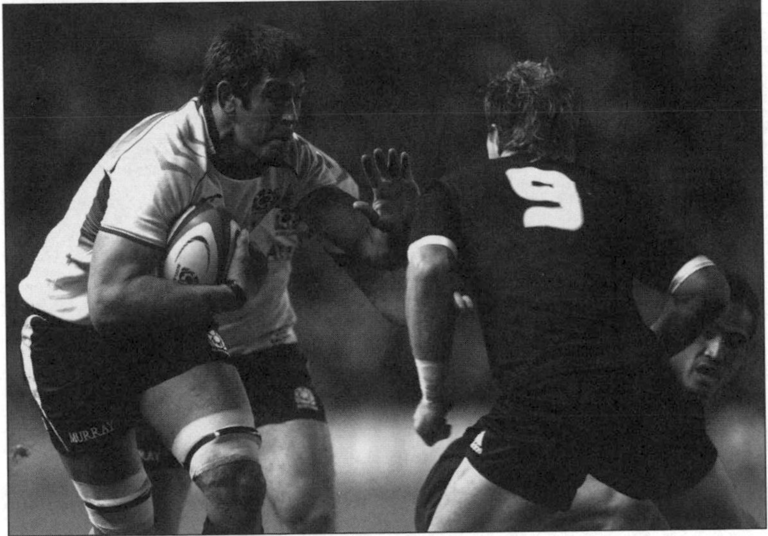

Nathan Hines went through the 75-cap barrier at the World Cup.

SCOTLAND INTERNATIONAL PLAYERS

(UP TO 31 OCTOBER 2011)

Note: Years given for International Championship matches are for second half of season; eg 1972 means season 1971–72. Years for all other matches refer to the actual year of the match. Entries in square brackets denote matches played in RWC Finals.

Abercrombie, C H (United Services) 1910 I, E, 1911 F, W, 1913 F, W
Abercrombie, J G (Edinburgh U) 1949 F, W, I, 1950 F, W, I, E
Agnew, W C C (Stewart's Coll FP) 1930 W, I
Ainslie, R (Edinburgh Inst FP) 1879 I, E, 1880 I, E, 1881 E, 1882 I, E
Ainslie, T (Edinburgh Inst FP) 1881 E, 1882 I, E, 1883 W, I, E, 1884 W, I, E, 1885 W, I 1, 2
Aitchison, G R (Edinburgh Wands) 1883 I
Aitchison, T G (Gala) 1929 W, I, E
Aitken, A I (Edinburgh Inst FP) 1889 I
Aitken, G G (Oxford U) 1924 W, I, E, 1925 F, W, I, E, 1929 F
Aitken, J (Gala) 1977 E, I, F, 1981 F, W, E, I, NZ 1, 2, R, A, 1982 E, I, F, W, 1983 F, W, E, NZ, 1984 W, E, I, F, R
Aitken, R (London Scottish) 1947 W
Allan, B (Glasgow Acads) 1881 I
Allan, J (Edinburgh Acads) 1990 NZ 1, 1991, W, I, R, [J, I, WS, E, NZ]
Allan, J L (Melrose) 1952 F, W, I, 1953 W
Allan, J L F (Cambridge U) 1957 I, E
Allan, J W (Melrose) 1927 F, 1928 I, 1929 F, W, I, E, 1930 F, E, 1931 F, W, I, E, 1932 SA, W, I, 1934 I, E
Allan, R C (Hutchesons' GSFP) 1969 I
Allardice, W D (Aberdeen GSFP) 1947 A, 1948 F, W, I, 1949 F, W, I, E
Allen, H W (Glasgow Acads) 1873 E
Anderson, A H (Glasgow Acads) 1894 I
Anderson, D G (London Scottish) 1889 I, 1890 W, I, E, 1891 W, E, 1892 W, E
Anderson, E (Stewart's Coll FP) 1947 I, E
Anderson, J W (W of Scotland) 1872 E
Anderson, T (Merchiston Castle School) 1882 I
Angus, A W (Watsonians) 1909 W, 1910 F, W, E, 1911 W, I, 1912 F, W, I, E, SA, 1913 F, W, 1914 E, 1920 F, W, I, E
Ansbro, J A (Northampton, London Irish) 2010 SA, Sm, 2011 F, W, E, It1, I2, [R, E]
Anton, P A (St Andrew's U) 1873 E
Armstrong, G (Jedforest, Newcastle) 1988 A, 1989 W, E, I, F, Fj, R, 1990 I, F, W, E, NZ 1, 2, Arg, 1991 F, W, E, I, R, [J, I, WS, E, NZ], 1993 I, F, W, E, 1994 E, I, 1996 NZ, 1, 2, A, 1997 W, SA (R), 1998 It, I, F, W, E, SA (R), 1999 W, E, I, F, Arg, R, [SA, U, Sm, NZ]
Arneil, R J (Edinburgh Acads, Leicester and Northampton) 1968 I, E, A, 1969 F, W, I, E, SA, 1970 F, W, I, E, A, 1971 F, W, I, E (2[1C]), 1972 F, W, E, NZ
Arthur, A (Glasgow Acads) 1875 E, 1876 E
Arthur, J W (Glasgow Acads) 1871 E, 1872 E
Asher, A G G (Oxford U) 1882 I, 1884 W, I, E, 1885 W, 1886 I, E
Auld, W (W of Scotland) 1889 W, 1890 W
Auldjo, L J (Abertay) 1878 E

Bain, D McL (Oxford U) 1911 E, 1912 F, W, E, SA, 1913 F, W, I, E, 1914 W, I
Baird, G R T (Kelso) 1981 A, 1982 E, I, F, W, A 1, 2, 1983 I, F, W, E, NZ, 1984 W, E, I, F, A, 1985 I, W, E, 1986 F, W, E, I, R, 1987 E, 1988 I
Balfour, A (Watsonians) 1896 W, I, E, 1897 E
Balfour, L M (Edinburgh Acads) 1872 E
Bannerman, E M (Edinburgh Acads) 1872 E, 1873 E
Bannerman, J M (Glasgow HSFP) 1921 F, W, I, E, 1922 F, W, I, E, 1923 F, W, I, E, 1924 F, W, I, E, 1925 F, W, I, E, 1926 F, W, I, E, 1927 F, W, I, E, A, 1928 F, W, I, E, 1929 F, W, I, E
Barclay, J A (Glasgow Warriors) 2007 [NZ], 2008 F, W, Arg 2, NZ, SA, C, 2009 W, F, It, I, Fj, A, 2010 F, W, It, E, I, Arg 1, 2, NZ, SA, Sm, 2011 F, W, I1, E, It1, 2, [R, Arg, E]
Barnes, I A (Hawick) 1972 W, 1974 F (R), 1975 E (R), NZ, 1977 I, F, W
Barrie, R W (Hawick) 1936 E
Bearne, K R F (Cambridge U, London Scottish) 1960 F, W
Beattie, J A (Hawick) 1929 F, W, 1930 W, 1931 F, W, I, E, 1932 SA, W, I, E, 1933 W, E, I, 1934 I, E, 1935 W, I, E, NZ, 1936 W, I, E
Beattie, J R (Glasgow Acads) 1980 I, F, W, E, 1981 F, W, E, I, 1983 F, W, E, NZ, 1984 E (R), R, A, 1985 I, 1986 F, W, E, I, R, 1987 I, F, W, E
Beattie, J W (Glasgow Warriors) 2006 R, PI, 2007 F, 2008 Arg 1, 2009 Fj, A, Arg, 2010 F, W, It, E, I, Arg 1, 2, 2011 I1, 2
Beattie, R S (Newcastle, Bristol) 2000 NZ 1, 2(R), Sm (R), 2003 E(R), It(R), I 2, [J(R), US, Fj]
Bedell-Sivright, D R (Cambridge U, Edinburgh U) 1900 W, 1901 W, I, E, 1902 W, I, E, 1903 W, I, 1904 W, I, E, 1905 NZ, 1906 W, I, E, SA, 1907 W, I, E, 1908 W, I
Bedell-Sivright, J V (Cambridge U) 1902 W
Begbie, T A (Edinburgh Wands) 1881 I, E
Bell, D L (Watsonians) 1975 I, F, W, E
Bell, J A (Clydesdale) 1901 W, I, E, 1902 W, I, E
Bell, L H I (Edinburgh Acads) 1900 E, 1904 W, I
Berkeley, W V (Oxford U) 1926 F, 1929 F, W, I
Berry, C W (Fettesian-Lorettonians) 1884 I, E, 1885 W, I 1, 1887 I, W, E, 1888 W, I
Bertram, D M (Watsonians) 1922 F, W, I, E, 1923 F, W, I, E, 1924 W, I, E
Beveridge, G (Glasgow) 2000 NZ 2(R), US (R), Sm (R), 2002 Fj(R), 2003 W 2, 2005 R(R)
Biggar, A G (London Scottish) 1969 SA, 1970 F, I, E, A, 1971 F, W, I, E (2[1C]), 1972 F, W
Biggar, M A (London Scottish) 1975 I, F, W, E, 1976 W, E, I, 1977 I, F, W, 1978 I, F, W, E, NZ, 1979 W, E, I, F, NZ, 1980 I, F, W, E
Birkett, G A (Harlequins, London Scottish) 1975 NZ
Bishop, J M (Glasgow Acads) 1893 I
Bisset, A A (RIE Coll) 1904 W
Black, A W (Edinburgh U) 1947 F, W, 1948 E, 1950 W, I, E
Black, W P (Glasgow HSFP) 1948 F, W, I, E, 1951 E
Blackadder, W F (W of Scotland) 1938 E
Blaikie, C F (Heriot's FP) 1963 I, E, 1966 E, 1968 A, 1969 F, W, I, E
Blair, M R L (Edinburgh) 2002 C, US, 2003 F(t+R), W 1(R), SA 2(R), It 2, I 2, [US], 2004 W(R), E(R), It(R), F(R), I(R), Sm(R), A1(R), 3(R), J(R), A4(R), SA(R), 2005 I(t&R), It(R), W(R), E, R, Arg, Sm(R), NZ(R), 2006 F, W, E, I, It(R), SA 1, 2, R, PI(R), A, 2007 I2, SA, [Pt, R, It, Arg], 2008 F, W, I, E, It, Arg 1, 2, NZ, SA, C, 2009 W, F, It, I, E, Fj(R), 2010 W(R), It(R), I(R), Arg 1(R), 2(R), NZ, Sm(R), 2011 F(R), W(R), I1, E(R), It1(R), 2, [R, Arg(R), E]
Blair, P C B (Cambridge U) 1912 SA, 1913 F, W, I, E
Bolton, W H (W of Scotland) 1876 E
Borthwick, J B (Stewart's Coll FP) 1938 W, I
Bos, F H ten (Oxford U, London Scottish) 1959 E, 1960 F, W, SA, 1961 F, SA, W, I, E, 1962 F, W, I, E, 1963 F, W, I, E
Boswell, J D (W of Scotland) 1889 W, I, 1890 W, I, E, 1891 W, I, E, 1892 W, I, E, 1893 I, E, 1894 I, E
Bowie, T C (Watsonians) 1913 I, E, 1914 I, E
Boyd, G M (Glasgow HSFP) 1926 E
Boyd, J L (United Services) 1912 E, SA

Boyle, A C W (London Scottish) 1963 F, W, I
Boyle, A H W (St Thomas's Hospital, London Scottish) 1966 A, 1967 F, NZ, 1968 F, W, I
Brash, J C (Cambridge U) 1961 E
Breakey, R W (Gosforth) 1978 E
Brewis, N T (Edinburgh Inst FP) 1876 E, 1878 E, 1879 I, E, 1880 I, E
Brewster, A K (Stewart's-Melville FP) 1977 E, 1980 I, F, 1986 E, I, R
Brotherstone, S J (Melrose, Brive, Newcastle) 1999 I (R), 2000 F, W, E, US, A, Sm, 2002 C (R)
Brown, A H (Heriot's FP) 1928 E, 1929 F, W
Brown, A R (Gala) 1971 E (2[1C]), 1972 F, W, E
Brown, C H C (Dunfermline) 1929 E
Brown, D I (Cambridge U) 1933 W, E, I
Brown, G L (W of Scotland) 1969 SA, 1970 F, W (R), I, E, A, 1971 F, W, I, E (2[1C]), 1972 F, W, E, NZ, 1973 E (R), P, 1974 W, E, I, F, 1975 I, F, W, E, A, 1976 F, W, E, I
Brown, J A (Glasgow Acads) 1908 W, I
Brown, J B (Glasgow Acads) 1879 I, E, 1880 I, E, 1881 I, E, 1882 I, E, 1883 W, I, E, 1884 W, I, E, 1885 I 1, 2, 1886 W, I, E
Brown, K D R (Borders, Glasgow Warriors, Saracens) 2005 R, Sm(R), NZ(R), 2006 SA 1(R), 2(R), R, PI, A, 2007 E, W, It, I1, 2(R), SA, [Pt(R), R(R), NZ, It(R), Arg(R)], 2008 F(R), W, I, E(R), It(R), Arg 1(R), 2(R), 2009 W(R), F(R), It(R), E(R), 2010 F, W, It, E, I, Arg 1, 2, NZ, SA, Sm, 2011 F, W, I1, E, It1, 2, [R, Gg, Arg]
Brown, P C (W of Scotland, Gala) 1964 F, NZ, W, I, E, 1965 I, E, SA, 1966 A, 1969 I, E, 1970 W, E, 1971 F, W, I, E (2[1C]), 1972 F, W, E, NZ, 1973 F, W, I, E, P
Brown, T G (Heriot's FP) 1929 W
Brown, W D (Glasgow Acads) 1871 E, 1872 E, 1873 E, 1874 E, 1875 E
Brown, W S (Edinburgh Inst FP) 1880 I, E, 1882 I, E, 1883 W, E
Browning, A (Glasgow HSFP) 1920 I, 1922 F, W, I, 1923 W, I, E
Bruce, C R (Glasgow Acads) 1947 F, W, I, E, 1949 F, W, I, E
Bruce, N S (Blackheath, Army and London Scottish) 1958 F, A, I, E, 1959 F, W, I, E, 1960 F, W, I, E, SA, 1961 F, SA, W, I, E, 1962 F, W, I, E, 1963 F, W, I, E, 1964 F, NZ, W, I, E
Bruce, R M (Gordonians) 1947 A, 1948 F, W, I
Bruce-Lockhart, J H (London Scottish) 1913 W, 1920 E
Bruce-Lockhart, L (London Scottish) 1948 E, 1950 F, W, 1953 I, E
Bruce-Lockhart, R B (Cambridge U and London Scottish) 1937 I, 1939 I, E
Bryce, C C (Glasgow Acads) 1873 E, 1874 E
Bryce, R D H (W of Scotland) 1973 I (R)
Bryce, W E (Selkirk) 1922 W, I, E, 1923 F, W, I, E, 1924 F, W, I, E
Brydon, W R C (Heriot's FP) 1939 W
Buchanan, A (Royal HSFP) 1871 E
Buchanan, F G (Kelvinside Acads and Oxford U) 1910 F, 1911 F, W
Buchanan, J C R (Stewart's Coll FP) 1921 W, I, E, 1922 W, I, E, 1923 F, W, I, E, 1924 F, W, I, E, 1925 F, I
Buchanan-Smith, G A E (London Scottish, Heriot's FP) 1989 Fj (R), 1990 Arg
Bucher, A M (Edinburgh Acads) 1897 E
Budge, G M (Edinburgh Wands) 1950 F, W, I, E
Bullmore, H H (Edinburgh U) 1902 I
Bulloch, A J (Glasgow) 2000 US, A, Sm, 2001 F (t+R), E
Bulloch, G C (West of Scotland, Glasgow) 1997 SA, 1998 It, I, F, W, E, Fj, A 1, SA, 1999 W, E, It, I, F, Arg, [SA, U, Sm, NZ], 2000 It, I, W (R), NZ 1, 2, A (R), Sm (R), 2001 F, W, E, It, I, Tg, Arg, NZ, 2002 E, It, I, F, W, C, US, R, SA, Fj, 2003 I 1, F, W 1, E, It 1, SA 1, 2, It 2(R), W2, I 2, [US, F, Fj, A], 2004 W, E, It, F, I, Sm, A1, 2, 3, J, A4, SA, 2005 F, I, It, W, E
Burnell, A P (London Scottish, Montferrand) 1989 E, I, F, Fj, R, 1990 I, F, W, E, Arg, 1991 F, W, E, I, R, [J, Z, I, WS, E, NZ], 1992 E, I, F, W, 1993 I, F, W, E, NZ, 1994 W, E, I, F, Arg 1, 2, SA, 1995 [Iv, Tg (R), F (R)], WS, 1998 E, SA, 1999 W, E, It, I, F, Arg, [Sp, Sm (R), NZ]
Burnet, P J (London Scottish and Edinburgh Acads) 1960 SA
Burnet, W (Hawick) 1912 E
Burnet, W A (W of Scotland) 1934 W, 1935 W, I, E, NZ, 1936 W, I, E
Burnett, J N (Heriot's FP) 1980 I, F, W, E
Burns, G G (Watsonians, Edinburgh) 1999 It (R), 2001 Tg (R), NZ (R), 2002 US (R)
Burrell, G (Gala) 1950 F, W, I, 1951 SA

Cairns, A G (Watsonians) 1903 W, I, E, 1904 W, I, E, 1905 W, I, E, 1906 W, I, E
Cairns, B J (Edinburgh) 2008 Arg 1, 2, NZ, SA, C, 2009 W, Arg
Calder, F (Stewart's-Melville FP) 1986 F, W, E, I, R, 1987 I, F, W, E, [F, Z, R, NZ], 1988 I, F, W, E, 1989 W, E, I, F, R, 1990 I, F, W, E, NZ 1, 2, 1991 R, [J, I, WS, E, NZ]
Calder, J H (Stewart's-Melville FP) 1981 F, W, E, I, NZ 1, 2, R, A, 1982 E, I, F, W, A 1, 2, 1983 I, F, W, E, NZ, 1984 W, E, I, F, A, 1985 I, F, W
Callam, D A (Edinburgh) 2006 R(R), PI(R), A, 2007 E, W, It, I1, F(R), SA, [NZ], 2008 F
Callander, G J (Kelso) 1984 R, 1988 I, F, W, E, A
Cameron, A (Glasgow HSFP) 1948 W, 1950 I, E, 1951 F, W, I, E, SA, 1953 I, E, 1955 F, W, I, E, 1956 F, W, I
Cameron, A D (Hillhead HSFP) 1951 F, 1954 F, W
Cameron, A W C (Watsonians) 1887 W, 1893 W, 1894 I
Cameron, D (Glasgow HSFP) 1953 I, E, 1954 F, NZ, I, E
Cameron, N W (Glasgow U) 1952 E, 1953 F, W
Campbell, A J (Hawick) 1984 I, F, R, 1985 I, F, W, E, 1986 F, W, E, I, R, 1988 F, W, A
Campbell, G T (London Scottish) 1892 W, I, E, 1893 I, E, 1894 W, I, E, 1895 W, I, E, 1896 W, I, E, 1897 I, 1899 I, 1900 E
Campbell, H H (Cambridge U, London Scottish) 1947 I, E, 1948 I, E
Campbell, J A (W of Scotland) 1878 E, 1879 I, E, 1881 I, E
Campbell, J A (Cambridge U) 1900 I
Campbell, N M (London Scottish) 1956 F, W
Campbell, S J (Dundee HSFP) 1995 C, I, F, W, E, R, [Iv, NZ (R)], WS (t), 1996 I, F, W, E, 1997 A, SA, 1998 Fj (R), A 2(R)
Campbell-Lamerton, J R E (London Scottish) 1986 F, 1987 [Z, R(R)]
Campbell-Lamerton, M J (Halifax, Army, London Scottish) 1961 F, SA, W, I, 1962 F, W, I, E, 1963 F, W, I, E, 1964 I, E, 1965 F, W, I, E, SA, 1966 F, W, I, E
Carmichael, A B (W of Scotland) 1967 I, NZ, 1968 F, W, I, E, A, 1969 F, W, I, E, SA, 1970 F, W, I, E, A, 1971 F, W, I, E (2[1C]), 1972 F, W, E, NZ, 1973 F, W, I, E, P, 1974 W, E, I, F, 1975 I, F, W, E, NZ, A, 1976 F, W, E, I, 1977 E, I (R), F, W, 1978 I
Carmichael, J H (Watsonians) 1921 F, W, I
Carrick, J S (Glasgow Acads) 1876 E, 1877 E
Cassels, D Y (W of Scotland) 1880 E, 1881 I, 1882 I, E, 1883 W, I, E
Cathcart, C W (Edinburgh U) 1872 E, 1873 E, 1876 E
Cawkwell, G L (Oxford U) 1947 F
Chalmers, C M (Melrose) 1989 W, E, I, F, Fj, 1990 I, F, W, E, NZ 1, 2, Arg, 1991 F, W, E, I, R, [J, Z (R), I, WS, E, NZ], 1992 E, I, F, W, A 1, 2, 1993 I, F, W, E, NZ, 1994 W, SA, 1995 C, I, F, W, E, R, [Iv, Tg, F, NZ], WS, 1996 A, It, 1997 W, I, F, A (R), SA, 1998 It, I, F, W, E, 1999 Arg (R)
Chalmers, T (Glasgow Acads) 1871 E, 1872 E, 1873 E, 1874 E, 1875 E, 1876 E
Chambers, H F T (Edinburgh U) 1888 W, I, 1889 W, I
Charters, R G (Hawick) 1955 W, I, E
Chisholm, D H (Melrose) 1964 I, E, 1965 E, SA, 1966 F, I, E, A, 1967 F, W, NZ, 1968 F, W, I
Chisholm, R W T (Melrose) 1955 I, E, 1956 F, W, I, E, 1958 F, W, A, I, 1960 SA
Church, W C (Glasgow Acads) 1906 W
Clark, R L (Edinburgh Wands, Royal Navy) 1972 F, W, E, NZ, 1973 F, W, I, E, P
Clauss, P R A (Oxford U) 1891 W, I, E, 1892 W, E, 1895 I
Clay, A T (Edinburgh Acads) 1886 W, I, E, 1887 I, W, E, 1888 W
Clunies-Ross, A (St Andrew's U) 1871 E
Coltman, S (Hawick) 1948 I, 1949 F, W, I, E
Colville, A G (Merchistonians, Blackheath) 1871 E, 1872 E
Connell, G C (Trinity Acads and London Scottish) 1968 E, A, 1969 F, E, 1970 F
Cooper, M McG (Oxford U) 1936 W, I
Corcoran, I (Gala) 1992 A 1(R)
Cordial, I F (Edinburgh Wands) 1952 F, W, I, E
Cotter, J L (Hillhead HSFP) 1934 I, E
Cottington, G S (Kelso) 1934 I, E, 1935 W, I, 1936 E
Coughtrie, S (Edinburgh Acads) 1959 F, W, I, E, 1962 W, I, E, 1963 F, W, I, E
Couper, J H (W of Scotland) 1896 W, I, 1899 I
Coutts, F H (Melrose, Army) 1947 W, I, E
Coutts, I D F (Old Alleynians) 1951 F, 1952 E
Cowan, R C (Selkirk) 1961 F, 1962 F, W, I, E
Cowie, W L K (Edinburgh Wands) 1953 E

Cownie, W B (Watsonians) 1893 W, I, E, 1894 W, I, E, 1895 W, I, E
Crabbie, G E (Edinburgh Acads) 1904 W
Crabbie, J E (Edinburgh Acads, Oxford U) 1900 W, 1902 I, 1903 W, I, 1904 E, 1905 W
Craig, A (Orrell, Glasgow) 2002 C, US, R, SA, Fj, 2003 I 1, F(R), W 1(R), E, It 1, SA 1, 2, W 2, I 2, [J, US, F], 2004 A3(R), 2005 F, I, It, W, E
Craig, J B (Heriot's FP) 1939 W
Craig, J M (West of Scotland, Glasgow) 1997 A, 2001 W (R), E (R), It
Cramb, R I (Harlequins) 1987 [R(R)], 1988 I, F, A
Cranston, A G (Hawick) 1976 W, E, I, 1977 E, W, 1978 F (R), W, E, NZ, 1981 NZ 1, 2
Crawford, J A (Army, London Scottish) 1934 I
Crawford, W H (United Services, RN) 1938 W, I, E, 1939 W, E
Crichton-Miller, D (Gloucester) 1931 W, I, E
Crole, G B (Oxford U) 1920 F, W, I, E
Cronin, D F (Bath, London Scottish, Bourges, Wasps) 1988 I, F, W, E, A, 1989 W, E, I, F, Fj, R, 1990 I, F, W, E, NZ 1, 2, 1991 F, W, E, I, R, [Z], 1992 A 2, 1993 I, F, W, E, NZ, 1995 C, I, F, [Tg, F, NZ], WS, 1996 NZ 1, 2, A, It, 1997 F (R), 1998 I, F, W, E
Cross, G D S (Edinburgh) 2009 W, 2010 E(R), 2011 I1(t&R), E(R), It1, I2, [R, Arg]
Cross, M (Merchistonians) 1875 E, 1876 E, 1877 I, E, 1878 E, 1879 I, E, 1880 I, E
Cross, W (Merchistonians) 1871 E, 1872 E
Cumming, R S (Aberdeen U) 1921 F, W
Cunningham, G (Oxford U) 1908 W, I, 1909 W, E, 1910 F, I, E, 1911 E
Cunningham, R F (Gala) 1978 NZ, 1979 W, E
Currie, L R (Dunfermline) 1947 A, 1948 F, W, I, 1949 F, W, I, E
Cusiter, C P (Borders, Perpignan, Glasgow Warriors) 2004 W, E, It, F, I, Sm, A1, 2, 3, J, A4, SA, 2005 F, I, It, W, Arg(R), Sm, NZ, 2006 F(R), W(R), E(R), I(R), It, R(R), PI, 2007 E, W, It, I1, F(R), I2(R), [R(R), NZ, It(R), Arg(R)], 2008 F(R), W(R), I(R), 2009 W(R), F(R), It(R), I(R), E(R), Fj, A, Arg, 2010 F, W, It, E, I, 2011 It2(R), [R(R), E(R)]
Cuthbert, J E (Bath) 2011 I2(R)
Cuthbertson, W (Kilmarnock, Harlequins) 1980 I, 1981 W, E, I, NZ 1, 2, R, A, 1982 E, I, F, W, A 1, 2, 1983 I, F, W, NZ, 1984 W, E, A

Dalgleish, A (Gala) 1890 W, E, 1891 W, I, 1892 W, 1893 W, 1894 W, I
Dalgleish, K J (Edinburgh Wands, Cambridge U) 1951 I, E, 1953 F, W
Dall, A K (Edinburgh) 2003 W 2(R)
Dallas, J D (Watsonians) 1903 E
Danielli, S C J (Bath, Borders, Ulster) 2003 It 2, W 2, [J(R), US, Fj, A], 2004 W, E, It, F, I, 2005 F, I, 2008 W(R), It, Arg 1, 2009 F, It, I, E, Fj, A, 2010 It, E(R), I(R), Arg 2, 2011 I1(R), E, It1, 2, [R, E]
Davidson, J A (London Scottish, Edinburgh Wands) 1959 E, 1960 I, E
Davidson, J N G (Edinburgh U) 1952 F, W, I, E, 1953 F, W, 1954 F
Davidson, J P (RIE Coll) 1873 E, 1874 E
Davidson, R S (Royal HSFP) 1893 E
Davies, D S (Hawick) 1922 F, W, I, E, 1923 F, W, I, E, 1924 F, E, 1925 W, I, E, 1926 F, W, I, E, 1927 F, W, I
Dawson, J C (Glasgow Acads) 1947 A, 1948 F, W, 1949 F, W, I, 1950 F, W, I, E, 1951 F, W, I, E, SA, 1952 F, W, I, E, 1953 E
Deans, C T (Hawick) 1978 F, W, E, NZ, 1979 W, E, I, F, NZ, 1980 I, F, 1981 F, W, E, I, NZ 1, 2, R, A, 1982 E, I, F, W, A 1, 2, 1983 I, F, W, E, NZ, 1984 W, E, I, F, A, 1985 I, F, W, E, 1986 F, W, E, I, R, 1987 I, F, W, E, [F, Z, R, NZ]
Deans, D T (Hawick) 1968 E
Deas, D W (Heriot's FP) 1947 F, W
De Luca, N J (Edinburgh) 2008 F, W, I(t&R), Arg 2(R), NZ, SA, C, 2009 F(R), It(R), I(R), E(R), Fj(R), A(R), Arg(R), 2010 It(R), E, I, Arg 1, 2(R), 2011 F, W, I1, E(R), It1(R), I2(R), It2, [Gg, Arg, E(R)]
Denton, D K (Edinburgh) 2011 I2(R)
Dewey, R E (Edinburgh, Ulster) 2006 R, 2007 E(R), W, It, I1, F, I2, SA, [Pt, R, NZ(R), It, Arg]
Dick, L G (Loughborough Colls, Jordanhill, Swansea) 1972 W (R), E, 1974 W, E, I, F, 1975 I, F, W, E, NZ, A, 1976 F, 1977 E
Dick, R C S (Cambridge U, Guy's Hospital) 1934 W, I, E, 1935 W, I, E, NZ, 1936 W, I, E, 1937 W, 1938 W, I, E
Dickinson, A G (Gloucester, Sale) 2007 [NZ], 2008 E(R), It(R), Arg 1(R), 2(t&R), NZ(R), SA(R), C(R), 2009 W(t&R), F, It(R), I, E, 2010 F, W, It(R), I(R), Arg 2(R), NZ(t&R), 2011 I2(R), It2, [R(R), Arg(R), E(R)]
Dickson, G (Gala) 1978 NZ, 1979 W, E, I, F, NZ, 1980 W, 1981 F, 1982 W (R)
Dickson, M R (Edinburgh U) 1905 I
Dickson, W M (Blackheath, Oxford U) 1912 F, W, E, SA, 1913 F, W, I
Di Rollo, M P (Edinburgh) 2002 US (R), 2005 R, Arg, Sm, NZ, 2006 F, E, I, It, SA 1, 2, R, PI, A, 2007 E, W, It, I1, F(R), [Pt, NZ]
Dobson, J (Glasgow Acads) 1911 E, 1912 F, W, I, E, SA
Dobson, J D (Glasgow Acads) 1910 I
Dobson, W G (Heriot's FP) 1922 W, I, E
Docherty, J T (Glasgow HSFP) 1955 F, W, 1956 E, 1958 F, W, A, I, E
Dods, F P (Edinburgh Acads) 1901 I
Dods, J H (Edinburgh Acads) 1895 W, I, E, 1896 W, I, E, 1897 I, E
Dods, M (Gala, Northampton) 1994 I (t), Arg 1, 2, 1995 WS, 1996 I, F, W, E
Dods, P W (Gala) 1983 I, F, W, E, NZ, 1984 W, E, I, F, R, A, 1985 I, F, W, E, 1989 W, E, I, F, 1991 I (R), R, [Z, NZ (R)]
Donald, D G (Oxford U) 1914 W, I
Donald, R L H (Glasgow HSFP) 1921 W, I, E
Donaldson, W P (Oxford U, W of Scotland) 1893 I, 1894 I, 1895 E, 1896 I, E, 1899 I
Don-Wauchope, A R (Fettesian-Lorettonians) 1881 E, 1882 E, 1883 W, 1884 W, I, E, 1885 W, I 1, 2, 1886 W, I, E, 1888 I
Don-Wauchope, P H (Fettesian-Lorettonians) 1885 I 1, 2, 1886 W, 1887 I, W, E
Dorward, A F (Cambridge U, Gala) 1950 F, 1951 SA, 1952 W, I, E, 1953 F, W, E, 1955 F, 1956 I, E, 1957 F, W, I, E
Dorward, T F (Gala) 1938 W, I, E, 1939 I, E
Douglas, B A F (Borders) 2002 R, SA, Fj, 2003 I 1, F, W 1, E, It 1, SA 1, 2, It 2, W 2, [J, US(t&R), F(R), Fj, A], 2004 W, E, It, F, I, Sm, A1, 2, 3, A4(R), SA(R), 2005 F(R), I(R), It(R), W(R), E(R), R, Arg, NZ, 2006 F, W, E, I, It, SA 1, 2(R)
Douglas, G (Jedforest) 1921 W
Douglas, J (Stewart's Coll FP) 1961 F, SA, W, I, E, 1962 F, W, I, E, 1963 F, W, I
Douty, P S (London Scottish) 1927 A, 1928 F, W
Drew, D (Glasgow Acads) 1871 E, 1876 E
Druitt, W A H (London Scottish) 1936 W, I, E
Drummond, A H (Kelvinside Acads) 1938 W, I
Drummond, C W (Melrose) 1947 F, W, I, E, 1948 F, I, E, 1950 F, W, I, E
Drybrough, A S (Edinburgh Wands, Merchistonians) 1902 I, 1903 I
Dryden, R H (Watsonians) 1937 E
Drysdale, D (Heriot's FP) 1923 F, W, I, E, 1924 F, W, I, E, 1925 F, W, I, E, 1926 F, W, I, E, 1927 F, W, I, E, A, 1928 F, W, I, E, 1929 F
Duff, P L (Glasgow Acads) 1936 W, I, 1938 W, I, E, 1939 W
Duffy, H (Jedforest) 1955 F
Duke, A (Royal HSFP) 1888 W, I, 1889 W, I, 1890 W, I
Dunbar, J P A (Leeds) 2005 F(R), It(R)
Duncan, A W (Edinburgh U) 1901 W, I, E, 1902 W, I, E
Duncan, D D (Oxford U) 1920 F, W, I, E
Duncan, M D F (W of Scotland) 1986 F, W, E, R, 1987 I, F, W, E, [F, Z, R, NZ], 1988 I, F, W, E, A, 1989 W
Duncan, M M (Fettesian-Lorettonians) 1888 W
Dunlop, J W (W of Scotland) 1875 E
Dunlop, Q (W of Scotland) 1971 E (2[1C])
Dykes, A S (Glasgow Acads) 1932 E
Dykes, J C (Glasgow Acads) 1922 F, E, 1924 I, 1925 F, W, I, 1926 F, W, I, E, 1927 F, W, I, E, A, 1928 F, I, 1929 F, W, I
Dykes, J M (Clydesdale, Glasgow HSFP) 1898 I, E, 1899 W, E, 1900 W, I, 1901 W, I, E, 1902 E

Edwards, D B (Heriot's FP) 1960 I, E, SA
Edwards, N G B (Harlequins, Northampton) 1992 E, I, F, W, A 1, 1994 W
Elgie, M K (London Scottish) 1954 NZ, I, E, W, 1955 F, W, I, E
Elliot, C (Langholm) 1958 E, 1959 F, 1960 F, 1963 E, 1964 F, NZ, W, I, E, 1965 F, W, I
Elliot, M (Hawick) 1895 W, 1896 E, 1897 I, E, 1898 I, E
Elliot, T (Gala) 1905 E
Elliot, T (Gala) 1955 W, I, E, 1956 F, W, I, E, 1957 F, W, I, E, 1958 W, A, I

Elliot, T G (Langholm) 1968 W, A, 1969 F, W, 1970 E
Elliot, W I D (Edinburgh Acads) 1947 F, W, E, A, 1948 F, W, I, E, 1949 F, W, I, E, 1950 F, W, I, E, 1951 F, W, I, E, SA, 1952 F, W, I, E, 1954 NZ, I, E, W
Ellis, D G (Currie) 1997 W, E, I, F
Emslie, W D (Royal HSFP) 1930 F, 1932 I
Eriksson, B R S (London Scottish) 1996 NZ 1, A, 1997 E
Evans, H L (Edinburgh U) 1885 I 1, 2
Evans, M B (Glasgow Warriors, Castres) 2008 C(R), 2009 W(R), F, It, I, E, 2010 F, W(t&R), It, E, I, Arg 1, 2, NZ, Sm(R), 2011 F, W, I1, E, It2, [R, Gg, Arg, E]
Evans, T H (Glasgow Warriors) 2008 Arg 1, NZ, SA, 2009 F, It, I, E, Arg, 2010 F, W
Ewart, E N (Glasgow Acads) 1879 E, 1880 I, E

Fahmy, E C (Abertillery) 1920 F, W, I, E
Fairley, I T (Kelso, Edinburgh) 1999 It, I (R), [Sp (R)]
Fasson, F H (London Scottish, Edinburgh Wands) 1900 W, 1901 W, I, 1902 W, E
Fell, A N (Edinburgh U) 1901 W, I, E, 1902 W, E, 1903 W, E
Ferguson, J H (Gala) 1928 W
Ferguson, W G (Royal HSFP) 1927 A, 1928 F, W, I, E
Fergusson, E A J (Oxford U) 1954 F, NZ, I, E, W
Finlay, A B (Edinburgh Acads) 1875 E
Finlay, J F (Edinburgh Acads) 1871 E, 1872 E, 1874 E, 1875 E
Finlay, N J (Edinburgh Acads) 1875 E, 1876 E, 1878 E, 1879 I, E, 1880 I, E, 1881 I, E
Finlay, R (Watsonians) 1948 E
Fisher, A T (Waterloo, Watsonians) 1947 I, E
Fisher, C D (Waterloo) 1975 NZ, A, 1976 W, E, I
Fisher, D (W of Scotland) 1893 I
Fisher, J P (Royal HSFP, London Scottish) 1963 E, 1964 F, NZ, W, I, E, 1965 F, W, I, E, SA, 1966 F, W, I, E, A, 1967 F, W, I, E, NZ, 1968 F, W, I, E
Fleming, C J N (Edinburgh Wands) 1896 I, E, 1897 I
Fleming, G R (Glasgow Acads) 1875 E, 1876 E
Fletcher, H N (Edinburgh U) 1904 E, 1905 W
Flett, A B (Edinburgh U) 1901 W, I, E, 1902 W, I
Forbes, J L (Watsonians) 1905 W, 1906 I, E
Ford, D St C (United Services, RN) 1930 I, E, 1931 E, 1932 W, I
Ford, J R (Gala) 1893 I
Ford, R W (Borders, Glasgow, Edinburgh) 2004 A3(R), 2006 W(R), E(R), PI(R), A(R), 2007 E(R), W(R), It(R), I1(R), F, I2, SA, [Pt(R), R, It, Arg], 2008 F, W, I, E, Arg 1, 2, NZ, SA, C, 2009 W, F, It, I, E, Fj, A, Arg, 2010 F, W, It, E, I, Arg 1, 2, NZ, SA, Sm, 2011 F, W, I1, E, It1, I2, [R, Gg, Arg, E]
Forrest, J E (Glasgow Acads) 1932 SA, 1935 E, NZ
Forrest, J G S (Cambridge U) 1938 W, I, E
Forrest, W T (Hawick) 1903 W, I, E, 1904 W, I, E, 1905 W, I
Forsayth, H H (Oxford U) 1921 F, W, I, E, 1922 W, I, E
Forsyth, I W (Stewart's Coll FP) 1972 NZ, 1973 F, W, I, E, P
Forsyth, J (Edinburgh U) 1871 E
Foster, R A (Hawick) 1930 W, 1932 SA, I, E
Fox, J (Gala) 1952 F, W, I, E
Frame, J N M (Edinburgh U, Gala) 1967 NZ, 1968 F, W, I, E, 1969 W, I, E, SA, 1970 F, W, I, E, A, 1971 F, W, I, E (2[1C]), 1972 F, W, E, 1973 P (R)
France, C (Kelvinside Acads) 1903 I
Fraser, C F P (Glasgow U) 1888 W, 1889 W
Fraser, J W (Edinburgh Inst FP) 1881 E
Fraser, R (Cambridge U) 1911 F, W, I, E
French, J (Glasgow Acads) 1886 W, 1887 I, W, E
Frew, A (Edinburgh U) 1901 W, I, E
Frew, G M (Glasgow HSFP) 1906 SA, 1907 W, I, E, 1908 W, I, E, 1909 W, I, E, 1910 F, W, I, 1911 I, E
Friebe, J P (Glasgow HSFP) 1952 E
Fullarton, I A (Edinburgh) 2000 NZ 1(R), 2, 2001 NZ (R), 2003 It 2(R), I 2(t), 2004 Sm(R), A1(R), 2
Fulton, A K (Edinburgh U, Dollar Acads) 1952 F, 1954 F
Fyfe, K C (Cambridge U, Sale, London Scottish) 1933 W, E, 1934 E, 1935 W, I, E, NZ, 1936 W, E, 1939 I

Gallie, G H (Edinburgh Acads) 1939 W
Gallie, R A (Glasgow Acads) 1920 F, W, I, E, 1921 F, W, I, E
Gammell, W B B (Edinburgh Wands) 1977 I, F, W, 1978 W, E
Geddes, I C (London Scottish) 1906 SA, 1907 W, I, E, 1908 W, E
Geddes, K I (London Scottish) 1947 F, W, I, E
Gedge, H T S (Oxford U, London Scottish, Edinburgh Wands) 1894 W, I, E, 1896 E, 1899 W, E
Gedge, P M S (Edinburgh Wands) 1933 I
Gemmill, R (Glasgow HSFP) 1950 F, W, I, E, 1951 F, W, I
Gibson, W R (Royal HSFP) 1891 I, E, 1892 W, I, E, 1893 W, I, E, 1894 W, I, E, 1895 W, I, E
Gilbert-Smith, D S (London Scottish) 1952 E
Gilchrist, J (Glasgow Acads) 1925 F
Gill, A D (Gala) 1973 P, 1974 W, E, I, F
Gillespie, J I (Edinburgh Acads) 1899 E, 1900 W, E, 1901 W, I, E, 1902 W, I, 1904 I, E
Gillies, A C (Watsonians) 1924 W, I, E, 1925 F, W, E, 1926 F, W, 1927 F, W, I, E
Gilmour, H R (Heriot's FP) 1998 Fj
Gilray, C M (Oxford U, London Scottish) 1908 E, 1909 W, E, 1912 I
Glasgow, I C (Heriot's FP) 1997 F (R)
Glasgow, R J C (Dunfermline) 1962 F, W, I, E, 1963 I, E, 1964 I, E, 1965 W, I
Glen, W S (Edinburgh Wands) 1955 W
Gloag, L G (Cambridge U) 1949 F, W, I, E
Godman, P J (Edinburgh) 2005 R(R), Sm(R), NZ(R), 2006 R, PI(R), A(t&R), 2007 W, It, 2008 Arg 2, NZ, SA, C, 2009 W, F, It, I, E, Fj, A, Arg, 2010 F, W(R), E(R)
Goodfellow, J (Langholm) 1928 W, I, E
Goodhue, F W J (London Scottish) 1890 W, I, E, 1891 W, I, E, 1892 W, I, E
Gordon, R (Edinburgh Wands) 1951 W, 1952 F, W, I, E, 1953 W
Gordon, R E (Royal Artillery) 1913 F, W, I
Gordon, R J (London Scottish) 1982 A 1, 2
Gore, A C (London Scottish) 1882 I
Gossman, B M (W of Scotland) 1980 W, 1983 F, W
Gossman, J S (W of Scotland) 1980 E (R)
Gowans, J J (Cambridge U, London Scottish) 1893 W, 1894 W, E, 1895 W, I, E, 1896 I, E
Gowlland, G C (London Scottish) 1908 W, 1909 W, E, 1910 F, W, I, E
Gracie, A L (Harlequins) 1921 F, W, I, E, 1922 F, W, I, E, 1923 F, W, I, E, 1924 F
Graham, G (Newcastle) 1997 A (R), SA (R), 1998 I, F (R), W (R), 1999 F (R), Arg (R), R, [SA, U, Sm, NZ (R)], 2000 I (R), US, A, Sm, 2001 I (R), Tg (R), Arg (R), NZ (R), 2002 E (R), It (R), I (R), F (R), W (R)
Graham, I N (Edinburgh Acads) 1939 I, E
Graham, J (Kelso) 1926 I, E, 1927 F, W, I, E, A, 1928 F, W, I, E, 1930 I, E, 1932 SA, W
Graham, J H S (Edinburgh Acads) 1876 E, 1877 I, E, 1878 E, 1879 I, E, 1880 I, E, 1881 I, E
Grant, D (Hawick) 1965 F, E, SA, 1966 F, W, I, E, A, 1967 F, W, I, E, NZ, 1968 F
Grant, D M (East Midlands) 1911 W, I
Grant, M L (Harlequins) 1955 F, 1956 F, W, 1957 F
Grant, T O (Hawick) 1960 I, E, SA, 1964 F, NZ, W
Grant, W St C (Craigmount) 1873 E, 1874 E
Gray, C A (Nottingham) 1989 W, E, I, F, Fj, R, 1990 I, F, W, E, NZ 1, 2, Arg, 1991 F, W, E, I, [J, I, WS, E, NZ]
Gray, D (W of Scotland) 1978 E, 1979 I, F, NZ, 1980 I, F, W, E, 1981 F
Gray, G L (Gala) 1935 NZ, 1937 W, I, E
Gray, R J (Glasgow Warriors) 2010 F(R), W(R), I(R), NZ, SA, Sm, 2011 F, I1, E, It1, I2, It2(R), [R, Gg(R), Arg, E]
Gray, S D (Borders, Northampton) 2004 A3, 2008 NZ(R), SA(R), C(R), 2009 W(R), It(R), I(R), E
Gray, T (Northampton, Heriot's FP) 1950 E, 1951 F, E
Greenlees, H D (Leicester) 1927 A, 1928 F, W, 1929 I, E, 1930 E
Greenlees, J R C (Cambridge U, Kelvinside Acads) 1900 I, 1902 W, I, E, 1903 W, I, E
Greenwood, J T (Dunfermline and Perthshire Acads) 1952 F, 1955 F, W, I, E, 1956 F, W, I, E, 1957 F, W, E, 1958 F, W, A, I, E, 1959 F, W, I
Greig, A (Glasgow HSFP) 1911 I
Greig, L L (Glasgow Acads, United Services) 1905 NZ, 1906 SA, 1907 W, 1908 W, I
Greig, R C (Glasgow Acads) 1893 W, 1897 I
Grieve, C F (Oxford U) 1935 W, 1936 E
Grieve, R M (Kelso) 1935 W, I, E, NZ, 1936 W, I, E
Grimes, S B (Watsonians, Newcastle) 1997 A (t+R), 1998 I (R), F (R), W (R), E (R), Fj, A 1, 2, 1999 W (R), E, It, I, F, Arg, R, [SA, U, Sm (R), NZ (R)], 2000 It, I, F (R), W, US, A, Sm (R), 2001 F (R), W (R), E (R), It, I (R), Tg, Arg, NZ, 2002 E, It, I, F (R), W (R), C, US, R, SA, Fj, 2003 I 1, F, W 1, E(R), It 1(R), W 2, I 2, [J, US, F, Fj, A], 2004 W, E, It, F, I, Sm, A1, J, A4, SA, 2005 F, I, It, W, E(R)

Grove, A (Worcester) 2009 Fj, A, Arg
Gunn, A W (Royal HSFP) 1912 F, W, I, SA, 1913 F

Hall, A J A (Glasgow) 2002 US (R)
Hall, D W H (Edinburgh, Glasgow Warriors) 2003 W 2(R), 2005 R(R), Arg, Sm(R), NZ(R), 2006 F, E, I, It(R), SA 1(R), 2, R, PI, A, 2007 E, W, It, I1, F(R), 2008 Arg 2(R), NZ(R), SA(R), C(R), 2009 W(R), F(R), It(R), I(R), E(R), Fj(R), A(R), Arg(R), 2010 SA(R), Sm(R), 2011 F(R), I2(R), It2(R), [Arg(R)]
Hamilton, A S (Headingley) 1914 W, 1920 F
Hamilton, C P (Newcastle) 2004 A2(R), 2005 R, Arg, Sm, NZ
Hamilton, H M (W of Scotland) 1874 E, 1875 E
Hamilton, J L (Leicester, Edinburgh, Gloucester) 2006 R(R), A(R), 2007 E, W, It(R), I1(R), F(R), I2, SA, [R, NZ(R), It, Arg], 2008 F, W, I(R), NZ, SA, C, 2009 W, F, I, E, 2010 W, It, E, I, Arg 1, 2, NZ, Sm(R), 2011 I2, [Gg, Arg]
Hannah, R S M (W of Scotland) 1971 I
Harrower, P R (London Scottish) 1885 W
Hart, J G M (London Scottish) 1951 SA
Hart, T M (Glasgow U) 1930 W, I
Hart, W (Melrose) 1960 SA
Harvey, L (Greenock Wands) 1899 I
Hastie, A J (Melrose) 1961 W, I, E, 1964 I, E, 1965 E, SA, 1966 F, W, I, E, A, 1967 F, W, I, NZ, 1968 F, W
Hastie, I R (Kelso) 1955 F, 1958 F, E, 1959 F, W, I
Hastie, J D H (Melrose) 1938 W, I, E
Hastings, A G (Cambridge U, Watsonians, London Scottish) 1986 F, W, E, I, R, 1987 I, F, W, E, [F, Z, R, NZ], 1988 I, F, W, E, A, 1989 Fj, R, 1990 I, F, W, E, NZ 1, 2, Arg, 1991 F, W, E, I, [J, I, WS, E, NZ], 1992 E, I, F, W, A 1, 1993 I, F, W, E, NZ, 1994 W, E, I, F, SA, 1995 C, I, F, W, E, R, [Iv, Tg, F, NZ]
Hastings, S (Watsonians) 1986 F, W, E, I, R, 1987 I, F, W, [R], 1988 I, F, W, A, 1989 W, E, I, F, Fj, R, 1990 I, F, W, E, NZ 1, 2, Arg, 1991 F, W, E, I, [J, Z, I, WS, E, NZ], 1992 E, I, F, W, A 1, 2, 1993 I, F, W, E, NZ, 1994 E, I, F, SA, 1995 W, E, R (R), [Tg, F, NZ], 1996 I, F, W, E, NZ 2, It, 1997 W, E (R)
Hay, B H (Boroughmuir) 1975 NZ, A, 1976 F, 1978 I, F, W, E, NZ, 1979 W, E, I, F, NZ, 1980 I, F, W, E, 1981 F, W, E, I, NZ 1, 2
Hay, J A (Hawick) 1995 WS
Hay-Gordon, J R (Edinburgh Acads) 1875 E, 1877 I, E
Hegarty, C B (Hawick) 1978 I, F, W, E
Hegarty, J J (Hawick) 1951 F, 1953 F, W, I, E, 1955 F
Henderson, A R (Glasgow Warriors) 2001 I (R), Tg (R), NZ (R), 2002 It, I, US (R), 2003 SA 1, 2, It 2, I 2, [US, F, Fj, A], 2004 W, E(t&R), It(R), F, I, Sm, A1, 2, 3, J, A4, SA, 2005 W(R), R, Arg, Sm, NZ, 2006 F, W, E, I, It, SA 1, 2, PI, A, 2007 E, It(R), I1(R), F, I2, SA, [NZ, It(R), Arg(R)], 2008 F, W, I, It(R)
Henderson, B C (Edinburgh Wands) 1963 E, 1964 F, I, E, 1965 F, W, I, E, 1966 F, W, I, E
Henderson, F W (London Scottish) 1900 W, I
Henderson, I C (Edinburgh Acads) 1939 I, E, 1947 F, W, E, A, 1948 I, E
Henderson, J H (Oxford U, Richmond) 1953 F, W, I, E, 1954 F, NZ, I, E, W
Henderson, J M (Edinburgh Acads) 1933 W, E, I
Henderson, J Y M (Watsonians) 1911 E
Henderson, M M (Dunfermline) 1937 W, I, E
Henderson, N F (London Scottish) 1892 I
Henderson, R G (Newcastle Northern) 1924 I, E
Hendrie, K G P (Heriot's FP) 1924 F, W, I
Hendry, T L (Clydesdale) 1893 W, I, E, 1895 I
Henriksen, E H (Royal HSFP) 1953 I
Hepburn, D P (Woodford) 1947 A, 1948 F, W, I, E, 1949 F, W, I, E
Heron, G (Glasgow Acads) 1874 E, 1875 E
Hill, C C P (St Andrew's U) 1912 F, I
Hilton, D I W (Bath, Glasgow) 1995 C, I, F, W, E, R, [Tg, F, NZ], WS, 1996 I, F, W, E, NZ 1, 2, A, It, 1997 W, A, SA, 1998 It, I (R), F, W, E, A 1, 2, SA (R), 1999 W (R), E (R), It (R), I (R), F, R (R), [SA (R), U (R), Sp], 2000 It (R), F (R), W (R), 2002 SA(R)
Hines, N J (Edinburgh, Glasgow, Perpignan, Leinster, Clermont-Auvergne) 2000 NZ 2(R), 2002 C, US, R(R), SA(R), Fj(R), 2003 W 1(R), E, It 1, SA 1, 2, It 2, W 2(R), I 2, [US, F(R), Fj, A], 2004 E(R), It(R), F(R), I(R), A3, J, A4, SA, 2005 F(R), I(R), It(R), W(R), E, 2006 E(R), I, It, SA 1, 2, R, PI, 2007 W(R), It, I1, F, I2, SA, [Pt, R, It, Arg], 2008 F, W, I, E, It, NZ, SA, C, 2009 I(R), E(R), Fj, A, Arg, 2010 F, It(R), E(R), NZ(R), SA, Sm, 2011 F, W, I1(R), E, It1, 2, [R(R), Gg, Arg(R), E(R)]
Hinshelwood, A J W (London Scottish) 1966 F, W, I, E, A, 1967 F, W, I, E, NZ, 1968 F, W, I, E, A, 1969 F, W, I, SA, 1970 F, W
Hinshelwood, B G (Worcester) 2002 C (R), R(R), SA(R), Fj, 2003 It 2, [J, US(R), Fj(R), A(R)], 2004 W, E, It, Sm, A1, 2, J, A4, SA, 2005 It(R)
Hodge D W (Watsonians, Edinburgh) 1997 F (R), A, SA (t+R), 1998 A 2(R), SA, 1999 W, Arg, R, [Sp, Sm (R)], 2000 F (R), W, E, NZ 1, 2, US (R), Sm (R), 2001 F (R), W, E, It, I (R), 2002 E, W (R), C, US
Hodgson, C G (London Scottish) 1968 I, E
Hogg, A (Edinburgh) 2004 W, E(R), It, F(R), I, Sm, A1, 2, 3, J, A4, SA, 2005 F, I, It, W, E, R, Arg, Sm, NZ, 2006 F, W, E, I, It, SA 1, 2, 2007 E(R), W(R), It(R), I1(R), F, I2, SA(t&R), [Pt, R, It, Arg], 2008 W(R), I, E, It, Arg 1, 2, NZ, SA, 2009 W
Hogg, C D (Melrose) 1992 A 1, 2, 1993 NZ (R), 1994 Arg 1, 2
Hogg, C G (Boroughmuir) 1978 F (R), W (R)
Holmes, S D (London Scottish) 1998 It, I, F
Holms, W F (RIE Coll) 1886 W, E, 1887 I, E, 1889 W, I
Horsburgh, G B (London Scottish) 1937 W, I, E, 1938 W, I, E, 1939 W, I, E
Howie, D D (Kirkcaldy) 1912 F, W, I, E, SA, 1913 F, W
Howie, R A (Kirkcaldy) 1924 F, W, I, E, 1925 W, I, E
Hoyer-Millar, G C (Oxford U) 1953 I
Huggan, J L (London Scottish) 1914 E
Hume, J (Royal HSFP) 1912 F, 1920 F, 1921 F, W, I, E, 1922 F
Hume, J W G (Oxford U, Edinburgh Wands) 1928 I, 1930 F
Hunter, F (Edinburgh U) 1882 I
Hunter, I G (Selkirk) 1984 I (R), 1985 F (R), W, E
Hunter, J M (Cambridge U) 1947 F
Hunter, M D (Glasgow High) 1974 F
Hunter, W J (Hawick) 1964 F, NZ, W, 1967 F, W, I, E
Hutchison, W R (Glasgow HSFP) 1911 E
Hutton, A H M (Dunfermline) 1932 I
Hutton, J E (Harlequins) 1930 E, 1931 F

Inglis, H M (Edinburgh Acads) 1951 F, W, I, E, SA, 1952 W, I
Inglis, J M (Selkirk) 1952 E
Inglis, W M (Cambridge U, Royal Engineers) 1937 W, I, E, 1938 W, I, E
Innes, J R S (Aberdeen GSFP) 1939 W, I, E, 1947 A, 1948 F, W, I, E
Ireland, J C H (Glasgow HSFP) 1925 W, I, E, 1926 F, W, I, E, 1927 F, W, I, E
Irvine, A R (Heriot's FP) 1972 NZ, 1973 F, W, I, E, P, 1974 W, E, I, F, 1975 I, F, W, E, NZ, A, 1976 F, W, E, I, 1977 E, I, F, W, 1978 I, F, E, NZ, 1979 W, E, I, F, NZ, 1980 I, F, W, E, 1981 F, W, E, I, NZ 1, 2, R, A, 1982 E, I, F, W, A 1, 2
Irvine, D R (Edinburgh Acads) 1878 E, 1879 I, E
Irvine, R W (Edinburgh Acads) 1871 E, 1872 E, 1873 E, 1874 E, 1875 E, 1876 E, 1877 I, E, 1878 E, 1879 I, E, 1880 I, E
Irvine T W (Edinburgh Acads) 1885 I 1, 2, 1886 W, I, E, 1887 I, W, E, 1888 W, I, 1889 I

Jackson, K L T (Oxford U) 1933 W, E, I, 1934 W
Jackson, R J H (Glasgow Warriors) 2010 NZ(R), Sm(R), 2011 F(R), I1, E, It1, I2, It2(R), [R, Arg, E]
Jackson, T G H (Army) 1947 F, W, E, A, 1948 F, W, I, E, 1949 F, W, I, E
Jackson, W D (Hawick) 1964 I, 1965 E, SA, 1968 A, 1969 F, W, I, E
Jacobsen, A F (Edinburgh) 2002 C (R), US, 2003 I 2, 2004 It, F, I, A3, J, A4, SA, 2005 R, Arg(R), Sm, 2006 R(R), PI(R), A(R), 2007 E(R), W(R), It(t&R), I1(R), F(R), I2, SA(R), [Pt], 2008 F, W, I, E, It, Arg 1, 2, NZ, SA, C, 2009 W, F, It, Fj, A, Arg, 2010 F(R), W(R), It, E, I, Arg 1, 2, NZ, SA, Sm, 2011 F, W, I1, E, It1, I2, [R, Gg, Arg, E]
Jamieson, J (W of Scotland) 1883 W, I, E, 1884 W, I, E, 1885 W, I 1, 2
Jardine, I C (Stirling County) 1993 NZ, 1994 W, E (R), Arg 1, 2, 1995 C, I, F, [Tg, F (t & R), NZ (R)], 1996 I, F, W, E, NZ 1, 2, 1998 Fj
Jeffrey, J (Kelso) 1984 A, 1985 I, E, 1986 F, W, E, I, R, 1987 I, F, W, E, [F, Z, R], 1988 I, W, A, 1989 W, E, I, F, Fj, R, 1990 I, F, W, E, NZ 1, 2, Arg, 1991 F, W, E, I, [J, I, WS, E, NZ]
Johnston, D I (Watsonians) 1979 NZ, 1980 I, F, W, E, 1981 R, A, 1982 E, I, F, W, A 1, 2, 1983 I, F, W, NZ, 1984 W, E, I, F, R, 1986 F, W, E, I, R
Johnston, H H (Edinburgh Collegian FP) 1877 I, E
Johnston, J (Melrose) 1951 SA, 1952 F, W, I, E
Johnston, W C (Glasgow HSFP) 1922 F
Johnston, W G S (Cambridge U) 1935 W, I, 1937 W, I, E
Joiner, C A (Melrose, Leicester) 1994 Arg 1, 2, 1995 C, I, F, W, E, R, [Iv, Tg, F, NZ], 1996 I, F, W, E, NZ 1, 1997 SA, 1998 It, I, A 2(R), 2000 NZ 1(R), 2, US (R)

Jones, P M (Gloucester) 1992 W (R)
Junor, J E (Glasgow Acads) 1876 E, 1877 I, E, 1878 E, 1879 E, 1881 I

Keddie, R R (Watsonians) 1967 NZ
Keith, G J (Wasps) 1968 F, W
Keller, D H (London Scottish) 1949 F, W, I, E, 1950 F, W, I
Kellock, A D (Edinburgh, Glasgow Warriors) 2004 A3(t&R), 2005 R(R), Arg(R), Sm(R), NZ(R), 2006 F, W, E, It(R), SA 1(R), 2, PI(R), A, 2007 E, 2008 Arg 1(t&R), 2(R), 2009 It, Fj, A, Arg, 2010 F, W, It, E, I, Arg 1, 2, 2011 F, W, I1, E, It1, I2(R), It2, [R, E]
Kelly, R F (Watsonians) 1927 A, 1928 F, W, E
Kemp, J W Y (Glasgow HSFP) 1954 W, 1955 F, W, I, E, 1956 F, W, I, E, 1957 F, W, I, E, 1958 F, W, A, I, E, 1959 F, W, I, E, 1960 F, W, I, E, SA
Kennedy, A E (Watsonians) 1983 NZ, 1984 W, E, A
Kennedy, F (Stewart's Coll FP) 1920 F, W, I, E, 1921 E
Kennedy, N (W of Scotland) 1903 W, I, E
Ker, A B M (Kelso) 1988 W, E
Ker, H T (Glasgow Acads) 1887 I, W, E, 1888 I, 1889 W, 1890 I, E
Kerr, D S (Heriot's FP) 1923 F, W, 1924 F, 1926 I, E, 1927 W, I, E, 1928 I, E
Kerr, G (Leeds, Borders, Glasgow, Edinburgh) 2003 I 1(R), F(R), W 1(R), E(R), SA 1, 2, W 2, [J(R), US, F], 2004 W(R), E(R), It(R), F(R), I(R), J, A4, SA, 2005 F, I, It, W, E, Arg, Sm(R), NZ, 2006 F, W, E, I, It, SA 1, 2, R, PI, A, 2007 E, W, It, I1, F, SA, [Pt(R), R, NZ(R), It, Arg], 2008 F(R), W(R), I(R)
Kerr, G C (Old Dunelmians, Edinburgh Wands) 1898 I, E, 1899 I, W, E, 1900 W, I, E
Kerr, J M (Heriot's FP) 1935 NZ, 1936 I, E, 1937 W, I
Kerr, R C (Glasgow) 2002 C, US, 2003 W 2
Kerr, W (London Scottish) 1953 E
Kidston, D W (Glasgow Acads) 1883 W, E
Kidston, W H (W of Scotland) 1874 E
Kilgour, I J (RMC Sandhurst) 1921 F
King, J H F (Selkirk) 1953 F, W, E, 1954 E
Kininmonth, P W (Oxford U, Richmond) 1949 F, W, I, E, 1950 F, W, I, E, 1951 F, W, I, E, SA, 1952 F, W, I, 1954 F, NZ, I, E, W
Kinnear, R M (Heriot's FP) 1926 F, W, I
Knox, J (Kelvinside Acads) 1903 W, I, E
Kyle, W E (Hawick) 1902 W, I, E, 1903 W, I, E, 1904 W, I, E, 1905 W, I, E, NZ, 1906 W, I, E, 1908 E, 1909 W, I, E, 1910 W

Laidlaw, A S (Hawick) 1897 I
Laidlaw, F A L (Melrose) 1965 F, W, I, E, SA, 1966 F, W, I, E, A, 1967 F, W, I, E, NZ, 1968 F, W, I, A, 1969 F, W, I, E, SA, 1970 F, W, I, E, A, 1971 F, W, I
Laidlaw, G D (Edinburgh) 2010 NZ(R), 2011 I2(R)
Laidlaw, R J (Jedforest) 1980 I, F, W, E, 1981 F, W, E, I, NZ 1, 2, R, A, 1982 E, I, F, W, A 1, 2, 1983 I, F, W, E, NZ, 1984 W, E, I, F, R, A, 1985 I, F, 1986 F, W, E, I, R, 1987 I, F, W, E, [F, R, NZ], 1988 I, F, W, E
Laing, A D (Royal HSFP) 1914 W, I, E, 1920 F, W, I, 1921 F
Lambie, I K (Watsonians) 1978 NZ (R), 1979 W, E, NZ
Lambie, L B (Glasgow HSFP) 1934 W, I, E, 1935 W, I, E, NZ
Lamond, G A W (Kelvinside Acads) 1899 W, E, 1905 E
Lamont, R P (Glasgow, Sale, Toulon) 2005 W, E, R, Arg, Sm, 2007 E(R), I1(R), F(R), I2, SA, [Pt, R, It, Arg], 2008 F, I, E, SA, C, 2009 Fj, A, Arg, 2010 W, NZ, 2011 It2, [Gg]
Lamont, S F (Glasgow, Northampton, Llanelli Scarlets) 2004 Sm, A1, 2, 3, J, A4, SA, 2005 F, I, It, W, E, R, Arg, Sm, NZ, 2006 F, W, E, I, It, SA1, R, PI, A, 2007 E, W, It, I1, F, I2, [Pt, R, It, Arg], 2008 NZ, 2009 W, Fj, A, Arg, 2010 F, W, It, E, I, Arg 1, 2, NZ, SA, Sm, 2011 F(R), W(R), I1, E, It1, I2, [R, Gg, Arg, E]
Laney, B J (Edinburgh) 2001 NZ, 2002 E, It, I, F, W, C, US, R, SA, Fj, 2003 I 1, F, SA 2(R), It 2(R), W 2, 2004 W, E, It, I(R)
Lang, D (Paisley) 1876 E, 1877 I
Langrish, R W (London Scottish) 1930 F, 1931 F, W, I
Lauder, W (Neath) 1969 I, E, SA, 1970 F, W, I, A, 1973 F, 1974 W, E, I, F, 1975 I, F, NZ, A, 1976 F, 1977 E
Laughland, I H P (London Scottish) 1959 F, 1960 F, W, I, E, 1961 SA, W, I, E, 1962 F, W, I, E, 1963 F, W, I, 1964 F, NZ, W, I, E, 1965 F, W, I, E, SA, 1966 F, W, I, E, 1967 E
Lawrie, J R (Melrose) 1922 F, W, I, E, 1923 F, W, I, E, 1924 W, I, E
Lawrie, K G (Gala) 1980 F (R), W, E
Lawson, A J M (Edinburgh Wands, London Scottish) 1972 F (R), E, 1973 F, 1974 W, E, 1976 E, I, 1977 E, 1978 NZ, 1979 W, E, I, F, NZ, 1980 W (R)
Lawson, R G M (Gloucester) 2006 A(R), 2007 E(R), W(R), It(R), I1(R), F, SA(R), [Pt(R), NZ(R)], 2008 E(R), Arg 1(R), 2(R), NZ(R), SA(R), C(R), 2009 A(R), Arg(R), 2010 E(R), Arg 1, 2, SA, Sm, 2011 F, W, I1(R), E, It1, I2, [Gg, Arg]
Lawson, S (Glasgow, Sale, Gloucester) 2005 R, Arg(R), Sm, NZ, 2006 F(R), W, I(R), It, SA 1, 2(R), R(R), 2007 [Pt, R(R), NZ, Arg(R)], 2008 It(R), 2010 F(R), W(R), E(R), I(R), Arg1(R), 2(R), NZ(R), 2011 W(R), I1(R), E(R), It1(R), 2, [R(R)]
Lawther, T H B (Old Millhillians) 1932 SA, W
Ledingham, G A (Aberdeen GSFP) 1913 F
Lee, D J (London Scottish, Edinburgh) 1998 I (R), F, W, E, Fj, A 1, 2, SA, 2001 Arg, 2004 It(R), F, I(R)
Lees, J B (Gala) 1947 I, A, 1948 F, W, E
Leggatt, H T O (Watsonians) 1891 W, I, E, 1892 W, I, 1893 W, E, 1894 I, E
Lely, W G (Cambridge U, London Scottish) 1909 I
Leslie, D G (Dundee HSFP, W of Scotland, Gala) 1975 I, F, W, E, NZ, A, 1976 F, W, E, I, 1978 NZ, 1980 E, 1981 W, E, I, NZ 1, 2, R, A, 1982 E, 1983 I, F, W, E, 1984 W, E, I, F, R, 1985 F, W, E
Leslie, J A (Glasgow, Northampton) 1998 SA, 1999 W, E, It, I, F, [SA], 2000 It, F, W, US, A, Sm, 2001 F, W, E, It, I, Tg, Arg, NZ, 2002 F, W
Leslie, M D (Glasgow, Edinburgh) 1998 SA (R), 1999 W, E, It, I, F, R, [SA, U, Sm, NZ], 2000 It, I, F, W, E, NZ 1, 2, 2001 F, W, E, It, 2002 It (R), I (R), F, W, R, SA, Fj(R), 2003 I 1, F, SA 1(R), 2 (R), It 2(R), W 2, [J(R), US(R)]
Liddell, E H (Edinburgh U) 1922 F, W, I, 1923 F, W, I, E
Lind, H (Dunfermline) 1928 I, 1931 F, W, I, E, 1932 SA, W, E, 1933 W, E, I, 1934 W, I, E, 1935 I, 1936 E
Lindsay, A B (London Hospital) 1910 I, 1911 I
Lindsay, G C (London Scottish) 1884 W, 1885 I 1, 1887 W, E
Lindsay-Watson, R H (Hawick) 1909 I
Lineen, S R P (Boroughmuir) 1989 W, E, I, F, Fj, R, 1990 I, F, W, E, NZ 1, 2, Arg, 1991 F, W, E, I, R, [J, Z, I, E, NZ], 1992 E, I, F, W, A 1, 2
Little, A W (Hawick) 1905 W
Logan, K M (Stirling County, Wasps) 1992 A 2, 1993 E(R), NZ(t), 1994 W, E, I, F, Arg 1, 2, SA, 1995 C, I, F, W, E, R, [Iv, Tg, F, NZ], WS, 1996 W (R), NZ 1, 2, A, It, 1997 W, E, I, F, A, 1998 I, F, SA (R), 1999 W, E, It, I, F, Arg, R, [SA, U, Sm, NZ], 2000 It, I, F, Sm, 2001 F, W, E, It, 2002 I (R), F (R), W, 2003 I 1, F, W 1, E, It 1, SA 1, 2, It 2, I 2, [J, US(R), F, Fj, A]
Logan, W R (Edinburgh U, Edinburgh Wands) 1931 E, 1932 SA, W, I, 1933 W, E, I, 1934 W, I, E, 1935 W, I, E, NZ, 1936 W, I, E, 1937 W, I, E
Longstaff, S L (Dundee HSFP, Glasgow) 1998 F (R), W, E, Fj, A 1, 2 1999 It (R), I (R), Arg (R), R, [U (R), Sp], 2000 It, I, NZ 1
Lorraine, H D B (Oxford U) 1933 W, E, I
Loudoun-Shand, E G (Oxford U) 1913 E
Low, M J (Glasgow Warriors) 2009 F(R), E(R), Fj, A, Arg, 2010 F, Arg 1, 2, SA(R), Sm(R), 2011 F(R), W(R), I1, E, It2
Lowe, J D (Heriot's FP) 1934 W
Lumsden, I J M (Bath, Watsonians) 1947 F, W, A, 1949 F, W, I, E
Lyall, G G (Gala) 1947 A, 1948 F, W, I, E
Lyall, W J C (Edinburgh Acads) 1871 E

Mabon, J T (Jedforest) 1898 I, E, 1899 I, 1900 I
Macarthur, J P (Waterloo) 1932 E
MacCallum, J C (Watsonians) 1905 E, NZ, 1906 W, I, E, SA, 1907 W, I, E, 1908 W, I, E, 1909 W, I, E, 1910 F, W, I, E, 1911 F, I, E, 1912 F, W, I, E
McClung, T (Edinburgh Acads) 1956 I, E, 1957 W, I, E, 1959 F, W, I, 1960 W
McClure, G B (W of Scotland) 1873 E
McClure, J H (W of Scotland) 1872 E
McCowan, D (W of Scotland) 1880 I, E, 1881 I, E, 1882 I, E, 1883 I, E, 1884 I, E
McCowat, R H (Glasgow Acads) 1905 I
McCrae, I G (Gordonians) 1967 E, 1968 I, 1969 F (R), W, 1972 F, NZ
McCrow, J W S (Edinburgh Acads) 1921 I
Macdonald, A E D (Heriot's FP) 1993 NZ
MacDonald, A R (Edinburgh) 2009 Arg, 2010 W(t&R), E(R), I(t)
McDonald, C (Jedforest) 1947 A
Macdonald, D C (Edinburgh U) 1953 F, W, 1958 I, E

Macdonald, D S M (Oxford U, London Scottish, W of Scotland) 1977 E, I, F, W, 1978 I, W, E
Macdonald, J D (London Scottish, Army) 1966 F, W, I, E, 1967 F, W, I, E
Macdonald, J M (Edinburgh Wands) 1911 W
Macdonald, J S (Edinburgh U) 1903 E, 1904 W, I, E, 1905 W
Macdonald, K R (Stewart's Coll FP) 1956 F, W, I, 1957 W, I, E
Macdonald, R (Edinburgh U) 1950 F, W, I, E
McDonald, W A (Glasgow U) 1889 W, 1892 I, E
Macdonald, W G (London Scottish) 1969 I (R)
MacDougall, B (Borders) 2006 W, SA2(R)
Macdougall, J B (Greenock Wands, Wakefield) 1913 F, 1914 I, 1921 F, I, E
McEwan, M C (Edinburgh Acads) 1886 E, 1887 I, W, E, 1888 W, I, 1889 W, I, 1890 W, I, E, 1891 W, I, E, 1892 E
MacEwan, N A (Gala, Highland) 1971 F, W, I, E (2[1C]), 1972 F, W, E, NZ, 1973 F, W, I, E, P, 1974 W, E, I, F, 1975 W, E
McEwan, W M C (Edinburgh Acads) 1894 W, E, 1895 W, E, 1896 W, I, E, 1897 I, E, 1898 I, E, 1899 I, W, E, 1900 W, E
MacEwen, R K G (Cambridge U, London Scottish) 1954 F, NZ, I, W, 1956 F, W, I, E, 1957 F, W, I, E, 1958 W
Macfadyen, D J H (Glasgow) 2002 C (R), US, 2004 Sm, A1, 2, 3, J, A4, SA, 2006 SA 1, 2(R)
Macfarlan, D J (London Scottish) 1883 W, 1884 W, I, E, 1886 W, I, 1887 I, 1888 I
McFarlane, J L H (Edinburgh U) 1871 E, 1872 E, 1873 E
McGaughey, S K (Hawick) 1984 R
McGeechan, I R (Headingley) 1972 NZ, 1973 F, W, I, E, P, 1974 W, E, I, F, 1975 I, F, W, E, NZ, A, 1976 F, W, E, I, 1977 E, I, F, W, 1978 I, F, W, NZ, 1979 W, E, I, F
McGlashan, T P L (Royal HSFP) 1947 F, I, E, 1954 F, NZ, I, E, W
MacGregor, D G (Watsonians, Pontypridd) 1907 W, I, E
MacGregor, G (Cambridge U) 1890 W, I, E, 1891 W, I, E, 1893 W, I, E, 1894 W, I, E, 1896 E
MacGregor, I A A (Hillhead HSFP, Llanelli) 1955 I, E, 1956 F, W, I, E, 1957 F, W, I
MacGregor, J R (Edinburgh U) 1909 I
McGuinness, G M (W of Scotland) 1982 A 1, 2, 1983 I, 1985 I, F, W, E
McHarg, A F (W of Scotland, London Scottish) 1968 I, E, A, 1969 F, W, I, E, 1971 F, W, I, E (2[1C]), 1972 F, E, NZ, 1973 F, W, I, E, P, 1974 W, E, I, F, 1975 I, F, W, E, NZ, A, 1976 F, W, E, I, 1977 E, I, F, W, 1978 I, F, W, NZ, 1979 W, E
McIlwham, G R (Glasgow Hawks, Glasgow, Bordeaux-Bègles) 1998 Fj, A 2(R), 2000 E (R), NZ 2(R), US (R), A (R), Sm (R), 2001 F (R), W (R), E (R), It (R), 2003 SA 2(R), It 2(R), W 2(R), I 2, [A(R)]
McIndoe, F (Glasgow Acads) 1886 W, I
MacIntyre, I (Edinburgh Wands) 1890 W, I, E, 1891 W, I, E
McIvor, D J (Edinburgh Acads) 1992 E, I, F, W, 1993 NZ, 1994 SA
Mackay, E B (Glasgow Acads) 1920 W, 1922 E
McKeating, E (Heriot's FP) 1957 F, W, 1961 SA, W, I, E
McKelvey, G (Watsonians) 1997 A
McKendrick, J G (W of Scotland) 1889 I
Mackenzie, A D G (Selkirk) 1984 A
Mackenzie, C J G (United Services) 1921 E
Mackenzie, D D (Edinburgh U) 1947 W, I, E, 1948 F, W, I
Mackenzie, D K A (Edinburgh Wands) 1939 I, E
Mackenzie, J M (Edinburgh U) 1905 NZ, 1909 W, I, E, 1910 W, I, E, 1911 W, I
McKenzie, K D (Stirling County) 1994 Arg 1, 2, 1995 R, [Iv], 1996 I, F, W, E, NZ 1, 2, A, It, 1998 A 1(R), 2
Mackenzie, R C (Glasgow Acads) 1877 I, E, 1881 I, E
Mackie, G Y (Highland) 1975 A, 1976 F, W, 1978 F
MacKinnon, A (London Scottish) 1898 I, E, 1899 I, W, E, 1900 E
Mackintosh, C E W C (London Scottish) 1924 F
Mackintosh, H S (Glasgow U, W of Scotland) 1929 F, W, I, E, 1930 F, W, I, E, 1931 F, W, I, E, 1932 SA, W, I, E
MacLachlan, L P (Oxford U, London Scottish) 1954 NZ, I, E, W
Maclagan, W E (Edinburgh Acads) 1878 E, 1879 I, E, 1880 I, E, 1881 I, E, 1882 I, E, 1883 W, I, E, 1884 W, I, E, 1885 W, I 1, 2, 1887 I, W, E, 1888 W, I, 1890 W, I, E
McLaren, A (Durham County) 1931 F
McLaren, E (London Scottish, Royal HSFP) 1923 F, W, I, E, 1924 F
McLaren, J G (Bourgoin, Glasgow, Bordeaux-Bègles, Castres) 1999 Arg, R, [Sp, Sm], 2000 It (R), F, E, NZ 1, 2001 F, W, E (R), I, Tg, Arg, NZ, 2002 E, It, I, F, W, 2003 W 1, E, It 1, SA 1(R), It 2, I 2(R), [J, F(R), Fj(t&R), A(R)]
McLauchlan, J (Jordanhill) 1969 E, SA, 1970 F, W, 1971 F, W, I, E (2[1C]), 1972 F, W, E, NZ, 1973 F, W, I, E, P, 1974 W, E, I, F, 1975 I, F, W, E, NZ, A, 1976 F, W, E, I, 1977 W, 1978 I, F, W, E, NZ, 1979 W, E, I, F, NZ
McLean, D I (Royal HSFP) 1947 I, E
Maclennan, W D (Watsonians) 1947 F, I
MacLeod, D A (Glasgow U) 1886 I, E
MacLeod, G (Edinburgh Acads) 1878 E, 1882 I
McLeod, H F (Hawick) 1954 F, NZ, I, E, W, 1955 F, W, I, E, 1956 F, W, I, E, 1957 F, W, I, E, 1958 F, W, A, I, E, 1959 F, W, I, E, 1960 F, W, I, E, SA, 1961 F, SA, W, I, E, 1962 F, W, I, E
MacLeod, K G (Cambridge U) 1905 NZ, 1906 W, I, E, SA, 1907 W, I, E, 1908 I, E
MacLeod, L M (Cambridge U) 1904 W, I, E, 1905 W, I, NZ
MacLeod, S J (Borders, Llanelli Scarlets, Edinburgh) 2004 A3, J(t&R), A4(R), SA(R), 2006 F(R), W(R), E, SA2(R), 2007 I2(R), [Pt(R), R(R), NZ, It(R), Arg(R)], 2008 F(R), W(R), I, E, It, Arg 1, 2, 2010 Arg 2(t&R), SA, 2011 W(R)
Macleod, W M (Fettesian-Lorettonians, Edinburgh Wands) 1886 W, I
McMillan, K H D (Sale) 1953 F, W, I, E
MacMillan, R G (London Scottish) 1887 W, I, E, 1890 W, I, E, 1891 W, E, 1892 W, I, E, 1893 W, E, 1894 W, I, E, 1895 W, I, E, 1897 I, E
MacMyn, D J (Cambridge U, London Scottish) 1925 F, W, I, E, 1926 F, W, I, E, 1927 E, A, 1928 F
McNeil, A S B (Watsonians) 1935 I
McPartlin, J J (Harlequins, Oxford U) 1960 F, W, 1962 F, W, I, E
Macphail, J A R (Edinburgh Acads) 1949 E, 1951 SA
Macpherson, D G (London Hospital) 1910 I, E
Macpherson, G P S (Oxford U, Edinburgh Acads) 1922 F, W, I, E, 1924 W, E, 1925 F, W, E, 1927 F, W, I, E, 1928 F, W, E, 1929 I, E, 1930 F, W, I, E, 1931 W, E, 1932 SA, E
Macpherson, N C (Newport) 1920 W, I, E, 1921 F, E, 1923 I, E
McQueen, S B (Waterloo) 1923 F, W, I, E
Macrae, D J (St Andrew's U) 1937 W, I, E, 1938 W, I, E, 1939 W, I, E
Madsen, D F (Gosforth) 1974 W, E, I, F, 1975 I, F, W, E, 1976 F, 1977 E, I, F, W, 1978 I
Mair, N G R (Edinburgh U) 1951 F, W, I, E
Maitland, G (Edinburgh Inst FP) 1885 W, I 2
Maitland, R (Edinburgh Inst FP) 1881 E, 1882 I, E, 1884 W, 1885 W
Maitland, R P (Royal Artillery) 1872 E
Malcolm, A G (Glasgow U) 1888 I
Manson, J J (Dundee HSFP) 1995 E (R)
Marsh, J (Edinburgh Inst FP) 1889 W, I
Marshall, A (Edinburgh Acads) 1875 E
Marshall, G R (Selkirk) 1988 A (R), 1989 Fj, 1990 Arg, 1991 [Z]
Marshall, J C (London Scottish) 1954 F, NZ, I, E, W
Marshall, K W (Edinburgh Acads) 1934 W, I, E, 1935 W, I, E, 1936 W, 1937 E
Marshall, T R (Edinburgh Acads) 1871 E, 1872 E, 1873 E, 1874 E
Marshall, W (Edinburgh Acads) 1872 E
Martin, H (Edinburgh Acads, Oxford U) 1908 W, I, E, 1909 W, E
Masters, W H (Edinburgh Inst FP) 1879 I, 1880 I, E
Mather, C G (Edinburgh, Glasgow) 1999 R (R), [Sp, Sm (R)], 2000 F (t), 2003 [F, Fj, A], 2004 W, E, F
Maxwell, F T (Royal Engineers) 1872 E
Maxwell, G H H P (Edinburgh Acads, RAF, London Scottish) 1913 I, E, 1914 W, I, E, 1920 W, E, 1921 F, W, I, E, 1922 F, E
Maxwell, J M (Langholm) 1957 I
Mayer, M J M (Watsonians, Edinburgh) 1998 SA, 1999 [SA (R), U, Sp, Sm, NZ], 2000 It, I
Mein, J (Edinburgh Acads) 1871 E, 1872 E, 1873 E, 1874 E, 1875 E
Melville, C L (Army) 1937 W, I, E
Menzies, H F (W of Scotland) 1893 W, I, 1894 W, E
Metcalfe, G H (Glasgow Hawks, Glasgow) 1998 A 1, 2, 1999 W, E, It, I, F, Arg, R, [SA, U, Sm, NZ], 2000 It, I, F, W, E, 2001 I, Tg, 2002 E, It, I, F, W (R), C, US, 2003 I 1, F, W 1, E, It 1, SA 1, 2, W 2, I 2, [US, F, Fj, A]
Metcalfe, R (Northampton, Edinburgh) 2000 E, NZ 1, 2, US (R), A (R), Sm, 2001 F, W, E
Methuen, A (London Scottish) 1889 W, I
Michie, E J S (Aberdeen U, Aberdeen GSFP) 1954 F, NZ, I, E, 1955 W, I, E, 1956 F, W, I, E, 1957 F, W, I, E
Millar, J N (W of Scotland) 1892 W, I, E, 1893 W, 1895 I, E
Millar, R K (London Scottish) 1924 I
Millican, J G (Edinburgh U) 1973 W, I, E
Milne, C J B (Fettesian-Lorettonians, W of Scotland) 1886 W, I, E

Milne, D F (Heriot's FP) 1991 [J(R)]
Milne, I G (Heriot's FP, Harlequins) 1979 I, F, NZ, 1980 I, F, 1981 NZ 1, 2, R, A, 1982 E, I, F, W, A 1, 2, 1983 I, F, W, E, NZ, 1984 W, E, I, F, A, 1985 F, W, E, 1986 F, W, E, I, R, 1987 I, F, W, E, [F, Z, NZ], 1988 A, 1989 W, 1990 NZ 1, 2
Milne, K S (Heriot's FP) 1989 W, E, I, F, Fj, R, 1990 I, F, W, E, NZ 2, Arg, 1991 F, W (R), E, [Z], 1992 E, I, F, W, A 1, 1993 I, F, W, E, NZ, 1994 W, E, I, F, SA, 1995 C, I, F, W, E, [Tg, F, NZ]
Milne, W M (Glasgow Acads) 1904 I, E, 1905 W, I
Milroy, E (Watsonians) 1910 W, 1911 E, 1912 W, I, E, SA, 1913 F, W, I, E, 1914 I, E
Mitchell, G W E (Edinburgh Wands) 1967 NZ, 1968 F, W
Mitchell, J G (W of Scotland) 1885 W, I 1, 2
Moffat, J S D (Edinburgh, Borders) 2002 R, SA, Fj(R), 2004 A3
Moir, C C (Northampton) 2000 W, E, NZ 1
Moncreiff, F J (Edinburgh Acads) 1871 E, 1872 E, 1873 E
Monteith, H G (Cambridge U, London Scottish) 1905 E, 1906 W, I, E, SA, 1907 W, I, 1908 E
Monypenny, D B (London Scottish) 1899 I, W, E
Moodie, A R (St Andrew's U) 1909 E, 1910 F, 1911 F
Moore, A (Edinburgh Acads) 1990 NZ 2, Arg, 1991 F, W, E
Morgan, D W (Stewart's-Melville FP) 1973 W, I, E, P, 1974 I, F, 1975 I, F, W, E, NZ, A, 1976 F, W, 1977 I, F, W, 1978 I, F, W, E
Morrison, G A (Glasgow Warriors) 2004 A1(R), 2(R), 3, J(R), A4(R), SA(R), 2008 W(R), E, It, Arg 1, 2, 2009 W, F, It, I, E, Fj, A, 2010 F, W, It, E, I, Arg 1, 2, NZ, SA, Sm, 2011 I2, It2, [Gg, Arg]
Morrison, I R (London Scottish) 1993 I, F, W, E, 1994 W, SA, 1995 C, I, F, W, E, R, [Tg, F, NZ]
Morrison, M C (Royal HSFP) 1896 W, I, E, 1897 I, E, 1898 I, E, 1899 I, W, E, 1900 W, E, 1901 W, I, E, 1902 W, I, E, 1903 W, I, 1904 W, I, E
Morrison, R H (Edinburgh U) 1886 W, I, E
Morrison, W H (Edinburgh Acads) 1900 W
Morton, D S (W of Scotland) 1887 I, W, E, 1888 W, I, 1889 W, I, 1890 I, E
Mowat, J G (Glasgow Acads) 1883 W, E
Mower, A L (Newcastle) 2001 Tg, Arg, NZ, 2002 It, 2003 I 1, F, W 1, E, It 1, SA 1, 2, W 2, I 2
Muir, D E (Heriot's FP) 1950 F, W, I, E, 1952 W, I, E
Munnoch, N M (Watsonians) 1952 F, W, I
Munro, D S (Glasgow High Kelvinside) 1994 W, E, I, F, Arg 1, 2, 1997 W (R)
Munro, P (Oxford U, London Scottish) 1905 W, I, E, NZ, 1906 W, I, E, SA, 1907 I, E, 1911 F, W, I
Munro, R (St Andrew's U) 1871 E
Munro, S (Ayr, W of Scotland) 1980 I, F, 1981 F, W, E, I, NZ 1, 2, R, 1984 W
Munro, W H (Glasgow HSFP) 1947 I, E
Murdoch, W C W (Hillhead HSFP) 1935 E, NZ, 1936 W, I, 1939 E, 1948 F, W, I, E
Murray, C A (Hawick, Edinburgh) 1998 E (R), Fj, A 1, 2, SA, 1999 W, E, It, I, F, Arg, [SA, U, Sp, Sm, NZ], 2000 NZ 2, US, A, Sm, 2001 F, W, E, It (R), Tg, Arg
Murray, E A (Glasgow, Northampton, Newcastle) 2005 R(R), 2006 R, PI, A, 2007 E, W, It, I1, F, I2, SA, [Pt, R, It, Arg], 2008 F, W, I, E, It, Arg 1, 2, NZ, SA, C, 2009 It, I, E, 2010 W, It, E, I, NZ, SA, Sm, 2011 F, W, It1(R), 2(R), [Gg, E]
Murray, G M (Glasgow Acads) 1921 I, 1926 W
Murray, H M (Glasgow U) 1936 W, I
Murray, K T (Hawick) 1985 I, F, W
Murray, R O (Cambridge U) 1935 W, E
Murray, S (Bedford, Saracens, Edinburgh) 1997 A, SA, 1998 It, Fj, A 1, 2, SA, 1999 W, E, It, I, F, Arg, R, [SA, U, Sm, NZ], 2000 It, I, F, W, E, NZ 1, US, A, Sm, 2001 F, W, E, It, I, Tg, Arg, NZ, 2002 E, It, I, F, W, R, SA, 2003 I 1, F, W 1, E, It 1, SA 1, 2, It 2, W 2, [J, F, A(R)], 2004 W, E, It, F, I, Sm, A1, 2, 2005 F, I, It, W, E, R, Arg, Sm, NZ, 2006 F, W, I, It, SA1, R, PI, A, 2007 E(t&R), W, It, I1, F, SA(R), [Pt, NZ]
Murray, W A K (London Scottish) 1920 F, I, 1921 F
Mustchin, M L (Edinburgh) 2008 Arg 1, 2, NZ(R), SA(R), C(R)

Napier, H M (W of Scotland) 1877 I, E, 1878 E, 1879 I, E
Neill, J B (Edinburgh Acads) 1963 E, 1964 F, NZ, W, I, E, 1965 F
Neill, R M (Edinburgh Acads) 1901 E, 1902 I
Neilson, G T (W of Scotland) 1891 W, I, E, 1892 W, E, 1893 W, 1894 W, I, 1895 W, I, E, 1896 W, I, E
Neilson, J A (Glasgow Acads) 1878 E, 1879 E
Neilson, R T (W of Scotland) 1898 I, E, 1899 I, W, 1900 I, E
Neilson, T (W of Scotland) 1874 E
Neilson, W (Merchiston Castle School, Cambridge U, London Scottish) 1891 W, E, 1892 W, I, E, 1893 I, E, 1894 E, 1895 W, I, E, 1896 I, 1897 I, E
Neilson, W G (Merchistonians) 1894 E
Nelson, J B (Glasgow Acads) 1925 F, W, I, E, 1926 F, W, I, E, 1927 F, W, I, E, 1928 I, E, 1929 F, W, I, E, 1930 F, W, I, E, 1931 F, W, I
Nelson, T A (Oxford U) 1898 E
Nichol, J A (Royal HSFP) 1955 W, I, E
Nichol, S A (Selkirk) 1994 Arg 2(R)
Nicol, A D (Dundee HSFP, Bath, Glasgow) 1992 E, I, F, W, A 1, 2, 1993 NZ, 1994 W, 1997 A, SA, 2000 I (R), F, W, E, NZ 1, 2, 2001 F, W, E, I (R), Tg, Arg, NZ
Nimmo, C S (Watsonians) 1920 E

Ogilvy, C (Hawick) 1911 I, E, 1912 I
Oliver, G H (Hawick) 1987 [Z], 1990 NZ 2(R), 1991 [Z]
Oliver, G K (Gala) 1970 A
Orr, C E (W of Scotland) 1887 I, E, W, 1888 W, I, 1889 W, I, 1890 W, I, E, 1891 W, I, E, 1892 W, I, E
Orr, H J (London Scottish) 1903 W, I, E, 1904 W, I
Orr, J E (W of Scotland) 1889 I, 1890 W, I, E, 1891 W, I, E, 1892 W, I, E, 1893 I, E
Orr, J H (Edinburgh City Police) 1947 F, W
Osler, F L (Edinburgh U) 1911 F, W

Park, J (Royal HSFP) 1934 W
Parks, D A (Glasgow Warriors, Cardiff Blues) 2004 W(R), E(R), F(R), I, Sm(t&R), A1, 2, 3, J, A4, SA, 2005 F, I, It, W, R, Arg, Sm, NZ, 2006 F, W, E, I, It(R), SA1, PI, A, 2007 E, I1, F, I2(R), SA(R), [Pt, R, NZ(R), It, Arg], 2008 F, W, I(R), E(R), It, Arg 1, 2(R), NZ(R), SA(t), C(R), 2010 W, It, E, I, Arg 1, 2, NZ, SA, Sm, 2011 F, W, I1(R), E(R), It1(R), 2, [R(R), Gg, Arg(R), E(R)]
Paterson, C D (Edinburgh, Gloucester) 1999 [Sp], 2000 F, W, E, NZ 1, 2, US, A, Sm, 2001 F, W, E, It, I, NZ, 2002 E, It, I, F, W, C, US, R, SA, Fj, 2003 I 1, F, W 1, E, It 1, SA 1, 2, It 2(R), W 2(R), I 2, [J, US, F, Fj, A], 2004 W, E, It, F, I, Sm, A3, J, A4, SA, 2005 F, I, It, W, E, R, Arg, Sm, NZ, 2006 F, W, E, I, It, SA 1, 2, R(R), PI, A, 2007 E, W, It, I1, F, I2, SA, [Pt(R), R, NZ, It, Arg], 2008 F(R), W, I, E, It, Arg 1, 2, NZ, SA, 2009 W(R), F(R), It(t&R), I, E, Fj(R), A(R), Arg(R), 2010 F, W, SA(R), 2011 I1, E, It1, I2, [R, Gg(R), Arg, E]
Paterson, D S (Gala) 1969 SA, 1970 I, E, A, 1971 F, W, I, E (2[1C]), 1972 W
Paterson, G Q (Edinburgh Acads) 1876 E
Paterson, J R (Birkenhead Park) 1925 F, W, I, E, 1926 F, W, I, E, 1927 F, W, I, E, A, 1928 F, W, I, E, 1929 F, W, I, E
Patterson, D (Hawick) 1896 W
Patterson, D W (West Hartlepool) 1994 SA, 1995 [Tg]
Pattullo, G L (Panmure) 1920 F, W, I, E
Paxton, I A M (Selkirk) 1981 NZ 1, 2, R, A, 1982 E, I, F, W, A 1, 2, 1983 I, E, NZ, 1984 W, E, I, F, 1985 I (R), F, W, E, 1986 W, E, I, R, 1987 I, F, W, E, [F, Z, R, NZ], 1988 I, E, A
Paxton, R E (Kelso) 1982 I, A 2(R)
Pearson, J (Watsonians) 1909 I, E, 1910 F, W, I, E, 1911 F, 1912 F, W, SA, 1913 I, E
Pender, I M (London Scottish) 1914 E
Pender, N E K (Hawick) 1977 I, 1978 F, W, E
Penman, W M (RAF) 1939 I
Peterkin, W A (Edinburgh U) 1881 E, 1883 I, 1884 W, I, E, 1885 W, I 1, 2
Peters, E W (Bath) 1995 C, I, F, W, E, R, [Tg, F, NZ], 1996 I, F, W, E, NZ 1, 2, A, It, 1997 A, SA, 1998 W, E, Fj, A 1, 2, SA, 1999 W, E, It, I
Petrie, A G (Royal HSFP) 1873 E, 1874 E, 1875 E, 1876 E, 1877 I, E, 1878 E, 1879 I, E, 1880 I, E
Petrie, J M (Glasgow) 2000 NZ 2, US, A, Sm, 2001 F, W, It (R), I (R), Tg, Arg, 2002 F (t), W (R), C, R(R), Fj, 2003 F(t+R), W 1(R), SA 1(R), 2 (R), It 2, W 2, I 2(R), [J, US, F(t&R), A(R)], 2004 It(R), I(R), Sm(R), A1(R), 2(t&R), 3(R), J, A4, SA(R), 2005 F, I, It, W, E(R), R, 2006 F(R), W(R), I(R), SA 2
Philip, T K (Edinburgh) 2004 W, E, It, F, I
Philp, A (Edinburgh Inst FP) 1882 E
Pinder, S J (Glasgow) 2006 SA 1(R), 2(R)
Pocock, E I (Edinburgh Wands) 1877 I, E
Pollock, J A (Gosforth) 1982 W, 1983 E, NZ, 1984 E (R), I, F, R, 1985 F
Polson, A H (Gala) 1930 E
Pountney, A C (Northhampton) 1998 SA, 1999 W (t+R), E (R), It (t+R), I (R), F, Arg, [SA, U, Sm, NZ], 2000 It, I, F, W, E, US, A, Sm, 2001 F, W, E, It, I, 2002 E, I, F, W, R, SA, Fj
Proudfoot, M C (Melrose, Glasgow) 1998 Fj, A 1, 2, 2003 I 2(R)

Purdie, W (Jedforest) 1939 W, I, E
Purves, A B H L (London Scottish) 1906 W, I, E, SA, 1907 W, I, E, 1908 W, I, E
Purves, W D C L (London Scottish) 1912 F, W, I, SA, 1913 I, E

Rea, C W W (W of Scotland, Headingley) 1968 A, 1969 F, W, I, SA, 1970 F, W, I, A, 1971 F, W, E (2[1C])
Redpath, B W (Melrose, Narbonne, Sale) 1993 NZ (t), 1994 E (t), F, Arg 1, 2, 1995 C, I, F, W, E, R, [Iv, F, NZ], WS, 1996 I, F, W, E. A (R), It, 1997 E, I, F, 1998 Fj, A 1, 2, SA, 1999 R (R), [U (R), Sp], 2000 It, I, US, A, Sm, 2001 F (R), E (R), It, I, 2002 E, It, I, F, W, R, SA, Fj, 2003 I 1, F, W 1, E, It 1, SA 1, 2, [J, US(R), F, Fj, A]
Reed, A I (Bath, Wasps) 1993 I, F, W, E, 1994 E, I, F, Arg 1, 2, SA, 1996 It, 1997 W, E, I, F, 1999 It (R), F (R), [Sp]
Reid, C (Edinburgh Acads) 1881 I, E, 1882 I, E, 1883 W, I, E, 1884 W, I, E, 1885 W, I 1, 2, 1886 W, I, E, 1887 I, W, E, 1888 W, I
Reid, J (Edinburgh Wands) 1874 E, 1875 E, 1876 E, 1877 I, E
Reid, J M (Edinburgh Acads) 1898 I, E, 1899 I
Reid, M F (Loretto) 1883 I, E
Reid, R E (Glasgow) 2001 Tg (R), Arg
Reid, S J (Boroughmuir, Leeds, Narbonne) 1995 WS, 1999 F, Arg, [Sp], 2000 It (t), F, W, E (t)
Reid-Kerr, J (Greenock Wand) 1909 E
Relph, W K L (Stewart's Coll FP) 1955 F, W, I, E
Rennie, R M (Edinburgh) 2008 I(R), 2010 NZ(R), SA(R), Sm(R), 2011 F(R), W(R), I2, It2(R), [R(R), Gg, E(R)]
Renny-Tailyour, H W (Royal Engineers) 1872 E
Renwick, J M (Hawick) 1972 F, W, E, NZ, 1973 F, 1974 W, E, I, F, 1975 I, F, W, E, NZ, A, 1976 F, W, E (R), 1977 I, F, W, 1978 I, F, W, E, NZ, 1979 W, E, I, F, NZ, 1980 I, F, W, E, 1981 F, W, E, I, NZ 1, 2, R, A, 1982 E, I, F, W, 1983 I, F, W, E, 1984 R
Renwick, W L (London Scottish) 1989 R
Renwick, W N (London Scottish, Edinburgh Wands) 1938 E, 1939 W
Richardson, J F (Edinburgh Acads) 1994 SA
Ritchie, G (Merchistonians) 1871 E
Ritchie, G F (Dundee HSFP) 1932 E
Ritchie, J M (Watsonians) 1933 W, E, I, 1934 W, I, E
Ritchie, W T (Cambridge U) 1905 I, E
Robb, G H (Glasgow U) 1881 I, 1885 W
Roberts, G (Watsonians) 1938 W, I, E, 1939 W, E
Robertson, A H (W of Scotland) 1871 E
Robertson, A W (Edinburgh Acads) 1897 E
Robertson, D (Edinburgh Acads) 1875 E
Robertson, D D (Cambridge U) 1893 W
Robertson, I (London Scottish, Watsonians) 1968 E, 1969 E, SA, 1970 F, W, I, E, A
Robertson, I P M (Watsonians) 1910 F
Robertson, J (Clydesdale) 1908 E
Robertson, K W (Melrose) 1978 NZ, 1979 W, E, I, F, NZ, 1980 W, E, 1981 F, W, E, I, R, A, 1982 E, I, F, A 1, 2, 1983 I, F, W, E, 1984 E, I, F, R, A, 1985 I, F, W, E, 1986 I, 1987 F (R), W, E, [F, Z, NZ], 1988 E, A, 1989 E, I, F
Robertson, L (London Scottish United Services) 1908 E, 1911 W, 1912 W, I, E, SA, 1913 W, I, E
Robertson, M A (Gala) 1958 F
Robertson, R D (London Scottish) 1912 F
Robson, A (Hawick) 1954 F, 1955 F, W, I, E, 1956 F, W, I, E, 1957 F, W, I, E, 1958 W, A, I, E, 1959 F, W, I, E, 1960 F
Rodd, J A T (United Services, RN, London Scottish) 1958 F, W, A, I, E, 1960 F, W, 1962 F, 1964 F, NZ, W, 1965 F, W, I
Rogerson, J (Kelvinside Acads) 1894 W
Roland, E T (Edinburgh Acads) 1884 I, E
Rollo, D M D (Howe of Fife) 1959 E, 1960 F, W, I, E, SA, 1961 F, SA, W, I, E, 1962 F, W, E, 1963 F, W, I, E, 1964 F, NZ, W, I, E, 1965 F, W, I, E, SA, 1966 F, W, I, E, A, 1967 F, W, E, NZ, 1968 F, W, I
Rose, D M (Jedforest) 1951 F, W, I, E, SA, 1953 F, W
Ross, A (Kilmarnock) 1924 F, W
Ross, A (Royal HSFP) 1905 W, I, E, 1909 W, I
Ross, A R (Edinburgh U) 1911 W, 1914 W, I, E
Ross, E J (London Scottish) 1904 W
Ross, G (Edinburgh, Leeds) 2001 Tg, 2002 R, SA, Fj(R), 2003 I 1, W 1(R), SA 2(R), It 2, I 2, [J], 2004 Sm, A1(R), 2(R), J(R), SA(R), 2005 It(R), W(R), E, 2006 F(R), W(R), E(R), I(R), It, SA 1(R), 2
Ross, G T (Watsonians) 1954 NZ, I, E, W
Ross, I A (Hillhead HSFP) 1951 F, W, I, E
Ross, J (London Scottish) 1901 W, I, E, 1902 W, 1903 E
Ross, K I (Boroughmuir FP) 1961 SA, W, I, E, 1962 F, W, I, E, 1963 F, W, E
Ross, W A (Hillhead HSFP) 1937 W, E
Rottenburg, H (Cambridge U, London Scottish) 1899 W, E, 1900 W, I, E
Roughead, W N (Edinburgh Acads, London Scottish) 1927 A, 1928 F, W, I, E, 1930 I, E, 1931 F, W, I, E, 1932 W
Rowan, N A (Boroughmuir) 1980 W, E, 1981 F, W, E, I, 1984 R, 1985 I, 1987 [R], 1988 I, F, W, E
Rowand, R (Glasgow HSFP) 1930 F, W, 1932 E, 1933 W, E, I, 1934 W
Roxburgh, A J (Kelso) 1997 A, 1998 It, F (R), W, E, Fj, A 1(R), 2(R)
Roy, A (Waterloo) 1938 W, I, E, 1939 W, I, E
Russell, R R (Saracens, London Irish) 1999 R, [U (R), Sp, Sm (R), NZ (R)], 2000 I (R), 2001 F (R), 2002 F (R), W (R), 2003 W 1(R), It 1(R), SA 1 (R), 2 (R), It 2, I 2(R), [J, F(R), Fj(t), A(R)], 2004 W(R), E(R), F(R), I(R), J(R), A4(R), SA(R), 2005 It(R)
Russell, W L (Glasgow Acads) 1905 NZ, 1906 W, I, E
Rutherford, J Y (Selkirk) 1979 W, E, I, F, NZ, 1980 I, F, E, 1981 F, W, E, I, NZ 1, 2, A, 1982 E, I, F, W, A 1, 2, 1983 E, NZ, 1984 W, E, I, F, R, 1985 I, F, W, E, 1986 F, W, E, I, R, 1987 I, F, W, E, [F]

Sampson, R W F (London Scottish) 1939 W, 1947 W
Sanderson, G A (Royal HSFP) 1907 W, I, E, 1908 I
Sanderson, J L P (Edinburgh Acads) 1873 E
Schulze, D G (London Scottish) 1905 E, 1907 I, E, 1908 W, I, E, 1909 W, I, E, 1910 W, I, E, 1911 W
Scobie, R M (Royal Military Coll) 1914 W, I, E
Scotland, K J F (Heriot's FP, Cambridge U, Leicester) 1957 F, W, I, E, 1958 E, 1959 F, W, I, E, 1960 F, W, I, E, 1961 F, SA, W, I, E, 1962 F, W, I, E, 1963 F, W, I, E, 1965 F
Scott, D M (Langholm, Watsonians) 1950 I, E, 1951 W, I, E, SA, 1952 F, W, I, 1953 F
Scott, J M B (Edinburgh Acads) 1907 E, 1908 W, I, E, 1909 W, I, E, 1910 F, W, I, E, 1911 F, W, I, 1912 W, I, E, SA, 1913 W, I, E
Scott, J S (St Andrew's U) 1950 E
Scott, J W (Stewart's Coll FP) 1925 F, W, I, E, 1926 F, W, I, E, 1927 F, W, I, E, A, 1928 F, W, E, 1929 E, 1930 F
Scott, M (Dunfermline) 1992 A 2
Scott, R (Hawick) 1898 I, 1900 I, E
Scott, S (Edinburgh, Borders) 2000 NZ 2 (R), US (t+R), 2001 It (R), I (R), Tg (R), NZ (R), 2002 US (R), R(R), Fj(R), 2004 Sm(R), A1(R)
Scott, T (Langholm, Hawick) 1896 W, 1897 I, E, 1898 I, E, 1899 I, W, E, 1900 W, I, E
Scott, T M (Hawick) 1893 E, 1895 W, I, E, 1896 W, E, 1897 I, E, 1898 I, E, 1900 W, I
Scott, W P (W of Scotland) 1900 I, E, 1902 I, E, 1903 W, I, E, 1904 W, I, E, 1905 W, I, E, NZ, 1906 W, I, E, SA, 1907 W, I, E
Scoular, J G (Cambridge U) 1905 NZ, 1906 W, I, E, SA
Selby, J A R (Watsonians) 1920 W, I
Shackleton, J A P (London Scottish) 1959 E, 1963 F, W, 1964 NZ, W, 1965 I, SA
Sharp, A V (Bristol) 1994 E, I, F, Arg 1, 2 SA
Sharp, G (Stewart's FP, Army) 1960 F, 1964 F, NZ, W
Shaw, G D (Sale) 1935 NZ, 1936 W, 1937 W, I, E, 1939 I
Shaw, I (Glasgow HSFP) 1937 I
Shaw, J N (Edinburgh Acads) 1921 W, I
Shaw, R W (Glasgow HSFP) 1934 W, I, E, 1935 W, I, E, NZ, 1936 W, I, E, 1937 W, I, E, 1938 W, I, E, 1939 W, I, E
Shedden, D (W of Scotland) 1972 NZ, 1973 F, W, I, E, P, 1976 W, E, I, 1977 I, F, W, 1978 I, F, W
Shepherd, R J S (Melrose) 1995 WS, 1996 I, F, W, E, NZ 1, 2, A, It, 1997 W, E, I, F, SA, 1998 It, I, W (R), Fj (t), A 1, 2
Shiel, A G (Melrose, Edinburgh) 1991 [I (R), WS], 1993 I, F, W, E, NZ, 1994 Arg 1, 2, SA, 1995 R, [Iv, F, NZ], WS, 2000 I, NZ 1(R), 2
Shillinglaw, R B (Gala, Army) 1960 I, E, SA, 1961 F, SA
Simmers, B M (Glasgow Acads) 1965 F, W, 1966 A, 1967 F, W, I, 1971 F (R)
Simmers, W M (Glasgow Acads) 1926 W, I, E, 1927 F, W, I, E, A, 1928 F, W, I, E, 1929 F, W, I, E, 1930 F, W, I, E, 1931 F, W, I, E, 1932 SA, W, I, E
Simpson, G L (Kirkcaldy, Glasgow) 1998 A 1, 2, 1999 Arg (R), R, [SA, U, Sm, NZ], 2000 It, I, NZ 1(R), 2001 I, Tg (R), Arg (R), NZ
Simpson, J W (Royal HSFP) 1893 I, E, 1894 W, I, E, 1895 W, I, E, 1896 W, I, 1897 E, 1899 W, E
Simpson, R S (Glasgow Acads) 1923 I
Simson, E D (Edinburgh U, London Scottish) 1902 E, 1903 W, I, E, 1904 W, I, E, 1905 W, I, E, NZ, 1906 W, I, E, 1907 W, I, E
Simson, J T (Watsonians) 1905 NZ, 1909 W, I, E, 1910 F, W, 1911 I

Simson, R F (London Scottish) 1911 E
Sloan, A T (Edinburgh Acads) 1914 W, 1920 F, W, I, E, 1921 F, W, I, E
Sloan, D A (Edinburgh Acads, London Scottish) 1950 F, W, E, 1951 W, I, E, 1953 F
Sloan, T (Glasgow Acads, Oxford U) 1905 NZ, 1906 W, SA, 1907 W, E, 1908 W, 1909 I
Smeaton, P W (Edinburgh Acads) 1881 I, 1883 I, E
Smith, A R (Oxford U) 1895 W, I, E, 1896 W, I, 1897 I, E, 1898 I, E, 1900 I, E
Smith, A R (Cambridge U, Gosforth, Ebbw Vale, Edinburgh Wands) 1955 W, I, E, 1956 F, W, I, E, 1957 F, W, I, E, 1958 F, W, A, I, 1959 F, W, I, E, 1960 F, W, I, E, SA, 1961 F, SA, W, I, E, 1962 F, W, I, E
Smith, C J (Edinburgh) 2002 C, US (R), 2004 Sm(t&R), A1(R), 2(R), 3(R), J(R), 2005 Arg(R), Sm, NZ(R), 2006 F(R), W(R), E(R), I(R), It(R), SA 1(R), 2, R(R), 2007 I2(R), [R(R), NZ, It(R), Arg(R)], 2008 E(R), It(R)
Smith, D W C (London Scottish) 1949 F, W, I, E, 1950 F, W, I, 1953 I
Smith, E R (Edinburgh Acads) 1879 I
Smith, G K (Kelso) 1957 I, E, 1958 F, W, A, 1959 F, W, I, E, 1960 F, W, I, E, 1961 F, SA, W, I, E
Smith, H O (Watsonians) 1895 W, 1896 W, I, E, 1898 I, E, 1899 W, I, E, 1900 E, 1902 E
Smith, I R (Gloucester, Moseley) 1992 E, I, W, A 1, 2, 1994 E (R), I, F, Arg 1, 2, 1995 [Iv], WS, 1996 I, F, W, E, NZ 1, 2, A, It, 1997 E, I, F, A, SA
Smith, I S (Oxford U, Edinburgh U) 1924 W, I, E, 1925 F, W, I, E, 1926 F, W, I, E, 1927 F, I, E, 1929 F, W, I, E, 1930 F, W, I, 1931 F, W, I, E, 1932 SA, W, I, E, 1933 W, E, I
Smith I S G (London Scottish) 1969 SA, 1970 F, W, I, E, 1971 F, W, I
Smith, M A (London Scottish) 1970 W, I, E, A
Smith, R T (Kelso) 1929 F, W, I, E, 1930 F, W, I
Smith, S H (Glasgow Acads) 1877 I, 1878 E
Smith, T J (Gala) 1983 E, NZ, 1985 I, F
Smith T J (Watsonians, Dundee HSFP, Glasgow, Brive, Northampton) 1997 E, I, F, 1998 SA, 1999 W, E, It, I, Arg, R, [SA, U, Sm, NZ], 2000 It, I, F, W, E, NZ 1, 2, US, A, Sm, 2001 F, W, E, It, I, Tg, Arg, NZ, 2002 E, It, I, F, W, R, SA, Fj, 2003 I 1, F, W 1, E, It 1, 2, [J, US, F, Fj, A], 2004 W, E, Sm, A1, 2, 2005 F, I, It, W, E
Sole, D M B (Bath, Edinburgh Acads) 1986 F, W, 1987 I, F, W, E, [F, Z, R, NZ], 1988 I, F, W, E, A, 1989 W, E, I, F, Fj, R, 1990 I, F, W, E, NZ 1, 2, Arg, 1991 F, W, E, I, R, [J, I, WS, E, NZ], 1992 E, I, F, W, A 1, 2
Somerville, D (Edinburgh Inst FP) 1879 I, 1882 I, 1883 W, I, E, 1884 W
Southwell, H F G (Edinburgh, Stade Français) 2004 Sm(t&R), A1, 2, 3(R), J, A4, SA, 2005 F, I, It, W, E, R(R), Arg(R), Sm(R), NZ, 2006 F, W, E, I, It, SA 1, 2, 2006 R, PI(t&R), A(R), 2007 E, W, It, I1, SA(R), [Pt(R), R(R), NZ, It(R), Arg(R)], 2008 F(R), W, I, E, It, Arg 2, NZ(R), SA(R), 2009 W, F, It, E(R), 2010 F(R), It, E, I, Arg 1, 2, NZ, SA, Sm, 2011 F, W
Speirs, L M (Watsonians) 1906 SA, 1907 W, I, E, 1908 W, I, E, 1910 F, W, E
Spence, K M (Oxford U) 1953 I
Spencer, E (Clydesdale) 1898 I
Stagg, P K (Sale) 1965 F, W, E, SA, 1966 F, W, I, E, A, 1967 F, W, I, E, NZ, 1968 F, W, I, E, A, 1969 F, W, I (R), SA, 1970 F, W, I, E, A
Stanger, A G (Hawick) 1989 Fj, R, 1990 I, F, W, E, NZ 1, 2, Arg, 1991 F, W, E, I, R, [J, Z, I, WS, E, NZ], 1992 E, I, F, W, A 1, 2, 1993 I, F, W, E, NZ, 1994 W, E, I, F, SA, 1995 R, [Iv], 1996 NZ 2, A, It, 1997 W, E, I, F, A, SA, 1998 It, I (R), F, W, E
Stark, D A (Boroughmuir, Melrose, Glasgow Hawks) 1993 I, F, W, E, 1996 NZ 2(R), It (R), 1997 W (R), E, SA
Steel, J F (Glasgow) 2000 US, A, 2001 I, Tg, NZ
Steele, W C C (Langholm, Bedford, RAF, London Scottish) 1969 E, 1971 F, W, I, E (2[1C]), 1972 F, W, E, NZ, 1973 F, W, I, E, 1975 I, F, W, E, NZ (R), 1976 W, E, I, 1977 E
Stephen, A E (W of Scotland) 1885 W, 1886 I
Steven, P D (Heriot's FP) 1984 A, 1985 F, W, E
Steven, R (Edinburgh Wands) 1962 I
Stevenson, A K (Glasgow Acads) 1922 F, 1923 F, W, E
Stevenson, A M (Glasgow U) 1911 F
Stevenson, G D (Hawick) 1956 E, 1957 F, 1958 F, W, A, I, E, 1959 W, I, E, 1960 W, I, E, SA, 1961 F, SA, W, I, E, 1963 F, W, I, 1964 E, 1965 F
Stevenson, H J (Edinburgh Acads) 1888 W, I, 1889 W, I, 1890 W, I, E, 1891 W, I, E, 1892 W, I, E, 1893 I, E
Stevenson, L E (Edinburgh U) 1888 W
Stevenson, R C (London Scottish) 1897 I, E, 1898 E, 1899 I, W, E
Stevenson, R C (St Andrew's U) 1910 F, I, E, 1911 F, W, I
Stevenson, W H (Glasgow Acads) 1925 F
Stewart, A K (Edinburgh U) 1874 E, 1876 E
Stewart, A M (Edinburgh Acads) 1914 W
Stewart, B D (Edinburgh Acads, Edinburgh) 1996 NZ 2, A, 2000 NZ 1, 2
Stewart, C A R (W of Scotland) 1880 I, E
Stewart, C E B (Kelso) 1960 W, 1961 F
Stewart, J (Glasgow HSFP) 1930 F
Stewart, J L (Edinburgh Acads) 1921 I
Stewart M J (Northampton) 1996 It, 1997 W, E, I, F, A, SA, 1998 It, I, F, W, Fj (R), 2000 It, I, F, W, E, NZ 1(R), 2001 F, W, E, It, I, Tg, Arg, NZ, 2002 E, It, I, F, W, C, US, R(R)
Stewart, M S (Stewart's Coll FP) 1932 SA, W, I, 1933 W, E, I, 1934 W, I, E
Stewart, W A (London Hospital) 1913 F, W, I, 1914 W
Steyn, S S L (Oxford U) 1911 E, 1912 I
Strachan, G M (Jordanhill) 1971 E (C) (R), 1973 W, I, E, P
Strokosch, A K (Edinburgh, Gloucester) 2006 A(R), 2008 I, E, It, Arg 1, 2, C, 2009 F, It, I, E, Fj, A, Arg, 2010 It(R), Arg 1(R), 2(R), 2011 E(R), It1(R), I2, [Gg, Arg, E]
Stronach, R S (Glasgow Acads) 1901 W, E, 1905 W, I, E
Stuart, C D (W of Scotland) 1909 I, 1910 F, W, I, E, 1911 I, E
Stuart, L M (Glasgow HSFP) 1923 F, W, I, E, 1924 F, 1928 E, 1930 I, E
Suddon, N (Hawick) 1965 W, I, E, SA, 1966 A, 1968 E, A, 1969 F, W, I, 1970 I, E, A
Sutherland, W R (Hawick) 1910 W, E, 1911 F, E, 1912 F, W, E, SA, 1913 F, W, I, E, 1914 W
Swan, J S (Army, London Scottish, Leicester) 1953 E, 1954 F, NZ, I, E, W, 1955 F, W, I, E, 1956 F, W, I, E, 1957 F, W, 1958 F
Swan, M W (Oxford U, London Scottish) 1958 F, W, A, I, E, 1959 F, W, I
Sweet, J B (Glasgow HSFP) 1913 E, 1914 I
Symington, A W (Cambridge U) 1914 W, E

Tait, A V (Kelso, Newcastle, Edinburgh) 1987 [F(R), Z, R, NZ], 1988 I, F, W, E, 1997 I, F, A, 1998 It, I, F, W, E, SA, 1999 W (R), E, It, I, F, Arg, R, [A, U, NZ]
Tait, J G (Edinburgh Acads) 1880 I, 1885 I 2
Tait, P W (Royal HSFP) 1935 E
Taylor, E G (Oxford U) 1927 W, A
Taylor, R C (Kelvinside-West) 1951 W, I, E, SA
Taylor, S M (Edinburgh, Stade Français) 2000 US, A, 2001 E, It, I, NZ (R), 2002 E, It, I, F, W, C, US, R, SA, Fj, 2003 I 1, F, W 1, E, It 1, SA 1, 2, It 2, I 2, [J, US, F, Fj, A], 2004 W, E, It, F, I, 2005 It, W, E, Arg, Sm, NZ, 2006 F, W, E, I, It, PI, A, 2007 E, W, It, I1, F, I2, [Pt, R, It, Arg], 2008 E, It, C, 2009 W, F, It, I, E
Telfer, C M (Hawick) 1968 A, 1969 F, W, I, E, 1972 F, W, E, 1973 W, I, E, P, 1974 W, E, I, 1975 A, 1976 F
Telfer, J W (Melrose) 1964 F, NZ, W, I, E, 1965 F, W, I, 1966 F, W, I, E, 1967 W, I, E, 1968 E, A, 1969 F, W, I, E, SA, 1970 F, W, I
Tennent, J M (W of Scotland) 1909 W, I, E, 1910 F, W, E
Thom, D A (London Scottish) 1934 W, 1935 W, I, E, NZ
Thom, G (Kirkcaldy) 1920 F, W, I, E
Thom, J R (Watsonians) 1933 W, E, I
Thomson, A E (United Services) 1921 F, W, E
Thomson, A M (St Andrew's U) 1949 I
Thomson, B E (Oxford U) 1953 F, W, I
Thomson, F M A (Glasgow Warriors) 2007 I2(t&R), SA(R), [NZ(R)], 2008 F(R), W(R), I(R), E(R), It
Thomson, I H M (Heriot's FP, Army) 1951 W, I, 1952 F, W, I, 1953 I, E
Thomson, J S (Glasgow Acads) 1871 E
Thomson, R H (London Scottish, PUC) 1960 I, E, SA, 1961 F, SA, W, I, E, 1963 F, W, I, E, 1964 F, NZ, W
Thomson, W H (W of Scotland) 1906 SA
Thomson, W J (W of Scotland) 1899 W, E, 1900 W
Timms, A B (Edinburgh U, Edinburgh Wands) 1896 W, 1900 W, I, 1901 W, I, E, 1902 W, E, 1903 W, E, 1904 I, E, 1905 I, E
Tod, H B (Gala) 1911 F
Tod, J (Watsonians) 1884 W, I, E, 1885 W, I 1, 2, 1886 W, I, E
Todd, J K (Glasgow Acads) 1874 E, 1875 E
Tolmie, J M (Glasgow HSFP) 1922 E
Tomes, A J (Hawick) 1976 E, I, 1977 E, 1978 I, F, W, E, NZ, 1979 W, E, I, F, NZ, 1980 F, W, E, 1981 F, W, E, I, NZ 1, 2,

R, A, 1982 E, I, F, W, A 1, 2, 1983 I, F, W, 1984 W, E, I, F, R, A, 1985 W, E, 1987 I, F, E (R), [F, Z, R, NZ]

Torrie, T J (Edinburgh Acads) 1877 E

Townsend, G P J (Gala, Northampton, Brive, Castres, Borders) 1993 E (R), 1994 W, E, I, F, Arg 1, 2, 1995 C, I, F, W, E, WS, 1996 I, F, W, E, NZ 1, 2, A, It, 1997 W, E, I, F, A, SA, 1998 It, I, F, W, E, Fj, A 1, 2, SA (R), 1999 W, E, It, I, F, [SA, U, Sp (R), Sm, NZ], 2000 It, I, F, W, E, NZ 1, 2, US, A, Sm, 2001 F, It, I, Arg, NZ, 2002 E, It, I, F, W, R(R), SA(R), Fj, 2003 I 1(R), F, W 1, E, It 1, SA 1, 2, W 2, [J(R), US, F, Fj, A]

Traynor, K (Edinburgh) 2009 Fj(R), A(R), Arg(R)

Tukalo, I (Selkirk) 1985 I, 1987 I, F, W, E, [F, Z, R, NZ], 1988 F, W, E, A, 1989 W, E, I, F, Fj, 1990 I, F, W, E, NZ 1, 1991 I, R, [J, Z, I, WS, E, NZ], 1992 E, I, F, W, A 1, 2

Turk, A S (Langholm) 1971 E (R)

Turnbull, D J (Hawick) 1987 [NZ], 1988 F, E, 1990 E (R), 1991 F, W, E, I, R, [Z], 1993 I, F, W, E, 1994 W

Turnbull, F O (Kelso) 1951 F, SA

Turnbull, G O (W of Scotland) 1896 I, E, 1897 I, E, 1904 W

Turnbull, P (Edinburgh Acads) 1901 W, I, E, 1902 W, I, E

Turner, F H (Oxford U, Liverpool) 1911 F, W, I, E, 1912 F, W, I, E, SA, 1913 F, W, I, E, 1914 I, E

Turner, J W C (Gala) 1966 W, A, 1967 F, W, I, E, NZ, 1968 F, W, I, E, A, 1969 F, 1970 E, A, 1971 F, W, I, E (2[1C])

Usher, C M (United Services, Edinburgh Wands) 1912 E, 1913 F, W, I, E, 1914 E, 1920 F, W, I, E, 1921 W, E, 1922 F, W, I, E

Utterson, K N (Borders) 2003 F, W 1, E(R)

Valentine, A R (RNAS, Anthorn) 1953 F, W, I

Valentine, D D (Hawick) 1947 I, E

Veitch, J P (Royal HSFP) 1882 E, 1883 I, 1884 W, I, E, 1885 I 1, 2, 1886 E

Vernon, R J (Glasgow Warriors, Sale) 2009 Fj(R), A(R), Arg(R), 2010 NZ, SA(R), Sm, 2011 F(R), W, I1(R), E(R), It1(R), 2, [R, Arg(R), E]

Villar, C (Edinburgh Wands) 1876 E, 1877 I, E

Waddell, G H (London Scottish, Cambridge U) 1957 E, 1958 F, W, A, I, E, 1959 F, W, I, E, 1960 I, E, SA, 1961 F, 1962 F, W, I, E

Waddell, H (Glasgow Acads) 1924 F, W, I, E, 1925 I, E, 1926 F, W, I, E, 1927 F, W, I, E, 1930 W

Wade, A L (London Scottish) 1908 E

Wainwright, R I (Edinburgh Acads, West Hartlepool, Watsonians, Army, Dundee HSFP) 1992 I (R), F, A 1, 2, 1993 NZ, 1994 W, E, 1995 C, I, F, W, E, R, [Iv, Tg, F, NZ], WS, 1996 I, F, W, E, NZ 1, 2, 1997 W, E, I, F, SA, 1998 It, I, F, W, E, Fj, A 1, 2

Walker, A (W of Scotland) 1881 I, 1882 E, 1883 W, I, E

Walker, A W (Cambridge U, Birkenhead Park) 1931 F, W, I, E, 1932 I

Walker, J G (W of Scotland) 1882 E, 1883 W

Walker, M (Oxford U) 1952 F

Walker, N (Borders, Ospreys) 2002 R, SA, Fj, 2007 W(R), It(R), F, I2(R), SA, [R(R), NZ], 2008 F, W, I, E, C, 2010 NZ(R), SA, Sm, 2011 F, W, I1, It1, I2, It2(R)

Wallace, A C (Oxford U) 1923 F, 1924 F, W, E, 1925 F, W, I, E, 1926 F

Wallace, W M (Cambridge U) 1913 E, 1914 W, I, E

Wallace, M I (Glasgow High Kelvinside) 1996 A, It, 1997 W

Walls, W A (Glasgow Acads) 1882 E, 1883 W, I, E, 1884 W, I, E, 1886 W, I, E

Walter, M W (London Scottish) 1906 I, E, SA, 1907 W, I, 1908 W, I, 1910 I

Walton, P (Northampton, Newcastle) 1994 E, I, F, Arg 1, 2, 1995 [Iv], 1997 W, E, I, F, SA (R), 1998 I, F, SA, 1999 W, E, It, I, F (R), Arg, R, [SA (R), U (R), Sp]

Warren, J R (Glasgow Acads) 1914 I

Warren, R C (Glasgow Acads) 1922 W, I, 1930 W, I, E

Waters, F H (Cambridge U, London Scottish) 1930 F, W, I, E, 1932 SA, W, I

Waters, J A (Selkirk) 1933 W, E, I, 1934 W, I, E, 1935 W, I, E, NZ, 1936 W, I, E, 1937 W, I, E

Waters, J B (Cambridge U) 1904 I, E

Watherston, J G (Edinburgh Wands) 1934 I, E

Watherston, W R A (London Scottish) 1963 F, W, I

Watson, D H (Glasgow Acads) 1876 E, 1877 I, E

Watson, W S (Boroughmuir) 1974 W, E, I, F, 1975 NZ, 1977 I, F, W, 1979 I, F

Watt, A G J (Glasgow High Kelvinside) 1991 [Z], 1993 I, NZ, 1994 Arg 2(t & R)

Watt, A G M (Edinburgh Acads) 1947 F, W, I, A, 1948 F, W

Weatherstone, T G (Stewart's Coll FP) 1952 E, 1953 I, E, 1954 F, NZ, I, E, W, 1955 F, 1958 W, A, I, E, 1959 W, I, E

Webster, S L (Edinburgh) 2003 I 2(R), 2004 W(R), E, It, F, I, Sm, A1, 2, 2005 It, NZ(R), 2006 F(R), W(R), E(R), I(R), It(R), SA 1(R), 2, R, PI, A, 2007 W(R), I2, SA, [Pt, R, NZ, It, Arg], 2008 F, I, E, It, Arg 1(R), 2, C, 2009 W

Weir, G W (Melrose, Newcastle) 1990 Arg, 1991 R, [J, Z, I, WS, E, NZ], 1992 E, I, F, W, A 1, 2, 1993 I, F, W, E, NZ, 1994 W (R), E, I, F, SA, 1995 F (R), W, E, R, [Iv, Tg, F, NZ], WS, 1996 I, F, W, E, NZ 1, 2, A, It (R), 1997 W, E, I, F, 1998 It, I, F, W, E, SA, 1999 W, Arg (R), R (R), [SA (R), Sp, Sm, NZ], 2000 It (R), I (R), F

Welsh, R (Watsonians) 1895 W, I, E, 1896 W

Welsh, R B (Hawick) 1967 I, E

Welsh, W B (Hawick) 1927 A, 1928 F, W, I, 1929 I, E, 1930 F, W, I, E, 1931 F, W, I, E, 1932 SA, W, I, E, 1933 W, E, I

Welsh, W H (Edinburgh U) 1900 I, E, 1901 W, I, E, 1902 W, I, E

Wemyss, A (Gala, Edinburgh Wands) 1914 W, I, 1920 F, E, 1922 F, W, I

West, L (Edinburgh U, West Hartlepool) 1903 W, I, E, 1905 I, E, NZ, 1906 W, I, E

Weston, V G (Kelvinside Acads) 1936 I, E

White, D B (Gala, London Scottish) 1982 F, W, A 1, 2, 1987 W, E, [F, R, NZ], 1988 I, F, W, E, A, 1989 W, E, I, F, Fj, R, 1990 I, F, W, E, NZ 1, 2, 1991 F, W, E, I, R, [J, Z, I, WS, E, NZ], 1992 E, I, F, W

White, D M (Kelvinside Acads) 1963 F, W, I, E

White, J P R (Glasgow, Sale, Clermont-Auvergne) 2000 E, NZ 1, 2, US (R), A (R), Sm, 2001 F (R), I, Tg, Arg, NZ, 2002 E, It, I, F, W, C, US, SA(R), Fj, 2003 F(R), W 1, E, It 1, SA 1, 2, It 2, [J, US(R), F, Fj(R), A], 2004 W(R), E, It, F, I, Sm, A1, 2, J(R), A4(R), SA, 2005 F, I, E, Arg, Sm, NZ, 2006 F, W, E, I, It, SA 1, 2, R, 2007 I2, SA, [Pt, R, It, Arg], 2008 F, W, E(R), It(R), NZ, SA, 2009 W, F, It, I, E, Fj(R), A(R), Arg(R)

White, T B (Edinburgh Acads) 1888 W, I, 1889 W

Whittington, T P (Merchistonians) 1873 E

Whitworth, R J E (London Scottish) 1936 I

Whyte, D J (Edinburgh Wands) 1965 W, I, E, SA, 1966 F, W, I, E, A, 1967 F, W, I, E

Will, J G (Cambridge U) 1912 F, W, I, E, 1914 W, I, E

Wilson, A W (Dunfermline) 1931 F, I, E

Wilson, A W (Glasgow) 2005 R(R)

Wilson, G A (Oxford U) 1949 F, W, E

Wilson, G R (Royal HSFP) 1886 E, 1890 W, I, E, 1891 I

Wilson, J H (Watsonians) 1953 I

Wilson, J S (St Andrew's U) 1931 F, W, I, E, 1932 E

Wilson, J S (United Services, London Scottish) 1908 I, 1909 W

Wilson, R (London Scottish) 1976 E, I, 1977 E, I, F, 1978 I, F, 1981 R, 1983 I

Wilson, R L (Gala) 1951 F, W, I, E, SA, 1953 F, W, E

Wilson, R W (W of Scotland) 1873 E, 1874 E

Wilson, S (Oxford U, London Scottish) 1964 F, NZ, W, I, E, 1965 W, I, E, SA, 1966 F, W, I, A, 1967 F, W, I, E, NZ, 1968 F, W, I, E

Wood, A (Royal HSFP) 1873 E, 1874 E, 1875 E

Wood, G (Gala) 1931 W, I, 1932 W, I, E

Woodburn, J C (Kelvinside Acads) 1892 I

Woodrow, A N (Glasgow Acads) 1887 I, W, E

Wotherspoon, W (W of Scotland) 1891 I, 1892 I, 1893 W, E, 1894 W, I, E

Wright, F A (Edinburgh Acads) 1932 E

Wright, H B (Watsonians) 1894 W

Wright, K M (London Scottish) 1929 F, W, I, E

Wright, P H (Boroughmuir) 1992 A 1, 2, 1993 F, W, E, 1994 W, 1995 C, I, F, W, E, R, [Iv, Tg, F, NZ], 1996 W, E, NZ 1

Wright, R W J (Edinburgh Wands) 1973 F

Wright, S T H (Stewart's Coll FP) 1949 E

Wright, T (Hawick) 1947 A

Wyllie, D S (Stewart's-Melville FP) 1984 A, 1985 W (R), E, 1987 I, F, [F, Z, R, NZ], 1989 R, 1991 R, [J (R), Z], 1993 NZ (R), 1994 W (R), E, I, F

Young, A H (Edinburgh Acads) 1874 E

Young, E T (Glasgow Acads) 1914 E

Young, R G (Watsonians) 1970 W

Young, T E B (Durham) 1911 F

Young, W B (Cambridge U, London Scottish) 1937 W, I, E, 1938 W, I, E, 1939 W, I, E, 1948 E

MELROSE AND AYR TAKE CENTRE STAGE

By Iain Spragg

It was all change in Scotland in the Premiership as Melrose dethroned Currie as champions after the SRU had introduced a new, experimental league format, but it was a familiar story in the Premier Cup as Ayr successfully defended their status as kings of the knockout game with a second successive victory in the final at Murrayfield.

In the league, the SRU abandoned a traditional league structure in favour of a two-stage campaign in which the 24 clubs in Premiership One and Two split into three leagues of eight after October, and it was Melrose who emerged the strongest to claim the title for first time in 14 years and in the process give the Borders region a champion club for the first time since Hawick triumphed back in 2002.

Craig Chalmer's side wrapped up the championship at the end of April with a 29–20 win over Ayr at Greenyards and so delivered a degree of revenge for defeat to the Millbrae club in the cup final in Edinburgh seven days earlier – the side's second reverse in the final against Ayr in the space of 12 months.

Melrose's decisive victory came chiefly courtesy of 19 points from the boot of fly-half Scott Wight, as well tries from Garry Elder and Ross Miller, and revived memories of the club's glory days when they were champions five times between 1992 and 1997.

"This is a great result for Melrose and for the Borders," said Chalmers, who was part of the all-conquering Melrose side in the 1990s. "We kept our heads and kicked our kicks. I think Scott Wight controlled things very well and the referee was very strong.

"I'm a greedy so-and-so and I wanted to win the cup final as well, but this was the title we really needed to win, this is the one that we have been working towards. It evoked all sorts of memories of 1997, and of course it was nice to win it in front of our own crowd."

Melrose dominated the early stages of the Premiership One season, winning nine of their 11 games to ensure they were one of the eight sides to qualify for the new-look Premiership A division and, although they suffered a 22–18 reverse to Currie in November in Edinburgh in their second game, Chalmer's team responded with a series of impressive victories, including a 45–23 defeat of Hawick and a 69–11 demolition of Boroughmuir.

Currie, however, were hot on their heels, and after the morale-boosting 22–18 win at Malleny Park they swept all before them to finish with seven victories from seven, averaging nearly 40 points per game and, had the league been decided solely on those results, Ally Donaldson's side would have been crowned champions.

However, the points all the Premiership A sides had accumulated in Premiership One action were also taken into account. Melrose had topped that table with 46 points, while Currie won just five of their 11 games earlier in the season and amassed a more modest 36 points, and when it came to the business end of the season that 10-point cushion was enough to ensure Chalmer's side received the silverware.

In the cup, the traditional knockout format remained unscathed, and after two high-scoring semi-finals Melrose and Ayr booked their places in the final for a repeat of their Murrayfield encounter 12 months earlier.

The first semi saw Melrose avenge their league defeat against Currie with a 43–25 blitz of Donaldson's side at Malleny Park as the visitors ran in five tries, which added to the 18 points from the boot of Wight, was enough to send Chalmer's charges through to the final for a fourth consecutive season.

"We didn't defend well enough," said a disappointed Donaldson after the game. "We gave away too many soft scores, pure and simple. We thought the game was turning our way just after half-time when we got ahead, but it didn't work out like that."

A fortnight later Ayr played their semi-final against Boroughmuir at Meggetland in an action-packed match that featured six tries, three yellow cards, one red and a narrow but dramatic 25–21 victory for the visitors.

The match turned on a controversial decision in the 72nd minute when Boroughmuir's Steven Reddick was sent off for what the referee judged to be a high tackle, and moments after the dismissal Ayr scored to take the lead for the first time and the home side were unable to respond.

"We couldn't have asked for more in the first half when we got ourselves ahead," said Boroughmuir captain Malcolm Clapperton. "But in the second we never really had control of the ball, and once we went a man down near the finish, there was no way back."

The final in mid-April was a feast of attacking rugby and drama and the result was in doubt for almost 80 minutes, but despite concerted pressure from Melrose for the final 20 minutes of the clash, twice going over the line but failing to ground the ball, it was Ayr's defence that stoically held firm to record a 25–21 success.

Ayr outscored Melrose four tries to two, and the difference between the two sides ultimately proved to be Scotland Under-20 outside centre Mark Bennett, whose superb two-try salvo deservedly earned the teenager the Man of the Match award and Ayr their second successive cup triumph.

Melrose replied with scores from Nick Beavon and replacement Hayden Mitchell but tries for Ayr from Steve Manning and captain Damien Kelly were enough to ensure Kenny Murray's team were in a position to weather the late storm from their opponents.

"I thought it was touch and go for a while, but we eventually pulled through," said Murray after the final whistle. "If we had kicked a few more kicks I think we might have got out of reach. I think we played quite well in the first half but playing 20 minutes with just 14 men was tough. We said at half time that we needed to keep our discipline if we wanted to win this match and I think we did that in the second half."

"The boys showed true grit and I'm really proud of them. Up to the last two scores I thought it could have gone either way, but we took our chances, pressed on and got the tries."

SCOTTISH RBS PREMIERSHIP 2010–11 RESULTS

PREMIER ONE

21 August 2010: **Glasgow** 41 **West of Scotland** 15, **Heriots** 39 **Watsonians** 14, **Dundee** 34 **Stirling** 37, **Melrose** 32 **Currie** 29, **Selkirk** 12 **Boroughmuir** 34, **Hawick** 22 **Ayr** 36. 28 August: **Boroughmuir** 19 **Hawick** 13, **Watsonians** 11 **Glasgow** 34, **Stirling** 10 **Heriots** 24, **Currie** 32 **Dundee** 32, **Ayr** 20 **Melrose** 17, **West of Scotland** 26 **Selkirk** 22. 4 September: **Boroughmuir** 41 **West of Scotland** 21, **Selkirk** 23 **Watsonians** 20, **Glasgow** 46 **Stirling** 26, **Heriots** 20 **Currie** 16, **Dundee** 23 **Ayr** 31, **Hawick** 14 **Melrose** 19. 11 September: **Stirling** 50 **Selkirk** 26, **Watsonians** 17 **Boroughmuir** 33, **Melrose** 39 **Dundee** 33, **Ayr** 25 **Heriots** 16, **Currie** 17 **Glasgow** 17, **West of Scotland** 12 **Hawick** 45. 18 September: **West of Scotland** 39 **Watsonians** 26, **Selkirk** 16 **Currie** 35, **Heriots** 26 **Melrose** 25, **Hawick** 33 **Dundee** 35, **Glasgow** 19 **Ayr** 15, **Boroughmuir** 29 **Stirling** 18. 25 September: **Watsonians** 19 **Hawick** 34, **Stirling** 31 **West of Scotland** 27, **Melrose** 23 **Glasgow** 17, **Dundee** 48 **Heriots** 24, **Currie** 34 **Boroughmuir** 19, **Ayr** 49 **Selkirk** 14. 2 October: **West of Scotland** 38 **Currie** 38, **Watsonians** 15 **Stirling** 13, **Selkirk** 24 **Melrose** 29, **Hawick** 17 **Heriots** 20, **Glasgow** 25 **Dundee** 24, **Boroughmuir** 14 **Ayr** 14. 9 October: **Stirling** 27 **Hawick** 25, **Melrose** 49 **Boroughmuir** 11, **Heriots** 20 **Glasgow** 22, **Dundee** 52 **Selkirk** 14, **Currie** 40 **Watsonians** 20, **Ayr** 38 **West of Scotland** 17. 16 October: **West of Scotland** 26 **Melrose** 59, **Watsonians** 17 **Ayr** 52, **Stirling** 30 **Currie** 43, **Selkirk** 17 **Heriots** 43, **Hawick** 13 **Glasgow** 23, **Boroughmuir** 30 **Dundee** 20. 23 October: **Melrose** 45 **Watsonians** 19, **Heriots** 24 **Boroughmuir** 20, **Hawick** 11 **Currie** 9, **Glasgow** 92 **Selkirk** 0, **Dundee** 92 **West of Scotland** 7, **Ayr** 43 **Stirling** 19. 30 October: **West of Scotland** 29 **Heriots** 64, **Watsonians** 30 **Dundee** 39, **Stirling** 20 **Melrose** 24, **Selkirk** 0 **Hawick** 25, **Currie** 24 **Ayr** 12, **Boroughmuir** 10 **Glasgow** 39.

PREMIER TWO

21 August: **Kirkcaldy** 23 **Peebles** 28, **Gala** 44 **Kelso** 10, **GHA** 25 **Jed-Forest** 34, **Biggar** 39 **Hillhead/Jordan** 23, **Aberdeen** 16 **Edinburgh** 24, **Falkirk** 37 **Stewarts** 35. 28 August: **Kelso** 25 **Kirkcaldy** 14, **Stewarts** 23 **Aberdeen** 36, **Edinburgh** 38 **Biggar** 18, **Hillhead/Jordan** 20 **GHA** 13, **Jed-Forest** 11 **Gala** 13, **Peebles** 21 **Falkirk** 21. 4 September: **Peebles** 31 **Kelso** 17, **Kirkcaldy** 16 **Jed-Forest** 16, **Gala Hillhead/Jordan** 9, **GHA** 10 **Edinburgh** 29, **Biggar** 41 **Gala** 21, **Falkirk** 29 **Aberdeen** 28. 11 September: **Hillhead/Jordan** 23 **Kirkcaldy** 20, **Jed-Forest** 18 **Peebles** 21, **Aberdeen** 32 **Biggar** 23, **Stewarts** 59 **GHA** 6, **Edinburgh** 32 **Gala** 21, **Kelso** 23 **Falkirk** 28. 18 September: **Kelso** 18 **Jed-Forest** 22, **Peebles** 29 **Hillhead/Jordan** 27, **Kirkcaldy** 20 **Edinburgh** 22, **Gala** 41 **Stewarts** 28, **GHA** 10 **Aberdeen** 17, **Falkirk** 53 **Biggar** 23. 25 September: **Stewarts** 24 **Kirkcaldy** 23, **Edinburgh** 7 **Peebles** 29, **Hillhead/Jordan** 52 **Kelso** 30, **Biggar** 19 **GHA** 37, **Aberdeen** 15 **Gala** 15, **Jed-Forest** 44 **Falkirk** 24. 2 October: **Jed-Forest** 29 **Hillhead/Jordan** 32, **Kelso** 14 **Edinburgh** 25, **Peebles** 21 **Stewarts** 15, **Kirkcaldy** 6 **Aberdeen** 58, **Gala** 27 **Biggar** 25, **Falkirk** 28 **GHA** 9. 9 October: **Biggar** 32 **Kirkcaldy** 21, **Aberdeen** 18 **Peebles** 13, **Stewarts** 17 **Kelso** 7, **Edinburgh** 20 **Jed-Forest** 18, **GHA** 16 **Gala** 28, **Hillhead/Jordan** 17 **Falkirk** 13. 16 October: **Hillhead/Jordan** 21 **Edinburgh** 34, **Jed-Forest** 34 **Stewarts** 15, **Kelso** 22 **Aberdeen** 48, **Peebles** 15 **Biggar** 12, **Kirkcaldy** 35 **GHA** 20, **Falkirk** 16 **Gala** 34. 23 October: **Gala** 36 **Kirkcaldy** 14, **GHA** 39 **Peebles** 21, **Biggar** 26 **Kelso** 17, **Aberdeen** 39 **Jed-Forest** 23, **Stewarts** 16 **Hillhead/Jordan** 41, **Falkirk** 25 **Edinburgh** 31. 30 October: **Edinburgh** 69 **Stewarts** 8, **Hillhead/Jordan** 29 **Aberdeen** 33, **Jed-Forest** 26 **Biggar** 18, **Kelso** 32 **GHA** 12, **Peebles** 14 **Gala** 18, **Kirkcaldy** 35 **Falkirk** 15.

PREMIER A

12 November: **Glasgow** 37 **Boroughmuir** 10. 13 November: **Melrose** 55 **Heriots** 36, **Currie** 58 **Hawick** 25, **Ayr** 17 **Dundee** 24. 20 November: **Heriots** 22 **Hawick** 17, **Currie** 22 **Melrose** 18, **Ayr** 19 **Glasgow** 11. 29 January: **Melrose** 45 **Hawick** 23, **Dundee** 20 **Glasgow** 37, **Currie** 46 **Heriots** 7, **Ayr** 31 **Boroughmuir** 20.19 February: **Heriots** 20 **Glasgow** 32, **Hawick** 6 **Ayr** 7, **Currie** 47 **Dundee** 3, **Boroughmuir** 6 **Melrose** 32. 26 February: **Dundee** 23 **Hawick** 25. 5 March: **Heriots** 34 **Dundee** 17, **Hawick** 10 **Boroughmuir** 39, **Glasgow** 13 **Melrose** 23. 19 March: **Boroughmuir** 6 **Dundee** 5. 26 March: **Boroughmuir** 26 **Heriots** 10. 2 April: **Melrose** 69 **Dundee** 11, **Heriots** 20 **Ayr** 38, **Boroughmuir** 15 **Currie** 43. 12 April: **Glasgow** 17 **Hawick** 19. 23 April: **Melrose** 29 **Ayr** 20, **Glasgow** 10 **Currie** 13. 30 April: **Ayr** 12 **Currie** 41.

FINAL TABLES

PREMIER A

	P	W	D	L	F	A	BP	Pts
Melrose	7	6	0	1	271	131	4	**74**
Currie	7	7	0	0	270	90	5	**69**
Ayr	7	4	0	3	144	151	3	**63**
Glasgow	7	3	0	4	157	124	5	**62**
Heriots	7	2	0	5	149	231	2	**48**
Boroughmuir	7	3	0	4	122	168	2	**44**
Dundee	7	1	0	6	103	235	2	**40**
Hawick	7	2	0	5	125	211	2	**31**

PREMIER B

	P	W	D	L	F	A	BP	Pts
Stirling	7	6	0	1	187	106	5	**29**
Edinburgh	7	6	0	1	155	122	4	**28**
Gala	7	4	0	3	156	90	6	**22**
Aberdeen	7	4	0	3	194	143	5	**21**
Watsonians	7	4	0	3	168	142	4	**20**
Selkirk	7	3	0	4	172	164	3	**15**
Peebles	7	1	0	6	80	228	1	**5**
West	7	0	0	7	124	241	3	**3**

SCOTTISH RBS PREMIERSHIP C Winners: Jed-Forest
SCOTTISH RBS PREMIERSHIP THREE Winners: Whitecraigs
SCOTTISH RBS NATIONAL ONE Winners: Lasswade
SCOTTISH RBS NATIONAL TWO Winners: Hawick YM
SCOTTISH RBS NATIONAL THREE Winners: Marr

SCOTTISH RBS NATIONAL CUP 2010–11 RESULTS

QUARTER-FINALS

19 March, 2011

Boroughmuir 6 **Dundee** 5
Hawick 21 **Currie** 34

20 March, 2011

Heriots 24 **Melrose** 39

26 March, 2011

Glasgow 18 **Ayr** 29

SEMI-FINALS

26 March, 2011

Currie 25 **Melrose** 43

9 April, 2011

Boroughmuir 21 **Ayr** 25

FINAL

17 April, Murrayfield, Edinburgh

MELROSE 21 (1G, 3PG, 1T) AYR 25 (1G, 1PG, 3T)

MELROSE: F Thomson; C Anderson, J Murray, J Helps, A Dodds; S Wight (captain), R Chrystie; N Beavon, W Mitchell, G Holborn, G Elder, R Miller, J Dalziel, G Runciman, G Dodds *Substitutions*: N Little for Holborn (42mins); G Innes for Mitchell (60 mins); H Mitchell for Elder (60 mins); C Murray for Helps (62 mins); B Colvine for Christie (75 mins)

SCORERS: *Tries:* Beavon, H Mitchell *Conversion:* Wight *Penalty Goals*: *Wight (3)*

AYR: G Anderson; S Manning, M Bennett, M Stewart, C Taylor; R Curle, AJ McFarlane; G Reid, S Adair, A Kelly, S Sutherland, D Kelly (captain), R Colhoun, P Burke, A Dunlop. *Substitutions*: D Stewart for Sutherland (51 mins); G Sykes for A Kelly (64 mins); G Tippett for Dunlop (79mins)

SCORERS: *Tries:* Manning, Bennett (2), Kelly *Conversion:* Curle *Penalty Goal:* Curle

REFEREE: C Rudkin (Scotland)

SOUTH AFRICA

SOUTH AFRICA'S 2010–11 TEST RECORD

OPPONENTS	DATE	VENUE	RESULT
Ireland	6 Nov	A	**Won** 23–21
Wales	13 Nov	A	**Won** 29–25
Scotland	20 Nov	A	**Lost** 17–21
England	27 Nov	A	**Won** 21–11
Australia	23 Jul	A	**Lost** 20–39
New Zealand	30 Jul	A	**Lost** 7–40
Australia	13 Aug	H	**Lost** 9–14
New Zealand	20 Aug	H	**Won** 18–5
Wales	11 Sept	N	**Won** 17–16
Fiji	17 Sept	N	**Won** 49–3
Namibia	22 Sept	N	**Won** 87–0
Samoa	30 Sept	N	**Won** 13–5
Australia	9 Oct	N	**Lost** 9–11

END OF THE ROAD

By Iain Spragg

Stu Forster/ Getty Images

The Springboks kicked off with a victory over Wales but went out in the quarter-finals.

After four eventful years as the Webb Ellis Cup holders, South Africa were deposed as world champions at the quarter-final stage by Australia in Wellington, bringing a disappointing end to the controversial and frequently compelling reign of Peter de Villiers as Springbok head coach.

The first black man to lead South Africa following his appointment in 2008 as Jake White's replacement, de Villiers enjoyed notable success with his side on the pitch, but his tenure was also marked by significant failures, culminating in the Springboks' defeat to the Wallabies and their surrender of the Webb Ellis Cup. His well-documented outbursts during his three years in charge only served to further divide public opinion on a coach who certainly did things his own way.

His greatest triumphs were the long-awaited 2–1 series victory over the British & Irish Lions in 2009, which was quickly followed by a first

Tri-Nations title in six years, but South Africa also finished bottom of the Tri-Nations table in de Villiers' three other southern hemisphere campaigns and recorded a modest four wins in 16 games in the process.

Rugby World Cup 2011 potentially offered a degree of redemption after two lean years for the Springboks and their coach, but they were unable to reproduce the irrepressible form that had seen them crowned champions four years earlier and, despite dominating both territory and possession against Australia in the Wellington Regional Stadium, they went down to an 11–9 defeat.

"There's a time to come and a time to go, and I think the journey for me is over," de Villiers reflected after going out of the tournament. "It was a brilliant journey and something you cannot take away from me. To work with people like this, people that are passionate about their country, people who always put their bodies on the line and try to bring hope to poor people back home who will never have the privilege that most of you guys have. It didn't go our way, we didn't take all our chances. The guys are quiet. We never expected this, so it was not a really good mood in the changing room."

Experience was the key component of the squad de Villiers named for New Zealand, with 12 of the side that beat England in the World Cup Final in Paris in 2007 pressed into action once again, and the Springbok veterans certainly had to call on all their collective nous as South Africa crossed swords with Wales in their Pool D opener in Wellington.

Wales' one and only win against the Springboks in 25 previous meetings had come in 1999, but de Villiers' side only narrowly avoided a repeat of that defeat in the Wellington Regional Stadium.

The champions initially appeared to be on course for a routine victory when Frans Steyn went over in the second minute, but Wales slowly clawed their way back into contention with three penalties from James Hook, and when No. 8 Toby Faletau scored a try in the 54th minute South Africa suddenly found themselves 16–10 adrift.

Alarm bells ringing, the Springboks rallied and the decisive score came 15 minutes from time when substitute Francois Hougaard cruised over under the posts after good work from Fourie du Preez. Morné Steyn landed the straightforward conversion and de Villiers escaped with a 17–16 win.

"The nerves for this game were unbelievable because of the pressure of what this game meant for the pool," admitted South Africa skipper John Smit. "Our greatest reward is that we have come through by a point, and fought our way back from a pretty sticky situation. Wales played some good rugby and kept us in our half, but we took the chance when we got it. Close game, nice to get through it."

The Fijians in Wellington were South Africa's next challenge, but there was no repeat of the drama of the Wales game as South Africa helped themselves to six tries in a 49–3 romp against the Pacific Islanders.

The result suggested the team was beginning to build a head of steam, and that impression was strengthened when South Africa met Namibia in the North Harbour Stadium.

The match was always going to be a mismatch between one of the game's true heavyweights and the African minnows, and so it proved as the Springboks ran in 12 unanswered tries, all of which were converted, in an 87–0 romp.

The final scoreline could have been even more comprehensive had South Africa not squandered further scoring opportunities, but Bryan Habana did cross to end his 11-match scoring drought and register his 39th Test try, eclipsing Joost van der Westhuizen's previous record of 38.

"I think other people were more worried about the record than I was," Habana said. "I've said it my whole career – it's always been about the Springbok team. It's never been about the number of tries I've been able to score, it's about contributing, and I'm disappointed that I haven't been able to contribute for the last couple of Tests.

"Hopefully now everyone can stop worrying about it and I can concentrate on playing rugby. It's been a great honour and privilege to break records and pass someone like Joost. Hopefully I can keep using my God-given talent to contribute to Springbok rugby."

South Africa's final pool match was against Samoa and, although they successfully doused the flames of a valiant challenge, winning 13–5 to secure top spot in Pool D, it was a performance that raised more questions than it answered about the champions' true potential in New Zealand.

"Everybody called this the pool of death," de Villiers said. "We knew this was going to be tough. The guys that we played against are quite high up in the rankings, but now it is all systems go. I think we're ready for the next phase.

"We'll never find a more physical game in this tournament. I think we played complete rugby. In the first half we attacked with everything we could, and in the second half our defence never let us down."

The Springboks prepared for their quarter-final in the knowledge they had lost their last three Tri-Nations clashes with Robbie Deans' Wallabies, and de Villiers' instinct was to go with his tried and tested troops for the last-eight showdown. He recalled Smit to the pack in place of Bismarck du Plessis and selected a starting XV with 836 caps between them, surpassing the previous South African record of 815 for the team picked to face Wales earlier in the tournament.

With the benefit of hindsight, it is difficult to see how they lost the quarter-final. The Springboks enjoyed 76 per cent of territory over the 80 minutes of action, but they were unable to convert it into points when it mattered most. Australia defended heroically, but it was South Africa who played the majority of the match on the front foot.

The opening score of the contest came on 10 minutes when Australian captain James Horwill crashed over for the only try of the match from close range after good work from Pat McCabe. A James O'Connor penalty six minutes later stretched the Wallaby lead, but a Steyn penalty two minutes before half-time cut the arrears and de Villiers' side trailed 8–3 at the break.

South Africa continued to exert the pressure after the restart, and a second successful Steyn penalty and then a drop-goal edged his side 9–8 in front as the match entered its final quarter. The Springboks should have closed out the game, but they conceded a cheap penalty at the lineout with nine minutes left on the clock and O'Connor stepped up to land what was the decisive kick.

Like every other previous winner of the tournament before them, South Africa had failed to defend their World Cup crown, and the defeat signalled the end of de Villiers' tenure. It also closed the book on the international careers of Smit and veteran lock Victor Matfield, who had amassed 221 Test caps between them.

"It is a sad occasion," admitted Smit after his final appearance for his country. "You never prepare for how it ends because you want it to be a fairytale, you want it to be a final, but it hasn't worked out that way. It would be silly to take that seven years and judge it by what happened today.

"I have been blessed to be in charge of these guys and run out with them, and blessed to be captain of the Springboks. I am devastated today. It is the end of a chapter, and I am proud of the guys I have played with and really proud to have been a Springbok. It is the first time I have lost a game on the scoreboard and won it every other way from a statistical point of view, so it makes it even harder to accept."

SOUTH AFRICA INTERNATIONAL STATISTICS

MATCH RECORDS UP TO 31 OCTOBER 2011

MOST CONSECUTIVE TEST WINS

17 1997 *A*2, *It*, *F* 1, 2, *E*, *S*, 1998 *I* 1, 2, *W* 1, *E* 1, *A* 1, *NZ* 1, 2, *A* 2, *W* 2, *S*, *I* 3

15 1994 *Arg* 1, 2, *S*, *W* 1995 *WS*, *A*, *R*, *C*, *WS*, *F*, *NZ*, *W*, *It*, *E*, 1996 *Fj*

MOST CONSECUTIVE TESTS WITHOUT DEFEAT

Matches	Wins	Draws	Period
17	17	0	1997 to 1998
16	15	1	1994 to 1996
15	12	3	1960 to 1963

MOST POINTS IN A MATCH

BY THE TEAM

Pts	Opponents	Venue	Year
134	Uruguay	E London	2005
105	Namibia	Cape Town	2007
101	Italy	Durban	1999
96	Wales	Pretoria	1998
87	Namibia	Albany	2011
74	Tonga	Cape Town	1997
74	Italy	Port Elizabeth	1999
72	Uruguay	Perth	2003
68	Scotland	Murrayfield	1997
64	USA	Montpellier	2007
63	Argentina	Johannesburg	2008
62	Italy	Bologna	1997
61	Australia	Pretoria	1997

BY A PLAYER

Pts	Player	Opponents	Venue	Year
35	P C Montgomery	Namibia	Cape Town	2007
34	J H de Beer	England	Paris	1999
31	P C Montgomery	Wales	Pretoria	1998
31	M Steyn	N Zealand	Durban	2009
30	T Chavhanga	Uruguay	E London	2005
29	G S du Toit	Italy	Port Elizabeth	1999
29	P C Montgomery	Samoa	Paris	2007
28	G K Johnson	W Samoa	Johannesburg	1995
26	J H de Beer	Australia	Pretoria	1997
26	P C Montgomery	Scotland	Murrayfield	1997
26	M Steyn	Italy	East London	2010
25	J T Stransky	Australia	Bloemfontein	1996
25	C S Terblanche	Italy	Durban	1999

MOST TRIES IN A MATCH

BY THE TEAM

Tries	Opponents	Venue	Year
21	Uruguay	E London	2005
15	Wales	Pretoria	1998
15	Italy	Durban	1999
15	Namibia	Cape Town	2007
12	Tonga	Cape Town	1997
12	Uruguay	Perth	2003
12	Namibia	Albany	2011
11	Italy	Port Elizabeth	1999
10	Ireland	Dublin	1912
10	Scotland	Murrayfield	1997

BY A PLAYER

Tries	Player	Opponents	Venue	Year
6	T Chavhanga	Uruguay	E London	2005
5	C S Terblanche	Italy	Durban	1999
4	C M Williams	W Samoa	Johannesburg	1995
4	P W G Rossouw	France	Parc des Princes	1997
4	C S Terblanche	Ireland	Bloemfontein	1998
4	B G Habana	Samoa	Paris	2007
4	J L Nokwe	Australia	Johannesburg	2008

MOST CONVERSIONS IN A MATCH

BY THE TEAM

Cons	Opponents	Venue	Year
13	Italy	Durban	1999
13	Uruguay	E London	2005
12	Namibia	Cape Town	2007
12	Namibia	Albany	2011
9	Scotland	Murrayfield	1997
9	Wales	Pretoria	1998
9	Argentina	Johannesburg	2008
8	Italy	Port Elizabeth	1999
8	USA	Montpellier	2007
7	Scotland	Murrayfield	1951
7	Tonga	Cape Town	1997
7	Italy	Bologna	1997
7	France	Parc des Princes	1997
7	Italy	Genoa	2001
7	Samoa	Pretoria	2002
7	Samoa	Brisbane	2003
7	England	Bloemfontein	2007
7	Italy	East London	2010

BY A PLAYER

Cons	Player	Opponents	Venue	Year
12	P C Montgomery	Namibia	Cape Town	2007
9	P C Montgomery	Wales	Pretoria	1998
9	A D James	Argentina	Johannesburg	2008
8	P C Montgomery	Scotland	Murrayfield	1997
8	G S du Toit	Italy	Port Elizabeth	1999
8	G S du Toit	Italy	Durban	1999
7	A O Geffin	Scotland	Murrayfield	1951
7	J M F Lubbe	Tonga	Cape Town	1997
7	H W Honiball	Italy	Bologna	1997
7	H W Honiball	France	Parc des Princes	1997
7	A S Pretorius	Samoa	Pretoria	2002
7	J N B van der Westhuyzen	Uruguay	E London	2005
7	P C Montgomery	England	Bloemfontein	2007

MOST PENALTIES IN A MATCH

BY THE TEAM

Penalties	Opponents	Venue	Year
8	Scotland	Port Elizabeth	2006
8	N Zealand	Durban	2009
7	France	Pretoria	1975
7	France	Cape Town	2006
7	Australia	Cape Town	2009
6	Australia	Bloemfontein	1996
6	Australia	Twickenham	1999
6	England	Pretoria	2000
6	Australia	Durban	2000
6	France	Johannesburg	2001
6	Scotland	Johannesburg	2003
6	N Zealand	Bloemfontein	2009
6	Australia	Bloemfontein	2010

BY A PLAYER

Pens	Player	Opponents	Venue	Year
8	M Steyn	N Zealand	Durban	2009
7	P C Montgomery	Scotland	Port Elizabeth	2006
7	P C Montgomery	France	Cape Town	2006
7	M Steyn	Australia	Cape Town	2009
6	G R Bosch	France	Pretoria	1975
6	J T Stransky	Australia	Bloemfontein	1996
6	J H de Beer	Australia	Twickenham	1999
6	A J J van Straaten	England	Pretoria	2000
6	A J J van Straaten	Australia	Durban	2000
6	P C Montgomery	France	Johannesburg	2001
6	L J Koen	Scotland	Johannesburg	2003
6	M Steyn	Australia	Bloemfontein	2010

MOST DROPPED GOALS IN A MATCH

BY THE TEAM

Drops	Opponents	Venue	Year
5	England	Paris	1999
4	England	Twickenham	2006
3	S America	Durban	1980
3	Ireland	Durban	1981
3	Scotland	Murrayfield	2004

BY A PLAYER

Drops	Player	Opponents	Venue	Year
5	J H de Beer	England	Paris	1999
4	A S Pretorius	England	Twickenham	2006
3	H E Botha	S America	Durban	1980
3	H E Botha	Ireland	Durban	1981
3	J N B van der Westhuyzen	Scotland	Murrayfield	2004
2	B L Osler	N Zealand	Durban	1928
2	H E Botha	NZ Cavaliers	Cape Town	1986
2	J T Stransky	N Zealand	Johannesburg	1995
2	J H de Beer	N Zealand	Johannesburg	1997
2	P C Montgomery	N Zealand	Cardiff	1999
2	F P L Steyn	Australia	Cape Town	2007

CAREER RECORDS

MOST CAPPED PLAYERS

Caps	Player	Career Span
111	J W Smit	2000 to 2011
110	V Matfield	2001 to 2011
102	P C Montgomery	1997 to 2008
89	J H van der Westhuizen	1993 to 2003
80	J P du Randt	1994 to 2007
77	M G Andrews	1994 to 2001
76	J P Botha	2002 to 2011
74	B G Habana	2004 to 2011
73	C J van der Linde	2002 to 2011
72	J de Villiers	2002 to 2011
69	J H Smith	2003 to 2010
69	J Fourie	2003 to 2011
68	S W P Burger	2003 to 2011
66	A G Venter	1996 to 2001
64	B J Paulse	1999 to 2007
63	D J Rossouw	2003 to 2011
62	P F du Preez	2004 to 2011
54	A-H le Roux	1994 to 2002
52	J C van Niekerk	2001 to 2010
51	P A van den Berg	1999 to 2007
51	R Pienaar	2006 to 2011
47	J T Small	1992 to 1997
47	E R Januarie	2005 to 2010
47	F P L Steyn	2006 to 2011
47	P J Spies	2006 to 2011
43	J Dalton	1994 to 2002
43	P W G Rossouw	1997 to 2003
42	G H Teichmann	1995 to 1999
42	R B Skinstad	1997 to 2007
42	A D James	2001 to 2011
42	J-P R Pietersen	2006 to 2011
42	B W du Plessis	2007 to 2011

MOST CONSECUTIVE TESTS

Tests	Player	Span
46	J W Smit	2003 to 2007
39	G H Teichmann	1996 to 1999
28	V Matfield	2008 to 2010
26	A H Snyman	1996 to 1998
26	A N Vos	1999 to 2001
25	S H Nomis	1967 to 1972
25	A G Venter	1997 to 1999
25	A-H le Roux	1998 to 1999

MOST TESTS AS CAPTAIN

Tests	Captain	Span
83	J W Smit	2003 to 2011
36	G H Teichmann	1996 to 1999
29	J F Pienaar	1993 to 1996
22	D J de Villiers	1965 to 1970
18	C P J Krigé	1999 to 2003
17	V Matfield	2007 to 2011
16	A N Vos	1999 to 2001
15	M du Plessis	1975 to 1980
12	R B Skinstad	2001 to 2007
11	J F K Marais	1971 to 1974

MOST POINTS IN TESTS

Points	Player	Tests	Career
893	P C Montgomery	102	1997 to 2008
410	M Steyn	34	2009 to 2011
312	H E Botha	28	1980 to 1992
240	J T Stransky	22	1993 to 1996
221	A J J van Straaten	21	1999 to 2001
200	B G Habana	74	2004 to 2011
190	J H van der Westhuizen	89	1993 to 2003
181	J H de Beer	13	1997 to 1999
171	A S Pretorius	31	2002 to 2007
160	J Fourie	69	2003 to 2011
156	H W Honiball	35	1993 to 1999
154	A D James	42	2001 to 2011
145	L J Koen	15	2000 to 2003
135*	B J Paulse	64	1999 to 2007
130	P J Visagie	25	1967 to 1971

* includes a penalty try

MOST TRIES IN TESTS

Tries	Player	Tests	Career
40	B G Habana	74	2004 to 2011
38	J H van der Westhuizen	89	1993 to 2003
32	J Fourie	69	2003 to 2011
27*	B J Paulse	64	1999 to 2007
25	P C Montgomery	102	1997 to 2008
21	P W G Rossouw	43	1997 to 2003
20	J T Small	47	1992 to 1997
19	D M Gerber	24	1980 to 1992
19	C S Terblanche	37	1998 to 2003
19	J de Villiers	72	2002 to 2011
14	C M Williams	27	1993 to 2000

* includes a penalty try

MOST CONVERSIONS IN TESTS

Cons	Player	Tests	Career
153	P C Montgomery	102	1997 to 2008
52	M Steyn	34	2009 to 2011
50	H E Botha	28	1980 to 1992
38	H W Honiball	35	1993 to 1999
33	J H de Beer	13	1997 to 1999
31	A S Pretorius	31	2002 to 2007
30	J T Stransky	22	1993 to 1996
26	A D James	42	2001 to 2011
25	G S du Toit	14	1998 to 2006
23	A J J van Straaten	21	1999 to 2001
23	L J Koen	15	2000 to 2003
20	P J Visagie	25	1967 to 1971

MOST PENALTY GOALS IN TESTS

Penalties	Player	Tests	Career
148	P C Montgomery	102	1997 to 2008
85	M Steyn	34	2009 to 2011
55	A J J van Straaten	21	1999 to 2001
50	H E Botha	28	1980 to 1992
47	J T Stransky	22	1993 to 1996
31	L J Koen	15	2000 to 2003
28	A D James	42	2001 to 2011
27	J H de Beer	13	1997 to 1999
25	H W Honiball	35	1993 to 1999
25	A S Pretorius	31	2002 to 2007
23	G R Bosch	9	1974 to 1976
19	P J Visagie	25	1967 to 1971
19	F P L Steyn	47	2006 to 2011

MOST DROPPED GOALS IN TESTS

Drops	Player	Tests	Career
18	H E Botha	28	1980 to 1992
8	J H de Beer	13	1997 to 1999
8	A S Pretorius	31	2002 to 2007
7	M Steyn	34	2009 to 2011
6	P C Montgomery	102	1997 to 2008
5	J D Brewis	10	1949 to 1953
5	P J Visagie	25	1967 to 1971
4	B L Osler	17	1924 to 1933

TRI-NATIONS RECORDS

RECORD	DETAIL		SET
Most points in season	158	in six matches	2009
Most tries in season	18	in four matches	1997
Highest score	61	61–22 v Australia (h)	1997
Biggest win	45	53–8 v Australia (h)	2008
Highest score conceded	55	35–55 v N Zealand (a)	1997
Biggest defeat	49	0–49 v Australia (a)	2006
Most appearances	44	V Matfield	2001 to 2011
Most points in matches	210	P C Montgomery	1997 to 2008
Most points in season	95	M Steyn	2009
Most points in match	31	M Steyn	v N Zealand (h), 2009
Most tries in matches	9	J Fourie	2005 to 2011
Most tries in season	4	J L Nokwe	2008
Most tries in match	4	J L Nokwe	v Australia (h) 2008
Most cons in matches	26	P C Montgomery	1997 to 2008
Most cons in season	12	J H de Beer	1997
Most cons in match	6	J H de Beer	v Australia (h), 1997
Most pens in matches	49	M Steyn	2009 to 2011
Most pens in season	23	M Steyn	2009
Most pens in match	8	M Steyn	v N Zealand (h), 2009

MISCELLANEOUS RECORDS

RECORD	HOLDER	DETAIL
Longest Test Career	J P du Randt	1994–2007
Youngest Test Cap	A J Hartley	18 yrs 18 days in 1891
Oldest Test Cap	J N Ackermann	37 yrs 34 days in 2007

CAREER RECORDS OF SOUTH AFRICA INTERNATIONAL PLAYERS

(UP TO 31 OCTOBER 2011)

PLAYER	DEBUT	CAPS	T	C	P	D	PTS
BACKS :							
G G Aplon	2010 v W	16	5	0	0	0	25
B A Basson	2010 v W	6	0	0	0	0	0
J L de Jongh	2010 v W	10	3	0	0	0	15
J de Villiers	2002 v F	72	19	0	0	0	95
P F du Preez	2004 v I	62	13	0	0	0	65
J Fourie	2003 v U	69	32	0	0	0	160
B G Habana	2004 v E	74	40	0	0	0	200
F Hougaard	2009 v It	15	3	0	0	0	15
A A Jacobs	2001 v It	34	7	0	0	0	35
A D James	2001 v F	42	3	26	28	1	154
Z Kirchner	2009 v BI	14	1	0	0	0	5
P Lambie	2010 v I	11	0	3	0	0	6
C McLeod	2011 v NZ	1	0	0	0	0	0
L N Mvovo	2010 v S	4	1	0	0	0	5
O M Ndungane	2008 v It	9	2	0	0	0	10
J L Nokwe	2008 v Arg	4	5	0	0	0	25
W Olivier	2006 v S	34	1	0	0	0	5
R Pienaar	2006 v NZ	51	6	19	17	0	119
J-P R Pietersen	2006 v A	42	12	0	0	0	60
F P L Steyn	2006 v I	47	9	5	19	3	121
M Steyn	2009 v BI	34	6	52	85	7	410
FORWARDS :							
W S Alberts	2010 v W	9	3	0	0	0	15
J P Botha	2002 v F	76	7	0	0	0	35
S B Brits	2008 v It	3	0	0	0	0	0
H W Brüssow	2008 v E	20	1	0	0	0	5

S W P Burger	2003 v Gg	68	13	0	0	0	65
K R Daniel	2010 v I	1	0	0	0	0	0
J R Deysel	2009 v It	4	0	0	0	0	0
B W du Plessis	2007 v A	42	5	0	0	0	25
J N du Plessis	2007 v A	30	1	0	0	0	5
M D Greyling	2011 v A	2	0	0	0	0	0
A J Hargreaves	2010 v W	4	0	0	0	0	0
A F Johnson	2011 v A	3	0	0	0	0	0
R Kankowski	2007 v W	19	1	0	0	0	5
W Kruger	2011 v A	2	0	0	0	0	0
L-F P Louw	2010 v W	10	2	0	0	0	10
V Matfield	2001 v It	110	7	0	0	0	35
G Mostert	2011 v NZ	2	0	0	0	0	0
T Mtawarira	2008 v W	32	2	0	0	0	10
G J Muller	2006 v S	24	0	0	0	0	0
M C Ralepelle	2006 v NZ	21	1	0	0	0	5
D J Rossouw	2003 v U	63	10	0	0	0	50
J W Smit	2000 v C	111	8	0	0	0	40
J H Smith	2003 v S	69	12	0	0	0	60
P J Spies	2006 v A	47	7	0	0	0	35
G G Steenkamp	2004 v S	38	6	0	0	0	30
G J Stegmann	2010 v I	6	0	0	0	0	0
J A Strauss	2008 v A	9	0	0	0	0	0
C J van der Linde	2002 v S	73	4	0	0	0	20
P R van der Merwe	2010 v F	11	1	0	0	0	5

Ryan Pierse/Getty Images

John Smit ended his South Africa career on 111 caps, before heading to Saracens.

SOUTH AFRICAN INTERNATIONAL PLAYERS (UP TO 31 OCTOBER 2011)

Note: Years given for International Championship matches are for second half of season; eg 1972 means season 1971–72. Years for all other matches refer to the actual year of the match. Entries in square brackets denote matches played in RWC Finals.

Ackermann, D S P (WP) 1955 BI 2, 3, 4, 1956 A 1, 2, NZ 1, 3, 1958 F 2
Ackermann, J N (NT, BB, N) 1996 Fj, A 1, NZ 1, A 2, 2001 F 2(R), It 1, NZ 1(R), A 1, 2006 I, E1, 2, 2007 Sm, A2
Aitken, A D (WP) 1997 F 2(R), E, 1998 I 2(R), W 1(R), NZ 1, 2(R), A 2(R)
Alberts, W S (NS) 2010 W2(R), S(t&R), E(R), 2011 NZ2, [W(R), Fj(R), Nm, Sm(t&R), A(t&R)]
Albertyn, P K (SWD) 1924 BI 1, 2, 3, 4
Alexander, F A (GW) 1891 BI 1, 2
Allan, J (N) 1993 A 1(R), Arg 1, 2(R), 1994 E 1, 2, NZ 1, 2, 3, 1996 Fj, A 1, NZ 1, A 2, NZ 2
Allen, P B (EP) 1960 S
Allport, P H (WP) 1910 BI 2, 3
Anderson, J W (WP) 1903 BI 3
Anderson, J H (WP) 1896 BI 1, 3, 4
Andrew, J B (Tvl) 1896 BI 2
Andrews, E P (WP) 2004 I1, 2, W1(t&R), PI, NZ1, A1, NZ2, A2, W2, I3, E, 2005 F1, A2, NZ2(t), Arg(R), F3(R), 2006 S1, 2, F, A1(R), NZ1(t), 2007 A2(R), NZ2(R)
Andrews, K S (WP) 1992 E, 1993 F 1, 2, A 1(R), 2, 3, Arg 1(R), 2, 1994 NZ 3
Andrews, M G (N) 1994 E 2, NZ 1, 2, 3, Arg 1, 2, S, W, 1995 WS, [A, WS, F, NZ], W, It, E, 1996 Fj, A 1, NZ 1, A 2, NZ 2, 3, 4, 5, Arg 1, 2, F 1, 2, W, 1997 Tg (R), BI 1, 2, NZ 1, A 1, NZ 2, A 2, It, F 1, 2, E, S, 1998 I 1, 2, W 1, E 1, A 1, NZ 1, 2, A 2, W 2, S, I 3, E 2, 1999 NZ 1, 2(R), A 2(R), [S, U, E, A 3, NZ 3], 2000 A 2, NZ 2, A 3, Arg, I, W, E 3, 2001 F 1, 2, It 1, NZ 1, A 1, 2, NZ 2, F 3, E
Antelme, J G M (Tvl) 1960 NZ 1, 2, 3, 4, 1961 F
Apsey, J T (WP) 1933 A 4, 5, 1938 BI 2
Aplon, G G (WP) 2010 W1, F, It 1, 2, NZ1(R), 2(R), A1, NZ3, A3(R), I, W2, S, E, 2011 A1, 2(R), [Nm]
Ashley, S (WP) 1903 BI 2
Aston, F T D (Tvl) 1896 BI 1, 2, 3, 4
Atherton, S (N) 1993 Arg 1, 2, 1994 E 1, 2, NZ 1, 2, 3, 1996 NZ 2
Aucamp, J (WT) 1924 BI 1, 2

Baard, A P (WP) 1960 I
Babrow, L (WP) 1937 A 1, 2, NZ 1, 2, 3
Badenhorst, C (OFS) 1994 Arg 2, 1995 WS (R)
Bands, R E (BB) 2003 S 1, 2, Arg (R), A 1, NZ 1, A 2, NZ 2, [U, E, Sm(R), NZ(R)]
Barnard, A S (EP) 1984 S Am 1, 2, 1986 Cv 1, 2
Barnard, J H (Tvl) 1965 S, A 1, 2, NZ 3, 4
Barnard, R W (Tvl) 1970 NZ 2(R)
Barnard, W H M (NT) 1949 NZ 4, 1951 W
Barry, D W (WP) 2000 C, E 1, 2, A 1(R), NZ 1, A 2, 2001 F 1, 2, US (R), 2002 W 2, Arg, Sm, NZ 1, A 1, NZ 2, A 2, 2003 A 1, NZ 1, A 2, [U, E, Sm, NZ], 2004 PI, NZ1, A1, NZ2, A2, W2, I3, E, Arg(t), 2005 F1, 2, A1, NZ2, W(R), F3(R), 2006 F
Barry, J (WP) 1903 BI 1, 2, 3
Bartmann, W J (Tvl, N) 1986 Cv 1, 2, 3, 4, 1992 NZ, A, F, 1, 2
Basson, B A (GW, BB) 2010 W1(R), It 1(R), I, W2, 2011 A1, NZ1
Bastard, W E (N) 1937 A 1, NZ 1, 2, 3, 1938 BI 1, 3
Bates, A J (WT) 1969 E, 1970 NZ 1, 2, 1972 E
Bayvel, P C R (Tvl) 1974 BI 2, 4, F 1, 2, 1975 F 1, 2, 1976 NZ 1, 2, 3, 4
Beck, J J (WP) 1981 NZ 2(R), 3(R), US
Bedford, T P (N) 1963 A 1, 2, 3, 4, 1964 W, F, 1965 I, A 1, 2, 1968 BI 1, 2, 3, 4, F 1, 2, 1969 A 1, 2, 3, 4, S, E, 1970 I, W, 1971 F 1, 2
Bekker, A (WP) 2008 W1, 2(R), It(R), NZ1(R), 2(t&R), A1(t&R), Arg(R), NZ3, A2, 3, W3(R), S(R), E(R), 2009 BI 1(R), 2(R), NZ2(R), A1(R), 2(R), F(t&R), It, I, 2010 It2, NZ1(R), 2(R)
Bekker, H J (WP) 1981 NZ 1, 3
Bekker, H P J (NT) 1952 E, F, 1953 A 1, 2, 3, 4, 1955 BI 2, 3, 4, 1956 A 1, 2, NZ 1, 2, 3, 4
Bekker, M J (NT) 1960 S
Bekker, R P (NT) 1953 A 3, 4
Bekker, S (NT) 1997 A 2(t)
Bennett, R G (Border) 1997 Tg (R), BI 1(R), 3, NZ 1, A 1, NZ 2
Bergh, W F (SWD) 1931 W, I, 1932 E, S, 1933 A 1, 2, 3, 4, 5, 1937 A 1, 2, NZ 1, 2, 3, 1938 BI 1, 2, 3
Bestbier, A (OFS) 1974 F 2(R)
Bester, J J N (WP) 1924 BI 2, 4
Bester, J L A (WP) 1938 BI 2, 3
Beswick, A M (Bor) 1896 BI 2, 3, 4
Bezuidenhout, C E (NT) 1962 BI 2, 3, 4
Bezuidenhout, C J (MP) 2003 NZ 2(R), [E, Sm, NZ]
Bezuidenhout, N S E (NT) 1972 E, 1974 BI 2, 3, 4, F 1, 2, 1975 F 1, 2, 1977 Wld
Bierman, J N (Tvl) 1931 I
Bisset, W M (WP) 1891 BI 1, 3
Blair, R (WP) 1977 Wld
Bobo, G (GL, WP) 2003 S 2(R), Arg, A 1(R), NZ 2, 2004 S(R), 2008 It
Boome, C S (WP) 1999 It 1, 2, W, NZ 1(R), A 1, NZ 2, A 2, 2000 C, E 1, 2, 2003 S 1(R), 2(R), Arg (R), A 1(R), NZ 1(R), A 2, NZ 2(R), [U(R), Gg, NZ(R)]
Bosch, G R (Tvl) 1974 BI 2, F 1, 2, 1975 F 1, 2, 1976 NZ 1, 2, 3, 4
Bosman, H M (FS) 2005 W, F3, 2006 A1(R)
Bosman, N J S (Tvl) 1924 BI 2, 3, 4
Botha, B J (N, Ulster) 2006 NZ2(R), 3, A3, I(R), E1, 2, 2007 E1, Sm, A1, NZ1, Nm(R), S(t&R), [Sm(R), E1, Tg(R), US], 2008 W2, 2009 It(R), I, 2010 W1, F, It 2(R), NZ1(R), 2(R), A1
Botha, D S (NT) 1981 NZ 1
Botha, G van G (BB) 2005 A3(R), F3(R), 2007 E1(R), 2(R), Sm(R), A1(R), NZ1, A2, NZ2(R), Nm, S, [Tg]
Botha, H E (NT) 1980 S Am 1, 2, BI 1, 2, 3, 4, S Am 3, 4, F, 1981 I 1, 2, NZ 1, 2, 3, US, 1982 S Am 1, 2, 1986 Cv 1, 2, 3, 4, 1989 Wld 1, 2, 1992 NZ, A, F 1, 2, E
Botha, J A (Tvl) 1903 BI 3
Botha, J P (BB) 2002 F, 2003 S 1, 2, A 1, NZ 1, A 2(R), [U, E, Gg, Sm, NZ], 2004 I1, PI, NZ1, A1, NZ2, A2, W2, I3, E, S, Arg, 2005 A1, 2, 3, NZ1, A4, NZ2, Arg, W, F3, 2007 E1, 2, A1, NZ1, Nm, S, [Sm, E1, Tg, US(R), Fj, Arg, E2], W, 2008 W1, 2, It, NZ1, 2, A1, Arg, W3, S, E, 2009 BI 1, 2, NZ1, 2, A1, 2, 3, NZ3, F, It, 2010 It 1, 2, NZ1, I, W2, S, E, 2011 A2, NZ2, [Fj, Nm]
Botha, J P F (NT) 1962 BI 2, 3, 4
Botha, P H (Tvl) 1965 A 1, 2
Boyes, H C (GW) 1891 BI 1, 2

Brand, G H (WP) 1928 NZ 2, 3, 1931 W, I, 1932 E, S, 1933 A 1, 2, 3, 4, 5, 1937 A 1, 2, NZ 2, 3, 1938 BI 1
Bredenkamp, M J (GW) 1896 BI 1, 3
Breedt, J C (Tvl) 1986 Cv 1, 2, 3, 4, 1989 Wld 1, 2, 1992 NZ, A
Brewis, J D (NT) 1949 NZ 1, 2, 3, 4, 1951 S, I, W, 1952 E, F, 1953 A 1
Briers, T P D (WP) 1955 BI 1, 2, 3, 4, 1956 NZ 2, 3, 4
Brink D J (WP) 1906 S, W, E
Brink, R (WP) 1995 [R, C]
Brits, S B (WP) 2008 It(R), NZ2(R), A1
Britz, G J J (FS, WP) 2004 I1(R), 2(R), W1(R), PI, A1, NZ2, A2(R), I3(t), S(t&R), Arg(R), 2005 U, 2006 E2(R), 2007 NZ2(R)
Britz, W K (N) 2002 W 1
Brooks, D (Bor) 1906 S
Brosnihan, W (GL, N) 1997 A 2, 2000 NZ 1(t+R), A 2(t+R), NZ 2(R), A 3(R), E 3(R)
Brown, C B (WP) 1903 BI 1, 2, 3
Brüssow, H W (FS) 2008 E(R), 2009 BI 1, 2(R), 3, NZ1, 2, A1, 2, 3, NZ3, F, It, I, 2011 A2, NZ2, [W, Fj, Nm(R), Sm, A]
Brynard, G S (WP) 1965 A 1, NZ 1, 2, 3, 4, 1968 BI 3, 4
Buchler, J U (Tvl) 1951 S, I, W, 1952 E, F, 1953 A 1, 2, 3, 4, 1956 A 2
Burdett, A F (WP) 1906 S, I
Burger, J M (WP) 1989 Wld 1, 2
Burger, M B (NT) 1980 BI 2(R), S Am 3, 1981 US (R)
Burger, S W P (WP) 1984 E 1, 2, 1986 Cv 1, 2, 3, 4
Burger, S W P (WP) 2003 [Gg(R), Sm(R), NZ(R)], 2004 I1, 2, W1, PI, NZ1, A1, NZ2, A2, W2, I3, E, 2005 F1, 2, A1, 2(R), 3(R), NZ1, A4, NZ2, Arg(R), W, F3, 2006 S1, 2, 2007 E1, 2, A1, NZ1, Nm, S, [Sm, US, Fj, Arg, E2], W, 2008 It(R), NZ1, 2, A1, NZ3, A2, 3, W3, S, E, 2009 BI 2, A2(R), 3(R), NZ3, F, I, 2010 F, It2, NZ1, 2, A1, NZ3, A2, 3, 2011 [W, Fj, Nm, Sm, A]
Burger, W A G (Bor) 1906 S, I, W, 1910 BI 2

Carelse, G (EP) 1964 W, F, 1965 I, S, 1967 F 1, 2, 3, 1968 F 1, 2, 1969 A 1, 2, 3, 4, S
Carlson, R A (WP) 1972 E
Carolin, H W (WP) 1903 BI 3, 1906 S, I
Carstens, P D (NS) 2002 S, E, 2006 E1(t&R), 2(R), 2007 E1, 2(t&R), Sm(R), 2009 BI 1(R), 3(t)
Castens, H H (WP) 1891 BI 1
Chavhanga, T (WP) 2005 U, 2007 NZ2(R), 2008 W1, 2
Chignell, T W (WP) 1891 BI 3
Cilliers, G D (OFS) 1963 A 1, 3, 4
Cilliers, N V (WP) 1996 NZ 3(t)
Claassen, J T (WT) 1955 BI 1, 2, 3, 4, 1956 A 1, 2, NZ 1, 2, 3, 4, 1958 F 1, 2, 1960 S, NZ 1, 2, 3, W, I, 1961 E, S, F, I, A 1, 2, 1962 BI 1, 2, 3, 4
Claassen, W (N) 1981 I 1, 2, NZ 2, 3, US, 1982 S Am 1, 2
Claassens, M (FS) 2004 W2(R), S(R), Arg(R), 2005 Arg(R), W, F3, 2007 A2(R), NZ2(R)
Clark, W H G (Tvl) 1933 A 3
Clarkson, W A (N) 1921 NZ 1, 2, 1924 BI 1
Cloete, H A (WP) 1896 BI 4
Cockrell, C H (WP) 1969 S, 1970 I, W
Cockrell, R J (WP) 1974 F 1, 2, 1975 F 1, 2, 1976 NZ 1, 2, 1977 Wld, 1981 NZ 1, 2(R), 3, US
Coetzee, D (BB) 2002 Sm, 2003 S 1, 2, Arg, A 1, NZ 1, A 2, NZ 2, [U, E, Sm(R), NZ(R)], 2004 S(R), Arg(R), 2006 A1(R)
Coetzee, J H H (WP) 1974 BI 1, 1975 F 2(R), 1976 NZ 1, 2, 3, 4
Conradie, J H (WP) 2002 W 1, 2, Arg (R), Sm, NZ 1, A 1, NZ 2(R), A 2(R), S, E, 2004 W1(R), PI, NZ2, A2, 2005 Arg, 2008 W1, 2(R), NZ1(R)
Cope, D K (Tvl) 1896 BI 2
Cotty, W (GW) 1896 BI 3
Crampton, G (GW) 1903 BI 2
Craven, D H (WP) 1931 W, I, 1932 S, 1933 A 1, 2, 3, 4, 5, 1937 A 1, 2, NZ 1, 2, 3, 1938 BI 1, 2, 3, **Cronjé, G** (BB) 2003 NZ 2, 2004 I2(R), W1(R)
Cronjé, J (BB, GL) 2004 I1, 2, W1, PI, NZ1, A1, NZ2(R), A2(t&R), S(t&R), Arg, 2005 U, F1, 2, A1, 3, NZ1(R), 2(t), Arg, W, F3, 2006 S2(R), F(R), A1(t&R), NZ1, A2, NZ2, A3(R), I(R), E1, 2007 A2(R), NZ2, Nm
Cronje, P A (Tvl) 1971 F 1, 2, A 1, 2, 3, 1974 BI 3, 4
Crosby, J H (Tvl) 1896 BI 2
Crosby, N J (Tvl) 1910 BI 1, 3
Currie, C (GW) 1903 BI 2

D'Alton, G (WP) 1933 A 1
Dalton, J (Tvl, GL, Falcons) 1994 Arg 1(R), 1995 [A, C], W, It, E, 1996 NZ 4(R), 5, Arg 1, 2, F 1, 2, W, 1997 Tg (R), BI 3, NZ 2, A 2, It, F 1, 2, E, S, 1998 I 1, 2, W 1, E 1, A 1, NZ 1, 2, A 2, W 2, S, I 3, E 2, 2002 W 1, 2, Arg, NZ 1, A 1, NZ 2, A 2, F, E
Daneel, G M (WP) 1928 NZ 1, 2, 3, 4, 1931 W, I, 1932 E, S
Daneel, H J (WP) 1906 S, I, W, E
Daniel, K R (NS) 2010 I(R)
Davidson, C D (N) 2002 W 2(R), Arg, 2003 Arg, NZ 1(R), A 2
Davids, Q (WP) 2002 W 2, Arg (R), Sm (R), 2003 Arg, 2004 I1(R), 2, W1, PI(t&R), NZ1(R)
Davison, P M (EP) 1910 BI 1
De Beer, J H (OFS) 1997 BI 3, NZ 1, A 1, NZ 2, A 2, F 2(R), S, 1999 A 2, [S, Sp, U, E, A 3]
De Bruyn, J (OFS) 1974 BI 3
De Jongh, H P K (WP) 1928 NZ 3
De Jongh, J L (WP) 2010 W1, F(R), It 1(R), 2, A1(R), NZ3, 2011 A1, NZ1, [Fj(R), Nm(R)]
De Klerk, I J (Tvl) 1969 E, 1970 I, W
De Klerk, K B H (Tvl) 1974 BI 1, 2, 3(R), 1975 F 1, 2, 1976 NZ 2(R), 3, 4, 1980 S Am 1, 2, BI 2, 1981 I 1, 2
De Kock, A N (GW) 1891 BI 2
De Kock, D (Falcons) 2001 It 2(R), US
De Kock, J S (WP) 1921 NZ 3, 1924 BI 3
De Kock, N A (WP) 2001 It 1, 2002 Sm (R), NZ 1(R), 2, A 2, F, 2003 [U(R), Gg, Sm(R), NZ(R)]
Delport, G M (GL, Worcester) 2000 C (R), E 1(t+R), A 1, NZ 1, A 2, NZ 2, A 3, Arg, I, W, 2001 F 2, It 1, 2003 A 1, NZ 2, [U, E, Sm, NZ]
Delport, W H (EP) 1951 S, I, W, 1952 E, F, 1953 A 1, 2, 3, 4
De Melker, S C (GW) 1903 BI 2, 1906 E
Devenish, C E (GW) 1896 BI 2
Devenish, G St L (Tvl) 1896 BI 2
Devenish, G E (Tvl) 1891 BI 1
De Villiers, D I (Tvl) 1910 BI 1, 2, 3
De Villiers, D J (WP, Bol) 1962 BI 2, 3, 1965 I, NZ 1, 3, 4, 1967 F 1, 2, 3, 4, 1968 BI 1, 2, 3, 4, F 1, 2, 1969 A 1, 4, E, 1970 I, W, NZ 1, 2, 3, 4
De Villiers, H A (WP) 1906 S, W, E
De Villiers, H O (WP) 1967 F 1, 2, 3, 4, 1968 F 1, 2, 1969 A 1, 2, 3, 4, S, E, 1970 I, W
De Villiers, J (WP, Munster) 2002 F, 2004 PI, NZ1, A1, NZ2, A2, W2(R), E, 2005 U, F1, 2, A1, 2, 3, NZ1, A4, NZ2, Arg, W, F3, 2006 S1, NZ2, 3, A3, I, E1, 2, 2007 E1, 2, A1, NZ1, Nm, [Sm], 2008 W1, 2, It, NZ1, 2, A1, Arg, NZ3, A2, 3, W3, S, E, 2009 BI 1, 2, NZ1, 2, A1, 2, 3, NZ3, I(R), 2010 F(t&R), It1, 2, NZ1, 2, 3, A2, 3, I, W2, S, E, 2011 A2, NZ2, [W, Sm(R), A]
De Villiers, P du P (WP) 1928 NZ 1, 3, 4, 1932 E, 1933 A 4, 1937 A 1, 2, NZ 1
Devine, D (Tvl) 1924 BI 3, 1928 NZ 2
De Vos, D J J (WP) 1965 S, 1969 A 3, S
De Waal, A N (WP) 1967 F 1, 2, 3, 4
De Waal, P J (WP) 1896 BI 4
De Wet, A E (WP) 1969 A 3, 4, E
De Wet, P J (WP) 1938 BI 1, 2, 3
Deysel, J R (NS) 2009 It(R), 2011 A1(R), NZ1, A2(R)
Dinkelmann, E E (NT) 1951 S, I, 1952 E, F, 1953 A 1, 2
Dirksen, C W (NT) 1963 A 4, 1964 W, 1965 I, S, 1967 F 1, 2, 3, 4, 1968 BI 1, 2
Dlulane, V T (MP) 2004 W2(R)
Dobbin, F J (GW) 1903 BI 1, 2, 1906 S, W, E, 1910 BI 1, 1912 S, I, W
Dobie, J A R (Tvl) 1928 NZ 2
Dormehl, P J (WP) 1896 BI 3, 4
Douglass, F W (EP) 1896 BI 1
Drotské, A E (OFS) 1993 Arg 2, 1995 [WS (R)], 1996 A 1(R), 1997 Tg, BI 1, 2, 3(R), NZ 1, A 1, NZ 2(R), 1998 I 2(R), W 1(R), I 3(R), 1999 It 1, 2, W, NZ 1, A 1, NZ 2, A 2, [S, Sp (R), U, E, A 3, NZ 3]

Dryburgh, R G (WP) 1955 BI 2, 3, 4, 1956 A 2, NZ 1, 4, 1960 NZ 1, 2
Duff, B R (WP) 1891 BI 1, 2, 3
Duffy, B A (Bor) 1928 NZ 1
Du Plessis, B W (NS) 2007 A2(t&R), NZ2, Nm(R), S(R), [Sm(R), E1(R), US(R), Arg(R), E2(t)], W(R), 2008 W1(R), 2(R), It, NZ1(R), 2, Arg, NZ3, A2, 3, W3, S, 2009 BI 1, 2, 3(R), NZ1, 2, A1, 2, 3, NZ3, F, I(R), 2010 I, W2, S, E, 2011 A2(R), NZ2, [W(R), Fj(R), Sm, A(R)]
Du Plessis, C J (WP) 1982 S Am 1, 2, 1984 E 1, 2, S Am 1, 2, 1986 Cv 1, 2, 3, 4, 1989 Wld 1, 2
Du Plessis, D C (NT) 1977 Wld, 1980 S Am 2
Du Plessis, F (Tvl) 1949 NZ 1, 2, 3
Du Plessis, J N (FS, NS) 2007 A2, NZ2, [Fj, Arg(t&R)], W, 2008 A3(R), E, 2009 NZ1(t), 2(R), A1(R), 2(R), NZ3(R), 2010 W1(R), F(R), It 1, 2, NZ1, 3, A2, 3, I, W2, S, E, 2011 A2, NZ2, [W, Fj, Sm, A]
Du Plessis, M (WP) 1971 A 1, 2, 3, 1974 BI 1, 2, F 1, 2, 1975 F 1, 2, 1976 NZ 1, 2, 3, 4, 1977 Wld, 1980 S Am 1, 2, BI 1, 2, 3, 4, S Am 4, F
Du Plessis, M J (WP) 1984 S Am 1, 2, 1986 Cv 1, 2, 3, 4, 1989 Wld 1, 2
Du Plessis, N J (WT) 1921 NZ 2, 3, 1924 BI 1, 2, 3
Du Plessis, P G (NT) 1972 E
Du Plessis, T D (NT) 1980 S Am 1, 2
Du Plessis, W (WP) 1980 S Am 1, 2, BI 1, 2, 3, 4, S Am 3, 4, F, 1981 NZ 1, 2, 3, 1982 S Am 1, 2
Du Plooy, A J J (EP) 1955 BI 1
Du Preez, F C H (NT) 1961 E, S, A 1, 2, 1962 BI 1, 2, 3, 4, 1963 A 1, 1964 W, F, 1965 A 1, 2, NZ 1, 2, 3, 4, 1967 F 4, 1968 BI 1, 2, 3, 4, F 1, 2, 1969 A 1, 2, S, 1970 I, W, NZ 1, 2, 3, 4, 1971 F 1, 2, A 1, 2, 3
Du Preez, G J D (GL) 2002 Sm (R), A 1(R)
Du Preez, J G H (WP) 1956 NZ 1
Du Preez, P F (BB) 2004 I1, 2, W1, PI(R), NZ1, A1, NZ2(R), A2(R), W2, I3, E, S, Arg, 2005 U(R), F1, 2(R), A1(R), 2(R), 3, NZ1(R), A4(R), 2006 S1, 2, F, A1(R), NZ1, A2, NZ2, 3, A3, 2007 Nm, S, [Sm, E1, US, Fj, Arg, E2], 2008 Arg(R), NZ3, A2, 3, W3, 2009 BI 1, 2, 3, NZ1, 2, A1, 2, 3, NZ3, F, It, I, 2011 A2, NZ2, [W, Fj, Nm(R), Sm, A]
Du Preez, R J (N) 1992 NZ, A, 1993 F 1, 2, A 1, 2, 3
Du Preez, W H (FS) 2009 It
Du Rand, J A (R, NT) 1949 NZ 2, 3, 1951 S, I, W, 1952 E, F, 1953 A 1, 2, 3, 4, 1955 BI 1, 2, 3, 4, 1956 A 1, 2, NZ 1, 2, 3, 4
Du Randt, J P (OFS, FS) 1994 Arg 1, 2, S, W, 1995 WS, [A, WS, F, NZ], 1996 Fj, A 1, NZ 1, A 2, NZ 2, 3, 4, 1997 Tg, BI 1, 2, 3, NZ 1, A 1, NZ 2, A 2, It, F 1, 2, E, S, 1999 NZ 1, A 1, NZ 2, A 2, [S, Sp (R), U, E, A 3, NZ 3], 2004 I1, 2, W1, PI, NZ1, A1, NZ2, A2, W2, I3, E, S(R), Arg(R), 2005 U(R), F1, A1, NZ1, A4, NZ2, Arg, W(R), F3, 2006 S1, 2, F, A1, NZ1, A2, NZ2, 3, A3, 2007 Sm, NZ1, Nm, S, [Sm, E1, US, Fj, Arg, E2]
Du Toit, A F (WP) 1928 NZ 3, 4
Du Toit, B A (Tvl) 1938 BI 1, 2, 3
Du Toit, G S (GW, WP) 1998 I 1, 1999 It 1, 2, W (R), NZ 1, 2, 2004 I1, W1(R), A1(R), S(R), Arg, 2006 S1(R), 2(R), F(R)
Du Toit, P A (NT) 1949 NZ 2, 3, 4, 1951 S, I, W, 1952 E, F
Du Toit, P G (WP) 1981 NZ 1, 1982 S Am 1, 2, 1984 E 1, 2
Du Toit, P S (WP) 1958 F 1, 2, 1960 NZ 1, 2, 3, 4, W, I, 1961 E, S, F, I, A 1, 2
Duvenhage, F P (GW) 1949 NZ 1, 3

Edwards, P (NT) 1980 S Am 1, 2
Ellis, J H (SWA) 1965 NZ 1, 2, 3, 4, 1967 F 1, 2, 3, 4, 1968 BI 1, 2, 3, 4, F 1, 2, 1969 A 1, 2, 3, 4, S, 1970 I, W, NZ 1, 2, 3, 4, 1971 F 1, 2, A 1, 2, 3, 1972 E, 1974 BI 1, 2, 3, 4, F 1, 2, 1976 NZ 1
Ellis, M C (Tvl) 1921 NZ 2, 3, 1924 BI 1, 2, 3, 4
Els, W W (OFS) 1997 A 2(R)
Engelbrecht, J P (WP) 1960 S, W, I, 1961 E, S, F, A 1, 2, 1962 BI 2, 3, 4, 1963 A 2, 3, 1964 W, F, 1965 I, S, A 1, 2, NZ 1, 2, 3, 4, 1967 F 1, 2, 3, 4, 1968 BI 1, 2, F 1, 2, 1969 A 1, 2
Erasmus, F S (NT, EP) 1986 Cv 3, 4, 1989 Wld 2
Erasmus, J C (OFS, GL) 1997 BI 3, A 2, It, F 1, 2, S, 1998 I 1, 2, W 1, E 1, A 1, NZ 2, A 2, S, W 2, I 3, E 2, 1999 It 1, 2, W, A 1, NZ 2, A 2, [S, U, E, A 3, NZ 3], 2000 C, E 1, A 1, NZ 1, 2, A 3, 2001 F 1, 2
Esterhuizen, G (GL) 2000 NZ 1(R), 2, A 3, Arg, I, W (R), E 3(t)
Etlinger, T E (WP) 1896 BI 4

Ferreira, C (OFS) 1986 Cv 1, 2
Ferreira, P S (WP) 1984 S Am 1, 2
Ferris, H H (Tvl) 1903 BI 3
Fleck R F (WP) 1999 It 1, 2, NZ 1(R), A 1, NZ 2(R), A 2, [S, U, E, A 3, NZ 3], 2000 C, E 1, 2, A 1, NZ 1, A 2, NZ 2, A 3, Arg, I, W, E 3, 2001 F 1(R), 2, It 1, NZ 1, A 1, 2, 2002 S, E
Floors, L (FS) 2006 E2
Forbes, H H (Tvl) 1896 BI 2
Fortuin, B A (FS) 2006 I, 2007 A2
Fourie, C (EP) 1974 F 1, 2, 1975 F 1, 2
Fourie, J (GL, WP) 2003 [U, Gg, Sm(R), NZ(R)], 2004 I2, E(R), S, Arg, 2005 U(R), F2(R), A1(R), 2, 3, NZ1, A4, NZ2, Arg, W, F3, 2006 S1, A1, NZ1, A2, NZ2, 3, A3, 2007 Sm(R), A1, NZ1, Nm, S, [Sm, E1, US, Fj, Arg, E2], W, 2008 Arg(R), W3(R), S(R), E(R), 2009 BI 1(R), 2(R), 3, NZ1, 2, A1, 2, 3, NZ3, F, It, I, 2010 W1, F, It2, NZ1, 2, A1, 2, 3, 2011 A2, NZ2, [W, Fj, Nm, Sm, A]
Fourie, T T (SET) 1974 BI 3
Fourie, W L (SWA) 1958 F 1, 2
Francis, J A J (Tvl) 1912 S, I, W, 1913 E, F
Frederickson, C A (Tvl) 1974 BI 2, 1980 S Am 1, 2
Frew, A (Tvl) 1903 BI 1
Froneman, D C (OFS) 1977 Wld
Froneman, I L (Bor) 1933 A 1
Fuls, H T (Tvl, EP) 1992 NZ (R), 1993 F 1, 2, A 1, 2, 3, Arg 1, 2
Fry, S P (WP) 1951 S, I, W, 1952 E, F, 1953 A 1, 2, 3, 4, 1955 BI 1, 2, 3, 4
Fynn, E E (N) 2001 F 1, It 1(R)
Fyvie, W (N) 1996 NZ 4(t & R), 5(R), Arg 2(R)

Gage, J H (OFS) 1933 A 1
Gainsford, J L (WP) 1960 S, NZ 1, 2, 3, 4, W, I, 1961 E, S, F, A 1, 2, 1962 BI 1, 2, 3, 4, 1963 A 1, 2, 3, 4, 1964 W, F, 1965 I, S, A 1, 2, NZ 1, 2, 3, 4, 1967 F 1, 2, 3
Garvey, A C (N) 1996 Arg 1, 2, F 1, 2, W, 1997 Tg, BI 1, 2, 3(R), A 1(t), It, F 1, 2, E, S, 1998 I 1, 2, W 1, E1, A 1, NZ 1, 2 A 2, W 2, S, I 3, E 2, 1999 [Sp]
Geel, P J (OFS) 1949 NZ 3
Geere, V (Tvl) 1933 A 1, 2, 3, 4, 5
Geffin, A O (Tvl) 1949 NZ 1, 2, 3, 4, 1951 S, I, W
Geldenhuys, A (EP) 1992 NZ, A, F 1, 2
Geldenhuys, S B (NT) 1981 NZ 2, 3, US, 1982 S Am 1, 2, 1989 Wld 1, 2
Gentles, T A (WP) 1955 BI 1, 2, 4, 1956 NZ 2, 3, 1958 F 2
Geraghty, E M (Bor) 1949 NZ 4
Gerber, D M (EP, WP) 1980 S Am 3, 4, F, 1981 I 1, 2, NZ 1, 2, 3, US, 1982 S Am 1, 2, 1984 E 1, 2, S Am 1, 2, 1986 Cv 1, 2, 3, 4, 1992 NZ, A, F 1, 2, E
Gerber, H J (WP) 2003 S 1, 2
Gerber, M C (EP) 1958 F 1, 2, 1960 S
Gericke, F W (Tvl) 1960 S
Germishuys, J S (OFS, Tvl) 1974 BI 2, 1976 NZ 1, 2, 3, 4, 1977 Wld, 1980 S Am 1, 2, BI 1, 2, 3, 4, S Am 3, 4, F, 1981 I 1, 2, NZ 2, 3, US
Gibbs, B (GW) 1903 BI 2
Goosen, C P (OFS) 1965 NZ 2
Gorton, H C (Tvl) 1896 BI 1
Gould, R L (N) 1968 BI 1, 2, 3, 4
Grant, P J (WP) 2007 A2(R), NZ2(R), 2008 W1(t&R), It(R), A1(R)
Gray, B G (WP) 1931 W, 1932 E, S, 1933 A 5
Greeff, W W (WP) 2002 Arg (R), Sm, NZ 1, A 1, NZ 2, A 2, F, S, E, 2003 [U, Gg]
Greenwood, C M (WP) 1961 I
Greyling, M D (BB) 2011 A1, NZ1
Greyling, P J F (OFS) 1967 F 1, 2, 3, 4, 1968 BI 1, F 1, 2, 1969 A 1, 2, 3, 4, S, E, 1970 I, W, NZ 1, 2, 3, 4, 1971 F 1, 2, A 1, 2, 3, 1972 E
Grobler, C J (OFS) 1974 BI 4, 1975 F 1, 2
Guthrie, F H (WP) 1891 BI 1, 3, 1896 BI 1

Habana, B G (GL, BB, WP) 2004 E(R), S, Arg, 2005 U, F1, 2, A1, 2, 3, NZ1, A4, NZ2, Arg, W, F3, 2006 S2, F, A1, NZ1, A2, NZ2, 3, I, E1, 2, 2007 E1, 2, S, [Sm, E1, Tg(R), US, Fj, Arg, E2], W, 2008 W1, 2, It, NZ1, 2, A1, NZ3, W3, S, E, 2009 BI 1, 2, NZ1, 2, A1, 2, 3, NZ3, F, It, I, 2010 F, It 1, 2, NZ1, 2, A1, NZ3, A2, 3, I, W2, 2011 A2, NZ2, [W, Nm, Sm, A]
Hahn, C H L (Tvl) 1910 BI 1, 2, 3
Hall, D B (GL) 2001 F 1, 2, NZ 1, A 1, 2, NZ 2, It 2, E, US, 2002 Sm, NZ 1, 2, A 2
Halstead, T M (N) 2001 F 3, It 2, E, US (R), 2003 S 1, 2
Hamilton, F (EP) 1891 BI 1
Hargreaves, A J (NS) 2010 W1(R), It 1(R), 2011 A1, NZ1
Harris, T A (Tvl) 1937 NZ 2, 3, 1938 BI 1, 2, 3
Hartley, A J (WP) 1891 BI 3
Hattingh, H (NT) 1992 A (R), F 2(R), E, 1994 Arg 1, 2
Hattingh, L B (OFS) 1933 A 2
Heatlie, B H (WP) 1891 BI 2, 3, 1896 BI 1, 4, 1903 BI 1, 3
Hendricks, M (Bol) 1998 I 2(R), W 1(R)
Hendriks, P (Tvl) 1992 NZ, A, 1994 S, W, 1995 [A, R, C], 1996 A 1, NZ 1, A 2, NZ 2, 3, 4, 5
Hepburn, T B (WP) 1896 BI 4
Heunis, J W (NT) 1981 NZ 3(R), US, 1982 S Am 1, 2, 1984 E 1, 2, S Am 1, 2, 1986 Cv 1, 2, 3, 4, 1989 Wld 1, 2
Hill, R A (R) 1960 W, I, 1961 I, A 1, 2, 1962 BI 4, 1963 A 3
Hills, W G (NT) 1992 F 1, 2, E, 1993 F 1, 2, A 1
Hirsch, J G (EP) 1906 I, 1910 BI 1
Hobson, T E C (WP) 1903 BI 3
Hoffman, R S (Bol) 1953 A 3
Holton, D N (EP) 1960 S
Honiball, H W (N) 1993 A 3(R), Arg 2, 1995 WS (R), 1996 Fj, A 1, NZ 5, Arg 1, 2, F 1, 2, W, 1997 Tg, BI 1, 2, 3(R), NZ 1(R), A 1(R), NZ 2, A 2, It, F 1, 2, E, 1998 W 1(R), E 1, A 1, NZ 1, 2, A 2, W 2, S, I 3, E 2, 1999 [A 3(R), NZ 3]
Hopwood, D J (WP) 1960 S, NZ 3, 4, W, 1961 E, S, F, I, A 1, 2, 1962 BI 1, 2, 3, 4, 1963 A 1, 2, 4, 1964 W, F, 1965 S, NZ 3, 4
Hougaard, D J (BB) 2003 [U(R), E(R), Gg, Sm, NZ], 2007 Sm, A2, NZ2
Hougaard, F (BB) 2009 It(R), 2010 A1(R), NZ3, A2, 3, W2(R), S, E(t&R), 2011 A2(t), NZ2(R), [W(R), Fj(R), Nm, Sm(R), A(R)]
Howe, B F (Bor) 1956 NZ 1, 4
Howe-Browne, N R F G (WP) 1910 BI 1, 2, 3
Hugo, D P (WP) 1989 Wld 1, 2
Human, D C F (WP) 2002 W 1, 2, Arg (R), Sm (R)
Hurter, M H (NT) 1995 [R, C], W, 1996 Fj, A 1, NZ 1, 2, 3, 4, 5, 1997 NZ 1, 2, A 2

Immelman, J H (WP) 1913 F

Jackson, D C (WP) 1906 I, W, E
Jackson, J S (WP) 1903 BI 2
Jacobs, A A (Falcons, NS) 2001 It 2(R), US, 2002 W 1(R), Arg, Sm (R), NZ 1(t+R), A 1(R), F, S, E (R), 2008 W1, 2, NZ1, 2, Arg, NZ3, A2, 3, W3, S, E, 2009 BI 1, 2, NZ2(R), A1(R), 2(R), 3(R), NZ3(R), F, It, 2010 I(R), E(R), 2011 A1(R), NZ1
James, A D (N, Bath, GL) 2001 F 1, 2, NZ 1, A 1, 2, NZ 2, 2002 F (R), S, E, 2006 NZ1, A2, NZ2, 3(R), E1, 2007 E1, 2, A1, NZ1, Nm, S, [Sm, E1, US, Fj, Arg, E2], 2008 W1, 2, NZ1, 2, A1, Arg, NZ3, A2, 3, 2010 It1, 2(R), NZ1(R), A1(R), 2(R), 2011 A2, [W(R)]
Jansen, E (OFS) 1981 NZ 1
Jansen, J S (OFS) 1970 NZ 1, 2, 3, 4, 1971 F 1, 2, A 1, 2, 3, 1972 E
Jantjes, C A (GL, WP) 2001 It 1, A 1, 2, NZ 2, F 3, It 2, E, US, 2005 Arg, W, 2007 W(R), 2008 W1, 2, It, NZ1, 2(R), A1, Arg, NZ3(R), A2, 3, W3, S, E
Januarie, E R (GL, WP) 2005 U, F2, A1, 2, 3(R), NZ1, A4, NZ2, 2006 S1(R), 2(R), F(R), A1, I, E1, 2, 2007 E1, 2, Sm, Nm(R), [Sm(R), Tg], W, 2008 W2, It, NZ1, 2, A1, Arg, NZ3(R), A2(R), 3(R), W3(R), S, E, 2009 BI 1(R), NZ1(R), 2(R), A1(R), 2(R), NZ3(R), 2010 W1, F, It 1, 2, NZ1, 2, 3(R)
Jennings, C B (Bor) 1937 NZ 1
Johnson, A F (FS) 2011 A1, NZ1(t&R), 2(t&R)
Johnson, G K (Tvl) 1993 Arg 2, 1994 NZ 3, Arg 1, 1995 WS, [R, C, WS]
Johnstone, P G A (WP) 1951 S, I, W, 1952 E, F, 1956 A 1, NZ 1, 2, 4
Jones, C H (Tvl) 1903 BI 1, 2
Jones, P S T (WP) 1896 BI 1, 3, 4
Jordaan, N (BB) 2002 E (R)
Jordaan, R P (NT) 1949 NZ 1, 2, 3, 4
Joubert, A J (OFS, N) 1989 Wld 1(R), 1993 A 3, Arg 1, 1994 E 1, 2, NZ 1, 2(R), 3, Arg 2, S, W, 1995 [A, C, WS, F, NZ], W, It, E, 1996 Fj, A 1, NZ 1, 3, 4, 5, Arg 1, 2, F 1, 2, W, 1997 Tg, BI 1, 2, A 2
Joubert, M C (Bol, WP) 2001 NZ 1, 2002 W 1, 2, Arg (R), Sm, NZ 1, A1, NZ 2, A 2, F (R), 2003 S 2, Arg, A 1, 2004 I1, 2, W1, PI, NZ1, A1, NZ2, A2, W2, I3, E, S, Arg, 2005 U, F1, 2, A1
Joubert, S J (WP) 1906 I, W, E
Julies, W (Bol, SWD, GL) 1999 [Sp], 2004 I1, 2, W1, S, Arg, 2005 A2(R), 3(t), 2006 F(R), 2007 Sm, [Tg]

Kahts, W J H (NT) 1980 BI 1, 2, 3, S Am 3, 4, F, 1981 I 1, 2, NZ 2, 1982 S Am 1, 2
Kaminer, J (Tvl) 1958 F 2
Kankowski, R (NS) 2007 W, 2008 W2(R), It, A1(R), W3(R), S(R), E(R), 2009 BI3, NZ3(R), F, It, 2010 W1(R), It 1(R), NZ2(R), A1, 3(R), S, 2011 A1(R), NZ1(R)
Kayser, D J (EP, N) 1999 It 2(R), A 1(R), NZ 2, A 2, [S, Sp (R), U, E, A 3], 2001 It 1(R), NZ 1(R), A 2(R), NZ 2(R)
Kebble, G R (N) 1993 Arg 1, 2, 1994 NZ 1(R), 2
Kelly, E W (GW) 1896 BI 3
Kempson, R B (N, WP, Ulster) 1998 I 2(R), W 1, E 1, A 1, NZ 1, 2 A 2, W 2, S, I 3, E 2, 1999 It 1, 2, W, 2000 C, E 1, 2, A 1, NZ 1, A 2, 3, Arg, I, W, E 3, 2001 F 1, 2(R), NZ 1, A 1, 2, NZ 2, 2003 S 1(R), 2(R), Arg, A 1(R), NZ 1(R), A 2
Kenyon, B J (Bor) 1949 NZ 4
Kipling, H G (GW) 1931 W, I, 1932 E, S, 1933 A 1, 2, 3, 4, 5
Kirchner, Z (BB) 2009 BI 3, F, It, I, 2010 W1(R), F, It1, NZ1, 2, A1, I, W2(R), S, E
Kirkpatrick, A I (GW) 1953 A 2, 1956 NZ 2, 1958 F 1, 1960 S, NZ 1, 2, 3, 4, W, I, 1961 E, S, F
Knight, A S (Tvl) 1912 S, I, W, 1913 E, F
Knoetze, F (WP) 1989 Wld 1, 2
Koch, A C (Bol) 1949 NZ 2, 3, 4, 1951 S, I, W, 1952 E, F, 1953 A 1, 2, 4, 1955 BI 1, 2, 3, 4, 1956 A 1, NZ 2, 3, 1958 F 1, 2, 1960 NZ 1, 2
Koch, H V (WP) 1949 NZ 1, 2, 3, 4
Koen, L J (GL, BB) 2000 A 1, 2001 It 2, E, US, 2003 S 1, 2, Arg, A 1, NZ 1, A 2, NZ 2, [U, E, Sm(R), NZ(R)]
Kotze, G J M (WP) 1967 F 1, 2, 3, 4
Krantz, E F W (OFS) 1976 NZ 1, 1981 I 1
Krige, C P J (WP) 1999 It 2, W, NZ 1, 2000 C (R), E 1(R), 2, A 1(R), NZ 1, A 2, NZ 2, A 3, Arg, I, W, E 3, 2001 F 1, 2, It 1(R), A 1(t+R), It 2(R), E (R), 2002 W 2, Arg, Sm, NZ 1, A 1, NZ 2, A 2, F, S, E, 2003 Arg, A 1, NZ 1, A 2, NZ 2, [E, Sm, NZ]
Krige, J D (WP) 1903 BI 1, 3, 1906 S, I, W
Kritzinger, J L (Tvl) 1974 BI 3, 4, F 1, 2, 1975 F 1, 2, 1976 NZ 4
Kroon, C M (EP) 1955 BI 1
Kruger, P E (Tvl) 1986 Cv 3, 4
Kruger, R J (NT, BB) 1993 Arg 1, 2, 1994 S, W, 1995 WS, [A, R, WS, F, NZ], W, It, E, 1996 Fj, A 1, NZ 1, A 2, NZ 2, 3, 4, 5, Arg 1, 2, F 1, 2, W, 1997 Tg, BI 1, 2, NZ 1, A 1, NZ 2, 1999 NZ 2, A 2(R), [Sp, NZ 3(R)]
Kruger, T L (Tvl) 1921 NZ 1, 2, 1924 BI 1, 2, 3, 4, 1928 NZ 1, 2
Kruger, W (BB) 2011 A1, NZ1
Kuhn, S P (Tvl) 1960 NZ 3, 4, W, I, 1961 E, S, F, I, A 1, 2, 1962 BI 1, 2, 3, 4, 1963 A 1, 2, 3, 1965 I, S

Labuschagne, J J (GL) 2000 NZ 1(R), 2002 W 1, 2, Arg, NZ 1, A 1, NZ 2, A2, F, S, E
La Grange, J B (WP) 1924 BI 3, 4
Lambie, P (NS) 2010 I(R), W2(R), S(R), E(R), 2011 A1(R), NZ1, 2, [Fj, Nm, Sm, A]
Larard, A (Tvl) 1896 BI 2, 4
Lategan, M T (WP) 1949 NZ 1, 2, 3, 4, 1951 S, I, W, 1952 E, F, 1953 A 1, 2

Laubscher, T G (WP) 1994 Arg 1, 2, S, W, 1995 It, E
Lawless, M J (WP) 1964 F, 1969 E (R), 1970 I, W
Ledger, S H (GW) 1912 S, I, 1913 E, F
Leonard, A (WP, SWD) 1999 A 1, [Sp]
Le Roux, A H (OFS, N) 1994 E 1, 1998 I 1, 2, W 1(R), E 1(R), A 1(R), NZ 1(R), 2(R), A 2(R), W 2(R), S (R), I 3(R), E 2(t+R), 1999 It 1(R), 2(R), W (R), NZ 1(R), A 1(R), NZ 2(R), A 2(R), [S(R), Sp, U (R), E (R), A 3(R), NZ 3(R)], 2000 E 1(t+R), 2(R), A 1(R), 2(R), NZ 2, A 3(R), Arg (R), I (t), W (R), E 3(R), 2001 F 1(R), 2, It 1, NZ 1(R), A 1(R), 2(R), NZ 2(R), F 3, It 2, E, US (R), 2002 W 1(R), 2(R), Arg, NZ 1(R), A 1(R), NZ 2(R), A 2(R)
Le Roux, H P (Tvl) 1993 F 1, 2, 1994 E 1, 2, NZ 1, 2, 3, Arg 2, S, W, 1995 WS [A, R, C (R), WS, F, NZ], W, It, E, 1996 Fj, NZ 2, Arg 1, 2, F 1, 2, W
Le Roux, J H S (Tvl) 1994 E 2, NZ 1, 2
Le Roux, M (OFS) 1980 BI 1, 2, 3, 4, S Am 3, 4, F, 1981 I 1
Le Roux, P A (WP) 1906 I, W, E
Little, E M (GW) 1891 BI 1, 3
Lobberts, H (BB) 2006 E1(R), 2007 NZ2(R)
Lochner, G P (WP) 1955 BI 3, 1956 A 1, 2, NZ 1, 2, 3, 4, 1958 F 1, 2
Lochner, G P (EP) 1937 NZ 3, 1938 BI 1, 2
Lockyear, R J (GW) 1960 NZ 1, 2, 3, 4, 1960 I, 1961 F
Lombard, A C (EP) 1910 BI 2
Lombard, F (FS) 2002 S, E
Lötter, D (Tvl) 1993 F 2, A 1, 2
Lotz, J W (Tvl) 1937 A 1, 2, NZ 1, 2, 3, 1938 BI 1, 2, 3
Loubscher, R I P (EP, N) 2002 W 1, 2003 S 1, [U(R), Gg]
Loubser, J A (WP) 1903 BI 3, 1906 S, I, W, E, 1910 BI 1, 3
Lourens, M J (NT) 1968 BI 2, 3, 4
Louw, F H (WP) 2002 W 2(R), Arg, Sm
Louw, J S (Tvl) 1891 BI 1, 2, 3
Louw, L-F P (WP, Bath) 2010 W1, F, It 1, 2, NZ1, 2, 3(R), 2011 [Fj(t), Nm(t&R), A(R)]
Louw, M J (Tvl) 1971 A 2, 3
Louw, M M (WP) 1928 NZ 3, 4, 1931 W, I, 1932 E, S, 1933 A 1, 2, 3, 4, 5, 1937 A 1, 2, NZ 2, 3, 1938 BI 1, 2, 3
Louw, R J (WP) 1980 S Am 1, 2, BI 1, 2, 3, 4 S Am 3, 4, F, 1981 I 1, 2, NZ 1, 3, 1982 S Am 1, 2, 1984 E 1, 2, S Am 1, 2
Louw, S C (WP) 1933 A 1, 2, 3, 4, 5, 1937 A 1, NZ 1, 2, 3, 1938 BI 1, 2, 3
Lubbe, E (GW) 1997 Tg, BI 1
Luyt, F P (WP) 1910 BI 1, 2, 3, 1912 S, I, W, 1913 E
Luyt, J D (EP) 1912 S, W, 1913 E, F
Luyt, R R (W P) 1910 BI 2, 3, 1912 S, I, W, 1913 E, F
Lyons, D J (EP) 1896 BI 1
Lyster, P J (N) 1933 A 2, 5, 1937 NZ 1

McCallum, I D (WP) 1970 NZ 1, 2, 3, 4, 1971 F 1, 2, A 1, 2, 3, 1974 BI 1, 2
McCallum, R J (WP) 1974 BI 1
McCulloch, J D (GW) 1913 E, F
MacDonald, A W (R) 1965 A 1, NZ 1, 2, 3, 4
Macdonald, D A (WP) 1974 BI 2
Macdonald, I (Tvl) 1992 NZ, A, 1993 F 1, A 3, 1994 E 2, 1995 WS (R)
McDonald, J A J (WP) 1931 W, I, 1932 E, S
McEwan, W M C (Tvl) 1903 BI 1, 3
McHardy, E E (OFS) 1912 S, I, W, 1913 E, F
McKendrick, J A (WP) 1891 BI 3
McLeod, C (NS) 2011 NZ1(R)
Maku, B G (BB) 2010 It1(R)
Malan, A S (Tvl) 1960 NZ 1, 2, 3, 4, W, I, 1961 E, S, F, 1962 BI 1, 1963 A 1, 2, 3, 1964 W, 1965 I, S
Malan, A W (NT) 1989 Wld 1, 2, 1992 NZ, A, F 1, 2, E
Malan, E (NT) 1980 BI 3(R), 4
Malan, G F (WP) 1958 F 2, 1960 NZ 1, 3, 4, 1961 E, S, F, 1962 BI 1, 2, 3, 1963 A 1, 2, 4, 1964 W, 1965 A 1, 2, NZ 1, 2
Malan, P (Tvl) 1949 NZ 4
Mallett, N V H (WP) 1984 S Am 1, 2
Malotana, K (Bor) 1999 [Sp]
Mans, W J (WP) 1965 I, S
Marais, C F (WP) 1999 It 1(R), 2(R), 2000 C, E 1, 2, A 1, NZ 1, A 2, NZ 2, A 3, Arg (R), W (R)
Marais, F P (Bol) 1949 NZ 1, 2, 1951 S, 1953 A 1, 2
Marais, J F K (WP) 1963 A 3, 1964 W, F, 1965 I, S, A 2, 1968 BI, 1, 2, 3, 4, F 1, 2, 1969 A 1, 2, 3, 4, S, E, 1970 I, W, NZ 1, 2, 3, 4, 1971 F 1, 2, A 1, 2, 3, 1974 BI 1, 2, 3, 4, F 1, 2
Maré, D S (Tvl) 1906 S
Marsberg, A F W (GW) 1906 S, W, E
Marsberg, P A (GW) 1910 BI 1
Martheze, W C (GW) 1903 BI 2, 1906 I, W
Martin, H J (Tvl) 1937 A 2
Matfield, V (BB) 2001 It 1(R), NZ 1, A 2, NZ 2, F 3, It 2, E, US, 2002 W 1, Sm, NZ 1, A 1, NZ 2(R), 2003 S 1, 2, Arg, A 1, NZ 1, A 2, NZ 2, [U, E, Sm, NZ], 2004 I1, 2, W1, NZ2, A2, W2, I3, E, S, Arg, 2005 F1, 2, A1, 2, 3, NZ1, A4, NZ2, Arg, W, F3, 2006 S1, 2, F, A1, NZ1, A2, NZ2, 3, A3, 2007 E1, 2, A1, NZ1, Nm, S, [Sm, E1, Tg(R), US, Fj, Arg, E2], 2008 W1(R), 2, It, NZ1, 2, A1, Arg, NZ3, A2, 3, W3, S, E, 2009 BI 1, 2, 3, NZ1, 2, A1, 2, 3, NZ3, F, It(R), I, 2010 W1, F, It 1, NZ1, 2, A1, NZ3, A2, 3, I, W2, S, E, 2011 A2, NZ2, [W, Sm, A]
Mellet, T B (GW) 1896 BI 2
Mellish, F W (WP) 1921 NZ 1, 3, 1924 BI 1, 2, 3, 4
Mentz, H (N) 2004 I1, W1(R)
Merry, J (EP) 1891 BI 1
Metcalf, H D (Bor) 1903 BI 2
Meyer, C du P (WP) 1921 NZ 1, 2, 3
Meyer, P J (GW) 1896 BI 1
Meyer, W (OFS, GL) 1997 S (R), 1999 It 2, NZ 1(R), A 1(R), 2000 C (R), E 1, NZ 1(R), 2(R), Arg, I, W, E 3, 2001 F 1(R), 2, It 1, F 3(R), It 2, E, US (t+R), 2002 W 1, 2, Arg, NZ 1, 2, A 2, F
Michau, J M (Tvl) 1921 NZ 1
Michau, J P (WP) 1921 NZ 1, 2, 3
Millar, W A (WP) 1906 E, 1910 BI 2, 3, 1912 I, W, 1913 F
Mills, W J (WP) 1910 BI 2
Moll, T (Tvl) 1910 BI 2
Montini, P E (WP) 1956 A 1, 2
Montgomery, P C (WP, Newport, N, Perpignan) 1997 BI 2, 3, NZ 1, A 1, NZ 2, A 2, F 1, 2, E, S, 1998 I 1, 2, W 1, E 1, A 1, NZ 1, 2, A 2, W 2, S, I 3, E 2, 1999 It 1, 2, W, NZ 1, A 1, NZ 2, A 2, [S, U, E, A 3, NZ 3], 2000 C, E 1, 2, A 1, NZ 1, A 2(R), Arg, I, W, E 3, 2001 F 1, 2(t), It 1, NZ 1, F 3(R), It 2(R), 2004 I2, W1, PI, NZ1, A1, NZ2, A2, W2, I3, E, S, 2005 U, F1, 2, A1, 2, 3, NZ1, A4, NZ2, Arg, W, F3, 2006 S1, 2, F, A1, NZ1, A2, NZ2, 2007 E1, 2, Sm(R), A1, NZ1, Nm, S, [Sm, E1, Tg(R), US, Fj, Arg, E2], 2008 W1(R), 2(R), NZ1(R), 2, Arg(R), NZ3, A2(R), 3(R)
Moolman, L C (NT) 1977 Wld, 1980 S Am 1, 2, BI 1, 2, 3, 4, S Am 3, 4, F, 1981 I 1, 2, NZ 1, 2, 3, US, 1982 S Am 1, 2, 1984 S Am 1, 2, 1986 Cv 1, 2, 3, 4
Mordt, R H (Z-R, NT) 1980 S Am 1, 2, BI 1, 2, 3, 4, S Am 3, 4, F, 1981 I 2, NZ 1, 2, 3, US, 1982 S Am 1, 2, 1984 S Am 1, 2
Morkel, D A (Tvl) 1903 BI 1
Morkel, D F T (Tvl) 1906 I, E, 1910 BI 1, 3, 1912 S, I, W, 1913 E, F
Morkel, H J (WP) 1921 NZ 1
Morkel, H W (WP) 1921 NZ 1, 2
Morkel, J A (WP) 1921 NZ 2, 3
Morkel, J W H (WP) 1912 S, I, W, 1913 E, F
Morkel, P G (WP) 1912 S, I, W, 1913 E, F, 1921 NZ 1, 2, 3
Morkel, P K (WP) 1928 NZ 4
Morkel, W H (WP) 1910 BI 3, 1912 S, I, W, 1913 E, F, 1921 NZ 1, 2, 3
Morkel, W S (Tvl) 1906 S, I, W, E
Moss, C (N) 1949 NZ 1, 2, 3, 4
Mostert, G (Stade Français) 2011 NZ1, A2(R)
Mostert, P J (WP) 1921 NZ 1, 2, 3, 1924 BI 1, 2, 4, 1928 NZ 1, 2, 3, 4, 1931 W, I, 1932 E, S
Mtawarira, T (NS) 2008 W2, It, A1(R), Arg, NZ3, A2, 3, W3, S, E, 2009 BI 1, 2, 3, NZ1, 2, A1, 2, 3, NZ3, F, It(R), I, 2010 I, W2, S, E, 2011 A2, NZ2(R), [W, Fj(R), Nm(R), Sm]
Muir, D J (WP) 1997 It, F 1, 2, E, S
Mujati, B V (WP) 2008 W1, It(R), NZ1(R), 2(t), A1(R), Arg(R), NZ3(R), A2(R), 3, W3(t), S(R), E(R)
Mulder, J C (Tvl, GL) 1994 NZ 2, 3, S, W, 1995 WS, [A, WS, F, NZ], W, It, E, 1996 Fj, A 1, NZ 1, A 2, NZ 2, 5, Arg 1, 2, F 1, 2, W, 1997 Tg, BI 1, 1999 It 1(R), 2, W, NZ 1, 2000 C(R), A 1, E 3, 2001 F 1, It 1
Muller, G H (WP) 1969 A 3, 4, S, 1970 W, NZ 1, 2, 3, 4, 1971 F 1, 2, 1972 E, 1974 BI 1, 3, 4

Muller, G J (NS, Ulster) 2006 S1(R), NZ1(R), A2, NZ2, 3, A3, I(R), E1, 2, 2007 E1(R), 2(R), Sm(R), A1(R), NZ1(R), A2, NZ2, Nm(R), [Sm(R), E1(R), Fj(t&R), Arg(t&R)], W, 2009 BI 3, 2011 [W(R)]
Muller, G P (GL) 2003 A 2, NZ 2, [E, Gg(R), Sm, NZ]
Muller, H L (OFS) 1986 Cv 4(R), 1989 Wld 1(R)
Muller, H S V (Tvl) 1949 NZ 1, 2, 3, 4, 1951 S, I, W, 1952 E, F, 1953 A 1, 2, 3, 4
Muller, L J J (N) 1992 NZ, A
Muller, P G (N) 1992 NZ, A, F 1, 2, E, 1993 F 1, 2, A 1, 2, 3, Arg 1, 2, 1994 E 1, 2, NZ 1, S, W, 1998 I 1, 2, W 1, E 1, A 1, NZ 1, 2, A 2, 1999 It 1, W, NZ 1, A 1, [Sp, E, A 3, NZ 3]
Murray, W M (N) 2007 Sm, A2, NZ2
Mvovo, L N (NS) 2010 S, E, 2011 A1, NZ1
Myburgh, F R (EP) 1896 BI 1
Myburgh, J L (NT) 1962 BI 1, 1963 A 4, 1964 W, F, 1968 BI 1, 2, 3, F 1, 2, 1969 A 1, 2, 3, 4, E, 1970 I, W, NZ 3, 4
Myburgh, W H (WT) 1924 BI 1

Naude, J P (WP) 1963 A 4, 1965 A 1, 2, NZ 1, 3, 4, 1967 F 1, 2, 3, 4, 1968 BI 1, 2, 3, 4
Ndungane, A Z (BB) 2006 A1, 2, NZ2, 3, A3, E1, 2, 2007 E2, Nm(R), [US], W(R)
Ndungane, O M (NS) 2008 It, NZ1, A3, 2009 BI 3, A3, NZ3, 2010 W1, 2011 NZ1(R), [Fj]
Neethling, J B (WP) 1967 F 1, 2, 3, 4, 1968 BI 4, 1969 S, 1970 NZ 1, 2
Nel, J A (Tvl) 1960 NZ 1, 2, 1963 A 1, 2, 1965 A 2, NZ 1, 2, 3, 4, 1970 NZ 3, 4
Nel, J J (WP) 1956 A 1, 2, NZ 1, 2, 3, 4, 1958 F 1, 2
Nel, P A R O (Tvl) 1903 BI 1, 2, 3
Nel, P J (N) 1928 NZ 1, 2, 3, 4, 1931 W, I, 1932 E, S, 1933 A 1, 3, 4, 5, 1937 A 1, 2, NZ 2, 3
Nimb, C F (WP) 1961 I
Nokwe, J L (FS) 2008 Arg, A2, 3, 2009 BI 3
Nomis, S H (Tvl) 1967 F 4, 1968 BI 1, 2, 3, 4, F 1, 2, 1969 A 1, 2, 3, 4, S, E, 1970 I, W, NZ 1, 2, 3, 4, 1971 F 1, 2, A 1, 2, 3, 1972 E
Nykamp, J L (Tvl) 1933 A 2

Ochse, J K (WP) 1951 I, W, 1952 E, F, 1953 A 1, 2, 4
Oelofse, J S A (Tvl) 1953 A 1, 2, 3, 4
Oliver, J F (Tvl) 1928 NZ 3, 4
Olivier, E (WP) 1967 F 1, 2, 3, 4, 1968 BI 1, 2, 3, 4, F 1, 2, 1969 A 1, 2, 3, 4, S, E
Olivier, J (NT) 1992 F 1, 2, E, 1993 F 1, 2 A 1, 2, 3, Arg 1, 1995 W, It (R), E, 1996 Arg 1, 2, F 1, 2, W
Olivier, W (BB) 2006 S1(R), 2, F, A1, NZ1, A2, NZ2(R), 3, A3, I(R), E1, 2, 2007 E1, 2, NZ1(R), A2, NZ2, [E1(R), Tg, Arg(R)], W(R), 2009 BI 3, NZ1(R), 2(R), F(R), It(R), I, 2010 F, It2(R), NZ1, 2, A1, 2011 A1, NZ1(R)
Olver, E (EP) 1896 BI 1
Oosthuizen, J J (WP) 1974 BI 1, F 1, 2, 1975 F 1, 2, 1976 NZ 1, 2, 3, 4
Oosthuizen, O W (NT, Tvl) 1981 I 1(R), 2, NZ 2, 3, US, 1982 S Am 1, 2, 1984 E 1, 2
Osler, B L (WP) 1924 BI 1, 2, 3, 4, 1928 NZ 1, 2, 3, 4, 1931 W, I, 1932 E, S, 1933 A 1, 2, 3, 4, 5
Osler, S G (WP) 1928 NZ 1
Otto, K (NT, BB) 1995 [R, C (R), WS (R)], 1997 BI 3, NZ 1, A 1, NZ 2, It, F 1, 2, E, S, 1998 I 1, 2, W 1, E 1, A 1, NZ 1, 2, A 2, W 2, S, I 3, E 2, 1999 It 1, W, NZ 1, A 1, [S (R), Sp, U, E, A 3, NZ 3], 2000 C, E 1, 2, A 1
Oxlee, K (N) 1960 NZ 1, 2, 3, 4, W, I, 1961 S, A 1, 2, 1962 BI 1, 2, 3, 4, 1963 A 1, 2, 4, 1964 W, 1965 NZ 1, 2

Pagel, G L (WP) 1995 [A (R), R, C, NZ (R)], 1996 NZ 5(R)
Parker, W H (EP) 1965 A 1, 2
Partridge, J E C (Tvl) 1903 BI 1
Paulse, B J (WP) 1999 It 1, 2, NZ 1, A 1, 2(R), [S (R), Sp, NZ 3], 2000 C, E 1, 2, A 1, NZ 1, A 2, NZ 2, A 3, Arg, W, E 3, 2001 F 1, 2, It 1, NZ 1, A 1, 2, NZ 2, F 3, It 2, E, 2002 W 1, 2, Arg, Sm (R), A 1, NZ 2, A 2, F, S, E, 2003 [Gg], 2004 I1, 2, W1, PI, NZ1, A1, NZ2, A2, W2, I3, E, 2005 A2, 3, NZ1, A4, F3, 2006 S1, 2, A1(R), NZ1, 3(R), A3(R), 2007 A2, NZ2
Payn, C (N) 1924 BI 1, 2
Pelser, H J M (Tvl) 1958 F 1, 1960 NZ 1, 2, 3, 4, W, I, 1961 F, I, A 1, 2
Pfaff, B D (WP) 1956 A 1
Pickard, J A J (WP) 1953 A 3, 4, 1956 NZ 2, 1958 F 2
Pienaar, J F (Tvl) 1993 F 1, 2, A 1, 2, 3, Arg 1, 2, 1994 E 1, 2, NZ 2, 3, Arg 1, 2, S, W, 1995 WS, [A, C, WS, F, NZ], W, It, E, 1996 Fj, A 1, NZ 1, A 2, NZ 2
Pienaar, R (NS, Ulster) 2006 NZ2(R), 3(R), A3(R), I(t), E1(R), 2007 E1(R), 2(R), Sm(R), A1, NZ1, A2, NZ2, Nm(R), S(R), [E1(t&R), Tg, US(R), Arg(R)], W, 2008 W1(R), It(R), NZ2(R), A1(R), 3(R), W3, S, E, 2009 BI 1, 2, 3(R), NZ1, A1(R), 2, 3, It(R), I(R), 2010 W1, F(R), It 1(R), 2(R), NZ1(R), 2(R), A1, I, W2, S(R), E, 2011 A1, NZ1, [Fj(R), Nm(R)]
Pienaar, Z M J (OFS) 1980 S Am 2(R), BI 1, 2, 3, 4, S Am 3, 4, F, 1981 I 1, 2, NZ 1, 2, 3
Pietersen, J-P R (NS) 2006 A3, 2007 Sm, A1, NZ1, A2, NZ2, Nm, S, [Sm, E1, Tg, US(R), Fj, Arg, E2], W, 2008 NZ2, A1, Arg, NZ3, A2, W3, S, E, 2009 BI 1, 2, NZ1, 2, A1, 2, F, It, I, 2010 NZ3, A2, 3, 2011 A2, NZ2, [W, Fj, Sm, A]
Pitzer, G (NT) 1967 F 1, 2, 3, 4, 1968 BI 1, 2, 3, 4, F 1, 2, 1969 A 3, 4
Pope, C F (WP) 1974 BI 1, 2, 3, 4, 1975 F 1, 2, 1976 NZ 2, 3, 4
Potgieter, D J (BB) 2009 I(t), 2010 W1, F(t&R), It 1, 2(R), A1(R)
Potgieter, H J (OFS) 1928 NZ 1, 2
Potgieter, H L (OFS) 1977 Wld
Powell, A W (GW) 1896 BI 3
Powell, J M (GW) 1891 BI 2, 1896 BI 3, 1903 BI 1, 2
Prentis, R B (Tvl) 1980 S Am 1, 2, BI 1, 2, 3, 4, S Am 3, 4, F, 1981 I 1, 2
Pretorius, A S (GL) 2002 W 1, 2, Arg, Sm, NZ 1, A 1, NZ 2, F, S (R), E, 2003 NZ 1(R), A 1, 2005 A2, 3, NZ1, A4, NZ2, Arg, 2006 NZ2(R), 3, A3, I, E1(t&R), 2, 2007 S(R), [Sm(R), E1(R), Tg, US(R), Arg(R)], W
Pretorius, J C (GL) 2006 I, 2007 NZ2
Pretorius, N F (Tvl) 1928 NZ 1, 2, 3, 4
Prinsloo, J (Tvl) 1958 F 1, 2
Prinsloo, J (NT) 1963 A 3
Prinsloo, J P (Tvl) 1928 NZ 1
Putter, D J (WT) 1963 A 1, 2, 4

Raaff, J W E (GW) 1903 BI 1, 2, 1906 S, W, E, 1910 BI 1
Ralepelle, M C (BB) 2006 NZ2(R), E2(R), 2008 E(t&R), 2009 BI 3, NZ1(R), 2(R), A2(R), NZ3(R), 2010 W1(R), F(R), It 1, 2(R) , NZ1(R), 2(R), A1(R), 2(R), 3(R), W2(R), 2011 A1(R), NZ1(R), [Nm(R)]
Ras, W J de Wet (OFS) 1976 NZ 1(R), 1980 S Am 2(R)
Rautenbach, S J (WP) 2002 W 1(R), 2(t+R), Arg (R), Sm, NZ 1(R), A 1, NZ 2(R), A 2(R), 2003 [U(R), Gg, Sm, NZ], 2004 W1, NZ1(R)
Reece-Edwards, H (N) 1992 F 1, 2, 1993 A 2
Reid, A (WP) 1903 BI 3
Reid, B C (Bor) 1933 A 4
Reinach, J (OFS) 1986 Cv 1, 2, 3, 4
Rens, I J (Tvl) 1953 A 3, 4
Retief, D F (NT) 1955 BI 1, 2, 4, 1956 A 1, 2, NZ 1, 2, 3, 4
Reyneke, H J (WP) 1910 BI 3
Richards, A R (WP) 1891 BI 1, 2, 3
Richter, A (NT) 1992 F 1, 2, E, 1994 E 2, NZ 1, 2, 3, 1995 [R, C, WS (R)]
Riley, N M (ET) 1963 A 3
Riordan, C A (Tvl) 1910 BI 1, 2
Robertson, I W (R) 1974 F 1, 2, 1976 NZ 1, 2, 4
Rodgers, P H (NT, Tvl) 1989 Wld 1, 2, 1992 NZ, F 1, 2
Rogers, C D (Tvl) 1984 E 1, 2, S Am 1, 2
Roos, G D (WP) 1910 BI 2, 3
Roos, P J (WP) 1903 BI 3, 1906 I, W, E
Rosenberg, W (Tvl) 1955 BI 2, 3, 4, 1956 NZ 3, 1958 F 1
Rossouw, C L C (Tvl, N) 1995 WS, [R, WS, F, NZ], 1999 NZ 2(R), A 2(t), [Sp, NZ 3(R)]
Rossouw, D H (WP) 1953 A 3, 4
Rossouw, D J (BB) 2003 [U, Gg, Sm(R), NZ], 2004 E(R), S, Arg, 2005 U, F1, 2, A1, W(R), F3(R), 2006 S1, 2, F, A1, I, E1, 2, 2007 E1, Sm, A1(R), NZ1, S, [Sm, E1, Tg, Fj, Arg, E2], 2008 W1(t&R), NZ3(R), A3(R), S(R), E, 2009 BI 1(R),

2(R), NZ1(R), 2(R), A1(R), 3(R), NZ3(R), F(R), It, I, 2010 W1, F, NZ1(R), 2, A1, NZ3(t&R), A2(R), 3, 2011 A1, NZ1, A2, NZ2(t&R), [W, Fj, Nm, Sm, A]

Rossouw, P W G (WP) 1997 BI 2, 3, NZ 1, A 1, NZ 2(R), A 2(R), It, F 1, 2, E, S, 1998 I 1, 2, W 1, E 1, A 1, NZ 1, 2, A 2, W 2, S, I 3, E 2, 1999 It 1, W, NZ 1, A 1(R), NZ 2, A 2, [S, U, E, A 3], 2000 C, E 1, 2, A 2, Arg (R), I, W, 2001 F 3, US, 2003 Arg

Rousseau, W P (WP) 1928 NZ 3, 4

Roux, F du T (WP) 1960 W, 1961 A 1, 2, 1962 BI 1, 2, 3, 4, 1963 A 2, 1965 A 1, 2, NZ 1, 2, 3, 4, 1968 BI 3, 4, F 1, 2 1969 A 1, 2, 3, 4, 1970 I, NZ 1, 2, 3, 4

Roux, J P (Tvl) 1994 E 2, NZ 1, 2, 3, Arg 1, 1995 [R, C, F (R)], 1996 A 1(R), NZ 1, A 2, NZ 3

Roux, O A (NT) 1969 S, E, 1970 I, W, 1972 E, 1974 BI 3, 4

Roux, W G (BB) 2002 F (R), S, E

Russell, R B (MP, N) 2002 W 1(R), 2, Arg, A 1(R), NZ 2(R), A 2, F, E (R), 2003 Arg (R), A 1(R), NZ 1, A 2(R), 2004 I2(t&R), W1, NZ1(R), W2(R), Arg(R), 2005 U(R), F2(R), A1(t), Arg(R), W(R), 2006 F

Samuels, T A (GW) 1896 BI 2, 3, 4

Santon, D (Bol) 2003 A 1(R), NZ 1(R), A 2(t), [Gg(R)]

Sauermann, J T (Tvl) 1971 F 1, 2, A 1, 1972 E, 1974 BI 1

Schlebusch, J J J (OFS) 1974 BI 3, 4, 1975 F 2

Schmidt, L U (NT) 1958 F 2, 1962 BI 2

Schmidt, U L (NT, Tvl) 1986 Cv 1, 2, 3, 4, 1989 Wld 1, 2, 1992 NZ, A, 1993 F 1, 2, A 1, 2, 3, 1994 Arg 1, 2, S, W

Schoeman, J (WP) 1963 A 3, 4, 1965 I, S, A 1, NZ 1, 2

Scholtz, C P (WP, Tvl) 1994 Arg 1, 1995 [R, C, WS]

Scholtz, H (FS) 2002 A 1(R), NZ 2(R), A 2(R), 2003 [U(R), Gg]

Scholtz, H H (WP) 1921 NZ 1, 2

Schutte, P J W (Tvl) 1994 S, W

Scott, P A (Tvl) 1896 BI 1, 2, 3, 4

Sendin, W D (GW) 1921 NZ 2

Sephaka, L D (GL) 2001 US, 2002 Sm, NZ 1, A 1, NZ 2, A 2, F, 2003 S 1, 2, A 1, NZ 1, A 2(t+R), NZ 2, [U, E(t&R), Gg], 2005 F2, A1, 2(R), W, 2006 S1(R), NZ3(t&R), A3(R), I

Serfontein, D J (WP) 1980 BI 1, 2, 3, 4, S Am 3, 4, F, 1981 I 1, 2, NZ 1, 2, 3, US, 1982 S Am 1, 2, 1984 E 1, 2, S Am 1, 2

Shand, R (GW) 1891 BI 2, 3

Sheriff, A R (Tvl) 1938 BI 1, 2, 3

Shimange, M H (FS, WP) 2004 W1(R), NZ2(R), A2(R), W2(R), 2005 U(R), A1(R), 2(R), Arg(R), 2006 S1(R)

Shum, E H (Tvl) 1913 E

Sinclair, D J (Tvl) 1955 BI 1, 2, 3, 4

Sinclair, J H (Tvl) 1903 BI 1

Skene, A L (WP) 1958 F 2

Skinstad, R B (WP, GL, N) 1997 E (t), 1998 W 1(R), E 1(t), NZ 1(R), 2(R), A 2(R), W 2(R), S, I 3, E 2, 1999 [S, Sp (R), U, E, A 3], 2001 F 1(R), 2(R), It 1, NZ 1, A 1, 2, NZ 2, F 3, It 2, E, 2002 W 1, 2, Arg, Sm, NZ 1, A 1, NZ 2, A 2, 2003 Arg (R), 2007 E2(t&R), Sm, NZ1, A2, [E1(R), Tg, US(R), Arg(R)]

Slater, J T (EP) 1924 BI 3, 4, 1928 NZ 1

Smal, G P (WP) 1986 Cv 1, 2, 3, 4, 1989 Wld 1, 2

Small, J T (Tvl, N, WP) 1992 NZ, A, F 1, 2, E, 1993 F 1, 2, A 1, 2, 3, Arg 1, 2, 1994 E 1, 2, NZ 1, 2, 3(t), Arg 1, 1995 WS, [A, R, F, NZ], W, It, E (R), 1996 Fj, A 1, NZ 1, A 2, NZ 2, Arg 1, 2, F 1, 2, W, 1997 Tg, BI 1, NZ 1(R), A 1(R), NZ 2, A 2, It, F 1, 2, E, S

Smit, F C (WP) 1992 E

Smit, J W (NS, Clermont-Auvergne) 2000 C (t), A 1(R), NZ 1(t+R), A 2(R), NZ 2(R), A 3(R), Arg, I, W, E 3, 2001 F 1, 2, It 1, NZ 1(R), A 1(R), 2(R), NZ 2(R), F 3(R), It 2, E, US (R), 2003 [U(R), E(t&R), Gg, Sm, NZ], 2004 I1, 2, W1, PI, NZ1, A1, NZ2, A2, W2, I3, E, S, Arg, 2005 U, F1, 2, A1, 2, 3, NZ1, A4, NZ2, Arg, W, F3, 2006 S1, 2, F, A1, NZ1, A2, NZ2, 3, A3, I, E1, 2, 2007 E1, 2, Sm, A1, [Sm, E1, Tg(R), US, Fj, Arg, E2], W, 2008 W1, 2, NZ1, W3, S, E, 2009 BI 1, 2, 3, NZ1, 2, A1, 2, 3, NZ3, F, It, I, 2010 W1, F, It 2, NZ1, 2, A1, NZ3, A2, 3, 2011 A1, NZ1, A2, NZ2(R), [W, Fj, Nm, Sm(R), A]

Smith, C M (OFS) 1963 A 3, 4, 1964 W, F, 1965 A 1, 2, NZ 2

Smith, C W (GW) 1891 BI 2, 1896 BI 2, 3

Smith, D (GW) 1891 BI 2

Smith D J (Z-R) 1980 BI 1, 2, 3, 4

Smith, G A C (EP) 1938 BI 3

Smith, J H (FS) 2003 S 1(R), 2(R), A 1, NZ 1, A 2, NZ 2, [U, E, Sm, NZ], 2004 W2, 2005 U(R), F2(R), A2, 3, NZ1, A4, NZ2, Arg, W, F3, 2006 S1, 2, F, A1, NZ1, A2, I, E2, 2007 E1, 2, A1, Nm, S, [Sm, E1, Tg(t&R), US, Fj, Arg, E2], W, 2008 W1, 2, It, NZ1, 2, A1, Arg, NZ3, A2, 3, W3, S, 2009 BI 1, 2, 3, NZ1, 2, A1, 2, 3, 2010 NZ3, A2, 3, I, W2, S, E

Smith, P F (GW) 1997 S (R), 1998 I 1(t), 2, W 1, NZ 1(R), 2(R), A 2(R), W 2, 1999 NZ 2

Smollan, F C (Tvl) 1933 A 3, 4, 5

Snedden, R C D (GW) 1891 BI 2

Snyman, A H (NT, BB, N) 1996 NZ 3, 4, Arg 2(R), W (R), 1997 Tg, BI 1, 2, 3, NZ 1, A 1, NZ 2, A 2, It, F 1, 2, E, S, 1998 I 1, 2, W 1, E 1, A 1, NZ 1, 2, A 2, W 2, S, I 3, E 2, 1999 NZ 2, 2001 NZ 2, F 3, US, 2002 W 1, 2003 S 1, NZ 1, 2006 S1, 2

Snyman, D S L (WP) 1972 E, 1974 BI 1, 2(R), F 1, 2, 1975 F 1, 2, 1976 NZ 2, 3, 1977 Wld

Snyman, J C P (OFS) 1974 BI 2, 3, 4

Sonnekus, G H H (OFS) 1974 BI 3, 1984 E 1, 2

Sowerby, R S (N) 2002 Sm (R)

Spies, J J (NT) 1970 NZ 1, 2, 3, 4

Spies, P J (BB) 2006 A1, NZ2, 3, A3, I, E1, 2007 E1(R), 2, A1, 2008 W1, 2, A1, Arg, NZ3, A2, 3, W3, S, E, 2009 BI 1, 2, 3(R), NZ1, 2, A1, 2, 3, NZ3, 2010 F, It 1, 2, NZ1, 2, A1, NZ3, A2, 3, I, W2, E, 2011 A2, NZ2, [W, Fj, Nm, Sm, A]

Stander, J C J (OFS) 1974 BI 4(R), 1976 NZ 1, 2, 3, 4

Stapelberg, W P (NT) 1974 F 1, 2

Starke, J J (WP) 1956 NZ 4

Starke, K T (WP) 1924 BI 1, 2, 3, 4

Steenekamp, J G A (Tvl) 1958 F 1

Steenkamp, G G (FS, BB) 2004 S, Arg, 2005 U, F2(R), A2, 3, NZ1(R), A4(R), 2007 E1(R), 2, A1, [Tg, Fj(R)], 2008 W1, 2(R), NZ1, 2, A1, W3(R), S(R), 2009 BI 1(R), 3(R), 2010 F, It 1, 2, NZ1, 2, A1, NZ3, A2, 3, 2011 A2(R), NZ2, [W(R), Fj, Nm, Sm(R), A]

Stegmann, A C (WP) 1906 S, I

Stegmann, G J (BB) 2010 I, W2, S, E, 2011 A1, NZ1

Stegmann, J A (Tvl) 1912 S, I, W, 1913 E, F

Stewart, C (WP) 1998 S, I 3, E 2

Stewart, D A (WP) 1960 S, 1961 E, S, F, I, 1963 A 1, 3, 4, 1964 W, F, 1965 I

Steyn, F P L (NS, Racing Metro) 2006 I, E1, 2, 2007 E1(R), 2(R), Sm, A1(R), NZ1(R), S, [Sm(R), E1, Tg(R), US, Fj, Arg, E2], W, 2008 W2(R), It, NZ1(R), 2(R), A1, NZ3(R), A2(R), W3(R), S(R), E(R), 2009 BI 1, 2, 3(t&R), NZ1, 2, A1, 2(R), 3(R), NZ3, 2010 W1, A2, 3, W2, S, E, 2011 A2, [W, Fj, Nm, Sm]

Steyn, M (BB) 2009 BI 1(t&R), 2(R), 3, NZ1(R), 2, A1, 2, 3, NZ3, F, It, I, 2010 F, It 1, 2, NZ1, 2, A1, NZ3, A2, 3, I, W2, S, E, 2011 A1, NZ1, A2(R), NZ2, [W, Fj, Nm, Sm, A]

Stofberg, M T S (OFS, NT, WP) 1976 NZ 2, 3, 1977 Wld, 1980 S Am 1, 2, BI 1, 2, 3, 4, S Am 3, 4, F, 1981 I 1, 2, NZ 1, 2, US, 1982 S Am 1, 2, 1984 E 1, 2

Strachan, L C (Tvl) 1932 E, S, 1937 A 1, 2, NZ 1, 2, 3, 1938 BI 1, 2, 3

Stransky, J T (N, WP) 1993 A 1, 2, 3, Arg 1, 1994 Arg 1, 2, 1995 WS, [A, R (t), C, F, NZ], W, It, E, 1996 Fj (R), NZ 1, A 2, NZ 2, 3, 4, 5(R)

Straeuli, R A W (Tvl) 1994 NZ 1, Arg 1, 2, S, W, 1995 WS, [A, WS, NZ (R)], E (R)

Strauss, C P (WP) 1992 F 1, 2, E, 1993 F 1, 2, A 1, 2, 3, Arg 1, 2, 1994 E 1, NZ 1, 2, Arg 1, 2

Strauss, J A (WP) 1984 S Am 1, 2

Strauss, J A (FS) 2008 A1(R), Arg(R), NZ3(R), A2(R), 3(R), 2009 F(R), It, 2010 S(R), E(R)

Strauss, J H P (Tvl) 1976 NZ 3, 4, 1980 S Am 1

Strauss, S S F (GW) 1921 NZ 3

Strydom, C F (OFS) 1955 BI 3, 1956 A 1, 2, NZ 1, 4, 1958 F 1, **Strydom, J J** (Tvl, GL) 1993 F 2, A 1, 2, 3, Arg 1, 2, 1994 E 1, 1995 [A, C, F, NZ], 1996 A 2(R), NZ 2(R), 3, 4, W (R), 1997 Tg, BI 1, 2, 3, A 2

Strydom, L J (NT) 1949 NZ 1, 2

Styger, J J (OFS) 1992 NZ (R), A, F 1, 2, E, 1993 F 2(R), A 3(R)

Suter, M R (N) 1965 I, S
Swanepoel, W (OFS, GL) 1997 BI 3(R), A 2(R), F 1(R), 2, E, S, 1998 I 2(R), W 1(R), E 2(R), 1999 It 1, 2(R), W, A 1, [Sp, NZ 3(t)], 2000 A 1, NZ 1, A 2, NZ 2, A 3
Swart, J (WP) 1996 Fj, NZ 1(R), A 2, NZ 2, 3, 4, 5, 1997 BI 3(R), It, S (R)
Swart, J J N (SWA) 1955 BI 1
Swart, I S (Tvl) 1993 A 1, 2, 3, Arg 1, 1994 E 1, 2, NZ 1, 3, Arg 2(R), 1995 WS, [A, WS, F, NZ], W, 1996 A 2

Taberer, W S (GW) 1896 BI 2
Taylor, O B (N) 1962 BI 1
Terblanche, C S (Bol, N) 1998 I 1, 2, W 1, E 1, A 1, NZ 1, 2, A 2, W 2, S, I 3, E 2, 1999 It 1(R), 2, W, A 1, NZ 2(R), [Sp, E (R), A 3(R), NZ 3], 2000 E 3, 2002 W 1, 2, Arg, Sm, NZ 1, A 1, 2(R), 2003 S 1, 2, Arg, A 1, NZ 1, A 2, NZ 2, [Gg]
Teichmann, G H (N) 1995 W, 1996 Fj, A 1, NZ 1, A 2, NZ 2, 3, 4, 5, Arg 1, 2, F 1, 2, W, 1997 Tg, BI 1, 2, 3, NZ 1, A 1, NZ 2, A 2, It, F 1, 2 E, S, 1998 I 1, 2, W 1, E 1, A 1, NZ 1, 2, A 2, W 2, S, I 3, E 2, 1999 It 1, W, NZ 1
Theron, D F (GW) 1996 A 2(R), NZ 2(R), 5, Arg 1, 2, F 1, 2, W, 1997 BI 2(R), 3, NZ 1(R), A 1, NZ 2(R)
Theunissen, D J (GW) 1896 BI 3
Thompson, G (WP) 1912 S, I, W
Tindall, J C (WP) 1924 BI 1, 1928 NZ 1, 2, 3, 4
Tobias, E G (SARF, Bol) 1981 I 1, 2, 1984 E 1, 2, S Am 1, 2
Tod, N S (N) 1928 NZ 2
Townsend, W H (N) 1921 NZ 1
Trenery, W E (GW) 1891 BI 2
Tromp, H (NT) 1996 NZ3, 4, Arg 2(R), F 1(R)
Truter, D R (WP) 1924 BI 2, 4
Truter, J T (N) 1963 A 1, 1964 F, 1965 A 2
Turner, F G (EP) 1933 A 1, 2, 3, 1937 A 1, 2, NZ 1, 2, 3, 1938 BI 1, 2, 3
Twigge, R J (NT) 1960 S
Tyibilika, S (N) 2004 S, Arg, 2005 U, A2, Arg, 2006 NZ1, A2, NZ2

Ulyate, C A (Tvl) 1955 BI 1, 2, 3, 4, 1956 NZ 1, 2, 3
Uys, P de W (NT) 1960 W, 1961 E, S, I, A 1, 2, 1962 BI 1, 4, 1963 A 1, 2, 1969 A 1(R), 2
Uys, P J (Pumas) 2002 S

Van Aswegen, H J (WP) 1981 NZ 1, 1982 S Am 2(R)
Van Biljon, L (N) 2001 It 1(R), NZ 1, A 1, 2, NZ 2, F 3, It 2(R), E (R), US, 2002 F (R), S, E (R), 2003 NZ 2(R)
Van Broekhuizen, H D (WP) 1896 BI 4
Van Buuren, M C (Tvl) 1891 BI 1
Van de Vyver, D F (WP) 1937 A 2
Van den Berg, D S (N) 1975 F 1, 2, 1976 NZ 1, 2
Van den Berg, M A (WP) 1937 A 1, NZ 1, 2, 3
Van den Berg, P A (WP, GW, N) 1999 It 1(R), 2, NZ 2, A 2, [S, U (t+R), E (R), A 3(R), NZ 3(R)], 2000 E 1(R), A 1, NZ 1, A 2, NZ 2(R), A 3(t+R), Arg, I, W, E 3, 2001 F 1(R), 2, A 2(R), NZ 2(R), US, 2004 NZ1, 2005 U, F1, 2, A1(R), 2(R), 3(R), 4(R), Arg(R), F3(R), 2006 S2(R), A1(R), NZ1, A2(R), NZ2(R), A3(R), I, E1(R), 2(R), 2007 Sm, A2(R), NZ2, Nm(t&R), S(R), [Tg, US], W(R)
Van den Bergh, E (EP) 1994 Arg 2(t & R)
Van der Linde, A (WP) 1995 It, E, 1996 Arg 1(R), 2(R), F 1(R), W (R), 2001 F 3(R)
Van der Linde, C J (FS, Leinster, WP, GL) 2002 S (R), E(R), 2004 I1(R), 2(R), PI(R), A1(R), NZ2(t&R), A2(R), W2(R), I3(R), E(t&R), S, Arg, 2005 U, F1(R), 2, A1(R), 3, NZ1, A4, NZ2, Arg, W, F3, 2006 S2(R), F(R), A1, NZ1, A2, NZ2, I, E1, 2, 2007 E1(R), 2, A1(R), NZ1(R), A2, NZ2, Nm, S, [Sm, E1(R), Tg, US(R), Arg, E2], W, 2008 W1(t&R), It, NZ1, 2, A1, Arg, NZ3, A2, 2009 F(R), I(t), 2010 W1, It1(R) , NZ2, A1(t&R), NZ3(R), A2(R), 3(R), I(R), W2(R), S(R), E(R), 2011 A1(t&R), NZ1(R), 2(R), [Nm]
Van der Merwe, A J (Bol) 1955 BI 2, 3, 4, 1956 A 1, 2, NZ 1, 2, 3, 4, 1958 F 1, 1960 S, NZ 2
Van der Merwe, A V (WP) 1931 W
Van der Merwe, B S (NT) 1949 NZ 1
Van der Merwe, H S (NT) 1960 NZ 4, 1963 A 2, 3, 4, 1964 F
Van der Merwe, H S (GL) 2007 W(t+R)
Van der Merwe, J P (WP) 1970 W
Van der Merwe, P R (SWD, WT, GW) 1981 NZ 2, 3, US, 1986 Cv 1, 2, 1989 Wld 1
Van der Merwe, P R (BB) 2010 F(R), It 2(R), A1(R), NZ3, A2, 3(R), I(R), W2(R), S(R), E(R), 2011 A1
Vanderplank, B E (N) 1924 BI 3, 4
Van der Schyff, J H (GW) 1949 NZ 1, 2, 3, 4, 1955 BI 1
Van der Watt, A E (WP) 1969 S (R), E, 1970 I
Van der Westhuizen, J C (WP) 1928 NZ 2, 3, 4, 1931 I
Van der Westhuizen, J H (WP) 1931 I, 1932 E, S
Van der Westhuizen, J H (NT, BB) 1993 Arg 1, 2, 1994 E 1, 2(R), Arg 2, S, W, 1995 WS, [A, C (R), WS, F, NZ], W, It, E, 1996 Fj, A 1, 2(R), NZ 2, 3(R), 4, 5, Arg 1, 2, F 1, 2, W, 1997 Tg, BI 1, 2, 3, NZ 1, A 1, NZ 2, A 2, It, F 1, 1998 I 1, 2, W 1, E 1, A 1, NZ 1, 2, A 2, W 2, S, I 3, E 2, 1999 NZ 2, A 2, [S, Sp (R), U, E, A 3, NZ 3], 2000 C, E 1, 2, A 1(R), NZ 1(R), A 2(R), Arg, I, W, E 3, 2001 F 1, 2, It 1(R), NZ 1, A 1, 2, NZ 2, F 3, It 2, E, US (R), 2003 S 1, 2, A 1, NZ 1, A 2(R), NZ 2, [U, E, Sm, NZ]
Van der Westhuyzen, J N B (MP, BB) 2000 NZ 2(R), 2001 It 1(R), 2003 S 1(R), 2, Arg, A 1, 2003 [E, Sm, NZ], 2004 I1, 2, W1, PI, NZ1, A1, NZ2, A2, W2, I3, E, S, Arg, 2005 U, F1, 2, A1, 4(R), NZ2(R), 2006 S1, 2, F, A1
Van Druten, N J V (Tvl) 1924 BI 1, 2, 3, 4, 1928 NZ 1, 2, 3, 4
Van Heerden, A J (Tvl) 1921 NZ 1, 3
Van Heerden, F J (WP) 1994 E 1, 2(R), NZ 3, 1995 It, E, 1996 NZ 5(R), Arg 1(R), 2(R), 1997 Tg, BI 2(t+R), 3(R), NZ 1(R), 2(R), 1999 [Sp]
Van Heerden, J L (NT, Tvl) 1974 BI 3, 4, F 1, 2, 1975 F 1, 2, 1976 NZ 1, 2, 3, 4, 1977 Wld, 1980 BI 1, 3, 4, S Am 3, 4, F
Van Heerden, J L (BB) 2003 S 1, 2, A 1, NZ 1, A 2(t), 2007 A2, NZ2, S(R), [Sm(R), E1, Tg, US, Fj(R), E2(R)]
Van Jaarsveld, C J (Tvl) 1949 NZ 1
Van Jaarsveldt, D C (R) 1960 S
Van Niekerk, J A (WP) 1928 NZ 4
Van Niekerk, J C (GL, WP, Toulon) 2001 NZ 1(R), A 1(R), NZ 2(t+R), F 3(R), It2, US, 2002 W 1(R), 2(R), Arg (R), Sm, NZ 1, A 1, NZ 2, A 2, F, S, E, 2003 A 2, NZ 2, [U, E, Gg, Sm], 2004 NZ1(R), A1(t), NZ2, A2, W2, I3, E, S, Arg(R), 2005 U(R), F2(R), A1(R), 2, 3, NZ1, A4, NZ2, 2006 S1, 2, F, A1, NZ1(R), A2(R), 2008 It(R), NZ1, 2, Arg(R), A2(R), 2010 W1
Van Reenen, G L (WP) 1937 A 2, NZ 1
Van Renen, C G (WP) 1891 BI 3, 1896 BI 1, 4
Van Renen, W (WP) 1903 BI 1, 3
Van Rensburg, J T J (Tvl) 1992 NZ, A, E, 1993 F 1, 2, A 1, 1994 NZ 2
Van Rooyen, G W (Tvl) 1921 NZ 2, 3
Van Ryneveld, R C B (WP) 1910 BI 2, 3
Van Schalkwyk, D (NT) 1996 Fj (R), NZ 3, 4, 5, 1997 BI 2, 3, NZ 1, A 1
Van Schoor, R A M (R) 1949 NZ 2, 3, 4, 1951 S, I, W, 1952 E, F, 1953 A 1, 2, 3, 4
Van Straaten, A J J (WP) 1999 It 2(R), W, NZ 1(R), A 1, 2000 C, E 1, 2, NZ 1, A 2, NZ 2, A 3, Arg (R), I (R), W, E 3, 2001 A 1, 2, NZ 2, F 3, It 2, E
Van Vollenhoven, K T (NT) 1955 BI 1, 2, 3, 4, 1956 A 1, 2, NZ 3
Van Vuuren, T F (EP) 1912 S, I, W, 1913 E, F
Van Wyk, C J (Tvl) 1951 S, I, W, 1952 E, F, 1953 A 1, 2, 3, 4, 1955 BI 1
Van Wyk, J F B (NT) 1970 NZ 1, 2, 3, 4, 1971 F 1, 2, A 1, 2, 3, 1972 E, 1974 BI 1, 3, 4, 1976 NZ 3, 4
Van Wyk, S P (WP) 1928 NZ 1, 2
Van Zyl, B P (WP) 1961 I
Van Zyl, C G P (OFS) 1965 NZ 1, 2, 3, 4
Van Zyl, D J (WP) 2000 E 3(R)
Van Zyl, G H (WP) 1958 F 1, 1960 S, NZ 1, 2, 3, 4, W, I, 1961 E, S, F, I, A 1, 2, 1962 BI 1, 3, 4
Van Zyl, H J (Tvl) 1960 NZ 1, 2, 3, 4, I, 1961 E, S, I, A 1, 2
Van Zyl, P J (Bol) 1961 I
Veldsman, P E (WP) 1977 Wld
Venter, A G (OFS) 1996 NZ 3, 4, 5, Arg 1, 2, F 1, 2, W, 1997 Tg, BI 1, 2, 3, NZ 1, A 1, NZ 2, It, F 1, 2, E, S, 1998 I 1, 2, W 1, E 1, A 1, NZ 1, 2, A 2, W 2, S (R), I 3(R), E 2(R), 1999

It 1, 2(R), W (R), NZ 1, A 1, NZ 2, A 2, [S, U, E, A 3, NZ 3], 2000 C, E 1, 2, A 1, NZ 1, A 2, NZ 2, A 3, Arg, I, W, E 3, 2001 F 1, It 1, NZ 1, A 1, 2, NZ 2, F 3(R), It 2(R), E (t+R), US (R)

Venter, A J (N) 2000 W (R), E 3(R), 2001 F 3, It 2, E, US, 2002 W 1, 2, Arg, NZ 1(R), 2, A 2, F, S (R), E, 2003 Arg, 2004 PI, NZ1, A1, NZ2(R), A2, I3, E, 2006 NZ3, A3

Venter, B (OFS) 1994 E 1, 2, NZ 1, 2, 3, Arg 1, 2, 1995 [R, C, WS (R), NZ (R)], 1996 A 1, NZ 1, A 2, 1999 A 2, [S, U]

Venter, F D (Tvl) 1931 W, 1932 S, 1933 A 3

Versfeld, C (WP) 1891 BI 3

Versfeld, M (WP) 1891 BI 1, 2, 3

Vigne, J T (Tvl) 1891 BI 1, 2, 3

Viljoen, J F (GW) 1971 F 1, 2, A 1, 2, 3, 1972 E

Viljoen, J T (N) 1971 A 1, 2, 3

Villet, J V (WP) 1984 E 1, 2

Visagie, I J (WP) 1999 It 1, W, NZ 1, A 1, NZ 2, A 2, [S, U, E, A 3, NZ 3], 2000 C, E 2, A 1, NZ 1, A 2, NZ 2, A 3, 2001 NZ 1, A 1, 2, NZ 2, F 3, It 2(R), E (t+R), US, 2003 S 1(R), 2(R), Arg

Visagie, P J (GW) 1967 F 1, 2, 3, 4, 1968 BI 1, 2, 3, 4, F 1, 2, 1969 A 1, 2, 3, 4, S, E, 1970 NZ 1, 2, 3, 4, 1971 F 1, 2, A 1, 2, 3

Visagie, R G (OFS, N) 1984 E 1, 2, S Am 1, 2, 1993 F 1

Visser, J de V (WP) 1981 NZ 2, US

Visser, M (WP) 1995 WS (R)

Visser, P J (Tvl) 1933 A 2

Viviers, S S (OFS) 1956 A 1, 2, NZ 2, 3, 4

Vogel, M L (OFS) 1974 BI 2(R)

Von Hoesslin, D J B (GW) 1999 It 1(R), 2, W (R), NZ 1, A 1(R)

Vos, A N (GL) 1999 It 1(t+R), 2, NZ 1(R), 2(R), A 2, [S (R), Sp, E (R), A 3(R), NZ 3], 2000 C, E 1, 2, A 1, NZ 1, A 2, NZ 2, A 3, Arg, I, W, E 3, 2001 F 1, 2, It 1, NZ 1, A 1, 2, NZ 2, F 3, It 2, E, US

Wagenaar, C (NT) 1977 Wld

Wahl, J J (WP) 1949 NZ 1

Walker, A P (N) 1921 NZ 1, 3, 1924 BI 1, 2, 3, 4

Walker, H N (OFS) 1953 A 3, 1956 A 2, NZ 1, 4

Walker, H W (Tvl) 1910 BI 1, 2, 3

Walton, D C (N) 1964 F, 1965 I, S, NZ 3, 4, 1969 A 1, 2, E

Wannenburg, P J (BB) 2002 F (R), E, 2003 S 1, 2, Arg, A 1(t+R), NZ 1(R), 2004 I1, 2, W1, PI(R), 2006 S1(R), F, NZ2(R), 3, A3, 2007 Sm(R), NZ1(R), A2, NZ2

Waring, F W (WP) 1931 I, 1932 E, 1933 A 1, 2, 3, 4, 5

Watson, L A (WP) 2007 Sm, 2008 W1, 2, It, NZ1(R), 2(R), Arg, NZ3(R), A2(R), 3(t&R)

Wegner, N (WP) 1993 F 2, A 1, 2, 3

Wentzel, M van Z (Pumas) 2002 F (R), S

Wessels, J J (WP) 1896 BI 1, 2, 3

Whipp, P J M (WP) 1974 BI 1, 2, 1975 F 1, 1976 NZ 1, 3, 4, 1980 S Am 1, 2

White, J (Bor) 1931 W, 1933 A 1, 2, 3, 4, 5, 1937 A 1, 2, NZ 1, 2

Wiese, J J (Tvl) 1993 F 1, 1995 WS, [R, C, WS, F, NZ], W, It, E, 1996 NZ 3(R), 4(R), 5, Arg 1, 2, F 1, 2, W

Willemse, A K (GL) 2003 S 1, 2, NZ 1, A 2, NZ 2, [U, E, Sm, NZ], 2004 W2, I3, 2007 E1, 2(R), Sm, A1, NZ1, Nm, S(R), [Tg]

Williams, A E (GW) 1910 BI 1

Williams, A P (WP) 1984 E 1, 2

Williams, C M (WP, GL) 1993 Arg 2, 1994 E 1, 2, NZ 1, 2, 3, Arg 1, 2, S, W, 1995 WS, [WS, F, NZ], It, E, 1998 A 1(t), NZ 1(t), 2000 C (R), E 1(t), 2(R), A 1(R), NZ 2, A 3, Arg, I, W (R)

Williams, D O (WP) 1937 A 1, 2, NZ 1, 2, 3, 1938 BI 1, 2, 3

Williams, J G (NT) 1971 F 1, 2, A 1, 2, 3, 1972 E, 1974 BI 1, 2, 4, F 1, 2, 1976 NZ 1, 2

Wilson, L G (WP) 1960 NZ 3, 4, W, I, 1961 E, F, I, A 1, 2, 1962 BI 1, 2, 3, 4, 1963 A 1, 2, 3, 4, 1964 W, F, 1965 I, S, A 1, 2, NZ 1, 2, 3, 4

Wolmarans, B J (OFS) 1977 Wld

Wright, G D (EP, Tvl) 1986 Cv 3, 4, 1989 Wld 1, 2, 1992 F 1, 2, E

Wyness, M R K (WP) 1962 BI 1, 2, 3, 4, 1963 A 2

Zeller, W C (N) 1921 NZ 2, 3

Zimerman, M (WP) 1931 W, I, 1932 E, S

LIONS CLAIM TENTH CURRIE CROWN

Gallo Images

The Lions go wild at the end of the 2011 ABSA Currie Cup final.

The Golden Lions comprehensively dismantled the Natal Sharks in the final of the 2011 ABSA Currie Cup, despatching the defending champions 42–16 in Johannesburg to end the province's 12-year drought in the competition and lift the famous trophy for a tenth time.

The Lions had fallen in the final in both 2002 and 2007 but made no mistake in front of their own supporters at Coca-Cola Park with a dominant display that underlined their superiority in the tournament over the 14 games of the regular season, irresistible form which John Mitchell's side carried with them into the knockout phase.

Man of the Match for the new champions was fly-half Elton Jantjies, who provided 24 points with the boot and, despite losing Springbok prop CJ van der Linde late in the first half after he was sent to the sin-bin for dangerous play, the Lions simply blew the Sharks away.

"When we were down to 14 men, we remained calm and the guys didn't drop in their performance," Mitchell said after the final whistle. "I'm very proud of how the team handled those incidents very well as we adapted to the situation. These past few weeks have been phenomenal. The fact that we played in front of a packed Coca-Cola Park showed how well the guys were playing, and the support has been great.

"People assumed I was crazy to take the job as Lions coach, but I love a challenge and my dream was to restore the pride that was once here in Johannesburg. I know it's been a frustrating number of years for all Lions fans, who probably had to turn the telly upside down to see their team on top of the log."

Beaten just three and four times respectively in the regular season, the Lions and the Sharks were joined by third-place Free State and fourth-place Western Province in the semi-finals, but it was to be first against second in the Johannesburg showdown.

The Sharks had comfortably beaten Western Province in the 2010 final, but they went from champions to whipping boys in the space of 12 months as Mitchell's team ran riot. The floodgates opened on 25 minutes when wing Michael Killiam went over for the first try of the match and, with Jantjies keeping the scoreboard ticking over for the home side, there was no way back for the Sharks.

Further tries from Patrick Cillies and Jaco Taute strengthened the Lions' grip on the trophy, and when the full-time whistle sounded they had won the Currie Cup on home soil for the first time since 1950. Their winning margin of 26 points was the second heaviest in the history of the competition, surpassed only by the Blue Bulls' 39–9 rout of Western Province in 1980.

"We were outplayed in every area of the game and were beaten by the better team," conceded Sharks coach John Plumtree. "They were backed by a massive crowd, they attacked and defended well and when they got in front it was always going to be difficult for us. We weren't able to stop them today. I think they were probably the more cohesive side."

ABSA CURRIE CUP 2011 RESULTS

SEMI-FINALS

Natal Sharks 20 **Free State** 13	**Golden Lions** 29 **Western Province** 20

FINAL

Golden Lions 42 **Natal Sharks** 16

TONGA

TONGA'S 2010–11 TEST RECORD

OPPONENT	DATE	VENUE	RESULT
USA	8 Jun	N	**Won** 44–13
Fiji	2 Jul	A	**Won** 45–21
Japan	9 Jul	N	**Lost** 27–28
Samoa	13 Jul	N	**Won** 29–19
Fiji	13 Aug	A	**Lost** 12–27
Fiji	19 Aug	A	**Won** 32–20
New Zealand	9 Sep	A	**Lost** 41–10
Canada	14 Sep	N	**Lost** 20–25
Japan	21 Sep	N	**Won** 31–18
France	1 Oct	N	**Won** 19–14

TONGA CLIMB TO NEW HIGH

By Tom Chick

Alex Livesey/Getty Images

Tonga celebrate their incredible win over the eventual runners-up, France.

Tonga left Rugby World Cup 2011 at the end of the pool stages having endured one of the most fascinating journeys of all the 20 participating teams.

Two wins from their four pool matches, automatic qualification for Rugby World Cup 2015 in England and a new high of ninth in the IRB World Rankings would see many regarding it as a job well done for the Sea Eagles.

Not those in the immediacy of the Tongan camp though, having come agonisingly close to what would have been a first-ever quarter-final berth in rugby's showpiece tournament with their passion and determination.

When the full-time whistle blew in their final Pool A match with France, there was an air of hysteria amongst fans and players alike at Wellington Regional Stadium as Isitolo Maka's side recorded a 19–14 win against the eventual runners-up in what was arguably the biggest upset of RWC 2011.

But their second victory in New Zealand, following a first win over Japan since 2006 in their previous match, meant their earlier 25–20 defeat to Canada was an even harder pill to swallow, having led 20–13 with less than 15 minutes to go, and on reflection a missed opportunity.

"The boys are talking about those moments, those what-ifs, those missed passes that could have been tries," admitted Siale Piutau, reflecting on what could have been following the victory over France, knowing victory against Canada would have seen Tonga, not Les Bleus reach the quarter-finals.

Before Tonga's campaign began with the privilege, if somewhat unenviable task, of facing the hosts and eventual champions New Zealand in the opening match of the tournament, at Eden Park on 9 September, they were greeted at Auckland Airport by thousands of fans in a sea of red.

Those very Tongan fans were in full force throughout the tournament, offering their own colour and passion from the stands, and after the opening match with the hosts Sione Kalamafoni admitted, "it feels like coming from Tonga to Tonga – everybody's wearing red."

But following a breathtaking opening ceremony and the traditional pre-match rituals, it was unsurprisingly New Zealand who were quicker and stronger in the opening encounters.

The result was all but sealed by half-time thanks to full-back Israel Dagg and wing Richard Kahui both crossing for two tries, but Tonga were able to avoid becoming the first side that failed to score in the first half of a RWC opening match with a Kurt Morath penalty in the dying seconds.

Continually cheered on by their rapturous support at Eden Park, the Tongans tore into the All Blacks in the second half and eventually scored a consolation try – only their second-ever try against New Zealand – through replacement prop Alisona Taumalolo in the 41–10 defeat.

It was the first time Tonga had reached double figures against New Zealand and was also their smallest loss against the All Blacks and New Zealand's lowest score against the Ikale Tahi, which were positives Tonga would build on in the rest of their campaign.

"I thought the ABs started very well, and it seemed that every time we made a mistake they scored. You can't afford mistakes against a team like the All Blacks," captain Finau Maka said after the match.

"But we came out firing, and I thought we defended well. It gave us confidence and we grew during the second half. Momentum is important, and to score a try when we were dominating was a real boost. That gave us a lot of confidence, and we can look forward to our next game against Canada in a good frame of mind."

Five days later Tonga had the opportunity to use those positives against the Canucks in Whangarei, but it was Kieran Crowley's side who recorded their first RWC 2011 victory and third against Tonga in the history of the tournament.

Canada had to battle to wrestle the initiative from Tonga after two tries from Piutau had helped the Sea Eagles to a 20–13 lead midway through the second half, but tries from Aaron Carpenter and Phil Mackenzie ensured Canada recorded their biggest ever RWC comeback.

Piutau had become the first Tongan to score two tries in a RWC match, but as coach Maka suggested Canada "kept fighting until the end" and that Tonga "made some silly mistakes that cost us the game."

With a seven-day break until their next match with Japan, five Sea Eagles took the opportunity to visit Paihia Primary School in the Bay of Islands to inspire a new generation of youngsters. "When I was young, I was sitting where you are now," scrum-half Taniela Moa told an audience of transfixed school children. "Former All Black Michael Jones came to talk to us and that inspired me to play rugby."

All of that inspiration was needed in their third match with Japan, one that had Isitolo Maka calling it their very own "World Cup final" on its eve, and that "nothing would be better than beating Japan", Tonga not having done so since 2006.

It was a match that Japan coach John Kirwan also had long had his eye on winning, but it was fly-half Morath and a personal tally of 16 points that helped to finally deliver a result Tonga had deserved, a 31–18 victory, much to the delight of the crowd in Whangarei. The 31 points were the most Tonga had scored in any RWC match, and having missed just one of his seven kicks Morath, who ended the tournament as the third top points scorer with 45 behind South Africa's Morné Steyn (62) and Australia's James O'Connor (52), was "pretty happy to get the win."

"We sort of let ourselves down in the first two games, and it was about getting a bit of respect back for us and the Tongan community, just to go out there and put it on the paddock finally," he added. "I still think there is a bit of room for improvement, but we are getting better which is good."

Tonga and their colourful army of supporters had 10 days to wait before their final Pool A match of RWC 2011 against France. "We've got one more game left and we've got nothing to lose. I'm sure our win [against Japan] will give us big confidence to take them on next week," said coach Maka.

"I know the coach, I've played against him, I know all the players. So it will be good to see them again and hopefully that will help us. But the French, when they are on, they can beat anyone in the world, so I just hope that they aren't on."

Buoyed by a boisterous welcome at the Wellington Parish Church where over 350 ex-pats crammed into the inner-city church hall to wish their national team luck, Tonga delivered the shock of the tournament.

By playing an "enormous" match and putting "their lives on this one match", according to Les Bleus scrum-half Dimitri Yachvili, Tonga were able to beat France 19–14 and deliver a last boost for their fans and one which would go down in history. "We did this for the fans – the last 40 minutes. We have the best fans in the world," insisted Kisi Pulu.

Sukanaivalu Hufanga scored Tonga's only try of the match, with Morath kicking the conversion and a further four penalties, and their reward for causing one of the biggest upsets in RWC history was a place in the top 10 of the IRB World Rankings for the first time.

"We're delighted with ourselves. The boys are over the moon that they won the game. It was a target to win tonight and we did well to win the game," said Aleki Lutui. "To beat France, it's a big, big thing for Tongan rugby and our history. We've been confident and we have a lot of young guys and we're always believing in ourselves that we could upset one of the biggest teams in the world."

The Ikale Tahi's deserved win lifted them to ninth in the IRB World Rankings, equalling the highest position occupied by Pacific rivals Fiji and Samoa since the rankings were introduced in October 2003. RWC 2011 will long love in the memories of Tongan rugby, although possibly with a little tinge of regret at what might have been.

TONGA INTERNATIONAL STATISTICS

MATCH RECORDS UP TO 31 OCTOBER 2011

WINNING MARGIN

Date	Opponent	Result	Winning Margin
21/03/2003	Korea	119–0	**119**
08/07/2006	Cook Islands	90–0	**90**
01/01/1979	Solomon Islands	92–3	**89**
10/02/2007	Korea	83–3	**80**
15/03/2003	Korea	75–0	**75**

MOST POINTS IN A MATCH

BY THE TEAM

Date	Opponent	Result	Points
21/03/2003	Korea	119–0	**119**
01/01/1979	Solomon Islands	92–3	**92**
08/07/2006	Cook Islands	90–0	**90**
06/12/2002	Papua New Guinea	84–12	**84**
10/02/2007	Korea	83–3	**83**

BY A PLAYER

Date	Player	Opponent	Points
21/03/2003	Pierre Hola	Korea	**39**
10/02/2007	Fangatapu Apikotoa	Korea	**28**
04/05/1999	Sateki Tuipulotu	Korea	**27**
21/03/2003	Benhur Kivalu	Korea	**25**
06/12/2002	Pierre Hola	Papua New Guinea	**24**

MOST TRIES IN A MATCH

BY THE TEAM

Date	Opponent	Result	Tries
21/03/2003	Korea	119–0	**17**
08/07/2006	Cook Islands	90–0	**14**
10/02/2007	Korea	83–3	**13**
24/06/2006	Cook Islands	77–10	**13**

BY A PLAYER

Date	Player	Opponent	Tries
21/03/2003	Benhur Kivalu	Korea	**5**
08/06/2011	Viliame Iongi	USA	**4**

MOST CONVERSIONS IN A MATCH

BY THE TEAM

Date	Opponent	Result	Cons
21/03/2003	Korea	119–0	**17**
08/07/2006	Cook Islands	90–0	**10**

BY A PLAYER

Date	Player	Opponent	Cons
21/03/2003	Pierre Hola	Korea	**17**
08/07/2006	Fangatapu Apikotoa	Cook Islands	**9**
10/02/2007	Fangatapu Apikotoa	Korea	**9**
06/12/2002	Pierre Hola	Papua New Guinea	**9**
05/07/1997	Kusitafu Tonga	Cook Islands	**9**

MOST PENALTIES IN A MATCH

BY THE TEAM

Date	Opponent	Result	Pens
10/11/2001	Scotland	20–43	**5**
28/06/2008	Samoa	15–20	**5**
13/07/2011	Samoa	29–19	**5**
19/08/2011	Fiji	32–20	**5**

BY A PLAYER

Date	Player	Opponent	Pens
13/07/2011	Kurt Morath	Samoa	**5**
19/08/2011	Kurt Morath	Fiji	**5**

MOST DROPPED GOALS IN A MATCH

BY THE TEAM

1 on 8 Occasions

BY A PLAYER

1 on 8 Occasions

MOST CAPPED PLAYERS

Name	Caps
'Elisi Vunipola	**41**
Benhur Kivalu	**38**
Pierre Hola	**37**
Manu Vunipola	**35**
Aleki Lutui	**33**

LEADING TRY SCORERS

Name	Tries
Siua Taumalolo	**12**
Fepikou Tatafu	**11**
Benhur Kivalu	**10**

LEADING CONVERSIONS SCORERS

Name	Cons
Pierre Hola	**65**
Sateki Tuipulotu	**33**
Fangatapu Apikotoa	**31**
Kurt Morath	**31**

LEADING PENALTY SCORERS

Name	Pens
Kurt Morath	**40**
Pierre Hola	**35**
Sateki Tuipulotu	**32**

LEADING DROPPED GOAL SCORERS

Name	DGs
Pierre Hola	**3**

LEADING POINTS SCORERS

Name	Points
Pierre Hola	**289**
Sateki Tuipulotu	**190**
Kurt Morath	**187**
Siua Taumalolo	**108**

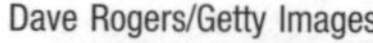

Dave Rogers/Getty Images

Pierre Hola still reigns supreme as Tonga's leading Test points scorer.

TONGA INTERNATIONAL PLAYERS (UP TO 31 OCTOBER 2011)

Note: Years given for International Championship matches are for second half of season; eg 1972 means season 1971–72. Years for all other matches refer to the actual year of the match. Entries in square brackets denote matches played in RWC Finals.

I Afeaki 1995 *F*, *S*, *Iv*, 1997 *Fj*, 2001 *S*, *W*, 2002 *J*, *Fj*, *Sa*, *Fj*, 2003 *Kor*, *Kor*, *I*, *Fj*, *Fj*, *It*, *C*, 2004 *Sa*, *Fj*, 2005 *It*, 2007 *Sa*, *SA*, *E*
P Afeaki 1983 *Fj*, *Sa*
S Afeaki 2002 *Fj*, *Sa*, *Fj*, *PNG*, *PNG*, 2003 *Kor*, *Kor*, *I*, *Fj*, *It*, *W*, *NZ*
V Afeaki 1997 *Sa*, 2002 *Sa*, *Fj*
JL Afu 2008 *J*, *Sa*, *Fj*, 2009 *Fj*, *Sa*, *J*, 2011 *US*
T Afu Fifita 1924 *Fj*, *Fj*, *Fj*
A Afu Fungavaka 1982 *Sa*, 1984 *Fj*, *Fj*, 1985 *Fj*, 1986 *W*, *Fj*, *Fj*, 1987 *C*, *W*, *I*, *Sa*, *Fj*
S 'Aho 1974 *S*, *W*
T Ahoafi 2007 *AuA*, *Sa*
P Ahofono 1990 *Sa*
K Ahota'e'iloa 1999 *Sa*, *F*, *Fj*, 2000 *C*, *Fj*, *J*
M Ahota'e'iloa 2010 *Sa*, *Fj*, *J*
S Aisake 1934 *Fj*
M Akau'ola 1934 *Fj*
P 'Ake 1926 *Fj*, *Fj*, *Fj*
A Alatini 2001 *S*, 2002 *J*, *Sa*, *Fj*, 2003 *I*, *Fj*
M Alatini 1969 *M*, 1972 *Fj*, *Fj*, 1973 *M*, *A*, *A*, *Fj*, 1974 *S*, *W*, *C*, 1975 *M*, 1977 *Fj*
PF Alatini 1995 *Sa*
S Alatini 1994 *Sa*, *Fj*, 1998 *Sa*, *Fj*, 2000 *NZ*, *US*
S Alatini 1977 *Fj*, 1979 *NC*, *M*, *E*
T Alatini 1932 *Fj*
V 'Alipate 1967 *Fj*, 1968 *Fj*, *Fj*, *Fj*, 1969 *M*
A Amone 1987 *W*, *I*, *Sa*, *Fj*
A Amore 1988 *Fj*
T Anitoni 1995 *J*, *Sa*, *Fj*, 1996 *Sa*, *Fj*
V Anitoni 1990 *Sa*
F Apikotoa 2004 *Sa*, *Fj*, 2005 *Fj*, *Sa*, *Fj*, *Sa*, *It*, *F*, 2006 *Coo*, *Coo*, 2007 *Kor*, *AuA*, *J*, *JAB*, 2008 *J*, *Sa*, *Fj*, 2009 *Fj*, *J*, 2010 *Fj*, *CHL*
T Apitani 1947 *Fj*, *Fj*
S Asi 1987 *C*
T Asi 1996 *Sa*
H 'Asi 2000 *C*
S Ata 1928 *Fj*
S Atiola 1987 *Sa*, *Fj*, 1988 *Fj*, *Fj*, 1989 *Fj*, *Fj*, 1990 *Fj*, *J*
H Aulika 2011 *Fj*, *Fj*, *C*, *J*, *F*

K Bakewa 2002 *PNG*, *PNG*, 2003 *Fj*
O Beba 1932 *Fj*, *Fj*, *Fj*
O Blake 1983 *M*, *M*, 1987 *Sa*, *Fj*, 1988 *Sa*, *Fj*, *Fj*
T Bloomfield 1973 *M*, *A*, *A*, *Fj*, 1986 *W*
D Briggs 1997 *W*
J Buloka 1932 *Fj*, *Fj*

D Edwards 1998 *A*, 1999 *Geo*, *Geo*, *Kor*, *US*, *Sa*, *F*, *Fj*, *C*, *NZ*, *It*, *E*
T Ete'aki 1984 *Fj*, 1986 *W*, *Fj*, *Fj*, 1987 *C*, *W*, *I*, 1990 *Fj*, *J*, *Sa*, *Kor*, *Sa*, 1991 *Sa*

U Fa'a 1994 *Sa*, *W*, 1995 *J*, 1998 *Sa*, *A*, *Fj*
L Fa'aoso 2004 *Sa*, *Fj*, 2005 *Fj*, *Sa*, *Fj*, *Sa*, 2007 *US*, *E*, 2009 *Pt*, 2011 *Fj*, *J*, *Fj*
P Fa'apoi 1963 *Fj*
V Fa'aumu 1986 *Fj*, *Fj*
O Faingaanuku 2011 *US*
T Fainga'anuku 1999 *NZ*, *It*, *E*, 2000 *C*, *Fj*, *J*, *NZ*, 2001 *Fj*, *Sa*, *Fj*, *Sa*
S Faka 'osi'folau 1997 *Z*, *Nm*, *SA*, *Fj*, *Sa*, *Coo*, *W*, 1998 *A*, *Fj*, 1999 *Geo*, *Kor*, *Fj*, 2001 *Sa*
DAT Fakafanua 2010 *CHL*
P Fakalelu 2005 *It*, 2006 *Coo*, *Coo*, 2009 *Sa*, *J*
J Fakalolo 1926 *Fj*, *Fj*, *Fj*
P Fakana 1963 *Fj*, *Fj*
F Fakaongo 1993 *S*, *Fj*, 1995 *Iv*, *Sa*, *Fj*, 2000 *Fj*, *J*, *NZ*, *Sa*, 2001 *S*, *W*, 2002 *J*, *Fj*, *Sa*
V Fakatou 1998 *Sa*, *A*, *Fj*, 1999 *Kor*, *NZ*
V Fakatulolo 1975 *M*
S Fakaua 2005 *Sa*
P Faka'ua 1967 *Fj*, *Fj*, *Fj*, 1968 *Fj*, *Fj*, *Fj*, 1969 *M*, *M*, 1972 *Fj*
N Fakauho 1977 *Fj*, *Fj*
P Fakava 1988 *Sa*, *Fj*
FP Faletau 1999 *Geo*, *Kor*, *Kor*, *J*, *US*, *Sa*, *F*, *Fj*, *C*
K Faletau 1988 *Sa*, *Fj*, 1989 *Fj*, *Fj*, 1990 *Sa*, 1991 *Fj*, 1992 *Fj*, 1997 *Nm*, *SA*, *Fj*, *Sa*, *Coo*, *W*, 1999 *Sa*, *F*, *Fj*, *C*
M Fanga'uta 1982 *Fj*
K Fangupo 2009 *Pt*
MU Fangupo 2009 *Sa*, *J*, 2010 *J*, *CHL*
F Faotusa 1990 *Sa*
LAHN Fatafehi 2009 *Fj*, *Sa*, *Pt*, 2010 *Sa*, *Fj*, *J*, 2011 *Fj*, *NZ*, *C*, *J*, *F*
IT Fatani 1992 *Fj*, 1993 *Sa*, *S*, *Fj*, *A*, *Fj*, 1997 *Fj*, *Coo*, 1999 *Geo*, *Kor*, *Kor*, *J*, *US*, *Sa*, *F*, *Fj*, *C*, *NZ*, *It*, *E*, 2000 *C*, *Fj*, *J*, *NZ*, *Sa*, *US*
O Faupula 1924 *Fj*, *Fj*, *Fj*
SLJ Faupula 2010 *CHL*
AOM Feao 2010 *Sa*, *Fj*
S Fe'ao 1995 *F*, *S*
SL Fekau 1983 *M*, *M*
K Feke 1988 *Fj*, *Fj*, 1989 *Fj*, 1990 *Fj*, *Sa*
SH Fekitoa 2010 *Sa*, *J*
T Feleola 1934 *Fj*
M Felise 1987 *W*, *I*
I Fenukitau 1993 *Sa*, *S*, *Fj*, *A*, *Fj*, 1994 *Sa*, *Fj*, 1995 *J*, *J*, *F*, *S*, 2002 *J*, *Fj*, *Sa*, 2003 *It*, *W*, *NZ*, *C*
Fetu'ulele 1967 *Fj*
K Fielea 1987 *C*, *W*, *I*, *Sa*, *Fj*, 1990 *J*, *Sa*, *Kor*, *Sa*, 1991 *Sa*
L Fifita 1934 *Fj*
P Fifita 1983 *Fj*
P Fifita 2003 *C*
S Fifita 1974 *S*, *W*, *C*, 1975 *M*
T Fifita 1984 *Fj*, *Fj*, 1986 *W*, *Fj*, *Fj*, 1987 *C*, *W*, *I*, 1991 *Sa*, *Fj*, *Fj*
T Fifita 2001 *Fj*, *Fj*, 2003 *Fj*, 2006 *J*, 2008 *J*
V Fifita 1982 *Fj*
V Fifita 2005 *F*
F Filikitonga 1990 *Fj*, *Sa*
L Filiiava 1960 *M*
M Filimoehala 1968 *Fj*, 1974 *W*, *C*, 1975 *M*, *M*
OAML Filipine 2000 *C*, 2006 *J*, *Fj*, *Coo*, *Sa*, 2007 *US*, *SA*, 2008 *J*
M Filise 1986 *Fj*, *Fj*
T Filise 2001 *Fj*, *Fj*, *S*, *W*, 2002 *Sa*, *Fj*, 2004 *Sa*, *Fj*, 2005 *Fj*, *Sa*, *Fj*, *Sa*, 2007 *Fj*, *Sa*, *E*, 2011 *NZ*, *J*
S Filo 2004 *Sa*, *Fj*
I Finau 1987 *Sa*, *Fj*, 1990 *Fj*, *J*, *Sa*
M Finau 1979 *NC*, *M*, *E*, *Sa*, 1980 *Sa*, 1984 *Fj*
M Finau 2007 *AuA*, 2008 *J*, 2009 *Fj*, *J*, 2010 *J*, *CHL*
S Finau 1998 *Sa*, 1999 *Geo*, *Sa*, *F*, *Fj*, *C*, *E*, 2001 *Fj*, *Fj*, *S*, 2005 *It*, *F*
S Finau 1989 *Fj*, *Fj*, 1990 *Fj*, *J*, *Sa*, *Kor*, *Sa*
S Finau 1924 *Fj*, *Fj*, *Fj*, 1926 *Fj*, *Fj*, *Fj*
T Finau 1967 *Fj*
T Finau 1924 *Fj*, *Fj*, *Fj*
V Finau 1987 *Sa*, *Fj*
I Fine 2007 *Kor*, *AuA*, *JAB*, *Sa*

K Fine 1987 *C, W, I*, 1988 *Fj*
L Fineanganofo 1924 *Fj, Fj, Fj*
J Finisi 1932 *Fj, Fj, Fj*
S Finisi 1928 *Fj*
P Fisi'iahi 1992 *Sa*
K Fisilau 1999 *J, US*, 2000 *C*, 2005 *Fj, Sa, It*
S Fisilau 2010 *Sa, Fj, J*, 2011 *Fj, J, Sa, Fj, NZ, J*
K Fokofuka 1995 *Sa*
K Folea 1991 *Fj*
S Foliaki 1973 *A, A*, 1977 *Fj*
Fololisi 1991 *Fj*
U Fono 2005 *Sa, Fj, It, F*
H Fonua 1973 *M, A, A, Fj*, 1974 *S, W, C*
O Fonua 2009 *Fj, Sa, Pt*
S Fonua 1928 *Fj, Fj, Fj*
SO Fonua 2002 *Sa, Sa*, 2003 *It, W, NZ, C*, 2007 *Kor, AuA, J, JAB, Fj, Sa*
T Fonua 2007 *Kor*
K Fotu 1990 *Fj, Sa, Kor, Sa*
L Fotu 1991 *Sa*, 1992 *Fj*, 1993 *S, Fj*
R Fotu 1979 *M*, 1983 *Fj, Sa*
S Fotu 1968 *Fj, Fj, Fj*, 1969 *M, M*
S Fotu 1947 *Fj*
TK Fotu 1987 *C*, 1988 *Sa, Fj*, 1989 *Fj*, 1990 *J*
P Fua'ava 1985 *Fj*
T Fuataimi 1928 *Fj*, 1932 *Fj, Fj, Fj*
F Fukofuka 1926 *Fj, Fj, Fj*, 1928 *Fj*
SM Fukofuka 2010 *Sa, Fj*
T Fukofuka 1993 *Fj*, 1995 *J, J, F, S, Iv, Fj*
A Fungavaka 1982 *Fj*
L Fusimalohi 1987 *Fj*, 1988 *Fj*, 1990 *J, Sa*

W Gibbons 2002 *PNG*, 2003 *Fj*

F Hafoka 1932 *Fj, Fj, Fj*
I Hafoka 1928 *Fj, Fj*, 1932 *Fj, Fj, Fj*, 1934 *Fj*
K Hafoka 1967 *Fj, Fj*, 1968 *Fj, Fj, Fj*
M Hafoka 1977 *Fj, Fj*, 1979 *M*, 1980 *Sa*
S Hafoka 1997 *W*
T Hafoka 1987 *Fj*
VA Hakalo 2006 *J, Coo, Sa*, 2010 *CHL*
S Hala 1999 *Geo, Geo, Kor*, 2002 *J, Fj, Sa, Sa, Fj*, 2003 *Kor, Kor*
H Halaeua 2010 *Fj, J*
M Halafatu 1989 *Fj*
KM Halafihi 2010 *Sa, J*
T Halafihi 1982 *Sa, Fj*, 1983 *Sa*, 1985 *Fj*
S Halahingano 1924 *Fj, Fj, Fj*
T Halaifonua 2009 *Fj, J*
A Halangahu 2007 *Kor*, 2011 *US*
C Halangi 2002 *Fj*
T Halasika 1988 *Fj, Fj*
C Hala'ufia 2000 *C*, 2001 *Fj, Sa, Fj, Sa, W*, 2002 *Sa*, 2004 *Sa, Fj*, 2005 *Fj, Fj, Sa, It, F*, 2006 *J, Fj, Coo, Sa, Coo*, 2007 *JAB, Fj*, 2009 *Fj*
S Hala'ufia 1977 *Fj*, 1979 *NC, M, E, Sa*, 1981 *Fj*
L Halavatau 1982 *Sa, Fj*
N Hau 2002 *Sa*
T Haumono 1924 *Fj, Fj, Fj*, 1926 *Fj, Fj, Fj*, 1928 *Fj*, 1932 *Fj, Fj, Fj*
SP Havea 2000 *NZ, US*, 2004 *Sa, Fj*, 2005 *Fj, Sa, Fj, Sa, It, F*, 2006 *J, Fj, Coo, Sa*, 2007 *Kor, JAB, Fj, Sa, US, SA, E*, 2008 *J, Sa, Fj*, 2010 *CHL*, 2011 *US, J, Sa*
T Havea 1924 *Fj, Fj, Fj*
AP Havili 2000 *C, Fj, J, Sa, US*, 2001 *Fj, Sa, Fj*, 2007 *AuA, J, JAB, US, SA, E*
M Havili 1987 *Sa*, 1988 *Fj*
P Havili 1981 *Fj, Fj, Fj*
KP Hehea 2006 *J, Fj, JAB, Coo, Sa, Coo*, 2007 *US, Sa, SA*, 2008 *Sa, Fj*, 2009 *Pt*, 2011 *Fj, J, Sa, Fj, NZ, J, F*
SE Hehepoto 1972 *Fj*, 1973 *M, A, A, Fj*
M Hekeheke 1986 *Fj, Fj*, 1988 *Fj*
Helehele 1985 *Fj*
T Helu 1967 *Fj, Fj*
WFUA Helu 2010 *Fj, J*, 2011 *US, Fj, J, Sa, Fj, C*
T Hikila 2010 *CHL*
O Hiko 1979 *E*
RP Hola 1998 *Sa, A, Fj*, 2001 *W*, 2002 *J, Fj, Sa, Sa, Fj, PNG, PNG*, 2003 *Kor, Kor, I, Fj, It, W, NZ, C*, 2005 *Fj*, 2006 *J, Fj, JAB, Coo, Sa, Coo*, 2007 *Sa, US, Sa, SA, E*, 2008 *J, Sa, Fj*, 2009 *Sa, J, Pt*
S Hola 1979 *Fj*
L Hopoate 1986 *W*
V Hosea 1967 *Fj, Fj*

F Hufanga 1973 *M*
S Hufanga 2003 *Fj, W, NZ, C*, 2004 *Sa, Fj*, 2005 *It, F*, 2006 *J, Fj, JAB*, 2007 *Fj, US, Sa, SA, E*, 2008 *Sa*, 2009 *Pt*, 2011 *US, Sa, Fj, Fj, NZ, J, F*

F Ika 1988 *Sa, Fj, Fj, Fj*, 1989 *Fj, Fj*
S Ika 2008 *J*, 2009 *Sa, J*
R Iloalahia 2010 *CHL*
M Ilolahia 1947 *Fj*
Inoke 1947 *Fj*
K 'Inoke 1967 *Fj, Fj, Fj*, 1968 *Fj, Fj, Fj*, 1969 *M, M*, 1972 *Fj*, 1973 *A*, 1975 *M*
V Iongi 2011 *US, Fj, J, Sa, Fj, Fj, NZ, C, F*
K 'Iongi 1967 *Fj, Fj, Fj*, 1968 *Fj, Fj, Fj*, 1969 *M, M*, 1972 *Fj*, 1973 *M, A, Fj*
T 'Isitolo 1995 *Iv, Sa, Fj*

M Kafatolu 2002 *J, Fj, Sa*
PNA Kaho 2011 *US*
T Kaho 1973 *A*
J Kaihau 1932 *Fj, Fj*
P Kaihau 1975 *M*, 1977 *Fj, Fj, Fj*
S Kaihau 1934 *Fj*
M Kaihea 1999 *Geo, Kor, Kor, J, Sa, F*
L Kainga 1928 *Fj, Fj*
L Kaiqa 1928 *Fj*
'A Kaitu'u 2000 *C*
J Kalaivalu 1996 *Sa*
SM Kalamafoni 2007 *Kor, AuA, J, JAB, Fj, Sa*, 2010 *Sa, Fj, J*, 2011 *Fj, J, Sa, Fj, Fj, NZ, C, J, F*
N Kalaniuvalu 1963 *Fj*
R Kapeli 1992 *Sa, Fj*, 1993 *Fj, A*
S Kapeli 2005 *Sa*
T Kapeli 1982 *Sa*
PF Kata 2009 *Pt*, 2010 *Sa, Fj, J*
FKM Katoa 2009 *J*
L Katoa 1996 *Sa, Fj*, 1997 *Nm, Fj, Sa*
P Katoa 1977 *Fj, Fj, Fj*, 1979 *NC, M, E, Sa, Fj*, 1981 *Fj, Fj, Fj*
P Katoa 1924 *Fj*
T Kaufana 1947 *Fj*
T Kaufusi 2007 *Kor, AuA, J, JAB, Fj, Sa*, 2009 *Sa, J*
L Kauhalaniua 1984 *Fj*
S Kauhenga 2002 *Sa, Sa, Fj*, 2003 *Fj*, 2006 *J*, 2007 *SA*, 2008 *J*, 2009 *Sa, J, Pt*, 2011 *US*
S Kava 1967 *Fj*
T Kavapalu 1967 *Fj*, 1968 *Fj, Fj, Fj*, 1969 *M, M*, 1972 *Fj*, 1973 *M, A, Fj*, 1974 *W*, 1975 *M, M*
A Kefu 1926 *Fj, Fj, Fj*, 1928 *Fj, Fj*
F Kefu 1972 *Fj, Fj*, 1973 *A*, 1974 *W, C*, 1975 *M*
M Kefu 1959 *Fj*, 1960 *M*, 1963 *Fj, Fj*
E Kelemeni 1967 *Fj, Fj, Fj*
K Kioa 1959 *Fj*, 1960 *M*
P Kiole 1977 *Fj, Fj*, 1979 *M, E, Fj*, 1980 *Sa*
S Kiole 2005 *Fj, Fj, Sa*, 2007 *AuA, J, JAB, Fj, Sa*, 2008 *Fj*
FT Kitekei'aho 1987 *C, W, I*
T kitekei'aho 1979 *Fj*
DJB Kivalu 1998 *Sa, A*, 1999 *Geo, Geo, Kor, Sa, F, Fj, C, NZ, It, E*, 2000 *C, Fj, J, NZ, Sa, US*, 2002 *J, Sa, Sa, Fj, PNG, PNG*, 2003 *Kor, Kor, Fj, Fj, It, W, NZ, C*, 2004 *Sa, Fj*, 2005 *Fj, Sa, Fj, Sa*
T Kolo 1993 *A*, 1995 *Sa, Fj*
OPV Koloamatangi 2011 *US*
C Koloi 1999 *US*
S Koloi 1998 *Sa, Fj*, 1999 *Geo, Geo, Kor, Kor, J, C, NZ, It, E*, 2000 *NZ, Sa, US*, 2001 *Sa*
K Kolokihakaufiji 2010 *CHL*
E Koloto 1986 *W*

F Lagilagi 1991 *Fj*
Jione Laiseni 1932 *Fj, Fj*
E Langi 2003 *NZ*
F Langi 1990 *Fj, J*
P Langi 1986 *W, Fj*
F Lani 1986 *Fj*
TA Latailakepa 1992 *Sa, Fj*, 1993 *Sa*
K Latu 1987 *Fj*
MKM Latu 2011 *J*
O Latu 2006 *J, Fj, JAB, Coo, Sa, Coo*, 2007 *Kor, AuA, J, JAB, Fj, Sa, US, Sa, SA, E*, 2008 *J, Sa, Fj*, 2009 *Fj, Sa, J*
P Latu 1994 *W*, 1995 *J, J, F, S, Iv, Sa, Fj*
S Latu 1984 *Fj, Fj*
S Latu 1992 *Fj*, 1993 *Fj, A*
S Latu 1972 *Fj*, 1973 *M, A, A, Fj*, 1974 *S, W, C*, 1975 *M, M*

U Latu 1997 *W*, 1998 *Sa*, 2002 *PNG*, *PNG*, 2003 *Kor*, *Kor*, *I*, *It*, *W*, *NZ*, *C*
U Latufeku 1959 *Fj*, 1960 *M*, 1963 *Fj*, 1968 *Fj*, *Fj*, *Fj*
P Latukefu 1995 *J*, *J*, *S*, *Iv*, *Sa*, *Fj*, 1998 *A*, *Fj*
T Latukefu 1967 *Fj*, *Fj*, *Fj*, 1968 *Fj*, *Fj*, *Fj*
M Latunipulu 1926 *Fj*, *Fj*, *Fj*
F Latusela 2003 *Kor*, *Kor*
F Lauei 1985 *Fj*
H Lavaka 1996 *Sa*, 1997 *SA*, *Fj*, *Sa*, *Coo*, *W*, 2003 *I*, *Fj*, *Fj*, *It*, *W*, *NZ*, *C*
K Lavaka 1996 *Fj*
M Lavaka 1993 *S*, *Fj*, *A*, *Fj*
S Lavaka 2008 *J*
T Lavaki 1990 *J*, *Kor*, 1993 *S*
F Lavemai 1984 *Fj*, *Fj*, 1985 *Fj*, 1986 *W*
M Lavulo 1979 *E*
T Lea'aetoa 2002 *PNG*, *PNG*, 2003 *Kor*, *Kor*, *I*, *It*, *W*, *NZ*, *C*, 2005 *It*, *F*, 2006 *J*, *Fj*, *JAB*, *Coo*, *Sa*, *Coo*, 2008 *J*, *Sa*, *Fj*, 2011 *US*, *Fj*, *Fj*, *Fj*
J Leba 1932 *Fj*, *Fj*, *Fj*
G Leger 2001 *S*, *W*, 2002 *J*, *Fj*, *Sa*, *Sa*, *Fj*, 2003 *Kor*, *Kor*, *I*, *Fj*, *It*, *NZ*, *C*
T Leger 1967 *Fj*, *Fj*
T Leha 1983 *M*, *M*
S Leilani 1981 *Fj*, 1983 *Fj*, *Sa*
FVMH Lemoto 2007 *Fj*
S Lepa 1928 *Fj*, *Fj*
A Liava'a 1979 *E*, 1981 *Fj*, *Fj*, *Fj*, 1983 *Fj*, *Sa*, *M*, *M*, 1984 *Fj*, *Fj*, 1985 *Fj*, 1987 *C*, *W*, *I*
S Liava'a 1979 *M*, *E*, 1981 *Fj*, *Fj*
V Likio 1947 *Fj*, *Fj*
L Lile 2002 *Sa*, *Fj*, 2003 *Fj*
VF Lilo 2007 *Kor*, *J*, *JAB*, *US*, *Sa*, *SA*, *E*, 2008 *J*, *Sa*, *Fj*, 2009 *Fj*, *Sa*, *J*, *Pt*, 2010 *Sa*, *Fj*, *J*, 2011 *Fj*, *J*, *Sa*, *Fj*, *NZ*, *J*, *F*
J Lino 1926 *Fj*, *Fj*, *Fj*
M Liongitau 1924 *Fj*, *Fj*, *Fj*
S Lisala 2005 *Sa*, *Fj*
S Lo'amanu 1926 *Fj*, *Fj*, *Fj*, 1928 *Fj*, *Fj*, *Fj*
T Lokotui 2001 *W*, 2011 *Fj*, *J*, *Sa*, *Fj*, *C*, *J*, *F*
S Lolo 1993 *Sa*
T Lolo'ahea 1987 *Sa*, 1990 *J*, *Sa*, *Kor*, *Sa*, 1991 *Sa*, *Fj*, *Fj*
L Lolohea 2007 *JAB*
P Lolohea 1983 *M*, *M*
K Lomu 1979 *Fj*
W Lose 1995 *F*, *S*, *Iv*
L Loto'ahea 1994 *Sa*
T Loto'ahea 1987 *Fj*, 1988 *Fj*, *Fj*, 1989 *Fj*, *Fj*, 1993 *S*, *Fj*, 1994 *W*, *Fj*
T Lovo 1982 *Sa*, 1986 *W*, *Fj*, *Fj*, 1987 *Sa*, 1988 *Fj*, 1989 *Fj*, *Fj*, 1990 *Sa*
S Lu'au 2007 *AuA*
I Lupina 1969 *M*, 1972 *Fj*
T Lutua 1990 *Kor*, 1992 *Fj*, 1994 *Sa*, *W*, *Fj*, 1995 *J*, *J*, *Iv*
V Lutua 1981 *Fj*, *Fj*, *Fj*, 1987 *W*, *I*, 1988 *Fj*, *Fj*
AA Lutui 1999 *Geo*, *J*, *Sa*, *F*, 2001 *Fj*, *Fj*, *S*, *W*, 2004 *Sa*, *Fj*, 2005 *Fj*, *Sa*, *Fj*, *Sa*, 2006 *Fj*, *JAB*, 2007 *AuA*, *J*, *JAB*, *Fj*, *Sa*, *US*, *Sa*, *SA*, *E*, 2010 *Sa*, *Fj*, *J*, 2011 *Fj*, *Fj*, *NZ*, *J*, *F*

F Ma'afa 1981 *Fj*, *Fj*
F Ma'afu 1985 *Fj*, 1986 *Fj*, *Fj*, 1988 *Sa*, *Fj*, *Fj*, *Fj*
P Ma'afu 1979 *M*, *E*, *Sa*, *Fj*, 1980 *Sa*, 1981 *Fj*, *Fj*, 1983 *M*, *M*
P Ma'afu 1959 *Fj*, 1960 *M*, 1963 *Fj*
T Ma'afu 1983 *M*, *M*
VS Ma'afu 2011 *US*, *J*, *Sa*, *Fj*, *Fj*, *NZ*, *C*, *J*, *F*
V Ma'ake 1973 *M*, *A*, *A*, *Fj*, 1974 *S*, *W*, *C*, 1975 *M*, *M*, 1977 *Fj*, *Fj*, *Fj*, 1979 *NC*, *M*, *E*, *Sa*, *Fj*, 1980 *Sa*
AI Ma'asi 2009 *Fj*, *Sa*, *J*, 2011 *US*, *J*, *Sa*, *Fj*, *C*, *J*
V Ma'asi 1997 *W*, 2000 *C*, *J*, *Sa*, *US*, 2001 *Fj*, *Fj*, *Sa*, *S*, *W*, 2002 *J*, *Fj*, *Sa*, *Sa*, 2003 *I*, *Fj*, *Fj*, *It*, *W*, *NZ*, *C*, 2005 *Fj*, *Sa*, *It*, *F*, 2008 *J*, *Sa*, *Fj*, 2009 *Fj*, *Sa*, *J*
S Mafana 1959 *Fj*, 1960 *M*, 1963 *Fj*, *Fj*
A Mafi 1995 *Iv*
F Mafi 1993 *A*, *Fj*, 1994 *Sa*, *W*, *Fj*, 1995 *J*, *J*, *F*, 1996 *Sa*, *Fj*, 1998 *Sa*, *A*, 1999 *Geo*, *Geo*, *Kor*, *J*, *US*, *NZ*, *It*, *E*
S Mafi 1969 *M*, *M*, 1972 *Fj*, *Fj*, *Fj*, 1973 *M*, *A*, *A*, *Fj*, 1974 *S*, *W*, *C*, 1975 *M*, *M*
S Mafi 1988 *Fj*, 1989 *Fj*, 1990 *Fj*, *Kor*, 1993 *Sa*
S Mafi 2010 *Sa*, *Fj*, *J*
S Mafile'o 1995 *Iv*, *Sa*, *Fj*, 1997 *Z*, *Nm*, *SA*, 2002 *J*, 2003 *Kor*, *Kor*, *I*, *Fj*
R Mahe 2005 *Sa*, *It*, *F*, 2006 *Fj*, *JAB*, *Coo*, *Coo*, 2007 *Kor*
S Mahe 1981 *Fj*, *Fj*, *Fj*
F Mahoni 1993 *Sa*, *A*, *Fj*, 1995 *J*, *J*, *F*, *Sa*, *Fj*, 1996 *Sa*, *Fj*, 1999 *Geo*, *J*

A Mailangi 2010 *J*
F Mailangi 1968 *Fj*, *Fj*, *Fj*, 1969 *M*
F Mailangi 1928 *Fj*, *Fj*
L Mailangi 1959 *Fj*, 1960 *M*, 1963 *Fj*, *Fj*
P Mailefihi 1979 *E*, 1982 *Fj*
AK Ma'ilei 2002 *J*, *Fj*, *Sa*, *Sa*, *Fj*, *PNG*, *PNG*, 2003 *Kor*, *Kor*, 2005 *Fj*, *Sa*, *F*, 2010 *Sa*, *J*, 2011 *Fj*, *J*, *Fj*, *Fj*, *NZ*, *J*, *F*
T Mak 1988 *Fj*
A Maka 2005 *F*
F Maka 2007 *US*, *Sa*, *SA*, *E*, 2011 *Fj*, *NZ*, *C*, *F*
L Maka 1997 *Z*, 1999 *Geo*, *J*, *US*, *F*, *NZ*, *It*, *E*, 2000 *C*, *Fj*, *J*, *NZ*, *US*, 2002 *J*, *Sa*, *Sa*, *Fj*, 2003 *Kor*, *Kor*
P Maka 1985 *Fj*
T Maka 1979 *NC*, *Sa*, 1981 *Fj*, *Fj*
V Maka 1983 *Fj*, *Sa*, 1984 *Fj*, *Fj*
H Makahoi 1974 *C*, 1975 *M*, *M*, 1977 *Fj*, *Fj*, *Fj*, 1979 *Sa*, *Fj*, 1980 *Sa*
S Makalo 1975 *M*
M Makasini 2005 *Fj*, *Sa*, *Fj*, *Sa*
T Makisi 1983 *M*, *M*, 1989 *Fj*, *Fj*
Malu 1947 *Fj*
M Malu 1979 *NC*, *Sa*
MV Malupo 2009 *Sa*, 2011 *US*, *Sa*
L Manako 2000 *NZ*, *Sa*
T Manako 1995 *J*, *J*
T Manako 2000 *J*
C Manu 1987 *Sa*, *Fj*, 1989 *Fj*, *Fj*
E Manu 1996 *Sa*, *Fj*, 1999 *Kor*, *J*, *US*
F Manukia 1993 *A*, *Fj*, 1994 *Sa*, *W*, *Fj*, 1995 *J*, *J*
M Manukia 1993 *Sa*, *S*, *Fj*, *A*, *Fj*, 1994 *Fj*
T Mapa 1967 *Fj*, *Fj*
P Mapakaitolo 1977 *Fj*, *Fj*
VP Mapakaitolo 2009 *Fj*, *J*, 2011 *US*
S Martens 1998 *A*, *Fj*, 1999 *Geo*, *Geo*, *Kor*, *Kor*, *J*, *US*, *Sa*, *F*, *Fj*, *C*, *NZ*, *It*, *E*, 2001 *S*, *W*, 2002 *Fj*, *Sa*, *Sa*, *Fj*, 2003 *Kor*, *Kor*, *It*, *W*, *NZ*, *C*, 2009 *Fj*, *Sa*, *J*
S Masi 1989 *Fj*
F Masila 1990 *J*, 1991 *Fj*, 1993 *Sa*, *S*, *A*, *Fj*, 1994 *W*, 1995 *F*, *Fj*, 1998 *Sa*, *A*
Masili 1991 *Fj*
SK Masima 2005 *Fj*
T Matakaiongo 1997 *W*
S Matangi 2000 *J*, *Sa*, 2001 *Fj*, *Sa*, 2002 *Fj*, *PNG*, 2004 *Sa*, *Fj*
S Matapule 1973 *M*, 1975 *M*
SH Mata'u 2007 *AuA*, 2008 *J*
S Mateaki 1928 *Fj*, *Fj*
P Mateo 2010 *CHL*
K Ma'u 1981 *Fj*, 1983 *Fj*, *Sa*, *M*, 1984 *Fj*, *Fj*
T Ma'u 1947 *Fj*, *Fj*
V Ma'u 1947 *Fj*
O Misa 2004 *Sa*, *Fj*
S Misa 1926 *Fj*, *Fj*, *Fj*
S Moa 1928 *Fj*
U Moa 1998 *A*, *Fj*, 1999 *Geo*
UV Moa 2011 *Fj*, *Fj*, *NZ*, *C*, *J*, *F*
V Moa 1993 *Sa*, *S*, 1998 *Sa*
F Moala 1982 *Sa*, *Fj*, 1983 *Fj*, *Sa*, *M*, *M*, 1984 *Fj*, *Fj*, 1985 *Fj*
F Moala 1982 *Sa*, 1983 *Sa*, 1985 *Fj*
F Moala 1963 *Fj*, *Fj*, 1968 *Fj*, *Fj*, *Fj*
K Moala 1959 *Fj*, 1960 *M*, 1963 *Fj*, 1967 *Fj*, *Fj*
M Moala 1986 *W*, *Fj*, *Fj*
M Moala 2004 *Sa*, *Fj*, 2009 *Pt*
P Moala 1982 *Sa*, 1986 *W*, *Fj*, *Fj*, 1987 *Sa*, *Fj*
P Moala 1981 *Fj*, *Fj*, *Fj*
S Moala 1988 *Fj*
T Moala 1972 *Fj*
V Moala'eua 1977 *Fj*, *Fj*, *Fj*, 1979 *NC*, *M*, *Sa*, *Fj*, 1981 *Fj*, *Fj*
V Moeaki 1934 *Fj*
Mofuike 1986 *Fj*
S Mohi 1986 *W*, *Fj*, *Fj*, 1987 *C*, *W*, *I*
S Moimoi 2001 *W*
S Moli 1992 *Fj*
F Molitika 2000 *C*, *J*, 2001 *Fj*, *Sa*, *S*, 2005 *It*, *F*
MK Molitika 1997 *Nm*, *SA*, *Fj*, *Sa*, *Coo*, *W*, 2000 *NZ*, *Sa*, *US*, 2001 *S*, 2005 *It*, 2006 *Fj*, *JAB*, *Coo*, *Sa*, 2007 *E*
DW Morath 2010 *Sa*, *Fj*, 2011 *US*
KS Morath 2009 *Pt*, 2010 *Sa*, *Fj*, *J*, 2011 *US*, *Fj*, *J*, *Sa*, *Fj*, *NZ*, *C*, *J*, *F*
S Moto'apuaka 1980 *Sa*, 1987 *C*
K Motu'apuaka 1972 *Fj*
S Motu'apuaka 1969 *M*, *M*, 1972 *Fj*
S Motu'apuka 1979 *Fj*
S Motuliki 1967 *Fj*
Mounga 1947 *Fj*

E Mo'ungaloa 1924 *Fj, Fj, Fj*
F Muller 1967 *Fj*, 1968 *Fj, Fj, Fj*, 1969 *M, M*, 1972 *Fj, Fj*

S Na'a Tovo 1924 *Fj, Fj, Fj*
T Na'aniumotu 2006 *J, JAB, Coo, Sa, Coo*, 2010 *CHL*
F Naitoko 2005 *Sa*
S Napa'a 1934 *Fj*
S Nau 2000 *C, Fj, J*, 2001 *Fj*, 2003 *Fj*, 2005 *It, F*, 2006 *JAB, Coo, Sa*
N Naufahu 2001 *Fj, Sa, Fj, W*, 2002 *J, Sa, Sa, Fj, PNG, PNG*, 2003 *Kor, Kor, I, W, C*
S Nauvai 1960 *M*
T Ngaluafe 1974 *S, W, C*, 1975 *M, M*
J Ngauamo 2003 *Kor, I, Fj, It, C*, 2005 *It*
MM Ngauamo 2002 *PNG, PNG*, 2003 *Kor, I, Fj, It, W, NZ, C*, 2005 *F*, 2006 *Fj, JAB*, 2008 *Sa, Fj*
S Ngauamo 1997 *Coo*, 1998 *A*
T Nisa 1991 *Fj*, 1992 *Fj*
U Niuila 1990 *Sa*
S Nuku 1981 *Fj, Fj, Fj*, 1984 *Fj, Fj*

L Ofa 1983 *Fj, Sa, M, M*, 1984 *Fj*
A Olosoni 2010 *Sa, Fj, J*
I Omani 1928 *Fj*, 1932 *Fj, Fj, Fj*
M 'Otai 1995 *J, J, F, S, Iv*
M 'Ota'ota 2000 *C*, 2005 *Fj, Sa, Fj*

E Paea 2011 *US*
H Paea 2007 *Kor*
L Pahulu 1973 *A, Fj*, 1974 *S*
V Pahulu 1967 *Fj, Fj, Fj*, 1968 *Fj, Fj, Fj*, 1969 *M, M*, 1973 *M*
P Palavi 1924 *Fj, Fj, Fj*
U Palavi 1960 *M*, 1963 *Fj, Fj*
J Pale 2001 *S, W*, 2002 *J, Fj, Sa, Sa, Fj*, 2003 *Fj*
M Pale 1998 *A*, 1999 *Geo*, 2002 *J, Fj*, 2006 *J, Coo, Sa*
SW Palei 2009 *J*
S Palenapa 1990 *Fj, J, Sa, Kor, Sa*, 1996 *Sa, Fj*
D Palu 2002 *PNG, PNG*, 2003 *Kor, Kor, I, Fj, It, C*, 2006 *J, JAB, Coo*, 2007 *AuA, J, JAB*
P Palu 1979 *NC*, 1981 *Fj*
TM Palu 2008 *J*
TT Palu 2011 *Sa, Fj, Fj, C, F*
S Panelapa 1988 *Fj*
H Pau'u 1983 *Fj, Sa*
T Pau'u 1992 *Fj*
J Payne 2002 *PNG, PNG*, 2003 *Kor, Kor, I, Fj, It, W, NZ, C*
D Penisini 1997 *Nm, Coo*, 1999 *Geo, Kor, C*
'O Pepa 1928 *Fj, Fj, Fj*
H Petelo 1982 *Fj*
H Pierra 2005 *Sa*
O Pifeleti 1983 *Fj, Sa, M, M*, 1984 *Fj, Fj*, 1985 *Fj*, 1989 *Fj, Fj*, 1990 *Sa*, 1991 *Sa, Fj, Fj*
T Piukala 1934 *Fj*
SV Piutau 2011 *Fj, Fj, NZ, C, J, F*
H Pohiva 1997 *W*, 1998 *Sa, Fj*
VV Pola 2010 *Fj, CHL*
THN Pole 2007 *Kor, AuA, J, JAB, Fj, Sa, US, Sa, E*, 2008 *Sa, Fj*, 2009 *Fj, Sa, J*
S Pone 2008 *Sa, Fj*
S Pongi 1990 *Sa*
SE Poteki 2007 *Kor*
VT Poteki 2007 *Kor*
S Pouanga 1947 *Fj, Fj*
E Pou'uhila 1988 *Fj*
SKV Puafisi 2011 *J, Sa*
ST Puloka 1928 *Fj, Fj*, 1934 *Fj*
K Pulu 2002 *Fj, PNG, PNG*, 2003 *Kor, Kor, I, Fj, It, W, NZ*, 2005 *Fj, Sa, Fj, Sa*, 2006 *J*, 2007 *US, Sa, SA, E*, 2008 *Fj*, 2009 *Sa, J*, 2011 *US, NZ, C, F*
M Pulumu 1979 *NC, Sa, Fj*, 1980 *Sa*, 1981 *Fj, Fj, Fj*
T Pulumufila 1974 *S, W, C*

H Saafi 2000 *NZ*
K Sakalia 2010 *CHL*
T Samiu 1947 *Fj*
Sanilaita 1981 *Fj*
S Satui 2009 *Pt*
A Saulala 1991 *Fj*
C Schaumkel 1992 *Sa, Fj*, 1997 *SA, Fj*
S Selupe 1963 *Fj, Fj*, 1967 *Fj, Fj*, 1969 *M, M*, 1972 *Fj*, 1973 *M, A, Fj*
S Selupe 1967 *Fj*, 1969 *M*, 1972 *Fj*
S Selupe 1924 *Fj, Fj, Fj*, 1928 *Fj*
T Siale 1997 *Nm, Sa*
M Sifa 1947 *Fj*
S Sika 1968 *Fj, Fj, Fj*, 1969 *M, M*
AH Sikalu 2007 *AuA, J*, 2010 *Sa, Fj*
T Sime 1963 *Fj*
T Sitanilei 1932 *Fj*
J Sitoa 1998 *A*
E Siua 2009 *Pt*, 2010 *CHL*, 2011 *US*
PIL Siulangapo 2010 *CHL*
T Soaiti 1932 *Fj, Fj, Fj*
T Soane 1982 *Sa, Fj*, 1983 *Fj, Sa*, 1984 *Fj, Fj*, 1985 *Fj*
L Stanley 1985 *Fj*
L Susimalofi 1989 *Fj*

L Tafa 2007 *J*
S Tahaafe 1987 *C*
P Taholo 1983 *M*
S Tai 1997 *W*, 1998 *A*
U Tai 1969 *M*, 1972 *Fj*
E Taione 1999 *It, E*, 2000 *Fj, J*, 2001 *S, W*, 2005 *F*, 2006 *JAB, Sa*, 2007 *Fj, Sa, US, Sa, SA, E*, 2008 *Sa, Fj*, 2009 *Fj*
K Take 1989 *Fj*
E Talakai 1993 *Sa, S, Fj, Fj*, 1995 *S, Iv, Sa, Fj*
H Taliai 1934 *Fj*
P Tanginoa 1995 *Fj*, 1997 *W*, 1998 *Sa, A*, 1999 *Geo*
T Tanginoa 2007 *AuA, J*
F Taniela 1982 *Fj*
I Tapueluelu 1990 *Fj, J, Sa, Sa*, 1993 *Sa, S*, 1999 *Kor, Kor, J, US, NZ, It, E*
F Tatafu 1996 *Fj*, 1997 *Z, Nm, Fj, Sa, Coo, W*, 1999 *Geo, Kor, Kor, J, Sa, Fj, C, NZ, E*, 2002 *J, Fj, Sa, PNG, PNG*
S Tatafu 1967 *Fj*
T Tatafu 1963 *Fj*
V Tau 1999 *US*
A Taufa 1993 *A*, 1995 *J, J, F, S*
AN Taufa 2010 *Sa, Fj, J*, 2011 *Fj, J, C*
E Taufa 2007 *Sa*, 2008 *J, Sa, Fj*
I Taufa 1972 *Fj*
S Taufa 1984 *Fj*
S Taufa 2005 *Fj, Sa, Fj, Sa*
T Taufa 1990 *Fj*
T Taufahema 1998 *Sa, A, Fj*, 1999 *Sa, F, NZ, It*, 2000 *C, Fj, J, NZ, Sa*, 2001 *Fj, Sa, Fj, S, W*
M Taufateau 1983 *M, M*, 1984 *Fj*, 1987 *Fj*
V Taufatofua 1926 *Fj, Fj, Fj*
A Ta'ufo'ou 1997 *Nm, SA, Fj, Sa, Coo*
E Ta'ufo'ou 2000 *C, Fj, J, NZ, Sa, US*
N Taufo'ou 1996 *Sa, Fj*, 1997 *Nm, SA, Fj, Sa, Coo, W*, 1998 *Sa, A, Fj*, 1999 *Geo, Kor, F, Fj, NZ, It, E*, 2000 *NZ, Sa, US*
E Taukafa 2002 *PNG, PNG*, 2003 *Kor, Kor, I, Fj, Fj, It, W, NZ, C*, 2005 *Fj, Sa, It, F*, 2006 *J, Fj, Coo, Sa, Coo*, 2007 *US, Sa, SA, E*, 2008 *Sa, Fj*, 2011 *Fj, J, Sa, Fj, NZ, C*
S Taukapo 2005 *Sa*
P Taukolo 1982 *Sa, Fj*
P Taula 2009 *Fj, Pt*, 2010 *Sa, Fj, J*
FKA Taumalolo 2011 *Fj, J, Sa, Fj, NZ, C, J, F*
S Taumalolo 1996 *Sa, Fj*, 1997 *Z, Nm, SA, Coo, W*, 1999 *Geo, Geo, Sa, F, Fj, C, NZ*, 2000 *NZ, Sa, US*, 2001 *Fj, Sa, S, W*, 2006 *J*, 2007 *JAB, Fj, Sa*
P Taumiuvao 1986 *Fj*
N Taumoefolau 1979 *NC, E, Sa, Fj*
P Taumoepeau 1928 *Fj, Fj, Fj*
SS Taumoepeau 2011 *US*
T Taumoepeau 1999 *Geo, Kor, Kor, J, US, NZ, E*, 2000 *Fj, J, NZ, Sa, US*, 2001 *Fj, Sa, Sa, S, W*, 2002 *J, Fj, Sa*, 2006 *J, Fj, JAB, Coo, Sa, Coo*, 2007 *AuA, J, Fj, Sa*
T Taumoepeau 1988 *Fj*
V Taumoepeau 1994 *Sa, W*, 1995 *Sa, Fj*
P Taumoua 2007 *J*
S Taupeaafe 1994 *W, Fj*, 1998 *Sa, A, Fj*, 1999 *Kor, J, NZ, It, E*, 2000 *NZ, US*, 2001 *Fj, Sa*
F Tautau'a 2007 *Kor*
S Tavo 1959 *Fj*, 1960 *M*, 1963 *Fj, Fj*, 1967 *Fj, Fj, Fj*, 1968 *Fj, Fj, Fj*, 1969 *M, M*
M Te Pou 1998 *A, Fj*, 1999 *Geo, Geo, Kor, Kor, J, US, F, NZ, It*, 2001 *S, W*
Telanisi 1967 *Fj*
SF Telefoni 2008 *J, Sa, Fj*, 2009 *Pt*, 2011 *Fj*
Teri 1991 *Fj*
Teutau 1991 *Fj*
SLN Timani 2008 *J*, 2009 *Fj*, 2011 *US, Fj, Fj, NZ, C*
D Tiueti 1997 *Fj, Sa, W*, 1999 *Geo, Geo, Kor, Sa, F, Fj, C, NZ, It, E*, 2000 *C, Fj, J, NZ, Sa, US*, 2001 *S, W*
T Tofua 1924 *Fj, Fj, Fj*, 1926 *Fj, Fj, Fj*
T Toga 1968 *Fj*

T Tohi 1997 *Nm, SA*
T Toke 2007 *Kor, J, JAB, Fj, Sa, US, Sa*, 2009 *Fj*, 2010 *Sa, Fj, J*
M Toloke 2010 *CHL*
V Toloke 1995 *J, Sa, Fj*, 1996 *Sa, Fj*, 1999 *Geo, Geo, Kor, Kor, US, NZ, E*, 2000 *NZ, Sa, US*, 2002 *J, Sa, Sa*
M Toma 1988 *Sa, Fj, Fj*, 1991 *Sa, Fj, Fj*
G Tonga 1997 *Z, W*
K Tonga 1996 *Fj*, 1997 *Nm, SA, Fj, Sa, Coo*, 1999 *Geo, Geo, Kor*, 2001 *Fj, Sa*
K Tonga 2003 *Fj, C*, 2004 *Sa, Fj*, 2005 *Fj, Fj*
K Tonga 1947 *Fj, Fj*
M Tonga 2001 *Fj, Sa, Fj, Sa*, 2003 *Kor, Kor*
M Tonga 1947 *Fj, Fj*
P Tonga 1973 *A*
S Tonga 2005 *Sa, Fj, Sa*
T Tonga 1990 *Sa*
S Tonga Simiki 1924 *Fj*, 1926 *Fj, Fj, Fj*
H Tonga'uiha 2005 *Fj, Sa, Sa*, 2006 *J, Fj, JAB, Coo, Sa, Coo*, 2007 *Kor, AuA, J, JAB, Fj, Sa, E*, 2008 *J, Sa, Fj*, 2009 *Fj, Sa, J*, 2011 *J, Sa*
SL Tonga'uiha 2005 *It, F*, 2007 *JAB, US, Sa, SA, E*, 2011 *Fj, NZ, C, J, F*
'O Topeni 2000 *J*
J Tuamoheloa 2003 *Fj*
S Tuamoheloa 2003 *Fj, C*, 2005 *Fj*
T Tuavao 1986 *Fj*
N Tufui 1990 *Fj, J, Sa, Sa*, 1992 *Fj*, 1994 *Fj*, 1995 *S, Iv*
S Tufui 1926 *Fj, Fj, Fj*, 1928 *Fj, Fj, Fj*, 1932 *Fj, Fj, Fj*, 1934 *Fj*
TH Tu'ifua 2003 *Fj, It, W, NZ*, 2006 *J, Fj, JAB, Coo, Sa*, 2007 *Fj, Sa, US, Sa, SA, E*
P Tu'ihalamaka 1972 *Fj*, 1973 *M, A, A, Fj*, 1974 *S, C*, 1975 *M, M*, 1977 *Fj, Fj*, 1979 *NC*, 1981 *Fj, Fj, Fj*, 1987 *C*
S Tu'ihalamaka 1999 *Kor, Kor, J, US*, 2001 *Sa, Fj*
Tu'ikolovatu 1983 *Fj*
JML Tuineau 2011 *Fj, J, Sa, Fj, NZ, J, F*
T Tu'ineua 1992 *Fj*, 1993 *Sa, S, Fj, A, Fj*
E Tu'ipolotu 1926 *Fj, Fj, Fj*, 1928 *Fj, Fj*
S Tu'ipolotu 1981 *Fj*
S Tu'ipolotu 1947 *Fj, Fj*
K Tuipulotu 1994 *Fj*, 1997 *Fj, Sa, Coo*
S Tuipulotu 1993 *Fj*, 1994 *Sa, W, Fj*, 1995 *J, J, F, S, Iv*, 1999 *Kor, F, Fj, C, It, E*, 2001 *S*, 2003 *Fj, Fj, It, NZ*
K Tu'ipulotu 1994 *W*, 1997 *SA, Fj, Coo, W*, 1999 *Kor, Kor, J, US, Fj, It, E*, 2000 *Fj, J*, 2001 *Fj*
M Tu'ipulotu 1977 *Fj, Fj, Fj*
P Tu'ipulotu 1979 *Sa*, 1980 *Sa*
SM Tu'ipulotu 1997 *W*, 1998 *Sa, A*, 1999 *Sa, F, NZ, E*, 2000 *C, NZ, Sa, US*, 2001 *Fj, Fj, Sa*, 2005 *Fj, Sa, It, F*, 2006 *J, Fj, JAB, Coo, Sa*, 2007 *US, Sa, SA, E*, 2008 *J, Sa*
V Tu'ipulotu 1977 *Fj, Fj, Fj*, 1979 *M, E, Fj*
J Tu'itavake 1932 *Fj*
L Tu'itavake 1959 *Fj*, 1960 *M*, 1963 *Fj, Fj*
P Tu'itavake 1995 *Fj*
I Tuivai 1993 *Sa*
K Tuivailala 1987 *Sa*, 1988 *Sa, Fj, Fj*, 1989 *Fj, Fj*, 1990 *Fj, J, Sa, Kor*, 1991 *Fj*
K Tuivailala 1988 *Fj*
M Tuku'aho 1979 *Fj*
M Tuku'aho 1979 *NC, Sa*, 1980 *Sa*, 1982 *Sa*
T Tulia 2002 *PNG*, 2003 *Kor, Kor, I, Fj*, 2004 *Sa, Fj*, 2005 *Fj, Sa*
A Tulikaki 1993 *S*
S Tulikifanga 1997 *SA, Fj, Sa, Coo*
S Tunufa'i 1934 *Fj*
F Tupi 1973 *A, A, Fj*, 1974 *S, W*, 1975 *M, M*
H Tupou 1982 *Sa, Fj*, 1983 *M, M*, 1984 *Fj, Fj*, 1987 *C, W, I*
IM Tupou 2006 *Coo, Coo*, 2007 *Kor, AuA, J, JAB, US, Sa, SA*, 2008 *J*, 2009 *Fj, Sa*
J Tupou 1994 *Fj*
M Tupou 2005 *Fj, Fj, Sa*, 2010 *CHL*
P Tupou 1984 *Fj*, 1986 *W*, 1988 *Fj*
S Tupou 1975 *M*
M Tu'ungafasi 1986 *W, Fj*, 1987 *W, I*
L Tu'uta 1928 *Fj, Fj*
T Tu'utu Kakato 1987 *C, W, I*, 1990 *Sa, Kor*, 1991 *Sa, Fj*, 1992 *Fj*

A Uasi 1993 *S*, 1994 *Sa, Fj*
L Uhatafe 1987 *Sa, Fj*
V Uhi 1997 *Z, Nm, SA, Fj, Sa, Coo*
S Ula 1959 *Fj*, 1960 *M*, 1963 *Fj, Fj*
T Ula 2011 *Fj*
L Ulufonua 2002 *PNG*, 2003 *Kor, Kor, Fj*
T Unga 1934 *Fj*

S Vaea 1974 *S, W, C*, 1975 *M*, 1977 *Fj, Fj*
S Vaea 1928 *Fj, Fj, Fj*
L Vaeno 1986 *Fj*
S Vaeno 1991 *Sa*
S Va'enuku 2003 *Fj, It, W, NZ*, 2004 *Sa, Fj*, 2005 *Sa, Fj, Sa, It*, 2007 *AuA, Sa*
T Va'enuku 1991 *Sa, Fj*, 1992 *Sa, Fj*, 1993 *S, Fj, A, Fj*, 1994 *Sa, W, Fj*, 1995 *F, S, Iv*
U Va'enuku 1995 *F, S, Iv*
L Va'eono 1987 *W*
L Vaeuo 1985 *Fj*
S Vaha'akolo 1990 *J, Kor*
SK Vahafolau 2007 *J, Fj, Sa*, 2008 *Sa, Fj*, 2009 *Pt*, 2011 *Fj, Sa, Fj, Fj, NZ, C, J, F*
N Vahe 1977 *Fj, Fj*
S Vai 1981 *Fj, Fj*, 1988 *Sa, Fj*
A Vaihu 1975 *M*
T Vaikona 2006 *J, Fj, JAB, Coo*
H Vaingalo 1988 *Fj*
F Vainikolo 2011 *Fj, Fj, C, J*
SAF Vaioleti 2010 *CHL*
T Vaioleti 2005 *F*, 2010 *CHL*
SFK Vaiomounga 2009 *Pt*, 2010 *Sa, Fj, J*, 2011 *Fj, Sa, Fj, C, J*
L Vaipulu 1987 *C*
JW Vaka 2004 *Sa, Fj*, 2005 *Sa*, 2007 *US, Sa, SA, E*, 2009 *Fj, Sa, J*
PM Vakaloa 2009 *Pt*
P Vakamalolo 1993 *Sa*
I Vaka'uta 1959 *Fj*, 1963 *Fj, Fj*
S Vaka'uta 1924 *Fj, Fj, Fj*
V Vaka'uta 1959 *Fj*, 1960 *M*
V Vake 1932 *Fj*
VL Vaki 2001 *Fj, Sa, Fj, Sa, S, W*, 2002 *J, Fj, Sa, Sa, Fj, PNG*, 2003 *I, Fj, Fj, It, W, NZ, C*, 2005 *Fj, Sa, It, F*, 2006 *JAB, Coo, Sa, Coo*, 2007 *US, Sa, SA, E*, 2008 *Fj*
Valeli 1947 *Fj*
F Valu 1973 *M, A, A, Fj*, 1974 *S, W, C*, 1975 *M, M*, 1977 *Fj, Fj, Fj*, 1979 *NC, M, E, Sa, Fj*, 1980 *Sa*, 1981 *Fj*, 1983 *Fj, Sa, M, M*, 1987 *C, W, I*
V Vanisi 1969 *M, M*
L Vano 1986 *Fj*
A Vasi 1993 *Fj*
I Vave 1973 *A, A, Fj*, 1974 *S, C*
T Vave 1993 *A*
M Vea 1992 *Fj*
S Veehala 1987 *Sa, Fj*, 1988 *Fj, Fj*, 1989 *Fj*, 1990 *J, Kor*, 1991 *Sa, Fj, Fj*
J Vikilani 1932 *Fj, Fj*
T Vikilani 1992 *Fj*, 1994 *Sa, W*
T Viliame 1979 *M*
O Vitelefi 1986 *W*
F Vuna 1977 *Fj, Fj, Fj*, 1979 *NC, M, Sa*, 1981 *Fj*
V Vuni 1932 *Fj, Fj, Fj*, 1934 *Fj*
A Vunipola 1982 *Fj*
E Vunipola 1990 *Fj, Kor*, 1993 *Sa, S, Fj, A, Fj*, 1994 *Sa, W*, 1995 *J, J, F, S, Iv*, 1996 *Sa, Fj*, 1997 *Z*, 1999 *Geo, Geo, Kor, Kor, J, F, Fj, NZ, It, E*, 2000 *C, Fj, J, NZ, Sa, US*, 2001 *Fj, Sa, Fj, Sa, S*, 2004 *Sa, Fj*, 2005 *F*
F Vunipola 1988 *Fj*, 1991 *Sa, Fj, Fj*, 1994 *Sa, W, Fj*, 1995 *J, J, F, S, Iv, Sa, Fj*, 1996 *Sa, Fj*, 1997 *SA, Fj, Coo*, 1998 *Sa, Fj*, 1999 *Geo, Kor, Kor, Fj, C, NZ, E*, 2000 *NZ, Sa, US*, 2001 *Sa*
K Vunipola 1982 *Sa, Fj*, 1983 *Fj, Sa, M, M*
M Vunipola 1987 *W, Sa*, 1988 *Sa, Fj, Fj, Fj*, 1989 *Fj, Fj*, 1990 *Kor*, 1991 *Fj, Fj*, 1992 *Sa*, 1993 *Sa, S, Fj, A, Fj*, 1994 *Sa, W*, 1995 *J, J, F, S, Sa, Fj*, 1996 *Sa, Fj*, 1997 *Nm, SA, Coo*, 1999 *Geo, Kor, Kor, US, Fj*
S Vunipola 1977 *Fj*, 1981 *Fj*, 1982 *Sa*
V Vunipola 1982 *Fj*
VS Vunipola 2004 *Sa, Fj*, 2005 *It*
S Vunipoli 1960 *M*, 1963 *Fj*

B Woolley 1998 *Sa, Fj*, 1999 *Geo, Geo, Kor, J, US, Sa, C, It*

USA

USA'S 2010–11 TEST RECORD

OPPONENT	DATE	VENUE	RESULT
Portugal	13 Nov	A	**Won** 22–17
Georgia	27 Nov	A	**Lost** 17–19
Tonga	8 Jun	N	**Lost** 13–44
Russia	18 Jun	N	**Won** 32–25
Canada	6 Aug	A	**Lost** 22–28
Canada	13 Aug	H	**Lost** 7–27
Japan	21 Aug	A	**Lost** 14–20
Ireland	11 Sep	N	**Lost** 10–22
Russia	15 Sep	N	**Won** 13–6
Australia	23 Sep	N	**Lost** 5–67
Italy	27 Sep	N	**Lost** 10–27

USA WIN THEIR 'WORLD CUP FINAL'

By Ian Gilbert

Mike Hewitt/Getty Images

The USA players are unable to contain their joy at their victory over Russia.

Trivia buffs will know that USA are the reigning Olympic rugby champions, having landed gold in 1924 – the last time the sport figured on the programme. In the years since that triumph, USA have faced three of their Pool C opponents – Australia, Ireland and Italy – 16 times without once winning.

But, crucially, the Eagles' other opponent at Rugby World Cup 2011, Russia, had lost all three of the sides' fixtures, and their clash in New Plymouth represented the USA's clearest chance of a victory at the tournament. With their inspirational captain, the charismatic Todd Clever, to the fore, USA won 13–6 with scrum-half Mike Petri scoring the only try.

That was game two, but the Eagles had opened their RWC campaign against Ireland. Tenacious defence forced the Irish to summon all their big-game nous, and players such as Man of the Match Paul O'Connell saw them home 22–10 – the second-closest margin in the eight fixtures between the two countries.

Clever was central to most of the good things that USA did, and coach Eddie O'Sullivan – a former coach of Ireland – said, "He's an inspirational captain and he had a massive game today. He led the team well, and we needed someone out there to do that."

The USA's first two matches were in New Plymouth, and there was good reason for the locals to take the Eagles to their heart, with the Ireland fixture coinciding with the tenth anniversary of the September 11 terrorist attacks.

Hours before the match at Stadium Taranaki the USA players and support staff joined hundreds for a 9/11 memorial service at St Andrew's church. The Reverend Kim Francis had been contacted by the US Embassy in New Zealand to suggest a memorial service.

New Yorker Petri, the Eagles vice-captain, was at high school in Manhattan when the World Trade Center was attacked. "Ten years ago, that was a dark day for everyone. You never forget something like that. It's a huge honour for us to represent our country on that day," Petri said.

The Ireland match was also significant for other milestones. Prop Mike MacDonald became the USA's most-capped player with a tally of 63 Test matches. "You can say a lot of things now, but in the heat of the moment the emotion is going to hit," he said.

There was also a family celebration for the Suniula brothers, centre Andrew Suniula and fly-half Roland, when they were named in the starting XV, becoming the first siblings to take the field at Rugby World Cup 2011. Andrew was a protégé of All Blacks head coach Graham Henry when he was headmaster at Kelston Boys High School in Auckland.

The Irish scrum made the big difference that night, shunting the USA eight at will, yet the passion and determination of their opponents meant Ireland were never able to pull away. The Eagles fixed up their malfunctioning set-piece for Russia, and that was the foundation for the narrow 13–6 victory, their first on the RWC stage since 2003.

The free-running Australians came next, a wounded Wallabies outfit coming off the back of a surprise defeat by Ireland. The Tri-Nations champions were stung into action, taking out their frustrations on USA to win 67–5 in Wellington.

The Eagles did at least have the satisfaction of scoring the first try against the Wallabies in the tournament when No. 8 JJ Gagiano dived over, and the USA just shaded the possession and territory too.

Tim Usasz felt the Eagles learned from the Australians' clinical finishing: "That's the difference when you play the big teams, they really punish you for your mistakes. We came here to be measured against the best and we will learn from it."

Finally came Italy in Nelson. O'Sullivan fielded his strongest XV, saying, "I'm not saying we'll beat Italy. That would be an arrogant thing to say, but I think we can test Italy and see what they've got."

At Trafalgar Park, however, the Eagles forwards were subdued by the Italian pack as four matches in 17 days took their toll. The Azzurri forwards turned on the power to win 27–10 and take the bonus point needed to keep their own quarter-final hopes alive – although that was rendered futile by their subsequent defeat by Ireland. USA's Biarritz speedster Takudzwa Ngwenya was seen as a danger man by the Italians, who limited his opportunities effectively.

O'Sullivan was phlegmatic after that final game. "We set up a strategy coming in that we'd try and get two major performances against Tier 1 nations and win against Russia," O'Sullivan said. "We certainly achieved our goal."

The Americans were so well-received in their travels around the North Island that O'Sullivan and his players were humbled by the sincerity of the support. O'Sullivan was determined that his charges, hailing from a country where rugby is a minority sport, would see the importance of the game to New Zealanders.

"The public reaction has been extraordinary, and that's something that a lot of our guys wouldn't have experienced before, and it's something I was anxious that they would experience," he said.

"On the bus ride up from Whanganui to New Plymouth, we passed a school [Hawera High School]. All the kids were out waving US flags. That blew a lot of guys away. We didn't even get to stop at that school, but it really was extraordinary that this school took the time to come out of class and wait for the bus to pass. That was fantastic. These kids didn't even get to meet the team, but they wanted to be out to welcome us through their town, even if it was at 30 miles an hour."

And, while the squad are roughly equally divided between keen amateurs and contracted professionals, the Eagles could count on one thing: the best backroom boys in the business.

Heading the medical team was Michael Keating, who has worked with the Chicago Blackhawks in the National Hockey League. "We're not the greatest rugby team in the world, but we are the best at medicine and in particular sports medicine," said Keating.

Camaraderie and medical care aside, the role of captain Clever was also integral. Now playing with Suntory in Japan, Clever was the first American to play Super Rugby in his stint with South Africa's Lions. O'Sullivan's parting words after the Italy match illustrated the importance of his captain. "He's been a huge leader for the team, not just tonight but throughout the tournament. He's been outstanding. I'm probably going to embarrass him now, but such is life."

USA INTERNATIONAL STATISTICS

MATCH RECORDS UP TO 31 OCTOBER 2011

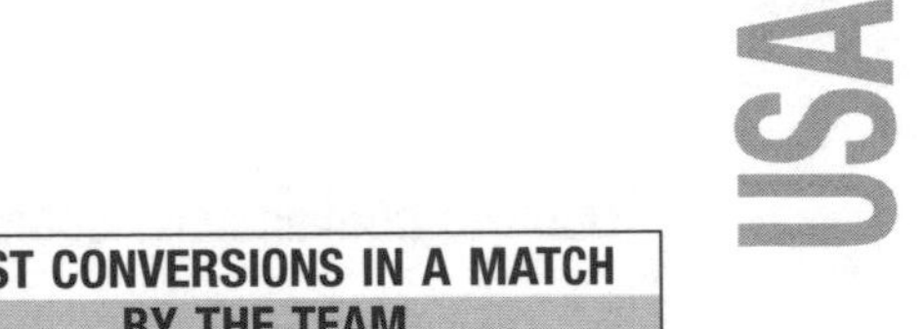

WINNING MARGIN

Date	Opponent	Result	Winning Margin
01/07/2006	Barbados	91–0	**91**
06/07/1996	Japan	74–5	**69**
07/11/1989	Uruguay	60–3	**57**
12/03/1994	Bermuda	60–3	**57**

MOST POINTS IN A MATCH

BY THE TEAM

Date	Opponent	Result	Points
01/07/2006	Barbados	91–0	**91**
06/07/1996	Japan	74–5	**74**
17/05/2003	Japan	69–27	**69**
12/04/2003	Spain	62–13	**62**
08/04/1998	Portugal	61–5	**61**

BY A PLAYER

Date	Player	Opponent	Points
07/11/1989	Chris O'Brien	Uruguay	**26**
31/05/2004	Mike Hercus	Russia	**26**
01/07/2006	Mike Hercus	Barbados	**26**
12/03/1994	Chris O'Brien	Bermuda	**25**
06/07/1996	Matt Alexander	Japan	**24**

MOST TRIES IN A MATCH

BY THE TEAM

Date	Opponent	Result	Tries
01/07/2006	Barbados	91–0	**13**
17/05/2003	Japan	69–27	**11**
07/11/1989	Uruguay	60–3	**11**
06/07/1996	Japan	74–5	**11**

BY A PLAYER

Date	Player	Opponent	Tries
06/07/1996	Vaea Anitoni	Japan	**4**
07/06/1997	Brian Hightower	Japan	**4**
08/04/1998	Vaea Anitoni	Portugal	**4**

MOST CONVERSIONS IN A MATCH

BY THE TEAM

Date	Opponent	Result	Cons
01/07/2006	Barbados	91–0	**13**
07/11/1989	Uruguay	60–3	**8**
06/07/1996	Japan	74–5	**8**

BY A PLAYER

Date	Player	Opponent	Cons
01/07/2006	Mike Hercus	Barbados	**13**
06/07/1996	Matt Alexander	Japan	**8**
07/11/1989	Chris O'Brien	Uruguay	**7**
17/05/2003	Mike Hercus	Japan	**7**

MOST PENALTIES IN A MATCH

BY THE TEAM

Date	Opponent	Result	Pens
18/09/1996	Canada	18–23	**6**

BY A PLAYER

Date	Player	Opponent	Pens
18/09/1996	Matt Alexander	Canada	**6**
21/09/1996	Matt Alexander	Uruguay	**5**
02/10/1993	Chris O'Brien	Australia	**5**
20/10/2003	Mike Hercus	Scotland	**5**
22/05/1999	Kevin Dalzell	Fiji	**5**
09/06/1984	Ray Nelson	Canada	**5**

MOST DROPPED GOALS IN A MATCH

BY THE TEAM

Date	Opponent	Result	DGs
27/11/2010	Georgia	17–19	**2**

BY A PLAYER

1 on 18 Occasions

MOST CAPPED PLAYERS

Name	Caps
Mike MacDonald	65
Luke Gross	62
Alec Parker	57
Dave Hodges	53

LEADING TRY SCORERS

Name	Tries
Vaea Anitoni	26
Paul Emerick	15
Todd Clever	11
Philip Eloff	10
Riaan van Zyl	10

LEADING CONVERSIONS SCORERS

Name	Cons
Mike Hercus	90
Matt Alexander	45
Chris O'Brien	24
Nese Malifa	17

LEADING PENALTY SCORERS

Name	Pens
Mike Hercus	76
Matt Alexander	55
Mark Williams	35

LEADING DROPPED GOAL SCORERS

Name	DGs
Mike Hercus	4

LEADING POINTS SCORERS

Name	Points
Mike Hercus	465
Matt Alexander	286
Chris O'Brien	144
Mark Williams	143
Vaea Anitoni	130

Nick Wilson/Getty Images

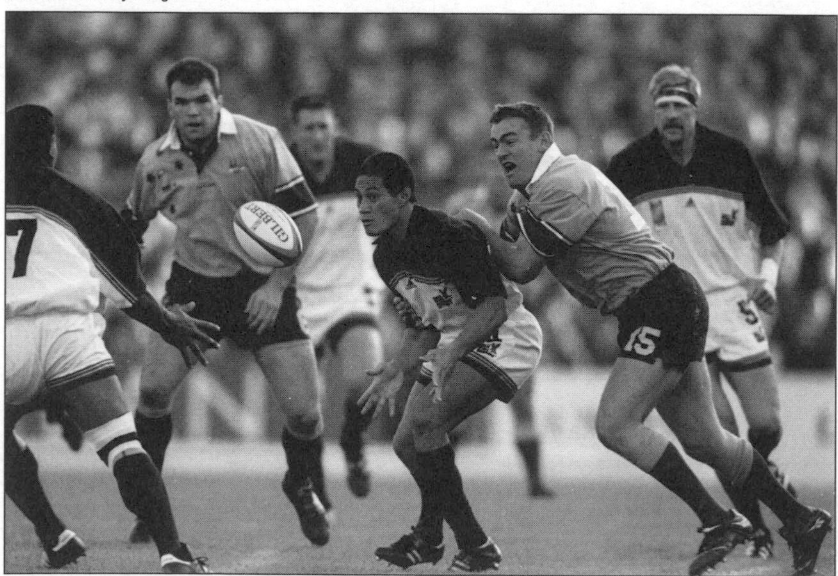

No one has scored more tries for the USA than Vaea Anitoni.

USA INTERNATIONAL PLAYERS (UP TO 31 OCTOBER 2011)

Note: Years given for International Championship matches are for second half of season; eg 1972 means season 1971–72. Years for all other matches refer to the actual year of the match. Entries in square brackets denote matches played in RWC Finals.

M Alexander 1995 *C*, 1996 *I*, *C*, *HK*, *J*, *HK*, *J*, *Ar*, *C*, *Ur*, 1997 *W*, *C*, *HK*, *J*, *J*, *HK*, *C*, *W*, *W*, 1998 *Pt*, *Sp*, *J*, *HK*, *C*
S Allen 1996 *J*, 1997 *HK*, *J*, *J*, *C*, *W*, *W*
T Altemeier 1978 *C*
D Anderson 2002 *S*
B Andrews 1978 *C*, 1979 *C*
VN Anitoni 1992 *C*, 1994 *C*, *Ar*, *Ar*, *I*, 1995 *C*, 1996 *I*, *C*, *C*, *HK*, *J*, *HK*, *J*, *Ar*, *C*, *Ur*, 1997 *W*, *C*, *J*, *HK*, *C*, *W*, *W*, 1998 *Pt*, *Sp*, *J*, *HK*, *C*, *C*, *J*, *HK*, *Fj*, *Ar*, *C*, *Ur*, 1999 *Tg*, *Fj*, *J*, *C*, *Sa*, *E*, *I*, *R*, *A*, 2000 *Fj*, *Sa*
S Auerbach 1976 *A*
M Aylor 2006 *IrA*, *M*, *C*, *Bar*, *Ur*, *Ur*, 2007 *S*, *C*, *Sa*, *SA*, 2008 *IrA*

A Bachelet 1993 *C*, *A*, 1994 *Ber*, *C*, *Ar*, *Ar*, *I*, 1995 *C*, 1996 *I*, *C*, *C*, *HK*, *J*, *HK*, *J*, *Ar*, *C*, 1997 *W*, *C*, *HK*, *J*, *J*, *HK*, *C*, *W*, *W*, 1998 *Pt*, *Sp*, *J*, *HK*, *C*, *C*, *J*
R Bailey 1979 *C*, 1980 *NZ*, 1981 *C*, *SA*, 1982 *C*, 1983 *C*, *A*, 1987 *Tun*, *C*, *J*, *E*
B Barnard 2006 *IrA*, *M*, *Bar*, *C*
JI Basauri 2007 *S*, *E*, *Tg*, 2008 *Ur*, *J*, *J*, 2010 *Pt*, *Geo*, 2011 *Tg*, *Rus*, *C*, *A*
D Bateman 1982 *C*, *E*, 1983 *A*, 1985 *J*, *C*
P Bell 2006 *IrA*, *M*, *C*, *Bar*, *C*, *Ur*, *Ur*
W Bernhard 1987 *Tun*
CM Biller 2009 *I*, *W*, *Geo*, *C*, *C*, 2010 *Rus*, *Pt*, *Geo*, 2011 *Tg*, *Rus*, *C*, *C*, *J*, *I*, *Rus*, *It*
TW Billups 1993 *C*, *A*, 1994 *Ber*, *C*, *Ar*, *Ar*, *I*, 1995 *C*, 1996 *I*, *C*, *C*, *HK*, *HK*, *J*, *Ar*, *C*, *Ur*, 1997 *W*, *C*, *HK*, *HK*, *W*, *W*, 1998 *Pt*, *Sp*, *J*, *HK*, *C*, *C*, *J*, *HK*, *Fj*, *Ar*, *C*, *Ur*, 1999 *Tg*, *Fj*, *J*, *C*, *Sa*, *E*, *I*, *R*, *A*
A Blom 1998 *Sp*, *J*, *HK*, *C*, *C*, *HK*, *Fj*, *Ar*, *Ur*, 1999 *Sa*, 2000 *J*, *C*, *I*
H Bloomfield 2007 *E*, *Tg*, *SA*, 2008 *E*, *C*
R Bordley 1976 *A*, *F*, 1977 *C*, *E*, 1978 *C*
J Boyd 2008 *IrA*, 2009 *I*
S Bracken 1994 *Ar*, 1995 *C*
G Brackett 1976 *A*, *F*, 1977 *E*
N Brendel 1983 *A*, 1984 *C*, 1985 *J*, *C*, 1987 *Tun*, *E*
D Briley 1979 *C*, 1980 *W*, *C*, *NZ*
J Buchholz 2001 *C*, 2002 *S*, 2003 *Sp*, *EngA*, *Ar*, *Fj*, *J*, *F*, 2004 *C*
B Burdette 2006 *Ur*, *Ur*, 2007 *E*, *S*, *C*, *E*, *Tg*, *Sa*, *SA*
J Burke 2000 *C*, *I*
JR Burke 1990 *C*, *J*, 1991 *J*, *J*, *S*, *C*, *F*, *NZ*, 1992 *C*
J Burkhardt 1983 *C*, 1985 *C*
E Burlingham 1980 *NZ*, 1981 *C*, *SA*, 1982 *C*, *E*, 1983 *C*, *A*, 1984 *C*, 1985 *C*, 1986 *J*, 1987 *Tun*, *C*, *J*, *E*

C Campbell 1993 *C*, *A*, 1994 *Ber*, *C*, *Ar*
D Care 1998 *Pt*, *J*, *C*
M Carlson 1987 *W*, *C*
M Caulder 1984 *C*, 1985 *C*, 1989 *C*
R Causey 1977 *C*, 1981 *C*, *SA*, 1982 *C*, *E*, 1984 *C*, 1986 *J*, 1987 *E*
W Chai 1993 *C*
R Chapman 2011 *J*
D Chipman 1976 *A*, 1978 *C*
JE Clark 1979 *C*, 1980 *C*
J Clarkson 1986 *J*, 1987 *Tun*, *C*, *J*, *E*
J Clayton 1999 *C*, *R*, *A*, 2000 *J*, *C*, *I*, *Fj*, *Tg*, *Sa*, *S*, *W*
TS Clever 2003 *Ar*, 2005 *C*, *R*, *W*, *ArA*, *C*, 2006 *IrA*, *M*, *C*, *Bar*, *C*, *Ur*, *Ur*, 2007 *E*, *S*, *C*, *E*, *Tg*, *Sa*, *SA*, 2008 *E*, *IrA*, *C*, *Ur*, *J*, *J*, 2009 *Geo*, *C*, *C*, *Ur*, *Ur*, 2010 *Pt*, *Geo*, 2011 *Tg*, *Rus*, *C*, *C*, *I*, *Rus*, *It*
R Cooke 1979 *C*, 1980 *W*, *C*, *NZ*, 1981 *C*, *SA*
B Corcoran 1989 *Ur*, *Ar*, 1990 *Ar*
J Coulson 1999 *A*
M Crick 2007 *E*, *S*, *C*, 2008 *E*, *IrA*, *C*, *Ur*, *J*, *J*
R Crivellone 1983 *C*, 1986 *C*, 1987 *C*
K Cross 2003 *Sp*, *Sp*, *J*, *C*, *EngA*, *EngA*, *Ar*, *C*, *Fj*, *S*, 2004 *C*, *Rus*
C Culpepper 1977 *E*, 1978 *C*
C Curtis 1997 *C*, *HK*, *J*, 1999 *Sa*, 2001 *Ar*

P Dahl 2009 *I*, *W*
B Daily 1989 *Ur*, *Ar*, 1990 *Ar*, *C*, *A*, *J*, 1991 *J*, *J*, *S*, *F*, *F*, *It*
K Dalzell 1996 *Ur*, 1998 *Sp*, *C*, *HK*, *C*, *Ur*, 1999 *Tg*, *Fj*, *J*, *C*, *Sa*, *E*, *I*, *R*, *A*, 2000 *J*, *C*, *I*, *Fj*, *Tg*, *Sa*, *S*, *W*, 2001 *C*, *E*, *SA*, 2002 *S*, *C*, *C*, *CHL*, *Ur*, 2003 *Sp*, *Sp*, *J*, *C*, *EngA*, *C*, *Ur*, *Fj*, *S*, *J*, *F*
PJ Danahy 2009 *Ur*, 2010 *Rus*, 2011 *Tg*, *Rus*, *J*, *A*
G De Bartolo 2008 *E*, *C*, *Ur*, *J*, *J*, 2009 *W*
MG de Jong 1990 *C*, 1991 *J*, *J*, *S*, *C*, *F*, *F*, *It*, *E*
M Deaton 1983 *A*, 1984 *C*, 1985 *J*
M Delai 1996 *I*, *HK*, *J*, 1997 *HK*, 1998 *HK*, 2000 *J*, *C*, *I*, *Fj*, *Tg*, *Sa*, *S*, *W*, 2001 *C*, *Ar*, *Ur*
D Dickson 1986 *J*, 1987 *A*
C Doherty 1987 *W*
D Dorsey 2001 *SA*, 2002 *S*, *C*, *C*, *CHL*, *Ur*, *CHL*, *Ur*, 2003 *Sp*, *Sp*, *J*, *C*, *EngA*, *Ar*, *C*, *Ur*, *Fj*, *S*, *J*, *F*, 2004 *C*, *Rus*, *C*, *F*
G Downes 1992 *HK*
BG Doyle 2008 *E*, *IrA*, *C*
R Duncanson 1977 *E*

P Eloff 2000 *J*, *C*, *I*, *Fj*, *Tg*, *Sa*, *S*, *W*, 2001 *C*, *Ar*, *Ur*, *E*, *SA*, 2002 *S*, *C*, *CHL*, *Ur*, 2003 *Sp*, *Sp*, *J*, *C*, *EngA*, *C*, *Ur*, *Fj*, *S*, *J*, *F*, 2006 *Bar*, *C*, *Ur*, *Ur*, 2007 *Tg*, *Sa*, *SA*
PL Emerick 2003 *Sp*, *EngA*, *Ar*, *C*, *Ur*, *Fj*, *S*, *J*, 2004 *C*, *F*, *I*, *It*, 2005 *C*, *R*, *W*, *ArA*, *C*, 2006 *C*, *Bar*, *C*, *Ur*, *Ur*, 2007 *S*, *C*, *E*, 2008 *E*, *IrA*, *C*, *Ur*, *J*, *J*, 2009 *Geo*, *C*, *C*, *Ur*, *Ur*, 2010 *Rus*, *Pt*, *Geo*, 2011 *Tg*, *Rus*, *C*, *C*, *J*, *I*, *Rus*, *It*
TV Enosa 2011 *Tg*, *Rus*, *C*, *C*, *J*, *A*
C Erskine 2006 *C*, *Ur*, *Ur*, 2007 *E*, *Tg*, *Sa*, *SA*, 2008 *Ur*, *J*, *J*
V Esikia 2006 *IrA*, *M*, *Bar*, *C*, *Ur*, *Ur*, 2007 *E*, *E*, *Tg*, *Sa*, *SA*, 2008 *E*, *IrA*
J Everett 1984 *C*, 1985 *J*, 1986 *J*, *C*, 1987 *Tun*, *J*, *E*
W Everett 1985 *J*, 1986 *J*, *C*

M Fabling 1995 *C*
M Fanucchi 1979 *C*, 1980 *W*
R Farley 1989 *I*, *Ur*, *Ar*, 1990 *Ar*, *C*, *A*, *J*, 1991 *J*, *J*, *S*, *C*, *F*, *F*, *It*, *E*, 1992 *C*
P Farner 1999 *Tg*, *Fj*, *J*, *C*, 2000 *J*, *C*, *I*, *Fj*, *Tg*, *Sa*, *S*, *W*, 2002 *C*, *C*, *CHL*, *Ur*, *CHL*, *Ur*
D Fee 2002 *C*, *C*, *CHL*, *Ur*, *CHL*, *Ur*, 2003 *Sp*, *Sp*, *J*, *C*, *EngA*, *C*, *Ur*, *Fj*, *S*, *J*, *F*, 2004 *C*, *Rus*, *C*, *F*, *I*, *It*, 2005 *C*, *R*, *W*, *ArA*, *C*

O Fifita 2000 *Fj, Tg, Sa, S, W*, 2001 *C, Ar, Ur, E, SA*, 2002 *C, C*, 2003 *Sp, EngA, EngA, Ar, S*
S Finkel 1981 *C*, 1983 *C, A*, 1986 *C*, 1987 *A, E*
AW Flay 1990 *J*, 1991 *J, J, S, F, It, E*
R Flynn 2000 *C, I, Fj, Tg, Sa, W*, 2001 *C, Ar*
J Fowler 1980 *W, C, NZ*, 1981 *C, SA*, 1982 *C, E*
W Fraumann 1976 *F*, 1977 *E*
A Freeman 1995 *C*, 1996 *I*
M French 2005 *W, ArA*, 2006 *IrA, M, Ur, Ur*, 2007 *E, C*
EC Fry 2011 *Tg, Rus, C, C, J, A*
B Furrow 1998 *C, C, J, HK*

JR Gagiano 2008 *Ur, J, J*, 2009 *I, W, Geo, C, C, Ur, Ur*, 2010 *Rus, Pt*, 2011 *J, A*
M Gale 1992 *C*
B Geraghty 1993 *C*
J Gillam 2000 *Tg*
D Gillies 1998 *Ar*, 1999 *Tg*
D Gonzalez 1990 *A*, 1993 *C*
G Goodman 1992 *C*
J Gouws 2003 *EngA, EngA, Ar, C, Ur, S, F*, 2004 *I, It*
J Grant 1981 *SA*
R Grant 2000 *Tg*
S Gray 1976 *F*, 1977 *E*, 1979 *C*, 1980 *W, NZ*, 1981 *SA*
R Green 1994 *I*, 1995 *C*, 1996 *I, C, C, HK, J, HK, J*, 1998 *Fj, Ar*
M Griffin 2003 *Sp, J, EngA*, 2004 *Rus, C, F*, 2005 *C, R*
J Grobler 1996 *Ar, C, Ur*, 1997 *C, J, J*, 1998 *J, Fj, C, Ur*, 1999 *Fj, J, C, Sa, E, I, R, A*, 2000 *J, C, I, Tg, Sa, S, W*, 2001 *C, Ar, Ur, E, SA*, 2002 *C, CHL, Ur*
LJ Gross 1996 *I, C, C, HK, J, HK, J, C, Ur*, 1997 *C, HK, J, J, HK, C, W, W*, 1998 *Pt, Sp, J, HK, C, C, J, HK, Fj, Ar, C, Ur*, 1999 *Tg, Fj, J, C, Sa, E, I, R, A*, 2000 *Fj, Tg, Sa, S, W*, 2001 *C, Ar, E, SA*, 2002 *S, C*, 2003 *Sp, Sp, J, C, EngA, EngA, Ar, C, Ur, Fj, S, J, F*
D Guest 1976 *F*, 1977 *C*
I Gunn 1982 *E*

T Hall 2011 *Tg*
M Halliday 1977 *E*, 1978 *C*, 1980 *W, C*, 1982 *C, E*
C Hansen 2005 *C*, 2006 *IrA, M, C*
J Hanson 1977 *C, E*, 1980 *W, C*, 1981 *C*, 1983 *C, A*
J Hartman 1983 *A*, 1984 *C*
J Hartman 2005 *C, ArA*
MTB Hawkins 2010 *Rus*
CC Hawley 2009 *Geo*, 2011 *Tg, Rus, C, A*
W Hayward 1991 *J, C*
GM Hein 1987 *Tun, C, J, A, E, W, C*, 1988 *R, USS*, 1989 *I, C, Ur, Ar*, 1990 *Ar, A*, 1991 *J, F, F, It, NZ, E*, 1992 *HK*, 1993 *C, A*, 1994 *Ber*
R Helu 1981 *C, SA*, 1982 *C, E*, 1983 *C, A*, 1985 *J, C*, 1987 *Tun, C, J, A*
B Henderson 1977 *C*
M Hercus 2002 *S, C, C, CHL, Ur, CHL, Ur*, 2003 *Sp, Sp, J, C, Ur, Fj, S, J, F*, 2004 *C, Rus, C, F, I, It*, 2005 *C, R, W, ArA, C*, 2006 *Bar, C, Ur, Ur*, 2007 *E, Tg, Sa, SA*, 2008 *E, IrA, C, Ur, J, J*, 2009 *I, W, Geo, C, C, Ur, Ur*
SJ Hiatt 1993 *A*, 1998 *Ar, C*
KG Higgins 1985 *J, C*, 1986 *J, C*, 1987 *Tun, C, J, A, E, W, C*, 1988 *C, R, USS*, 1989 *I, C, Ur, Ar*, 1990 *Ar, A, J*, 1991 *J, J, S, C, F, It, E*
B Hightower 1997 *W, J, HK, C, W, W*, 1998 *Fj, C, Ur*, 1999 *Tg, Fj, J, C, Sa, I, R, A*
D Hobson 1991 *J*
M Hobson 2005 *R*
DT Hodges 1996 *Ur*, 1997 *W, W*, 1998 *Pt, Sp, J, HK, C, J, HK, Fj, Ar, C, Ur*, 1999 *Tg, Fj, J, C, Sa, E, I, R, A*, 2000 *J, C, I, Fj, Tg, Sa, S, W*, 2001 *C, Ar, Ur, E, SA*, 2002 *S, C, C, CHL, Ur, CHL, Ur*, 2003 *Sp, J, C, EngA, Fj, S, J, F*, 2004 *C, F*
C Hodgson 2002 *S, C, CHL, CHL*, 2003 *Sp, Sp, J, C, EngA, C*, 2004 *C, Rus*
J Hollings 1979 *C*, 1980 *NZ*
J Holtzman 1995 *C*, 1997 *HK, J*, 1998 *Ar*
J Hopkins 1996 *HK*
D Horton 1986 *C*, 1987 *A, C*
B Horwath 1984 *C*, 1985 *J, C*, 1986 *C*, 1987 *A, W*, 1990 *J*
B Hough 1991 *C*, 1992 *HK*, 1994 *Ar*
B Howard 1998 *HK, Fj, Ar*, 1999 *Sa*
C Howard 1980 *NZ*
J Hullinger 2006 *IrA, C, Bar, Ur, Ur*

M Inns 1985 *J, C*, 1986 *C*
R Isaac 1989 *C, Ar*

D Jablonski 1977 *C*, 1978 *C*, 1979 *C*, 1980 *W*
DW James 1990 *C, A*, 1993 *C, A*, 1994 *Ber, C, Ar, Ar, I*
WL Jefferson 1985 *J, C*, 1986 *C*, 1987 *W, C*, 1989 *I*
J Jellaco 1982 *C, E*
D Jenkinson 1984 *C*, 1985 *C*, 1986 *J*
NS Johnson 2009 *I, W, Geo, C, C, Ur*, 2010 *Rus, Pt, Geo*, 2011 *Tg, Rus, C, C, J, I, Rus, A, It*
PW Johnson 1987 *C, A, W, C*, 1988 *C, R, USS*, 1989 *I, C, Ar*, 1990 *A*, 1991 *F, F, NZ*, 1992 *HK, C*
WD Johnson 2009 *I, W, Ur, Ur*
S Jones 2005 *ArA*, 2006 *Ur*
G Judge 1991 *C*, 1992 *HK*

M Kane 2000 *J, I, Fj*, 2004 *C, F*, 2005 *ArA, C*
J Kelleher 1978 *C*, 1979 *C*
T Kelleher 2000 *C, I*, 2001 *C, Ar, Ur*
J Keller 1992 *HK, C*
J Kelly 2006 *M, C, Bar*
S Kelso 1977 *C, E*, 1978 *C*
D Kennedy 1997 *HK*, 1998 *Pt, Sp, J, HK*
J Keyter 2000 *W*, 2001 *SA*, 2002 *S, C, C, CHL, Ur, CHL, Ur*, 2003 *C, EngA, Ar, C, Ur, S, F*
F Khasigian 1976 *A*
K Khasigian 1998 *Ar*, 1999 *J, E, I, R, A*, 2000 *J, C, I, Fj, Sa, S, W*, 2001 *C, Ar, Ur, E, SA*, 2002 *S, C, C, CHL, Ur, CHL, Ur*, 2003 *Sp, Sp, J, C, EngA, Ar, C, Ur, Fj, S, J, F*
K Kjar 2001 *Ar, SA*, 2002 *S, C, C, CHL, Ur, CHL*, 2003 *EngA, EngA, Ar, S, J*, 2005 *ArA, C*, 2006 *C*, 2007 *E, S, C*
T Klein 1976 *A*, 1977 *C*, 1978 *C*
S Klerck 2003 *Ar, Ur, J*, 2004 *C, Rus, C, I, It*
T Kluempers 1996 *J*, 2000 *W*, 2001 *C, Ar, Ur*
J Knutson 1988 *USS*

CD Labounty 1998 *C, J*
A Lakomskis 2002 *CHL, Ur*, 2004 *I, It*
G Lambert 1981 *C, SA*, 1982 *C, E*, 1984 *C*, 1985 *C*, 1987 *Tun, C, J, A, E*, 1988 *C, R, USS*, 1989 *C, Ur, Ar*, 1990 *Ar*
S Laporta 1989 *Ur, Ar*
M Laulaupealu 2008 *E, IrA, C*
SC LaValla 2010 *Rus, Pt*, 2011 *Tg, Rus, C, J, Rus, A, It*
S Lawrence 2006 *C, Bar, C, Ur, Ur*
R Le Clerc 1998 *C, Ur*
B Le May 2008 *J*
PW LeClerc 1996 *HK, J*, 1997 *W, J, HK, C*, 1998 *C*, 1999 *Tg, Fj, J, C, Sa*
R Lehner 1995 *C*, 1996 *C, C, HK, J, HK, J, Ar, C*, 1997 *W, C, J, J, HK, C, W, W*, 1998 *Pt, Sp, J, HK, C, C, Ar, Ur*, 1999 *Tg, Fj, J, Sa, E, I, R*, 2000 *J, C, I, Fj, Tg, Sa*
O Lentz 2006 *IrA, M, Bar*, 2007 *E, Tg, Sa, SA*
J Lett 2008 *E, IrA, C*
WN Leversee 1988 *R*, 1989 *I, Ur*, 1990 *Ar, C, A, J*, 1991 *J, J, S, F, It*, 1994 *Ar, I*, 1996 *Ar*
R Lewis 1990 *C*, 1991 *S*
M L'Huillier 1999 *E, A*
R Liddington 2003 *Ar, C, S*, 2004 *Rus, C*
J Lik 2005 *C, R, ArA*
S Lipman 1988 *C, R, USS*, 1990 *C, J*, 1991 *F, It, NZ, E*
C Lippert 1989 *C, Ur, Ar*, 1990 *Ar, C, A, J*, 1991 *J, S, C, F, F, It, NZ*, 1993 *A*, 1994 *Ber, C, Ar, Ar, I*, 1996 *HK, J, Ar, C, Ur*, 1997 *C, HK, J, J, HK, W, W*, 1998 *J, HK, C, C, J, HK*
M Liscovitz 1977 *C, E*, 1978 *C*
R Lockerem 1996 *C, Ur*
J Lombard 1977 *C, E*, 1979 *C*
C Long 2003 *Sp*
J Lopez 1978 *C*
I Loveseth 1983 *A*
RA Lumkong 1994 *Ber, C, Ar, Ar, I*, 1996 *C, C, HK, J, HK, J, Ar, C, Ur*, 1997 *W*, 1998 *Pt, Sp, J, HK, C, C, J, HK, Fj, C, Ur*, 1999 *E, R, A*

D Lyle 1994 *I*, 1995 *C*, 1996 *I, C, C, HK, J, HK, J*, 1997 *W, C, HK, J, J, HK, C, W, W*, 1999 *Tg, Fj, J, C, Sa, E, I, R*, 2000 *S, W*, 2001 *C, Ar, E, SA*, 2002 *CHL, Ur*, 2003 *Sp, Sp, J, C, EngA, C, Ur, Fj, S, J, F*

MS MacDonald 2000 *Fj*, 2001 *C, Ar, Ur, E, SA*, 2002 *S, C, C, CHL, Ur, CHL, Ur*, 2003 *Sp, Sp, J, C, EngA, EngA, C, Ur, Fj, S, J, F*, 2004 *C, Rus, F, I, It*, 2005 *C, R, W, ArA, C*, 2006 *IrA, C, Bar, C, Ur, Ur*, 2007 *S, C, E, Tg, Sa, SA*, 2008 *E, IrA, C, Ur, J, J*, 2009 *I, W, Geo, C, C*, 2010 *Pt, Geo*, 2011 *C, J, I, Rus, It*
C Mackay 2008 *J*, 2009 *I, W*
A Magleby 2000 *W*, 2001 *Ar, Ur, E*
A Malifa 2009 *I, W, Geo, C*
VL Malifa 2007 *E, S, C, E, SA*, 2008 *IrA, C, Ur, J, J*, 2009 *Ur, Ur*, 2010 *Rus, Pt, Geo*, 2011 *Tg, Rus, C, C, J, I, A, It*
P Malloy 1995 *C*
L Manga 1986 *J*, 1989 *Ar*, 1991 *J, C, NZ, E*, 1992 *HK, C*
M Mangan 2005 *C, R, W, ArA, C*, 2006 *IrA, M, C, Bar, C, Ur*, 2007 *E, S, C, E, Tg, SA*
S Manoa 2010 *Geo*
J McBride 1998 *Pt, Sp, C, Fj, Ar, C, Ur*, 2000 *J, C, I, Tg, Sa*
BR McClenahan 2009 *W, Ur*, 2011 *A*
T McCormack 1989 *Ur, Ar*, 1990 *Ar, C*
G McDonald 1989 *I*, 1996 *I, C*
A McGarry 2002 *S, CHL*
M McLeod 1997 *J, HK, C*
T Meek 2006 *IrA, M, C, Bar*
H Mexted 2006 *Bar, Ur, Ur*, 2007 *E, S, C, E, Sa*
J Meyersieck 1982 *C*, 1983 *C, A*, 1985 *J*, 1986 *C*
J Mickel 1986 *C*
K Miles 1982 *C, E*
C Miller 2002 *CHL, Ur*
M Moeakiola 2007 *E, Tg, Sa, SA*, 2008 *E, IrA, C, Ur, J, J*, 2009 *I, W, Geo, C, C, Ur, Ur*, 2010 *Rus, Pt, Geo*, 2011 *Tg, Rus, C, I, Rus, It*
B Monroe 1985 *C*
A Montgomery 1986 *C*, 1987 *W, C*, 1988 *C*, 1989 *I, C*
B Morrison 1979 *C*, 1980 *W*
C Morrow 1997 *W, C, HK, C, W, W*, 1998 *Pt, C, C*, 1999 *Tg, C, E*
T Moser 1980 *W*
N Mottram 1990 *Ar, J*, 1991 *J, S, C, F, NZ, E*, 1992 *C*
F Mounga 1998 *C, J, HK, Fj, C, Ur*, 1999 *Sa, E, I, R, A*, 2003 *Sp, J*, 2004 *F, I, It*, 2005 *R*, 2007 *E, C, Sa*
D Murphy 1976 *F*

J Naivalu 2000 *Sa, S, W*, 2001 *C, Ur, E*, 2004 *C, Rus, C, F*
J Naqica 2001 *E, SA*, 2002 *S, C, C, CHL, Ur*, 2003 *Ar*
J Nash 2006 *M, C*
RB Nelson 1983 *C, A*, 1984 *C*, 1985 *C*, 1986 *J*, 1987 *C, J, A, E*, 1988 *R, USS*, 1989 *I, Ur, Ar*, 1990 *Ar, C, A, J*, 1991 *J, S, C, F, F, It, E*
T Ngwenya 2007 *E, Tg, Sa, SA*, 2008 *IrA, C, Ur, J, J*, 2009 *Geo, C, C, Ur, Ur*, 2010 *Rus, Pt, Geo*, 2011 *C, C, I, Rus, It*
C Nicolau 2002 *C*, 2003 *J, C, EngA*
S Niebauer 1976 *A*, 1979 *C*, 1980 *W, C, NZ*, 1981 *C, SA*, 1982 *C, E*
D Niu 1999 *Tg, Fj, J, C, E, I, R, A*

CP O'Brien 1988 *C, R, USS*, 1989 *I, C, Ur, Ar*, 1990 *Ar, A, J*, 1991 *S, C, F, F, NZ, E*, 1992 *HK*, 1993 *C, A*, 1994 *Ber*
T O'Brien 1980 *NZ*, 1983 *C, A*
M O'Donnell 1976 *F*
C Okezie 1979 *C*, 1980 *C, NZ*, 1981 *C*, 1982 *C, E*
M Ording 1976 *A, F*, 1977 *E*, 1978 *C*
M Ormsby 1983 *C*
A Osborne 2007 *C*
C Osentowski 2004 *It*, 2005 *C, R, W*, 2006 *IrA, M, C, Bar, C, Ur, Ur*, 2007 *E, S, C, E, Tg, Sa, SA*
K Oxman 1976 *A*

S Paga 1998 *C, C*, 1999 *C, Sa, E, I, R, A*, 2002 *CHL, Ur, CHL, Ur*, 2003 *J*, 2004 *C, Rus, F*
TD Palamo 2007 *SA*, 2008 *J*
MJ Palefau 2005 *C, R, W, ArA, C*, 2006 *IrA, M, C*, 2007 *E, S*, 2008 *E*
AF Paoli 1982 *E*, 1983 *C*, 1985 *J*, 1986 *J, C*, 1987 *C, J, A, W, C*, 1988 *C, R, USS*, 1989 *I, C, Ur, Ar*, 1991 *J, F, It*
AJ Parker 1996 *HK, J, HK, J, Ar, C, Ur*, 1997 *W*, 1998 *Pt, Sp, J, HK, C, C, J, HK, Fj*, 1999 *Fj, C, Sa, E, I, R, A*, 2002 *CHL, Ur, CHL, Ur*, 2003 *Sp, Sp, C, EngA, C, Ur, Fj, S, F*, 2004 *C, Rus, C, I, It*, 2005 *W*, 2006 *C, Ur, Ur*, 2007 *E, Tg, Sa, SA*, 2008 *Ur, J*, 2009 *Geo, C, C, Ur, Ur*
D Parks 1980 *C*
E Parthmore 1977 *E*
J Paterson 2011 *J, I, Rus, It*
DT Payne 2007 *S, SA*
J Peter 1987 *W, C*
T Petersen 1993 *C*
MZ Petri 2007 *SA*, 2008 *E, IrA, C, Ur, J, J*, 2009 *I, W, Geo, C, C, Ur, Ur*, 2010 *Rus, Pt, Geo*, 2011 *Tg, Rus, C, C, J, I, Rus, A, It*
A Petruzzella 2004 *C, F, I*, 2005 *W, ArA, C*, 2006 *IrA, M, Bar*
MD Pidcock 1991 *C, NZ, E*
ST Pittman 2008 *Ur, J*, 2009 *Geo, C, C*, 2010 *Rus, Pt, Geo*, 2011 *Tg, Rus, C, C, J, I, Rus, A, It*
M Purcell 1980 *W*, 1981 *C, SA*, 1982 *C, E*, 1983 *C, A*, 1984 *C*, 1986 *J, C*, 1987 *Tun, C, J, E*
TJ Purpura 2010 *Rus*
J Pye 2005 *ArA, C*

P Quinn 2007 *E*, 2008 *Ur, J, J*

RR Randell 1993 *A*, 1994 *Ber, C, Ar, I*, 1995 *C*, 1996 *I, HK, J, Ar, C*, 1997 *C*
J Raven 1998 *C, J*
E Reed 1999 *A*, 2001 *Ur, E, SA*, 2002 *S, C, C*
AM Ridnell 1987 *A*, 1988 *C, R, USS*, 1991 *J, S, C, F, F, It, NZ, E*, 1992 *HK*, 1993 *C*
J Rissone 1996 *I, C, C, HK, Ur*
R Rosser 2006 *Ur, Ur*
VR Rouse 2010 *Rus*
D Rowe 2005 *R, W*
A Russell 2006 *C, Ur*
A Ryland 2005 *C, R, W, C*

R Samaniego 1992 *HK*
L Sanft 1996 *J*
J Santos 1995 *C*, 1996 *C, C, HK*
A Satchwell 2002 *S*, 2003 *Ur*
A Saulala 1997 *C, HK, C, W, W*, 1998 *Pt, Sp, HK, C, J, HK*, 1999 *Tg, Fj, J, C, Sa, E, A*, 2000 *Fj, Tg*
M Saunders 1987 *Tun, C, J, A, E, W, C*, 1988 *C, R, USS*, 1989 *I, C*
MH Sawicki 1990 *Ar, J*, 1991 *J, F, NZ*
MA Scharrenberg 1993 *A*, 1994 *Ber, C, Ar, Ar*, 1995 *C*, 1996 *I, J, HK, J, Ar, C, Ur*, 1997 *W, C, HK, J, J, HK, C, W, W*, 1998 *Pt, Sp, J, HK, C, C, Ar, C, Ur*, 1999 *Tg, Fj, J, C, Sa, I, R, A*
J Scheitlin 1979 *C*
CJ Schlereth 1993 *C*, 1994 *I*, 1998 *J*
G Schneeweis 1976 *A*, 1977 *E*
B Schoener 2006 *IrA, M, C*
E Schram 1993 *A*, 1994 *Ber, C, Ar, Ar*, 1996 *J, Ar*
J Schraml 1991 *C*, 1992 *HK*, 1993 *C*
K Schubert 2000 *J, C, I, Fj, Tg, Sa*, 2001 *C, Ar, Ur, E, SA*, 2002 *S, C, C, CHL, Ur, CHL, Ur*, 2003 *Sp, Sp, J, C, EngA, Ar, C, Ur, Fj, S, J, F*, 2004 *C, Rus, C, F, I, It*, 2005 *C, R, W, ArA, C*, 2006 *IrA, M, C, Bar, C*, 2008 *IrA, C*
RE Schurfeld 1992 *HK, C*, 1993 *A*, 1994 *Ber, C*
T Scott 1976 *F*
BH Scully 2011 *Rus, C, C, J, I, Rus, A, It*
T Selfridge 1976 *A, F*, 1977 *C*, 1980 *W, C*
D Shanagher 1980 *NZ*, 1981 *C, SA*, 1982 *C, E*, 1984 *C*, 1985 *J*, 1986 *J*, 1987 *W*
RC Shaw 2008 *IrA, C*
P Sheehy 1991 *NZ, E*, 1992 *HK, C*
M Sherlock 1977 *C*
MM Sherman 2003 *EngA, Ar, F*, 2004 *Rus*, 2005 *C, W, ArA*
W Shiflet 1983 *C, A*, 1985 *J*, 1987 *A*
K Shuman 1997 *HK, J, J, W*, 1998 *J, HK, C, C, J, Ar*, 1999 *Tg, Fj, J, E, I, R, A*, 2000 *J, C, I, Fj, Tg, Sa, S, W*, 2001 *Ar, Ur, E, SA*

M Siano 1989 *I, C, Ur, Ar*
L Sifa 2008 *Ur, J*, 2009 *I, W, Ur, Ur*, 2010 *Rus*, 2011 *A*
MK Sika 1993 *C, A*, 1994 *Ber, C, Ar, Ar, I*, 1996 *C, C, J, HK, J, Ar, C, Ur*, 1997 *J, W*
S Sika 2003 *Fj, J, F*, 2004 *C, F, I, It*, 2005 *W, C*, 2006 *IrA, M*, 2007 *S, C, E, Tg, Sa, SA*, 2008 *IrA, C, Ur*, 2009 *Geo, C*
C Slaby 2008 *E, C*
H Smith 2008 *Ur, J, J*, 2009 *I, W, Geo, C, C, Ur, Ur*, 2010 *Geo*, 2011 *C, C, J, I, Rus, A, It*
M Smith 1988 *C*
T Smith 1980 *C*, 1981 *C, SA*, 1982 *E*
B Smoot 1992 *C*
J Sprague 2009 *Ur, Ur*
M Stanaway 1997 *C, HK, J, C*, 1998 *HK*
LE Stanfill 2005 *C*, 2006 *C*, 2007 *E, S, C, E, Tg, Sa, SA*, 2008 *E, IrA*, 2009 *I, W, Geo, C, C, Ur, Ur*, 2010 *Rus, Pt, Geo*, 2011 *Tg, Rus, C, C, J, I, Rus, A, It*
D Steinbauer 1992 *C*, 1993 *C*
J Stencel 2006 *C*
D Stephenson 1976 *A, F*, 1977 *C*
I Stevens 1998 *C*
P Still 2000 *S, W*, 2001 *C, Ar, Ur, E, SA*
W Stone 1976 *F*
D Straehley 1983 *C*, 1984 *C*
G Sucher 1998 *C, J, HK, Fj, C, Ur*, 1999 *Tg, Fj, J, C, Sa, E, I, R, A*
A Suniula 2008 *J*, 2010 *Rus, Pt, Geo*, 2011 *Tg, Rus, C, C, J, I, Rus, It*
RPJ Suniula 2009 *I, W, C, C*, 2011 *Tg, C, C, J, I, Rus, It*
B Surgener 2001 *SA*, 2002 *C, Ur*, 2003 *Sp, EngA, EngA*, 2004 *C, F, I, It*, 2005 *W*
E Swanson 1976 *A*
C Sweeney 1976 *A, F*, 1977 *C, E*
M Swiderski 1976 *A*
K Swiryn 2009 *I, W, C, C, Ur, Ur*, 2010 *Pt, Geo*, 2011 *Tg, Rus, C, J, A*
B Swords 1980 *W, C, NZ*
KR Swords 1985 *J, C*, 1986 *C*, 1987 *Tun, C, J, A, W, C*, 1988 *C, R, USS*, 1989 *I, C, Ur, Ar*, 1990 *Ar, C, A, J*, 1991 *J, J, S, C, F, F, It, NZ, E*, 1992 *C*, 1993 *C, A*, 1994 *Ber, C, Ar, Ar*

TK Takau 1994 *Ar, Ar, I*, 1996 *C, C, HK, J, HK*, 1997 *C, HK, J, HK, W, W*, 1998 *Sp, HK, C, C, J, HK, Ur*, 1999 *E, I, R, A*
R Tardits 1993 *A*, 1994 *Ber, C, Ar, Ar, I*, 1995 *C*, 1996 *I, C, C, J, Ar*, 1997 *W, C*, 1998 *Sp, HK, Fj*, 1999 *Tg, Fj, J, C, Sa, I, R*
J Tarpoff 2002 *S, C, C, CHL*, 2003 *Sp, Sp, C, EngA, EngA*, 2006 *IrA, M, C, Bar*
P Thiel 2009 *Ur, Ur*, 2010 *Rus, Pt, Geo*, 2011 *Tg, C, C, J, I, A, It*
M Timoteo 2000 *Tg*, 2001 *C, Ar, Ur, SA*, 2002 *S, C, C, CHL, Ur, CHL*, 2003 *Sp, Sp, J, EngA, Ar, C, F*, 2004 *C, Rus, C, F, I, It*, 2005 *C, R*, 2006 *IrA, M, C, Bar*
AEO Tuilevuka 2006 *IrA, M, C*, 2009 *I, W, Geo, C, Ur, Ur*, 2010 *Rus*
STV Tuilevuka 2010 *Pt*
A Tuipulotu 2004 *C, Rus, C, I, It*, 2005 *C, R, W*, 2006 *C, Bar, C, Ur, Ur*, 2007 *E, S, C, Tg, Sa*, 2008 *E*
CE Tunnacliffe 1991 *F, NZ, E*, 1992 *HK*

TD Usasz 2009 *I, W, Geo, C, C, Ur, Ur*, 2010 *Rus, Pt, Geo*, 2011 *Tg, Rus, C, C, J, I, Rus, A, It*

Vaka 1987 *C*
JL Van Der Giessen 2008 *E, C, Ur, J, J*, 2009 *I, W, Geo, C, C, Ur, Ur*, 2010 *Rus, Pt*, 2011 *Tg, Rus, C, C, I, Rus, It*
M van der Molen 1992 *C*
R van Zyl 2003 *Sp, Sp, J, C, EngA, C, Ur, Fj, S, J, F*, 2004 *C, F*
F Viljoen 2004 *Rus, C, F, I, It*, 2005 *C, R, W, ArA, C*, 2006 *IrA, M, C, Ur, Ur*, 2007 *E, S, C*
T Vinick 1986 *C*, 1987 *A, E*
J Vitale 2006 *C, Ur*, 2007 *E*, 2008 *IrA*
BG Vizard 1986 *J, C*, 1987 *Tun, C, J, A, E, W, C*, 1988 *C, R, USS*, 1989 *I, C*, 1990 *C, A*, 1991 *J, J, S, C, F, It*
C Vogl 1996 *C, C*, 1997 *W, C, HK, J, J, HK, C*, 1998 *HK, Fj, Ar*

J Waasdorp 2003 *J, EngA, Ar, Ur, J, F*, 2004 *C, Rus, C, F, I, It*, 2005 *C, ArA, C*
D Wack 1976 *F*, 1977 *C*, 1978 *C*, 1980 *C*
B Waite 1976 *F*
J Walker 1996 *I, C, HK, J, Ar, C, Ur*, 1997 *W, J, HK, C, W, W*, 1998 *Sp, J, HK, C, C, J, HK, Ar, C, Ur*, 1999 *Tg, J*
L Walton 1980 *C, NZ*, 1981 *C, SA*
A Ward 1980 *NZ*, 1983 *C*
B Warhurst 1983 *C, A*, 1984 *C*, 1985 *J, C*, 1986 *J*, 1987 *Tun, C, J*
M Waterman 1992 *C*
J Welch 2008 *J, J*, 2009 *I, Geo, C*
G Wells 2000 *J, C, I, Fj, Tg, Sa, S, W*, 2001 *C, Ar, Ur, E*
T Whelan 1982 *E*, 1987 *C*, 1988 *C, R, USS*
EA Whitaker 1990 *J*, 1991 *F, F, It, NZ*
B Wiedemer 2007 *E*, 2008 *E, IrA, C*
L Wilfley 2000 *I, Tg, W*, 2001 *Ar, Ur, SA*, 2002 *S, C, C, CHL, Ur, CHL, Ur*, 2003 *Sp, Sp, J, C, EngA, EngA, S*
JP Wilkerson 1991 *E*, 1993 *A*, 1994 *C*, 1996 *C, Ur*, 1997 *W, C, HK, J, J, C, W, W*, 1998 *Pt, Sp, J, HK*
B Williams 1988 *C, R, USS*, 1989 *C*, 1992 *C*
C Williams 1990 *C, A, J*, 1991 *J, S, C*
D Williams 2004 *C, Rus, C, F, I, It*, 2005 *ArA*, 2006 *Ur, Ur*, 2007 *E, C*
MA Williams 1987 *W, C*, 1988 *C, R, USS*, 1989 *I, Ur, Ar*, 1990 *Ar, C, A*, 1991 *J, J, F, F, It, NZ, E*, 1992 *HK*, 1994 *C, Ar, Ar, I*, 1996 *I, C, C, HK*, 1997 *W*, 1998 *Fj, Ar, Ur*, 1999 *Tg, J, C, Sa, E, I*
G Wilson 1978 *C*, 1980 *W, C*, 1981 *C, SA*
M Wyatt 2003 *Ar, C, Ur, J, F*, 2004 *C, Rus, C, F, I, It*, 2005 *W, ArA, C*, 2006 *C*
CT Wyles 2007 *E, S, C, E, Tg, Sa, SA*, 2008 *E, IrA, C, Ur, J, J*, 2009 *I, W, Geo, C, C, Ur, Ur*, 2010 *Rus, Pt, Geo*, 2011 *Rus, A, It*

D Younger 2000 *J, C, I, Fj*
S Yungling 1997 *HK, W*

R Zenker 1987 *W, C*

WALES

WALES' 2010–11 TEST RECORD

OPPONENTS	DATE	VENUE	RESULT
Australia	6 Nov	H	**Lost** 16–25
South Africa	13 Nov	H	**Lost** 25–29
Fiji	19 Nov	H	**Drew** 16–16
New Zealand	27 Nov	H	**Lost** 25–37
England	4 Feb	H	**Lost** 19–26
Scotland	12 Feb	A	**Won** 24–6
Italy	26 Feb	A	**Won** 24–16
Ireland	12 Mar	H	**Won** 19–13
France	19 Mar	A	**Lost** 28–9
England	6 Aug	A	**Lost** 23–19
England	13 Aug	H	**Won** 19–9
Argentina	20 Aug	H	**Won** 28–13
South Africa	11 Sep	N	**Lost** 16–17
Samoa	18 Sep	N	**Won** 17–10
Namibia	26 Sep	N	**Won** 81–7
Fiji	2 Oct	N	**Won** 66–0
Ireland	8 Oct	N	**Won** 22–10
France	15 Oct	N	**Lost** 8–9
Australia	21 Oct	N	**Lost** 18–21

SEMI-FINAL HEARTBREAK

By Paul Morgan

Stu Forster/Getty Images

Wales enjoyed a sensational Rugby World Cup campaign to finish fourth.

Wales' quest to reach the final of the World Cup for the first time in the Principality's history came to a dramatic and hugely controversial end as Warren Gatland's side were narrowly beaten 9–8 by France in Auckland in a match that will forever be remembered for the first-half dismissal of flanker Sam Warburton.

The Welsh skipper was sent off by Alain Rolland in the 18th minute after a dangerous tackle on France wing Vincent Clerc and, although the 14 men in red who remained on the pitch battled valiantly despite their numerical disadvantage, it was France who scraped through to the final to face the All Blacks.

Wales had last reached the semi-final stage of the tournament at the inaugural World Cup in 1987, but their hopes of becoming only the third side from the northern hemisphere to progress to the final were dashed when Warburton, one of the players of 2011, trudged disconsolately off the pitch at Eden Park.

The back row forward did lift Clerc in the tackle, but in the aftermath of his side's heartbreaking defeat the young captain was adamant that there was nothing deliberate or premeditated in the challenge.

"There was no intent," Warburton insisted as the semi-final post mortem began. "I went to compete for the ball after, and I thought it was a normal tackle. The next thing I know I'm walking off into the stands. Obviously I'm gutted with the red card, but there was nothing malicious. It felt that as soon as I hit him his body weight took control of what happened.

"All the boys are so disappointed with the result, but I thought the courage and bravery they showed was second to none. Afterwards in the changing room you really don't take too much information in because you are devastated."

Gatland unveiled his World Cup squad at the end of August. The headline news was the omission of veteran flanker Martyn Williams and the appointment of Warburton as captain in place of the injured Matthew Rees, and it quickly became apparent a youthful-looking Wales squad were capable of making a real impact in New Zealand.

They kicked off the tournament with the daunting prospect of facing champions South Africa in Wellington, but the Welsh were far from overawed and came within a whisker of a famous upset.

Initially the game seemed to be following a prearranged script when Frans Steyn bustled over after just two minutes, but Wales refused to buckle and slowly worked their way back into contention with three penalties from James Hook. They then took the lead in the 54th minute when No. 8 Toby Faletau broke through to score and, with Hook adding the conversion, Wales suddenly found themselves 16–10 to the good. The lead, however, lasted 15 minutes, and when substitute Francois Hougaard raced over, a try crucially converted by Morne Steyn, the Springboks were defending a 17–16 advantage. A late Rhys Priestland drop-goal and Hook penalty attempt both sailed wide and South Africa held on for the win.

"I'm very proud of the effort the players put in," Gatland insisted. "We did everything but win the game. It is about taking your opportunities. We didn't start well and held off them in those first couple of minutes, but after that we dominated territory and possession and played some great rugby. We put ourselves in with a chance to win, but in the end we weren't quite good enough. But we got a bonus point out of it, and we will take a massive amount from it. We have been knocking on the door for a while, and if we get over that hurdle it will be good for us for the rest of the tournament."

The next hurdle was Samoa in Hamilton and, although Wales did

Hannah Johnston/Getty Images

Rhys Priestland was one of the great Test discoveries of 2011.

successfully negotiate the obstacle, it was not without a degree of anxiety.

The first try of the match went to the Samoans on the stroke of half-time courtesy of prop Antony Perenise and, although Hook and Priestland had both kept the scoreboard ticking over for Wales with penalties, they could not quite shake off the challenge of the South Sea Islanders until the 67th minute when Shane Williams showed all his predatory instincts to score his 55th Test try and give Gatland's side a degree of breathing space. The match finally finished 17–10 and Wales escaped with the win they craved.

"Samoa are very physical, and it was a tough game for us," Warburton said. "We wanted to keep the ball in play as much as we could and back our fitness levels towards the end of the match. Both sides didn't disappoint; we knew it was going to be an immensely tough battle."

Wales finally got into their attacking stride in their final two Pool D clashes, demolishing Namibia 81–7 in New Plymouth courtesy of a Williams hat-trick and brace from George North and then crushed Fiji 66–0 in Hamilton, and the stage was set for an all northern hemisphere quarter-final clash with Ireland in Wellington.

Wales had lost two of their previous three meetings with the Irish, but they always looked capable of improving on that statistic once

Williams had squeezed over in the corner in the second minute and, although Ireland did battle back to level the encounter at 10–10 apiece in the 45th minute after a Keith Earls try, Gatland's side continued to exude a quiet confidence.

They took the match by the scruff of the neck just six minutes after Earls' try when Mike Phillips expertly dived over, and when Jonathan Davies crashed through the Irish defence late on the contest was over and Wales were comfortable 22–10 winners.

"It's an historic win," Phillips said. "The boys have been outstanding in the lead up to this game. We have so much respect for the Irish boys, and I feel sorry for them. They are great players and outstanding gentlemen, but we were superb today."

Wales were the first to register in what was to be a low-scoring but epic semi-final at Eden Park when Hook landed a seventh-minute touchline penalty after Thierry Dusautoir was caught offside, but that was comprehensively overshadowed by Warburton's red card 11 minutes later.

France were on terms on 21 minutes when Morgan Parra landed his first three-pointer of the game, and he extended the French lead to 9–3 with successful efforts in the 33rd and 50th minutes to leave Welsh hopes hanging by a thread.

Wales were actually playing well despite going down to 14 men, and when Phillips cut through on the blind side of a ruck and dived over for the only try of the match on 58 minutes they were within a single point of France.

Stephen Jones missed the conversion, but it was Wales who were playing all the rugby now, and six minutes from time Leigh Halfpenny was presented with a penalty chance on halfway after another French offside. But his kick dipped below the crossbar and Wales were out of the World Cup.

"We just feel like the destiny of the result was taken out of our hands with the red card," Gatland said. "He's lifted him, that's a yellow card, but he's not driven him into the ground. Does that mean every time there's a tackle where you lift someone off the ground it's a red card? Why spoil the semi-final with a red card? He's not a dirty player.

"I'm just gutted. We were down to 14, but we showed great character and I'm proud of our efforts. But we can't go to just one tournament and do well, we have got to kick on from here. I feel let down, I thought this team were good enough to go on and take the final, but it was not to be. We just feel that ultimately the result wasn't in our control."

Gatland handed the captain's armband to prop Gethin Jenkins for the bronze-medal match with Australia at Eden Park in the absence of the suspended Warburton, but once again Wales came heartbreakingly close to victory only to ultimately lose by a narrow margin.

The Wallabies scored first on 10 minutes when Berrick Barnes sliced through the defence, but a Hook penalty sent Gatland's side in at half-time trailing 7–3. Nine minutes after the break Williams scored his 57th try for his country in his 86th Test and his final World Cup appearance after a neat dribble and touchdown, but two penalties from James O'Connor restored Australia's advantage and they got what proved the decisive score five minutes from time when No. 8 Ben McCalman strolled over on the blindside. A late try from Halfpenny gave the Wales support something to cheer, but Gatland and his side had to be content with a fourth-place finish.

"I'm proud of the way we finished," Jenkins said. "We've just come up short again today, but we've enjoyed the tournament. It's a shame we couldn't finish it off with the win. We talked about creating history and to come fourth, while it's not as good as third, is still an improvement on the last couple of World Cups. To get to the semis is a great achievement for this group of players."

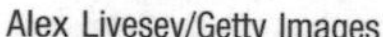

Alex Livesey/Getty Images

Shane Williams ended the World Cup with the 57th Test try of an illustrious career.

WALES INTERNATIONAL STATISTICS

MATCH RECORDS UP TO 31 OCTOBER 2011

MOST CONSECUTIVE TEST WINS

11 1907 *I*, 1908 *E, S, F, I, A*, 1909 *E, S, F, I*, 1910 *F*
10 1999 *F1, It, E, Arg 1, 2, SA, C, F2, Arg 3, J*
8 1970 *F*, 1971 *E, S, I, F*, 1972 *E, S, F*
8 2004 *J*, 2005 *E, It, F, S, I, US, C*

MOST CONSECUTIVE TESTS WITHOUT DEFEAT

Matches	Wins	Draws	Period
11	11	0	1907 to 1910
10	10	0	1999 to 1999
8	8	0	1970 to 1972
8	8	0	2004 to 2005

MOST POINTS IN A MATCH

BY THE TEAM

Pts	Opponents	Venue	Year
102	Portugal	Lisbon	1994
98	Japan	Cardiff	2004
81	Romania	Cardiff	2001
81	Namibia	New Plymouth	2011
77	USA	Hartford	2005
72	Japan	Cardiff	2007
70	Romania	Wrexham	1997
66	Romania	Cardiff	2004
66	Fiji	Hamilton	2011
64	Japan	Cardiff	1999
64	Japan	Osaka	2001
61	Canada	Cardiff	2006
60	Italy	Treviso	1999
60	Canada	Toronto	2005
58	Fiji	Cardiff	2002
57	Japan	Bloemfontein	1995
55	Japan	Cardiff	1993

BY A PLAYER

Pts	Player	Opponents	Venue	Year
30	N R Jenkins	Italy	Treviso	1999
29	N R Jenkins	France	Cardiff	1999
28	N R Jenkins	Canada	Cardiff	1999
28	N R Jenkins	France	Paris	2001
28	G L Henson	Japan	Cardiff	2004
27	N R Jenkins	Italy	Cardiff	2000
27	C Sweeney	USA	Hartford	2005
26	S M Jones	Romania	Cardiff	2001
24	N R Jenkins	Canada	Cardiff	1993
24	N R Jenkins	Italy	Cardiff	1994
24	G L Henson	Romania	Wrexham	2003
23	A C Thomas	Romania	Wrexham	1997
23	N R Jenkins	Argentina	Llanelli	1998
23	N R Jenkins	Scotland	Murrayfield	2001
22	N R Jenkins	Portugal	Lisbon	1994
22	N R Jenkins	Japan	Bloemfontein	1995
22	N R Jenkins	England	Wembley	1999
22	S M Jones	Canada	Cardiff	2002
22	J W Hook	England	Cardiff	2007
22	D R Biggar	Canada	Toronto	2009

MOST TRIES IN A MATCH

BY THE TEAM

Tries	Opponents	Venue	Year
16	Portugal	Lisbon	1994
14	Japan	Cardiff	2004
12	Namibia	New Plymouth	2011
11	France	Paris	1909
11	Romania	Wrexham	1997
11	Romania	Cardiff	2001
11	USA	Hartford	2005
11	Japan	Cardiff	2007
10	France	Swansea	1910
10	Japan	Osaka	2001
10	Romania	Cardiff	2004
9	France	Cardiff	1908
9	Japan	Cardiff	1993
9	Japan	Cardiff	1999
9	Japan	Tokyo	2001
9	Canada	Toronto	2005
9	Canada	Cardiff	2006
9	Fiji	Hamilton	2011

BY A PLAYER

Tries	Player	Opponents	Venue	Year
4	W Llewellyn	England	Swansea	1899
4	R A Gibbs	France	Cardiff	1908
4	M C R Richards	England	Cardiff	1969
4	I C Evans	Canada	Invercargill	1987
4	N Walker	Portugal	Lisbon	1994
4	G Thomas	Italy	Treviso	1999
4	S M Williams	Japan	Osaka	2001
4	T G L Shanklin	Romania	Cardiff	2004
4	C L Charvis	Japan	Cardiff	2004

MOST CONVERSIONS IN A MATCH

BY THE TEAM

Cons	Opponents	Venue	Year
14	Japan	Cardiff	2004
11	Portugal	Lisbon	1994
11	USA	Hartford	2005
10	Romania	Cardiff	2001
9	Namibia	New Plymouth	2011
9	Fiji	Hamilton	2011
8	France	Swansea	1910
8	Japan	Cardiff	1999
8	Romania	Cardiff	2004
8	Canada	Cardiff	2006
7	France	Paris	1909
7	Japan	Osaka	2001
7	Japan	Cardiff	2007

BY A PLAYER

Cons	Player	Opponents	Venue	Year
14	G L Henson	Japan	Cardiff	2004
11	N R Jenkins	Portugal	Lisbon	1994
11	C Sweeney	U S A	Hartford	2005
10	S M Jones	Romania	Cardiff	2001
8	J Bancroft	France	Swansea	1910
8	N R Jenkins	Japan	Cardiff	1999
8	J Hook	Canada	Cardiff	2006
7	S M Jones	Japan	Osaka	2001
7	S M Jones	Romania	Cardiff	2004
6	J Bancroft	France	Paris	1909
6	G L Henson	Romania	Wrexham	2003
6	C Sweeney	Canada	Toronto	2005
6	S M Jones	Namibia	New Plymouth	2011

MOST PENALTIES IN A MATCH

BY THE TEAM

Pens	Opponents	Venue	Year
9	France	Cardiff	1999
8	Canada	Cardiff	1993
7	Italy	Cardiff	1994
7	Canada	Cardiff	1999
7	Italy	Cardiff	2000
6	France	Cardiff	1982
6	Tonga	Nuku'alofa	1994
6	England	Wembley	1999
6	Canada	Cardiff	2002
6	England	Cardiff	2009
6	Canada	Toronto	2009
6	New Zealand	Cardiff	2010

BY A PLAYER

Pens	Player	Opponents	Venue	Year
9	N R Jenkins	France	Cardiff	1999
8	N R Jenkins	Canada	Cardiff	1993
7	N R Jenkins	Italy	Cardiff	1994
7	N R Jenkins	Canada	Cardiff	1999
7	N R Jenkins	Italy	Cardiff	2000
6	G Evans	France	Cardiff	1982
6	N R Jenkins	Tonga	Nuku'alofa	1994
6	N R Jenkins	England	Wembley	1999
6	S M Jones	Canada	Cardiff	2002
6	D R Biggar	Canada	Toronto	2009
6	S M Jones	New Zealand	Cardiff	2010

MOST DROPPED GOALS IN A MATCH

BY THE TEAM

Drops	Opponents	Venue	Year
3	Scotland	Murrayfield	2001
2	Scotland	Swansea	1912
2	Scotland	Cardiff	1914
2	England	Swansea	1920
2	Scotland	Swansea	1921
2	France	Paris	1930
2	England	Cardiff	1971
2	France	Cardiff	1978
2	England	Twickenham	1984
2	Ireland	Wellington	1987
2	Scotland	Cardiff	1988
2	France	Paris	2001

BY A PLAYER

Drops	Player	Opponents	Venue	Year
3	N R Jenkins	Scotland	Murrayfield	2001
2	J Shea	England	Swansea	1920
2	A Jenkins	Scotland	Swansea	1921
2	B John	England	Cardiff	1971
2	M Dacey	England	Twickenham	1984
2	J Davies	Ireland	Wellington	1987
2	J Davies	Scotland	Cardiff	1988
2	N R Jenkins	France	Paris	2001

MOST CAPPED PLAYERS

Caps	Player	Career Span
104	S M Jones	1998 to 2011
100	G Thomas	1995 to 2007
99	M E Williams	1996 to 2011
94	C L Charvis	1996 to 2007
92	G O Llewellyn	1989 to 2004
87	N R Jenkins	1991 to 2002
86	S M Williams	2000 to 2011
82	G D Jenkins	2002 to 2011
76	D J Peel	2001 to 2011
75	A R Jones	2003 to 2011
72	I C Evans	1987 to 1998
70	T G L Shanklin	2001 to 2010
67	J J Thomas	2003 to 2011
64	I M Gough	1998 to 2010
60	W M Phillips	2003 to 2011
59	R Howley	1996 to 2002
59	J W Hook	2006 to 2011
59	A-W Jones	2006 to 2011
58	G R Jenkins	1991 to 2000
57	D J Jones	2001 to 2009
57	R P Jones	2004 to 2011
55	J P R Williams	1969 to 1981
54	R N Jones	1986 to 1995
53	G O Edwards	1967 to 1978
53	I S Gibbs	1991 to 2001
52	L S Quinnell	1993 to 2002
52	M Taylor	1994 to 2005
51	D Young	1987 to 2001

MOST CONSECUTIVE TESTS

Tests	Player	Span
53	G O Edwards	1967 to 1978
43	K J Jones	1947 to 1956
39	G Price	1975 to 1983
38	T M Davies	1969 to 1976
33	W J Bancroft	1890 to 1901

MOST TESTS AS CAPTAIN

Tests	Captain	Span
28	I C Evans	1991 to 1995
27	R P Jones	2008 to 2010
22	R Howley	1998 to 1999
22	C L Charvis	2002 to 2004
21	G Thomas	2003 to 2007
19	J M Humphreys	1995 to 2003
18	A J Gould	1889 to 1897
14	D C T Rowlands	1963 to 1965
14	W J Trew	1907 to 1913

MOST POINTS IN TESTS

Points	Player	Tests	Career
1049	N R Jenkins	87	1991 to 2002
917	S M Jones	104	1998 to 2011
326	J W Hook	59	2006 to 2011
304	P H Thorburn	37	1985 to 1991
285	S M Williams	86	2000 to 2011
211	A C Thomas	23	1996 to 2000
200	G Thomas	100	1995 to 2007
166	P Bennett	29	1969 to 1978
157	I C Evans	72	1987 to 1998

MOST TRIES IN TESTS

Tries	Player	Tests	Career
57	S M Williams	86	2000 to 2011
40	G Thomas	100	1995 to 2007
33	I C Evans	72	1987 to 1998
22	C L Charvis	94	1996 to 2007
20	G O Edwards	53	1967 to 1978
20	T G R Davies	46	1966 to 1978
20	T G L Shanklin	70	2001 to 2010
18	G R Williams	44	2000 to 2005
17	R A Gibbs	16	1906 to 1911
17	J L Williams	17	1906 to 1911
17	K J Jones	44	1947 to 1957

MOST CONVERSIONS IN TESTS

Cons	Player	Tests	Career
153	S M Jones	104	1998 to 2011
130	N R Jenkins	87	1991 to 2002
43	P H Thorburn	37	1985 to 1991
40	J W Hook	59	2006 to 2011
38	J Bancroft	18	1909 to 1914
30	A C Thomas	23	1996 to 2000
29	G L Henson	33	2001 to 2011
25	C Sweeney	35	2003 to 2007
20	W J Bancroft	33	1890 to 1901
20	I R Harris	25	2001 to 2004

MOST PENALTY GOALS IN TESTS

Penalties	Player	Tests	Career
235	N R Jenkins	87	1991 to 2002
186	S M Jones	104	1998 to 2011
70	P H Thorburn	37	1985 to 1991
58	J W Hook	59	2006 to 2011
36	P Bennett	29	1969 to 1978
35	S P Fenwick	30	1975 to 1981
32	A C Thomas	23	1996 to 2000
22	G Evans	10	1981 to 1983

MOST DROPPED GOALS IN TESTS

Drops	Player	Tests	Career
13	J Davies	32	1985 to 1997
10	N R Jenkins	87	1991 to 2002
8	B John	25	1966 to 1972
7	W G Davies	21	1978 to 1985
6	S M Jones	104	1998 to 2011
4	J W Hook	59	2006 to 2011

INTERNATIONAL CHAMPIONSHIP RECORDS

RECORD	DETAIL		SET
Most points in season	151	in five matches	2005
Most tries in season	21	in four matches	1910
Highest score	49	49–14 v France	1910
Biggest win	39	47–8 v Italy	2008
Highest score conceded	60	26–60 v England	1998
Biggest defeat	51	0–51 v France	1998
Most appearances	51	M E Williams	1998–2010
Most points in matches	467	S M Jones	2000–2011
Most points in season	74	N R Jenkins	2001
Most points in match	28	N R Jenkins	v France, 2001
Most tries in matches	22	S M Williams	2000–2011
Most tries in season	6	M C R Richards	1969
	6	S M Williams	2008
Most tries in match	4	W Llewellyn	v England, 1899
	4	M C R Richards	v England, 1969
Most cons in matches	69	S M Jones	2000–2011
Most cons in season	12	S M Jones	2005
Most cons in match	8	J Bancroft	v France, 1910
Most pens in matches	100	S M Jones	2000–2011
Most pens in season	16	P H Thorburn	1986
	16	N R Jenkins	1999
Most pens in match	7	N R Jenkins	v Italy, 2000
Most drops in matches	8	J Davies	1985–1997
Most drops in season	5	N R Jenkins	2001
Most drops in match	3	N R Jenkins	v Scotland, 2001

MISCELLANEOUS RECORDS

RECORD	HOLDER	DETAIL
Longest Test Career	G O Llewellyn	1989 to 2004
	M E Williams	1996 to 2011
Youngest Test Cap	T W J Prydie	18 yrs 25 days in 2010
Oldest Test Cap	T H Vile	38 yrs 152 days in 1921

CAREER RECORDS OF WALES INTERNATIONAL PLAYERS

(UP TO 31 OCTOBER 2011)

PLAYER BACKS :	DEBUT	CAPS	T	C	P	D	PTS
D R Biggar	2008 v C	8	0	8	12	0	52
A M Bishop	2008 v SA	15	0	0	0	0	0
A G Brew	2007 v I	8	2	0	0	0	10
L M Byrne	2005 v NZ	46	10	0	0	0	50
C D Czekaj	2005 v C	9	2	0	0	0	10
J J V Davies	2009 v C	21	5	0	0	0	25
S L Halfpenny	2008 v SA	26	9	0	10	0	75
W T M Harries	2010 v NZ	2	0	0	0	0	0
G L Henson	2001 v J	33	3	29	18	1	130
J W Hook	2006 v Arg	59	12	40	58	4	326
T James	2007 v E	10	2	0	0	0	10
S M Jones	1998 v SA	104	7	153	186	6	917
T D Knoyle	2010 v NZ	6	0	0	0	0	0
G P North	2010 v SA	15	9	0	0	0	45
D J Peel	2001 v J	76	5	0	0	0	25
W M Phillips	2003 v R	60	8	0	0	0	40
R Priestland	2011 v S	9	0	12	5	0	39
T W J Prydie	2010 v It	4	1	0	0	0	5
R S Rees	2010 v E	9	1	0	0	0	5
J H Roberts	2008 v S	38	4	0	0	0	20
T G L Shanklin	2001 v J	70	20	0	0	0	100
M L Stoddart	2007 v SA	8	5	0	0	0	25
L D Williams	2011 v Arg	4	2	0	0	0	10
M S Williams	2011 v Bb	7	4	0	0	0	20
S M Williams	2000 v F	86	57	0	0	0	285

FORWARDS :

S A Andrews	2011 v Bb	1	0	0	0	0	0
H Bennett	2003 v I	48	0	0	0	0	0
R J Bevington	2011 v Bb	6	0	0	0	0	0
L B Burns	2011 v Bb	7	1	0	0	0	5
L C Charteris	2004 v SA	32	0	0	0	0	0
B S Davies	2009 v S	31	0	0	0	0	0
T T Faletau	2011 v Bb	10	2	0	0	0	10
I M Gough	1998 v SA	64	1	0	0	0	5
R M Hibbard	2006 v Arg	15	0	0	0	0	0
P James	2003 v R	31	0	0	0	0	0
G D Jenkins	2002 v R	82	4	0	0	0	20
A R Jones	2003 v E	75	2	0	0	0	10
A-W Jones	2006 v Arg	59	7	0	0	0	35
D L Jones	2000 v Sm	13	0	0	0	0	0
R P Jones	2004 v SA	57	2*	0	0	0	10
D J Lydiate	2009 v Arg	19	0	0	0	0	0
C Mitchell	2009 v C	11	0	0	0	0	0
K J Owens	2011 v Nm	1	0	0	0	0	0
A T Powell	2008 v SA	22	1	0	0	0	5
M Rees	2005 v US	47	2	0	0	0	10
J J Thomas	2003 v A	67	7	0	0	0	35
J C Tipuric	2011 v Arg	1	0	0	0	0	0
J Turnbull	2011 v S	3	0	0	0	0	0
S K Warburton	2009 v US	23	2	0	0	0	10
M E Williams	1996 v Bb	99	14	0	0	1	73
J V Yapp	2005 v E	21	0	0	0	0	0

* Ryan Jones's figures include a penalty try awarded against Canada in 2006

WALES INTERNATIONAL PLAYERS
(UP TO 31 OCTOBER 2011)

Note: Years given for International Championship matches are for second half of season; eg 1972 means season 1971–72. Years for all other matches refer to the actual year of the match. Entries in square brackets denote matches played in RWC Finals.

Ackerman, R A (Newport, London Welsh) 1980 NZ, 1981 E, S, A, 1982 I, F, E, S, 1983 S, I, F, R, 1984 S, I, F, E, A, 1985 S, I, F, E, Fj
Alexander, E P (Llandovery Coll, Cambridge U) 1885 S, 1886 E, S, 1887 E, I
Alexander, W H (Llwynypia) 1898 I, E, 1899 E, S, I, 1901 S, I
Allen, A G (Newbridge) 1990 F, E, I
Allen, C P (Oxford U, Beaumaris) 1884 E, S
Andrews, F (Pontypool) 1912 SA, 1913 E, S, I
Andrews, F G (Swansea) 1884 E, S
Andrews, G E (Newport) 1926 E, S, 1927 E, F, I
Andrews, S A (Cardiff Blues) 2011 Bb(R)
Anthony, C T (Swansea, Newport, Gwent Dragons) 1997 US 1(R), 2(R), C (R), Tg (R), 1998 SA 2, Arg, 1999 S, I (R), 2001 J 1, 2, I (R), 2002 I, F, It, E, S, 2003 R (R)
Anthony, L (Neath) 1948 E, S, F
Appleyard, R C (Swansea) 1997 C, R, Tg, NZ, 1998 It, E (R), S, I, F
Arnold, P (Swansea) 1990 Nm 1, 2, Bb, 1991 E, S, I, F 1, A, [Arg, A], 1993 F (R), Z 2, 1994 Sp, Fj, 1995 SA, 1996 Bb (R)
Arnold, W R (Swansea) 1903 S
Arthur, C S (Cardiff) 1888 I, M, 1891 E
Arthur, T (Neath) 1927 S, F, I, 1929 E, S, F, I, 1930 E, S, I, F, 1931 E, S, F, I, SA, 1933 E, S
Ashton, C (Aberavon) 1959 E, S, I, 1960 E, S, I, 1962 I
Attewell, S L (Newport) 1921 E, S, F

Back, M J (Bridgend) 1995 F (R), E (R), S, I
Badger, O (Llanelli) 1895 E, S, I, 1896 E
Baker, A (Neath) 1921 I, 1923 E, S, F, I
Baker, A M (Newport) 1909 S, F, 1910 S
Bancroft, J (Swansea) 1909 E, S, F, I, 1910 F, E, S, I, 1911 E, F, I, 1912 E, S, I, 1913 I, 1914 E, S, F
Bancroft, W J (Swansea) 1890 S, E, I, 1891 E, S, I, 1892 E, S, I, 1893 E, S, I, 1894 E, S, I, 1895 E, S, I, 1896 E, S, I, 1897 E, 1898 I, E, 1899 E, S, I, 1900 E, S, I, 1901 E, S, I
Barlow, T M (Cardiff) 1884 I
Barrell, R J (Cardiff) 1929 S, F, I, 1933 I
Bartlett, J D (Llanelli) 1927 S, 1928 E, S
Bassett, A (Cardiff) 1934 I, 1935 E, S, I, 1938 E, S
Bassett, J A (Penarth) 1929 E, S, F, I, 1930 E, S, I, 1931 E, S, F, I, SA, 1932 E, S, I
Bateman, A G (Neath, Richmond, Northampton) 1990 S, I, Nm 1, 2, 1996 SA, 1997 US, S, F, E, R, NZ, 1998 It, E, S, I, 1999 S, Arg 1, 2, SA, C, [J, A (R)], 2000 It, E, S, I, Sm, US, SA, 2001 E (R), It (t), R, I, Art (R), Tg
Bater, J (Ospreys) 2003 R (R)
Bayliss, G (Pontypool) 1933 S
Bebb, D I E (Carmarthen TC, Swansea) 1959 E, S, I, F, 1960 E, S, I, F, SA, 1961 E, S, I, F, 1962 E, S, F, I, 1963 E, F, NZ, 1964 E, S, F, SA, 1965 E, S, I, F, 1966 F, A, 1967 S, I, F, E
Beckingham, G (Cardiff) 1953 E, S, 1958 F
Bennett, A M (Cardiff) 1995 [NZ] SA, Fj
Bennett, H (Ospreys) 2003 I 2(R), S 2(R), [C(R), Tg(R)], 2004 S(R), F(R), Arg 1(R), 2, SA1(R), 2006 Arg 2, PI(R), 2007 E2, [J(R)], SA, 2008 E, S, It(R), F, 2009 S(R), E(R), F(R), It, I(R), NZ(R), Sm, Arg(R), A(R), 2010 E(R), S(R), F, I(R), It(R), NZ1(R), 2(R), A(R), SA2(R), Fj, NZ3(R), 2011 Bb, E2, 3(R), Arg(R) , [SA, Sm, Fj, I, F, A]
Bennett, I (Aberavon) 1937 I
Bennett, P (Cardiff Harlequins) 1891 E, S, 1892 S, I
Bennett, P (Llanelli) 1969 F (R), 1970 SA, S, F, 1972 S (R), NZ, 1973 E, S, I, F, A, 1974 S, I, F, E, 1975 S (R), I, 1976 E, S, I, F, 1977 I, F, E, S, 1978 E, S, I, F
Bergiers, R T E (Cardiff Coll of Ed, Llanelli) 1972 E, S, F, NZ, 1973 E, S, I, F, A, 1974 E, 1975 I
Bevan, G W (Llanelli) 1947 E
Bevan, J A (Cambridge U) 1881 E
Bevan, J C (Cardiff, Cardiff Coll of Ed) 1971 E, S, I, F, 1972 E, S, F, NZ, 1973 E, S
Bevan, J D (Aberavon) 1975 F, E, S, A
Bevan, S (Swansea) 1904 I
Bevington, R J (Ospreys) 2011 Bb, E2(R), 3(R), Arg(R), [Nm(R), A(R)]
Beynon, B (Swansea) 1920 E, S
Beynon, G E (Swansea) 1925 F, I
Bidgood, R A (Newport) 1992 S, 1993 Z 1, 2, Nm, J (R)
Biggar, D R (Ospreys) 2008 C(R), 2009 C, US(R), Sm, 2010 NZ1(R), 2, A(R), Fj
Biggs, N W (Cardiff) 1888 M, 1889 I, 1892 I, 1893 E, S, I, 1894 E, I
Biggs, S H (Cardiff) 1895 E, S, 1896 S, 1897 E, 1898 I, E, 1899 S, I, 1900 I
Birch, J (Neath) 1911 S, F
Birt, F W (Newport) 1911 E, S, 1912 E, S, I, SA, 1913 E
Bishop, A M (Ospreys) 2008 SA2(R), C, A(R), 2009 S(R), C, US, Arg(R), A(R), 2010 I(R), It(R), NZ1, A, SA2(t), Fj, NZ3(R)
Bishop, D J (Pontypool) 1984 A
Bishop, E H (Swansea) 1889 S
Blackmore, J H (Abertillery) 1909 E
Blackmore, S W (Cardiff) 1987 I, [Tg (R), C, A]
Blake, J (Cardiff) 1899 E, S, I, 1900 E, S, I, 1901 E, S, I
Blakemore, R E (Newport) 1947 E
Bland, A F (Cardiff) 1887 E, S, I, 1888 S, I, M, 1890 S, E, I
Blyth, L (Swansea) 1951 SA, 1952 E, S
Blyth, W R (Swansea) 1974 E, 1975 S (R), 1980 F, E, S, I
Boobyer, N (Llanelli) 1993 Z 1(R), 2, Nm, 1994 Fj, Tg, 1998 F, 1999 It (R)
Boon, R W (Cardiff) 1930 S, F, 1931 E, S, F, I, SA, 1932 E, S, I, 1933 E, I
Booth, J (Pontymister) 1898 I
Boots, J G (Newport) 1898 I, E, 1899 I, 1900 E, S, I, 1901 E, S, I, 1902 E, S, I, 1903 E, S, I, 1904 E
Boucher, A W (Newport) 1892 E, S, I, 1893 E, S, I, 1894 E, 1895 E, S, I, 1896 E, I, 1897 E
Bowcott, H M (Cardiff, Cambridge U) 1929 S, F, I, 1930 E, 1931 E, S, 1933 E, I
Bowdler, F A (Cross Keys) 1927 A, 1928 E, S, I, F, 1929 E, S, F, I, 1930 E, 1931 SA, 1932 E, S, I, 1933 I
Bowen, B (S Wales Police, Swansea) 1983 R, 1984 S, I, F, E, 1985 Fj, 1986 E, S, I, F, Fj, Tg, WS, 1987 [C, E, NZ], US, 1988 E, S, I, F, WS, 1989 S, I
Bowen, C A (Llanelli) 1896 E, S, I, 1897 E
Bowen, D H (Llanelli) 1883 E, 1886 E, S, 1887 E
Bowen, G E (Swansea) 1887 S, I, 1888 S, I
Bowen, W (Swansea) 1921 S, F, 1922 E, S, I, F
Bowen, Wm A (Swansea) 1886 E, S, 1887 E, S, I, 1888 M, 1889 S, I, 1890 S, E, I, 1891 E, S
Brace, D O (Llanelli, Oxford U) 1956 E, S, I, F, 1957 E, 1960 S, I, F, 1961 I
Braddock, K J (Newbridge) 1966 A, 1967 S, I
Bradshaw, K (Bridgend) 1964 E, S, I, F, SA, 1966 E, S, I, F
Brew, A G (Newport Gwent Dragons, Ospreys) 2007 I(R), A2, E2, 2010 Fj, 2011 Bb, E3(R), Arg(R), [Nm]
Brew, N R (Gwent Dragons) 2003 R
Brewer, T J (Newport) 1950 E, 1955 E, S
Brice, A B (Aberavon) 1899 E, S, I, 1900 E, S, I, 1901 E, S, I, 1902 E, S, I, 1903 E, S, I, 1904 E, S, I
Bridges, C J (Neath) 1990 Nm 1, 2, Bb, 1991 E (R), I, F 1, A

Bridie, R H (Newport) 1882 I
Britton, G R (Newport) 1961 S
Broster, B G J (Saracens) 2005 US(R), C
Broughton, A S (Treorchy) 1927 A, 1929 S
Brown, A (Newport) 1921 I
Brown, J (Cardiff) 1925 I
Brown, J A (Cardiff) 1907 E, S, I, 1908 E, S, F, 1909 E
Brown, M (Pontypool) 1983 R, 1986 E, S, Fj (R), Tg, WS
Bryant, D J (Bridgend) 1988 NZ 1, 2, WS, R, 1989 S, I, F, E
Bryant, J (Celtic Warriors) 2003 R (R)
Buchanan, D A (Llanelli) 1987 [Tg, E, NZ, A], 1988 I
Buckett, I M (Swansea) 1994 Tg, 1997 US 2, C
Budgett, N J (Ebbw Vale, Bridgend) 2000 S, I, Sm (R), US, SA, 2001 J 1(R), 2, 2002 I, F, It, E, S
Burcher, D H (Newport) 1977 I, F, E, S
Burgess, R C (Ebbw Vale) 1977 I, F, E, S, 1981 I, F, 1982 F, E, S
Burnett, R (Newport) 1953 E
Burns, J (Cardiff) 1927 F, I
Burns, L B (Newport Gwent Dragons) 2011 Bb(R), E2(R), 3, [Sm(R), Nm, Fj(R), A(R)]
Bush, P F (Cardiff) 1905 NZ, 1906 E, SA, 1907 I, 1908 E, S, 1910 S, I
Butler, E T (Pontypool) 1980 F, E, S, I, NZ (R), 1982 S, 1983 E, S, I, F, R, 1984 S, I, F, E, A
Byrne, L M (Llanelli Scarlets, Ospreys, Clermont-Auvergne) 2005 NZ(R), Fj, SA, 2006 E(t&R), S(t&R), I, It, F, Arg 1, 2, PI, 2007 F1, A1, E2, 2008 E, S, It, I, F, SA3, NZ, A, 2009 S, E, F, It, I, 2010 E, S, F, I, It, SA1, NZ1, 2, SA2, Fj, NZ3, 2011 E1(R), S, It, I, F, Arg, [Nm, Fj]

Cale, W R (Newbridge, Pontypool) 1949 E, S, I, 1950 E, S, I, F
Cardey, M D (Llanelli) 2000 S
Carter, A J (Newport) 1991 E, S
Cattell, A (Llanelli) 1883 E, S
Challinor, C (Neath) 1939 E
Charteris, L C (Newport Gwent Dragons) 2004 SA2(R), R, 2005 US, C, NZ(R), Fj, 2007 SA(R), 2008 C, NZ(R), 2009 S(R), F(R), It, I(R), US(R), NZ, Sm, Arg, A, 2010 E, F(R), I, It, 2011 Bb, E2(R), 3, [SA, Sm, Nm(R), Fj, I, F, A]
Charvis, C L (Swansea, Tarbes, Newcastle, Newport Gwent Dragons) 1996 A 3(R), SA, 1997 US, S, I, F, 1998 It (R), E, S, I, F, Z (R), SA 1, 2, Arg, 1999 S, I, F 1, It, E, Arg 1, SA, F 2, [Arg 3, A], 2000 F, It (R), E, S, I, Sm, US, SA, 2001 E, S, F, It, R, I, Arg, Tg, A, 2002 E (R), S, SA 1, 2, R, Fj, C, NZ, 2003 It, E 1(R), S 1(R), I 1, F, A, NZ, E 2, S 2, [C, Tg, It, NZ, E], 2004 S, F, E, It, Arg 1, 2, SA1, 2, R, NZ, J, 2005 US, C, NZ, SA, A, 2006 E, S, I, It, 2007 A1, 2, E2, Arg(R), F2(R), [C(t&R), A, J, Fj], SA
Clapp, T J S (Newport) 1882 I, 1883 E, S, 1884 E, S, I, 1885 E, S, 1886 S, 1887 E, S, I, 1888 S, I
Clare, J (Cardiff) 1883 E
Clark, S S (Neath) 1882 I, 1887 I
Cleaver, W B (Cardiff) 1947 E, S, F, I, A, 1948 E, S, F, I, 1949 I, 1950 E, S, I, F
Clegg, B G (Swansea) 1979 F
Clement, A (Swansea) 1987 US (R), 1988 E, NZ 1, WS (R), R, 1989 NZ, 1990 S (R), I (R), Nm 1, 2, 1991 S (R), A (R), F 2, [WS, A], 1992 I, F, E, S, 1993 I (R), F, J, C, 1994 S, I, F, Sp, C (R), Tg, WS, It, SA, 1995 F, E, [J, NZ, I]
Clement, W H (Llanelli) 1937 E, S, I, 1938 E, S, I
Cobner, T J (Pontypool) 1974 S, I, F, E, 1975 F, E, S, I, A, 1976 E, S, 1977 F, E, S, 1978 E, S, I, F, A 1
Cockbain, B J (Celtic Warriors, Ospreys) 2003 R, [C, It, NZ, E], 2004 S, I, F, E, Arg 1, 2, SA2, NZ, 2005 E, It, F, S, I, US, C(R), NZ, Fj, 2007 F1(t&R), A1
Coldrick, A P (Newport) 1911 E, S, I, 1912 E, S, F
Coleman, E O (Newport) 1949 E, S, I
Coles, F C (Pontypool) 1960 S, I, F
Collins, J E (Aberavon) 1958 A, E, S, F, 1959 E, S, I, F, 1960 E, 1961 F
Collins, R G (S Wales Police, Cardiff, Pontypridd) 1987 E (R), I, [I, E, NZ], US, 1988 E, S, I, F, R, 1990 E, S, I, 1991 A, F 2, [WS], 1994 C, Fj, Tg, WS, R, It, SA, 1995 F, E, S, I
Collins, T J (Mountain Ash) 1923 I
Conway-Rees, J (Llanelli) 1892 S, 1893 E, 1894 E
Cook, T (Cardiff) 1949 S, I
Cooper, G J (Bath, Celtic Warriors, Newport Gwent Dragons, Gloucester, Cardiff Blues) 2001 It, J 1, 2, 2003 E 1, S 1, I 1, F(R), A, NZ, E 2, [C, Tg, It(t&R), NZ, E], 2004 S, I, F, E, It, R(R), NZ(R), J, 2005 E(R), It(R), F(R), NZ(R), Fj, SA, A, 2006 E(R), PI(R), 2007 A1(R), E2, [J(R)], 2008 SA1, 2, 3, NZ, A, 2009 C, US(R), NZ, Arg, 2010 E, S
Cooper, V L (Llanelli) 2002 C, 2003 I 2(R), S 2
Cope, W (Cardiff, Blackheath) 1896 S
Copsey, A H (Llanelli) 1992 I, F, E, S, A, 1993 E, S, I, J, C, 1994 E (R), Pt, Sp (R), Fj, Tg, WS (R)
Cornish, F H (Cardiff) 1897 E, 1898 I, E, 1899 I
Cornish, R A (Cardiff) 1923 E, S, 1924 E, 1925 E, S, F, 1926 E, S, I, F
Coslett, T K (Aberavon) 1962 E, S, F
Cowey, B T V (Welch Regt, Newport) 1934 E, S, I, 1935 E
Cresswell, B R (Newport) 1960 E, S, I, F
Cummins, W (Treorchy) 1922 E, S, I, F
Cunningham, L J (Aberavon) 1960 E, S, I, F, 1962 E, S, F, I, 1963 NZ, 1964 E, S, I, F, SA
Czekaj, C D (Cardiff Blues) 2005 C, 2006 Arg 1(R), 2007 I, S, A1, 2, 2009 C, 2010 A(R), SA2(R)

Dacey, M (Swansea) 1983 E, S, I, F, R, 1984 S, I, F, E, A, 1986 Fj, Tg, WS, 1987 F (R), [Tg]
Daniel, D J (Llanelli) 1891 S, 1894 E, S, I, 1898 I, E, 1899 E, I
Daniel, L T D (Newport) 1970 S
Daniels, P C T (Cardiff) 1981 A, 1982 I
Darbishire, G (Bangor) 1881 E
Dauncey, F H (Newport) 1896 E, S, I
Davey, C (Swansea) 1930 F, 1931 E, S, F, I, SA, 1932 E, S, I, 1933 E, S, 1934 E, S, I, 1935 E, S, I, NZ, 1936 S, 1937 E, I, 1938 E, I
David, R J (Cardiff) 1907 I
David, T P (Llanelli, Pontypridd) 1973 F, A, 1976 I, F
Davidge, G D (Newport) 1959 F, 1960 S, I, F, SA, 1961 E, S, I, 1962 F
Davies, A (Cambridge U, Neath, Cardiff) 1990 Bb (R), 1991 A, 1993 Z 1, 2, J, C, 1994 Fj, 1995 [J, I]
Davies, A C (London Welsh) 1889 I
Davies, A E (Llanelli) 1984 A
Davies, B (Llanelli) 1895 E, 1896 E
Davies, B (Llanelli Scarlets) 2006 I(R)
Davies, B S (Cardiff Blues) 2009 S(R), It(R), C, NZ(R), Sm(R), 2010 E(t&R), S(R), F, I, It, SA1, NZ1, 2, A, SA2, Fj(R), NZ3, 2011 E1, S, It, I, F, E2, Arg, [SA(R), Sm(R), Nm, Fj, I(R), F(R), A]
Davies, C (Cardiff) 1947 S, F, I, A, 1948 E, S, F, I, 1949 F, 1950 E, S, I, F, 1951 E, S, I
Davies, C (Llanelli) 1988 WS, 1989 S, I (R), F
Davies, C A H (Llanelli, Cardiff) 1957 I, 1958 A, E, S, I, 1960 SA, 1961 E
Davies, C H (Swansea, Llanelli) 1939 S, I, 1947 E, S, F, I
Davies, C L (Cardiff) 1956 E, S, I
Davies, C R (Bedford, RAF) 1934 E
Davies, D B (Llanelli) 1907 E
Davies, D B (Llanelli) 1962 I, 1963 E, S
Davies, D E G (Cardiff) 1912 E, F
Davies, D G (Cardiff) 1923 E, S
Davies, D H (Neath) 1904 S
Davies, D H (Bridgend) 1921 I, 1925 I
Davies, D H (Aberavon) 1924 E
Davies, D I (Swansea) 1939 E
Davies, D J (Neath) 1962 I
Davies, D M (Somerset Police) 1950 E, S, I, F, 1951 E, S, I, F, SA, 1952 E, S, I, F, 1953 I, F, NZ, 1954 E
Davies, E (Maesteg) 1919 NZA
Davies, E G (Cardiff) 1928 F, 1929 E, 1930 S
Davies, E P (Aberavon) 1947 A, 1948 I
Davies, G (Swansea) 1900 E, S, I, 1901 E, S, I, 1905 E, S, I
Davies, G (Cambridge U, Pontypridd) 1947 S, A, 1948 E, S, F, I, 1949 E, S, F, 1951 E, S
Davies, H (Swansea) 1898 I, E, 1901 S, I
Davies, H (Bridgend) 1984 S, I, F, E
Davies, H G (Llanelli) 1921 F, I, 1925 F
Davies, H J (Neath) 1912 E, S
Davies, H J (Newport) 1924 S
Davies, H J (Cambridge U, Aberavon) 1959 E, S
Davies, H S (Treherbert) 1923 I
Davies, I T (Llanelli) 1914 S, F, I
Davies, J (Neath, Llanelli, Cardiff) 1985 E, Fj, 1986 E, S, I, F, Fj, Tg, WS, 1987 F, E, S, I, [I, Tg (R), C, E, NZ, A], 1988 E, S, I, F, NZ 1, 2, WS, R, 1996 A 3, 1997 US (t), S (R), F (R), E
Davies, Rev J A (Swansea) 1913 S, F, I, 1914 E, S, F, I
Davies, J D (Neath, Richmond) 1991 I, F 1, 1993 F (R), Z 2, J, C, 1994 S, I, F, E, Pt, Sp, C, WS, R, It, SA, 1995 F, E, [J, NZ, I] SA, 1996 It, E, S, I, F 1, A 1, Bb, F 2, It, 1998 Z, SA 1
Davies, J H (Aberavon) 1923 I
Davies, J J V (Scarlets) 2009 C, US, Sm(R), Arg, A, 2010 NZ1(R), 2, 2011 E1, S, I, F, Bb, E2, Arg, [SA, Sm, Nm, Fj(R), I, F, A]
Davies, L (Swansea) 1939 S, I
Davies, L (Bridgend) 1966 E, S, I
Davies, L B (Neath, Cardiff, Llanelli) 1996 It, E, S, I, F 1, A 1, Bb,

F 2, It (R), 1997 US 1, 2, C, R, Tg, NZ (R), 1998 E (R), I, F, 1999 C, 2001 I, 2003 It
Davies, L M (Llanelli) 1954 F, S, 1955 I
Davies, M (Swansea) 1981 A, 1982 I, 1985 Fj
Davies, Mefin (Pontypridd, Celtic Warriors, Gloucester) 2002 SA 2(R), R, Fj, 2003 It, S 1(R), I 1(R), F, A(R), NZ(R), I 2, R, [Tg, NZ(R), E(R)], 2004 S, F, It(R), Arg 1, 2(R), SA1, 2(R), R, NZ, J, 2005 E, It, F, S, I, C(R), NZ, SA(R), A(t), 2006 S(R), I(R), It(R), F(R), 2007 A2
Davies, M J (Blackheath) 1939 S, I
Davies, N G (London Welsh) 1955 E
Davies, N G (Llanelli) 1988 NZ 2, WS, 1989 S, I, 1993 F, 1994 S, I, E, Pt, Sp, C, Fj, Tg (R), WS, R, It, 1995 E, S, I, Fj, 1996 E, S, I, F 1, A 1, 2, Bb, F 2, 1997 E
Davies, P T (Llanelli) 1985 E, Fj, 1986 E, S, I, F, Fj, Tg, WS, 1987 F, E, I, [Tg, C, NZ], 1988 WS, R, 1989 S, I, F, E, NZ, 1990 F, E, S, 1991 I, F 1, A, F 2, [WS, Arg, A], 1993 F, Z 1, Nm, 1994 S, I, F, E, C, Fj (R), WS, R, It, 1995 F, I
Davies, R H (Oxford U, London Welsh) 1957 S, I, F, 1958 A, 1962 E, S
Davies, S (Swansea) 1992 I, F, E, S, A, 1993 E, S, I, Z 1(R), 2, Nm, J, 1995 F, [J, I], 1998 I (R), F
Davies, T G R (Cardiff, London Welsh) 1966 A, 1967 S, I, F, E, 1968 E, S, 1969 S, I, F, NZ 1, 2, A, 1971 E, S, I, F, 1972 E, S, F, NZ, 1973 E, S, I, F, A, 1974 S, F, E, 1975 F, E, S, I, 1976 E, S, I, F, 1977 I, F, E, S, 1978 E, S, I, A 1, 2
Davies, T J (Devonport Services, Swansea, Llanelli) 1953 E, S, I, F, 1957 E, S, I, F, 1958 A, E, S, F, 1959 E, S, I, F, 1960 E, SA, 1961 E, S, F
Davies, T M (London Welsh, Swansea) 1969 S, I, F, E, NZ 1, 2, A, 1970 SA, S, E, I, F, 1971 E, S, I, F, 1972 E, S, F, NZ, 1973 E, S, I, F, A, 1974 S, I, F, E, 1975 F, E, S, I, A, 1976 E, S, I, F
Davies, W (Cardiff) 1896 S
Davies, W (Swansea) 1931 SA, 1932 E, S, I
Davies, W A (Aberavon) 1912 S, I
Davies, W G (Cardiff) 1978 A 1, 2, NZ, 1979 S, I, F, E, 1980 F, E, S, NZ, 1981 E, S, A, 1982 I, F, E, S, 1985 S, I, F
Davies, W T H (Swansea) 1936 I, 1937 E, I, 1939 E, S, I
Davis, C E (Newbridge) 1978 A 2, 1981 E, S
Davis, M (Newport) 1991 A
Davis, W E N (Cardiff) 1939 E, S, I
Dawes, S J (London Welsh) 1964 I, F, SA, 1965 E, S, I, F, 1966 A, 1968 I, F, 1969 E, NZ 2, A, 1970 SA, S, E, I, F, 1971 E, S, I, F
Day, H C (Newport) 1930 S, I, F, 1931 E, S
Day, H T (Newport) 1892 I, 1893 E, S, 1894 S, I
Day, T B (Swansea) 1931 E, S, F, I, SA, 1932 E, S, I, 1934 S, I, 1935 E, S, I
Deacon, J T (Swansea) 1891 I, 1892 E, S, I
Delahay, W J (Bridgend) 1922 E, S, I, F, 1923 E, S, F, I, 1924 NZ, 1925 E, S, F, I, 1926 E, S, I, F, 1927 S
Delaney, L (Llanelli) 1989 I, F, E, 1990 E, 1991 F 2, [WS, Arg, A], 1992 I, F, E
Delve, G L (Bath, Gloucester) 2006 S(R), I(R), Arg 1(R), 2(R), 2008 S(R), It(R), I(R), SA1(R), 2, 2010 I, It(R)
Devereux, D B (Neath) 1958 A, E, S
Devereux, J A (S Glamorgan Inst, Bridgend) 1986 E, S, I, F, Fj, Tg, WS, 1987 F, E, S, I, [I, C, E, NZ, A], 1988 NZ 1, 2, R, 1989 S, I
Diplock, R S (Bridgend) 1988 R
Dobson, G A (Cardiff) 1900 S
Dobson, T (Cardiff) 1898 I, E, 1899 E, S
Donovan, A J (Swansea) 1978 A 2, 1981 I (R), A, 1982 E, S
Donovan, R E (S Wales Police) 1983 F (R)
Douglas, M H J (Llanelli) 1984 S, I, F
Douglas, W M (Cardiff) 1886 E, S, 1887 E, S
Dowell, W H (Newport) 1907 E, S, I, 1908 E, S, F, I
Durston, A P R (Bridgend) 2001 J 1, 2
Dyke, J C M (Penarth) 1906 SA
Dyke, L M (Penarth, Cardiff) 1910 I, 1911 S, F, I

Edmunds, D A (Neath) 1990 I (R), Bb
Edwards, A B (London Welsh, Army) 1955 E, S
Edwards, B O (Newport) 1951 I
Edwards, D (Glynneath) 1921 E
Edwards, G O (Cardiff, Cardiff Coll of Ed) 1967 F, E, NZ, 1968 E, S, I, F, 1969 S, I, F, E, NZ 1, 2, A, 1970 SA, S, E, I, F, 1971 E, S, I, F, 1972 E, S, F, NZ, 1973 E, S, I, F, A, 1974 S, I, F, E, 1975 F, E, S, I, A, 1976 E, S, I, F, 1977 I, F, E, S, 1978 E, S, I, F
Eidman, I H (Cardiff) 1983 S, R, 1984 I, F, E, A, 1985 S, I, Fj, 1986 E, S, I, F
Elliott, J (Cardiff) 1894 I, 1898 I, E
Elsey, W J (Cardiff) 1895 E
Emyr, Arthur (Swansea) 1989 E, NZ, 1990 F, E, S, I, Nm 1, 2, 1991 F 1, 2, [WS, Arg, A]
Evans, A (Pontypool) 1924 E, I, F
Evans, B (Llanelli) 1933 E, S, 1936 E, S, I, 1937 E
Evans, B R (Swansea, Cardiff Blues) 1998 SA 2(R), 1999 F 1, It, E, Arg 1, 2, C, [J (R), Sm (R), A (R)], 2000 Sm, US, 2001 J 1(R), 2002 SA 1, 2, R(R), Fj, C, NZ, 2003 It, E 1, S 1, I 2, R, 2004 F(R), E(t), It(R)
Evans, B S (Llanelli) 1920 E, 1922 E, S, I, F
Evans, C (Pontypool) 1960 E
Evans, D (Penygraig) 1896 S, I, 1897 E, 1898 E
Evans, D B (Swansea) 1926 E
Evans, D B (Swansea) 1933 S
Evans, D D (Cheshire, Cardiff U) 1934 E
Evans, D J (Scarlets) 2009 C, US
Evans, D P (Llanelli) 1960 SA
Evans, D W (Cardiff) 1889 S, I, 1890 E, I, 1891 E
Evans, D W (Oxford U, Cardiff, Treorchy) 1989 F, E, NZ, 1990 F, E, S, I, Bb, 1991 A (R), F 2(R), [A (R)], 1995 [J (R)]
Evans, E (Llanelli) 1937 E, 1939 S, I
Evans, F (Llanelli) 1921 S
Evans, G (Cardiff) 1947 E, S, F, I, A, 1948 E, S, F, I, 1949 E, S, I
Evans, G (Maesteg) 1981 S (R), I, F, A, 1982 I, F, E, S, 1983 F, R
Evans, G D (Llanelli Scarlets) 2006 PI(R)
Evans, G L (Newport) 1977 F (R), 1978 F, A 2(R)
Evans, G R (Cardiff) 1889 S
Evans, G R (Llanelli) 1998 SA 1, 2003 I 2, S 2, [NZ]
Evans, H I (Swansea) 1922 E, S, I, F
Evans, Ian (Ospreys) 2006 Arg 1, 2, A, C, NZ, 2007 [J(R), Fj], SA, 2008 E(R), S, It, F(R), SA1(R), 2(R), 3, NZ
Evans, I (London Welsh) 1934 S, I
Evans, I C (Llanelli, Bath) 1987 F, E, S, I, [I, C, E, NZ, A], 1988 E, S, I, F, NZ 1, 2, 1989 I, F, E, 1991 E, S, I, F 1, A, F 2, [WS, Arg, A], 1992 I, F, E, S, A, 1993 E, S, I, F, J, C, 1994 S, I, E, Pt, Sp, C, Fj, Tg, WS, R, 1995 E, S, I, [J, NZ, I], SA, Fj, 1996 It, E, S, I, F 1, A 1, 2, Bb, F 2, A 3, SA, 1997 US, S, I, F, 1998 It
Evans, I L (Llanelli) 1991 F 2(R)
Evans, J (Llanelli) 1896 S, I, 1897 E
Evans, J D (Cardiff) 1958 I, F
Evans, J E (Llanelli) 1924 S
Evans, J H (Pontypool) 1907 E, S, I
Evans, J R (Newport) 1934 E
Evans, J W (Blaina) 1904 E
Evans, O J (Cardiff) 1887 E, S, 1888 S, I
Evans, P D (Llanelli) 1951 E, F
Evans, R (Bridgend) 1963 S, I, F
Evans, R L (Llanelli) 1993 E, S, I, F, 1994 S, I, F, E, Pt, Sp, C, Fj, WS, R, It, SA, 1995 F, [NZ, I (R)]
Evans, R T (Newport) 1947 F, I, 1950 E, S, I, F, 1951 E, S, I, F
Evans, S (Swansea, Neath) 1985 F, E, 1986 Fj, Tg, WS, 1987 F, E, [I, Tg]
Evans, T D (Swansea) 1924 I
Evans, T G (London Welsh) 1970 SA, S, E, I, 1972 E, S, F
Evans, T H (Llanelli) 1906 I, 1907 E, S, I, 1908 I, A, 1909 E, S, F, I, 1910 F, E, S, I, 1911 E, S, F, I
Evans, T P (Swansea) 1975 F, E, S, I, A, 1976 E, S, I, F, 1977 I
Evans, T W (Llanelli) 1958 A
Evans, V (Neath) 1954 I, F, S
Evans, W F (Rhymney) 1882 I, 1883 S
Evans, W G (Brynmawr) 1911 I
Evans, W H (Llwynypia) 1914 E, S, F, I
Evans, W J (Pontypool) 1947 S
Evans, W R (Bridgend) 1958 A, E, S, I, F, 1960 SA, 1961 E, S, I, F, 1962 E, S, I
Everson, W A (Newport) 1926 S

Faletau, T T (Newport Gwent Dragons) 2011 Bb, E2, 3, [SA, Sm, Nm, Fj, I, F, A]
Faulkner, A G (Pontypool) 1975 F, E, S, I, A, 1976 E, S, I, F, 1978 E, S, I, F, A 1, 2, NZ, 1979 S, I, F
Faull, J (Swansea) 1957 I, F, 1958 A, E, S, I, F, 1959 E, S, I, 1960 E, F
Fauvel, T J (Aberavon) 1988 NZ 1(R)
Fear, A G (Newport) 1934 S, I, 1935 S, I
Fender, N H (Cardiff) 1930 I, F, 1931 E, S, F, I
Fenwick, S P (Bridgend) 1975 F, E, S, A, 1976 E, S, I, F, 1977 I, F, E, S, 1978 E, S, I, F, A 1, 2, NZ, 1979 S, I, F, E, 1980 F, E, S, I, NZ, 1981 E, S
Finch, E (Llanelli) 1924 F, NZ, 1925 F, I, 1926 F, 1927 A, 1928 I
Finlayson, A A J (Cardiff) 1974 I, F, E
Fitzgerald, D (Cardiff) 1894 S, I
Ford, F J V (Welch Regt, Newport) 1939 E

Ford, I R (Newport) 1959 E, S
Ford, S P (Cardiff) 1990 I, Nm 1, 2, Bb, 1991 E, S, I, A
Forster, J A (Newport Gwent Dragons) 2004 Arg 1
Forward, A (Pontypool, Mon Police) 1951 S, SA, 1952 E, S, I, F
Fowler, I J (Llanelli) 1919 NZA
Francis, D G (Llanelli) 1919 NZA, 1924 S
Francis, P W (Maesteg) 1987 S
Funnell, J S (Ebbw Vale) 1998 Z (R), SA 1
Fury, W L (London Irish) 2008 SA1(R), 2(R)

Gabe, R T (Cardiff, Llanelli) 1901 I, 1902 E, S, I, 1903 E, S, I, 1904 E, S, I, 1905 E, S, I, NZ, 1906 E, I, SA, 1907 E, S, I, 1908 E, S, F, I
Gale, N R (Swansea, Llanelli) 1960 I, 1963 E, S, I, NZ, 1964 E, S, I, F, SA, 1965 E, S, I, F, 1966 E, S, I, F, A, 1967 E, NZ, 1968 E, 1969 NZ 1(R), 2, A
Gallacher, I S (Llanelli) 1970 F
Garrett, R M (Penarth) 1888 M, 1889 S, 1890 S, E, I, 1891 S, I, 1892 E
Geen, W P (Oxford U, Newport) 1912 SA, 1913 E, I
George, E E (Pontypridd, Cardiff) 1895 S, I, 1896 E
George, G M (Newport) 1991 E, S
Gething, G I (Neath) 1913 F
Gibbs, A (Newbridge) 1995 I, SA, 1996 A 2, 1997 US 1, 2, C
Gibbs, I S (Neath, Swansea) 1991 E, S, I, F 1, A, F 2, [WS, Arg, A], 1992 I, F, E, S, A, 1993 E, S, I, F, J, C, 1996 It, A 3, SA, 1997 US, S, I, F, Tg, NZ, 1998 It, E, S, SA 2, Arg, 1999 S, I, F 1, It, E, C, F 2, [Arg 3, J, Sm, A], 2000 I, Sm, US, SA, 2001 E, S, F, It
Gibbs, R A (Cardiff) 1906 S, I, 1907 E, S, 1908 E, S, F, I, 1910 F, E, S, I, 1911 E, S, F, I
Giles, R (Aberavon) 1983 R, 1985 Fj (R), 1987 [C]
Gill, I A R (Saracens) 2010 I(R)
Girling, B E (Cardiff) 1881 E
Goldsworthy, S J (Swansea) 1884 I, 1885 E, S
Gore, J H (Blaina) 1924 I, F, NZ, 1925 E
Gore, W (Newbridge) 1947 S, F, I
Gough, I M (Newport, Pontypridd, Newport Gwent Dragons, Ospreys) 1998 SA 1, 1999 S, 2000 F, It (R), E (R), S, I, Sm, US, SA, 2001 E, S, F, It, Tg, A, 2002 I (R), F (R), It, S, 2003 R, 2005 It(R), US(R), SA, A, 2006 E, S, I, It, F, Arg 1, 2, A, C, NZ, 2007 I, S(R), F1, It, E1, Arg, F2, [C, A, Fj(R)], 2008 E, S, It, I, F, SA1, 2, 3(R), C, A, 2009 S, E, F, I, C(R), US, 2010 I(R), It(R), Fj
Gould, A J (Newport) 1885 E, S, 1886 E, S, 1887 E, S, I, 1888 S, 1889 I, 1890 S, E, I, 1892 E, S, I, 1893 E, S, I, 1894 E, S, 1895 E, S, I, 1896 E, S, I, 1897 E
Gould, G H (Newport) 1892 I, 1893 S, I
Gould, R (Newport) 1882 I, 1883 E, S, 1884 E, S, I, 1885 E, S, 1886 E, 1887 E, S
Graham, T C (Newport) 1890 I, 1891 S, I, 1892 E, S, 1893 E, S, I, 1894 E, S, 1895 E, S
Gravell, R W R (Llanelli) 1975 F, E, S, I, A, 1976 E, S, I, F, 1978 E, S, I, F, A 1, 2, NZ, 1979 S, I, 1981 I, F, 1982 F, E, S
Gray, A J (London Welsh) 1968 E, S
Greenslade, D (Newport) 1962 S
Greville, H G (Llanelli) 1947 A
Griffin, Dr J (Edinburgh U) 1883 S
Griffiths, C R (Llanelli) 1979 E (R)
Griffiths, D (Llanelli) 1888 M, 1889 I
Griffiths, G (Llanelli) 1889 I
Griffiths, G M (Cardiff) 1953 E, S, I, F, NZ, 1954 I, F, S, 1955 I, F, 1957 E, S
Griffiths, J (Swansea) 2000 Sm (R)
Griffiths, J L (Llanelli) 1988 NZ 2, 1989 S
Griffiths, M (Bridgend, Cardiff, Pontypridd) 1988 WS, R, 1989 S, I, F, E, NZ, 1990 F, E, Nm 1, 2, Bb, 1991 I, F 1, 2, [WS, Arg, A], 1992 I, F, E, S, A, 1993 Z 1, 2, Nm, J, C, 1995 F (R), E, S, I, [J, I], 1998 SA 1
Griffiths, V M (Newport) 1924 S, I, F
Gronow, B (Bridgend) 1910 F, E, S, I
Gwilliam, J A (Cambridge U, Newport) 1947 A, 1948 I, 1949 E, S, I, F, 1950 E, S, I, F, 1951 E, S, I, SA, 1952 E, S, I, F, 1953 E, I, F, NZ, 1954 E
Gwynn, D (Swansea) 1883 E, 1887 S, 1890 E, I, 1891 E, S
Gwynn, W H (Swansea) 1884 E, S, I, 1885 E, S

Hadley, A M (Cardiff) 1983 R, 1984 S, I, F, E, 1985 F, E, Fj, 1986 E, S, I, F, Fj, Tg, 1987 S (R), I, [I, Tg, C, E, NZ, A], US, 1988 E, S, I, F
Halfpenny, S L (Cardiff Blues) 2008 SA3, C, NZ, 2009 S, E, F, NZ, Sm, Arg, A, 2010 E(R), S, F, I, SA1, NZ1, 2, 2011 I, F, Arg, [Sm(R), Nm, Fj, I, F, A]
Hall, I (Aberavon) 1967 NZ, 1970 SA, S, E, 1971 S, 1974 S, I, F
Hall, M R (Cambridge U, Bridgend, Cardiff) 1988 NZ 1(R), 2, WS, R, 1989 S, I, F, E, NZ, 1990 F, E, S, 1991 A, F 2, [WS, Arg, A], 1992 I, F, E, S, A, 1993 E, S, I, 1994 S, I, F, E, Pt, Sp, C, Tg, R, It, SA, 1995 F, S, I, [J, NZ, I]
Hall, W H (Bridgend) 1988 WS
Hancock, F E (Cardiff) 1884 I, 1885 E, S, 1886 S
Hannan, J (Newport) 1888 M, 1889 S, I, 1890 S, E, I, 1891 E, 1892 E, S, I, 1893 E, S, I, 1894 E, S, I, 1895 E, S, I
Harding, A F (London Welsh) 1902 E, S, I, 1903 E, S, I, 1904 E, S, I, 1905 E, S, I, NZ, 1906 E, S, I, SA, 1907 I, 1908 E, S
Harding, C T (Newport) 1888 M, 1889 S, I
Harding, G F (Newport) 1881 E, 1882 I, 1883 E, S
Harding, R (Swansea, Cambridge U) 1923 E, S, F, I, 1924 I, F, NZ, 1925 F, I, 1926 E, I, F, 1927 E, S, F, I, 1928 E
Harries, W T M (Newport Gwent Dragons) 2010 NZ2(R), A
Harris, C A (Aberavon) 1927 A
Harris, D J E (Pontypridd, Cardiff) 1959 I, F, 1960 S, I, F, SA, 1961 E, S
Harris, I R (Cardiff) 2001 Arg, Tg, A, 2002 I, It (R), E, S (R), Fj(R), C(R), NZ(R), 2003 It, E 1(R), S 1(R), I 1(R), F, I 2, S 2, [C, Tg, It, E], 2004 S, I, F, It
Hathway, G F (Newport) 1924 I, F
Havard, Rev W T (Llanelli) 1919 NZA
Hawkins, F J (Pontypridd) 1912 I, F
Hayward, B I (Ebbw Vale) 1998 Z (R), SA 1
Hayward, D J (Newbridge) 1949 E, F, 1950 E, S, I, F, 1951 E, S, I, F, SA, 1952 E, S, I, F
Hayward, D J (Cardiff) 1963 E, NZ, 1964 S, I, F, SA
Hayward, G (Swansea) 1908 S, F, I, A, 1909 E
Hellings, D (Llwynypia) 1897 E, 1898 I, E, 1899 S, I, 1900 E, I, 1901 E, S
Henson, G L (Swansea, Ospreys, Toulon) 2001 J 1(R), R, 2003 NZ(R), R, 2004 Arg 1, 2, SA1, 2, R, NZ, J, 2005 E, It, F, S, I, 2006 I(R), F(R), A, NZ(R), 2007 A1(t&R), 2(R), SA, 2008 E, S, It, I, F, 2009 F(R), It, I, 2011 Bb, E3
Herrerá, R C (Cross Keys) 1925 S, F, I, 1926 E, S, I, F, 1927 E
Hiams, H (Swansea) 1912 I, F
Hibbard, R M (Ospreys) 2006 Arg 1(R), 2(R), 2007 A1(R), 2(R), 2008 SA1(R), 2, C, 2009 C, US(R), 2011 E1(R), S(R), It(R), I(R), F(R), Arg
Hickman, A (Neath) 1930 E, 1933 S
Hiddlestone, D D (Neath) 1922 E, S, I, F, 1924 NZ
Hill, A F (Cardiff) 1885 S, 1886 E, S, 1888 S, I, M, 1889 S, 1890 S, I, 1893 E, S, I, 1894 E, S, I
Hill, S D (Cardiff) 1993 Z 1, 2, Nm, 1994 I (R), F, SA, 1995 F, SA, 1996 A 2, F 2(R), It, 1997 E
Hinam, S (Cardiff) 1925 I, 1926 E, S, I, F
Hinton, J T (Cardiff) 1884 I
Hirst, G L (Newport) 1912 S, 1913 S, 1914 E, S, F, I
Hodder, W (Pontypool) 1921 E, S, F
Hodges, J J (Newport) 1899 E, S, I, 1900 E, S, I, 1901 E, S, 1902 E, S, I, 1903 E, S, I, 1904 E, S, 1905 E, S, I, NZ, 1906 E, S, I
Hodgson, G T R (Neath) 1962 I, 1963 E, S, I, F, NZ, 1964 E, S, I, F, SA, 1966 S, I, F, 1967 I
Hollingdale, B G (Swansea) 1912 SA, 1913 E
Hollingdale, T H (Neath) 1927 A, 1928 E, S, I, F, 1930 E
Holmes, T D (Cardiff) 1978 A 2, NZ, 1979 S, I, F, E, 1980 F, E, S, I, NZ, 1981 A, 1982 I, F, E, 1983 E, S, I, F, 1984 E, 1985 S, I, F, E, Fj
Hook, J W (Ospreys, Perpignan) 2006 Arg 1(R), 2, A(R), PI, C, NZ(R), 2007 I, S, F1, It, E1, A1, 2, Arg, F2, [C, A(R), J, Fj], SA, 2008 E, S, It(R), I(R), F, SA1(R), 2, 3(R), C, NZ(R) , 2009 S(R), F(R), It, NZ, Sm, Arg, A, 2010 E, S, F, I, It, SA1, A, SA2, Fj, NZ3, 2011 E1, S, It, I, F, E3, Arg, [SA, Sm, I(R), F, A]
Hopkin, W H (Newport) 1937 S
Hopkins, K (Cardiff, Swansea) 1985 E, 1987 F, E, S, [Tg, C (R)], US
Hopkins, P L (Swansea) 1908 A, 1909 E, I, 1910 E
Hopkins, R (Maesteg) 1970 E (R)
Hopkins, T (Swansea) 1926 E, S, I, F
Hopkins, W J (Aberavon) 1925 E, S
Horsman, C L (Worcester) 2005 NZ(R), Fj, SA, A, 2006 PI, 2007 I, F1, It, E1, A2(R), E2, F2, [J, Fj]
Howarth, S P (Sale, Newport) 1998 SA 2, Arg, 1999 S, I, F 1, It, E, Arg 1, 2, SA, C, F 2, [Arg 3, J, Sm, A], 2000 F, It, E
Howells, B (Llanelli) 1934 E
Howells, W G (Llanelli) 1957 E, S, I, F
Howells, W H (Swansea) 1888 S, I
Howley, R (Bridgend, Cardiff) 1996 E, S, I, F 1, A 1, 2, Bb, F 2, It, A 3, SA, 1997 US, S, I, F, E, Tg (R), NZ, 1998 It, E, S, I, F, Z, SA 2, Arg, 1999 S, I, F 1, It, E, Arg 1, 2, SA, C, F 2, [Arg 3, J, Sm, A], 2000 F, It, E, Sm, US, SA, 2001 E, S, F, R, I, Arg, Tg, A, 2002 I, F, It, E, S
Hughes, D (Newbridge) 1967 NZ, 1969 NZ 2, 1970 SA, S, E, I

Hughes, G (Penarth) 1934 E, S, I
Hughes, H (Cardiff) 1887 S, 1889 S
Hughes, K (Cambridge U, London Welsh) 1970 I, 1973 A, 1974 S
Hullin, W G (Cardiff) 1967 S
Humphreys, J M (Cardiff, Bath) 1995 [NZ, I], SA, Fj, 1996 It, E, S, I, F 1, A 1, 2, Bb, It, A 3, SA, 1997 S, I, F, E, Tg (R), NZ (R), 1998 It (R), E (R), S (R), I (R), F (R), SA 2, Arg, 1999 S, Arg 2(R), SA (R), C, [J (R)], 2003 E 1, I 1
Hurrell, R J (Newport) 1959 F
Hutchinson, F O (Neath) 1894 I, 1896 S, I
Huxtable, R (Swansea) 1920 F, I
Huzzey, H V P (Cardiff) 1898 I, E, 1899 E, S, I
Hybart, A J (Cardiff) 1887 E

Ingledew, H M (Cardiff) 1890 I, 1891 E, S
Isaacs, I (Cardiff) 1933 E, S

Jackson, T H (Swansea) 1895 E
James, C R (Llanelli) 1958 A, F
James, D (Swansea) 1891 I, 1892 S, I, 1899 E
James, D M (Cardiff) 1947 A, 1948 E, S, F, I
James, D R (Treorchy) 1931 F, I
James, D R (Bridgend, Pontypridd, Llanelli Scarlets) 1996 A 2(R), It, A 3, SA, 1997 I, Tg (R), 1998 F (R), Z, SA 1, 2, Arg, 1999 S, I, F 1, It, E, Arg 1, 2, SA, F 2, [Arg 3, Sm, A], 2000 F, It (R), I (R), Sm (R), US, SA, 2001 E, S, F, It, R, I, 2002 I, F, It, E, S (R), NZ(R), 2005 SA, A, 2006 I, F, 2007 E2, Arg, [J]
James, E (Swansea) 1890 S, 1891 I, 1892 S, I, 1899 E
James, J B (Bridgend) 1968 E
James, P (Ospreys) 2003 R, 2009 NZ, Sm, Arg, A, 2010 E, S, F, I, It(t&R), SA1, NZ1, 2, A(R), SA2, Fj, NZ3(R), 2011 E1, S, It, I, F, Bb, E2, 3, Arg, [SA, Sm, Fj(R), F(R), A]
James, T (Cardiff Blues, Wasps) 2007 E2(R), SA(R), 2008 SA2(R), 2009 C, US, Sm, Arg(R), A(R), 2010 E, NZ3
James, T O (Aberavon) 1935 I, 1937 S
James, W (Gloucester) 2007 E2, Arg(R), F2(R), [J]
James, W J (Aberavon) 1983 E, S, I, F, R, 1984 S, 1985 S, I, F, E, Fj, 1986 E, S, I, F, Fj, Tg, WS, 1987 E, S, I
James, W P (Aberavon) 1925 E, S
Jarman, H (Newport) 1910 E, S, I, 1911 E
Jarrett, K S (Newport) 1967 E, 1968 E, S, 1969 S, I, F, E, NZ 1, 2, A
Jarvis, L (Cardiff) 1997 R (R)
Jeffery, J J (Cardiff Coll of Ed, Newport) 1967 NZ
Jenkin, A M (Swansea) 1895 I, 1896 E
Jenkins, A E (Llanelli) 1920 E, S, F, I, 1921 S, F, 1922 F, 1923 E, S, F, I, 1924 NZ, 1928 S, I
Jenkins, D M (Treorchy) 1926 E, S, I, F
Jenkins, D R (Swansea) 1927 A, 1929 E
Jenkins, E (Newport) 1910 S, I
Jenkins, E M (Aberavon) 1927 S, F, I, A, 1928 E, S, I, F, 1929 F, 1930 E, S, I, F, 1931 E, S, F, I, SA, 1932 E, S, I
Jenkins, G D (Pontypridd, Celtic Warriors, Cardiff Blues) 2002 R, NZ(R), 2003 E 1(R), S 1(R), I 1, F, A, NZ, I 2(R), E 2, [C, Tg, It(R), NZ(R), E(R)], 2004 S(R), I(R), F, E, It, Arg 1(R), 2(R), SA1, 2(R), R, NZ, J, 2005 E, It, F, S, I, 2006 E(R), S(R), I(R), It(R), F(R), A, C, NZ(R), 2007 I, S(R), F1, It, E1, 2(R), Arg(R), F2(R), [C, A, J(R), Fj], SA, 2008 E(R), S(R), It, I, F, SA1, 2, 3, NZ, A, 2009 S, E, F, It(R), I, NZ, Sm, Arg, A, 2010 S(R), It, A, NZ3, 2011 [Sm(R), Nm, Fj, I, F, A]
Jenkins, G R (Pontypool, Swansea) 1991 F 2, [WS (R), Arg, A], 1992 I, F, E, S, A, 1993 C, 1994 S, I, F, E, Pt, Sp, C, Tg, WS, R, It, SA, 1995 F, E, S, I, [J], SA (R), Fj (t), 1996 E (R), 1997 US, US 1, C, 1998 S, I, F, Z, SA 1(R), 1999 I (R), F 1, It, E, Arg 1, 2, SA, F 2, [Arg 3, J, Sm, A], 2000 F, It, E, S, I, Sm, US, SA
Jenkins, J C (London Welsh) 1906 SA
Jenkins, J L (Aberavon) 1923 S, F
Jenkins, L H (Mon TC, Newport) 1954 I, 1956 E, S, I, F
Jenkins, N R (Pontypridd, Cardiff) 1991 E, S, I, F 1, 1992 I, F, E, S, 1993 E, S, I, F, Z 1, 2, Nm, J, C, 1994 S, I, F, E, Pt, Sp, C, Tg, WS, R, It, SA, 1995 F, E, S, I, [J, NZ, I], SA, Fj, 1996 F 1, A 1, 2, Bb, F 2, It, A 3(R), SA, 1997 S, I, F, E, Tg, NZ, 1998 It, E, S, I, F, SA 2, Arg, 1999 S, I, F 1, It, E, Arg 1, 2, SA, C, F 2, [Arg 3, J, Sm, A], 2000 F, It, E, I (R), Sm (R), US (R), SA, 2001 E, S, F, It, 2002 SA 1(R), 2(R), R
Jenkins, V G J (Oxford U, Bridgend, London Welsh) 1933 E, I, 1934 S, I, 1935 E, S, NZ, 1936 E, S, I, 1937 E, 1938 E, S, 1939 E
Jenkins, W J (Cardiff) 1912 I, F, 1913 S, I
John, B (Llanelli, Cardiff) 1966 A, 1967 S, NZ, 1968 E, S, I, F, 1969 S, I, F, E, NZ 1, 2, A, 1970 SA, S, E, I, 1971 E, S, I, F, 1972 E, S, F
John, D A (Llanelli) 1925 I, 1928 E, S, I
John, D E (Llanelli) 1923 F, I, 1928 E, S, I
John, E R (Neath) 1950 E, S, I, F, 1951 E, S, I, F, SA, 1952 E, S, I, F, 1953 E, S, I, F, NZ, 1954 E
John G (St Luke's Coll, Exeter) 1954 E, F
John, J H (Swansea) 1926 E, S, I, F, 1927 E, S, F, I
John, P (Pontypridd) 1994 Tg, 1996 Bb (t), 1997 US (R), US 1, 2, C, R, Tg, 1998 Z (R), SA 1
John, S C (Llanelli, Cardiff) 1995 S, I, 1997 E (R), Tg, NZ (R), 2000 F (R), It (R), E (R), Sm (R), SA (R), 2001 E (R), S (R), Tg (R), A, 2002 I, F, It (R), S (R)
Johnson, T A W (Cardiff) 1921 E, F, I, 1923 E, S, F, 1924 E, S, NZ, 1925 E, S, F
Johnson, W D (Swansea) 1953 E
Jones , A E (SEE Emyr)
Jones, A H (Cardiff) 1933 E, S
Jones, A M (Llanelli Scarlets) 2006 E(t&R), S(R)
Jones, A R (Ospreys) 2003 E 2(R), S 2, [C(R), Tg(R), It, NZ, E], 2004 S, I, Arg 1, 2, SA1, 2, R, NZ, J(t&R), 2005 E, It, F, S, I, US, NZ, Fj(R), SA(t&R), A(R), 2006 E, S, I, It, F, Arg 1, 2, A, PI(R), C, NZ, 2007 S, It(R), E1(R), A1, Arg, [C, A], 2008 E, S, I, F, SA1, 3, NZ, A, 2009 S, E, F, I, 2010 E, S, F, I, It, SA1, NZ1, 2, A, SA2, Fj, NZ3, 2011 F, Arg, [SA, Sm, Fj, I, F]
Jones, A W (Mountain Ash) 1905 I
Jones, A-W (Ospreys) 2006 Arg 1, 2, PI, C(R), NZ(R), 2007 I, S, F1, It, E1, 2, Arg, F2, [C, A, J, Fj], SA, 2008 E, I, F, SA1, 2, 3, NZ, A, 2009 S, E, F, It, I, NZ, Sm, Arg, A, 2010 E, S, SA1(R), NZ1, 2, A, SA2, NZ3, 2011 E1, S, It, I, F, Bb(R), E2, 3, Arg, [SA, Sm, Nm, Fj(R), I, F, A(R)]
Jones, B J (Newport) 1960 I, F
Jones, B L (Devonport Services, Llanelli) 1950 E, S, I, F, 1951 E, S, SA, 1952 E, I, F
Jones, C (Harlequins) 2007 A1(R), 2
Jones, C W (Cambridge U, Cardiff) 1934 E, S, I, 1935 E, S, I, NZ, 1936 E, S, I, 1938 E, S, I
Jones, C W (Bridgend) 1920 E, S, F
Jones, D (Aberavon) 1897 E
Jones, D (Treherbert) 1902 E, S, I, 1903 E, S, I, 1905 E, S, I, NZ, 1906 E, S, SA
Jones, D (Neath) 1927 A
Jones, D (Cardiff) 1994 SA, 1995 F, E, S, [J, NZ, I], SA, Fj, 1996 It, E, S, I, F 1, A 1, 2, Bb, It, A 3
Jones, D A R (Llanelli Scarlets) 2002 Fj, C, NZ, 2003 It(R), E 1, S 1, I 1, F, NZ, E 2, [C, Tg, It, NZ(R), E], 2004 S, I, F, E, It, Arg 2, SA1, 2, R, NZ, J, 2005 E, Fj, 2006 F(R), 2008 SA1, 2(R), C, NZ(R), A(R), 2009 S, E(R), F(R), It, I, C, US, NZ(R)
Jones, D C J (Swansea) 1947 E, F, I, 1949 E, S, I, F
Jones, D J (Neath, Ospreys) 2001 A (R), 2002 I (R), F (R), 2003 I 2, S 2, [C, It], 2004 S, E, It, Arg1, 2, SA1(R), 2, R(R), NZ(t&R), J, 2005 US, C, NZ, SA, A, 2006 E, S, I, It, F, Arg 1, 2, A(R), PI, C(R), NZ, 2007 I(R), S, F1(R), It(R), E1(R), Arg, F2, [C(R), A(R), J, Fj(R)], SA(R), 2008 E, S, It(R), I(R), F(t&R), SA1(R), 2(R), 2009 C, US, NZ(R), Arg(R), A(R)
Jones, D K (Llanelli, Cardiff) 1962 E, S, F, I, 1963 E, F, NZ, 1964 E, S, SA, 1966 E, S, I, F
Jones, D L (Newport) 1926 E, S, I, F, 1927 E
Jones, D L (Ebbw Vale, Celtic Warriors, Cardiff Blues) 2000 Sm, 2003 R (R), 2004 SA1, 2008 S(R), It(R), 2009 C, US, 2010 F, SA1, NZ2(R), A(R), SA2(R), Fj
Jones, D P (Pontypool) 1907 I
Jones, E H (Swansea, Neath) 1930 I, F
Jones, E L (Llanelli) 1930 F, 1933 E, S, I, 1935 E
Jones, E L (Llanelli) 1939 S
Jones, G (Ebbw Vale) 1963 S, I, F
Jones, G (Llanelli) 1988 NZ 2, 1989 F, E, NZ, 1990 F
Jones, G G (Cardiff) 1930 S, 1933 I
Jones, G H (Bridgend) 1995 SA
Jones, H (Penygraig) 1902 S, I
Jones, H (Neath) 1904 I
Jones, H J (Neath) 1929 E, S
Jones, I C (London Welsh) 1968 I
Jones, I E (Llanelli) 1924 E, S, 1927 S, F, I, A, 1928 E, S, I, F, 1929 E, S, F, I, 1930 E, S
Jones, J (Aberavon) 1901 E
Jones, J (Bedwellty) (Abertillery) 1914 E, S, F, I
Jones, J (Swansea) 1924 F
Jones, J (Aberavon) 1919 NZA, 1920 E, S, 1921 S, F, I
Jones, J A (Cardiff) 1883 S
Jones, J P (Tuan) (Pontypool) 1913 S
Jones, J P (Jack) (Pontypool) 1908 A, 1909 E, S, F, I, 1910 F, E, 1912 E, F, 1913 F, I, 1920 F, I, 1921 E
Jones, K D (Cardiff) 1960 SA, 1961 E, S, I, 1962 E, F, 1963 E, S, I, NZ
Jones, K J (Newport) 1947 E, S, F, I, A, 1948 E, S, F, I, 1949 E, S, I, F, 1950 E, S, I, F, 1951 E, S, I, F, SA, 1952 E, S, I, F,

WALES

1953 E, S, I, F, NZ, 1954 E, I, F, S, 1955 E, S, I, F, 1956 E, S, I, F, 1957 S

Jones, K P (Ebbw Vale) 1996 Bb, F 2, It, A 3, 1997 I (R), E, 1998 S, I, F (R), SA 1

Jones, K W J (Oxford U, London Welsh) 1934 E

Jones, Matthew (Ospreys) 2005 C(R)

Jones, M A (Neath, Ebbw Vale) 1987 S, 1988 NZ 2(R), 1989 S, I, F, E, NZ, 1990 F, E, S, I, Nm 1, 2, Bb, 1998 Z

Jones, M A (Llanelli Scarlets) 2001 E (R), S, J 1, 2002 R, Fj, C, NZ, 2003 It, I 1, A, NZ, E 2, [C, Tg, It, E], 2006 E, S, I, It, Arg 1, 2, PI, C, NZ, 2007 S, F1, It, E1, Arg, F2, [C, A, Fj], SA, 2008 E, It, I, F, SA1, 2, C, A, 2009 E, It, I, US

Jones, P E R (Newport) 1921 S

Jones, P L (Newport) 1912 SA, 1913 E, S, F, 1914 E, S, F, I

Jones, R (Llwynypia) 1901 I

Jones, R (Northampton) 1926 E, S, F

Jones, R (London Welsh) 1929 E

Jones, R B (Cambridge U) 1933 E, S

Jones, R E (Coventry) 1967 F, E, 1968 S, I, F

Jones, R G (Llanelli, Cardiff) 1996 It, E, S, I, F 1, A 1, 1997 US (R), S (R), US 1, 2, R, Tg, NZ

Jones, R H (Swansea) 1901 I, 1902 E, 1904 E, S, I, 1905 E, 1908 F, I, A, 1909 E, S, F, I, 1910 F, E

Jones, R L (Llanelli) 1993 Z 1, 2, Nm, J, C

Jones, R N (Swansea) 1986 E, S, I, F, Fj, Tg, WS, 1987 F, E, S, I, [I, Tg, E, NZ, A], US, 1988 E, S, I, F, NZ 1, WS, R, 1989 I, F, E, NZ, 1990 F, E, S, I, 1991 E, S, F 2, [WS, Arg, A], 1992 I, F, E, S, A, 1993 E, S, I, 1994 I (R), Pt, 1995 F, E, S, I, [NZ, I]

Jones, R P (Ospreys) 2004 SA2, NZ(R), J, 2005 E(R), F, S, I, US, 2006 A, C, NZ, 2007 I, S, F1, It, E1, 2008 E, S, It, I, F, SA1, 2, 3, C, NZ, A, 2009 E, F, It(R), I, C, US, NZ, Sm, Arg, 2010 E, S, F, It, SA1, NZ1, 2, SA2(R), Fj, NZ3, 2011 E1(R), S, It, I, F, Bb, E2(R), [Nm, Fj, F(R), A]

Jones, S (Neath, Newport Gwent Dragons) 2001 J 1(R), 2004 SA2, R(R), NZ(R), J(R)

Jones, S M (Llanelli Scarlets, Clermont Auvergne) 1998 SA 1(R), 1999 C (R), [J (R)], 2000 It (R), S, I, 2001 E, F (R), J 1, 2, R, I, Arg, Tg, A, 2002 I, F, It, S, SA 1, 2, R(R), Fj, C, NZ, 2003 S 1, I 1, F, A, NZ, E 2, [Tg, It(R), NZ, E], 2004 S, I, F, E, It, SA2, R, NZ, 2005 E, It, F, S, I, NZ, SA, A, 2006 E, S, I, It, F, A, NZ, 2007 I, S, F1, It, [C(R), A, J, Fj], 2008 S(R), It, I, F(R), SA1, 2, 3, NZ, A, 2009 S, E, F, It(R), I, NZ, Arg, A, 2010 E, S, F, I, It, SA1, NZ1, 2(R), A, SA2, Fj(R), NZ3, 2011 E1, S(R), It, F(R), Bb, [Nm, Fj(R), F(R), A(t&R)]

Jones, S T (Pontypool) 1983 S, I, F, R, 1984 S, 1988 E, S, F, NZ 1, 2

Jones, T (Newport) 1922 E, S, I, F, 1924 E, S

Jones, T B (Newport) 1882 I, 1883 E, S, 1884 S, 1885 E, S

Jones, T I (Llanelli) 1927 A, 1928 E, S, I, F

Jones, W (Cardiff) 1898 I, E

Jones, W D (Llanelli) 1948 E

Jones, W H (Llanelli) 1934 S, I

Jones, W I (Llanelli, Cambridge U) 1925 E, S, F, I

Jones, W J (Llanelli) 1924 I

Jones, W K (Cardiff) 1967 NZ, 1968 E, S, I, F

Jones, W R (Swansea) 1927 A, 1928 F

Jones-Davies, T E (London Welsh) 1930 E, I, 1931 E, S

Jones-Hughes, J (Newport) 1999 [Arg 3(R), J], 2000 F

Jordan, H M (Newport) 1885 E, S, 1889 S

Joseph, W (Swansea) 1902 E, S, I, 1903 E, S, I, 1904 E, S, 1905 E, S, I, NZ, 1906 E, S, I, SA

Jowett, W F (Swansea) 1903 E

Judd, S (Cardiff) 1953 E, S, I, F, NZ, 1954 E, F, S, 1955 E, S

Judson, T H (Llanelli) 1883 E, S

Kedzlie, Q D (Cardiff) 1888 S, I

Keen, L (Aberavon) 1980 F, E, S, I

Knight, P (Pontypridd) 1990 Nm 1, 2, Bb (R), 1991 E, S

Knill, F M D (Cardiff) 1976 F (R)

Knoyle, T D (Scarlets) 2010 NZ1(R), 2011 S(R), Bb(R), E2(R), Arg, [Nm]

Lamerton, A E H (Llanelli) 1993 F, Z 1, 2, Nm, J

Lane, S M (Cardiff) 1978 A 1(R), 2, 1979 I (R), 1980 S, I

Lang, J (Llanelli) 1931 F, I, 1934 S, I, 1935 E, S, I, NZ, 1936 E, S, I, 1937 E

Law, V J (Newport) 1939 I

Lawrence, S D (Bridgend) 1925 S, I, 1926 S, I, F, 1927 E

Legge, W S G (Newport) 1937 I, 1938 I

Leleu, J (London Welsh, Swansea) 1959 E, S, 1960 F, SA

Lemon, A W (Neath) 1929 I, 1930 S, I, F, 1931 E, S, F, I, SA, 1932 E, S, I, 1933 I

Lewis, A J L (Ebbw Vale) 1970 F, 1971 E, I, F, 1972 E, S, F, 1973 E, S, I, F

Lewis, A L P (Cardiff) 1996 It, E, S, I, A 2(t), 1998 It, E, S, I, F, SA 2, Arg, 1999 F 1(R), E (R), Arg 1(R), 2(R), SA (R), C (R), [J (R), Sm (R), A (R)], 2000 Sm (R), US (R), SA (R), 2001 F (R), J 1, 2, 2002 R(R)

Lewis, B R (Swansea, Cambridge U) 1912 I, 1913 I

Lewis, C P (Llandovery) 1882 I, 1883 E, S, 1884 E, S

Lewis, D H (Cardiff) 1886 E, S

Lewis, E J (Llandovery) 1881 E

Lewis, E W (Llanelli, Cardiff) 1991 I, F 1, A, F 2, [WS, Arg, A], 1992 I, F, S, A, 1993 E, S, I, F, Z 1, 2, Nm, J, C, 1994 S, I, F, E, Pt, Sp, Fj, WS, R, It, SA, 1995 E, S, I, [J, I], 1996 It, E, S, I, F 1

Lewis, G (Pontypridd, Swansea) 1998 SA 1(R), 1999 It (R), Arg 2, C, [J], 2000 F (R), It, S, I, Sm, US (t+R), 2001 F (R), J 1, 2, R, I

Lewis, G W (Richmond) 1960 E, S

Lewis, H (Swansea) 1913 S, F, I, 1914 E

Lewis, J G (Llanelli) 1887 I

Lewis, J M C (Cardiff, Cambridge U) 1912 E, 1913 S, F, I, 1914 E, S, F, I, 1921 I, 1923 E, S

Lewis, J R (S Glam Inst, Cardiff) 1981 E, S, I, F, 1982 F, E, S

Lewis, M (Treorchy) 1913 F

Lewis, P I (Llanelli) 1984 A, 1985 S, I, F, E, 1986 E, S, I

Lewis, R A (Abertillery) 1966 E, S, I, F, A, 1967 I

Lewis, T W (Cardiff) 1926 E, 1927 E, S

Lewis, W (Llanelli) 1925 F

Lewis, W H (London Welsh, Cambridge U) 1926 I, 1927 E, F, I, A, 1928 F

Lewis-Roberts, E T (Sale) 2008 C(R)

Llewellyn, D S (Ebbw Vale, Newport) 1998 SA 1(R), 1999 F 1(R), It (R), [J (R)]

Llewellyn, G D (Neath) 1990 Nm 1, 2, Bb, 1991 E, S, I, F 1, A, F 2

Llewellyn, G O (Neath, Harlequins, Ospreys, Narbonne) 1989 NZ, 1990 E, S, I, 1991 E, S, A (R), 1992 I, F, E, S, A, 1993 E, S, I, F, Z 1, 2, Nm, J, C, 1994 S, I, F, E, Pt, Sp, C, Tg, WS, R, It, SA, 1995 F, E, S, I, [J, NZ, I], 1996 It, E, S, I, F 1, A 1, 2, Bb, F 2, It, A 3, SA, 1997 US, S, I, F, E, US 1, 2, NZ, 1998 It, E, 1999 C (R), [Sm], 2002 E (R), SA 1, 2, R(R), Fj, C, NZ, 2003 E 1(R), S 1(R), I 1, F, A, NZ, I 2, S 2(R), [C, Tg, It, E(R)], 2004 S, F(R), E(R), It, Arg 1, 2, SA1, R, NZ

Llewellyn, P D (Swansea) 1973 I, F, A, 1974 S, E

Llewellyn, W (Llwynypia) 1899 E, S, I, 1900 E, S, I, 1901 E, S, I, 1902 E, S, I, 1903 I, 1904 E, S, I, 1905 E, S, I, NZ

Llewelyn, D B (Newport, Llanelli) 1970 SA, S, E, I, F, 1971 E, S, I, F, 1972 E, S, F, NZ

Lloyd, A (Bath) 2001 J 1

Lloyd, D J (Bridgend) 1966 E, S, I, F, A, 1967 S, I, F, E, 1968 S, I, F, 1969 S, I, F, E, NZ 1, A, 1970 F, 1972 E, S, F, 1973 E, S

Lloyd, D P M (Llanelli) 1890 S, E, 1891 E, I

Lloyd, E (Llanelli) 1895 S

Lloyd, G L (Newport) 1896 I, 1899 S, I, 1900 E, S, 1901 E, S, 1902 S, I, 1903 E, S, I

Lloyd, R (Pontypool) 1913 S, F, I, 1914 E, S, F, I

Lloyd, T (Maesteg) 1953 I, F

Lloyd, T J (Neath) 1909 F, 1913 F, I, 1914 E, S, F, I

Loader, C D (Swansea) 1995 SA, Fj, 1996 F 1, A 1, 2, Bb, F 2, It, A 3, SA, 1997 US, S, I, F, E, US 1, R, Tg, NZ

Lockwood, T W (Newport) 1887 E, S, I

Long, E C (Swansea) 1936 E, S, I, 1937 E, S, 1939 S, I

Luscombe, H N (Newport Gwent Dragons, Harlequins) 2003 S 2(R), 2004 Arg 1, 2, SA1, 2, R, J, 2005 E, It, S(t&R), 2006 E, S, I, It, F, 2007 I

Lydiate, D J (Newport Gwent Dragons) 2009 Arg(R), A, 2010 A, Fj, NZ3, 2011 E1, S, It, I, F, Bb, E2, 3, Arg, [SA, Sm, I, F, A]

Lyne, H S (Newport) 1883 S, 1884 E, S, I, 1885 E

McBryde, R C (Swansea, Llanelli, Neath, Llanelli Scarlets) 1994 Fj, SA (t), 1997 US 2, 2000 I (R), 2001 E, S, F, It, R, I, Arg, Tg, A, 2002 I, F, It, E, S (R), SA 1, 2, C, NZ, 2003 A, NZ, E 2, S 2, [C, It, NZ, E], 2004 I, E, It, 2005 It(R), F(R), S(R), I(R)

McCall, B E W (Welch Regt, Newport) 1936 E, S, I

McCarley, A (Neath) 1938 E, S, I

McCusker, R J (Scarlets) 2010 SA1(R), NZ1(R), 2(R)

McCutcheon, W M (Swansea) 1891 S, 1892 E, S, 1893 E, S, I, 1894 E

McIntosh, D L M (Pontypridd) 1996 SA, 1997 E (R)

Madden, M (Llanelli) 2002 SA 1(R), R, Fj(R), 2003 I 1(R), F(R)

Maddock, H T (London Welsh) 1906 E, S, I, 1907 E, S, 1910 F

Maddocks, K (Neath) 1957 E

Main, D R (London Welsh) 1959 E, S, I, F

Mainwaring, H J (Swansea) 1961 F

Mainwaring, W T (Aberavon) 1967 S, I, F, E, NZ, 1968 E

Major, W C (Maesteg) 1949 F, 1950 S

Male, B O (Cardiff) 1921 F, 1923 S, 1924 S, I, 1927 E, S, F, I, 1928 S, I, F
Manfield, L (Mountain Ash, Cardiff) 1939 S, I, 1947 A, 1948 E, S, F, I
Mann, B B (Cardiff) 1881 E
Mantle, J T (Loughborough Colls, Newport) 1964 E, SA
Margrave, F L (Llanelli) 1884 E, S
Marinos, A W N (Newport, Gwent Dragons) 2002 I (R), F, It, E, S, SA 1, 2, 2003 R
Marsden-Jones, D (Cardiff) 1921 E, 1924 NZ
Martin, A J (Aberavon) 1973 A, 1974 S, I, 1975 F, E, S, I, A, 1976 E, S, I, F, 1977 I, F, E, S, 1978 E, S, I, F, A 1, 2, NZ, 1979 S, I, F, E, 1980 F, E, S, I, NZ, 1981 I, F
Martin, W J (Newport) 1912 I, F, 1919 NZA
Mason, J E (Pontypridd) 1988 NZ 2(R)
Mathews, Rev A A (Lampeter) 1886 S
Mathias, R (Llanelli) 1970 F
Matthews, C M (Bridgend) 1939 I
Matthews, J (Cardiff), 1947 E, A, 1948 E, S, F, 1949 E, S, I, F, 1950 E, S, I, F, 1951 E, S, I, F
May, P S (Llanelli) 1988 E, S, I, F, NZ 1, 2, 1991 [WS]
Meek, N N (Pontypool) 1993 E, S, I
Meredith, A (Devonport Services) 1949 E, S, I
Meredith, B V (St Luke's Coll, London Welsh, Newport) 1954 I, F, S, 1955 E, S, I, F, 1956 E, S, I, F, 1957 E, S, I, F, 1958 A, E, S, I, 1959 E, S, I, F, 1960 E, S, F, SA, 1961 E, S, I, 1962 E, S, F, I
Meredith, C C (Neath) 1953 S, NZ, 1954 E, I, F, S, 1955 E, S, I, F, 1956 E, I, 1957 E, S
Meredith, J (Swansea) 1888 S, I, 1890 S, E
Merry, J A (Pill Harriers) 1912 I, F
Michael, G M (Swansea) 1923 E, S, F
Michaelson, R C B (Aberavon, Cambridge U) 1963 E
Millar, W H (Mountain Ash) 1896 I, 1900 E, S, I, 1901 E, S, I
Mills, F M (Swansea, Cardiff) 1892 E, S, I, 1893 E, S, I, 1894 E, S, I, 1895 E, S, I, 1896 E
Mitchell, C (Ospreys, Exeter) 2009 C(R), US(R), Sm(R), 2010 NZ2(R), 2011 E1, S, It, I, E2, 3, [Nm]
Moon, R H StJ B (Llanelli) 1993 F, Z 1, 2, Nm, J, C, 1994 S, I, F, E, Sp, C, Fj, WS, R, It, SA, 1995 E (R), 2000 S, I, Sm (R), US (R), 2001 E (R), S (R)
Moore, A P (Cardiff) 1995 [J], SA, Fj, 1996 It
Moore, A P (Swansea) 1995 SA (R), Fj, 1998 S, I, F, Z, SA 1, 1999 C, 2000 S, I, US (R), 2001 E (R), S, F, It, J 1, 2, R, I, Arg, Tg, A, 2002 F, It, E, S
Moore, S J (Swansea, Moseley) 1997 C, R, Tg
Moore, W J (Bridgend) 1933 I
Morgan, C H (Llanelli) 1957 I, F
Morgan, C I (Cardiff) 1951 I, F, SA, 1952 E, S, I, 1953 S, I, F, NZ, 1954 E, I, S, 1955 E, S, I, F, 1956 E, S, I, F, 1957 E, S, I, F, 1958 E, S, I, F
Morgan, C S (Cardiff Blues) 2002 I, F, It, E, S, SA 1, 2, R(R), 2003 F, 2005 US
Morgan, D (Swansea) 1885 S, 1886 E, S, 1887 E, S, I, 1889 I
Morgan, D (Llanelli) 1895 I, 1896 E
Morgan, D E (Llanelli) 1920 I, 1921 E, S, F
Morgan, D R R (Llanelli) 1962 E, S, F, I, 1963 E, S, I, F, NZ
Morgan, E (Swansea) 1914 E, S, F, I
Morgan, E (London Welsh) 1902 E, S, I, 1903 I, 1904 E, S, I, 1905 E, S, I, NZ, 1906 E, S, I, SA, 1908 F
Morgan, F L (Llanelli) 1938 E, S, I, 1939 E
Morgan, G R (Newport) 1984 S
Morgan, H J (Abertillery) 1958 E, S, I, F, 1959 I, F, 1960 E, 1961 E, S, I, F, 1962 E, S, F, I, 1963 S, I, F, 1965 E, S, I, F, 1966 E, S, I, F, A
Morgan, H P (Newport) 1956 E, S, I, F
Morgan, J L (Llanelli) 1912 SA, 1913 E
Morgan, K A (Pontypridd, Swansea, Newport Gwent Dragons) 1997 US 1, 2, C, R, NZ, 1998 S, I, F, 2001 J 1, 2, R, I, Arg, Tg, A, 2002 I, F, It, E, S, SA 1, 2, 2003 E 1, S 1, [C, It], 2004 J(R), 2005 E(R), It(R), F, S, I, US, C, NZ, Fj, 2006 A, Pl, NZ, 2007 I, S, It, E1, Arg, F2, [C, A(R), J]
Morgan, M E (Swansea) 1938 E, S, I, 1939 E
Morgan, N H (Newport) 1960 S, I, F
Morgan, P E J (Aberavon) 1961 E, S, F
Morgan, P J (Llanelli) 1980 S (R), I, NZ (R), 1981 I
Morgan, S (Cardiff Blues) 2007 A2(R)
Morgan, T (Llanelli) 1889 I
Morgan, W G (Cambridge U) 1927 F, I, 1929 E, S, F, I, 1930 I, F
Morgan, W I (Swansea) 1908 A, 1909 E, S, F, I, 1910 F, E, S, I, 1911 E, F, I, 1912 S
Morgan, W L (Cardiff) 1910 S
Moriarty, R D (Swansea) 1981 A, 1982 I, F, E, S, 1983 E, 1984 S, I, F, E, 1985 S, I, F, 1986 Fj, Tg, WS, 1987 [I, Tg, C (R), E, NZ, A]
Moriarty, W P (Swansea) 1986 I, F, Fj, Tg, WS, 1987 F, E, S, I, [I, Tg, C, E, NZ, A], US, 1988 E, S, I, F, NZ 1
Morley, J C (Newport) 1929 E, S, F, I, 1930 E, I, 1931 E, S, F, I, SA, 1932 E, S, I
Morris, D R (Neath, Swansea, Leicester) 1998 Z, SA 1(R), 2(R), 1999 S, I, It (R), 2000 US, SA, 2001 E, S, F, It, Arg, Tg, A, 2004 Arg 1(R), 2(R), SA1(R)
Morris, G L (Swansea) 1882 I, 1883 E, S, 1884 E, S
Morris, H T (Cardiff) 1951 F, 1955 I, F
Morris, J I T (Swansea) 1924 E, S
Morris, M S (S Wales Police, Neath) 1985 S, I, F, 1990 I, Nm 1, 2, Bb, 1991 I, F 1, [WS (R)], 1992 E
Morris, R R (Swansea, Bristol) 1933 S, 1937 S
Morris, S (Cross Keys) 1920 E, S, F, I, 1922 E, S, I, F, 1923 E, S, F, I, 1924 E, S, F, NZ, 1925 E, S, F
Morris, W (Llanelli) 1896 S, I, 1897 E
Morris, W D (Neath) 1967 F, E, 1968 E, S, I, F, 1969 S, I, F, E, NZ 1, 2, A, 1970 SA, S, E, I, F, 1971 E, S, I, F, 1972 E, S, F, NZ, 1973 E, S, I, A, 1974 S, I, F, E
Morris, W G H (Abertillery) 1919 NZA, 1920 F, 1921 I
Morris, W J (Newport) 1965 S, 1966 F
Morris, W J B (Pontypool) 1963 S, I
Moseley, K (Pontypool, Newport) 1988 NZ 2, R, 1989 S, I, 1990 F, 1991 F 2, [WS, Arg, A]
Murphy, C D (Cross Keys) 1935 E, S, I
Mustoe, L (Cardiff) 1995 Fj, 1996 A 1(R), 2, 1997 US 1, 2, C, R (R), 1998 E (R), I (R), F (R)

Nash, D (Ebbw Vale) 1960 SA, 1961 E, S, I, F, 1962 F
Newman, C H (Newport) 1881 E, 1882 I, 1883 E, S, 1884 E, S, 1885 E, S, 1886 E, 1887 E
Nicholas, D L (Llanelli) 1981 E, S, I, F
Nicholas, T J (Cardiff) 1919 NZA
Nicholl, C B (Cambridge U, Llanelli) 1891 I, 1892 E, S, I, 1893 E, S, I, 1894 E, S, 1895 E, S, I, 1896 E, S, I
Nicholl, D W (Llanelli) 1894 I
Nicholls, E G (Cardiff) 1896 S, I, 1897 E, 1898 I, E, 1899 E, S, I, 1900 S, I, 1901 E, S, I, 1902 E, S, I, 1903 I, 1904 E, 1905 I, NZ, 1906 E, S, I, SA
Nicholls, F E (Cardiff Harlequins) 1892 I
Nicholls, H C W (Cardiff) 1958 I
Nicholls, S H (Cardiff) 1888 M, 1889 S, I, 1891 S
Norris, C H (Cardiff) 1963 F, 1966 F
Norster, R L (Cardiff) 1982 S, 1983 E, S, I, F, 1984 S, I, F, E, A, 1985 S, I, F, E, Fj, 1986 Fj, Tg, WS, 1987 F, E, S, I, [I, C, E], US, 1988 E, S, I, F, NZ 1, WS, 1989 F, E
North, G P (Scarlets) 2010 SA2, Fj, NZ3, 2011 F, Bb, E2, 3, Arg, [SA, Sm, Nm(R), Fj, I, F, A]
Norton, W B (Cardiff) 1882 I, 1883 E, S, 1884 E, S, I

Oakley, R L (Gwent Dragons) 2003 I 2, S 2(R)
O'Connor, A (Aberavon) 1960 SA, 1961 E, S, 1962 F, I
O'Connor, R (Aberavon) 1957 E
O'Neil, W (Cardiff) 1904 S, I, 1905 E, S, I, 1907 E, I, 1908 E, S, F, I
O'Shea, J P (Cardiff) 1967 S, I, 1968 S, I, F
Oliver, G (Pontypool) 1920 E, S, F, I
Osborne, W T (Mountain Ash) 1902 E, S, I, 1903 E, S, I
Ould, W J (Cardiff) 1924 E, S
Owen, A D (Swansea) 1924 E
Owen, G D (Newport) 1955 I, F, 1956 E, S, I, F
Owen, M J (Pontypridd, Newport Gwent Dragons) 2002 SA 1, 2, R, C(R), NZ(R), 2003 It, I 2, S 2, 2004 S(R), I(R), F, E, It, Arg 1, 2, SA2, R, NZ, J, 2005 E, It, F, S, I, NZ, Fj, SA, A, 2006 E, S, I, It, F, Pl, 2007 A1(R), 2, E2, [C(R), A(R), J(R), Fj(R)]
Owen, R M (Swansea) 1901 I, 1902 E, S, I, 1903 E, S, I, 1904 E, S, I, 1905 E, S, I, NZ, 1906 E, S, I, SA, 1907 E, S, 1908 F, I, A, 1909 E, S, F, I, 1910 F, E, 1911 E, S, F, I, 1912 E, S
Owens, K J (Scarlets) 2011 [Nm(R)]

Packer, H (Newport) 1891 E, 1895 S, I, 1896 E, S, I, 1897 E
Palmer, F C (Swansea) 1922 E, S, I
Parfitt, F C (Newport) 1893 E, S, I, 1894 E, S, I, 1895 S, 1896 S, I
Parfitt, S A (Swansea) 1990 Nm 1(R), Bb
Parker, D S (Swansea) 1924 I, F, NZ, 1925 E, S, F, I, 1929 F, I, 1930 E
Parker, E T (Swansea) 1919 NZA, 1920 E, S, I, 1921 E, S, F, I, 1922 E, S, I, F, 1923 E, S, F
Parker, S T (Pontypridd, Celtic Warriors, Newport Gwent Dragons, Ospreys) 2002 R, Fj, C, NZ, 2003 E 2, [C, It, NZ], 2004 S, I, Arg 1, 2, SA1, 2, NZ, 2005 Fj, SA, A, 2006 Pl, C, NZ, 2007 A1, 2, F2(t&R), [C, A], SA, 2008 E, S(R), It(R), SA1
Parker, W J (Swansea) 1899 E, S

Parks, R D (Pontypridd, Celtic Warriors) 2002 SA 1(R), Fj(R), 2003 I 2, S 2
Parsons, G (Newport) 1947 E
Pascoe, D (Bridgend) 1923 F, I
Pask, A E I (Abertillery) 1961 F, 1962 E, S, F, I, 1963 E, S, I, F, NZ, 1964 E, S, I, F, SA, 1965 E, S, I, F, 1966 E, S, I, F, A, 1967 S, I
Payne, G W (Army, Pontypridd) 1960 E, S, I
Payne, H (Swansea) 1935 NZ
Peacock, H (Newport) 1929 S, F, I, 1930 S, I, F
Peake, E (Chepstow) 1881 E
Pearce, P G (Bridgend) 1981 I, F, 1982 I (R)
Pearson, T W (Cardiff, Newport) 1891 E, I, 1892 E, S, 1894 S, I, 1895 E, S, I, 1897 E, 1898 I, E, 1903 E
Peel, D J (Llanelli Scarlets, Sale) 2001 J 2(R), R (R), Tg (R), 2002 I (R), It (R), E (R), S (R), SA 1, 2, R, Fj, C, NZ, 2003 It, S 1(R), I 1(R), F, NZ(R), I 2, S 2, [C(R), Tg(R), It, NZ(R), E(R)], 2004 S(R), I(R), F(R), E(R), It(R), Arg 1, 2, SA1, 2, R, NZ, 2005 E, It, F, S, I, 2006 E, S, I, It, A, C, NZ, 2007 I, S, F1, It, E1, Arg, F2, [C, A, Fj], SA, 2008 S(R), It, SA3(R), C(R), NZ(R), 2009 S(R), E(R), F(R), C(R), US, Sm, Arg(R), A, 2010 I(R), It(R), 2011 E1(R), F(R)
Pegge, E V (Neath) 1891 E
Perego, M A (Llanelli) 1990 S, 1993 F, Z 1, Nm (R), 1994 S, I, F, E, Sp
Perkins, S J (Pontypool) 1983 S, I, F, R, 1984 S, I, F, E, A, 1985 S, I, F, E, Fj, 1986 E, S, I, F
Perrett, F L (Neath) 1912 SA, 1913 E, S, F, I
Perrins, V C (Newport) 1970 SA, S
Perry, W J (Neath) 1911 E
Phillips, A J (Cardiff) 1979 E, 1980 F, E, S, I, NZ, 1981 E, S, I, F, A, 1982 I, F, E, S, 1987 [C, E, A]
Phillips, B (Aberavon) 1925 E, S, F, I, 1926 E
Phillips, D H (Swansea) 1952 F
Phillips, H P (Newport) 1892 E, 1893 E, S, I, 1894 E, S
Phillips, H T (Newport) 1927 E, S, F, I, A, 1928 E, S, I, F
Phillips, K H (Neath) 1987 F, [I, Tg, NZ], US, 1988 E, NZ 1, 1989 NZ, 1990 F, E, S, I, Nm 1, 2, Bb, 1991 E, S, I, F 1, A
Phillips, L A (Newport) 1900 E, S, I, 1901 S
Phillips, R D (Neath) 1987 US, 1988 E, S, I, F, NZ 1, 2, WS, 1989 S, I
Phillips, W D (Cardiff) 1881 E, 1882 I, 1884 E, S, I
Phillips, W M (Llanelli Scarlets, Cardiff Blues, Ospreys, Bayonne) 2003 R, 2004 Arg 1(R), 2(R), J(R), 2005 US, C, NZ, Fj(R), SA(R), 2006 S(R), It(R), F, Arg 1, 2, PI, C(R), NZ(R), 2007 I(R), F1(R), E1(R), A1, 2, F2(R), [C(R), A(R), J, Fj(R)], SA(R), 2008 E, S, It(R), I, F, 2009 S, E, F, It, I, 2010 It, SA1, NZ1, 2, A, SA2, Fj(R), NZ3, 2011 E1, S, It, I, F, Bb, E2, 3, [SA, Sm, Fj, I, F, A]
Pickering, D F (Llanelli) 1983 E, S, I, F, R, 1984 S, I, F, E, A, 1985 S, I, F, E, Fj, 1986 E, S, I, F, Fj, 1987 F, E, S
Plummer, R C S (Newport) 1912 S, I, F, SA, 1913 E
Pook, T R (Newport) 1895 S
Popham, A J (Leeds, Llanelli Scarlets) 2003 A (R), I 2, R, S 2, [Tg, NZ], 2004 I(R), It(R), SA1, J(R), 2005 C, Fj(R), 2006 E(R), It(R), F, Arg 1, 2, PI, NZ(R), 2007 I, S, F1, It, E1, 2(R), Arg, F2, [C, A(t), J, Fj], SA(R), 2008 E(R)
Powell, A T (Cardiff Blues, Wasps, Sale) 2008 SA3, C(R), NZ, A, 2009 S, E, F, It, NZ, Sm, Arg, A, 2010 E, S, SA2, NZ3(R), 2011 E1, Arg, [Sm(R), Nm(R), Fj(R), A(R)]
Powell, G (Ebbw Vale) 1957 I, F
Powell, J (Cardiff) 1923 I
Powell, J A (Cardiff) 1906 I
Powell, R D (Cardiff) 2002 SA 1(R), 2(R), C(R)
Powell, R W (Newport) 1888 S, I
Powell, W C (London Welsh) 1926 S, I, F, 1927 E, F, I, 1928 S, I, F, 1929 E, S, F, I, 1930 S, I, F, 1931 E, S, F, I, SA, 1932 E, S, I, 1935 E, S, I
Powell, W J (Cardiff) 1920 E, S, F, I
Price, B (Newport) 1961 I, F, 1962 E, S, 1963 E, S, F, NZ, 1964 E, S, I, F, SA, 1965 E, S, I, F, 1966 E, S, I, F, A, 1967 S, I, F, E, 1969 S, I, F, NZ 1, 2, A
Price, G (Pontypool) 1975 F, E, S, I, A, 1976 E, S, I, F, 1977 I, F, E, S, 1978 E, S, I, F, A 1, 2, NZ, 1979 S, I, F, E, 1980 F, E, S, I, NZ, 1981 E, S, I, F, A, 1982 I, F, E, S, 1983 E, I, F
Price, M J (Pontypool, RAF) 1959 E, S, I, F, 1960 E, S, I, F, 1962 E
Price, R E (Weston-s-Mare) 1939 S, I
Price, T G (Llanelli) 1965 E, S, I, F, 1966 E, A, 1967 S, F
Priday, A J (Cardiff) 1958 I, 1961 I
Priestland, R (Scarlets) 2011 S(R), Bb(R), E2, 3, [SA, Sm, Nm(R), Fj, I]
Pritchard, C C (Newport, Pontypool) 1904 S, I, 1905 NZ, 1906 E, S
Pritchard, C C (Pontypool) 1928 E, S, I, F, 1929 E, S, F, I
Pritchard, C M (Newport) 1904 I, 1905 E, S, NZ, 1906 E, S, I, SA, 1907 E, S, I, 1908 E, 1910 F, E
Proctor, W T (Llanelli) 1992 A, 1993 E, S, Z 1, 2, Nm, C, 1994 I, C, Fj, WS, R, It, SA, 1995 S, I, [NZ], Fj, 1996 It, E, S, I, A 1, 2, Bb, F 2, It, A 3, 1997 E(R), US 1, 2, C, R, 1998 E (R), S, I, F, Z, 2001 A
Prosser, D R (Neath) 1934 S, I
Prosser, F J (Cardiff) 1921 I
Prosser, G (Pontypridd) 1995 [NZ]
Prosser, I G (Neath) 1934 E, S, I, 1935 NZ
Prosser, T R (Pontypool) 1956 S, F, 1957 E, S, I, F, 1958 A, E, S, I, F, 1959 E, S, I, F, 1960 E, S, I, F, SA, 1961 I, F
Prothero, G J (Bridgend) 1964 S, I, F, 1965 E, S, I, F, 1966 E, S, I, F
Pryce-Jenkins, T J (London Welsh) 1888 S, I
Prydie, T W J (Ospreys) 2010 It, SA1, NZ1, 2
Pugh, C H (Maesteg) 1924 E, S, I, F, NZ, 1925 E, S
Pugh, J D (Neath) 1987 US, 1988 S (R), 1990 S
Pugh, P (Neath) 1989 NZ
Pugh, R (Ospreys) 2005 US(R)
Pugsley, J (Cardiff) 1910 E, S, I, 1911 E, S, F, I
Pullman, J J (Neath) 1910 F
Purdon, F T (Newport) 1881 E, 1882 I, 1883 E, S

Quinnell, D L (Llanelli) 1972 F (R), NZ, 1973 E, S, A, 1974 S, F, 1975 E (R), 1977 I (R), F, E, S, 1978 E, S, I, F, A 1, NZ, 1979 S, I, F, E, 1980 NZ
Quinnell, J C (Llanelli, Richmond, Cardiff) 1995 Fj, 1996 A 3(R), 1997 US (R), S (R), I (R), E (R), 1998 SA 2, Arg, 1999 I, F 1, It, E, Arg 1, 2, SA, C, F 2, [Arg 3, J, A], 2000 It, E, 2001 S (R), F (R), It (R), J 1, 2, R (R), I (R), Arg, 2002 I, F
Quinnell, L S (Llanelli, Richmond) 1993 C, 1994 S, I, F, E, Pt, Sp, C, WS, 1997 US, S, I, F, E, 1998 It, E, S (R), Z, SA 2, Arg, 1999 S, I, F 1, It, E, Arg 1, 2, SA, C, F 2, [Arg 3, Sm, A], 2000 F, It, E, Sm, US, SA, 2001 E, S, F, It, Arg, Tg, A, 2002 I, F, It, E, R, C(R)

Radford, W J (Newport) 1923 I
Ralph, A R (Newport) 1931 F, I, SA, 1932 E, S, I
Ramsay, S (Treorchy) 1896 E, 1904 E
Randall, R J (Aberavon) 1924 I, F
Raybould, W H (London Welsh, Cambridge U, Newport) 1967 S, I, F, E, NZ, 1968 I, F, 1970 SA, E, I, F (R)
Rayer, M A (Cardiff) 1991 [WS (R), Arg, A (R)], 1992 E (R), A, 1993 E, S, I, Z 1, Nm, J (R), 1994 S (R), I (R), F, E, Pt, C, Fj, WS, R, It
Rees, A (Maesteg) 1919 NZA
Rees, A (Maesteg) 1962 E, S, F
Rees, A M (London Welsh) 1934 E, 1935 E, S, I, NZ, 1936 E, S, I, 1937 E, S, I, 1938 E, S
Rees, B I (London Welsh) 1967 S, I, F
Rees, C F W (London Welsh) 1974 I, 1975 A, 1978 NZ, 1981 F, A, 1982 I, F, E, S, 1983 E, S, I, F
Rees, D (Swansea) 1900 E, 1903 E, S, 1905 E, S
Rees, D (Swansea) 1968 S, I, F
Rees, E B (Swansea) 1919 NZA
Rees, H E (Neath) 1979 S, I, F, E, 1980 F, E, S, I, NZ, 1983 E, S, I, F
Rees, H T (Cardiff) 1937 S, I, 1938 E, S, I
Rees, J (Swansea) 1920 E, S, F, I, 1921 E, S, I, 1922 E, 1923 E, F, I, 1924 E
Rees, J I (Swansea) 1934 E, S, I, 1935 S, NZ, 1936 E, S, I, 1937 E, S, I, 1938 E, S, I
Rees, L M (Cardiff) 1933 I
Rees, M (Llanelli Scarlets) 2005 US, 2006 Arg 1, A, C, NZ(R), 2007 I(R), S(t&R), F1, It, E1, A1, Arg, F2, [C, A, Fj], 2008 E(R), S(R), It, I, F(R), SA1, 3, NZ, A, 2009 S, E, F, It(R), I, NZ, Sm(R), Arg, A, 2010 I, It, SA1, NZ1, 2, A, SA2, NZ3, 2011 E1, S, It, I, F
Rees, P (Llanelli) 1947 F, I
Rees, P M (Newport) 1961 E, S, I, 1964 I
Rees, R (Swansea) 1998 Z
Rees, R S (Cardiff Blues) 2010 E(R), S(R), F, I, NZ2(R), A(R), SA2(R), Fj, NZ3(R)
Rees, T A (Llandovery) 1881 E
Rees, T E (London Welsh) 1926 I, F, 1927 A, 1928 E
Rees, T J (Newport) 1935 S, I, NZ, 1936 E, S, I, 1937 E, S
Rees-Jones, G R (Oxford U, London Welsh) 1934 E, S, 1935 I, NZ, 1936 E
Reeves, F C (Cross Keys) 1920 F, I, 1921 E
Reynolds, A D (Swansea) 1990 Nm 1, 2(R), 1992 A (R)
Rhapps, J (Penygraig) 1897 E
Rice-Evans, W (Swansea) 1890 S, 1891 E, S
Richards, D S (Swansea) 1979 F, E, 1980 F, E, S, I, NZ, 1981 E, S, I, F, 1982 I, F, 1983 E, S, I, R (R)

Richards, E G (Cardiff) 1927 S
Richards, E I (Cardiff) 1925 E, S, F
Richards, E S (Swansea) 1885 E, 1887 S
Richards, H D (Neath) 1986 Tg (R), 1987 [Tg, E (R), NZ]
Richards, K H L (Bridgend) 1960 SA, 1961 E, S, I, F
Richards, M C R (Cardiff) 1968 I, F, 1969 S, I, F, E, NZ 1, 2, A
Richards, R (Aberavon) 1913 S, F, I
Richards, R C (Cross Keys) 1956 F
Richards, T B (Swansea)1960 F
Richards, T L (Maesteg) 1923 I
Richards, W C (Pontypool) 1922 E, S, I, F, 1924 I
Richardson, S J (Aberavon) 1978 A 2(R), 1979 E
Rickards, A R (Cardiff) 1924 F
Ring, J (Aberavon) 1921 E
Ring, M G (Cardiff, Pontypool) 1983 E, 1984 A, 1985 S, I, F, 1987 I, [I, Tg, A], US, 1988 E, S, I, F, NZ 1, 2, 1989 NZ, 1990 F, E, S, I, Nm 1, 2, Bb, 1991 E, S, I, F 1, 2, [WS, Arg, A]
Ringer, J (Bridgend) 2001 J 1(R), 2(R)
Ringer, P (Ebbw Vale, Llanelli) 1978 NZ, 1979 S, I, F, E, 1980 F, E, NZ
Roberts, C R (Neath) 1958 I, F
Roberts, D E A (London Welsh) 1930 E
Roberts, E (Llanelli) 1886 E, 1887 I
Roberts, E J (Llanelli) 1888 S, I, 1889 I
Roberts, G J (Cardiff) 1985 F (R), E, 1987 [I, Tg, C, E, A]
Roberts, H M (Cardiff) 1960 SA, 1961 E, S, I, F, 1962 S, F, 1963 I
Roberts, J (Cardiff) 1927 E, S, F, I, A, 1928 E, S, I, F, 1929 E, S, F, I
Roberts, J H (Cardiff Blues) 2008 S, SA1, 2, 3, C(R), NZ, A, 2009 S, E, F, It, I(R), NZ, Sm, Arg, A, 2010 E, S, F, I, It, SA1, NZ1, 2, 2011 E1, S, It, I, F, E2, 3, Arg, [SA, Sm, Fj, I, F, A]
Roberts, M (Scarlets) 2008 C, 2009 NZ(R), A(t&R)
Roberts, M G (London Welsh) 1971 E, S, I, F, 1973 I, F, 1975 S, 1979 E
Roberts, T (Newport, Risca) 1921 S, F, I, 1922 E, S, I, F, 1923 E, S
Roberts, W (Cardiff) 1929 E
Robins, J D (Birkenhead Park) 1950 E, S, I, F, 1951 E, S, I, F, 1953 E, I, F
Robins, R J (Pontypridd) 1953 S, 1954 F, S, 1955 E, S, I, F, 1956 E, F, 1957 E, S, I, F
Robinson, I R (Cardiff) 1974 F, E
Robinson, J P (Cardiff Blues) 2001 J 1(R), 2(R), Arg (R), Tg (R), A, 2002 I, Fj(R), C, NZ, 2003 A, NZ, I 2, S 2, 2006 Arg 1, 2, 2007 I, S, F1(R), A1, 2, Arg(t&R), F2, [J]
Robinson, M F D (Swansea) 1999 S, I, F 1, Arg 1
Robinson, N J (Cardiff Blues) 2003 I 2, R, 2004 Arg 1(R), 2, SA1, 2005 US, C, NZ(R), Fj, 2006 S(R), Arg 1, 2, 2009 US
Rocyn-Jones, D N (Cambridge U) 1925 I
Roderick, W B (Llanelli) 1884 I
Rogers, P J D (London Irish, Newport, Cardiff) 1999 F 1, It, E, Arg 1, 2, SA, C, F 2, [Arg 3, J, Sm, A], 2000 F, It, E, S, I, SA
Rosser, M A (Penarth) 1924 S, F
Rowland, E M (Lampeter) 1885 E
Rowlands, C F (Aberavon) 1926 I
Rowlands, D C T (Pontypool) 1963 E, S, I, F, NZ, 1964 E, S, I, F, SA, 1965 E, S, I, F
Rowlands, G (RAF, Cardiff) 1953 NZ, 1954 E, F, 1956 F
Rowlands, K A (Cardiff) 1962 F, I, 1963 I, 1965 I, F
Rowles, G A (Penarth) 1892 E
Rowley, M (Pontypridd) 1996 SA, 1997 US, S, I, F, R
Roy, W S (Cardiff) 1995 [J (R)]
Russell, S (London Welsh) 1987 US

Samuel, D (Swansea) 1891 I, 1893 I
Samuel, J (Swansea) 1891 I
Samuel, T F (Mountain Ash) 1922 S, I, F
Scourfield, T B (Torquay Athletic) 1930 F
Scrine, F G (Swansea) 1899 E, S, 1901 I
Selley, T J (Llanelli Scarlets) 2005 US(R)
Shanklin, J L (London Welsh) 1970 F, 1972 NZ, 1973 I, F
Shanklin, T G L (Saracens, Cardiff Blues) 2001 J 2, 2002 F, It, SA 1(R), 2(R), R, Fj, 2003 It, E 1, S 1, I 1, F(t+R), A, NZ, S 2, [Tg, NZ], 2004 I(R), F(R), E, It(R), Arg 1(R), 2, SA1, 2(R), R, NZ, J, 2005 E, It, F, S, I, 2006 A, C, NZ, 2007 S(R), F1, It, E1, 2, Arg, [C, A, J(R), Fj], SA, 2008 E(R), S, It, I, F, SA1, 2, 3, C, NZ, A, 2009 S, E, F, It(R), I, NZ, Sm, 2010 It(R), A, SA2, Fj(R), NZ3
Shaw, G (Neath) 1972 NZ, 1973 E, S, I, F, A, 1974 S, I, F, E, 1977 I, F
Shaw, T W (Newbridge) 1983 R
Shea, J (Newport) 1919 NZA, 1920 E, S, 1921 E
Shell, R C (Aberavon) 1973 A (R)
Sidoli, R A (Pontypridd, Celtic Warriors, Cardiff Blues) 2002 SA 1(R), 2(R), R, Fj, NZ, 2003 It, E 1, S 1, I 1, F, A, NZ, E 2, [C(R), Tg, It(R), NZ, E], 2004 I, It(R), 2005 E, It, F, S, I, C, NZ, Fj(R), SA, A, 2006 E, S, I, It, F, PI, C(R), 2007 I(t&R), S, A1, 2, E2
Simpson, H J (Cardiff) 1884 E, S, I
Sinkinson, B D (Neath) 1999 F 1, It, E, Arg 1, 2, SA, F 2, [Arg 3, J, Sm, A], 2000 F, It, E, 2001 R (R), I, Arg (R), Tg, A, 2002 It (R)
Skrimshire, R T (Newport) 1899 E, S, I
Skym, A (Llanelli) 1928 E, S, I, F, 1930 E, S, I, F, 1931 E, S, F, I, SA, 1932 E, S, I, 1933 E, S, I, 1935 E
Smith, J S (Cardiff) 1884 E, I, 1885 E
Smith, R (Ebbw Vale) 2000 F (R)
Sowden-Taylor, R (Cardiff Blues) 2005 It(R), C(R), NZ(R), 2007 A2(R), SA, 2008 C, 2009 C, US
Sparks, B A (Neath) 1954 I, 1955 E, F, 1956 E, S, I, 1957 S
Spiller, W (Cardiff) 1910 S, I, 1911 E, S, F, I, 1912 E, F, SA, 1913 E
Spratt, J P (Ospreys) 2009 C(R), US(R)
Squire, J (Newport, Pontypool) 1977 I, F, 1978 E, S, I, F, A 1, NZ, 1979 S, I, F, E, 1980 F, E, S, I, NZ, 1981 E, S, I, F, A, 1982 I, F, E, 1983 E, S, I, F
Stadden, W J (Cardiff) 1884 I, 1886 E, S, 1887 I, 1888 S, M, 1890 S, E
Stephens, C (Bridgend) 1998 E (R), 2001 J 2(R)
Stephens, C J (Llanelli) 1992 I, F, E, A
Stephens, G (Neath) 1912 E, S, I, F, SA, 1913 E, S, F, I, 1919 NZA
Stephens, I (Bridgend) 1981 E, S, I, F, A, 1982 I, F, E, S, 1984 I, F, E, A
Stephens, Rev J G (Llanelli) 1922 E, S, I, F
Stephens, J R G (Neath) 1947 E, S, F, I, 1948 I, 1949 S, I, F, 1951 F, SA, 1952 E, S, I, F, 1953 E, S, I, F, NZ, 1954 E, I, 1955 E, S, I, F, 1956 S, I, F, 1957 E, S, I, F
Stock, A (Newport) 1924 F, NZ, 1926 E, S
Stoddart, M L (Llanelli Scarlets) 2007 SA, 2008 SA1(R), C, 2011 E1, S, It, Bb, E2
Stone, P (Llanelli) 1949 F
Strand-Jones, J (Llanelli) 1902 E, S, I, 1903 E, S
Sullivan, A C (Cardiff) 2001 Arg, Tg
Summers, R H B (Haverfordwest) 1881 E
Sutton, S (Pontypool, S Wales Police) 1982 F, E, 1987 F, E, S, I, [C, NZ (R), A]
Sweeney, C (Pontypridd, Celtic Warriors, Newport Gwent Dragons) 2003 It(R), E 1, NZ(R), I 2, S 2, [C, It, NZ(t&R), E(t)], 2004 I(R), F(R), E(R), It(R), Arg 1, SA1(R), 2(R), R(R), J, 2005 It(R), F(t), S(R), US, C, NZ, Fj(R), SA(t&R), A(R), 2006 PI, C(R), 2007 S(t), A2(R), E2, F2(R), [J(R)], SA(R)
Sweet-Escott, R B (Cardiff) 1891 S, 1894 I, 1895 I

Tamplin, W E (Cardiff) 1947 S, F, I, A, 1948 E, S, F
Tanner, H (Swansea, Cardiff) 1935 NZ, 1936 E, S, I, 1937 E, S, I, 1938 E, S, I, 1939 E, S, I, 1947 E, S, F, I, 1948 E, S, F, I, 1949 E, S, I, F
Tarr, D J (Swansea, Royal Navy) 1935 NZ
Taylor, A R (Cross Keys) 1937 I, 1938 I, 1939 E
Taylor, C G (Ruabon) 1884 E, S, I, 1885 E, S, 1886 E, S, 1887 E, I
Taylor, H T (Cardiff) 1994 Pt, C, Fj, Tg, WS (R), R, It, SA, 1995 E, S, [J, NZ, I], SA, Fj, 1996 It, E, S, I, F 1, A 1, 2, It, A 3
Taylor, J (London Welsh) 1967 S, I, F, E, NZ, 1968 I, F, 1969 S, I, F, E, NZ 1, A, 1970 F, 1971 E, S, I, F, 1972 E, S, F, NZ, 1973 E, S, I, F
Taylor, M (Pontypool, Swansea, Llanelli Scarlets, Sale) 1994 SA, 1995 F, E, SA (R), 1998 Z, SA 1, 2, Arg, 1999 I, F 1, It, E, Arg 1, 2, SA, F 2, [Arg 3, J, Sm, A], 2000 F, It, E, S, Sm, US, 2001 E, S, F, It, 2002 S, SA 1, 2, 2003 E 1, S 1, I 1, F, A, NZ, E 2, [C(R), Tg, NZ, E], 2004 F, E, It, R(R), 2005 I, US, C, NZ
Thomas, A C (Bristol, Swansea) 1996 It, E, S, I, F 2(R), SA, 1997 US, S, I, F, US 1, 2, C, R, NZ (t), 1998 It, E, S (R), Z, SA 1, 2000 Sm, US, SA (R)
Thomas, A R F (Newport) 1963 NZ, 1964 E
Thomas, A G (Swansea, Cardiff) 1952 E, S, I, F, 1953 S, I, F, 1954 E, I, F, 1955 S, I, F
Thomas, B (Neath, Cambridge U) 1963 E, S, I, F, NZ, 1964 E, S, I, F, SA, 1965 E, 1966 E, S, I, 1967 NZ, 1969 S, I, F, E, NZ 1, 2
Thomas, B M G (St Bart's Hospital) 1919 NZA, 1921 S, F, I, 1923 F, 1924 E
Thomas, C J (Newport) 1888 I, M, 1889 S, I, 1890 S, E, I, 1891 E, I
Thomas, C R (Bridgend) 1925 E, S
Thomas, D J (Swansea) 1904 E, 1908 A, 1910 E, S, I, 1911 E, S, F, I, 1912 E
Thomas, D J (Swansea) 1930 S, I, 1932 E, S, I, 1933 E, S, 1934 E, 1935 E, S, I

Thomas, D L (Neath) 1937 E
Thomas, D L (Aberavon) 1961 I
Thomas, E (Newport) 1904 S, I, 1909 S, F, I, 1910 F
Thomas, E J R (Mountain Ash) 1906 SA, 1908 F, I, 1909 S
Thomas, G (Newport) 1888 M, 1890 I, 1891 S
Thomas, G (Bridgend, Cardiff, Celtic Warriors, Toulouse, Cardiff Blues) 1995 [J, NZ, I], SA, Fj, 1996 F 1, A 1, 2, Bb, F 2, It, A 3, 1997 US, S, I, F, E, US 1, 2, C, R, Tg, NZ, 1998 It, E, S, I, F, SA 2, Arg, 1999 F 1(R), It, E, Arg 2, SA, F 2, [Arg 3, J (R), Sm, A], 2000 F, It, E, S, I, US (R), SA, 2001 E, F, It, J 1, 2, R, Arg, Tg, A, 2002 E, R, Fj, C, NZ, 2003 It, E 1, S 1, I 1, F, I 2, E 2, [C, It, NZ(R), E], 2004 S, I, F, E, It, SA2, R, NZ, 2005 E, It, F, NZ, SA, A, 2006 E, S, A, C, 2007 It(t&R), E1, A1, 2, E2, Arg, F2, [C(R), A, Fj]
Thomas, G M (Bath, Ospreys, Llanelli Scarlets, Newport Gwent Dragons) 2001 J 1, 2, R, I (R), Arg, Tg (R), A (R), 2002 S (R), SA 2(R), R(R), 2003 It(R), E 1, S 1, F, E 2(R), R, 2006 Arg 1, 2, Pl, 2007 I(t&R), A1, 2, 2010 NZ1, 2
Thomas, H M (Llanelli) 1912 F
Thomas, H W (Swansea) 1912 SA, 1913 E
Thomas, H W (Neath) 1936 E, S, I, 1937 E, S, I
Thomas, I (Bryncethin) 1924 E
Thomas, I D (Ebbw Vale, Llanelli Scarlets) 2000 Sm, US (R), SA (R), 2001 J 1, 2, R, I, Arg (R), Tg, 2002 It, E, S, SA 1, 2, Fj, C, NZ, 2003 It, E 1, S 1, I 1, F, A, NZ, E 2, [Tg, NZ, E], 2004 I, F, 2007 A1, 2, E2
Thomas, J D (Llanelli) 1954 I
Thomas, J J (Swansea, Ospreys) 2003 A, NZ(R), E 2(R), R, [It(R), NZ, E], 2004 S(t&R), I, F, E, Arg 2(R), SA1(R), R(t&R), J, 2005 E(R), It, F(R), S(R), US, C, NZ, 2006 It(R), F(R), A, Pl(R), C, NZ, 2007 S(R), F1(R), It(R), E1(R), A1, 2, Arg, F2, [C, A], SA, 2008 E, S, It, I, F, SA1, 2, 2009 It, Sm(R), Arg(R), A(R), 2010 E(R), S, F, I, It, SA1, NZ1, 2, A, SA2, Fj, NZ3(R), 2011 E1(R), S(R), I(R), F(R), Arg(R)
Thomas, L C (Cardiff) 1885 E, S
Thomas, M C (Newport, Devonport Services) 1949 F, 1950 E, S, I, F, 1951 E, S, I, F, SA, 1952 E, S, I, F, 1953 E, 1956 E, S, I, F, 1957 E, S, 1958 E, S, I, F, 1959 I, F
Thomas, N (Bath) 1996 SA (R), 1997 US 1(R), 2, C (R), R, Tg, NZ, 1998 Z, SA 1
Thomas, R (Swansea) 1900 E, S, I, 1901 E
Thomas, R (Pontypool) 1909 F, I, 1911 S, F, 1912 E, S, SA, 1913 E
Thomas, R C C (Swansea) 1949 F, 1952 I, F, 1953 S, I, F, NZ, 1954 E, I, F, S, 1955 S, I, 1956 E, S, I, 1957 E, 1958 A, E, S, I, F, 1959 E, S, I, F
Thomas, R L (London Welsh) 1889 S, I, 1890 I, 1891 E, S, I, 1892 E
Thomas, R M (Newport Gwent Dragons) 2006 Arg 2(R), 2007 E2(R), SA, 2008 It, SA2, C, 2009 It
Thomas, S (Llanelli) 1890 S, E, 1891 I
Thomas, S G (Llanelli) 1923 E, S, F, I
Thomas, T R (Cardiff Blues) 2005 US(R), C, NZ(R), Fj, SA, A, 2006E, S, I, It, F, Pl, C(R), NZ, 2007 I, S, F1(R), It(R), E1(R), 2(R), F2(R), [C(R), A(R), J, Fj(R)], SA(R), 2008 SA2(R)
Thomas, W D (Llanelli) 1966 A, 1968 S, I, F, 1969 E, NZ 2, A, 1970 SA, S, E, I, F, 1971 E, S, I, F, 1972 E, S, F, NZ, 1973 E, S, I, F, 1974 E
Thomas, W G (Llanelli, Waterloo, Swansea) 1927 E, S, F, I, 1929 E, 1931 E, S, SA, 1932 E, S, I, 1933 E, S, I
Thomas, W H (Llandovery Coll, Cambridge U) 1885 S, 1886 E, S, 1887 E, S, 1888 S, I, 1890 E, I, 1891 S, I
Thomas, W J (Cardiff) 1961 F, 1963 F
Thomas, W J L (Llanelli, Cardiff) 1995 SA, Fj, 1996 It, E, S, I, F 1, 1996 Bb (R), 1997 US
Thomas, W L (Newport) 1894 S, 1895 E, I
Thomas, W T (Abertillery) 1930 E
Thompson, J F (Cross Keys) 1923 E
Thorburn, P H (Neath) 1985 F, E, Fj, 1986 E, S, I, F, 1987 F, [I, Tg, C, E, NZ, A], US, 1988 S, I, F, WS, R (R), 1989 S, I, F, E, NZ, 1990 F, E, S, I, Nm 1, 2, Bb, 1991 E, S, I, F 1, A
Tipuric, J C (Ospreys) 2011 Arg(R)
Titley, M H (Bridgend, Swansea) 1983 R, 1984 S, I, F, E, A, 1985 S, I, Fj, 1986 F, Fj, Tg, WS, 1990 F, E
Towers, W H (Swansea) 1887 I, 1888 M
Travers, G (Pill Harriers, Newport) 1903 E, S, I, 1905 E, S, I, NZ, 1906 E, S, I, SA, 1907 E, S, I, 1908 E, S, F, I, A, 1909 E, S, I, 1911 S, F, I
Travers, W H (Newport) 1937 S, I, 1938 E, S, I, 1939 E, S, I, 1949 E, S, I, F
Treharne, E (Pontypridd) 1881 E, 1883 E
Trew, W J (Swansea) 1900 E, S, I, 1901 E, S, 1903 S, 1905 S, 1906 S, 1907 E, S, 1908 E, S, F, I, A, 1909 E, S, F, I, 1910 F, E, S, 1911 E, S, F, I, 1912 S, 1913 S, F
Trott, R F (Cardiff) 1948 E, S, F, I, 1949 E, S, I, F
Truman, W H (Llanelli) 1934 E, 1935 E
Trump, L C (Newport) 1912 E, S, I, F
Turnbull, B R (Cardiff) 1925 I, 1927 E, S, 1928 E, F, 1930 S
Turnbull, J (Scarlets) 2011 S(R), Bb(R), E3(R)
Turnbull, M J L (Cardiff) 1933 E, I
Turner, P (Newbridge) 1989 I (R), F, E

Uzzell, H (Newport) 1912 E, S, I, F, 1913 S, F, I, 1914 E, S, F, I, 1920 E, S, F, I
Uzzell, J R (Newport) 1963 NZ, 1965 E, S, I, F

Vickery, W E (Aberavon) 1938 E, S, I, 1939 E
Vile, T H (Newport) 1908 E, S, 1910 I, 1912 I, F, SA, 1913 E, 1921 S
Vincent, H C (Bangor) 1882 I
Voyle, M J (Newport, Llanelli, Cardiff) 1996 A 1(t), F 2, 1997 E, US 1, 2, C, Tg, NZ, 1998 It, E, S, I, F, Arg (R), 1999 S (R), I (t), It (R), SA (R), F 2(R), [J, A (R)], 2000 F (R)

Wakeford, J D M (S Wales Police) 1988 WS, R
Waldron, R G (Neath) 1965 E, S, I, F
Walker, N (Cardiff) 1993 I, F, J, 1994 S, F, E, Pt, Sp, 1995 F, E, 1997 US 1, 2, C, R (R), Tg, NZ, 1998 E
Waller, P D (Newport) 1908 A, 1909 E, S, F, I, 1910 F
Walne, N J (Richmond, Cardiff) 1999 It (R), E (R), C
Walters, N (Llanelli) 1902 E
Wanbon, R (Aberavon) 1968 E
Warburton, S K (Cardiff Blues) 2009 US(R), Sm, A(R), 2010 S(R), I(R), It, SA1, A, NZ3, 2011 E1, S, It, I, F, Bb, E2, 3, [SA, Sm, Nm, Fj, I, F]
Ward, W S (Cross Keys) 1934 S, I
Warlow, D J (Llanelli) 1962 I
Waters, D R (Newport) 1986 E, S, I, F
Waters, K (Newbridge) 1991 [WS]
Watkins, D (Newport) 1963 E, S, I, F, NZ, 1964 E, S, I, F, SA, 1965 E, S, I, F, 1966 E, S, I, F, 1967 I, F, E
Watkins, E (Neath) 1924 E, S, I, F
Watkins, E (Blaina) 1926 S, I, F
Watkins, E V (Cardiff) 1935 NZ, 1937 S, I, 1938 E, S, I, 1939 E, S
Watkins, H V (Llanelli) 1904 S, I, 1905 E, S, I, 1906 E
Watkins, I J (Ebbw Vale) 1988 E (R), S, I, F, NZ 2, R, 1989 S, I, F, E
Watkins, L (Oxford U, Llandaff) 1881 E
Watkins, M J (Newport) 1984 I, F, E, A
Watkins, M J (Llanelli Scarlets) 2003 It(R), E 1(R), S 1(R), I 1(R), R, S 2, 2005 US(R), C(R), Fj, SA(R), A, 2006 E, S, I, It, F, Arg 1, 2(R)
Watkins, S J (Newport, Cardiff) 1964 S, I, F, 1965 E, S, I, F, 1966 E, S, I, F, A, 1967 S, I, F, E, NZ, 1968 E, S, 1969 S, I, F, E, NZ 1, 1970 E, I
Watkins, W R (Newport) 1959 F
Watts, D (Maesteg) 1914 E, S, F, I
Watts, J (Llanelli) 1907 E, S, I, 1908 E, S, F, I, A, 1909 S, F, I
Watts, W H (Newport) 1892 E, S, I, 1893 E, S, I, 1894 E, S, I, 1895 E, I, 1896 E
Watts, W J (Llanelli) 1914 E
Weatherley, D J (Swansea) 1998 Z
Weaver, D S (Swansea) 1964 E
Webb, A (Jim) (Abertillery) 1907 S, 1908 E, S, F, I, A, 1909 E, S, F, I, 1910 F, E, S, I, 1911 E, S, F, I, 1912 E, S
Webb, J (Newport) 1888 M, 1889 S
Webbe, G M C (Bridgend) 1986 Tg (R), WS, 1987 F, E, S, [Tg], US, 1988 F (R), NZ 1, R
Webster, R E (Swansea) 1987 [A], 1990 Bb, 1991 [Arg, A], 1992 I, F, E, S, A, 1993 E, S, I, F
Wells, G T (Cardiff) 1955 E, S, 1957 I, F, 1958 A, E, S
Westacott, D (Cardiff) 1906 I
Wetter, J J (Newport) 1914 S, F, I, 1920 E, S, F, I, 1921 E, 1924 I, NZ
Wetter, W H (Newport) 1912 SA, 1913 E
Wheel, G A D (Swansea) 1974 I, E (R), 1975 F, E, I, A, 1976 E, S, I, F, 1977 I, E, S, 1978 E, S, I, F, A 1, 2, NZ, 1979 S, I, 1980 F, E, S, I, 1981 E, S, I, F, A, 1982 I
Wheeler, P J (Aberavon) 1967 NZ, 1968 E
Whitefoot, J (Cardiff) 1984 A (R), 1985 S, I, F, E, Fj, 1986 E, S, I, F, Fj, Tg, WS, 1987 F, E, S, I, [I, C]
Whitfield, J J (Newport) 1919 NZA, 1920 E, S, F, I, 1921 E, 1922 E, S, I, F, 1924 S, I
Whitson, G K (Newport) 1956 F, 1960 S, I
Wilkins, G (Bridgend) 1994 Tg
Williams, A (Ospreys, Bath) 2003 R (R), 2005 v US(R), C(R), 2006 Arg 2(R), 2007 A2(R)

Williams, B (Llanelli) 1920 S, F, I
Williams, B H (Neath, Richmond, Bristol) 1996 F 2, 1997 R, Tg, NZ, 1998 It, E, Z (R), SA 1, Arg (R), 1999 S (R), I, It (R), 2000 F (R), It (R), E (t+R), 2001 R (R), I (R), Tg (R), A (R), 2002 I (R), F (R), It (R), E (R), S
Williams, B L (Cardiff) 1947 E, S, F, I, A, 1948 E, S, F, I, 1949 E, S, I, 1951 I, SA, 1952 S, 1953 E, S, I, F, NZ, 1954 S, 1955 E
Williams, B R (Neath) 1990 S, I, Bb, 1991 E, S
Williams, C (Llanelli) 1924 NZ, 1925 E
Williams, C (Aberavon, Swansea) 1977 E, S, 1980 F, E, S, I, NZ, 1983 E
Williams, C D (Cardiff, Neath) 1955 F, 1956 F
Williams, D (Ebbw Vale) 1963 E, S, I, F, 1964 E, S, I, F, SA, 1965 E, S, I, F, 1966 E, S, I, A, 1967 F, E, NZ, 1968 E, 1969 S, I, F, E, NZ 1, 2, A, 1970 SA, S, E, I, 1971 E, S, I, F
Williams, D (Llanelli) 1998 SA 1(R)
Williams, D A (Bridgend, Swansea) 1990 Nm 2(R), 1995 Fj (R)
Williams, D B (Newport, Swansea) 1978 A 1, 1981 E, S
Williams, E (Neath) 1924 NZ, 1925 F
Williams, E (Aberavon) 1925 E, S
Williams, F L (Cardiff) 1929 S, F, I, 1930 E, S, I, F, 1931 F, I, SA, 1932 E, S, I, 1933 I
Williams, G (London Welsh) 1950 I, F, 1951 E, S, I, F, SA, 1952 E, S, I, F, 1953 NZ, 1954 E
Williams, G (Bridgend) 1981 I, F, 1982 E (R), S
Williams, G J (Bridgend, Cardiff Blues) 2003 It(R), E 1(R), S 1, F(R), E 2(R), 2009 C(R), US, 2010 E, S
Williams, G M (Aberavon) 1936 E, S, I
Williams, G P (Bridgend) 1980 NZ, 1981 E, S, A, 1982 I
Williams, G R (Cardiff Blues) 2000 I, Sm, US, SA, 2001 S, F, It, R (R), I (R), Arg, Tg (R), A (R), 2002 F (R), It (R), E (R), S, SA 1, 2, R, Fj, C, NZ, 2003 It, E 1, S 1, I 1, F, A, NZ, E 2, [Tg, It(R)], 2004 S, I, F, E, It, Arg1, R, J, 2005 F(R), S, US, C
Williams, H R (Llanelli) 1954 S, 1957 F, 1958 A
Williams, J F (London Welsh) 1905 I, NZ, 1906 S, SA
Williams, J J (Llanelli) 1973 F (R), A, 1974 S, I, F, E, 1975 F, E, S, I, A, 1976 E, S, I, F, 1977 I, F, E, S, 1978 E, S, I, F, A 1, 2, NZ, 1979 S, I, F, E
Williams, J L (Cardiff) 1906 SA, 1907 E, S, I, 1908 E, S, I, A, 1909 E, S, F, I, 1910 I, 1911 E, S, F, I
Williams, J L (Blaina) 1920 E, S, F, I, 1921 S, F, I
Williams, J P R (London Welsh, Bridgend) 1969 S, I, F, E, NZ 1, 2, A, 1970 SA, S, E, I, F, 1971 E, S, I, F, 1972 E, S, F, NZ, 1973 E, S, I, F, A, 1974 S, I, F, 1975 F, E, S, I, A, 1976 E, S, I, F, 1977 I, F, E, S, 1978 E, S, I, F, A 1, 2, NZ, 1979 S, I, F, E, 1980 NZ, 1981 E, S
Williams, L D (Cardiff Blues) 2011 Arg(R), [Nm(R), Fj(R), A(R)]
Williams, L H (Cardiff) 1957 S, I, F, 1958 E, S, I, F, 1959 E, S, I, 1961 F, 1962 E, S
Williams, M E (Pontypridd, Cardiff Blues) 1996 Bb, F 2, It (t), 1998 It, E, Z, SA 2, Arg, 1999 S, I, C, J, [Sm], 2000 E (R), 2001 E, S, F, It, 2002 I, F, It, E, S, SA 1, 2, Fj, C, NZ, 2003 It, E 1, S 1, I 1, F, A, NZ, E 2, [C, Tg(R), It, E(R)], 2004 S, I, F(t&R), E(R), It, SA2(t&R), R(R), NZ(R), J(R), 2005 E, It, F, S, I, Fj, SA, A, 2006 E, S, I, It, F, A, C, NZ, 2007 I, S, F1, It, E1, Arg, F2, [C, A, J, Fj], 2008 E, S, It, I, F, SA3, NZ, A, 2009 S, E, F, I, NZ, Arg, A, 2010 E, S, F, I, A(R), SA2, NZ3(R), 2011 Arg
Williams, M S (Scarlets) 2011 Bb(R), E2(R), 3(R), Arg(R) , [Nm, Fj, A(R)]
Williams, M T (Newport) 1923 F
Williams, O (Llanelli) 1947 E, S, A, 1948 E, S, F, I
Williams, O L (Bridgend) 1990 Nm 2
Williams, R D G (Newport) 1881 E
Williams, R F (Cardiff) 1912 SA, 1913 E, S, 1914 I
Williams, R H (Llanelli) 1954 I, F, S, 1955 S, I, F, 1956 E, S, I, 1957 E, S, I, F, 1958 A, E, S, I, F, 1959 E, S, I, F, 1960 E
Williams, S (Llanelli) 1947 E, S, F, I, 1948 S, F
Williams, S A (Aberavon) 1939 E, S, I
Williams, S M (Neath, Cardiff, Northampton) 1994 Tg, 1996 E (t), A 1, 2, Bb, F 2, It, A 3, SA, 1997 US, S, I, F, E, US 1, 2(R), C, R (R), Tg (R), NZ (t+R), 2002 SA 1, 2, R, Fj(R), 2003 It, E 1, S 1, F(R)
Williams, S M (Neath, Ospreys) 2000 F (R), It, E, S, I, Sm, SA (R), 2001 J 1, 2, I, 2003 R, [NZ, E], 2004 S, I, F, E, It, Arg 1, 2, SA1, 2, NZ, J, 2005 E, It, F, S, I, NZ, Fj, SA, A, 2006 E, S, It, F, Arg 1, 2, A, Pl(R), C, NZ, 2007 F1, It, E1, F2, [C, A, J, Fj], 2008 E, S, It, I, F, SA1, 2, 3, NZ, A, 2009 S, F, It, I, NZ, Arg, A, 2010 E, S, F, I, It, A, SA2, 2011 E1, S, It, I, E2, 3, [SA, Sm, I, F, A]
Williams, T (Pontypridd) 1882 I
Williams, T (Swansea) 1888 S, I
Williams, T (Swansea) 1912 I, 1913 F, 1914 E, S, F, I
Williams, T (Swansea) 1921 F
Williams, T G (Cross Keys) 1935 S, I, NZ, 1936 E, S, I, 1937 S, I
Williams, W A (Crumlin) 1927 E, S, F, I
Williams, W A (Newport) 1952 I, F, 1953 E
Williams, W E O (Cardiff) 1887 S, I, 1889 S, 1890 S, E
Williams, W H (Pontymister) 1900 E, S, I, 1901 E
Williams, W L T (Llanelli, Cardiff) 1947 E, S, F, I, A, 1948 I, 1949 E
Williams, W O G (Swansea, Devonport Services) 1951 F, SA, 1952 E, S, I, F, 1953 E, S, I, F, NZ, 1954 E, I, F, S, 1955 E, S, I, F, 1956 E, S, I
Williams, W P J (Neath) 1974 I, F
Williams-Jones, H (S Wales Police, Llanelli) 1989 S (R), 1990 F (R), I, 1991 A, 1992 S, A, 1993 E, S, I, F, Z 1, Nm, 1994 Fj, Tg, WS (R), It (t), 1995 E (R)
Willis, W R (Cardiff) 1950 E, S, I, F, 1951 E, S, I, F, SA, 1952 E, S, 1953 S, NZ, 1954 E, I, F, S, 1955 E, S, I, F
Wiltshire, M L (Aberavon) 1967 NZ, 1968 E, S, F
Windsor, R W (Pontypool) 1973 A, 1974 S, I, F, E, 1975 F, E, S, I, A, 1976 E, S, I, F, 1977 I, F, E, S, 1978 E, S, I, F, A 1, 2, NZ, 1979 S, I, F
Winfield, H B (Cardiff) 1903 I, 1904 E, S, I, 1905 NZ, 1906 E, S, I, 1907 S, I, 1908 E, S, F, I, A
Winmill, S (Cross Keys) 1921 E, S, F, I
Wintle, M E (Llanelli) 1996 It
Wintle, R V (London Welsh) 1988 WS (R)
Wooller, W (Sale, Cambridge U, Cardiff) 1933 E, S, I, 1935 E, S, I, NZ, 1936 E, S, I, 1937 E, S, I, 1938 S, I, 1939 E, S, I
Wyatt, C P (Llanelli) 1998 Z (R), SA 1(R), 2, Arg, 1999 S, I, F 1, It, E, Arg 1, 2, SA, C (R), F 2, [Arg 3, J (R), Sm, A], 2000 F, It, E, US, SA, 2001 E, R, I, Arg (R), Tg (R), A (R), 2002 I, It (R), E, S (R), 2003 A(R), NZ(t+R), E 2, [Tg(R), NZ(R)]
Wyatt, G (Pontypridd, Celtic Warriors) 1997 Tg, 2003 R (R)
Wyatt, M A (Swansea) 1983 E, S, I, F, 1984 A, 1985 S, I, 1987 E, S, I

Yapp, J V (Cardiff Blues) 2005 E(R), It(R), F(R), S(R), I(R), C(R), Fj, 2006 Arg 1(R), 2008 C, NZ(R), 2009 S(R), It, C, US, 2010 SA1(R), NZ1(R), SA2(R), 2011 E1(t&R), S(R), I(R), F(R)
Young, D (Swansea, Cardiff) 1987 [E, NZ], US, 1988 E, S, I, F, NZ 1, 2, WS, R, 1989 S, NZ, 1990 F, 1996 A 3, SA, 1997 US, S, I, F, E, R, NZ, 1998 It, E, S, I, F, 1999 I, E (R), Arg 1(R), 2(R), SA, C (R), F 2, [Arg 3, J, Sm, A], 2000 F, It, E, S, I, 2001 E, S, F, It, R, I, Arg
Young, G A (Cardiff) 1886 E, S
Young, J (Harrogate, RAF, London Welsh) 1968 S, I, F, 1969 S, I, F, E, NZ 1, 1970 E, I, F, 1971 E, S, I, F, 1972 E, S, F, NZ, 1973 E, S, I, F
Young, P (Gwent Dragons) 2003 R (R)

LLANELLI CLAIM CROWN

Claudio Villa/Getty Images

Young Wales star Steve Shingler was on target when Llanelli lifted the Principality Premiership.

In the Principality's first season of play-off rugby in 2009–10, it was a dominant Neath side who were the undisputed kings of the club game as the All Blacks topped the table and then dramatically dispatched Swansea in the inaugural Premiership Play-Off Final. In 2010–11, however, it was an altogether different story as Llanelli were eventually crowned champions, despite the Parc y Scarlets side finishing a distant third in the final table.

Coached by Kevin George, Llanelli were not widely tipped to get past Neath in the semi-finals, let alone defeat Pontypridd, the runaway league 'winners' after 26 games, in the second final. However, they timed their end-of-season surge to perfection to emerge 24–18 victors at Sardis Road and lift the trophy despite finishing the match with 13 players after late yellow cards for fly-half Steve Shingler and replacement hooker Rhys Lawrence.

In the process, George's side denied Pontypridd a famous double after their 35–24 victory over Aberavon in the final of the SWALEC Cup two and a half weeks earlier at the Millennium Stadium.

"The first half was great," George said after Llanelli's triumph in the Play-Off Final. "I think it went as we planned. Never been in a game like that before where you can have so many yellow cards, and it was very difficult, but it was great television viewing… perhaps not the spectacle and the game Ponty and us were hoping for.

"To go to Neath and then come to Pontypridd and win the title is fantastic, and the experience the young players have gained from this will teach them how to deal with the passion and crowds at the big occasions. The whole point of this team is to support the Scarlets and get the younger boys through. We've played 80 boys this season, we've played five 17-year-olds, we've played eight 18-year-olds, giving junior international players the chance to experience these things."

Llanelli smelt success at the House of Pain when full-back Dan Newton crashed over in the opening minutes, and further scores from centre Nic Reynolds and wing Lee Williams were enough to secure victory, despite Huw Dowden and Rhys Downes replying for the home side.

For Ponty, defeat was a bitter pill to swallow having finished 16 points clear of Llanelli in the regular season, but a degree of consolation had already been forthcoming after their triumph in the SWALEC Cup, a competition they had unexpectedly crashed out of 12 months earlier at the semi-final stage at the hands of Carmarthen.

A year later, however, they made no mistake against Aberavon in a thrilling encounter in Cardiff. Scrum-half Lewis Jones was the star of the show with two of Pontypridd's four tries on the day, and although Aberavon crossed the whitewash three times themselves they were unable to prevent Ponty from lifting the trophy for a fourth time in the club's history.

"It was my first chance of playing at the Millennium Stadium, and everything was, as expected, to a high standard, the facilities and the surface. It was not a full house, but it certainly felt that way – there was a lot of noise and the crowd generated a great atmosphere," Jones said.

"I couldn't have imagined scoring two tries before the game. I'm usually more of a provider than a finisher, and getting the two touch-downs was the icing on the cake. I came into the club as third-choice scrum-half and was determined to work hard and to take any chances that came my way."

PRINCIPALITY PREMIERSHIP 2010–11 RESULTS

28 August 2010: **Cardiff** 61 **Carmarthen** 18, **Llandovery** 16 **Swansea** 37, **Newport** 40 **Llanelli** 36, **Pontypool** 27 **Bedwas** 17, **Pontypridd** 23 **Cross Keys** 15, **Wanderers** 3 **Neath** 52, **Tonmawr** 18 **Aberavon** 19. 4 September: **Aberavon** 31 **Pontypool** 26, **Bedwas** 22 **Neath** 21, **Carmarthen** 14 **Newport** 30, **Cross Keys** 20 **Cardiff** 21, **Llanelli** 43 **Llandovery** 10, **Swansea** 34 **Tonmawr** 34, **Wanderers** 15 **Pontypridd** 47. 11 September: **Aberavon** 25 **Bedwas** 24, **Cardiff** 23 **Llanelli** 26, **Neath** 16 **Cross Keys** 9, **Newport** 20 **Swansea** 38, **Pontypool** 61 **Wanderers** 29, **Pontypridd** 20 **Carmarthen** 18, **Tonmawr** 31 **Llandovery** 7. 18 September: **Aberavon** 22 **Pontypridd** 40, **Bedwas** 35 **Cardiff** 34, **Carmarthen** 23 **Swansea** 34, **Cross Keys** 23 **Llandovery** 17, **Llanelli** 83 **Tonmawr** 32 **Wanderers** 31 **Newport** 39. 22 September: **Newport** 34 **Carmarthen** 10, **Pontypridd** 83 **Wanderers** 8. 25 September: **Cardiff** 26 **Aberavon** 28, **Llandovery** 31 **Wanderers** 7, **Llanelli** 43 **Carmarthen** 10, **Newport** 17 **Bedwas** 16, **Pontypridd** 24 **Pontypool** 13, **Swansea** 34 **Cross Keys** 28, **Tonmawr** 16 **Neath** 23. 2 October: **Aberavon** 41 **Newport** 25, **Bedwas** 18 **Llandovery** 15, **Carmarthen** 29 **Tonmawr** 28, **Cross Keys** 27 **Llanelli** 19, **Neath** 16 **Pontypridd** 13, **Pontypool** 22 **Cardiff** 17, **Wanderers** 24 **Swansea** 49. 9 October: **Carmarthen** 16 **Cross Keys** 25, **Llandovery** 16 **Aberavon** 34, **Neath** 44 **Cardiff** 10, **Swansea** 48 **Bedwas** 21, **Wanderers** 13 **Llanelli** 23, **Tonmawr** 23 **Pontypridd** 38, **Newport** 20 **Pontypool** 8. 16 October: **Bedwas** 36 **Cross Keys** 27, **Carmarthen** 19 **Pontypool** 29, **Wanderers** 19 **Tonmawr** 42, **Neath** 28 **Aberavon** 21. 23 October: **Aberavon** 27 **Swansea** 12, **Bedwas** 3 **Llanelli** 28, **Cross Keys** 28 **Tonmawr** 33, **Pontypool** 26 **Llandovery** 26, **Pontypridd** 16 **Cardiff** 16, **Wanderers** 24 **Carmarthen** 10. 24 October: **Newport** 12 **Neath** 31. 30 October: **Carmarthen** 17 **Bedwas** 10, **Cross Keys** 59 **Wanderers** 20, **Llandovery** 21 **Neath** 34, **Llanelli** 28 **Aberavon** 18, **Newport** 18 **Pontypridd** 23, **Swansea** 41 **Pontypool** 14, **Tonmawr** 30 **Cardiff** 30. 2 November: **Neath** 33 **Carmarthen** 7. 5 November: **Cardiff** 15 **Swansea** 11, **Pontypridd** 19 **Llanelli** 13, **Tonmawr** 9 **Bedwas** 17. 6 November: **Newport** 11 **Llandovery** 21. 9 November: **Cross Keys** 11 **Carmarthen** 16, **Aberavon** 34 **Llandovery** 14, **Bedwas** 29 **Swansea** 25, **Cardiff** 13 **Neath** 20, **Llanelli** 58 **Wanderers** 26, **Pontypool** 15 **Newport** 22, **Pontypridd** 31 **Tonmawr** 8. 13 November: **Llandovery** 21 **Cardiff** 24, **Swansea** 28 **Pontypridd** 39. 14 November: **Aberavon** 56 **Wanderers** 16, **Tonmawr** 19 **Newport** 12. 15 November: **Llanelli** 19 **Neath** 12. 20 November: **Bedwas** 22 **Wanderers** 10, **Cardiff** 25 **Cross Keys** 34, **Neath** 26 **Llandovery** 25, **Pontypool** 15 **Swansea** 38, **Pontypridd** 28 **Newport** 15, **Tonmawr** 24 **Carmarthen** 12. 4 December: **Llanelli** 32 **Cardiff** 16. 11 December: **Aberavon** 18 **Tonmawr** 29. 27 December: **Llanelli** 40 **Swansea** 27. 29 December: **Bedwas** 18 **Pontypridd** 30. **Cardiff** 29 **Wanderers** 23. 2 January: **Tonmawr** 7 **Llanelli** 26. 3 January: **Cardiff** 21 **Bedwas** 22, **Llandovery** 18 **Cross Keys** 25, **Neath** 43 **Pontypool** 20, **Newport** 26 **Wanderers** 20, **Swansea** 46 **Carmarthen** 19, **Pontypridd** 32 **Aberavon** 21. 8 January: **Aberavon** 27 **Cardiff** 14, **Bedwas** 25 **Newport** 28, **Carmarthen** 11 **Llanelli** 15, **Cross Keys** 21 **Swansea** 16, **Neath** 19 **Tonmawr** 10, **Wanderers** 41 **Llandovery** 33. 15 January: **Bedwas** 6 **Aberavon** 20. 18 January: **Cardiff** 24 **Pontypool** 12. 12 February: **Pontypool** 27 **Carmarthen** 11, **Aberavon** 59 **Llanelli** 15, **Neath** 48 **Bedwas** 18, **Wanderers** 8 **Cross Keys** 24, **Swansea** 27 **Newport** 18. 15 February: **Carmarthen** 6 **Pontypridd** 3. 16 February: **Wanderers** 13 **Cardiff** 29. 23 February: **Wanderers** 14 **Pontypool** 12. 26 February: **Cardiff** 11 **Tonmawr** 7, **Carmarthen** 34 **Llandovery** 7, **Newport** 24 **Cross Keys** 10, **Pontypridd** 24 **Bedwas** 10. 1 March: **Pontypool** 3 **Neath** 25. 5 March: **Aberavon** 46 **Carmarthen** 40, **Cross Keys** 23 **Newport** 23, **Neath** 41 **Wanderers** 35, **Tonmawr** 26 **Swansea** 22, **Bedwas** 32 **Pontypool** 19. 8 March: **Llandovery** 23 **Llanelli** 26. 10 March: **Pontypridd** 28 **Neath** 8. 11 March: **Pontypool** 18 **Cross Keys** 16, **Swansea** 18 **Llandovery** 19. 12 March: **Carmarthen** 50 **Wanderers** 25. 13 March: **Llanelli** 33 **Newport** 25. 15 March **Pontypool** 18 **Pontypridd** 29. 19 March: **Bedwas** 21 **Carmarthen** 26, **Cardiff**

42 **Newport** 16, **Cross Keys** 41 **Aberavon** 10, **Neath** 35 **Swansea** 15, **Pontypool** 46 **Llanelli** 40, **Pontypridd** 41 **Llandovery** 3. 22 March: **Llandovery** 26 **Pontypool** 16, **Swansea** 57 **Wanderers** 7, **Cross Keys** 17 **Neath** 21. 23 March: **Cardiff** 6 **Pontypridd** 20. 24 March: **Llanelli** 32 **Bedwas** 7, **Cross Keys** 15 **Pontypridd** 19. 29 March: **Neath** 35 **Newport** 12, **Swansea** 7 **Llanelli** 34. 30 March: **Carmarthen** 11 **Aberavon** 23, **Tonmawr** 37 **Pontypool** 25. 2 April: **Aberavon** 21 **Cross Keys** 25, **Cardiff** 25 **Llandovery** 26, **Neath** 37 **Llanelli** 28, **Newport** 35 **Tonmawr** 31, **Pontypridd** 34 **Swansea** 7, **Wanderers** 30 **Bedwas** 36. 5 April: **Carmarthen** 29 **Cardiff** 22, **Llandovery** 24 **Tonmawr** 28. 9 April: **Cross Keys** 47 **Bedwas** 15, **Llanelli** 47 **Pontypool** 45, **Newport** 27 **Cardiff** 21. 12 April: **Swansea** 10 **Neath** 32, **Llandovery** 10 **Bedwas** 17, **Pontypool** 29 **Aberavon** 38. 13 April: **Tonmawr** 23 **Wanderers** 9. 14 April: **Llanelli** 25 **Pontypridd** 30. 16 April: **Bedwas** 21 **Tonmawr** 28, **Carmarthen** 24 **Neath** 22, **Cross Keys** 22 **Pontypool** 10, **Llandovery** 18 **Newport** 29, **Swansea** 34 **Cardiff** 36, **Wanderers** 19 **Aberavon** 75. 19 April: **Swansea** 46 **Aberavon** 44, **Tonmawr** 7 **Cross Keys** 31, **Llandovery** 17 **Pontypridd** 33. 23 April: **Llandovery** 47 **Carmarthen** 38, **Llanelli** 57 **Cross Keys** 13, **Newport** 42 **Aberavon** 41, **Pontypool** 28 **Tonmawr** 34. 25 April: **Aberavon** 15 **Neath** 11.

FINAL TABLE

	P	W	D	L	F	A	BP	PTS
Pontypridd	26	23	1	2	767	382	13	**107**
Neath	26	21	0	5	733	426	16	**100**
Llanelli	26	19	0	7	869	586	15	**91**
Aberavon	26	17	0	9	814	633	15	**83**
Swansea	26	12	1	13	761	670	22	**72**
Cross Keys	26	13	1	13	636	543	14	**68**
Newport	26	14	1	11	620	657	8	**66**
Tonmawr	26	12	2	12	614	651	13	**65**
Cardiff	26	10	2	14	611	613	15	**59**
Bedwas	26	11	0	15	517	666	10	**54**
Carmarthen	26	9	0	17	518	710	7	**43**
Pontypool	26	7	1	18	584	721	8	**38**
Llandovery	26	6	1	19	511	719	12	**38**
Wanderers	26	3	0	23	489	1067	9	**21**

PRINCIPALITY PREMIERSHIP PLAY-OFF SEMI-FINAL

12 May, 2011

Neath 5 **Llanelli** 46

FINAL

19 May 2010, Sardis Road, Pontypridd

PONTYPRIDD 18 (1G, 1T, 2PG)
LLANELLI 24 (3G, 1PG)

PONTYPRIDD: A Thomas; G Wyatt, G Dacey, D Lockyer, O Williams; S Humberstone, L Jones; S Williams, K Dacey, R Harford, C Locke, R Savage, D Waters, W O'Connor, C Dicomidis (captain).

SUBSTITUTES: R Downes, D Gunter, L Williams, H Dowden, E Siggery, C Hill, S Hobbs.

SCORERS: *Tries:* Dowden, Downes *Conversion:* Gunter *Penalty Goals:* Humberstone (2)

LLANELLI: D Newton; D Ford, N Reynolds, J Lewis, L Williams; S Shingler, G Davies; P John, C Hawkins (captain), S Gardiner, A Powell, D Day, D Eager, M Gilbert, N Cudd

SUBSTITUTES: S Hopkins, R Lawrence, R Jones, N White, A Powell, J James, C Keenan

SCORERS: *Tries:* Newton, Reynolds, Williams *Conversions:* Shingler (3) *Penalty Goal:* Shingler

REFEREE: D Jones (WRU)

LEAGUE ONE EAST

Winners: Ebbw Vale

LEAGUE ONE WEST

Winners: Bridgend

LEAGUE ONE NORTH

Winners: Caernarfon

LEAGUE TWO EAST

Winners: Mountain Ash

LEAGUE TWO WEST

Winners: Ammanford

LEAGUE TWO NORTH

Winners: Bala

LEAGUE THREE EAST

Winners: Rhymney

LEAGUE THREE SOUTH EAST

Winners: Abercynon

LEAGUE THREE SOUTH WEST

Winners: Glynneath

LEAGUE THREE WEST

Winners: Crymych

LEAGUE FOUR EAST

Winners: Senghenydd

LEAGUE FOUR SOUTH EAST

Winners: Rhiwbina

LEAGUE FOUR SOUTH WEST

Winners: Maesteg Harlequins

LEAGUE FOUR WEST

Winners: Tenby United

LEAGUE FIVE SOUTH EAST

Winners: Penygraig

LEAGUE FIVE SOUTH CENTRAL

Winners: Resolven

LEAGUE FIVE SOUTH WEST

Winners: Trebanos

LEAGUE FIVE WEST

Winners: Furnace United

LEAGUE SIX EAST

Winners: Abertysswg Falcons

LEAGUE SIX SOUTH EAST

Winners: Hafodyrynys

LEAGUE SIX CENTRAL

Winners: Cymru Caerdydd

LEAGUE SIX WEST

Winners: Nantgaredig

SWALEC CUP 2010–11 RESULTS

QUARTER-FINALS

26 March 2011

Merthyr 30 **Pontypridd** 38

Tonmawr 13 **Llandovery** 23

Swansea 39 **Newport** 34

27 March 2011

Cardiff 17 **Aberavon** 19

SEMI-FINALS

9 April 2011

Llandovery 12 **Aberavon** 18

Pontypridd 33 **Swansea** 22

FINAL

2 May 2011, Millennium Stadium, Cardiff

ABERAVON 24 (3G, 1PG) PONTYPRIDD 35 (3G, 1T, 2PG, 1DG)

ABERAVON: M Jarvis; R Carter, W Price, A Beck, R Thomas; J Davies, D Davies; N White, M Breeze, A Edwards, I Moore, S Williams, J King, N Strong, C Davies (captain)

SUBSTITUTES: L Gadd, D Pritchard, D Thomas, A Bray, J Jones, R Morris, L Howell

SCORERS: *Tries:* Carter, Williams, Strong *Conversions:* Jarvis (3) *Penalty Goal:* Jarvis

PONTYPRIDD: A Thomas; G Wyatt, G Dacey, D Lockyer, O Williams; S Humberstone, L Jones; S Williams. K Dacey, R Harford, C Hill, R Savage, D Waters, W O'Connor, C Dicomidis (captain)

SUBSTITUTES: C Clayton; D Gunter, G Lucas, K Knaggs, C Locke, E Siggery H Dowden

SCORERS: *Tries:* Jones (2), Waters, Savage *Conversions:* Humberstone (3) *Penalty Goals:* Humberstone (2) *Dropped goal:* Humberstone

REFEREE: G Morris (WRU)

The Combined Teams

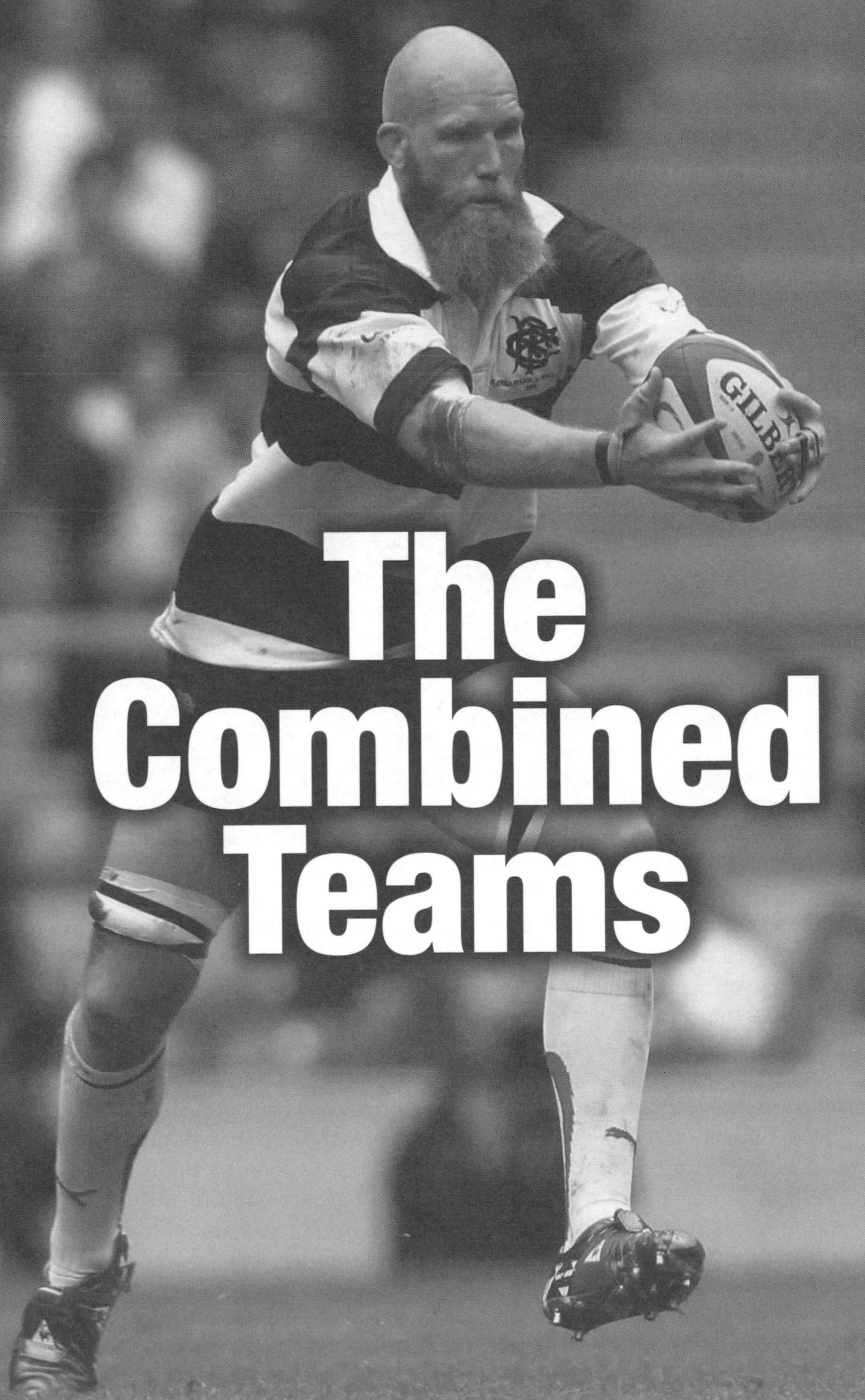

UNBEATEN BAA-BAAS ON TOP

Dave Rogers/Getty Images

The Barbarians won a thrilling game at Twickenham.

The Barbarians celebrated their induction into the International Rugby Board's Hall of Fame by recording six wins out six in their 120th season, claiming the notable scalps of South Africa, England and Wales in the process.

The Baa-Baas and late founder William Percy Carpmael were honoured at half-time of their 38–32 victory over England at Twickenham when IRB vice chairman Bill Beaumont presented club president Micky Steele-Bodger and chairman John Spencer with a commemorative cap and gold pin in recognition of the team's contribution to rugby.

"It is a great honour to be inducting the Barbarians, one of the most recognisable teams in the game, into the IRB Hall of Fame along with its founder William Percy Carpmael," said Beaumont, who himself turned out for the famous invitational side 15 times between 1975 and 1981. "I had the huge privilege of playing for the Barbarians alongside some of the greats of the game. It was a special experience, and I have many wonderful memories and made friends for life through the club.

"It is especially pleasing to see that the values that this club was founded on, values of fair play, camaraderie and fellowship, are as central to the Barbarians now as they were when William Percy Carpmael turned a dream into a reality."

The new season began in November with the clash against the Combined Services XV at the Army Rugby Stadium in Aldershot under the watchful eye of former England coach Brian Ashton, and the 2,000 assembled spectators were certainly treated to an entertaining spectacle as the Baa-Baas triumphed 46–21.

New Zealand Maori fly-half Willie Walker was the star of the show in the annual Remembrance Day fixture with two of the visitors' eight tries, while the Services side also crossed three times.

"I thoroughly enjoyed it," Ashton said after the match. "The game was a great spectacle, and 67 points on the scoreboard proves that. But fair play to the Combined Services; they continued to play throughout and they produced some cracking rugby in the second period, our defence was scrambling at times. I have done a bit of work with the Forces, so I know what they are about."

Next up were the touring Springboks at Twickenham. The Baa-Baas selected a team featuring six Australians and five New Zealanders, and it was Wallabies Drew Mitchell and James O'Connor who did the initial damage with three first-half tries. South Africa hit back through Odwa Ndungane, but Italy's Quintin Geldenhuys went over in the corner to restore the invitational side's 14-point lead and a 26–20 victory was secured.

"It's a strange feeling when you hear the national anthem of the team you've coached, but I take my hat off to these guys," said the Baa-Baas coach Nick Mallett, who also coached South Africa between 1997 and 2000. "The first 30 minutes was some of the best rugby I've seen in the November Tests. We cut South Africa to pieces in the first half-hour and left a couple more tries out there. We got some great ball in the first half, but then South Africa put us under pressure in the second."

A 45–36 win over Richmond at the Athletic Ground in April maintained the Barbarians' unblemished winning record, and seven days later they followed it up with a 43–35 success over Bedford in the 84th annual Mobbs Memorial match at Goldington Road to make it four wins from four.

England and Wales now stood between the Baa-Baas and a perfect record for the season. The English named a youthful-looking side for the non-cap clash at HQ, while the Baa-Baas were captained by Italian

No 8 Sergio Parisse, and the early exchanges strongly suggested it would be the home side celebrating at the final whistle.

Scores from Henry Trinder, Ugo Monye and James Simpson-Daniel eased the hosts into a 24–7 lead after just 26 minutes. The Barbarians rallied with four unanswered tries from Frédéric Michalak, Tim Visser, George Smith and Joe van Niekerk, but England hit back with a Tom Johnson score and, with the clock running down, the visitors trailed 32–31.

There was, however, enough time for one more crucial score, and it went to the Baa-Baas when Dutch wing Visser finished off an incisive move begun by Fijian substitute Joe Tekori in the last passage of play in the match. Ruan Pienaar converted and the Baa-Baas were 38–32 winners.

The final match of the Baa-Baas' season was equally dramatic as they crossed swords with Wales at the Millennium Stadium, and once again a last-minute score was to prove the difference between the two sides.

The home side opened the scoring when the recalled Gavin Henson provided the telling pass for wing George North to race over, but the visitors hit back through Tekori after Brock James had intercepted a wayward pass from Mike Phillips. Fijian flyer Isa Nacewa scored a second try for the Baa-Baas before Morgan Stoddard benefitted from a charge-down to reply for Wales.

Further scores from Parisse and powerful French centre Mathieu Bastareaud for the Barbarians and Phillips and Aled Brew for the Welsh kept the scoreboard ticking over, but the defining moment was yet to come.

It came in the final minute when substitute Willie Mason, playing in only his second game of rugby union, offloaded superbly in the tackle for Nacewa to race over from long range. James converted, and once again the last-gasp Baa-Baas were victorious, this time emerging 31–28 winners.

"Obviously Willie [Mason] is coming from a league background, and if you look at the two tries he set up they were typical league tries where you are running across people's faces and you get in the big right-hand offload," said Baa-Baas coach Dai Young.

"It's a big call to step up and play rugby union at the age of 31, but he certainly has the physicality, there is no doubt about that. He has the aptitude in both attack and defence, and it's just a matter of learning the game. You could see how excited he was just to get on the field. He sprinted onto the pitch, and he had a big part in that final 15 minutes or so."

BRITISH & IRISH LIONS INTERNATIONAL STATISTICS

MATCH RECORDS UP TO 31 OCTOBER 2011

MOST CONSECUTIVE TEST WINS

6	1891	SA 1, 2, 3,	1896 *SA* 1, 2, 3
3	1899	*A* 2, 3, 4	
3	1904	*A* 1, 2, 3	
3	1950	*A* 1, 2,	1955 *SA* 1
3	1974	*SA* 1, 2, 3	

MOST CONSECUTIVE TESTS WITHOUT DEFEAT

Matches	Wins	Draws	Period
6	6	0	1891 to 1896
6	4	2	1971 to 1974

MOST POINTS IN A MATCH

BY THE TEAM

Pts	Opponents	Venue	Year
31	Australia	Brisbane	1966
29	Australia	Brisbane	2001
28	S Africa	Pretoria	1974
28	S Africa	Johannesburg	2009
26	S Africa	Port Elizabeth	1974
25	S Africa	Cape Town	1997
25	Argentina	Cardiff	2005
25	S Africa	Pretoria	2009
24	Australia	Sydney	1950
24	Australia	Sydney	1959

BY A PLAYER

Pts	Player	Opponents	Venue	Year
20	J P Wilkinson	Argentina	Cardiff	2005
20	S M Jones	S Africa	Pretoria	2009
18	A J P Ward	S Africa	Cape Town	1980
18	A G Hastings	N Zealand	Christchurch	1993
18	J P Wilkinson	Australia	Sydney	2001
17	T J Kiernan	S Africa	Pretoria	1968
16	B L Jones	Australia	Brisbane	1950

MOST TRIES IN A MATCH

BY THE TEAM

Tries	Opponents	Venue	Year
5	Australia	Sydney	1950
5	S Africa	Johannesburg	1955
5	Australia	Sydney	1959
5	Australia	Brisbane	1966
5	S Africa	Pretoria	1974

BY A PLAYER

Tries	Player	Opponents	Venue	Year
2	A M Bucher	Australia	Sydney	1899
2	W Llewellyn	Australia	Sydney	1904
2	C D Aarvold	N Zealand	Christchurch	1930
2	J E Nelson	Australia	Sydney	1950
2	M J Price	Australia	Sydney	1959
2	M J Price	N Zealand	Dunedin	1959
2	D K Jones	Australia	Brisbane	1966
2	T G R Davies	N Zealand	Christchurch	1971
2	J J Williams	S Africa	Pretoria	1974
2	J J Williams	S Africa	Port Elizabeth	1974
2	T Croft	S Africa	Durban	2009
2	S M Williams	S Africa	Johannesburg	2009

MOST CONVERSIONS IN A MATCH

BY THE TEAM

Cons	Opponents	Venue	Year
5	Australia	Brisbane	1966
4	S Africa	Johannesburg	1955
3	Australia	Sydney	1950
3	Australia	Sydney	1959
3	Australia	Brisbane	2001
3	S Africa	Durban	2009

BY A PLAYER

Cons	Player	Opponents	Venue	Year
5	S Wilson	Australia	Brisbane	1966
4	A Cameron	S Africa	Johannesburg	1955
3	J P Wilkinson	Australia	Brisbane	2001
3	S M Jones	S Africa	Durban	2009

MOST PENALTIES IN A MATCH

BY THE TEAM

Pens	Opponents	Venue	Year
6	N Zealand	Christchurch	1993
6	Argentina	Cardiff	2005
5	S Africa	Pretoria	1968
5	S Africa	Cape Town	1980
5	Australia	Sydney	1989
5	S Africa	Cape Town	1997
5	S Africa	Durban	1997
5	S Africa	Pretoria	2009

BY A PLAYER

Pens	Player	Opponents	Venue	Year
6	A G Hastings	N Zealand	Christchurch	1993
6	J P Wilkinson	Argentina	Cardiff	2005
5	T J Kiernan	S Africa	Pretoria	1968
5	A J P Ward	S Africa	Cape Town	1980
5	A G Hastings	Australia	Sydney	1989
5	N R Jenkins	S Africa	Cape Town	1997
5	N R Jenkins	S Africa	Durban	1997
5	S M Jones	S Africa	Pretoria	2009

MOST DROPPED GOALS IN A MATCH

BY THE TEAM

Drops	Opponents	Venue	Year
2	S Africa	Port Elizabeth	1974

BY A PLAYER

Drops	Player	Opponents	Venue	Year
2	P Bennett	S Africa	Port Elizabeth	1974

CAREER RECORDS

MOST CAPPED PLAYERS

Caps	Player	Career Span
17	W J McBride	1962 to 1974
13	R E G Jeeps	1955 to 1962
12	C M H Gibson	1966 to 1971
12	G Price	1977 to 1983
10	A J F O'Reilly	1955 to 1959
10	R H Williams	1955 to 1959
10	G O Edwards	1968 to 1974

MOST CONSECUTIVE TESTS

Tests	Player	Span
15	W J McBride	1966 to 1974
12	C M H Gibson	1966 to 1971
12	G Price	1977 to 1983

MOST TESTS AS CAPTAIN

Tests	Captain	Span
6	A R Dawson	1959
6	M O Johnson	1997 to 2001

MOST POINTS IN TESTS

Points	Player	Tests	Career
67	J P Wilkinson	6	2001 to 2005
66	A G Hastings	6	1989 to 1993
53	S M Jones	6	2005 to 2009
44	P Bennett	8	1974 to 1977
41	N R Jenkins	4	1997 to 2001
35	T J Kiernan	5	1962 to 1968
30	S Wilson	5	1966
30	B John	5	1968 to 1971

MOST TRIES IN TESTS

Tries	Player	Tests	Career
6	A J F O'Reilly	10	1955 to 1959
5	J J Williams	7	1974 to 1977
4	W Llewellyn	4	1904
4	M J Price	5	1959

MOST CONVERSIONS IN TESTS

Cons	Player	Tests	Career
7	J P Wilkinson	6	2001 to 2005
7	S M Jones	6	2005 to 2009
6	S Wilson	5	1966
4	J F Byrne	4	1896
4	C Y Adamson	4	1899
4	B L Jones	3	1950
4	A Cameron	2	1955

MOST PENALTY GOALS IN TESTS

Penalties	Player	Tests	Career
20	A G Hastings	6	1989 to 1993
16	J P Wilkinson	6	2001 to 2005
13	N R Jenkins	4	1997 to 2001
12	S M Jones	6	2005 to 2009
11	T J Kiernan	5	1962 to 1968
10	P Bennett	8	1974 to 1977
7	S O Campbell	7	1980 to 1983

MOST DROPPED GOALS IN TESTS

Drops	Player	Tests	Career
2	P F Bush	4	1904
2	D Watkins	6	1966
2	B John	5	1968 to 1971
2	P Bennett	8	1974 to 1977
2	C R Andrew	5	1989 to 1993

SERIES RECORDS

RECORD	HOLDER	DETAIL
Most team points		79 in S Africa 1974
Most team tries		10 in S Africa 1955 & 1974
Most points by player	N R Jenkins	41 in S Africa 1997
Most tries by player	W Llewellyn	4 in Australia 1904
	J J Williams	4 in S Africa 1974

MAJOR TOUR RECORDS

RECORD	DETAIL	YEAR	PLACE
Most team points	842	1959	Australia, NZ & Canada
Most team tries	165	1959	Australia, NZ & Canada
Highest score & biggest win	116–10	2001	v W Australia President's XV
Most individual points	188 by B John	1971	Australia & N Zealand
Most individual tries	22 by A J F O'Reilly	1959	Australia, NZ & Canada
Most points in match	37 by A G B Old	1974 v SW Districts	Mossel Bay, S Africa
Most tries in match	6 by D J Duckham	1971 v W Coast/Buller	Greymouth, N Zealand
	6 by J J Williams	1974 v SW Districts	Mossel Bay, S Africa

MISCELLANEOUS RECORDS

RECORD	HOLDER	DETAIL
Longest Test Career	W J McBride	13 seasons, 1962–1974
Youngest Test Cap	A J F O'Reilly	19 yrs 91 days in 1955
Oldest Test Cap	N A Back	36 yrs 160 days in 2005

BRITISH & IRISH LIONS INTERNATIONAL PLAYERS (UP TO 31 OCTOBER 2011)

From 1891 onwards.

* Indicates that the player was uncapped at the time of his first Lions Test but was subsequently capped by his country.

Aarvold, C D (Cambridge U, Blackheath and England) 1930 NZ 1, 2, 3, 4, A
Ackerman, R A (London Welsh and Wales) 1983 NZ 1, 4 (R)
Ackford, P J (Harlequins and England) 1989 A 1, 2, 3
Adamson, C Y (Durham City) 1899 A 1, 2, 3, 4
Alexander, R (NIFC and Ireland) 1938 SA 1, 2, 3
Andrew, C R (Wasps and England) 1989 A 2, 3, 1993 NZ 1, 2, 3
Arneil, R J (Edinburgh Acads and Scotland) 1968 SA 1, 2, 3, 4
Archer, H A (Guy's H and *England) 1908 NZ 1, 2, 3
Ashcroft, A (Waterloo and England) 1959 A 1, NZ 2
Aston, R L (Cambridge U and England) 1891 SA 1, 2, 3
Ayre-Smith, A (Guy's H) 1899 A 1, 2, 3, 4
Back, N A (Leicester and England) 1997 SA 2(R), 3, 2001 A 2, 3, 2005 NZ 1
Bainbridge, S J (Gosforth and England) 1983 NZ 3, 4
Baird, G R T (Kelso and Scotland) 1983 NZ 1, 2, 3, 4
Baker, A M (Newport and Wales) 1910 SA 3
Baker, D G S (Old Merchant Taylors' and England) 1955 SA 3, 4
Balshaw, I R (Bath and England) 2001 A 1(R), 2(R), 3(R)
Bassett, J A (Penarth and Wales) 1930 NZ 1, 2, 3, 4, A
Bateman, A G (Richmond and Wales) 1997 SA 3(R)
Bayfield, M C (Northampton and England) 1993 NZ 1, 2, 3
Beamish, G R (Leicester, RAF and Ireland) 1930 NZ 1, 2, 3, 4, A
Beattie, J R (Glasgow Acads and Scotland) 1983 NZ 2(R)
Beaumont, W B (Fylde and England) 1977 NZ 2, 3, 4, 1980 SA 1, 2, 3, 4
Bebb, D I E (Swansea and Wales) 1962 SA 2, 3, 1966 A 1, 2, NZ 1, 2, 3, 4
Bedell-Sivright, D R (Cambridge U and Scotland) 1904 A 1
Bell, S P (Cambridge U) 1896 SA 2, 3, 4
Belson, F C (Bath) 1899 A 1
Bennett, P (Llanelli and Wales) 1974 SA 1, 2, 3, 4, 1977 NZ 1, 2, 3, 4
Bentley, J (Newcastle and England) 1997 SA 2, 3
Bevan, J C (Cardiff Coll of Ed, Cardiff and Wales) 1971 NZ 1
Bevan, T S (Swansea and Wales) 1904 A 1, 2, 3, NZ
Black, A W (Edinburgh U and Scotland) 1950 NZ 1, 2
Black, B H (Oxford U, Blackheath and England) 1930 NZ 1, 2, 3, 4, A
Blakiston, A F (Northampton and England) 1924 SA 1, 2, 3, 4
Bowcott, H M (Cambridge U, Cardiff and Wales) 1930 NZ 1, 2, 3, 4, A
Bowe, T J (Ospreys and Ireland) 2009 SA 1, 2, 3
Boyd, C A (Dublin U and *Ireland) 1896 SA 1
Boyle, C V (Dublin U and Ireland) 1938 SA 2, 3
Brand, T N (NIFC and *Ireland) 1924 SA 1, 2
Bresnihan, F P K (UC Dublin and Ireland) 1968 SA 1, 2, 4
Bromet, E (Cambridge U) 1891 SA 2, 3
Bromet, W E (Oxford U and England) 1891 SA 1, 2, 3
Brophy, N H (UC Dublin and Ireland) 1962 SA 1, 4
Brown, G L (W of Scotland and Scotland) 1971 NZ 3, 4, 1974 SA 1, 2, 3, 1977 NZ 2, 3, 4
Bucher, A M (Edinburgh Acads and Scotland) 1899 A 1, 3, 4
Budge, G M (Edinburgh Wands and Scotland) 1950 NZ 4
Bulger, L Q (Lansdowne and Ireland) 1896 SA 1, 2, 3, 4
Bulloch, G C (Glasgow and Scotland) 2001 A l(t), 2005 NZ 3(R)
Burcher, D H (Newport and Wales) 1977 NZ 3
Burnell, A P (London Scottish and Scotland) 1993 NZ 1
Bush, P F (Cardiff and *Wales) 1904 A 1, 2, 3, NZ
Butterfield, J (Northampton and England) 1955 SA 1, 2, 3, 4
Byrne, J F (Moseley and England) 1896 SA 1, 2, 3, 4
Byrne, J S (Leinster and Ireland) 2005 Arg, NZ 1, 2(R), 3
Byrne, L M (Ospreys and Wales) 2009 SA 1
Calder, F (Stewart's-Melville FP and Scotland) 1989 A 1, 2, 3
Calder, J H (Stewart's-Melville FP and Scotland) 1983 NZ 3
Cameron, A (Glasgow HSFP and Scotland) 1955 SA 1, 2
Campbell, S O (Old Belvedere and Ireland) 1980 SA 2(R), 3, 4, 1983 NZ 1, 2, 3, 4
Campbell-Lamerton, M J (Halifax, Army and Scotland) 1962 SA 1, 2, 3, 4, 1966 A 1, 2, NZ 1, 3
Carey, W J (Oxford U) 1896 SA 1, 2, 3, 4
Carleton, J (Orrell and England) 1980 SA 1, 2, 4, 1983 NZ 2, 3, 4
Carling, W D C (Harlequins and England) 1993 NZ 1
Catt, M J (Bath and England) 1997 SA 3
Cave, W T C (Cambridge U and *England) 1903 SA 1, 2, 3
Chalmers, C M (Melrose and Scotland) 1989 A 1
Chapman, F E (Westoe, W Hartlepool and *England) 1908 NZ 3
Charvis, C L (Swansea and Wales) 2001 A 1(R), 3(R)
Clarke, B B (Bath and England) 1993 NZ 1, 2, 3
Clauss, P R A (Oxford U and Scotland) 1891 SA 1, 2, 3
Cleaver, W B (Cardiff and Wales) 1950 NZ 1, 2, 3
Clifford, T (Young Munster and Ireland) 1950 NZ 1, 2, 3, A 1, 2
Clinch, A D (Dublin U and Ireland) 1896 SA 1, 2, 3, 4
Cobner, T J (Pontypool and Wales) 1977 NZ 1, 2, 3
Colclough, M J (Angoulême and England) 1980 SA 1, 2, 3, 4, 1983 NZ 1, 2, 3, 4
Collett, G F (Cheltenham) 1903 SA 1, 2, 3
Connell, G C (Trinity Acads and Scotland) 1968 SA 4
Cookson, G (Manchester) 1899 A 1, 2, 3, 4
Cooper, G J (Newport Gwent Dragons and Wales) 2005 Arg
Corry, M E (Leicester and England) 2001 A 1, 2(t+R), 3, 2005 Arg, NZ 1, 2(R), 3(R)
Cotton, F E (Loughborough Colls, Coventry and England) 1974 SA 1, 2, 3, 4, 1977 NZ 2, 3, 4
Coulman, M J (Moseley and England) 1968 SA 3
Cove-Smith, R (Old Merchant Taylors' and England) 1924 SA 1, 2, 3, 4
Cowan, R C (Selkirk and Scotland) 1962 SA 4
Crean, T J (Wanderers and Ireland) 1896 SA 1, 2, 3, 4
Croft, T R (Leicester and England) 2009 SA 1, 2, 3(t&R)
Cromey, G E (Queen's U, Belfast and Ireland) 1938 SA 3
Crowther, S N (Lennox) 1904 A 1, 2, 3, NZ
Cueto, M J (Sale and England) 2005 NZ 3
Cunningham, W A (Lansdowne and Ireland) 1924 SA 3
Cusiter, C P (Borders and Scotland) 2005 Arg (R)
Dallaglio, L B N (Wasps and England) 1997 SA 1, 2, 3
Dancer, G T (Bedford) 1938 SA 1, 2, 3
D'Arcy, G (Leinster and Ireland) 2005 Arg
Davey, J (Redruth and England) 1908 NZ 1
Davidson, I G (NIFC and Ireland) 1903 SA 1
Davidson, J W (London Irish and Ireland) 1997 SA 1, 2, 3
Davies, C (Cardiff and Wales) 1950 NZ 4
Davies, D M (Somerset Police and Wales) 1950 NZ 3, 4, A 1
Davies, D S (Hawick and Scotland) 1924 SA 1, 2, 3, 4
Davies, H J (Newport and Wales) 1924 SA 2
Davies, T G R (Cardiff, London Welsh and Wales) 1968 SA 3, 1971 NZ 1, 2, 3, 4
Davies, T J (Llanelli and Wales) 1959 NZ 2, 4

Davies, T M (London Welsh, Swansea and Wales) 1971 NZ 1, 2, 3, 4, 1974 SA 1, 2, 3, 4
Davies, W G (Cardiff and Wales) 1980 SA 2
Davies, W P C (Harlequins and England) 1955 SA 1, 2, 3
Dawes, S J (London Welsh and Wales) 1971 NZ 1, 2, 3, 4
Dawson, A R (Wanderers and Ireland) 1959 A 1, 2, NZ 1, 2, 3, 4
Dawson, M J S (Northampton, Wasps and England) 1997 SA 1, 2, 3, 2001 A 2(R), 3, 2005 NZ 1(R), 3(R)
Dibble, R (Bridgwater Albion and England) 1908 NZ 1, 2, 3
Dixon, P J (Harlequins and England) 1971 NZ 1, 2, 4
Dobson, D D (Oxford U and England) 1904 A 1, 2, 3, NZ
Dodge, P W (Leicester and England) 1980 SA 3, 4
Dooley, W A (Preston Grasshoppers and England) 1989 A 2, 3
Doran, G P (Lansdowne and Ireland) 1899 A 1, 2
Down, P J (Bristol and *England) 1908 NZ 1, 2, 3
Doyle, M G (Blackrock Coll and Ireland) 1968 SA 1
Drysdale, D (Heriot's FP and Scotland) 1924 SA 1, 2, 3, 4
Duckham, D J (Coventry and England) 1971 NZ 2, 3, 4
Duggan, W P (Blackrock Coll and Ireland) 1977 NZ 1, 2, 3, 4
Duff, P L (Glasgow Acads and Scotland) 1938 SA 2, 3
Easterby, S H (Llanelli Scarlets and Ireland) 2005 NZ 2, 3
Edwards, G O (Cardiff and Wales) 1968 SA 1, 2, 1971 NZ 1, 2, 3, 4, 1974 SA 1, 2, 3, 4
Edwards, R W (Malone and Ireland) 1904 A 2, 3, NZ
Ellis, H A (Leicester and England) 2009 SA 3(R)
Evans, G (Maesteg and Wales) 1983 NZ 3, 4
Evans, G L (Newport and Wales) 1977 NZ 2, 3, 4
Evans, I C (Llanelli and Wales) 1989 A 1, 2, 3, 1993 NZ 1, 2 3, 1997 SA 1
Evans, R T (Newport and Wales) 1950 NZ 1, 2, 3, 4, A 1, 2
Evans, T P (Swansea and Wales) 1977 NZ 1
Evans, W R (Cardiff and Wales) 1959 A 2, NZ 1, 2, 3
Evers, G V (Moseley) 1899 A 2, 3, 4
Farrell, J L (Bective Rangers and Ireland) 1930 NZ 1, 2, 3, 4, A
Faull, J (Swansea and Wales) 1959 A 1, NZ 1, 3, 4
Fenwick, S P (Bridgend and Wales) 1977 NZ 1, 2, 3, 4
Fitzgerald, C F (St Mary's Coll and Ireland) 1983 NZ 1, 2, 3, 4
Fitzgerald, L M (Leinster and Ireland) 2009 SA 2
Flutey, R J (Wasps and England) 2009 SA 3
Ford, R W (Edinburgh and Scotland) 2009 SA 3(R)
Foster, A R (Queen's U, Belfast and Ireland) 1910 SA 1, 2
Francombe, J S (Manchester) 1899 A 1
Gabe, R T (Cardiff and Wales) 1904 A 1, 2, 3, NZ
Gibbs, I S (Swansea and Wales) 1993 NZ 2, 3, 1997 SA 1, 2, 3
Gibbs, R A (Cardiff and Wales) 1908 NZ 1, 2
Gibson, C M H (Cambridge U, NIFC and Ireland) 1966 NZ 1, 2, 3, 4, 1968 SA 1(R), 2, 3, 4, 1971 NZ 1, 2, 3, 4
Gibson, G R (Northern and England) 1899 A 1, 2, 3, 4
Gibson, T A (Cambridge U and *England) 1903 SA 1, 2, 3
Giles, J L (Coventry and England) 1938 SA 1, 3
Gillespie, J I (Edinburgh Acads and Scotland) 1903 SA 1, 2, 3
Gould, J H (Old Leysians) 1891 SA 1
Gravell, R W R (Llanelli and Wales) 1980 SA 1(R), 2, 3, 4
Graves, C R A (Wanderers and Ireland) 1938 SA 1, 3
Gray, H G S (Scottish Trials) 1899 A 1, 2
Greenwood, J T (Dunfermline and Scotland) 1955 SA 1, 2, 3, 4
Greenwood, W J H (Harlequins and England) 2005 NZ 1(R), 3
Greig, L L (US and *Scotland) 1903 SA 1, 2, 3
Grewcock, D J (Bath and England) 2001 A 1, 2, 3, 2005 Arg, NZ 1(R)
Grieve, C F (Oxford U and Scotland) 1938 SA 2, 3
Griffiths, G M (Cardiff and Wales) 1955 SA 2, 3, 4
Griffiths, V M (Newport and Wales) 1924 SA 3, 4
Guscott, J C (Bath and England) 1989 A 2, 3, 1993 NZ 1, 2, 3, 1997 SA 1, 2, 3
Hall, M R (Bridgend and Wales) 1989 A 1
Hammond, J (Cambridge U, Blackheath) 1891 SA 1, 2, 3, 1896 SA 2, 4
Hancock, P F (Blackheath and England) 1891 SA 1, 2, 3, 1896 SA 1, 2, 3, 4
Hancock, P S (Richmond and *England) 1903 SA 1, 2, 3
Handford, F G (Manchester and England) 1910 SA 1, 2, 3
Harding, A F (London Welsh and Wales) 1904 A 1, 2, 3, NZ, 1908 NZ 1, 2, 3
Harding, R (Cambridge U, Swansea and Wales) 1924 SA 2, 3, 4
Harris, S W (Blackheath and England) 1924 SA 3, 4
Harrison, E M (Guy's H) 1903 SA 1
Hastings, A G (London Scottish, Watsonians and Scotland) 1989 A 1, 2, 3, 1993 NZ 1, 2, 3
Hastings, S (Watsonians and Scotland) 1989 A 2, 3
Hay, B H (Boroughmuir and Scotland) 1980 SA 2, 3, 4
Hayes, J J (Munster and Ireland) 2005 Arg, 2009 SA 3(R)
Hayward, D J (Newbridge and Wales) 1950 NZ 1, 2, 3
Healey, A S (Leicester and England) 1997 SA 2(R), 3(R)
Heaslip, J P R (Leinster and Ireland) 2009 SA 1, 2, 3
Henderson, N J (Queen's U, Belfast, NIFC and Ireland) 1950 NZ3
Henderson, R A J (Wasps and Ireland) 2001 A 1, 2, 3
Henderson, R G (Northern and Scotland) 1924 SA 3, 4
Hendrie, K G P (Heriot's FP and Scotland) 1924 SA 2
Henson, G L (Neath-Swansea Ospreys and Wales) 2005 NZ 2
Hewitt, D (Queen's U, Belfast, Instonians and Ireland) 1959 A 1, 2, NZ 1, 3, 4, 1962 SA 4
Hickie, D A (Leinster and Ireland) 2005 Arg
Higgins, R (Liverpool and England) 1955 SA 1
Hill, R A (Saracens and England) 1997 SA 1, 2, 2001 A 1, 2, 2005 NZ 1
Hind, G R (Guy's H and *England) 1908 NZ 2, 3
Hinshelwood, A J W (London Scottish and Scotland) 1966 NZ 2, 4, 1968 SA 2
Hodgson, J McD (Northern and *England) 1930 NZ 1, 3
Holmes, T D (Cardiff and Wales) 1983 NZ 1
Hopkins, R (Maesteg and Wales) 1971 NZ 1(R)
Horgan, S P (Leinster and Ireland) 2005 Arg (R), NZ 1(R), 2(R), 3(R)
Horrocks-Taylor, J P (Leicester and England) 1959 NZ 3
Horton, A L (Blackheath and England) 1968 SA 2, 3, 4
Howard, W G (Old Birkonians) 1938 SA 1
Howie, R A (Kirkcaldy and Scotland) 1924 SA 1, 2, 3, 4
Howley, R (Cardiff and Wales) 2001 A 1, 2
Hulme, F C (Birkenhead Park and England) 1904 A 1
Irvine, A R (Heriot's FP and Scotland) 1974 SA 3, 4, 1977 NZ 1, 2, 3, 4, 1980 SA 2, 3, 4
Irwin, D G (Instonians and Ireland) 1983 NZ 1, 2, 4
Isherwood, G A M (Old Alleynians, Sale) 1910 SA 1, 2, 3
Jackett, E J (Falmouth, Leicester and England) 1908 NZ 1, 2, 3
Jackson, F S (Leicester) 1908 NZ 1
Jackson, P B (Coventry and England) 1959 A 1, 2, NZ 1, 3, 4
James, D R (Llanelli and Wales) 2001 A 1, 2, 3
Jarman, H (Newport and Wales) 1910 SA 1, 2, 3
Jarman, J W (Bristol and *England) 1899 A 1, 2, 3, 4
Jeeps, R E G (Northampton and *England) 1955 SA 1, 2, 3, 4, 1959 A 1, 2, NZ 1, 2, 3, 1962 SA 1, 2, 3, 4
Jenkins, G D (Cardiff Blues and Wales) 2005 NZ 1, 2, 3, 2009 SA 1, 2
Jenkins, N R (Pontypridd, Cardiff and Wales) 1997 SA 1, 2, 3, 2001 A 2(R)
Jenkins, V G J (Oxford U, London Welsh and Wales) 1938 SA 1
John, B (Cardiff and Wales) 1968 SA 1, 1971 NZ 1, 2, 3, 4
John, E R (Neath and Wales) 1950 NZ 1, 2, 3, 4, A 1, 2
Johnson, M O (Leicester and England) 1993 NZ 2, 3, 1997 SA 1, 2, 3, 2001 A 1, 2, 3
Johnston, R (Wanderers and Ireland) 1896 SA 1, 2, 3
Jones, A R (Ospreys and Wales) 2009 SA 1(R), 2
Jones, A-W (Ospreys and Wales) 2009 SA 1, 2(R), 3(R)
Jones, B L (Devonport Services, Llanelli and Wales) 1950 NZ 4, A 1, 2
Jones, D K (Llanelli, Cardiff and Wales) 1962 SA 1, 2, 3, 1966 A 1, 2, NZ 1
Jones, E L (Llanelli and *Wales) 1938 SA 1, 3
Jones, I E (Llanelli and Wales) 1930 NZ 1, 2, 3, 4, A
Jones, J P "Jack" (Newport and *Wales) 1908 NZ 1, 2, 3, 1910 SA 1, 2, 3
Jones J P "Tuan" (Guy's H and *Wales) 1908 NZ 2, 3
Jones K D (Cardiff and Wales) 1962 SA 1, 2, 3, 4
Jones K J (Newport and Wales) 1950 NZ 1, 2, 4
Jones R N (Swansea and Wales) 1989 A 1, 2, 3
Jones, R P (Neath-Swansea Ospreys and Wales) 2005 NZ 1(R), 2, 3
Jones, S M (Clermont Auvergne, Llanelli Scarlets and Wales) 2005 NZ 1, 2(R), 3, 2009 SA 1, 2, 3
Jones S T (Pontypool and Wales) 1983 NZ 2, 3, 4
Judkins, W (Coventry) 1899 A 2, 3, 4
Kay, B J (Leicester and England) 2005 Arg (R), NZ 1
Keane, M I (Lansdowne and Ireland) 1977 NZ 1

Kearney, R D J (Leinster and Ireland) 2009 SA 1(R), 2, 3
Kennedy, K W (CIYMS, London Irish and Ireland) 1966 A 1, 2, NZ 1, 4
Kiernan, M J (Dolphin and Ireland) 1983 NZ 2, 3, 4
Kiernan, T J (Cork Const and Ireland) 1962 SA 3, 1968 SA 1, 2, 3, 4
Kininmonth, P W (Oxford U, Richmond and Scotland) 1950 NZ 1, 2, 4
Kinnear, R M (Heriot's FP and *Scotland) 1924 SA1, 2, 3, 4
Kyle, J W (Queen's U, Belfast, NIFC and Ireland) 1950 NZ 1, 2, 3, 4, A 1, 2
Kyrke, G V (Marlborough N) 1908 NZ 1
Laidlaw, F A L (Melrose and Scotland) 1966 NZ 2, 3
Laidlaw, R J (Jedforest and Scotland) 1983 NZ 1(R), 2, 3, 4
Lamont, R A (Instonians and Ireland) 1966 NZ 1, 2, 3, 4
Lane, M F (UC Cork and Ireland) 1950 NZ 4, A 2
Larter, P J (Northampton, RAF and England) 1968 SA 2
Laxon, H (Cambridge U) 1908 NZ 1
Leonard, J (Harlequins and England) 1993 NZ 2, 3, 1997 SA 1(R), 2001 A 1(R), 2(R)
Lewis, R A (Abertillery and Wales) 1966 NZ 2, 3, 4
Lewsey, O J (Wasps and England) 2005 NZ 1, 2, 3
Llewellyn, W (Llwynypia, Newport and Wales) 1904 A 1, 2, 3, NZ
Lynch, J F (St Mary's Coll and Ireland) 1971 NZ 1, 2, 3, 4
McBride, W J (Ballymena and Ireland) 1962 SA 3, 4, 1966 NZ 2, 3, 4, 1968 SA 1, 2, 3, 4, 1971 NZ 1, 2, 3, 4, 1974 SA 1, 2, 3, 4
Macdonald, R (Edinburgh U and Scotland) 1950 NZ 1, A 2
McEvedy, P F (Guy's H) 1904 A 2, 3, NZ, 1908 NZ 2, 3
McFadyean, C W (Moseley and England) 1966 NZ 1, 2, 3, 4
McGeechan, I R (Headingley and Scotland) 1974 SA 1, 2, 3, 4, 1977 NZ 1, 2, 3(R), 4
McGown, T M W (NIFC and Ireland) 1899 A 1, 2, 3, 4
McKay, J W (Queen's U, Belfast and Ireland) 1950 NZ 1, 2, 3, 4, A 1, 2
McKibbin, H R (Queen's U, Belfast and Ireland) 1938 SA 1, 2, 3
Mackie, O G (Wakefield Trinity and *England) 1896 SA 1, 2, 3, 4
Maclagan, W E (London Scottish and Scotland) 1891 SA 1, 2, 3
McLauchlan, J (Jordanhill and Scotland) 1971 NZ 1, 2, 3, 4, 1974 SA 1, 2, 3, 4
McLeod, H F (Hawick and Scotland) 1959 A 1, 2, NZ 1, 2, 3, 4
McLoughlin, R J (Gosforth, Blackrock Coll and Ireland) 1966 A 1, 2, NZ, 4
Macmillan, R G (London Scottish and Scotland) 1891 SA 1, 2, 3
MacNeill, H P (Oxford U and Ireland) 1983 NZ 1, 2, 4 (R)
Macpherson, N C (Newport and Scotland) 1924 SA 1, 2, 3, 4
Macrae, D J (St Andrew's U and Scotland) 1938 SA 1
McVicker, J (Collegians and Ireland) 1924 SA 1, 3, 4
Magee, A M (Bective R and Ireland) 1896 SA 1, 2, 3, 4
Magee, J M (Bective R) 1896 SA 2, 4
Marques, R W D (Harlequins and England) 1959 A 2, NZ 2
Marsden-Jones, D (London Welsh and Wales) 1924 SA 1, 2
Marshall, H (Blackheath and *England) 1891 SA 2, 3
Martin, A J (Aberavon and Wales) 1977 NZ 1
Martelli, E (Dublin U) 1899 A 1
Martindale, S A (Kendal and England) 1930 A
Massey, B F (Hull and ER) 1904 A 3
Matthews, J (Cardiff and Wales) 1950 NZ 1, 2, 3, 4, A 1, 2
Maxwell, R B (Birkenhead Park) 1924 SA 1
Mayfield, W E (Cambridge U) 1891 SA 2, 3
Mayne, R B (Queen's U, Belfast and Ireland) 1938 SA 1, 2, 3
Meares, A W D (Dublin U and *Ireland) 1896 SA 3, 4
Mears, L A (Bath and England) 2009 SA 1
Meredith, B V (Newport and Wales) 1955 SA 1, 2, 3, 4, 1962 SA 1, 2, 3, 4
Meredith, C C (Neath and Wales) 1955 SA 1, 2, 3, 4
Millar, S (Ballymena and Ireland) 1959 A 1, 2, NZ 2, 1962 SA 1, 2, 3, 4, 1968 SA 1, 2
Miller, E R P (Leicester and England) 1997 SA 2(R)
Milliken, R A (Bangor and Ireland) 1974 SA 1, 2, 3, 4
Milne, K S (Heriot's FP and Scotland) 1993 NZ 1
Mitchell, W G (Richmond and England) 1891 SA 1, 2, 3
Monye, Y C C (Harlequins and England) 2009 SA 1, 3
Moody, L W (Leicester and England) 2005 Arg, NZ 2, 3
Moore, B C (Nottingham, Harlequins and England) 1989 A 1, 2, 3, 1993 NZ 2, 3
Morgan, C I (Cardiff and Wales) 1955 SA 1, 2, 3, 4
Morgan, D W (Stewart's-Melville FP and Scotland) 1977 NZ 3(R), 4
Morgan, E (London Welsh, Guy's H and Wales) 1904 A 1, 2, 3, NZ
Morgan, E (Swansea and *Wales) 1908 NZ 2, 3
Morgan, G J (Clontarf and Ireland) 1938 SA 3
Morgan, H J (Abertillery and Wales) 1959 NZ.3, 4, 1962 SA 2, 3
Morgan, M E (Swansea and Wales) 1938 SA 1, 2
Morgan, W L (Cardiff and *Wales) 1908 NZ 2, 3
Morley, J C (Newport and Wales) 1930 NZ 1, 2, 3
Morris, C D (Orrell and England) 1993 NZ 1, 2, 3
Morris, D R (Swansea and Wales) 2001 A 3(R)
Morrison, M C (Royal HSFP and Scotland) 1903 SA 1, 2, 3
Mortimer, W (Marlborough N and *England) 1896 SA 1, 2, 3, 4
Mulcahy, W A (UC Dublin and Ireland) 1959 A 1, NZ 4, 1962 SA 1, 2, 3, 4
Mullen, K D (Old Belvedere and Ireland) 1950 NZ 1, 2, A 2
Mulligan, A A (Wanderers, London Irish and Ireland) 1959 NZ 4
Mullin, B J (London Irish and Ireland) 1989 A 1
Mullineux, M (Blackheath) 1896 SA 1, 1899 A 1
Mullins, R C (Oxford U) 1896 SA 1, 3
Murphy, G E A (Leicester and Ireland) 2005 Arg, NZ 3
Murphy, N A A (Cork Const and Ireland) 1959 A 2, NZ 1, 2, 4, 1966 A 1, 2, NZ 2, 3
Murray, P F (Wanderers and Ireland) 1930 NZ 1, 2, 4, A
Neale, M E (Bristol, Blackheath and *England) 1910 SA 1, 2, 3
Neary, A (Broughton Park and England) 1977 NZ 4
Neill, R M (Edinburgh Acads and Scotland) 1903 SA 2, 3
Nelson, J E (Malone and Ireland) 1950 NZ 3, 4, A 1, 2
Nicholls, E G (Cardiff and Wales) 1899 A 1, 2, 3, 4
Nicholson, B E (Harlequins and England) 1938 SA 2
Nicholson, E T (Birkenhead Park and *England) 1899 A 3, 4
Norris, C H (Cardiff and Wales) 1966 NZ 1, 2, 3
Norster, R L (Cardiff and Wales) 1983 NZ 1, 2, 1989 A 1
Novis, A L (Blackheath and England) 1930 NZ 2, 4, A
O'Brien, A B (Guy's H) 1904 A 1, 2, 3, NZ
O'Callaghan, D P (Munster and Ireland) 2005 Arg, NZ 2, 3, 2009 SA 1(R)
O'Connell, P J (Munster and Ireland) 2005 NZ 1, 2, 3, 2009 SA 1, 2, 3
O'Donnell, R C (St Mary's Coll and Ireland) 1980 SA I
O'Driscoll, B G (Blackrock Coll, Leinster and Ireland) 2001 A 1, 2, 3, 2005 NZ 1, 2009 SA 1, 2
O'Driscoll, J B (London Irish and Ireland) 1980 SA 1, 2, 3, 4, 1983 NZ 2, 4
O'Gara, R J R (Munster and Ireland) 2005 NZ 3(R), 2009 SA 2(R)
O'Neill, H O'H (Queen's U, Belfast and Ireland) 1930 NZ 1, 2, 3, 4, A
O'Reilly, A J F (Old Belvedere and Ireland) 1955 SA 1, 2, 3, 4, 1959 A 1, 2, NZ 1, 2, 3, 4
Oldham, W L (Coventry and England) 1908 NZ 1
Orr, P A (Old Wesley and Ireland) 1977 NZ 1
O'Shea, J P (Cardiff and Wales) 1968 SA 1
Owen, M J (Newport Gwent Dragons and Wales) 2005 Arg
Parker, D S (Swansea and Wales) 1930 NZ 1, 2, 3, 4, A
Pask, A E I (Abertillery and Wales) 1962 SA 1, 2, 3, 1966 A 1, 2, NZ 1, 3, 4
Patterson, C S (Instonians and Ireland) 1980 SA 1, 2, 3
Patterson, W M (Sale and *England) 1959 NZ 2
Paxton, I A M (Selkirk and Scotland) 1983 NZ 1, 2, 3, 4
Pedlow, A C (CIYMS and Ireland) 1955 SA 1, 4
Peel, D J (Llanelli Scarlets and Wales) 2005 NZ 1, 2, 3
Perry, M B (Bath and England) 2001 A 1, 2, 3
Phillips, W M (Ospreys and Wales) 2009 SA 1, 2, 3
Pillman, C H (Blackheath and England) 1910 SA 2, 3
Piper, O J S (Cork Const and Ireland) 1910 SA 1
Poole, H (Cardiff) 1930 NZ 3
Popplewell, N J (Greystones and Ireland) 1993 NZ 1, 2, 3
Preece, I (Coventry and England) 1950 NZ 1
Prentice, F D (Leicester and England) 1930 NZ 2, A
Price, B (Newport and Wales) 1966 A 1, 2, NZ 1, 4
Price, G (Pontypool and Wales) 1977 NZ 1, 2, 3, 4, 1980 SA 1, 2, 3, 4, 1983 NZ 1, 2, 3, 4
Price, M J (Pontypool and Wales) 1959 A 1, 2, NZ 1, 2, 3
Prosser, T R (Pontypool and Wales) 1959 NZ, 4
Pullin, J V (Bristol and England) 1968 SA 2, 3, 4, 1971 NZ 1, 2, 3, 4

Quinnell, D L (Llanelli and *Wales) 1971 NZ. 3, 1977 NZ 2, 3, 1980 SA 1, 2
Quinnell, L S (Llanelli and Wales) 2001 A 1, 2, 3
Ralston, C W (Richmond and England) 1974 SA 4
Reed, A I (Bath and Scotland) 1993 NZ 1
Rees, H E (Neath and *Wales) 1977 NZ 4
Rees, M (Llanelli Scarlets and Wales) 2009 SA 1(R), 2, 3
Reeve, J S R (Harlequins and England) 1930 NZ 1, 3, 4, A
Regan, M P (Bristol and England) 1997 SA 3
Reid, T E (Garryowen and Ireland) 1955 SA 2, 3
Renwick, J M (Hawick and Scotland) 1980 SA 1
Rew, H (Blackheath, Army and England) 1930 NZ 1, 2, 3, 4
Reynolds, F J (Old Cranleighans and England) 1938 SA 1, 2
Richards, D (Leicester and England) 1989 A 1, 2, 3, 1993 NZ 1, 2, 3
Richards, D S (Swansea and Wales) 1980 SA 1
Richards, M C R (Cardiff and Wales) 1968 SA 1, 3, 4
Richards, T J (Bristol and Australia) 1910 SA 1, 2
Rimmer, G (Waterloo and England) 1950 NZ 3
Ringland, T M (Ballymena and Ireland) 1983 NZ 1
Risman, A B W (Loughborough Colls and England) 1959 A 1, 2, NZ 1, 4
Ritson, J A S (Northern and *England) 1908 NZ 1
Robbie, J C (Greystones and Ireland) 1980 SA 4
Roberts, J H (Cardiff Blues and Wales) 2009 SA 1, 2
Robins, J D (Birkenhead Park and Wales) 1950 NZ 1, 2, 3, A 1, 2
Robins, R J (Pontypridd and Wales) 1955 SA 1, 2, 3, 4
Robinson, J T (Sale and England) 2001 A 1, 2, 3, 2005 NZ 1, 2
Rodber, T A K (Northampton and England) 1997 SA 1, 2
Rogers, D P (Bedford and England) 1962 SA 1, 4
Rogers, R J (Bath) 1904 NZ
Rotherham, A (Cambridge U and *England) 1891 SA 1, 2, 3
Rowlands, K A (Cardiff and Wales) 1962 SA 1, 2, 4
Rowntree, G C (Leicester and England) 2005 Arg, NZ 2(t+R), 3(R)
Rutherford, D (Gloucester and England) 1966 A 1
Rutherford, J Y (Selkirk and Scotland) 1983 NZ 3
Saunders, S M (Guy's H) 1904 A 1, 2
Savage, K F (Northampton and England) 1968 SA 1, 2, 3, 4
Scotland, K J F (Cambridge U, Heriot's FP and Scotland) 1959 A 1, 2, NZ 1, 3, 4
Scott, W P (West of Scotland and Scotland) 1903 SA 1, 2, 3
Sealy, J (Dublin U and *Ireland) 1896 SA 1, 2, 3, 4
Sharp, R A W (Oxford U, Redruth and England) 1962 SA 3, 4
Shaw, S D (Wasps and England) 2009 SA 2, 3
Sheridan, A J (Sale and England) 2009 SA 2(t&R), 3
Simpson, C (Cambridge U) 1891 SA 1
Skrimshire, R T (Newport and Wales) 1903 SA 1, 2, 3
Slattery, J F (Blackrock Coll and Ireland) 1974 SA 1, 2, 3, 4
Slemen, M A C (Liverpool and England) 1980 SA 1
Smith, A R (Edinburgh Wands, London Scottish and Scotland) 1962 SA 1, 2, 3
Smith, D F (Richmond and England) 1910 SA 1, 2, 3
Smith, D W C (London Scottish and Scotland) 1950 A 1
Smith, G K (Kelso and Scotland) 1959 A 1, 2, NZ 1, 3
Smith, I S (Oxford U, London Scottish and Scotland) 1924 SA 1, 2
Smith, O J (Leicester and England) 2005 Arg
Smith, T J (Watsonians, Northampton and Scotland) 1997 SA 1, 2, 3, 2001 A 1, 2, 3
Smith, T W (Leicester) 1908 NZ 2, 3
Smyth, R S (Dublin U and Ireland) 1903 SA 1, 2, 3
Smyth, T (Malone, Newport and Ireland) 1910 SA 2, 3
Sole, D M B (Edinburgh Acads and Scotland) 1989 A 1, 2, 3
Spong, R S (Old Millhillians and England) 1930 NZ 1, 2, 3, 4, A
Spoors, J A (Bristol) 1910 SA 1, 2, 3
Squire, J (Newport, Pontypool and Wales) 1977 NZ 4, 1980 SA 1, 2, 3, 4, 1983 NZ 1
Squires, P J (Harrogate and England) 1977 NZ 1
Stagg, P K (Oxford U, Sale and Scotland) 1968 SA 1, 3, 4
Stanger-Leathes, C F (Northern and *England) 1904 A 1
Steele, W C C (Bedford, RAF and Scotland) 1974 SA 1, 2
Stephens, I (Bridgend and Wales) 1983 NZ 1
Stephens, J R G (Neath and Wales) 1950 A 1, 2
Stevenson, R C (St Andrew's U and Scotland) 1910 SA 1, 2, 3
Stimpson, T R G (Newcastle and England) 1997 SA 3(R)
Stout, F M (Gloucester and England) 1899 A 1, 2, 3, 4, 1903 SA 1, 2, 3
Surtees, A A (Cambridge U) 1891 SA 1, 2, 3
Swannell, B I (Northampton and *Australia) 1899 A 2, 3, 4, 1904 A 1, 2, 3, NZ
Tait, A V (Newcastle and Scotland) 1997 SA 1, 2
Tanner, H (Swansea and Wales) 1938 SA 2
Taylor, A R (Cross Keys and Wales) 1938 SA 1, 2
Taylor, J (London Welsh and Wales) 1971 NZ 1, 2, 3, 4
Taylor, R B (Northampton and England) 1968 SA 1, 2, 3, 4
Teague, M C (Gloucester, Moseley and England) 1989 A 2, 3, 1993 NZ 2(t)
Tedford, A (Malone and Ireland) 1903 SA 1, 2, 3
Telfer, J W (Melrose and Scotland) 1966 A 1, 2, NZ 1, 2, 4, 1968 SA 2, 3, 4
Thomas, G (Toulouse and Wales) 2005 NZ 1, 2, 3
Thomas, M C (Devonport Services, Newport and Wales) 1950 NZ 2, 3, A 1, 1959 NZ 1
Thomas, R C C (Swansea and Wales) 1955 SA 3, 4
Thomas, W D (Llanelli and *Wales) 1966 NZ 2, 3, 1968 SA 3(R), 4, 1971 NZ 1, 2, 4 (R)
Thompson, C E K (Lancashire) 1899 A 2, 3, 4
Thompson, R (Cambridge U) 1891 SA 1, 2, 3
Thompson, R H (Instonians, London Irish and Ireland) 1955 SA 1, 2, 4
Thompson, S G (Northampton and England) 2005 Arg (R), NZ 1(R), 2
Timms, A B (Edinburgh U and Scotland) 1899 A 2, 3, 4
Todd, A F (Blackheath and *England) 1896 SA 1, 2, 3, 4
Townsend, G P J (Northampton and Scotland) 1997 SA 1, 2
Trail, D H (Guy's H) 1904 A 1, 2, 3, NZ
Travers, W H (Newport and Wales) 1938 SA 2, 3
Tucker, C C (Shannon and Ireland) 1980 SA 3, 4
Turner, J W C (Gala and Scotland) 1968 SA 1, 2, 3, 4
Underwood, R (RAF, Leicester and England) 1989 A 1, 2, 3, 1993 NZ 1, 2, 3
Underwood, T (Newcastle and England) 1997 SA 3
Unwin, E J (Rosslyn Park, Army and England) 1938 SA 1, 2
Uttley, R M (Gosforth and England) 1974 SA 1, 2, 3, 4
Vassall, H H (Blackheath and England) 1908 NZ 1, 2, 3
Vickery, P J (Gloucester, Wasps and England) 2001 A 1, 2, 3, 2009 SA 1, 3
Vile, T H (Newport and *Wales) 1904 A 2, 3, NZ
Voyce, A T (Gloucester and England) 1924 SA 3, 4
Waddell, G H (Cambridge U, London Scottish and Scotland) 1962 SA 1, 2
Waddell, H (Glasgow Acads and Scotland) 1924 SA 1, 2, 4
Wainwright, R I (Watsonians and Scotland) 1997 SA 3
Walker, E F (Lennox) 1903 SA 2, 3
Walker, S (Instonians and Ireland) 1938 SA 1, 2, 3
Wallace, D P (Munster and Ireland) 2009 SA 1, 2, 3(R)
Wallace, Jos (Wanderers and Ireland) 1903 SA 1, 2, 3
Wallace, P S (Saracens and Ireland) 1997 SA 1, 2, 3
Wallace, W (Percy Park) 1924 SA 1
Waller, P D (Newport and Wales) 1910 SA 1, 2, 3
Ward, A J P (Garryowen and Ireland) 1980 SA 1
Waters, J A (Selkirk and Scotland) 1938 SA 3
Watkins, D (Newport and Wales) 1966 A 1, 2, NZ 1, 2, 3, 4
Watkins, S J (Newport and Wales) 1966 A 1, 2, NZ 3
Webb, J (Abertillery and Wales) 1910 SA 1, 2, 3
Welsh, W B (Hawick and Scotland) 1930 NZ 4
Weston, M P (Richmond, Durham City and England) 1962 SA 1, 2, 3, 4, 1966 A 1, 2
Wheeler, P J (Leicester and England) 1977 NZ 2, 3, 4, 1980 SA 1, 2, 3, 4
White, D B (London Scottish and Scotland) 1989 A 1
White, J M (Leicester and England) 2005 Arg (R), NZ 1, 2, 3
Whitley, H (Northern and *England) 1924 SA 1, 3, 4
Whittaker, T S (Lancashire) 1891 SA 1, 2, 3
Wilkinson, J P (Newcastle and England) 2001 A 1, 2, 3, 2005 Arg, NZ 1, 2
Willcox, J G (Oxford U, Harlequins and England) 1962 SA 1, 2, 4
Williams, B L (Cardiff and Wales) 1950 NZ 2, 3, 4, A 1, 2
Williams, C (Swansea and Wales) 1980 SA 1, 2, 3, 4
Williams, D (Ebbw Vale and Wales) 1966 A 1, 2, NZ 1, 2, 4
Williams, D B (Cardiff and *Wales) 1977 NZ 1, 2, 3

Williams, J F (London Welsh and Wales) 1908 NZ 3
Williams, J J (Llanelli and Wales) 1974 SA 1, 2, 3, 4, 1977 NZ 1, 2, 3
Williams, J L (Cardiff and Wales) 1908 NZ 1, 2
Williams, J P R (London Welsh and Wales) 1971 NZ 1, 2, 3, 4, 1974 SA 1, 2, 3, 4
Williams, M E (Cardiff Blues and Wales) 2005 NZ 3(R), 2009 SA 1(R), 2(R), 3
Williams, R H (Llanelli and Wales) 1955 SA 1, 2, 3, 4, 1959 A 1, 2, NZ 1, 2, 3, 4
Williams, S H (Newport and *England) 1910 SA 1, 2, 3
Williams, S M (Ospreys and Wales) 2005 Arg, NZ 2, 2009 SA 2(R), 3
Williams, W O G (Swansea and Wales) 1955 SA 1, 2, 3, 4
Willis, W R (Cardiff and Wales) 1950 NZ 4, A 1, 2
Wilson, S (London Scottish and Scotland) 1966 A 2, NZ 1, 2, 3, 4
Windsor, R W (Pontypool and Wales) 1974 SA 1, 2, 3, 4, 1977 NZ 1
Winterbottom, P J (Headingley, Harlequins and England) 1983 NZ 1, 2, 3, 4, 1993 NZ, 1, 2, 3
Wood, B G M (Garryowen and Ireland) 1959 NZ 1, 3
Wood, K B (Leicester) 1910 SA 1, 3
Wood, K G M (Harlequins and Ireland) 1997 SA 1, 2, 2001 A 1, 2, 3
Woodward, C R (Leicester and England) 1980 SA 2, 3
Worsley, J P R (Wasps and England) 2009 SA3
Wotherspoon, W (Cambridge U and Scotland) 1891 SA 1
Young, A T (Cambridge U, Blackheath and England) 1924 SA 2
Young, D (Cardiff and Wales) 1989 A 1, 2, 3
Young, J (Harrogate, RAF and Wales) 1968 SA 1
Young, J R C (Oxford U, Harlequins and England) 1959 NZ 2
Young, R M (Queen's U, Belfast, Collegians and Ireland) 1966 A 1, 2, NZ 1, 1968 SA 3

Adrian Murrell/Getty Images

Sir Clive Woodward won two Lions caps in 1980.

Cross-Border Tournaments

LEINSTER CROWNED KINGS OF EUROPE

By Joe Schmidt, the winning coach

Michael Steele/Getty Images

Leinster are rightly thrilled with their second Heineken Cup trophy.

The opportunity simply to coach a side in the Heineken Cup is a huge privilege, but to lead Leinster to the trophy is something I will never forget for the rest of my life, let alone my coaching career in rugby.

It really is difficult to put into words exactly how it felt when the whistle went in the final at the Millennium Stadium, but safe to say it was a day of high emotion and, at times, complete despair.

The way we beat Northampton in the final, coming back from a 22–6 deficit at half-time, may have made for a great spectacle for the supporters who made the journey to Cardiff, and the huge television audience, but it took years off me and I would definitely have preferred a more straightforward and much less stressful victory. But then again, the Heineken Cup is one of rugby's great prizes, and I don't suppose it should ever come that easily.

I thought nothing could ever surpass Clermont finally lifting the Bouclier de Brennus in 2010 when I was coach at the Parc des Sports Marcel Michelin. The club had waited 100 years to be crowned champions of France for the first time, and the sense of relief when we finally laid that ghost to rest was enormous, but in terms of the sense of occasion, the match against the Saints in Cardiff was even bigger.

The atmosphere inside the Millennium Stadium was like nothing else I've ever experienced, and the contrast between the two halves of rugby verged on the ridiculous at times. I can confidently predict that there will not be a final like that again for many, many years.

Leinster's path to the final, I felt, was a difficult one and when we were drawn with my old team Clermont, plus Saracens and Racing Metro, in Pool Two, I knew instantly we would have a real fight on our hands. The reigning champions of France, the champions-elect of England and a dangerous Racing side all added up to a huge challenge and, although we did eventually top the group, it was not without a few wobbles along the way.

In fact, we were lucky to escape with the win against Sarries at Wembley in round two, and after losing to Clermont on the road next up we were in real danger of missing out on the business end of the tournament. To their credit, the boys rallied for three important wins on the bounce, but it proves how fine the margins can be in such a fiercely contested competition.

The knockout stages were certainly no easier and, after working so hard to ensure we had home advantage in the quarter-finals, I have to admit I was disappointed to get Leicester. They don't come more physical than the Tigers, and it was a brutally tough match which we were delighted to eventually win 17–10.

Our 32–23 semi-final victory over Toulouse was in contrast an altogether more expansive and open affair, and I thought it was a fantastic game of rugby. We knew it would be a different beast in comparison to the Leicester match, and we made the conscious decision before kick-off to take more risks because we felt it would be an encounter where fortune favoured the brave.

There were some breathtaking and prolonged passages of play, and I hope anyone who watched the match appreciated the way both teams tried to play the game.

The final was packed with drama, and Northampton simply bullied us physically in the first half. It was the onslaught we had talked about before the game, but we didn't practise what we preached, and the Saints deserved their three tries and 22–6 lead. They blew us off the pitch, and I'm sure they would have wanted the match to continue rather than coming in after the first 40 minutes.

A lot of people have asked me what was said in the dressing room at half-time to spark such a famous comeback. Obviously words were said, but I can honestly say that the mood among the players was calm, I'd say an air of quiet resolve, and no-one started throwing the tea cups around or banging the walls.

I was disappointed rather than angry with the performance in the first 40, and I talked about the need to keep hold of the ball and to improve our defence. I didn't need to shout, and everyone listened as we plotted our fightback.

Some of the players also had their say, and Johnny Sexton in particular stood up and told the team it was time for everyone to keep believing in themselves. Jamie Heaslip spoke well and Leo Cullen was the voice of reason, but I have to say Johnny was magnificent for such a young man, and he set exactly the right tone.

He certainly backed his words up with his actions in that second half, and he grew up in front of our eyes in the Millennium Stadium with his two tries, his kicking and his all-round performance. It was a wonderful example of a player grabbing a game by the scruff of the neck and refusing to accept defeat. He should be very proud of the way he performed.

Looking at the tournament more generally, I was impressed with the brand of quick, incisive rugby the Scarlets played in the competition, and the number of phases and the tempo both Clermont and Toulouse produced was really refreshing and entertaining.

In terms of the individuals on show, I thought Ben Foden was superb for Northampton. His try-saving tackle on Brian O'Driscoll in the final was incredible, he scored for his side at the other end, he was brilliant under the high ball and he really is now the complete player.

Soane Tonga'uiha was a huge presence in the scrum for the Saints in Cardiff. You might have to wait a long time to see such a destructive performance like that up front again, and the lock Courtney Lawes was a real presence around the park as well.

Elsewhere, the hooker Schalk Brits at Saracens really caught the eye. He's a solid enough scrummager but a real handful in the loose and he really led from the front.

As a Kiwi and having coached with the Blues in Auckland, I regularly get asked to compare the standard of the Heineken Cup and Super Rugby and my answer is always the same – it's like comparing apples and oranges.

To my mind, they are incomparable because they're played on such different surfaces and at different times of the year, and this inevitably means the two tournaments will produce very different styles of rugby.

A popular view is Super Rugby teams are generally more ambitious and more adventurous, but I think that does a disservice to the Heineken Cup sides who do try and play an expansive game. There's no difference in the mind set, it's simply that European pitches in the middle of winter make it harder to execute.

And in terms of the spectacle, it's impossible to deny that the Heineken Cup is great viewing. The final was unforgettable, but there were more great games earlier in the competition, and the way that Aironi pinched a win for Italy and the fact Sarries, who went on to win the Premiership in England, finished bottom of the pool just goes to prove how unpredictable the tournament can be.

Stu Forster/Getty Images

Four-times champions Toulouse only made it as far as the semi-finals this time around.

HEINEKEN CUP 2010–11 RESULTS

ROUND ONE

8 October, 2010	
Glasgow 21 **Dragons** 13	**Northampton** 18 **Castres** 14
Ulster 30 **Aironi** 6	
9 October, 2010	
Treviso 29 **Leicester** 34	**Scarlets** 43 **Perpignan** 34
Leinster 38 **Racing Metro** 22	**Blues** 18 **Edinburgh** 17
Toulon 19 **Ospreys** 14	**London Irish** 23 **Munster** 17
Clermont 25 **Saracens** 10	
10 October, 2010	
Bath 11 **Biarritz** 12	**Toulouse** 18 **Wasps** 16

ROUND TWO

15 October, 2010	
Castres 27 **Blues** 20	**Ospreys** 27 **London Irish** 16
16 October, 2010	
Aironi 6 **Bath** 22	**Munster** 45 **Toulon** 18
Edinburgh 27 **Northampton** 31	**Dragons** 19 **Toulouse** 40
Racing Metro 16 **Clermont** 9	**Saracens** 23 **Leinster** 25
17 October, 2010	
Wasps 38 **Glasgow** 26	**Biarritz** 35 **Ulster** 15
Perpignan 35 **Treviso** 14	**Leicester** 46 **Scarlets** 10

ROUND THREE

10 December, 2010

Glasgow 16 **Toulouse** 28

11 December, 2010

Aironi 28 **Biarritz** 27
Perpignan 24 **Leicester** 19
Ulster 22 **Bath** 18
Scarlets 35 **Treviso** 27
Saracens 21 **Racing Metro** 24
Castres 21 **Edinburgh** 16
Northampton 23 **Blues** 15

12 December, 2010

Dragons 16 **Wasps** 23
Munster 22 **Ospreys** 16
Clermont 20 **Leinster** 13
London Irish 13 **Toulon** 19

ROUND FOUR

17 December, 2010

Biarritz 34 **Aironi** 3
Racing Metro 14 **Saracens** 19

18 December, 2010

Bath 22 **Ulster** 26
Treviso 15 **Scarlets** 38
Ospreys 19 **Munster** 15
Toulon 38 **London Irish** 17
Leinster 24 **Clermont** 8

19 December, 2010

Wasps 37 **Dragons** 10
Blues 19 **Northampton** 23
Leicester 22 **Perpignan** 22

20 December, 2010

Edinburgh 24 **Castres** 22

21 December, 2010

Toulouse 36 **Glasgow** 10

ROUND FIVE

14 January, 2011

Blues 14 **Castres** 9
Clermont 28 **Racing Metro** 17
Northampton 37 **Edinburgh** 0

15 January, 2011

Treviso 9 **Perpignan** 44
Leinster 43 **Saracens** 20
Toulouse 17 **Dragons** 3
Bath 55 **Aironi** 16
Ulster 9 **Biarritz** 6
Scarlets 18 **Leicester** 32

16 January, 2011

Glasgow 20 **Wasps** 10
London Irish 24 **Ospreys** 12
Toulon 32 **Munster** 16

ROUND SIX

21 January, 2011

Racing Metro 11 **Leinster** 36

Saracens 14 **Clermont** 24

22 January, 2011

Aironi 6 **Ulster** 43

Biarritz 26 **Bath** 19

Munster 28 **London Irish** 14

Ospreys 29 **Toulon** 17

Castres 12 **Northampton** 23

Edinburgh 14 **Blues** 21

23 January, 2011

Leicester 62 **Treviso** 15

Perpignan 37 **Scarlets** 5

Dragons 16 **Glasgow** 23

Wasps 21 **Toulouse** 16

POOL TABLES

POOL ONE

	P	W	D	L	F	A	BP	PTS
Northampton	6	6	0	0	155	87	1	25
Blues	6	3	0	3	107	113	2	14
Castres	6	2	0	4	105	115	3	11
Edinburgh	6	1	0	5	98	150	4	8

POOL TWO

	P	W	D	L	F	A	BP	PTS
Leinster	6	5	0	1	179	104	4	24
Clermont	6	4	0	2	114	94	3	19
Racing	6	2	0	4	104	151	1	9
Saracens	6	1	0	5	107	155	2	6

POOL THREE

	P	W	D	L	F	A	BP	PTS
Toulon	6	4	0	2	143	134	1	17
Munster	6	3	0	3	143	122	4	16
Ospreys	6	3	0	3	117	113	2	14
London Irish	6	2	0	4	107	141	1	9

POOL FOUR

	P	W	D	L	F	A	BP	PTS
Biarritz	6	4	0	2	140	85	6	22
Ulster	6	5	0	1	145	93	2	22
Bath	6	2	0	4	147	108	6	14
Aironi	6	1	0	5	65	211	0	4

POOL FIVE

	P	W	D	L	F	A	BP	PTS
Perpignan	6	4	1	1	196	112	4	22
Leicester	6	4	1	1	215	118	4	22
Scarlets	6	3	0	3	149	191	3	15
Treviso	6	0	0	6	109	248	1	1

POOL SIX

	P	W	D	L	F	A	BP	PTS
Toulouse	6	5	0	1	155	85	2	22
Wasps	6	4	0	2	145	106	3	19
Glasgow	6	3	0	3	116	141	0	12
Dragons	6	0	0	6	77	161	2	2

QUARTER-FINALS

9 April, 2011	
Perpignan 29 Toulon 25	Leinster 17 Leicester 10
10 April, 2011	
Northampton 23 Ulster 13	Biarritz 20 Toulouse 27

SEMI-FINALS

30 April, Aviva Stadium, Dublin

LEINSTER 32 (2G, 6PG) TOULOUSE 23 (2G, 2PG, 1DG)

LEINSTER: I Nacewa; S Horgan, B O'Driscoll, G D'Arcy, L Fitzgerald; J Sexton, E Reddan; C Healy, R Strauss, M Ross, L Cullen (captain), N Hines, K McLaughlin, S O'Brien, J Heaslip

SUBSTITUTIONS: S Jennings for McLaughlin (52 mins); H Van der Merwe for Healy (52 mins); I Boss for Reddan (52 mins); F McFadden for Fitzgerald (temp 56–67 mins); S Wright for Ross (73 mins)

SCORERS: *Tries:* Heaslip, O'Driscoll *Conversions:* Sexton (2) *Penalty Goals:* Sexton (6)

YELLOW CARD: O'Driscoll (36 mins)

TOULOUSE: C Heymans; V Clerc, F Fritz, C Poitrenaud, M Medard; D Skrela, J Doussain; J-B Poux, W Servat, C Johnston, Y Maestri, P Albacete, J Bouilhou (captain), Y Nyanga, L Picamoles

SUBSTITUTIONS: T Dusautoir for Nyanga (44 mins); D Human for Poux (44 mins); Y Jauzion for Fritz (60 mins); G Lamboley for Maestri (60 mins); S Sowerby for Picamoles (64 mins); N Bezy for Skrela (67 mins); J Falefa for Johnston (67 mins); V Lacombe for Servat (77 mins)

SCORERS: *Tries:* Fritz, Picamoles *Conversions:* Skrela (2) *Penalty Goals:* Skrela, Bezy *Dropped Goal:* Skrela

REFEREE: D Pearson (England)

1 May, Stadium: MK, Milton Keynes

NORTHAMPTON 23 (2G, 3PG) PERPIGNAN 7 (1G)

NORTHAMPTON: B Foden; C Ashton, J Clarke, J Downey, P Diggin; S Myler, L Dickson; S Tonga'uiha, D Hartley (captain), B Mujati, C Lawes, C Day, P Dowson, C Clark, R Wilson

SUBSTITUTIONS: M Sorenson for Day (73 mins); J Ansbro for Clarke (76 mins); T Mercey for Mujati (76 mins); S Commins for Dickson (79 mins); A Waller for Tonga'uiha (79 mins); B Sharman for Hartley (79 mins); M Easter for Clark (79)

SCORERS: *Tries:* Foden, Clarke *Conversions:* Myler (2) *Penalty Goals:* Myler (3)

PERPIGNAN: J Porical; A Plante, D Marty, G Hume, J Candelon; N Laharrague, D Mele; P Freshwater, G Guirado, N Mas (captain), R Alvarez, R Tchale-Watchou, G Le Corvec, B Guiry, D Chouly

SUBSTITUTIONS: H Tuilagi for Le Corvec (50 mins); J Schuster for Freshwater (60 mins); G Vilaceca for Alvarez (67 mins); J Michel for Porical (70 mins); M Edmonds for Laharrague (72 mins); K Boulogne for Mele (72 mins); C Geli for Guirado (73 mins); K Pulu for Mas (73 mins)

SCORERS: *Try:* Guirado *Conversion:* Porical

REFEREE: G Clancy (Ireland)

FINAL

21 May, Millennium Stadium, Cardiff

LEINSTER 33 (3G, 4PG) NORTHAMPTON 22 (2G, 1PG)

LEINSTER: I Nacewa; S Horgan, B O'Driscoll, G D'Arcy, L Fitzgerald; J Sexton, E Reddan; C Healy, R Strauss, M Ross, L Cullen (captain), N Hines, K McLaughlin, S O'Brien, J Heaslip

SUBSTITUTIONS: S Jennings for McLaughlin (41 mins); H Van der Merwe for Healy (61 mins); F McFadden for D'Arcy (67 mins); I Boss for Reddan (71 mins); I Madigan for Sexton (77 mins); SD Toner for Strauss (77); S Wright for Ross (77 mins); J Harris-Wright for Hines (77 mins)

SCORERS: *Tries:* Sexton (2) Hines *Conversions:* Sexton (3) *Penalty Goals:* Sexton (4)

NORTHAMPTON: B Foden; C Ashton, J Clarke, J Downey, P Diggin; S Myler, L Dickson; S Tonga'uiha, D Hartley (captain), B Mujati, C Lawes, C Day, C Clark, P Dowson, R Wilson

SUBSTITUTIONS: M Easter for Wilson (62 mins); S Geraghty for Myler (66 mins); T Mercey for Mujati (66 mins); A Waller for Tonga'uiha (66 mins); J Ansbro for Downey (66 mins); B Sharman for Hartley (69 mins); S Commins for Ashton (77 mins); M Sorenson for Day (77 mins)

SCORERS: *Tries:* Dowson, Foden, Hartley *Conversions:* Myler (2) *Penalty Goal:* Myler

YELLOW CARDS: Mujati (26 mins), Dowson (59 mins)

REFEREE: R Poite (France)

QUINS COMPLETE HAT-TRICK

By Iain Spragg

Dave Rogers/Getty Images

The Quins players start their victorious lap of honour.

Harlequins wrote a new chapter in the European rugby history books as they claimed the Amlin Challenge Cup after a nerve-shredding victory in the final over Stade Français, becoming the first side to lift the trophy three times in the 15-year history of the competition.

The Londoners were the European Shield champions in 2001 and the victors in the Parker Pen Challenge Cup three years later, and they made it a hat-trick of triumphs in European rugby's second-tier tournament in 2011 with a dramatic 19–18 win over the Parisians at the Cardiff City Stadium, surpassing two-time winners Sale and Clermont Auvergne in the process.

Harlequins certainly left it late against their French opponents and trailed 18–12 with just seven minutes remaining, only for England scrum-half Danny Care to create the space for Argentinean wing Gonzalo Camacho to speed over. New Zealand fly-half Nick Evans slotted over a seemingly nerveless touchline conversion and Harlequins were champions for a third time.

"It is massive for the club, but it is for the players and the supporters," said director of rugby Conor O'Shea, who marked his first full season in charge at The Stoop with a trophy. "Next year we want to kick on in the Premiership undoubtedly, but we had a lot of guys playing in their first final here and now they have got Stade in their locker.

"We didn't play well tonight. We were alright in the first half but didn't get a lead. I wouldn't say we imploded at the start of the second half, but we off-loaded in the wrong parts of the pitch. But we have played some great rugby and lost this season and there have been some pretty heartbreaking games. This team said they wanted to play a certain way and they didn't totally deliver it. But they did deliver silverware, and I am delighted for them."

Harlequins reached the knockout stages of the Challenge Cup after topping Pool One, and they were joined in the last eight by fellow group winners Brive, Montpellier, Stade Français and La Rochelle. The quintet were in turn joined by Clermont, Wasps and Munster, who had failed to progress from their respective groups in the Heineken Cup, to complete the quarter-final line-up.

The all-French clash between La Rochelle and Clermont opened the last-eight proceedings at the Stade Marcel Deflandre, and a try apiece from wings Kini Murimurivalu and Aurélien Rougerie was enough to secure a 23–12 win for Clermont.

A day later, it was an all-English encounter as Harlequins welcomed London neighbours Wasps to The Stoop, and 22 points from Evans' boot proved decisive as O'Shea's side emerged 32–22 winners. Stade then beat Montpellier 32–28 at Stade Charlety before Brive and Munster served up an avalanche of points in their last-eight clash in France. The two sides conjured up 79 points and nine tries between them at the Stade Municipal, but it was the Irishmen who eventually found themselves on the right side of a 42–37 scoreline.

The first semi-final was a strictly French affair as Stade entertained reigning Top 14 champions Clermont, and the heavyweight meeting did not disappoint. Interception tries from Julian Arias and Guillaume Boussés sent the Parisians on their way, but it was the five penalties and two conversions from fly-half Lionel Beauxis that proved the difference between the two sides as Stade eventually edged a thrilling match 29–25.

"When he's on song he's unstoppable," said Stade head coach Michael Cheika in tribute to Beauxis after one of his last matches for the club before joining Toulouse ahead of the new season. "His goal-kicking was absolutely out of this world. He's just so natural. He's a great player and Toulouse are lucky to be getting him because he's class."

The second semi-final presented Quins with the daunting task of travelling to Ireland to face Munster in their own backyard. Only Leicester had come away from Thomond Park with victory in 41 previous European fixtures, but a superb early onslaught from the visitors made a massive upset a real possibility.

First-half tries from second-row George Robson and Care had Munster reeling and, although full-back Felix Jones replied for the home side, Quins went in at half-time 14–7 up. Two Rory Clegg penalties after the restart stretched the lead and, despite Nick Easter's red card and a late try from Doug Howlett, the English side held out for a 20–12 triumph and one of the most famous results in the club's history.

"The way that we played didn't give us any opportunity whatsoever to get a result," bemoaned Munster head coach Tony McGahan after his side's shock defeat. "We really stood off them and showed an inability to make first-up tackles.

"I don't think we got through more than two phases in the first half and we conceded 11 turnovers. We failed to put any doubts in their mind. If they show the same spirit and execution in the final that they showed today, then I don't think they will have any problems."

The final began relatively tentatively as Evans and Beauxis traded early penalties, but after the first 40 minutes the match hung in the balance with Harlequins enjoying a precarious 9–6 advantage. However, the complexion of the match changed as Stade surged into a 15–9 lead courtesy of another two Beauxis penalties and a Mathieu Bastareaud drop-goal, but the defining moment was yet to come as Camacho dived over to drag the Londoners to within a single point. It was now all up to Evans, who held his nerve superbly to convert from wide out on the right touchline and break French hearts.

AMLIN CHALLENGE CUP 2010–11 RESULTS

ROUND ONE	
7 October, 2010	
Newcastle 22 **Bourgoin** 16	**Stade Français** 57 **Crociati** 6
8 October, 2010	
Agen 26 **Gloucester** 19	**Sale** 97 **El Salvador** 11
Brive 32 **Padova** 6	
9 October, 2010	
Bucharest 9 **Leeds** 23	**Rovigo** 3 **La Rochelle** 38
Cavalieri 23 **Connacht** 21	**Exeter** 13 **Montpellier** 20
10 October, 2010	
Bayonne 16 **Harlequins** 12	
ROUND TWO	
14 October, 2010	
Montpellier 32 **Newcastle** 8	
15 October, 2010	
Bourgoin 19 **Exeter** 34	**Connacht** 16 **Bayonne** 13
16 October, 2010	
Bucharest 20 **Crociati** 19	**Harlequins** 55 **Cavalieri** 17
Padova 9 **Sale** 56	**El Salvador** 3 **Brive** 116
Gloucester 90 **Rovigo** 7	**La Rochelle** 30 **Agen** 23
17 October, 2010	
Leeds 13 **Stade Français** 22	
ROUND THREE	
9 December, 2010	
Montpellier 39 **Bourgoin** 14	
11 December, 2010	
Bucharest 20 **Stade Français** 29	**Exeter** 36 **Newcastle** 10
Padova 37 **El Salvador** 10	**La Rochelle** 6 **Gloucester** 13
Rovigo 10 **Agen** 33	**Brive** 18 **Sale** 9
12 December, 2010	
Leeds 55 **Crociati** 6	**Harlequins** 20 **Connacht** 9
Bayonne 65 **Cavalieri** 7	

ROUND FOUR	
16 December, 2010	
Stade Français 35 **Bucharest** 7	
17 December, 2010	
Connacht 9 **Harlequins** 15	
18 December, 2010	
Agen 61 **Rovigo** 11	**Bourgoin** 36 **Montpellier** 18
19 December, 2010	
El Salvador 37 **Padova** 16	**Crociati** 6 **Leeds** 46
Newcastle 26 **Exeter** 24	**Gloucester** 18 **La Rochelle** 24
20 December, 2010	
Cavalieri 7 **Bayonne** 31	**Sale** 13 **Brive** 15
ROUND FIVE	
13 January, 2011	
Agen 17 **La Rochelle** 28	
14 January, 2011	
Brive 52 **El Salvador** 3	**Newcastle** 0 **Montpellier** 6
Sale 54 **Padova** 0	
15 January, 2011	
Cavalieri 16 **Harlequins** 48	**Bayonne** 21 **Connacht** 35
Crociati 16 **Bucharest** 12	**Exeter** 17 **Bourgoin** 6
Rovigo 7 **Gloucester** 55	
16 January, 2011	
Stade Français 39 **Leeds** 10	
ROUND SIX	
20 January, 2011	
Gloucester 60 **Agen** 7	**La Rochelle** 71 **Rovigo** 17
22 January, 2011	
El Salvador 5 **Sale** 50	**Harlequins** 39 **Bayonne** 17
Padova 20 **Brive** 24	**Montpellier** 32 **Exeter** 30
Connacht 83 **Cavalieri** 7	
23 January, 2011	
Bourgoin 28 **Newcastle** 0	**Leeds** 26 **Bucharest** 6
Crociati 17 **Stade Français** 34	

GROUP TABLES

POOL ONE

	P	W	D	L	F	A	BP	PTS
Harlequins	6	5	0	1	189	84	4	24
Connacht	6	3	0	3	173	99	3	15
Bayonne	6	3	0	3	163	116	3	15
Cavalieri	6	1	0	5	77	303	0	4

POOL TWO

	P	W	D	L	F	A	BP	PTS
Brive	6	6	0	0	257	54	3	27
Sale	6	4	0	2	279	58	5	21
Padova	6	1	0	5	88	213	2	11
El Salvador	6	1	0	5	69	368	0	0

POOL THREE

	P	W	D	L	F	A	BP	PTS
Montpellier	6	5	0	1	147	101	1	21
Exeter	6	3	0	3	154	113	4	16
Bourgoin	6	2	0	4	119	130	3	11
Newcastle	6	2	0	4	66	142	1	9

POOL FOUR

	P	W	D	L	F	A	BP	PTS
Stade Français	6	6	0	0	216	73	5	29
Leeds	6	4	0	2	173	88	3	19
Bucharest	6	1	0	5	74	148	1	5
Crociati	6	1	0	5	70	224	1	5

POOL FIVE

	P	W	D	L	F	A	BP	PTS
La Rochelle	6	5	0	1	197	91	4	24
Gloucester	6	4	0	2	255	77	5	21
Agen	6	3	0	3	167	158	3	15
Rovigo	6	0	0	6	55	348	0	0

Jamie McDonald/Getty Images

Munster lost an epic semi-final to Harlequins.

QUARTER-FINALS

7 April, 2011	
La Rochelle 13 Clermont 23	
8 April, 2011	
Harlequins 32 Wasps 22	Stade Français 32 Montpellier 28
9 April, 2011	
Brive 37 Munster 42	

SEMI-FINALS

29 April, Stade Charlety, Paris

STADE FRANÇAIS 29 (2G, 5PG)
CLERMONT AUVERGNE 25 (2G, 1T, 2PG)

STADE FRANÇAIS: H Southwell; J Arias, M Bastareaud, G Tiesi, G Boussés; L Beauxis, J Dupuy; R Roncero, L Sempere, D Attoub, T Palmer, P Pape, J Haskell, A Burban, S Parisse (captain)

SUBSTITUTIONS: J Leguizamon for Burban (17 mins); R Bonfils for Sempere (24 mins); R Slimani for Attoub (50 mins); Attoub for Slimani (68 mins); O Phillips for Arias (77 mins); D Weber for Roncero (77mins)

SCORERS: *Tries:* Arias, Bousses *Conversions:* Beauxis (2) *Penalty Goals:* Beauxis (5)

YELLOW CARD: Arias (52 mins)

CLERMONT: T Pisi; W Fofana, A Rougerie (captain), M Joubert, K Murimurivalu; B Russell, M Parra; V Debaty, W Wepener, D Zirakashvili, J Pierre, T Privat, J Cudmore, J Bardy, E Vermuelen

SUBSTITUTIONS: G Canale for Joubert (temp 37–40 mins); A Audebert for Bardy (44 mins); S Lauaki for Pierre (47 mins); M Ledesma for Wepener (58 mins); A Floch for Pisi (60 mins); Canale for Joubert (61 mins); K Senio for Russell (67 mins); L Faure for Debaty (67 mins); M Scelzo for Zirakashvili (67 mins)

SCORERS: *Tries:* Pisi, Russell, Cudmore *Conversions:* Parra (2) *Penalty Goals:* Parra (2)

REFEREE: N Owens (Wales)

30 April, Thomond Park, Limerick

MUNSTER 12 (1G, 1T)
HARLEQUINS 20 (2G, 2PG)

MUNSTER: F Jones; D Howlett, L Mafi, P Warwick, K Earls; R O'Gara (captain), C Murray; W Du Preez, D Varley, T Buckley, D O'Callaghan, M O'Driscoll, D Leamy, D Wallace, J Coughlan

SUBSTITUTIONS: S Tuitupou for Warwick (40 mins); P O'Connell for O'Driscoll (40 mins); J Hayes for Buckley (40 mins); P Stringer for Murray (54 mins); M Horan for Du Preez (54 mins); J Murphy for Earls (63 mins); D Ryan for O'Callaghan (68 mins); M Sherry for Varley (74 mins)

SCORERS: *Tries:* Jones, Howlett *Conversion:* O'Gara

YELLOW CARD: O'Callaghan (47 mins)

HARLEQUINS: M Brown; G Camacho, G Lowe, J Turner-Hall, U Moyne; N Evans, D Care; J Marler, J Gray, J Johnson, O Kohn, G Robson, M Fa'asavalu, C Robshaw (captain), N Easter

SUBSTITUTIONS: R Clegg for Evans (40 mins); C Jones for Marler (71 mins); T Vallejos for Kohn (72 mins)

SCORERS: *Tries:* Robson, Care *Conversions:* Evans, Care *Penalty Goals:* Clegg (2)

YELLOW CARD: Easter (47 mins)

RED CARD: Easter (70 mins)

REFEREE: R Poite (France)

FINAL

20 May, Cardiff City Stadium, Cardiff

HARLEQUINS 19 (1G, 4PG)
STADE FRANÇAIS 18 (4PG, 2PG)

HARLEQUINS: M Brown; G Camacho, G Lowe, J Turner-Hall, U Monye; N Evans, D Care; J Marler, J Gray, J Johnston, O Kohn, G Robson, M Fa'asavalu, C Robshaw (captain), N Easter

SUBSTITUTIONS: W Skinner for Fa'asavalu (60 mins); R Chisholm for Lowe (75 mins)

SCORERS: *Tries:* Camacho *Conversion:* Evans *Penalty Goals:* Evans (4)

STADE FRANÇAIS: M Rodriguez; J Arias, M Bastareaud, G Bousses, D Camara; L Beauxis, J Dupuy; R Roncero, R Bonfils, D Attoub, T Palmer, P Pape, J Haskell, A Burban, S Parisse (captain)

SUBSTITUTIONS: J Leguizamon for Burban (37 mins)

SCORERS: *Penalty Goals:* Beauxis (4) *Dropped Goals:* Bastareaud, Rodriguez

REFEREE: G Clancy (Ireland)

SIX OF THE BEST

By Iain Spragg

Jamie McDonald/Getty Images

England celebrate winning the final Churchill Cup beating Canada in the final.

It was the end of a brief but successful era in international rugby in 2011 as England Saxons won the ninth and final Churchill Cup tournament, bringing down the curtain on a competition that had begun eight years earlier with the mission statement of bringing high-profile Test rugby to Canada and the USA on an annual basis.

The first Churchill Cup was staged in Vancouver in 2003, but on the same day as England's second string defeated the Canucks 37–6 in the swansong final at Sixways – and with both Canada and the USA now included on the IRB's tour schedule – the organisers announced the competition had served its purpose.

"The Churchill Cup has provided what we had all hoped for – regular international competition for USA and Canada in a showpiece event, which has been hosted in 17 venues and included 13 participating nations," said the RFU's Paul Vaughan, an executive member of the cup board. "It has also given us refereeing and coaching opportunities for all three Unions and ultimately strengthened the relationship between us."

Although it was the strengthening of the game in North America which was the driving force behind the Churchill Cup's birth, it is fitting that it is England, the competition's most successful nation, who have emerged its final victors.

Champions in its inaugural year in the guise of England A, the Saxons won six of the nine tournaments staged, and had it not been for Ireland A's triumph in 2009 in America, England would have claimed the last five titles in succession.

The Saxons reached the last-ever final with considerable ease, despatching the USA Eagles 87–8 at Franklin's Gardens before beating Tonga 41–14 at Kingsholm eight days later. In contrast, the Canadians were made to work much harder for both their group stage victories over Italy A (26–12) and Russia (34–18).

Any hopes the Canucks harboured of pulling off a major shock in the final and beating the Saxons in Worcester eventually evaporated after initial stubborn resistance, and two tries from wing Miles Benjamin plus further scores from opposite wing Charlie Sharples, flanker James Gaskell and fellow back rower Jamie Gibson were enough to overcome the Canadian challenge.

"We knew exactly what Canada were going to bring to the party," Saxons coach Stuart Lancaster said after the match. "We knew it would take the full 80 minutes to break them down, and it was a good performance. If you had said beforehand we would win 37–6, I would have taken it. Canada are a fit side and well organised. We dropped off a bit either side of half-time, but the more experienced players stepped up and we finished it off well.

"It is objective achieved, and alongside that to give some lads an opportunity for further development and try to push some forward – short-term for the World Cup training squad, but also long term. We need to continue to create development opportunities for players to play for England. We need to bridge the gap between Premiership rugby and international rugby and also give players an opportunity to come out of their club sides and work with different coaches and different players."

Canada replied with a drop-goal from fly-half Ander Monro and a penalty from winger James Pritchard but were unable to prevent the Saxons scoring 22 unanswered second-half points for victory. "It's a disappointing way to end," admitted flanker Chauncey O'Toole. "I don't really feel we put our best foot forward today, but we'll learn from it."

In the Plate Final, Italy A faced Tonga for third place, and it was eventually the Azzurri forward power up front that prevailed as the Europeans won 27–18.

The Italians opened the scoring with the match's first try from fly-half Riccardo Bocchino, and they led 10–3 at half-time. They stretched their advantage after the break with a try from centre Andrea Pratichetti, but Tonga hit back with an eye-catching long-range effort from Viliami Iongi to cut the deficit.

The result still hung in the balance until Giovanbattista Venditti scored Italy's third try, rendering Mateo Malupo's late effort for the Tongans no more than a consolation score.

"We improved a lot today, and we put in a good performance," said Italy A captain Marco Bortolami after the match. "We have some young players and they need experience. It was terrible against Canada but better against Tonga, and today was a real improvement."

In the Bowl Final, the Eagles faced Russia in a dress rehearsal for their Rugby World Cup pool stage clash in New Zealand later in the year. On this occasion it was the Americans who emerged slender 32–25 winners after a match that ebbed and flowed throughout.

The first half of the match at Sixways ended all square at 8–8 after centre Paul Emerick had touched down for the Eagles, but wing Vladimir Ostroushko struck back for the Bears, and there was nothing to separate the sides.

After the break, Russia took the lead with a try from second row Alexander Voytov, only for USA captain Todd Clever to reply with a 70-metre interception score, but when Vasily Artemyev scored a third try for the Bears the two teams were again deadlocked at 25–25.

The match needed a decisive intervention, and it finally came from substitute Taivalu Enosa, who raced over late on to give the States a morale-boosting victory.

"We are delighted to finish the Churchill Cup with a solid win," said USA head coach Eddie O'Sullivan. "It was hard work, as we expected it would be, and heavy rain before the kick-off made handling difficult. It was a game that could have gone either way, especially when it opened up in the second half. But I think we showed great heart and composure to take a late lead and close out the game. There were some great individual performances throughout the team."

For Russia, defeat was a valuable if steep learning curve ahead of their rematch with the Americans at the World Cup. "If we could have kept hold of the ball more we could have won," admitted coach Kingsley Jones. "The USA were smarter than us at the breakdown. We are taking two steps forward and one step back, but we need to take the positives out of this tournament."

CHURCHILL CUP 2011 RESULTS

GROUP PHASE

4 June, Franklin's Gardens, Northampton	
Italy A 12	**Canada** 26
England Saxons 87	**USA** 8
8 June, Moseley Road, Hersham	
Tonga 44	**USA** 13
Canada 34	**Russia** 18
12 June, Kingsholm, Gloucester	
England Saxons 41	**Tonga** 14
Italy A 24	**Russia** 19

GROUP TABLES

POOL A

P	W	D	L	F	A	BP	PTS	
Saxons	2	2	0	0	128	22	2	**10**
Tonga	2	1	0	1	58	54	1	**5**
USA	2	0	0	2	21	131	0	**0**

POOL B

P	W	D	L	F	A	BP	PTS	
Canada	2	2	0	0	60	30	1	**9**
Italy A	2	1	0	1	36	45	0	**4**
Russia	2	0	0	2	37	58	1	**1**

CHURCHILL CUP FINAL

18 June, Sixways, Worcester

ENGLAND SAXONS 37 (3G, 2T, 2PG)
CANADA 6 (1PG, 1DG)

SAXONS: M Brown; C Sharples, H Trinder, B Twelvetrees, M Benjamin; R Clegg, P Hodgson; M Mullan, D Paice, M Stevens, M Botha, G Kitchener, J Gaskell, T Johnson, J Crane (captain)

SUBSTITUTIONS: A Goode for Brown (53 mins); J Gibson for Kitchener (64 mins); N Catt for Mullan (70 mins); M Young for Hodgson (73 mins); T Ojo for Benjamin (74 mins); C Fearns for Johnson (74 mins); J Gray for Paice (76 mins)

SCORERS: *Tries:* Gaskell, Benjamin (2), Sharples, Gibson *Conversions:* Clegg (3) *Penalty Goals:* Clegg (2)

CANADA: M Evans; C Hearn, P Mackenzie, R Smith, J Pritchard; A Monro, S White; H Buydens, P Riordan (captain), J Marshall, B Erichsen, J Cudmore, J Sinclair, C O'Toole, A Carpenter

SUBSTITUTIONS: C Trainor for Hearn (53 mins); T Hotson for Erichsen (64 mins); N Dala for Carpenter (64 mins); N Hirayama for Monro (68 mins); A Tiedemann for Buydens (70 mins); S Franklin for Marshall (70 mins); J Mackenzie for White (74 mins)

SCORERS: *Penalty Goal:* Pritchard *Dropped Goal:* Monro

REFEREE: R Poite (France)

CHURCHILL CUP PLATE FINAL

18 June, Sixways, Worcester

TONGA 18 (1G, 1T, 2PG) ITALY A 27 (3G, 2PG)

ITALY A: D Gerber; G Venditi, A Pratichetti, M Pratichetti, A Esposito; R Bocchino, T Tebaldi; M Aguero, T D'Apice, F Staibano, J Furno, M Bortolami (captain), L Petillo, F Minto, M Vosawai

SUBSTITUTIONS: D Chistolini for Staibano (40 mins); De Marchi for Aguero (57 mins); N Belardo for Esposito (65 mins); V Bernabò for Minto (65 mins); G Toniolatti for Gerber (67 mins); A Manici for D'Apice (75 mins); R Trevisan for Bortolami (75 mins)

SCORERS: *Tries:* Bocchino, Pratichetti, Venditti *Conversions:* Tebaldi (3) *Penalty Goals:* Tebaldi (2)

TONGA: M Malupo; V Helu, S Hufanga, T Sili, V Iongi; E Paea, S Havea; O Fainga'anuku, A Halangahu, K Pulu (captain), J Afu, E Kauhenga, S Timani, P Kaho, P Mapakaitolo

SUBSTITUTIONS: T Ula for Mapakaitolo (28 mins); K Morath for Helu (41 mins); M Latu for Fainga'anuku (44 mins); P Koloamatangi for Kaho (53 mins); S Fonua for Sili (54 mins); D Morath for Havea (75 mins); S Telefoni for Halangahu (75 mins)

SCORERS: *Tries:* Iongi, Malupo *Penalty Goals:* Paea, K Morath *Conversion:* K Morath

REFEREE: N Owens (Wales)

CHURCHILL CUP BOWL FINAL

18 June, Sixways, Worcester

USA 32 (3G, 1T, 2PG) RUSSIA 25 (2G, 1T, 2PG)

USA: B Scully; C Hawley, P Emerick, A Suniula, K Swiryn; N Malifa, M Petri; M Moeakiola, C Biller, S Pittman, J van der Giessen, S LaValla, I Basauri, T Clever (captain), L Stanfill

SUBSTITUTIONS*:* T Enosa for Halwey (57 mins); N Johnson for Basauri (62 mins); T Usasz for Petri (62 mins); E Fry for Moeakiola (68 mins)

SCORERS: *Tries:* Emerick, Suniula, Clever, Enosa *Conversions:* Malifa (3)

Penalty Goals: Malifa (2)

RUSSIA: I Klyuchnikov; V Artemyev, M Babaev, A Makovetskiy, V Ostroushko; Y Kushnarev, A Shakirov; S Popov, V Korshunov (captain), I Prishchepenko, A Voytov, D Antonov, A Temnov, A Garbuzov, V Grachev

SUBSTITUTIONS*:* V Gresev for Garbuzov (35 mins); A Panasenko for Garbuzov (62 mins); A Chernyshev for Prischepenko (73 mins)

SCORERS: *Tries:* Ostroushko, Voytov, Artemyev *Conversions:* Kushnarev (2) *Penalty Goals:* Kushnarev (2)

REFEREE: D Pearson (England)

Jamie McDonald/Getty Images

The USA are clearly delighted with their Bowl Final victory over Russia.

GLOUCESTER GET HOME

By Iain Spragg

Dave Rogers/Getty Images

Gloucester celebrate winning the trophy.

It was a welcome case of third time lucky for Gloucester in the LV= Cup as Bryan Redpath's side erased the painful memories of defeat in the competition's previous two finals, demolishing Newcastle 34–7 in a one-sided encounter at Franklin's Gardens to finally claim the Anglo-Welsh Cup title.

The Cherry and Whites had been humiliated 50–12 by Cardiff in the 2009 final at Twickenham, and 12 months later they were denied the trophy again after a 30–24 reverse against Northampton, but they made no mistake in 2011 with a convincing four-try romp over the Falcons that went some way to dispelling the impression the club was destined to remain perennial bridesmaids.

It was Gloucester's first domestic silverware since their triumph over Northampton in the Powergen Cup final eight years earlier and the first trophy for Redpath following his appointment as Dean Ryan's successor as Gloucester head coach in the summer of 2009.

"We were always in control of the territory and possession, and even though we were a little bit loose and didn't play as well as we could have done, we managed to put them to bed in the second half and win the silverware," said wing Charlie Sharples, the scorer of Gloucester's third try.

"That was the biggest thing. They had nothing to lose at the end, throwing it about a little bit, but they only got the one try, so the defence wasn't too bad and we're thrilled to get the win.

"It's a huge milestone. We're still aware of the task we've got left and we still very much want to be in contention for winning the Premiership, but it's nice to put the LV= Cup to bed after three years and have it sitting on the mantelpiece."

Gloucester qualified for the knockout stages of the LV= Cup with relative ease, winning three of their four Pool Three fixtures to reach the semi-finals. They did lose their tournament opener 18–12 to the Dragons at Rodney Parade in November but recovered with three consecutive wins.

They were joined by Pool One winners Newcastle, who bounced back from defeats to Premiership rivals Harlequins and Bath to beat Exeter and qualify.

In Pool Two, the Dragons edged out Saracens for a place in the last four, despite both sides finishing on 12 points courtesy of the Welsh side's higher try count in their four matches, while in Pool Four Harlequins topped the group with an impressive unbeaten record and an average of over 30 points per game.

The first semi-final saw Quins entertain the Falcons at The Stoop, and it proved to be a match that began in explosive fashion and ended with high drama.

The start could not have been better for the home side when scrum-half Karl Dickson scampered over for a try inside the first minute, and two penalties from Rory Clegg ensured Harlequins' first-half dominance was rewarded with a 13–6 lead at the break.

A Jimmy Gopperth try for Newcastle, which he converted, dragged them back into contention, but when Mike Brown edged the Londoners further in front the game seemed to be up for Newcastle. There was, however, time for one last roll of the dice, and fortune favoured the Falcons when substitute wing Tane Tu'ipulotu went over in injury-time, wrapping up an amazing 21–20 victory with the very last play of the match.

"You can count on one hand as you go through your career the amount of times you win a game like that," said head coach Alan Tait. "They had thrown everything at us. I had hardly sat in my seat and they were 7–0 up and Ugo Monye dropped a scoring opportunity as well.

"You ride your luck, but I have to praise our lads for the effort they put in; they never say die. They have really battled, and I am sure this will give a massive lift to the club.

"It's a great honour to play in finals, and we have worked really hard for it. I feel for the Harlequins boys because it is a hard pill to swallow. But we didn't win it with a penalty. We won it with a try that was worthy of winning a game of rugby."

Two days later Gloucester and the Dragons crossed swords at Kingsholm, but there was to be no repeat of the first semi-final's last-gasp dramatics as the Cherry and Whites ran in seven tries to record a thumping 45–7 win over the Welsh region.

The undisputed star of the show was home wing Sharples with a dazzling four-try salvo that simply blew away the Dragons' hopes of reaching the final, while the other Gloucester tries came from flanker Andy Hazell, centre Eliota Fuimaono-Sapolu and fly-half Nicky Robinson.

In fact, all three of those tries came in the first half before Sharples had himself crossed for the first time early after the break. The wing went over three more times in the next 20 minutes as the Cherry and Whites romped to victory.

"We are very disappointed with that performance," said caretaker Dragons coach Darren Edwards in the immediate aftermath of his side's mauling. "We were well beaten, but what we have done is expose some young players to a game like that and hopefully that bodes well for the future.

"We struggled with the intensity of the game, and we didn't get a real foothold in it. We gave the ball away too cheaply, and nine of our first 10 errors were due to handling. That is the fine line in games like this."

A week later Gloucester took to the pitch at Franklin's Gardens to tackle the Falcons knowing an unwelcome hat-trick of final defeats potentially awaited them, but if there were nerves among Redpath's starting XV, they did not show as the Cherry and Whites warmed instantly to their task, and when wing Tom Voyce dashed over as early as the sixth minute, a score converted by Robinson, they were well on their way.

A Robinson penalty before the break ensured Gloucester retreated to the dressing room at half-time with a 10–0 lead, and just before the hour mark Fuimaono-Sapolu was both instigator and finisher of a fine move through the Cherry and White back-line that resulted in a second try.

In their semi-final, the Falcons had mounted a fine second-half fight-back against Harlequins to snatch victory from the jaws of defeat but, now trailing 17–0 to Gloucester, there was to be no repeat of their great escape.

Perhaps inevitably, the third Gloucester try came from the prolific Sharples and although wing Luke Eves did give the final scoreline a degree of respectability with Newcastle's only try of the match, it was Redpath's team which had the final word when substitute hooker Darren Dawidiuk crashed over.

Victory booked the Cherry and Whites' place in the Heineken Cup for the following season and finally ended their dismal sequence of defeat in the competition, although Robinson admitted after the game that Gloucester were never fully able to relax.

"It wasn't the perfect performance, but it's hard to get that in a final," he said after landing 14 points with the boot. "We were edgy at times but the scoreboard shows we were pretty dominant in a lot of aspects of the match.

"We struggled a bit for periods, but we managed to create something out of nothing and within a 10-minute period we scored a couple of tries and that put the game to bed. Once we got that 20-point lead, it was always going to be difficult for Newcastle to come back."

For Newcastle, the LV= Cup campaign had proved a distraction to their struggles in the Premiership, but Tait was the first to admit his side were beaten by the better team on the day.

"I shook Bryan's hand after the game and the first thing I said to him was 'it was probably a job too far for us'," Tait said. "Full credit to what they are doing at Gloucester. They looked the part even in the warm-up. They are a good outfit.

"We got stuck into the game, and I still thought we had a bit of a chance at half-time because I knew we were still strong. We just didn't play in the right areas, and when they got us to 20–0 we started to play the old Barbarians stuff that doesn't really work at this level."

LV= CUP 2010–11 GROUP TABLES

POOL ONE

	P	W	D	L	F	A	BP	PTS
Newcastle	4	2	0	2	61	59	1	9
Wasps	4	1	0	3	50	101	1	4
Blues	4	0	1	3	56	104	0	2
Leicester	4	0	0	4	60	141	0	0

POOL THREE

	P	W	D	L	F	A	BP	PTS
Gloucester	4	3	0	1	119	52	4	16
Northampton	4	2	1	1	108	86	1	11
Sale	4	2	0	2	89	109	1	9
Scarlets	4	2	0	2	93	89	1	9

POOL TWO

	P	W	D	L	F	A	BP	PTS
Dragons	4	3	0	1	75	69	0	12
Saracens	4	2	1	1	116	72	2	12
London Irish	4	1	0	3	75	125	1	5
Leeds	4	0	0	4	70	143	2	2

POOL FOUR

	P	W	D	L	F	A	BP	PTS
Harlequins	4	4	0	0	123	65	1	17
Ospreys	4	3	0	1	110	51	2	14
Bath	4	3	0	1	82	55	2	14
Exeter	4	2	1	1	90	56	1	11

SEMI-FINALS

11 March, Twickenham Stoop, London

HARLEQUINS 20 (2G, 2PG)
NEWCASTLE FALCONS 21 (1G, 1T, 3PG)

HARLEQUINS: M Brown; T Williams, G Lowe, J Turner-Hall, U Monye; R Clegg, K Dickinson; J Marler, M Cairns, J Andress, O Kohn, P Browne, M Fa'asavalu, W Skinner, C Robshaw (captain)

SUBSTITUTIONS: J Gray for Cairns (38 mins); M Lambert for Andress (67 mins); T Vallejos for Fa'asavalu (64 mins); C York for Skinner (17)

SCORERS: *Tries:* Dickson, Brown *Conversions:* Clegg (2) *Penalty Goals:* Clegg (2)

NEWCASTLE: M Tait; D Williams, L Eves, J Fitzpatrick, G Bobo; J Gopperth, M Young; J Golding, M Thompson, E Murray, J Hudson (captain), A Van der Heijden, T Swinson, B Wilson, A Hogg

SUBSTITUTIONS: R Vickers for Thompson (41); T Tu'ipulotu for Williams (47 mins); H Charlton for Young (57 mins); G Shiels for Golding (57 mins); K Brookes for Murray (65 mins), M Wilson for B Wilson (73 mins)

SCORERS: *Tries:* Gopperth, Tu'ipulotu *Conversions:* Gopperth *Penalty Goals:* Gopperth (3)

REFEREE: N Owens (Wales)

13 March, Kingsholm, Gloucester

GLOUCESTER 45 (5G, 2T) DRAGONS 17 (1G, 2T)

GLOUCESTER: O Morgan; C Sharples, H Trinder, E Fuimaono-Sapolu, T Voyce; N Robinson, J Pasqualin; N Wood, O Azam, R Harden, J Hamilton, A Brown, P Buxton, A Hazell, L Narraway (captain)

SUBSTITUTIONS: Y Thomas for Wood (40 mins); J May for Trinder (47 mins); W James for Hamilton (51 mins); F Burns for Morgan (54 mins); A Qera for Hazell (55 mins); D Dawidiuk for Narraway (57 mins); T Taylor for Pasqualin (60 mins); S Knight for Harden (66 mins)

SCORERS: *Tries:* Hazell, Fuimaono-Sapolu, Robinson, Sharples (4) *Conversions:* Robinson (5)

DRAGONS: M Thomas; W Harries, T Riley, P Leach, A Brew; J Tovey, W Evans; P Price, L Burns, D Way, L Charteris (captain), A Jones, A Coombs, L Evans, T Faletau

SUBSTITUTIONS: S Jones for Burns (42 mins); A Hughes for Riley (46 mins); J Groves for L Evans (65 mins); A Brown for A Jones (67mins); M Jones for M Thomas (70 mins); J Evans for W Evans (74 mins); H Gustafson for Price (75 mins), P Palmer for Way (78 mins)

SCORERS: *Tries:* Jones, Brew, Groves *Conversion:* Tovey

REFEREE: C Berdos (France)

FINAL

20 March, Franklin's Gardens, Northampton

GLOUCESTER 34 (4G, 2PG) NEWCASTLE 7 (1G)

Gloucester: O Morgan; C Sharples, T Molenaar, E Fuimaono-Sapolu, T Voyce; N Robinson, J Pasqualin; N Wood, O Azam, R Harden, J Hamilton, A Brown, A Qera, A Hazell, L Narraway (captain)

SUBSTITUTIONS: M Cox for Hazell (41 mins); H Trinder for Molenaar (56 mins); F Burns for Morgan (60 mins); W James for Hamilton (64 mins); S Knight for Harden (71 mins); T Taylor for Fuimaono-Sapolu (74 mins); D Dawidiuk for Azam (78 mins)

SCORERS: *Tries:* Voyce, Fuimaono-Sapolu, Sharples, Dawidiuk *Conversions:* Robinson(4) *Penalty Goals:* Robinson (2)

NEWCASTLE: A Tait; L Fielden, T Tu'ipulotu, J Fitzpatrick, L Eves; J Gopperth, M Young; J Golding, M Thompson, K Brookes, J Hudson (captain), A Van der Heijden, T Swinson, B Wilson, A Hogg

SUBSTITUTIONS: R Vickers for Thompson (46 mins); G Bobo for Fitzpatrick (53 mins); T Catterick for Fielden (61 mins); M Wilson for van der Heijden (62 mins); G Shiels for Golding (65 mins); J Hall for Brookes (68 mins); H Charlton for Young (69 mins); F Levi for Swinson (71 mins)

SCORERS: *Try:* Eves *Conversion:* Gopperth

REFEREE: D Pearson (England)

REDS COMPLETE SUPER RUGBY REDEMPTION

Chris Hyde/Getty Images

The Reds complete an amazing transformation by winning the first Super Rugby title.

In May 2007 the Reds travelled to Cape Town for their Super Rugby clash with the Bulls and, after the darkest 80 minutes in the history of the proud Queensland side, they returned home licking their wounds after a humiliating 92–3 mauling on South African soil.

For a team that won the last two Super 10 titles of the game's amateur era, registering the record losing margin in Super Rugby in the Loftus Versfeld was the painful nadir of a five-year nightmare between 2004 and 2009 in which they finished in the bottom three of the table every season.

And yet within four years of their 13-try capitulation in Cape Town, the Reds were crowned Super 15 champions after overcoming the Crusaders 18–13 in the final in Brisbane, completing one of the greatest revivals in the game.

In the process, the Reds joined two-time champions Brumbies as only the second Australian winners of the southern hemisphere's premier club tournament and ended New Zealand and South Africa's six-year stranglehold on the silverware.

The Reds' resurgence began in earnest in October 2009 when they made former Wallaby prop Ewen McKenzie their seventh coach in 11 years, and within two seasons their desperate hope of reviving the franchise's fortunes were realised as they triumphed in their trans-Tasman clash with the Crusaders in the Suncorp Stadium, watched by a record Australian Super Rugby crowd of 52,113.

"The lowest point in Queensland rugby history was probably that Bulls defeat back in Pretoria, something I was unfortunately a part of," said Reds captain James Horwill after the final whistle in Brisbane. "That's probably the lowest point we've ever been. Now we're arguably at the highest point we've ever been. It's pretty special. To be part of that, it's pretty cool to be honest. It's credit to the whole organisation. The players have probably been the figurehead of that. There's been a lot of work around the brand of the Reds.

"We knew the Crusaders would just keep coming. I don't know what to say – I'm lost for words. All year people have doubted us, saying we couldn't go the distance, but we have shown we can do it. It means the world to me to lead this side. We never gave in. We're just like a big family. We dig deep for each other, and I think that was evident tonight against a very good Crusaders side."

The champions-elect began their campaign in February with a narrow 21–20 win over Western Force in Brisbane, but they were brought down to earth with a considerable bump just six days later when they travelled to Sydney to face the Waratahs in the ANZ Stadium.

McKenzie's side had not won a Super Rugby fixture in Sydney since 2003, and they were unable to break the sequence in 2011 as the Waratahs ran in four unanswered tries through Drew Mitchell, Dave Dennis, Lachie Turner and Benn Robinson for a 30–6 bonus point victory.

Defeat hardly constituted a crisis, but the Reds nonetheless closed ranks immediately, embarking on an impressive seven-match winning run that established their title credentials.

Arguably the most impressive result in that sequence came in mid-March when the Bulls, the champions in 2009 and 2010, were the visitors to the Suncorp Stadium but were despatched with some aplomb by their Australian hosts.

The Reds outscored the South Africans six tries to three courtesy of Quade Cooper, Radike Samo, Luke Morahan (2), Digby Ioane and Horwill, and had it not been for the late score from Bjorn Basson for the Bulls they would not have registered what was a flattering 39–30 defeat.

An agonising 28–26 defeat to the Hurricanes in Wellington a fortnight later proved to be little more than a temporary setback and, once the Crusaders were beaten 17–16 at the end of May, there was no stopping the Reds as they finished top of the table and ensured home advantage in the semi-finals.

The Stormers finished second to wrap up an automatic place in the last four, while the Crusaders, Blues, Waratahs and Sharks all qualified for the play-offs. Both play-offs saw the home side emerge victorious, and so it was the Blues and the Crusaders who progressed into the semi-finals.

The Reds' last-four clash with the Blues in early July was a feast of attacking rugby, orchestrated in chief by Cooper at fly-half, and the New Zealanders simply had no answer to the repeated Australian thrusts.

Wing Rod Davies completed a superb hat-trick, centre Ben Tapuai added a fourth try which was supplemented by 10 points from the boot of Cooper, and the Reds raced to a 30–13 win in Brisbane.

"I'm not going to take any coaching credit for that," said McKenzie after his number 10's virtuoso display. "That was just pure Quade. I'm still working out how he set up Tapuai's try. And it wasn't just his attack, he worked very, very hard in defence. I said it during the week, the bigger the stage the more he likes it."

Later the same day the Stormers and Crusaders crossed swords in Cape Town in the second semi-final, with the Kiwis looking to book their place in a 10th final in 13 years and the South Africans hoping to make a second successive final. After 80 minutes, it was the New Zealanders who were celebrating.

First-half tries from wing Sean Maitland and centre Robbie Fruean provided the platform for the Crusaders' 29–10 win, but not for the first time it was the kicking of Dan Carter that proved pivotal as the fly-half kicked 19 points for the seven-time champions.

"We'll sit and do a bit of soul-searching after that," admitted Stormers coach Allister Coetzee. "They were outstanding. Our own tactics were naïve, and as a coaching staff and group we take responsibility. We played too much rugby in our own half again, and that wasn't the plan.

"They exploited it well, and points came from turnovers they capitalised on. It was another learning experience for us. I know it's difficult to digest, but you do learn from big games like this one, and we look forward to next season."

The final in the Suncorp Stadium was a nerve-jangling yet supremely entertaining contest which ebbed and flowed but was ultimately settled by a moment of sublime individual skill by scrum-half Will Genia.

A full 32 minutes had been played before the Reds finally drew first blood with a Cooper penalty, but the lead lasted a mere three minutes as Carter collected his own clever grubber kick to score the opening try of the match in the corner. The All Black duly converted, but moments before the break Cooper landed a second penalty and the Crusaders' lead was cut to a precarious 7–6.

The second half saw Carter slot a 48th-minute penalty, but the tide began to turn in the Reds' favour two minutes later when Ioane scored a brilliant long-range try. Cooper added the extra two points, but Carter's second penalty of the battle on 54 minutes left the two protagonists locked at 13–13.

The tension was palpable as the clock ticked down, but the Australian contingent in the record Suncorp crowd experienced a collective surge of relief in the 67th minute when Genia scored a dazzling try. Collecting the ball near his own 10-metre line, the Wallaby danced past the first three tackles and was suddenly free deep in enemy territory. The Crusaders cover desperately scrambled across, but Genia cleverly used the supporting Cooper as a dummy runner and raced onwards towards the line, sliding over despite a late, despairing tackle.

Cooper missed with the conversion, but it was to prove academic as there were no more scores, and the Reds' remarkable transformation from the whipping boys of Super Rugby to champions was complete.

"Although we didn't get the result we were after, I would like to mention it's been a tough year. Every time we have taken the field this year, hopefully we have done you proud back in Christchurch and put a smile on your face," said Crusaders captain Richie McCaw in reference to the earthquake that struck Christchurch. "I know it's been a tough time at home, but we can hold our heads up high and maybe next year.

"It was an epic final. It came down to one or two opportunities. They made us pay, and that is what footie is all about. The Reds scored their try and they took advantage of turnovers. It came down to one or two things.

"We are definitely proud of the way the guys have stuck to their task all year. We were ready to play in the final, but we just weren't good enough. I guess in some ways we are pleased with the season, but we are bitterly disappointed at losing out."

SUPER RUGBY 2011 RESULTS

18 February: **Hurricanes** 9 **Highlanders** 14, **Rebels** 0 **Waratahs** 43. 19 February: **Blues** 24 **Crusaders** 22, **Brumbies** 28 **Chiefs** 20, **Sharks** 24 **Cheetahs** 9, **Lions** 20 **Bulls** 24. 20 February: **Reds** 21 **Force** 20. 25 February: **Highlanders** 23 **Chiefs** 13, **Rebels** 25 **Brumbies** 24, **Cheetahs** 23 **Bulls** 25. 26 February: **Hurricanes** 0 **Crusaders** 0, **Waratahs** 30 **Reds** 6, **Sharks** 26 **Blues** 12, **Stormers** 19 **Lions** 16. 4 March: **Crusaders** 33 **Waratahs** 18, **Lions** 32 **Blues** 41. 5 March: **Chiefs** 38 **Rebels** 10, **Brumbies** 25 **Reds** 31, **Force** 12 **Sharks** 39, **Stormers** 21 **Cheetahs** 15, **Bulls** 28 **Highlanders** 35. 11 March: **Crusaders** 52 **Brumbies** 10, **Rebels** 32 **Sharks** 34, **Stormers** 18 **Highlanders** 6. 12 March: **Hurricanes** 29 **Chiefs** 26, **Force** 22 **Blues** 22, **Cheetahs** 20 **Lions** 25. 18 March 2011: **Chiefs** 15 **Sharks** 9, **Reds** 53 **Rebels** 3. 19 March: **Highlanders** 13 **Crusaders** 44, **Blues** 41 **Hurricanes** 17, **Waratahs** 3 **Cheetahs** 23, **Lions** 15 **Force** 27, **Bulls** 13 **Stormers** 23. 25 March: **Rebels** 42 **Hurricanes** 25. 26 March: **Reds** 41 **Cheetahs** 8, **Chiefs** 13 **Blues** 16, **Brumbies** 22 **Waratahs** 29, **Stormers** 51 **Force** 16, **Bulls** 30 **Lions** 23. 27 March: **Crusaders** 44 **Sharks** 28. 1 April: **Highlanders** 26 **Brumbies** 20, **Waratahs** 23 **Chiefs** 16. 2 April: **Blues** 29 **Cheetahs** 22, **Hurricanes** 14 **Bulls** 26, **Force** 25 **Rebels** 26, **Lions** 25 **Reds** 30, **Sharks** 6 **Stormers** 16. 8 April: **Highlanders** 24 **Cheetahs** 21. 9 April: **Crusaders** 27 **Bulls** 0, **Brumbies** 17 **Hurricanes** 16, **Force** 3 **Waratahs** 31, **Stormers** 6 **Reds** 19, **Sharks** 27 **Lions** 3. 15 April: **Chiefs** 16 **Crusaders** 34, **Rebels** 18 **Highlanders** 40. 16 April: **Blues** 31 **Waratahs** 17, **Reds** 39 **Bulls** 30, **Lions** 19 **Stormers** 33, **Cheetahs** 47 **Hurricanes** 50. 17 April: **Brumbies** 19 **Force** 27. 22 April: **Blues** 40 **Rebels** 23. 23 April: **Crusaders** 18 **Highlanders** 26, **Reds** 19 **Waratahs** 15, **Force** 26 **Bulls** 21, **Sharks** 40 **Hurricanes** 24, **Lions** 30 **Chiefs** 34. 29 April: **Highlanders** 10 **Blues** 15, **Cheetahs** 47 **Brumbies** 36. 30 April: **Hurricanes** 28 **Reds** 26, **Waratahs** 28 **Rebels** 9, **Force** 30 **Crusaders** 42, **Bulls** 43 **Chiefs** 27, **Stormers** 32 **Sharks** 12. 6 May: **Hurricanes** 11 **Blues** 17, **Rebels** 18 **Reds** 33, **Lions** 19 **Cheetahs** 53. 7 May: **Chiefs** 20 **Highlanders** 7, **Waratahs** 20 **Force** 15, **Stormers** 14 **Crusaders** 20, **Sharks** 34 **Brumbies** 16. 13 May: **Highlanders** 13 **Hurricanes** 6, **Reds** 37 **Blues** 31. 14 May: **Chiefs** 30 **Stormers** 23, **Brumbies** 20 **Lions** 29, **Bulls** 47 **Rebels** 10, **Cheetahs** 33 **Crusaders** 20. 20 May: **Blues** 26 **Stormers** 28. 21 May: **Crusaders** 25 **Chiefs** 19, **Waratahs** 29 **Lions** 12, **Force** 13 **Brumbies** 13, **Cheetahs** 41 **Rebels** 21, **Sharks** 23 **Bulls** 32. 27 May: **Hurricanes** 34 **Force** 28. 28 May: **Highlanders** 22 **Lions** 26, **Brumbies** 3 **Stormers** 16, **Sharks** 26 **Waratahs** 21, **Bulls** 32 **Cheetahs** 21, **Reds** 17 **Crusaders** 16. 3 June: **Highlanders** 14 **Force** 21, **Rebels** 3 **Stormers** 40, **Bulls** 23 **Waratahs** 17. 4 June: **Hurricanes** 38 **Lions** 27, **Blues** 11 **Chiefs** 16, **Reds** 14 **Brumbies** 22, **Cheetahs** 18 **Sharks** 23. 10 June: **Chiefs** 18 **Hurricanes** 18, **Brumbies** 32 **Rebels** 17. 11 June: **Crusaders** 23 **Blues** 16, **Waratahs** 33 **Highlanders** 7, **Force** 21 **Reds** 24, **Lions** 30 **Sharks** 30, **Stormers** 16 **Bulls** 19. 17 June: **Blues** 33 **Highlanders** 16, **Rebels** 24 **Force** 27. 18 June: **Chiefs** 11 **Reds** 19, **Crusaders** 16 **Hurricanes** 9, **Waratahs** 41 **Brumbies** 7, **Bulls** 23 **Sharks** 26, **Cheetahs** 34 **Stormers** 44.

FINAL TABLE

	P	W	D	L	BYE	F	A	BP	PTS
Reds	16	13	0	3	2	429	309	6	**66**
Stormers	16	12	0	4	2	400	257	7	**63**
Crusaders	16	11	1	4	2	436	273	7	**61**
Blues	16	10	1	5	2	405	335	10	**60**
Waratahs	16	10	0	6	2	398	252	9	**57**
Sharks	16	10	1	5	2	407	339	7	**57**
Bulls	16	10	0	6	2	416	370	6	**54**
Highlanders	16	8	0	8	2	296	343	5	**45**
Hurricanes	16	5	2	9	2	328	398	10	**42**
Chiefs	16	6	1	9	2	332	348	6	**40**
Cheetahs	16	5	0	11	2	435	437	12	**40**
Force	16	5	2	9	2	333	416	5	**37**
Brumbies	16	4	1	11	2	314	437	7	**33**
Lions	16	3	1	12	2	351	477	7	**29**
Rebels	16	3	0	13	2	281	570	4	**24**

PLAY-OFFS

24 February

Blues 26 **Waratahs** 13

25 February

Crusaders 36 **Sharks** 8

SEMI-FINALS

2 July, Suncorp Stadium, Brisbane

REDS 30 (2G, 1PG, 2T, 1DG) BLUES 13 (1G, 2PG)

REDS: J Lance; R Davies, A Faingaa, B Tapuai, D Ioane; Q Cooper, W Genia; B Daley, S Faingaa, G Holmes, R Simmons, J Horwill (captain), S Higginbotham, B Robinson, R Samo

SUBSTITUTIONS: J Schatz for Samo (24 mins); A Wallace-Harrison for Simmons (60 mins); J Hanson for S Faingaa (65 mins); L Gill for Robinson (65 mins); W Chambers for Tapuai (76 mins); I Prior for Genia (76 mins); G Shepherdson for Holmes (78 mins)

SCORERS: *Tries*: Davies (3), Tapuai *Conversion*: Cooper (2) *Penalty Goal*: Cooper (2) *Dropped Goal:* (2)

BLUES: J Payne; J Rokocoko, B Stanley, L McAlister, L Munro; S Brett, A Mathewson; C Faumuina, K Mealamu (captain), J Afoa, C Lowrey , A Williams, J Kaino, L Braid, P Saili

SUBSTITUTIONS: R Ranger for Munro (39 mins); C Smylie for Mathewson (50 mins); DJ Braid for L Braid (58 mins); S Stowers for McAlister (tem 59 to 64 mins); T McCartney for Faumuina (65 mins); J King for Saili (73 mins)

SCORERS: *Try*: Lowrey *Conversion*: Brett *Penalty Goals*: McAlister

REFEREE J Kaplan (South Africa)

2 July, Newlands, Cape Town

STORMERS 10 (1G, 1PG)
CRUSADERS 29 (2G, 5PG)

STORMERS: C Jantjies; G Aplon, J Fourie, J de Villiers, B Habana; P Grant, L Schreuder; W Blaauw, T Liebenberg, B Harris, R Elstadt, A Bekker, S Burger (captain), F Louw, N Koster

SUBSTITUTIONS: S Brits for Burger (40 mins); J de Jongh for Jantjes (52 mins); S Kitshoff for Blaauw (52 mins); D Fourie for Liebenberg (59 mins); N Groom for Schreuder (64 mins); A van Zyl for Elstadt (64 mins); J Sadie for Aplon (75 mins)

SCORERS *Try*: Habana *Conversion*: Grant *Penalty Goal*: Grant

Crusaders: T Marshall; S Maitland, R Fruean, SB Williams, Z Guildford; D Carter, A Ellis; W Crockett, C Flynn, O Franks, B Thorn, S Whitelock, G Whitelock, R McCaw (captain), K Read

SUBSTITUTIONS: K Fotuali'i for Ellis (17 mins); B Franks for O Franks (55 mins); M Todd for G Whitelock (59 mins); L Romano for Thorn (68 mins); Q MacDonald for Flynn (72 mins); R Crotty for Fruean (75 mins); M Berquist for Carter (75 mins)

SCORERS *Tries*: Fruean, Maitland *Conversions*: Carter (2) *Penalty Goals*: Carter (5)

REFEREE C Joubert (South Africa)

FINAL

9 July, Suncorp Stadium, Brisbane

REDS 18 (1G, 2PG, 1T) CRUSADERS 13 (1G 2PG)

REDS: J Lance; R Davies, A Faingaa, B Tapuai, D Ioane; Q Cooper, W Genia; B Daley, S Faingaa, G Holmes, R Simmons, J Horwill (captain), S Higginbotham, B Robinson, R Samo

SUBSTITUTIONS: L Gill for Robinson (59 mins); A Wallace-Hamilton for Simmons (60 mins); J Hanson for S Faingaa (62 mins)

SCORERS *Tries*: Ioane, Genia *Conversion*: Cooper *Penalty Goals*: Cooper (2)

CRUSADERS: T Marshall; S Maitland, R Fruean, SB Williams, Z Guildford; D Carter, A Ellis; W Crockett, C Flynn, O Franks, B Thorn, S Whitelock, G Whitelock, R McCaw (captain), K Read

SUBSTITUTIONS: M Todd for G Whitelock (54 mins); K Fotuali'i for Ellis (59 mins); B Franks for O Franks (64 mins); L Romano for Thorn (71 mins); R Crotty for Fruean (73 mins)

SCORERS *Try*: Carter *Conversion*: Carter *Penalty Goals*: Carter (2)

REFEREE B Lawrence (New Zealand)

MUNSTER VICTORIOUS AS LEAGUE GETS TOUGHER

By Tom Shanklin

The 2010–11 season marked the 10th anniversary of the Magners League, or the Celtic League as it was originally known, and I would definitely argue that the tournament has really come into its own since its inception and is now an unqualified success. Other competitions might generate a little more hype in the media, but the Magners League has developed into a really tough nut to crack and a genuine prize for those who play in it.

I remember making my debut in the competition in the 2003–04 season. I was selected on the right wing to play against Munster at Musgrave Park and, while I was delighted to be given the opportunity to impress, it wasn't the happiest of introductions to the tournament – the Blues were well beaten 31–10, and I spent 10 minutes in the sin bin for coming in from the side at the breakdown. I've got to say I did have some better performances after that.

Since my debut, the tournament has really developed season by season. I played in front of about 5,000 at Musgrave Park back in 2003, but the crowds have grown steadily since then, the competition has been marketed significantly better off the pitch and the intensity on the pitch has increased.

If I had to give one example of the overall improvement it would be the dramatic decrease in the number of games perceived as easy fixtures, matches the bigger clubs could bank on winning without really breaking sweat. In the early days, and with due respect to them, we'd consider teams like Connacht and Glasgow easy fixtures home and away, but

Dino Panato/Getty Images

Coach Tony McGahan led Munster to the final Magners League title.

that's just not the case these days. Glasgow had a disappointing campaign in 2010–11, but they reached the semi-final the previous year and for me that encapsulated an increasingly level playing field. There just aren't the walkovers there used to be.

I know there were some doubts about the introduction of the Italian sides, Aironi and Treviso, for the 2010–11 season but, despite finishing bottom and third bottom respectively, I thought there were plenty of encouraging signs from both. Nine victories for Treviso, including a famous win over Munster, was fantastic in their first season and, although Aironi could record only one win, they lost four other games by a single point and definitely have something to build on in their second year. The Magners League was certainly a more interesting product with the Italian sides involved.

Exposure to the league can only help strengthen Italian rugby but, conversely, I also believe the tournament will benefit from their arrival because it helps expand its reach across Europe, bringing Magners rugby to a new group of supporters.

Congratulations to Munster on winning the title in 2011 for a third time. They have been one of the dominant forces in the competition since it began and after finishing 14 points clear of the chasing pack in the regular season, I think justice was done with their 19–9 win over Leinster in the final.

I remain unconvinced of the merits of the play-offs, but I do have to admit that the format maintained interest in the league long after it became clear Munster wouldn't be caught at the top. If it had been a traditional first-past-the-post system, it would have all been over as a meaningful competition by February.

Munster were the strongest side over the course of the season, but there's no doubt their task in the final at Thomond Park was made considerably easier by the fact the game came seven days after Leinster's epic, rollercoaster victory over Northampton in the Heineken Cup final. That was a brutal and mentally draining game, and I'm sure it took a lot out of the Leinster boys. Munster were then lying in wait for them, relatively fresh and focused, and I'm sure that gave them a certain edge in what was always going to be a tight match.

Munster were champions, Leinster the runners-up and second place in the table with Ulster in third, and I think that reflects the increasing strength in depth in Irish rugby at the moment. I really don't think there's much to choose between the full-strength XVs of the top six or seven clubs, but the Irish teams continue to cope with injuries and international call-ups better than the rest.

It was a disappointing season for the Blues and the rest of the Welsh sides. The Ospreys made the semi-finals, but collectively the Welsh clubs didn't really threaten to break the Irish stranglehold. From a Cardiff perspective, they were too slow out of the blocks and I've always believed that you have to be top or thereabouts of the Magners by Christmas if you want to have a realistic chance of winning it.

However, a big positive for Welsh rugby was the emergence of George North and Rhys Priestland at the Scarlets, and it was a huge endorsement of the Magners League that they were to cut their teeth in the tournament, force their way into the Wales set-up and then go on and make a real impact at the World Cup in New Zealand.

That is exactly what a strong domestic competition should be all about. It's got to give opportunities to young players to prove themselves, but it also has to provide a high standard of rugby that prepares those youngsters for the step up to international level. The Magners has proved it can do both.

It was an even tougher year for the Scottish sides, with Glasgow and Edinburgh both finishing in the bottom half of the table. As I said earlier, Glasgow were semi-finalists the previous season while Edinburgh were runners-up in 2009, but in 2010–11 they both unfortunately went backwards.

Edinburgh have certainly missed Andy Robinson since he took the Scotland job, but both teams continue to struggle as soon as they have to rotate their squads. Saying that, Tim Visser was very impressive on the wing for Edinburgh, and it is no mean feat to score 14 tries in a single season.

I've already mentioned the two Italian sides. I'm sure they will improve, and there's no doubt joining the Magners League will help both clubs attract new players. I know plenty of players who would love to live and work in Italy but have been discouraged in the past because, a few Heineken Cup games aside, the general level of rugby wasn't up to scratch. That's changing now, and I expect to see Aironi and Treviso looking towards Wales, Scotland and Ireland for new signings in the future.

If I did have to take issue with one aspect of the Magners League, however, it would have to be the standard of refereeing. The best officials, the likes of Wayne Barnes and Alain Rolland, are top class, but I think the gap between the leading referees and the rest is still too big. Any tournament benefits from strong refereeing but can suffer if there are too many below-par officials, and I think the Magners League deserves strong, consistent referees.

Dino Panato/Getty Images

Benetton Treviso (right) picked up an impressive nine wins, but Aironi finished bottom with just one victory.

3 September, 2010: **Glasgow** 22 **Leinster** 19, **Ulster** 27 **Ospreys** 26. 4 September: **Connacht** 40 **Dragons** 17, **Treviso** 34 **Scarlets** 28, **Blues** 34 **Edinburgh** 23, **Munster** 33 **Aironi** 17. 10 September: **Edinburgh** 13 **Munster** 16, **Ospreys** 32 **Treviso** 16. 11 September: **Scarlets** 35 **Connacht** 33, **Aironi** 15 **Ulster** 22, **Leinster** 34 **Blues** 23. 12 September: **Dragons** 23 **Glasgow** 11. 17 September: **Glasgow** 17 **Connacht** 19, **Scarlets** 49 **Aironi** 10, **Ulster** 29 **Edinburgh** 21. 18 September: **Treviso** 29 **Leinster** 13, **Blues** 43 **Dragons** 21, **Munster** 22 **Ospreys** 10. 24 September: **Treviso** 7 **Blues** 19, **Dragons** 14 **Scarlets** 27, **Edinburgh** 32 **Leinster** 24, **Glasgow** 29 **Munster** 43. 25 September: **Ospreys** 38 **Aironi** 6, **Connacht** 15 **Ulster** 15. 30 September: **Blues** 22 **Connacht** 6. 1 October: **Treviso** 20 **Dragons** 13, **Ulster** 19 **Glasgow** 17. 2 October: **Aironi** 9 **Edinburgh** 10, **Leinster** 13 **Munster** 9, **Scarlets** 18 **Ospreys** 21. 22 October: **Edinburgh** 21 **Ulster** 16, **Munster** 39 **Treviso** 13, **Blues** 10 **Scarlets** 16. 23 October: **Connacht** 6 **Leinster** 18, **Dragons** 36 **Aironi** 5. 24 October: **Glasgow** 31 **Ospreys** 23. 29 October: **Aironi** 3 **Blues** 20, **Ulster** 6 **Munster** 16, **Scarlets** 18 **Glasgow**1 4. 30 October: **Treviso** 24 **Connacht** 17, **Leinster** 19 **Edinburgh** 18, **Ospreys** 16 **Dragons** 21. 5 November: **Edinburgh** 21 **Treviso** 9, **Glasgow** 33 **Aironi** 8. 19 November: **Connacht** 15 **Ospreys** 16, **Leinster** 27 **Dragons** 6. 21 November: **Blues** 15 **Ulster** 37, **Munster** 27 **Scarlets** 26. 26 November: **Treviso** 9 **Ulster** 19, **Dragons** 20 **Munster** 6, **Edinburgh** 24 **Connacht** 19. 27 November: **Blues** 38 **Glasgow** 6, **Aironi** 17 **Scarlets** 34. 28 November: **Ospreys** 19 **Leinster** 15. 3 December: **Scarlets** 17 **Leinster** 17. 4 December: **Munster** 16 **Blues** 9, **Ospreys** 33 **Edinburgh** 16. 24 December: **Treviso** 15 **Aironi** 10. 27 December: **Ulster** 13 **Leinster** 30, **Ospreys** 60 **Scarlets** 17, **Glasgow** 30 **Edinburgh** 18, **Connacht** 12 **Munster** 16. 31 December: **Aironi** 15 **Treviso** 16, **Blues** 27 **Ospreys** 25. 1 January, 2011: **Leinster** 30 **Connacht** 8, **Scarlets** 21 **Dragons** 15, **Munster** 35 **Ulster** 10. 2 January: **Edinburgh** 28 **Glasgow** 17. 6 January: **Dragons** 17 **Connacht** 16. 7 January: **Ulster** 32 **Treviso** 13, **Blues** 24 **Aironi** 13, **Leinster** 15 **Ospreys** 10. 8 January: **Edinburgh** 16 **Scarlets** 21, **Munster** 22 **Glasgow** 20. 10 February: **Leinster** 21 **Aironi** 16. 11 February: **Glasgow** 15 **Blues** 26. 12 February: **Dragons** 30 **Edinburgh** 22, **Connacht** 17 **Scarlets** 13. 13 February: **Treviso** 19 **Munster** 18, **Ospreys** 23 **Ulster** 22. 18 February: **Connacht** 37 **Glasgow** 8, **Scarlets** 16 **Ulster** 18, **Munster** 23 **Edinburgh** 13.19 February: **Treviso** 18 **Ospreys** 34, **Blues** 11 **Leinster** 3. 20 February: **Aironi** 3 **Dragons** 18. 24 February: **Scarlets** 11 **Edinburgh** 3. 25 February: **Ulster** 32 **Blues** 13, **Leinster** 30 **Treviso** 5, **Glasgow** 16 **Dragons** 16. 27 February: **Aironi** 10 **Munster** 20, **Ospreys** 33 **Connacht** 18. 4 March: **Connacht** 31 **Treviso** 25, **Ulster** 23 **Aironi** 10, **Edinburgh** 11 **Blues** 16, **Leinster** 26 **Scarlets** 15. 5 March: **Ospreys** 37 **Glasgow** 6, **Munster** 38 **Dragons** 17. 11 March: **Connacht** 11 **Aironi** 6. 18 March: **Ulster** 25 **Dragons** 23, **Glasgow** 25 **Treviso** 17. 25 March: **Blues** 15 **Munster** 16, **Glasgow** 19 **Ulster** 22. 26 March: **Aironi** 25 **Connacht** 13, **Edinburgh** 23 **Ospreys** 16. 27 March: **Dragons** 16 **Leinster** 26, **Scarlets** 22 **Treviso** 16. 1 April: **Ulster** 20 **Scarlets** 18, **Connacht** 27 **Edinburgh** 23. 2 April: **Aironi** 16 **Glasgow** 17, **Ospreys** 21 **Blues** 21, **Munster** 24 **Leinster** 23. 3 April: **Dragons** 33 **Treviso** 10. 15 April: **Dragons** 32 **Ospreys** 28, **Connacht** 12 **Blues** 26, **Edinburgh** 35 **Aironi** 15. 16 April: **Treviso** 19 **Glasgow** 16, **Scarlets** 6 **Munster** 13, **Leinster** 34 **Ulster** 26. 21 April: **Blues** 29 **Treviso** 9. 22 April: **Ulster** 27 **Connacht** 16, **Edinburgh** 27 **Dragons** 15, **Glasgow** 29 **Scarlets** 37. 23 April: **Aironi** 8 **Leinster** 20, **Ospreys** 20 **Munster** 22. 29 April: **Dragons** 28 **Blues** 15. 6 May: **Aironi** 10 **Ospreys** 12, **Treviso** 31 **Edinburgh** 6, **Dragons** 13 **Ulster** 20, **Leinster** 38 **Glasgow** 3, **Munster** 22 **Connacht** 6, **Scarlets** 38 **Blues** 23.

FINAL TABLE

	P	W	D	L	F	A	BP	PTS
Munster	22	19	0	3	496	327	7	**83**
Leinster	22	15	1	6	495	336	8	**70**
Ulster	22	15	1	6	480	418	5	**67**
Ospreys	22	12	1	9	553	418	13	**63**
Scarlets	22	12	1	9	503	453	12	**62**
Blues	22	13	1	8	479	392	6	**60**
Dragons	22	10	1	11	444	462	7	**49**
Edinburgh	22	9	0	13	421	460	7	**43**
Connacht	22	7	1	14	394	459	9	**39**
Treviso	22	9	0	13	374	502	2	**38**
Glasgow	22	6	1	15	401	543	7	**33**
Aironi	22	1	0	21	247	517	8	**12**

SEMI–FINALS

13 May, RDS, Dublin

LEINSTER 18 (1G, 2PG, 1T) ULSTER 3 (1PG)

LEINSTER: I Nacewa; F McFadden, B O'Driscoll, G D'Arcy, L Fitzgerald; J Sexton, I Boss; C Healy, R Strauss, M Ross, L Cullen (captain), N Hines, S O'Brien, S Jennings, J Heaslip *Substitutions:* E Reddan for Boss (31 mins); S Wright for Ross (32 mins) D Kearney for O'Driscoll (40 mins); I Madigan for Sexton (55 mins); J Harris-Wright for Strauss (55 mins); H van der Merwe for Healy (60 mins); D Toner for Cullen (72 mins); K McLaughlin for O'Brien (72 mins)

SCORERS: *Tries:* McFadden, Fitzgerald *Conversion:* McFadden *Penalty Goals:* Sexton (2)

ULSTER: A D'Arcy; C Gilroy, D Cave, N Spence, S Danielli; I Humphreys, R Pienaar; T Court, R Best (captain), D Fitzpatrick, J Muller, T Barker, P Wannenburg, C Henry, R Diack *Substitutions:* J Cronin for Fitzpatrick (42 mins); P Marshall for Humphreys (58 mins); A Kyriacou for Court (75 mins); T Anderson for Best (75 mins); P McAllister for Danielli (75 mins); C Gaston for Wannenburg (75 mins); I Whitten for Cave (77 mins)

SCORERS: *Penalty Goal:* Pienaar

REFEREE: G Clancy (Ireland)

14 May, Thomond Park, Limerick

MUNSTER 18 (1G, 2PG, 1T)
OSPREYS 11 (2PG, 1T)

MUNSTER: F Jones, D Howlett, D Barnes, L Mafi, K Earls, R O'Gara, C Murray; M Horan, D Varley, J Hayes, D O'Callaghan, P O'Connell (captain), D Ryan, D Wallace, J Coughlan *Substitutions:* P Stringer for Murray (56 mins); W du Preez for Horan (56 mins); M Sherry for Varley (56 mins); D Leamy for Coughlan (61 mins); S Archer for Hayes (62 mins); S Zebo for Barnes (74 mins); N Ronan for Leamy (74 mins)

SCORERS: *Tries:* Barnes (2) *Conversion:* O'Gara *Penalty Goals:* O'Gara (2)

OSPREYS: R Fussell, T Bowe, A Bishop, J Hook, N Walker, D Biggar, R Webb; P James, H Bennett, A Jones, I Gough, A Wyn Jones (captain), R Jones, J Tipuric, J Thomas *Substitutions:* A Beck for Hook (39 mins); R Hibbard for Bennett (48 mins); J Collins for Gough (48 mins); T Isaacs for Webb (54 mins); M Holah for R Jones (64 mins); C Griffiths for A Jones (72 mins); T Smith for Tipuric (74 mins)

SCORERS: *Try:* Fussell *Penalty Goals:* Biggar (2)

REFEREE: N Owens (Wales)

FINAL

28 May, Thomond Park, Limerick

MUNSTER 19 (2G, 1T) LEINSTER 9 (3PG)

MUNSTER: F Jones; D Howlett, D Barnes, L Mafi, K Earls; R O'Gara, C Murray; M Horan, D Varley, J Hayes, D O'Callaghan, P O'Connell (captain), D Ryan, D Wallace, J Coughlan *Substitutions:* W du Preez for Horan (53 mins); M Sherry for Varley (59 mins): D Leamy for O'Callaghan (68 mins); P Warwick for Jones (75 mins)

SCORERS: *Tries:* Howlett, Earls, Penalty *Try*; *Conversions:* O'Gara (2)

LEINSTER: I Nacewa; S Horgan, B O'Driscoll, F McFadden, L Fitzgerald; J Sexton, E Reddan; H van der Merwe, R Strauss, M Ross, L Cullen (captain), N Hines, S O'Brien, S Jennings, J Heaslip *Substitutions:* C Healy for van der Merwe (59 mins); K McLaughlin for O'Brien (59 mins); S Wright for Ross (69 mins); A Dundon for Jennings (70 mins): P O'Donohoe for Reddan (77 mins)

SCORERS: *Penalty Goals:* Sexton (3)

YELLOW CARD: O'Callaghan (48 mins)

REFEREE: N Owens (Wales)

JAPAN CLAIM FIRST TITLE

By Indra Singh

IRB

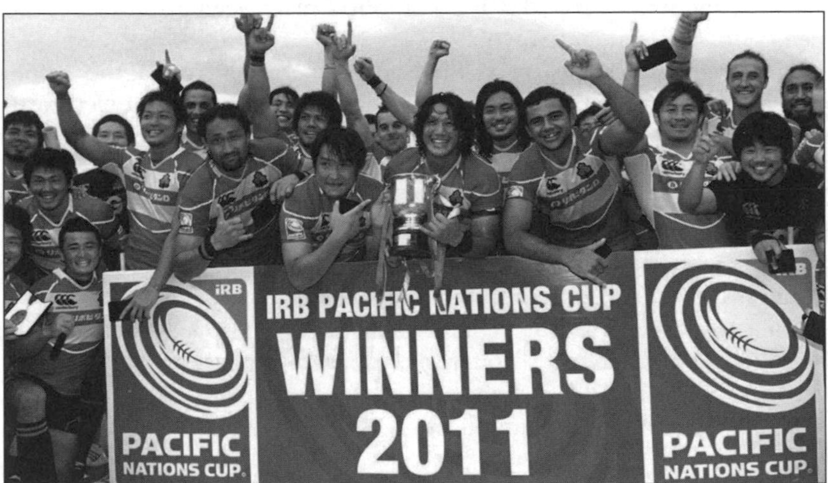

Japan celebrate their triumph in the Pacific Nations Cup.

The first-ever non-Oceana champion of the IRB Pacific Nations Cup was crowned in July at Churchill Park in Fiji as Japan created history to lift its maiden title and engrave a new name on the trophy for the second year in succession.

With only defending champions Samoa, the Junior All Blacks and New Zealand Maori having won the previous five installments, the John

Kirwan-coached Japan made it an emotional win and injected a huge confidence boost to the Brave Blossoms with Rugby World Cup just two months away.

Japan were due to host the tournament, but because of the devastating earthquake and Tsunami in March, only the opening round match between them and Samoa was played in Tokyo, with the rest of the matches moving to Fiji.

The win bought an emotional response from players and management alike, who dedicated their victory to the people of Japan and elevated their status to serious contenders in the region and beyond.

Despite their eventual win, Japan did not make the best start to the tournament, recording a loss to Samoa at home 34–15 in the opening round, and looked unlikely to add the PNC to their Asian Five Nations triumph earlier in the year.

However, a thrilling 28–27 win over Tonga at the National Stadium in the Fijian capital of Suva gave the side the much-needed points and self belief.

Heading into the nail-biting last day of matches, all four teams were still in contention to take the title, and Kirwan's brigade headed into the third and final match day lying in fourth place needing a bonus-point victory to secure their crown.

The drama started early as the two Pacific rivals Tonga and Samoa gave it their all in the final quest for the title. Tonga emerged victorious, recording a 29–19 win to put one hand on the trophy before Japan broke their hearts.

Tonga's earlier win meant hosts Fiji started their match against Japan knowing that this year's overall title was beyond their reach; however, Japan taught the hosts a harsh lesson in forward play, beating Sam Domoni's men 24–13 despite the noisy home crowd.

An early Seremaia Bai penalty gave them a 3–0 lead before wing Napolioni Nalaga burst through the Japanese defence to make it 8–0, but indiscipline would cost them.

Skipper Dominiko Waqaniburotu was sent to the sin bin for foul play before Fiji received the first of two red cards in the match, Sisa Koyamaibole sent off for dangerous play, and despite a rich advantage in the possession stakes, further indiscipline and errors restricted their scoring in the first half.

After the restart, Fiji's woes continued as Bai was sent to the sin bin, before Japan full-back Go Aruga scored an unconverted try to make it 8–5.

Fiji hit back with Nalaga's second try for a 13–5 lead, at which point

Tonga were sitting pretty with one hand on the trophy, but Japan kicked on and started their own quest for the title.

Ryan Nicholas went over for a try, which replacement Shaun Webb converted to make it 13–12, before Fiji's second red card – to centre Seru Rabeni for a high tackle – gifted the Japanese a two-man advantage which they used to put Shota Horie in for their third try and a 17–13 lead.

Shortly afterwards Fiji were reduced to 12 men when replacement Waisea Luveniyali was sin binned, and Japan rattled the Fijians with sterling forward play before replacement Yuta Imamura scored the crucial fourth bonus-point try for Japan. Webb added the extras for the 24–13 win.

"This is big for Japan Rugby, and Fiji gave us the chance as their discipline let them down," said Kirwan.

"However, I salute my players for the effort, and they did what I asked them at the break. Now it is the World Cup and there is still a lot of work to be done."

The tournament gave fans a pre-Rugby World Cup treat with Japan and Tonga and Fiji and Samoa all in action. Tonga and Japan met again at the Rugby World Cup as they were together in Pool A, while Fiji and Samoa were in Pool D.

For the first time in the history of the tournament, no one team was ruled out of winning the title until the last day, and Tonga hurt the most, as the side would have engraved their name on the trophy if not for unforced errors giving the narrow win to Japan in round two.

The Friendly Islanders scored the most points in the competition with 72, while Fiji was next on 57, Samoa 52 and Japan 43 and then went on to record an historic Rugby World Cup pool.

The side also scored eight tries, the most by any team, while impressive fly-half Kurt Morath was, for the second year in a row, the top points scorer with 37, having kicked six penalties and seven conversions.

Japan's Kosuke Honde and Ryu Holani, together with Fiji's Sekonaia Kalou and Alesana Tuilagi, all scored two tries each. Fijian full-back Taniela Rawaqa remains the top all-time points scorer with 103, while Japan's James Arlidge is on 96 and Morath close behind on 95.

The tournament proved to be the final selection ground for the four coaches before naming their Rugby World Cup squads. A number of new players were thrown into the mix to show their worth, while there was a return for some veterans like Fiji's all-time top points scorer, Nicky Little.

"We have played well in the PNC, but there is still lots of work to be done for World Cup,' said Tonga coach Isitolo Maka at the time, and clearly the work was done to mark a memorable Rugby World Cup for the Tongans who entered the top 10 of the IRB World Rankings for the first time ever on the back of their historic pool win over France.

Both the PNC and rugby's showpiece tournament in New Zealand reflected the significant growth and improved performance of all the Pacific Island teams. The seventh installment of the Pacific Nations Cup in 2012 is a mouth-watering prospect.

02/07/2011	**Tonga** 45–21 **Fiji**	Churchill Park, **Lautoka**
02/07/2011	**Japan** 15–34 **Samoa**	PCMRG, **Tokyo**
09/07/2011	**Tonga** 27–28 **Japan**	National Stadium, **Suva**
09/07/2011	**Samoa** 18–36 **Fiji**	National Stadium, **Suva**
13/07/2011	**Tonga** 29–19 **Samoa**	Churchill Park, **Lautoka**
13/07/2011	**Japan** 24–13 **Fiji**	Churchill Park, **Lautoka**

Team	P	W	D	L	PF	PA	TF	TA	BP	PTS
Tonga	3	2	0	1	101	68	10	7	2	**10**
Japan	3	2	0	1	67	74	10	9	2	**10**
Samoa	3	1	0	2	71	80	7	9	1	**5**
Fiji	3	1	0	2	70	87	9	11	1	**5**

HAT-TRICK FOR THE WARRIORS

By Karen Bond

IRB

Warriors hit the heights.

The winner's name on the IRB Pacific Rugby Cup may have remained the same for the third successive year, with the Fiji Warriors again lifting the trophy, but the exciting new format in 2011 meant the team playing under this banner was a little different.

The Warriors, who last year became the only side to successfully defend the title, were no longer one of two representative sides from Fiji tackling the best locally based players in Samoa and Tonga in a six-team tournament.

Instead, they were the Fiji A side and had eight different opponents to face – their equivalents in Tonga and Samoa as well as the development teams of six Super Rugby outfits, three in Australia and three in New Zealand.

The new-look competition was split into three series, the first in Australia, followed by one in New Zealand before the climax in Fiji, with only the three "core" Pacific Island teams capable of lifting the trophy in 2011.

The introduction of the six Super Rugby development sides – Junior Waratahs, Brumby Runners, QAS Reds Academy, Crusader Knights and the Chiefs and Hurricanes Development XVs – raised the competition to a new level and provided "money can't buy" experience for the Islanders.

"Most of our players had never played at that level," Samoa A manager Ryan Schuster admitted after the tournament ended. "Even though the results were [sometimes] one-sided, it did not reflect the effort put in by the players. The opposition capitalised on the little mistakes to score.

"I think we should continue this format – it will help the Pacific nations. We have learned a lot this year and hope to improve next year. The players have enjoyed this tournament. In previous years we were just playing amongst ourselves, but this format has a bright future."

The Pacific Rugby Cup kicked off on 19 February with Fiji Warriors preventing an Australian clean sweep, Taniela Rawaqa's late penalty snatching a 27–26 victory over the Reds Academy at Ballymore.

Four days later there was better news, with the Warriors edging past the Junior Waratahs 15–12, Samoa A overcoming the Reds Academy 23–20 and Tonga A fighting back to draw 22–22 with the Brumby Runners.

The final day of the Australian Series also yielded two victories for the "core" teams, Samoa A proving too strong for the Junior Waratahs in winning 35–12 and Tonga A picking up a first win, 23–22 over the Reds Academy following Edmond Paea's late penalty.

Fiji Warriors surrendered their perfect record with a narrow 30–28 loss to the Brumby Runners in Canberra, leaving the title race finely poised as the competition moved across the Tasman with both they and Samoa A on nine points, three more than Tonga A.

The opening weekend in New Zealand brought the Islanders back down to earth after a positive Australian leg with three heavy losses, the Crusader Knights – playing at Carisbrook in a match moved after the devastating earthquake in Christchurch – and Chiefs Development XV scoring half centuries against the Warriors and Tonga A respectively.

Samoa A faired a little better in only losing 33–0 to the Hurricanes Development XV, but four days later they came within a whisker of beating the Crusader Knights in Timaru, only for Tom Taylor's last-gasp conversion of Rhys Llewellyn's try to condemn them to a 22–21 loss.

Fiji Warriors fell 25–10 to the Chiefs Development XV, while Tonga A got acquainted with Hutt Recreation Park, one of their nation's bases at Rugby World Cup 2011, exactly six months before they opened the tournament against hosts New Zealand.

The Samoans finally picked up the only win on New Zealand soil when they edged the Chiefs Development XV 18–17 in Pukekohe, albeit only after Trent Renata missed two late kicks for the hosts, and entered the final Series – a round robin between the "core" teams – with a five-point advantage over Fiji Warriors.

This meant that the Warriors returned home knowing that only back-to-back victories over Tonga A and Samoa A would keep alive hopes of keeping the silverware in Fijian hands, and even then this wouldn't be enough if the Samoans beat their Tongan rivals.

The Warriors ticked off the first task, thanks largely to the Rawaqa's reliable boot, the full-back kicking all the points in a 21–14 victory at Churchill Park in Lautoka. However, it could have been a different story had the Tongans not missed four kicks at goal.

Samoa A were also left ruing four missed kicks after slipping to a 23–12 loss against the Warriors, who scored 10 points late on – including a second try for wing Apisalome Waqatabu – to move three points clear in the standings.

The Fijians had to keep their fingers crossed and pray for a Tongan victory four days later at Lawaqa Park in Sigatoka. Their nerves were certainly put through the wringer with a proverbial game of two halves, Tonga A going in 8–0 at half-time before their opponents came surging back to lead 13–8.

However, just as it seemed the Tongans would pay for squandering several try-scoring opportunities in the first half, they mounted one last attack and were awarded a penalty. Paea kicked to touch, and from the resulting lineout they sucked the defence in and swung the ball wide for Ahofono Alovili to score. Paea then held his nerve to land the conversion to secure the win and confirm the Warriors as champions.

"What has been the beauty of this new structure is that the best locally based players in Fiji, Samoa and Tonga, some of whom will go to the World Cup, have now had an opportunity to play the best up-and-coming players in Australia and New Zealand," said William Glenwright, IRB Regional General Manager for Oceania.

"Eight high-quality games, six of which were against Super Rugby development teams. You can't buy that level of experience, particularly in a World Cup year, and I think it is great for the national coaches to be able to test the local players in that sort of environment."

IRB PACIFIC RUGBY CUP 2011 RESULTS:

AUSTRALIA SERIES		
19/02/11	Junior Waratahs 28–18 Tonga A	Foreshaw Rugby Park
19/02/11	Brumby Runners 29–13 Samoa A	Canberra Stadium
19/02/11	QAS Reds Academy 26–27 Fiji Warriors	Ballymore
23/02/11	Junior Waratahs 12–15 Fiji Warriors	St Marys League Club
23/02/11	Brumby Runners 22–22 Tonga A	Vikings Park
23/02/11	QAS Reds Academy 20–23 Samoa A	Ballymore
28/02/11	Junior Waratahs 12–35 Samoa A	St Marys League Club
28/02/11	QAS Reds Academy 22–23 Tonga A	Ballymore
28/02/11	Brumby Runners 30–28 Fiji Warriors	Vikings Park

NEW ZEALAND SERIES		
04/03/11	Crusaders Knights 55–7 Fiji Warriors	Carisbrook
04/03/11	Chiefs Development XV 50–13 Tonga A	Growers Stadium
05/03/11	Hurricanes Development XV 33–0 Samoa A	Porirua Park
09/03/11	Chiefs Development XV 25–10 Fiji Warriors	Blake Park
09/03/11	Crusaders Knights 22–21 Samoa A	Alpine Energy Stadium
09/03/11	Hurricanes Development XV 41–10 Tonga A	Hutt Recreation Ground
14/03/11	Hurricanes Development XV 27–13 Fiji Warriors	Carisbrook
14/03/11	Crusaders Knights 36–18 Tonga A	Lincoln University
14/03/11	Chiefs Development XV 17–18 Samoa A	Growers Stadium

PACIFIC ISLAND SERIES		
19/03/11	Fiji Warriors 21–14 Tonga A	Churchill Park
22/03/11	Fiji Warriors 23–12 Samoa A	Churchill Park
26/03/11	Tonga A 15–13 Samoa A	Lawaqa Park

FINAL STANDINGS

	P	W	D	L	F	A	BP	PTS
Fiji Warriors	8	4	0	4	144	201	1	**17**
Samoa A	8	3	0	5	135	171	2	**15**
Tonga A	8	2	1	5	133	233	1	**11**

JAPAN DEDICATE TITLE TO PEOPLE BACK HOME

By Tom Chick

Hannah Johnston/Getty Images

John Kirwan led Japan to another HSBC Asian 5 Nations title.

Japan had extra motivation to secure a fourth successive HSBC Asian 5 Nations title in 2011 after dedicating the campaign to those back home who had been affected by the devastating earthquake and tsunami which struck in March.

The Brave Blossoms succeeded in lifting the Japanese spirits with another dominant campaign, scoring 307 points and conceding just 35 in beating Hong Kong, Kazakhstan, the United Arab Emirates and Sri Lanka to remain the only side to win the competition since its inception in 2008.

"We set two main goals for the HSBC Asian 5 Nations 2011 at the beginning of this tour," explained Japan coach John Kirwan. "First, defending the championship title and second, remembering the 11 March tragedy and sending a sort of spiritual message to the people who are suffering from the earthquake, tsunami and nuclear issue in the Tohoku region."

The 2011 installment of the Top 5 began on 23 April, with newly promoted Sri Lanka and the UAE, who replaced the disbanded Arabian Gulf in the top tier of Asian rugby, playing out a 13–13 draw in Colombo, while Kazakhstan suffered a 23–10 defeat to Hong Kong in Almaty.

Kazakhstan were unable to find the form that had seen them finish second in 2010 throughout this year's tournament and were on the wrong end of a surprise 24–10 defeat to the UAE a week later thanks to a 14-point haul from fly-half Jonathon Grady in the first-ever international match played in Abu Dhabi.

It was the UAE's first-ever victory in international rugby and left them top of the standings in their debut campaign.

"It feels fantastic," admitted UAE coach Bruce Birtwistle afterwards. "It is great to get our first win at home under the UAE banner, and I'm extremely proud of the effort of the entire team."

But, as the only Asian side competing at Rugby World Cup 2011 in New Zealand, Japan were always heavy favourites to defend the title, and they duly got their campaign off to a winning start on 30 April.

With coach Kirwan admitting his side had "plenty of work to do" after witnessing a "poor performance" in the 45–22 victory over Hong Kong, Japan went on to score 172 unanswered points in their next two matches against Kazakhstan and the UAE to retain the distinctive trophy with a match still remaining.

Takeshi Kizu scored four of Japan's nine tries against Kazakhstan in a 61–0 victory in the Thailand capital Bangkok, before James Arlidge caught the eye against the UAE at The Sevens in Dubai on 13 May, scoring the first of his side's 17 tries after just three minutes at the beginning of a 29-point haul for the fly-half.

With the title secured, Japan would not take their foot off the pedal and scored a further 14 tries to finish in emphatic style with a 90–13 victory against Sri Lanka in Colombo on 21 May and stretch their unbeaten run in the competition to 16 matches.

Alisi Tupuailai stole the headlines in Japan's final match, the centre scoring five tries to tie the record of team-mate Kosuke Endo for the most in an Asian 5 Nations match, and his quintet also took his tally for the season to nine, the most ever scored by an individual in a single Top 5 campaign.

"It is great to defend our title," admitted captain Takashi Kikutani, who scored twice in the Sri Lanka win. "In our team we have two players whose families were affected by the 11 March disasters. Thus, at the beginning of the tour, we were determined to play hard in the four matches, not only for ourselves, but also for the people of Tohoku and Japan."

With the title already Japan's before the final round of matches, many eyes were on the Hong Kong Football Club where Hong Kong and the UAE both had their sights set on securing victory to finish second in the standings.

In reality, there was only going to be one winner once the match got underway, with Hong Kong dominating the set pieces and the breakdown, enjoying a wealth of possession to run in ten tries for their biggest win in Asian 5 Nations history, Nick Hewson and Ross Armour both scoring twice in the 62–3 victory.

"We have to sustain this result," said Hong Kong coach Dai Rees. "Finishing second in Asia probably means nothing if you look down the road to qualifying for the 2015 World Cup. What matters is that we keep improving as we have done over the last few years. Last year we finished third and now we are second. We have to continue to improve."

Sri Lanka's defeat to Japan saw them relegated to Division I and, although their stay in the Top 5 may have been brief, they have shown their potential in a sport enjoying huge growth in the country and will be favourites to secure another title to return to Asia's elite tier for 2013.

Their place in 2012 will be taken by Korea, who return to the Top 5 at the first attempt after a 58–19 victory over Singapore in the Division I final thanks to two tries apiece from Wong Yong Kim, Sung Soo Kim, Nam Wook Kim and Kwang Min Kim.

In the other tiers of the A5N pyramid, Chinese Taipei were triumphant in Division II after they beat Thailand 22–10 in the final and will replace Malaysia in Division I, while China will take India's place in Division II following a 28–18 victory over Guam.

In Division IV, the curtain raiser to Japan's victory over the UAE was the final between Qatar and Lebanon. Qatar created their own piece of history with a first-ever Test victory, over top seeds Jordan, and then followed it up by beating Lebanon 29–14 to win the title and remain unbeaten in Test rugby. In Division V Laos beat Cambodia 11–7 in the last of the action in this year's A5N to take the title 32–26 on aggregate.

HSBC ASIAN 5 NATIONS 2011 RESULTS

TOP 5

Sri Lanka 13–13 **United Arab Emirates**, **Kazakhstan** 10–23 **Hong Kong**, **United Arab Emirates** 24–10 **Kazakhstan**, **Hong Kong** 22–45 **Japan**, **Sri Lanka** 3–48 **Hong Kong**, **Kazakhstan** 0–61 **Japan**, **United Arab Emirates** 0–111 **Japan**, **Kazakhstan** 34–18 **Sri Lanka**, **Sri Lanka** 13–90 **Japan**, **Hong Kong** 62–3 **Kazakhstan**

DIVISION I

Singapore 52–17 **Malaysia**, **Korea** 34–20 **Philippines**, **Malaysia** 20–86 **Philippines**, **Korea** 58–19 **Singapore**

DIVISON II

Chinese Taipei 34–31 **Iran**, **India** 24–37 **Thailand**, **Iran** 30–19 **India**, **Chinese Taipei** 22–10 **Thailand**

DIVISION III

Pakistan 10–37 **Guam**, **China** 32–23 **Indonesia**, **Pakistan** 19–20 **Indonesia**, **Guam** 18–28 **China**

DIVISION IV

Uzbekistan 15–34 **Lebanon**, **Jordan** 8–26 **Qatar**, **Uzbekistan** 14–17 **Jordan**, **Lebanon** 14–29 **Qatar**

DIVISION V

Cambodia 19–21 **Laos**, **Laos** 11–7 **Cambodia**

TOP 5 – FINAL STANDINGS

	P	W	D	L	F	A	BP	PTS
Japan	4	4	0	0	307	35	4	**24**
Hong Kong	4	3	0	1	155	61	2	**17**
UAE	4	1	1	2	40	196	0	**8**
Kazakhstan	4	1	0	3	54	126	1	**6**
Sri Lanka	4	0	1	3	47	185	0	**3**

KINGS RULE IN ROMANIA

By Karen Bond

IRB

The South African Kings emerged triumphant with some great rugby.

The IRB Nations Cup took on added significance in 2011 with three of the six participating teams using the tournament to fine-tune their preparations for the Rugby World Cup in New Zealand just three months later. One of these, Namibia, arrived as the defending champions after their surprise success last year, while Georgia and hosts Romania were themselves hoping to challenge for the title.

For the fifth successive year the Nations Cup was held in the Romanian capital of Bucharest with Portugal, hosts of the inaugural tournament in 2006, the Argentina Jaguars and the South African Kings completing the six-team field for the competition played at the stadionul National Arcul de Triumf from 10–19 June.

The South African Kings, on their first foray overseas, would ultimately become their country's third Nations Cup winners with an unbeaten record following wins over Georgia, Romania and Portugal. The Alan Solomons-coached outfit did not have it all their own way, but with No. 8 Luke Watson in outstanding form and wing Siyanda Grey scoring a record six tries for the tournament, the Kings followed in the footsteps of the Emerging Springboks coached by Peter de Villiers in 2007 and the Chester Williams-coached Emerging South Africa a year later.

The opening day kicked off with defending champions Namibia taking on Romania but, despite the presence of 11 of their 2010 vintage, the Africans failed to take their chances and it was the host nation who edged a tight affair 13–11. "At the end of the day, a win is a win, though we did not play to our full potential and made too many unforced errors, both individual and as a team," was the verdict of Romania captain Marius Tincu.

Rain had begun to fall shortly after the opening match, but it did not stop the desire of both Georgia and the South African Kings to play running rugby. Georgia scored the first try through Irakli Chkhikvadze, but the Kings ultimately ran out 31–17 winners, with Watson leading from the front and Grey scoring a hat-trick of tries.

The final match of the day was a thrilling encounter between Portugal and the Jaguars. Los Lobos produced an inspired performance to mark the Portuguese National Day, full of pride and guts to upset the Jaguars 25–21. The lead changed hands several times, but the never-say-die attitude of the Portuguese, who tackled like men possessed, snatched an unexpected victory with a well-taken try by replacement Jacques Le Roux.

Four days later two of the unbeaten sides came face to face, with Romania and the Kings playing out a dramatic encounter full of great intensity and passion in the dusk of a balmy Bucharest afternoon. Romania dominated the early exchanges, but the South Africans shifted up a gear in the second half and ran out 27–23 winners before a vocal capacity crowd.

While the Kings went to the top of the standings with two wins from two, the other two matches produced first victories of the tournament for Namibia and Georgia, both by narrow margins. The Namibians adapted better to the heavy rain to win a hard and uncompromising affair with Portugal 29–23, while Georgia also had cause to celebrate after battling to a 14–13 win over the Jaguars to the delight of coach Richie Dixon. "We have achieved what we wanted – that is to see several young players at work in significant areas for the RWC squad, and I am delighted with their work rate . . . the fact that we won is really a bonus."

Four nations went into the final day with a shot at the title, although if the South African Kings ran out winners over Portugal in the opening match then the results for Romania and Namibia against the Jaguars and Georgia respectively would only suffice to determine the final standings. Despite the loss of Watson after he was taken ill on the eve of the match, the Kings battled past the committed Portuguese to triumph 39–12, their third try by flanker Jacques Potgieter taking the IRB Nations Cup through the 2,000-point mark since it began in Lisbon in 2006.

"This was a good win, the third of the tournament, and I am happy for the boys," admitted Kings captain and former South Africa Sevens star Mzwandile Stick. "We had lost our way in the first half, but a few words from the coach at half-time and we regained structure after the break. It was very hot and this was a very intense, physical tournament. I am delighted."

Portugal coach Errol Brain was nonetheless delighted by "the progress of this young team" and admitted "this is the kind of rugby Portuguese rugby needs to make progress and I am very happy for the boys". Los Lobos would ultimately finish fifth, above Romania on point differential after the hosts were felled 37–13 by the Jaguars in the final match of the tournament.

It was the Jaguars' first win of the 2011 tournament and came after they began to pinch ball at the breakdown with regularity and launch lightning counter-attacks in the second half, wrapping up the bonus point with Joaquin Tuculet's try. This, allied with two losing bonus points after narrow losses to Portugal and Georgia, enabled the Argentina Jaguars to sneak into third place in the standings.

Georgia were the others winners on the final day, recovering from a 15–10 deficit at half-time to claim victory in the 50th match in IRB Nations Cup history, with Revaz Gigauri's try and the boot of Malkhaz Urjukashvili making the 2010 champions pay for some wayward kicking. Dixon was quick to pay tribute to his charges for "showing the true Georgian spirit" in the second half to seal the 23–18 victory and the runners-up spot behind the South African Kings.

IRB NATIONS CUP 2011 RESULTS

10/06/11	Romania 13–11 Namibia	stadionul National Arcul de Triumf
10/06/11	Georgia 17–31 South African Kings	stadionul National Arcul de Triumf
10/06/11	Argentina Jaguars 21–25 Portugal	stadionul National Arcul de Triumf
15/06/11	Georgia 14–13 Argentina Jaguars	stadionul National Arcul de Triumf
15/06/11	Romania 23–27 South African Kings	stadionul National Arcul de Triumf
15/06/11	Portugal 23–29 Namibia	stadionul National Arcul de Triumf
19/06/11	Portugal 12–39 South African Kings	stadionul National Arcul de Triumf
19/06/11	Georgia 23–18 Namibia	stadionul National Arcul de Triumf
19/06/11	Romania 13–37 Argentina Jaguars	stadionul National Arcul de Triumf

FINAL STANDINGS

	P	W	D	L	F	A	BP	PTS
South African Kings	3	3	0	0	97	52	1	**13**
Georgia	3	2	0	1	54	62	0	**8**
Argentina Jaguars	3	1	0	2	71	52	3	**7**
Namibia	3	1	0	2	58	59	2	**6**
Portugal	3	1	0	2	49	75	1	**5**
Romania	3	1	0	2	60	89	1	**5**

MAJOR RUGBY TOURS 2010–2011

By Chris Rhys

BLEDISLOE CUP

30 October, So Kon Po Stadium, Hong Kong Australia 26 (3G 1T) New Zealand 24 (3G 1PG)

AUSTRALIA: KJ Beale (NSW Waratahs); JD O'Connor (Western Force), AP Ashley-Cooper (Brumbies), MJ Giteau (Brumbies), DA Mitchell (NSW Waratahs); QS Cooper (Queensland Reds), SW Genia (Queensland Reds); BA Robinson (NSW Waratahs), ST Moore (Brumbies), BE Alexander (Brumbies), MD Chisholm (Brumbies), NC Sharpe (western Force), RD Elsom (Brumbies)(capt), BJ McCalman (Western Force), DW Pocock (Western Force) **SUBSTITUTIONS**: JA Slipper (Queensland Reds) for Robinson (51 mins), SM Faingaa (Queensland Reds) for Moore (62 mins), BS Barnes (NSW Waratahs) for Giteau (63 mins), DW Mumm (NSW Waratahs) for Chisholm (72 mins), L Burgess (NSW Waratahs) for Genia (76 mins) **SCORERS**: *Tries:* Cooper, Ashley-Cooper, Mitchell, O'Connor *Conversions*: Giteau, O'Connor (2)

NEW ZEALAND: JM Muliaina (Waikato); CS Jane (Wellington), CG Smith (Wellington), MA Nonu (Wellington), JT Rokocoko (Auckland); DW Carter (Canterbury), QJ Cowan (Southland); TD Woodcock (North Harbour), KF Mealamu (Auckland), OT Franks (Canterbury), BC Thorn (Canterbury), TJS Donnelly (Otago), J Kaino (Auckland), KJ Read (Canterbury), RH McCaw (Canterbury)(capt) **SUBSTITUTIONS**: I Toeava (Auckland) for Jane (51 mins), SR Donald (Auckland) & IF Afoa (Auckland) for Carter & O Franks (60 mins), SL Whitelock (Canterbury) for Donnelly (61 mins), AS Mathewson (Wellington) for Cowan (72 mins) **SCORERS**: *Tries*: Cowan, Jane, Nonu *Conversions*: Carter (3) *Penalty goal*: Carter **REFEREE**: ACP Rolland (Ireland)

AUSTRALIA TO EUROPE 2010

TOUR PARTY

FULL BACKS: KJ Beale (NSW Waratahs)

THREEQUARTERS: DA Mitchell (NSW Waratahs), AP Ashley-Cooper (Brumbies), RD Davies (Queensland Reds), PJ Hynes (Queensland Reds), LD Turner (NSW Waratahs), L Morahan (Queensland Reds), BS Barnes (NSW Waratahs), AS Faingaa (Queensland Reds), MJ Giteau (Brumbies), PJ McCabe (Queensland Reds), JD O'Connor (Western Force) **HALF BACKS**: SW Genia (Queensland Reds). L Burgess (NSW Waratahs), N Phipps (Melbourne Rebels), QS Cooper (Queensland Reds) **FORWARDS**: ST Moore (Brumbies), H Edmonds (Brumbies), SM Faingaa (Queensland Reds), S'UT Polota-Nau (NSW Waratahs), BA Robinson (NSW Waratahs), SL Ma'afu (Brumbies), BE Alexander (Brumbies), BP Daley (Queensland Reds), J Slipper (Queensland Reds), V Humphries (Queensland Reds), DW Mumm (NSW Waratahs), NC Sharpe (Western Force), RA Simmons (Queensland Reds), MD Chisholm (Brumbies), DW Pocock (Western Force), M Hodgson (Western Force), P McCutcheon (NSW Waratahs), RD Elsom (Brumbies), RN Brown (Western Force), S Higginbotham (Queensland Reds), B McCalman (Western Force)

TEAM MANAGER RH Egerton **COACH** RM Deans **ASSISTANT COACHES** RW Williams, EP Noriega, DV Nucifora **CAPTAIN** RD Elsom

6 November, Millennium Stadium, Cardiff Wales 16 (1G 3PG) Australia 25 (2G 2PG 1T)

WALES: JW Hook (Ospreys); WTM Harries (Newport Gwent Dragons), TGL Shanklin (Cardiff Blues), AM Bishop (Ospreys), SM Williams (Ospreys); SM Jones (Scarlets), WM Phillips (Ospreys); GD Jenkins (Cardiff Blues), M Rees (Scarlets)(capt), AR Jones (Ospreys), BS Davies (Cardiff Blues), A-W Jones (Ospreys), DJ Lydiate (Newport Gwent Dragons), J Thomas (Ospreys), S Warburton (Cardiff Blues) **SUBSTITUTIONS**: ME Williams (Cardiff Blues), RS Rees (Cardiff Blues) & DR Biggar (Ospreys) for Warburton, Phillips & SM Jones (65 mins), P James (Ospreys) for Jenkins (70 mins), DL Jones (Cardiff Blues), H Bennett (Ospreys) & CD Czekaj (Cardiff Blues) for A-W Jones, M Rees & Shanklin (74 mins) **SCORERS**: *Try:* RS Rees *Conversion*: Biggar *Penalty goals*: SM Jones (3)

AUSTRALIA: Beale; O'Connor, Ashley-Cooper, Giteau, Mitchell; Cooper, Genia; Robinson, SM Faingaa, Alexander, Chisholm, Sharpe, Elsom (capt), McCalman, Pocock **SUBSTITUTIONS**: Edmonds for SM

Faingaa (54 mins), Slipper for Alexander (61 mins), Barnes for Giteau (67 mins), Burgess & Mumm for Genia & Chisholm (74 mins) **SCORERS**: *Tries*: Pocock, Beale, Alexander *Conversions*: O'Connor (2) *Penalty goals*: O'Connor (2) **REFEREE**: W Barnes (England)

9 November, Leicester Leicester Tigers 15 (5PG) Australia XV 26 (2G 3PG 1DG)

Leicester Tigers: Scorers: *Penalty goals*: Twelvetrees (5)

Australia XV: **Scorers:** *Tries*: Turner, Higginbotham *Conversions*: Barnes (2) *Penalty goals*: Barnes (3) *Dropped goal*: Barnes

13 November, Twickenham England 35 (2G 7PG) Australia 18 (1G 2PG 1T)

ENGLAND: BJ Foden (Northampton Saints); CJ Ashton (Northampton Saints), MJ Tindall (Gloucester Rugby), SE Hape (Bath Rugby), MJ Cueto (Sale Sharks); TGAL Flood (Leicester Tigers), BR Youngs (Leicester Tigers); AJ Sheridan (Sale Sharks), DM Hartley (Northampton Saints), DR Cole (Leicester Tigers), CL Lawes (Northampton Saints), TP Palmer (Stade Francais), TR Croft (Leicester Tigers), NJ Easter (Harlequins), LW Moody (Bath Rugby)(capt) **SUBSTITUTIONS**: DS Care (Harlequins) for Youngs (53 mins), DA Armitage (London Irish) for Tindall (62 mins), DG Wilson (Bath Rugby) for Sheridan (65 mins), SG Thompson (Leeds Carnegie) for Hartley (69 mins), SD Shaw (London Wasps) for Palmer (70 mins), CC Hodgson (Sale Sharks) & CH Fourie (Leeds Carnegie) for Flood & Easter (77 mins) **SCORERS**: *Tries:* Ashton (2) *Conversions*: Flood (2) *Penalty goals*: Flood (7)

AUSTRALIA: Beale; O'Connor, Ashley-Cooper, Giteau, Mitchell; Cooper, Genia; Robinson, Moore, Alexander, Chisholm, Sharpe, Elsom (capt), McCalman, Pocock **SUBSTITUTIONS**: Burgess for Genia (47 mins), Slipper for Robinson (53 mins), Mumm for Chisholm (55 mins), Brown for McCalman (57 mins), Barnes for Giteau (58 mins) **SCORERS**: *Tries*: Beale (2) *Conversion*: O'Connor *Penalty goals*: O'Connor (2) **REFEREE**: C Joubert (South Africa)

16 November, Thomond Park, Limerick Munster 15 (3PG 2DG) Australia XV 6 (2PG)

Munster: Scorers: *Penalty goals*: Warwick (3) *Dropped goals*: Warwick (2)

Australia XV: Scorers: *Penalty goals: Barnes (2)*

20 November, Stadio Artemio Franchi, Florence Italy 14 (3PG 1T) Australia 32 (2G 6PG)

ITALY: L McLean (Treviso); T Benvenuti (Treviso), G-J Canale (ASM Clermont Auvergne), A Sgarbi (Treviso), Mi Bergamasco (Racing Metro); L Orquera (CA Brive), E Gori (Treviso); A Lo Cicero (Racing Metro), F Ongaro (Aironi), M-L Castrogiovanni (Leicester Tigers), C-A del Fava (Aironi), Q Geldenhuys (Aironi), A Zanni (Treviso), SM Parisse (Stade Francais)(capt), P Derbyshire (Treviso) **SUBSTITUTIONS**: C Festuccia (Racing Metro) for Ongaro (48 mins), L Cittadini (Treviso) & RJ Barbieri (Treviso) for Castrogiovanni & Zanni (54 mins), P Canavosio (Aironi) & A Masi (Racing Metro) for Gori & Sgarbi (60 mins), S Dellape (Racing Metro) & R Bocchino (Aironi) for Del Fava & Gori (68 mins) **SCORERS**: *Try:* Barbieri *Penalty goals:* Mi Bergamsco (2), Orquera

AUSTRALIA: Beale; Turner, Ashley-Cooper, Barnes, Mitchell; Cooper, Burgess; Slipper, Moore, Alexander, Simmons, Sharpe, Elsom (capt), McCalman, Pocock **SUBSTITUTIONS**: Polota-Nau & Robinson for Moore & Slipper (67 mins), Chisholm & Hodgson for Sharpe & Pocock (68 mins), McCabe for Ashley-Cooper (78 mins) **SCORERS**: *Tries*: Mitchell, Elsom *Conversions*: Barnes (2) *Penalty goals*: Barnes (6) **REFEREE**: C Berdos (France)

27 June, November, Stade de France, Paris France 16 (1G 3PG) Australia 59 (6G 4PG 1T)

FRANCE: J Porical (USA Perpignan); Y Huget (Aviron Bayonnais), A Rougerie (ASM Clermont Auvergne), Y Jauzion (Stade Toulousain), A Palisson (CA Brive); D Traille (Biarritz Olympique), M Parra (ASM Clermont Auvergne); T Domingo (ASM Clermont Auvergne), W Servat (Stade Toulousain), N Mas (USA Perpignan), J Pierre (ASM Clermont Auvergne), J Thion (Biarritz Olympique), T Dusautoir (Stade Toulousain)(capt), S Chabal (Racing Metro), F Ouedraogo (RC Montpellier-Herault) **SUBSTITUTIONS**: G Guirado (USA Perpignan) for Servat (34 mins), M Andreu (Castres Olympique) for Palisson (41 mins), J Schuster (USA Perpignan) for Domingo (50 mins), F Estebanez (CA Brive) for Jauzion (53 mins), J Bonnaire (ASM Clermont Auvergne) for Chabal (60 mins), R Millo-Chluski (Stade Toulousain) for Thion (68 mins), D Yachvili (Biarritz Olympique) for Parra (72 mins) **SCORERS**: *Try:* Penalty try *Conversion*: Parra *Penalty goals*: Parra (3)

AUSTRALIA: Beale; O'Connor, Ashley-Cooper, Barnes, Mitchell; Cooper, Genia; Slipper, Moore, Alexander, Simmons, Sharpe, Elsom (capt), McCalman, Pocock **SUBSTITUTIONS**: Robinson for Alexander (35 mins), Higginbotham for McCalman (63 mins), Chisholm for Sharpe (63 mins), Polota-Nau for Moore (72 mins), Burgess, Turner & Giteau for Genia, Ashley-Cooper & Barnes (74 mins) **SCORERS**: *Tries*: Mitchell (3), Ashley-Cooper, Robinson, Genia, O'Connor *Conversions*: O'Connor (6) *Penalty goals*: O'Connor (4) **REFEREE**: BJ Lawrence (New Zealand)

NEW ZEALAND TO EUROPE 2010

TOUR PARTY

FULL BACKS: JM Muliaina (Waikato)

THREEQUARTERS: HE Gear (Wellington), CS Jane (Wellington), I Toeava (Auckland), JT Rokocoko (Auckland), MA Nonu (Wellington), CG Smith (Wellington), SB Williams (Canterbury)

HALF BACKS: QJ Cowan (Southland), AM Ellis (Canterbury), AS Mathewson (Wellington), DW Carter (Canterbury), SR Donald (Waikato)

FORWARDS: KF Mealamu (Auckland), HTP Elliot (Hawke's Bay), AK Hore (Taranaki), TD Woodcock (North Harbour), B Franks (Tasman), OT Franks (Canterbury), IF Afoa (Auckland), * N Tialata (Wellington), AF Boric (North Harbour), TJS Donnelly (Otago), BC Thorn (Canterbury), SL Whitelock (Canterbury), DJ Braid (Auckland), J Kaino (Auckland), RH McCaw (Canterbury), LJ Messam (Waikato), KJ Read (Canterbury)

* Replacement on tour

TEAM MANAGER D Shand **COACH:** G Henry **ASSISTANT COACHES** S Hansen, W Smith **CAPTAIN** RH McCaw

6 November, Twickenham England 16 (1G 3PG) New Zealand 26 (2G 4PG)

ENGLAND: BJ Foden (Northampton Saints); CJ Ashton (Northampton Saints), MJ Tindall (Gloucester Rugby), SE Hape (Bath Rugby), MJ Cueto (Sale Sharks); TGAL Flood (Leicester Tigers), BR Youngs (Leicester Tigers); AJ Sheridan (Sale Sharks), SG Thompson (Leeds Carnegie), DR Cole (Leicester Tigers), CL Lawes (Northampton Saints), TP Palmer (Stade Francais), TR Croft (Leicester Tigers), NJ Easter (Harlequins), LW Moody (Bath Rugby)(capt) **SUBSTITUTIONS**: DM Hartley (Northampton Saints) for Thompson (50 mins), DG Wilson (Bath Rugby) for Sheridan (57 mins), DMJ Attwood (Gloucester Rugby) for Palmer (63 mins), CH Fourie (Leeds Carnegie) for Moody (66 mins), DA Armitage (London Irish) for Cueto (67 mins), DS Care (Harlequins) for Youngs (72 mins) **SCORERS**: *Try:* Hartley *Conversion*: Flood *Penalty goals*: Flood (3)

NEW ZEALAND: Muliaina; Rokocoko, SB Williams, Nonu, Gear; Carter, Mathewson; Woodcock, Mealamu, O Franks, Thorn, Whitelock, Kaino, Read, McCaw (capt) **SUBSTITUTIONS**: Ellis for Mathewson (50 mins), Toeava for Rokocoko (57 mins), Boric for Whitelock (67 mins), Afoa for O Franks (74 mins) **SCORERS**: *Tries*: Gear, Read *Conversions*: Carter (2) *Penalty goals:* Carter (4) **REFEREE**: R Poite (France)

13 November, Murrayfield Scotland 3 (1PG) New Zealand 49 (7G)

SCOTLAND: HGF Southwell (Stade Francais); RP Lamont (RC Toulon), MD Evans (Glasgow), GA Morrison (Glasgow), SF Lamont (Scarlets); DA Parks (Cardiff Blues), MRL Blair (Edinburgh)(capt), AF Jacobsen (Edinburgh), RW Ford (Edinburgh), EA Murray (Northampton Saints), JL Hamilton (Gloucester Rugby), RJ Gray (Glasgow), KDR Brown (Saracens), RJ Vernon (Glasgow), JA Barclay (Glasgow) **SUBSTITUTIONS**: GD Laidlaw (Edinburgh) for Blair (38 mins), N Walker (Ospreys) & NJ Hines (Leinster) for R Lamont & Hamilton (40 mins), S Lawson (Gloucester Rugby), RM Rennie (Edinburgh) & AG Dickinson (Gloucester Rugby) for Ford, Brown & Murray (64 mins), RJH Jackson (Glasgow) for Parks (67 mins) **SCORER**: *Penalty goal*: Parks

NEW ZEALAND: Muliaina; Toeava, Smith, SB Williams, Gear; Carter, Cowan; Woodcock, Elliot, O Franks, Thorn, Whitelock, Messam, Read, McCaw (capt) **SUBSTITUTIONS**: Donald for Carter (50 mins), Afoa for O Franks (53 mins), Boric & Braid for Thorn & McCaw (57 mins), Ellis for Cowan (58 mins), Hore for Elliot (60 mins) **SCORERS**: *Tries*: Gear (2), Muliaina (2), Carter, Smith, Ellis *Conversions*: Carter (5), Donald (2) **REFEREE**: D Pearson (England)

20 November, Aviva Stadium, Dublin Ireland 18 (1G 2PG 1T) New Zealand 38 (3G 4PG 1T)

IRELAND: RDJ Kearney (Leinster); TJ Bowe (Ospreys), BG O'Driscoll (Leinster)(capt), GWD D'Arcy (Leinster), LM Fitzgerald (Leinster): J Sexton (Leinster), EG Reddan (Leinster); CE Healy (Leinster), R Best (Ulster), TG Court (Ulster), DP O'Callaghan (Munster), MR O'Driscoll (Munster), SPH Ferris (Ulster), JPR Heaslip (Leinster), DP Wallace (Munster) **SUBSTITUTIONS**: S Cronin (Connacht) for Best (22 mins), KG Earls (Munster) for Fitzgerald (46 mins), D Toner (Leinster), PA Stringer (Munster) & JJ Hayes (Munster) for M O'Driscoll, Reddan & Court (63 mins), RJR O'Gara (Munster) for Kearney (74 mins) **SCORERS**: *Tries:* Ferris, B O'Driscoll *Conversion*: Sexton *Penalty goals*: Sexton (2)

NEW ZEALAND: Muliaina; Jane, Smith, Nonu, Gear; Carter, Ellis, Woodcock, Elliot, O Franks, Boric, Donnelly, Kaino, Read, McCaw (capt) **SUBSTITUTIONS**: Whitelock for Donnelly (40 mins), SB Williams, Hore & Mathewson for Nonu, Elliot & Ellis (58 mins), Afoa for O Franks (65 mins) **SCORERS**: *Tries*: Read (2), Boric, Whitelock *Conversions*: Carter (3) *Penalty goals*: Carter (4) **REFEREE**: M Jonker (South Africa)

27 November, Millennium Stadium, Cardiff Wales 25 (1G 6PG) New Zealand 37 (3G 2PG 2T)

WALES: LM Byrne (Ospreys); GP North (Scarlets), TGL Shanklin (Cardiff Blues), JW Hook (Ospreys), T James (Cardiff Blues); SM Jones (Scarlets), WM Phillips (Ospreys); GD Jenkins (Cardiff Blues), M Rees (Scarlets)(capt), AR Jones (Ospreys), BS Davies (Cardiff Blues), A-W Jones (Ospreys), DJ Lydiate (Newport Gwent Dragons), RP Jones (Ospreys), S Warburton (Cardiff Blues) **SUBSTITUTIONS**: A Powell (London Wasps) & J Thomas (Ospreys) for Lydiate & R Jones (48 mins), ME Williams (Cardiff Blues) for Warburton (74 mins), AM Bishop (Ospreys) for Shanklin (77 mins), H Bennett (Ospreys), P James (Ospreys) & RS Rees (Cardiff Blues) for M Rees, Jenkins & Phillips (78 mins) **SCORERS**: *Try:* Byrne *Conversion:* SM Jones *Penalty goals*: SM Jones (6)

NEW ZEALAND: Muliaina; Toeava, Smith, SB Williams, Gear; Carter, Cowan; Woodcock, Mealamu, O Franks, Thorn, Whitelock, Kaino, Read, McCaw (capt) **SUBSTITUTIONS**: Braid for Read (38 mins), Nonu for SB Williams (48 mins), Boric for Whitelock (53 mins), Afoa for O Franks (62 mins), Hore for Mealamu (74 mins), Donald & Ellis for Carter & Cowan (77 mins) **SCORERS**: *Tries*: Gear (2), Muliaina, Toeava, Afoa *Conversions*: Carter (3) *Penalty goals*: Carter (2) **REFEREE**: DA Lewis (Ireland)

SOUTH AFRICA TO EUROPE 2010

TOUR PARTY

FULL BACKS: GG Aplon (Western Province), Z Kirchner (Blue Bulls)

THREEQUARTERS: BA Basson (Blue Bulls), BG Habana (Western Province), L Mvovo (Sharks), J de Jongh (Western Province), J de Villiers (Western Province), E Jantjies (Lions), FPL Steyn (Racing Metro), AA Jacobs (Sharks)

HALF BACKS: R Pienaar (Ulster), F Hougaard (Blue Bulls), M Steyn (Blue Bulls), P Lambie (Sharks)

FORWARDS: BW du Plessis (Sharks), MC Ralepelle (Blue Bulls), A Strauss (Cheetahs), JN du Plessis (Sharks), T Mtawarira (Sharks), CJ van der Linde (Cheetahs), C Oesthuizen (Cheetahs), PR van der Merwe (Blue Bulls), JP Botha (Blue Bulls), V Matfield (Blue Bulls), A Hargreaves (Sharks), WS Alberts (Sharks), GJ Stegmann (Blue Bulls), K Daniel (Sharks), R Kankowski (Sharks), JH Smith (Cheetahs), PJ Spies (Blue Bulls)

* Replacement on tour

HEAD COACH P de Villiers **CAPTAIN** V Matfield

6 November, Aviva Stadium, Dublin Ireland 21 (1G 3PG 1T) South Africa 23 (2G 3PG)

IRELAND: RDJ Kearney (Leinster); TJ Bowe (Ospreys), BG O'Driscoll (Leinster)(capt), GWD D'Arcy (Leinster), LM Fitzgerald (Leinster): J Sexton (Leinster), EG Reddan (Leinster); CE Healy (Leinster), R Best (Ulster), TD Buckley (Munster), DP O'Callaghan (Munster), MR O'Driscoll (Munster), SPH Ferris (Ulster), JPR Heaslip (Leinster), DP Wallace (Munster) **SUBSTITUTIONS**: TG Court (Ulster) for Buckley (50 mins), D Ryan (Munster) for M O'Driscoll (62 mins), RJR O'Gara (Munster) & PA Stringer (Munster) for Sexton & Reddan (65 mins), KG Earls (Munster) for Kearney (74 mins) **SCORERS**: *Tries*: Bowe, Kearney *Conversion:* O'Gara *Penalty goals*: Sexton (3)

SOUTH AFRICA: Aplon; Basson, Kirchner, De Villiers, Habana; M Steyn, Pienaar, Mtawarira, B du Plessis, J du Plessis, Botha, Matfield (capt), Smith, Spies, Stegmann **SUBSTITUTIONS**: Lambie for M Steyn (58 mins), Daniel for Stegmann (65 mins), Jacobs for De Villiers (66 mins), Van der Linde & Van der Merwe for J du Plessis & Botha (70 mins) **SCORERS**: *Tries:* Smith, Aplon *Conversions*: M Steyn, Lambie *Penalty goals*: M Steyn (3) **REFEREE**: N Owens (Wales)

13 November, Millennium Stadium, Cardiff Wales 25 (2G 2PG 1T) South Africa 29 (2G 5PG)

WALES: LM Byrne (Ospreys); GP North (Scarlets), TGL Shanklin (Cardiff Blues), JW Hook (Ospreys), SM Williams (Ospreys); SM Jones (Scarlets), WM Phillips (Ospreys); P James (Ospreys), M Rees (Scarlets) (capt), AR Jones (Ospreys), BS Davies (Cardiff Blues), A-W Jones (Ospreys), A Powell (London Wasps), J Thomas (Ospreys), ME Williams (Cardiff Blues) **SUBSTITUTIONS**: AM Bishop (Ospreys) for Shanklin (temp 38–40 mins), CD Czekaj (Cardiff Blues) for SM Williams (40 mins), RP Jones (Ospreys) for Powell (59 mins), RS Rees (Cardiff Blues) for Phillips (69 mins), H Bennett (Ospreys) & JV Yapp (Cardiff Blues) for M Rees & James (70 mins), DL Jones (Cardiff Blues) for A-W Jones (74 mins) **SCORERS**: *Tries*: North (2), Hook *Conversions*: SM Jones (2) *Penalty goals*: SM Jones (2)

SOUTH AFRICA: Aplon; Basson, F Steyn, De Villers, Habana; M Steyn, Pienaar; Mtawarira, B du Plessis, J du Plessis, Botha, Matfield (capt), Smith, Spies, Stegmann **SUBSTITUTIONS**: Alberts for Stegmann (46 mins), Van der Merwe & Hougaard for Botha & Pienaar (59 mins), Lambie for M Steyn (64 mins), Kirchner & Ralepelle for Habana & B du Plessis (73 mins), Van der Linde for J du Plessis (75 mins) **SCORERS**: *Tries:* Alberts, Matfield *Conversions*: M Steyn (2) *Penalty goals*: M Steyn (5) **REFEREE**: SR Walsh (Australia)

20 November, Murrayfield Scotland 21 (6PG 1DG) South Africa 17 (4PG 1T)

SCOTLAND: HGF Southwell (Stade Francais); N Walker (Ospreys), JA Ansbro (Northampton Saints), GA Morrison (Glasgow), SF Lamont (Scarlets); DA Parks (Cardiff Blues), RGM Lawson (Gloucester Rugby) (capt), AF Jacobsen (Edinburgh), RW Ford (Edinburgh), EA Murray (Northampton Saints), RJ Gray (Glasgow), SJ MacLeod (Edinburgh), NJ Hines (Leinster), KDR Brown (Saracens), JA Barclay (Glasgow) **SUBSTITUTIONS**: RJ Vernon (Glasgow) for MacLeod (34 mins), DWH Hall (Glasgow) & MJ Low (Glasgow) for Ford & Murray (68 mins), CD Paterson (Edinburgh) for Walker (73 mins), RM Rennie (Edinburgh) for Brown (78 mins) **SCORER**: *Penalty goals*: Parks (6) *Dropped goal*: Parks

SOUTH AFRICA: Kirchner; Aplon, F Steyn, De Villers, Mvovo; M Steyn; Hougaard; Mtawarira, B du Plessis, J du Plessis, Botha, Matfield (capt), Smith, Kankowski, Stegmann **SUBSTITUTIONS**: Alberts for Smith (temp 20–25 mins) & Stegmann (46 mins), Pienaar for Hougaard (47 mins), Lambie for M Steyn (63 mins), Van der Merwe for Botha (64 mins), Van der Linde for Mtawarira (71 mins), Strauss for B Du Plessis (78 mins) **SCORERS**: *Try:* Alberts *Penalty goals*: M Steyn (4) **REFEREE**: SJ Dickinson (Australia)

27 November, Twickenham England 11 (2PG 1T) South Africa 21 (1G 3PG 1T)

ENGLAND: BJ Foden (Northampton Saints); CJ Ashton (Northampton Saints), MJ Tindall (Gloucester Rugby), SE Hape (Bath Rugby), MJ Cueto (Sale Sharks); TGAL Flood (Leicester Tigers), BR Youngs (Leicester Tigers); AJ Sheridan (Sale Sharks), DM Hartley (Northampton Saints), DR Cole (Leicester Tigers), CL Lawes (Northampton Saints), TP Palmer (Stade Francais), TR Croft (Leicester Tigers), NJ Easter (Harlequins), LW Moody (Bath Rugby)(capt) **SUBSTITUTIONS**: CH Fourie (Leeds Carnegie) for Croft (21 mins), CC Hodgson (Sale Sharks) for Flood (33 mins), DS Care (Harlequins) for Youngs (61 mins), DG Wilson (Bath Rugby) & SD Shaw (London Wasps) for Cole & Lawes (67 mins), SG Thompson (Leeds Carnegie) & MA Banahan (Bath Rugby) for Hartley & Ashton (72 mins) **SCORERS**: *Try:* Foden *Penalty goals*: Flood (2)

SOUTH AFRICA: Kirchner; Aplon, F Steyn, De Villiers, Mvovo; M Steyn, Pienaar; Mtawarira, B du Plessis, J du Plessis, Botha, Matfield (capt), Smith, Spies, Stegmann **SUBSTITUTIONS**: Jacobs & Alberts for Kirchner & Stegmann (46 mins), Van der Linde for J du Plessis (52 mins), Van der Merwe for Botha (66 mins), Hougaard for Aplon (temp 59–67 mins) & De Villiers (67 mins), Strauss & Lambie for B du Plessis & Aplon (78 mins) **SCORERS**: *Tries:* Alberts, Mvovo *Conversion*: M Steyn *Penalty goals*: M Steyn (3) **REFEREE**: G Clancy (Ireland)

4 December, Twickenham Barbarians 26 (3G 1T) South Africa XV 20 (1G 1PG 2T)

Barbarians: Scorers: *Tries*: DA Mitchell (2), JD O'Connor, Q Geldenhuys *Conversions*: JD O'Connor (3)
South Africa XV: Scorers: *Tries*: O Ndungane, JP Botha, B Maku *Conversion*: Jantjies *Penalty goal*: Jantjies

ARGENTINA TO EUROPE 2010

TOUR PARTY

FULL BACKS: M Rodriguez (Stade Franacias)

THREEQUARTERS: H Agulla (Leicester Tigers), G Camacho (Harlequins), L Gonzalez Amorosino (Leicester Tigers), L Borges (RC Albi), M Bustos Moyano (RC Montpellier-Herault), R Carballo (Begles-Bordeaux), G Tiesi (Stade Francais), S Fernandez (RC Montpellier-Herault), M Bosch (Biarritz Olympique),

HALF BACKS: A Lalanne (London Irish), N Vergallo (Stade Toulousain), F Contepomi (RC Toulon), A Figuerola (CA Brive)

FORWARDS: M Ledesma (ASM Clermont Auvergne), A Creevy (ASM Clermont Auvergne), E Guinazu (Biarritz Olympique), M Scelzo (ASM Clermont Auvergne), R Roncero (Stade Francais), J Figallo (RC Montpellier-Herault), M Ayerza (Leicester Tigers), S Guzman (Tucuman RC), M Galarza (Leinster), E Lozada (Edinburgh), M Carizza (Biarritz Olympique), P Albacete (Stade Toulousain), A Galindo (Racing Metro), M de Acheval (Alumni), G Fessia (Cordoba Athletic), JM Fernandez-Lobbe (RC Toulon). * JF Cabello (Tucuman RC)

* Replacement on tour

TEAM MANAGER A Cubelli **COACH** S Phelan **CAPTAIN** F Contepomi

13 November, Stadio Marc Antonio Bentegodi, Verona Italy 16 (1G 3PG) Argentina 22 (1G 5PG)

ITALY: L McLean (Treviso); T Benvenuti (Treviso), G-J Canale (ASM Clermont Auvergne), A Masi (Racing Metro), Mi Bergamasco (Racing Metro); C Gower (Aviron Bayonnais) T Tebaldi (Aironi); S Perugini (Aironi), L Ghiraldini (Treviso), M-L Castrogiovanni (Leicester Tigers), C-A del Fava (Aironi), Q Geldenhuys (Aironi), A Zanni (Treviso), S Parisse (Stade Francais)(capt), R Barbieri (Treviso) **SUBSTITUTIONS**: F Ongaro (Aironi) for Ghiraldini (58 mins), P Derbyshire (Treviso), P Canavosio (Aironi) & A Lo Cicero (Racing Metro) for Zanni, Tebaldi & Perugini (62 mins), S Dellape (Racing Metro) for De Fava (70 mins), L Orquera (CA Brive) for Gower (73 mins), A Sgarbi (Treviso) for Benvenuti (75 mins) **SCORERS**: *Try*: Penalty try *Conversion*: Mi Bergamasco *Penalty goals*: Mi Bergamasco (3)

ARGENTINA: Rodriguez; Camacho, Tiesi, Fernandez, Amorosino; F Contepomi (capt), Vergallo; Roncero, Ledesma, Scelzo, Carizza, Galarza, Fessia, JM Fernandez-Lobbe, De Acheval **SUBSTITUTIONS**: Galindo for Fernandez-Lobbe (34 mins), Lozada for Carizza (47 mins), Creevy & Figallo for Ledesma & Scelzo (62 mins), Ayerza for Roncero (78 mins) **SCORERS**: *Try:* Rodriguez *Conversion*: F Contepomi *Penalty goals*: F Contepomi (5) **REFEREE**: CJ Pollock (New Zealand)

20 November, Stade de la Mosson, Montpellier France 15 (4PG 1DG) Argentina 9 (3PG)

FRANCE: A Palisson (CA Brive); Y Huget (Aviron Bayonnais), A Rougerie (ASM Clermont Auvergne), Y Jauzion (Stade Toulousain), M Andreu (Castres Olympique); D Traille (Biarritz Olympique), M Parra (ASM Clermont Auvergne); T Domingo (ASM Clermont Auvergne), W Servat (Stade Toulousain). N Mas (USA Perpignan), J Pierre (ASM Clermont Auvergne), L Nallet (Racing Metro), T Dusautoir (Stade Toulousain) (capt), S Chabal (Racing Metro), J Bonnaire (ASM Clermont Auvergne) **SUBSTITUTIONS**: L Ducalcon (Castres Olympique) for Domingo (55 mins), J Thion (Biarritz Olympique) for Pierre (56 mins), I Harinordoquy (Biarritz Olympique) for Chabal (63 mins), G Guirado (USA Perpignan) for Servat (65 mins), D Yachvili (Biarritz Olympique), F Estebanez (CA Brive) & J Porical (USA Perpignan) for Parra, Traille & Rougerie (77 mins) **SCORERS**: *Penalty goals*: Parra (4) *Dropped goal*: Traille

ARGENTINA: Rodriguez; Camacho, Tiesi, Fernandez, Amorosino; F Contepomi (capt), Vergallo; Roncero, Ledesma, Scelzo, Galarza, Albacete, Fessia, JM Fernandez-Lobbe, De Acheval **SUBSTITUTIONS**: Cabello for De Acheval (40 mins), Creevy for Ledesma (63 mins), Galindo, Bosch & Scelzo for Fessia, Fernandez & Roncero (65 mins) **SCORER**: *Penalty goals*: F Contepomi (3) **REFEREE**: JI Kaplan (South Africa)

28 November, Aviva Stadium, Dublin Ireland 29 (2G 5PG) Argentina 9 (3PG)

IRELAND: GEA Murphy (Leicester Tigers); TJ Bowe (Ospreys), BG O'Driscoll (Leinster)(capt), GWD D'Arcy (Leinster), AD Trimble (Ulster); J Sexton (Leinster), PA Stringer (Munster); CE Healy (Leinster), S Cronin (Connacht), TD Buckley (Munster), DP O'Callaghan (Munster), MR O'Driscoll (Munster), SPH Ferris (Ulster), JPR Heaslip (Leinster), DP Wallace (Munster) **SUBSTITUTIONS**: DP Leamy (Munster) for Ferris (60 mins), TG Court (Ulster) for Buckley (63 mins), D Varley (Munster) for Cronin (64 mins), KG Earls (Munster) for B O'Driscoll (68 mins), RJR O'Gara (Munster) for Sexton (69 mins), D Toner (Leinster) for M O'Driscoll (71 mins), EG Reddan (Leinster) for Stringer (75 mins) **SCORERS**: *Tries*: Ferris, D'Arcy *Conversions*: Sexton, O'Gara *Penalty goals*: Sexton (5)

ARGENTINA: Rodriguez; Agulla, Tiesi, Bosch, Amorosino; F Contepomi (capt), Vergallo; Roncero, Ledesma, Scelzo, Galarza, Albacete, Fessia, JM Fernandez-Lobbe, Cabello **SUBSTITUTIONS**: Ayerza for Roncero (43 mins), Figallo for Scelzo (49 mins), Borges for Tiesi (60 mins), Creevy for Ledesma (61 mins), Lalanne for Vergallo (69 mins), Guzman for Galarza (75 mins) **SCORER**: *Penalty goals*: F Contepomi (3) **REFEREE**: SM Lawrence (South Africa)

SAMOA TO JAPAN & EUROPE 2010

TOUR PARTY

FULL BACKS: PB Williams (Sale Sharks), L Lui (Moata'a)

THREEQUARTERS: D Lemi (London Wasps), AT Tuilagi (Leicester Tigers), F Otto (Scopa), M Pesamino (Vailele), S Sinoti (Hawke's Bay), GT Pisi (Taranaki), SJ Mapusua (London Irish), J Helleur (Auckland), GL Williams (ASM Clermont Auvergne), U Setu (Sunnybank)

HALF BACKS: KF Fotuali'i (Hawke's Bay), T Lavea (ASM Clermont Auvergne), AJ Poluleuligaga (Exeter Chiefs), U Mai (El Salvador), B Va'aulu (CS Bourgoin-Jallieu)

FORWARDS: MM Schwalger (Taranaki), TT Paulo (ASM Clermont Auvergne), S Fualau (Canterbury), CAI Johnston (Stade Toulousain), AI Perenise (Hawke's Bay), S Taulafo (London Wasps), N Leleimalefaga (RC Montpellier-Herault), S Lemalu (Counties Manakau), L Mulipola (Don Bosco), FHL Levi (Newcastle Falcons), KG Thompson (Southland), JI Tekori (Castres Olympique), D Leo (Begles-Bordeaux) A Aiono (Marist), M Timoteo (Vaiala), O Treviranus (Malie), M Salave'a (RC Narbonne), C Slade (Exeter Chiefs), GJ Stowers (London Irish), R Muagututia (Scopa), F Selesele (Moata'a)

* Replacement on tour

TEAM MANAGER MT Vaea **COACH:** FT Tafua **ASSISTANT COACHES** T Coventry, B McLean, M Casey CAPTAIN MM Schwalger

30 October, Tokyo Japan 10 (1G 1PG) Samoa 13 (1G 2PG)

JAPAN: Scorers: *Try*: K Holani *Conversion*: J Arlidge *Penalty goal*: J Arlidge
SAMOA: Scorers: *Try*: K Fotuali'i *Conversion*: Lui *Penalty goals*: Lui (2)

13 November, Aviva Stadium, Dublin Ireland 20 (2G 2PG) Samoa 10 (1G 1PG)

IRELAND: LM Fitzgerald (Leinster); TJ Bowe (Ospreys), BG O'Driscoll (Leinster)(capt), PW Wallace (Ulster), AD Trimble (Ulster); RJR O'Gara (Munster), PA Stringer (Munster); TG Court (Ulster), S Cronin (Connacht), JJ Hayes (Munster), DP O'Callaghan (Munster), D Toner (Leinster), DP Leamy (Munster), JPR Heaslip (Leinster), S O'Brien (Leinster) **SUBSTITUTIONS**: SPH Ferris (Ulster) & R Best (Ulster) for Heaslip & Cronin (60 mins), CE Healy (Leinster) for Hayes (62 mins), D Ryan (Munster) for Toner (67 mins), IJ Boss (Ulster) for Stringer (76 mins) **SCORERS**: *Tries*: Heaslip, O'Gara *Conversions*: O'Gara (2) *Penalty goals*: O'Gara (2)
SAMOA: P Williams: Lemi, G Pisi, Mapusua, A Tuilagi; Lavea, Fotuali'i; Taulafo, Schwalger (capt), Perenise, Levi, Thompson, Treviranus, Stowers, Salavea **SUBSTITUTIONS**: Polu for Lavea (68 mins), Tekori & Aiono for Levi & Treviranus (71 mins), Lemalu for Taulafo (76 mins), G Williams for Pisi (76 mins) **SCORERS**: *Try;* A Tuilagi *Conversion*: P Williams *Penalty goal*: P Williams **REFEREE**: KW Brown (New Zealand)

20 November, Twickenham England 26 (2G 4PG) Samoa 13 (1PG 2T)

ENGLAND: BJ Foden (Northampton Saints); CJ Ashton (Northampton Saints), MA Banahan (Bath Rugby), SE Hape (Bath Rugby), MJ Cueto (Sale Sharks); TGAL Flood (Leicester Tigers), BR Youngs (Leicester Tigers); AJ Sheridan (Sale Sharks), DM Hartley (Northampton Saints), DG Wilson (Bath Rugby), CL Lawes (Northampton Saints), TP Palmer (Stade Francais), JAW Haskell (London Wasps), NJ Easter (Harlequins)(capt), CH Fourie (Leeds Carnegie) **SUBSTITUTIONS**: SG Thompson (Leeds Carnegie) & DR Cole (Leicester Tigers) for Hartley & Wilson (55 mins), DMJ Attwood (Gloucester Rugby), TR Croft (Leicester Tigers) & DR Care (Harlequins) for Lawes, Haskell & Youngs (67 mins), CC Hodgson (Sale Sharks) & DA Armitage (London Irish) for Hape & Ashton (74 mins) **SCORERS**: *Tries*: Banahan, Croft *Conversions*: Flood (2) *Penalty goals*: Flood (4)
SAMOA: P Williams: Lemi, G Pisi, Mapusua, A Tuilagi; Lavea, Fotuali'i; Taulafo, Schwalger (capt), Perenise, Levi, Thompson, Treviranus, Stowers, Salavea **SUBSTITUTIONS**: Johnston for Taulafo (temp 12–19 mins), Tekori for Thompson (40 mins), Paulo for Schwalger (48 mins), Otto for Lemi (59 mins), Aiono, Polu & Johnston for Treviranus, Lavea & Perenise (67 mins) **SCORERS**: *Tries:* P Williams, Otto *Penalty goal*: P Williams **REFEREE**: P Fitzgibbon (Ireland)

27 November, Pittodrie Stadium, Aberdeen Scotland 19 (1G 3PG 1DG) Samoa 16 (1G 3PG)

SCOTLAND: HGF Southwell (Stade Francais); N Walker (Ospreys), JA Ansbro (Northampton Saints), GA Morrison (Glasgow), SF Lamont (Scarlets); DA Parks (Cardiff Blues), RGM Lawson (Gloucester Rugby) (capt), AF Jacobsen (Edinburgh), RW Ford (Edinburgh), EA Murray (Northampton Saints), RJ Gray (Glasgow), NJ Hines (Leinster), KDR Brown (Saracens), RJ Vernon (Glasgow), JA Barclay (Glasgow) **SUBSTITUTIONS**: MRL Blair (Edinburgh) for Lawson (58 mins), RJH Jackson (Edinburgh), MB Evans (Glasgow), MJ Low (Glasgow) & JL Hamilton (Gloucester Rugby) for Parks, Murray, Ansbro & Gray (58 mins), DWH Hall (Glasgow) & RM Rennie (Edinburgh) for Ford & S Lamont (73 mins) **SCORERS**: *Try:* Walker *Conversion*: Parks *Penalty goals*: Parks (2), Jackson *Dropped goal*: Parks
SAMOA: P Williams: Lemi, G Pisi, Mapusua, A Tuilagi; Lavea, Fotuali'i; Taulafo, Schwalger (capt), Johnston, Levi, Thompson, Treviranus, Stowers, Salavea **SUBSTITUTIONS**: Perenise for Johnston (60 mins), Tekori & Paulo for Thompson & Schwalger (60 mins), Aiono for Treviranus (65 mins), Otto & Leo for Lemi & Salavea (73 mins) **SCORERS**: *Try:* Fotuali'I *Conversion*: P Williams *Penalty goal*: P Williams (3) **REFEREE**: SR Walsh (Australia)

FIJI TO EUROPE 2010

TOUR PARTY

FULL BACKS: JL Matavesi (Exeter Chiefs), NAS Ligairi (CA Brive)
THREEQUARTERS: R Ratu (RC Aurillac), S Radidi (Nadali), M Tagicakibau, (Saracens) N Nalaga (Nadroga), V Goneva (US Colomiers), S Naqelevuki (Western Province), AJ Vulivuli (Racing Metro), S Rabeni (Leicester Tigers), * GV Lovubalavu (RC Toulon)
HALF BACKS: N Kenatale (Tailevu), S Taka (Veilomani), T Rawaqa (Saunaka), S Bai (Castres Olympique)
FORWARDS: T Tuapati (Woodlands), V Veikoso (Nadi), S Somoca (Sigatoka Bulls), DT Manu (Scarlets), GC Dewes (Esher), C Ma'afu (Eastern Suburbs), V Rarawa (Duavata), I Rawaqa (World Fighting Bulls), RWG Lewaravu (Sale Sharks), S Kalou (Kaikorai), S Naevo (NEC), M Ravulo (North Harbour), A Qera (Gloucester Rugby), J Naikadawa (Kaite), S Koyamaibole (Sale Sharks), J Qovu (Racing Metro),

* Replacement on tour
TEAM MANAGER T Waqa **COACH** S Domoni **CAPTAIN** DT Manu

13 November, Stade de la Beaujoire, Nantes France 34 (2G 5PG 1T) Fiji 12 (4PG)

FRANCE: J Porical (USA Perpignan); J Arias (Stade Francais), D Marty (USA Perpignan), F Estabanez (CA Brive), M Medard (Stade Toulousain): D Traille (Biarritz Olympique), D Yachvili (Biarritz Olympique); J Schuster (USA Perpignan), G Guirado (USA Perpignan), L Ducalcon (Castres Olympique); R Millo-Chluski (Stade Toulousain), J Thion (Biarritz Olympique), F Ouedraogo (RC Montpellier-Herault), I Harinordoquy (Biarritz Olympique)(capt), A Lapandry (ASM Clermont Auvergne) **SUBSTITUTIONS**: B Noirot (Racing Metro) & S Chabal (Racing Metro) for Guirado & Harinordoquy (54 mins), D Skrela (Stade Toulousain) & J Pierre (ASM Clermont Auvergne) for Traille & Millo-Chluski (67 mins), M Parra (ASM Clermont Auvergne) & A Palisson (CA Brive) for Yachvili & Medard (75 mins) **SCORERS**: *Tries*: Marty, Medard, Penalty try *Conversions*: Yachvili (2) *Penalty goals*: Yachvili (5)

FIJI: Ligairi; Naqelevuki, Vulivuli, Rabeni, Nalaga; Bai, Kenatale; Dewes, Tuapati, Manu (capt), Lewaravu, Qovu, Naevo, Koyamaibole, Qera **SUBSTITUTIONS**: Lovubalavu for Nakelevuqi (57 mins), Ravulo & Matevesi for Qera & Ligairi (68 mins), Veikoso & Kalou for Tuapati & Lewaravu (71 mins), Taka for Kenatale (75 mins) **SCORER**: *Penalty goals*: Bai (4) **REFEREE**: A Small (England)

19 November, Millennium Stadium, Cardiff Wales 16 (1G 3PG) Fiji 16 (1G 3PG)

WALES: LM Byrne (Ospreys); GP North (Scarlets), JW Hook (Ospreys), AM Bishop (Ospreys), AG Brew (Newport Gwent Dragons); DR Biggar (Ospreys), RS Rees (Cardiff Blues); P James (Ospreys), H Bennett (Ospreys), AR Jones (Ospreys), IM Gough (Ospreys), DL Jones (Cardiff Blues), RP Jones (Ospreys), J Thomas (Ospreys), DJ Lydiate (Newport Gwent Dragons) **SUBSTITUTIONS**: BS Davies (Cardiff Blues), WM Phillips (Ospreys), SM Jones (Scarlets) & TGL Shanklin (Cardiff Blues) for Gough, Rees, Biggar & Bishop (49 mins) **SCORERS**: *Try:* Penalty try *Conversion*: SM Jones *Penalty goals*: Biggar (2), SM Jones

FIJI: Matavesi; Goneva, Vulivuli, Lovobalavu, M Tagicakibau; Bai, Kenatale; Ma'afu, Veikoso, Manu (capt), Rawaqa, Qovu, Naevo, Koyamaibole, Ravulo **SUBSTITUTIONS**: Ratu & Qera for M Tagicakibau & Koyamaibole (49 mins), Tuapati for Veikoso (52 mins), Taka for Kenatale (54 mins), Dewes for Ma'afu (58 mins), T Rawaqa for Vulivuli (66 mins), Kalou for Ravulo (74 mins) **SCORERS**: *Try:* Vulivuli *Conversion*: Bai *Penalty goal*: Bai (3) **REFEREE**: J Garces (France)

27 November, Stadio Alberto Braglia, Modena Italy 24 (8PG) Fiji 16 (1G 3PG)

ITALY: L McLean (Treviso); A Masi (Racing Metro), G-J Canale (ASM Clermont Auvergne), A Sgarbi (Treviso), Mi Bergamasco (Racing Metro); L Orquera (CA Brive), E Gori (Treviso); S Perugini (Aironi), F Ongaro (Aironi), M-L Castrogiovanni (Leicester Tigers), C-A del Fava (Aironi), Q Geldenhuys (Aironi), A Zanni (Treviso), SM Parisse (Stade Francais)(capt), R Barbieri (Treviso) **SUBSTITUTIONS**: S Dellape (Racing Metro) for Del Fava (7 mins), C Festuccia (Racing Metro) & R Bocchino (Aironi) for Ongaro & Orquera (50 mins), T Benvenuti (Treviso) for Masi (57 mins), A lo Cicero (Racing Metro) for Perugini (60 mins), P Derbyshire (Treviso) for Barbieri (69 mins) **SCORER**: *Penalty goals*: Mi Bergamasco (8)

FIJI: Ligairi; Goneva, Vulivuli, Lovobalavu, Nalaga; Bai, Kenatale; Ma'afu, Tuapati, Manu (capt), Lewaravu, Qovu, Naevo, Koyamaibole, Qera **SUBSTITUTIONS**: Kalou for Koyamaibole (53 mins), Rabeni for Goneva (60 mins), Rarawa & Naikadawa for Ma'afu & Qera (69 mins), Veikoso for Tuapati (74 mins) **SCORERS**: *Try:* Tuapati *Conversion*: Bai *Penalty goals*: Bai (3) **REFEREE**: D Pearson (England)

2011 SUMMER TESTS

4 June, Millennium Stadium, Cardiff Wales 28 (4G) Barbarians 31 (3G 2T)

WALES: ML Stoddart (Scarlets); GP North (Scarlets), JJV Davies (Scarlets), GL Henson (unattached), AG Brew (Newport Gwent Dragons); SM Jones (Scarlets), WM Phillips (Ospreys); RJ Bevington (Ospreys), H Bennett (Ospreys), P James (Ospreys), RP Jones (Ospreys), LC Charteris (Newport Gwent Dragons), DJ Lydiate (Newport Gwent Dragons), TT Faletau (Newport Gwent Dragons), S Warburton (Cardiff Blues)(capt) **SUBSTITUTIONS**: A-W Jones (Ospreys), TD Knoyle (Scarlets), S Williams (Scarlets), SA Andrews (Cardiff Blues) for RP Jones, Phillips, Henson & Bevington (61 mins), J Turnbull (Scarlets) for Lydiate (63 mins), L Burns (Newport Gwent Dragons) for Bennett (64 mins), R Priestland (Scarlets) for SM Jones (66 mins) **SCORERS**: *Tries*: North, Stoddart, Phillips, Brew *Conversions*: SM Jones (4)

BARBARIANS: IK Nacewa (Fiji); PH Sackey (England), RSR Rabeni (Fiji), M Bastareaud, DC Howlett (New Zealand); BR James (ASM Clermont Auvergne), S Tillous-Borde (France); ID Thomas (Wales), S Bruno (France), CJ Hayman (New Zealand), JI Tekori (Samoa), PD Tito (Cardiff Blues), JC van Niekirk (South

Africa), SM Parisse (Italy)(capt), ME Williams (Wales) **SUBSTITUTIONS**: LL Ghiraldini (Italy) for Bruno (54 mins), GB Smith (Australia) for ME Williams (55 mins), EB Lund (Biarritz Olympique) for Tito (56 mins), B Baby (France) for Sackey (61 mins), LD Williams (Cardiff Blues) for Tillous-Borde (64 mins), D Kubriashvili (Georgia) & W Mason (RC Toulon) for Hayman & Rabeni (65 mins) **SCORERS**: *Tries:* Tekori, Nacewa (2), Parisse, Bastareaud *Conversions*: James (3) **REFEREE**: ACP Rolland (Ireland)

17 July, Stadium Australia, Sydney Australia 23 (2G 3PG) Samoa 32 (3G 2PG 1T)

AUSTRALIA: MA Gerrard (Melbourne Rebels); RD Davies (Queensland Reds), AP Ashley-Cooper (Brumbies), PJ McCabe (Brumbies), DAN Ioane (Queensland Reds); MJ Giteau (Western Force); N Phipps (Melbourne Rebels); SM Kepu (NSW Waratahs), ST Moore (Brumbies), BE Alexander (Brumbies), S Timani (NSW Waratahs), NC Sharpe (Western Force), RD Elsom (Brumbies)(capt), BJ McCalman (Western Force), M Hodgson (Western Force) **SUBSTITUTIONS**: BS Robinson (Queensland Reds) for Hodgson (50 mins), DJ Vickerman (NSW Waratahs) for Sharpe (51 mins), KJ Beale (NSW Waratahs) for Gerrard (55 mins), SW Genia (Queensland Reds) for Phipps (56 mins), S Higginbotham (Queensland Reds) for McCalman (59 mins) **SCORERS**: *Tries*: Ioane, Giteau *Conversions*: Giteau (2) *Penalty goals*: Giteau (3)

SAMOA: PB Williams (Sale Sharks); SLK Tagicakibau (London Irish), GT Pisi (Northampton Saints), SJ Mapusua (Kubota Spears), AT Tuilagi (Leicester Tigers); T Pisi (Suntory Sungoliath), K Fotuali'i (Crusaders); S Taulafo (London Wasps), MM Schwalger (Taranaki) (capt), AI Perenise (Hurricanes), KG Thompson (Hawke's Bay), D Leo (London Wasps), T Tu'ifua (Newcastle Falcons), GJ Stowers (London Irish), M Fa'asavalu (Harlequins) **SUBSTITUTIONS**: E Fuimaono-Sapolu (Gloucester Rugby) for G Pisi (58 mins), CAI Johnston (Stade Toulousain) for Taulafo (65 mins), F Levi (Newcastle Falcons) for Thompson (69 mins), B Helleur (North Harbour) for T Pisi (72 mins), TT Paulo (ASM Clermont-Auvergne) for Schwalger (78 mins), M Salavea (RC Narbonne) for Tu'ifua (78 mins) **SCORERS**: *Tries:* A Tuilagi, P Williams, Thompson, G Pisi *Conversions*: T Pisi (3) *Penalty goals*: T Pisi (2) **REFEREE**: M Jonker (South Africa)

22 July, Otago Stadium, Dunedin New Zealand 60 (7G 2PG 1T) Fiji 14 (2G)

NEW ZEALAND: JM Muliaina (Waikato); ZR Guildford (Hawke's Bay), CG Smith (Wellington), MA Nonu (Wellington), SW Sivivatu (Waikato); CR Slade (Canterbury), QJ Cowan (Southland); WWV Crockett (Canterbury), AK Hore (Taranaki), BJ Franks (Tasman), JMRA Hoeata (Taranaki), AJ Williams (Auckland), AJ Thomson (Otago), LJ Messam (Waikato), RH McCaw (Canterbury)(capt) **SUBSTITUTIONS**: BR Smith (Otago) for Sivivatu (50 mins), SL Whitelock (Canterbury) & PAT Weepu (Wellington) for Hoeata & Cowan (53 mins), DW Carter (Canterbury) for Slade (64 mins), J Kaino (Auckland) for Messam (65 mins), CR Flynn (Canterbury) and IF Afoa (Auckland) for Hore & Crockett (66 mins) **SCORERS**: *Tries*: Sivivatu, Slade, Hore, Thomson, CG Smith, Weepu, Penalty try, Muliaina *Conversions*: Slade (4), Carter (3) *Penalty goals*: Slade (2)

FIJI: ILR Keresoni (RC Perigreux); T Nagusa (RC Montpellier-Herault), AJ Vulivuli (Racing Metro), RS Fatiaki (Worcester Warriors), NV Nalaga (Nadroga); S Bai (Castres Olympique), N Kenatale (Nadroga), GDC Ma'afu (Eastern Suburbs), S Koto (RC Narbonne), DT Manu (Scarlets)(capt), S Kalou (Kaikorai), R Nasiga (Nadroga), DM Waqaniburotu (Fraser Tech), SM Matadigo (RC Montpellier-Herault), A Qera (Gloucester Rugby) **SUBSTITUTIONS**: V Goneva (US Colomiers) for Nagusa (55 mins), M Ravulo (North Harbour) for Qera (60 mins), V Buatava (Badia) for Kenatale (64 mins), JU Domolailai (Lomavata) & S Somoca (Sigatoka Bulls) for Nasiga & Ma'afu (69 mins), V Veikoso (Nadi) & RT Rawaqa (Saunaka) for Koto & Nalaga (78 mins) **SCORERS**: *Tries:* Kenatale, Goneva *Conversions*: Bai (2) **REFEREE**: SJ Dickinson (Australia)

6 August, Murrayfield Scotland 10 (1G 1PG) Ireland 6 (2PG)

SCOTLAND: CD Paterson (Edinburgh); N Walker (Ospreys), JA Ansbro (London Irish), GA Morrison (Glasgow), SF Lamont (Scarlets); RJH Jackson (Glasgow), RGM Lawson (Gloucester Rugby)(capt), AF Jacobsen (Edinburgh), RW Ford (Edinburgh), G Cross (Edinburgh), JL Hamilton (Gloucester Rugby), RJ Gray (Glasgow), AK Strokosch (Gloucester Rugby), J Beattie (Glasgow), RM Rennie (Edinburgh) **SUBSTITUTIONS**: JE Cuthbert (Bath Rugby) for Walker (21 mins), AG Dickinson (Sale Sharks), D Denton (Edinburgh) & AD Kellock (Glasgow) for Jacobsen, Beattie & Hamilton (57 mins), NJ de Luca (Edinburgh), GD Laidlaw (Edinburgh) & DWH Hall (Glasgow) for Paterson, Lawson & Ford (70 mins) **SCORERS**: *Try*: Ansbro *Conversion*: Jackson *Penalty goal*: Paterson

IRELAND: RDJ Kearney (Leinster); AD Trimble (Ulster), F McFadden (Leinster), PW Wallace (Ulster), LM Fitzgerald (Leinster), J Sexton (Leinster), T O'Leary (Munster); TG Court (Ulster), S Cronin (Leinster), TD Buckley (Sale Sharks), D Ryan (Munster), LFM Cullen (Leinster) (capt), MP McCarthy (Connacht), DP Leamy (Munster), N Ronan (Munster) **SUBSTITUTIONS**: K McLaughlin (Leinster) for Ryan (52 mins), J Flannery (Munster), IJ Boss (Leinster) & JJ Hayes (Munster) for Cronin, O'Leary & Buckley (60 mins), MR O'Driscoll (Munster) for Cullen (61 mins), F Jones (Munster) & MJ Horan (Munster) for Fitzgerald & Court (62 mins) **SCORERS**: *Penalty goals*: Sexton (2) **REFEREE**: W Barnes (England)

6 August, Twickenham England 23 (2G 1PG 2DG) Wales 19 (2G 1T)

ENGLAND: DA Armitage (London Irish); MA Banahan (Bath Rugby), EMS Tuilagi (Leicester Tigers), RJ Flutey (London Wasps), MJ Cueto (Sale Sharks); JP Wilkinson (RC Toulon), DS Care (Harlequins); AR Corbisiero (London Irish), DM Hartley (Northampton Saints), MJH Stevens (Saracens), SD Shaw (London Wasps), TP Palmer (Stade Francais), TR Croft (Leicester Tigers), JAW Haskell (Ricoh Black Rams), LW Moody (Bath Rugby)(capt) **SUBSTITUTIONS**: REP Wigglesworth (Saracens), LA Mears (Bath Rugby), DG Wilson (Bath Rugby) & MJ Botha (Saracens) for Care, Hartley, Stevens & Shaw (57 mins), C Sharples (Gloucester Rugby) for Tuilagi (59 mins), TA Wood (Northampton Saints) for Moody (60 mins), CC Hodgson (Saracens) for Wilkinson (76 mins) **SCORERS**: *Tries*: Haskell, Tuilagi *Conversions*: Wilkinson (2) *Penalty goal*: Wilkinson *Dropped goals*: Wilkinson (2)

WALES: ML Stoddart (Scarlets); GP North (Scarlets), JJV Davies (Scarlets), JH Roberts (Cardiff Blues), SM Williams (Ospreys); R Priestland (Scarlets), WM Phillips (Aviron Bayonnais); P James (Ospreys), H Bennett (Ospreys), C Mitchell (Exeter Chiefs), BS Davies (Cardiff Blues), A-W Jones (Ospreys), DJ Lydiate (Newport Gwent Dragons), TT Faletau (Newport Gwent Dragons), S Warburton (Cardiff Blues)(capt) **SUBSTITUTIONS**: S Williams (Scarlets) for Stoddart (48 mins), RP Jones (Ospreys) for Faletau (54 mins), TD Knoyle (Scarlets) for Phillips (61 mins), L Burns (Newport Gwent Dragons) for Bennett (64 mins), RJ Bevington (Ospreys) and LC Charteris (Newport Gwent Dragons) for James & A-W Jones (65 mins) **SCORERS**: *Tries:* North (2), SM Williams *Conversions*: Priestland (2) **REFEREE**: SR Walsh (Australia)

6 August, BMO Stadium, Toronto Canada 28 (2G 3PG 1T) USA 22 (2G 1PG 1T)

Canada: Scorers: *Tries*: E Fairhurst, P MacKenzie, J Sinclair *Conversions*: J Pritchard (2) *Penalty goals*: J Pritchard (3)

USA: Scorers: *Tries:* T Clever (2), T Ngwenya *Conversions*: T Enosa, M Malifa *Penalty goal*: M Malifa

13 August, Churchill Park, Laukota Fiji 27 (3G 2PG) Tonga 12 (1G 1T)

Fiji: Scorers: *Tries*: V Goneva, K Murimurivalu, R Nasiga *Conversions*: S Bai (3) *Penalty goals*: Bai (2)

Tonga: Scorers: *Tries:* V Iongi (2) *Conversion*: S Fisliau

13 August, Millennium Stadium, Cardiff Wales 19 (1G 4PG) England 9 (3PG)

WALES: JW Hook (USA Perpignan); GP North (Scarlets), JH Roberts (Cardiff Blues), GL Henson (unattached), SM Williams (Ospreys); R Priestland (Scarlets), WM Phillips (Aviron Bayonnais); P James (Ospreys), L Burns (Newport Gwent Dragons), C Mitchell (Exeter Chiefs), LC Charteris (Newport Gwent Dragons), A-W Jones (Ospreys), DJ Lydiate (Newport Gwent Dragons), TT Faletau (Newport Gwent Dragons), S Warburton (Cardiff Blues)(capt) **SUBSTITUTIONS**: S Williams (Scarlets) for Henson (31 mins), AG Brew (Newport Gwent Dragons) for Priestland (40 mins), H Bennett (Ospreys) for Burns (52 mins), J Turnbull (Scarlets) for A-W Jones (60 mins), RJ Bevington (Ospreys) for James (69 mins) **SCORERS**: *Try*: Hook *Conversion:* Hook *Penalty goals*: Priestland (2), Hook (2)

ENGLAND: BJ Foden (Northampton Saints); MA Banahan (Bath Rugby), MJ Tindall (Gloucester Rugby) (capt), SE Hape (London Irish), MJ Cueto (Sale Sharks); TGAL Flood (Leicester Tigers), REP Wigglesworth (Saracens); AR Corbisiero (London Irish), SG Thompson (London Wasps), DR Cole (Leicester Tigers), LP Deacon (Leicester Tigers), CL Lawes (Northampton Saints), TA Wood (Northampton Saints), NJ Easter (Harlequins), CH Fourie (Sale Sharks) **SUBSTITUTIONS**: DS Care (Harlequins) for Wigglesworth (29 mins), JAW Haskell (Ricoh Black Rams) for Fourie (50 mins), LA Mears (Bath Rugby), MJH Stevens (Saracens) & DA Armitage (London Irish) for Thompson, Corbisiero & Tindall (59 mins), TP Palmer (Stade Francais) & CC Hodgson (Sale Sharks) for Deacon & Flood (67 mins) **SCORER**: *Penalty goals*: Flood (3) **REFEREE**: ACP Rolland (Ireland)

13 August, Stadio Dino Manuzzi, Cesena Italy 31 (4G 1PG) Japan 24 (3G 1PG)

ITALY: L McLean (Treviso); G Toniolatti (Aironi), A Sgarbi (Treviso), M Pratichetti (Aironi), T Benvenuti (Treviso); R Bocchino (Aironi), E Gori (Treviso); A lo Cicero (Racing Metro), LL Ghiraldini (Treviso), L Cittadini (Treviso), Q Geldenhuys (Aironi), M Bortolami (Aironi), A Zanni (Treviso), SM Parisse (Stade Francais)(capt), Ma Bergamasco (Stade Francais) **SUBSTITUTIONS**: C van Zyl (Treviso) for Geldenhuys (31 mins), P Canavosio (Aironi) for Gori (49 mins), P Derbyshire (Treviso) & M-L Castrogiovanni (Leicester Tigers) for Zanni & Cittadini (53 mins), L Orquera (Aironi) & G-J Canale (ASM Clermont Auvergne) for Bocchino & Sgarbi (56 mins), T D'Apice (Aironi) for Ghiraldini (76 mins) **SCORERS**: *Tries*: Pratichetti, Ghiraldini, Gori, Lo Cicero *Conversions*: Bocchino (3), Orquera *Penalty goal*: Orquera

JAPAN: S Webb (Coca Cola West Red Sparks); K Endo (Toyota Verblitz), K Taira (Suntory Sungoliath), R Nicholas (Suntory Sungoliath), T Usuzuki (Toshiba Brave Lupus); J Arlidge (Nottingham), F Tanaka (Sanyo Wild Knights); H Hirashima (Kobe Steel), S Horie (Sanyo Wild Knights), K Hatakeyama (Suntory Sungoliath),

J Ives (Sanyo Wild Knights), T Kitagawa (Toyota Verblitz), T Kikutani (Toyota Verblitz)(capt), K Holani (Sanyo Wild Knights), M Leitch (Toshiba Brave Lupus) **SUBSTITUTIONS**: L Thompson (Kintetsu Liners) for Ives (17 mins), N Fujita (Honda Heat) for Hatakeyama (52 mins), A Tupuailei (Canon Eagles) for Taira (53 mins), A Hiwasa (Suntory Sungoliath) for Tanaka (69 mins), T Nishihara (Panasonic Wild Knights) for Kikutani (77 mins) **SCORERS**: *Tries:* Usuzuki, Taira, Penalty try *Conversions*: Arlidge (3) *Penalty goal*: Arlidge **REFEREE**: R Poite (France)

13 August, Stade Chaban-Delmas, Bordeaux France 19 (1G 4PG) Ireland 12 (4PG)

FRANCE: D Traille (Biarritz Olympique); V Clerc (Stade Toulousain), D Marty (USA Perpignan), M Mermoz (USA Perpignan), A Palisson (RC Toulon); F Trinh-Duc (RC Montpellier-Herault), D Yachvili (Biarritz Olympique); S Marconnet (Biarritz Olympique), D Szarzewski (Stade Francais), L Ducalcon (Castres Olympique); J Pierre (ASM Clermont Auvergne),R Millo-Chluski (Stade Toulousain), J Thion (Biarritz Olympique), T Dusautoir (Stade Toulousain)(capt), I Harinordoquy (Biarritz Olympique), R Lakafia (Castres Olympique) **SUBSTITUTIONS**: D Skrela (ASM Clermont Auvergne) for Mermoz (26 mins), G Guirado (USA Perpignan) & J-B Poux (Stade Toulousain) for Szarzewski & Marconnet (54 mins), L Nallet (Racing Metro) for Millo-Chluski (58 mins), M Medard (Stade Toulousain) & J Bonnaire (ASM Clermont Auvergne) for Traille & Harinordoquy (64 mins), M Parra (ASM Clermont Auvergne) for Yachvili (77 mins) **SCORERS**: *Tries*: Clerc *Conversion*: Yachvili *Penalty goals*: Yachvili (4)

IRELAND: RDJ Kearney (Leinster); AD Trimble (Ulster), KG Earls (Munster), PW Wallace (Ulster), LM Fitzgerald (Leinster); RJR O'Gara (Munster), EG Reddan (Leinster); CE Healy (Leinster), R Best (Ulster), MR Ross (Leinster), DF O'Callaghan (Munster), LFM Cullen (Leinster)(capt), R Ryan (Munster), DP Leamy (Munster), S O'Brien (Leinster) **SUBSTITUTIONS**: F Jones (Munster) for Kearney (46 mins), PJ O'Connell (Munster), JPR Heaslip (Leinster) & TD Buckley (Sale Sharks) for Cullen, Leamy & Healy (50 mins), J Flannery (Munster) & C Murray (Munster) for Best & Reddan (60 mins), F McFadden (Leinster) for Trimble (67 mins) **SCORER**: *Penalty goals*: O'Gara (4) **REFEREE**: SR Walsh (Australia)

13 August, Infinity Park, Glendale USA 7 (1G) Canada 27 (3G 2PG)

USA: Scorers: *Try*: B Scully *Conversion*: M Malifa

Canada: Scorers: *Tries:* A Carpenter, P MacKenzie, DTH van der Merwe *Conversions*: J Pritchard (3) *Penalty goals*: J Pritchard (2)

19 August, Churchill Park, Lautoka Fiji 20 (2G 2PG) Tonga 32 (1G 5PG 2T)

Fiji: Scorers: *Tries*: L Nakarawa, R Nasiga *Conversions*: W Luveniyali (2) *Penalty goals*: W Luveniyali (2)

Tonga: Scorers: *Tries:* A Fatafehi, V Lilo, F Vainikolo *Conversion*: K Morath *Penalty goals*: K Morath (5)

20 August, Millennium Stadium, Cardiff Wales 28 (2G 3PG 1T) Argentina 13 (1G 2PG)

WALES: LM Byrne (ASM Clermont Auvergne); SL Halfpenny (Cardiff Blues), JJV Davies (Scarlets), JH Roberts (Cardiff Blues), GP North (Scarlets): JW Hook (USA Perpignan), TD Knoyle (Scarlets), P James (Ospreys), RM Hibbard (Ospreys), AR Jones (Ospreys), BS Davies (Cardiff Blues), A-W Jones (Ospreys), DJ Lydiate (Newport Gwent Dragons), A Powell (Sale Sharks), ME Williams (Cardiff Blues)(capt) **SUBSTITUTIONS**: J Thomas (Ospreys) & AG Brew (Newport Gwent Dragons) for Lydiate & Byrne (57 mins), LD Williams (Cardiff Blues), H Bennett (Ospreys) & J Tipuric (Ospreys) for Hibbard, Knoyle & ME Williams (61 mins), RJ Bevington (Ospreys) for AR Jones (62 mins), S Williams (Scarlets) for Roberts (66 mins) **SCORERS**: *Tries*: Powell, A-W Jones, North *Conversions*: Hook (2) *Penalty goals*: Hook (3)

ARGENTINA: M Rodriguez (Stade Francais); G Camacho (Exeter Chiefs), M Bosch (Biarritz Olympique), S Fernandez (RC Montpellier-Herault), H Agulla (Leicester Tigers), F Contepomi (Stade Francais)(capt), N Vergallo (Stade Toulousain), R Roncero (Stade Francais), M Ledesma (ASM Clermont Auvergne), J Figallo (RC Montpellier-Herault), M Carizza (Biarritz Olympique), P Albacete (Stade Toulousain), JF Cabello (Tucuman), JM Fernandez Lobbe (RC Toulon), JM Leguizamon (Lyon OU) **SUBSTITUTIONS**: M Scelzo (SU Agen) & JJ Imhoff (Duendes) for Figallo & Camacho (40 mins), A Creevy (RC Montpellier-Herault) for Ledesma (50 mins), A Campos (unattached) for Leguizamon (66 mins), M Galarza (Pampas) for Carizza (69 mins) **SCORERS**: *Try:* Scelzo *Conversion:* F Contepomi *Penalty goals*: F Contepomi (2) **REFEREE**: R Poite (France)

20 August, Murrayfield Scotland 23 (2G 3PG) Italy 12 (1G 1T)

SCOTLAND: RP Lamont (RC Toulon); MB Evans (Castres Olympique), NJ de Luca (Edinburgh), GA Morrison (Glasgow), SCJ Danielli (Ulster); DA Parks (Cardiff Blues), MRL Blair (Edinburgh); AG Dickinson (Sale Sharks), S Lawson (Gloucester Rugby), M Low (Glasgow), NJ Hines (ASM Clermont Auvergne), AD Kellock (Glasgow)(capt) KDR Brown (Saracens), RJ Vernon (Sale Sharks), JA Barclay (Glasgow) **SUBSTITUTIONS**:

EA Murray (Newcastle Falcons) for Low (54 mins), N Walker (Ospreys) for Danielli (55 mins), RJH Jackson (Glasgow), RJ Gray (Glasgow) & CP Cusiter (Glasgow) for Parks, Hines & Blair (61 mins), DWH Hall (Glasgow) for S Lawson (70 mins), RM Rennie (Edinburgh) for Vernon (74 mins) **SCORERS**: *Tries*: Dickinson, Blair *Conversions*: Parks (2) *Penalty goals*: Parks (3)

ITALY: A Masi (Aironi); T Benvenuti (Treviso), G-J Canale (ASM Clermont Auvergne), G Garcia (Treviso), Mi Bergamasco (Racing Metro); L Orquers (Aironi), F Semenzato (Treviso); A lo Cicero (Racing Metro), F Ongaro (Aironi), M-L Castrogiovanni (Leicester Tigers), C-A del Fava (Aironi), C van Zyl (Treviso), P Derbyshire (Treviso), SM Parisse (Stade Francais)(capt), JR Barbieri (Treviso) **SUBSTITUTIONS**: T D'Apice (Aironi) for Ongaro (40 mins), J Furno (Aironi) for Del Fava (51 mins), R Bocchino (Aironi) for Orquera (56 mins), A Zanni (Treviso) for Derbyshire (62 mins), L Cittadini (Treviso) for Lo Cicero (71 mins), E Gori (Treviso) for Canale (74 mins) **SCORERS**: *Tries:* Benvenuti, Semenzato *Conversion*: Mi Bergamasco **REFEREE**: D Pearson (England)

20 August, Aviva Stadium, Dublin Ireland 22 (2G 1PG 1T) France 26 (2G 3PG 1DG)

IRELAND: F Jones (Munster); AD Trimble (Ulster), BG O'Driscoll (Leinster)(capt), GWD D'Arcy (Leinster), KG Earls (Munster); J Sexton (Leinster), T 'O'Leary (Munster); CE Healy (Leinster), R Best (Ulster), MR Ross (Leinster), DF O'Callaghan (Munster), PJ O'Connell (Munster), S O'Brien (Leinster), JPR Heaslip (Leinster), S Jennings (Leinster) **SUBSTITUTIONS**: TG Court (Ulster) for Healy (50 mins), EG Reddan (Leinster) for O'Leary (53 mins), J Flannery (Munster) & SPH Ferris (Ulster) for Best & Jennings (60 mins), RJR O'Gara (Munster) for D'Arcy (67 mins), LM Fitzgerald (Leinster) for Jones (68 mins), MP McCarthy (Connacht) for O'Callaghan (75 mins) **SCORERS**: *Tries*: Healy, Sexton, O'Brien *Conversions*: O'Gara (2) *Penalty goal*: Sexton

FRANCE: C Heymans (Aviron Bayonnais); M Medard (Stade Toulousain), A Rougerie (ASM Clermont Auvergne), F Estebanez (Racing Metro), A Palisson (RC Toulon); D Skrela (ASM Clermont Auvergne), M Parra (ASM Clermont Auvergne); J-B Poux (Stade Toulousain), D Szarzewski (Stade Francais), N Mas (USA Perpignan), P Pape (Stade Francais), L Nallet (Racing Metro)(capt), F Ouedraogo (RC Montpellier-Herault), L Picamoles (Stade Toulousain), J Bonnaire (ASM Clermont Auvergne) **SUBSTITUTIONS**: F Trinh-Duc (RC Montpellier-Herault) for Skrela (13 mins), F Barcella (Biarritz Olympique) for Poux (40 mins), G Guirado (USA Perpignan) for Szarzewski (53 mins), J Pierre (ASM Clermont Auvergne) for Pape (60 mins), V Clerc (Stade Toulousain) for Rougerie (72 mins), D Yachvili (Biarritz Olympique) for Parra (78 mins) **SCORERS**: *Tries:* Heymans, Trinh-Duc *Conversions*: Parra (2) *Penalty goals*: Parra (3) *Dropped goal:* Trinh-Duc **REFEREE**: C Joubert (South Africa)

27 August, Aviva Stadium, Dublin Ireland 9 (3PG) England 20 (2G 2PG)

IRELAND: GEA Murphy (Leicester Tigers); TJ Bowe (Ospreys), KG Earls (Munster), GWD D'Arcy (Leinster), AD Trimble (Ulster); RJR O'Gara (Munster), EG Reddan (Leinster); CE Healy (Leinster), J Flannery (Munster), MR Ross (Leinster), DF O'Callaghan (Munster), PJ O'Connell (Munster)(capt), SPH Ferris (Ulster), JPR Heaslip (Leinster), DP Wallace (Munster) **SUBSTITUTIONS**: DP Leamy (Munster) for Wallace (21 mins), D Ryan (Munster) for Heaslip (34 mins), R Best (Ulster) for Flannery (50 mins), J Sexton (Leinster) and C Murray (Munster) for O'Gara & Reddan (61 mins), TG Court (Ulster) for Healy (70 mins), F McFadden (Leinster) for Trimble (72 mins) **SCORER**: *Penalty goals*: O'Gara (3)

ENGLAND: BJ Foden (Northampton Saints); CJ Ashton (Northampton Saints), EMS Tuilagi (Leicester Tigers), MJ Tindall (Gloucester Rugby)(capt), MJ Cueto (Sale Sharks); JP Wilkinson (RC Toulon), REP Wigglesworth (Saracens); AJ Sheridan (Sale Sharks), SG Thompson (London Wasps), DR Cole (Leicester Tigers), LP Deacon (Leicester Tigers), CL Lawes (Northampton Saints), TR Croft (Leicester Tigers), JAW Haskell (Ricoh Black Rams), CH Fourie (Sale Sharks) **SUBSTITUTIONS**: TP Palmer (Stade Francais) & DA Armitage (London Irish) for Fourie & Cueto (21 mins), DM Hartley (Northampton Saints) for Thompson (51 mins), MJH Stevens (Saracens) for Sheridan (56 mins), SD Shaw (London Wasps) for Deacon (62 mins), TGAL Flood (Leicester Tigers) for Tindall (74 mins) **SCORERS**: *Tries:* Tuilagi, Armitage *Conversions*: Wilkinson (2) *Penalty goals*: Wilkinson (2) **REFEREE**: N Owens (Wales)

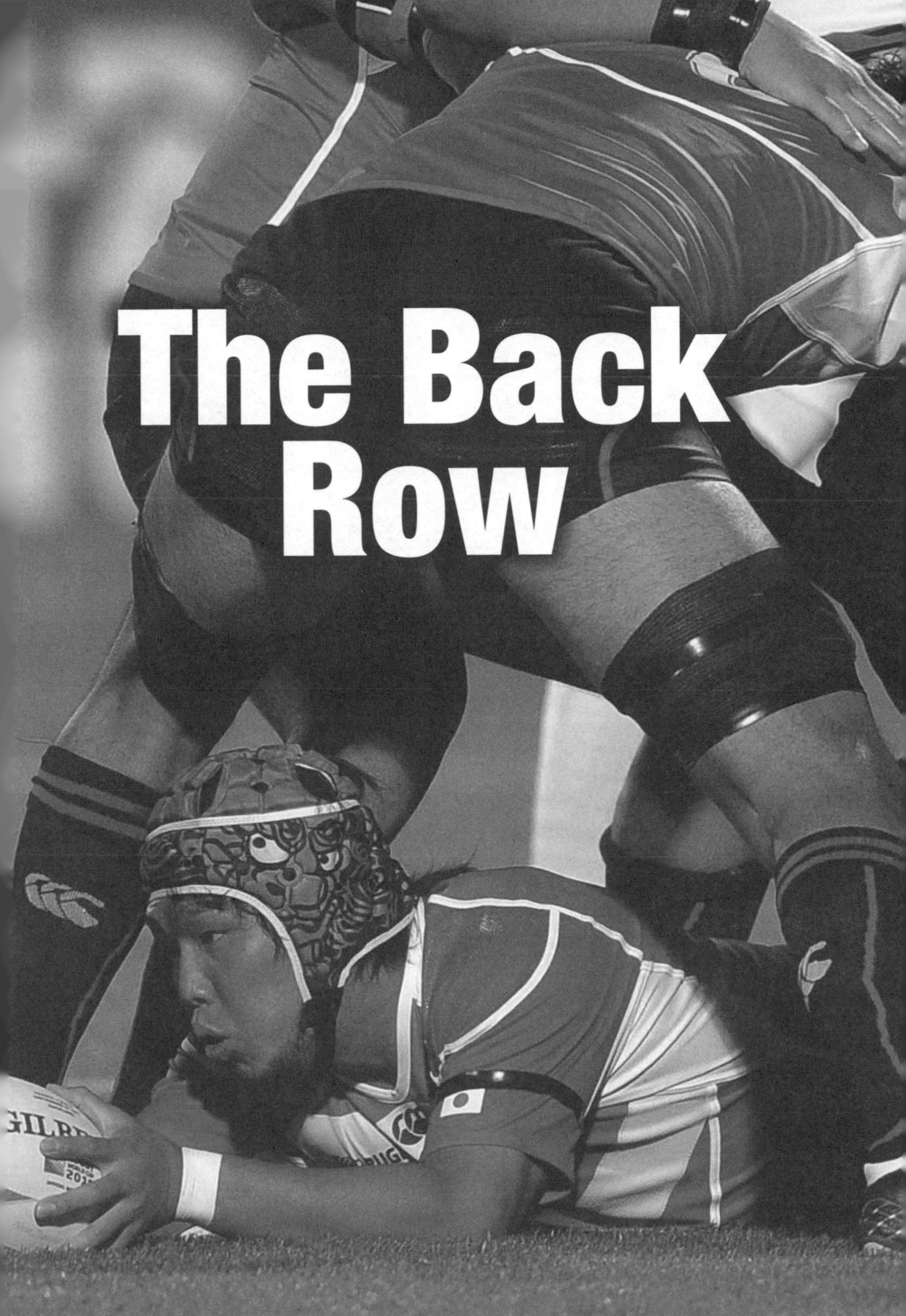

The Back Row

BIG FIVE SETS THE AGENDA

By Paddy O'Brien, IRB Referee Manager

Phil Walter/Getty Images

Referee George Clancy oversees a scrum in the Tri-Nations clash between New Zealand and the All Blacks.

At the Rugby World Cup 2011 we made some key changes to the way we look at officiating. The two most significant were the appointment of 10 referees for the tournament and the establishment of the Big Five to create the template for them to work with within matches.

In recent years we'd had the Experimental Law Variation (ELV) process, which had its supporters and its detractors, and the result was the debate about whether the game needed to be changed law-wise, or whether some of the laws we had needed to be refereed more strictly.

Apart from a couple of tinkerings with the laws, we came up with the Big Five for referees, coaches and players to focus on:

1. Tackle Area

Referee this area strictly. The tackler and assisted tacklers must release, tackled player must let the ball go and arriving players must come through the gate on their feet, so we get a contest. By applying that strictly, players started conforming and we got quick ball. Teams didn't have to take quick ball, but we gave the teams who did want it the option.

2. Offside
We wanted this clearly refereed around the ruck and maul. The key is to give teams the space to use if they want it. Also we wanted to be strict on offsides from kicks, again to do with space.

3. Scrum
All of us have a view on how we can fix the scrum, but at the moment we have what we have. So we put in some key triggers for the referees:

- We want the front-rowers to be square on engagement.
- We want tightheads to bind on the body not the arm and for all the props to be square, with the loosehead not driving in downwards. All of the teams bought into this.

4. Obstruction at the maul.
We said the maul is an integral part of the game, but it should be able to be defended, so the ball carrier should be able to be tackled at the formation.

5. Foul Play
Foul play should not be a referee problem, but a player problem.

By the referees team agreeing the Big Five and then going to the coaches, it meant everyone bought into it. It was crucial we didn't wander off those key elements and stuck to our guns.

If we get this right, refereed to the law, then the game will be ok. And I think that the Rugby World Cup 2011 showed that if they are applied properly we get competitive and better rugby.

There will always be referee error, but I believe if you have a template to work off you are halfway there. We have made it simpler for the referee. Before, there was too much subjective refereeing, but we are saying they can't let things go. That doesn't take away game management by a referee, as they have other elements like advantage.

The key thing for me was that after round one some teams were not compliant, but by round two we had a competition in every game I watched, and you could see players checking to see if they were onside or not. They still go offside when they are desperate, but that is to be expected, and we'll penalise. This template will get us away from this notion a few years ago that there was a northern and southern hemisphere style of refereeing.

I know some readers will wonder why the put-in at the scrum was not in the Big Five. We brought this up with the coaches, and I'd like to see a change in the engagement procedure that would help bring back hooking, because at the moment the hooker is just another prop – he doesn't hook the ball back any more.

At the moment the scrum is all about the hit. I'd like to see the scrum change to a hooking contest and a strength contest. You need a controlled engagement, but perhaps after that on a blow of a whistle or a command we then scrum.

The work rate of a referee at scrum time is massive. He has so much to look for, so if we can have a more controlled engagement no referee can have an excuse on crooked feeds. Then we will start picking hookers again.

Legacy is another crucial thing for me, and now we need Steve Walsh, Craig Joubert, Nigel Owens and Wayne Barnes to go back to their respective countries and spread the word so a Heineken Cup match is refereed this season the same as a Super Rugby game.

We have to spread the word and make sure there is no watering down of the Big Five. What do they say about no pain no gain? It may take four or five weeks of pain in a particular competition, but we have to stick to it, as we will get there in the end. But we have to follow the same template as otherwise we are not being fair on the players.

The other big change for Rugby World Cup 2011 was the selection of a more streamlined panel of 10 referees for the tournament. This meant that we had a close group of referees and we were able to keep very tight control on all the issues at the tournament, working together to reach a solution if necessary. I only get one crack every four years to set the agenda and it's crucial that we ensure the highest levels of consistency.

We have also encouraged coaches to come back to us with comments after World Cup matches, but not that many have. The difference is if a coach asks me to look at Steve Walsh's game, I say Steve Walsh will look at his own game and will reply to that query. What the coaches want is Steve Walsh's view and not mine. Coaches still meet the referee before matches, but it is a lot shorter and more of a focus on the Big Five.

In terms of objectives, I don't believe you need to see lots of tries scored to have quality rugby. Look at New Zealand v Australia in the World Cup semi-final, which is a case in point.

I'm delighted to say that there are some tremendous young referees coming through, as we have one eye on the Rugby World Cup 2015. We saw some great referees at the Junior World Championship, and now we plan to give them more exposure at a higher level.

INTERNATIONAL REFEREES

DISMISSALS IN MAJOR INTERNATIONAL MATCHES

Up to 31 October 2011 in major international matches. These cover all matches for which the eight senior members of the International Board have awarded caps, and also all matches played in Rugby World Cup final stages.

A E Freethy	sent off	C J Brownlie (NZ)	E v NZ	1925
K D Kelleher	sent off	C E Meads (NZ)	S v NZ	1967
R T Burnett	sent off	M A Burton (E)	A v E	1975
W M Cooney	sent off	J Sovau (Fj)	A v Fj	1976
N R Sanson	sent off	G A D Wheel (W)	W v I	1977
N R Sanson	sent off	W P Duggan (I)	W v I	1977
D I H Burnett	sent off	P Ringer (W)	E v W	1980
C Norling	sent off	J-P Garuet (F)	F v I	1984
K V J Fitzgerald	sent off	H D Richards (W)	NZ v W	*1987
F A Howard	sent off	D Codey (A)	A v W	*1987
K V J Fitzgerald	sent off	M Taga (Fj)	Fj v E	1988
O E Doyle	sent off	A Lorieux (F)	Arg v F	1988
B W Stirling	sent off	T Vonolagi (Fj)	E v Fj	1989
B W Stirling	sent off	N Nadruku (Fj)	E v Fj	1989
F A Howard	sent off	K Moseley (W)	W v F	1990
F A Howard	sent off	A Carminati (F)	S v F	1990
F A Howard	sent off	A Stoop (Nm)	Nm v W	1990
A J Spreadbury	sent off	A Benazzi (F)	A v F	1990
C Norling	sent off	P Gallart (F)	A v F	1990
C J Hawke	sent off	F E Mendez (Arg)	E v Arg	1990
E F Morrison	sent off	C Cojocariu (R)	R v F	1991
J M Fleming	sent off	P L Sporleder (Arg)	WS v Arg	*1991
J M Fleming	sent off	M G Keenan (WS)	WS v Arg	*1991
S R Hilditch	sent off	G Lascubé(F)	F v E	1992
S R Hilditch	sent off	V Moscato (F)	F v E	1992
D J Bishop	sent off	O Roumat (Wld)	NZ v Wld	1992
E F Morrison	sent off	J T Small (SA)	A v SA	1993
I Rogers	sent off	M E Cardinal (C)	C v F	1994
I Rogers	sent off	P Sella (F)	C v F	1994
D Mené	sent off	J D Davies (W)	W v E	1995
S Lander	sent off	F Mahoni (Tg)	F v Tg	*1995
D T M McHugh	sent off	J Dalton (SA)	SA v C	*1995
D T M McHugh	sent off	R G A Snow (C)	SA v C	*1995
D T M McHugh	sent off	G L Rees (C)	SA v C	*1995
J Dumé	sent off	G R Jenkins (W)	SA v W	1995
W J Erickson	sent off	V B Cavubati (Fj)	NZ v Fj	1997
W D Bevan	sent off	A G Venter (SA)	NZ v SA	1997

C Giacomel	sent off	R Travaglini (Arg)	F v Arg	1997
W J Erickson	sent off	D J Grewcock (E)	NZ v E	1998
S R Walsh	sent off	J Sitoa (Tg)	A v Tg	1998
R G Davies	sent off	M Giovanelli (It)	S v It	1999
C Thomas	sent off	T Leota (Sm)	Sm v F	1999
C Thomas	sent off	G Leaupepe (Sm)	Sm v F	1999
S Dickinson	sent off	J–J Crenca (F)	NZ v F	1999
E F Morrison	sent off	M Vunibaka (Fj)	Fj v C	*1999
A Cole	sent off	D R Baugh (C)	C v Nm	*1999
W J Erickson	sent off	N Ta'ufo'ou (Tg)	E v Tg	*1999
P Marshall	sent off	B D Venter (SA)	SA v U	*1999
P C Deluca	sent off	W Cristofoletto (It)	F v It	2000
J I Kaplan	sent off	A Troncon (It)	It v I	2001
R Dickson	sent off	G Leger (Tg)	W v Tg	2001
P C Deluca	sent off	N J Hines (S)	US v S	2002
P D O'Brien	sent off	M C Joubert (SA)	SA v A	2002
P D O'Brien	sent off	J J Labuschagne (SA)	E v SA	2002
S R Walsh	sent off	V Ma'asi (Tg)	Tg v I	2003
N Williams	sent off	S D Shaw (E)	NZ v E	2004
S J Dickinson	sent off	P C Montgomery (SA)	W v SA	2005
S M Lawrence	sent off	L W Moody (E)	E v Sm	2005
S M Lawrence	sent off	A Tuilagi (Sm)	E v Sm	2005
S R Walsh	sent off	S Murray (S)	W v S	2006
J I Kaplan	sent off	H T–Pole (Tg)	Sm v Tg	*2007
A C Rolland	sent off	J Nieuwenhuis (Nm)	F v Nm	*2007
N Owens	sent off	N Nalaga (Pl)	F v Pl	2008
W Barnes	sent off	J P R Heaslip (I)	NZ v I	2010
C Joubert	sent off	D A Mitchell (A)	A v NZ	2010
N Owens	sent off	P B Williams (Sm)	SA v Sm	*2011
A C Rolland	sent off	S K Warburton (W)	W v F	*2011

** Matches in Rugby World Cup final stages*

OBITUARIES

By Adam Hathaway

BRIAN BOOBBYER, who died on 17 January 2011 aged 82, won nine caps for England in the centre and was also an outstanding cricketer but turned his back on both sports at the age of 24 to travel abroad and work with Frank Buchman's Moral Re-Armament movement. As a schoolboy batsman, he once went an entire season at Durston House prep school without being dismissed and went on to play for Oxford University for four years. Middlesex were interested in him but his Christian faith won the day. In rugby, while doing his national service, he played for Rosslyn Park and made his England debut against Wales in 1950 and got the only score in a 3–0 win over Ireland the following year. After a tour to Japan following his last term at Oxford, Boobbyer stayed on to work with an international MRA group to help with post-war reconciliation and never played rugby or cricket at the top level again. He travelled all over the world and in 2005 his family published the best of his talks and writings in a book, *Like a Cork out of a Bottle*, which was a reference to a description of his style of rugby found in a book on the history of the Varsity match.

HANNES BOTHA, who died on 30 August 2011 aged 74, was a South African forward who won three caps for the Springboks in 1962 against the touring British Lions. A career soldier, he rose to the rank of Brigadier, and although a second row by nature he played at flanker in the three wins against the Lions in the second, third and fourth Tests. Schooled in Pretoria, his military career started in Stellenbosch and the military academy at Saldanha, while at the same time playing in the second row for Boland. He moved to Pretoria in 1960 and played for Northern Transvaal and represented the Junior Springboks against Wilson Whineray's All Blacks the same year. He was then picked for Avril Malan's, South African side that toured Europe – he had been a school mate of Malan's, playing at lock while Malan played at No 8, but the roles were reversed for South Africa, even though he did not play a Test on the tour. After playing against the Lions, he transferred to Tempe, near Bloemfontein, and made 16 appearances for Orange Free State. His day job began to take precedent over rugby and he was an aide de camp to the state president.

608 **CLIFF BRITTLE**, who died on 11 September 2011 aged 69, was a rugby administrator and businessman, the RFU chairman from 1996 to 1998, one of the most turbulent periods in that body's history, and later chairman of the Management Board. He was previously Staffordshire's coach and their RFU Committee member from 1989. Under his chairmanship the RFU appointed Clive Woodward as England coach, at Fran Cotton's recommendation, and withstood calls for his removal a couple of years later. He also helped in signing Jason Robinson from rugby league. In 2003 one newspaper claimed England's World Cup win was down to three people – Brittle, Woodward and Cotton. Brittle played centre at Longton High School, Old Longtonians, Stoke-on-Trent and Sale, and for Staffordshire, and coached the Staffordshire County Championship side. With his brother Rob, he ran a plant hire business based in Stoke-on-Trent until it was sold in 1987 and he moved to the Isle of Man. Cotton, an ally of Brittle's and a member of the RFU's Management Board until resigning over the treatment of Brittle, said, "Cliff had rugby close to his heart and cared deeply about the game at every level. He was impatient to secure the best for English rugby and all involved in it at the very difficult time when the game went professional. I am sure many of us will remember him as a visionary and as a true friend."

RFU

Cliff Brittle was RFU chairman from 1996 to 1998.

DAVE BROCKHOFF, who died on 16 June 2011 aged 83, was a former flanker and coach who played for Australia 26 times, including eight Tests, between 1949 and 1953 and was part of the side which won the Bledisloe Cup in 1949. A four-time rugby blue at Sydney University, he played for Eastern Suburbs until 1961, was appointed coach of the side in 1963 and had three periods in charge of the New South Wales Waratahs. He made a huge impact as a coach with the Wallabies and some credit Brockhoff with restoring credibility to the Australian shirt during his colourful reign from 1974 to 1979. Firstly, his side beat England in two violent Test matches in 1975 and they won the Bledisloe Cup in his final game by beating the All Blacks at the Sydney Cricket Ground. That was a first triumph on home soil since 1934. His team talks were the stuff of legend and he constantly fought with the Australian Rugby Union which was not comfortable with his aggressive coaching style. Even late on his life he would be at Sydney Airport to wish departing Wallabies or Waratahs the best on their latest overseas trip and was there when they returned. He was described, on his death, by the *Sydney Morning Herald* as 'the heart and soul of Australian rugby, the Wallabies and the Waratahs'.

BOB BURRELL, who died on 13 April 2011 aged 87, was one of Scottish rugby's great characters, an international referee, president of Gala RFC and a renowned after-dinner speaker. Burrell took charge of five internationals in the 1960s, making his debut with the whistle in Ireland's 1966 match with Wales at Lansdowne Road, and was invited to referee the Varsity match before taking charge of a Test, which was a rare honour. Before becoming an official, Burrell played in the centre for Gala, where is brother Dod (later president of the SRU and manager of the 1977 British Lions) was also in the side. He played 140 games before refereeing took over, and when he gave that up Burrell took to the after-dinner circuit, where he once won the title of Wit of the Year. In his business life he looked after the sponsorship interests of Keyline Builders' Merchants and served on the Gala RFC committee, becoming president in 1989 until 1991. He was made a life member of Gala in 2004. His grandson, Edinburgh, Scotland A and Scotland Sevens forward Roddy Grant was a recent source of pride.

MICK CREMIN, who died on 13 January 2011 aged 87, was an Australian fly-half who played three Tests for the Wallabies and 19 matches in total between 1946 and 1948. Nicknamed 'Smiler', Cremin was a graduate of the Sydney Boys' High School and Sydney University, played for Randwick and New South Wales and was one of the most influential players in Australia immediately after the Second World War. He made his Test debut against the All Blacks in Dunedin where Australia were beaten 31–8, and his last against the same opposition was in Brisbane the next year when the Wallabies lost 13–5. He did get one over the New Zealanders, however, when, in 1947, he helped mastermind New South Wales' shock win over the touring All Blacks at the Sydney Cricket Ground. He captained Australia in six non-Test tour matches, played for Randwick for nine years from 1940, making 132 first grade appearances, and was captain from 1944 to 1947. He kept involved with rugby after retiring from playing by coaching the Northern Suburbs club in Sydney.

ALBERT FERRASSE, who died on 28 July 2011 aged 93, was a championship-winning second row with Agen but was more famous for his role as an administrator. Ferrasse was the first French chairman of the International Rugby Board, where he sat in 1980 and 1987, and helped to promote the idea of a Rugby World Cup, eventually presenting New Zealand captain David Kirk with the trophy at the end of the first tournament. He was an IRB Council Member from 1979 to 1992. As a player he won the French Championship in 1945 before turning his attention to refereeing, taking charge of the 1959 French final and then administration. He was president of Agen from 1963 to 1985 and of the French Federation between 1968 and 1991. In 2001, Ferrasse was presented with the IRB Chairman's Award in recognition of his service to the development and growth of rugby. He was also made a commander of the l'Ordre National de la Légion d'Honneur for services to French Rugby and established the Albert Ferrasse Foundation in 1990 to care for injured players. IRB chairman Bernard Lapasset said: "A man of great stature, Albert Ferrasse's contribution to French, European and world rugby was massive. He was a visionary, a pioneer and a great champion of the game."

TOMMY GENTLES, who died on 4 July 2011 aged 77, was a South African scrum-half and reputedly the smallest player ever to play for the Springboks. Gentles stood just 1.60m (5ft 3in) but still played six times for his national side between 1955 and 1958. It was Gentles, as was the custom in those days for scrum-halves, who was holding the ball up for Jack van der Schyff for his fateful missed kick against the British Lions at Ellis Park in 1955 which meant the Boks lost the first Test match by a solitary point. He played three of the four games against the tourists, went on the 1956 South African trip to Australia and New Zealand, playing twice against the All Blacks, and was vice-captain when South Africa lost to the French tourists in the second Test of 1958. Aged

24, he turned to rugby league – with Wigan and then Leeds – but did not enjoy the experience, especially as professionals were ostracized by the union game in those days and he was once kicked out of the clubhouse of his former club Villagers when he went there for a drink. Away from rugby he was a successful insurance broker.

ANDY HURST, who died in March 2011 aged 76, was a Wasps and Henley winger who played once for England, in the 1962 match against Scotland at Murrayfield which ended in a 3–3 draw. Born in Cairo, his family moved to England when he was a youngster and after attending the Dragon School, Oxford, and Abbotsholme, Staffordshire, Oxford University and serving in the Royal Navy he became a solicitor, founding the company of ACB Hurst and Co in Henley in 1971 where he worked until he was 73. A popular figure in Henley where he frequently campaigned on local issues, his full name was Andrew Charles Brunel Hurst as he was the great, great nephew of the famous engineer Isambard Kingdom Brunel.

MOSS KEANE, who died on 5 October 2010 aged 62, was a legendary and hugely popular figure in Irish rugby despite not taking up the sport until his early 20s. Keane's standing in the sport in his homeland was underlined when more than 800 people attended his funeral and partied for 48 hours in his memory. It was a fitting send-off to one of the more distinctive characters in rugby. Four years after his first game of rugby union, Keane was making his debut, at second row, for Ireland in Paris, a first cap in a run of 51 in which he was never dropped. Keane represented Kerry at Gaelic football at under-21 level before being introduced to rugby at University College Cork, playing under a false name, Moss Fenton, to prevent detection by the Gaelic Athletic Association. Keane was a member of the Munster side that beat the All Blacks in 1978, won Triple Crowns with Ireland in 1974 and 1982 and was a Test player on the 1977 Lions tour to New Zealand. A larger-than-life character, he earned a master's degree in dairy science and worked for the ministry of agriculture, playing for Lansdowne until retiring from rugby in 1985. He was diagnosed with cancer in 2008.

JOHN LAW OBE, who died on 21 September 2010 aged 94, was secretary of the Scottish Rugby Union from 1954 to 1983 and a captain in the Highland Light Infantry in the Second World War. He was behind the SRU's championing of short tours around world rugby and the electric blanket used to protect the pitch at Murrayfield. His love of rugby came from his time at Kelvinside Academy where he played as a second row, and he left school to qualify as a lawyer at Glasgow University.

DAVID MARQUES, who died on 29 September 2010 aged 77, was capped 23 times by England at second row and played two Tests for the Lions on the 1959 Lions tour to Australia and New Zealand. Renowned as being the epitome of the English gentleman, he formed a record-setting partnership at lock with fellow Harlequin John Currie, with the pair appearing in 22 consecutive England internationals between 1956 and 1961, helping the team to the Grand Slam in 1957, and played for the London club for 11 seasons. Schooled at Tonbridge, he was part of the first XV of 1949 that were unbeaten during the season and also featured the future England cricketer Colin Cowdrey. Off the pitch he was renowned as a gentle giant, stepping off the plane on the Lions tour in the boiling heat of Darwin decked out in the suit, bowler hat and umbrella of a city gent. He worked for the family firm, making street lights, was a crew member of *Sovereign*, the 1964 America's Cup challenger, a magistrate and a governor of Haileybury College and a church warden.

GRAEME MOODY, who died in a surfing accident on 24 August 2011 aged 60, was a known as the voice of the All Blacks on New Zealand's airwaves. Moody was a sports reporter and commentator on NewsTalk ZB for 35 years, covering Olympic Games, Rugby World Cups, Commonwealth Games and America's Cup yachting. Moody studied at Wellington Polytech and started his career on the Whakatane Beacon before switching to radio with Radio 1XX. His career highlights included reporting on the Springboks controversial tour to New Zealand in 1981 and the Rugby World Cup 1995 final when he had to describe the All Blacks' defeat to a devastated nation. New Zealand coach Graham Henry described Moody, who was twice voted New Zealand Radio Best Sports Commentator as 'a top bloke'.

HOWARD NICHOLLS, who died on 2 March 2011 aged 79, won one cap on the wing for Wales in the 1958 victory over Ireland at Lansdowne Road, a match that also marked Cliff Morgan's last appearance for the Welsh. Born in Maesteg, Nicholls played for his local club as well as Bridgend, Cardiff and Crawshays at club level – as a wing or centre – racking up 150 games for Cardiff between 1952 and 1959 in which he scored 68 tries. In 1957–58 he was the side's top try-scorer, touching down 20 times, and also played in Cardiff's famous 14–11 win over the touring Australians at the Arms Park in 1957. That was a vintage era for Cardiff, with the likes of Morgan, Bleddyn Williams, Gordon Wells and Rex Willis all turning out for the club. Nicholls was also a keen schoolboy cricketer at the Hereford Cathedral School where he played in the same teams as Peter and Dick Richardson who batted for Worcestershire and England. A butcher by trade, he ran a shop in Maesteg, which he took over from his father, until retiring in 1988, and was a keen bird photographer, having many pictures published in specialist magazines. His father-in-law was Arthur Hugh Jones, who played on the wing for Wales in 1933.

BRIAN POPE, who died on 19 August 2011 aged 100, was England's oldest surviving international player until his death, and the RFU marked his century with a special presentation of a framed match report from his playing days. Born in Barnet in 1911, Pope attended Uppingham School and then Cambridge University where he won his blue in the 8–3 defeat to Oxford in 1932. By then he was already an international, having played scrum-half for England in 1931 against Wales, Scotland and France. After the extraordinary 10-try affair in Edinburgh, which Scotland won 28–19; England went to Paris on Easter Monday for what would turn out to be France's last Championship match until 1947 due to arguments over professionalism. England led three times and scored three tries to two in the 14–13 defeat (under modern scoring values they would have been 19–16 winners). Pope, whose club was Blackheath FC, later served in the RAF in the Second World War and was an underwriting company director, working on the Lloyds Insurance market. He played golf well into his 90s and scored a hole-in-one at Royal St George's Maiden hole aged 92.

ISAIA RASILA, who died on 9 October 2010 aged 41, played at two Rugby World Cups, in 1999 and 2003, for Fiji. In all he won 38 caps for his country as a hooker, winning his first against Western Samoa in 1992, and captaining Fiji on five occasions. Born in Vunavutu, he played for Nadroga when they dominated Fijian rugby from 1994 to 1998, and represented the side more than 80 times.

ALLAN ROY, who died on 16 April 2011 aged 99, was a Waterloo and Scotland second row who won six caps for his country in 1938 and 1939. Born in Ainsdale, Southport, he played in Scotland's Triple Crown-clinching win over England at Twickenham in his first year as an international in the game known as Wilson Shaw's match when the fly-half scored two tries and made one in a 21–16 win. He was an ever-present the next year when all three internationals – France were not in the championships – were lost, and the outbreak of war ruined his chances of further honours. Roy's family came from Tayside but moved to Merseyside in 1900, and he attended Liverpool University with designs on becoming an architect. However, he joined the family business and during the Second World War served with Cameron Highlanders in Burma. When the conflict ended, golf took over as sporting passion. He played off scratch and was a leading member of the Lancashire county team as well as reviving and expanding the family business, diversifying into paper bag manufacture, launderettes and the exportation of snooker tables.

JOHNNY SIMPSON, who died on 17 November 2010 aged 88, was a New Zealand prop who played 33 games for the All Blacks, including nine Tests in the late 1940s. Simpson, known as the 'Iron Man', formed a noted front row partnership with fellow prop Kevin Skinner and hooker Has Catley. He was part of the renowned New Zealand Army side that toured Britain after the Second World War, playing 18 of 33 matches, including wins over England, Scotland and Wales. His first taste of action with New Zealand was on their 1947 tour to Australia and he played in all four Tests on the 1949 trip to South Africa. Simpson was touted as a possible captain of the 1953–54 All Black tour of Europe but, with a third child due, he put his family first. On retirement he was an assistant coach with Auckland, an hotelier in Paraparaumu and an accomplished lawn bowls player.

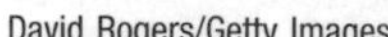

David Rogers/Getty Images

Former RFU President, Peter Trunkfield, who died in 2011.

PETER TRUNKFIELD, who died on 27 December 2010 aged 80, was a hugely popular figure in English rugby, president of the RFU in 1998–99, a period that coincided with Lawrence Dallaglio's infamous loss of the England captaincy, a legendary liaison officer for southern hemisphere touring sides and a stalwart of the Buckinghamshire Rugby Union and Marlow RUFC. He was able to talk to everyone at any level of the game, a skill that came in useful during the political upheaval at the RFU in the 1990s and the row that could have ended up with England being thrown out of the-then Five Nations. Trunkfield played for Bletchley in his youth but it was off the field that he became a giant of the game.

TOM WALKINSHAW, who died from cancer on 12 December 2010 aged 64, was best known in rugby as the owner of Gloucester, where he took over in 1997, and as the chairman of Premier Rugby from 1998–2002 where he oversaw the introduction of the salary cap and a rise in attendances at domestic games. He was also heavily involved in the discussions with the RFU about player release to England which is now enshrined in the eight-year agreement between the clubs and Twickenham. During his reign at Gloucester, Kingsholm was redeveloped and the week before he died he texted coach Bryan Redpath to congratulate him on a win. Born in Midlothian, Walkinshaw's other passion was motor sport. He founded

Mark Thompson/Getty Images

Rugby lost motor racing boss Tom Walkinshaw in 2011.

Tom Walkinshaw Racing in 1976 and won a European touring car title in 1984. When he was involved with the Benetton team he helped recruit Michael Schumacher and the influential designer Ross Brawn. After Schumacher won the world title Walkinshaw moved on to run Ligier and then Arrows, where he was influential in Damon Hill joining the team in 1997. Arrows folded in 2002 and Walkinshaw turned to Australia and an association with the car manufacturer Holden, which he took over in 2008. Walkinshaw's son, Ryan, is now on the board at Gloucester.

COLIN WHITE, who died on 19 January 2011 aged 63, made the first of his four England Test appearances at prop in the side that beat the All Blacks 15–9 at Twickenham in 1983 at the age of 34. White was a tree-surgeon by trade and was handicapped after he chopped off three fingers in a chainsaw accident, and it was felt, especially in the North East, where he played for Gosforth, that four caps was insufficient reward for his ability. White was part of the Gosforth side, known as 'the Green Machine' that won two John Player Cup finals at Twickenham, in 1976 and 1977, and was the team captain for the 1981 final against Leicester. He also propped for the North in their 21–9 win over the 1979 All Blacks at Otley, where the likes of Graham Mourie, Murray Mexted and Stu Wilson lost the only game of their 11-match tour. Later in life White was involved in the coaching set-up at Northern RFC and served as chairman of rugby at Gosforth.

DYSON 'TUG' WILSON, who died on 20 April 2011 aged 84, won eight caps in the England back row between 1953 and 1955, was a British Lion in 1955 and at different times an undercover policeman, fisherman, yachtsman, boxer, farmer and a writer. Born in the Western Cape in 1926, Wilson's parents moved to England when he was eight, and he was one of half-a-dozen South African-born players who represented England in the 1950s. At club level he played for Harlequins and was captain of Middlesex, but his international career was hampered by the presence of outstanding back row players such as John Kendall-Carpenter, Reg Higgins, Don White, Vic Roberts and Peter Robbins. After rugby he ran two unsegregated restaurants in Rhodesia – the Curry House and the Bombay Duck – much to the chagrin of Ian Smith's government, took a fair around the mining towns of Zambia before working on a fishing boat, back in England, in Cornwall. Wilson crossed the Atlantic twice in yachts – once with his wife and children – before settling on a farm on the Lizard where he raised cattle, played squash to an old age and amused friends with tales of his adventures. He was buried in a wood he had created on his farm.

THE DIRECTORY

MEMBER UNIONS OF THE INTERNATIONAL RUGBY BOARD

ANDORRA Federació Andorrana de Rugby
www.far.ad

ARGENTINA Union Argentina de Rugby
www.uar.com.ar

AUSTRALIA Australian Rugby Union
www.rugby.com.au

AUSTRIA Osterreichischer Rugby Verband
www.rugby-austria.at

BAHAMAS Bahamas Rugby Football Union
www.rugbybahamas.com

BARBADOS Barbados Rugby Football Union
www.rugbybarbados.com

BELGIUM Fédération Belge de Rugby
www.rugby.be

BERMUDA Bermuda Rugby Union
www.bermudarfu.com

BOSNIA & HERZEGOVINA Ragbi Savez Republike Bosne i Hercegovine
www.zeragbi.blogspot.com

BOTSWANA Botswana Rugby Union

BRAZIL Confederação Brazileria de Rugby
www.brasilrugby.com.br

BULGARIA Bulgarian Rugby Federation
www.bfrbg.org

CAMEROON Fédération Camerounaise de Rugby
www.fecarugby.org

CANADA Rugby Canada
www.rugbycanada.ca

CAYMAN Cayman Rugby Union
www.caymanrugby.com

CHILE Federación de Rugby de Chile
www.feruchi.cl

CHINA Chinese Rugby Football Association
www.rugbychina.com

CHINESE TAIPEI Chinese Taipei Rugby Football Union
www.rocrugby.org.tw

COLOMBIA Pro Federacion Colombiana de Rugby
www.fecorugby.co

COOK ISLANDS Cook Islands Rugby Union
www.rugby.co.ck

CROATIA Hrvatski Ragbijaski Savez
www.rugby.hr

CZECH REPUBLIC Ceska Rugbyova Unie
www.rugbyunion.cz

DENMARK Dansk Rugby Union
www.rugby.dk

ENGLAND Rugby Football Union
www.rfu.com

FIJI Fiji Rugby Union
www.fijirugby.com

FINLAND Suomen Rugbyliitto
www.rugby.fi

FRANCE Fédération Française de Rugby
www.ffr.fr

GEORGIA Georgian Rugby Union
www.rugby.ge

GERMANY Deutscher Rugby Verband
www.rugby.de

GUAM Guam Rugby Football Union

GUYANA Guyana Rugby Football Union

HONG KONG Hong Kong Rugby Football Union
www.hkrugby.com

HUNGARY Magyar Rögbi Szövetség
www.mrgsz.hu

INDIA Indian Rugby Football Union
www.rugbyindia.in

IRELAND Irish Rugby Football Union
www.irishrugby.ie

ISRAEL Israel Rugby Union
www.rugby.org.il

ITALY Federazione Italiana Rugby
www.federugby.it

IVORY COAST Fédération Ivoirienne de Rugby

JAMAICA Jamaica Rugby Football Union

JAPAN Japan Rugby Football Union
www.jrfu.org

KAZAKHSTAN Kazakhstan Rugby Football Federation
www.kaz-rugby.kz

KENYA Kenya Rugby Football Union
www.kenyarfu.com

KOREA Korea Rugby Union
www.rugby.or.kr

LATVIA Latvijas Regbija Federäcija
www.rugby.lv

LITHUANIA Lietuvos Regbio Federacija
www.lrf.lt

LUXEMBOURG Fédération Luxembourgeoise de Rugby
www.rugby.lu

MADAGASCAR Fédération Malagasy de Rugby

MALAYSIA Malaysia Rugby Union
www.mru.org.my

MALTA Malta Rugby Football Union
www.maltarugby.com

MAURITIUS Rugby Union Mauritius
www.rugbymauritius.com

MEXICO Federación Mexicana de Rugby
www.mexrugby.com

MOLDOVA Federatia de Rugby din Moldovei
www.rugby.md

MONACO Fédération Monégasque de Rugby
www.monaco-rugby.com

MOROCCO Fédération Royale Marocaine de Rugby
www.frm-rugby.ma

NAMIBIA Namibia Rugby Union

NETHERLANDS Nederlands Rugby Bond
www.rugby.nl

NEW ZEALAND New Zealand Rugby Football Union
www.allblacks.com

NIGERIA Nigeria Rugby Football Federation
www.nrff-ng.com

NIUE ISLANDS Niue Rugby Football Union

NORWAY Norges Rugby Forbund
www.rugby.no

PAKISTAN Pakistan Rugby Union
www.pakistanrugby.com

PAPUA NEW GUINEA Papua New Guinea Rugby Football Union

PARAGUAY Union de Rugby del Paraguay
www.urp.org.py

PERU Federación Peruana de Rugby
www.rugbyperu.org

PHILIPPINES The Philippines Rugby Football Union
www.prfu.com

POLAND Polski Związek Rugby
www.pzrugby.pl

PORTUGAL Federação Portuguesa de Rugby
www.fpr.pt

ROMANIA Federatia Romana de Rugbi
www.frr.ro

RUSSIA Rugby Union of Russia
www.rugby.ru

SAMOA Samoa Rugby Union
www.samoarugbyunion.ws

SCOTLAND Scottish Rugby Union
www.scottishrugby.org

SENEGAL Fédération Sénégalaise de Rugby
www.senegal-rugby.com

SERBIA Rugby Union of Serbia
www.rugbyserbia.org.rs

SINGAPORE Singapore Rugby Union
www.singaporerugby.com

SLOVENIA Rugby Zveza Slovenije
www.rugby.si

SOLOMON ISLANDS Solomon Islands Rugby Union Federation

SOUTH AFRICA South African Rugby Union
www.sarugby.co.za

SPAIN Federación Española de Rugby
www.ferugby.com

SRI LANKA Sri Lanka Rugby Football Union
www.srilankarugby.com

ST. VINCENT & THE GRENADINES St. Vincent & The Grenadines Rugby Union Football

SWAZILAND Swaziland Rugby Union
www.swazilandrugby.com

SWEDEN Svenska Rugby Forbundet
www.rugby.se

SWITZERLAND Fédération Suisse de Rugby
www.suiseerugby.com

TAHITI Fédération Tahitienne de Rugby de Polynésie Française
www.tahitirugbyunion.com

THAILAND Thai Rugby Union
www.thairugbyunion.com

TONGA Tonga Rugby Football Union

TRINIDAD & TOBAGO Trinidad and Tobago Rugby Football Union
www.ttrfu.com

TUNISIA Fédération Tunisienne de Rugby

UGANDA Uganda Rugby Football Union
www.ugandarugby.com

UKRAINE National Rugby Federation of Ukraine
www.rugby.org.ua

URUGUAY Union de Rugby del Uruguay
www.uru.org.uy

USA USA Rugby
www.usarugby.org

VANUATU Vanuatu Rugby Football Union

VENEZUELA Federación Venezolana de Rugby Amateur

WALES Welsh Rugby Union
www.wru.co.uk

ZAMBIA Zambia Rugby Football Union

ZIMBABWE Zimbabwe Rugby Union
www.zimbabwerugby.com

REGIONAL ASSOCIATIONS

ARFU Asian Rugby Football Union
www.arfu.com

CAR Confédération Africaine de Rugby
www.confederation-africaine-rugby.com

CONSUR Confederacion Sudamericana de Rugby
www.consur.org

FIRA-AER FIRA-Association Européenne de Rugby
www.fira-aer-rugby.com

FORU Federation of Oceania Rugby Unions
www.oceaniarugby.com

NACRA North America Caribbean Rugby Association
www.nacrugby.com

ASSOCIATE MEMBERS

AMERICAN SAMOA American Samoa Rugby Football Union

ARMENIA Rugby Federation of Armenia
www.armrugby.am

AZERBAIJAN Azerbaijan Rugby Union
www.rugby.az

BRITISH VIRGIN ISLANDS British Virgin Islands Rugby Union
www.bvirugby.com

BURUNDI Fédération Burundaise de Rugby

CAMBODIA Cambodia Federation of Rugby
www.cambodiarugby.org

GHANA Ghana Rugby Union

Greece Hellenic Federation of Rugby

INDONESIA Persatuan Rugby Union Indonesia
www.indonesianrugby.com

IRAN Iran Rugby Federation
www.iranrc.org

KYRGYZSTAN Kyrgyzstan Rugby Union

LAO Lao Rugby Federation
www.laorugby.com

MALI Fédération Malienne de Rugby

MAURITANIA Fédération Mauritanienne de Rugby

MONGOLIA Mongolia Rugby Union

RWANDA Fédération Rwandaise de Rugby
www.rwandarugby.org

ST. LUCIA St. Lucia Rugby Football Union

TANZANIA Tanzania Rugby Union

TOGO Fédération Togolaise de Rugby
www.fetogrugby.com

UZBEKISTAN Uzbekistan Rugby Union
www.rugby.uz

Acknowledgements

The 2012 Edition of the *IRB World Rugby Yearbook* was produced at breakneck speed, after Rugby World Cup 2011, so I need to offer my thanks to a number of people who were key players in its production.

In the same way that the World Cup goes from first game to last on the back of an army of staff working day and night, it is the same with the *IRB World Rugby Yearbook*.

Now in its sixth season since it returned from the wilderness, it is only in your hands due to the huge efforts of a large number of people.

First to Dom Rumbles, the IRB's Head of Communications, who had the vision to appreciate how important the Yearbook is in a world where we are bombarded by an increasingly large number of spurious statistics and articles. The Yearbook cuts through them to provide a definitive, and official, guide to the rugby world.

Andrea Wiggins and Karen Bond, working with Dom at the IRB, made the Yearbook happen, pure and simple. Their workload is increased tenfold in a Rugby World Cup year, so their diligence and commitment is a credit to them.

But we would never have hit our punishing deadlines without the dedication of Julie Garvock at Palimpsest Book Production, who continues to set new benchmarks when it comes to book production. Hats off to Julie.

The Yearbook wouldn't be worth buying without John Griffiths' world-famous statistics or the writing team, which was headed by Iain Spragg, and this year included a number of new faces.

And lastly (but certainly not least) to the publishers at Vision Sports Publishing, where we had a new and welcome addition to the team in the shape of Alex Morton, who joined Jim Drewett and Toby Trotman, who continue to have the drive to put the Yearbook into the vital position it holds in the rugby world.

We thank you for buying this 2012 edition, and hope you enjoy it, but if you have any comments please do not hesitate to email me at paulrugbymorgan@hotmail.com. We'd love to hear your suggestions for future editions.

PAUL MORGAN – Joint Editor